The Zohar

by
Rav Shimon bar Yochai
From The Book of Avraham

with
The Sulam Commentary

by
Rav Yehuda Ashlag

The First Ever Unabridged
English Translation with Commentary

Published by
The Kabbalah Centre International Inc.
Dean Rav S. P. Berg Shlita

Edited and Compiled by
Rabbi Michael Berg

With a small change in consciousness
we can remove all family separations

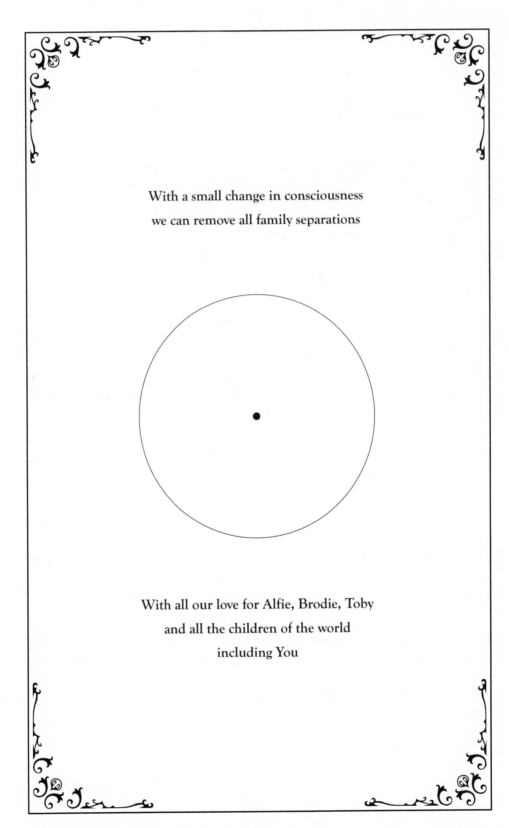

With all our love for Alfie, Brodie, Toby
and all the children of the world
including You

APPLYING THE POWER OF THE ZOHAR

The Zohar is a book of great mystical power and wisdom. It is Universally recognized as the definitive work on the Kabbalah – and it is also so Much more.

The Zohar is a wellspring of spiritual energy, a fountainhead of metaphysical power that not only reveals and explains, but literally brings blessing, protection, and well-being into the lives of all those who read or peruse its sacred texts. All that is required is worthy desire, the certainty of a trusting heart, and an open and receptive mind. Unlike other books, including the great spiritual texts of other traditions, The Zohar is written in a kind of code, through which metaphors, parables, and cryptic language at first conceal but ultimately reveal the forces of creation.

As electrical current is concealed in wire and cable before disclosing itself as an illuminated light bulb, the spiritual Light of the Creator is wrapped in allegory and symbolism throughout the Aramaic text of the Zohar. And while many books contain information and knowledge, the Zohar both expresses and embodies spiritual Light. The very letters on its pages have the power to bring spiritual wisdom and positive energy into every area of our lives.

As we visually scan the Aramaic texts and study the accompanying insights that appear in English, spiritual power is summoned from above – and worlds tremble as Light is sent forth in response.

It's primary purpose is not only to help us acquire wisdom, but to draw Light from the Upper Worlds and to bring sanctification into our lives. Indeed, the book itself is the most powerful of all tools for cleansing the soul and connecting to the Light of the Creator. As you open these pages, therefore, do not make understanding in the conventional sense your primary goal.

Although you may not have a knowledge of Aramaic, look first at the Aramaic text before reading the English. Do not be discouraged by difficulties with comprehension. Instead, open your heart to the spiritual transformation the Zohar is offering you.

Ultimately, the Zohar is an instrument for refining the individual soul – for removing darkness from the earth – and for bringing well being and blessing to our fellow man.

Its purpose is not only to make us intellectually wise, but to make us spiritually pure.

Torah

Also known as the Five Books of Moses, the Torah is considered to be the physical body of learning, whereas the Zohar is the internal soul. The literal stories of the Torah conceal countless hidden secrets.` The Zohar is the Light that illuminates all of the Torah's sublime mysteries.

Beresheet	Genesis
Shemot	Exodus
Vayikra	Leviticus
Bemidbar	Numbers
Devarim	Deuteronomy

Prophets

Amos	Amos
Chagai	Haggai
Chavakuk	Habakkuk
Hoshea	Hosea
Malachi	Malachi
Melachim	Kings
Michah	Micah
Nachum	Nahum
Ovadyah	Obadiah
Shmuel	Samuel
Shoftim	Judges
Tzefanyah	Zephaniah
Yechezkel	Ezekiel
Yehoshua	Joshua
Yeshayah	Isaiah
Yirmeyah	Jeremiah
Yoel	Joel
Yonah	Jonah
Zecharyah	Zechariah

Writings

Daniel	Daniel
Divrei Hayamim	Chronicles
Eicha	Lamentations
Ester	Esther
Ezra	Ezra
Nechemiah	Nehemiah
Iyov	Job
Kohelet	Ecclesiastes
Mishlei	Proverbs
Rut	Ruth

Sir Hashirim	Songs of Songs
Tehilim	Psalms

The Ten Sfirot – Emanations

To conceal the blinding *Light* of the Upper World, and thus create a tiny point into which our universe would be born, ten *curtains* were fabricated. These ten *curtains* are called Ten Sfirot. Each successive Sfirah further reduces the emanation of *Light*, gradually dimming its brilliance to a level almost devoid of *Light* – our physical world known as *Malchut*. The only remnant of Light remaining in this darkened universe is a *pilot light* which sustains our existence. This Light is the life force of a human being and the force that gives birth to stars, sustains suns and sets everything from swirling galaxies to busy ant hills in motion. Moreover, the Ten Sfirot act like a prism, refracting the Light into many *colors* giving rise to the diversity of life and matter in our world.

The Ten Sfirot are as follows:

Keter	Crown
Chochmah	Wisdom
Binah	Understanding
Da'at	Knowledge
Zeir Anpin	Small Face,

(includes the next six Sfirot):

Chesed	Mercy (Chassadim - plural)
Gvurah	Judgment (Gvurot - Plural)
Tiferet	Splendor
Netzach	Victory (Eternity)
Hod	Glory
Yesod	Foundation
Malchut	Kingdom

The Partzufim - Spiritual forms

One complete structure of the Ten Sfirot creates a *Partzuf* or Spiritual Form. Together, these forces are the building blocks of all reality. As water and sand combine to create cement, the Ten Sfirot

VII

combine to produce a Spiritual Form [*Partzuf*]. Each of the Spiritual Forms below are therefore composed of one set of Ten Sfirot.

These Spiritual Forms are called:

Atik	Ancient
Atik Yomin	Ancient of Days
Atika Kadisha	Holy Ancient
Atik of Atikin	Anceint of Ancients
Aba	Father
Arich Anpin	Long Face
Ima	Mother
Nukva	Female
Tevunah	Intelligence
Yisrael Saba	Israel Grandfather
Zachar	Male

These names are not meant to be understood literally. Each represents a unique spiritual force and building block, producing a substructure and foundation for all the worlds make up reality.

The Five Worlds

All of the above Spiritual Forms [*Partzufim*] create one spiritual world. There are Five Worlds in total that compose all reality, therefore, five sets of the above Spiritual Forms are required.

Our physical world corresponds to the world of: Asiyah – Action

Adam Kadmon	Primordial Man
Atzilut	Emanation
Briyah	Creation
Yetzirah	Formation
Asiyah	Action

The Five Levels of the soul

Nefesh	First, Lowest level of Soul
Ruach	Second level of Soul
Neshamah	Third level of Soul
Chayah	Fourth level of Soul
Yechidah	Highest, fifth level of Soul

Names of God

As a single ray of white sunlight contains the seven colors of the spectrum, the one Light of the Creator embodies many diverse spiritual forces. These different forces are called *Names of God*. Each Name denotes a specific attribute and spiritual power. The Hebrew letters that compose these Names are the interface by which these varied Forces act upon our physical world. The most common Name of God is the Tetragrammaton (the four letters, *Yud Hei Vav Hei* יהוה.) Because of the enormous power that the Tetragrammaton transmits, we do not utter it aloud. When speaking of the Tetragrammaton, we use the term *Hashem* which means, *The Name*.

Adonai, El, Elohim, Hashem, Shadai, Eheyeh, Tzevaot, Yud Hei Vav Hei

People

Er	The son of Noach
Rabbi Elazar	The son of Rabbi Shimon bar Yochai
Rabbi Shimon bar Yochai	Author of the Zohar
Shem, Cham, Yefet	Noach's children
Shet	Seth
Ya'akov	Jacob
Yishai	Jesse (King David's father)
Yitzchak	Isaac
Yosef	Joseph
Yitro	Jethro
Yehuda	Judah

Angels

Angels are distinct energy components, part of a vast communication network running through the upper worlds. Each unique Angel is responsible for transmitting various forces of influence into our physical universe.

Adriel, Ahinael, Dumah (name of Angel in charge of the dead), Gabriel, Kadshiel, Kedumiel, Metatron, Michael, Rachmiel,

Raphael, Tahariel, Uriel

Nations

Nations actually represent the inner attributes and character traits of our individual self. The nation of Amalek refers to the doubt and uncertainty that dwells within us when we face hardship and obstacles. Moab represents the dual nature of man. Nefilim refers to the sparks of Light that we have defiled through our impure actions, and to the negative forces that lurk within the human soul as a result of our own wrongful deeds.

Amalek, Moab, Nefilim

General

Aba	Father
	Refers to the male principle and positive force in our universe. Correlates to the proton in an atom.
Arvit	The Evening prayer
Chayot	Animals
Chupah	Canopy (wedding ceremony)
Et	The
Avadon	Hell
Gehenom	Hell
Sheol	Hell
	The place a soul goes for purification upon leaving this world.
Ima	Mother
	The female principle and minus force in our universe. Correlates to the electron in an atom.
Kiddush	Blessing over the wine
Klipah	Shell (negativity)
Klipot	Shells (Plural)
Kriat Sh'ma	The Reading of the Sh'ma
Mashiach	Messiah
Minchah	The Afternoon prayer
Mishnah	Study
Mochin	Brain, Spiritual levels of Light
Moed	A designated time or holiday
Negev	The south of Israel
Nukva	Female

Partzuf	Face
Shacharit	The Morning prayer
Shamayim	Heavens (sky)
Shechinah	The Divine presence, The female aspect of the Creator
Tefilin	Phylacteries
The Dinur river	The river of fire
Tzadik	Righteous person
Zion	Another name for Jerusalem
Yisrael	The land of Israel
	The nation of Israel or an individual Israelite
Zohar	Splendor

The Hebrew vowels

Chirik אַ, Cholam וֹא אֹ, Kamatz אָ, Patach אַ, Segol אֶ, Sh'va אְ, Shuruk וּא אֻ, Tzere אֵ.

The Twelve Tribes

Asher, Dan, Ephraim, Gad, Issachar, Judah, Levi, Menasheh, Naphtali, Reuben, Shimon, Zebulun

Jewish Holidays

Rosh Hashanah	The Jewish New Year
Yom Kippur	Day of Atonement
Sukkot	Holiday of the Booths
Shmini Atzeret	The day of Convocation
Simchat Torah	Holiday on which we dance with the Torah
Pesach	Passover
Shavout	Holiday of the Weeks

כרך י

פרשת יתרו, משפטים

Vol. X

Yitro, Mishpatim

A Prayer from The Ari

To be recited before the study of the Zohar

Ruler of the universe, and Master of all masters, The Father of mercy and forgiveness, we thank You, our God and the God of our fathers, by bowing down and kneeling, that You brought us closer to Your Torah and Your holy work, and You enable us to take part in the secrets of Your holy Torah. How worthy are we that You grant us with such big favor, that is the reason we plead before You, that You will forgive and acquit all our sins, and that they should not bring separation between You and us.

And may it be your will before You, our God and the God of our fathers, that You will awaken and prepare our hearts to love and revere You, and may You listen to our utterances, and open our closed heart to the hidden studies of Your Torah, and may our study be pleasant before Your Place of Honor, as the aroma of sweet incense, and may You emanate to us Light from the source of our soul to all of our being. And, may the sparks of your holy servants, through which you revealed Your wisdom to the world, shine.

May their merit and the merit of their fathers, and the merit of their Torah, and holiness, support us so we shall not stumble through our study. And by their merit enlighten our eyes in our learning as it stated by King David, The Sweet Singer of Israel: "Open my eyes, so that I will see wonders from Your Torah" (Tehilim 119:18). Because from His mouth God gives wisdom and understanding.

"May the utterances of my mouth and the thoughts of my heart find favor before You, God, my Strength and my Redeemer" (Tehilim 19:15).

YITRO

Name of Articels

1. "When Jethro...heard"

A Synopsis

Rabbi Chizkiyah begins a discussion to do with raising up the hands. It is important to raise them only in prayer and blessing, as the ten fingers correspond to the ten potentates who receive blessings, and to the ten sayings. The lesson turns to the King and priest above, and the King and priest below, and we learn that there is a King and a priest of the Other Side as well. The number ten is additionally significant, as God struck the Pharaoh with ten plagues. About Jethro, we now learn that he gave advice to Moses on the administration of justice following the laws of God, and Moses listened to him. Though the people had seen the miracles done by Moses, they gave up their idol worship and believed in Moses' God only after Jethro, who was a powerful priest of Midian, acknowledged the greatness of Hashem. We read of the three advisors to the Pharaoh: Jethro, Job and Bilaam. Bilaam was a sorcerer, but Job had fear, and we are told of the great power of fear to draw down the spirit from above, whether it be Holy or from the Other side. While Job converted to worship of the Holy One due to the fear generated by his witnessing of the miracles, Jethro did not convert until after the drowning in the Red Sea. However, Bilaam neither repented nor converted; we are told that even in the Other Side there is a small streak of light that comes from the Holy side, and Bilaam knew how to use this. In the same way, Moses saw a fine streak of darkness from the Other Side. So we learn that all things connect to one another, the pure and the impure.

‏1. וַיִּשְׁמַע יִתְרוֹ כֹהֵן מִדְיָן חֹתֵן מֹשֶׁה אֵת כָּל אֲשֶׁר עָשָׂה וְגוֹ'. רַבִּי חִזְקִיָּה פָּתַח וְאָמַר, וַיִּשָּׂא אַהֲרֹן אֶת יָדָו. כְּתִיב יָדוֹ חַד, בְּגִין דְּבָעֵי לְאָרְמָא יְמִינָא עַל שְׂמָאלָא, וְהָא אוֹקִימְנָא רָזָא.‏

1. "When Jethro, the priest of Midian, Moses's father-in-law, heard of all that Hashem had done for Moses..." (Shemot 18:1). Rabbi Chizkiyah opened the discussion, saying: "And Aaron lifted up his hands" (Vayikra 9:22). "His hands" is spelled without *Yud*, thus meaning one hand only. And this is the reason: one should lift up his right hand above his left hand. And we have already explained this secret.

‏2. אַשְׁכַּחְנָא בְּסִפְרָא דִּשְׁלֹמֹה מַלְכָּא, דְּכָל מַאן דְּאָרִים יְדוֹי לְעֵילָא,‏

וְלָאו אִינּוּן בִּצְלוֹתִין וּבְעוּתִין, הַאי אִיהוּ בַּר נָשׁ, דְּאִתְלַטְיָיא מֵעֲשָׂרָה שׁוּלְטָנִין מִמְּנָן. וְאִינּוּן עֲשָׂרָה שַׁלִּיטִין אֲשֶׁר הָיוּ בָּעִיר. אִלֵּין אִינּוּן עֲשָׂרָה דִּי מִמְּנָן עַל פְּרִישׁוּ דִּידִין לְעֵילָא לְנַטְלָא הַהוּא צְלוֹתָא, אוֹ הַהִיא בִּרְכָתָא, וְיָהֲבֵי בֵּיהּ חֵילָא, לְאִתְיַקְרָא שְׁמָא קַדִּישָׁא, וְאִתְבְּרַךְ מִתַּתָּא. כֵּיוָן דְּמִתַּתָּא אִתְבְּרַךְ, מֵהַהוּא פְּרִישׁוּ דִּידִין לְעֵילָא, כְּדֵין אִתְבְּרְכָא מֵעֵילָא, וְאִתְיְקַר מִכָּל סִטְרִין.

2. I found this in the book of King Solomon: anyone who desires to raise his hands upwards, without any prayer or request in them, will be cursed by ten potentates. These are "ten rulers who are in a city" (Kohelet 7:19). These ten potentates are designated for those who spread their hands upwards, to receive this prayer or that blessing and to bestow upon them powers through which the Holy Name is exalted and blessed from below. When the Name is blessed from below, through the spreading of the hands upwards, it then receives blessings from above. Thus, it is exalted from all sides.

3. וְאִלֵּין עֲשָׂרָה מִמְּנָן, זְמִינִין לְנַטְלָא מֵאִינּוּן בִּרְכָאן דִּלְעֵילָא, וּלְאַרְקָא לְתַתָּא, וּלְבָרְכָא לְהַהוּא דִּמְבָרֵךְ לֵיהּ, דִּכְתִיב וַאֲנִי אֲבָרְכֵם.

3. These ten appointed potentates are there to receive the blessings from above and propel them below, to bless those who are deserving of these blessings. As it is written: "And I will bless them" (Bemidbar 6:27).

4. בְּג״כ, יִסְתַּמַּר בַּר נָשׁ, בְּשַׁעֲתָא דְּיָרִים יְדוֹי לְעֵילָא, לְמֶהֱוֵי בִּצְלוֹ, אוֹ בְּבִרְכָאן אוֹ בְּבָעוּתָא, וְלָא יָרִים יְדוֹי לְמַגָּנָא, בְּגִין דְּאָלֵּין עֲשָׂרָה אִינּוּן זְמִינִין, וּמִתְעֲרִין. לְגַבֵּי הַהוּא פְּרִישׁוּ דִּידִין, וְאִי הוּא לְמַגָּנָא, אִינּוּן עֲשָׂרָה לַטְיִין לֵיהּ, בִּמְאָתָן וְאַרְבְּעִין וּתְמַנְיָא לָוְוטִין. וְהַאי אִיהוּ דִּכְתִיב בֵּיהּ, וַיֶּאֱהַב קְלָלָה וַתְּבוֹאֵהוּ.

4. Consequently, man must be careful that, at the time when he raises his hands upwards, they are raised in prayer, in blessing, or in entreaty. And he must not raise his hands idly, since those ten potentates are ready and are roused towards the spreading of the hands, and if it is in vain, these ten will

curse it with two hundred and forty-eight curses. This is what is written: "For he loved cursing, and it came to him" (Tehilim 109:17).

5. וּכְדֵין, רוּחַ מְסָאֲבָא שַׁרְיָא עַל אִינוּן יְדִין, דְּאִיהוּ אָרְחֵיהּ לְמִשְׁרֵי עַל אֲתָר רֵיקַנְיָא, וּבִרְכָּתָא לָא שַׁרְיָא בַּאֲתָר רֵיקַנְיָא. וְעַ״ד כְּתִיב, הֲרִימוֹתִי יָדִי אֶל ה׳ אֵל עֶלְיוֹן, דְּמִתַּרְגְּמִינָן בִּצְלוּ.

5. And thus, an impure spirit rests on these hands for its way is to rest in empty places. But blessings do not rest in empty places. Therefore, it is written: "I have raised my hand to Hashem, the most high El" (Beresheet 14:22), which is translated into Aramaic as 'with prayer'.

6. וּבְהַאי פְּרִישׁוּ דְּיָדִין, אִית רָזִין עִלָּאִין, בְּשַׁעֲתָא דְּאִתְפְּרִישׁוּ, וְאִזְדְּקָפוּ לְעֵילָא, אוֹקִיר בַּר נָשׁ לְקוּדְשָׁא בְּרִיךְ הוּא, בְּכַמָּה רָזִין עִלָּאִין. אַחְזֵי לִיחֲדָא רָזָא דְּעֶשֶׂר אֲמִירָן, בְּגִין לְיַחֲדָא כֹּלָּא, וּלְאִתְבָּרְכָא שְׁמָא קַדִּישָׁא כַּדְקָא חֲזֵי, וְאַחְזֵי לִיחֲדָא רָזָא דִּרְתִיכִין פְּנִימָאִין, וּרְתִיכִין דִּלְבַר, בְּגִין דְּיִתְבָּרֵךְ שְׁמָא קַדִּישָׁא בְּכָל סִטְרִין, וְיִתְיַחֵד כֹּלָּא כַּחֲדָא, עֵילָא וְתַתָּא.

6. This lifting of the hands has supreme secrets. At the time that one spreads out his hands and lifts them upwards, man glorifies the Holy One, blessed be He, with many supernal secrets, and is worthy of uniting the ten sayings in order to unify the whole and bless the Holy Name properly. He also unites the inner Chariots OF ATZILUT and the outer Chariots OUTSIDE ATZILUT so that the Holy Name may be blessed from all sides, and all becomes one above and below.

7. פָּתַח וְאָמַר, וְלֹא יֵרָאוּ פָנַי רֵיקָם, דָּא אִיהוּ רָזָא דִּזְקִיפוּ דְּאֶצְבְּעָן, כַּד זָקִיף לוֹן בַּר נָשׁ לְעֵילָא, דְּבָעֵי דְּלָא לְאִזְדַּקְּפָא בְּרֵיקַנְיָא, אֶלָּא בִּצְלוּ וּבְבָעוּתִין וּבְבִרְכָּאן. וְעַ״ד וְלֹא יֵרָאוּ פָנַי רֵיקָם. וְלֹא יֵרָאוּ לְפָנַי לָא כְּתִיב, אֶלָּא פָנַי, רָזָא דִּזְקִיפוּ דְּאֶצְבְּעָן, דְּלָא אִצְטְרִיכוּ לְזַקְפָא לְמַגָּנָא, כְּמָה דְּאִתְּמַר.

7. He opened the discussion, saying: "and none shall appear before Me empty" (Shemot 23:15). This is the secret of the raising of the fingers. For when man spreads his fingers upwards, he should not do so in vain, but only with prayer, supplications and blessings. This is the secret of: "and none shall appear before Me (lit. 'My face') empty." It does not say, 'and none shall appear before Me', but rather (lit.) "My face," which refers to the secret of the raising of the fingers – that it should not be done without an intention, as we said.

‎8. עֲשָׂרָה שַׁלִּיטִין דְּקָאמְרָן, אִינּוּן עֶשֶׂר אֲמִירָן לְתַתָּא, בְּרָזָא דְּאַתְוָון רְשִׁימִין כְּגַוְונָא דִּלְעֵילָא, וְאִלֵּין קַיְּימִין בְּקַדְמֵיתָא עַל הַהוּא זְקִיפָן דְּאֶצְבְּעָאן. וּבְהָא כָּל סִטְרָא דִּקְדוּשָׁה אִתְאֲחַד לְעֵילָא, לְאַרְמָא כְּדֵין כָּל סִטְרִין אַחֲרָנִין אִתְכַּפְיָין כֻּלְּהוּ, וְאוֹדָן לְמַלְכָּא קַדִּישָׁא.

8. The ten rulers of which we spoke are the lower ten sayings, according to the secret of the inscribed letters correlating to those above; and at first, they have control of the raising of the fingers. And through this, the whole side of Holiness is united above; thus, the Other Side yields all and acknowledges the Holy King.

‎9. תָּא חֲזֵי, בְּרָזָא דִּקְדוּשָׁה אִיהוּ מֶלֶךְ, וְכֹהֵן וּמְשַׁמֵּשׁ תְּחוֹתֵיהּ, בֵּין לְעֵילָא בֵּין לְתַתָּא. אִית מֶלֶךְ לְעֵילָא, דְּאִיהוּ רָזָא דְּקֹדֶשׁ הַקֳּדָשִׁים, וְאִיהוּ מֶלֶךְ עִלָּאָה, וּתְחוֹתֵיהּ אִית כֹּהֵן רָזָא דְּאוֹר קַדְמָאָה, דְּקָא מְשַׁמֵּשׁ קַמֵּיהּ, וְדָא אִיהוּ כֹּהֵן דְּאִקְרֵי גָּדוֹל, סִטְרָא דִּימִינָא.

9. Come and behold: in the secret doctrine of Holiness, there is a king and a priest who serves under him, both above and below. The King above is the secret of Holy of Holies, NAMELY BINAH. He is the King above; and under him there is a priest, the secret of primeval light who ministers before him, WHICH IS THE SFIRAH OF CHESED. He is the priest who is called 'great', at the right side.

‎10. אִית מֶלֶךְ לְתַתָּא, דְּאִיהוּ כְּגַוְונָא דְּהַהוּא מֶלֶךְ עִלָּאָה, וְאִיהוּ מֶלֶךְ עַל כֹּלָּא דִּלְתַתָּא. וּתְחוֹתֵיהּ אִית כֹּהֵן דִּמְשַׁמֵּשׁ לֵיהּ, רָזָא דְּמִיכָאֵל

-6-

כַּהֲנָא רַבָּא, דְּאִיהוּ לִימִינָא. וְדָא אִיהוּ רָזָא דִּמְהֵימָנוּתָא שְׁלֵימָתָא, סְטְרָא דִּקְדוּשָׁה.

10. There is a king below, NAMELY MALCHUT, in the likeness of the King above, and he is the king over all that is below, NAMELY THE WORLDS OF BRIYAH, YETZIRAH AND ASIYAH. And under him there is a priest who ministers to him, whom we signify as Michael, the High Priest at his right hand, NAMELY CHESED. This is the true secret of Faith, the side of Holiness.

11. בְּסִטְרָא אַחֲרָא, דְּלָאו אִיהוּ סְטְרָא דִּקְדוּשָׁה, אִית רָזָא דְּאִיהוּ מֶלֶךְ, וְהָא אוּקִימְנָא דְּאִקְרֵי מֶלֶךְ זָקֵן וּכְסִיל, וּתְחוֹתֵיהּ אִית כֹּהֵן אוֹן, וְדָא הוּא רָזָא דִּכְתִיב, וַיֹּאמֶר אֶפְרַיִם אַךְ עָשַׁרְתִּי מָצָאתִי אוֹן לִי, בְּגִין דְּחֵילָא דָּא, שַׁלְטָא עַל הַהוּא עוֹבָדָא דַּעֲבַד יָרָבְעָם. וְאִלְמָלֵא דְּאַשְׁכַּח חֵילָא דָּא, לָא יָכִיל לְאַצְלָחָא בְּהַהוּא עוֹבָדָא.

11. On the Other Side, meaning the side which is not Holy, there is a secret, which is a king, and we have established that he is called "an old and foolish king" (Kohelet 4:13). THIS IS THE EVIL INCLINATION. And under him there is the priest of On, as it is written in the verse: "And Efraim said: 'Yet I am become rich, I have found wealth (Heb. *ON*) for myself'" (Hoshea 12:9). THIS IS THE PRIEST OF THE OTHER SIDE, because this power, On, ruled over an act of idolatry committed by Jerobaam. And if there had not been such power, he would not have been able to succeed in his act.

12. רָזָא דְּמִלָּה, בְּשַׁעֲתָא דְּהַאי מֶלֶךְ וְהַאי כֹּהֵן אִתְכַּפְיָין, וְאִתְבָּרוּ, כְּדֵין כָּל סִטְרִין אַחֲרָנִין אִתְכַּפְיָין, וְאוֹדָן לֵיהּ לְקוּדְשָׁא בְּרִיךְ הוּא, כְּדֵין קוּדְשָׁא בְּרִיךְ הוּא שָׁלִיט בִּלְחוֹדוֹי עֵילָא וְתַתָּא, כד"א, וְנִשְׂגַּב יְיָ' לְבַדּוֹ בַּיּוֹם הַהוּא.

12. The essence of this matter is as follows. When this king and this priest OF THE OTHER SIDE yield, and their power is broken, then all the other sides yield and acknowledge the sovereignty of the Holy One, blessed be He. Then the Holy One, blessed be He, alone rules both above and below, as

it is written: "And Hashem alone shall be exalted on that day" (Yeshayah 2:11).

13. כְּגַוְונָא דָּא, וְרָזָא דָּא מַמָּשׁ, עָבַד קוּדְשָׁא בְּרִיךְ הוּא בְּאַרְעָא, דְּתָבַר מֶלֶךְ זָקֵן וּכְסִיל, וְדָא הוּא פַּרְעֹה, בְּשַׁעֲתָא דְּאָתָא מֹשֶׁה לְפַרְעֹה, וְאָמַר, אֱלֹהֵי הָעִבְרִים נִקְרָא עָלֵינוּ, פָּתַח וְאָמַר, לֹא יָדַעְתִּי אֶת יְיָ', וּבָעָא קוּדְשָׁא בְּרִיךְ הוּא דְּיִתְיָקַר שְׁמֵיהּ בְּאַרְעָא, כְּמָה דְּאִיהוּ יַקִּירָא לְעֵילָּא. כֵּיוָן דְּאַלְקֵי לֵיהּ וּלְעַמֵּיהּ, אָתָא וְאוֹדֵי לֵיהּ לְקוּדְשָׁא בְּרִיךְ הוּא.

13. The Holy One, blessed be He, acted in a similar manner and with this exact secret here on earth in breaking the old and foolish king, namely Pharaoh. In the hour that Moses came to Pharaoh and said to him: "the Elohim of the Hebrews had met with us" (Shemot 5:3), he replied: "I know not Hashem" (Ibid. 2). The Holy One, blessed be He, desired that His name be glorified on earth as it is glorified above AND HE STRUCK HIM WITH TEN PLAGUES. After He struck him and his nation, Pharoah came and acknowledged the Holy One, blessed be He.

14. וּלְבָתַר אִתְּבַר וְאִתְכַּפְיָיא הַהוּא כֹּהֵן אוֹן, יִתְרוֹ, דִּמְשַׁמֵּשׁ תְּחוֹתֵיהּ, עַד דְּאָתָא וְאוֹדֵי לֵיהּ לְקוּדְשָׁא בְּרִיךְ הוּא, וְאָמַר בָּרוּךְ יְיָ' אֲשֶׁר הִצִּיל אֶתְכֶם וְגוֹ', עַתָּה יָדַעְתִּי כִּי גָדוֹל יְיָ' וְגוֹ', וְדָא הוּא כֹּהֵן אוֹן, סִטְרָא אַחֲרָא, דְּאִיהוּ סְטַר שְׂמָאלָא. וְדָא אִיהוּ רָזָא דְּאָמְרָה רָחֵל, כַּד חָמָאת דְּמִיתַת, כְּמָה דִּכְתִּיב, בֶּן אוֹנִי. וּבְגִין דָּא אוֹחֵי יַעֲקֹב, וְאָמַר בֶּן יָמִין, וְלָא בֶן אוֹנִי, סְטַר יְמִינָא, וְלָא שְׂמָאלָא.

14. Afterwards, He broke and humbled the priest of On, Jethro, that served under him, until he came and acknowledged the Holy One, blessed be He, saying "Blessed be Hashem, who has delivered you... Now I know that Hashem is great" (Shemot 18:10-11). And this is the priest of On, from the Other Side, which is the left side. And this is the secret Rachel communicated when she saw death. She said: "*Ben-Oni* (lit. 'son of my sorrow')" (Beresheet 35:18), and because of this Jacob hastened to say, "Benjamin (lit. 'son of the right')" the right side and not the left side.

15. וְכֵיוָן דְּהַהוּא מֶלֶךְ וְכֹהֵן אוֹדוּ לְקוּדְשָׁא בְּרִיךְ הוּא, וְאִתְכַּפְרוּ קַמֵּיהּ, כְּדֵין אִסְתַּלַּק קוּדְשָׁא בְּרִיךְ הוּא בִּיקָרֵיהּ עַל כֹּלָּא, עֵילָּא וְתַתָּא, וְעַד דְּאִסְתַּלַּק קוּדְשָׁא בְּרִיךְ הוּא בִּיקָרֵיהּ, כַּד אוֹדָן אִלֵּין קַמֵּיהּ, לָא אִתְיְיהִיבַת אוֹרַיְיתָא. עַד לְבָתַר דְּאָתָא יִתְרוֹ, וְאוֹדֵי וְאָמַר, עַתָּה יָדַעְתִּי כִּי גָדוֹל יְיָ׳ מִכָּל הָאֱלֹהִים. בָּרוּךְ יְיָ׳ אֲשֶׁר הִצִּיל אֶתְכֶם וְגוֹ׳. כְּדֵין אִסְתַּלַּק קוּדְשָׁא בְּרִיךְ הוּא בִּיקָרֵיהּ, עֵילָּא וְתַתָּא, וּלְבָתַר יָהַב אוֹרַיְיתָא בִּשְׁלִימוּ, דְּשֻׁלְטָנוּ עַל כֹּלָּא.

15. When the king and that priest acknowledged the Holy One, blessed be He, and were humbled before Him, the Holy One, blessed be He, was then above everyone in glory, above and below. And before the Holy One, blessed be He, rose in glory before these acknowledged, the Torah was not yet given. It was only after Jethro came and acknowledged Him by saying, "I now know that Hashem is supreme over all other Elohim." "Blessed be Hashem, who has delivered you." Then the Holy One, blessed be He, rose in glory above and below. And only afterwards was the Torah given in full, expressing His sovereignty over all.

16. ר״א פָּתַח וְאָמַר, יוֹדוּךָ עַמִּים אֱלֹהִים יוֹדוּךָ עַמִּים כֻּלָּם, ת״ח, דָּוִד מַלְכָּא קָם וְשַׁבַּח וְאוֹדֵי לְמַלְכָּא קַדִּישָׁא. וְהוּא אִשְׁתַּדַּל בְּאוֹרַיְיתָא, בְּהַהִיא שַׁעֲתָא כַּד רוּחַ צָפוֹן אִתְּעַר, וַהֲוָה בָּטַשׁ בְּאִינּוּן נִימִין דְּכִנּוֹרָא, וְכִנּוֹרָא הֲוָה מְנַגֵּן וְאָמַר שִׁירָה וְכוּ׳, וּמַה שִׁירָה הֲוָה קָאָמַר.

16. Rabbi Elazar opened the discussion with the following verse: "Let the peoples praise You, Elohim, let all the peoples give thanks to You" (Tehilim 67:3). Come and behold: King David rose and praised and thanked the Holy King. He was studying the Torah at that moment when the north wind rose and struck the strings of his harp, and the harp made music. HE ASKS: Now what was the song of the harp?

17. תָּא חֲזֵי, בְּשַׁעֲתָא דְּקוּדְשָׁא בְּרִיךְ הוּא אִתְּעַר לְגַבֵּי כָּל אִינּוּן רְתִיכִין, לְמֵיהַב לוֹן טַרְפָּא, כְּמָה דְּאוּקִימְנָא דִּכְתִיב, וַתָּקָם בְּעוֹד לַיְלָה וַתִּתֵּן טֶרֶף לְבֵיתָהּ וְחֹק לְנַעֲרוֹתֶיהָ. כְּדֵין, כֻּלְּהוּ בְּחֶדוּ, פַּתְחֵי וְאַמְרֵי,

אֱלֹהִים יְחָנֵּנוּ וִיבָרְכֵנוּ יָאֵר פָּנָיו אִתָּנוּ סֶלָה. כַּד רוּחַ צָפוֹן אִתְּעַר וְנָחִית לְעָלְמָא, נָשִׁיב וְאָמַר, לָדַעַת בָּאָרֶץ דַּרְכֶּךָ בְּכָל גּוֹיִם יְשׁוּעָתֶךָ. כִּנּוֹר בְּשַׁעֲתָא דְּאִיהוּ מְנַגְּנָא בֵּיהּ בְּהַהוּא, רוּחָא, פָּתַח וְאָמַר יוֹדוּךָ עַמִּים כֻּלָּם דָּוִד כַּד הֲוָה קָם, וְאִתְּעַר עֲלֵיהּ רוּחַ קֻדְשָׁא, פָּתַח וְאָמַר, אֶרֶץ נָתְנָה יְבוּלָהּ יְבָרְכֵנוּ אֱלֹהִים אֱלֹהֵינוּ יְבָרְכֵנוּ אֱלֹהִים וְיִירְאוּ אוֹתוֹ כָּל אַפְסֵי אָרֶץ. בְּגִין לְאַמְשָׁכָא טִיבוּ דְקוּדְשָׁא בְּרִיךְ הוּא, מֵעֵילָּא לְתַתָּא. לְבָתַר אָתָא דָוִד בְּרוּחַ קֻדְשָׁא, וְסִדֵּר לוֹן כַּחֲדָא, אִסְתַּכַּל בְּכֹלָּא בְּהַאי קְרָא דִכְנּוֹרָא, דְּשְׁלִימוּ דִּיקָרָא דְקוּדְשָׁא בְּרִיךְ הוּא עֵילָּא וְתַתָּא.

17. AND HE RESPONDS: Come and behold. In the hour that the Holy One, blessed be He, is roused towards the Chariots to give them nourishment, as it is written: "She rises while it is night and gives food to her household and a portion to her maidens" (Mishlei 31:15), then everyone opens joyfully: "Elohim be gracious to us and bless us; and cause His face to shine upon us Selah" (Tehilim 67:2). And when the north wind is awakened and descends upon the world, it blows, saying: "that Your way may be known upon earth, Your salvation among all nations" (Ibid. 3). And the harp, at the hour that it is played by that wind, opens and says, "let all the peoples give thanks to you." When he was awakened and roused by the Holy Spirit, David said: "The earth has yielded her increase; and Elohim, even our Elohim shall bless us. Elohim shall bless us; and let all the ends of the earth fear Him" (Ibid. 8), so as to draw down the goodness of the Holy One, blessed be He, from above downwards. Later, David, roused by the Holy Spirit, arranged all the songs into one, AS IT IS WRITTEN, "ELOHIM WILL BLESS US..." He observed this scriptural verse of the harp, "LET ALL THE PEOPLES GIVE THANKS TO YOU" (IBID. 5), for the glorification of the Holy One, blessed be He, is above and below, NAMELY "AND LET ALL THE ENDS OF THE EARTH FEAR HIM."

18. בְּשַׁעֲתָא דִּשְׁאַר עַמִּין אִתְכַּפְיָין, אַתְיָין וְאוֹדָאן לֵיהּ לְקוּדְשָׁא בְּרִיךְ הוּא, כֵּיוָן דְּאִינּוּן אִתְכַּפְיָין, וְאוֹדָן לֵיהּ, כְּדֵין אִשְׁתְּלִים יְקָרָא דְקוּדְשָׁא בְּרִיךְ הוּא עֵילָּא וְתַתָּא. בְּשַׁעֲתָא דְּאָתָא מֹשֶׁה לְפַרְעֹה וְאָמַר לֵיהּ יְיָ' אֱלֹהֵי הָעִבְרִים נִקְרָא עָלֵינוּ וְגוֹ', פָּתַח אִיהוּ וְאָמַר לֹא יָדַעְתִּי אֶת יְיָ'.

-10-

18. The hour when the other nations yielded came, and they acknowledged the Holy One, blessed be He. Once they yielded and acknowledged Him, the glory of the Holy One, blessed be He, became complete above and below. In the hour that Moses came to Pharaoh and said to him, "the Elohim of the Hebrews had met with us," Pharaoh replied, "I know not Hashem..."

19. וּבָעָא קוּדְשָׁא בְּרִיךְ הוּא, דְּיִתְיָיִקַר שְׁמֵיהּ בְּאַרְעָא, כְּמָה דְּאִיהוּ יַקִּירָא לְעֵילָּא, כֵּיוָן דְּאַלְקֵי לֵיהּ וּלְעַמֵּיהּ, אָתָא וְאוֹדֵי לֵיהּ לְקוּדְשָׁא בְּרִיךְ הוּא, דִּכְתִּיב, יְיָ' הַצַּדִּיק. אִיהוּ דַּהֲוָה מַלְכָּא קְרוֹפִינוֹס דְּכָל עָלְמָא, כֵּיוָן דְּאִיהוּ אוֹדֵי, כָּל שְׁאַר מַלְכִין אוֹדוּן, דִּכְתִּיב, אָז נִבְהֲלוּ אַלּוּפֵי אֱדוֹם.

19. When the Holy One, blessed be He, desired that His name be glorified on earth as it is above, after He struck him and his nation, he came and acknowledged the Holy One, blessed be He, as it is written: "Hashem is righteous" (Shemot 9:27). The instant he, who was the most important king in the world, acknowledged Him, all the other kings acknowledged, as it is written: "then the chiefs of Edom shall be amazed" (Shemot 15:15).

20. אָתָא יִתְרוֹ, כּוֹמָרָא עִלָּאָה וְרַבְרְבָא, רַב מְמָנָא דְּכָל טַעֲוָון אַחֲרָנִין, וְאוֹדֵי לֵיהּ לְקוּדְשָׁא בְּרִיךְ הוּא, וְאָמַר עַתָּה יָדַעְתִּי כִּי גָדוֹל יְיָ' מִכָּל הָאֱלֹהִים, כְּדֵין אִסְתַּלָּק וְאִתְיָיִקַר קוּדְשָׁא בְּרִיךְ הוּא בִּיקָרֵיהּ עֵילָּא וְתַתָּא, וּלְבָתַר יָהַב אוֹרַיְיתָא בִּשְׁלִימוּ, דְּשַׁלְטָנוּ עַל כֹּלָּא.

20. Jethro came, the great and supreme priest, appointed ruler over the whole pagan world, and acknowledged the Holy One, blessed be He, saying: "I now know that Hashem is supreme over all Elohim." Then the Holy One, blessed be He, was exalted in His glory from above and below, and afterwards He gave the Torah in the completeness of His dominion.

21. אר"ש לְרַ' אֶלְעָזָר בְּרֵיהּ, ע"ד כְּתִיב, יוֹדוּךָ עַמִּים אֱלֹהִים עַמִּים כּוּלָם. אָתָא רַ' אֶלְעָזָר וְנָשִׁיק יְדוֹי. בָּכָה רַ' אַבָּא וְאָמַר, כְּרַחֵם אָב עַל בָּנִים. מַאן יְרַחֵם עַל רַ' אֶלְעָזָר, וּלְאַשְׁלְמָא מִלּוֹי, בַּר רְחִימוּ דְמָר, זַכָּאָה חוּלְקָנָא, דְּזָכֵינָא לְמִשְׁמַע מִלִּין אִלֵּין קַמֵּיהּ, דְּלָא נִכְסוֹף

בְּהוּ לְעָלְמָא דְּאָתֵי.

21. Rabbi Shimon said to his son, Rabbi Elazar: Regarding this it is written, "Let all peoples praise You, O Elohim; let all the peoples give thanks to You." Then Rabbi Elazar came and kissed the hand of his father. Rabbi Aba wept and said: "As a father pities his children" (Tehilim 103:13). Who will have pity on Rabbi Elazar and bring his words to completion, except by the love of my master? How happy can we consider ourselves that we were privileged to hear these words so that we shall not be ashamed through them in the World to Come!

22. אָמַר רַבִּי אַבָּא, הָא כֹּהֵן אוֹן לָא כְּתִיב בְּיִתְרוֹ, כֹּהֵן מִדְיָן כְּתִיב. א״ל, כֹּלָא אִיהוּ חַד. בְּקַדְמֵיתָא חָמוּי דְּיוֹסֵף, כֹּהֵן אוֹן אִקְרֵי. וּלְבָתַר חָמוּי דְּמֹשֶׁה, כֹּהֵן מִדְיָן. וְכֹלָא רָזָא חֲדָא, דְּהָא אִלֵּין תְּרֵין מֹשֶׁה וְיוֹסֵף. בְּדַרְגָּא דְּרָזָא חֲדָא קַיְימִין, בְּרָזָא דְּאָת וָ״ו, תְּרֵין וָוִין כַּחֲדָא. וּמַה דְּאִתְּמַר כֹּהֵן מִדְיָן, רָזָא דָּא אֵשֶׁת מִדְיָנִים.

22. Rabbi Aba said: It was not written that Jethro was a priest of On, but rather of Midian. He said to him: It is all one. At first the father-in-law of Joseph was called a priest of On; afterwards, the father-in-law of Moses was called a priest of Midian. For all are of the same secret. THE PRIEST OF MIDIAN IS SIMILAR TO THE PRIEST OF ON. For these two, Moses and Joseph, are at the same grade of secret, the secret of the letter *Vav* THAT IS FULLY SPELLED WITH two *Vavs* together; THE FIRST *VAV* REFERS TO MOSES, TIFERET; THE SECOND *VAV* IS JOSEPH, YESOD. And what is said of the priest of Midian is the secret of a contentious (Heb. *Midianim*) woman.

23. אָרִים יְדוֹי עַל רֵישֵׁיה ר׳ אַבָּא וּבָכָה, אָמַר, נְהִירוּ דְּאוֹרַיְיתָא סַלְקָא הַשְׁתָּא עַד רוֹם רְקִיעָא דְּכָרְסַיָיא עִלָּאָה, לְבָתַר דְּיִסְתַּלַק מֹר מֵעָלְמָא, מַאן יַנְהִיר נְהִירוּ דְּאוֹרַיְיתָא. וַוי לְעָלְמָא דְּיִשְׁתְּאַר יָתוֹם מִינָךְ. אֲבָל מִלִּין דְּמֹר יִתְנְהִירוּ בְּעָלְמָא עַד דְּיֵיתֵי מַלְכָּא מְשִׁיחָא וּכְדֵין כְּתִיב, וּמָלְאָה הָאָרֶץ דֵּעָה אֶת יְיָ׳ וְגוֹ׳.

23. Rabbi Aba raised his hands to his head and cried, saying: The light of the Torah now reaches the highest throne in heaven. When the master passes

away from earth, who will light the lamp of the Torah? Woe to the world which will be orphaned from you. However, the words of the master will shine in the world until there comes the King Messiah, and then it is written: "the earth shall be full of the knowledge of Hashem" (Yeshayah 11:9).

24. וַיִּשְׁמַע יִתְרוֹ כֹּהֵן וְגוֹ', רַבִּי חִיָּיא אָמַר, הַאי קְרָא אִית לְאִסְתַּכְּלָא בֵּיהּ, בְּקַדְמֵיתָא כְּתִיב, אֵת כָּל אֲשֶׁר עָשָׂה אֱלֹהִים לְמֹשֶׁה, וּלְבָתַר כְּתִיב כִּי הוֹצִיא יְיָ'. אֶלָּא רָזָא דָא אֵת כָּל אֲשֶׁר עָשָׂה אֱלֹהִים, דָּא שְׁמָא דְאָגִין עַל מֹשֶׁה וְעַל יִשְׂרָאֵל, וְלָא אִתְעֲדֵי מִנַּיְיהוּ בְּגָלוּתָא. וּלְבָתַר, שְׁמָא עִלָּאָה אַפִּיק לוֹן מִמִּצְרַיִם. דְּהָא שְׁמָא קַדִּישָׁא דְּאַפִּיק לוֹן, בְּרָזָא דְיוֹבְלָא הֲוָה.

24. "When Jethro..." Rabbi Chiya said: We should look further into this verse. In the first instance it is written: "Everything that Elohim did for Moses" (Shemot 18:1). Later it is written: "and that Hashem has brought Yisrael out" (Ibid.). HE ANSWERS: This is the secret. "Everything that Elohim did," WHICH IS MALCHUT, is the Name that protected Moses and Yisrael, and did not move from them in exile. Later it was the Supreme Name which brought them out of Egypt, for the Name that brought them forth FROM EGYPT is the principle of Jubilee, WHICH IS BINAH.

25. ד"א אֵת כָּל אֲשֶׁר עָשָׂה אֱלֹהִים לְמֹשֶׁה, כַּד אִתְרְמֵי לְנַהֲרָא, וְכַד שֵׁזִיב לֵיהּ מֵחַרְבָּא דְּפַרְעֹה, וּלְיִשְׂרָאֵל עַמּוֹ, דִּכְתִיב, וַיִּשְׁמַע אֱלֹהִים אֶת נַאֲקָתָם. וּכְתִיב וְכַאֲשֶׁר יְעַנּוּ אוֹתוֹ כֵּן יִרְבֶּה וְכֵן יִפְרֹץ.

25. Another interpretation. "Everything that Elohim did for Moses," refers to when he was thrown into the river and was saved from the sword of Pharaoh. And "for Yisrael, His people," is as it is written: "And Elohim heard their groaning" (Shemot 2:24), and: "But the more they afflicted them, the more they multiplied and grew" (Shemot 1:12).

26. וַיִּשְׁמַע יִתְרוֹ כֹּהֵן מִדְיָן. רַבִּי יוֹסֵי פָּתַח, פְּדוּת שָׁלַח לְעַמּוֹ צִוָּה לְעוֹלָם בְּרִיתוֹ קָדוֹשׁ וְנוֹרָא שְׁמוֹ. מַאי שְׁנָא, בְּכָל שְׁאָר קְרָאֵי, דִּבְכֻלְּהוּ, תְּרֵין תֵּיבִין מֵאַלְפָא בֵּיתָא, וּבְהַאי קְרָא, וּבִקְרָא דַאֲבַתְרֵיהּ, תְּלַת תְּלַת.

אֶלָּא, בְּגִין לְאַשְׁלְמָא שִׁית סְטְרִין, בְּהַאי אַלְפָא בֵּיתָא, הַאי לָקֳבֵל תְּלַת פּוּרְקָנִין דְּיִשְׂרָאֵל, בַּר פּוּרְקָנָא קַדְמָאָה. קְרָא אַחֲרָא, לָקֳבֵל תּוֹרָה נְבִיאִים וּכְתוּבִים. וְכֹלָּא תַּלְיָא בְּהַאי חָכְמָה.

26. "When Jethro, the priest of Midian…" Rabbi Yosi began the discussion, saying: "He sent redemption to His people. He has commanded His covenant forever. Holy and revered is His Name" (Tehilim 111:9). HE ASKS: Why is there a difference? In all other verses, each verse has two letters in alphabetical order, SUCH AS THE VERSE BEFORE, WHICH IS SPELLED WITH TWO LETTERS, *SAMECH* AND *AYIN*. HOWEVER, in this verse, and the verse following it, there are three each. IN THIS VERSE, THERE ARE THREE LETTERS AND THE VERSE FOLLOWING HAS THREE LETTERS. THE REPLY: This is in order to complete six aspects by the alphabet, WHICH ARE THE THREE REDEMPTIONS OF YISRAEL AND THE THREE DIVISIONS OF THE SCRIPTURES – THE TORAH, THE PROPHETS AND THE WRITINGS. THIS VERSE corresponds to the three redemptions of Yisrael, BABYLON, GREECE AND EDOM, apart from the first redemption FROM EGYPT, WHICH HAD ALREADY TAKEN PLACE. The last verse corresponds to the Torah, the Prophets and the Writings. And everything is dependent upon this wisdom. SINCE THE TORAH, THE PROPHETS AND THE WRITINGS DEPEND AND COME FROM WISDOM, THE FOLLOWING VERSE THEREFORE BEGINS WITH: "THE BEGINNING OF CHOCHMAH."

27. פְּדוּת שָׁלַח לְעַמּוֹ, כַּד פָּרִיק קוּדְשָׁא בְּרִיךְ הוּא לְיִשְׂרָאֵל, מִגָּלוּתָא דְּמִצְרַיִם, וְעָבֵד לוֹן נִסִּין וּגְבוּרָן. צִוָּה לְעוֹלָם בְּרִיתוֹ, כַּד אָתָא יִתְרוֹ, וְקַבִּיל לֵיהּ קוּדְשָׁא בְּרִיךְ הוּא, וְקָרִיב לֵיהּ לְפוּלְחָנֵיהּ. וּמִתַּמָּן, אִתְקְרִיבוּ כָּל אִינּוּן גִּיּוֹרִין, תְּחוֹת גַּדְפוֹי דִּשְׁכִינְתָּא, מִתַּמָּן וּלְהָלְאָה, קָדוֹשׁ וְנוֹרָא שְׁמוֹ. דְּהָא כְּדֵין אִתְקַדָּשׁ שְׁמֵיהּ דְּקוּדְשָׁא בְּרִיךְ הוּא, דְּהָא יִתְקַדַּשׁ שְׁמָא קַדִּישָׁא, כַּד אִתְּבַר, וְאִתְכַּפְיָא סִטְרָא אַחֲרָא, כְּמָה דַּהֲוָה בְּיִתְרוֹ.

27. Another interpretation of: "He sent redemption to His people," is when the Holy One, blessed be He, brought forth Yisrael from the land of Egypt and caused mighty deeds and miracles. "He had commanded His covenant forever." This is when Jethro came and was received by the Holy One, blessed be He, who brought him closer to His worship, and so all proselytes

were brought near under the wings of the Shechinah. From then onward, "holy and revered is His name." For then the Holy Name of the Holy One, blessed be He, became hallowed. The Holy Name becomes further hallowed when the Other Side becomes broken and yielding, as it was with Jethro.

28. וַיִּשְׁמַע יִתְרוֹ וְגוֹ', וְכִי יִתְרוֹ שָׁמַע, וְכָל עָלְמָא לֹא שַׁמְעוּ, וְהָא כְּתִיב, שָׁמְעוּ עַמִּים יִרְגָּזוּן. אֶלָּא, כָּל עָלְמָא שָׁמְעוּ, וְלָא אִתְּבָּרוּ, וְאִיהוּ שָׁמַע וְאִתְּבַּר, וְאִתְכַּפְיָא מִקַּמֵּיהּ דְּקוּדְשָׁא בְּרִיךְ הוּא, וְאִתְקְרַב לְדַחַלְתֵּיהּ.

28. "When Jethro…" HE ASKS: Only Jethro heard, while the rest of the world did not hear? Is it not written: "The people shall hear, and be afraid" (Shemot 15:14)? HE ANSWERS: Indeed, the whole world did hear, but they were not broken. THEREFORE, IT WAS AS IF THEY DID NOT HEAR. But he heard, and was broken and yielded before the Holy One, blessed be He, and was brought near to fearing Him. THEREFORE HIS IS INDEED A HEARING.

29. רַבִּי אַבָּא אָמַר, בְּכַמָּה אֲתַר תָּנֵינָן, דְּקוּדְשָׁא בְּרִיךְ הוּא, כָּל מַה דְּעָבֵד לְעֵילָא וְתַתָּא כֹּלָא אִיהוּ קְשׁוֹט, וְעוֹבָדָא דִּקְשׁוֹט. וְלֵית לָךְ מִלָּה בְּעָלְמָא דְּבָעֵי בַּר נָשׁ לְדַחְיָא לֵיהּ מִנֵּיהּ, וּלְאַנְהָגָא בֵּיהּ קְלָנָא, דְּהָא כֻּלְּהוּ עוֹבָדָא דִּקְשׁוֹט אִינּוּן, וְכֹלָּא אִצְטְרִיךְ בְּעָלְמָא.

29. Rabbi Aba said: In many places we have learned that whatever the Holy One, blessed be He, does above or below, is all true and His works are true. And there is nothing in the world that man needs to reject or find despicable, for all are works of truth, and are all needed in the world.

30. דְּהָא זִמְנָא חֲדָא, הֲוָה ר' אֶלְעָזָר אָזִיל בְּאָרְחָא, וַהֲוָה אָזִיל עַמֵּיהּ ר' חִזְקִיָּה, חָמוּ חַד חִוְיָא, קָם ר' חִזְקִיָּה לְמִקְטְלֵיהּ. א"ל ר' אֶלְעָזָר, שְׁבִיק לֵיהּ לָא תִּקְטְלִינֵיהּ. א"ל, וְהָא מִלָּה בִּישָׁא אִיהוּ, דְּקָטִיל בְּנֵי נָשָׁא. א"ל לְר' חִזְקִיָּה, וְהָא כְּתִיב אִם יִשּׁוֹךְ הַנָּחָשׁ בְּלֹא לָחַשׁ. לָא נָשִׁיךְ חִוְיָא לְבַר נָשׁ, עַד דִּלְחֲשִׁין לֵיהּ מִלְּעֵילָא, וְאַמְרֵי לֵיהּ זִיל קְטִיל לֵיהּ לִפְלָנַיָּא.

30. It once happened that Rabbi Elazar was walking along the road, accompanied by Rabbi Chizkiyah. They saw a snake and Rabbi Chizkiyah rose to kill it. Rabbi Elazar said to him: Leave it alone, do not kill it. He replied to him: But this is an evil thing that kills human beings. He said to Rabbi Chizkiyah: But it is written, "If the serpent bites and can not be charmed (lit. 'without a charm')" (Kohelet 10:11). The snake does not bite a person unless it is whispered to from above and ordered, 'Go and kill that person'!

31. וְלִזְמְנִין כְּמָה דְּעָבֵיד הַאי, הָכִי נָמֵי שֵׁזִיב לְבַר נָשׁ, מְמַלְלִין אַחֲרָנִין, וְעַל יְדוֹי אַרְחִישׁ קוּדְשָׁא בְּרִיךְ הוּא נִיסָא לִבְנֵי נָשָׁא, וְכֹלָּא בִּידָא דְּקוּדְשָׁא בְּרִיךְ הוּא תַּלְיָא, וְכֹלָּא אִיהוּ עוֹבָדֵי יְדוֹי, וְאִצְטְרִיךְ עָלְמָא לְהוּ, וְאִי לָאו דְּאִיצְטְרִיךְ לוֹן עָלְמָא, לָא עֲבֵד לוֹן קוּדְשָׁא בְּרִיךְ הוּא. וְע"ד לָא בָּעֵי בַּר נָשׁ לְאַנְהָגָא בְּהוּ קָלָנָא בְּמִלֵּי דְעָלְמָא. בְּמִלּוֹי וּבְעוֹבָדוֹי דְּקוּדְשָׁא בְּרִיךְ הוּא עאכ"ו.

31. At times, just as it does this, so does it save man from other things. And thus, by its hand does the Holy One perform a miracle for men. Everything is in the hands of the Holy One, blessed be He, for it is all His creation. The world needs them. For if the world did not need them, the Holy One, blessed be He, would not have created them. Therefore man must not conduct himself in a despicable manner with things of the world; how much more so with the words or the acts of the Holy One, blessed be He.

32. פָּתַח וְאָמַר, וַיַּרְא אֱלֹהִים אֶת כָּל אֲשֶׁר עָשָׂה וְהִנֵּה טוֹב מְאֹד. וַיַּרְא אֱלֹהִים: דָּא אֱלֹהִים חַיִּים. וַיַּרְא: דְּאִסְתַּכַּל לְאַנְהָרָא לוֹן, וּלְאַשְׁגָּחָא לוֹן. אֶת כָּל אֲשֶׁר עָשָׂה כֹּלָּא בִּכְלָלָא חֲדָא, עֵילָא וְתַתָּא. וְהִנֵּה טוֹב: דָּא סִטְרָא דִּימִינָא. מְאֹד: דָּא סִטְרָא דִּשְׂמָאלָא, וְהָא אוֹקִמוּהָ, טוֹב: דָּא מַלְאַךְ חַיִּים מְאֹד: דָּא מַלְאַךְ הַמָּוֶת. וְכֹלָּא רָזָא חֲדָא. רָזָא הוּא, לְאִינוּן דְּמִסְתַּכְּלֵי בְּרָזָא דְחָכְמְתָא.

32. He opened the discussion with the verse: "And Elohim saw everything that He had made and, behold, it was very good" (Beresheet 1:31). "And Elohim saw," refers to living Elohim, WHICH IS BINAH; "And Elohim

saw," MEANS He was intent upon giving them Light, and guarding them; "everything that He had made," is everything united, above and below; "very," is the left side; "good," is the right side. As it was already established, "very," is the Angel of Death; "good," is the Angel of Life. It is all one secret, a secret to those who observe the mystery of Wisdom.

33. וַיַּרְא אֱלֹהִים אֶת כָּל אֲשֶׁר עָשָׂה. בְּכָל עוֹבָדָא דִּבְרֵאשִׁית, כְּתִיב, וַיַּרְא אֱלֹהִים כִּי טוֹב, וְהָכָא וַיַּרְא אֱלֹהִים אֶת כָּל אֲשֶׁר עָשָׂה. אֱלֹהִים לְתַתָּא, שָׁלִיט עַל תַּתָּאֵי. אֱלֹהִים לְעֵילָּא, שָׁלִיט עַל עִלָּאֵי. דָּא אִיהוּ רָזָא דֶּאֱלֹהִים חַיִּים, דְּאַנְהִיר וְאַדְלִיק כָּל אִינּוּן בּוֹצִינִין עִלָּאִין וְתַתָּאִין, וּמִתַּמָּן נָפְקִין כָּל אִינּוּן נְהוֹרִין לְאַנְהָרָא.

33. "And Elohim saw everything that He had made." HE ASKS: Throughout the works of Creation, it is written: "And Elohim saw that it was good." But here, it is written: "And Elohim saw everything He had made." HE ANSWERS: The lower Elohim, MALCHUT, rules those below. The Elohim above, BINAH, rules those above. ELOHIM ABOVE, THAT RULES THOSE ABOVE, is an aspect of the Living Elohim, WHICH IS BINAH. HENCE, "AND ELOHIM SAW EVERYTHING HE HAD MADE," as He illuminated and lit all candles above and below, and from there all lights emerge to illuminate.

תוספתא

34. בְּטְמִירוּ דִּטְמִירִין, אִתְרְשִׁים רְשִׁימוּ חַד, דְּלָא אִתְחֲזֵי וְלָא אִתְגַּלְיָא. הַהוּא רְשִׁימוּ, רָשִׁים וְלָא רָשִׁים. מָארֵי דְּסָכְלְתָנוּ, וּפִקְחִין דְּעַיְינִין, לָא יַכְלִין לְמֵיקַם בֵּיהּ. אִיהוּ קִיּוּמָא דְּכֹלָּא. הַהוּא רְשִׁימוּ אִיהוּ זְעֵיר, דְּלָא אִתְחֲזְיָא וְלָא אִתְגַּלְיָא. קַיְימָא בִּרְעוּתָא, לְקַיְימָא כֹּלָּא. לְנַטְלָא מַה דְּנַטְלָא, מִמַּה דְּלֵית בֵּיהּ רְשִׁימוּ, וְלָא רְעוּתָא, דְּלָא אִתְחֲזֵי.

Tosefta (addendum)

34. Upon the most hidden of all that is hidden, one imprint was impressed that is neither seen, nor revealed. This impression is an impression yet not

an impression. Those of understanding and open eyes, GIFTED IN WISDOM, can not understand its nature. It maintains everything. This impression is so small as to be unseen and not revealed, existing there by the will to sustain all. It receives whatever it receives from that which has no impression or will, and is not visible.

35. הַהוּא רְשִׁימוּ בָּעָא לְאַחֲפָיָא גַּרְמֵיה, וְעָבַד לֵיה לְגַרְמֵיה, לְאִתְטַמְּרָא בֵּיה, חַד הֵיכָלָא. הַהוּא הֵיכָלָא אַפִּיק לֵיה מִגַּרְמֵיה, וּמָתַח לֵיה בִּמְתִיחוּ רַב וְסַגִּיא לְכָל סִטְרִין, אוֹקִיר לֵיה בִּלְבוּשֵׁי יְקָר, פָּתַח לֵיה חַמְשִׁין תַּרְעִין.

35. This impression desired to veil itself, and created for itself a chamber with which to be covered. It drew it from itself, and extended it with great expansion from all sides and adorned it with valuable attire, thereby opening up in it fifty gates.

36. לְגוֹ בְּגוֹ, אִתְטָמַר וְאִתְגְּנִיז הַהוּא רְשִׁימוּ. כֵּיוָן דְּאִתְגְּנִיז בֵּיה, וְעָאל בְּגַוֵּיה, אִתְמַלְיָא נְהוֹרָא. מֵהַהוּא נְהִירוּ, נַבְעִין נְהוֹרִין, וְנִצוֹצִין נָפְקִין מֵאִינּוּן תַּרְעִין, וְנָהֲרִין כֹּלָּא.

36. In the innermost part IN THAT CHAMBER, that impression was treasured and concealed. After being concealed, it was penetrated by light. From this light there issued forth lights and sparks, and it emerged through the gates of the chamber and shone upon everything.

37. הַהוּא הֵיכָלָא אִתְחַפְיָיא בְּשִׁית יְרִיעָן. אִינּוּן שִׁית יְרִיעָן, אִינּוּן חֲמֵשׁ. לְגוֹ בְּגוֹ אִינּוּן יְרִיעָן, קַיְּימָא חַד יְרִיעָא מְרַקְמָא, בְּהַהוּא יְרִיעָה אִתְחַפְיָיא הַהוּא הֵיכָלָא, מִנֵּיה אַשְׁגַּח וְחָמָא לְכֹלָּא.

37. This chamber is cloaked, THAT IS TO SAY, CLOTHED with six screens. Yet these six screens are but five. In the innermost part of these screens, there prevails one embroidered screen. It is with this screen that the chamber is covered AND CLOTHED. From within, it monitors and sees everything.

38. הַאי הֵיכְלָא אִיהוּ פְּקִיחָא דְעַיְינִין, דְלָא נָיִים. אִיהוּ אַשְׁגַּח תָּדִיר
לְאַנְהָרָא לְתַתָּא, מִגּוֹ נְהִירוּ דְּהַהוּא רְשִׁימוּ. הַהוּא סָכְלְתָנוּ, חָכְמְתָא
טְמִירְתָּא, רְעוּ דִרְעוּתִין הֲוֵי גָּנִיז וְטָמִיר, וְלָא אִתְגַּלְיָא, קַיְימָא וְלָא
קַיְימָא. בְּרִיךְ הוּא מְטָמִיר דְּטָמִירוּ, בְּרִיךְ הוּא לְעָלַם וּלְעָלְמֵי עַד אָמֵן.

(ע״כ תוספתא)

38. This chamber is the opening of eyes – so that it does not sleep. It is
forever attentive to shed light below, out of the light of the impression. This
understanding, this concealed wisdom and the will of wills, is concealed and
cloaked, and not revealed; it exists yet does not exist. Blessed be it from the
concealed of all the concealed. Blessed be it forever and eternally, Amen.

(End of Tosefta)

39. תָּא חֲזֵי, יִתְרוֹ הוּא דְּיָהַב עֵיטָא לְמֹשֶׁה, עַל תִּקוּנָא דְּדִינִין, הָכִי
אִצְטְרִיךְ. וְרָזָא דָּא דְּאוֹדֵי לֵיהּ לְקוּדְשָׁא בְּרִיךְ הוּא, וְסִדֵּר קַמֵּיהּ תִּקוּנָא
דְּדִינוֹי, לְאַחֲזָאָה מַה דִּכְתִיב, כִּי הַמִּשְׁפָּט לֵאלֹהִים הוּא, וְלָא לְסִטְרָא
אָחֳרָא. וְדִינִין לְיִשְׂרָאֵל אִתְיְיהִיבוּ, וְלָא לְאָחֳרָא, דִּכְתִיב חֻקָּיו וּמִשְׁפָּטָיו
לְיִשְׂרָאֵל. וְת״ח, לָא יַנְהִיג בַּר נָשׁ קְלָנָא בְּאָחֳרָא, וּמִלָּה דְּהֶדְיוֹטָא,
מִלָּה אִיהוּ. דְּהָא בְּמֹשֶׁה כְּתִיב, וַיִּשְׁמַע מֹשֶׁה לְקוֹל חוֹתְנוֹ וְגוֹ׳.

39. Come and behold: it was Jethro who gave advice to Moses on the
administration of justice. And this is how it should be. And this is the secret
of acknowledging the Holy One, blessed be He, and arranging openly the
administration of justice: to teach what is written, "for the Judgment is
Elohim's" (Devarim 1:17), and not of the Other Side. And these laws were
given to Yisrael and to none other, as it is written: "His statutes and His
judgments to Yisrael" (Tehilim 147:19). Come and behold: man must not
despise another, and the words from a layman are still words, as it is written
of Moses, "And Moses hearkened to the voice of his father-in-law."

40. וַיִּשְׁמַע יִתְרוֹ וְגוֹ׳. פָּתַח וְאָמַר עַל כֵּן אוֹדְךָ בַגּוֹיִם יְיָ׳ וּלְשִׁמְךָ
אֲזַמֵּרָה. דָּוִד מַלְכָּא אָמַר דָּא בְּרוּחַ קֻדְשָׁא, בְּשַׁעֲתָא דְּחָמָא, דְּהָא יְקָרָא

דְּקוּדְשָׁא בְּרִיךְ הוּא, לָא אִסְתָּלִיק בִּסְלִיקוּ וְלָא אִתְיָיקְרָא בְּעָלְמָא, אֶלָּא מִסְטְרָא דִשְׁאַר עַמִּין. וְאִי תֵּימָא, הָא קוּדְשָׁא בְּרִיךְ הוּא לָא אִתְיָיקַר בְּעָלְמָא, אֶלָּא בְּגִינֵיהוֹן דְּיִשְׂרָאֵל. הָכִי הוּא וַדַּאי, דְּהָא יִשְׂרָאֵל אִינּוּן הֲווֹ יְסוֹדָא דִשְׁרָגָּא לְאַנְהֲרָא, אֲבָל כַּד שְׁאַר עַמִּין אָתָאן וְאוֹדָן לֵיהּ, בִּשְׁעַבּוּדָא דִּיקָרָא דְּקוּדְשָׁא בְּרִיךְ הוּא, כְּדֵין אִתּוֹסַף יְסוֹדָא דִשְׁרָגָּא, וְאִתְתַּקַּף עַל כָּל עוֹבָדוֹי. בַּחֲבוּרָא חֲדָא, וְשַׁלִּיט קוּדְשָׁא בְּרִיךְ הוּא בִּלְחוֹדוֹי עֵילָא וְתַתָּא.

40. "When Jethro…heard" He opened the discussion, saying: "Therefore I will give thanks to You, Hashem, among the nations, and sing praises to Your Name" (Tehilim 18:50). King David said this, in the spirit of Holiness, when he saw that only the other nations exalted and glorified the Holy One, blessed be He, in the world. But if you say that the Holy One, blessed be He, exalts Himself in the world only for Yisrael, this is certainly so. For Yisrael is the base of the shine of the candle. Yet when the other nations come forth to acknowledge Him through worship of the glory of the Holy One, blessed be He, then the base of the candle increases and is strengthened. And then the Holy One, blessed be He, rules alone, above and below.

41. כְּגַוְונָא דָא, כָּל עָלְמָא, דְּחִילוּ וְאֵימָתָא נָפַל עָלַיְיהוּ מִקַּמֵּי קוּדְשָׁא בְּרִיךְ הוּא. וְכֵיוָן דְּאָתָא יִתְרוֹ, דְּאִיהוּ כּוֹמְרָא עִלָּאָה, דְּכָל טַעֲוָון אַחֲרָנִין, כְּדֵין אִתְתַּקַּף יְקָרָא דְּקוּדְשָׁא בְּרִיךְ הוּא עַל כֹּלָּא.

41. It happened that great fear and terror of the Holy One, blessed be He, fell upon the entire world WHEN THEY HEARD OF THE MIRACLES OCCURRING DURING THE EXODUS FROM EGYPT. And when Jethro came, the High Priest of the heathen deities, then the glory of the Holy One, blessed be He, was strengthened and He ruled over all.

42. בְּגִין, דְּכָל עָלְמָא, כַּד שָׁמְעוּ שֵׁמַע גְּבוּרְתֵּיהּ דְּקוּדְשָׁא בְּרִיךְ הוּא, זָעוּ. וְכֻלְּהוּ הֲווֹ מִסְתַּכְּלָן בְּיִתְרוֹ, דְּאִיהוּ חַכִּים וְרַב מְמָנָא דְּכָל טַעֲוָון דְּעָלְמָא, כֵּיוָן דְּחָמוּ, דְּאִיהוּ אָתָא וּפָלַח לֵיהּ לְקוּדְשָׁא בְּרִיךְ הוּא, וְאָמַר

עַתָּה יָדַעְתִּי כִּי גָדוֹל יְיָ' מִכָּל הָאֱלֹהִים, כְּדֵין כֻּלְהוּ אִתְרַחֲקוּ
מִפּוּלְחָנֵיהוֹן, וְיָדְעוּ דְּלֵית בְּהוּ מַמָּשׁוּ. כְּדֵין אִתְיַיקַר יְקָרָא דִּשְׁמָא
קַדִּישָׁא דְּקוּדְשָׁא בְּרִיךְ הוּא, בְּכָל סִטְרִין. וְעַל דָּא אִתְרְשִׁים פַּרְשָׁתָא
דָּא בְּאוֹרַיְיתָא, וְשֵׁירוּתָא דְּפַרְשָׁתָּא הֲוָה בֵּיהּ בְּיִתְרוֹ.

42. For when the people of the entire world heard of the wonders of the
Holy One, blessed be He, they trembled. Then they looked up to Jethro, who
was the wisest and was appointed over all of the heathen deities. When they
saw that he came to worship the Holy One, blessed be He, saying: "Now I
know that Hashem is greater than all the Elohim," they gave up their idol
worship, realizing their idols were worthless. At that time, the glory of the
Holy Name of the Holy One, blessed be He, was exalted on all sides.
Therefore this scriptural chapter has been recorded in the Torah, with
Jethro's name at its beginning.

43. יִתְרוֹ חַד מֵחַכִּימִין דְּפַרְעֹה הֲוָה. תְּלַת חַכִּימִין הֲווֹ לֵיהּ לְפַרְעֹה, חַד
יִתְרוֹ, וְחַד אִיּוֹב, וְחַד בִּלְעָם. חַד יִתְרוֹ: דְּלָא הֲוָה פּוּלְחָנָא וּמְמַנָּא
וְשַׁמְּשָׁא וְכֹכְבָא דְּשָׁלִיט עַל שׁוּלְטָנֵיהּ, דְּלָא הֲוָה יָדַע פּוּלְחָנָא דְּאִתְחֲזֵי
לֵיהּ, וְהַהוּא שִׁמּוּשָׁא דִּילֵיהּ. בִּלְעָם, הֲוָה חַרְשָׁא בְּכָל מִינֵי חֲרָשִׁין בֵּין
בְּעוֹבָדָא בֵּין בְּמִלָּה.

43. Jethro was one of the advisors to Pharaoh. Pharaoh had three advisors:
Jethro, Job and Bilaam. One was Jethro, and there was no worship,
appointed minister, sun or star that ruled over his empire that he did not
know its appropriate service. Bilaam was a sorcerer in all manner of
enchantments, whether by act or by word.

44. אִיּוֹב הֲוָה דָּחִיל בִּדְחִילוּ, וּבַהַהוּא דְּחִילוּ דִּילֵיהּ הֲוָה עָקָרָא דִּילֵיהּ, בְּגִין
דְּמִלָּה דִּלְעֵילָא בֵּין דִּקְדוּשָׁה, בֵּין דְּסִטְרָא אַחֲרָא, לָא יָכִיל בַּר נָשׁ
לְאַמְשְׁכָא רוּחָא דִּלְעֵילָא לְתַתָּא וּלְמִקְרַב גַּבֵּיהּ, אֶלָּא בִּדְחִילוּ. וְיכַוֵּין
לִבֵּיהּ וּרְעוּתֵיהּ בִּדְחִילוּ וּתְבִירוּ דְּלִבָּא, וּכְדֵין יַמְשִׁיךְ לְתַתָּא רוּחָא
דִּלְעֵילָא וּרְעוּתָא דְּאִצְטְרִיךְ.

44. Job had fear. This reverence was his mainstay, IT WAS THE ESSENCE OF HIS STRENGTH. For a word above, whether it be Holy or of the Other Side, man can draw down the spirit from above and unite with it below, only with fear, by concentrating his heart and mind with fear, broken-heartedly. And only then can he draw down the spirit of above, and the needed wish.

45. וְאִי לָא יְשַׁוֵּי לְבֵּיהּ וּרְעוּתֵיהּ בִּדְחִילוּ לְהַהוּא סִטְרָא, לָא יָכִיל לְאִתְדַּבְּקָא בֵּיהּ רְעוּתֵיהּ, בַּר לְהָנֵי טוֹפְסֵי דְּקִיקִין, וְלָא בְּכֻלְּהוּ, בְּגִין דְּאִית בְּהוּ שָׁלְטָנִין, דְּאִצְטְרִיךְ לְגַבַּיְיהוּ, רְעוּתָא דְּלִבָּא וּדְחִילוּ. כ"ש אִינוּן מִלִּין עִלָּאִין, דְּאִצְטְרִיךְ דְּחִילוּ וְאֵימָתָא וּרְעוּתָא יַתִּיר.

45. And if he does not direct his heart and mind in fear to that side, then his mind cannot cling to it, only with diminutive images, and not even with all of them, since they are ruled by those who require meditation of the heart and fear, and even more so in the case of those supernal objects who require much more fear, terror, and intention.

46. יִתְרוֹ אִצְטְרִיךְ פּוּלְחָנֵיהּ דְּהַהוּא סִטְרָא תָּדִיר, בֵּין בְּזִמְנָא דְּאִצְטְרִיךְ לֵיהּ לְבַר נָשׁ, בֵּין בְּזִמְנָא דְּלָא אִצְטְרִיךְ לֵיהּ, בְּגִין דְּהַהוּא סִטְרָא יְהֵא דָּבִיק לְגַבֵּיהּ, בְּשַׁעֲתָא דְּאִצְטְרִיךְ לֵיהּ. בִּלְעָם אִתְדָּבַּק בְּאִינוּן חֲרָשִׁין, כְּמָה דְּאִתְּמַר.

46. Jethro had to worship that side continuously, whether his worshippers needed him or not, so that that side would cleave to him when he needed it. Bilaam was connected with that sorcery, as was stated before.

47. אִיּוֹב בְּסַגִּיאוּ דְּהַהוּא דְּחִילוּ דִּילֵיהּ אַהֲדַר בְּמִצְרַיִם לְמִדְחַל מִקַּמֵּיהּ דְּקוּדְשָׁא בְּרִיךְ הוּא, כַּד חָמָא אִינוּן גְּבוּרָן וְנִסִּין, דְּעָבַד קוּדְשָׁא בְּרִיךְ הוּא בְּמִצְרַיִם. יִתְרוֹ, לָא אַהֲדַר בְּכָל דָּא, עַד דְּנָפְקוּ יִשְׂרָאֵל מִמִּצְרַיִם, וְכָל אִינוּן קִשְׁרִין וְטִפְסִין דְּקָשִׁירוּ מִצְרָאֵי, לָא הֲווֹ כְּלוּם, וְנַפְקוּ. וּלְבָתַר דְּטָבַע לוֹן בְּיַמָּא, כְּדֵין תָּב, וְאַהֲדַר לְפוּלְחָנָא דְּקָבָּ"ה.

47. Due to an overpowering sense of fear within him, when Job witnessed

the miracles and mighty works the Holy One, blessed be He, had performed in Egypt, he returned to Egypt to worship the Holy One, blessed be He, in fear. Jethro did not convert to the worship of the Holy One, blessed be He, until the exodus from Egypt. All of the bonds and images that the Egyptians made were to no avail, for still they departed. And only when they drowned in the sea did Jethro convert to worship the Holy One, blessed be He.

48. בִּלְעָם לָא תָּב, וְלָא אַהְדָּר, דִּטְנוּפָא דְסִטְרָא אַחֲרָא הֲוָה מִתְדַּבַּק בֵּיה, וְעִם כָּל דָּא אִסְתַּכְּלוּתָא דְמֶרְחִיק הֲוָה מִסְתַּכֵּל, בְּגוֹ הַהוּא טְנוּפָא וְאִתְדַּבְּקוּתָא דְסִטְרָא אַחֲרָא. דְּהָא בְּסִטְרָא אַחֲרָא אִית נְהִירוּ דָּקִיק חַד, דְנָהִיר סַחֲרָנֵיה, כד״א וְנֹגַהּ לוֹ סָבִיב. וְדָא אִסְתַּכְּלוּתָא זְעֵיר הֲוָה מִסְתַּכֵּל מֵרְחִיק, וְלָא בְּכֻלְּהוּ מִלִּין.

48. Bilaam did not repent or convert, since the impurities of the Other Side still clung to him. And yet, he observed from a distance, and prophesied through the impurities and the clinging to the Other Side. For in the Other Side there is one small thread of light that surrounds it, as it is written: "And a brightness was about it" (Yechezkel 1:27). And he saw through this small brightness from afar, though not in all matters.

49. וְכַד הֲוָה מִסְתַּכֵּל מִלָּה זְעֵיר מֵהַהוּא נְהִירוּ, כְּבָתַר כּוֹתְלָא הֲוָה, אָמַר וְלָא יָדַע מַאי קָאָמַר. וַהֲוָה מִסְתַּכֵּל בְּהַהוּא נְהִירוּ בִּסְתִּימוּ דְּעֵינָא, וְאִתְגַּלְגֵּל עֵינָא, וְחָזֵי בַּר נָשׁ נְהוֹרָא סְתִימָא, וְלָא חֲזֵי. וְרָזָא דָּא שְׁתוּם הָעָיִן, וְאוּקְמוּהָ שְׁתוּם: סָתוּם, וְכֹלָּא חַד.

49. And when he perceived this small streak of light, it was as if from behind a wall, and he spoke, yet did not know what he said. He perceived this light as if with the white part of the eye – as when the eye rolls and one sees covered light, yet does see. And this is the secret of: "whose eyes are opened" (Bemidbar 24:15). And we learned that "opened (Heb. *satum*, spelled with the Hebrew letter *sin*)" MEANS closed (Heb. *satum*, with the Hebrew letter *Samech*). And all pertains to the same thing.

50. דְּהָא לֵית סִטְרָא אַחֲרָא, דְּלֵית בֵּיה נְהִירוּ זְעֵיר דָּקִיק מִסִּטְרָא דִקְדוּשָׁה, כְּגַוְונָא דִרוֹב חֶלְמִין, דִּבְסַגִּיאוּת תַּבְנָא, אִית חַד גַּרְעִינָא

-23-

דְּחָטִין. בַּר אִלֵּין טַפְסֵי דְּקִיקִין חֲצִיפִין, דְּכֻלְּהוּ מְסָאֲבֵי יַתִּיר. וּבְהוּ הֲוָה בִּלְעָם יוֹדַע.

50. There can always be found a small streak of light that comes from the side of Holiness, as in most dreams, where in a pile of straw there is one grain of wheat. Except for those minor images that are most unclean. And it was in these, that Bilaam knew.

51. זַכָּאָה חוּלָקֵיה דְּמֹשֶׁה, דְּאִיהוּ לְעֵילָא בְּכָל קְדוּשִׁין עִלָּאִין, וְאִסְתַּכַּל, בְּמַה דְּלָא אִתְיְיהִיב רְשׁוּ לְבַר נָשׁ אַחֲרָא בְּעָלְמָא לְאִסְתַּכְּלָא. וּכְמָה דְּבִלְעָם הֲוָה חָמֵי נְהִירוּ זְעֵיר דָּקִיק כְּמִבָּתַר כּוֹתְלָא, מִגּוֹ הַהוּא סִטְרָא אַחֲרָא. אוּף הָכִי מֹשֶׁה, מִגּוֹ נְהִירוּ עִילָּאָה רַב וְסַגִּי, הֲוָה חָמֵי לְתַתָּא כְּמִבָּתַר כּוֹתְלָא, חַד חֲשׁוֹכָא דָּקִיק, דְּאִתְחֲזֵי לֵיה. וְלָאו בְּכָל זִמְנָא, כְּמָה דְּבִלְעָם לָא הֲוָה מִסְתַּכֵּל הַהוּא נְהִירוּ בְּכָל זִמְנָא.

51. Happy is the lot of Moses, who is high above all other supernal sanctities. For he perceived that which no other man on earth was ever given permission to observe. And just as Bilaam saw a small light, fine and thin, as if behind a wall, from within the Other Side, so through the great supernal light of Holiness did Moses see below, as if from behind a wall, a fine streak of darkness. And he did not see it always, just as Bilaam did not always see that light.

52. זַכָּאָה חוּלָקֵיה דְּמֹשֶׁה נְבִיאָה מְהֵימְנָא, מַה כְּתִיב בֵּיה, וַיֵּרָא מַלְאַךְ יְיָ' אֵלָיו בְּלַבַּת אֵשׁ מִתּוֹךְ הַסְּנֶה. הַסְּנֶה וַדַּאי הֲוָה בְּגוֹ הַהוּא קְדוּשָׁה וְאִתְדַּבַּק בֵּיה. דְּכֹלָּא אִתְדְּבַק דָּא בְּדָא, טָהוֹר וְטָמֵא, לֵית טָהוֹר אֶלָּא מִגּוֹ טָמֵא.

52. Happy is the lot of Moses, the faithful prophet. For it is written about him: "And an Angel of Hashem appeared to him in a flame of fire out of the midst of a bush" (Shemot 3:2). "...a bush..." REFERS TO A KLIPAH, which was in Holiness and was connected to it. For all things connect one to another, the pure and the impure. There is no purity except from within impurity.

53. וְרָזָא דָּא, מִי יִתֵּן טָהוֹר מִטָּמֵא. קְלִיפָה וּמוֹחָא דָא בְּדָא סַלְקָא. וְדָא קְלִיפָה לָא יִתְעֲדֵי וְלָא יִתְּבַר, עַד זִמְנָא דִיקוּמוּן מֵתִין מֵעַפְרָא, כְּדֵין יִתְּבַר קְלִיפָה, וּנְהִירוּ יַנְהִיר בְּעָלְמָא בְּלָא סְתִימוּ מִגּוֹ מוֹחָא. זַכָּאִין אִינּוּן צַדִּיקַיָּא בְּעָלְמָא דֵין וּבְעָלְמָא דְּאָתֵי.

53. And this is the principle of: "Who can bring a clean thing out of an unclean?" (Iyov 14:4). The shell (Heb. *Klipah*) and the fruit are correlated, one with the other. And this Klipah will never be broken or be gone until the dead rise from the dust. Then the Klipah will be broken and the light will shine into the world, without any covering, from the inner part. Happy are the righteous in this world and in the World to Come.

2. "and her two sons"

A Synopsis

Three of the rabbis are wondering why the title verse says "her sons" instead of 'the sons of Moses'. Their comprehension is corrected by Rabbi Shimon, who tells them that the sons referred to belong to Jethro, not Moses, and that Jethro brought his whole family that they might enter under the wings of the Shechinah, who was joined celestially with Moses.

54. וְאֵת שְׁנֵי בָנֶיהָ, אָמַר רַבִּי חִיָּיא, וְכִי בָנֶיהָ וְלֹא בָּנָיו שֶׁל מֹשֶׁה. אֶלָּא, בְּגִין דְּאִיהִי אִשְׁתַּדְלַת אֲבַתְרַיְיהוּ, בְּלָא בַּעְלָהּ, קָרָא לוֹן אוֹרַיְיתָא בָּנֶיהָ, וְלֹא בָּנָיו. א״ר יוֹסֵי, אע״ג דִּבְנוֹי דְּמֹשֶׁה הֲווֹ. מִלָּה דִּקְשׁוֹט בָּנֶיהָ וַדַּאי. ר׳ אֶלְעָזָר אָמַר, הָא מֹשֶׁה הֲוָה מִזְדַּוֵּוג בַּאֲתָר אָחֳרָא קַדִּישָׁא עִלָּאָה, וְלָאו יְקָרָא דִילֵיהּ לְמִקְרֵי לוֹן בָּנָיו. הַשְׁתָּא אַף עַל גַּב דִּבְנוֹי הֲווֹ, בְּגִין יְקָרָא דְּהַהוּא אֲתָר דְּאִזְדַּוַּוג בֵּיהּ, קָרָא לוֹן בָּנֶיהָ הָכָא, לְבָתַר קָרָא לוֹן בָּנָיו מ״ט, בְּגִין דְּהַהוּא שַׁעֲתָא דְּמָטוּ, הֲוָה מֹשֶׁה מְמַלֵּל בִּשְׁכִינְתָּא. לְבָתַר דְּאִתְפְּרַשׁ וְנָפַק לְגַבֵּי חָמוּי, כְּדֵין כְּתִיב וַיָּבֹא יִתְרוֹ חֹתֵן מֹשֶׁה וּבָנָיו וְאִשְׁתּוֹ וְגוֹ׳.

54. "...and her two sons..." (Shemot 18:3). Rabbi Chiya said: Why are they called "her sons" and not 'the sons of Moses'? HE ANSWERS: Because she raised them without her husband, the Torah calls them "her sons," and not 'his sons'. Rabbi Yosi said: Even though they were the sons of Moses, THEY WERE, BY A SECRET PRINCIPLE, most certainly her sons. BECAUSE, Rabbi Elazar said: Moses united himself in another holy, celestial place, and it would not have been respectful to call them his sons. Now, even though they were his sons, because of the dignity of the place in which he united, WHICH WAS THE SHECHINAH, they were here called "her sons." Afterwards, they were called "his sons." What is the reason? Because when they reached MOSES, Moses was talking to the Shechinah. Later, when he separated FROM THE SHECHINAH and went out to meet his father-in-law, then it is written: "And Jethro, Moses's father-in-law, came, with his sons" (Ibid. 5).

55. אָמַר ר׳ שִׁמְעוֹן, אֶלְעָזָר אֶלְעָזָר, אֲנָא חֲמֵינָא בְּפַרְשָׁתָא דָא, דְּאַתְּ

שָׁארֵי מִלָּה כַּדְקָא יֵאוֹת, וְסִיּוּמָא לָאו הָכִי. וַדַּאי בְּגִין יְקָרָא דִּשְׁכִינְתָּא, אִזְדַּוְּוגַת עִלָּאָה דְּאִזְדָּוַּוג בֵּיה בְּמֹשֶׁה, כְּתִיב בָּנֶיהָ. וְאִי תֵימָא, וְהָא כְּתִיב וַיָּבֹא יִתְרוֹ חֹתֵן מֹשֶׁה וּבָנָיו וְאִשְׁתּוֹ אֶל מֹשֶׁה. אֶלָּא אִיהוּ כְּלָלָא חֲדָא. וּבָנָיו, בָּנָיו דְּיִתְרוֹ, דְּהָא לְבָתַר דְּאָתָא מֹשֶׁה לְגַבֵּיה, הֲווֹ לֵיה בְּנִין.

55. Rabbi Shimon said: Elazar, Elazar. I see in this portion that the beginning of your interpretation is quite proper, but the ending is not the way you interpret it. Certainly, because of the respect of the Shechinah, who was joined celestially with Moses, it is written "her sons." And though it is written, "And Jethro, Moses's father-in-law, came, with his sons and his wife to Moses," IT STATES "HIS SONS," which is inclusive, and the words "his sons," refer to the sons of Jethro. For after Moses came to him, he had sons.

56. וְהָכִי הֲוָה בְּיַעֲקֹב, דְּכֵיוָן דְּאָתָא לְגַבֵּיה דְּלָבָן, וְשַׁוֵּי דִּיוֹרֵיה בֵּיה, הֲווֹ לֵיה בְּנִין. אוּף הָכָא מֹשֶׁה, כֵּיוָן דְּשַׁוֵּי דִּיוֹרֵיה בְּיִתְרוֹ, הֲווֹ לֵיה לְיִתְרוֹ בְּנִין וְכָל בֵּיתֵיה אַיְיתֵי עִמֵּיה, לְמֵיעַל לוֹן תְּחוֹת גַּדְפֵּי דִּשְׁכִינְתָּא, וְיִתְרוֹ אָמַר לְמֹשֶׁה, אֲנִי חֹתֶנְךָ יִתְרוֹ בָּא אֵלֶיךָ וְאִשְׁתְּךָ וּשְׁנֵי בָנֶיהָ עִמָּה, וּשְׁנֵי בָנֶיהָ כְּתִיב, וְלָא כְּתִיב וּשְׁנֵי בָנֶיךָ. בְּנִין הֲווֹ לֵיה לְיִתְרוֹ, דִּכְתִיב וּבְנֵי קֵינִי חֹתֵן מֹשֶׁה עָלוּ מֵעִיר הַתְּמָרִים וּבְנוֹי שָׁבַק עִם מֹשֶׁה.

56. And so it was with Jacob. When he came to Laban and dwelt in his house, Laban had sons. Also here, when Moses dwelt with Jethro, he too had sons. And Jethro brought his whole family, so they might all enter together under the wings of the Shechinah. And Jethro said to Moses: "I, your father-in-law Jethro, am come to you, and your wife, and her two sons with her." And it is not written 'your two sons'. WHAT DO WE LEARN FROM THIS? That Jethro had children, as it is written: "And the children of the Kenite, Moses's father-in-law went up out of the city of palm trees" (Shoftim 1:16). And he left his sons with Moses.

3. "and Jethro, Moses's father-in-law, came"

A Synopsis

The discussion turns around the verse, "And many nations shall go and say, 'Come and let us go up to the mountain of Hashem'," and we learn that the mountain is symbolic of conversion, to proselytize the soul.

57. וַיָּבֹא יִתְרוֹ חֹתֵן מֹשֶׁה. פָּתַח וְאָמַר, וְהָלְכוּ עַמִּים רַבִּים וְאָמְרוּ לְכוּ וְנַעֲלֶה אֶל הַר יְיָ' וְגו'. הַאי קְרָא אוּקְמוּהָ בְּכַמָּה אֲתָר. אֲבָל זִמְנִין שְׁאַר עַמִּין לְמֶהַךְ וּלְכַתְּתָא רַגְלַיְיהוּ, לְמֵיעַל תְּחוֹת גַּדְפֵּי דִשְׁכִינְתָּא. לְכוּ וְנַעֲלֶה כָּל טַעֲוָון דְּעָלְמָא אִית לוֹן יְרִידָה, וְקוּדְשָׁא בְּרִיךְ הוּא מַאן דְּאִתְדַּבָּק בֵּיהּ, אִית בֵּיהּ עֲלִיָּה.

57. "And Jethro, Moses' father-in-law came" (Shemot 18:5). He opened the discussion with the verse: "And many nations shall go and say, 'Come and let us go up to the mountain of Hashem'" (Yeshayah 2:3). This verse is explained in many places. Yet, the time will come when the other nations will strive to come under the wings of the Shechinah. "…let us go up…" All idol worshippers of the world pertain to descent, but those who cleave to the Holy One, blessed be He, will achieve an ascent. THEREFORE, IT IS WRITTEN: "LET US GO UP."

58. אֶל הַר יְיָ', דָּא אַבְרָהָם, דִּכְתִיב אֲשֶׁר יֵאָמֵר הַיּוֹם בְּהַר יְיָ' יֵרָאֶה, דְּהָא אַבְרָהָם קְרֵי לֵיהּ הַר. מַה הַר הֶפְקֵירָא לְכָל מַאן דְּבָעֵי בְּעָלְמָא, אוּף אֲתָר דָּא קַדִּישָׁא, הֶפְקֵירָא לְקַבְּלָא לְכָל מַאן דְּבָעֵי בְּעָלְמָא. אֶל בֵּית, דָּא יַעֲקֹב, דְּקָרָא לְהַאי אֲתָר בַּיִת, דִּכְתִיב אֵין זֶה כִּי אִם בֵּית אֱלֹהִים.

58. "…the mountain of Hashem…" refers to Abraham, as written: "as it is said to this day: In the mount Hashem will appear" (Beresheet 22:14). For Abraham called it 'a mountain'. Just as the mountain is abandoned property, free to all who care for it, so is this holy place, THE TEMPLE, open to all those who desire it on earth. "…to the house…" (Yeshayah 2:3) is Jacob, who called this place a "house," as it is written: "this is no other than the house of Elohim" (Beresheet 28:17).

59. ד"א, הַר וּבַיִת, אע"ג דְּכֹלָּא חַד דַּרְגָּא, סְלִיקוּ לְדָא מִן דָּא, הַר, לִשְׁאַר עַמִּין, כַּד אָתָאן לְאָעֲלָא תְּחוֹת גַּדְפּוֹי. בַּיִת, לְיִשְׂרָאֵל, לְמֶהֱוֵי עִמְּהוֹן כְּאִתְּתָא בְּבַעְלָהּ. בְּדִיּוּרָא חַד בְּחֶדְוָוה, וּרְבִיעָא עֲלַיְיהוּ כְּאִימָא עַל בְּנִין.

59. Another interpretation. Though "mountain" and "house" pertain to the same grade, one is higher than the other. A "mountain" is for the rest of the nations who come to enter under its wings. A "house" is to the nation of Yisrael like a wife to her husband in one household – united in happiness, it adheres to them like a mother over her children.

60. תָּא חֲזֵי, מַה כְּתִיב הָכָא בְּיִתְרוֹ, וַיָּבֹא יִתְרוֹ חֹתֵן מֹשֶׁה וּבָנָיו וְאִשְׁתּוֹ אֶל מֹשֶׁה וְגוֹ', כֵּיוָן דִּכְתִיב אֶל מֹשֶׁה, אֲמַאי כְּתִיב אֶל הַמִּדְבָּר. אֶלָּא עִקָּרָא דְּכֹלָּא לְמָה דַּהֲוָה אָתֵי, אֶל הַמִּדְבָּר. וּמַאן אִיהוּ, הַר אֱלֹהִים, דְּדָא אִיהוּ אֲתָר לְגַיּוֹרֵי לְאִתְגַּיְירָא. וְעַל דָּא כְּתִיב, אֶל מֹשֶׁה, אֶל הַמִּדְבָּר, לְמֹשֶׁה, לְגַיְירָא לוֹן, וּלְאַעֲלָא לוֹן תְּחוֹת גַּדְפֵי שְׁכִינְתָּא. אֶל הַמִּדְבָּר הֲווֹ אַתְיָין, דְּאִיהוּ הַר הָאֱלֹהִים, לְמֶעְבַּד נַפְשַׁיְיהוּ.

60. Come and behold: what is written here regarding Jethro? "…and Jethro, Moses's father-in-law, came, with his sons and his wife to Moses into the wilderness." HE ASKS: Since it is written, "to Moses," why does the verse add, "into the wilderness"? HE ANSWERS: What is important is what Jethro came to the desert for. And what is it? It is a mountain of Elohim, and it is a place for a stranger to convert. Therefore, it is written "…to Moses into the wilderness." "To Moses," to proselytize them and bring them under the wings of the Shechinah. "Into the wilderness," they would come. For the mountain of Elohim is to proselytize the soul, THAT IS, TO RECEIVE FROM THENCE THE NEFESH OF THE CONVERT.

61. וּבְגִין כַּךְ קַיְימָא הַהוּא אֲתָר, בְּרָזָא דְּהַר דְּכָל מַאן דְּאָתֵי זָכֵי בֵּיהּ. וְאִקְרֵי גֵּר צֶדֶק. וְהָא אוּקִימְנָא, גֵּר, אַף עַל גַּב דְּאִתְדַּבַּק בַּאֲתָר דָּא עִלָּאָה קַדִּישָׁא, כֵּיוָן דְּשָׁבַק עַמֵּיהּ וַאֲבָהָתוֹי גֵּר. צֶדֶק אִקְרֵי, כְּמַאן דְּשַׁוֵּי מְדוֹרֵיהּ בַּאֲתָר דְּלָא יָדַע מִקַּדְמַת דְּנָא.

61. On account of this, the location stands as a mystery called "mountain," and everyone who comes there is credited with the title: "a convert of righteousness." We have explained that he is called a convert. Even though he united on high, with the celestial and holy, because he left his own country and kin, HE IS CALLED "A CONVERT." He is called "a convert of righteousness" since he set up his dwelling in a place he did not know before, WHICH IS IN THE SHECHINAH, CALLED 'RIGHTEOUSNESS'.

4. "This is the book"

A Synopsis

We learn that the book in "This is the book of the generations of Adam" is actually two books, an upper and a lower, and comprises Male and Female together. They also incorporate the secret of 'keep' and 'remember'. Lastly we are also told that the book refers to the secret of the features of human beings by which the descendants of man can be recognized.

62. רַבִּי יִצְחָק וְרַבִּי יוֹסִי, הֲווֹ יַתְבֵי יוֹמָא חַד וְלָעָאן בְּאוֹרַיְיתָא בִּטְבֶרְיָא. אַעֲבַּר רַבִּי שִׁמְעוֹן, אָמַר לוֹן בְּמַאי עַסְקִיתוּ, אָמְרוּ לֵיהּ, בְּהַאי קְרָא דְּאוֹלִיפְנָא מִנֵּיהּ דְּמָר, אָמַר לוֹן מַאי אִיהוּ. אָמְרוּ לֵיהּ, הַאי דִּכְתִּיב זֶה סֵפֶר תּוֹלְדוֹת אָדָם בְּיוֹם בְּרוֹא אֱלֹהִים אָדָם בִּדְמוּת אֱלֹהִים עָשָׂה אוֹתוֹ. וְהָא אִתְּמַר, דְּאַחֲמֵי קוּדְשָׁא בְּרִיךְ הוּא לְאָדָם הָרִאשׁוֹן, כָּל אִינּוּן דָּרִין דַּהֲווֹ זְמִינִין לְמֵיתֵי לְעָלְמָא, וְכָל אִינּוּן פַּרְנָסִין, וְכָל אִינּוּן חַכִּימִין, דַּהֲווֹ זְמִינִין בְּכָל דָּרָא וְדָרָא.

62. Rabbi Yitzchak and Rabbi Yosi were sitting and studying the Torah in Tiberias. Rabbi Shimon passed before them. He asked them: With what are you occupied? They answered him: The verse which we have learned from our master. He said to them: Which is that? They responded: That which is written, "This is the book of the generations of Adam. In the day that Elohim created man, in the likeness of Elohim He made him" (Beresheet 5:1). And after all, we have learned that the Holy One, blessed be He, showed to Adam all those generations that in the future will be born onto earth, and all the leaders and all the sages that in the future will be present in each and every generation.

63. וְרָזָא אוֹלִיפְנָא, זֶה סֵפֶר. אִית סֵפֶר וְאִית סֵפֶר. סֵפֶר לְעֵילָּא, סֵפֶר לְתַתָּא. סֵפֶר לְתַתָּא אִקְרֵי סֵפֶר הַזִּכָּרוֹן, סֵפֶר דְּהַהוּא זִכָּרוֹן, וְדָא חַד צַדִּיק, וְאִקְרֵי זֶה. וּבְגִין דְּלָא לְאַפְרְשָׁא לוֹן, דְּאִינּוּן תָּדִיר כַּחֲדָא בְּיִחוּדָא חֲדָא, כְּתִיב, זֶה סֵפֶר תְּרֵין דַּרְגִּין דְּאִינּוּן חַד, כְּלָלָא דְּכַר וְנוּקְבָּא.

63. And this is a secret we have learned. "This is the Book," NAMELY there are two books. There is an upper book and there is a lower book. The lower book is called 'the Book of the Remembrance', WHICH MEANS the Book of that Remembrance, which is a certain Righteous one, NAMELY YESOD, called "this (Heb. *zeh*)." AND MALCHUT IS HIS BOOK. In order not to separate them, since they are always together and form one, it is therefore written: "This (Heb. *zeh*) is the book" – two levels which are one, the principle of Male and Female. FOR "THIS" IS MASCULINE, YESOD, AND THE "BOOK" IS FEMININE, MALCHUT.

64. וְדָא אִיהוּ כְּלָלָא חֲדָא, דְּכָל אִינּוּן נִשְׁמָתִין וְרוּחִין דְּפַרְחִין בִּבְנֵי נָשָׁא, כְּלָלָא דְּכָל תּוֹלָדוֹת, אִינּוּן בְּרָזָא תוֹלְדוֹת אָדָם וַדַּאי. דְּהָא מֵהַהוּא צַדִּיק דְּקָאמַר, פַּרְחִין אִינּוּן נִשְׁמָתִין בְּתִיאוּבְתָּא חֲדָא, וְדָא אִיהוּ שַׁקְיוּ דְּגִנְתָּא דְּאַשְׁקֵי הַהוּא נָהָר דְּנָפִיק מֵעֵדֶן, דִּכְתִּיב וְנָהָר יוֹצֵא מֵעֵדֶן לְהַשְׁקוֹת אֶת הַגָּן. וְדָא אִיהוּ רָזָא דְּאָדָם, דִּכְתִּיב תּוֹלְדוֹת אָדָם.

64. And this is one principle: all those souls and spirits that fly into human beings, which consist of all the descendants, are assuredly in the secret of the generations of Adam, NAMELY THE DESCENDANTS OF THE UPPER MAN, REFERRING TO ZEIR ANPIN. This is because from this said Righteous all the souls fly forth with one desire. And this is the watering of the Garden that this river, which went forth from Eden, gives, as it is written: "And a river went out of Eden to water the Garden" (Beresheet 2:10). THE EXPLANATION: FROM YESOD FLOWED THE SOULS AND SPIRITS OF THE GARDEN, WHICH IS MALCHUT, and this is the secret of Adam, as it is written: "the generations of Adam."

65. לְבָתַר בְּיוֹם בְּרוֹא אֱלֹהִים אָדָם, דָּא אָדָם דִּלְתַתָּא, דְּהָא תְּרֵין אָדָם כְּתִיבֵי בְּהַאי קְרָא, חַד רָזָא דִּלְעֵילָּא, וְחַד רָזָא דִּלְתַתָּא, אָדָם דְּאִיהוּ רָזָא דִּלְעֵילָּא, אִיהוּ בְּגִנְזוֹי, דְּגָנִיז קְרָא, בִּדְכַר וְנוּקְבָּא בְּרָזָא חֲדָא, דִּכְתִּיב זֶה סֵפֶר, דָּא כְּלָלָא דְּכַר וְנוּקְבָּא כַּחֲדָא. כֵּיוָן דְּעָבְדוּ תּוֹלְדוֹת כַּחֲדָא, קָרָא לוֹן אָדָם, דִּכְתִּיב תּוֹלְדוֹת אָדָם.

65. Afterwards, THE WORDS, "In the day that Elohim created man," refer to the lower man, because there are two men mentioned in this verse. One

refers to the secret OF ADAM from above, and one refers to the secret OF ADAM from below. Adam, in the secret of above, WHICH IMPLIES ZEIR ANPIN, is within the mystery of that verse concealed in Male and Female, in one secret. As it is stated, "This is the book," which comprises Male and Female together, AS STATED BEFORE. When they together produced offspring, they were openly called 'man' (Adam), as is written "the generations of Adam."

66. לְבָתַר דְּאִתְגַּלְיָיא מִלְתָא, מִגּוֹ סְתִימוּ עִלָּאָה קַדְמָאָה דִּקְרָא, בָּרָא אָדָם לְתַתָּא, דִּכְתִיב בְּיוֹם בְּרוֹא אֱלֹהִים אָדָם בִּדְמוּת אֱלֹהִים עָשָׂה אוֹתוֹ. בִּדְמוּת דְּאָדָם אִיהוּ כְּהַאי חֵיזוּ דְּאִתְחֲזֵי דְּיוּקְנִין בֵּיה, וְאִינּוּן דְּיוּקְנִין לָא קַיְימִין בְּהַהוּא חֵיזוּ בְּדִיוּקְנָא בְּקִיוּמָא, אֶלָּא מִתְעַבְרָן מִינֵּיה, אוֹף הָכִי בִּדְמוּת אֱלֹהִים.

66. After it was revealed from the first supernal mystery of the verse, NAMELY, IT WAS REVEALED THAT "THIS IS THE BOOK" ALLUDES TO THE SUPERNAL MAN, WHOSE GENERATIONS ARE THE SOULS AND SPIRITS OF HUMAN BEINGS AS WAS MENTIONED BEFORE, He created the lower man as it is written: "In the day that Elohim created man, in the likeness of Elohim He made him." "In the likeness," MEANS Adam was like a mirror with figures that appear in it; the figures do not stay fixed in the mirror for very long, but fade away from it. It is also HERE, "in the likeness of Elohim."

67. ד"א, בִּדְמוּת אֱלֹהִים, דִּיוּקְנָא דְּשַׁיְיפִין דְּכַר וְנוּקְבָא, בְּרָזָא דְּאָחוֹר וָקֶדֶם. אָחוֹר: בְּרָזָא דְּשָׁמוֹר. וָקֶדֶם: בְּרָזָא דְּזָכוֹר. וּבְאִלֵּין תַּלְיָין כָּל פִּקוּדֵי אוֹרַיְיתָא, שִׁית מְאָה וּתְלֵיסַר פִּקּוּדֵי אוֹרַיְיתָא, כְּלָלָא דְּכֹלָּא. וְתָנֵינָן, אָחוֹר לְעוֹבָדָא דִּבְרֵאשִׁית, וָקֶדֶם לְעוֹבָדָא דְּמֶרְכָּבָה. וְכֹלָּא דָּא בְּדָא תַּלְיָא. בִּדְמוּת אֱלֹהִים, בְּהַהוּא דִּיוּקְנָא מַמָּשׁ, וְהָא אוֹקִים לֵיה מֹר.

67. Another interpretation: "In the likeness of Elohim," MEANS the shape of the limbs of male and female, in the secret of back and front. The back is of the secret of "keep," FOR THAT IS A FEMININE ASPECT. The front is the male, in the secret of "remember," WHICH IS ZEIR ANPIN. And on these all

the commandments of the Torah depend, 613 commandments of the Torah, that are all inclusive. We have learned THAT MAN WAS CREATED after the Creation and before the act of the divine Chariot. And one is dependent upon the other. "In the likeness of Elohim," is in the exact shape OF MALCHUT. So it was explained to me by my master.

68. תּוּ, זֶה סֵפֶר תּוֹלְדוֹת אָדָם: לְדִיּוּקְנִין, בְּרָזֵי דְּדִיּוּקְנִין דְּב״ן, לְאִשְׁתְּמוֹדָעָא בְּאִינוּן תּוֹלְדוֹת דְּב״ן, דִּיּוּקְנָא דְּרָזִין דְּב״ן, בְּשַׂעְרָא, בְּמִצְחָא, בְּעַיְינִין, בְּאַנְפִּין. בְּשִׂפְוָון, וּבְשִׁרְטוּטֵי יְדִין, וּבְאוֹדְנִין. בְּאִלֵּין שֶׁבַע בְּנֵי נָשָׁא אִשְׁתְּמוֹדְעָן.

68. More about, "This is the book of the generations of Adam." This refers to the secret of the features of human beings, the features with which to recognize the descendants of man, and the hidden meanings of these human features: the hair, the forehead, the eyes, the face, the lips, the lines on the hand, and the ears. With these seven human beings can be recognized.

5. And you shall behold the secret of the hair

A Synopsis
This section describes the traits and motivations of persons with different types of hair. We are told that the mysteries of the varied types of hair are for those who are wise in Torah, who recognize what is hidden in human beings, and are in the image of Elohim. It is they who sit in judgment.

69. בְּשַׂעְרָא. הַאי מַאן דְּשַׂעֲרֵיה קָמִיט, וְסָלִיק לְעֵילָּא עַל רֵישֵׁיה, מָארֵיה דִּרְגִּיזוּ. לְבֵיה קָמִיט כְּטוּפְסָא, לָאו כַּשְׁרָאן עוֹבָדוֹי. בְּשׁוּתָּפוּ אִתְרְחַק מִנֵּיה.

69. One is recognized by the hair. All who have creased hair, MEANING CURLY HAIR, that is swept upwards, AND DOES NOT HANG DOWN FROM THE HEAD, IS OF an angry disposition. His heart is wrinkled like a rag, SIGNIFYING HIS HEART IS FULL OF FEAR. His actions are not good. In partnership, one must stay away from him.

70. שַׂעֲרָא שְׁעִיעַ יַתִּיר, וְתָלֵי לְתַתָּא, טָב אִיהוּ לְשׁוּתָּפוּ. וּרְוְוחָא אִשְׁתְּכַח בֵּיה. וְאִיהוּ בִּלְחוֹדוֹי לָאו הָכִי. מָארֵי דְּרָזִין אִיהוּ בְּאִינּוּן רָזִין עִלָּאִין. בְּרָזִין זְעִירִין לָא קַיְּימָא בְּהוּ. עוֹבָדוֹי כַּשְׁרָאן וְלָא כַּשְׁרָאן.

70. If his hair is unusually smooth, and hangs low, then it is good to associate with him, for gain is found within him. IN OTHER WORDS, ONE BENEFITS FROM AN ASSOCIATION WITH HIM. However, when he is alone (THAT IS, WITHOUT A COMPANION) it is not so. THERE IS NO SUCCESS WITH HIM. He can keep secrets of great importance, yet, in secrets of minor importance, he is not reliable. His actions are SOMETIMES good, AND SOMETIMES not good.

71. וְאִי תָּלֵי לְתַתָּא, וְלָא שְׁעִיעַ, לְבֵיה לָא דָּחִיל, מָארֵיה דִּזְדוֹנָא אִיהוּ. כָּסִיף בְּעוֹבָדִין דְּכַשְׁרָן, וְיָאָן קַמֵּיה, וְלָא עָבֵיד. וְכַד אִיהוּ סִיב, אַהֲדָר לְמֶהֱוֵי דָּחִיל וְיָאָן עוֹבָדוֹי. וְהָנֵי מִילֵי, בְּמִילֵי דְּעָלְמָא. אֲבָל בְּמִילֵי דִּשְׁמַיָּא, יִצְלַח מַאן דְּיִקְרַב בֵּיה. לָא יִתְגַּלּוּן לֵיה רָזִין עִלָּאִין,

אֲבָל רָזִין זְעִירִין טָב אִיהוּ לְנַטְרָא לוֹן, מִמִּלָה זְעֵירָא עָבֵיד רַב, וּמִלּוֹי אִשְׁתְּמָעוּ. וְרָזָא דָּא זַיִ"ן, בְּאִינוּן אַתְוָון דְּשִׁיעוּרָא דְמַר.

71. If his hair hangs low and is not smooth, he has no fear in his heart. He is a malicious person. He desires good deeds, and thinks well of them, but he does not accomplish THEM. When he reaches old age, he returns to fear HASHEM, and his actions are proper. And these things pertain to the secular world, FOR THEN HE IS A MALICIOUS PERSON AND DOES NOT ACCOMPLISH GOOD DEEDS. But in esoteric matters, everyone benefits who associates with him. Do not reveal important secrets to him, but he will safeguard minor secrets. He can make big things from little things, and his words will be heard with respect. He is under the letter of *Zayin*, according to the letters taught by our master.

72. שַׂעֲרָא אוּכְמָא יַתִּיר צָהִיב, אַצְלַח בְּכָל עוֹבָדוֹי בְּמִלֵּי דְּעָלְמָא, וּבִסְחוֹרָא, וּבִדְדָמֵי לוֹן. וַתְרָן אִיהוּ דָּא אַצְלַח לְחוֹדוֹי. מַאן דְּמִתְחַבֵּר בַּהֲדֵיהּ, לָא אַצְלַח לְיוֹמִין סַגִּיאִין, אֶלָּא אַצְלַח מִיַּד, וְהַהִיא אַצְלָחוּתָא פַּרְחָא מִנֵּיהּ. וְרָזָא דָּא דְּאִיהוּ בִּכְלָלָא דְּאָת ז'.

72. If the hair is black and extremely shiny, he will succeed in all his actions, specifically in worldly matters – THIS IS MALCHUT, CALLED 'WORLD' – and in commerce, WHICH IS THE ABUNDANCE OF MALCHUT, ACCORDING TO THE SECRET OF THE VERSE: "SHE IS LIKE THE MERCHANT SHIPS" (MISHLEI 31:5). He is benevolent, but he succeeds only when alone, WITHOUT AN ASSOCIATE. And whosoever joins him as an associate will not succeed for long, but will have only immediate success, and that success shall fly from him. This secret is included in the letter *Zayin*.

73. שַׂעֲרָא אוּכְמָא דְּלָא צָהִיב, לְזִמְנִין אַצְלַח, לְזִמְנִין לָא אַצְלַח. דָּא אִיהוּ לְשׁוּתָפוּ וּלְאִשְׁתַּדְּלָא בַּהֲדֵיהּ, טָב לִזְמַן קָרִיב, וְלָא לִזְמַן רָחִיק, דְּהָא לִזְמַן רָחִיק יַחֲשׁוֹב מַחֲשָׁבִין. וּבְגִין דְּלָא יִתְפָּרְשׁוּן מִנֵּיהּ, הֲוֵי טָב לִזְמַן קָרִיב. דָּא יִצְלַח בְּאוֹרַיְיתָא. אִי יִשְׁתַּדַּל אֲבַתְרָהָא. וְיִצְלָחוּן בֵּיהּ אַחֲרָנִין. לֵית לֵיהּ רָזָא, לִזְמַן רָחִיק. דָּחִיק לִבָּא אִיהוּ. יֶחֱמֵי בְּשַׂנְאוֹי.

לָא יַכְלִין לֵיהּ שַׂנְאוֹי, וְאִיהוּ דָּחִיק לַבָּא, וְאִיהוּ בְּרָזָא דְּאָת י', דְּלָא
קַיְּימָא בִּכְלָלָא דְּאָת ז', אֶלָּא י' בִּלְחוֹדוֹי, בְּרָזָא דְּאַתְוָון דְּקִיקִין.

73. If his hair is black and not shiny, at times he will be successful and at times he will not succeed. It is good to associate and work with him for a short time, but not for a lengthy time, for during lengthy times he tends to think. So in order not to be parted from him, he is good for a short time. Such a one succeeds in Torah studies if he perseveres after it. And others will likewise succeed by him. He can not keep secrets for a long time. He is mean-hearted. He shall see his enemies, and they shall not prevail against him. He is mean (Heb. *tzar*)-hearted, as in the esoteric principle of the letter *Yud*, WHICH IS SMALL AND NARROW (HEB. *TZAR*) – and he is not included in the letter *Zayin*, AS STATED PREVIOUSLY, but the in letter *Yud*, in the secret of small letters.

74. שַׂעֲרָא דִּמְרִיט, יִצְלַח בְּעוֹבָדוֹי, וְרַמָּאָה אִיהוּ כַּפִין בְּבֵיתֵיהּ. אִתְחֲזֵי
דְּחִיל חַטָּאָה לְבַר, לָאו הָכִי לְגוֹ. דָּא עַד לָא סִיב. אִי שַׂעֲרֵיהּ מְרִיט,
לְבָתַר דְּסִיב, אִתְהַפַּךְ מִכַּמָּה דַּהֲוָה בְּקַדְמֵיתָא, הֵן לְטַב הֵן לְבִישׁ.

74. If his hair is balding, he will succeed in business, but he is a swindler. There is a scarcity of food in his house. On the surface, it seems he fears sin, but it is not so within. And all this is so before he comes to old age. But if he becomes bald in his old age, he becomes the opposite of what he was before, for good or for bad.

75. וְהָנֵי מִילֵי שַׂעֲרָא דִּמְרִיט בֵּין עֵינוֹי, ע"ג מוֹחָא, בַּאֲתָר דְּאָנַח
תְּפִלִּין. וְאִי בַּאֲתָר אַחֲרָא דְּרֵישָׁא, לָאו הָכִי. וְלָאו אִיהוּ רַמָּאָה, אֶלָּא
מָארֵיהּ דְּלִישָׁנָא בִּישָׁא. בִּלְחִישׁוּ, בְּלָא אֲרָמוּת קָלָא. לִזְמְנִין דָּחִיל
חַטָּאָה אִיהוּ, לִזְמְנִין לָא. וְדָא אִיהוּ בְּרָזָא דְּאָת ז', כַּד כָּלִיל אָת י'.

75. The stated words refer to hair balding on the forehead, between the eyes, at the place where the Tefilin are placed. However, at another spot on the head, it is not so. He is not a swindler, but an evil gossiper, one who gossips quietly without raising his voice. At times he is fears sin, and at times he does not. Thus, he is under the secret of the letter *Zayin*, when it includes the letter *Yud*.

76. עַד הָכָא, רָזִין דְּשַׂעֲרָא לְמָרֵי מִדִּין, דְּיַדְעֵי אָרְחֵי וְרָזֵי דְּאוֹרַיְיתָא, לְאִשְׁתְּמוֹדְעָא טְמִירוּ דִּבְנֵי נָשָׁא, דְּאִינּוּן בְּצֶלֶם אֱלֹהִים סָתוּם שְׁמָא, דְּאִתְפְּרַשׁ לְכַמָּה אָרְחִין.

76. Until this point, the mysteries of the varied types of hair are for those who sit in judgment, know the ways and mysteries of the Torah, recognize what is hidden in human beings, and are in the image of Elohim, in whom this nomenclature, ELOHIM, is concealed – which is explained in many ways.

6. And you shall behold the secret of the forehead

A Synopsis

This part examines the shape, size and slope of the forehead, together with the minute details of the furrows in the forehead; it uses these facts to explain the persons who have these sets of characteristics. The secret of the forehead is under the letter Nun, that is Gvurah.

77. בְּרָזָא דְּמִצְחָא, בְּאָת נ', דְּאִיהוּ שְׁלִימוּ דְּאָת זַיִ"ן, לִזְמְנִין אִתְכְּלִילַת בְּרָזָא דְּאָת ז', וּלְזִמְנִין אִיהוּ בִּלְחוֹדָהָא. מִצְחָא דְּאִיהוּ דָּקִיק וְחַד, בְּלָא עִגּוּלָא דָּא הוּא בַּר נָשׁ דְּלָא מִתְיַישְׁבָא בְּדַעְתֵּיהּ, חָשִׁיב דְּאִיהוּ חַכִּים, וְלָא יָדַע. אִתְבְּהִיל בְּרוּחֵיהּ. נָשִׁיךְ בְּלִישָׁנֵיהּ כְּחִוְיָא.

77. The secret of the forehead. This is under the letter *Nun*, WHICH IS GVURAH, which is the perfection of the letter *Zayin* – WHICH IS MALCHUT, SINCE MALCHUT WAS BUILT FROM THE LEFT COLUMN, WHICH IS GVURAH. Sometimes THE *NUN* is included in the letter *Zayin*, and at times it stands by itself. A forehead which is small, rises sharply, and is not round, signifies a man who is not settled in his mind. He thinks he is wise, but knows little. He is frightened in spirit, and has a serpent's tongue.

78. קָמִיטִין דְּמִצְחֵיהּ רַבְרְבָן, וְלָאו אִינּוּן בְּזִוּוּגָא. בְּשַׁעֲתָא דְּמַלִּיל אִתְעֲבֵידוּ אִינּוּן קָמִיטִין בְּמִצְחֵיהּ, וְלָאו בְּזִוּוּגָא. רְשִׁימִין אַחֲרָנִין דִּי בְּמִצְחֵיהּ כֻּלְּהוּ בְּזִוּוּגָא. דָּא, בָּעֵי דְּלָא לְאִזְדַּוְּוגָא לֵיהּ, אֶלָּא זִמְנָא זְעֵירָא, וְלָא זִמְנָא סַגִּי. כָּל מַה דְּעָבֵד וְחָשַׁב, אִיהוּ לְתוֹעַלְתֵּיהּ, וְלָא חַיִּישׁ לְתוֹעַלְתָּא דְּאַחֲרָנִין. לָאו אִיהוּ מָארֵי דְּרָזִין כְּלָל. דָּא אִיהוּ, הוֹלֵךְ רָכִיל מְגַלֶּה סוֹד, וְלָא חָשִׁיב מִלּוֹי כְּלָל. דָּא אִיהוּ בְּרָזָא דְּאָת נ' דְּכְלִילָא בְּאָת ז', וְלָא אִקְרֵי נֶאֱמָן רוּחַ בְּקִיּוּמָא.

78. IF the furrows in his forehead are large and are not joined ONE WITH THE OTHER, and if when he speaks these same furrows are formed, but not joined, while the other lines in his forehead are all joined, ONE WITH THE OTHER, then one is not to associate with him for more than a brief period, and not for a lengthy time. Whatever he does and thinks is only for his own

advantage, and he has no concern for the benefit of others. He can not keep a secret at all. Of him it is said: "A talebearer reveals secrets" (Mishlei 11:13). His words are not meaningful. This is the mystery of the letter *Nun*, which is included in the letter *Zayin*. He does not have a reliable disposition.

79. מִצְחָא דָּקִיק בְּעִגּוּלָא, דָּא אִיהוּ בַּר נָשׁ חַכִּימָא, בְּמָה דְּאִסְתַּכַּל. לְזִמְנִין אִתְבְּהִיל בְּרוּחֵיה. רְחִימוּ דִּילֵיה בְּחֶדְוָה. רַחֲמָן אִיהוּ עַל כֹּלָּא, אִסְתָּכַּל בְּמִלִּין סַגִּיאִין. אִי יִשְׁתָּדַּל בְּאוֹרַיְיתָא לֶהֱוֵי חַכִּים יַתִּיר.

79. IF his forehead is small and rounded, he makes intelligent observations, yet, he is fearful in spirit. His love is joyous. He is kindhearted to everyone. He has interests in many things. If he studies the Torah, he will become quite wise.

80. תְּלַת קְמִיטִין עִלָּאִין רַבְרְבִין בְּמִצְחֵיה בְּשַׁעֲתָא דְּאִיהוּ מַלִּיל. תְּלַת קְמִיטִין קָרִיב לְעֵינָא חַד. וּתְלַת קְמִיטִין עַל עֵינָא אַחֲרָא. בָּכֵי בְּשַׁעֲתָא דְּאַרְגִּיז. דָּא אִיהוּ טָב יַתִּיר מִכַּמָּה דְּאִתְחֲזֵי. אַרְמֵי בָּתַר כַּתְפוֹי כָּל מִלִּין דְּעָלְמָא, בֵּין בְּעוֹבָדוֹי, בֵּין בְּמִלִּין אַחֲרָנִין, וְלָא חָיֵישׁ. אַצְלַח בְּאוֹרַיְיתָא. כָּל בַּר נָשׁ דְּיִשְׁתַּדַּל בַּהֲדֵיה יַתִּיר מִמִּלִּין אַחֲרָנִין דְּעָלְמָא, לְזִמְנִין אִתְדְּבַק רְעוּתֵיה בְּקֻדְשָׁא בְּרִיךְ הוּא, וּלְזִמְנִין לָא. בְּדִינָא לָא אַצְלַח. אִתְרְחַק אִיהוּ מִן דִּינָא. וְרָזָא דָּא אָת נ' בִּלְחוֹדוֹי, דְּלָא אִתְכְּלִילַת בְּאָת ז'. וּבְגִין דְּלָא אִתְכְּלִילַת בְּאָת ז', אִתְרְחַק מִן דִּינָא, וְלָא קָאֵים בֵּיה, וּרְחִימוּתָא אִיהוּ סִטְרָא דִּילֵיה.

80. IF three large wrinkles are in his forehead at the time when he speaks, and three wrinkles are near one eye, and three wrinkles are near the other eye, and he cries at the time he is angry, then he is better than he appears to be. Whether it be in deeds or in words, he throws over his shoulders all secular matters, and cares not for them. He will have success in the study of the Torah. In fact, anyone who engages with him will profit even in secular matters, FOR WHICH HE ATTACHES NO IMPORTANCE. At times he clings to the will of the Holy One, blessed be He, and at times he does not. In legal matters, he has no success; he stays far away from legal judgments. And this is the secret of the letter *Nun* by itself, not included in the *Zayin*. Since it is

not included in the letter *Zayin*, he keeps his distance from the law and does not stay there. Rather, love is his side.

81. מִצְחָא דְּאִיהוּ בְּלָא עֲגוּלָא, וְאִיהוּ רַבְרְבָא. הַאי אִיהוּ בַּר נָשׁ דְּכָל זִמְנִין כַּד קָאֵים, וְכַד אָזִיל, כָּפִיף רֵישֵׁיהּ. הַאי אִתְפְּלִיג לִתְרֵין לִסְטְרִין, וְאִינּוּן סִטְרֵי שַׁגְעוֹנָא. סִטְרָא חֲדָא אִיהוּ שַׁגְעוֹנָא דְּאִתְחֲזֵי, וּבְנֵי נָשָׁא אַחֲרָנִין יַדְעִין שַׁגְעוֹנָא, דְּאִשְׁתְּמוֹדְעָא קָמֵי כֹּלָּא. וְאִיהוּ טִפְּשָׁא.

81. IF his forehead is not rounded but is large, this is a man who, whether he stands or walks, always bends his head. This type can be divided into two aspects of madness. One aspect is a noticeable madness, evident to all who observe and recognize it. He is the fool.

82. בְּמִצְחֵיהּ אִית ד' קָמִיטִין רַבְרְבִין, לְזִמְנִין בְּשַׁעֲתָא דְּמַלִּיל קָמִיט לוֹן בְּמִצְחֵיהּ, וּלְזִמְנִין דְּאִתְפְּשַׁט מִצְחֵיהּ בְּמַשְׁכֵיהּ, וְלָא אִתְחֲזוֹן. אִינּוּן קָמִיטִין אִתְחֲזוֹן, קָמִיטִין אַחֲרָנִין רַבְרְבִין בְּסִטְרָא דְּעֵינוֹי, חַיִּיךְ לְמַגְנָא. פּוּמֵיהּ רַבְרְבָא. לָאו אִיהוּ בַּר נָשׁ לְתוֹעַלְתָּא. סִטְרָא אַחֲרָא אִיהוּ. שַׁגְעוֹנָא דְּאִתְכַּסֵּי בֵּיהּ, וּבְנֵי נָשָׁא לָא מִסְתַּכְּלָן בֵּיהּ. וְאִיהוּ אִתְחַכַּם בְּמַה דְּאִשְׁתַּדַּל, וַאֲפִילוּ בְּאוֹרַיְיתָא, אֲבָל לָא לִשְׁמָהּ, אֶלָּא בְּגִין לְאִתְגָּאָה בִּפְנֵי עַמָּא. וְכֹלָּא בִּלְחִישׁוּ וּבְגֵאוּת לִבָּא, לְאַחֲזָאָה דְּאִיהוּ זַכָּאָה וְלָאו הָכִי. כָּל מִלּוֹי לָאו אִינּוּן לִשְׁמָא דְּקוּדְשָׁא בְּרִיךְ הוּא, אֶלָּא בְּגִין בְּנֵי נָשָׁא. וְחָשִׁיב מַחֲשָׁבִין, וְאַנְהִיג גַּרְמֵיהּ. כְּמִנְהָגָא דִּלְבַר, דְּיִסְתַּכְּלוּן בֵּיהּ. הַאי אִיהוּ בְּרָזָא דְּאָת נ', דִּי בִּכְלָלָא דְּאָת ז'.

82. IF he has four large wrinkles on his forehead – and sometimes when he speaks they appear on his forehead, while at other times the skin on his forehead is stretched so the wrinkles are not seen; there are wrinkles that are seen, and THEN other large wrinkles close to his eyes; he laughs freely WITHOUT REASON; and his mouth is large, this man has no worth, and is of the Other Side. Madness is concealed in him and people do not notice it. And he gets wiser in everything he does, even in the study of Torah – but not for its own sake but only to boast before people. And his custom is to be clandestine and conceited. He appears to be pious, but is not so. Everything

he says is not for the sake of the Holy One, blessed be He, but for man. His thoughts and his behavior are for external appearance, to draw attention to himself. This is the mystery of the letter *Nun,* which is included in the letter *Zayin.*

83. מִצְחָא דְּאִיהוּ בְּעגּוּלָא רַבְרְבָא, פְּקִיחָא אִיהוּ, הֶכְרְנוּ דְּכֹלָּא בֵּיהּ. יָדַע בְּכָל מַה דְּאִשְׁתַּדַּל, אֲפִילוּ בְּלָא אוּמָנָא דְּיוֹלִיף לֵיהּ. אַצְלַח בְּכָל מַה דְּאִשְׁתַּדַּל. וּבְמָמוֹנָא, לְזִמְנִין אַצְלַח, לְזִמְנִין לָא. מִמִּלָּה זְעֵירָא אִסְתָּכַל בְּמִלִּין סַגִּיאִין. נָבוֹן אִקְרֵי. לָא חָיִישׁ לְמִלִּין דְּעָלְמָא, וַאֲפִילוּ דְּיִנְדַע דְּיִתְבְּסִיף בְּהוּ לָא חָיִישׁ לוֹן, וְלָא שָׁוֵי עַל לִבֵּיהּ. רָכִיךְ לִבָּא אִיהוּ.

83. IF the forehead is rounded and large, he is clever. He remembers everything. He acquires wisdom from whatever he works hard at, and even without a trainer to teach him. He succeeds at whatever he endeavors. However, in money matters, sometimes he succeeds, and sometimes he does not. From little things, he can infer great things. He is called 'wise'. He does not concern himself with mundane matters, even when he knows that he may be embarrassed by not concerning himself with these matters. He pays no attention to them. He is soft-hearted.

84. תְּרֵין קְמִיטִין עִלָּאִין רַבְרְבִין בְּמִצְחֵיהּ. חַד קְמִיטָא עַל עֵינָא חַד, וְחַד קְמִיטָא עַל עֵינָא אַחֲרָא. וְאִשְׁתְּכָחוּ תְּלַת קְמִיטִין רַבְרְבִין בְּמִצְחֵיהּ, בְּאִלֵּין דְּעַיְינִין, בַּר קְמִיטָא תַּתָּאָה, דְּאִיהוּ אִתְפְּלַג עַל עַיְינִין. דָּא חָשִׁיב מַחֲשָׁבִין לְגוֹ וְלָא לְבַר. בְּגִין דְּלָא חָשִׁיב לִבְנֵי נָשָׁא בְּעוֹבָדוֹי, וְדָחִיל אִיהוּ לְפוּם שַׁעֲתָא, וְלָא יַתִּיר. לְפַיּוּסָא, אִתְפַּיְיסָא בְּעוֹבָדוֹי דִּלְבַר מִקַּמֵי בְּ"נ, לָאו אִינּוּן, אֶלָּא לְזִמְנִין כְּרַבְיָא, וּלְזִמְנִין בְּחָכְמָה. דָּא אִיהוּ בְּרָזָא דְּאָת נ', דְּאִיהוּ בִּלְחוֹדוֹי, דְּלָא אִתְכְּלִיל בְּאָת ז'. וְחֶלְשָׁא אִיהוּ, דְּלָא אִתְכְּלִיל בְּאִלֵּין אַתְוָון קַדְמָאֵי, אֶלָּא אִסְתְּמִיךְ לְאָת ס' לְאִתְכְּלָלָא בֵּיהּ. וְלָא בְּאַתְוָון קַדְמָאֵי. עַד הָכָא רָזִין דְּחָכְמָתָא דְּמִצְחָא.

84. IF there are two large wrinkles set high upon his forehead, one wrinkle

over one eye, and one wrinkle over another eye, and there are also three large wrinkles in his forehead, those above his eyes, and apart FROM THEM a lower furrow split above the eyes, this signifies deep inner thought, not revealed on the outside because people do not pay attention to his actions. He is in fear for a short time only, but never more than that. As for pleasing, he is only concerned with his outward actions before people, and these, HIS ACTIONS, are nothing more than childish at times, and at times they are wise. This stands in the mystery of the letter *Nun* when it is alone and is not included in the letter *Zayin*. But it is weak because it has not been included in the original letters, but is supported by the letter *Samech* to be included with it, but not with the original letters. Until this point are the secrets of wisdom of the forehead.

7. And you shall behold the secret of the eyes

A Synopsis
The secret of the eyes is found in the secret of the letter Samech. Here one must discern the color of the eyes, and the way the eye rests in the socket. The eyebrows are also examined.

85. בְּרָזָא דְּעַיְינִין, בְּרָזָא דְּאָת ס', בְּהַהוּא גַּוְונָא דְּסַחֲרָא לְבַר, וּכְמָה דְּיָתְבָא עֵינָא, דְּיָתְבָא עַל שְׁלִימוּ, דְּלָא שְׁקִיעַ, הַאי לָאו רַמָּאָה הִיא, וְרָחִיק מֵרַמָּאוּתָא, דְּלָא אִית בֵּיהּ כְּלָל.

85. As for the secret of the eyes, they may be found in the secret of the letter *Samech*. ONE MUST DISCERN the color that encircles the eyes from the outside, and the way the eye rests in its fullness, and that it is not immersed deeply in its socket. Such a one is not deceptive, and has not a trace of fraudulence.

86. גַּוְונֵי דְּעַיְינִין אִינּוּן ד'. חִוָּורוּ לְבַר, דְּסַחֲרָא עֵינָא, כְּגַוְונָא דְּכָל בַּר נָשׁ. לְגוֹ מִנֵּיהּ אוּכָמָא דְּסַחֲרָא, וְאִתְכְּלִיל חִוָּורוּ וְאוּכָמוּ כַּחֲדָא. לְגוֹ מִנֵּיהּ יְרוֹקָא. וְאִתְכְּלִיל בְּאוּכָמָה. לְגוֹ מִנֵּיהּ הַהוּא בַּת עֵינָא, נְקוּדָא אוּכָמָא. דָּא אִיהוּ בַּר נָשׁ דְּחַיִּיךְ תָּדִיר, וְחַדֵּי בְּחֶדּוּ. וְחָשִׁיב מַחֲשָׁבִין לְטַב, וְלָא אִשְׁתְּלִימוּ אִינּוּן מַחֲשָׁבִין, בְּגִין דְּסַלִּיק לוֹן מִיַּד מֵרְעוּתֵיהּ. אִשְׁתַּדַּל בְּמִילֵּי דְּעָלְמָא. וְכַד אִשְׁתַּדַּל בְּמִילֵּי דִּשְׁמַיָּא, אַצְלַח. הַאי אִצְטְרִיךְ לְאִתַּתְקְּפָא בֵּיהּ לְאִשְׁתַּדְּלָא בְּאוֹרַיְיתָא, דְּהָא יִצְלַח בָּהּ.

86. There are four colors to be found in the eyes: A) There is the white outside, that circles the eye, common to every person. THAT IS, THERE IS NO DIFFERENCE IN THIS ASPECT FROM PERSON TO PERSON. B) Enclosed within it is a black color that encircles, and the black and white merge together, WHICH ALLUDES TO CHESED AND GVURAH, WHICH INCLUDE ONE WITH THE OTHER. C) Within this is a greenish color, ALLUDING TO TIFERET, included in the black. D) The innermost is the pupil of the eye, which is a black dot. THIS ALLUDES TO MALCHUT. This is a person who is always laughing and full of cheer. He has good intentions, but his intentions are never accomplished, since they slip from his mind. He is occupied with

worldly matters, but when occupied with spiritual matters, he will succeed. Therefore, he should be encouraged to occupy himself with the Torah, for he will succeed in it.

87. גְּבִינֵי עֵינוֹי רַבְרְבִין, וְכַסְיָין לְתַתָּא. בְּאִינּוּן גְּוָונִין דְּעֵינָא אִית רְשִׁימִין סוּמָקִין דְּקִיקִין בְּאַרְכָּא. אִינּוּן רְשִׁימִין אִקְרוּן אַתְוָון זְעִירִין דְּעֵינָא. בְּגִין דְּאִינּוּן גְּוָונִין דְּעֵינָא. אִי נָהֲרִין בִּנְהִירוּ, הַהוּא נְהִירוּ סָלִיק אַתְוָון לְאִתְחֲזָאָה, לְאִינּוּן מָארֵי דְּמַדִּין. בְּאִינּוּן רְשִׁימִין אַחֲרָנִין דְּקִיקִין, וְהַאי אִיהוּ בְּאָת ס׳, וּכְלִילָא בְּאָת ה׳.

87. IF his eyebrows are thick, inclining downwards, AND IF in the color of his eyes there are red lined impressions, these impressions are called "small letters of the eyes" because when these colors of the eye shine in the light, the light causes the letters to be revealed to those who judge, together with the other, small impressions. This is in the shape of the letter *Samech*, and is included in the letter *Hei*.

88. עַיְינִין יְרוֹקִין דְּסַחֲרִין בְּחִוְּורוּ, וּמִתְעָרְבִין אִינּוּן יְרוֹקִין, בְּהַהוּא חִוְּורוּ. רַחֲמָנָא אִיהוּ, וְאִיהוּ חָשִׁיב תָּדִיר לְתוֹעַלְתֵּיה, וְלָא חָשִׁיב לְנִזְקָא דְּאַחֲרָנִין כְּלוּם.

88. Green eyes that are surrounded in white, with the green blended in the white, implies that he is a merciful man, yet he thinks always for his own benefit. The harm of others does not concern him at all.

89. גְּוָונָא אוּכָמָא לָא אִתְחֲזֵי בֵּיה. חָמִיד אִיהוּ וְלָא מִסִּטְרָא בִּישָׁא. וְאִי סַלְקָא בִּידֵיהּ מִסִּטְרָא בִּישָׁא, לָא יָתוּב מִנֵּיהּ. מְהֵימָנָא אִיהוּ בְּמַה דְּאִשְׁתְּמוֹדְעָא. וּבַמֶּה דְּלָא אִשְׁתְּמוֹדְעָא לָאו מְהֵימָנָא אִיהוּ. מָארֵיהּ דְּרָזִין אִיהוּ, בְּמִלָּה דְּאִיהוּ רָזָא, עַד דְּיִשְׁמַע לְהַהוּא רָזָא בְּאֲתָר אַחֲרָא. כֵּיוָן דְּשָׁמַע לֵיה גַּלֵּי כֹּלָּא. וְלָאו עִמֵּיה רָזָא כְּלָל, דְּכָל מִלּוֹי לָאו אִינּוּן בִּשְׁלִימוּ. גְּוָונֵי עֵינוֹי סָחֲרָן בְּחִוְּורוּ וּבִירוֹקָא. דָּא אִיהוּ בְּרָזָא דְּאָת ה׳, וְאִתְכְּלִיל בְּאָת ז׳, וּבְאָת ס׳.

89. IF the black color is not noticeable in his eyes, he is greedy, but not in an evil way. But if an opportunity should arise for him to accomplish evil, he will not turn from it. He can be trustworthy when speaking of things he knows, yet not trustworthy in things he does not know. He can keep a secret as long as it is a secret, until he hears the secret at another place. Once he hears about it, he reveals everything and it is no longer a secret with him at all, because nothing he does is perfect. The eye color encircled with white and green is the secret of the letter *Hei* when included with the letters *Zayin* and *Samech*.

90. עַיְינִין צְהִיבִין יְרוֹקִין, שַׁגְעוֹנָא אִית בֵּיה. וּבְגִין שַׁגְעוֹנֵיה אִיהוּ פּוּם מְמַלֵּל רַבְרְבָן, וְעָבֵיד גַּרְמֵיה כְּבַר נָשׁ רַב, בְּרַבְרְבָנוּ. וּמַאן דְּאִתְתַּקַּף בֵּיה, נָצַח לֵיה. לָא אִתְחֲזֵי לְרָזִין דְּאוֹרַייְתָא, דְּהָא לָא שָׁכִיךְ בְּלִבֵּיה, בְּאִינּוּן רָזִין. דְּעָבֵיד גַּרְמֵיה רַב בְּהוּ. דָּא אִיהוּ בְּרָזָא דְּאָת ה׳, וְאִתְכְּלִיל בְּאָת ז׳ בִּלְחוֹדוֹי, וְאִתְרְחַק מֵאָת ס׳. וּבְגִין דְּאִיהוּ עָבֵד גַּרְמֵיה בְּרַבְרְבָנוּ, אִתְרְחַק מִנֵּיה מֵאָת ס׳, וְלָא אִתְקְרִיב בַּהֲדֵיה. דָּא כַּד אִיהוּ מַלִּיל, עָבֵיד קְמִיטִין סַגִּיאִין בְּמִצְחֵיה.

90. IF his eyes are yellowish-green, he has madness about him, and because of this madness his mouth speaks in a bombastic manner, and he carries a self-importance about himself, and whoever attacks him, conquers him. He is not worthy of the Torah secrets, since in his heart he can not keep silent about such secrets, AND HE REVEALS THEM TO OTHERS so that through them he can make himself seem a bigger MAN. This is the mystery of the letter *Hei*, which is only included in the letter *Zayin*, and is removed from the letter *Samech*. It is because he conducts himself with pride that he is far removed from the letter *Samech* and can not approach it. When he speaks, he produces many wrinkles on his forehead.

91. עַיְינִין חִוָּורִן, דְּסַחֲרָן זְעֵיר בִּירוֹקָא, מָארֵיה דְּרוּגְזָא, וְרַחֲמָנָא אִיהוּ לְרוּב זִמְנִין. וְכַד אִתְמְלֵי רוּגְזָא, לֵית בֵּיה רְחִימוּ כְּלָל, וְאִתְהַפָּךְ לְאַכְזָרִיּוּת. לָאו אִיהוּ מָארֵיה דְּרָזִין, דָּא אִיהוּ בְּרָזָא דְּאָת ה׳, דְּאִתְכְּלִיל בְּאָת ס׳.

91. One with white eyes, encircled lightly with green, has an angry disposition, but for the most part, he is kind-hearted. However, when he is full of anger he has no love in him whatsoever, and becomes cruel. He can not be trusted with a secret. This belongs to the mystery of the letter *Hei,* which is included in the letter *Samech.*

92. עַיְינִין יְרוֹקִין וְחִוּוֹרִין כַּחֲדָא, וּזְעֵיר מִגָּוֶון אוּכָם בְּהוּ, דָּא אִיהִי מָארֵיהּ דְּרָזִין, וְאַצְלַח בְּהוּ. וְאִי שָׁארֵי בְּאַצְלָחוּתָא אַצְלַח וְסָלִיק. שַׂנְאוֹי לָא יַכְלִין לֵיהּ, וְאִיהוּ שַׁלִּיט עֲלַיְיהוּ בְּשׁוּלְטָנוּ, וְאִתְכַּפְיָין קַמֵיהּ. דָּא אִיהוּ בְּרָזָא דְּאָת כ', דְּאִתְכְּלִיל בְּרָזָא דְּאָת ס'. וְעַ"ד אִיהוּ שַׁלִּיט, אִי שָׁארֵי בֵּיהּ. עַד הָכָא רָזִין דְּעַיְינִין לְאִינוּן מָארֵי דְּחָכְמְתָא.

92. He with eyes that are green and white together with a little black color in them, can be trusted with secrets and is successful in utilizing them. If he begins with success, then he will continue to succeed further. His enemies can not prevail against him and he rules over them entirely, and they are submissive to him. This is under the sign of the letter *Caf*, which is included in the letter *Samech.* Thus, he rules once he starts TO RULE. Thus far are the mysteries of the eyes, which are revealed to the wise.

8. And you shall behold the secret of the face

8. And you shall behold the secret of the face

A Synopsis

The secret of the face is for those who master inner wisdom. We learn that the features of the face are recognized not by outward impressions, but rather from the spirit and the impressions of inner secrets. The impressions of all 22 letters are engraved into the spirit, and these impressions enter into the face, to be seen only by those with wisdom. Also, the spirit projects the image of the face of a man, a lion, an ox and an eagle, all for a time.

93. רָזָא דְאַנְפִּין, לְאִינוּן מָארֵי דְחָכְמָתָא פְּנִימָאָה. דְיוּקְנִין דְּאַנְפִּין, לָאו אִינוּן בִּרְשִׁימִין דִּלְבַר, אֶלָּא בְּגוֹ רְשִׁימָא דְּרָזִין פְּנִימָאִין. דְּדִיוּקְנִין דְּאַנְפִּין, מִתְהַפְּכָן מִגּוֹ דְיוּקְנִין דִּרְשִׁימוּ דְּאַנְפִּין, סְתִימִין בְּרוּחָא דְּשַׁרְיָא לְגוֹ. וּמִגּוֹ הַהוּא רוּחָא, אִתְחֲזֵי לְבַר דְיוּקְנִין דְּאַנְפִּין, דְּאִשְׁתְּמוֹדְעָן לְגַבֵּי אִינוּן חַכִּימִין.

93. The secret of the face is for those who master inner wisdom. The features of the face are not RECOGNIZED by the outward impressions ON THE SKIN OF THE FACE, AS WAS SAID OF THE FOREHEAD, but by the impressions of inner secrets. For the features of the face are inverted AND APPEAR by force of impressions of the face, which are concealed in the spirit that dwells within. And from this spirit, the features of the face appear outside, which are recognizable only to the wise OF INTERNAL WISDOM, AS MENTIONED ABOVE.

94. דְיוּקְנִין דְּאַנְפִּין אִשְׁתְּמוֹדְעָן מִגּוֹ רוּחָא. רוּחָא אִית בְּבַר נָשׁ, דְּרָזִין דְּאַתְוָון חֲקִיקִין בֵּיהּ. וְכֻלְּהוּ אַתְוָון סְתִימִין גּוֹ הַהוּא רוּחָא, וּלְפוּם שַׁעֲתָא סַלְקִין רְשִׁימִין דְּאִינוּן אַתְוָון לְגוֹ אַנְפִּין. וּכְמָה דְאִינוּן אַתְוָון סַלְקִין, הָכִי אִתְחֲזוֹן אַנְפִּין, בְּדִיוּקְנִין רְשִׁימִין לְפוּם שַׁעֲתָא, בְּחֵיזוּ דְּלָא קַיְימָא. בַּר אִינוּן מָארֵי דְחָכְמָתָא דְּאִתְקַיְימָן בְּהוֹ, וְלָא אִתְנְשֵׁי מִנַּיְיהוּ.

94. The features of the face are recognized from the spirit. There is in man a spirit on which the secret of the letters are engraved, and all 22 letters are enclosed in that spirit. According to the seasons OF MAN, the impressions of

these very same letters enter into the face. And as these letters come up, so does the face appear with these engraved impressions according to the time OF MAN. But this appearance does not last long, FOR THESE FEATURES SOON PASS. Only men of Wisdom see them, and they exist never to be forgotten by them.

95. הַהוּא אֲתָר דְּאִקְרֵי עָלְמָא דְּאָתֵי, וּמִתַּמָּן נַפְקָא רָזָא דְּאוֹרַיְיתָא, בְּכֻלְּהוּ אַתְוָון דְּאִינּוּן כ״ב אַתְוָון, כְּלָלָא דְּכֹלָּא. וְהַהוּא נַהֲרָא דְּנָפִיק מֵעֵדֶן, נָטִיל כֹּלָּא. וְכַד פַּרְחָן מִנֵּיהּ אִינּוּן רוּחִין וְנִשְׁמָתִין, כֻּלְּהוּ מִצְטַיְּירָן בְּצִיּוּרָא דְּאִינּוּן אַתְוָון, וְהָכִי נַפְקֵי כֻּלְּהוּ. וּבְג״כ, רוּחָא דְּבַר נָשׁ דְּמִצְטַיְּירָא בְּצִיּוּרָא דְּאַתְוָון, עָבֵיד צִיּוּרָא בְּאַנְפִּין.

95. There is a place which is called the 'World to Come', WHICH IS BINAH. From there issues forth the secret of the Torah, WHICH IS ZEIR ANPIN THAT EMANATES FROM BINAH, with all its letters, consisting of 22 letters that comprise everything. And the river that goes forth from Eden, WHICH IS ZEIR ANPIN, receives everything. When the spirits and the souls soar from it, all are stamped with the imprint of these same letters. And everything emerges in this manner. Therefore, the spirit of man is stamped with the imprint of these letters, and the imprint forms a shape on the face OF MAN.

96. א״ל ר״ש, אִי הָכִי צִיּוּרָא דְּאִימָּא, לָא מִצְטַיְּירָא גּוֹ הַהוּא רוּחָא, אָמְרוּ, הָכִי שְׁמַעֲנָא מִנֵּיהּ דְּמֹר, דְּצִיּוּרָא דְּאַתְוָון מִסִּטְרָא דִּלְעֵילָּא, וְצִיּוּרָא דְּאִימָּא מִצְטַיְּירָא בְּהַהוּא רוּחָא לְתַתָּא. צִיּוּרָא דְּאַתְוָון אִתְגְּנִיזוּ לְגוֹ, וְצִיּוּרָא דְּאִימָּא בָּלִיט לְבַר.

96. Rabbi Shimon said to him: If so, the image of the mother OF THE SPIRIT, NAMELY MALCHUT, is not shaped from within that spirit, AS THE LETTERS COME FROM THE FATHER OF THE SPIRIT – NAMELY ZEIR ANPIN, AS MENTIONED. They replied to him: So we heard from our master, that the form of letters comes from above, FROM ZEIR ANPIN and the form of the mother – NAMELY MALCHUT CONTAINING FOUR FACES, LION, OX, AND SO ON – is formed in that spirit below. And the form of the letters, THAT COME FROM ZEIR ANPIN, are concealed within, and the form of Ima projects outwardly.

97. צִיּוּרָא דְּאִימָא, פְּנֵי אָדָ"ם, פְּנֵי אַרְיֵ"ה, פְּנֵי שׁוֹ"ר, פְּנֵי נֶשֶׁ"ר. וְרוּחָא עָבֵיד צִיּוּרָא דְּכֻלְּהוּ לְבַר לְפוּם שַׁעֲתָא, בְּגִין דְּכָל מַה דְּאִיהוּ מִסִּטְרָא דְּרוּחָא בָּלְטָא לְבַר, וְאִתְחֲזֵי וְאִתְגְּנִיז. וְכָל הָנֵי דְּיוּקְנִין, אִתְחַזְיָין, מִתְצַיְּירָן בְּצִיּוּרָא דְּאַתְוָון אע"ג דְּאִינּוּן גְּנִיזִין. אִלֵּין אַרְבַּע דְּיוּקְנִין אִתְחַזְיָין לְפוּם שַׁעֲתָא, לְאִינּוּן מָארֵי דְּעַיְינִין, דְּיַדְעִין בְּרָזָא דְּחָכְמְתָא לְאִסְתַּכְּלָא בְּהוּ.

97. The form of Ima, WHICH IS MALCHUT, is the face of a man, the face of a lion, the face of an ox and the face of an eagle. And the spirit projects the image of all of them for a time, for everything belonging on the side of the spirit projects itself to the outside, and when it becomes visible, is IMMEDIATELY concealed. All these forms which become visible and are designed in the shape of letters, COME FROM ZEIR ANPIN, even though they are concealed FROM WITHIN, AS PREVIOUSLY MENTIONED. These four forms are visible for a time to those who have eyes to see, AND THESE ARE MEN OF WISDOM who comprehend, by the mystery of wisdom, how to contemplate them.

98. צִיּוּר"א קַדְמָאָ"ה, כַּד אָזִיל בַּר נָשׁ בְּאֹרַח קְשׁוֹט, אִינּוּן דְּיַדְעִין בְּרָזִין דְּמָארֵיהוֹן מִסְתַּכְּלָן בֵּיהּ, בְּגִין דְּהַהוּא רוּחָא דִּלְגוֹ, מִתְתַּקְנָא בֵּיהּ, וּבָלִיט לְבַר, צִיּוּרָא דְּכֹלָּא. וְהַהוּא צִיּוּרָא אִיהוּ צִיּוּרָא דְּאָדָם, וְדָא אִיהוּ צִיּוּרָא שְׁלִים יַתִּיר מִכָּל צִיּוּרִין. וְדָא אִיהוּ צִיּוּרָא, דְּאַעְבַּר לְפוּם שַׁעֲתָא, קָמֵי עֵינַיְיהוּ דְּחַכִּימֵי לִבָּא. הַאי כַּד מִסְתַּכְּלָן בְּאַנְפֹּוי לְבַר, אִינּוּן אַנְפִּין דְּקַיְימָן קַמֵּיהּ, עַיְינִין דְּלִבָּא רָחִים לוֹן.

98. The first form is as follows. When a man walks in the way of Truth, those who know the secret of their Master discern him, because the spirit within is established in him and projects the design to the outside, WHICH INCLUDES the full design; that form becomes the form of man. This form is the most perfect of all other designs, and this is the design that passes for a time before the eyes of the wise-hearted. When they look at his appearance from the outside, at that face that is before them, the eyes of the heart are moved to love him.

99. אַרְבַּע סִימָנִין דְּאַתְוָון אִית בְּהוּ, שׁוּרְיְיקָא חַד בָּלִיט בִּשְׁכִיבוּ, בְּסִטְרָא דִּימִינָא, וְשׁוּרְיְיקָא חַד דְּכָלִיל תְּרֵין אַחֲרָנִין דַּאֲחִידָן בֵּיהּ, בְּסִטְרָא דִּשְׂמָאלָא. וְאִלֵּין ד' סִימָנִים, אִינּוּן ד' אַתְוָון, דְּאִקְרוּן עֵדוּת וְסִימָנָא דָּא ע'. הַהוּא שׁוּרְיְיקָא דְּסְטַר יְמִינָא, דְּבָלִיט בִּשְׁכִיבוּ. ד' וְאִינּוּן תְּרֵין אַתְוָון דְּמִתְחַבְּרָן בֵּיהּ ו"ת, אִינּוּן הַהִיא שׁוּרְיְיקָא דְּכָלִיל תְּרֵין אַחֲרָנִין, וְדָא אִיהוּ רָזָא דִּכְתִיב עֵדוּת בִּיהוֹסֵף שָׂמוֹ דְּכָל מַאן דְּחָמָא לֵיהּ הֲוָה רָחִים לֵיהּ בְּלִבּוֹי, וּבִרְחִימוּ אִשְׁתְּלִים.

99. Four letter signs are impressed on it. One vein is conspicuous on his face in a depression, THAT IS TO SAY, IT IS NOT PROJECTED ON THE OUTSIDE, LIKE A CONSPICUOUS GROOVE, from the right side. There is another vein that includes and seizes two others that are attached to it from the left side OF THE FACE. These four signs are the four letters *Ayin, Vav, Dalet,* and *Tav* (Heb. *edut,* lit. 'testimony'). The sign *Ayin* is the vein on the right side and is conspicuous in its sunken position. The *Dalet* and the two letters attached to it, *Vav* and *Tav,* form a vein which includes two other veins ON THE LEFT SIDE OF THE FACE. This is the secret of the phrase: "This He ordained in Joseph for testimony" (Tehilim 81:6), for everyone who saw him loved him in their heart, and in this love he was perfected.

100. זַרְעָא דְּדָוִד מִתְהַפְּכָן בֵּיהּ חֵיזוּ דִּגְוָונִין, וּבְג"כ טָעָה שְׁמוּאֵל, דִּכְתִיב אַל תַּבֵּט אֶל מַרְאֵהוּ, בְּגִין דְּסִטְרָא אַחֲרָא הֲוָה בֵּיהּ בֶּאֱלִיאָב, דְּלָא הֲוָה הָכִי בְּדָוִד, דְּיוּקְנִין דְּדָוִד טְמִירִין אִינּוּן, דְּהָא דְּיוּקְנִין דְּסִטְרָא אַחֲרָא, אִתְכְּלִיל גּוֹ דְּיוּקְנִין, וְהַהוּא דְּיוּקָנָא דְּסְטַר אַחֲרָא אִתְחֲזֵי בֵּיהּ בְּקַדְמֵיתָא, דְּאַעְבַּר עַל עַיְינִין לְפוּם שַׁעֲתָא, וּבָהִיל לִבָּא וְדָחִיל, וּלְבָתַר וְטוֹב רוֹאִי וַיְיָ' עִמּוֹ. וְדָא אִיהוּ עֵדוּת לְגַבֵּיהּ.

100. In the seed of David, the colors are reversed. This is why Samuel erred, as it is written: "look not on his countenance" (I Shmuel 16:7), since the Other Side was in Eliav, which was not so in David. For the features of David were covered, for the forms of the Other Side were included in his own features. And it is the form of the Other Side that is seen first, passing over the eyes temporarily and frightening the heart, yet afterwards: "a comely person, and Hashem is with him" (Ibid. 19). This gives testimony about him.

101. דִּיּוּקְנָא דָּא דְּאָדָם, כְּלִיל כָּל דִּיּוּקְנִין, וְכֻלְּהוּ כְּלִילָן בֵּיהּ, הַאי לָא בָּהִיל בְּרוּחֵיהּ. בְּשַׁעֲתָא דְּרוּגְזֵיהּ אִיהוּ בְּנַיְיחָא, וּמִלּוֹי בְּנַיְיחָא, וּמִיָּד אִתְפָּיַיס.

101. The image of man includes all forms, and all forms include his. Such a man is not frightened in spirit, in times of anger he is calm, his words are calming and he is quickly appeased.

102. זַרְעָא דְּדָוִד דְּאִתְחֲזֵי בֵּיהּ הַהוּא דִּיּוּקְנָא בְּקַדְמֵיתָא, דְּאַעֲבַר לְפוּם שַׁעֲתָא עַל עַיְינִין, בְּרוּגְזֵיהּ בְּנַיְיחָא, מִיָּד אִתְפָּיַיס. אֲבָל נָטִיר דְּבָבוּ כְּנָחָשׁ לְסוֹפָא. בְּגִין דְּהַהוּא סִטְרָא גַּרְמָא לֵיהּ, דְּסַחֲרָא בְּכָל סִטְרִין. אֲבָל מוֹחָא דִּבְגוֹ קְלִיפָה וְלִבָּא מִתְיַשְּׁרָא, וְיַצִּיבָא דָּא לְאִינּוּן זַכָּאִין. אֲבָל חַיָּיבִין לָא מִתְעַבְּרָן מֵהַהוּא דִּיּוּקְנָא קַדְמָאָה בִּישָׁא, וְאִתְחַבְּרָן בֵּיהּ בְּכֹלָּא.

102. In the seed of David – where the image OF THE OTHER SIDE is seen at first and passes briefly before the eyes, AS PREVIOUSLY DISCUSSED – he is self-controlled in anger, and quickly appeased. Yet, he must guard a serpentine hatred in the end. For it is that side that brought THIS about, surrounding itself on all sides UNTIL IT TAKES ITS REVENGE, but the fruit that is enclosed in its shell and the heart become righteous. This is true for righteous people, but in evil people, the original evil form is not turned aside from them, being fully attached to them.

103. צִיּוּר"א תְּנִיינָ"א, אִי הַהוּא בַּר נָשׁ לָא אָזִיל כָּל כַּךְ בְּאָרְחָא בִּישָׁא, וְאַסְטֵי מֵהַהוּא אָרְחָא, וְתָב לְמָארֵיהּ, לָא דְּהוּא רְגִילָא בְּאָרְחוֹי דִּמְתַקְּנָן, אֶלָּא אִיהוּ דַּהֲוָה בְּאִינּוּן אוֹרְחֵי מִתְעֲדֵי, וְסָטֵי מִנַּיְיהוּ וְתָב לְמָארֵיהּ. הַאי אִיהוּ רוּחָא טָבָא שָׁארֵי לְמִשְׁרֵי עֲלוֹי, וּלְאִתַּתְקְפָא עַל זוּהֲמָא קַדְמָאָה דַּהֲוָה בֵּיהּ, וּבָלִיט לְבַר, בְּאִסְתַּכְּלוּתָא, דְּעַיְינִין לְפוּם שַׁעֲתָא, כְּחַד דִּיּוּקְנָא דְּאַרְיֵה דְּאִתְגַּבַּר הַאי בְּשַׁעֲתָא דְּחָמֵי לֵיהּ, הַהוּא חֵיזוּ גָּרִים לֵיהּ לְאַעֲבָּר בְּלִבֵּיהּ אַרְיֵה דְּמִתְגַּבְּרָא לְפוּם שַׁעֲתָא.

103. This is the second form. If a man does not walk much in the ways of wickedness, turning aside from this path and returning to His Master, this means that a good spirit is beginning to rest upon him, overpowering the first impurities that were upon him. It is projected outside, observed by the eyes temporarily, in the form of a powerful lion. At the time when THIS IMAGE is seen, this appearance causes the spirit of a powerful lion to prevail in his heart – THAT IS TO SAY, HIS HEART PREVAILS OVER THE EVIL SIDE.

104. הַאי מִסְתַּכְּלָן בְּאַנְפּוֹי לְבָתַר, אִינּוּן אַנְפִּין דְּלָבָּא לָא רָחִים לוֹן לְפוּם שַׁעֲתָא, וּמִיַּד תָּב לְבֵיהּ וְרָחִים לֵיהּ. כַּד מִסְתַּכְּלָן בֵּיהּ אַכְסִיף, וְחָשִׁיב דְּכֹלָּא יַדְעִין בֵּיהּ. אַנְפּוֹי חַפְיָין דָּמָא לְפוּם שַׁעֲתָא, מִתְהַפְּכָן לְחִוּוָרָא אוֹ לִירוֹקָא.

104. With reference to him, WHO HAS THE IMAGE OF A POWERFUL LION, when they discern his face afterwards, it is a face that the heart does not love immediately, but an instant later, the heart returns to love it. When people look at him, he becomes embarrassed and thinks everyone knows his ways; THAT IS TO SAY, IT SEEMS TO HIM THAT EVERYONE KNOWS WHAT HE THINKS AND DOES IN SECRET. AND IN HIS SHAME, blood rushes to his face for a short time, AND AFTERWARDS it reverses its colors to white or green.

105. תְּלַת שׁוּרְיָיקֵן אִית בְּאַנְפּוֹי. חַד לִימִינָא, דְּדָא אִתְפָּשַׁט בְּאַנְפּוֹי וְאִתְאֲחִיד בֵּיהּ. חַד דְּסַלְקָא לְחוֹטְמֵיה לְעֵילָא, וּתְרֵין לִשְׂמָאלָא. וְחַד דְּאִתְפָּשַׁט לְתַתָּא מֵאִינּוּן תְּרֵין, וְאָחִיד בְּהַאי וּבְהַאי. וְאִלֵּין אִינּוּן אַתְוָון דְּמִתְחַקְּקָן בְּאַנְפּוֹי, וְאִינּוּן בַּלְטִין דְּלָא שְׁכִיבִין. וְכַד מִתְיַישְׁבָא וְאַרְגִּיל בְּאֹרַח קְשׁוֹט, שְׁכִיבִין.

105. Three fine veins are on his face. There is one on the right. This is traced on the face, which grips it. Another proceeds upward to the bridge of the nose. There are two on the left, and one that branches downward from these two attaches itself to this one and that one. These letters which are carved upon his face protrude and are not sunken. But when he becomes settled, and gradually becomes accustomed to walking in the way of Truth, they sink.

‎106. וְרָזָא דְּאִינּוּן אַתְוָון אִיהוּ קָרִיב. דָּא הֲוָה רָחִיק, וְהַשְׁתָּא אִינּוּן
אַתְוָון בָּלְטִין בְּאַנְפּוֹי, וְסָהֲדִין בֵּיהּ בִּבְהִילוּ. וְסִימָנָא דָּא ק' מִסְּטַר
יְמִינָא אַתְוָון אַחֲרָנִין מִסְּטַר שְׂמָאלָא, ואע"ג דְּשׁוּרְיָיקֵי אַחֲרָנִין אִתְחֲזוּן
בְּאַנְפּוֹי, לָא בָּלְטִין לְבַר כְּהָנֵי. בַּר בְּזִמְנָא דַּהֲוָה אָזִיל בְּעֲקִימוּ.

106. The secret of these letters. He is near (Heb. *karov*, Kof Resh Vav Bet). He was far, and when HE CAME NEAR, the letters protruded in his face to give hasty testimony. And this is the mark of *Kof*, which is on the right side OF THE FACE. The other letters, WHICH ARE *RESH VAV BET*, are on the left side OF THE FACE. And even though other veins are seen in his face, they do not protrude on the outside as these do, except when he walks on the path of evil – THEN THESE ALSO PROTRUDE.

‎107. הַאי אִיהוּ זַרְעָא דְּדָוִד, אִתְהַפַּךְ מֶחֱזוּ דָּא. בְּקַדְמֵיתָא אִתְחֲזֵי
בְּדִיּוּקְנָא דְּאָדָם, וּלְבָתַר קַיְּימָא בְּדִיּוּקְנָא דְּאַרְיֵה, וְאִתְפְּרַשׁ בְּדִיּוּקְנָא
דְּסִטְרָא אַחֲרָא, וּבְכֹלָּא, מִתְהַפְּכָא מִשְּׁאָר בְּנֵי נָשָׁא.

107. This appearance is different in one who is from the seed of David. First he appears in the form of man, then that of a lion. He then separates from the Other Side. And in all things, he is the reverse of other men.

‎108. צִיּוּר"א תְּלִי"תָאה, אִי הַהוּא בַּר נָשׁ אָזִיל בְּאָרְחָא דְּלָא
מִתְתַּקְנָא, וְסָטֵי אוֹרְחוֹי מֵאָרְחֵי דְּאוֹרַיְיתָא, הַהוּא רוּחָא קַדִּישָׁא
אִסְתַּלָּק מִנֵּיהּ, וְרוּחָא אַחֲרָא אִתְחֲזֵי בֵּיהּ, וְדִיּוּקְנָא אַחֲרָא, וּבָלִיט לְבַר,
בְּאִסְתַּכְּלוּתָא דְּעַיְינִין דְּחַכִּימֵי לִבָּא, לְפוּם שַׁעֲתָא דְּיוּקְנָא דְּשׁוֹר.
בְּשַׁעֲתָא דְּחָמָאן לֵיהּ, מַעֲבְרָן בְּלִבַּיְיהוּ הַהוּא דְּיוּקְנָא, וְאִסְתַּכְּלָן בֵּיהּ.

108. This is the third form. If a man walks in a path that is not correct and his ways lead him away from the path of the Torah, that Holy Spirit is removed from him and another spirit is seen in him; another image which is protruding, observable to the eyes of the wise-hearted as the form of an ox. At the moment that he is observed BY THE WISE OF HEART, they pass the image OF AN OX across their hearts, and contemplate it.

109. ג' קוּרְטָמֵי סוּמָקֵי בְּאַנְפּוֹי, בְּסִטְרָא דִּימִינָא, וְאִינּוּן שׁוּרְיָיקֵי סוּמָקֵין דְּקִיקִין. וּתְלַת בִּשְׂמָאלָא, וְאִלֵּין אִינּוּן אַתְוָון דְּבַלְטִין בֵּיהּ. חַד אִיהוּ שׁוּרְיָיקָא דָּקִיק בְּעֲגוּלָא, וּתְרֵין דְּקִיקִין אַחֲרָנִין עֲלֵיהּ, וְכֻלְּהוּ בְּעֲגוּלָא. וּכְדֵין שְׁקִיעִין עֵינוֹי.

109. On the right side of his face there are three red kernels OF WILD CROCUS, and these red veins are small. And there are three on the left side OF HIS FACE. These are the letters, which are prominent in him. One vein FROM THE THREE ON THE RIGHT AND THE LEFT SIDE is small and spherical. And two other thin veins above are also circular. The eyes of this person are sunken INTO HIS FOREHEAD.

110. וְרָזָא דְּאִינּוּן אַתְוָון. חַד אִיהוּ כ', תְּרֵין אַחֲרָנִין ר"ת אִינּוּן. וְכֵן לְסְטַר שְׂמָאלָא, וְסִימָנָא דָּא הַהוּא דִּכְתִיב, הַכָּרַת פְּנֵיהֶם עָנְתָה בָּם וְאִלֵּין אַתְוָון בַּלְטִין בְּאַנְפִּין, עַל כָּל שְׁאַר שׁוּרְיָיקִין. וְאִי תָּב מִשְּׂמָאלָא לִימִינָא, אִתְכַּפְיָא הַהוּא רוּחָא וְאִתְתַּקַּף רוּחָא דְּקֻדְשָׁא, וְאִלֵּין שׁוּרְיָיקִין שְׁכִיבוּ, וְאַחֲרָנִין בַּלְטִין לְבַר, כְּמָה דְּאִתְּמַר.

110. This is the secret of these letters. One OF THE THREE is the letter *Caf*, the other two veins form the letters *Resh* and *Tav*. So it is WITH THE THREE VEINS on the left side: ONE OF THEM IS THE LETTER *CAF* AND THE OTHERS *RESH* AND *TAV*. And these letters form that which is written: "The sight of their countenance (Heb. *hakarat, Hei-Caf-Resh-Tav*) witnesses against them" (Yeshayah 3:9). And these are the letters that protrude in the face more than all other sinews. But if he returns REPENTING, turning away from the left AND COMING to THE SIDE OF the right, then that spirit yields and the spirit of Holiness prevails. Then these veins sink and others protrude on the outside, as we have studied.

111. זַרְעָא דְּדָוִד אִיהוּ בְּהִפּוּכָא, אִתְחַזְיָיא בְּדִיּוּקְנָא דְּאַרְיֵה בְּקַדְמֵיתָא, וּלְבָתַר אִתְהַדַּר בְּדִיּוּקְנָא דְּשׁוֹר. תְּרֵין שׁוּרְיָיקִין אוּכָמִין בְּאַנְפּוֹי, חַד מִימִינָא, וְחַד מִשְּׂמָאלָא, וְאִלֵּין אִינּוּן אַתְוָון, חַד אִקְרֵי ד', וְחַד אִקְרֵי ע', וְכֹלָּא מִתְהַפְּכָא מִשְּׁאַר בְּנֵי נָשָׁא.

111. It is the opposite with the seed of David. The image of the lion is seen first, and afterwards it turns to the image of an ox. Two dark veins are visible in his face, one from the right and one from the left, and these are the letters: one was called '*Dalet*' and the other called '*Ayin*'. And in everything it is the opposite from other men.

112. צִיוּר״א רְבִיעָ״אה, דָּא אִיהוּ צִיּוּרָא דְּבַר נָשׁ, דְּקַיְּימָא תָּדִיר לְאִתְתַּקְּנָא עַל רָזָא דְּמִלְּקַדְמִין, הַאי אִיהוּ חֵיזוּ לְחַכִּימֵי לִבָּא בְּדִיּוּקְנָא דְּנֶשֶׁר. הַהוּא רוּחָא דִּילֵיהּ אִיהוּ רוּחָא חַלָּשָׁא. הַאי לָא אַחְזֵי בְּאַנְפִּין אַתְוָון דְּבַלְטִין לְבַר, דְּהָא אִתְאֲבִידוּ מִנֵּיהּ, וְאִשְׁתְּקָעוּ בְּזִמְנָא אַחֲרָא דְּמִלְּקַדְמִין, דְּאִסְתָּלָקוּ מִנֵּיהּ, וְעַל דָּא לָא בַּלְטִין בֵּיהּ.

112. The fourth image is the form of a man, always standing ready to amend a secret past, AND DOING NO MORE DAMAGE. This is seen by the wise of heart in the form of an eagle. His spirit is a spirit of weakness. He does not exhibit on his face letters that protrude outwardly, since these were lost and sunk in his early days. Since they left him, they are no longer protruding.

113. וְרָזָא דִּילֵיהּ, עֵינוֹי לָא נְהִרִין בִּנְצִיצוּ, כַּד אִיהוּ בְּחֶדְוָה. וּבְזִמְנָא דְּסָפַר שְׂעַר רֵישֵׁיהּ וְדִיקְנֵיהּ. בְּגִין דְּרוּחֵיהּ לָא נָהִיר לֵיהּ בְּאַתְוָון, וְאִשְׁתְּקַע נְצִיצוּ דִּילֵיהּ דַּהֲוָה בְּקַדְמֵיתָא. לָא קַיְּימָא בְּאִסְתַּכְּלוּתָא דְּאַנְפִּין לְאִסְתַּכְּלָא. וְרָזָא דְּהַאי וְשַׁבֵּחַ אֲנִי אֶת הַמֵּתִים שֶׁכְּבָר מֵתוּ מִן הַחַיִּים אֲשֶׁר הֵמָּה חַיִּים עֲדֶנָה. זַרְעָא דְּדָוִד, סוֹד יְיָ' לִירֵאָיו וּבְרִיתוֹ לְהוֹדִיעָם.

113. This is the secret of him. His eyes do not sparkle with brightness, even when he is joyful, nor at those times when he trims the hair on his head and his beard. This is because his spirit does not shine in those letters, and the sparks of light which he had at the beginning have now declined. It can not be observed when one looks at his face BECAUSE THERE ARE NO PROTRUDING LETTERS, AS WAS MENTIONED BEFORE. And this is the secret as it is written: "So I praised the dead that are already dead more than the living that are yet alive" (Kohelet 4:2). However, pertaining to the seed of David, "the counsel (also: 'secret') of Hashem is with them that fear Him: and He will reveal to them His covenant" (Tehilim 25:14).

114. בְּרוּחָא דְּבַר נָשׁ, אִצְטַיָּירוּ אַתְוָון, כְּמָה דְּאִתְּמַר, וְאִיהוּ בָּלִיט לוֹן
לְבַר, וְאִתְמְסַר חָכְמְתָא דָּא לְחַכִּימֵי לִבָּא לְמִנְדַע וּלְאִשְׁתְּמוֹדְעָא, רוּחָא
קַיְימָא בְּרָזָא דְּזֶה סֵפֶר, וְכֹלָּא בְּרָזָא דָּא קַיְימָא, בַּר חֵיזוּ דְּאַנְפִּין
דְּאִתְּדָן בְּגַוְוונָא אַחֲרָא, כְּפוּם שׁוּלְטָנוּ דְּרוּחָא, אוֹ מָארֵיהּ דְּרוּחָא. זַכָּאִין
אִינּוּן חַכִּימִין דְּכֹלָּא אִתְמְסַר לוֹן לְמִנְדַּע. עַד הָכָא רָזָא דְּאַנְפִּין.

114. In the spirit of man, letters are impressed, as we have learned, which protrude through to the outside ON THE FACE. And this wisdom has been given to the wise to comprehend and to recognize. The spirit can be approached through the concealed significance of the phrase, "This is the book" (Beresheet 5:11). Everything is approached through this mystery except for facial features, which we judge by another method, according to the rule of the spirit or man of spirit. Happy are those wise ones who are privileged to be entrusted with this knowledge. Until this point is the secret of faces.

9. And you shall behold the secret of the lips

A Synopsis
The secret of the lips is in the letter Pe, and we read of the qualities of men with different types of lips.

115. מִכָּאן וּלְהָלְאָה בְּרָזָא דְּשִׂפְוָון, בְּאָת פ׳ דְּכָלִיל בְּרָזָא דְּאָת ס׳. שִׂפְוָון רַבְרְבָן, דָּא אִיהוּ בַּר נָשׁ מַלִּיל בְּלִישָׁנָא בִּישָׁא, וְלָא אַכְסִיף, וְלָא דָחִיל, מָארֵי דְּמַחֲלוֹקֶת, רְכִילָא אִיהוּ בֵּין הַאי לְהַאי. וּמְשַׁלֵּחַ מְדָנִים בֵּין אַחִים. לָאו אִיהוּ מָארֵיהּ דְּרָזִין, וְכַד אִשְׁתַּדַּל בְּאוֹרַיְיתָא מְכַסֶּה רָזִין, אֲבָל מָארֵיהּ דְּלִישָׁנָא בִּישָׁא, וְלָא שָׁוֵי דְּחִילוּ בְּלִבֵּיהּ.

115. From here forward is the secret of the lips, of the letter *Pe*, which is included in the secret of the letter *Samech*. Big lips denote a man who spreads malicious gossip without shame or fear. He is a person who causes dissension and slander between one another, THAT IS TO SAY, BETWEEN MAN AND HIS NEIGHBOR. He is "one that sows discord among brethren" (Mishlei 6:19), and he can not keep a secret. When he endeavors in the Torah, he can keep hidden secrets. Yet he still is a malicious gossiper without any fear in his heart.

116. וְסִימָנָא דָּא, אָת פ׳ דְּכָלִיל בְּאָת ר׳ וְלָא אִתְכְּלִיל בְּאָת ס׳. הַאי אִיהוּ דְּאִתְחֲזֵי דְּאִיהוּ זַכָּאָה, וְלָא דָחִיל חַטָּאָה אִיהוּ, וְלָא בָּעֵי לְאִשְׁתַּדְּלָא אֲבַתְרֵיהּ, בְּגִין דְּכָל מִלּוֹי אִינּוּן בְּפוּמָא וְלָא בְּגוּפָא.

116. This sign, the letter *Pe,* is included in the letter *Resh* but not in the letter *Samech*. Such a one seems to be righteous but he has no fear of transgressing. One should have no dealings with him, because whatever he does proceeds out of his mouth alone and not from his body.

117. שִׂפְוָון עַתִּיקִין בְּעַתִּיקוּ, וְלָאו דְּקִיקִין. הַאי אִיהוּ בַּר נָשׁ מָארֵיהּ דְּרוּגְזָא יַתִּיר. מָארֵיהּ דְּזָדוֹנָא. לָא יָכִיל לְמִסְבַּל מִלָּה. מָארֵי דְּלִישָׁנָא בִּישָׁא בְּפַרְהֶסְיָא, בְּלָא כְּסוּפָא כְּלָל. לְזִמְנִין אִשְׁתַּדַּל בְּלֵיצָנוּתָא. הַאי אִיהוּ בַּר נָשׁ דְּבָעֵי לְאִתְרַחֲקָא מִנֵּיהּ.

117. Lips that are dry and shriveled and not thin signify a man with a quick temper. He is malicious. He is intolerant with everything. Openly, he spreads malicious gossip without shame. At times he is frivolous, and scoffs at others. This is a man from whom you must remain at a distance.

118. אִתְמְלֵי דִּיקְנֵיהּ בְּשַׂעְרָא, הַהוּא, לִישָׁנָא בִּישָׁא, אוֹרֵי עָלֵיהּ בְּפַרְהֶסְיָא, לֵית לֵיהּ כִּסּוּפָא. אִשְׁתָּדַּל בְּמַחְלוֹקֶת. אַצְלַח בְּמִלֵּי דְּעָלְמָא. חָמֵי בְּשַׂנְאוֹי. דָּא אִיהוּ קוֹרֵץ בְּעֵינָיו, עַל דָּא אִתְּמַר הֶעֵז אִישׁ רָשָׁע בְּפָנָיו. דָּא אִיהוּ בְּרָזָא דְּאָת פ׳ בִּלְחוֹדוֹי. דְּלָא אִתְכְּלִיל בְּאָת ס׳ כְּלָל. וּלְזִמְנִין אִתְחַבָּר בְּאָת ר׳ בְּהַאי אָת ר׳ אִתְכְּלִיל.

118. If his beard becomes full, according to evil speech, such a one speaks openly to everyone. He has no shame and he concerns himself with causing strife. Yet, he is successful in worldly matters. He gazes upon his enemies, and he "winks with his eyes" (Ibid. 13). Concerning him, it is said: "A wicked man hardens his face" (Mishlei 21:29). He stands under the mystery of the letter *Pe* alone, when it is not included in the *Samech* at all. Yet at times it is joined to the letter *Resh*. It is included in this letter *Resh*.

10. And you shall behold the secret of the ears

A Synopsis

The size and shape of ears is correlated to certain human characteristics, the ears being of the letter Yud. From here, we are told that the Zohar will speak about the mysteries of the verse, "This is the book," in its supreme spiritual level in the context of times and seasons of this world.

119. בְּרָזָא דְּאוּדְנִין, מַאן דְּאוּדְנוֹי רַבְרְבִין, טִפְּשָׁא בְּלִיבֵּיה וְשִׁגְעוֹנָא בְּרוּחֵיה. מַאן דְּאוּדְנוֹי זְעִירִין, וְקַיְימִין עַל קִיּוּמָא. פְּקִיחָא דְּלִבָּא בְּאִתְעָרוּתָא אִיהוּ. צָבֵי לְאִשְׁתַּדְּלָא בְּכֹלָּא. וְרָזָא דָּא אָת י' דְּאִתְכְּלִיל בְּכָל שְׁאַר אַתְוָון.

119. The mystery of the ears. One whose ears are large has foolishness in his heart and madness in his spirit. One whose ears are small and preserve a proper shape, when awakened, is wise-hearted. He will concern himself with everything. This type is under the letter *Yud*, which is included in all other letters.

120. עַד הָכָא, רָזִין דְּדִיּוּקְנִין דְּבַר נָשׁ. מִכָּאן וּלְהָלְאָה, רָזִין אַחֲרָנִין בְּאַתְוָון דְּמָר, דְּלָא קַיְימִין גּוֹ פַּרְצוּפָא, אֶלָּא לְמִנְדַּע רָזִין דְּהַאי פְּסוּקָא, גּוֹ דַּרְגִּין עִלָּאִין, בְּזִמְנִין וּתְקִיפִין דְּהַאי עָלְמָא, וְלָא זָכֵינָן בְּהוּ.

120. Until this point is the secret of the shapes of man. From here forward we will concern ourselves with other mysteries of our master RABBI SHIMON which have no standing with regard to the countenance. Rather, we will endeavor to learn the mysteries of the verse, "THIS IS THE BOOK," in its supreme spiritual level in the context of times and seasons of this world, of WHICH UNTIL NOW we were not worthy of knowing.

121. אָמַר ר' שִׁמְעוֹן, בְּנַי, זַכָּאִין אַתּוּן בְּעָלְמָא, דֵּין, וּבְעָלְמָא דְּאָתֵי, וְזַכָּאִין עֵינַי, דְּיִזְכּוּן לְמֶיחֱמֵי דָּא, כַּד אֵיעוּל לְהַהוּא עָלְמָא דְּאָתֵי. בְּגִין נִשְׁמָתִי קָרֵי לְעַתִּיק יוֹמִין, הַאי קְרָא, תַּעֲרוֹךְ לְפָנַי שֻׁלְחָן נֶגֶד צוֹרְרָי דְּשַׁנְתָּ בַשֶּׁמֶן רֹאשִׁי כּוֹסִי רְוָיָה. וְקוּדְשָׁא בְּרִיךְ הוּא קָרֵי עֲלָן, פִּתְחוּ

שְׁעָרִים וְיָבֹא גוֹי צַדִּיק שֹׁמֵר אֱמוּנִים.

121. Rabbi Shimon said: My children, you are worthy in this world and you are worthy in the World to Come. Blessed are my eyes that will be worthy to see this when I enter the World to Come. For the sake of my soul, I call to Atik Yomin ('Ancient of Days') this verse: "You prepare a table before me in the presence of my enemies: You anoint my head with oil; my cup runs over" (Tehilim 23:5). And the Holy One, blessed be He, calls to us: "Open the Gates, that the righteous nation that keeps faithfulness may enter in" (Yeshayah 26:2).

11. And you shall behold the secret of the lines of the hands

A Synopsis

We are told that God impressed spiritual mysteries upon the palm and fingers of a person. The mystery of the palm is of the letter Caf. The skin, bones and sinews are compared to things in the supernal realms. Returning to a discussion of the face, we read that it is only possible to discern a person fully when the face is without anger, but is shining and serene. Much reference is made in this whole section to the firmament, the heavens and the stars. At the end we learn that Moses had no need of these signs by which the wise recognize the wise, for he was informed by the Holy Spirit; King Solomon knew these things and was able to judge because of his throne, but King Messiah will judge by the fragrance. And these three were able to judge the world without witnesses. All others who are wise in these signs must warn people, and try to heal them.

122. אוֹף אִינּוּן פָּתְחוּ וְאָמְרוּ, כְּתִיב וִידֵי אָדָם מִתַּחַת כַּנְפֵיהֶם, הַאי קְרָא אוּקְמוּהָ חַבְרַיָּיא, דְּאִינּוּן יְדִין לְקַבְּלָא מָארֵיהוֹן דִּתְיוּבְתָּא דְּתָבָאן לְגַבֵּי קוּדְשָׁא בְּרִיךְ הוּא. אֲבָל יְדֵי אָדָם, אִלֵּין אִינּוּן דִּיּוּקְנִין וְרָזִין עִלָּאִין, דְּשַׁוֵּי קוּדְשָׁא בְּרִיךְ הוּא בְּבַר נָשׁ, וְסָדֵר לוֹן בְּאֶצְבְּעָן לְבַר וּלְגוֹ. וּבְהַהוּא כַּ"ף.

122. They opened the discussion with a discourse on the verse: "and they had the hands of a man under their wings" (Yechezkel 1:8). This verse, the friends explained, are the hands to receive penitents who return to the Holy One, blessed be He. "...the hands of a man..." are the forms and spiritual mysteries which the Holy One, Blessed be He, impressed upon man and arranged in his fingers, outwardly and inwardly, and in his palm. THAT IS, THE PALM OF HIS HAND.

123. וְקוּדְשָׁא בְּרִיךְ הוּא כַּד בָּרָא לֵיה לְבַר נָשׁ, סָדֵר בֵּיה, כָּל דִּיּוּקְנִין דְּרָזִין עִלָּאִין, דְּעָלְמָא דִּלְעֵילָּא, וְכָל דִּיּוּקְנִין דְּרָזִין תַּתָּאִין, דְּעָלְמָא דִּלְתַתָּא, וְכֹלָּא מִתְחַקְּקָא בב"נ, דְּאִיהוּ קָאִים בְּצֶלֶם אֱלֹהִים, בְּגִין דְּאִקְרֵי יְצִיר כַּ"ף.

123. When the Holy One, blessed be He, created man, He arranged in him all the forms of the supernal mysteries of the world above, WHICH IS BINAH, and all the images of the lower mysteries of the world below, WHICH IS MALCHUT. And all is carved in man and found in the image of Elohim, because he is called "the creation of the palm," WHICH IS THE PALM OF THE HOLY ONE, BLESSED BE HE.

124. וְרָזָא דְּכַ״ף, דְּאָת דָּא דְּאִקְרֵי כַּ״ף, דִּכְתִּיב, וַיִּבְרָא אֱלֹהִים אֶת הָאָדָם בְּצַלְמוֹ, דָּא אִיהוּ רָזָא דְּאָת כַּ״ף. אָת דָּא, אִית בֵּיהּ רָזִין עִלָּאִין, וְדִיּוּקְנִין עִלָּאִין. בְּהַאי כַּ״ף תַּלְיָין עֶשֶׂר אֲמִירָן מִימִינָא וּמִשְׂמָאלָא, חָמֵשׁ מִימִינָא, וְחָמֵשׁ מִשְׂמָאלָא, וְאִינוּן חַד בְּרָזָא חֲדָא.

124. And the mystery of the palm (Heb. *caf*) is of the letter which is called '*Caf*', as it is written: "And Elohim created Man in His own image" (Beresheet 1:27). This is the secret of the letter *Caf*. This letter has supernal secrets and spiritual forms. This *Caf*, WHICH IS THE PALM OF THE HAND, contains ten sayings from right and left – five in the right PALM and five in the left PALM. And all are one, in one secret – THE RIGHT AND THE LEFT ARE UNITED INTO ONE.

125. תָּנֵינָן כְּתִיב וְגַם אֲנִי אַכֶּה כַפִּי אֶל כַּפִּי, דְּלֶהֱווֹ דָא עִם דָּא בְּפַלּוּגְתָּא וְיִסְתַּלְּקוּ בִּרְכָּאן מֵעַלְמָא, הוֹאִיל וְגָאוּתָא דְּיִשְׂרָאֵל אִתְיְהִיבַת לְעַמִּין. כַּד מִתְחַבְּרָן כַּחֲדָא, כְּתִיב, כַּף אַחַת עֲשָׂרָה זָהָב מְלֵאָה קְטֹרֶת רֶמֶז לְחִבּוּרָא חֲדָא. וְכַד הֲווֹ בְּחִבּוּרָא חֲדָא, כְּתִיב, וַיִּבְרָא אֱלֹהִים אֶת הָאָדָם בְּצַלְמוֹ וְגוֹ'. וַיִּבְרָא אֱלֹהִים דָּא סְלִיקוּ דְּמַחֲשָׁבָה בְּרָזָא פְנִימָאָה. אֶת הָאָדָם: רָזָא דְּכַר וְנוּקְבָּא כַּחֲדָא, בְּצֶלֶם אֱלֹהִים רָזָא דְּכַף.

125. It is written: "I will also smite My one palm upon the other" (Yechezkel 21:22). ITS EXPLANATION is that this one and that one shall be in conflict so that blessings will be removed from this world, and the pride of Yisrael will be given over to the other nations. THIS IS BECAUSE FROM THE UNIFICATION OF RIGHT AND LEFT THERE CONTINUE FROM THE LEFT THE THREE FIRST SFIROT TO YISRAEL, WHICH IS THEIR PRIDE. WHEN THEY ARE DIVIDED, THE OTHER NATIONS SUCKLE FROM THE LEFT

COLUMN, AND THE PRIDE OF YISRAEL IS GIVEN OVER TO THE HEATHEN NATIONS. And when they are joined together, it is written: "One spoon (Heb. *caf*) of ten shekels of gold, full of incense" (Bemidbar 7:14). This is an indication of one connection, WHICH MEANS THE TEN FROM THE RIGHT AND THE LEFT ARE UNITED IN ONE PALM (HEB. *CAF*). And when they are united in one connection, it is written: "And Elohim created man in His own image..." "And Elohim created," implies the departure of thought through the inner mystery; "man," is the secret of Male and Female together, SINCE *ET* (ENG. 'THE'), WHICH COMES BEFORE THE WORD "MAN," IS FEMALE, AND "MAN" (HEB. *ADAM*) IS MALE. "In the image of Elohim," is the mystery of *Caf*, THAT IS, WHEN TWO RIGHT AND LEFT PALMS WERE UNIFIED INTO ONE *CAF*, WHEN ALL SUPERNAL MOCHIN EMANATE FROM THEM.

126. כַּד אִתְבְּרֵי אָדָם, מַה כְּתִיב, בֵּיהּ, עוֹר וּבָשָׂר תַּלְבִּישֵׁנִי וְגוֹ'. אִי הָכִי הָאָדָם מַהוּ. אִי תֵּימָא, דְּאֵינוּ אֶלָּא עוֹר וּבָשָׂר עֲצָמוֹת וְגִידִים, לָאו הָכִי, דְּהָא וַדַּאי הָאָדָם לָאו אִיהוּ אֶלָּא נִשְׁמָתָא. וְאִלֵּין דְּקָאָמַר עוֹר וּבָשָׂר עֲצָמוֹת וְגִידִים, כֻּלְּהוּ לָא הֲווֹ אֶלָּא מַלְבּוּשָׁא בִּלְחוֹדוֹי, מָאנִין אִינּוּן דְּבַר נָשׁ, וְלָאו אִינּוּן אָדָם. וְכַד הַאי אָדָם אִסְתַּלָּק, אִתְפָּשַׁט מֵאִנּוּן מָאנִין דְּקָא לְבִישׁ.

126. When man was created, what is written concerning him: "You have clothed me with skin and flesh..." (Iyov 10:11). HE ASKS: If so, what is man IN HIS ESSENCE? AND HE ANSWERS: If you think THAT MAN is nothing more than skin, flesh, bones and sinews, this is not so. For certainly man is but his soul. And skin, flesh, bones, and sinews, are all only the clothing. These are the implements of man, and not man HIMSELF. And when man passes away, he divests himself of all these implements that he wore.

127. עוֹר דְּאִתְלַבַּשׁ בֵּיהּ בַּר נָשׁ. וְכָל אִינּוּן עֲצָמוֹת וְגִידִים, כֻּלְּהוּ בְּרָזָא דְּחָכְמְתָא עִלָּאָה כְּגַוְונָא דִּלְעֵילָּא. עוֹר כְּגַוְונָא דִּלְעֵילָּא, כְּמָה דְּאוֹלִיף מֹר, בְּאִינּוּן יְרִיעוֹת, דִּכְתִיב נוֹטֶה שָׁמַיִם כַּיְרִיעָה. עוֹרוֹת אֵלִים מְאָדָּמִים וְעוֹרוֹת תְּחָשִׁים. אִינּוּן מַלְבּוּשִׁין דִּלְעֵילָּא, דִּמְסַכְּכֵי לְמַלְבּוּשָׁא, אִתְפַּשְׁטוּתָא דִּשְׁמַיִם, דְּאִיהוּ מַלְבּוּשָׁא דִּלְבַר. יְרִיעוֹת אִינּוּן מַלְבּוּשָׁא

דִּלְגוֹ, וְאִיהוּ קְרוּמָא דְּסָכִיךְ עַל בִּשְׂרָא.

127. The skin with which man has been clothed and all these bones and sinews, are all in the mystery of the supernal wisdom corresponding to that which is above. AND HE EXPLAINS THAT the skin, corresponding to that which is above, is, as we have learned, in connection with the curtains, as it is written: "who stretches out the heavens like a curtain" (Tehilim 104:1), "rams' skins dyed red, and badgers' skins" (Shemot 25:5). These are the garments up above that cover the garments which are like the extensions of the heavens, which is the outer garment. The curtains are the inner garments, corresponding to the skin that protects the flesh. AND THUS IT IS SAID, "WHO STRETCHES OUT THE HEAVENS LIKE A CURTAIN," AS THE CURTAINS ARE THE INNER GARMENTS, AND ON THESE ARE THE HEAVENLY GARMENTS FROM THE OUTSIDE.

128. עֲצָמוֹת וְגִידִים, אִינּוּן רְתִיכִין, וְכָל אִינּוּן חַיָּילִין, דְּקַיְימִין לְגוֹ. וְכֻלְּהוּ מַלְבּוּשִׁין לִפְנִימָאָה, רָזָא דְּאָדָם עִלָּאָה, דְּאִיהוּ פְּנִימָאָה.

128. The bones and the sinews are the Chariots and all the hosts, which are appointed inward. THAT IS, THEY ARE ALL AN INNER ASPECT AND THE FIRST THREE SFIROT OF THE OUTER PART OF THE GRADE, FOR THE SINEWS ARE THE Neshamah OF THE GARMENT, AND THE BONES ARE AN ASPECT OF Chayah OF THE GARMENT. And all of these are garments to that which is inward, which is also the mystery of the supernal man who is the innermost TO THEM.

129. אוּף הָכִי רָזָא לְתַתָּא, אָדָם אִיהוּ פְּנִימָאָה לְגוֹ. מַלְבּוּשִׁין דִּילֵיהּ כְּגַוְונָא דִּלְעֵילָּא. עֲצָמוֹת וְגִידִין, כְּגַוְונָא דְּקָאמְרָן בְּאִינּוּן רְתִיכִין וּמַשִׁירְיָין. בָּשָׂר אִיהוּ סָכִיךְ עַל אִינּוּן מַשִׁירְיָין וּרְתִיכִין, וְקַיְימָא לְבַר, וְדָא רָזָא דְּאִתְמַשְׁכָא לְסִטְרָא אַחֲרָא. עוֹר דְּסָכִיךְ עַל כֹּלָּא, דָּא אִיהוּ כְּגַוְונָא דְּאִינּוּן רְקִיעִין, דְּסָכִיכוּ עַל כֹּלָּא. וְכֻלְּהוּ מַלְבּוּשִׁין לְאִתְלַבְּשָׁא בְּהוּ. פְּנִימָאָה דִּלְגוֹ רָזָא דְּאָדָם. וְכֹלָּא רָזָא, לְתַתָּא כְּגַוְונָא דִּלְעֵילָּא. וְעַל דָּא וַיִּבְרָא אֱלֹקִים אֶת הָאָדָם בְּצַלְמוֹ בְּצֶלֶם אֱלֹקִים, וְרָזָא דְּאָדָם לְתַתָּא כֹּלָּא אִיהוּ בְּרָזָא דִּלְעֵילָּא.

129. The same secret is found here below. Man is the inner of the innermost and his garments correspond to that which is above. The bones and the sinews are similar to what we have said regarding the Chariots and hosts, THAT ARE CALLED 'BONES' AND 'SINEWS'. The flesh is a covering to those hosts and Chariots THAT ARE CALLED 'BONES' AND 'SINEWS', and appears itself outwardly TO THEM. And this is the secret THAT THE FLESH is being drawn FROM HIM to the Other Side. The skin, which covers all, corresponds to the firmaments which cover everything. And all of these are garments to be worn by him, the innermost being the mystery of man. And all is a secret. For what is below corresponds to the above. And thus it is written: "And Elohim created man in His own image, in the image of Elohim" (Beresheet 1:97). For the mystery of man below corresponds entirely to the secret above.

130. בְּהַאי רְקִיעָא דִלְעֵילָא, דִמְסַכֵּךְ עַל כֹּלָא, אִתְרְשִׁימוּ בֵּיה רְשִׁימִין, לְאִתְחֲזָאָה וּלְמִנְדַע בְּאִינּוּן רְשִׁימִין, דְּאִתְקְבִיעוּ בֵּיה מִלִּין וְרָזִין סְתִימִין. וְאִינּוּן רְשִׁימִין דְּכֹּכְבַיָּא וּמַזָלֵי, דְּאִתְרְשִׁימוּ וְאִתְקְבִיעוּ בְּהַאי רְקִיעָא, דְּסָכִיךְ לְבַר. אוּף הָכִי עוֹר, דְּאִיהוּ סְכוּכָא לְבַר בְּבַר נָשׁ, דְּאִיהוּ רְקִיעָא דְּסָכִיךְ עַל כֹּלָא, אִית בֵּיה רְשִׁימִין וְשִׂרְטוּטִין, וְאִינּוּן כֹּכְבַיָּא וּמַזָלֵי דְּהַאי עוֹר. לְאִתְחֲזָאָה בְּהוּ, וּלְמִנְדַע בְּהוּ, מִלִּין וְרָזִין סְתִימִין, בְּכֹכְבַיָּא וּמַזָלְיָא, לְעַיְינָא בְּהוּ חַכִּימֵי לִבָּא, וּלְאִסְתַּכְּלָא בְּהוּ לְמִנְדַע אִסְתַּכְּלוּתָא בְּאַנְפִּין, בְּרָזִין דְּקָאָמְרָן, וְרָזָא דָא, הוֹבְרֵי שָׁמַיִם הַחוֹזִים בַּכֹּכָבִים.

130. In this firmament up above, which covers everything, impressions were set in it to show and know, through these impressions, things and concealed secrets. These are the shapes of the stars and constellations recorded and fixed in this firmament, which covers externally. Similarly, the skin which covers man FROM THE OUTSIDE is like the firmament that covers all, having lines and impressions – which is CONSIDERED TO BE AN ASPECT OF THE stars and constellations of this skin. One may perceive in them hidden things and deep mysteries of the stars and constellations, THAT ARE THE IMPRESSIONS AND LINES IN THE SKIN, through which the wise of heart may study them, and discern the secrets hidden within, as we have stated. And this is the secret of: "the astrologers, the stargazers" (Yeshayah 47:13).

131. וְדָא אִיהוּ, כַּד אִינּוּן נְהִירִין וְקַיְימִין, בְּלָא רוּגְזָא. בְּזִמְנָא דְּרוּגְזָא שַׁלְטָא עֲלֵיהּ דְּבַר נָשׁ, דִּינָא אַחֲרָא אִתְמְסַר לְמִנְדַּע בֵּיהּ. בַּמֶּה דְּלָא אִתְיְיהִיב לְשַׁלְטָאָה, לְמִנְדַּע בְּזִמְנָא דְּדִינָא שַׁלְטָא בִּרְקִיעָא.

131. And this can be discerned only when the face shines and remains without anger, FOR ONLY THEN CAN WE OBSERVE AND DISCERN, AS MENTIONED PREVIOUSLY. At the time when anger rules over man, another Judgment is applied. And why was this Judgment not allowed to control man? IT IS POSSIBLE to know at the time when Judgment rules the firmament.

132. אֲבָל אִסְתַּכְּלוּתָא דְּאַנְפִּין עַל אֹרַח קְשׁוֹט, בְּשַׁעֲתָא דְּאַנְפִּין נְהִירִין, וְקַיְימָא בַּר נָשׁ עַל קִיוּמָא, וְאִינּוּן רְשִׁימִין אִתְחֲזוּן בְּאֹרַח קְשׁוֹט, דִּכְדֵין בְּהַהוּא אִסְתַּכְּלוּתָא יָכִיל לְאִתְדָּנָא עַל בּוּרְיֵיהּ יַתִּיר, וְאַף עַל גַּב דִּבְכֹלָּא כָּל אִינּוּן חַכִּימִין יַכְלִין לְאִסְתַּכְּלָא.

132. But the face is observed in its truthful way, when the face shines and man is secure. THEN these impressions are seen in a truthful way, and with this discernment one is able to judge better, with clarification – although there are many STYLES the wise can utilize to discern.

133. שִׂרְטוּטֵי יְדִין וְשִׂרְטוּטֵי אֶצְבְּעָן, לְגוֹ, כֻּלְּהוּ קַיְימִין בְּרָזִין אַחֲרָנִין, לְמִנְדַּע בְּמִלִּין סְתִימִין. וְאִלֵּין אִינּוּן כֹּכְבַיָּא, דִּנְהִירִין לְאִסְתַּכְּלָא גּוֹ מַזָּלֵי, בִּטְסִירִין עִלָּאִין.

133. The lines of the hands and the lines of the fingers from the inside are all set under other secrets with which to discern concealed matters. And these are the stars that shine so as to reveal the interiors of the constellations in high ministers.

134. אֶצְבְּעָן קַיְימֵי בְּרָזִין עִלָּאִין. טוּפְרֵי אֶצְבְּעָאן, דְּקַיְימִין דַּחֲפְיָן, לְבַר, הוּא אוּקְמוּהָ בְּאִינּוּן רָזִין, דַּהֲווֹ פָּנִים דִּלְבַר, וּבֵהוּ אִית רָזִין, לְאִינּוּן חֲרָשִׁין, דְּמִסְתַּכְּלֵי בְּטוּפְרֵי, בִּנְהִירוּ דְּמִלָּה אַחֲרָא, דְּשַׁלְטָא בְּהוּ,

וְאִינּוּן חֲרָשִׁין קָא מְסָאֲבֵי לְהַהוּא אֲתָר.

134. There are supernal secrets in the fingers. The nails of the fingers cover them from the outside. They are explained through these inner secrets that are manifested on the outside. These contain secrets to those wizards who contemplate the fingernails, in the light of other principles that govern them, and these magicians defile that place.

135. בְּטוּפְרִין אִית זִמְנִין, דְּנַהֲרִין בְּהוּ כְּכָבִין חִוָּורִין דְּקִיקִין, וְאִלֵּין אִינּוּן כְּתוֹלַדְהָ דִּטְלוּפְחִין, וְאִינּוּן שְׁקִיעִין כְּהַאי מַסְמְרָא עַל לוּחָא. וְלָאו אִינּוּן כְּאִינּוּן חִוָּורן דְּלָא שְׁקִיעִין, אֶלָּא דְּקַיְימִין לְעֵילָא. בְּהָנֵי דְּלָא שְׁקִיעִין, לֵית בְּהוּ מַמָּשָׁא. אֲבָל הָנֵי דְּשְׁקִיעִין חִוָּורִין כְּתוֹלַדְהָ דִּטְלוּפְחִין אִית בְּהוּ מַמָּשָׁא, וְאִית סִימָנָא טָבָא לֵיהּ לְבַר נָשׁ בְּהוּ, וְיַצְלַח בְּהַהוּא זִמְנָא. אוֹ גְּזֵרָה אִתְגְּזַר עֲלֵיהּ וְאִשְׁתְּזִיב מִינָהּ.

135. In the nails, there are times when little white stars shine from them – THAT IS, LITTLE WHITE SPOTS ARE SEEN IN THE NAILS, which are similar to birthmarks, the shape of lentils – and they are sunk IN THE NAILS as if nailed to a board. And they are different to those other white SPOTS that are not sunken, but are fixed above ON THE NAILS; those that are not sunken have no meaning. But those that are white and immersed like birthmarks the shape of lentils, have meaning, and they are a good omen for man, and he will succeed during this time. Or if a judgment was imposed upon him he will be rescued from it.

136. שִׁרְטוּטֵי יְדִין בְּרָזִין עִלָּאִין, בְּאֶצְבְּעָן לְגוֹ. בִּידִין שִׁרְטוּטִין רַבְרְבִין, שִׁרְטוּטִין זְעֵירִין דְּקִיקִין עִלָּאִין בִּימִינָא. בְּאִינּוּן אֶצְבְּעָן דִּבְהוּ שִׁרְטוּטִין זְעֵירִין. בְּאֶצְבְּעָא זְעֵירָא דִּימִינָא, אִית רְשִׁימִין דְּקִיקִין. אֶצְבְּעָא דָּא, קַיְימָא תָּדִיר עַל עוֹבָדִין דִּבְסִטַר אַחֲרָא.

136. The lines of the hands are among the supernal mysteries, along with the fingers from the inside, THAT IS, NOT ON THE SIDE OF THE NAILS, BUT THE SIDE OF THE FLESH. In the hands, there are large lines and small, thin upper lines in the right. In the little finger on the right, there are thin

impressions. This finger is fixed permanently on acts by the Other Side.

137. בְּהַאי אֶצְבְּעָא קַיְימִין שִׂרְטוּטִין, אִינּוּן דְּאֶצְבְּעָא אִתְכְּפִיל בְּהוּ. הֲנֵי לָאו אִינּוּן לְאִסְתַּכְּלָא, אֶלָּא אִי אִי אִתּוֹסְפָן בֵּיהּ. אִי אִתּוֹסְפָן תְּרֵין אוֹחֲרָנִין, עַל הַהוּא שִׂרְטוּטָא דְּאִתְכְּפַל בְּהוּ. אָרְחָא לָא אִזְדָּמַן לֵיהּ. וְאִי יַעֲבֹד לָא יִצְלַח.

137. In this finger, we find lines that are formed when the finger is folded, DURING THE CLOSING OF THE HAND. We do not observe these, except if added to BY OTHER LINES. If two other lines are added to the line THAT THE FINGER formed when doubled over, a way of opportunity will not be opened to him. And if he does initiate an opportunity, he will not succeed.

138. בַּר אִי קַיְימָן בְּאָרְכָּא, בֵּין רְשִׁימָא, לִרְשִׁימָא, בְּזִמְנָא דְּיִתְמְשַׁךְ מַשְׁכָא לַאֲחוֹרָא, וְאִשְׁתָּאֲרוּ אִינּוּן רְשִׁימִין דְּאִשְׁתְּמוֹדְעָן. הַאי יִצְלַח בְּאָרְחָא. וְסִימָן דָּא, תְּלַת תְּלַת בְּפוּתְיָא. וְאַרְבַּע בְּאָרְכָּא. וְרָזָא דָּא ז' מֵאַתְוָון זְעִירִין.

138. In the case where the lines are fixed lengthwise between impressions, BETWEEN THE IMPRESSIONS FORMED WHEN THE FINGER IS FOLDED OVER, at the time when the skin of the finger is pulled backwards – AND WITH ALL THIS, these recognizable impressions remain AND ARE NOT ERASED DUE TO THE PULLING OF THE SKIN, such a person will succeed in his ways. The sign for this is three lines in width, and four in length. This is the secret of *Zayin* from the small letters. FOR IN THE HEBREW ALPHABET THERE ARE THREE STYLES OF LETTERS: LARGE, MEDIUM, AND SMALL. AND THE *ZAYIN* HERETOFORE MENTIONED REFERS TO THE SMALLEST STYLE OF LETTERS.

139. רְשִׁימָא חַד בְּאָרְכָּא, וּתְרֵין תְּרֵין בְּפוּתְיָא. מֵאָרְחָא, יִשְׁמַע מִלִּין בִּזְמַן קָרִיב, וְלֵית לֵיהּ בְּהוּ תּוֹעַלְתָּא. אַרְבַּע רְשִׁימִין בְּאָרְכָּא, וְד' רְשִׁימִין בְּפוּתְיָא, אָרְחָא אִזְדָּמַן לֵיהּ בְּטֹרַח סַגִּי, וּלְסוֹפָא לְתוֹעַלְתָּיהּ. וְרָזָא דָּא ז' מֵאַתְוָון אֶמְצָעַיְין, דְּבֵין זְעִירִין וְרַבְרְבִין.

139. IF there is one impression that is a lengthwise line, and there are two widthwise lines, then along his travels he will hear of things in the near future, but they will not benefit him. If there are impressions that are four lengthwise lines and four widthwise lines, an opportunity will come his way, and through hard effort the results will be to his benefit. And this is the mystery of *Zayin* from the medium size letters of the Hebrew alphabet, those between the large LETTERS and the smaller LETTERS.

140. חָמֵשׁ זְעִירִין רְשִׁימִין בְּפוּתְיָא לְתַתָּא, וְאַרְבַּע בְּפוּתְיָא לְעֵילָּא, וְאַרְבַּע בְּאַרְכָּא נַיְיחָא לֵיהּ בְּבֵיתֵיהּ, וְעַצְלָא אִיהוּ. וְאָרְחָא הֲוַת מִתַּתְקְנָא קַמֵּיהּ, וְלָא בָּעֵי לְמֶעְבַּד. וְאִי יַעֲבֵד, יִצְלַח בְּהַהוּא אָרְחָא, אֲבָל לָא עָבֵיד לֵיהּ, וְעַצְלָא הֲוֵי וְרָזָא דָּא ז' דְּאִיהִי פְּעוּטָה.

140. If there are five small impressions in width at the bottom, and four in width at the top, and four lengthwise, he has peace in the house, and he is lazy. An opportunity may present itself for him, but he does not wish to take advantage of it. Had he taken advantage, he would have succeeded along this path. But he takes no advantage of it because he is lazy. And this is the mystery of the small *Zayin*.

141. בְּאֶצְבְּעָא דְּאֶמְצָעִיתָא, הַאי אֶצְבְּעָא קַיְּימָא, לְמֶעְבַּד עוֹבָדָא הַהוּא דְּחָשִׁיב. אִי שִׁרְטוּטָא חֲדָא קַיְּימָא בְּאַרְכָּא, בֵּין שִׁרְטוּטֵי דְּפוּתְיָא, הַאי חָשַׁב מַחֲשָׁבִין, וְאִסְתַּלְּקָן מִנֵּיהּ, וְדָחִיל וְלָא עָבֵיד, וְהַהִיא מַחֲשָׁבָה לָא אִתְעֲבֵיד כְּלָל.

141. The middle finger is the finger that stands TO SHOW IF he should manifest the action of which he thought. If one line is fixed lengthwise between lines at width, he thinks thoughts, but they are gone from him; he fears and he does not CARRY THEM OUT, and these thoughts amount to nothing.

142. אִי תְּרֵין שִׁרְטוּטִין בְּאַרְכָּא, דְּקַיְּימִין כַּד אִתְפָּשַׁט מַשְׁכָא לַאֲחוֹרָא. הַאי לָאו בֵּיהּ מַחֲשָׁבִין, וְחָשִׁיב מַחֲשָׁבִין לְפוּם שַׁעֲתָא, וְאִתְעֲבֵיד, וְלָא מַחֲשָׁבָה דְּהִרְהֵר בֵּיהּ כְּלָל, אֶלָּא מַחֲשָׁבָה דְּאִיהוּ בְּבֶהֱלוּ וּזְעִירָא, אֲבָל הִרְהוּרָא וּמַחֲשָׁבָה לָא.

142. If two lines are fixed lengthwise EVEN when the skin of the finger is pulled backwards, AND THEY ARE NOT CANCELED DUE TO THE PULL OF THE SKIN, he has no real thoughts, but only thinks superficial thoughts of the moment and accomplishes them. But he does not have contemplative thoughts, rather impulsive and petty thoughts, but no contemplative thoughts.

143. וְאִי תְּלַת רְשִׁימִין בְּאָרְכָּא. וּבְפוּתְיָא תְּרֵין אוֹ תְּלַת, כַּד אִתְפָּשַׁט מַשְׁכָא לַאֲחוֹרָא. הַאי אִיהוּ ב״נ דְּאִיהוּ פְּקִיחָא, וְחָשִׁיב מַחֲשָׁבִין, וְכָל אִינּוּן מַחֲשָׁבִין דְּאִינּוּן לְסִטַר קוּדְשָׁא בְּרִיךְ הוּא אִתְקַיְּימָן בִּידֵיהּ, וּמַחֲשָׁבִין אַחֲרָנִין לָאו הָכִי.

143. If there are three impressions in length and two or three impressions in width, after he stretches the skin OF THE FINGER backwards, he is a man who is wise and contemplative. And all those thoughts that are on the side of the Holy One, Blessed be He, will be fulfilled by his hands, but not so with other thoughts.

144. אִי אַרְבַּע אוֹ חֲמִשָׁה בְּאָרְכָּא, בְּאִתְפָּשְׁטוּ דְמַשְׁכָא כִּדְקָאמְרָן, כַּד שַׁרְיָאן עַל פּוּתְיָא, בִּתְלַת, אוֹ בְּאַרְבַּע, אוֹ מִתְּרֵין וּלְהָלְאָה. דָּא בַּר נָשׁ דְּמַחֲשָׁבוֹי לְאַבְאָשָׁא, וְאִשְׁתְּבַח בְּהוּ. וְדִיקְנָה וּגְבִינֵי עֵינוֹי סוּמָקִין, מְחַשֵּׁב לְבִישׁ וְאִשְׁתְּבַח בְּהוּ. קָצְרָא דְּיוֹמִין אִיהוּ. פְּקִיחָא אִיהוּ. וְאַכְנַע תָּדִיר לְמִכִּילָן דְּבִישׁ. אַצְלַח. וּלְסוֹפָא דְּיוֹמִין זְעִירִין אִסְתַּלָּק מֵעָלְמָא.

144. If there are four or five IMPRESSIONS in length after the skin OF THE FINGER is stretched, as previously stated, and they rest on three or four, or even two or more IMPRESSIONS OF THE lines in width, such a person has thoughts which tend to be evil and he glories in such thoughts. And when the beard and eyebrows are red, he thinks evil and glories in it for a brief time. He is cunning, and he always yields to these evil characteristics. Thus, he succeeds. After a brief period, he dies.

145. אַסְוָותָא לְהַאי תְּיוּבְתָּא. כְּדֵין אִשְׁתְּכָחוּ תְּלַת רְשִׁימִין, אוֹ אַרְבַּע, וְשַׁרְיָין עַל תְּרֵין. תְּלַת רְשִׁימִין אוֹ ד׳ בְּאָרְכָּא וְשַׁרְיָין עַל תְּרֵין בְּפוּתְיָא. דְּהָא כְּפוּם מִנְהֲגָא דְּבַר נָשׁ, הָכִי מִתְחַלְּפֵי שִׂרְטוּטִין, מִזְּמַן לִזְמַן. וְרָזָא

דָּא הַמּוֹצִיא בְּמִסְפָּר צְבָאָם וְגוֹ', מֵרֹב אוֹנִים וְאַמִיץ כֹּחַ וְגוֹ'.

145. The remedy for this is repentance. And then we find three or four impressions resting on two, THAT IS, three or four impressions in length resting on two impressions in width, since, according to the habit of man, lines are changed from time to time. This secret is derived from the verse: "that brings out their host by number; He calls them all by names; because of the greatness of His might, and because He is strong in power" (Yeshayah 40:26).

146. כְּמָה דְּקוּדְשָׁא בְּרִיךְ הוּא אַחְלַף חַיָּילִין וּזְמַנִּין בְּכֹכְבֵי שְׁמַיָּא, יוֹמָא דָּא כָּךְ, וּלְיוֹמָא אָחֳרָא כָּךְ. כְּפוּם דְּאָדָם דִּלְגוֹ כָּל עוֹבָדוֹי. הָכִי אִתְחֲזוּן בְּהַאי רְקִיעָא. וְהָכִי אִתְחֲזֵי בְּהַאי מַשְׁכָא דְּהַאי אָדָם תַּתָּאָה. דְּאִיהוּ רְקִיעָא, עוֹר דְּחַפְיָא עַל כֹּלָּא.

146. As the Holy One, blessed be He, changes hosts and seasons in the stars in the heavens – this day, so, and another day, thus, all according to the SUPERNAL man who is the inner aspect of his actions as they appear in these heavens, the same is seen on the skin of man below, since his skin, which covers everything, is a firmament.

147. וְכֹלָּא כְּפוּם גַּוְונָא דְּאָדָם דִּלְגוֹ, דְּהַאי לְזִמְנִין קָאִים בְּדִינָא, לְזִמְנִין בְּרַחֲמֵי, כְּהַהוּא גַּוְונָא מַמָּשׁ אַחֲזֵי לְבַר. לְזִמְנִין כְּהַאי גַּוְונָא, וּלְזִמְנִין כְּהַאי גַּוְונָא כְּגַוְונָא דָּא לְתַתָּא בְּהַאי אָדָם, כְּמָה דְּאֲמָרָן, לְזִמְנִין כְּהַאי גַּוְונָא, וּלְזִמְנִין כְּהַאי גַּוְונָא, וְרָזָא דָּא אָת ז' אִתְכְּלִיל בֵּיהּ אָת י'.

147. And all is according to the kind of inner man who is at times under Judgment and at times under Mercy. This is exactly the same sight outside, OVER THE FIRMAMENT, that at times appears in this mode, and at other times in that mode. This is also similar to that man, as we have stated previously, that is at times SEEN ON HIS SKIN in this way and at other times in that way. This is the secret sign of the letter *Zayin* when it is included in the letter *Yud*.

148. וְרָזִין אִלֵּין בְּאֶצְבְּעָן דִּימִינָא, בְּזְעֵירָא וּבְרַבְרְבָא. וְסִימָן כַּקָּטֹן
כַּגָּדוֹל תִּשְׁמָעוּן. אֵלּוּ תְּרֵין אֶצְבְּעָן בְּרָזִין אִלֵּין, וְהָכִי אִינּוּן בְּרָזִין
דְּאוֹלִיפְנָא מִנֵּיהּ דְּמֹר, בְּרָזֵי דְּרַב יֵיסָא סָבָא. מִכָּאן וּלְהָלְאָה שִׂרְטוּטִין
אַחֲרָנִין, דְּאִקְרוּן כֻּלְּהוּ תוֹלְדוֹת, וְאִינּוּן תּוֹלְדוֹת אָדָם, כְּמָה דִּכְתִּיב,
תּוֹלְדוֹת הַשָּׁמַיִם, וְהָא אִתְּמַר, דְּכֹלָּא רָזָא דָּא. כְּגַוְונָא דָּא תּוֹלְדוֹת
אָדָם, בְּכָל אִינּוּן דִּיּוּקְנִין דְּאַנְפִּין, וּבְכָל אִינּוּן דְּקָאַמְרָן. וּבְאִלֵּין
תּוֹלְדוֹת דְּשִׂרְטוּטֵי יְדִין, דְּאִתְחַזְיָין בְּרָזִין פְּנִימָאִין, כְּמָה דְּאִתְחֲזֵי.

148. And these secrets are in the fingers of the right hand – the little FINGER and the large one, THAT IS, THE MIDDLE FINGER. The indication is: "but hear the small as well as the great" (Devarim 1:17). These two fingers are connected to these secrets. These are the mysteries which we have learned from our master, from the secrets of Rav Yesa Saba (the elder). From now and onward, other lines, are all called 'descendants', which refers to the descendants of Adam, as it has been written: "the generations of the heavens" (Beresheet 2:4). As we have learned, all is this secret. Similar to this are the descendants of man in all the shapes of the face, and in all that we discussed before, and in those descendants of the lines of the hands that are seen through inner secrets, as is fit.

149. זֶה סֵפֶר תּוֹלְדוֹת אָדָם, לְשִׂרְטוּטִין, סִימָן זר״ה פס״ץ. רָזִין
לְחַכִּימֵי לִבָּא, רזהס״ף, חָמֵשׁ אַתְוָון, בְּחָמֵשׁ תַּרְעִין, לְמִנְדַּע חָכְמָה
בְּסוּכְלְתָנוּ.

149. "This is the book of the generations of Adam" (Beresheet 5:1). This refers to the lines. To the signs Zayin-Resh-Hei-Pe-Samech-Tzadi, WHICH ARE THE LETTERS OF "THIS IS THE BOOK (HEB. zeh-SEFER, ZAYIN-HEI, SAMECH-PE-RESH)," TZADI HAS BEEN ADDED. The secrets to the wise in heart are Resh-Zayin-Hei-Samech-final Pe; Five letters in five gates for the gain of Wisdom by understanding.

150. תַּרְעָא קַדְמָאָה, ר׳. בִּידָא אִית שִׂרְטוּטִין דְּקִיקִין, וְשִׂרְטוּטִין
רַבְרְבִין. וְכֻלְּהוּ מִתְעָרְבֵי דָּא עִם דָּא. שִׂרְטוּטִין רַבְרְבִין דְּאִית בִּידָא, כַּד
אִינּוּן תְּרֵין בְּאַרְכָּא, וּתְרֵין בְּפוּתְיָא, וְאָחִידוּ דָּא בְּדָא, דָּא אִיהוּ בְּרָזָא

דְּאָת ה', וּבְרָזָא דְּאָת ר' וְדָחֵי לְאָת ז', וְנָטִיל אִלֵּין תְּרֵין אַתְוָון. בְּפוּתְיָא נָטִיל ה', בְּאַרְכָּא נָטִיל ר', וְסִימָן דִּילֵיהּ ה"ר.

150. The First Gate is *Resh*. In the hand, there are thin lines and great lines. And all these lines mingle with one another. The great lines that are in the hand, when they are two in length, and two in width, and merge with each other are the secret of the letter *Hei*, and the letter *Resh*. It rejects the letter *Zayin*, and seizes these two letters. At its width, it takes the letter *Hei*; at its length, it takes the letter *Resh*. Its sign is *Hei-Resh*.

151. דָּא אִית לֵיהּ בִּידָא שְׂמָאלָא כְּהַאי גַּוְונָא בְּאִלֵּין שִׂרְטוּטִין רַבְרְבִין. אֲבָל אִינּוּן שִׂרְטוּטִין זְעִירִין דְּנָטִיל יְמִינָא, לָא נָטִיל שְׂמָאלָא. דִּימִינָא נָטִיל, חַד שִׂרְטוּטָא דָּקִיק לְעֵילָּא בְּאַרְכָּא, וְחַד שִׂרְטוּטָא דָּקִיק לְתַתָּא, דְּאָחִיד בֵּין אִינּוּן תְּרֵין שִׂרְטוּטִין רַבְרְבָן. בְּפוּתְיָא אִית חַד שִׂרְטוּטָא דָּקִיק, דְּאָחִיד לְתַתָּא בְּאִינּוּן תְּרֵין דְּשַׁרְיָא עֲלֵיהּ. וּבִשְׂמָאלָא לָאו הָכִי, וְרָזָא דִּילֵיהּ אִיהוּ בִּימִינָא, וְלָאו בִּשְׂמָאלָא.

151. There are those who have similar lines TO THOSE ON THE RIGHT HAND ALSO in the left hand, particularly with the great lines. But it is with small lines that the right hand receives, while the left hand does not receive. For the right hand receives one thin line in length above, and one thin line below, which is seized between two great lines THAT ARE FOUND THERE. In the width there is one thin line that touches below two lines resting upon it. But in the left hand, this is not so. Thus, the secret is in the right hand and not the left.

152. הַאי אִיהוּ בַּר נָשׁ, דְּלִזְמְנִין תָּאִיב בְּבֵיתָא, וּלְזְמְנִין בְּאָרְחָא, דָּא לָא שָׁכִיךְ לְבֵיהּ בְּהַאי וּבְהַאי. כַּד אִיהוּ בְּבֵיתָא תָּאִיב בְּאָרְחָא, וְכַד אִיהוּ בְּאָרְחָא, תָּאִיב בְּבֵיתָא. אַצְלַח תָּדִיר בְּאָרְחָא, וּלְזְמְנִין בְּבֵיתָא. דָּא אַצְלַח בְּאוֹרַיְיתָא, וּבְרָזֵי דְּאוֹרַיְיתָא אִי אִשְׁתְּדַל בְּהוּ. הַאי חָמֵי בְּשַׂנְאוֹי, תּוֹעַלְתָּא לְסַגִּיאִין בֵּיהּ. עַצְלָא אִיהוּ בְּמִלֵּי דְּעָלְמָא. אִי אִתְּעַר, אִתְּעָרוּן לְאוֹטָבָא לֵיהּ מִלְעֵילָּא. זָכֵי בְּמִלּוֹי. דָּא אִיהוּ חֲמִידָא וּמְפַזֵּר מָמוֹנָא. טַב עֵינָא אִיהוּ. צְלוֹתֵיהּ אִשְׁתְּמַע. נָחִית וְסָלִיק בְּמָמוֹנָא.

152. This is a man who adores BEING at home at times, and on the road at times. His heart is not at ease with either. When he is at home, he yearns for the road; and when he is on the road, he yearns for home. He is always successful on the road, and at times at home. This person is successful in the Torah and in the mysteries of the Torah if he puts effort into them. He gazes on his enemies. Many will benefit from him. He is lazy in worldly matters. Yet, if he is stimulated FROM BELOW, then they will stimulate to improve him from above. He gains merit through his words. He is precious and spends his money. He has a good eye. His prayers are heard. In regards to money, he has ups and downs THAT IS, IN HIS POSSESSIONS.

153. דָּא אִיהוּ דִּלְזִמְנִין מִתְבַּר לִבֵּיהּ לְגַבֵּיהּ מָארֵיהּ. וּכְדֵין אִשְׁתְּכָחוּ תְּלַת שִׂרְטוּטִין זְעִירִין, דִּמְעַבְּרָן בְּהַהוּא שִׂרְטוּטָא דָּקִיק, דְּאִתּוֹסָף עַל אִינּוּן תְּרֵין דִּפוּתְיָא, וְרָזָא דָּא ה' דְּמִתְחַבְּרָא עִם ר'. דָּא אָרְחָא, דָּא בֵּיתָא. דָּא חֶדְוָה, דָּא עֲצִיבוּ, דָּא תּוֹעַלְתָּא, דָּא עַצְלָא, דָּא טַב עֵינָא, דָּא חֲמִידָא, וּמְפַזֵּר מָמוֹנָא. דָּא מִתְבַּר לִבֵּיהּ, וְתָב לְמָארֵיהּ.

153. There are times when his heart is broken before his Master. And then we find three small lines crossing the thin line that was added to the two lines in width. And this is the secret. The *Hei* is joined with the *Resh*. HE GIVES A BRIEF REVIEW OF THE WORDS, WHICH IS GOOD FOR THE MEMORY. It is the road. It is home. It is delight. It is sadness. It is beneficial. He is lazy. He is good-eyed. He is precious and scatters his money. It implies a broken heart, and the return to his Master.

154. תַּרְעָא תִּנְיָינָא, ז'. בִּימִינָא, בְּקַסְטִירוּ דְּקוּלְטָא, רְשִׁימִין שְׁכִיחֵי, כַּד אִשְׁתְּכָחוּ תְּלַת שִׂרְטוּטִין רַבְרְבִין בְּפוּתְיָא, וּתְרֵין רַבְרְבִין בְּאָרְכָּא, וְחַד מֵאִינּוּן דְּאָרְכָּא, אָחִיד בְּאִינּוּן תְּרֵין דִּפוּתְיָא, וְחַד אַחֲרָא לָא אָחִיד בְּהוּ. הַאי אִית פַּסְלוּ בְּזַרְעֵיהּ, מִסְּטְרָא דַּאֲבוֹי, אוֹ מִסְּטְרָא דְּאִמֵּיהּ.

154. The second gate is *Zayin*. In the right HAND, in the part that accepts AND RECEIVES, NAMELY IN THE PALM OF THE HAND, there are impressions. When three great lines in width and two great lines are found, and one of those in length touches two in width, while the other one does not touch them, this implies a defect in the seed, either from the side of the father or the side of the mother.

155. וּכְדֵין מִשְׁתַּכְּחֵי לְתַתָּא מֵאִנּוּן תְּלַת שִׂרְטוּטִין דְּפוּתְיָא, תְּרֵין שִׂרְטוּטִין דְּקִיקִין, דַּאֲחִידָן בְּהוּ לְתַתָּא. הַאי אִיהוּ בַּר נָשׁ, מְתַקֵּן עוֹבָדוֹי, קַמֵּי בְּנֵי נָשָׁא, וְלִבֵּיהּ לָא קְשׁוֹט. וּלְזִמְנָא דְּסִיב, אַהֲדָר לְאִתְתַּקְנָא. כְּדֵין אִשְׁתְּכָחוּ אִינּוּן תְּרֵין שִׂרְטוּטִין בְּאָרְכָּא, אֲחִידָן בְּאִינּוּן דְּפוּתְיָא, דָּא עִם דָּא. וּתְרֵין אַחֲרָנִין עִמְּהוֹן בְּאֶמְצָעִיתָא, דְּקִיקִין, וְדָא בְּאָרְכָּא. וּתְלַת דְּקִיקִין בְּפוּתְיָא, וְרָזָא דָּא ז' דְּמִתְחַבְּרָא בְּאָת ר'.

155. And then we find below the three lines in width, two thin lines that touch them from below. This signifies a man who amends his actions in front of other people, yet his heart is not true. And at the time of his old age he repents to correct his actions. Then we find the two lines in length touch those in width, this one with that one, and two others, thin lines, with them in the middle – lengthwise – and also three thin lines in width. And this is the mystery of the *Zayin* that is linked to the letter *Resh*.

156. וְכַד אִיהוּ סִיב וְתָב כִּדְקָאמְרָן, אִתְתַּקָּן אִיהוּ בְּרָזָא דְּאָת ר', וְאִתְחַבָּר בְּאָת ז'. לְבָתַר כַּד הַאי אִתְתַּקָּן, אִיהוּ תָּדִיר בִּלְחִישׁוּ, וְכָל עוֹבָדוֹי בִּלְחִישׁוּ. אֲבָל לָאו אִיהוּ בְּקִיּוּמָא כַּדְקָא חֲזֵי בְּגִין דְּהַהוּא פְּסִלוּ, עַד לָא אִתְיָיאָשָׁא בֵּיהּ.

156. When he reaches old age and repents, as we have said, he is corrected under the secret of the letter *Resh*, and is joined with the letter *Zayin*. Afterwards, when matters have been corrected, he is always in silence and all his actions are secretive. But he is not established fully in this, because this defect, WHICH IS STILL IN HIS SEED, has not given him up AND STIMULATES HIM TO EVIL.

157. וּלְבָתַר דְּאִתְיָיאָשָׁא. הַהוּא פְּסִילוּ, כְּדֵין אִשְׁתְּכָחוּ שִׂרְטוּטִין בִּידָא יְמִינָא, אַרְבַּע וְחָמֵשׁ. אַרְבַּע בְּאָרְכָּא, חָמֵשׁ בְּפוּתְיָא. וְרָזָא דָּא ז', וְאִתְחַבָּר בְּאָת ה'. הַאי לְזִמְנִין אַצְלַח, לְזִמְנִין לָא אַצְלַח. אַצְלַח בְּאוֹרַיְיתָא, וּלְסוֹף יוֹמוֹי, אַצְלַח אֲפִילוּ בְּמָמוֹנָא.

157. But after this defective seed gives up, then we find four and five lines in his right hand, four lines in length and five in width. And this secret is *Zayin* that is linked to the letter sign *Hei*. This implies that at times he succeeds in matters, and at times he does not succeed. He will succeed in Torah learning. And toward the end of his life, he will even succeed even in financial matters.

158. תַּרְעָא תְּלִיתָאָה, ה'. בִּימִינָא, כַּד אִשְׁתְּכָחוּ חָמֵשׁ שִׂרְטוּטִין בְּפוּתְיָא, וּתְלַת בְּאַרְכָּא, וְאִשְׁתְּכַח הַהוּא שִׂרְטוּטָא דְּאֶמְצָעִיתָא מֵאִינוּן תְּלַת, דָּא אִיהוּ בְּרָזָא דְּאָת ה', וְאִסְתְּמִיךְ בְּאוֹת ס'.

158. The third gate is *Hei*. In the right hand, when there are five lines in width, and three in length, and there is a middle line RECOGNIZED ESPECIALLY among the three lines IN LENGTH, this is the secret of the letter *Hei*, which is supported by the letter *Samech*.

159. בְּזִמְנָא דְּאִשְׁתְּכַח הַהוּא שִׂרְטוּטָא דְּאֶמְצָעִיתָא, דְּעָאל וְאָחִיד גּוֹ אִינּוּן חָמֵשׁ שִׂרְטוּטִין דְּפוּתְיָא, דָּא אִיהוּ בַּר נָשׁ עָצִיב וְרָגִיז גּוֹ בֵּיתֵיהּ, וּבְגוֹ בְּנֵי נָשָׁא לָאו הָכִי. קַמְצָן אִיהוּ בְּבֵיתֵיהּ, וְרָגִיז וְכָפִין, וּלְזִמְנִין לָא. לְבַר מִבֵּיתֵיהּ לָאו הָכִי. אַצְלַח בְּעוֹבְדֵי עָלְמָא. כַּד אִשְׁתָּדַּל בְּאוֹרַיְיתָא אִסְתְּכַּל זְעֵיר וְאִתְהַדָּר בָּהּ. מְהֵימָנָא אִיהוּ, אֲבָל לָאו כָּל זִמְנָא. וְהַהוּא זִמְנָא דְּלָאו מְהֵימָנָא, אַחְזֵי גַּוֶון קְשׁוֹט, וְלָא קְשׁוֹט בִּשְׁלִימוּ. בְּדִינָא יִצְלַח. מְהֵימָנָא אִיהוּ בְּרָזִין דְּאוֹרַיְיתָא, דָּא אִיהוּ בְּרָזָא דְּאָת ה', וְאִתְחַבָּר בְּאָת ס'.

159. If this middle line FROM THE THREE LINES IN LENGTH is found to enter and to touch those five lines in width, it signifies a man who is sad and angry in his house. But this is not so with other men. He is a miser in his house, he is angry and hungry, yet at other times he is not. Outside of his house, he is not this way. He succeeds in worldly matters. When he is occupied with Torah, he observes a little, and then goes back to it. He is truthful, but not always. And at those times that he is not truthful, he appears to be truthful. He is successful in judgments. He is faithful to the secrets of the Torah. And this is the sign of the letter *Hei* and is linked to the letter *Samech*.

160. וְאִי אַרְבַּע שִׂרְטוּטִין בְּפוּתְיָא, וְחָמֵשׁ בְּאַרְכָּא, תְּרֵין מֵאִינּוּן דְּאָרְכָּא, עָאלִין גּוֹ אִינּוּן אַרְבַּע, דָּא אִיהוּ בַּר נָשׁ חַדֵי בְּבֵיתֵיהּ, וְאִתְחֲזֵי עָצִיב לְבָּא לְבַר, וְלָאו הָכִי דְּכֵיוָן דְּמַלִּיל עִם בְּנֵי נָשָׁא, אַחְזֵי חֶדוּ וְאִתְכְּוָון בְּמִלּוֹי.

160. If there are four lines in width, and five lines in length, and two of those in length enter in the midst of those four IN WIDTH, it signifies a man who is happy in his house, but appears to be of sad heart on the outside. Yet, this is not true for as soon as he speaks with people, he shows happiness and speaks with intent.

161. תְּלַת שִׂרְטוּטִין זְעִירִין עָאלִין גּוֹ אִינּוּן דְּאָרְכָּא, דָּא אִית לֵיהּ חַד רְשִׁימוּ אוּכָם בְּגוּפֵיהּ, וּתְלַת שַׂעֲרִין תַּלְיָין בְּהַהוּא רְשִׁימוּ, וְהַהוּא רְשִׁימוּ אִיהוּ כְּעִגּוּלָא, וְחַד תְּבִירָא בְּרֵישֵׁיהּ. וּלְהַאי רְשִׁימָא, קָרָאן לֵיהּ חַכִּימֵי לִבָּא, דְּיַדְעִין רָזִין אִלֵּין, רֵישׁ נִשְׁרָא. רְשִׁימוּ דָּא, אִתְחֲזֵי לְזִמְנִין, בֵּין כַּתְפוֹי. וּלְזִמְנִין, בִּדְרוֹעָא יְמִינָא. וּלְזִמְנִין, עַל יְדָא יְמִינָא בְּאֶצְבְּעוֹי.

161. Three small lines enter in the midst of those lines in length. And this person has a black spot on his body, and three hairs hang from this spot. The spot is round, and a break is in the top OF THE SPOT. This impression is called by the wise in heart, who know these mysteries, the name of 'Eagle Head'. This impression is sometimes seen between his shoulders, and at times on his right arm, and at times on his right hand on his fingers.

162. אִי רְשִׁימָא דָּא רֵישׁ נִשְׁרָא, אִיהוּ בְּאֹרַח מֵישָׁר בְּתִקּוּנוֹי, יִסְתַּלַּק לְעוּתְרָא וְלִיקָרָא. וְאִי הַהוּא רֵישׁ נִשְׁרָא אִתְהַפַּךְ לַאֲחוֹרָא, יִזְכֶּה לִבְנִין לְזִמְנִין. אֲבָל כַּד אִיהוּ סִיב, יִזְכֶּה לְעוּתְרָא יַתִּיר, וְלִיקָר סַגְיָא, יַתִּיר מֵעוּלְמוֹי, וְיַצְלַח בְּאוֹרַיְיתָא, אִי אִשְׁתְּדַּל בָּהּ.

162. If this impression, which we call Eagle Head, is in a manner that is well set, then he will be raised to wealth and honor. But if this Eagle Head is

turned backwards, he will at times be worthy of children. As he grows older, he will be worthy of great wealth and great honor, more than when he was a youth. He will also succeed in the Torah if he occupies himself with it.

163. רֵישׁ נִשְׁרָא דָא, אִתְחֲזֵי לְזִמְנִין אוּכָמָא, וּלְזִמְנִין גָּוֶון דְּלָא סוּמָק זְעֵיר, דְּלָא אִצְטְבַּע כָּל כָּךְ. לְזִמְנִין בְּשַׂעֲרִין לְזִמְנִין שְׁעִיעַ, וְכֹלָּא חַד סִימָנָא אִיהוּ, וּבְחַד דִּינָא אִתְדָּן.

163. This Eagle Head looks black at times, and at times it is a color that is only slightly red, for it was not dyed much. And WE LOOK AT THE HAIR HANGING FROM IT, for at times they are straight. And everything is under one sign, and judged according to the same law.

164. וְאִי הַהוּא גָּוֶון סוּמָק אִצְטְבַע יַתִּיר, וְקָאִים בִּגְוָונֵיהּ, זְמַן זְעֵיר הוּא דְּאִצְטְבַע, בְּגִין דְּאִלֵּין גַּוְונִין, לְזִמְנִין קַיְימִין נְהִירִין, וּלְזִמְנִין חֲשׁוּכִין. וְאִי אִצְטְבַע הַהוּא סוּמָק וְנָהִיר, כְּדֵין אִית בִּידָא שְׂמָאלָא, תְּלַת שִׂרְטוּטִין בְּאַרְכָּא, וּתְלַת בְּפוּתְיָא, וְחַד דָּקִיק עַל אִינּוּן דְּפוּתְיָא, וְחַד דָּקִיק עַל אִינּוּן דְּאַרְכָּא. וּבִידָא יְמִינָא אִתּוֹסָף חַד בְּפוּתְיָא בִּלְחוֹדוֹי. הַאי בַּר נָשׁ שָׁכִיב בַּנִדָּה, וְלָא תָב מִינֵּהּ לְמָארֵיהּ.

164. If this red color is significantly red and maintains its color; and if it is only a brief time since it became colored; and – since these colors are found shining at times, and at other times are dim – if this red color becomes bright and shining; and he has in his left hand three lines in length, and three lines in width; and there is one thin line on those width lines and one thin line on those length lines; and in the right hand, one thin line alone is added to the width, then he is a man who slept with a menstruant woman and did not repent to his Master.

165. וְכַד תָּב בִּתְיוּבְתָּא, אִשְׁתָּארוּ אִינּוּן שִׂרְטוּטִין בִּידָא שְׂמָאלָא, וְהַהוּא דְּאִתּוֹסָף בִּימִינָא, אִתְעֲדֵי מִנֵּיהּ, וְאִתְעֲדֵי הַהוּא סוּמָקָא, דְּלָא אִתְחֲזֵי נָהִיר כָּל כָּךְ מִנֵּיהּ. וּלְזִמְנִין דְּאַף עַל גַּב דְּתָב, לָא אַעֲדִיו מִנֵּיהּ הַהוּא סוּמָקָא, עַד זְמַן. הַאי אִיהוּ בְּרָזָא דְּאָת ה', וְאִתְעֲדֵי אָת ס',

וְעָאל תְּחוֹתוֹי אָת ץ', וְאִתְחַבָּר אָת ה' בְּאָת ץ'. הַאי בָּעֵי תִּקּוּנָא
לְנַפְשֵׁיה בִּבְהִילוּ. חַכִּימָא דְּלִבָּא דְּחָמֵי לֵיה, חוֹבָתָא אִית עָלֵיה, לוֹמַר
לֵיה זִיל אַסֵי לְנַפְשָׁךָ.

165. And when he repents, the lines in the left hand remain. And the line
that was added in the right hand is gone. And the red color is also gone, for
the brightness does not shine as much. And at times, even though he
repents, the redness is not removed for a time. This is in the mystery of the
letter *Hei*. And the letter *Samech* is removed, and instead the letter final
Tzadi has been substituted, and the letter *Hei* is linked to final *Tzadi*. This
person quickly needs a correction of the spirit. It is incumbent upon the wise
of heart, who observe him, to say to him: "Go and heal yourself."

166. וְאִי תְּלַת שִׂרְטוּטִין בְּאַרְכָּא, וְחַד בְּפוּתְיָא, דָּא אִיהוּ בְּרָזָא דְּאָת
ה' בִּלְחוֹדֵיה. וּלְזִמְנִין אִתְחַבָּר בְּרָזָא דְּאָת ז'. הַאי אִיהוּ בַּר נָשׁ תָּאִיב
בָּתַר בִּצְעִין דְּעָלְמָא. וְאִי לָאו, רָדִיף בָּתַר נָשִׁין, וְתֵיאוּבְתֵּיה נְאוּפִים.
וְאע"ג דְּתָאִיב לִבְצֵעִין דְּעָלְמָא, הַאי לָא אַעֲדִיו מִנֵּיה, וְלָא אַכְסִיף.
עֵינוֹי שְׁקִיעִין וּמַלִּיל בְּהוּ.

166. Three lines in length and one in width is the secret of the letter *Hei* by
itself. And at times it is linked to the mystery of the letter *Zayin*. This
signifies a man who lusts and is greedy for profit in the world. And if not,
then he chases women with the lust for committing adultery. And even
though he lusts and is greedy for gain in the world, this is not removed from
him, and he is not ashamed. His eyes are sunken, and he speaks with them.
THAT IS, AT THE TIME OF SPEAKING HE WINKS WITH HIS EYES.

167. אִי תָּב לְמָארֵיה מִתְחַלְּפֵי שִׂרְטוּטִין. תְּלַת בְּפוּתְיָא וְחַד לְאָרְכָּא,
וְאִינוּן תְּרֵין דְּקִיקִין קַיְימִין בְּקִיּוּמָא, כְּדֵין רְעוּ דִּילֵיה יַתִּיר בְּאִתְּתֵיה,
וְאִתְדְּבַק בָּהּ. חַד דָּקִיק יַתִּיר, עָאל בֵּין אִינוּן תְּרֵין דְּקִיקִין. כְּדֵין
אִתְחַבָּר אָת ה' בְּאָת ז'.

167. If he returns to his Master, the lines are changed – three in width, and

one in length. The two thin lines remain. This implies that he desires his wife more, and attaches himself to her. One especially thin line enters between two thin lines. Then the letter *Hei* joins itself to the letter *Zayin*.

168. וְאִי שִׂרְטוּטָא חַד בְּאַרְכָּא וְאַרְבַּע בְּפוּתְיָא, וּתְלַת דְּקִיקִין קַיְימִין עַל הַהוּא חַד, וְחַד עַל אִינּוּן אַרְבַּע. עַל דְּרוֹעָא שְׂמָאלָא, אִית לֵיהּ תְּלַת קַסְטְרִין דְּקִיקִין, דְּאִתְיְלִידוּ בֵּיהּ מִיּוֹמִין זְעִירִין, וְחַד שַׂעֲרָא תַּלְיָא, בְּהַהוּא חַד דְּרֵישָׁא. הַאי אִיהוּ רָדִיף בָּתַר נְאוּפָא דְּאֵשֶׁת חַבְרֵיהּ. מָארֵיהּ דְּזָדוֹנָא אִיהוּ. אַגְזִים בְּעֵינָא שְׂמָאלָא, בְּלָא מִלּוּלָא כְּלַל, וְאַשְׁלִים. וּבְגִין דְּאִיהוּ מָארֵיהּ זְדוֹנָא, לָא חָיֵישׁ לִיקָרָא דְּמָארֵיהּ, לְאָתָבָא קַמֵּיהּ. לְבָתַר קָטִיל חִוְיָא לֵיהּ, אוֹ בַּר נָשׁ סוּמָקָא.

168. If: one line is in length and four lines are in width; and three thin lines remain on the same one THAT IS IN LENGTH; and one line on the four THAT ARE IN WIDTH; on the left arm are three thin lines that just appeared a few days previously; and a single hair hangs on that one THAT IS at their top, then he is one eager to commit adultery with his neighbor's wife. He is malicious. He frightens with his left eye, without uttering a word, and completes – THAT IS, HE COMPLETES HIS WORK AND DOES NOT HAVE TO SPEAK. Because he is malicious, returning to his Master does not concern him. Afterwards a serpent or a red man, will kill him.

169. וְאִי אַרְבַּע בְּאַרְכָּא, וּתְלַת בְּפוּתְיָא, וְאִינּוּן דְּסַלְקִין לְעֵילָא אַעֲדִיו מִנֵּיהּ. הַאי, תָּבַר לִבֵּיהּ לְגַבֵּי מָארֵיהּ, וְתָב בְּתִיוּבְתָּא. כְּדֵין אִיהוּ בְּרָזָא דְּאָת פ', וְאִתְחֲבָּר בְּאָת ה'. עַל אַלֵּין, וְעַל אִינּוּן דִּכְוָותֵיהּ, כְּתִיב, שָׁלוֹם שָׁלוֹם לָרָחוֹק וְלַקָּרוֹב.

169. If there are four in length, and three in width, and those lines that go up are removed from him, this implies he breaks his heart before his Master and repents. This is under the principle of the letter *Pe,* and is joined with the letter *Hei*. Of these it is written: "Peace, peace both for far and near." (Yeshayah 57:19).

170. עַד הָכָא, כָּל אִינּוּן רָזִין דְּתוֹלְדוֹת אָדָם, דְּאִינּוּן תּוֹלְדוֹת,

דְּאִתְיְלִידוּ בֵּיהּ מִזְמַן לִזְמַן, כְּפוֹם אָרְחוֹי דְּבַר נָשׁ. זַכָּאָה חוּלָקֵיהוֹן דְּאִינּוּן דְּיַתְבִין קַמֵּיהּ דְּמֹר, וְזָכוּ לְמִשְׁמַע מִפּוּמֵיהּ רָזִין דְּאוֹרַיְיתָא. זַכָּאָה אִינּוּן בְּהַאי עָלְמָא, וְזַכָּאִין אִינּוּן לְעָלְמָא דְּאָתֵי. אָמַר ר׳ שִׁמְעוֹן, זַכָּאִין אַתּוּן חַבְרַיָּא, דְּכָל רָזִין לָא אָנִיס לְכוּ, כַּמָּה דּוּכְתִּין עִלָּאִין אִזְדַּמְּנָן לְכוּ לְעָלְמָא דְּאָתֵי.

170. Until this point are all the secrets of the generations of Adam, which is the history of those born to him from time to time, according to the nature of man. Happy is the lot of those who sit before my master, RABBI SHIMON, who are worthy to hear from his lips the secrets of the Torah. Happy are those in this world, and happy are those in the World to Come. Rabbi Shimon said: Happy are you, friends that no secret has disappeared from you. How many supernal places await you in the World to Come!

171. פָּתַח וְאָמַר וְאַתָּה תֶחֱזֶה מִכָּל הָעָם אַנְשֵׁי חַיִל יִרְאֵי אֱלֹהִים אַנְשֵׁי אֱמֶת שׂוֹנְאֵי בָצַע, הַאי קְרָא אוּקְמוּהָ. אֲבָל וְאַתָּה תֶחֱזֶה, תִּבְחַר לָא כְּתִיב. אֶלָּא תֶחֱזֶה: לְפוּם חֵיזוּ דְּעַיְינִין. בְּמַאי. בְּדִיּוּקְנָא דְּבַר נָשׁ בְּאִלֵּין שִׁית סִטְרִין דְּקָאָמַרְתּוּן וְכֹלָּא בְּהַאי קְרָא. וְאַתָּה תֶחֱזֶה, חַד, בְּשַׂעֲרָא. מִכָּל הָעָם, תְּרֵין, בְּמִצְחָא. אַנְשֵׁי חַיִל, תְּלַת, בְּאַנְפִּין. יִרְאֵי אֱלֹהִים, אַרְבַּע, בְּעַיְינִין. אַנְשֵׁי אֱמֶת, חָמֵשׁ, בְּשִׂפְוָון. שׂוֹנְאֵי בָצַע, שִׁית, בִּידִין, בְּשִׂרְטוּטֵיהוֹן.

171. He opened with the quote, "Moreover (lit. 'and') you shall provide (lit. 'behold') out of all the people able men, such as fear Elohim, men of truth, hating unjust gain" (Shemot 18:21). HE ASKS: But it is written: "you shall behold" instead of, 'you shall choose'. AND HE ANSWERS: "you shall behold" according to sight. In what? In the image of man, in those six characteristics that we previously discussed, and everything is in that verse. "...you shall behold..." is the first, of the hair; "out of all the people" is the second, of the brow; "able men" is third, of the face; "such as fear Elohim" is the fourth, of the eyes; "men of truth" is the fifth, of the lips; "hating unjust gain" is sixth, of the hands and their lines.

172. דְּאִלֵּין אִינּוּן סִימָנִין, לְאִשְׁתְּמוֹדְעָא בְּהוּ בְּנֵי נָשָׁא, לְאִינּוּן דְּרוּחַ

חָכְמְתָא שַׁרְיָא עֲלַיְיהוּ. וע"כד, מֹשֶׁה לָא אִצְטְרִיךְ דָּא, אֶלָּא מַה כְּתִיב, וַיִּבְחַר מֹשֶׁה אַנְשֵׁי חַיִל מִכָּל יִשְׂרָאֵל. בְּגִין דְּרוּחָא קוּדְשָׁא הֲוָה אָתֵי לְגַבֵּיהּ, וְאוֹדַע לֵיהּ, וּבֵיהּ הֲוָה חָמֵי כֹּלָּא.

172. For all these are the signs by which we recognize men on whom the spirit of Wisdom rests. Yet Moses had no need of them, for as it is written: "And Moses chose able men out of all Yisrael" (Ibid. 25). For the Holy Spirit came to him and informed him. And through this he could see it all.

173. מְנָא לָן, דִּכְתִּיב כִּי יִהְיֶה לָהֶם דָּבָר בָּא אֵלַי. בָּאִים אֵלַי לָא כְּתִיב, אֶלָּא בָּא אֵלַי, דָּא רוּחַ קוּדְשָׁא, דַּהֲוָה אָתֵי לְגַבֵּיהּ, וּבֵיהּ הֲוָה יָדַע, וְלָא אִצְטְרִיךְ לְכָל דָּא לְאַסְתַּכְּלָא וּלְעַיְינָא, אֶלָּא לְפוּם שַׁעֲתָא הֲוָה יָדַע מֹשֶׁה.

173. From where do we learn this? From the verse: "When they have a matter, they come (lit. 'he comes') to me" (Ibid. 16). It is not written 'they come', but "he comes." This is the Holy Spirit that came to him, and that is how he knew. Therefore, Moses had no need to observe and ponder all this, since he knew instantly.

174. כה"ג, יָדַע שְׁלֹמֹה מַלְכָּא, יָדַע בְּכוּרְסְיֵיהּ, דְּרוּחַ קוּדְשָׁא שַׁרְיָא עֲלֵיהּ, דְּכָל מַאן דְּקָרִיב לְכוּרְסְיֵיהּ, דְּחִילוּ וְאֵימָתָא נָפִיל עֲלֵיהּ, וּבֵיהּ הֲוָה דָּאִין דִּינָא בְּלָא סָהֲדִין. בְּגִין דְּדִיּוּקְנִין הֲווֹ בְּכוּרְסְיֵיהּ, וְכָל מַאן דְּמִקְרֵב בְּשִׁקְרָא, מְכַשְׁכְּשָׁא הַהוּא דִּיּוּקְנָא, וַהֲוָה יָדַע שְׁלֹמֹה מַלְכָּא, דְּבִשְׁקְרָא קָאָתֵי. בְּגִין כַּךְ, אֵימָתָא דְּכוּרְסְיֵיהּ הֲוָה נָפִיל עַל כֹּלָּא, וְכֻלְּהוּ אִשְׁתְּכָחוּ זַכָּאִין קָמֵיהּ.

174. Similarly, King Solomon also knew. He knew through his throne, for the Holy Spirit rested upon it. Trembling and fear overcame everyone who came near his throne. And he could judge them without witnesses. Since there were images in his throne, the image would knock if anyone approached with a falsehood, and King Solomon would know that he came with a lie. Because of this the fear of the throne fell upon all, and all were found righteous before him.

175. מַלְכָּא מְשִׁיחָא בְּרֵיחָא, כד״א וַהֲרִיחוֹ בְּיִרְאַת יְיָ׳ וְלֹא לְמַרְאֵה עֵינָיו יִשְׁפּוֹט וְגוֹ׳. וּתְלַת אִלֵּין, דָּנוּ עָלְמָא, בְּלָא סָהֲדִין וְהַתְרָאָה. שְׁאַר בְּנֵי עָלְמָא עַל פּוּם סָהֲדִין, עַל מֵימָר אוֹרַיְיתָא. חַכִּימִין דְּאִשְׁתְּמוֹדְעָן בְּאִינּוּן דִּיּוּקְנִין, עֲלַיְיהוּ לְאַזְהָרָא לִבְנֵי עָלְמָא, וּלְמֵיהַב אַסְוָותָא לִבְנֵי נָשָׁא, וּלְאַסֵּי נַפְשַׁיְיהוּ. זַכָּאִין אִינּוּן בְּהַאי עָלְמָא, וְזַכָּאִין אִינּוּן בְּעָלְמָא דְּאָתֵי.

175. King Messiah will judge by the fragrance, as it is written: "and his delight (lit. 'smell') shall be in the fear of Hashem; and he shall not judge after the sight of his eyes..." (Yeshayah 11:3). And these three, NAMELY MOSES, KING SOLOMON, AND KING MESSIAH judged the world without witnesses and without warning. The rest of the world must judge by word of witnesses and by word of the Torah. It is incumbent upon those who are wise in these images to warn people and give them succor, and to heal them. Happy are they in this world, and happy are they in the World to Come.

12. And you shall behold the secret of secrets

A Synopsis

Rabbi Shimon tells us of the secrets of the book of Adam and the secret book of King Solomon. He reveals that the Tree of Life is the book, so that the concealed wisdom was transmitted to Adam in the shapes and visages of people; Solomon inherited this wisdom and wrote it in his book, while Moses learned the wisdom from the Shechinah. Rabbi Shimon reiterates that the six aspects of man to be observed are the hair, the eyes, the nose, the lips, the face and the hands, especially the lines in the hands. He compares the skin that covers everything to the skin of the firmament, with which God created the stars and constellations, and says that the appearance of the stars and planets are everchanging, as is the appearance of the skin of man. This is followed by another long description of the six aspects and how they manifest in people of different character. In the Mishnah we learn that when the time came to create man, the light was bestowed from Keter to Binah to Zeir Anpin, and thus brought forth the souls of man. The Ruach is the result of the mating of Zeir Anpin and Malchut, and it takes on hues from the sun and moon, from water and fire, wind and earth. Rabbi Shimon explains further about the creation of the body of man, and the Nefesh and the Ruach, and says that the actions of the Nefesh inside the body appear on the skin outside.

רזא דרזין

176. וְאַתָּה תֶחֱזֶה מִכָּל הָעָם. זֶה סֵפֶר תּוֹלְדוֹת אָדָם. דָּא סֵפֶר מֵאִינּוּן סִפְרִין, סְתִימִין וַעֲמִיקִין, אָמַר ר' שִׁמְעוֹן, אֲרִימִית יְדַי בִּצְלוּ לְמַאן דִּבְרָא עָלְמָא, דְּאַף עַל גַּב דִּבְהַאי קְרָא גָּלוּ קַדְמָאֵי סְתִימִין עִלָּאִין, אִית לְאִסְתַּכְּלָא וּלְעַיְינָא בְּרָזִין דְּסִפְרָא דְּאָדָם קַדְמָאָה, דְּמִתַּמָּן אִתְמַשְׁכָא סִפְרָא גְּנִיזָא דִּשְׁלֹמֹה מַלְכָּא.

Raza deRazin - secret of secrets

176. "Moreover (lit. 'and') you shall provide (lit. 'behold') out of all the people" (Shemot 18:21). "This is the book of the generations of Adam" (Beresheet 5:1), which is to say this book is from those books that are sealed and are profoundly deep. Rabbi Shimon said: I have raised my hand in prayer to the One who created the world. Even though in this scriptural

verse the ancient ones revealed higher hidden things, yet we must further study and ponder the secrets of the book of Adam, as from that point continues the secret book of King Solomon.

177. זֶה: דְּתַלְיָא בֵּיה כֹּלָּא. זֶה: אִילָנָא דְחַיֵּי. זֶה: וְלָא אַחֲרָא דְּגַלֵּי. זֶה: כְּמָה דְּאַתְּ אָמֵר, הַחֹדֶשׁ הַזֶּה לָכֶם רֹאשׁ חֳדָשִׁים, זֶה נִיסָן וְלָא אַחֲרָא.

177. HE EXPOUNDS UPON THE VERSE: "THIS IS THE BOOK." "This" indicates that everything is dependent on it. "This" is the Tree of Life, THAT IS, TIFERET. "This" REVEALS, and there is none other to reveal. "This," is as it is written: "This month shall be to you the beginning of months," (Shemot 12:2) WHICH MEANS THAT "This" refers to *Nissan* and no other month. AND ALSO, "THIS" REVEALS AND NONE OTHER.

178. זֶה סֵפֶר, לְאַשְׁגָּחָא וּלְגַלָּאָה תּוֹלְדוֹת אָדָם, אִילָנָא דְּגַלֵּי תּוֹלְדוֹת אָדָם. וְעָבֵיד אִיבִין לְאַפָּקָא לְעָלְמָא. זֶה סֵפֶר, לְמִנְדַּע חָכְמְתָא סְתִימָא וַעֲמִיקָא, דְּאִתְמְסַר לְאָדָם קַדְמָאָה, בְּדִיּוּקְנָא דִּבְנֵי נָשָׁא, חָכְמְתָא דָּא אִתְמְסַר לִשְׁלֹמֹה מַלְכָּא, וְיָרִית לָהּ וְכָתַב בְּסִפְרֵיה.

178. It is this book that we contemplate to reveal the generations of man. IT IS a tree that reveals the generations of Adam that will bear fruit, THAT IS, THAT WILL GIVE BIRTH TO SOULS, to bring them out into the world. "This is the book" from which may be known the concealed and profound wisdom that was transmitted to the First Man in the shapes of people. This wisdom was transmitted to King Solomon , who inherited it and wrote it in his book.

179. אוֹלִיפְנָא, דְּמֹשֶׁה אִתְקְשֵׁי בְּדָא, עַד דְּאָתַת שְׁכִינְתָּא וְאוֹלִיפַת לֵיה, וְהִיא חָמָאת וּבְרִירַת לְכָל אִינוּן גּוּבְרִין דְּאִתְחֲזוּן בְּפַרְצוּפָא, וְתַמָּן אוֹלִיף מֹשֶׁה חָכְמְתָא דָּא, וְעַיֵּיל בְּגַוֵּיה, הַה"ד וְאַתָּה תֶחֱזֶה מִכָּל הָעָם. הַהוּא דִּכְתִיב בֵּיה וְאַתָּה הוּא וּשְׁנוֹתֶיךָ לֹא יִתָּמּוּ. וְאַתָּה מְחַיֶּה אֶת כֻּלָּם. וְאַתָּה יְיָ' מָגֵן בַּעֲדִי.

179. We have been taught that Moses found this difficult until the Shechinah came and taught it to him. She perceived and sorted out all those

people who could be seen AND RECOGNIZED by their countenances, and Moses thereby learned this wisdom, and was brought into it. Therefore it is written: "And You shall behold," that of which it is written "and You are the same, and Your years shall never end." (Tehilim 102: 27) "...and You do preserve them all..." (Nechemyah 9:6) "and You, Hashem, are a shield for me" (Tehilim 3:4). JUST AS IN ALL THESE WORDS "AND YOU" IS TO BE EXPLAINED AS THE SHECHINAH, SO HERE, "AND YOU SHALL BEHOLD," REFERS TO THE SHECHINAH.

180. וְאַתָּה תֶחֱזֶה, וְתִסְתַּכַּל בְּהַא. אַנְתְּ, וְלָא אַחֲרָא, לְמִנְדַּע וּלְאִסְתַּכְּלָא בְּשִׁתִּין רִבּוֹא. בְּשִׁית סִטְרִין אִית לְאִסְתַּכְּלָא. בְּדִיּוּקְנִין דִּבְנֵי נָשָׁא, וּלְמִנְדַּע חָכְמְתָא עַל בּוּרְיֵיהּ. וְאִלֵּין אִינּוּן בְּשַׂעֲרָא. בְּעַיְינִין. בְּחוֹטָמָא. בְּשִׂפְוָון. בְּאַפִּין. בִּיְדִין. בְּאִינּוּן שִׂרְטוּטִין דִּיְדִין. וּבְשִׁית סִטְרִין אִלֵּין, כְּתִיב וְאַתָּה תֶחֱזֶה.

180. "And You," NAMELY THE SHECHINAH, "shall behold" and observe it. You and none other, to know and to contemplate six hundred thousand. In six aspects you are to contemplate the images of man and to clearly know this wisdom. These are: the hair, the eyes, the nose, the lips, the face, and the hands, especially the lines in the hands. Of the six aspects, it is written: "And you shall behold."

181. וְאַתָּה תֶחֱזֶה, בְּשַׂעֲרָא בְּקַמְטִין דְּמִצְחָא, בְּאִלֵּין קְרִיצִין דְּעַל עַיְינִין. מִכָּל הָעָם, בְּעַיְינִין. בְּדוּקִין דְּעֵינָא, וּבְקַמְטִין דִּתְחוֹת עֵינָא. אַנְשֵׁי חָיִל, דִּבְהוּ חֵילָא לְמֵיקָם בְּהֵיכָלִין דְּמַלְכָּא. בְּצְהִיבוּ דְּאַפִּין. בְּאַפִּין, בְּקַמְטִין דְּאַפִּין. בִּרְשִׁימוּ דִּבְהוּ בְּדִיקְנָא. שִׂנְאֵי בָצַע, בִּיְדִין, בְּשִׂרְטוּטֵי יְדִין, רְשִׁימִין דִּבְהוּ. וְכֻלְּהוּ שִׁית סִטְרִין רְמִיזִין הָכָא, דְּאִתְמְסָרוּ לְמֹשֶׁה, לְאִסְתַּכְּלָא וּלְמִנְדַּע חָכְמְתָא סְתִימָאָה, וְחָכְמְתָא דָא, יָרְתָּן זַכָּאֵי קְשׁוֹט כַּדְקָא יָאוֹת, זַכָּאָה חוּלָקֵהוֹן.

181. "And you shall behold," THAT IS, in the hair, the creases on the brow, and the eyebrows. "...out of all the people..." IS TO BE INTERPRETED AS with eyes, in the membranes in the eyes, and in the folds under the eyes. "...able men..." REFERS TO those who have the strength to stand in the

palace of the King. They are recognized by the brightness on their faces, by their face, by the wrinkles on their faces, and by the marks in their beards. "…hating unjust gain…" REFERS TO the hands, and the lines in the hands, and the marks in them. All these six aspects implied here, IN THE SCRIPTURAL VERSE, were transmitted to Moses to contemplate and from which to learn concealed wisdom. This wisdom is inherited by those who are properly righteous and truthful. Happy is their lot.

182. כְּתִיב עוֹר וּבָשָׂר תַּלְבִּישֵׁנִי וְגוֹ', כְּגַוְונָא דָא עָבֵד קוּדְשָׁא בְּרִיךְ הוּא לְעֵילָא, דַּרְגִּין עַל דַּרְגִּין, אַלֵּין עַל אִלֵּין, סְתִימִין גּוֹ סְתִימִין, וְחַיָּילִין וּרְתִיכִין, אַלֵּין עַל אִלֵּין, הָכִי עָבֵיד בְּכָל אִינּוּן, עַרְקִין וְגִידִין, וְאַלֵּין אִינּוּן גַּרְמִין, וְקַיְימִין בְּקִיּוּמָא דְּדַרְגִּין עִלָּאִין, וְאִלֵּין אִקְרוּן בָּשָׂר, דַּרְגִּין וְשַׁלְטָנוּתָא דְּקֵץ כָּל בָּשָׂר, וְכָל אִינּוּן דְּאִתְהֲנוּן מִתְּנָנָא דִּבְשָׂר, דְּרֵיחִין דְּקָרְבְּנִין, וְאַחֲרָנִין דְּשַׁלְטִין בַּבָּשָׂר. וְעֵילָא מִכֻּלְּהוּ עוֹר, מַשְׁכָא דְּחָפֵי עַל כֹּלָּא.

182. It is written: "You have clothed me with skin and flesh…" (Iyov 10:11). In a similar fashion, the Holy One, blessed be He, made levels upon levels above, these upon those, concealed ones within others concealed, hosts and Chariots, the one over the other. Similarly, He made in all these arteries and tendons THAT HE MADE IN THEM LEVEL UPON LEVEL…and these are the bones that exist on higher levels. And those OF THE LEVELS are called 'flesh', being the levels of the domain of the end of all flesh. And all these benefit from the smoke of the flesh, from the scent of the sacrificial offerings, and from others things associated with flesh. And above all these is the skin. This is the hide that covers everything.

183. כְּגַוְונָא דְּעָבֵד קוּדְשָׁא בְּרִיךְ הוּא כֹּכָבִים וּמַזָּלוֹת בְּמַשְׁכָא דִּרְקִיעָא, לְאִסְתַּכְּלָא בְּהוּ, וְאִינּוּן אוֹתוֹת הַשָּׁמַיִם, וּלְמִנְדַּע בְּהוּ חָכְמְתָא. הָכִי עָבֵד קוּדְשָׁא בְּרִיךְ הוּא בִּבְנֵי נָשָׁא, רְשִׁימִין וְקָמִיטִין בְּהַהוּא פַּרְצוּפָא דְּאָדָם, כְּאִינּוּן כֹּכָבִים וּמַזָּלוֹת, לְמִנְדַּע וּלְאִסְתַּכְּלָא בְּהוּ חָכְמְתָא סַגְיָא, וּלְאִתְנַהֲגָא בְּהוּ גּוּפָא.

183. The Holy One, blessed be He, created the stars and the constellations

with the skin of the firmament, as they are the signs of the heavens so that we may observe them to know the wisdom from them. Similarly, the Holy One, blessed be He, created man with marks and wrinkles in THE SKIN OF the face of man, which are similar to the stars and constellations IN THE FIRMAMENT, through which to know and to perceive great wisdom, applying it to the body.

184. כְּמָה דְמִתְחַלְּפֵי בְּמַשְׁכָא דִרְקִיעָא, חֵיזוּ דְּכֹכְבַיָּא וּמַזָּלֵי, לְפוּם עוֹבָדִין דְּעָלְמָא, הָכִי מִתְחַלְּפִין חֵיזוּ דִרְשִׁימִין וְקִמְטִין בְּמַשְׁכָא דְּב"נ, לְפוּם עוֹבָדוֹי מִזְּמַן לִזְמַן. וּמִלִּין אִלֵּין לָא אִתְמְסָרוּ אֶלָּא לְזַכָּאֵי קְשׁוֹט, לְמִנְדַּע וּלְאַלְּפָא חָכְמָתָא סַגִּיא.

184. Just as the appearance of the stars and constellations change in the firmament according to worldly events, so does the appearance of the marks and wrinkles on the skin of man change according to the actions of man from time to time. This wisdom was given only for the true righteous to learn and to know this great knowledge.

185. זֶה סֵפֶר תּוֹלְדוֹת אָדָם, מִזְּמַן לִזְמַן, לְפוּם עוֹבָדוֹי דְאָדָם, הָכִי אִתְיְלִידוּ, וְאִתְרְשִׁימוּ וְאִתְחַלְּפוּ בֵּיהּ רְשִׁימִין מִזְּמַן לִזְמַן. דְּהָא בְּזִמְנָא דְרוּחָא קַדִּישָׁא שַׁרְיָא בְּגַוֵּיהּ, הָכִי עָבֵיד תּוֹלְדוֹת, וְאַחְזֵי רְשִׁימִין הַהוּא רוּחַ לְבַר.

185. "This is the book of the generations of Adam." From time to time, according to the actions of man, marks are born, changed and etched upon the skin of man. For when the Holy Spirit rests within him, it produces offspring, and shows these marks of the Outside Spirit.

186. וּבְזִמְנָא דְּמִתְעַבְרָא וְזָז מִנֵּיהּ רוּחַ קַדְשָׁא, וְאַתְיָא רוּחַ מְסָאֲבָא, וְהַהוּא רוּחַ מְסָאֲבָא הוּא מְכַשְׁכְּשָׁא בְּגַוֵּיהּ, וְאַחְזֵי לְבַר חֵיזוּ וּרְשִׁימִין יְדִיעָאן, דְּאִשְׁתְּמוֹדְעָן בֵּיהּ בְּקַמְטִין בְּמַשְׁכָא לְבַר. וְאע"ג דְּשַׂעֲרָא וּמִצְחָא וְחוֹטָמָא וְעַיְינִין, וְכָל אִנּוּן סִימָנִין, קַיְימִין עַל קִיּוּמַיְיהוּ.

186. And when the Holy Spirit removes itself from him and the Spirit of

Defilement comes, this Spirit of Defilement pulsates within him and appears on his exterior with familiar marks. It is recognizable in the wrinkles of his exterior skin, even if the hair, the brow, and the nose remain unchanged.

187. זר״ה פס״ץ, אָת דָּא דְּמִתְחַלְּפָא תָּדִיר בְּהָא חָכְמְתָא. בְּאָת זַי״ן, מִלָּה דְּקַיְּימָא בְּשַׂעֲרָא הֲוָה וְסִימָנִיךְ זַי״ן, וּמָאנֵי קְרָבָא דְּשִׁמְשׁוֹן, בְּשַׂעֲרָא. וְדָא הוּא נִזְרָא דְּאֱלֹהִים עָלֵיה.

187. *Zayin-Resh-Hei-Pe-Samech*-final *Tzadi*. This letter, REFERRING TO THE FINAL *TZADI,* is always exchangeable in this wisdom. TO CLARIFY, THE MAIN ONES ARE THE FIVE LETTERS: ZAYIN, *RESH, HEI, PE, SAMECH.* THESE LETTERS FORM THE WORDS "*ZEH SEFER* ('THIS BOOK')." THE FINAL *TZADI* JOINS WITH THEM, ALWAYS TO BE EXCHANGED WITH THESE LETTERS. The letter *Zayin* is that letter that is found in the hair of man; this is derived from *Zayin,* NAMELY WEAPONS (Heb. *ZAYIN*). And the weapons of Shimshon were in his hair, FOR IN HIS HAIR WAS ALL HIS BRAVERY. This was the crown of Elohim that was upon him.

188. שַׂעֲרָא דְּקַיְּימָא לְאִשְׁתְּמוֹדְעָא, וְתַלְיָא. דָּא קַיְּימָא בְּאָת ז׳, וְאִתְחֲבָּר בֵּיה אָת צ׳. דָּא עָאל וְאַפִּיק ס׳.

188. Hair that stands in a familiar way and hangs FROM THE TOP DOWN stands in the letter sign of *Zayin* and is joined by the letter *Tzadi*, which enters and takes out the letter *Samech*.

189. אִי שַׂעֲרָא דָּא תַּלְיָא וְאוּכָם, וּבְמִצְחָא תְּלָתָא שִׁרְטוּטִין מִסְּטְרָא דִּימִינָא, וּתְרֵין מִשְּׂמָאלָא, וְלָא מִתְחַבְּרָן אִלֵּין בְּאִלֵּין. בְּסְטַר יְמִינָא אִית תְּלָתָא רְשִׁימִין דְּקִיקִין, דְּעַבְרִין עֲלַיְיהוּ. וְאִינּוּן שְׁבִילִין לְמֶעֱבַר עַל אִינּוּן שִׁרְטוּטִין אַחֲרָנִין. וּבְסְטַר שְׂמָאלָא חָמֵשׁ, וְחַד מִנֵּיה זְעֵיר בְּאָרְכֵּיה. דָּא קַיְּימָא בְּגוֹ אָת ז׳ וְאָת ע׳. כְּדֵין תִּשְׁכַּח קְרִיצִין תַּקִּיפִין דְּעַל חוֹרֵי עֵינוֹי, דְּמִתְחַבְּרָן דָּא בְּדָא.

189. There is hair that hangs and is black, and in the forehead there are three lines on the right side, and two on the left side, and these ones are not joined together with the others. On the right side there are three thin marks that pass over them. These are paths to cross over other lines. On the left side, there are five lines. One of them is small in length. This is included in the letter *Zayin* and the letter final *Tzadi*. Then there are the strong eyebrows above the eye sockets that are joined together.

189. דָּא אִיהוּ בַּר נָשׁ מָארֵיהּ דְּרוּגְזָא, וְלָא בִּבְהִילוּ, וְנַיְיחָא דִּילֵיהּ בְּעָכּוּבָא. חָשִׁיב בְּגַרְמֵיהּ דְּאִיהוּ חַכִּים. וְלָאו הָכִי. זָקִיף רֵישָׁא לְאִסְתַּכְּלָא תָּדִיר. מָארֵי מָצוּתָא לְבַר. בְּבֵיתֵיהּ לָאו הָכִי. אוֹרַיְיתָא לָא חָשִׁיב לְאִסְתַּכְּלָא בָּהּ. מִלִּין דִּבְנֵי נָשָׁא חֲשִׁיבִין עֲלֵיהּ כְּמָטוֹל, וְאָתִיב מִלִּין תַּקִּיפִין עֲלַיְיהוּ.

190. Such a man is angry. Though not quick to become angry, he impedes his peace of mind. He holds himself to be wise, but he is not. He constantly holds his head up high to watch. He is quarrelsome in public, but not at home. He is not interested in Torah learning. He considers people's words as a burden, and answers them with emphatic words.

191. וְאִי מִתְפָּרְשָׁן קְרִיצִין דָּא מִן דָּא, מָטוּ וְלָא מָטוּ, כְּדֵין תִּשְׁכַּח בְּמִצְחָא לְסִטְרָא דִּימִינָא, תְּרֵין שִׂרְטוּטִין רַבְרְבִין וְחַד זְעֵירָא, וּתְרֵין רְשִׁימִין זְעִירִין דְּעָאלִין בֵּינַיְיהוּ לְפוּתְיָא. וְלִסְטַר שְׂמָאלָא תְּרֵין, חַד רַבְרְבָא, וְחַד זְעֵירָא, וְחַד רְשִׁימוּ זְעֵיר דְּעָאל בְּחַד וְלָא מָטֵי לְתִנְיָינָא.

191. If the eyebrows are separated one from the other, touching yet not touching ONE ANOTHER, then you will find on the right side of the forehead two large lines and one small one, and two small marks that have entered between them in width. And on the left side are two lines, one large, one small, and one small mark that has entered on one line but not the other.

192. דָּא אִיהוּ מָארֵיהּ דְּרוּגְזָא, לְפוּם שַׁעֲתָא אִתְמְלֵי רוּגְזָא, וּלְפוּם שַׁעֲתָא שָׁכִיךְ רוּגְזֵיהּ, וּמָארֵי קְטָטָא בְּבֵיתֵיהּ, וְלָאו בְּרוּחַ נַיְיחָא. זִמְנָא חֲדָא בְּיוֹמוֹי אָתִיב תּוּקְפִין לִבְנֵי נָשָׁא. אִסְתַּכַּל לְתַתָּא. מִצְחֵיהּ קָמִיט

בְּרוּגְזֵיה, וְדָמֵי כְּכַלְבָּא, וּמִיָּד שָׁכִיךְ וְאָתִיב רְכִיכִין. דָּא אִיהוּ בַּר נָשׁ, דְּרוּחָא דִּילֵיה וּרְעוּתָא דִּילֵיה, לְאִשְׁתַּדְּלָא בִּסְחוֹרָתָא וּמִנְדָּה בְּלוֹ וְהֲלָךְ וּבְאִשְׁתַּדְּלוּתֵיה, סָלִיק לְמָמוֹנָא. דְּהָא אִתְחַלַּף אָת צ' בְּאָת ס'.

192. This is a man of anger. He is angry one moment, and the next moment he forgets his anger. He is quarrelsome in his house, and he is not at peace in spirit. There was a time in his life when he was quite emphatic with people. He looks down. His forehead is creased at the time of his anger, similar to a dog, and when immediately it is forgotten, his response is soft. This is a man whose spirit and will is occupied with business. He vows to pay taxes, THAT IS TO PAY ALL KINDS OF TAXES TO THE KING, and in his endeavors TO DO BUSINESS he becomes wealthy, for the letter final *Tzadi* is replaced by a *Samech*.

193. וְאִי מִתְפָּרְשָׁן קְרִיצִין דָּא מִן דָּא, וְשַׂעֲרִין אַחֲרָנִין עַיְילִין בֵּין דָּא לְדָא זְעִירִין. דָּא נָטִיר דְּבָבוּ סַגִּי תָּדִיר. טַב אִיהוּ בְּבֵיתֵיה. וְחַדֵי וְעָצִיב בִּבְנֵי נָשָׁא, דָּא קַיְימָא בֵּין צ' וּבֵין ס'. טָמִיר מָמוֹנֵיה. לָא בָּעֵי לְאַגְלוּיֵי, וְלָאִתְגְּלֵי בְּעוֹבָדוֹי. קַמְצָן אִיהוּ. וְשַׂעֲרֵיה גָּבִיל דָּא עִם דָּא, וְתַלְיָיא. לָא חָשִׁיב גַּרְמֵיה לְמִלְבַּשׁ כַּדְקָא יָאוֹת. מַה דְּלָבִישׁ לָא אִתְתַּקַּן בֵּיה. מִצְחֵיה רַבְרְבָא, תְּלַת שִׂרְטוּטִין בִּימִינָא, וְאַרְבַּע בִּשְׂמָאלָא תְּרֵין רְשִׁימִין עַיְילִין בֵּינַיְיהוּ.

193. If the eyebrows are separated one from the other, and other small hairs intercross them, this is a person who has always a great, vindictive hatred. He is well behaved in his house. He is both happy and grievous with people. This lies between the final *Tzadi* and *Samech*. He conceals his money. He does not wish to reveal his doings, nor does he wish that anyone should reveal his doings. He is a miser, and his hairs hang in equal length, one to the other. He does not give any thought to the wearing of proper clothes. What he does wear does not fit him properly. His forehead is large, with three lines on the right side, four on the left side, and with two marks entering between them.

194. דָּא כַּד מַלִּיל פָּשִׁיט מַשְׁכָא דְּמִצְחָא, וְאִינּוּן שִׂרְטוּטִין לָא אִתְחַזוּן

כָּל כָּךְ. כָּפִיף רֵישֵׁיה אָזִיל. יְמִינָא מִנֵּיה שְׂמָאלָא. שְׂמָאלָא מִנֵּיה יְמִינָא. עָצִיב תָּדִיר אֲנִינָא אִיהוּ, מָארֵיה דְּלִישָׁנָא בִּישָׁא. חָשִׁיב גַּרְמֵיה חַכִּים בְּכָל עוֹבָדוֹי. מָארֵי דְּבָבוּ בְּכָל אִינּוּן דְּמִשְׁתַּדְּלָן בְּאוֹרַיְיתָא.

194. When he speaks, he stretches the skin of his forehead, and these lines can not be seen clearly. He bends his head down and walks. His right is like his left, and his left like his right. He is always depressed. He mourns. He has an evil tongue. He regards himself as one who is wise in all his deeds. He has a hatred for all who occupy themselves with Torah learning.

195. בִּדְרוֹעָא שְׂמָאלָא, אִית לֵיה רְשִׁימָא אוּכְמָא, וד' שַׂעֲרִין זְעֵירִין בָּה, וּתְרֵין רַבְרְבִין דְּתַלְיָין בֵּיה סוּמָקִין. שַׂעֲרָא שְׁעִיעַ וְתָלֵי, וְאִיהוּ, לָאו סוּמָק, וְלָאו אוּכָם, מִצְחָא דִּילֵיה לָא רַב וְלָא זְעֵיר. דָּא קַיְימָא בֵּין אָת ס', וּבֵין אָת ץ' כְּלִילָא בְּאָת ז'.

195. Another type is signified by a black mark on his left arm with four small hairs in it. Two large ones that are hanging on it are red. The hairs are smooth and hanging, neither red nor black, and his forehead is neither large nor small. This stands between the letter *Samech* and the letter final *Tzadi*. It is included in the letter *Zayin*.

196. חַד שִׂרְטוּטָא רַב בְּמִצְחֵיה, דְּאַזְלָא בְּפוּתְיָא, מִסְטְרָא דָּא לְסִטְרָא דָּא. תְּרֵין שִׂרְטוּטִין אַחֲרָנִין, אֲבָל לָא לָא רְשִׁימִין כ"כ, דְּהָא לָא קַיְימִין מִסְטְרָא דָּא לְסִטְרָא דָּא, בְּהַאי. אַרְבַּע קְמִיטִין זְעֵירִין קַיְימִין, בֵּין תְּרֵין קְרִיצִין, עַל רֵישָׁא דְּחוֹטָמָא לְעֵילָא.

196. There is one large line in his forehead that spans in width from this side to that side. There are two other lines not marked so emphatically, since they are not continuous from one side to the other side, AS IN THE CASE OF THE FIRST LINE. There are four small creases that stand between the two eyebrows at the top of the nose.

197. דָּא אִיהוּ מָארֵיה דְּחֶדְוָה, חַכִּים, פְּקִיחַ, וַותְרָן בְּמָמוֹנֵיה, בְּכָל מַה דְּאִשְׁתַּדַּל לְמִנְדַע אִיהוּ חַכִּים. לְפוּם שַׁעֲתָא רָגֵז, וּלְפוּם שַׁעֲתָא נָח

רוּגְזֵיהּ, לָא נָטַר דְּבָבוּ לְעָלְמִין. לְזִמְנָא טַב, וּלְזִמְנָא לָאו הָכִי כ״ב,
קָאֵים בְּמַתְקְלָא. כַּד תָּב לְמָארֵיהּ, מָארֵיהּ אָחִיד בִּידֵיהּ, וְסָלִיק לִיקָר
סַגִּיא. כֹּלָּא צְרִיכִין לֵיהּ. אָת ס׳ אַזְלָא לְדִידֵיהּ תָּדִיר יַתִּיר מֵאָת צ׳. כָּל
אִינּוּן דְּיָעֲטִין עָלֵיהּ עֵיטָא בִּישָׁא, לָא מַצְלִיחִין, וְלָא אִתְקַיָּים הַהוּא
עֵיטָא, וְלָא יַכְלִין לְאַבְאָשָׁא לֵיהּ. אִתְחֲזֵי רַמָּאָה וְלָאו הָכִי הוּא. אָת ס׳
וְאָת צ׳ מַגִּיחִין עָלֵיהּ, וּבג״כ סָלִיק וְנָחִית. כַּד תָּב לְמָארֵיהּ, אָת ס׳
נָצַח, וְאִתְעֲבִיד רְעוּתֵיהּ בְּכֹלָּא. רַחֲמָן אִיהוּ. וּבָכֵי כַּד אִתְמְלֵי רַחֲמִין.

197. This is a happy man. He is wise, intelligent, and lenient with his money. He becomes wise in whatever he endeavors to know. He can become angry in one moment, and the next moment his anger is calmed. He does not hold a vindictive hatred forever. At times he is well behaved, and at other times he is not as well behaved, but he is found in balance – THAT IS, NEITHER PARTICULARLY GOOD, NOR PARTICULARLY BAD. When he repents to his Master, his Master holds his hands and he is raised to great honor. Everyone needs him. The letter *Samech* goes with him always, more than the letter final *Tzadi*. All who counsel him with bad advice will not succeed, for the bad advice will not be fulfilled. And they can not injure him. He seems to be a charlatan, but it is not so. The letter *Samech* and the letter final *Tzadi* wrestle over him. Therefore, AT TIMES he is up AND AT TIMES he is down. When he repents before his Master, the letter *Samech* is victorious and fulfills his wish in everything. He is compassionate, and he cries when he is full of compassion.

198. חַד רְשׁוּמָא אִית לֵיהּ בִּדְרוֹעָא יְמִינָא, וְקַיְּימָא פַּרְצוּפָא, וְלֵית
עָלֵיהּ שַׂעֲרִין כְּלַל. וְאִי שַׂעֲרָא קְמִיטָא, וְלָא תָּלֵי תְּחוֹת אוּדְנִין, וְאִיהוּ
קָמִיט לְעֵילָּא מֵאוּדְנִין דָּא קַיְּימָא בְּמִלּוּלֵיהּ.

198. One mark is in the right arm, and his face is without any hair at all. But if there is hair which is curled, not dangling below the ears, but raised and curled above the ears, then he keeps his word.

199. מִצְחֵיהּ רַב וְלָאו כ״כ. שִׂרְטוּטִין דִּילֵיהּ חָמֵשׁ. תְּלַת עֲבָרִין
מִסִּטְרָא דָּא לְסִטְרָא דָּא, וּתְרֵין לָא עֲבָרִין. מָארֵי קְטָטָה אִיהוּ, וּבְבֵיתֵיהּ

יַתִּיר. כָּל עוֹבָדוֹי בִּבְהִילוּ, אִתְחֲזֵי טָב, וְלָאו הָכִי. שָׁבַח גַּרְמֵיהּ בְּמָה
דְּלָא אִית בֵּיהּ. דָּא קָאִים בְּאָת ז' לְחוֹד, וְסָלִיק לְמֵרָחִיק בְּאָת צ' לְחוֹד,
מָטֵי וְלָא מָטֵי אָת ס' לֵית בֵּיהּ כְּלָל. וַותְרָן בְּמִלּוּלֵיהּ וְלָא יַתִּיר, אָעִיל
גַּרְמֵיהּ בְּמָה דְּלָא אִתְחֲזֵי לֵיהּ, מַאן דְּאִשְׁתַּתַּף בַּהֲדֵיהּ, אִצְטְרִיךְ
לְאִסְתַּמְּרָא מֵחֲמִידוּ דִּילֵיהּ, אֲבָל אַצְלַח אִיהוּ בַּהֲדֵיהּ.

199. His forehead is large, but not huge. There are five lines on it. Three pass from this side to that side OF THE FOREHEAD, and two lines do not traverse. This man is a quarrelsome person, at home for the most part. All his actions are hurried, and though they seem beneficial, they are not. He lauds himself for what he does not have. This pertains to the letter *Zayin* itself, remotely aspiring to the letter *Tzadi* by itself, reaching yet not reaching. The letter *Samech* is not included in him at all. He is lenient in his speech, but no more than that. He brings more than he deserves to himself. One who partakes with him must be wary of his greed but will succeed with him.

200. שַׂעֲרָא דְּתָלֵי וְלָא שְׁעִיעַ, וְשַׂעֲרֵיהּ רַב. חָמֵשׁ שִׂרְטוּטִין בֵּיהּ, דְּמָטוּ
וְלָא מָטוּ דָּא לְדָא, עַיְינִין דִּילֵיהּ צְהִיבִין פְּקִחִין. דָּא כָּפִיף רֵישֵׁיהּ.
אִתְחֲזֵי טָב וְזַכָּאָה, וְלָאו הָכִי. שָׁבַח גַּרְמֵיהּ. אִי אִשְׁתְּדַּל בְּאוֹרַיְיתָא כְּבַר
נָשׁ רַב. תַּקִּיף בִּיצְרֵיהּ. כַּד מַלִּיל, אַקְמִיט חוֹטָמֵיהּ וּפָשִׁיט מַשְׁכָא
דְּמִצְחֵיהּ. כָּל עוֹבָדוֹי לְחֵיזוּ דִּבְנֵי נָשָׁא, אַצְלַח בְּמָמוֹנָא, רַמָּאָה אִיהוּ
בְּכָל עוֹבָדוֹי. מָארֵי דְּלִישָׁנָא בִּישָׁא. יָדַע לְאִסְתַּמְּרָא מִבְּנֵי נָשָׁא בְּכֹלָּא.
שִׁגְעוֹנָא בֵּיהּ, וְאִתְכַּסֵּי בְּמָה דְּאִיהוּ עָבֵיד. אָעִיל קַטְטִין בִּלְחִישׁוּ.

200. Another type is signified by hair that is dangling and is not flat. He has a profusion of hair and five lines in it; some are touching yet are not touching each other. His eyes are shining and alert. His head is bent low. He seems to be pleasant and honest, but is not so. He praises himself. If he occupies himself with Torah learning, he acts like a great man. He has strong desires. When he speaks, he wrinkles his nose, and stretches the skin of his forehead. All of his actions are for the sake of appearances in public. He succeeds in wealth. He is deceitful in all that he does. He is a slanderer. He knows how to defend himself from people in everything. He has madness in him, and conceals what he does SO THAT IT SHALL NOT BE

RECOGNIZED. He secretly brings strife BETWEEN FRIENDS.

201. אוּדְנוֹי רַבְרְבָן, קַיְימִין בְּקִיּוּמַיְיהוּ תְּחוֹת שַׂעֲרָא, דָּא קַיְימָא בְּאָת
ץ' וְאָת ז', וּבְגִין כַּךְ עוֹבָדוֹי לְחֵיזוּ בְּנֵי נָשָׁא. בֵּין כִּתְפוֹי תַּלְיָין תְּלַת
שַׂעֲרִין בְּלָא רְשִׁימָא כְּלָל. מַאן דְּאִשְׁתַּתַּף בַּהֲדֵיהּ לָא אַצְלַח. וְאִיהוּ
אַצְלַח בְּרַמָּאוּתָא דִּילֵיהּ, וְאִתְחֲזֵי זַכָּאָה לְאַחֲרָא, וְחָשִׁיב דְּעָבֵד
לָקֳבְלֵיהּ עוֹבָדֵי קְשׁוֹט.

201. He has big ears which are placed underneath his hair. He is established by the letter final *Tzadi* and the letter *Zayin*. Therefore, his actions are for the public. If three hairs hang between his shoulders, without any marks at all, one who partakes with him will not succeed. But he will succeed with his own deceit. He appears to be righteous with respect to another and thinks that his are truthful actions in dealing with him.

202. שַׂעֲרָא קְמִיטָא וְתָלֵי תְּחוֹת אוּדְנִין, אִי אִיהוּ רָוָוק, חַד שִׂרְטוּטָא
בְּמִצְחֵיהּ, וּתְלַת קְמִיטִין עַל רֵישָׁא דְּחוֹטְמִין, בֵּין קְרִיצִין דִּילֵיהּ.
מָארֵיהּ דְּחֶדְוָה אִיהוּ. פְּקִיחָא בְּכֹלָּא. רַמָּאָה. וַותְּרָן אִיהוּ עָבֵיד
וַותְּרָנוּתָא לְאִינּוּן דְּמִקְרְבִין בַּהֲדֵיהּ. דָּא קַיְימָא בְּאָת ס' וְאָת ז'. וְכַד
הֲוֵי סִיב, מִתְחַלְּפָן אַתְוָון, אָת ז' בְּרֵישָׁא, וְאָת ס' בַּהֲדֵיהּ. לָאו אִיהוּ
וַותְּרָן, אֶלָּא בְּבֵיתֵיהּ. אַצְלַח בְּמָמוֹנֵיהּ. רַמָּאָה לָא הֲוֵי. אַעֲדֵי גַרְמֵיהּ
מֵהַהוּא אָרְחָא.

202. If his hair is crimped and hangs beneath his ears; if he is unmarried; and if there is one line in his brow, and three creases at the top of his nose, between his eyebrows, then, he is a happy man, intelligent in all matters. He is deceitful. He concedes and gives in to those closest to him. This stands under the letter *Samech* and the letter *Zayin*. As he grows older, the letters are exchanged – the letter *Zayin* is at the beginning, followed by the letter *Samech*. He then no longer concedes, except in his home. He succeeds in wealth. He is no longer deceitful, having removed himself from that path.

203. עַל קְרִיצָא שְׂמָאלָא, אִית חַד רִישׁוּמָא זְעֵיר, דְּמָחָה לֵיהּ בַּר נָשׁ

בְּיוֹמֵי עוֹלֵימוֹי, אָטִים עֵינָא יְמִינָא. חָמֵשׁ קְמִיטִין עַל רֵישָׁא דְחוּטָמֵיהּ,
בְּפוּתְיֵיהּ בֵּין קְרִיצֵי עֵינוֹי. שַׁעֲרָא קְמִיטָא זְעֵיר עַל רֵישֵׁיהּ. קָמִיט
דְעַיְינִין. דָּא אִיהוּ בָּאת ז' בִּלְחוֹדוֹי. בְּלָא סָכְלְתָנוּ. שִׁגְעוֹנָא בְּלִבֵּיהּ.
בָּהִיל בְּעוֹבְדוֹי.

203. On his left eyebrow, there is a small mark where a man had hit him in
his youth. His right eye is closed. There are five furrows on top of his nose,
spanning the width between his eyebrows. His hair is curled slightly on his
head. He creases his eyes. This person stands in the letter *Zayin* alone. He
has no understanding. He has madness in his heart. He is hasty in his actions.

204. חַד שִׂרְטוּטָא עַל מִצְחֵיהּ. וְאַרְבַּע אַחֲרָנִין זְעֵירִין. לֵית בֵּיהּ
מְהֵימָנוּתָא, לָא יִשְׁתָּתַּף בַּר נָשׁ בַּהֲדֵיהּ, דְּלָא יִצְלַח. חַיָּיבָא אִיהוּ
לְמָארֵיהּ בְּכָל עוֹבְדוֹי. חַד תּוֹלְדוּתָא זְעֵירָא אִית לֵיהּ עַל יַרְכָא
שְׂמָאלָא. לְזִמְנִין אִתְמְחֵי, וּלְזִמְנִין אִתְיְילִיד. וְאִי אַרְבַּע שִׂרְטוּטִין עַל
מִצְחֵיהּ, כָּל הָנֵי אִית בֵּיהּ, אֲבָל לֵית בֵּהּ תּוֹלַדְתָּא. וְאִי תְּלַת רַבְרְבִין
וּתְלַת זְעֵירִין, שַׁפִּירוּ דְשַׁעֲרָא אִיהוּ, וְאִיהוּ בְּאֶמְצָעִיתָא. ע"כ רָזָא
דְשַׁעֲרָא.

204. He who has one line on his brow and four other small ones, has no
faith. One should not associate with him, since he will not be successful. He
sins against his Master in all his actions. He has one small birthmark on his
left thigh. At times, it disappears, at other times, it reappears. If he has four
lines on his brow, he has all these MENTIONED ABOVE, except for the
birthmark ON HIS LEFT THIGH. If he has three large lines and three small
ones ON HIS FOREHEAD, and they are in the center of the forehead, he has
beautiful hair. Until this point is the secret of the hair.

205. מִצְחָא מִתְפָּרְשָׁא בְּשַׂעֲרָא, וּמִצְחָא מִתְפָּרְשָׁא בְּעַיְינִין, עֵינָא
מִתְפָּרְשָׁא בְּשַׂעֲרָא, לד' סִטְרִין. בְּבַת עֵינָא, בִּגְווֹנִין דְעֵינָא, בְּחִוָּורוּ
דְעֵינָא, בְּאוּכָמוּ דְעֵינָא. כָּל אִסְתַּכְּלוּתָא לְאִסְתַּכְּלָא, בְּכָל אִינּוּן סִימָנִין
דְשִׁית דְּקָאמְרָן, לֵית לְהוּ אֶלָּא מִי"ג שְׁנִין וּלְעֵילָא, דְּאִתְפָּרְשָׁא רוּחַ

קַדְשָׁא מֵרוּחַ מְסָאֲבָא. בַּר בְּשִׁרְטוּטֵי בִּלְחוֹדוֹי, דְּשִׁרְטוּטִין בֵּין זְעֵירָא וּבֵין רַב מִתְחַלְּפֵי תָּדִיר וְכֵן בְּכֻלְּהוּ.

205. The forehead is to be made understandable through the hair and is to be defined through the eyes. The eyes are to be explained through the hair from four perspectives: in the pupil of the eye; in the colors of the eye; in the white of the eye; in the black pupil of the eye. All perceptions should be performed with the stated six signs, THE HAIR ON THE FOREHEAD, AND SO ON, AS MENTIONED PREVIOUSLY. These are to be applied to persons of at least thirteen years in age, when IN A MAN, the Holy Spirit has already separated itself from the Spirit of Uncleanliness. The exception is the lines, since these lines, whether small or large, are constantly changing. IT IS POSSIBLE TO DISTINGUISH IF THEY ARE FROM THE UNCLEANLINESS, OR FROM THE HOLINESS. And so it is with all of them, AS WILL BE DISCUSSED FURTHER.

206. כְּתִיב וַיִּבְחַר מֹשֶׁה אַנְשֵׁי חַיִל מִכָּל יִשְׂרָאֵל וְגוֹ', דְּאִילּוּ עַל אִינּוּן סִימָנִין אַחֲרָנִין בָּעָא וְלָא אַשְׁכַּח. וְכֵן הָבוּ לָכֶם אֲנָשִׁים חֲכָמִים וִידוּעִים לְשִׁבְטֵיכֶם. מַאי יְדוּעִים. דְּאִשְׁתְּמוֹדְעָאן בְּאִינּוּן סִימָנִין, וְאַשְׁכַּח, בַּר נְבוֹנִים דְּלָא אַשְׁכַּח.

206. It is written: "And Moses chose able men out of all Yisrael" (Shemot 18:25). For he was seeking other signs APART FROM "ABLE MEN," but did not find any. Also, "Take wise men, who are understanding and known among your tribes" (Devarim 1:13). What is the meaning of "known"? For they are known by those signs MENTIONED PREVIOUSLY. And he found them, but they were not men of understanding. THIS INDICATES THAT "ABLE MEN" AND "WISE MEN" ARE NEAR EACH OTHER IN QUALITY, SINCE HERE THE SCRIPTURES STATE, "AND MOSES CHOSE ABLE MEN," AND IN DEVARIM THE SCRIPTURES STATE, "SO I TOOK THE CHIEFS OF YOUR TRIBES, WISE MEN, AND KNOWN" (IBID. 15).

207. עֵינָא בְּרָזָא דְּאָת ר' וְאָת פ', דְּגְבִינִין חִוָּורִין וְשַׂעֲרָא סוּמְקָא. אִי גְּבִינִין דְּעֵינוֹי חִוָּורִין, דָּא הוּא בַּר נָשׁ דְּאִצְטְרִיכוּ בְּנֵי נָשָׁא לְאִסְתַּמְּרָא מִנֵּיהּ. כָּל מִלּוֹי בְּרָמָאוּתָא. פְּקִיחָא אִיהוּ. נָטִיר דְּבָבוּ. דָּא אִיהוּ בְּאָת ר'

בִּלְחוֹדוֹי. וְלָא אִתְחַבָּר בַּהֲדֵיה אָת פ׳. אָת דָּא, אַזְלָא וְשָׁאט עָלֵיה, וְלָא אִתְיַשָּׁבָא בֵּיה. עֵינוֹי דְּדָא שְׁקִיעִין, בָּהִיל בְּעוֹבָדוֹי. וְכֵן כָּל מַאן דְּעֵינוֹי שְׁקִיעִין, אִצְטְרִיךְ לְאִסְתַּמְּרָא מִנֵּיה בְּכָל עוֹבָדִין. רַמָאָה אִיהוּ, וּבְרַמָאוּתֵיה יָהִיב טַעֲמָא לְמִלּוֹי.

207. The eye is under the secret of the letter *Resh* and the letter *Pe*. The eyebrows are white, and the hair is red. If the eyebrows are white, this is a man of whom people must be wary. Everything he does is deceitful. He is shrewd. He harbors hatred. And all this is under the letter *Resh* alone, when it is not joined with the letter *Pe*. This letter, REFERRING TO *PE*, walks and rambles over him, and does not settle in him. His eyes are sunken. He is rushed in his actions. And so it is with all those whose eyes are recessed. We must be wary of all their actions. They are deceitful. And with their deceit, they give logic to their words.

208. מִצְחָא דִּילֵיה רַב, וְלָא עֲגוּלָא. תְּרֵין רְשִׁימִין רַבְרְבִין אַזְלִין בְּפוּתְיָא דְּמִצְחֵיה, מִסְטָר לִסְטָר, וְאַרְבַּע זְעִירִין. שַׂעֲרָא דִּילֵיה תַּלְיָא. קָרִיר מוֹחָא אִיהוּ. וְעַל דָּא פְּקִיחָא הֲוֵי אוּדְנוֹי זְעִירִין. בִּדְרוֹעוֹי שַׂעֲרָא רַב. נָקִיד אִיהוּ בְּנִקּוּדִין דִּרְשִׁימִין אוּכָּמִין. וְאִי רְשִׁימִין סוּמָקִין, תָּב לְזִמְנִין לְמֶעְבַּד טִיבוּ, וְאִתְקַיַּים בֵּיה זִמְנָא זְעֵירָא, וּלְזִמְנִין תָּב לְקִלְקוּלֵיה. חַמְדָּן אִיהוּ.

208. If his forehead is large, and not round shaped; and two broad marks sweep across the brow from side to side, and also four small marks; and his hair hangs, then he is cool-headed. Therefore, he is intelligent. His ears are small. He has hairy arms. He is covered with black spots. If he has red marks, he returns occasionally to do good. And so he remains for a brief time, and sometimes he returns to his evil ways. He is lustful.

209. זַרְעָא דְּדָוִד בְּהִפּוּכָא. דָּוִד מַלְכָּא יָרִית דָּא סוּמָקָא שַׁפִּירָא, לְמֶעְבַּד דִּינָא, וּלְמֶעְבַּד שַׁפִּירוּ דְּעוֹבָדוֹי. עֵינוֹי עַיְנִין דְּרַחֲמֵי, יַתְבִין עַל שְׁלִימוּ, סַלְקִין חִנָּא וְחִסְדָּא. חַד חוּטָא יְרוֹקָא אָזִיל בְּגַוַוויְיהוּ. בְּשַׁעֲתָא דְּאַגָּח קְרָבָא, הַהוּא חוּטָא אִתְהַפַּךְ וְאִתְהֲוֵי סוּמָקָא כְּוַורְדָּא. נָח רוּגְזֵיה

בְּקַרְבָא, תָּב הַהוּא חוּטָא כְּמִלְּקַדְּמִין. נִסִּין רַבְרְבִין הֲווֹ בְּעֵינוֹי. הֲווֹ
חֲדָאן. תְּאֵיבִין לְמֶחֱמֵי. נְקוּדִין בִּתְלַת גַּוְונִין, חֵדוּ דְלִבָּא הֲווֹ בְּלֵב כֹּלָּא,
חַיָּיבַיָּא דְּמִסְתַּכְּלִין בְּהוּ, הֲווֹ זָעִין וְדָחֲלִין, סַלְקִין בְּלִבַּיְיהוּ אֵימָתָא
וּדְחִילוּ.

209. It is the reverse with the seed of David. King David inherited this fine red to do judgment and to perform suitable deeds. His eyes were filled with compassion and were settled in fullness, projecting grace and kindness. And a green line ran through them. At the time he waged war, that line changed and became red as a rose. When his anger was calmed from the war, the line returned to its original. Great miracles were in his eyes. People were happy, and they longed to see them. THERE WERE IN THEM specks in three colors. Joy filled his whole heart. The evil-doers who observed them were greatly agitated, and great fright and terror arose in their hearts.

210. מִצְחָא דִּילֵיהּ רַב עֲגוּלָא בְּשַׁפִּירוּ, וְכָל אַתְוָון אִתְחַזְיָין וְסַלְקִין
בֵּיהּ, אִלֵּין סַלְקִין וְאִלֵּין נַחְתִּין. אִינּוּן דְּנַחְתִּין סַלְקִין, יַהֲבִין דּוּכְתָּא
אִלֵּין לְאִלֵּין. בְּגִין כָּךְ רְשִׁימִין דִּילֵיהּ סַלְקִין בְּאַרְכָּא לְעֵילָּא. גְּבִינִין
דְּעֵינוֹי רַחֲמִין לְרַחֲמָנוּתָא. לָא אוּכְמִין וְלָא סוּמָקִין, אֶלָּא בֵּין תְּרֵין
גַּוְונִין. בַּת עֵינָא דִּלְגוֹ, אַחֲזֵי כָּל דְּיוּקְנִין דְּעָלְמָא, חוּטָא סוּמָקָא סַחֲרָא
לֵיהּ, וְחֶדְוָוא סְחוֹר סְחוֹר כֹּלָּא.

210. Another type is he whose forehead is large and nicely rounded, and all the letters are visible and rising in it. Some rise and some descend; those that descend rise, and each one gives space to the other. Because of this, his impressions go upward in length ON HIS FOREHEAD. His eyebrows are filled with compassion. They are not black, nor are they red, but in fact they are between THESE two colors. The pupil of the eye, from within, projects all the worldly images. A red line surrounds it, and joy surrounds everything.

211. שֵׁירוּתָא, דְּחַיָּיבִין מְקָרְבִין לְמֶחֱמֵי, אִינּוּן חַיָּיבַיָּא חָמָאן לוֹן
חַיָּיכָאן, רַחֲמֵי חִנָּא וְחִסְדָּא. לְבָתַר תּוּקְפָּא וּדְחִילוּ וְאֵימָתָנוּ וְרוּגְזָא.
וְעֵינוֹי יוֹנִים לְגַבַּיְיהוּ. מַאי יוֹנִים. דְּעַבְדִין לוֹן אוֹנָאָה לְחַיָּיבַיָּא. כד"א

לֹא תוֹנוּ אִישׁ אֶת עֲמִיתוֹ וּכְתִיב עֵינֶיךָ יוֹנִים. מְקָרְבָן, וּמְרַחֲקָן. כָּל
דְּיוּקְנִין דְּעָלְמָא כֻּלְּהוּ כְּלִילָן בְּאַנְפּוֹי. שַׂעֲרָא דְּרֵישֵׁיהּ, הֲוָה רָשִׁים
בִּגְוָונֵי שִׁבְעָה זִינֵי דַּהֲבָא.

211. At first, when the evil doers approach to look at THE EYES, these same evil-doers laugh, for there is compassion, beauty and kindness IN THEM. Afterwards, THEY SEE IN THEM power and fear, terror and anger. And his eyes are like doves when turned towards them. What are dove's eyes? They are eyes that deceive the wicked, as it is written in scriptures: "you shall not defraud (Heb. *tonu*) one another" (Vayikra 25:14). And it is written: "you have dove's (Heb. *yonim*) eyes" (Shir Hashirim 4:1) that attract WHOEVER OBSERVES THEM, and repel THEM. All the images of the world are included in his face. The hairs on his head are blazed with the colors of seven kinds of gold.

212. חֲמֵינָא בְּסִפְרָא דְּאָדָם קַדְמָאָה, דְּאָמַר הָכִי דְּיוּקְנִין דִּמְשִׁיחָא
קַדְמָאָה, לְסִיהֲרָא, גַּוָון דִּילֵיהּ, זָהָב יְרַקְרַק בְּאַנְפּוֹי. גַּוָון דִּילֵיהּ, זָהָב
אוֹפִיר בְּדִיקְנֵיהּ. גַּוָון דִּילֵיהּ, זָהָב שְׁבָא בְּגַבִינוֹי. גַּוָון דִּילֵיהּ זָהָב
פַּרְוַיִם, בְּקָרִיצִין דְּעַל עֵינוֹי. גַּוָון דִּילֵיהּ, זָהָב סָגוּר בְּשַׂעֲרָא דְּרֵישֵׁיהּ.
גַּוָון דִּילֵיהּ, זָהָב מוּפַז עַל חַדוֹי בְּלוּחָא דְּעַל לִבֵּיהּ. גַּוָון דִּילֵיהּ זָהָב
תַּרְשִׁישׁ, עַל תְּרֵין דְּרוֹעִין. כָּל שִׁבְעָה גַּוָונִין אִלֵּין, הֲווֹ רְשִׁימִין, עַל כָּל
אִינּוּן דּוּכְתֵּי דְּשַׂעֲרוֹי.

212. I saw the following written in the book of Adam: the appearance of the first Messiah is as the moon – WHICH IS MALCHUT, MEANING OF THE SEED OF DAVID, SINCE THE SECOND MESSIAH IS MESSIAH, SON OF JOSEPH. His face will be greenish gold in appearance. The color of his beard will appear to be as the gold of *Ofir*. The appearance of his eyebrows is of *Sheva* gold. The appearance of the eyebrows, NAMELY IN THE EYELASHES, is of the gold of *Parvayim*. Pure gold is the appearance of his hair. The finest gold is the color on his chest, on the tablet of his heart. On both his arms is the color and appearance of *Tarshish* gold. All these seven colors are recorded in all the places of the hair.

213. בִּדְרוֹעָא יְמִינָא, הֲוָה חָקִיק וְרָשִׁים רְשׁוּמָא חֲדָא סָתִים מִבְּנֵי נָשָׁא,

מִגְדָּל חָקוּק בְּאַרְיֵה. וְאֶלֶף זְעֵירָא רָשִׁים בְּגַוֵּיהּ, וְסִימָנָא דָּא אֶלֶף הַמָּגֵן תָּלוּי עָלָיו. כָּל זִמְנָא דְּאַגַּח קְרָבָא, הַהוּא רְשִׁימָא סַלְקָא וּבָלְטָא, וְעַל מִגְדָּל מְכַשְׁכְּשָׁא הַאי אֶלֶף, וּכְדֵין אִתְתָּקַף לְאַגָּחָא קְרָבָא. כַּד עָאל בִּקְרָבָא מְכַשְׁכְּשָׁא הַהוּא אַרְיֵה, וּכְדֵין אִתְגַּבַּר כְּאַרְיֵה, וְנָצַח קְרָבִין. וְהַהוּא מִגְדָּל אִתְרְהִיט, וְסִימָנֵיהּ בּוֹ יָרוּץ צַדִּיק וְנִשְׂגָּב. וְנִשְׂגַּב דָּוִד מִשַׂנְאוֹי דְּלָא יַכְלִין לְגַבֵּיהּ. וּמִן סָמָנִין אִלֵּין וּרְשִׁימִין אִלֵּין, הֲווֹ רְשִׁימִין בִּדְרָעֵיהּ שְׂמָאלָא. רְשׁוּמָא דְּבַר נָשׁ אַחֲרָא לָאו כְּהַאי.

213. On his right arm, one impression was carved and marked, concealed from people. And this is a tower on which a lion was engraved. A small *Aleph* is marked within. And this is the sign "on which there hand a thousand (Heb. *elef*) bucklers" (Shir Hashirim 4:4). When he wages war, that mark always becomes erect and protrudes. And in the tower that *Aleph* pulsates, and he becomes powerful to wage a war. When he enters into war, the lion pulsates; he becomes as strong as a lion and wins the wars. In pulsating, that tower accelerates, and its sign is: "…the righteous runs into it and is safe…" (Mishlei 18:10). David is safe from his enemies; they can not overcome him. And some of these signs and impressions were registered on his left arm. No other individual ever had these marks AS THE SEED OF DAVID.

214. עַיְינִין צְהִיבִין פְּקִיעִין, שַׁגְעוֹנָא בְּלִבֵּיהּ. מִצְחָא רַב. שַׂעֲרוֹי סַגִּיאִין, תַּלְיִין, רְחִיקִין מִמַּשְׁכָא דְּרֵישָׁא. פְּקִיחָא אִיהוּ. פּוּם מְמַלֵּל רַבְרְבָן. שִׂפְוָון דִּילֵיהּ עֲתִיקִין מָארֵיהּ דְּלִישָׁנָא בִּישָׁא.

214. If the eyes are bright and protruding, he has madness in his heart. His forehead is large. Many hairs are hanging DOWNWARD, remote from the skin of the skull. He is wise. He boasts. His lips are wilted. He has the evil tongue.

215. בְּמִצְחֵיהּ תְּלַת שִׁרְטוּטִין, אִי בְּעֵינֵיהּ תְּרֵין שׁוּרְיְיקֵי סוּמָקֵי, דָּא הֲוָה בָּאת ר׳ בִּלְחוֹדוֹי, וְשׁוּרְיְיקָא זָהִיר לְגַבַּיְיהוּ. עֲבֵירָה אִזְדַּמְּנַת לְגַבֵּיהּ, וְאִשְׁתְּזִיב מִינָהּ.

215. Three lines are in his forehead. If there are two red veins in his eyes, then it is under the letter *Resh* only. An illuminating vein is present in them. An opportunity arose for him to commit a transgression and he was saved from it.

216. וְאִי שׁוּרְיָיקָא חֲדָא סוּמָקָא לְגוֹ בְּעֵינָא, קַיְימָא בְּאַרְכָּא, וּתְרֵין זְעִירִין תְּחוֹתֵיה, וְחַד דְּאַעֲבַּר בְּעֵינוֹי. דְּדֵין אִית לֵיה עֵיטָא בִּישָׁא, בְּאִתְּתָא אֲסוּרָה, וַעֲדַיִין עֵיטָא קַיְימָא. כְּדֵין תִּשְׁתְּכַח בְּמִצְחֵיה, חַד שִׂרְטוּטָא לְאַרְכָּא. מִקְרִיצָא יְמִינָא חַד שַׂעֲרָא וְאַרְבַּע זְעִירִין תְּחוֹתֵיה, וְחַד דְּאַעֲבַּר בֵּינַיְיהוּ לְפוּתְיֵיה.

216. If there is one red vein in his eye within, standing lengthwise, and two small veins beneath it, and one vein traverses the eye, he gives bad counsel pertaining to a woman prohibited to him. And if the counsel still exists, you will find one line lengthwise on his forehead. From his right eyebrow PROTRUDES one hair, and four small hairs underneath. And there is one hair that passes between them, widthwise.

217. וְאִי יִתְפְּרַשׁ מֵהַהוּא חַטָאָה, תִּשְׁכַּח בְּעֵינֵיה, תְּרֵין שׁוּרְיָיקֵי דְּקִיקִין, אַזְלִין בְּפוּתְיֵיה דְּעֵינָא, וְלָא אַעֲבַּר חַד בֵּינַיְיהוּ, וְכֵן בְּמִצְחָא. וּמִזְמַן דְּאִתְפְּרַשׁ מֵהַהוּא חוֹבָה, הוּא מִזְמַן ט׳ יוֹם, דְּהָא מִתַּמָּן וּלְהָלְאָה, יִתְמַחוּן רְשִׁימִין אִלֵּין, וְיִתְיֵילְדוּ אַחֲרָנִין.

217. If he withdrew from that transgression, then you will find in his eyes two thin veins passing along the width of the eye, but no other vein passes between them. It is the same with the forehead. The time of consideration for his withdrawal from this iniquity is nine days. From then on, these impressions are erased, and other impressions appear.

218. עַיְינִין דְּקִיקִין, וּמִתְהַפְּכָן זְעֵיר בְּסוּמָקָא. דָּא אִיהוּ פְּקִיחָא. כָּל מִלּוֹי בְּתִיוּבְתָּא. בְּמִצְחוֹי תִּשְׁכַּח רְשִׁימִין תְּלַת. חַד רַב, דְּאַעֲבַּר מִסְּטְרָא דָּא לְסִטְרָא דָּא. וּתְרֵין אַחֲרָנִין דְּלָא עַבְרִין. קְרִיצִין דְּעֵינוֹי רַבְרְבִין. מָארֵיה דְּקַשְׁיוּ אִיהוּ. כַּד מַלִּיל, קָמִיט בְּחוּטְמִין, בְּרוּגְזֵיה, אוֹ בְּקַשְׁיוּ דְּלִבֵּיה. זָקִיף שׂוּם בִּישׁ עֲלֵיה. בִּישׁ בְּעֵינֵי דְּכֹלָּא. כֹּלָּא שַׂנְאִין לֵיה.

אַצְלַח לְזִמְנִין וּלְזִמְנִין לָא.

218. Narrow eyes that become slightly red signify an understanding man. All his words are in argument. On his forehead you will find three impressions. A large one passes from one side to the other side. Two others do not pass this length. His eyebrows are large. He is stubborn. When he speaks or when his heart is hard, he wrinkles his nose in anger. He has a bad reputation. He is bad in the eyes of everyone, and all hate him. Sometimes he succeeds and sometimes he does not.

219. תְּלַת שַׂעֲרִין רַבְרְבִין בְּחַדּוֹי עַל לִבֵּיה. שִׂפְוָון דִּילֵיה עַתִּיקִין, מָארֵיה גָּאוּתָא בְּשִׁגְעוֹנָא. לִישָׁנָא בִישָׁא.

219. Three large hairs are on his breast, over his heart. His lips are parched. He is arrogant to the point of lunacy. He has an evil tongue.

220. שַׂעֲרוֹי שְׂעִיעִין רַבְרְבִין וְסַגִּיאִין. אַנְפּוֹי אַנְפִּין אֲרִיכִין זְעֵיר, וְעַגּוּלִין זְעֵיר, לְזִמְנִין אִתְחָרַט מִכָּל מַה דְּעָבֵד וְתָב לְקַלְקוּלֵיה. בְּעֵינֵיה תִּשְׁכַּח שׁוּרְיָיקֵי, תְּרֵין בְּעֵינָא דִּימִינָא, וְחַד בְּעֵינָא דִּשְׂמָאלָא. אוּדְנוֹי זְעֵירִין, קַיְימִין בְּקִיּוּמָא.

220. His hair is flat, long, and profuse. He has a slightly long and slightly rounded face; At times he regrets all he did but returns to his bad deeds. In his eyes, you will find two veins in his right eye, and one in his left eye. His ears are small and straight.

221. זַרְעָא דְּדָוִד בְּהִפּוּכָא. זַרְעָא דְּדָוִד כָּל סִימָנִין אִלֵּין לְטָב, וּלְמֶעְבַּד טִיבוּ. בַּר שִׂפְוָון רַבְרְבִין, דְּכָל מַאן דִּשְׂפְוָותֵיה רַבְרְבִין, מָארֵיה דְּלִישָׁנָא בִישָׁא אִיהוּ, בֵּין זַכָּאָה, בֵּין חַיָּיבָא. בַּר אִי צַדִּיק גָּמוּר הוּא. וּבְזַכְיוּ דִּילֵיה נָצַח וְנָטִיר גַּרְמֵיה.

221. The seed of David is the reverse. In the offspring of David all these signs are good signs and bring benefit, except for big lips. For all those who have big lips are slanderers, whether righteous or evil, unless he is a

thoroughly righteous man that succeeds by his merits and guards himself FROM THE EVIL TONGUE.

222. עַיְינִין יְרוֹקִין, זְעֵיר מִגַּוֵון סוּמָק אָזִיל בֵּינַיְיהוּ, בְּמִצְחֵיהּ תְּרֵין רְשׁוּמִין, מִסְטְרָא דָּא לְסִטְרָא דָּא, וְחַד לְעֵילָא זְעֵירָא, וְחַד לְתַתָּא. אִיהוּ בְּאָת פ׳ וְאָת ר׳. דָּא מִצְחֵיהּ רַב בְּעִגּוּלָא, אִיהוּ טָב לְכֹלָּא. יָהִיב מִכָּל מַה דְּאִית לֵיהּ לְכָל בַּר נָשׁ. וַתְרָן אִיהוּ. שַׂעֲרוֹי שְׁעִיעַ וְתָלֵי. בְּסִטְרָא יְמִינָא אִית לֵיהּ חִוָּורוּ דְשַׂעֲרֵי, מִיּוֹמָא דְּאִתְבְּרֵי.

222. IF the eyes are green with a little red mixed in, and on his forehead there are two impressions from this side to that side, one small mark above, and a small one on the bottom, he is under the letters *Pe* and *Resh*. This person's forehead is large and circular. He is good to all. He gives all of what he has to everybody. He is yielding. His hair is flat and hangs. On the right side, he has white hairs from the day he was born.

223. מַתְנִיתִין. בְּנֵי עָלְמָא מָארֵיהוֹן דְּסָכְלְתָנוּ, פְּקִיחִין עַיְינִין, מָארֵיהוֹן דִּמְהֵימְנוּתָא, דִּי הֲוָה גְּנִיזָא בְּכוּ. מַאן מִנְּכוֹן דְּסָלִיק וְנָחִית. מַאן דִּי רוּחַ אֱלָהִין קַדִּישִׁין בֵּיהּ. לֵיקוּם וְלִינְדַע, בְּשַׁעֲתָא דְּסָלִיק בִּרְעוּתָא דְּרֵישָׁא חִוָּורָא, לְמִבְרֵי אָדָם, בָּטַשׁ בְּגוֹ בּוּצִינָא חֲדָא, וּבָטַשׁ בּוּצִינָא בִּפְשִׁיטוּ דְּנָהִיר, וְהַהוּא פְּשִׁיטוּ דְּבוּצִינָא אַפִּיק נִשְׁמָתִין.

223. Mishnah. Men of the world, of understanding, of open eyes, REFERRING TO PEOPLE OF CHOCHMAH, people of Faith, THE SHECHINAH, which is treasured in you: of whoever among you ascended and descended – THAT IS, THE RECIPIENTS OF THE LIGHTS THAT ILLUMINATE FROM BELOW UPWARD, CALLED 'ASCENT' AND LIGHTS THAT ILLUMINATE FROM ABOVE DOWNWARD CALLED 'DESCENT' – he who has the Spirit of Holy Elohim in him shall rise and know that at the instant that the white head, WHICH IS KETER, so desired to create man, it bestowed light into one luminary, WHICH IS BINAH. And this luminary bestowed light through the extension of the luminary, WHICH IS ZEIR ANPIN, WHO BALANCES AND ILLUMINATES THE TWO COLUMNS, RIGHT AND LEFT, OF BINAH. And this extension of the luminary brought forth the souls OF MAN.

224. אוּף הָכִי בָּטַשׁ גּוֹ טִנָרָא חֲדָא תַּקִּיפָא, וְאַפִּיק הַהוּא טִינָרָא שַׁלְהוֹבָא חֲדָא מְלַהֲטָא, מְרֻקְמָא בְּכַמָה גְּווֹנִין, וְהַהוּא שַׁלְהוֹבָא סַלְקָא וְנַחְתָּא, עַד דְּהַהוּא פְּשִׁיטוּ בָּטַשׁ בֵּיהּ, וְתָב וְאִתְיְשַׁב בְּדוּכְתֵּיהּ, וְאִתְעָבֵיד רוּחָא דְחַיֵּיא.

224. Even so, the extension of the luminary, WHICH IS ZEIR ANPIN, united with and poured into one solid rock, WHICH IS MALCHUT. And that rock brought forth a scorching flame textured with a variety of hues. And that flame ascends and descends, until the extension OF THAT LUMINARY, WHICH IS ZEIR ANPIN, influences it – NAMELY, IT POURED INTO IT THE ASPECT OF THE CENTRAL COLUMN AND CHASSADIM, and THEN it returns and settles in its place and becomes the Ruach life, OF ADAM.

225. וְהַהוּא רוּחָא אִתְתְּחַם, וְנָטִיל חַד גְּווֹן מִשִּׁמְשָׁא. נָחִית לְתַתָּא, נָטִיל גְּווֹן חַד מִסִּיהֲרָא. סָטָא לִימִינָא, נָטַל גְּווֹן מַיָּיא, כָּלִיל בְּפוּמָא דְּאַרְיֵה חֲדָא. סָטָא לִשְׂמָאלָא, נָטַל גְּווֹן אֶשָׁא, כָּלִיל בְּפוּמָא דְּחַד שׁוֹר, סוּמָקָא כְּווֹרְדָא. סָטָא לְקַמֵיהּ, נָטַל גְּווֹן רוּחָא, כָּלִיל בְּפוּמָא דְּחַד נֶשֶׁר רַבְרְבָא, רַב גַּדְפִין, מָארֵיהּ דְּנוֹצָה, כָּל גְּווֹנִין בֵּיהּ מִתְחַמָּאן. סָטָא לַאֲחוֹרָא, נָטַל גְּווֹן עַפְרָא, כָּלִיל מד' סְטְרֵי עָלְמָא. בְּפוּמָא דְּאָדָם, וְכָל דִּיּוּקְנִין מִסְתַּכְּלָן לְגַבֵּיהּ.

225. This Ruach acquired boundaries OF TWELVE DIAGONAL LIMITS THAT IT RECEIVED FROM ZEIR ANPIN. It takes on one hue from the sun, FROM ZEIR ANPIN, WHICH IS GREEN IN COLOR. Then it descends to a lower level and takes on one color from the moon, MALCHUT, WHICH IS A HUE THAT RECEIVES FROM ALL THE HUES AND RECEIVES FROM FOUR LIVING CREATURES: THE LION, THE OX, THE EAGLE, AND MAN, IN THE LOWER CHARIOT. It moves to the right and takes on the hue of water, WHICH IS WHITE, that is included in the mouth of a lion, WHICH IS CHESED. It moves to the left and takes on the hue of fire, WHICH IS RED and is included in the mouth of an ox that is red like a rose, WHICH IS GVURAH. Moving to the front, it takes on the hue of the wind, GREEN, THAT IS included in the mouth of a large eagle with great wings and feathers in which all hues are seen – WHICH IS THE HUE OF PURPLE INCLUDED IN ALL THE HUES. THIS

IS TIFERET. Moving to the rear, it takes on the hue of earth THAT RECEIVES FROM ALL THE HUES – that is included in all four corners of the earth, CHESED, GVURAH, TIFERET AND MALCHUT – RECEIVING from the mouth of man's face, toward whom all images look. THIS IS MALCHUT.

226. אִתְיָישַׁב הַהוּא רוּחָא בְּהַהוּא עַפְרָא, וְאִתְלְבַּשׁ בֵּיהּ. כְּדֵין הַהוּא עַפְרָא, מְכַשְׁכְּשָׁא וְנָחַת לְתַתָּא, וְכָנַשׁ עַפְרָא מד' סִטְרִין דְּעָלְמָא, וְאִתְעֲבֵיד דִּיּוּקְנָא חֲדָא וּפַרְצוּפָא, וְהַהוּא רוּחָא אִתְטָמַר מִגּוֹ לְגוֹ. וְהַהוּא עַפְרָא דְּאִתְכְּנִישׁ מד' סִטְרִין בָּטַשׁ לְגַבֵּיהּ נֶפֶשׁ כְּלִילָא בְּרוּחָא.

226. This Ruach settled in this earth and was clothed in it. FOR THE SOIL IS MALCHUT, WHICH IS THE NEFESH OF ADAM. AND THE RUACH WAS CLOTHED IN THE NEFESH. Then that soil, WHICH IS THE NEFESH, swirled, descended and gathered soil from the four directions. And it was made into a form and a countenance, WHICH IS THE BODY OF THE FIRST MAN. The Ruach was concealed in the innermost. And the Nefesh poured bounty into that soil that assembled from the four winds, WHICH IS THE BODY, when it was included in the Ruach.

227. וְהַהוּא נֶפֶשׁ אִיהוּ יְסוֹדָא לְעוֹבָדֵי גוּפָא. כְּפוּם עוֹבָדִין דְּהַהוּא נֶפֶשׁ בְּגוּפָא, הָכִי אִתְחֲזֵי בְּמַשְׁכָא לְבַר. רוּחָא דָּא אִתְטָמַר לְגוֹ. וְהַהוּא אִתְחֲזֵי לְבַר, סָלִיק וְנָחִית, וּבָטַשׁ בְּאַנְפּוֹי, וְאַחְזֵי דִּיּוּקְנִין וּרְשִׁימִין. בָּטַשׁ בְּמִצְחֵיהּ, אַחְזֵי דִּיּוּקְנִין וּרְשִׁימִין בָּטַשׁ בְּעֵינוֹי, וְאַחְזֵי דִּיּוּקְנִין וּרְשִׁימִין. הה"ד הַכָּרַת פְּנֵיהֶם עָנְתָה בָּם.

227. This Nefesh is the origin of the actions of the body. According to the actions of that Nefesh inside the body, so shall it appear on the skin outside. The Ruach is concealed on the inside, and that, REFERRING TO THE NEFESH, is visible from the outside. It ascends and descends and strikes in his face, showing shapes and impressions. It strikes in his forehead, showing shapes and marks, it strikes in the eyes, showing shapes and marks, as it is written: "the sight of their face does witness against them" (Yeshayah 3:9).

228. בּוּצִינָא דְּאִתְמְשַׁךְ מִנֵּיהּ מְדִידוּ, דְּחַד חוּטָא יְרוֹקָא, שַׁלְהָבוּתָא דְּתֹהוּ. בָּטַשׁ בִּידוֹי בְּשַׁעֲתָא דְּבַר נָשׁ נָאִים, וְרָשִׁים רְשִׁימִין וְשִׂרְטוּטִין

בִּידֵיהּ, וּכְפוּם עוֹבָדִין דְּב״נ הָכִי אִתְרְשִׁים. וְאִלֵּין אַתְוָון מִתְהַפְּכָן מִתַּתָּא לְעֵילָּא, וְיַדְעֵי לוֹן חַבְרֵי קְשׁוֹט, בִּרְשִׁימוּ דְּאַתְוָון דְּבוּצִינָא, וְכָל אִלֵּין חֵילִין דִּלְגוֹ דְּב״נ, עַבְדִין רְשׁוּמִין וְשִׂרְטוּטִין אַתְוָון מִתְהַפְּכָן. מַאן דְּרָקִים דָּא, רָקִים בְּשִׁפּוּלֵי מַשְׁכְּנָא. כד״א, רֻקַּמְתִּי בְּתַחְתִּיּוֹת אָרֶץ. בְּרִיךְ הוּא בְּרִיךְ שְׁמֵיהּ לְעָלַם וּלְעָלְמֵי עָלְמִין.

228. The luminary from which measurement is drawn, IS of one green thread, WHICH IS THE CENTRAL COLUMN THAT HAS A GREEN COLOR. IT RECEIVED the flame of formlessness, NAMELY, THE FIRE OF MALCHUT OF THE ATTRIBUTE OF JUDGMENT. It strikes on the hands of man when he is asleep and records impressions and lines in his hands. According to the actions of man, so is his hand etched. These letters turn over in him from the bottom to top. This wisdom is known by those friends, who are RIGHTEOUS MEN OF Truth, through the imprint of the letters of the luminary – WHICH IS MALCHUT, AS PREVIOUSLY MENTIONED. All the inner resources of man manifest impressions, lines and letters that interchange. He who inscribes these also inscribes in the end of the tabernacle, WHICH IS MALCHUT CALLED 'TABERNACLE', as it is written: "and curiously wrought in the lowest parts of the earth" (Tehilim 139:15). THIS REFERS TO THE LOWEST PART OF MALCHUT, WHICH IS CALLED 'EARTH'. SHE IS ALSO FASHIONED FROM THE POWER OF THE FLAME OF THE ATTRIBUTE OF JUDGMENT, LIKE THE HANDS OF MAN. Blessed be He, and blessed be His Name forever and ever.

229. עַיְינִין חִוָּורָא, וְאֶבְרִין סוּמָקִין, בְּאַתְרֵיהּ דְּנָפִיק מִינֵּיהּ, דָּא אִיהוּ בְּאָת פ׳ וְאָת ר׳ כְּלִילָא כַּחֲדָא.

229. White eyes and slivers of red flesh where THE EYES protrude – NAMELY IN THE EYE SOCKETS, SO THAT WHEN HE ROTATES HIS EYES, THEY ARE VISIBLE – are from the letter *Pe* and the letter *Resh* when they are included together.

230. מִצְחֵיהּ רַב, תְּלַת שִׂרְטוּטִין סַלְּקִין בְּמִצְחֲיָה, שִׁית זְעִירִין אַחֲרָנִין. סוּמָק הוּא וְלָא סוּמָק, קַיְּימָא בֵּין תְּרֵין גְּווֹנִין. שַׂעֲרֵיהּ אוּף הָכִי. אַנְפּוֹי רַבְרְבָן. שַׂעֲרֵיהּ קָמִיט, וְלָא כ״ב. תָּלֵי זְעֵיר תְּחוֹת אוּדְנוֹי. טָב אִיהוּ,

מָארֵי דִּמְהֵימְנוּתָא, מָארֵי דְּרוּגְזָא תַּקִיף, בְּשַׁעֲתָא דְּאִתְרְגִיז.

230. Another type of person has a large forehead, and three lines that come up in his forehead, and six smaller ones, red yet not very red, and they stay between these two colors. The same is true for his hair. He has a large face. His hair is wrinkled, THAT IS, CURLY, but not too much. It hangs slightly below his ears. That PERSON is good. He has faith. The moment he becomes angry, it is an extremely intense anger.

231. הַהוּא סוּמָקָא דִּתְחוֹת עֵינָא, אִתְפָּשַׁט בְּעֵינֵיה. רוּגְזֵיה בִּיש. בְּשַׁעֲתָא דְּמַלִיל בְּרוּגְזֵיה סָתִים פּוּמֵיה, וְנָפִיק תְּנָנָא מִנְּחִירוֹי. וְלִזְמַן זְעֵיר נָח רוּגְזֵיה, וְלָא כָּל רוּגְזֵיה, עַד יוֹמָא אַחֲרָא, אוֹ תְּרֵין יוֹמִין. דָּא אַצְלַח לִזְמְנִין, וְלִזְמְנִין לָא. אֲבָל קָאֵים תָּדִיר בְּאַצְלָחוּתָא, בֵּין זְעֵיר וּבֵין רַב.

231. If that red below his eyes, IN THE EYE SOCKETS, AS MENTIONED BEFORE, spreads in his eyes, he has a bad temper. When he talks in anger, he closes his mouth, and his nostrils fume. After a short time, his anger subsides, but not completely until after a day or two. He is sometimes successful and sometimes not. But he usually succeeds, whether a little or much.

232. וְאִי סוּמָקָא דְּפוּם עֵינָא, זְעֵיר כְּחוּטָא, וְלָא אִתְפָּשַׁט בְּשַׁעֲתָא דְּרוּגְזֵיה בְּעֵינָא, וְאִית בֵּיה כָּל הָנֵי סִימָנִין. חַלְשָׁא בְּלִבָּא. וְאִיהוּ דָּחִיל מִכֹּלָּא, שֵׁינָתֵיה לָא אִתְיָישַׁב בֵּיה. חָשִׁיב תָּדִיר מַחֲשָׁבִין וְדָחִיל מִכֹּלְּהוּ. וְאַצְלַח לְכֹלָּא. מָארֵיה דְּגַרִיעַ. לָא חָשׁ לְגִיּוּפָא.

232. If the red inside his eye is fine as a thread, and does not spread in the time of his anger, if he has those signs he has a weak heart and is fearful of everything. His sleep is unsettled, He always has thoughts and is afraid of everything. He causes everybody WHO JOINS HIM to succeed. He is corrupt and does not refrain from adultery.

233. לִזְמְנִין תָּב בִּתְיוּבְתָּא וְדָחִיל. וּמִגּוֹ דְּחִילוּ, כְּדֵין תִּשְׁכַּח בְּעֵינֵיה יְמִינָא, הַהוּא סוּמָקָא דְּפוּם עֵינָא, בְּסוֹפָא בְּשִׁפּוּלֵי עֵינָא, וְחַד שׁוּרַיְיקָא

דְּקִיק סוּמָק בְּעֵינֵיה שְׂמָאלָא, וְאִי מִתְחַלְּפֵי מַה דִּימִינָא לִשְׂמָאלָא, וּמַה דִּשְׂמָאלָא לִימִינָא, כְּדֵין אִיהוּ בְּקַלְקוּלֵיה. וְתָב וְתָבַר גְּזִיזָא דְּבַרְדָּא, בְּגִין לְאַעְבְּרָא עֲבֵירָה.

233. Sometimes he repents and is afraid, and in his fright, you will find redness inside his right eye, at the rim of the eye, and one fine red vein on his left eye. And if they change – that which was in the right is in the left, and that which was in the left is in the right – then he is sinful, NOT HAVING REPENTED. He returned and broke a piece of ice, WHICH INTERRUPTED HIM FROM THE TRANSGRESSION in order to commit transgression.

234. תְּרֵין קְמִיטִין עַל רֵישָׁא דְּעֵינָא, וּתְלַת לְתַתָּא. וּבְרַגְלֵיה שְׂמָאלָא, בְּאֶצְבְּעָא דְּאֶמְצָעִיתָא, שִׁית שַׂעֲרִין, וּבְזִמְנָא אַחֲרָא חָמֵשׁ, וְהַשְׁתָּא שִׁית, חַד זְעֵירָא בֵּינַיְיהוּ. עַיְינִין אוּכָּמִין, וּקְרִיצִין דְּעַל עֵינוֹי רַבְרְבִין, סַגִּיאִין שַׂעֲרִין, אַלֵּין עַל אַלֵּין, וְאִינּוּן עַיְינִין אוּכָּמִין וְיָרוֹקָא, אָזִיל בְּגַוַּיְיהוּ, וְהַהוּא יְרוֹקָא אַטְבַּע יַתִּיר. הַאי אִית לֵיה חָמֵשׁ שִׂרְטוּטִין בְּמִצְחָא, תְּרֵין דְּעַבְרִין מִסְטַר לִסְטַר. וּתְלַת דְּלָא עַבְרִין וְכוּ'.

(עַיֵּין סוֹף הַסֵּפֶר עכ"מ)

234. Two furows on top of his eye, and three underneath. On his left foot, on the middle toe, there are six hairs and sometimes five. Presently he has six hairs, since one of them is short. He has black eyes, and his eyebrows have many hairs resting over each other. These eyes are black eyes interlaced with green, but the green is more recessed. That person has five lines on his forehead: two which traverse from side to side, and three which do not. (THE END IS MISSING)

(End of Raza deRazin)

13. "In the third month"

A Synopsis

This section tells us of the two lights of the right and the left called Gemini, that is the constellation that rules over the third month, Sivan. Uriel rules over this month, and we are told of his camps, each of which has keys of light issuing from the inner supernal Chasmal. Rabbi Shimon explains the significance of twins in terms of the birth of Jacob and Esau, and then says that the Torah itself is twins – the Written Torah and the Oral Torah – given in the third month to the triple nation of the Three Fathers. And finally he tells us that the Torah was given in three parts – the Torah, the Prophets and the Writings. But the important conclusion is that all is one.

235. בַּחֹדֶשׁ הַשְּׁלִישִׁי לְצֵאת בְּנֵי יִשְׂרָאֵל וְגוֹ', דְּשָׁלִיט בֵּיהּ אוריא"ל, רַב מְמָנָא, וּתְלַת מְאָה וְשִׁתִּין וְחָמֵשׁ רִבּוֹא מַשְׁרְיָין עֲמֵיהּ, כְּחוּשְׁבַּן יוֹמֵי שַׁתָּא. וְכֻלְּהוּ אִית לוֹן תְּלַת מְאָה וְשִׁתִּין וְחָמֵשׁ מַפְתְּחָן נְהוֹרִין, מֵהַהוּא נְהוֹרָא דְּנָפְקָא מִגּוֹ חַשְׁמַל עִלָּאָה פְּנִימָאָה גָּנִיז וְסָתִים, דִּי רָזִין דְּאַתְוָון קַדִּישִׁין עִלָּאִין דִּשְׁמָא קַדִּישָׁא, תַּלְיָין בֵּיהּ.

235. "In the third month, after the children of Yisrael went out of the land of Egypt" (Shemot 19:1). The Great Minister, Uriel, rules over THE THIRD MONTH, FOR NISSAN, IYAR AND SIVAN ARE COMPARED WITH CHESED, GVURAH AND TIFERET, AS MICHAEL RULES IN CHESED, GABRIEL IN GVURAH, AND URIEL RULES IN TIFERET. He is accompanied by 365 ten thousands of camps, corresponding to the number of days of the year, WHICH ARE 365 DAYS OF THE SOLAR YEAR. And all of them have 365 keys of light issuing from the inner supernal Chashmal (Eng. 'electrum'), which is treasured and concealed, and in which the mysteries of the holy supernal letters of the Holy Name are suspended.

236. וְאִיהוּ רָזָא דְּאִישׁ תָּם, מָארֵיהּ דְּבֵיתָא, אִישׁ הָאֱלֹהִים. תָּם: דְּתַמָּן סִיּוּמָא וְקִשּׁוּרָא דִּתְפִילִין, וְיַעֲקֹב אִישׁ תָּם הֲוָה. וּבְדִיּוּקְנֵיהּ, קַיְימָא רָזָא דְּחַשְׁמַל פְּנִימָאָה עִלָּאָה טָמִיר וְגָנִיז. וְכָל נְהוֹרִין סְתִימִין עִלָּאִין נָקִיט אִיהוּ, וְנָפְקֵי מִנֵּיהּ, וְכֻלְּהוּ מַשְׁרְיָין נַקְטֵי אִינּוּן מַפְתְּחָן דְּהַהוּא נְהוֹרָא דְּנָפִיק מִגּוֹ חַשְׁמַל.

236. This is the secret of "a plain man" (Beresheet 25:27), WHO IS JACOB, THE SECRET OF TIFERET – MEANING THAT he is the master of the house, a man of Elohim. "PLAIN" IS DERIVED FROM WHOLENESS, for there is the ending of the knot of the Tefilin, WHICH IS THE SECRET OF MALCHUT IS CALLED 'LEAH'. "...and Jacob was a plain man..." MEANING HER MAN. And the secret of the inner supreme Chashmal, which is concealed and treasured, has his shape. And he holds all the hidden supreme lights, and they issue forth from him. And all the camps OF THE ABOVE MENTIONED ANGEL URIEL hold the keys of that light that issues from the Chashmal.

237. וְהַהוּא נְהוֹרָא, כָּלִיל בִּתְרֵין נְהוֹרִין, וְאִינּוּן חַד. נְהוֹרָא קַדְמָאָה, אִיהוּ נְהוֹרָא חִוָּורָא, דְּלָא שַׁלְטָא בֵּיה עֵינָא, וְדָא אִיהוּ נְהוֹרָא דְּגָנִיז לְצַדִּיקַיָּיא. כד"א אוֹר זָרוּעַ לַצַּדִּיק וְגו'. נְהוֹרָא תִּנְיָינָא, אִיהוּ נְהוֹרָא מְנַצְצָא מְלַהֲטָא, בִּגְוֵון סוּמָק. וְאִתְכְּלִילוּ תְּרֵין נְהוֹרִין כְּחַד, וַהֲוֵו חַד.

237. And that light includes the two lights OF THE RIGHT AND THE LEFT and yet they are in it one LIGHT. The first light is a white one too bright for an eye to behold and this is the treasured light for the righteous as it is written: "Light is sown for the righteous" (Tehilim 97:11) and the second light is one which gleams and sparkles red, FOR IT IS THE SECRET OF THE LEFT LIGHT. And both of them are included as one in it, and they became one.

238. וְהַאי אוריא"ל רַב מְמָנָא, וְכָל אִינּוּן מַשִׁירְיָין, נַטְלֵי הַהוּא נְהוֹרָא, וּבְגִין דְּכָלִיל בִּתְרֵין, אִקְרֵי תְּאוֹמִי"ם. וְעַל דָּא שַׁלְטָא בֵּיה, הַהוּא מַזְּלָא דְּאִקְרֵי בְּרָזָא דִּילֵיה תְּאוֹמִים, וּבֵיה אִתְיְהִיבַת אוֹרַיְיתָא. וּמִכָּאן אִתְמַשְׁכָאן דַּרְגִּין לְתַתָּא, עַד דְּסַלְּקִין בִּשְׁמָהָן, לְאַנְהָרָא עָלְמָא.

238. Uriel the Arch Minister and all those camps WITH HIM take that light which is called 'Gemini' for it includes two lights. Therefore, that constellation rules over THIS MONTH, which is called 'Gemini', after its secret, in which the Torah was given and from which all the grades are drawn below until they rise through the Name to illuminate the world.

239. כָּל שְׁאַר מַזְּלֵי, לֵית לוֹן פֶּה וְלָשׁוֹן, וְהַאי אִית לֵיה פֶּה וְלָשׁוֹן

כְּלִילָן כַּחֲדָא. וְעַל דָּא בְּאוֹרַיְיתָא, וְהָגִיתָ בּוֹ יוֹמָם וְלַיְלָה כְּתִיב. יוֹמָם,
לָקֳבֵל לָשׁוֹן. לַיְלָה, לָקֳבֵל פֶּה. וְכֹלָּא כָּלִיל כַּחֲדָא. וּבְכֹלָּא סָלִיק
תְּאוֹמִים.

239. None of the other signs WHICH RULE IN OTHER MONTHS have a mouth
or tongue but this one, GEMINI, has a mouth and tongue included as one.
Therefore, it is written in regards to the Torah: "And you shall meditate
therein day and night" (Yehoshua 1:8). "Day" corresponds to the tongue,
WHICH IS ZEIR ANPIN, and "night" corresponds to the mouth, WHICH IS
MALCHUT, and all is included in THE SECRET OF the Gemini (Heb.
teomim).

240. תּוֹמִים כְּתִיב, וְעַל רָזָא דָּא כְּתִיב תּוֹמִים, וְהִנֵּה תוֹמִים בְּבִטְנָהּ. אִי
תֵּימָא דִּבְגִין תַּרְוַוייהוּ קָאָמַר. לָאו הָכִי, דְּהָא עֵשָׂו לָא סָלִיק בְּרָזָא דָּא.
אֶלָּא בְּגִין יַעֲקֹב קָאָמַר, וְשִׁבְחָא דָּא, דַּהֲוָה בִּמְעָהָא דְּהַהִיא צַדֶּקֶת, קָא
מְשַׁבַּח קְרָא. וּבְגִין דַּהֲוָה תַּמָּן הַהוּא רָשָׁע, אִסְתַּלַּק מִתַּמָּן אָלֶף.

240. It is written: "*Tomim*," WITHOUT THE LETTER *ALEPH*, and in relation
to this secret it is written "*Tomim*," in: "behold, there were twins (Heb.
tomim) in her womb" (Beresheet 25:24). And "*TOMIM*" is not said OF
JACOB AND ESAU, for Esau is not connected to this secret. It indicates that
it is said "*TOMIM*" of Jacob ALONE, FOR JACOB IS THE SECRET OF THE
CENTRAL COLUMN WHICH INCLUDES TWO LIGHTS, THE RIGHT AND THE
LEFT, AND AFTER THOSE TWO LIGHTS HE IS CALLED "*TOMIM*". WHEN
THE SCRIPTURE SAYS "BEHOLD *TOMIM*," IT INDICATES THAT HE, JACOB,
WAS IN HER WOMB. And the scripture praises Jacob for being in the womb
of that righteous woman, but because the wicked ESAU was there too, the
letter *Aleph* departed, AND IT IS WRITTEN "*TOMIM*" WITHOUT *ALEPH*.

241. וְכֹלָּא רָזָא חֲדָא. יַעֲקֹב נָטִיל בְּרָזָא דִּילֵיהּ, תְּרֵין יַרְחִין נִיסָ"ן
וְאִיָּי"ר, וְאִתְכְּלִיל אִיהוּ בְּרָזָא דְּסִיּוָן, דְּאִיהוּ תְּאוֹמִים. עֵשָׂו, נָטִיל בְּרָזָא
דִּילֵיהּ, תְּרֵין יַרְחִין תַּמּוּ"ז אָ"ב, וְאִיהוּ לָא אִשְׁתְּכַח, וְאִתְאֲבִיד, דְּהָא
אֱלוּ"ל לָאו דִּילֵיהּ הוּא, וַאֲפִילוּ אָ"ב, ט' יוֹם אִינּוּן דִּילֵיהּ, וְלָא יַתִּיר,
וְאִתְאֲבִיד, וְלָא אִשְׁתְּכַח, וְלָאו אִיהוּ בְּרָזָא דִּתְאוֹמִים, אֶלָּא אִתְפְּרַשׁ

לְחוֹדֵיהּ, וְסָטָא לְסִטְרָא אַחֲרָא בַּאֲפִיסָה וּשְׁמָמוּ, כד"א, הָאוֹיֵב תַּמּוּ חֳרָבוֹת לָנֶצַח.

241. All is one secret, for Jacob receives through his secret, TIFERET, THE CENTRAL COLUMN, the two months *Nissan* and *Iyar*, and he is included in the secret of THE MONTH *Sivan*, which is THE SIGN OF Gemini. THIS MEANS THAT BY BEING INCLUDED IN THE MONTH *SIVAN* – WHICH INCLUDES TWO MONTHS, *NISSAN* AND *IYAR*, WHICH ARE RIGHT AND LEFT – IT IS THEREFORE CALLED "TWINS," AND SINCE JACOB IS ALSO INCLUDED IN IT HE RECEIVES THOSE TWO MONTHS. Esau receives through his own inner meaning the two months, *Tammuz* and *Av*, but since he does not abide in THE CENTRAL COLUMN, WHICH IS *ELUL*, he therefore loses Elul, for Elul is not his. And he does not even have the whole MONTH of *Av*, but only nine days and no more, so it can be seen that he is not included in the secret of the twins – WHICH IS THE CENTRAL COLUMN. He separated himself and turned towards the Other Side in naught and desolation, as it is written: "The enemies are come to an end in perpetual ruins" (Tehilim 9:7).

242. וּבְגִין דְּיַעֲקֹב אִיהוּ תְּאוֹמִים, אִתְיְהִיבַת אוֹרַיְיתָא לִבְנוֹי בַּחֹדֶשׁ תְּאוֹמִים, וְאוֹרַיְיתָא בְּרָזָא דִּתְאוֹמִים, תּוֹרָה שֶׁבִּכְתָב, וְתוֹרָה שבע"פ. בַּחֹדֶשׁ תְּלִיתָאֵי, לְעַם תְּלִיתָאֵי, בְּדַרְגִּין תְּלִיתָאִין, תּוֹרָה תְּלִיתָאֵי: תּוֹרָה, נְבִיאִים, וּכְתוּבִים. וְכֹלָא חַד.

242. Because Jacob is in the sign of the twins, the Torah was given to his children in the months of the twins, being itself "twins" – WHICH IS the Written Torah and the Oral Torah. IT WAS GIVEN in the third month to the triple nation, WHICH INCLUDES three grades, NAMELY, THE 'THREE FATHERS'. THE TORAH WAS GIVEN in three parts: the Torah, the Prophets and the Writings, and all is one.

243. בַּחֹדֶשׁ הַשְּׁלִישִׁי וְגוֹ'. פָּרְשְׁתָּא דָּא בְּהַאי קְרָא אוּקְמוּהָ לֵיהּ לְעֵילָּא. תָּאנֵי רַבִּי חִיָּיא, בְּהַהוּא זִמְנָא דְּמָטוּ יִשְׂרָאֵל לְטוּרָא דְּסִינַי, כָּנִישׁ לְהוּ קוּדְשָׁא בְּרִיךְ הוּא לְזַרְעַיְין דְּיִשְׂרָאֵל, וְאַשְׁגַּח לֵיהּ בְּכֻלְּהוּ, וְלָא אַשְׁכַּח בְּכֻלְּהוּ זַרְעָא דְּיִשְׂרָאֵל פְּסֹלוּ, אֶלָּא כֻּלְּהוּ זַרְעָא קַדִּישָׁא,

כֻּלְּהוּ בְּנֵי קְשׁוֹט.

243. "In the third month…" We have already explained that chapter in the scripture above. Rabbi Chiya said that at the time that Yisrael approached Mount Sinai, the Holy One, blessed be He, gathered the seeds of the nation of Yisrael and examined them all. And He found no blemish in all the seeds of Yisrael but saw they were all of a holy seed and of Truth.

244. בְּהַהוּא זִמְנָא אָמַר קוּדְשָׁא בְּרִיךְ הוּא לְמֹשֶׁה, הַשְׁתָּא אֲנָא בָּעֵי לְמֵיהָב אוֹרַיְיתָא לְיִשְׂרָאֵל, מָשִׁיךְ לְהוּ בִּרְחִימוּתָא דַּאֲבָהָן, בִּרְחִימוּתָא דִּרְחִימְנָא לְהוּ, וּבְאַתְווֹן דַּעֲבָדִית לְהוּ. וְאַתְּ הֱוֵי לִי שְׁלוּחָא, וְאֵתִיב מִלִּין אִלֵּין. אָמַר ר' יוֹסִי אָמַר ר' יְהוּדָה, כַּךְ אָמַר קוּדְשָׁא בְּרִיךְ הוּא לְמֹשֶׁה, בְּמִלָּה דָּא הֱוֵי לִי שְׁלִיחָא מְהֵימְנָא, לְאַמְשָׁכָא יִשְׂרָאֵל אֲבַתְרָאי.

244. At that time, the Holy One, blessed be He, said to Moses: 'Now do I wish to give Yisrael the Torah. Draw them to Me by My love for the Patriarch and by the signs that I have made manifest to them. And you shall be My messenger. Therefore, go and tell them those words.' Rabbi Yosi said that Rabbi Yehuda said that those were the words that the Holy One, blessed be He, said to Moses, and continued: 'Thus, you shall be My faithful messenger by drawing Yisrael to go after Me.'

14. "And Moses went up to Elohim"

A Synopsis

This section offers several interpretations of "And Moses went up to Elohim and Hashem called to him out of the mountain, saying." One explanation is that Moses went up to the place where the Shechinah's wings are outspread. The discussion turns to the issue of perfection, and we hear that there is always awe or dread when in the presence of the perfection of all. The title verse is then applied first to Moses, then to God, and finally to the four bonds of earth, air, fire and water. Rabbi Shimon hears Rabbi Yesa tell of a dream where from Rabbi Yesa finally remembered and understood that Chochmah was above, Tiferet below, and Malchut the Sanctuary of God that lay between them. The last interpretation reminds us that whoever comes to be purified is always assisted.

245. וּמשֶׁה עָלָה אֶל הָאֱלֹהִים וַיִּקְרָא אֵלָיו יְיָ' מִן הָהָר וְגוֹ'. וּמשֶׁה עָלָה אֶל הָאֱלֹהִים, לְאַתְרָא דִּפְרִישָׁן גַּדְפוֹי דִּשְׁכִינְתָּא, כד"א וַיֵּט שָׁמַיִם וַיֵּרַד וְגוֹ'.

245. "And Moses went up to Elohim and Hashem called to him out of the mountain, saying" (Shemot 19:3). "And Moses went up to Elohim," MEANS THAT Moses went up to the place where the wings of the Shechinah are outspread, as it is written: "He bowed the heavens also and came down" (Tehilim 18:9).

246. תָּאנָא אָמַר ר' יְהוּדָה, כָּל זִמְנָא דִּגְלוּפֵי מַלְכָּא עִלָּאָה מִתְיַשְּׁרָן בְּאַתְרַיְיהוּ, עָלְמִין כֻּלְּהוּ בְּחֵידוּ, וְכָל עוֹבָדִין מִתְיַשְּׁרָן בְּקִיוּמַיְיהוּ. כד"א, אֶת מַעֲשֵׂה יְיָ' כִּי נוֹרָא הוּא. מַאי כִּי נוֹרָא הוּא. אָמַר ר' אֶלְעָזָר, שְׁלִימוּ דְּכֹלָּא. כד"א הָאֵל הַגָּדוֹל הַגִּבּוֹר וְהַנּוֹרָא. מַאי וְהַנּוֹרָא. דָּא יַעֲקֹב. וּכְתִיב, וְיַעֲקֹב אִישׁ תָּם, כְּתַרְגּוּמוֹ, גְּבַר שְׁלִים. שְׁלִים בְּכֹלָּא. כַּךְ כָּל עוֹבָדִין דְּקוּדְשָׁא בְּרִיךְ הוּא, שְׁלֵימִין בִּשְׁלִימוּ, בְּקִיוּמָא שְׁלִים.

246. We have learned that Rabbi Yehuda said that as long as the legislations of the Supernal King adhere to their proper places, MEANING THAT THEY BALANCE BETWEEN RIGHT AND LEFT, all the worlds are with joy and all the works are maintained properly, as it is written: "the work of

Hashem...that it is tremendous" (Shemot 34:10). What does "tremendous" mean? Rabbi Elazar said that it is the perfection of all, as it is written: "A great El, a mighty and a terrible" (Devarim 10:17). What does "terrible" mean? This is Jacob, THE CENTRAL COLUMN, for it is written: "And Jacob was a plain man" (Beresheet 25:27). "...plain..." means, according to the Aramaic translation, 'a complete man', perfect in all. Thus, all the deeds of the Holy One, blessed be He, are perfect in wholeness, and are perfectly maintained.

247. תַּנְיָא, רַבִּי יוֹסִי אוֹמֵר, יוֹמָא חַד הֲוָה קָאִימְנָא קַמֵּיהּ דְּר' יְהוּדָה סָבָא, שָׁאִילְנָא לֵיהּ, מַאי דִּכְתִיב, וַיִּירָא וַיֹּאמַר מַה נּוֹרָא וְגוֹ'. מַאי קָא חָמָא, דְּקָאָמַר דְּאִיהוּ נוֹרָא. אָמַר לִי, חָמָא שְׁלִימוּ דִּמְהֵימְנוּתָא קַדִּישָׁא, דַּהֲוָה שְׁכִיחַ בְּהַהוּא אֲתָר, כְּגַוְונָא דִּלְעֵילָּא. וּבְכָל אֲתָר דַּהֲוֵי שְׁלֵימוּתָא שְׁכִיחַ, אִקְרֵי נוֹרָא.

247. As we learned, Rabbi Yosi explained that one day, while he was standing before Rabbi Yehuda Saba (the elder), he asked him about the meaning of the verse: "And he was afraid and said: 'How dreadful is this place'" (Beresheet 28:17). What did Jacob see that frightened him and made him call it "dreadful"? Rabbi Yehuda explained that he saw there the perfection of the holy Faith, WHICH IS MALCHUT, that was frequent in that place as it is above, and any place wherein His perfection is found is called "dreadful."

248. אֲמֵינָא לֵיהּ, אִי הָכִי, אֲמַאי תַּרְגּוּמוֹ דְּחִילוּ, וְלָא שָׁלִים. אָמַר לִי, לֵית דְּחִילוּ אֶלָּא בַּאֲתָר דְּהֲוֵי שְׁלֵימוּתָא שְׁכִיחַ, וּבְכָל אֲתָר דְּהֲוֵי שְׁלֵימוּתָא שְׁכִיחַ, אִתְקְרֵי נוֹרָא. דִּכְתִיב, יְראוּ אֶת יְיָ' קְדוֹשָׁיו כִּי אֵין מַחְסוֹר לִירֵאָיו, מִמַּשְׁמַע דְּקָאָמַר כִּי אֵין מַחְסוֹר, בַּאֲתָר דְּלֵית מַחְסוֹר, שְׁלֵימוּתָא שְׁכִיחַ.

248. I asked him: If that is so, why then is the word "dreadful" translated into Aramaic as 'fear' and not as 'perfection'? FOR IF "DREADFUL" MEANS 'PERFECTION', HE SHOULD HAVE TRANSLATED IT AS "PERFECTION." He answered that there is no awe but in a place where perfection is found, and any place in which there is completeness is called "dreadful", as it is

written: "O fear Hashem you saints of His, for those who fear Him there is no lack" (Tehilim 34:10). We can learn from this verse, "there is no lack," THAT AWE IS COMPLETENESS, for wherever there is no deficiency there is completeness.

249. תָּאנָא מִי עָלָה שָׁמַיִם וַיֵּרַד, אָמַר ר' יוֹסֵי, דָּא הוּא מֹשֶׁה, דִּכְתִּיב וּמֹשֶׁה עָלָה אֶל הָאֱלֹהִים. מִי אָסַף רוּחַ בְּחָפְנָיו, דָּא הוּא אַהֲרֹן. דִּכְתִּיב, וּמִלֵּא חָפְנָיו קְטֹרֶת סַמִּים דַּקָּה. מִי צָרַר מַיִם בַּשִּׂמְלָה, דָּא אֵלִיָּהוּ. דִּכְתִּיב, אִם יִהְיֶה הַשָּׁנִים הָאֵלֶּה טַל וּמָטָר כִּי אִם לְפִי דְּבָרִי. מִי הֵקִים כָּל אַפְסֵי אָרֶץ, דָּא הוּא אַבְרָהָם. דִּכְתִּיב בֵּיהּ, אֵלֶּה תוֹלְדוֹת הַשָּׁמַיִם וְהָאָרֶץ בְּהִבָּרְאָם, אַל תִּקְרֵי בְּהִבָּרְאָם, אֶלָּא בְּאַבְרָהָם.

249. We studied: "Who has ascended up into heaven and come down" (Mishlei 30:4). Rabbi Yosi said that it is Moses, for it is written: "And Moses went up to Elohim" (Shemot 19:3). "Who has gathered the wind in His fists" (Mishlei 30:4)? It is Aaron, as it is written: "And his hands full of sweet incense beaten small" (Vayikra 16:12). "Who has bound the waters in a garment"? It is Eliyahu, as it is written: "There shall not be dew or rain these years but according to my word" (I Melachim 17:1). "Who has established all the ends of the earth"? It is Abraham, of whom it is written: "These are the generations of the heaven and of the earth when they were created (behibar'am)" (Beresheet 2:4). Do not pronounce it 'behibar'am', but "beAbraham (lit. 'by Abraham')," (spelled with the same letters).

250. הוּא תָּנֵי הַאי, וְהוּא אָמַר, מִי עָלָה שָׁמַיִם, דָּא קוּדְשָׁא בְּרִיךְ הוּא. דִּכְתִּיב בֵּיהּ עָלָה אֱלֹהִים בִּתְרוּעָה מִי אָסַף רוּחַ בְּחָפְנָיו, דָּא קוּדְשָׁא בְּרִיךְ הוּא, דִּכְתִּיב אֲשֶׁר בְּיָדוֹ נֶפֶשׁ כָּל חָי וְגוֹ'. מִי צָרַר מַיִם בַּשִּׂמְלָה דָּא קוּדְשָׁא בְּרִיךְ הוּא. דִּכְתִּיב בֵּיהּ צוֹרֵר מַיִם בְּעָבָיו. מִי הֵקִים כָּל אַפְסֵי אָרֶץ, דָּא קוּדְשָׁא בְּרִיךְ הוּא. דִּכְתִּיב בֵּיהּ, בְּיוֹם עֲשׂוֹת יְיָ' אֱלֹהִים אֶרֶץ וְשָׁמָיִם. תּוּ אָמַר, מִי עָלָה שָׁמַיִם וַיֵּרַד וְגוֹ', אִלֵּין אִינּוּן אַרְבַּע קְטִירֵי עָלְמָא, אֵשׁ רוּחַ מַיִם וְעָפָר.

250. He taught this, and said: "Who has ascended up into heaven?" The

Holy One, blessed be He, of whom it is written: "Elohim is gone up with a shout" (Tehilim 47:6). "Who gathered the wind in His fists"? The Holy One, blessed be He, of whom it is written: "In whose hands is the soul of every living thing" (Iyov 12:9). "Who has bound the waters in a garment"? The Holy One, blessed be He, of whom it is written: "He binds up the waters in His thick clouds" (Iyov 26:8). "Who has established all the ends of the earth"? The Holy One, blessed be He, of whom it is written: "In the day that Hashem Elohim made the earth and the heavens" (Beresheet 2:4). RABBI YOSI continued further and said: "Who went up into heaven and came down"? Those are the four bonds of the world: fire, air, water and earth.

251. אָמַר ר' יֵיסָא, אִתְחָזוּן מִלּוֹי דְּר' יוֹסִי, דְּלָא מִתְקַיְּימָאן. כַּד מָטוּ מִלִּין אִלֵּין לְגַבֵּיה דְּר' שִׁמְעוֹן, אָנַח יְדוֹי בְּרֵישֵׁיה דְּר' יוֹסִי וּבָרְכֵיה, וְאָמַר שַׁפִּיר קָא אָמַרְתְּ, וְהָכִי הוּא. אָמַר לֵיה מְנָא לָךְ. אָמַר הָכִי אוֹלִיפְנָא מֵאַבָּא, דַּהֲוָה אָמַר מִשְּׁמֵיה דְּרַב הַמְנוּנָא סָבָא.

251. Rabbi Yesa said: It is evident that Rabbi Yosi's interpretations of this verse have no hold, FOR THEY ARE INCOMPATIBLE WITH EACH OTHER. But when Rabbi Shimon heard them he put his hand on the head of Rabbi Yosi and blessed him, saying: Your interpretations are quite right and well said, and it is indeed so. Where have you learned THIS? And he answered: I have learned them from my father who heard it from Rav Hamnuna Saba (the elder).

252. יוֹמָא חַד הֲוָה יָתִיב ר' שִׁמְעוֹן בְּתַרְעָא דְּצִפּוֹרִי, אָמַר לֵיה ר' יֵיסָא, הַאי דְּאָמַר ר' יוֹסִי, מִי עָלָה שָׁמַיִם וַיֵּרַד וְגוֹ', זִמְנָא חֲדָא אָמַר, דָּא מֹשֶׁה. לְבָתַר אָמַר, דָּא קוּדְשָׁא בְּרִיךְ הוּא. לְבָתַר אָמַר, אִלֵּין ד' קְטִירִין אֵשׁ רוּחַ מַיִם וְעָפָר. וַחֲמֵינָא לֵיה לְמֹר דְּבָרְכֵיה.

252. One day, Rabbi Shimon was sitting at the gate of Tzipori when Rabbi Yesa said to him: That which Rabbi Yosi said, "Who ascended up into the heavens and came down," he applied once to Moses then to the Holy One, blessed be He, and finally he said that these are the four bonds, fire, air, water and earth – and I saw that my master blessed him!

253. אָמַר לֵיהּ וַדַּאי שַׁפִּיר קָא אָמַר, וְהָכִי הוּא, וְכֹלָּא חַד מִלָּה, וְכֻלְּהוּ
מִלֵּי אִתְקַיְּימוּ בְּקוּדְשָׁא בְּרִיךְ הוּא, וְכֻלְּהוּ בְּחַד מַתְקְלָא סַלְקָא.
אִתְרְגִישׁ ר' יֵיסָא בְּמִלּוֹי דְּר' שִׁמְעוֹן, וְאָמַר וַדַּאי הַאי הָכִי הוּא, וְהָכִי
אוֹלִיפְנָא מִקַּמֵּיהּ דְּמַר זִמְנָא אַחֲרָא. אֵלֶּה תּוֹלְדוֹת הַשָּׁמַיִם וְהָאָרֶץ
בְּהִבָּרְאָם, אַל תִּקְרֵי בְּהִבָּרְאָם, אֶלָּא בְּאַבְרָהָם. דִּכְתִיב, כִּי אָמַרְתִּי
עוֹלָם חֶסֶד יִבָּנֶה.

253. Rabbi Shimon replied: Assuredly, what he said is well spoken, and so it is. All are the same, and all things apply to the Holy One, blessed be He, and all of them amount to the same thing. Rabbi Yesa became excited by the words of Rabbi Shimon and he said: This is indeed so, and on another occasion I learned from my master the explanation of the verse: "These are the generations of the heavens and of the earth when they were created" (Heb. *behibar'am*). Do not read it as '*behibar'am*', but rather "*beabra'ham* ('in Abraham')" (with the same letters) – NAMELY, WITH CHESED OF ZEIR ANPIN, as it is written: "For I have said, the world is built by *Chesed* (Eng. 'kindness')" (Tehilim 89:3), – AND ALL THE OTHER NAMES: MOSES, AARON, ELIYAHU AND THE FOUR ELEMENTS, FIRE, AIR, WATER AND EARTH, AS ALL ARE THE NAMES OF THE HOLY ONE, BLESSED BE HE.

254. וְכֹלָּא שַׁפִּיר. אֲבָל סוֹפָא דִּקְרָא מַאי קָא מַיְירֵי דִּכְתִיב מַה שְּׁמוֹ
וּמַה שֶּׁם בְּנוֹ כִּי תֵדָע. מַה שְּׁמוֹ תִּינַח, מַה שֵּׁם בְּנוֹ מַהוּ. אָמַר לֵיהּ, רָזָא
דְּמִלָּה הָא אוֹלִיפְנָא לְר' אֶלְעָזָר בְּרִי. אָמַר לֵיהּ, לֵימָא לִי מַר, דְּהָא
בְּחֶלְמִי שָׁאִילְנָא קַמֵּיהּ דְּמַר הַאי מִלָּה, וְאָמַר לִי, וְאַנְשִׁינָא לָהּ. אָמַר
לֵיהּ, אִי אֵימָא תִּדְכַּר. אָמַר לֵיהּ וַדַּאי. דְּהָא מַה דְּאוֹלִיפְנָא קַמֵּי דְּמַר
יוֹמָא דָּא אַדְכַּרְנָא.

254. This is well said, but what is the meaning of the last part of the verse saying: "What is his name and what is His son's name that you should know" (Mishlei 30:4)? I can understand "What is His name," but what about "His son's name"? Rabbi Shimon replied: I have already taught the secret of this verse to my son Rabbi Elazar. He said to him: Please, tell me master, for I have asked you in a dream concerning it and I have forgotten the answer. He replied: Now if I tell you will you remember it? Rabbi Yesa

answered: Assuredly, for what my master teaches me by daytime I remember.

255. א"ל רָזָא דְמִלָה, הַיְינוּ דִכְתִיב בְּנִי בְכוֹרִי יִשְׂרָאֵל וּכְתִיב יִשְׂרָאֵל אֲשֶׁר בְּךָ אֶתְפָּאָר. וּבְרָזָא עִלָּאָה, וְהַאי אִקְרֵי בְּנוֹ. אָמַר יָנוּחַ דַעְתֵּיה דְּמֹר, דְּהָא רָזָא דָא יְדַעְנָא. אַדְהָכִי, לָא אִדְכַּר ר' יֵיסָא, חָלַשׁ דַּעְתֵּיה, אָזַל לְבֵיתֵיה, אַדְמוּךְ, אַחְזִיאוּ לֵיה בְּחֶלְמָא, חַד סִפְרָא דְּאַגַּדְתָּא, דַּהֲוָה כְּתִיב בֵּיה, חָכְמָה וְתִפְאֶרֶת בְּמִקְדָּשׁוֹ.

255. He said: The secret of it is connected with the verse, "Yisrael is My son, my firstborn" (Shemot 4:22), and, "Yisrael, in whom I will be glorified" (Yeshayah 49:3). And it is in the supernal secret of this verse THAT YISRAEL SIGNIFIES TIFERET and is called "His son." Rabbi Yesa replied: Be assured, my master, that I know this secret. Yet Rabbi Yesa could not remember WHAT HE WAS TOLD IN HIS DREAM, and distressed, he went home and slept. Then he had a dream in which he was shown a book of Agadah wherein it was written: "Chochmah and Tiferet are in His sanctuary."

256. אִתְּעַר, אָזַל לְגַבֵּיה דְּר"ש, נָשַׁק יְדוֹי, אָמַר, הָכִי חֲמֵינָא בְּחֶלְמָא. זִמְנָא אַחֲרָא חֲמֵינָא בְּחֶלְמָא, חַד סִפְרָא דְּאַגַּדְתָּא דְּאַחְזִיו קַמַּאי, וַהֲוָה כְּתִיב בֵּיה, חָכְמָה וְתִפְאֶרֶת בְּמִקְדָּשׁוֹ, חָכְמָה לְעֵילָא, תִּפְאֶרֶת לְתַתָּא. בְּמִקְדָּשׁוֹ לְגַבַּיְיהוּ. וְהָכִי חֲמֵינָא בְּחֶלְמָא זִמְנָא חֲדָא. וְהָכִי אַשְׁכַּחְנָא בְּפוּמָאי. א"ל ר' שִׁמְעוֹן, עַד כְּעַן רַבְיָא אַנְתְּ, לְמֵיעַל בֵּין מְחַצְדֵי חַקְלָא, וְהָא כֹּלָּא אַחְזִיאוּ לָךְ. וְדָא הוּא דִכְתִיב, מַה שְׁמוֹ וּמַה שֶּׁם בְּנוֹ כִּי תֵדָע. חָכְמָה שְׁמוֹ, תִּפְאֶרֶת בְּנוֹ.

256. When he awoke he went to Rabbi Shimon and kissed his hands saying: Thus I was shown in my dream, and some other time I saw in my dream a book of Agadah wherein it was written: "Chochmah and Tiferet in His sanctuary." "Chochmah" above, "Tiferet" below, and His sanctuary, WHICH IS MALCHUT, by them. This is what I saw once in my dream, and these words were on my lips. Then Rabbi Shimon said to him: Until now you were too young to be enumerated among the reapers of the field, MEANING

THOSE KNOWLEDGEABLE IN SECRETS, but now everything has been shown to you. And this is the meaning of the verse: "What is His name and what is his son's name that you should know." Chochmah is "His name" and Tiferet is "His son's name," FOR CHOCHMAH AND BINAH ARE ABA AND IMA OF TIFERET, AS IT IS KNOWN.

257. וּמֹשֶׁה עָלָה אֶל הָאֱלֹהִים, זַכָּאָה חוּלָקֵיה דְּמֹשֶׁה, דְּזָכֵי לִיקָרָא דָּא, דְּאוֹרַיְיתָא אַסְהִיד בְּגִינֵיה כָּךְ. ת"ח, מַה בֵּין מֹשֶׁה לִשְׁאַר בְּנֵי עָלְמָא. שְׁאַר בְּנֵי עָלְמָא, כַּד סַלְקִין, סַלְקִין לְעָתְרָא, סַלְקִין לִרְבוּ, סַלְקִין לְמַלְכוּ, אֲבָל מֹשֶׁה כַּד סָלִיק, מַה כְּתִיב בֵּיה, וּמֹשֶׁה עָלָה אֶל הָאֱלֹהִים, זַכָּאָה חוּלָקֵיה.

257. "And Moses went up to Elohim." Happy is the portion of Moses for being worthy of this honor to which the Torah itself testifies. Come and behold the difference between Moses and all other men of the world. When other men rise, they rise in richness or they rise to greatness or kingship, but of Moses it is written: "And Moses went up to Elohim." Blessed is his share.

258. ר' יוֹסֵי אָמַר, מִכָּאן אָמְרוּ חַבְרַיָּא, הַבָּא לִיטָהֵר מְסַיְּיעִין אוֹתוֹ, דִּכְתִיב וּמֹשֶׁה עָלָה אֶל הָאֱלֹהִים. מַה כְּתִיב בַּתְרֵיה, וַיִּקְרָא אֵלָיו יְיָ'. דְּמַאן דְּבָעֵי לְאִתְקַרְבָא, מְקַרְבִין לֵיה.

258. Rabbi Yosi said: From this verse the friends deduced that "he who comes to be purified is assisted," for it is written, "And Moses went up to Elohim," and afterwards it is written, "and Hashem called to him." Thus, he who desires to come nearer is brought nearer.

15. "Thus shall you say to the house of Jacob"

A Synopsis

Here we read of the happiness of those who are chosen by God to come near to Him. Those who reside in the Holy Land have the presence of God because the Shechinah always dwells there. In, "And Hashem called to him from the mountain, saying, 'Thus shall you say to the house of Jacob',," Hashem means to reveal wisdom to the children of Yisrael, and to tell them the truth about what He has done for them. We read how Rabbi Yosi and Rabbi Chiya fall in with a man who has the wisdom of herbs, and who cures them with one of his herbs of an ailment that they did not even know they had. He shows them the danger and the power of his herb, and they watch while it kills the serpent. In this way we learn the tremendous power inherent in everything that God created to grow on earth.

259. וַיִּקְרָא אֵלָיו יְיָ' מִן הָהָר לֵאמֹר כֹּה תֹאמַר לְבֵית יַעֲקֹב וְגוֹ'. ר' יִצְחָק פָּתַח, אַשְׁרֵי תִּבְחַר וּתְקָרֵב יִשְׁכֹּן חֲצֵרֶיךָ, זַכָּאָה חוּלָקֵיהּ דְּהַהוּא ב"נ, דְּקוּדְשָׁא בְּרִיךְ הוּא אִתְרְעֵי בֵּיהּ, וְקָרִיב לֵיהּ, לְמִשְׁרֵי בְּגוֹ הֵיכָלָא קַדִּישָׁא, דְּכָל מַאן דְּאִיהוּ אִתְרְעֵי בֵּיהּ לְפוּלְחָנֵיהּ, רָשִׁים הוּא מֵרְשִׁימִין דִּלְעֵילָּא, לְמִנְדַּע דְּהָא הוּא אִתְבְּחַר מִקַּמֵּיהּ דְּמַלְכָּא קַדִּישָׁא עִלָּאָה, לְמִשְׁרֵי בְּמָדוֹרוֹי. וְכָל מַאן דְּאִשְׁתְּכַח בֵּיהּ הַהוּא רְשִׁימָא, אַעֲבַר בְּכָל תַּרְעִין דִּלְעֵילָּא, וְלֵית דְּיִמְחֵי בִּידוֹי.

259. "And Hashem called to him from the mountain, saying, 'Thus shall you say to the house of Jacob'" (Shemot 19:3). Rabbi Yitzchak opened the discussion with the verse: "Happy is he whom You choose, and cause to approach to You, that he may dwell in Your court" (Tehilim 65:5). Happy is the portion of the man whom the Holy One, blessed be He, desires to bring near to Him to dwell in the Holy Palace, for he whom He desires to receive to worship Him is inscribed above, to make it known that he has been chosen by the Holy King to dwell in His appartment. And everyone who has upon him such a sign can pass through all the supernal gates without any hindrance.

260. ר' יְהוּדָה אָמַר, זַכָּאָה חוּלָקֵיהּ דְּמֹשֶׁה, דְּעֲלֵיהּ כְּתִיב אַשְׁרֵי תִּבְחַר וּתְקָרֵב, וּכְתִיב בֵּיהּ וּמֹשֶׁה נִגַּשׁ אֶל הָעֲרָפֶל וְנִגַּשׁ מֹשֶׁה לְבַדּוֹ אֶל יְיָ'

וְהֵם לָא יִגָּשׁוּ. כֹּה תֹאמַר לְבֵית יַעֲקֹב: אַלֵּין נוּקְבֵי, וְתַגֵּיד לִבְנֵי יִשְׂרָאֵל: אַלֵּין דּוּכְרִין.

260. Rabbi Yehuda said: Happy is the share of Moses, of whom it is written, "Happy is he whom You choose, and cause to approach to You," and of whom it is also written, "And Moses drew near to the mist" (Shemot 20:18), and, "And Moses alone shall come near Hashem: but they shall not come near" (Shemot 24:2). "Thus shall you say to the House of Jacob," are the wp,em, and "the children of Yisrael" are the men.

261. ר' שִׁמְעוֹן אָמַר, כֹּה תֹאמַר, כד"א כֹּה תְבָרְכוּ. וּכְתִיב, וַחֲסִידֶיךָ יְבָרְכוּכָה, כְּלוֹמַר יְבָרְכוּ כֹּה. כֹּה תֹאמַר לְבֵית יַעֲקֹב, בַּאֲמִירָה. וְהַיְינוּ מִסִּטְרָא דְּדִינָא. וְתַגֵּיד לִבְנֵי יִשְׂרָאֵל, כד"א, וַיַּגֵּד לָכֶם אֶת בְּרִיתוֹ. וּכְתִיב הִגַּדְתִּי הַיּוֹם לַיְיָ' אֱלֹהֶיךָ. לִבְנֵי יִשְׂרָאֵל, דּוּכְרִין, דְּאָתוּ מִסִּטְרָא דְּרַחֲמֵי.

261. Rabbi Shimon said: "Thus (Heb. *koh*) shall you say" has the same meaning as in the verse, "In this way (Heb. *koh*) shall you bless" (Bemidbar 6:22), and as in another verse, "And Your pious ones shall bless You (Heb. *yevarchuchah*)" (Tehilim 145:10), namely, bless (Heb. *yevarchu*) koh – KOH BEING MALCHUT WHICH IS CALLED 'KOH'. "Thus shall you say to the house of Jacob," meaning by "saying," from the side of Judgment. "...and tell the children of Yisrael..." is the same as in the verse, "And He declared (told) to you His Covenant" (Devarim 4:13), and as in the verse, "I profess (tell) this day to Hashem your Elohim" (Devarim 26:3), FOR "TELLING" PERTAINS TO MERCY. "...the children of Yisrael..." are the men who come from the side of Mercy, THEREFORE IT IS ADDRESSED TO THEM BY "TELLING."

262. א"ר יִצְחָק, הוֹאִיל וַאֲתֵינָא לְהַאי, מַה הוּא הִגַּדְתִּי הַיּוֹם לַיְיָ' אֱלֹהֶיךָ. לַיְיָ' אֱלֹהֵינוּ, מִבָּעֵי לֵיהּ. אָמַר לֵיהּ ר' שִׁמְעוֹן, וְכִי הַאי בִּלְחוֹדוֹי הוּא. וְהָא כְּתִיב כִּי יְיָ' אֱלֹהֶיךָ מְבִיאֲךָ אֶל אֶרֶץ טוֹבָה וְגוֹ'. אֲשֶׁר יְיָ' אֱלֹהֶיךָ נוֹתֵן לָךְ. כִּי יְיָ' אֱלֹהֶיךָ אֵשׁ אוֹכְלָה הוּא, וְכֻלְּהוּ הָכִי.

262. Rabbi Yitzchak said: Since we have come upon this verse, why is it

-124-

written: "I told this day to Hashem your Elohim," instead of 'Hashem our Elohim'? Rabbi Shimon replied: Not only this. For it is also written: "For Hashem your Elohim brings you into a good land" (Devarim 8:7), "that Hashem your Elohim gives you" (Devarim 7:16), and it is written, "For Hashem your Elohim is a consuming fire" (Devarim 4:24). And all of them are written the same way.

263. אֶלָּא הָכִי תָּנֵינָן, כָּל הַדָּר בְּאֶרֶץ יִשְׂרָאֵל דּוֹמֶה כְּמִי שֶׁיֵּשׁ לוֹ אֱלוֹהַּ. וְכָל הַדָּר בְּחוּצָה לָאָרֶץ דּוֹמֶה כְּמִי שֶׁאֵין לוֹ אֱלוֹהַּ. מַאי טַעֲמָא. מִשּׁוּם דְּזַרְעָא קַדִּישָׁא, לְאַרְעָא קַדִּישָׁא סַלְקָא. וּשְׁכִינְתָּא בְּאַתְרָהּ יָתְבָא. וְהַאי בְּהַאי תַּלְיָא. וּמֹשֶׁה לָא קָאָמַר אֱלֹהֶיךָ, אֶלָּא לְאִינּוּן דַּהֲווֹ זְמִינִין לְמֵיעַל לְאַרְעָא קַדִּישָׁא, וּלְקַבְּלָא אַפֵּי שְׁכִינְתָּא. וּמַה דְּלָא אָמַר אֱלֹהֵינוּ, מִשּׁוּם דְּהָא מֹשֶׁה לָא זָכָה לְמֵיעַל לְאַרְעָא, וּבְגִינֵי כַּךְ, אֱלֹהֶיךָ וַדַּאי בְּכָל אֲתָר, מִשּׁוּם דְּאִינּוּן הֲווֹ זְמִינִין לְמֵיעַל תַּמָּן.

263. We have learned that he who resides in the land of Yisrael has Elohim, and he who resides outside of it is as he who is without Elohim. The reason for this is that the holy seed comes to the Holy Land and the Shechinah dwells in Her place, and they depend on each other. Therefore, Moses did not say "your Elohim" except to those who were going to settle in the Holy Land and to receive the Shechinah. And Moses did not say 'our Elohim' since he did not merit to enter into the Holy Land. Therefore, it is written "your Elohim" in all these verses, for they were to enter there.

264. א"ל וַדַּאי הָכִי הוּא. אֲבָל הָכָא כְּתִיב, וּבָאתָ אֶל הַכֹּהֵן אֲשֶׁר יִהְיֶה בַּיָּמִים הָהֵם וְאָמַרְתָּ אֵלָיו הִגַּדְתִּי הַיּוֹם לַיְיָ' אֱלֹהֶיךָ, וְהָא אִינּוּן בְּאַרְעָא שַׁרְיָין, מַאי טַעֲמָא אֱלֹהֶיךָ, וְלֹא אֱלֹהֵינוּ. אֶלָּא אִינּוּן בַּעְיָין לְאַחְזָאָה וּלְאוֹדָעָה, דִּבְגִינֵי דְּחֶסֶד עִלָּאָה, זָכָאן לְכָל הַאי, וְשַׁרְיָין בְּאַרְעָא, וְעָאלָן לְהַהִיא אַרְעָא, וְעָבֵד עִמְּהוֹן כָּל אִינּוּן טָבָאן, וּבְגִינֵי כַּךְ, הֲווֹ אַמְרֵי מִלִּין אִלֵּין לַכֹּהֵן, דִּכְתִיב הִגַּדְתִּי הַיּוֹם לַיְיָ' אֱלֹהֶיךָ, מִשּׁוּם דְּאָתֵי מִסִּטְרָא דְּחֶסֶד.

264. He said to him: Assuredly it is so, but why is it written, "And you shall

come to the priest that shall be in those days, and say to him, 'I profess this day to Hashem your Elohim'" (Devarim 26:3)? If they were already in the Holy Land, why did he say "your Elohim" and not 'our Elohim'? AND HE ANSWERS that they show and praise the supernal Chesed, for it granted them all that merit to enter and dwell in that Holy Land, and performed by them all that goodness. Therefore, they said those words to the priest, as it is written: "I profess this day to the Hashem your Elohim," for he comes from the side of the Chesed.

265. כֹּה תֹאמַר לְבֵית יַעֲקֹב, לְהַהוּא אֲתָר דְּאִתְחֲזֵי לְהוּ. וְתַגֵּיד לִבְנֵי יִשְׂרָאֵל, בְּהַהוּא אֲתָר שְׁלִים דְּאִתְחֲזֵי לְהוּ, דְּהָא יַעֲקֹב וְיִשְׂרָאֵל, תְּרֵין דַּרְגִּין אִסְתָּלָקוּ, וּבְדַרְגָּא חַד סַלְקִין, אֶלָּא יִשְׂרָאֵל שְׁלֵימוּתָא דְּכֹלָּא אִקְרֵי. וְתַגֵּיד לִבְנֵי יִשְׂרָאֵל, לְאַחֲזָאָה חָכְמְתָא, וּלְאִשְׁתָּעֵי בְּרוּחַ חָכְמְתָא, טִיבוּ וּקְשׁוֹט דְּעָבֵד לוֹן קוּדְשָׁא בְּרִיךְ הוּא, דִּכְתִיב וַיַּגֵּד לָכֶם אֶת בְּרִיתוֹ.

265. "Thus shall you say to the house of Jacob," namely to that place which is appropriate TO THEIR GRADE; "And tell the children of Yisrael," namely to that place which is appropriate TO THEIR GRADE, for Jacob and Yisrael are two grades. JACOB IS THE LEVEL OF THE SIX ENDS AND YISRAEL IS THE GRADE OF THE FIRST THREE SFIROT, and both of them amount to one grade, WHICH IS ZEIR ANPIN, but Yisrael is called 'the completeness of all'. Therefore, it is written: "And tell the children of Yisrael," MEANING to reveal Wisdom to them and to tell them in the spirit of Wisdom the grace and the Truth of what the Holy One, blessed be He, has done for them, FOR "TELLING" ALLUDES TO CHOCHMAH, as it is written: "And He declared (told) to you His Covenant."

266. תָּנֵיָא, אָמַר ר' יוֹסֵי, זִמְנָא חֲדָא הֲוֵינָא אָזִיל בְּאָרְחָא, וַהֲוָה ר' חִיָּיא בְּרִי עִמִּי. עַד דַּהֲוֵינָא אָזְלִין, אַשְׁכַּחְנָא חַד גְּבַר, דַּהֲוָה לָקִיט בְּחַקְלָא, עֲשָׂבִין לְאַסְוָותָא. קְרִיבְנָא לְגַבֵּיהּ, אֲמֵינָא לֵיהּ, בַּר נָשׁ, קוּטְרָא דְּקוּטְרֵי דַּעֲשָׂבִין לָמָה. לָא זָקִיף רֵישֵׁיהּ, וְלָא אָמַר מִידֵי. אַהֲדַרְנָא זִמְנָא אַחֲרָא וַאֲמֵינָא הַאי, וְלָא אָמַר מִידֵי. אֲמֵינָא לֵיהּ לְרַבִּי חִיָּיא בְּרִי, אוֹ הַאי בַּר נָשׁ בַּר אָטִים אוּדְנִין, אוֹ שַׁטְיָא, אוֹ חַכִּימָא. יָתִיבְנָא

-126-

גַּבּוֹי. לְבָתַר לָקִיט אִינּוּן עֲשָׂבִין, וְאָחִיד לוֹן, וְחָפָא עֲלַיְיהוּ טַרְפֵּי גוּפְנִין.

266. We learned that Rabbi Yosi said: Once I was on my way accompanied by Rabbi Chiya, my son. While walking we came upon a man who was collecting medicinal herbs in the field. We drew near him and I asked him: Tell us, what are these bundles of herbs for? He gave no reply and did not even raise his head. I asked him again but he gave no answer. Then I said to Rabbi Chiya, my son: This man is either deaf or mad or wise. So we sat down near him. Afterwards he collected all the herbs and made them into bundles and covered each bundle with fig leaves.

267. אָמַר לָן, אֲנָא חֲמֵינָא דִּיוּדָאִין אָתוּן, וְיוּדָאִין אַמְרֵי עֲלַיְיהוּ, דְּאִינּוּן חַכִּימִין, אִי לָא דְּחַיְּיסָנָא עֲלַיְיכוּ הַשְׁתָּא, תֶּהֱווֹן רְחִיקָן מִבְּנֵי נָשָׁא כְּסִגִירָא דָּא, דְּמַרְחֲקִין לֵיהּ מִכֹּלָּא, דְּהָא אֲנָא חֲמֵינָא, דְּרֵיחָא דְּחַד עִשְׂבָּא דַּהֲוָה קָרִיב גַּבֵּיכוֹן, עָאל בְּגוּפַיְיכוּ, וְתֶהֱווֹן רְחִיקִין תְּלָתָא יוֹמִין. אֶלָּא אֲכִילוּ אִלֵּין תּוּמֵי בָּרָא וְתִתְסוּן.

267. He turned to us and said: I see that you are Jews and Jews are said to be clever people. If I did not have pity for you now, you would be expelled from people as lepers are, for I perceive the odor of a certain herb which has entered your body. You would be outcasts FROM MEN for three days. But now eat this wild garlic and you will be healed.

268. אֲכַלְנָא מִנַּיְיהוּ דַּהֲווֹ שְׁכִיחִין קַמָּן, וְאַדְמַכְנָא, וְאִתְקַטַּרְנָא בְּזֵיעָא, עַד עִידָן סַגִּי. לְבָתַר אִתְּעַרְנָא, אָמַר לָן הַהוּא גַּבְרָא, הַשְׁתָּא אֱלָהֲכוֹן עִמְּכוֹן, דְּאַשְׁכַּחְתּוּן לִי, דְּהָא אַסְוָותָא דְּגוּפַיְיכוֹן עַל יְדִי אִשְׁתְּלִים.

268. So we ate from these that were before us and fell into a sleep, and we were bathed in perspiration for a long time. When we awakened that man said: Now your Elohim is with you, for you have found me and the cure of your bodies is accomplished through me.

269. עַד דַּהֲוֵינָא אַזְלִין, אָמַר לוֹן, כָּל בַּר נָשׁ בָּעֵי לְאִשְׁתְּעֵי בְּבַר נָשׁ אַחֲרָא, כְּפוּם אָרְחוֹי, דְּהָא לְנוּקְבָּא כְּפוּם אָרְחוֹי. לְגַבְרָא כְּפוּם אָרְחוֹי.

לְגַבְרָא דְּגַבְרֵי כְּפוּם אָרְחוֹי. אֲמֵינָא לְרַבִּי חִיָּיא בְּרִי, הַיְינוּ דִּכְתִּיב, כֹּה תֹאמַר לְבֵית יַעֲקֹב וְתַגֵּיד לִבְנֵי יִשְׂרָאֵל.

269. As we went along he said to us: Every person must converse with his fellow according to their way. That is, to a woman according to her way, and to a man according to his way, and to a man among men according to his way. Then I was struck by this remark and said to Rabbi Chiya, my son: This accords with the verse, "Thus shall you say to the house of Jacob and tell the children of Yisrael."

270. אָמַר לָן, חֲמֵיתוּן דְּלָא זָקִיפְנָא רֵישָׁאי, וְלָא אִשְׁתָּעֵינָא בַּהֲדַיְיכוּ, מִשּׁוּם דְּאַבָּא חַכִּימָא בַּעֲשָׂבִין מִכָּל בְּנֵי דָּרָא הֲוָה. וְאוֹלִיפְנָא מֵאַבָּא אָרְחוֹי דְּכָל עֲשָׂבִין, דִּבְהוֹן קָשׁוֹט, וַאֲנָא בְּכָל שַׁתָּא מָדוֹרָאי בֵּינַיְיהוּ.

270. The man said to us: You probably noticed that I did not raise my head, nor did I speak to you. This is because my father was a greater expert in herbs than any one else at his time, and I have learned from him the powers and the uses of all the herbs that are true, and I spend the whole year among them.

271. וְהַאי עִשְׂבָּא דַּחֲמֵיתוּן, דַּחֲפֵינָא לֵיהּ בְּטַרְפֵּי דְּגוּפְנִין אִלֵּין, בְּבֵיתָאי אִית אֲתָר חַד, וְהוּא לְסְטַר צָפוֹן, וּבְהַהוּא אֲתָר נָעִיץ חַד רֵיחַיָּא, וּמֵעֵינָא דְּהַהוּא רֵיחַיָּא, נָפִיק חַד גְּבַר בִּתְרֵין רֵישִׁין, וְחַרְבָּא שִׁינָנָא בִּידֵיהּ וּבְכָל יוֹמָא קָא מְצַעֵר לָן. וַאֲנָא לָקִיטְנָא הַאי עִשְׂבָּא, וְזִילוּ אֲבַתְרָאי, וְתֶחֱמוּן חֵילֵיהּ דְּהַאי עִשְׂבָּא, וּמַה דִּי אֱלָהָא עִלָּאָה גַּלֵּי בְּעָלְמָא, וְלֵית מַאן דְּיֵדַע אָרְחוֹי. בְּכֹלָּא.

271. Now I will tell you of this herb you saw me cover with fig leaves. In a northern corner in my house there is a place in which there is a millstone from the hole of which a man with two heads emerges. He carries a sharp sword in his hands, and every day he distresses us. I gathered this herb on account of him. Now follow me and you shall see the power of this herb, and what the supreme Elohim has revealed in the world, and that there is no one that knows His ways.

272. אֲזִילְנָא אֲבַתְרֵיה, עַד דַּהֲוֵינָא אַזְלֵי בְּאָרְחָא, מָאִיךְ לְחַד נוּקְבָּא בְּעַפְרָא, וְשַׁוֵּי מֵהַהוּא עִשְׂבָּא בְּנוּקְבָּא, נָפַק חַד חִוְיָא וְרֵישָׁא דִּילֵיה סַגִּי. נָטַל חַד סַנְטִירָא, וְקָטִיר לֵיה כְּחַד גַּדְיָא. דָּחִילְנָא. אָמַר לוֹן זִילוּ אֲבַתְרָאי.

272. So we followed him. On the way to his house we saw him bending to a hole in the ground in which he deposited some of that herb, and a serpent with an enormous head issued. The man took a rope and bound the serpent as though it was a lamb. We were afraid, but the man told us to follow him.

273. עַד דְּמָטֵינָא לְבֵיתֵיה. חֲמֵינָא הַהוּא אֲתָר בַּחֲשׁוֹכָא, בָּתַר חַד כּוֹתְלָא. נָטַל חַד שְׁרַגָּא וְדָלִיק דְּלֵיקָא סַחֲרָנֵיה דְּהַהוּא אֲתָר דְּרֵיחַיָּא. אָמַר לוֹן, מִמַּה דְּתֶחֱמוּן לֹא תִּדְחֲלוּן וְלָא תִּשְׁתָּעוּן מִידֵי.

273. When we reached his house, we saw that place in the dark behind a wall. He took a candle and kindled a fire around that place of the millstone. Then he said to us: Do not be frightened at what you see and keep silent.

274. אַדְהָכִי, שָׁרֵי חִוְיָא מִקְּטְרוֹי, וְכָתַשׁ בְּקִיסְטָא מֵהַהוּא עִשְׂבָּא. וְשַׁוֵּי בְּרֵישֵׁיה דְּחִוְיָא. עָאל חִוְיָא בְּהַהוּא עֵינָא דְּרֵיחַיָּא, וּשְׁמַעְנָא קָלָא דְּכָל אֲתָר מִזְדַּעְזְעָא. בָּעֵינָן לְמֵיפַק, אָחִיד בִּידָנָא הַהוּא גַּבְרָא, אָמַר, לָא תִּדְחֲלוּן קְרִיבוּ גַּבָּאי.

274. While at that, he loosened the serpent's bonds and ground some of the herbs and sprinkled this upon the serpent's head. Then the serpent descended into the opening of that millstone and we heard a voice which caused the whole place to shake. We wanted to leave, but the man took hold of our hands saying: Fear not. Come close to me.

275. אַדְהָכִי, נָפַק חִוְיָא שָׁתִית דָּמָא, נָקִיט הַהוּא גַּבְרָא מֵהַהוּא עִשְׂבָּא, וְשַׁוֵּי בְּרֵישֵׁיה כִּבְקַדְמֵיתָא. עָאל בְּהַהוּא עֵינָא דְּרֵיחַיָּא. לְשַׁעֲתָא זְעֵירָא, חֲמֵינָא, דְּנָפִיק מֵהַהוּא עֵינָא חַד גַּבְרָא בִּתְרֵין רֵישִׁין, וְחִוְיָא שַׁרְיָא סַחֲרָנֵיה דְּקַדְלוֹי. עָאל בְּהַהוּא עֵינָא דְּרֵיחַיָּא וְנָפַק תְּלַת זִמְנֵי.

הוּא אָמַר, זְקִיטָא זְקִיטָא, וַוי לְאִימֵיה דִּלְהַהוּא אֲתָר אוֹבִיל לֵיה.

275. Meanwhile the serpent reappeared, and it was dripping blood. Again the man took some of that herb and sprinkled it upon the serpent's head. THE SERPENT entered the opening of that millstone. After a short time we saw a man with two heads came out from the millstone with a serpent wound about his neck. He come in and out of that millstone three times, saying: Chameleon, chameleon, woe to his mother who brought him to that place!

276. אַדְהָכִי, אִתְעֲקַר רֵיחַיָּא מֵאַתְרֵיה, וְנַפְקוּ, גַּבְרָא וְחִוְיָא, וְנָפְלוּ וּמִיתוּ תַּרְוַויְיהוּ. וַאֲנָן דָּחִילְנָא סַגִּי. אָמַר לוֹן הַהוּא גַּבְרָא, דָּא הוּא חֵילָא דְּעִשְׂבָּא דַּאֲנָא לָקִיטְנָא קָמַיְיכוּ, וּבְגִינֵי כַּךְ לָא אִשְׁתָּעֵינָא בַּהֲדַיְיכוּ, וְלָא זָקִיפְנָא רֵישָׁאי, בְּשַׁעֲתָא דְּקַרִיבְתּוּן גַּבָּאי.

276. Then the millstone was torn from its place and both the man and the serpent came out, fell down, and died. We were terrified. Then that man said: Thus is the power of the herb which I collected in your presence. This was the reason why I did not speak to you or raise my head when you approached me.

277. אָמַר לוֹן אִילוּ אִילוּ יַדְעִין בְּנֵי נָשָׁא חָכְמְתָא, דְּכָל מַה דְּנָטַע קוּדְשָׁא בְּרִיךְ הוּא בְּאַרְעָא, וְחֵילָא דְּכָל מַה דְּאִשְׁתְּכַח בְּעָלְמָא, יִשְׁתְּמוֹדְעוּן חֵילָא דְּמָארֵיהוֹן, בְּחָכְמְתֵיה סַגִּיאָה. אֲבָל לָא טָמִיר קב"ה חָכְמְתָא דָּא מִבְּנֵי נָשָׁא, אֶלָּא בְּגִין דְּלָא יִסְטוּן מֵאָרְחוֹי, וְלָא יִתְרַחֲצוּ בְּהַהִיא חָכְמְתָא וְיִנְשׁוּן לֵיה.

277. He said to us: If men only knew the wisdom of all that the Holy One, blessed be He, has planted in the earth, and all the power of all that which is to be found in the world, they would acknowledge the power of their Master in His great wisdom. But the Holy One, blessed be He, has purposely hidden this wisdom from men in order that they do not turn from His ways by trusting in that wisdom alone, thus forgetting Him.

278. כַּד אֲתֵינָא, וַאֲמֵינָא הָנֵי מִלֵּי קָמֵי דְּר"ש, אָמַר וַדַּאי חֲכִימָא הֲוָה.

וְת״ח, לֵית עִשְׂבָּא וְעִשְׂבָּא דְּאִתְיְילִיד בְּאַרְעָא, דְּלָא הֲוָה בֵּיהּ חָכְמְתָא
סַגִּיאָה, וְחֵילֵיהּ בִּשְׁמַיָּא סַגְיָא. תָּא חֲזֵי, מִן אֵזוֹבָא. דִּבְכָל אֲתָר דְּבָעֵי
קוּדְשָׁא בְּרִיךְ הוּא לְדַכָּאָה לְב״נ, בְּאֵזוֹבָא מִתְדְּכֵי. מ״ט. מִשּׁוּם דְּיִתְּעַר
חֵילֵיהּ דִּלְעֵילָא דְּאִתְפָּקְדָא עֲלוֹי, דְּהָא הַהוּא חֵילָא דְּאִתְפָּקְדָא עֲלוֹי
כַּד אִתְּעָרָא, מְבַעֲרָא רוּחַ מְסָאֲבָא, וְאִתְדְּכֵי בַּר נָשׁ. וְעָלָךְ אֲמֵינָא בְּרִיךְ
רַחֲמָנָא דְּשֵׁזְבָךְ.

278. When I came and recounted those things to Rabbi Shimon, he said: Surely that was a wise man, for observe that there is no grass or herb that grows on the earth in which much wisdom and great power in heaven is not manifested. Come and observe this from the hyssop, for whenever the Holy One, blessed be He, desires that men purify themselves, they have to do it by the hyssop. What is the reason? To arouse that power above that is appointed over, for when it is aroused, it exterminates the Spirit of Impurity and the defiled person is cleansed. And to you I say: Blessed be the Merciful One who delivered you.

16. "on eagles' wings"

A Synopsis

"You have seen what I did to Egypt and how I bore you on eagles' wings." This section tells us by way of analogy with the eagle that God is merciful to His own children, but uses severe judgment with the heathen nations. In the vision of Ezekiel the face of man includes the face of a lion and the face of an ox, with the face of the eagle – mercy – between them and combining them.

279. אַתֶּם רְאִיתֶם אֲשֶׁר עָשִׂיתִי לְמִצְרַיִם וָאֶשָּׂא אֶתְכֶם עַל כַּנְפֵי נְשָׁרִים. מַאי כַּנְפֵי נְשָׁרִים. א"ר יְהוּדָה בְּרַחֲמֵי. דִּכְתִיב כְּנֶשֶׁר יָעִיר קִנּוֹ וְגוֹ'. וְהַיְינוּ רָזָא דְּאָמַר ר' שִׁמְעוֹן, דֶּרֶךְ הַנֶּשֶׁר בַּשָּׁמַיִם. מַאי בַּשָּׁמַיִם. בְּרַחֲמֵי. מַה נֶּשֶׁר אִשְׁתְּכַח בְּרַחֲמֵי עַל בְּנוֹי, וְדִינָא לְגַבֵּי אַחֲרָנִין. כָּךְ קוּדְשָׁא בְּרִיךְ הוּא אִשְׁתְּכַח בְּרַחֲמֵי לְגַבֵּי יִשְׂרָאֵל, וְדִינָא לְגַבֵּי עַמִּין עעכו"ם.

279. "You have seen what I did to Egypt and how I bore you on eagles' wings" (Shemot 19:4). What does "eagles' wings" mean? Rabbi Yehuda said that "eagles' wings" means Mercy, as it is written in the verse: "As an eagle stirs up her nest" (Devarim 32:11), MEANING THAT "AN EAGLE" SIGNIFIES MERCY. And this is the secret in Rabbi Shimon's words: "The way of the vultures in the air" (Mishlei 30:19). "...in the air..." means with Mercy, FOR ZEIR ANPIN IS CALLED 'HEAVEN' AND HAS MERCY, FOR CHESED, GVURAH AND TIFERET ARE JUDGMENT AND MERCY. As the eagle watches mercifully over its own young but is cruel toward others, so is the Holy One, blessed be He, merciful towards Yisrael but judges the heathen nations severly.

280. ר' אֶלְעָזָר, הֲוָה אָזִיל מִקַפּוֹטְקִיָּא לְלוּד, וַהֲוָה אָזִיל ר' יוֹסֵי וְר' חִיָּיא עִמֵּיהּ, קָמוּ בִּנְהוֹרָא, כַּד נָהִיר יְמָמָא, וַהֲווֹ אַזְלֵי. אָמַר ר' חִיָּיא, חֲמֵינָא הַאי קְרָא דִּכְתִיב, וּפְנֵי אַרְיֵה אֶל הַיָּמִין לְאַרְבַּעְתָּן וּפְנֵי שׁוֹר מֵהַשְּׂמֹאל לְאַרְבַּעְתָּן וּפְנֵי נֶשֶׁר לְאַרְבַּעְתָּן הָא אַרְיֵה בִּימִינָא, שׁוֹר מִשְּׂמָאלָא, נֶשֶׁר בְּאָן אֲתַר דּוּכְתֵּיהּ.

280. Rabbi Elazar was once going from Cappadocia to Lod accompanied by

Rabbi Yosi and Rabbi Chiya. They had risen at sunrise and as the light appeared they started to walk. Rabbi Chiya said: I see the vision which is described in the verse, "And they four had the face of a lion, on the right side and they four had the face of an ox, on the left side, they four also had the face of an eagle" (Yechezkel 1:10), AND I WONDER, if the lion is on the right side and the ox is on the left one, where is the place of the eagle?

281. אָמַר לֵיהּ ר' אֶלְעָזָר, בְּאַתְרָא דְּיַעֲקֹב שַׁרְיָא. מ"ט. מִשּׁוּם דְּנֶשֶׁר בְּכֹלָּא אִשְׁתְּכַח, רַחֲמֵי לִבְנוֹי, דִּינָא לְגַבֵּי אַחֲרָנִין. כָּךְ קוּדְשָׁא בְּרִיךְ הוּא, אוֹבִיל לוֹן לְיִשְׂרָאֵל בְּרַחֲמֵי. וּבְדִינָא לְגַבֵּי אַחֲרָנִין, דִּכְתִיב וָאֶשָּׂא אֶתְכֶם עַל כַּנְפֵי נְשָׁרִים. וּכְתִיב כְּנֶשֶׁר יָעִיר קִנּוֹ.

281. Rabbi Elazar replied: Its place is where Jacob is, MEANING THE CENTRAL COLUMN. The reason for this is that the eagle combines everything, BOTH MERCY AND JUDGMENT – Mercy to its own young and Judgment to the others. So the Holy One, blessed be He, THE SECRET OF THE CENTRAL COLUMN, led Yisrael with love and dealt sternly with others, as it is written: "And bore you on eagles' wings," and, "As an eagle stirs up her nest."

282. מְנָלָן דְּנֶשֶׁר רַחֲמֵי אִקְרֵי. דִּכְתִיב דֶּרֶךְ הַנֶּשֶׁר בַּשָּׁמַיִם. בַּשָּׁמַיִם מַמָּשׁ. וּבְגִינֵי כָּךְ אַרְיֵה לִימִינָא. שׁוֹר לִשְׂמָאלָא. נֶשֶׁר בֵּינַיְיהוּ וְאָחִיד לוֹן. אָדָם כָּלִיל כֻּלְּהוּ, וְכֹלָּא אִתְכְּלִילָן בֵּיהּ, דִּכְתִיב וְעַל דְּמוּת הַכִּסֵּא דְּמוּת כְּמַרְאֵה אָדָם עָלָיו מִלְמַעְלָה.

282. We can learn that an eagle signifies Mercy, for it is written: "The way of the vultures (lit. 'eagle') in the air (lit. 'heaven')," actually 'in heaven', WHICH IS ZEIR ANPIN, THE PROPRIETOR OF MERCY. Therefore, the lion is on the right and the ox on the left, and the eagle is between them and combines both of them. "THE FACE OF a man" includes all of them and in it they are all comprised, FOR HE IS THE ASPECT OF MALCHUT WHICH RECEIVES FROM ALL OF THEM, as it is written: "Upon the likeness of the throne was the likeness as the appearance of a man above upon it" (Ibid. 26).

17. "And it came to pass, on the third day"

A Synopsis

The theme of mercy and judgment is continued in this section. Good deeds are necessary to deserve mercy, and this idea is explored through looking at the verse, "We have a little sister and she has no breasts, what shall we do for our sister in the day when she shall be spoken for." The "third day" of the title verse refers to Tiferet, that is Mercy.

283. וַיְהִי בַיּוֹם הַשְּׁלִישִׁי וְגוֹ'. ר' אַבָּא פָּתַח, אָחוֹת לָנוּ קְטַנָּה וְשָׁדַיִם אֵין לָהּ מַה נַּעֲשֶׂה לַאֲחוֹתֵנוּ בַּיּוֹם שֶׁיְּדוּבַּר בָּהּ. אָחוֹת לָנוּ קְטַנָּה, דָּא כְּנֶסֶת יִשְׂרָאֵל, דְּאִקְרֵי אָחוֹת לְקוּדְשָׁא בְּרִיךְ הוּא. וְשָׁדַיִם אֵין לָהּ, הַיְינוּ דְּתָנֵינָן, בְּשַׁעֲתָא דְּקָרִיבוּ יִשְׂרָאֵל לְטוּרָא דְּסִינַי, לָא הֲוָה בְּהוֹן זַכְוָון, וְעוֹבָדִין טָבִין, לְאַגָּנָא עָלַיְיהוּ, דִּכְתִיב וְשָׁדַיִם אֵין לָהּ. דְּהָא אִינוּן תִּקּוּנָא וְשַׁפִּירוּ דְּאִתְּתָא, וְלֵית שַׁפִּירוּ דְּאִתְּתָא אֶלָּא אִינוּן. מַה נַּעֲשֶׂה לַאֲחוֹתֵנוּ. מַה יִתְעֲבִיד מִינָּהּ, בְּשַׁעֲתָא דְּקוּדְשָׁא בְּרִיךְ הוּא, יִתְגְּלֵי בְּטוּרָא דְּסִינַי, לְמַלְּלָא בְּפִתְגָמֵי אוֹרַיְיתָא, וְיִפְרַח נִשְׁמָתְהוֹן מִנַּיְיהוּ.

283. "And it came to pass, on the third day" (Shemot 19:16). Rabbi Aba opened the discussion with the verse: "We have a little sister and she has no breasts, what shall we do for our sister in the day when she shall be spoken for" (Shir Hashirim 8:8). "A little sister" is the Congregation of Yisrael, which is called 'the sister of the Holy One, blessed be He'. "She has no breasts" is as we have learned, that when Yisrael approached Mount Sinai, they had in them no merits or good deeds to protect them, as it is written: "she has no breasts" – for they are the beauty of a woman, and a woman's beauty comes from them alone. "What shall we do for our sister," that is, what will be done with them when the Holy One, blessed be He, reveals Himself on Mount Sinai to proclaim the words of the Torah, for their souls will fly away from them.

284. אָמַר ר' יוֹסֵי. בְּהַהוּא שַׁעֲתָא דְּקָרִיבוּ יִשְׂרָאֵל לְטוּרָא דְּסִינַי, בְּהַהוּא לֵילְיָא וְנַגְהֵי, תְּלָתָא יוֹמִין דְּלָא אִזְדַּוְּוגוּ לְאִנְתְּתַיְיהוּ, אָתוּ מַלְאָכִין עִלָּאִין, וְקַבִּילוּ לְיִשְׂרָאֵל בְּאַחְוָותָא. אִינוּן מַלְאָכִין לְעֵילָּא,

וְיִשְׂרָאֵל מַלְאָכִין לְתַתָּא. אִינּוּן מְקַדְּשִׁין שְׁמָא עִלָּאָה לְעֵילָּא, וְיִשְׂרָאֵל מְקַדְּשִׁין שְׁמָא עִלָּאָה לְתַתָּא.

284. Rabbi Yosi said: At the time Yisrael approached Mount Sinai, together with that night and the following morning, it was three days altogether during which the people abstained from conjugal intercourse with their wives. The holy angels came and received them with fraternity, for they are angels above and Yisrael are angels below; they sanctify the Supreme Name above, while Yisrael sanctify the Supreme Name below.

285. וְאִתְעַטְּרוּ יִשְׂרָאֵל בְּשַׁבְעִין כִּתְרִין בְּהַהוּא לֵילְיָא. וּמַלְאֲכֵי עִלָּאֵי הֲווֹ אַמְרֵי אָחוֹת לָנוּ קְטַנָּה וְשָׁדַיִם אֵין לָהּ, דְּלֵית בְּהוּ זַכְוָון וְעוֹבָדִין טָבִין. מַה נַּעֲשֶׂה לַאֲחוֹתֵנוּ, כְּלוֹמַר מַה יְקָר וְרִבּוּ נַעֲבִיד לַאֲחַתְנָא דָּא בְּיוֹמָא דְּקוּדְשָׁא בְּרִיךְ הוּא יִתְגְּלֵי בְּטוּרָא דְּסִינַי לְמֵיהַב לְהוּ אוֹרַיְיתָא.

285. And Yisrael were crowned with seventy crowns on that night. Then the supernal angels said: "'We have a little sister and she has no breasts,'" for they have no merits and good deeds, so "what shall we do for our sister?" That is, how shall we honor her on the day when the Holy One, blessed be He, reveals Himself on Mount Sinai to give them the Torah?

286. וַיְהִי בַיּוֹם הַשְּׁלִישִׁי, כְּתִיב הֱיוּ נְכוֹנִים לִשְׁלֹשֶׁת יָמִים אַל תִּגְּשׁוּ אֶל אִשָּׁה וְהָיִינוּ בַיּוֹם הַשְּׁלִישִׁי. ר׳ שִׁמְעוֹן אָמַר, בְּשַׁעֲתָא דְּקוּדְשָׁא בְּרִיךְ הוּא בָּעָא לְאִתְגַּלָּאָה בְּטוּרָא דְּסִינַי, קָרָא קוּדְשָׁא בְּרִיךְ הוּא לְכָל פָּמַלְיָיא דִּילֵיהּ, אָמַר לוֹן, הַשְׁתָּא יִשְׂרָאֵל רַבְיָין, דְּלָא יַדְעִין נִימוּסֵי, וַאֲנָא בָּעֵי לְאִתְגְּלֵי עֲלַיְיהוּ, אִי אִתְגְּלֵי עֲלַיְיהוּ בְּחֵילָא דִּגְבוּרָה, לָא יַכְלִין לְמִסְבַּל. אֲבָל אִתְגְּלֵי עֲלַיְיהוּ בְּרַחֲמֵי, וִיקַבְּלוּן נִימוּסֵי, הה״ד, וַיְהִי בַיּוֹם הַשְּׁלִישִׁי. בַּיּוֹם הַשְּׁלִישִׁי וַדַּאי דְּאִיהוּ רַחֲמֵי מְנָלָן. דִּכְתִיב, וַיֵּט שָׁמַיִם וַיֵּרַד.

286. It is written: "Be ready by the third day, come not near a woman," (Shemot 19:15) and, "And it came to pass, on the third day." Rabbi Shimon said that at the time that the Holy One, blessed be He, desired to be revealed

on Mount Sinai, He gathered all His retinue and told them: 'Now Yisrael are like children who do not know My commandments, and I desire to be revealed before them with Mercy, and they will accept My Law.' Therefore it is written: "And it came to pass on the third day." Indeed, the manifestation took place on the third day, FOR IT IS THE DAY OF TIFERET, which is Mercy. And how do we know all that? It is written: "He bowed the heavens also, and came down" (II Shmuel 22:10), AND "HEAVENS" ARE TIFERET, WHICH IS MERCY, AS IS EXPLAINED ABOVE.

287. וּבְהַאי אִתְגְּלֵי קוּדְשָׁא בְּרִיךְ הוּא לְיִשְׂרָאֵל, אַקְדִּים לְהוּ רַחֲמֵי בְּקַדְמֵיתָא. וּלְבָתַר אִתְיְיהִיב לְהוּ אוֹרַיְיתָא, מִסִּטְרָא דִּגְבוּרָה. בְּיוֹם הַשְּׁלִישִׁי, דְּהָכִי אִתְחֲזֵי לְהוּ, דִּבְגִינֵי כַּךְ יִשְׂרָאֵל אִקְרוּן.

287. When the Holy One, blessed be He, revealed Himself before Yisrael, He extended Mercy at first and afterwards He gave them the Torah, from the side of Gvurah, on the third day. THUS, THEY INCLUDED BOTH MERCY AND JUDGMENT, as is appropriate for them. Hence, they are called 'Yisrael', FOR THE NAME 'YISAREL' CONSTITUTES MERCY AND JUDGMENT.

288. בִּהְיוֹת הַבֹּקֶר, דִּכְתִיב, בֹּקֶר לֹא עָבוֹת. הָא אִי הֲוָה עָבוֹת קַדְרוּתָא אִשְׁתְּכַח, וְלָא אִתְגַּלְיָיא חֶסֶ"ד. וְאֵימָתַי אִתְגַּלְיָיא חֶסֶ"ד. בַּבֹּקֶר. כד"א, הַבֹּקֶר אוֹר. דְּכַד נָהִיר צַפְרָא, חֶסֶ"ד אִשְׁתְּכַח בְּעָלְמָא, וְדִינִין מִתְעַבְּרָן. וּבְזִמְנָא דְּלָא נָהִיר בֹּקֶר, דִּינִין עַד כְּעַן לָא מִתְעַבְּרָן. דִּכְתִיב, בְּרָן יַחַד כֹּכְבֵי בֹקֶר וַיָּרִיעוּ כָּל בְּנֵי אֱלֹהִים. כֵּיוָן דְּאִתְעַבְּרָן אִינוּן כֹּכְבַיָּא וְנָהִיר שִׁמְשָׁא, בֵּיהּ שַׁעֲתָא כְּתִיב, בֹּקֶר לֹא עָבוֹת. וְחֶסֶ"ד אִתְעַר בְּעָלְמָא תַּתָּאָה, בְּהַהִיא שַׁעֲתָא כְּתִיב, בִּהְיוֹת הַבֹּקֶר. וְכֵיוָן דְּמִתְעַבְּרָן כֹּכְבַיָּא בֹּקֶר אִשְׁתְּכַח.

288. "When morning came." It is written: "In a morning without clouds" (II Shmuel 23:4), for if it was a cloudy morning, there would have been darkness in it and Chesed would not have been revealed. And when does Chesed reveal itself? In the morning, as it is written: "the morning was light" (Beresheet 44:3). Thus, as soon as the day breaks, Chesed is present in the world and Judgments are removed, but when the light of the morning

does not enter, Judgments are not removed, as it is written: "When the morning stars sang together and all the sons of Elohim shouted for joy" (Iyov 37:7), as soon as the stars fade away and the sun shines at that time, as it is written: "A morning without clouds." And Chesed is awakened in the lower world at that time, it is written: "When morning came," since the stars disappeared and morning appeared.

289. אָמַר ר' יוֹסֵי, בִּהְיוֹת הַבֹּקֶר שָׁארֵי קוּדְשָׁא בְּרִיךְ הוּא לְאִתְגַּלָּאָה בְּטוּרָא דְּסִינַי. תָּאנָא, בִּהְיוֹת הַבֹּקֶר, כַּד אִתְּעַר זְכוּתֵיה דְּאַבְרָהָם, דִּכְתִיב בֵּיה וַיַּשְׁכֵּם אַבְרָהָם בַּבֹּקֶר.

289. Rabbi Yosi said that "When morning came," the Holy One, blessed be He, started to reveal Himself on Mount Sinai. We learned that, "When morning came," means when the merit of Abraham is awakened, of whom it is written: "And Abraham went early in the morning" (Beresheet 19:26).

18. "There were thunders and lightnings"

A Synopsis

The rabbis offer various ideas about "voices." One of them says that it means two voices – water and wind – which became one; one of them says that it is one voice that never ceases; one of them says that it comes from three – wind, water and fire. The discussion moves to lightning and then to the "fiery law" that is the Torah. And we learn that the sound of the Shofar came forth to break the heavy dark cloud.

290. וַיְהִי קֹלת וּבְרָקִים, אָמַר רַבִּי אַבָּא, קֹלת כְּתִיב חָסֵר. תְּרֵין קָלִין דְּאַהֲדָרוּ לְחָד, דָּא נָפְקָא מִן דָּא, רוּחָא מִמַּיָּא. וּמַיָּא מֵרוּחָא. תְּרֵין דְּאִינּוּן חַד, וְחַד דְּאִיהוּ תְּרֵי.

290. "There were thunders (Heb. *kolot*) and lightnings" (Shemot 19:16). Rabbi Aba said that "*kolot*" is spelled without *VAV*, THE INDICATION OF THE PLURAL FORM, signifying that there were two thunders (lit. 'voices') that became one again, one emanating from the other – wind from water and water from wind, two that are one, and one that is two. THEREFORE THE WORD "*KOLOT*" IS WRITTEN WITHOUT *VAV*.

291. אָמַר רַבִּי יוֹסֵי, קֹלת חַד, וְאִיהוּ קָלָא רַבְרְבָא תַּקִּיפָא, דְּלָא פַּסְקַת לְעָלְמִין, הַהוּא דִּכְתִיב בֵּיהּ קוֹל גָּדוֹל וְלֹא יָסַף דְּהָא שְׁאָר קָלִין אִתְפַּסְּקָן, דְּתַנְיָא, בְּאַרְבְּעָה תְּקוּפִין בַּשַׁתָּא, קָלָא אִתְפַּסְּקַת, וּכְדֵין דִּינִין מִתְעָרִין בְּעָלְמָא. וְהַאי קָלָא דְּכָלִיל שְׁאָר קָלִין בֵּיהּ, לָא אִתְפְּסַק לְעָלְמִין, וְלָא אִתְעֲבַר מִקִּיּוּמָא שְׁלִים וְתוּקְפָּא דִּילֵיהּ. תָּאנָא, הַאי קָלָא, קָלָא דְּקָלִין, קָלָא דְּכָלִיל כָּל שְׁאָר קָלִין.

291. Rabbi Yosi said: "kolot," MEANS one; this voice is a great and strong one which never ceases, as it is written: "A great voice which was not heard again" (Devarim 5:19). This is because all the other voices do cease. As we learned, four times a year the voice ceases, and then Judgments are awakened in the world. But this voice, which includes the other voices, never ceases and never abates of its full existence and force. We have learned that this voice is the voice of voices, the voice which contains all other voices.

‎292. אָמַר ר' יְהוּדָה, לֵית קָלָא, אֶלָּא מִסִּטְרָא דְרוּחָא וּמַיָּא וְאֶשָּׁא. וְכֹלָּא עָבֵיד קָלָא, וְאִתְכְּלִיל דָּא בְּדָא, וְעַ"ד כְּתִיב קֹלֹת. וּבְרָקִים, א"ר יוֹסֵי, הַיְינוּ דִכְתִיב, בְּרָקִים לַמָּטָר עָשָׂה שֶׁלְּהוֹבָא בְּעוּטְרֵי, קְטִירָא דְרַחֲמֵי בְּחִיבָּתָא, דְלָא שְׁכִיחוּ.

292. Rabbi Yehuda said: There is no voice but the one which comes from wind, water and fire, THAT ARE THE THREE COLUMNS. And all this the voice performs, WHICH IS THE CENTRAL COLUMN. AND BY IT, THE COLUMNS are included in each other AND BECOME ONE. Therefore, the word "kolot" is spelled WITHOUT VAV, THE INDICATION OF THE PLURAL FORM. "…and lightning…": Rabbi Yosi cited that verse and explained: "He makes lightning for the rain" (Tehilim 135:7), MEANING THAT "LIGHTNING" IS THE COMBINATION OF FIRE AND WATER, AS LIGHTNING IN THE RAIN — for the flame OF THE LIGHTNING in the rain INDICATES THAT IT IS a union of Mercy with infrequent love.

‎293. תָּנָא, ר' יְהוּדָה אוֹמֵר, בְּסִטָר גְּבוּרָה, אוֹרַיְיתָא אִתְיְיהִיבַת. אָמַר רַבִּי יוֹסֵי, אִי הָכִי בְּסִטָר שְׂמָאלָא הֲוֵי. אָמַר לֵיהּ, אִתְהַדַּר לִימִינָא. דִּכְתִיב מִימִינוֹ אֵשׁ דָּת לָמוֹ. וּכְתִיב יְמִינְךָ יְיָ' נֶאְדָּרִי בַּכֹּחַ וְגוֹ'. אַשְׁכְּחָן שְׂמָאלָא דְּאִתְחֲזַר לִימִינָא, וִימִינָא לִשְׂמָאלָא, הָא גְּבוּרָה לִימִינָא.

293. Rabbi Yehuda said: We have learned that the Torah was given from the side of Gvurah. Rabbi Yosi said: In that case THE TORAH must be of the left side. He said: It returned to the right, as it is written: "From His right hand went a fiery law for them" (Devarim 33:2), and: "Your right hand, Hashem, is glorious in power" (Shemot 15:6). So we see that the left is included within the right, FOR IT IS WRITTEN: "FROM HIS RIGHT HAND A FIERY LAW FOR THEM"; and the right is included within the left FOR IT IS WRITTEN: "YOUR RIGHT HAND, HASHEM, IS GLORIOUS IN POWER." Thus, Gvurah, WHICH IS THE LEFT, is included within the right.

‎294. וְעָנָן כָּבֵד עַל הָהָר וְגוֹ', עֲנָנָא תַּקִּיף, דְּשַׁקִּיעַ בְּאַתְרֵיהּ, דְלָא נָטִיל. וְקֹל שֹׁפָר חָזָק מְאֹד, מִגּוֹ דַּעֲנָנָא תַּקִּיף הֲוָה, נָפִיק הַהוּא קָלָא, כד"א וַיְהִי כְּשָׁמְעֲכֶם אֶת הַקּוֹל מִתּוֹךְ הַחֹשֶׁךְ.

294. "And a heavy cloud upon the mountain" (Shemot 19:16) meaning, a very mighty cloud stuck in one place BECAUSE OF ITS HEAVINESS that does not move FROM PLACE TO PLACE AS DO OTHER CLOUDS. "And the sound of a shofar exceedingly loud" (Ibid.); that sound was very strong, for it issued from the midst of the heavy cloud IN ORDER TO BREAK IT, as it is written: "When you heard the voice out of the midst of the darkness" (Devarim 5:20).

295. אָמַר רַבִּי יְהוּדָה, תְּלַת חֲשׁוֹכֵי הֲווֹ, דִּכְתִיב חשֶׁךְ עָנָן וַעֲרָפֶל. וְהַהוּא קָלָא הֲוָה נָפִיק פְּנִימָאָה מִכֻּלְּהוּ. אָמַר רַבִּי יוֹסֵי, פְּנִימָאָה דְּכֹלָּא הֲוָה, דְּבֵיהּ כְּתִיב, קוֹל גָּדוֹל וְלֹא יָסָף.

295. Rabbi Yehuda said: There were three kinds of darkness, for it is written, "darkness, clouds and thick darkness" (Devarim 4:11). And that voice, NAMELY, THE VOICE OF THE SHOFAR, came forth as the innermost depths. Rabbi Yosi said that the innermost of all of them was THE VOICE of which it is written: "A great voice which was not heard again."

19. "and all the people saw the voices"

A Synopsis

Here the experience where Moses talked face to face with God on Mount Sinai is compared to Ezekiel's visions. It is pointed out that Ezekiel saw the Shechinah and the hand of God, but Moses was greater because he saw the head and body of Zeir Anpin. All the people who were on the mountain literally "saw the voice" as it was carved out of darkness, cloud and fog – and figuratively they saw what no one in succeeding generations would ever again see until the time of Messiah, and that was the supernal illumination that showed them all hidden and veiled knowledge.

296. אָמַר ר' אַבָּא כְּתִיב וְכָל הָעָם רֹאִים אֶת הַקּוֹלֹת. רֹאִים, שְׁמְעִים מִבָּעֵי לֵיהּ. אֶלָּא הָכִי תָּנֵינָן, אִינּוּן קָלִין, הֲווֹ מִתְגַּלְּפֵי בְּהַהוּא חֲשׁוֹכָא וַעֲנָנָא וְקַבָּלָא, וּמִתְחַזְיָין בְּהוֹ, כְּמָה דְאִתְחֲזֵי גּוּפָא, וְחָמָאן מַה דְחָמָאן, וְשַׁמְעִין מַה דְּשַׁמְעִין, מִגּוֹ הַהוּא חֲשׁוֹכָא וְקַבָּלָא וַעֲנָנָא, וּמִגּוֹ הַהוּא חֵיזוּ דַּהֲווֹ חָמָאן, הֲווֹ נְהִירִין בִּנְהִירוּ עִלָּאָה, וְיַדְעִין, מַה דְּלָא יָדְעוּ דָרִין אַחֲרָנִין, דְּאָתוּ בַּתְרַיְיהוּ.

296. Rabbi Aba said: It is written, "And all the people perceived the thunderings (lit. 'saw the voices')" (Shemot 20:15). HE ASKS: WHY IS IT WRITTEN "see," rather than 'hear'? AND HE ANSWERS that we have already learned that those voices were carved out upon the darkness, cloud and the fog, visible as a body is. And they saw whatever it was they saw, and heard what they heard from within the darkness, cloud and fog. And because they saw that sight they were illuminated with a supernal illumination and knew things beyond the understanding of all other generations to come.

297. וְכֻלְּהוּ, הֲווֹ חָמָאן אַפִּין בְּאַפִּין, הה"ד, פָּנִים בְּפָנִים דִּבֶּר יְיָ' עִמָּכֶם. וּמַאן הֲווֹ חָמָאן. תָּאנֵי רַבִּי יוֹסֵי, מִנְּהִירוּ דְּאִינּוּן קַלָּן, דְּלָא הֲוָה קוֹל, דְּלָא הֲוָה נָהִיר בִּנְהִירוּ, דְּמִסְתַּכְּלֵי בֵּיהּ כָּל גְּנִיזִין, וְכָל טְמִירִין, וְכָל דָרִין דְּיֵיתוּן עַד מַלְכָּא מְשִׁיחָא. וּבְגִינֵי כַּךְ כְּתִיב וְכָל הָעָם רֹאִים אֶת הַקּוֹלֹת, רֹאִים רְאִיָּה מַמָּשׁ.

297. All of them saw face to face, as it is written: "Hashem talked with you

face to face" (Devarim 5:4). And what did they see? Rabbi Yosi explains: From the illumination of those voices, as there was not a voice that did not shine, they could see all things hidden and veiled which will never be revealed to succeeding generations until the days of King Messiah. Therefore it is written: "And all the people see the voices," for they actually saw.

298. אָמַר רַבִּי אֶלְעָזָר, וְכָל הָעָם רֹאִים. רֹאִים: כְּמָה דַּאֲמֵינָא, דְּחָמוּ מִנְּהִירוּ דְּאִינּוּן קַלָּן, מַה דְּלָא חָמוּ דָּרִין בַּתְרָאִין אַחֲרָנִין. אֶת הַקּוֹלֹת: כד״א, וָאֶרְאֶה אֶת יי׳. וָאֶרְאֶה יי׳, לָא כְּתִיב, אֶלָּא אֶת יי׳. אוּף הָכָא, וְכָל הָעָם רֹאִים הַקּוֹלֹת לֹא נֶאֱמַר, אֶלָּא אֶת הַקּוֹלֹת.

298. Rabbi Elazar said: "And all the people see" means, as we have said, that they saw all those wonderful things that no generation after will ever see, by means of the illumination of those voices. "...the voices..." has the same meaning as in the verse: "I saw Hashem" (Yeshayah 6:1). It is written: "Hashem" preceded by the particle *Et*, WHICH MEANS THAT HE SAW THE SHECHINAH WHICH IS CALLED '*ET*'. In this verse too it is written: "And all the people see the voices," with the particle *Et* (lit. 'the'), TO INDICATE THAT THEY SAW THE SHECHINAH.

299. כְּגַוְונָא דָא, אֶת הַשָּׁמַיִם וְאֶת הָאָרֶץ, דְּהָא אָתִין דִּבְאוֹרַיְיתָא, לְאִסְתַּכְּלָא בְּחָכְמְתָא אִתְיְיהִיבוּ. כַּבֵּד אֶת אָבִיךָ וְאֶת אִמֶּךָ כַּבֵּד אֶת יי׳ מֵהוֹנֶךָ. וְכֻלְּהוּ לְאִתְכְּלָלָא בְּהוּ מִלָּה אַחֲרָא. אוּף הָכָא, אֶת הַקּוֹלֹת, לְאַסְגָּאָה הַהוּא קָלָא אַחֲרָא לְתַתָּא, דְּכָנִישׁ לוֹן לְגַבֵּיהּ, מַה דְּנָפִיק מִנַּיְיהוּ, דְּבֵיהּ חָמָאן וּמִסְתַּכְּלָן בְּחָכְמְתָא עִלָּאָה כָּל גִּנְזִין עִלָּאִין, וְכָל רָזִין טְמִירִין וּסְתִימִין, מַה דְּלָא אִתְגַּלְיָיא לְדָרִין בַּתְרָאִין, דְּאָתוּ בַּתְרַיְיהוּ, וְלָא לְדָרִין דְּיֵיתוּן לְעָלְמִין, עַד זִמְנָא דְּיֵיתֵי מַלְכָּא מְשִׁיחָא. דִּכְתִיב, כִּי עַיִן בְּעַיִן יִרְאוּ בְּשׁוּב יי׳ צִיּוֹן. וְאֶת הַלַּפִּידִים, בְּקַדְמֵיתָא בְּרָקִים, וְהַשְׁתָּא לַפִּידִים. כֹּלָּא חַד. אֲבָל מִדְּאִתְתַּקְּנוּ בְּתִקּוּנוֹי לְאִתְחֲזָאָה, אִתְקְרוּן הָכִי.

299. In the same manner we can explain the verse: "the heaven and the earth" (Beresheet 1:1), for all the "*Et* (lit. 'the')" particles mentioned in the

Torah enable us to have the perception of wisdom – as in the verse: "Honor (*et*) your father and (*et*) your mother" (Shemot 20:12) and the verse, "Honor (*et*) Hashem with your substance" (Mishlei 3:8). These verses ARE EXPLAINED as including something in addition. Here too, "the voices" include that other voice below, WHICH IS MALCHUT, which gathers into itself the other voices and that which emerges from them. In it, IN MALCHUT, the people saw and beheld, through sublime Wisdom, all the celestial treasures and all the hidden mysteries which were never revealed to succeeding generations or to any far away generations, and will not be revealed until the days of King Messiah. As it is written: "For they shall see eye to eye Hashem returning to Zion" (Yeshayah 52:8). HE ASKS: Why is "the lightning" called first "lightning (Heb. *berakim*)," (Shemot 19:16) and afterwards "lightning (Heb. *lapidim*)"? AND HE ANSWERS that both of them have one meaning, for when THE *BERAKIM* are quite formed and ready to appear, they are called *LAPIDIM*.

300. וְאֵת קוֹל הַשּׁוֹפָר. תָּאנֵי רַבִּי יִצְחָק, כְּתִיב אַחַת דִּבֶּר אֱלֹהִים שְׁתַּיִם זוּ שָׁמַעְתִּי, כד"א, אָנֹכִי, וְלֹא יִהְיֶה לְךָ.

300. "…the sound in the Shofar…" (Shemot 20:15). Rabbi Yitzchak says: It is written, "Elohim has spoken once: twice have I heard this" (Tehilim 62:12). This is similar to: "I am Hashem your Elohim," and, "You shall not make for yourself" (Shemot 20:2). "I AM" SIGNIFIES THE SECRET OF BINAH, AND "YOU SHALL NOT MAKE FOR YOURSELF" SIGNIFIES THE SECRET OF ZEIR ANPIN, AND BOTH OF THEM WERE UTTERED AT ONCE. IN THIS VERSE, TOO, THE SOUND IS ZEIR ANPIN AND THE SHOFAR IS BINAH, AND BOTH WERE UTTERED AT THE SAME TIME.

301. א"ר יְהוּדָה, קֹל בַּשּׁוֹפָר מִבָּעֵי לֵיהּ. הַשּׁוֹפָר לָמָה. אֶלָּא, הַהוּא קוֹל דְּאִקְרֵי שׁוֹפָר. דִּכְתִיב, וְהַעֲבַרְתָּ שׁוֹפַר תְּרוּעָה בַּחֹדֶשׁ הַשְּׁבִיעִי בֶּעָשׂוֹר לַחֹדֶשׁ בְּיוֹם הַכִּפּוּרִים, בְּדָא אִתְקְרֵי שׁוֹפָר.

301. Rabbi Yehuda said: It should have said 'the sound in the Shofar'; why DOES IT SAY "of the Shofar"? AND HE ANSWERS: That voice was called 'Shofar', as in the verse: "Then shall you cause the Shofar to sound on the tenth day of the seventh month, on the Day of Atonement" (Vayikra 25:9). On that YOM KIPPUR (DAY OF ATONEMENT) it is called 'Shofar', MEANING

THAT WHEN THE SOUND ISSUES FROM BINAH, THE SOUND IS CALLED 'SHOFAR'.

302. א״ר יוֹסֵי, מַה שׁוֹפָר, אַפִּיק קָלָא, אֶשָּׁא וְרוּחָא וּמַיָּא, אוּף הָכָא, כֹּלָּא אִתְכְּלִיל בְּהַאי, וּמִדָּא נָפְקִין קָלִין אַחֲרָנִין.

302. Rabbi Yosi said: As the PHYSICAL Shofar makes a sound WHICH INCLUDES fire, air and water, here too everything is included in it, FOR HERE IN THE SOUND THAT COMES OUT FROM THE SHOFAR, FIRE, WIND AND WATER ARE INCLUDED – WHICH ARE CHESED, GVURAH AND TIFERET, THE SECRET OF THE THREE COLUMNS. And from this sound other sounds emerge.

303. א״ר אֶלְעָזָר, קוֹל דְּנָפִיק מִשּׁוֹפָר, דְּמַשְׁמַע דְּשׁוֹפָר חַד, וְקוֹל נָפִיק מִנֵּיהּ, וְשׁוֹפָר בְּקְיוּמֵיהּ שְׁכִיחַ, וּבְגִינֵי כָּךְ כְּתִיב, קוֹל הַשֹּׁפָר.

303. Rabbi Elazar said that "THE SOUND OF THE SHOFAR" MEANS the sound which comes out from a Shofar, which means that there is one Shofar and a solitary sound comes out from it, FOR THE SOUND IS THE SECRET OF ZEIR ANPIN AND THE SHOFAR IS THE SECRET OF BINAH. The Shofar stands by itself SEPARATE FROM THE SOUND WHICH COMES OUT OF IT, therefore it is written: "the sound of the Shofar," AND NOT, 'THE SOUND IN THE SHOFAR'.

304. רַבִּי יְהוּדָה אָמַר הָכִי, קוֹל הַשֹּׁפָר, הַשֹּׁפָר כְּתִיב חָסֵר, כד״א, שְׁפַר קֳדָם דָּרְיָוֶשׁ. מִלְכִּי יִשְׁפַּר עֲלָךְ. שְׁפַר קָדָמַי לְהַחֲוָיָא.

304. Rabbi Yehuda said: In "the sound of the Shofar," the word "Shofar" is spelled without THE LETTER VAV, FOR IT HAS THE SAME MEANING AS IN THE VERSE, "It pleased (Heb. shafar) Daryavesh" (Daniel 6:1) and in the verse, "O king, let my counsel be acceptable (Heb. yishpar) to you" (Daniel 4:24) and the verse, "I thought it good (Heb. shefar) to report the signs and wonders" (Daniel 3:32) – MEANING THAT THESE ARE EXPRESSIONS WHICH SPEAK OF GLORY AND BEAUTY, WHICH ALLUDES TO ZEIR ANPIN, THE SECRET OF TIFERET.

305. רַבִּי שִׁמְעוֹן אָמַר, קוֹל הַשּׁוֹפָר, אַתְרָא דְּקָלָא נָפִיק מִנֵּיהּ, אִקְרֵי שׁוֹפָר. תּוּ אָמַר רַבִּי שִׁמְעוֹן, תָּא חֲזֵי, קוֹל הַשּׁוֹפָר: אַתְרָא דְּקָלָא, הַיְינוּ דִּכְתִיב, כִּי עַל כָּל מוֹצָא פִּי יְיָ' יִחְיֶה הָאָדָם. מַאי מוֹצָא פִּי יְיָ'. דָּא קוֹל הַשּׁוֹפָר, הוּא רַב מִכָּל שְׁאַר קַלֵּי תַּתָּאֵי, וְתַקִּיפָא מִכֻּלְּהוּ, דִּכְתִיב וְקוֹל שׁוֹפָר חָזָק מְאֹד, וְעַל כָּל שְׁאַר קָלִין לָא אִתְּמַר חָזָק מְאֹד. בְּהַאי קוֹל הַשּׁוֹפָר תַּלְיָא כֹּלָּא, וְדָא הוּא דְּאִקְרֵי קוֹל גָּדוֹל, דִּכְתִיב קוֹל גָּדוֹל וְלֹא יָסָף. וְאִקְרֵי קוֹל דְּמָמָה דַקָּה, נְהִירוּ דְּבוּצִינֵי, דְּהוּא זַךְ וְדַקִּיק, וְזָכִיךְ וְנָהִיר לְכֹלָּא.

305. Rabbi Shimon said that "the sound of the Shofar" MEANS THAT the place from which the sound comes out is called 'Shofar', FOR THE SOUND IS ZEIR ANPIN AND THE SHOFAR IS BINAH, AND ZEIR ANPIN ISSUES FROM BINAH, AS IS KNOWN. Rabbi Shimon continued and said: Come and behold: "the sound of the Shofar" refers to where the voice is, for it is written: "By every word that proceeds out of the mouth of Hashem does man live" (Devarim 7:3). What comes "out of the mouth of Hashem"? "...the sound of the Shofar..." which is greater than any other lower voices, and stronger than them all, as it is written: "the sound of a Shofar exceedingly loud" (Shemot 19:16). Of other voices it is not said "exceedingly loud (lit. 'very strong')." Everything depends on this sound of the Shofar, and it is called 'a great voice', as written: "a great voice which was not heard again" (Devarim 5:19), and it called "a still small voice" (I Melachim 19:12), which is the light of the luminaries, which is pure and subtle, and purifies and illuminates all things.

306. דְּמָמָה, מַהוּ דְּמָמָה. אָמַר ר"ש, דְּבָעֵי ב"נ לְמִשְׁתּוֹקָא מִנֵּיהּ, וּלְמֶחֱסַם פּוּמֵיהּ. כד"א, אָמַרְתִּי אֶשְׁמְרָה דְּרָכַי מֵחֲטוֹא בִלְשׁוֹנִי אֶשְׁמְרָה לְפִי מַחְסוֹם. דְּמָמָה אִיהִי שְׁתוּקָא דְּלָא אִשְׁתְּמַע לְבַר. וַיַּרְא הָעָם וַיָּנֻעוּ וַיַּעַמְדוּ מֵרָחֹק, דְּחָמוּ מַה דְּחָמוּ. וַיָּנוּעוּ כד"א וַיָּנֻעוּ אַמּוֹת הַסִּפִּים מִקּוֹל הַקּוֹרֵא.

306. IT IS WRITTEN: "still." What does "still" mean? Rabbi Shimon said that one must be silent WITH AWE and shut his mouth, as it is written: "I said, 'I will take heed of my ways that I sin not with my tongue: I will keep a curb

on my mouth" (Tehilim 39:2). The word "still" means silence in which no voice is heard outside. "When the people saw it, they were shaken and stood afar off," for what they saw FRIGHTENED THEM. The word "shaken (also: 'moved')" (Shemot 20:15), has the same meaning as in: "And the posts of the door moved at the voice of him" (Yeshayah 6:4).

307. תָּאנָא, מַה כְּתִיב בֵּיה בִּיחֶזְקֵאל, כַּד חָמָא גְּבוּרָן נִימוֹסֵי קוּדְשָׁא בְּרִיךְ הוּא, דִּכְתִּיב, וָאֵרֶא וְהִנֵּה רוּחַ סְעָרָה בָּאָה וְגו', רוּחַ סְעָרָה אֲמַאי. א"ר יוֹסֵי, לְתַבְרָא אַרְבַּע מַלְכְּוָון. א"ר יְהוּדָה, תָּנֵינָא, רוּחָא רַבָּה, דְּאִתְּעַר בְּנִימוּסֵי גְּבוּרָה דִּלְעֵילָא בָּאָה מִן הַצָּפוֹן. מִצָּפוֹן לָא כְּתִיב אֶלָּא מִן הַצָּפוֹן הַהוּא דְּאִשְׁתְּמוֹדַע לְעֵילָא, הַהוּא דְּטָמִיר וְגָנִיז לְעֵילָא.

307. We have learned that Ezekiel saw the might of the ways of the Holy One, blessed be He, as it is written: "And I looked and behold, a storm wind came out..." (Yechezkel 1:4) What is the storm wind for? Rabbi Yosi explained: To break the four kingdoms. Rabbi Yehuda said: We have learned that it is a great wind that was aroused through the mighty deeds above. And it "came out from the north." It is not written 'from north' but "the north," WITH THE DEFINITE ARTICLE, which indicates that specific wind which is hidden and kept above.

308. עָנָן גָּדוֹל וְאֵשׁ מִתְלַקַּחַת, דַּהֲוָה אָחִיד בֵּיה, וְלָא אָחִיד, אָחִיד בְּסִטְרוֹי, לְאִתְעָרָא דִּינָא, דִּתְנֵינָן, תְּלַת זִמְנִין בְּיוֹמָא, יַנְקָא הַהוּא דִּינָא קַשְׁיָא, בְּגֶרְדִּינוֹי גְּלִיפִין מִסְּטְרָא דִּגְבוּרָה, הה"ד וְאֵשׁ מִתְלַקַּחַת. בְּגִין לְאִתְעָרָא בְּעָלְמָא.

308. "...a great cloud and a fire flaring up..." (Ibid.) "...FLARING UP..." MEANS THAT it held yet held not to it, gripping its sides to arouse Judgment. We learned that three times a day Severe Judgment sucks from the supernal inscriptions that come from the side of Gvurah. Therefore it says, "and a fire flaring up," so that it would be roused in the world.

309. וּמַה מְבַסֵּם לֵיה, הַהוּא דִּכְתִּיב בֵּיה וְנֹגַהּ לוֹ סָבִיב. דְּהַהוּא זִיהֲרָא דְּאַסְחַר לֵיה מִכָּל סִטְרוֹי, מְבַסֵּם לֵיה, וּמַתְקִין לֵיה, בְּגִין דְּלָא לֶהֱוֵי

דִּינָא קַשְׁיָא, וְיֵיכְלוּן בְּנֵי נָשָׁא לְמִסְבְּלֵיהּ.

309. What mitigates this "FLARING UP FIRE" OF BINAH? "A brightness was about it" (Ibid.), for that splendor, WHICH IS CHOCHMAH, surrounds it and encircles it and mitigates it, so that the Judgment is not too hard for men to bear.

310. וּמִתּוֹכָהּ כְּעֵין הַחַשְׁמַל, תָּאנָא, וּמִתּוֹכָהּ: וּמִגַּוָּוהּ. כְּעֵין הַחַשְׁמַל, מַאי חַשְׁמַל. אָ"ר יְהוּדָה, חַיּוֹת אֵשָׁא מְמַלְּלָא.

310. "...and out of the midst of it, as it were the color of electrum" MEANS from its interior part. What is "electrum (Heb. *chashmal*)"? RABBI YEHUDA SAID: It is the speaking of fiery animals (Heb. CHAYOT ESH – *memalelot*), WHICH ARE FROM THE ASPECT OF THE MALE AND FEMALE, WHEN FACE TO FACE, WHICH ARE THEN CALLED 'VOICE' AND 'SPEECH'." HENCE, THEY TALK.

311. תָּאנָא, אָ"ר יוֹסֵי, חַשְׁמַל: מַה דַּהֲוָה לִבָּא לְאֵשָׁא, דִּכְתִיב מִתּוֹךְ הָאֵשׁ כְּעֵין הַחַשְׁמַל. וְלֹא הַחַשְׁמַל מִתּוֹךְ הָאֵשׁ, מִגּוֹ אֵשָׁא דְּאִיהִי לְגוֹ בְּאֵשָׁא. כְּעֵין הַחַשְׁמַל דְּאִיהִי בָּתַר אַרְבַּע דַּרְגִּין, דִּכְתִיב, רוּחַ סְעָרָה, עָנָן גָּדוֹל, וְאֵשׁ מִתְלַקַּחַת, וְנֹגַהּ לוֹ סָבִיב. וּמִתּוֹכָהּ כְּעֵין הַחַשְׁמַל מִתּוֹךְ הָאֵשׁ, הַהוּא דִּכְתִיב בֵּיהּ וְאֵשׁ מִתְלַקַּחַת.

311. Rabbi Yosi said: We have learned that *chashmal* MEANS the heart (Heb. *lev, Lamed-Bet*) of the fire, MEANING THE SECRET OF THE *LAMED-BET* (=32) PATHS OF CHOCHMAH – WHICH ARE THE LIVING CREATURES OF BINAH, WHICH IS THE SECRET OF THE "FIRE FLARING UP," as it is written: "out of the midst of it, as it were the color of electrum." It is written this way instead of JUST "the electrum," FOR "AS IT WERE (LIT. 'LIKE THE EYE')" ALLUDES TO THE LIGHT OF THE CHOCHMAH WHICH IS CALLED 'AN EYE'. "...out of the midst of the fire..." means from the inner part of the fire. "As it were the color of electrum" means that ELECTRUM is behind the four grades, for it is written: "a storm wind," "a great cloud," "a fire flaring up," and "a brightness was about it." "...out of the midst of the fire..." refers to that "fire flaring up," WHICH IS BINAH, AND IT DOES NOT MEAN OUT OF THE MIDST OF THE BRIGHTNESS.

312. תַּנְיָא רַבִּי יוֹסֵי בַּר רַבִּי יְהוּדָה אָמַר, חָמוּ יִשְׂרָאֵל הָכָא, מַה דְּלָא חָמָא יְחֶזְקֵאל בֶּן בּוּזִי, וְכֻלְּהוּ אִתְדַּבְּקוּ בְּחָכְמְתָא עִלָּאָה יַקִּירָא. חֲמִשָּׁה דַּרְגִּין דְּקָלִין, חָמוּ יִשְׂרָאֵל בְּטוּרָא דְּסִינַי. וּבַחֲמִשָּׁה אִלֵּין אִתְיְיהִיבַת אוֹרַיְיתָא. דַּרְגָּא חֲמִישָׁאָה הוּא, דִּכְתִיב קוֹל הַשּׁפָר. יְחֶזְקֵאל לָקֳבְלֵיהוֹן חָמָא חֲמִשָּׁה דַּרְגִּין דְּאִינּוּן לְבַר מֵאִלֵּין, דְּאִינּוּן רוּחַ סְעָרָה, עָנָן גָּדוֹל, וְאֵשׁ מִתְלַקַּחַת, וְנֹגַהּ לוֹ סָבִיב, וְעֵין הַחַשְׁמַל.

312. Rabbi Yosi, the son of Rabbi Yehuda, said that Yisrael at Mount Sinai saw what the prophet Ezekiel never saw, and they were all united with the divine, precious Wisdom. Yisrael saw five grades of voices on Mount Sinai, by which the Torah was given. The fifth grade was "the sound of the Shofar." Ezekiel saw but five lower grades outside THOSE FIVE VOICES, which were: "a storm wind," "a great cloud," "a fire flaring up," "a brightness was about it," and "as it were the color of electrum."

313. אָמַר רַבִּי אֶלְעָזָר, בְּיִשְׂרָאֵל כְּתִיב, פָּנִים בְּפָנִים דִּבֶּר יְיָ' וְגוֹ'. בִּיחֶזְקֵאל כְּתִיב, כְּעֵין, וּדְמוּת, כְּמַאן דְּחָמֵי בָּתַר כּוֹתָלִין סַגִּיאִין, כְּמַאן דְּחָמֵי בַּר נָשׁ בָּתַר כּוֹתָלָא. אָמַר רַבִּי יְהוּדָה, מַה דְּחָמוּ יִשְׂרָאֵל, לָא חָמָא נְבִיאָה אַחֲרָא, כ"ש מַה דְּחָמָא מֹשֶׁה, דְּלָא חָמָא נְבִיאָה אַחֲרָא. זַכָּאָה חוּלָקֵיהּ, דִּכְתִיב בֵּיהּ, וַיְהִי שָׁם עִם יְיָ' וְלֹא בְּחֵיזוּ אַחֲרָא, כְּמָה דִּכְתִיב, וּמַרְאֶה וְלֹא בְחִידוֹת.

313. Rabbi Elazar said: Of Yisrael, it is written, "Hashem talked with you face to face" (Devarim 5:4), and of Ezekiel it is written, "as it were," and "likeness," – like one who looks from behind many walls, like a man looking from behind a wall. Rabbi Yehuda said that what Yisrael saw on Mount Sinai no prophet ever saw, and much more so, what Moses saw no other prophet saw. Happy is his share, of whom it is written: "And he was there with Hashem" (Shemot 34:28), FOR THIS IS THE SECRET OF THE SHINING MIRROR, instead of a different mirror WHICH DOES NOT SHINE, as it is written: "manifestly and not in dark speeches" (Bemidbar 12:8) – NOT LIKE THE OTHER MIRRORS WHICH DO NOT ILLUMINATE AND SPEAK IN RIDDLES.

314. אָמַר רַבִּי יוֹסֵי, ת״ח, כְּתִיב, הָיֹה הָיָה דְּבַר יְיָ׳, נְבוּאָה לְשַׁעֲתָא
הָיְתָה. ר׳ יְהוּדָה אוֹמֵר, לְקִיּוּמָא הוּא דְּאָתָא, דְּאִצְטְרִיךְ לְמֶהֱוֵי
בְּגִינֵיהוֹן דְּיִשְׂרָאֵל, לְאִשְׁתְּמוֹדְעָא דְּהָא לָא שָׁבִיק לוֹן קוּדְשָׁא בְּרִיךְ
הוּא, וּבְכָל אֲתָר דְּמִתְפַּזְרִין יִשְׂרָאֵל בְּגָלוּתָא, עִמְהוֹן הוּא שַׁרְיָא.

314. Rabbi Yosi said: Come and behold. When the scripture said, "The word of Hashem came (Heb. *hayoh-hayah*)" (Yechezkel 1:3) it indicated that the prophecy was for that time alone. THEREFORE, IT IS WRITTEN THERE, "*HAYOH-HAYAH*." Rabbi Yehuda said that this was for support, for Yisrael to know that the Holy One, blessed be He, had not forsaken them and to prove to them that wherever they are spread in exile, He is with them.

315. אָמַר רַבִּי אֶלְעָזָר, הָיֹה הָיָה: דְּחָמָא וְלָא חָמָא, דְּקָאִים בְּאִינוּן
מִלִּין, וְלָא קָאִים. הה״ד וָאֵרֶא כְּעֵין חַשְׁמַל, וְלָא חַשְׁמַל אֲבָל יִשְׂרָאֵל,
מַה כְּתִיב בְּהוּ, וְכָל הָעָם רֹאִים אֶת הַקּוֹלֹת, כָּל חַד וְחַד חָמָא, כְּדְקָא
חֲזֵי לֵיהּ.

315. Rabbi Elazar remarked that the expression "*hayoh-haya* (lit. 'was being')" MEANS that he both saw and did not see, understood and did not understand, as it is written: "I saw something like the color of electrum" (Yechezkel 1:27). IT IS not WRITTEN, 'I SAW electrum', but of Yisrael, it is written: "And all the people see the voices," MEANING that each one of them saw according to what he was worthy of seeing.

316. דְּתַנְיָא, כָּל חַד וְחַד הֲוֵוֹ קַיְימִין שׁוּרִין שׁוּרִין, תְּחוּמִין תְּחוּמִין,
וּכְדְקָא אִתְחֲזֵי לְהוּ, חָמוּ כָּל חַד וְחַד. אָמַר ר״ש, רֵישֵׁי דְעַמָּא
בִּלְחוֹדַיְיהוּ, רֵישֵׁי דְשִׁבְטִין בִּלְחוֹדַיְיהוּ. נוּקְבֵי בִּלְחוֹדַיְיהוּ. ה׳ דַּרְגִּין
לִימִינָא, וְה׳ דַּרְגִּין לִשְׂמָאלָא. הה״ד אַתֶּם נִצָּבִים הַיּוֹם כֻּלְּכֶם לִפְנֵי יְיָ׳
אֱלֹהֵיכֶם רָאשֵׁיכֶם שִׁבְטֵיכֶם זִקְנֵיכֶם וְשׁוֹטְרֵיכֶם כֹּל אִישׁ וְגו׳, הָא ה׳
דַּרְגִּין לִימִינָא. וְה׳ דַּרְגִּין לִשְׂמָאלָא מַאן אִינּוּן. הַיְינוּ דִּכְתִיב, טַפְּכֶם,
נְשֵׁיכֶם, וְגֵרְךָ אֲשֶׁר בְּקֶרֶב מַחֲנֶיךָ, מֵחֹטֵב עֵצֶיךָ, עַד שֹׁאֵב מֵימֶיךָ. הָא ה׳
דַּרְגִּין לִשְׂמָאלָא.

316. We have learned that they stood in rows and in groups and divisions, and each one saw as befitted him. Rabbi Shimon said that the chiefs of the tribes STOOD by themselves and all the women by themselves. And five grades STOOD at the right and five grades at the left, as it is written: "You stand this day all of you before Hashem your Elohim, your captains of your tribes, your elders, and your officers, with all the men of Yisrael" (Devarim 29:9). These are the five grades to the right. And what are the five grades to the left? It is written: "your little ones, your wives, and your stranger that is in your camp, from the hewer of your wood to the drawer of your water" (Ibid. 10). These are the five grades to the left.

317. כֻּלְהוּ דַּרְגִּין אִתְתָּקָנוּ כְּגַוְונָא דִּלְעֵילָא. לָקֲבְלֵיהוֹן יַרְתּוּ יִשְׂרָאֵל אַחֲסָנַת עָלְמִין, עֶשֶׂר אֲמִירָן, דִּבְהוּ תַּלְיָין כָּל פִּקּוּדִין, וְכָל זַכְוָון, וְכָל יְרוּתַת אַחֲסָנָא, דְּאִינוּן חוּלָקָא טָבָא דְּיִשְׂרָאֵל.

317. All these grades were established in the likeness of above. Against them, Yisrael inherited an eternal possession, the Ten Commandments, from which are suspended all the precepts and merits, and all the inheritance of their portion, being the good portion of Yisrael.

318. תָּאנָא, בְּהַהִיא שַׁעֲתָא דְּקוּדְשָׁא בְּרִיךְ הוּא אִתְגַּלֵּי בְּטוּרָא דְּסִינַי, הֲווֹ חָמָאן כָּל יִשְׂרָאֵל, כְּמַאן דְּחָמֵי נְהוֹרָא בַּעֲשִׁישָׁתָא, וּמֵהַהוּא נְהוֹרָא הֲוָה חָמֵי כָּל חַד וְחַד, מַה דְּלָא חָמָא יְחֶזְקֵאל נְבִיאָה.

318. We have learned that at the time that the Holy One, blessed be He, revealed Himself on Mount Sinai, all of Yisrael looked as one who sees a light streaming through the glass of an oil-lamp. By means of that light each one of them saw more than the prophet Ezekiel.

319. מ"ט. מִשּׁוּם דְּאִינוּן קָלִין עִלָּאִין, אִתְגַּלְיָאוּ בְּחַד, כְּמָה דַּאֲמֵינָא, דִּכְתִיב, וְכָל הָעָם רוֹאִים אֶת הַקּוֹלוֹת. אֲבָל בִּיחֶזְקֵאל, שְׁכִינְתָּא אִתְגַּלֵּי בִּרְתִּיכוֹי, וְלָא יַתִּיר, וַהֲוָה חָמֵי, כְּמַאן דְּחָמֵי בָּתַר כּוֹתָלִין סַגִּיאִין.

319. How is this so? Because all the supernal voices were revealed at once, as it is written: "And all the people see the voices." But to Ezekiel the

Shechinah alone was revealed through Her Chariots, and he caught but glimpses of it as though through many walls.

320. אָמַר רַבִּי יְהוּדָה, זַכָּאָה חוּלָקָא דְּמֹשֶׁה, דִּכְתִיב בֵּיהּ, וַיֵּרֶד יְיָ׳ עַל הַר סִינַי וַיִּקְרָא יְיָ׳ לְמֹשֶׁה, זַכָּאָה דָּרָא, דִּכְתִיב בֵּיהּ, וַיֵּרֶד יְיָ׳ לְעֵינֵי כָל הָעָם עַל הַר סִינַי.

320. Rabbi Yehuda said: Happy is the portion of Moses. Of him, it is written: "And Hashem came down upon Mount Sinai…and Hashem called Moses" (Shemot 19:20). And happy are the generation of whom it is written: "Hashem will came down in the sight of all the people upon Mount Sinai."

321. ת״ח, כְּתִיב מִימִינוֹ אֵשׁ דָּת לָמוֹ, דְּהָא מִימִינָא אִתְגְּלֵי מַה דְּאִתְגְּלֵי. מַה בֵּין הַאי לְהַאי. אָמַר ר׳ יוֹסֵי, הָכָא בְּסִינַי, רֵישָׁא וְגוּפָא דְּמַלְכָּא, דִּכְתִיב וַיֵּט שָׁמַיִם וַיֵּרֶד, וּבַאֲתַר דְּאִית רֵישָׁא, אִית גוּפָא, אֲבָל בִּיחֶזְקֵאל כְּתִיב וַתְּהִי עָלָיו שָׁם יַד יְיָ׳, דְּאִתְגְּלֵי יְדָא, וְלָא גוּפָא. וְתָנֵינָן, אֲפִילוּ בִּידָא, יַד יְיָ׳ עִלָּאָה, יַד יְיָ׳ תַּתָּאָה.

321. Come and behold: whatever was revealed came from the right side, as it is written: "From His right hand went a fiery law for them" (Devarim 33:2). AND HE ASKS: What is the difference between this and the one WHICH EZEKIEL SAW? Rabbi Yosi answered that here, on Mount Sinai, the head and the body of the King were revealed, as it is written: "He bowed the heavens also and came down" (II Shmuel 22:10), FOR BEFORE THIS IT IS WRITTEN, "THERE WENT UP A SMOKE OUT OF HIS NOSTRILS AND FIRE OUT OF HIS MOUTH" (IBID. 9), MEANING THAT THERE WAS ONLY A HEAD OF WHICH NOSTRILS AND MOUTH ARE MENTIONED, and wherever there is a head, there is also a body. But of Ezekiel it is written: "And the hand of Hashem was there upon him" (Yechezkel 1:3). Only the hand was revealed, not the body, and we have learned that even the hand has two aspects: the supernal hand, WHICH IS THE HAND OF ZEIR ANPIN, and the lower hand, WHICH IS MALCHUT AND IS CALLED 'A HAND'. AND TO EZEKIEL THE LOWER HAND WAS REVEALED.

322. ת״ח, כְּתִיב נִפְתְּחוּ הַשָּׁמַיִם וָאֶרְאֶה מַרְאוֹת אֱלֹהִים. מַרְאוֹת כְּתִיב

חָסֵר, לְאִתְחֲזָאָה דִּבְגִין שְׁכִינְתָּא קָאָמַר, דְּהָא וָאֶרְאֶה מַרְאֹת חָסֵר, מַרְאֶה חַד. אָמַר ר' יֵיסָא, וְכִי שְׁכִינְתָּא לָאו כֹּלָּא. אָמַר רַבִּי יוֹסֵי, לָא דָּמֵי רֵישָׁא דְּמַלְכָּא, לְרַגְלוֹי דְּמַלְכָּא, אע"ג דְּכֹלָּא הֲוֵי בְּגוּפָא דְּמַלְכָּא.

322. Come and behold: in the verse, "The heavens were opened and I saw visions of Elohim" (Yechezkel 1:1), the word "visions" (Heb. MAR'OT) is written without THE LETTER VAV, AN INDICATION OF one mirror, which is the Shechinah. Rabbi Yesa asked: Is not the Shechinah all inclusive? Rabbi Yosi answered: The head of the King is not to be likened with His feet, WHICH IS THE SHECHINAH THAT CLOTHES HIM FROM THE CHEST DOWNWARDS, CALLED HIS 'FEET' – although everything is part of the body of the King.

323. תָּא חֲזֵי, בִּישַׁעְיָהוּ כְּתִיב, וָאֶרְא אֶת יְיָ', בִּיחֶזְקֵאל כְּתִיב, וָאֶרְאֶה מַרְאֹת אֱלֹהִים, הָכָא אֶת, הָתָם מַרְאֹת. מַה דְּחָמָא דָא, חָמָא דָא. זַכָּאָה חוּלָקֵיהּ דְּמֹשֶׁה, דְּלָא הֲוָה נְבִיאָה מְהֵימְנָא שְׁלֵימָא כְּווֹתֵיהּ.

323. Come and behold: It is said of Isaiah, "and I saw Hashem" (Yeshayah 6:1), WHICH IS THE SHECHINAH, CALLED "ET (LIT. 'THE')." And of Ezekiel it is written: "And I saw visions of Elohim." Here "Et" IS THE SHECHINAH, and there "visions" IS THE SHECHINAH, for what one saw, so did the other, NAMELY ONLY THE SHECHINAH. Happy is the portion of Moses. There was no prophet as perfect as he, FOR HE SAW THE ILLUMINATING MIRROR, WHICH IS ZEIR ANPIN.

324. וָאֶרְא אֶת יְיָ', אֶת דַּיְיקָא. וָאֶרְאֶה מַרְאֹת אֱלֹהִים, מַרְאֹת דַּיְיקָא. וּבְדַרְגָּא חַד הֲווֹ. אִי הָכִי, אֲמַאי לָא פָּרִישׁ יְשַׁעְיָה כּוּלֵי הַאי. אָמַר רַבִּי יוֹסֵי, דָּא כְּלִיל, דָּא פָּרִישׁ. מַאי טַעְמָא פָּרִישׁ כּוּלֵי הַאי יְחֶזְקֵאל. אֶלָּא, כֹּלָּא אִצְטְרִיךְ בְּגִינֵיהוֹן דְּיִשְׂרָאֵל, דְּיִנְדְּעוּן חֲבִיבוּתָא דְּחָבִיב לְהוּ קוּדְשָׁא בְּרִיךְ הוּא, דְּשְׁכִינְתֵּיהּ וּרְתִיכוֹי אַתְיָין לְדַיְירָא בֵּינַיְיהוּ בְּגָלוּתָא.

324. "…and I saw (et) Hashem." Et precisely REFERS TO THE SHECHINAH. "And I saw visions of Elohim," "vision" being precisely THE SHECHINAH.

ISAIAH AND EZEKIEL were BOTH in the same grade. AND HE ASKS: Why then did Isaiah not give a detailed description AS EZEKIEL DID? Rabbi Yosi answers: The one spoke in general, NAMELY ISAIAH, and the other in details, NAMELY EZEKIEL. Why did Ezekiel give such a detailed description? HE ANSWERS: EZEKIEL SPOKE IN A DETAILED MANNER in consideration of Yisrael, so that they would know that the Holy One, blessed be He, loved them and that the Shechinah with Her Chariots had gone down into exile to dwell with them.

325. א״ר חִיָּיא, בְּאֶרֶץ כַּשְׂדִּים, וְהָא כְּתִיב הֵן אֶרֶץ כַּשְׂדִּים זֶה הָעָם לֹא הָיָה, אֲמַאי אִתְגְּלֵי שְׁכִינְתָּא תַּמָּן. אִי תֵּימָא בְּגִינֵיהוֹן דְּיִשְׂרָאֵל, הֲוָה טָב דְּתִתְשְׁרֵי שְׁכִינְתָּא בְּגַוַּוְיְיהוּ, וְלָא יִתְגַּלְיָיא. אֶלָּא, הָכִי תָּאנָא, אִי לָאו דְּאִתְגַּלְיָיא לָא הֲווֹ יַדְעִין.

325. Rabbi Chiya asked: Why did the Shechinah reveal Herself in "the land of Casdim," FOR IT IS WRITTEN: "Behold the land of Casdim, this people was not" (Yeshayah 23:13). If it was for Yisrael's sake, surely She could have been present among them without being revealed? AND HE ANSWERS: We have learned that if She had not revealed Herself, they would not have known THAT SHE WAS WITH THEM.

326. וְהָא דְּאִתְגַּלְיָיא, מַה כְּתִיב, עַל נְהַר כְּבָר, עַל מַיָּא, בְּאֲתָר דְּלָא יִסְתְּאַב, וְלָא שַׁרְיָא מְסָאֲבוּתָא. וְהַהוּא נַהֲרָא, הֲוָה חַד מֵאַרְבַּע נָהֲרִין, דְּנָפְקִין מִגִּנְתָּא דְעֵדֶן, דִּכְתִיב עַל נְהַר כְּבָר. מַאי כְּבָר. דִּכְבָר הֲוָה. מֵאֲתָר דִּשְׁכִינְתָּא שַׁרְיָא עֲלוֹי. וּכְתִיב וַתְּהִי עָלָיו שָׁם יַד יְיָ׳, שָׁם, וְלָא בְּאֲתָר אַחֲרָא.

326. She revealed Herself, as written, "by the river K'var" (Yechezkel 1:1), meaning by the water, in a place where impurity can not dwell. That river was one of the four rivers which issued from the Garden of Eden, as written: "by the river K'var." What does "K'var" (lit. 'already') mean? That it already existed from a place upon which the Shechinah dwelt, as it is written: "And the hand of Hashem was there" (Ibid.), that is, there and not elsewhere.

327. אָמַר רַבִּי חִיָּיא, כְּתִיב וּמִתּוֹכָהּ דְּמוּת אַרְבַּע חַיּוֹת וְזֶה מַרְאֵיהֶן

דְּמוּת אָדָם לָהֶנָה. תָּאנָא בְּרָזָא עִלָּאָה, אַרְבַּע חֵיוָון אִית, דְּאִינְהוּ לְגוֹ
בְּגוֹ הֵיכָלָא קַדִּישָׁא, וְאִינּוּן קַדְמָאֵי, עַתִּיקִין דְּעַתִּיקָא קַדִּישָׁא, כְּלָלָא
דִּשְׁמָא עִלָּאָה. וִיחֶזְקֵאל חָמָא, דְּמוּת דִּרְתִיכִין עִלָּאִין, דְּהָא הוּא חָמָא,
מֵאֲתָר דְּלָא הֲוָה נָהִיר כָּל כָּךְ. תָּאנָא, כְּגַוְונָא דִלְעֵילָּא, אִית לְתַתָּא
מִנַּיְיהוּ, וְכֵן בְּכֻלְּהוּ עָלְמִין, כּוּלְּהוּ אֲחִידָן דָּא בְּדָא, וְדָא בְּדָא.

327. Rabbi Chiya said: It is written, "Also out of the midst of it came the likeness of four living creatures. And this was their appearance; they had the likeness of a man" (Yechezkel 1:5). And we have learned, according to the esoteric teaching, that there are four living creatures in the holy chamber, WHICH IS BINAH. They are the most ancient celestial beings WHICH ARE DERIVED from Atika Kadisha (the Holy Ancient One), and which include the Supernal Name, YUD HEI VAV HEI, FOR *YUD* IS A LION, *HEI* IS AN OX, *VAV* IS AN EAGLE, AND THE LAST *HEI* IS A MAN. AND THEY ARE THE SECRET OF THE THREE COLUMNS AND MALCHUT WHICH RECEIVES THEM. Ezekiel saw only the likeness of the supernal Chariots, because he saw them from a region which was not very bright, MEANING FROM THE WORLD OF YETZIRAH. As we have already learned, as there is above IN BINAH so it is below IN MALE AND FEMALE, and so in all the worlds, BRIYAH, YETZIRAH AND ASIYAH. And all of them are linked one with another, AND WHATEVER THERE IS IN THE UPPER WORLD, THERE IS ALSO IN THE LOWER ONE, AND HE SAW THEM IN THE WORLD OF YETZIRAH.

328. וְאִי תֵּימָא לְעֵילָּא יַתִּיר דְּחָמָא. תָּנֵינָן, מֹשֶׁה חָמָא בְּאַסְפָּקְלַרְיָא
דְּנָהֲרָא, וְכֻלְּהוּ נְבִיאֵי לָא חָמוּ אֶלָּא מִגּוֹ אַסְפָּקְלַרְיָא דְּלָא נָהֲרָא,
דִּכְתִיב וָאֶרְאֶה מַרְאֹת אֱלֹהִים. וּכְתִיב אִם יִהְיֶה נְבִיאֲכֶם יְיָ' בַּמַּרְאָה
אֵלָיו אֶתְוַדָּע וְגוֹ' לֹא כֵן עַבְדִּי מֹשֶׁה וְגוֹ', וּכְתִיב פֶּה אֶל פֶּה אֲדַבֶּר בּוֹ.

328. And you may think that he beheld them further above THE WORLD OF YETZIRAH. Yet we learned that Moses saw the vision from a bright mirror, WHICH IS ZEIR ANPIN, while other prophets derived their visions from a dull mirror, as written: "And I saw visions (Heb. *mar'ot*) of Elohim." The word *"MAR'OT"* is written WITHOUT THE LETTER *VAV*, WHICH INDICATES MALCHUT, and: "If there be a prophet among you, I, Hashem make Myself known to him in a vision... My servant Moses is not so...With him I speak

mouth to mouth" (Bemidbar 12:6-7).

329. א"ר יוֹסֵי, ת"ח, דִּנְבִיאִין כֻּלְהוּ לְגַבֵּיה, כְּנוּקְבָא לְגַבֵּי דְכוּרָא,
דִּכְתִיב פֶּה אֶל פֶּה אֲדַבֶּר בּוֹ וּמַרְאֶה. וְלִשְׁאָר נְבִיאִים כְּתִיב, בַּמַּרְאָה
אֵלָיו אֶתְוַדַּע. בַּמַּרְאָה וְלָא מַרְאֹת. כ"ש יְחֶזְקֵאל, דַּאֲפִילוּ מַרְאֶה לָא
כְּתִיב בֵּיה, אֶלָּא מַרְאֹת חָסֵר, וּכ"ש דִּכְתִיב בְּמֹשֶׁה, וְלָא בְחִידוֹת, אֶלָּא
כָּל מִלָּה עַל בּוּרְיֵיה. זַכָּאָה אִיהוּ דָרָא, דִּנְבִיאָה דָא שָׁרֵי בְּגַוַוייְהוּ.

329. Rabbi Yosi said: Come and behold. All the prophets are IN
COMPARISON WITH MOSES, like a female to a male, as written: "With him
I speak mouth to mouth, manifestly (Heb. *u'mar'eh*, lit: 'and a mirror')",
WHICH IS MOST CERTAINLY THE BRIGHT MIRROR (HEB. *MAR'AH*), AS IT
IS WRITTEN: WITH HIM I SPEAK "MOUTH TO MOUTH." Of all other
prophets it is said: "If there be a prophet among you, I, Hashem make
Myself known to him in a vision (Heb. *bemar'ah*)," MEANING THAT THEY
DERIVED THEIR VISION FROM A DULL MIRROR. AND IT IS WRITTEN,
"*bemar'ah*," (lit. 'a vision') and not '*mar'ot*', WITHOUT THE LETTER *VAV*.
All the more so of Ezekiel, as it is not written in relation to him '*mar'eh*'
but rather "*mar'ot*," without THE LETTER *VAV*, FOR HE SAW THE VISION
FROM THE WORLD OF YETZIRAH. This is all the more so for Moses, of
whom it is written: "and not in dark speeches," but showed him everything
clearly. Blessed, indeed, was the generation among whom this prophet
lived.

330. א"ר יוֹסֵי בְּרַבִּי יְהוּדָה, אַפִּין בְּאַפִּין חָמוּ יִשְׂרָאֵל זִיו יְקָרָא
דְּמַלְכֵּיהוֹן, וְלָא הֲוָה בְּהוֹן סוֹמִין, וְחִגְּרִין, וּקְטִיעִין, וְחֵרְשִׁין. סוֹמִין,
מַשְׁמַע דִּכְתִיב וְכָל הָעָם רוֹאִים. חִגְּרִין, דִּכְתִיב וַיִּתְיַצְּבוּ בְּתַחְתִּית הָהָר.
קְטִיעִין חֵרְשִׁין, וְנַעֲשֶׂה וְנִשְׁמָע. וּלְזִמְנָא דְּאָתֵי כְּתִיב אָז יְדַלֵּג כָּאַיָּל
פִּסֵחַ וְתָרוֹן לְשׁוֹן אִלֵּם.

330. Rabbi Yosi said, in the name of Rabbi Yehuda, that Yisrael saw the
precious glory of their King face to face, and there were neither blind nor
lame, nor deaf, nor any without hands among them. No blind, as it is
written, "And all the people perceived"; no lame, as it is written, "And they
stood at the foot of the mountain" (Shemot 19:17). There were no lame and

none without hands, as written, "And they said, 'All that Hashem has said will we do and obey" (Shemot 24:7); and of the days to come it says, "Then shall the lame man leap as a hart and the tongue of the dumb sing" (Yeshayah 35:6).

20. "And Elohim spoke"

A Synopsis

We are told here of God's admonitions to his chosen people so that they will merit the World to Come and be worthy of the heaven above, Zeir Anpin, and the earth above, Malchut. Rabbi Shimon explains that the heritage of Jacob bestowed through Isaac's blessing means that Jacob and all his descendants will be revived by the dew of heaven, that is, raised from the dead in the time to come. When Elohim spoke, each word rose and descended, was watered with the heavenly dew, encircled Yisrael and brought back their souls. Then it was engraved upon the tablets of stone, and each word was like a treasure house full of precious secrets and laws. He who occupies himself with the study of the Torah, of its secrets and laws, is saved from the fire of Gehenom, and this is due to the merit of Abraham, who pled for the children of Yisrael. Lastly we are told that the smoke that came out of Sinai was the Shechinah who manifested Herself there to the people.

331. וַיְדַבֵּר אֱלֹהִים אֶת כָּל הַדְּבָרִים הָאֵלֶּה לֵאמֹר. רַבִּי יְהוּדָה פָּתַח, מִי יְמַלֵּל גְּבוּרוֹת יְיָ' יַשְׁמִיעַ כָּל תְּהִלָּתוֹ. בְּכַמָּה אָרְחִין, אוֹרַיְיתָא אַסְהִידַת בְּבַר נָשׁ, דְּלָא יֵחוּב קַמֵּי מָארֵיה. בְּכַמָּה אָרְחִין, יָהִיב לֵיה עֵיטָא, דְּלָא יִסְטֵי מֵאָרְחוֹי לִימִינָא וְלִשְׂמָאלָא. בְּכַמָּה אָרְחִין יָהִיב לֵיה עֵיטָא, הֵיךְ יְתוּב קַמֵּי מָארֵיה, וְיִמְחוֹל לֵיה.

331. "And Elohim spoke all these words, saying" (Shemot 20:1). Rabbi Yehuda opened the discussion with that verse and said: "Who can utter the mighty acts of Hashem? Who can declare all His praise?" (Tehilim 106:2). In how many ways does the Torah admonish man not to sin before his Master. In how many ways does it counsel him not to turn from the way, either to the right or to the left, and in how many forms it shows him how to return to his Master so that He may forgive him.

332. דִּתְנָן, שִׁית מְאָה וּתְלַת עֲשַׂר זִינֵי עֵיטָא, יָהִיב אוֹרַיְיתָא לְבַר נָשׁ, לְמֶהֱוֵי שָׁלִים בְּמָארֵיה, בְּגִין דְּמָארֵיה בָּעָא לְאוֹטָבָא לֵיה בְּעָלְמָא דֵּין וּבְעָלְמָא דְּאָתֵי. וְיַתִּיר בְּעָלְמָא דְּאָתֵי, דְּהָא תָּנֵינָן, כָּל מַה דְּקוּדְשָׁא בְּרִיךְ הוּא אַשְׁלִים לֵיה לְבַר נָשׁ, מֵאִינוּן טָבָאן דְּזָכֵי בְּהוּ לְעָלְמָא דְּאָתֵי

אִשְׁתְּלִים בְּהוּ. מַאי טַעְמָא. מִשּׁוּם דְּעָלְמָא דְּאָתֵי דְּקוּדְשָׁא בְּרִיךְ הוּא הֲוֵי.

332. We have learned that the Torah has given a man 613 counsels in order that he may be perfect with his Master, for his Master desires only his good, both in this world and in the World to Come, but especially in the World to Come, since whatever good the Holy One, blessed be He, bestows upon man in this world is taken from the sum of good which he is entitled to receive in the World to Come. Why is that? Because the World to Come is the possession of the Holy One, blessed be He.

333. וְהָכִי תָּנֵינָן, הַאי עָלְמָא לְקַבְלֵיה דְּעָלְמָא דְּאָתֵי, לָא הֲוֵי אֶלָּא כְּפְרוֹזְדוֹר לְגַבֵּי טְרַקְלִין. וְכַד זָכֵי הַהוּא זַכָּאָה, בְּדִידֵיה זָכֵי. דְּתַנְיָא, כְּתִיב וְנַחֲלָה לֹא יִהְיֶה לּוֹ בְּקֶרֶב אֶחָיו. מ״ט. מִשּׁוּם דַּיְיָ׳ הוּא נַחֲלָתוֹ. זַכָּאָה חוּלְקֵיה, מַאן דְּזָכֵי לְאַחֲסָנָא אַחֲסַנְתָּא עִלָּאָה דָּא. זָכֵי בָּהּ בְּעָלְמָא דָּא, וּבְבֵיתָא דְּהַאי עָלְמָא. כַּךְ בְּעָלְמָא דְּאָתֵי, וּבְבֵיתָא עִלָּאָה קַדִּישָׁא, דִּכְתִיב וְנָתַתִּי לָהֶם בְּבֵיתִי וּבְחוֹמוֹתַי יָד וָשֵׁם, זַכָּאָה חוּלְקֵיה דְּהַהוּא זַכָּאָה, דְּמָדוֹרֵיה עִם מַלְכָּא בְּבֵיתֵיה.

333. We have learned that the comparison between this world and the World to Come is as an antechamber compared with the hall itself. The reward of the righteous is His very own, as it is written of the tribe of Levi: "Therefore shall they have no inheritance among their brethren." Why? Because "Hashem is their inheritance" (Devarim 18:2). Happy is the man who is entitled to receive such a supernal heritage, for he merits it in this world and in the house of this world, as well as in the World to Come and the heavenly, holy House, as it is written: "And to them will I give in My house and within My walls a memorial" (Yeshayah 56:5). Happy is the portion of the righteous for being worthy to dwell with the King in His own House.

334. ר' שִׁמְעוֹן אָמַר, זַכָּאָה חוּלְקֵיה דְּהַהוּא זַכָּאָה, דְּזָכֵי לְהַאי דִּכְתִיב, אָז תִּתְעַנַּג עַל יְיָ׳, עִם יְיָ׳ לָא כְּתִיב, אֶלָּא עַל יְיָ׳. מַאי עַל יְיָ׳. אֲתַר דְּעִלָּאִין וְתַתָּאִין אִתְמַשְׁכָן מִינֵיה, וְתָאֲבִין לְהַהוּא אֲתַר, דִּכְתִיב מֵאַיִן יָבֹא עֶזְרִי. וּכְתִיב, וְעַד עַתִּיק יוֹמַיָּא מְטָה וּקְדָמוֹהִי הַקְרְבוּהִי. וְתִיאוּבְתָּא

וְעִנּוּגָא דְצַדִּיקַיָּא, לְאִסְתַּכְּלָא לְהַהוּא זִיוָא, דְּכָל זִיוָא מִינֵּיה נָפְקָא, וְאִתְמַשְּׁכָן מִנֵּיה כָּל אִינּוּן כִּתְרִין.

334. Rabbi Shimon said: Happy is the portion of the righteous who is worthy of this, as it is written: "Then shall you delight yourself in (lit. 'above') Hashem" (Yeshayah 58:14). It is not written 'in Hashem', but "above Hashem," namely in the place from which the upper and the lower worlds are derived and for which they yearn, of which it is written: "From where (Heb. *ayin*) comes my help?" (Tehilim 121:1) REFERRING TO THE SFIRAH OF KETER, WHICH IS CALLED NOTHINGNESS (Heb. *AYIN*). And it is also written: "And came to the Ancient of Days and they brought him near before him" (Daniel 7:13) NAMELY KETER WHICH IS CALLED 'THE ANCIENT OF DAYS'. The desire and the delight of the righteous is to look at that splendor whence all lights issue and all celestial crowns, WHICH ARE THE SFIROT, are drawn.

335. תּוּ אר"ש, תָּנֵינָן בְּהַאי קְרָא אָז תִּתְעַנַּג עַל יְיָ', סוֹפֵיה דִּקְרָא מַה כְּתִיב, וְהִרְכַּבְתִּיךָ עַל בָּמוֹתֵי אָרֶץ, עַל הַהוּא אֲתָר דְּאִקְרֵי בָּמוֹתֵי אָרֶץ, אִיהוּ לְעֵילָא מֵהַאי אֶרֶץ, וְהַהוּא אֲתָר דְּאִקְרֵי בָּמֳתֵי אָרֶץ, הַיְינוּ שָׁמַיִם. וְהַיְינוּ דִּכְתִיב עַל בָּמֳתֵי אָרֶץ.

335. Rabbi Shimon continued: We learned of the verse, "Then shall you delight yourself in Hashem," that it ends with, "and I will cause you to ride upon the high places of the earth" (Yeshayah 58:14). This refers to the place called 'the high places of the earth', which is above "the earth," WHICH IS MALCHUT AND IS CALLED 'EARTH', and "heaven," NAMELY ZEIR ANPIN, as is written: "the high places of the earth," FOR HEAVEN IS ABOVE THE EARTH.

336. עַל יְיָ' אָמַר ר' אַבָּא, אָז תֵּשֵׁב לָא כְּתִיב, אֶלָּא אָז תִּתְעַנַּג עַל יְיָ', הַיְינוּ שָׁמַיִם. דִּכְתִיב, רוּמָה עַל הַשָּׁמַיִם אֱלֹהִים. וְהִרְכַּבְתִּיךָ עַל בָּמֳתֵי אָרֶץ, הַיְינוּ אֶרֶץ הַחַיִּים, מִמַּשְׁמַע דִּכְתִיב עַל בָּמוֹתַי, לְאַכְלְלָא צִיּוֹן וִירוּשָׁלַיִם, דְּאִקְרוּן בָּמֳתֵי אָרֶץ, וְהַיְינוּ שָׁמַיִם דִּלְעֵילָא, וְאֶרֶץ דִּלְעֵילָא. וּמִלָּה דְּאָמַר ר' שִׁמְעוֹן, הָכִי הוּא, וְכֹלָּא חַד, דִּכְתִיב וְעַד עַתִּיק יוֹמַיָּא

מִטָּה וְגוֹ', וְכָל הָנֵי מִילֵי לַאֲתַר חַד סַלְקִין.

336. Rabbi Aba continued with more explanations: It is not written, 'shall you sit' but rather, "shall you delight yourself in (lit. 'above') Hashem," namely "heaven," WHICH IS ZEIR ANPIN, for it is written: "Be You exalted, O Elohim, above the heavens" (Tehilim 57:12) THAT IS, ZEIR ANPIN. "And I will cause you to ride upon the high places of the earth," refers to the Land of the Living, WHICH IS MALCHUT CALLED 'EARTH'. The meaning of "upon the high places" is that it includes Zion and Jerusalem, FOR THEY ARE THE INSIDE AND THE OUTSIDE OF YESOD OF MALCHUT – meaning THAT THE VERSE SPEAKS OF the heaven above, WHICH IS ZEIR ANPIN, and the earth above, WHICH IS MALCHUT. And that which Rabbi Shimon spoke is thus, AS I SAID, and it is all one, as written: "And came to the Ancient of Days," and all amounts to the same.

337. אָמַר ר' אַבָּא לר"ש, לֵימָא לִי מֹר, הַאי קְרָא כּוּלֵיהּ, בְּמַאי אוֹקִימְנָא לֵיהּ, דִּכְתִיב אָז תִּתְעַנַּג עַל יְיָ' וְהִרְכַּבְתִּיךָ עַל בָּמֳתֵי אָרֶץ וְהַאֲכַלְתִּיךָ נַחֲלַת יַעֲקֹב אָבִיךָ. אָמַר לֵיהּ, הָא כֹּלָּא אִתְּמַר, דְּתַפְנוּקָא וְעִדּוּנָא עַל יְיָ' כְּתִיב, אֲתַר דְּאִיהוּ לְעֵילָא. וּכְתִיב וְעַד עַתִּיק יוֹמַיָּא מְטָה וְגוֹ'. עַל בָּמֳתֵי אָרֶץ כְּמָה דְּאִתְּמַר.

337. Rabbi Aba asked Rabbi Shimon: May my master explain the verse: "And I will cause you to ride upon the high places of the earth, and feed you with the heritage of Jacob your father." RABBI SHIMON answered him: It was already explained that the delight and pleasure are, as written, "above Hashem," which is above, NAMELY KETER. And it is written: "And came to the Ancient of Days and they brought him near before him." "Upon the high places of the earth" is as we said, THE LAND OF THE LIVING, NAMELY MALCHUT.

338. וְהַאֲכַלְתִּיךָ נַחֲלַת יַעֲקֹב אָבִיךָ. כְּמָה דִּכְתִיב וְיִתֶּן לְךָ הָאֱלֹהִים מִטַּל הַשָּׁמַיִם וְגוֹ', וְהַיְינוּ נַחֲלַת יַעֲקֹב. וּבִרְכָתָא דְּבָרִיךְ יִצְחָק לְיַעֲקֹב, עַל הַאי שָׁמַיִם קָאֲמַר. וּבִרְכֵיהּ בְּבִרְכָתָא, דִּזְמִינִין בְּנוֹי דְּיַעֲקֹב, לְאַחֲיָא בְּהַהוּא טַלָּא לְזִמְנָא דְּאָתֵי, דִּכְתִיב וְיִתֶּן לְךָ הָאֱלֹהִים. לְךָ וְלֹא לְאַחֲרָא.

מִטַּל הַשָּׁמַיִם, דְּבֵיהּ זְמִינִין מֵתַיָּא לְאַחֲיָא לְזִמְנָא דְּאָתֵי, דְּנָפִיק מֵעַתִּיקָא לִזְעֵירָא דְּאַפִּין, וְשַׁרְיָא בְּהַאי שָׁמַיִם. אִסְתָּכַּל ר' אַבָּא וְאָמַר, הַשְׁתָּא אִשְׁתְּמַע כֹּלָּא וְאִשְׁתְּכַח דְּבִרְכָתָא דְּיִצְחָק, עִלָּאָה מִמַּאי דַּחֲשִׁיבְנָא.

338. "And feed you with the heritage of Jacob your father," has the same meaning as the verse: "Therefore the Elohim give you of the dew of heaven" (Beresheet 27:28). "THE DEW OF HEAVEN" means the heritage of Jacob, and when Isaac blessed Jacob he alluded to heaven, WHICH IS ZEIR ANPIN, and he gave him the blessing that all the descendants of Jacob in the future will be revived by that dew, as it is written: "Therefore the Elohim give you." Only "you," and not to someone else. "The dew of heaven" is that by which the dead will be revived in the days to come, FOR THAT DEW ISSUES from Atika Kadisha (the Holy Ancient One) to Zeir Anpin, WHICH IS CALLED 'HEAVEN' and resides in heaven. Rabbi Aba thought OF THE VERSE and said: Now everything is clear, and I see that there is even more significance in Isaac's blessing than I had thought.

339. תָּאנָא מִי יְמַלֵּל גְּבוּרֹת יְיָ'. מִי יְמַלֵּל, מִי יְדַבֵּר מִבְּעֵי לֵיהּ. אָמַר ר' חִיָּיא, כד"א, וְקָטַפְתָּ מְלִילֹת בְּיָדֶךָ. גְּבוּרֹת יְיָ', דְּסַגִּיאִין אִינּוּן, וְנָפְקִין מִגְּבוּרָה חַד. וְתָאנָא, חַד גְּבוּרָה עִלָּאָה, עִטְרָא דְּעִטְּרִין, מִתְעַטְּרָא, וְנָפְקִין מִנֵּיהּ חַמְשִׁין תַּרְעִין. מִנְּהוֹן יְמִינָא, וּמִנְּהוֹן שְׂמָאלָא. וְכָל חַד וְחַד גְּבוּרָה אִתְקְרֵי, וְכָל חַד וְחַד מִתְעַטְּרָא, בְּקַרְדִּיטֵי גְּלִיפִין נְהוֹרִין, וְכֻלְּהוּ אִקְרוּן גְּבוּרֹת יְיָ'.

339. "Who can utter (Heb. *yemalel*) the mighty acts of Hashem?" (Tehilim 106:2). HE ASKS: Why does it say "utter" instead of 'tell'. Rabbi Chiya explained the answer by citing the verse: "then you may pluck the ears (Heb. *melilot*) with your hand" (Devarim 23:26). THEY ARE SO CALLED, FOR ONE HAS TO SEPARATE THE GRAINS FROM THE EAR BY PLUCKING (HEB. *MELILAH*) WITH THE HANDS, AND WHEN IT SAYS "UTTER" IT MEANS THAT ONE SHOULD SEPARATE AND CANCEL THE JUDGMENTS OF HASHEM. The word "*Gvurot* (lit. 'mighty acts')" of Hashem IS SPELLED WITHOUT THE LETTER *VAV* – THE INDICATION OF THE PLURAL FORM – AND implies that there are many *Gvurot* but all of them are coming from one

Gvurah. We have learned that there is one supernal Gvurah, the crown of the crowns, WHICH IS BINAH FROM WHICH JUDGMENTS ARE AROUSED and from which come fifty gates, some to the right and some to the left. And each one of them is called *'Gvurah'*, and each one of them is crowned with the lights of the supernal carvings, and all of them are called "the mighty acts of Hashem."

340. אָמַר רַבִּי חִיָּיא, גְּבוּרֹת יְיָ' חָסֵר כְּתִיב, דְּהָא כֻּלְּהוּ כְּלִילָן בְּדָא. יַשְׁמִיעַ כָּל תְּהִלָּתוֹ: דָּא הוּא שְׁכִינַת זִיו יְקָרֵיהּ דְּקוּדְשָׁא בְּרִיךְ הוּא, דִּכְתִּיב וּתְהִלָּתוֹ מָלְאָה הָאָרֶץ.

340. Rabbi Chiya said: THEREFORE, the word *Gvurot* is written without THE LETTER *VAV*, for all THE GVUROT are included within THE SUPERNAL GVURAH, WHICH IS BINAH. The closing part of the verse is: "Who can declare all His praise?" This indicates the Shechinah, which is the most precious glory of the Holy One, blessed be He, as it is expressed in the verse: "His glory covered the heavens and the earth was full of His praise" (Chavakuk 3:3).

341. אָמַר ר"ש, כְּתִיב וְנָהָר יוֹצֵא מֵעֵדֶן לְהַשְׁקוֹת אֶת הַגָּן וְגוֹ', שֵׁם הָאֶחָד פִּישׁוֹן וְגוֹ'. הָא אִלֵּין בִּשְׁמָהָן אִקְרוּן. וַהֲנֵי אַרְבַּע מֵהַהוּא נָהָר דְּנָפִיק אִתְמַשְׁכָּן. מַה שְׁמֵיהּ דְּהַהוּא נַהֲרָא דְּנָפִיק. אָמַר ר' שִׁמְעוֹן, יוּבַל שְׁמֵיהּ. דִּכְתִּיב, וְעַל יוּבַל יְשַׁלַּח שָׁרָשָׁיו, וּכְתִיב וְלֹא יָמִישׁ מֵעֲשׂוֹת פֶּרִי. מַאי טַעְמָא לֹא יָמִישׁ, מִשּׁוּם דְּעַל יוּבַל יְשַׁלַּח שָׁרָשָׁיו. וְעַל דָּא כְּתִיב וּכְמוֹצָא מַיִם אֲשֶׁר לֹא יְכַזְּבוּ מֵימָיו. וּבְגִין כָּךְ כְּתִיב יוֹצֵא, וְאֵינוֹ פּוֹסֵק.

341. Rabbi Shimon cited a verse: "And a river went out of Eden to water the Garden and from thence it was parted and branched into four streams, the name of the first is Pishon..." (Beresheet 2:10). Those RIVERS which came from that river which comes forth from Eden have names; but what is the name of the one which comes out OF EDEN? Rabbi Shimon says that its name is Yuval, for it is written: "And that spreads out its roots by the river (Heb. *yuval*)" (Yirmeyah 17:8), and, "Nor shall it cease from yielding fruit" (Ibid.). The reason that it shall not "cease from yielding fruit" is that it

spreads "its roots by the river," WHICH IS BINAH. Therefore it is written: "Like a spring of water whose waters fail not" (Yeshayah 58:11), FOR THE PLENTY WHICH COMES FORTH FROM THE BINAH NEVER CEASES. Therefore, it is written: "A river went OUT OF EDEN"; it comes out of it and never ceases.

342. תָּאנָא א"ר שִׁמְעוֹן כְּתִיב וַיְדַבֵּר אֱלֹהִים אֶת כָּל הַדְּבָרִים וְגוֹ', וַיְדַבֵּר, בְּגִין לְאַכְרְזָא מִילִין. דְּתָאנָא, בְּשַׁעֲתָא דְּקוּדְשָׁא בְּרִיךְ הוּא אִתְגְּלֵי, וְשָׁארֵי לְמַלְּלָא, עֲלָאִין וְתַתָּאִין אִתְחַלְחֲלוּ, וְנַפְקוּ נִשְׁמָתְהוֹן דְּיִשְׂרָאֵל.

342. Rabbi Shimon cited the verse: "And Elohim spoke all these words" (Shemot 20:1). IT SAYS "SPOKE" AND NOT 'SAID', BECAUSE "spoke" denotes announcing IN A LOUD VOICE, for we have learned that at the time that the Holy One, blessed be He, revealed Himself and began to speak, the celestial and the terrestrial beings began to tremble, and the souls of Yisrael left them.

343. וְתָאנָא הַהוּא מִלָּה, הֲוָה טָאס מִלְּעֵילָא לְתַתָּא, וּמִתְגַּלְּפָא בְּאַרְבַּע רוּחֵי עָלְמָא, וְסַלְקָא וְנַחְתָּא. כַּד סַלְקָא, אִשְׁתְּאָבָא מִטּוּרֵי דְּאַפַּרְסְמוֹנָא דַּכְיָא, וְאִשְׁתְּאָבָא בְּהַהוּא טַלָּא דִּלְעֵילָא, וְאַסְחַר בְּסַחֲרָנֵיהוֹן דְּיִשְׂרָאֵל, וְתָבַת בְּהוֹן נִשְׁמָתְהוֹן וְאַסְחַר וּמִתְגַּלְּפָא בַּאֲתַרֵיהּ, בְּלוּחֵי אַבְנָא. וְכֵן כָּל מִלָּה וּמִלָּה.

343. We have learned that that word soared from above downwards, being engraved upon the four winds of the universe on its way, and then rose once more and again descended. When it rose up it was filled from the mountains of pure balsam and was watered with the heavenly dew. Then it encircled Yisrael and brought back their souls. Then it turned back and was engraved upon the tablets of stone. And so it was with each and every word.

344. אָמַר רַבִּי שִׁמְעוֹן, כָּל מִלָּה וּמִלָּה הֲוָה מַלְיָא בְּכָל אִינּוּן טַעֲמִין, בְּכָל אִינּוּן מִלִּין גְּזֵרִין, אַגְרִין, וְעוֹנָשִׁין, רָזִין וְסִתְרִין כְּאַסְקוּפָא דָא, דְּאִיהִי מַלְיָא מִכֹּלָּא.

344. Rabbi Shimon said that every word contained all manner of legal implications and derivations, all the laws concerning reward and punishment, as well as all mysteries and hidden aspects, for each word was like a treasure house full of precious things.

345. וּבְשַׁעֲתָא דַּהֲוָה נָפִיק הַהוּא מִלָּה, אִתְחֲזֵי חַד. וְכַד הֲוָה מִתְגַּלְּפָא בְּאַתְרוֹי אִתְחֲזוּן בְּהַהוּא מִלָּה, שַׁבְעִין עַנְפִין, דְּסַלְקִין בְּגַוָּה, וְחַמְשִׁין כִּתְרִין חָסֵר חַד מֵהַאי גִּיסָא, וְחַמְשִׁין חָסֵר חַד מִגִּיסָא אַחֲרָא כְּפַטִּישָׁא דָא, בְּזִמְנָא דְּאִיהוּ בָּטַשׁ בְּטִנָרָא. כְּמָה דְאַתְּ אָמֵר וּכְפַטִּישׁ יְפוֹצֵץ סָלַע. וַהֲווֹ חָמָאן כָּל יִשְׂרָאֵל עֵינָא בְּעֵינָא, וַהֲווֹ חַדָּאן.

345. When one word was uttered it seemed as one, but when it was engraved in its place UPON THE TABLETS OF STONES, seventy branches were revealed in it, fifty crowns less one on one side, and fifty less one upon the other, like the hammer which breaks the rocks in a mountain, as it is written: "Like a hammer that breaks the rock in pieces" (Yirmeyah 23:29). And all of Yisrael saw eye to eye and rejoiced.

346. וְכֻלְּהוּ דָּרִין בַּתְרָאִין כֻּלְּהוּ אִזְדְּמָנוּ לְתַמָּן, וְכֻלְּהוּ קַבִּילוּ אוֹרַיְיתָא בְּטוּרָא דְּסִינַי, דִּכְתִּיב כִּי אֶת אֲשֶׁר יֶשְׁנוֹ פֹּה וְגו', וְאֶת אֲשֶׁר אֵינֶנּוּ פֹּה עִמָּנוּ הַיּוֹם. וְכֻלְּהוּ כָּל חַד וְחַד כַּדְקָא חֲזֵי לֵיהּ. וְכֻלְּהוּ חָמָאן וּמְקַבְּלִין מִלִּין.

346. The souls of all the generations to come were present there and all of them received the Torah on Mount Sinai, as it is written: "but with those that stands here with us this day...and also with those that are not here with us this day" (Devarim 29:14). They were all there, each according to his merit, and saw and received the words.

347. אֱלֹהִים: דָּא גְּבוּרָא. אֶת: דְּאִתְכְּלִיל בִּימִינָא, כְּמָה דְּתָנֵינָן אֶת הַשָּׁמַיִם, דְּאִיהוּ יְמִינָא. וְאֶת הָאָרֶץ, דְּאִיהוּ שְׂמָאלָא. דִּכְתִּיב, אַף יָדִי יָסְדָה אֶרֶץ וִימִינִי טִפְּחָה שָׁמָיִם. כָּל: לְאַכְלְלָא כָּל שְׁאָר כִּתְרִין. הַדְּבָרִים: מִתְקַשְּׁרָן דָּא בְּדָא הָאֵלֶּה: כָּל אִינּוּן טַעֲמִין, כָּל

אִינּוּן רָזִין, כָּל אִינּוּן סִתְרִין, גְּזֵרִין וְעוֹנָשִׁין.

347. "AND ELOHIM SPOKE ALL THESE (HEB. 'ET') WORDS, SAYING" (SHEMOT 20:1). THE NAME Elohim indicates Gvurah; 'Et' INDICATES that it was joined to the right. As we have learned, "the (Et) heaven" is the right and "and the earth" is the left, as written: "My hand also has laid the foundation of the earth and My right hand has spanned the heavens" (Yeshayah 48:13). The right side IS CHESED AND is called "Et (the)." The word "all" is IN ORDER to include all the other Sfirot. "These words" INDICATE that everything is included, one within the other. "These" INDICATES all the meanings, the secrets, the mysteries, decrees and penalties.

348. לֵאמֹר: לְמֶהֱוֵי יְרוּתָא לְכֹלָּא. דִּכְתִיב תּוֹרָה צִוָּה לָנוּ מֹשֶׁה מוֹרָשָׁה וְגוֹ'. דְּאִי תֵּימָא לְגַלָּאָה מַה דְּלָא אִצְטְרִיךְ לְגַלָּאָה לְכָל בַּ"נ, כְּתִיב אָנֹכִי יְיָ' אֱלֹהֶיךָ. כְּמָה דַּאֲנָא טְמִירָא וְסָתִים, כַּךְ יְהוֹן אִלֵּין מִלִּין טְמִירִין וּסְתִימִין בְּלִבָּךְ.

348. The word "saying" INDICATES THAT all that was said was an inheritance for everyone, as it is written: "Moses commanded us a Torah, the inheritance of the congregation of Jacob" (Devarim 33:4). You may say that IT SHOULD BE UNDERSTOOD LITERALLY, TO REVEAL TO EVERYONE AND to reveal what must not be revealed to anyone. However, it says: "I am Hashem your Elohim" (Shemot 20:1) WHICH INDICATES THAT as I am hidden and concealed, so should these words be covered and concealed in your heart.

349. ד"א וַיְדַבֵּר אֱלֹהִים, חַד. אֶת כָּל הַדְּבָרִים הָאֵלֶּה לֵאמֹר הָא חָמֵשׁ דַּרְגִּין אַחֲרָנִין. ר' יְהוּדָה אָמַר, וַיְדַבֵּר אֱלֹהִים: גְּבוּרָה. אֶת: יְמִינָא. כָּל: דָּא וְדָא אָמַר ר' יִצְחָק, לְאַכְלְלָא אַבְרָהָם דִּכְתִיב וַיְיָ' בֵּרַךְ אֶת אַבְרָהָם בַּכֹּל.

349. There is another interpretation of this verse. "And Elohim spoke" is one GRADE. "All (et) these words saying," are five more grades, FOR EACH WORD IS A GRADE. Rabbi Yehuda said that "And Elohim spoke" is Gvurah,

"*Et*" is the right side, WHICH IS CHESED, and "all" INCLUDES both GVURAH AND CHESED. Rabbi Yitzchak said that "ALL" includes Abraham, for it is written: "And Hashem had blessed Abraham in all things" (Beresheet 24:1).

350. הַדְּבָרִים: לְאַכְלָלָא שְׁאַר כִּתְרִין דְּאִתְכַּסְיָין. הָאֵלֶּה: אִינוּן דְּאִתְגַּלְיָין. וּכְתִיב וְכָל הָעָם רֹאִים אֶת הַקּוֹלֹת. לֵאמֹר: דָּא הוּא דִּכְתִּיב, אֵשֶׁת חַיִל עֲטֶרֶת בַּעְלָהּ. וּכְתִיב, לֵאמֹר הֵן יְשַׁלַּח אִישׁ אֶת אִשְׁתּוֹ.

350. The function of "words" is to include all the covered crowns. The word "these" includes all those which were revealed, as it is written: "And all the people see the voices," NAMELY THE REVEALED VISIONS INCLUDED IN "THESE." "Saying," REFERS TO THE SHECHINAH, as it is written: "A virtuous woman is a crown to her husband" (Mishlei 12:4), and: "It was said: 'If a man put away his wife'" (Yirmeyah 3:1). THE WORD "SAYING" IS CLOSE TO HER MAN, WHICH INDICATES THAT IT REFERS TO THE NUKVA OF ZEIR ANPIN, WHICH IS THE SHECHINAH.

351. אָמַר ר' יִצְחָק, אֲמַאי אִתְיְהִיבַת אוֹרַיְיתָא בְּאֶשָּׁא וַחֲשׁוֹכָא, דִּכְתִיב וְהָהָר בֹּעֵר בָּאֵשׁ עַד לֵב הַשָּׁמַיִם חֹשֶׁךְ עָנָן וַעֲרָפֶל. דְּכָל מַאן דְּיִשְׁתַּדַּל בְּאוֹרַיְיתָא, אִשְׁתְּזִיב מֵאֶשָּׁא אַחֲרָא דְּגֵיהִנָּם, וּמֵחֲשׁוֹכָא דִּמְחַשְׁכִין כָּל שְׁאַר עַמִּין לְיִשְׂרָאֵל, דְּבִזְכוּתֵיה דְּאַבְרָהָם אִשְׁתְּזִיבוּ יִשְׂרָאֵל מֵאֶשָּׁא דְּגֵיהִנָּם.

351. Rabbi Yitzchak asked: Why was the Torah given in fire and darkness, as it is written, "And the mountain burned with fire to the heart of heaven, with darkness clouds and thick darkness" (Devarim 4:11). AND HE ANSWERED THAT THE REASON IS that he who is occupied with the study of the Torah will be saved from the other fire of Gehenom, and from the darkness that the other nations bring upon Yisrael. It was the merit of Abraham which saved Yisrael from the fire of Gehenom.

352. דְּתַנְיָא אָמַר לֵיה קוּדְשָׁא בְּרִיךְ הוּא לְאַבְרָהָם, כָּל זִמְנָא דְּבָנֶיךָ יִשְׁתַּדְּלוּן בְּאוֹרַיְיתָא, יִשְׁתְּזִבוּן מֵאִלֵּין. וְאִי לָא, הָא נוּרָא דְּגֵיהִנָּם דְּשַׁלְטָא בְּהוּ, וְיִשְׁתַּעְבְּדוּן בֵּינֵי עֲמַמְיָא. א"ל, בִּתְרֵי קְטוֹרֵי לָא מִזְדַּקְפָן

-166-

מִלִּין, אֶלָּא אִי נִיחָא קַמָּךְ, יִשְׁתֵּזְבוּן מִנּוּרָא דְּגֵיהִנָּם, וְיִשְׁתַּעְבְּדוּן בֵּינֵי

עֲמַמְיָא, עַד דְּיִתוּבוּן גַּבָּךְ. אָמַר לֵיהּ יָאוֹת הוּא וַדַּאי, הה"ד אִם לֹא כִּי

צוּרָם מְכָרָם. מַאן הוּא צוּרָם. דָּא הוּא אַבְרָהָם. דִּכְתִיב הַבִּיטוּ אֶל צוּר

חֻצַּבְתֶּם. וַיְיָ' הִסְגִּירָם, דָּא קוּדְשָׁא בְּרִיךְ הוּא, דְּאִסְתְּכַּם עַל יְדוֹי.

352. As we have learned, the Holy One, blessed be He, said to Abraham: 'As long as your children shall study the Torah they will be saved FROM FIRE AND DARKNESS, but if they should turn from her and forget her paths, the fire of Gehenom will have dominion over them and they will be subjected to the nations'. Then ABRAHAM said to Him: 'May things not come to pass, THE FIRE OF GEHENOM AND EXILE, with these two knots. If it pleases You, let them escape from the fire of Gehenom and go into exile and become enslaved to other nations until they return to You'. THE HOLY ONE, BLESSED BE HE, answered him: 'So be it then', and so it was as it is written: "unless their Rock had sold them" (Devarim 32:30). Who is "their Rock"? Abraham, as it is written: "Look to the rock whence you are hewn" (Yeshayah 51:1). "And Hashem had shut them up" (Ibid.), refers to the Holy One, blessed be He, who agreed with him.

353. אָמַר ר' יְהוּדָה, מִיּוֹמָא דְּנָפְקוּ יִשְׂרָאֵל מִמִּצְרַיִם עַד יוֹמָא דְּאִתְיְהִיבַת אוֹרַיְיתָא, חַמְשִׁין יוֹמִין הֲווֹ. מ"ט אָמַר ר' יְהוּדָה, מִשּׁוּם אִינּוּן שְׁנֵי דְּיוֹבְלָא, דִּכְתִיב וְקִדַּשְׁתֶּם אֶת שְׁנַת הַחֲמִשִּׁים שָׁנָה.

353. Rabbi Yehuda said: Fifty days elapsed between the day Yisrael were led out from Egypt and the day the Torah was given to them. What was the reason? Rabbi Yehuda said: In order that the number of days should correspond to the number of years of Jubilee, WHICH IS BINAH, as it is written: "And you shall hallow the fiftieth year" (Vayikra 25:10), NAMELY, THE FIFTIETH GATE IN BINAH.

354. תָּאנָא, אר"ש, הַהוּא יוֹבְלָא אַפִּיק לוֹן לְיִשְׂרָאֵל מִמִּצְרַיִם. וְאִי תֵימָא דְּיוֹבְלָא מַמָּשׁ. אֶלָּא מִסִּטְרָא דְּיוֹבְלָא הֲוָה, וּמִסִּטְרָא דְּיוֹבְלָא אִתְּעַר דִּינָא עַל מִצְרָאֵי, וּבְגִינֵי כַּךְ חַמְשִׁין אִלֵּין דְּיוֹבְלָא הֲווֹ.

354. Rabbi Shimon said: We have learned that it was the Jubilee which led

Yisrael out from Egypt. If you believe that it is Jubilee itself, NAMELY
BINAH ITSELF, IT IS NOT SO. THE EXODUS occurred through the aspect of
Jubilee and from the aspect of the same Judgment was stirred up against the
Egyptians. Therefore, those fifty years are THE FIFTY GATES OF Jubilee,
WHICH IS BINAH.

355. תָּאנָא, לָקֳבֵל דָּא, חַמְשִׁין זִמְנִין אִתְּמַר וְאִדְכַּר בְּאוֹרַיְיתָא, נִמּוּסִין
דְּמִצְרַיִם, וְשִׁבְחֵי אִינּוּן כֻּלְּהוּ, אֲשֶׁר הוֹצֵאתִיךָ. וַיּוֹצִיאֲךָ. כִּי בְּיַד חֲזָקָה
הוֹצִיאֲךָ. וְכֻלְּהוּ זִמְנֵי, חַמְשִׁין אִינּוּן, וְלָא יַתִּיר, מִשּׁוּם דְּכֹלָּא בְּיוֹבְלָא
אִתְעֲטָּר, וּמִסִּטְרָא דְּיוֹבְלָא אָתָא כֹּלָּא. וּבְגִינֵי כַּךְ, אוֹרַיְיתָא דְּאָתֵי
מִגְּבוּרָה, אִתְעַטְּרַת בִּימִינָא. דִּכְתִיב מִימִינוֹ אֵשׁ דָּת לָמוֹ. וְתַנְיָא חֲמִשָׁא
קָלִין הֲווֹ. וְכֻלְּהוּ אִתְחֲזִיאוּ בְּהוּ, וְאִתְכְּלִילוּ בְּהוּ, וְאִתְעַטְּרוּ בְּדָא.

355. We have learned that the deeds in Egypt are mentioned fifty times in
the Torah, and in all of those times words of praise are said. For example:
"who have brought you out of the land of Egypt" (Shemot 20:2), and, "And
brought you out" (Devarim 4:37), and, "For by strength of hand Hashem
brought you out from this place..." (Shemot 13:3): fifty times exactly and no
more, since all is adorned with Jubilee, WHICH IS BINAH, and from the side
of Jubilee everything comes. AND THERE ARE FIFTY GATES TO BINAH.
Therefore, the Torah, which comes from Gvurah, is crowned in the right, as
it is written: "From His right hand went a fiery law for them" (Devarim
33:2). We have also learned that WHEN THE TORAH WAS GIVEN, there were
five voices: CHESED, GVURAH, TIFERET, NETZACH AND HOD IN BINAH,
and all of these were seen in them, included in them, and crowned IN
BINAH.

356. אָמַר ר' שִׁמְעוֹן, בְּהַהוּא זִמְנָא דְּקַבִּילוּ יִשְׂרָאֵל אוֹרַיְיתָא, יוֹבְלָא
דָּא אַעֲטַר בְּעִטְרוֹי לְקוּדְשָׁא בְּרִיךְ הוּא, כְּמַלְכָּא דְּאִתְעַטָּר בְּגוֹ חֵילֵיהּ.
דִּכְתִיב, צְאֶינָה וּרְאֶינָה בְּנוֹת צִיּוֹן בַּמֶּלֶךְ שְׁלֹמֹה בַּעֲטָרָה שֶׁעִטְּרָה לוֹ
אִמּוֹ. מַאן אִמּוֹ. דָּא יוֹבְלָא. וְיוֹבְלָא אִתְעַטָּר, בְּחֶדְוָה בִּרְחִימוּ בִּשְׁלִימוּ.
דִּכְתִיב אֵם הַבָּנִים שְׂמֵחָה. מַאן אֵם הַבָּנִים. אר"ש דָּא יוֹבְלָא.

356. Rabbi Shimon said: At the time that Yisrael received the Torah, that

Jubilee, WHICH IS BINAH, crowned the Holy One, blessed be He, WHO IS
ZEIR ANPIN, as a king is crowned in the midst of his hosts, as it is written:
"Go forth, O daughters of Zion, and behold King Solomon with the crown
with which his mother crowned him" (Shir Hashirim 3:11). Who is "his
mother"? It is Yovel, FOR BINAH IS CALLED 'JUBILEE' (HEB. YOVEL)
AND SHE IS THE MOTHER OF ZEIR ANPIN, CALLED 'SOLOMON'. The
Jubilee was crowned with joy, love and perfection, as it is written: "be a
joyful mother of children" (Tehilim 113:9). Who is the "mother of
children"? Rabbi Shimon said: This is Jubilee.

357. א"ר יְהוּדָה, ע"ד כְּתִיב, יִשְׂמַח אָבִיךָ וְאִמֶּךָ וְתָגֵל יוֹלַדְתֶּךָ. מַאן
אָבִיךָ וְאִמֶּךָ. א"ר יְהוּדָה, כְּמָה דְּאוּקְמוּהָ בְּסִפְרָא דִּצְנִיעוּתָא, דִּכְתִּיב,
עֶרְוַת אָבִיךָ וְעֶרְוַת אִמְּךָ לֹא תְגַלֵּה וַוי לְמַאן דְּגַלֵּי עֶרְיָיתְהוֹן.

357. Rabbi Yehuda said: Concerning this it is written, "Let your father and
your mother be glad and let her who bore you rejoice" (Mishlei 23:24). Who
are "your father and your mother"? They are as explained in Safra
deTz'niuta (lit. 'the Concealed Book'), relating to the verse: "The nakedness
of your father, or the nakedness of your mother, shall you not uncover"
(Vayikra 17:7). Woe to one who uncovers their nakedness, FOR THE
SECRET OF CHOCHMAH AND BINAH ARE CALLED 'FATHER' AND
'MOTHER'.

358. תָּאנָא, א"ר יִצְחָק, בְּשַׁעֲתָא דְּקוּדְשָׁא בְּרִיךְ הוּא אִתְגְּלֵי בְּטוּרָא
דְּסִינַי, אִזְדַּעְזַע טוּרָא. וּבְשַׁעֲתָא דְּסִינַי אִזְדַּעְזַע, כָּל שְׁאַר טוּרֵי עָלְמָא
אִזְדַּעְזְעוּ, וַהֲווֹ סַלְקִין וְנַחְתִּין, עַד דְּאוֹשִׁיט קוּדְשָׁא בְּרִיךְ הוּא יְדוֹי
עֲלַיְיהוּ, וְאִתְיַישְׁבוּ. וְקָלָא נָפְקָא וּמַכְרְזָא, מַה לְּךָ הַיָּם כִּי תָנוּס הַיַּרְדֵּן
תִּסּוֹב לְאָחוֹר הֶהָרִים תִּרְקְדוּ כְאֵילִים וְגוֹ'.

358. Rabbi Yitzchak said: We have learned that at the time that the Holy
One, blessed be He, revealed Himself on Mount Sinai, the mountain began
to shake and all the mountains on earth trembled and quaked, and they rose
and fell until the Holy One, blessed be He, stretched out His hand and
calmed them. And a voice was heard proclaiming: "What ails you, O you
sea, that you flee? O Jorden, that you are driven back? You mountains, that
you skip like rams..." (Tehilim 114:4-5).

359. וְאִינּוּן תָּבָאן וְאַמְרִין, מִלְפָנֵי אָדוֹן חוּלִי אָרֶץ. אָמַר ר' יִצְחָק, מִלְפָנֵי אָדוֹן, דָּא אִימָא, דִּכְתִיב אֵם הַבָּנִים שְׂמֵחָה. חוּלִי אָרֶץ, דָּא אִימָא תַּתָּאָה. מִלְפָנֵי אֱלוֹהַ יַעֲקֹב, דָּא הוּא אַבָּא, דִּכְתִיב, בְּנִי בְכֹרִי יִשְׂרָאֵל. וְעַל הַאי כְּתִיב בַּעֲטָרָה שֶׁעִטְּרָה לוֹ אִמּוֹ.

359. And they answered Him: "Tremble, you earth, at the presence of the Master." Rabbi Yitzchak said: "At the presence of the Master," refers to Ima, WHO IS BINAH, as it is written: "a joyful mother of children." "Tremble, you earth," refers to the lower Ima, WHO IS MALCHUT. "At the presence of the Eloha of Jacob," is Aba, WHO IS ZEIR ANPIN, LOWER ABA, as it is written: "Yisrael is My son, My firstborn" (Shemot 4:22), MEANING ZEIR ANPIN WHICH IS CALLED 'YISRAEL'. And of that it is written: "the crown with which his mother crowned him," "HIS MOTHER" BEING BINAH.

360. מַהוּ בַּעֲטָרָה. א"ר יִצְחָק, כְּמָה דִּכְתִיב, וְשָׁאוּל וַאֲנָשָׁיו עוֹטְרִים אֶת דָּוִד. מִשּׁוּם דְּמִתְעַטָּר, בְּחִוָּורָא בְּסוּמָקָא וּבִירוֹקָא, בְּכָל גְּוָונִין דִּכְלְהוּ כְּלִילָן בֵּיהּ, וְאִסְתַּחֲרָן בֵּיהּ. אָמַר ר' יְהוּדָה, בַּעֲטָרָה שֶׁעִטְּרָה לוֹ אִמּוֹ. מַאן עֲטָרָה. דִּכְתִיב, יִשְׂרָאֵל אֲשֶׁר בְּךָ אֶתְפָּאָר. וּכְתִיב וּבֵית תִּפְאַרְתִּי אֲפָאֵר.

360. HE ASKS: What is "the crown WITH WHICH HIS MOTHER CROWNED HIM"? and Rabbi Yitzchak replies: This resembles the verse, "For Saul and his men compassed David and his men round about" (I Shmuel 23:26), WHICH IS LIKE ENCIRCLING, for ZEIR ANPIN is crowned AND SURROUNDED BY IMA with white, red and green, all colors – THE SECRET OF THE THREE COLUMNS – all of which are included and encircled in it. Rabbi Yehuda asked: In the verse, "the crown with which his mother crowned him," what is the crown? It has the same meaning as in "Yisrael, in whom I will be glorified" (Yeshayah 49:3), and, "And I will glorify the house of My glory" (Yeshayah 60:7), NAMELY, THE FIRST THREE SFIROT WHICH ARE THE GLORY OF ZEIR ANPIN, WHICH IS CALLED 'YISRAEL' AND ALSO 'TIFERET'.

361. אָמַר ר' יִצְחָק, אוֹרַיְיתָא אִתְיְהִיבַת בְּאֶשָׁא אוּכְמָא, עַל גַּבֵּי אֶשָׁא חִוָּורָא, לְאַכְלְלָא יְמִינָא בִּשְׂמָאלָא, וּשְׂמָאלָא דְּאִתְחֲזַר יְמִינָא, דִּכְתִיב

מִימִינוֹ אֵשׁ דָּת לָמוֹ.

361. Rabbi Yitzchak said that the Torah was given in a black fire engraved upon a white fire, in order to include the right in the left. And the left was returned to the right, as it is written: "From His right hand went a fiery law for them."

362. א"ר אַבָּא, בְּשַׁעֲתָא דְּתָנָנָא דְּסִינַי הֲוָה נָפִיק, סָלִיק אֶשָּׁא, וּמִתְעַטֵּר בְּהַהוּא תָּנָנָא בְּאִתְגַּלְיָיא, כְּאִתְכְּלָא דָּא, וְסָלִיק וְנָחִית, וְכָל רֵיחִין וּבוּסְמִין דִּבְגִנְתָּא דְּעֵדֶן, הֲוָה סָלִיק הַהוּא תָּנָנָא, בְּחֵיזוּ דְּחִוָּור וְסוּמָק וְאוּכָם, הה"ד, מְקֻטֶּרֶת מֹר וּלְבוֹנָה מִכֹּל אַבְקַת רוֹכֵל.

362. Rabbi Aba said: When the smoke came out of Mount Sinai, a fire ascended and was crowned with it openly, AND LOOKED like cluster. And it flared high and dwindled again, and all the aromas of the Garden of Eden were blended in that smoke, having the colors white, red and black, as it is written: "Perfumed with myrrh and frankincense, with all powders of the merchant" (Shir Hashirim 3:6).

363. הַהוּא תָּנָנָא מַאן הֲוָה. אָמַר ר' יִצְחָק, שְׁכִינְתָּא דְּאִתְגַּלֵּי לְתַמָּן, כד"א, מִי זֹאת עוֹלָה מִן הַמִּדְבָּר כְּתִמְרוֹת עָשָׁן. אָמַר ר' יְהוּדָה, לָמָּה לָךְ כּוּלֵי הַאי הָא קְרָא שְׁלִים הוּא, דִּכְתִיב וְהַר סִינַי עָשַׁן כֻּלּוֹ מִפְּנֵי אֲשֶׁר יָרַד עָלָיו יְיָ' בָּאֵשׁ וַיַּעַל עֲשָׁנוֹ כְּעֶשֶׁן הַכִּבְשָׁן. זַכָּאָה עַמָּא דְּחָמָאן דָּא, וְיַדְעִין דָּא.

363. Rabbi Yitzchak said that the smoke was the Shechinah who manifested Herself there, as it is written in the verse: "Who is this coming out of the wilderness like columns of smoke" (Ibid.), WHICH ALLUDES TO THE SHECHINAH. Rabbi Yehuda said: Surely you do not have to go to great lengths to learn of it, for there is a whole description: "And Mount Sinai smoked in every part, because Hashem descended upon it in fire, and the smoke of it ascended like the smoke of a furnace" (Shemot 19:18). Blessed are the people who saw it and knew it.

21. "the tablets were the work of Elohim"

A Synopsis

We hear how the tablets of the Ten Commandments were of sapphire, and the letters were visible on both sides and composed of both black fire and white fire, from the left and the right. The rabbis are in some confusion about whether Elohim made the tablets specially or whether they were really 'just' sapphire as any other sapphire. Rabbi Shimon says the tablets were formed of the supernal dew which flows from Atika Kadisha, and that they pre-existed the creation of the world but were perfected on the sixth day of creation especially for this purpose. The miracle was that one could read one side from the other. We are told that the Torah actually literally restored the souls of Yisrael after they had flown away at the time that the people heard the words of God. The text now turns to the rule of Solomon, during which time the moon was full. When Zedekiah came, the moon waned and remained thus, so Malchut was removed far from Zeir Anpin, and became dark. The moon shone when Yisrael stood by Mount Sinai, and it shone when Judah was found worthy to receive the kingdom.

364. א״ר חִיָּיא, כַּד אִתְגְּלִיפוּ אַתְוָון בְּלוּחֵי אַבְנָא, הֲווֹ מִתְחַזְיָין בִּתְרֵין סִטְרִין, מִסִּטְרָא דָא, וּמִסִּטְרָא דָא, וְלוּחִין מֵאֶבֶן סַנְפִּירִינוֹן הֲווֹ, וְאִתְגְּלִיפוּ וְאִתְחַפְּיָין בְּאֶשָּׁא חִוּוּרָא, וְאַתְוָון הֲווֹ מֵאֶשָּׁא אוּכְמָא, וּמִתְגַּלְפָן בִּתְרֵין סִטְרִין, מִסִּטְרָא דָא וּמִסִּטְרָא דָא.

364. Rabbi Chiya said: When the letters were engraved upon the two tablets of stone, they were visible on both sides. The tablets were of sapphire, engraved and covered with white fire and the letters were of black fire, covered again, and engraved with white fire upon both sides.

365. אָמַר ר׳ אַבָּא, לוּחִין הֲווֹ בְּעֵינַיְיהוּ, וְאַתְוָון הֲווֹ טָאסִין, וּמִתְחַזְיָין בִּתְרֵין אֶשִּׁין, אֶשָּׁא חִוּוּרָא, וְאֶשָּׁא אוּכְמָא, לְאִתְחֲזָאָה כַּחֲדָא, יְמִינָא וּשְׂמָאלָא, דִּכְתִיב אֹרֶךְ יָמִים בִּימִינָהּ בִּשְׂמֹאלָהּ וְגו׳. וְהָא כְּתִיב מִימִינוֹ אֵשׁ דָּת לָמוֹ. אֶלָּא מִסִּטְרָא דִגְבוּרָה הֲוָה, וְאִתְכְּלִילַת בִּימִינָא. וּבְגִין כָּךְ אֶשָּׁא חִוּוּרָא וְאֶשָּׁא אוּכְמָא.

365. Rabbi Aba said that the two tablets remained as they were, THAT IS, COMPLETE, WITHOUT ANY CHANGE. And the letters soared in the air and could be seen with both black and white fire in order to demonstrate the union of the right and the left, FOR WHITE IS RIGHT AND BLACK IS LEFT, as it is written: "Length of days is in her right hand and in her left hand are riches and honor" (Mishlei 3:16). HE ASKS: Is it not written: "From His right hand went a fiery law to them" (Devarim 33:2)? AND HE ANSWERS THAT the Torah emanated from the side of Gvurah, WHICH IS THE LEFT, and was included in the right side. Therefore IT HAD IN IT black and white fire.

366. תָּאנָא, כְּתִיב וְהַלֻחֹת מַעֲשֵׂה אֱלֹהִים הֵמָה וגו', א"ר יְהוּדָה, וְהַלֻחֹת כְּתִיב, חַד. תְּרֵי הֲווֹ וּמִתְחַזְיָין חַד. וְעֶשֶׂר אֲמִירָן מִתְגַּלְּפֵי בְּהוּ. חָמֵשׁ כְּלִילָן בְּחָמֵשׁ, לְמֶהֱוֵי כֹּלָּא יְמִינָא. מַעֲשֵׂה אֱלֹהִים הֵמָּה וַדַּאי.

366. As we learned, it says "the tablets (Heb. *luchot*) were the work of Elohim" (Shemot 32:16). Rabbi Yehuda said that it is written "*luchot*," WITHOUT VAV, that is one (in singular), to indicate that although they were two, they appeared as one. And the Ten Commandments were engraved upon them, one section of five being included in the other section of five, so that all pertains to the right side. In this way they were indeed the very "work of Elohim."

367. רַבִּי יִצְחָק אָמַר, שֶׁל סַנְפִּירִינוֹן הֲווֹ, וּתְרֵין אַבְנִין הֲווֹ. וְאַבְנִין הֲווֹ סְתִימָאן. נָשִׁיב קוּדְשָׁא בְּרִיךְ הוּא בְּרוּחָא, וְאִתְפָּשַׁט וְאִתְגְּלִיפוּ תְּרֵין לוּחִין. ר' יְהוּדָה אָמַר, כְּעֵין סַנְפִּירִינוֹן הֲווֹ. מַשְׁמַע דִּכְתִיב מַעֲשֵׂה אֱלֹהִים הֵמָּה.

367. Rabbi Yitzchak said that the tablets were of sapphire, for there were originally two sapphire stones which were rough hewn, and the Holy One, blessed be He, caused a wind to blow upon them, and they were smoothed and transformed into two tablets. Rabbi Yehuda said that they only looked like sapphire, BUT WERE NOT OF REAL SAPPHIRE, and this is the meaning of the verse which describes them as "the work of Elohim." FOR IF THEY WERE OF SAPPHIRE, THEY WOULD HAVE BEEN LIKE OTHER PRECIOUS STONES AND NOT "THE WORK OF ELOHIM."

368. אָמַר לֵיהּ, אִי הָכִי, סַנְפִּירִינוֹן דָּא דְּהוּא אַבְנָא טָבָא יַקִּירָא מִשְׁאָר אַבְנִין, לָאו עוֹבָדָא דְּקוּדְשָׁא בְּרִיךְ הוּא אִינּוּן. א"ל, בְּמַאי אוֹקִימְנָא מַעֲשֵׂה אֱלֹהִים הֵמָּה. הֵמָּה דַּיְיקָא. אֶלָּא ת"ח, כְּתִיב וְהַלֻּחֹת מַעֲשֵׂה אֱלֹהִים. הַלֻּחֹת כְּתִיב, וְלָא כְּתִיב וְהָאֲבָנִים מַעֲשֵׂה אֱלֹהִים הֵמָּה.

368. He said to him: If this is so, the sapphire, which is a stone more precious than any other, is not the work of Elohim, YET THE WHOLE CREATION IS "THE WORK OF ELOHIM". So he explained to him: How then do we explain the words: "were the work of Elohim"? They were indeed so. THEY WERE A SPECIAL "WORK OF ELOHIM," NOT INCLUDED IN THE WORKS OF CREATION. Yet come and behold: it is written that "the tablets were the work of Elohim." It says "the tablets," not 'the stones were the work of Elohim', FOR HE BLEW UPON THE STONES, WHICH WERE OF REAL SAPPHIRE, AND THEY WERE TRANSFORMED INTO TWO TABLETS, AS MENTIONED ABOVE.

369. אָמַר ר' שִׁמְעוֹן, כֹּלָּא חַד הוּא, אֲבָל אִלֵּין תְּרֵין לוּחִין עַד לָא אִתְבְּרֵי עָלְמָא הֲווֹ, וְאִסְתַּלָּקוּ מֵעֶרֶב שַׁבָּת, וְעָבַד לוֹן קוּדְשָׁא בְּרִיךְ הוּא, וְעוֹבָדוֹי הֲווֹ.

369. Rabbi Shimon said: Both are the same, FOR BOTH RABBI YOSI'S AND RABBI YEHUDA'S WORDS LEAD TO THE SAME PLACE. These two tablets existed from before the creation of the world, but were perfected on the sixth day of Creation especially for this purpose. Thus, they were a particular work of the Holy One, blessed be He.

370. מִמַּה אִתְעֲבִידוּ. תָּאנָא, מֵהַהוּא טַלָּא עִלָּאָה, דְּנָגִיד מֵעַתִּיקָא קַדִּישָׁא. וְכַד נָגִיד וְאִתְמְשַׁךְ לַחֲקַל דְּתַפּוּחִין קַדִּישִׁין, נָטַל קוּדְשָׁא בְּרִיךְ הוּא תְּרֵין כְּפוֹרֵי מִנַּיְיהוּ, וְאִתְגְּלִידוּ, וְאִתְעֲבִידוּ תְּרֵין אַבְנִין יַקִּירִין. נָשַׁב בְּהוּ, וְאִתְפַּשְּׁטוּ לִתְרֵין לוּחִין, הה"ד מַעֲשֵׂה אֱלֹהִים הֵמָּה וְהַמִּכְתָּב מִכְתַּב אֱלֹהִים הוּא. כְּמָה דִכְתִיב, כְּתוּבִים בְּאֶצְבַּע אֱלֹהִים.

370. HE ASKS: Of what were they made? AND HE ANSWERS: We have learned that they were formed of the supernal dew which issues from Atika

-174-

Kadisa (the Holy Ancient One), BEING KETER. When this supernal dew was descending on the field of the holy apple trees, MALCHUT, the Holy One, blessed be He, took two drops, causing them to solidify and turn into two precious stones. He blew on them and they became flat like tablets, as it is written: "the work of Elohim, and the writing was the writing of Elohim," and "written with the finger of Elohim" (Devarim 9:10).

371. תָּאנָא, אֶצְבַּע אֱלֹהִים. הַהוּא אֶצְבַּע סָלִיק לַעֲשָׂרָה. כְּמָה דְאִתְּמַר, אֶצְבַּע אֱלֹהִים הִיא. וְכָל אֶצְבַּע וְאֶצְבַּע סָלִיק לַעֲשָׂרָה, עַד דְּאִתְעָבֵיד יְדָא שְׁלֵימָתָא, דִּכְתִּיב וַיַּרְא יִשְׂרָאֵל אֶת הַיָּד הַגְּדוֹלָה.

371. We learned that "the finger of Elohim" expanded into ten, FOR THE TEN FINGERS CORRESPOND TO THE TEN SFIROT AND EACH ONE OF THEM INCLUDES TEN SFIROT, as written: "written with the finger of Elohim." Each one of the fingers expanded into ten until a complete hand was formed, as it is written: "And Yisrael saw that great work (lit. 'hand')" (Shemot 14:31). THUS, HERE ALSO, "THE FINGER OF ELOHIM" IS EXPANDED INTO TEN.

372. אָמַר ר' יְהוּדָה, חָרוּת עַל הַלֻּחֹת, נְקִיבָן הֲווֹ אַבְנִין, וְאִתְחֲזִיאוּ לִתְרֵין סִטְרִין, חָרוּת גְּלוּפָא דִּגְלִיפִין. אָמַר ר' אַבָּא, מֵהַאי סִטְרָא אִתְחֲזֵי סִטְרָא אַחֲרָא, וְאִתְקְרֵי מֵהָכָא, מַה דִּכְתִּיב בְּסִטְרָא אַחֲרָא.

372. Rabbi Yehuda said: "engraved upon the tablets." THE LETTERS ON the stones were pierced so that the writing could be seen FROM ONE SIDE TO THE OTHER, AND THE WRITING was seen from both sides. "…engraved…" means that THE WRITING formed an engraving within an engraving, THROUGH ONE SIDE TO THE OTHER. According to Rabbi Aba, it was possible to see one side from the other side and to read the writing thereon.

373. רַבִּי אֶלְעָזָר אָמַר, בְּנֵס הֲווֹ כְּתִיבִין, דְּכָל בְּנֵי נָשָׁא, הֲווֹ אַמְרִין וְסָהֲדִין, דְּהָא מִכְתַּב אֱלֹהִים הוּא וַדַּאי, דְּהָא כָּל בְּנֵי עָלְמָא לָא יַכְלִין לְמִנְדַּע לוֹן כְּמָה דַּהֲווֹ.

373. Rabbi Elazar said: They were written miraculously in order that every

man would bear testimony that it was the writing of Elohim, for none of the people in the world could conceive them as they really were.

374. לְדַעְתַּיְיהוּ דְּאִינּוּן דְּאַמְרִין, נְקִיבִין הֲווֹ, מִי כְּתִיב חָרוּת בַּלֻּחֹת, עַל הַלֻּחֹת כְּתִיב. אֶלָּא הָכִי תָּאנָא, חֲמִשָּׁא קָלִין אִינּוּן לִימִינָא, וַחֲמִשָּׁא לִשְׂמָאלָא. וְאִינּוּן דִּשְׂמָאלָא כְּלִילָן בִּימִינָא. וּמָן יְמִינָא, אִתְחֲזוּן אִינּוּן דִּשְׂמָאלָא, וְהָכָא כֹּלָּא אִיהוּ יְמִינָא, וְאִתְכְּלִילָן אִלֵּין בְּאִלֵּין, מַאן דַּהֲוָה בְּסִטְרָא דָּא, חָמֵי לְסִטְרָא אַחֲרָא, וְקָרֵי לוֹן לְאִינּוּן אַתְווֹן. דְּהָא תָּנֵינָן, שְׂמָאלָא אִתְחֲזַר יְמִינָא, דִּכְתִּיב מִימִינוֹ אֵשׁ דָּת לָמוֹ, וּבְגִין כָּךְ מִכְתַּב אֱלֹהִים הוּא וַדַּאי.

374. HE ASKS: According to those who say they were pierced THROUGH, why does it not say that the writing was engraved 'in the tablets' instead of "upon the tablets"? AND HE ANSWERS: We have learned that five sounds were on the right and five on the left, and those of the left were included in the right, and from the right one could see those of the left. And here, UPON THE TABLETS, all was on the right, because THOSE FIVE COMMANDMENTS OF THE LEFT were included in those OF THE RIGHT. THEREFORE, he who stood at one side could see what was on the other side and read the letters, FOR THE MIRACLE WITH WHICH THE LETTERS WERE ENGRAVED WAS THAT ONE COULD READ ONE SIDE FROM THE OTHER. THIS DOES NOT APPLY TO THE FRONT AND BACK, BUT TO THE RIGHT AND LEFT SIDE, BECAUSE THEY WERE NOT ENGRAVED THROUGH. For we have learned that the left turned into the right, as it is written: "From His right hand went a fiery law for them." Therefore, assuredly it was "the work of Elohim."

375. הָא כֵּיצַד, מַאן דַּהֲוָה מִסִּטְרָא דָּא, הֲוָה קָרֵי בְּדָא, אָנֹכִי יְיָ' אֱלֹהֶיךָ. וּמֵאִלֵּין אַתְווֹן הֲוָה חָמֵי, וְקָרֵי לֹא תִרְצַח. הֲוָה קָרֵי לֹא יִהְיֶה לְךָ. וַהֲוָה חָמֵי וְקָרֵי, לֹא תִנְאָף. וַהֲוָה קָרֵי לֹא תִשָּׂא אֶת שֵׁם יְיָ' אֱלֹהֶיךָ לַשָּׁוְא. וַהֲוָה חָמֵי וְקָרֵי לֹא תִגְנֹב. וְכֹלָּא מִסִּטְרָא דָּא, וְכָךְ לְכֻלְּהוּ, וּכְדֵין מִסִּטְרָא אַחֲרָא, וְכֻלְּהוּ כְּלִילָן דָּא בְּדָא כַּה"ג. הה"ד מִכְתַּב אֱלֹהִים הוּא. מִכְתַּב אֱלֹהִים הוּא וַדַּאי.

375. HE EXPLAINS: Thus, he who stood on one would read "I am Hashem

your Elohim," and out of these letters he could see and read the words, "You shall not murder," and he read, "You shall not have," and could see and read the words, "You shall not commit adultery." He read "You shall not take the name of Hashem your Elohim in vain," and at the same time he could see and read the words, "You shall not steal." And it was thus with all the words from THE RIGHT side, and in the same way all those from the other side, and they were all included one within the other this way. Of this, it is said: "the writing of Elohim," for assuredly it was "the writing of Elohim" (Shemot 32:16).

376. וַיֵּרֶד מֹשֶׁה אֶל הָעָם וַיֹּאמֶר אֲלֵיהֶם. רַבִּי יוֹסֵי אָמַר, מַאי אֲמִירָא דָּא דִּכְתִיב וַיֹּאמֶר אֲלֵיהֶם, וְלָא כְּתִיב מַאי קָאָמַר. א"ר יִצְחָק, תָּא חֲזֵי, אָרְחָא דְּעָלְמָא הוּא, כַּד אָתֵי חֶדְוָותָא לְבַר נָשׁ, אוֹ כַּד אָתֵי צַעֲרָא, עַד לָא יָדַע מִנֵּיהּ לָא יָכִיל לְמִסְבַּל, דְּהָא לִבָּא אִתְפְּרַח לְשַׁעְתָּא. וְכַד יָדַע מִנֵּיהּ, קָאִים בְּקִיּוּמֵיהּ, וְיָכִיל לְמִסְבַּל. כָּל שֶׁכֵּן הָכָא, דְּהָא מֹשֶׁה אָמַר לוֹן כָּל מַה דַּהֲוָה לְבָתַר, וְאַתְקִיף לְבַיְיהוּ בְּמִלִּין, וְלָא יָכִילוּ לְמִסְבַּל. כ"ש אִי לָא אָמַר לוֹן מִידִי. ובג"כ וַיֹּאמֶר אֲלֵיהֶם בְּקַדְמֵיתָא, וְאִתְתַּקַּף לְבַיְיהוּ. וּלְבָתַר וַיְדַבֵּר אֱלֹהִים.

376. Rabbi Yosi said: What is the point of the remark, "And Moses went down to the people and said to them" (Shemot 19:25), if what he said to them is not written? Rabbi Yitzchak explained: Come and behold. When a person expects some good fortune or misfortune to befall him, before he knows what it is, he can not bear it, it is because his heart will fly out from him for a time. But once the best or the worst is known, he is relaxed and can endure it. It is all the more so in this case. When Moses prepared them for that which was about to take place, he strengthened their hearts with his words, for otherwise they would not be able to bear all that was about to come. Therefore, it is written: "and said to them," and right after that "And Elohim spoke" (Shemot 20:1).

377. וְעִם כָּל דָּא, לָא יָכִילוּ לְמִסְבַּל, דְּהָא תָּנֵינָן, אָמַר ר' יְהוּדָה אָמַר ר' חִיָּיא אָמַר ר' יוֹסֵי, כַּד שָׁמְעוּ מִלָּה דְּקוּדְשָׁא בְּרִיךְ הוּא, פָּרְחַת נִשְׁמָתַיְיהוּ, וְסַלְקָא נִשְׁמָתַיְיהוּ דְּיִשְׂרָאֵל, עַד כּוּרְסֵי יְקָרָא דִּילֵיהּ, לְאִתְדַּבְּקָא תַּמָּן.

377. Despite all this, they could not endure it, for as we have been taught from Rabbi Yehuda who said in the name of Rabbi Chiya, in the name of Rabbi Yosi: When they heard the words of the Holy One, blessed be He, their souls flew from them and ascended up to the Throne of Glory in order to cleave to it.

378. אָמְרָה אוֹרַיְיתָא קַמֵּיה דְּקוּדְשָׁא בְּרִיךְ הוּא, וְכִי לְמַגָּנָא הֲוֵינָא מִתְרֵי אַלְפֵי שְׁנִין, עַד לָא אִתְבְּרֵי עָלְמָא, לְמַגָּנָא כְּתִיב בָּה, וְאִישׁ אִישׁ מִבְּנֵי יִשְׂרָאֵל וּמִן הַגֵּר הַגָּר בְּתוֹכָם וְאֶל בְּנֵי יִשְׂרָאֵל תְּדַבֵּר לֵאמֹר. כִּי לִי בְנֵי יִשְׂרָאֵל עֲבָדִים. אָן אִינוּן בְּנֵי יִשְׂרָאֵל. בָּה שַׁעֲתָא, אָהַדְרַת אוֹרַיְיתָא נִשְׁמָתַיְיהוּ דְּיִשְׂרָאֵל, כָּל חַד וְחַד לְאַתְרֵיה. אוֹרַיְיתָא אִתְקִיפַת, וַאֲחִידַת בְּהוּ בְּנִשְׁמָתַיְיהוּ, לְאַהַדְּרָא לְהוּ לְיִשְׂרָאֵל הה"ד תּוֹרַת יְיָ' תְּמִימָה מְשִׁיבַת נָפֶשׁ. מְשִׁיבַת נֶפֶשׁ מַמָּשׁ.

378. The Torah said to the Holy One, blessed be He: 'Was it for nothing that I was fashioned two thousand years before the creation of the world? Is it all in vain that in Me it is inscribed: "Whatever man there be of the house of Yisrael, or of the strangers who sojourn among you" (Vayikra 17:8); "And you shall speak to the children of Yisrael, saying" (Vayikra 24:15); and "For to Me the children of Yisrael are servants" (Vayikra 25:55). Where, then, are these children of Yisrael?' At that hour, the Torah returned their souls to the children of Yisrael, every one of them to its own place. The Torah strengthened and took hold of the souls and gave them back to Yisrael, as it is written: "The Torah of Hashem is perfect, restoring the soul" (Tehilim 19:8). "…restoring…" literally, AS IT RESTORED THE SOULS OF YISRAEL AFTER THEY FLEW AWAY FROM THEM.

379. תָּאנָא, כְּתִיב וַיֵּשֶׁב שְׁלֹמֹה עַל כִּסֵּא יְיָ' לְמֶלֶךְ, כְּמָה דִכְתִיב, שֵׁשׁ מַעֲלוֹת לַכִּסֵּא. ר' אַבָּא אָמַר, דְּקָיְימָא סִיהֲרָא בְּאַשְׁלָמוּתָא. דְּתָנֵינָן, בְּיוֹמוֹי דִשְׁלֹמֹה, קָיְימָא סִיהֲרָא בְּאַשְׁלָמוּתָא.

379. We have learned that the verses: "Then Solomon sat on the throne of Hashem as king," (I Divrei Hayamim 29:23) and, "The throne had six steps" (I Melachim 10:19) CORRESPOND TO THE SIX SFIROT: CHESED, GVURAH, TIFERET, NETZACH, HOD AND YESOD. THEREFORE, IT IS CALLED "THE

THRONE OF HASHEM." Rabbi Aba said that the moon was then full; as we learned that in the days of King Solomon, the moon was in its fullness – MEANING THAT THE NUKVA OF ZEIR ANPIN, WHICH IS CALLED 'MOON', WAS IN HER FULLNESS.

380. אֵימָתַי בְּאַשְׁלָמוּתָא. דְּקַיְימָא בַּחֲמִשָּׁה עָשָׂר, כְּמָה דְּתָנֵינָן, אַבְרָהָם. יִצְחָק. יַעֲקֹב. יְהוּדָה. פֶּרֶץ. חֶצְרוֹן. רָם. עֲמִינָדָב. נַחְשׁוֹן. שַׂלְמוֹן. בּוֹעַז. עוֹבֵד. יִשַׁי. דָּוִד. שְׁלֹמֹה. כַּד אָתָא שְׁלֹמֹה, קַיְימָא סִיהֲרָא בְּאַשְׁלָמוּתָא. הַהַ"ד, וַיֵּשֶׁב שְׁלֹמֹה עַל כִּסֵּא יְיָ' לְמֶלֶךְ. וּכְתִיב שֵׁשׁ מַעֲלוֹת לַכִּסֵּא. כֹּלָא כְּגַוְונָא דִּלְעֵילָא.

380. HE ASKS: When was the moon, WHICH IS MALCHUT, in its fullness? AND HE ANSWERS: When it was established by fifteen KINGS, as we learned: Abraham, Isaac, Jacob, Judah, Peretz, Chetzron, Ram, Aminadav, Nachshon, Shalmon, Boaz, Oved, Yishai, David, and Solomon. When Solomon sat on his throne, the moon, WHICH IS MALCHUT was in its fullness. Therefore, it is written: "Then Solomon sat on the Throne of Hashem as king," WHICH IS MALCHUT. It is also written: "The throne had six steps," CORRESPONDING TO THE SIX SFIROT OF MALCHUT: CHESED, GVURAH, TIFERET, NETZACH, HOD AND YESOD, having the same model as above.

381. בְּיוֹמוֹי דְּצִדְקִיָּה, קַיְימָא סִיהֲרָא בִּפְגִימוּתָא, וְאִתְפְּגִים. כַּד"א, וְיָרֵחַ לֹא יַגִּיהַּ אוֹרוֹ. דְּתָנֵינָן, בְּיוֹמוֹי דְּצִדְקִיָּה, אִתְפְּגִים סִיהֲרָא, וְאִתְחַשְּׁכוּ אַנְפַּיְיהוּ דְּיִשְׂרָאֵל.

381. In the days of Zedekiah, the moon, WHICH IS MALCHUT, was waning and was defective, as it is written: "And the moon shall not shed her light" (Yeshayah 13:10). For as we have learned, in the days of Tidkiyahu the moon was in its wane and the face of Yisrael was darkened.

382. פּוּק וְחָשִׁיב, רְחַבְעָם. אֲבִיָּה. אָסָא. יְהוֹשָׁפָט. יְהוֹרָם. אֲחַזְיָהוּ. יוֹאָשׁ. אֲמַצְיָהוּ. עוּזִיָּהוּ. יוֹתָם. אָחָז. יְחִזְקִיָּהוּ. מְנַשֶּׁה. אָמוֹן. יֹאשִׁיָּהוּ.

צִדְקִיָּהוּ. וְכַד אָתָא צִדְקִיָּהוּ אִתְפְּגִים סִיהֲרָא וְקַיְימָא עַל פְּגִימוּתָא. דִּכְתִיב וְאֶת עֵינֵי צִדְקִיָּה עִוֵּר. בֵּיהּ זִמְנָא הִשְׁלִיךְ מִשָּׁמַיִם אֶרֶץ. הַאי אֶרֶץ אִתְעֲבָרָא מִקַמֵּי שָׁמַיִם, וְאִתְרַחֲקַת מִנֵּיהּ, וְאִתְחֲשָׁכָא הַאי אֶרֶץ.

382. Come and behold: Rechavam, Aviyah, Asa, Yehoshafat, Yehoram, Achazyahu, Yoash, Amatzyahu, Uziyahu, Yotam, Achaz, Yechizkiyahu, Menasheh, Amon, Yoshiyahu. When Zedekiah came, the moon waned and remained thus, for it is written: "Then he put out the eyes of Zedekiah" (Yirmeyah 52:11). Then "Hashem...cast down from heaven (to) earth" (Eichah 2:1), meaning that the earth, WHICH IS MALCHUT, was removed far from heaven, WHICH IS ZEIR ANPIN, and became dark.

383. תָּאנָא, בְּשַׁעֲתָא דְּקַיְימוּ יִשְׂרָאֵל עַל טוּרָא דְּסִינַי שָׁארֵי סִיהֲרָא לְאַנְהֲרָא, דִּכְתִיב, וַיֵּט שָׁמַיִם וַיֵּרַד. מַהוּ וַיֵּרַד. דְּקָרִיב שִׁמְשָׁא לְגַבֵּי סִיהֲרָא, וְשָׁרֵי לְאַנְהֲרָא סִיהֲרָא. דִּכְתִיב דֶּגֶל מַחֲנֵה יְהוּדָה מִזְרָחָה.

383. We have learned that when Yisrael stood by Mount Sinai the moon began to shine, as it is written: "He bowed the heavens also, and came down" (II Shmuel 22:10) meaning that the sun, WHICH IS ZEIR ANPIN AND IS CALLED 'HEAVENS', approached the moon, WHICH IS MALCHUT. And the moon began to shine, as is expressed in the verse: "And on the east side towards the rising of the sun shall they of the standard of the camp of Judah pitch by their hosts" (Bemidbar 2:3). "JUDAH" IS THE CHARIOT OF MALCHUT, AND "THE EAST SIDE" SIGNIFIES SHINING AND ILLUMINATION.

384. בְּטוּרָא דְּסִינַי, אִתְמָנָא יְהוּדָה, רוֹפִינַס בְּמַלְכוּתָא, דִּכְתִיב, וִיהוּדָה עוֹד רָד עִם אֵל וְעִם קְדוֹשִׁים נֶאֱמָן. מַהוּ וְעִם קְדוֹשִׁים נֶאֱמָן. כַּד אָמַר קב"ה לְיִשְׂרָאֵל, וְאַתֶּם תִּהְיוּ לִי מַמְלֶכֶת כֹּהֲנִים וְגוֹי קָדוֹשׁ, נֶאֱמָן הֲוָה יְהוּדָה לְקַבְּלָא מַלְכוּתָא, וְשָׁארֵי סִיהֲרָא לְאַנְהֲרָא.

384. On Mount Sinai Judah was appointed chief in the kingdom, as it is written: "But Judah still rules with El, and is faithful with Holy Ones" (Hoshea 12:1), "...faithful with Holy Ones..." meaning that when the Holy

One, blessed be He, said to Yisrael: "And you shall be to Me a kingdom of priests, and a holy nation" (Shemot 19:6), Judah was found trustworthy to receive the kingship. Then the moon, WHICH IS MALCHUT, began to shine.

22. "I am Hashem your Elohim"

A Synopsis

We are told that the Torah includes all the Sfirot, and that we must never forsake it. The commandments of the Torah cling to the body of Zeir Anpin, so that when a person sins he transgresses against the body of the King. When the Torah was given, Binah and her children, Male and Female, were in perfect harmony, but if a person sins it removes the mother from her children. Rabbi Elazar now tells us that God created heaven and earth simultaneously, one with His right hand and the other with His left. In the grade called 'righteous', the newly created heavens longed for the earth, as a man longs to join with a woman, and a holy river of oil comes from the head of the King and pours itself out upon the earth just as the male injects seed into the female. Rabbi Yitzchak now asks where Hashem went when He came down upon Mount Sinai. Rabbi Yosi said He came lower and lower down through the grades until he reached earth, and He went toward the Shechinah who stood there. Hence Zeir Anpin descended and united with the Shechinah.

385. אָנֹכִי יְיָ' אֱלֹהֶיךָ אֲשֶׁר הוֹצֵאתִיךָ וְגוֹ' ר' אֶלְעָזָר פָּתַח, שְׁמַע בְּנִי מוּסַר אָבִיךָ וְאַל תִּטּוֹשׁ תּוֹרַת אִמֶּךָ. שְׁמַע בְּנִי מוּסַר אָבִיךָ: דָּא קוּדְשָׁא בְּרִיךְ הוּא וְאַל תִּטּוֹשׁ תּוֹרַת אִמֶּךָ: דָּא כְּנֶסֶת יִשְׂרָאֵל. מַאן כ"י. דָּא בִּינָה. כְּמָה דִּכְתִיב, לְהָבִין אִמְרֵי בִינָה.

385. "I am Hashem your Elohim who have brought you out..." (Shemot 20:2). Rabbi Elazar opened the discussion with the verse: "My son, hear the instruction of your father and do not forsake the Torah of your mother" (Mishlei 1:8). "My son, hear the instruction of your father," refers to the Holy One, blessed be He, MEANING, ZEIR ANPIN; "do not forsake the Torah of your mother" refers to the Congregation of Yisrael, which is Binah, as it is written: "To perceive the words of understanding (Heb. Binah)" (Mishlei 1:1).

386. ר' יְהוּדָה אָמַר, מוּסַר אָבִיךָ: דָּא הִיא חָכְמָה. וְאַל תִּטּוֹשׁ תּוֹרַת אִמֶּךָ: דָּא הִיא בִינָה. ר' יִצְחָק אָמַר, הָא וְהָא, חַד מִלָּה אִתְפָּרְשׁוּ. דְּתָנֵינָן, אוֹרַיְיתָא מֵחָכְמָה דִּלְעֵילָּא נָפְקַת. ר' יוֹסֵי אָמַר, מִבִּינָה נָפְקַת,

דְּכְתִיב לְהָבִין אִמְרֵי בִינָה, וּכְתִיב וְאַל תִּטּוֹשׁ תּוֹרַת אִמֶּךָ.

386. According to Rabbi Yehuda, "the instruction of your father" is Chochmah CALLED ABA (ENG. 'FATHER'), and "do not forsake the Torah of your mother," is Binah. Rabbi Yitzchak said that both of the interpretations mean the same thing, for as we have learned, the Torah emanated from the supernal Chochmah, AND CHOCHMAH (LIT. 'WISDOM') IS DIVIDED INTO THE RIGHT, CALLED 'ABA', AND THE LEFT, CALLED 'IMA'. Rabbi Yosi said that THE TORAH emanated from Binah, for it is written: "To perceive the words of understanding," and also, "Do not forsake the Torah of your mother," AND BINAH IS CALLED 'IMA' (ENG. 'MOTHER').

387. אָמַר ר' יְהוּדָה, אוֹרַיְיתָא מֵחָכְמָה וּבִינָה אִתְכְּלִילַת, דִּכְתִיב, שְׁמַע בְּנִי מוּסַר אָבִיךָ וְאַל תִּטּוֹשׁ תּוֹרַת אִמֶּךָ. ר' אַבָּא אָמַר, בְּכֹלָּא אִתְכְּלִילַת, דְּכֵיוָן דִּבְאִלֵּין תְּרֵין אִתְכְּלִילַת, אִתְכְּלִילַת בְּכֹלָּא. בְּחֶסֶד, בְּדִינָא בְּרַחֲמֵי. בְּכֻלְּהוּ שְׁלִימוּתָא דְּאִצְטְרִיךְ מִלָּה. אִי מַלְכָּא וּמַטְרוֹנִיתָא מִסְתַּכְּמִין, כֹּלָּא מִסְתַּכְּמִין. בַּאֲתָר דְּאִלֵּין מִשְׁתַּכְּחִין, כֹּלָּא מִשְׁתַּכְּחִין.

387. Rabbi Yehuda said: The Torah includes both Chochmah and Binah, as it is written, "My son, hear the instruction of your father and do not forsake the Torah of your mother." Rabbi Aba said that the Torah contains all THE SFIROT, since once it combines both CHOCHMAH AND BINAH, it combines all THE SFIROT, FOR CHOCHMAH AND BINAH INCLUDE ALL THE SFIROT: Chesed, Judgment and Mercy – BEING CHESED, GVURAH AND TIFERET – in all required perfection. When the King and the Queen are joined WITH IT, all the others are joined WITH IT, for wherever CHOCHMAH AND BINAH are found, all the others are found as well.

388. ר' יוֹסֵי אָמַר, אָנֹכִי: דָּא שְׁכִינְתָּא. כְּמָה דִּכְתִיב, אָנֹכִי אֵרֵד עִמְּךָ מִצְרַיְמָה. יְיָ' אֱלֹהֶיךָ: ר' יִצְחָק אָמַר, אָנֹכִי: דָּא שְׁכִינְתָּא. וּפָסְקָא טַעֲמָא. כד"א אָנֹכִי עָשִׂו בְּכוֹרֶךָ. יְיָ' אֱלֹהֶיךָ: דָּא קוּדְשָׁא בְּרִיךְ הוּא. כְּמָה דִּכְתִיב, מִן הַשָּׁמַיִם הִשְׁמִיעֲךָ אֶת קוֹלוֹ. וּכְתִיב אַתֶּם רְאִיתֶם כִּי

מִן הַשָּׁמַיִם דִּבַּרְתִּי עִמָּכֶם. מִן הַשָּׁמַיִם מִן הַשָּׁמַיִם מַמָּשׁ דָּא קוּדְשָׁא בְּרִיךְ הוּא.

388. Rabbi Yosi said: "I" (Shemot 20:2) is the Shechinah, as it is written: "I will go down with you into Egypt" (Beresheet 46:4). Rabbi Yitzchak said that "I," which is the Shechinah, is separated by a trope; AFTER THE WORD "I" THERE IS A TONAL PAUSE BETWEEN IT AND THE NEXT WORDS, "HASHEM YOUR ELOHIM," THE SAME as in "I am Esau your firstborn" (Beresheet 27:19), WHICH MEANS, I AM WHO I AM; ESAU IS YOUR FIRSTBORN. THEREFORE, "Hashem your Elohim" is the Holy One, blessed be He, THAT IS, ZEIR ANPIN, as it is said: "Out of heaven He made you hear His voice" (Devarim 4:36), AND 'HEAVEN' IS ZEIR ANPIN. It is also written: "You have seen that I have talked with you from heaven" (Shemot 20:19): "From heaven" indeed, for this is the Holy One, blessed be He, NAMELY ZEIR ANPIN.

389. אֲשֶׁר הוֹצֵאתִיךָ מֵאֶרֶץ מִצְרַיִם. אֲשֶׁר: אֲתָר דְּכֹלָּא מְאַשְּׁרִין לֵיהּ. הוֹצֵאתִיךָ מֵאֶרֶץ מִצְרַיִם: דָּא יוֹבְלָא. כְּמָה דְתָנֵינָן, מִסִּטְרָא דְּיוֹבְלָא נָפְקוּ יִשְׂרָאֵל מִמִּצְרַיִם. וּבְגִין כָּךְ, חַמְשִׁין זִמְנִין אִדְכַּר יְצִיאַת מִצְרַיִם בְּאוֹרַיְיתָא. חַמְשִׁין יוֹמִין לְקַבְּלָא אוֹרַיְיתָא. חַמְשִׁין שְׁנִין לְחֵירוּ דַּעֲבָדִין.

389. "...who (Heb. *asher*) have brought you out of the land of Egypt." (Shemot 20:2). *Asher* MEANS a place which everyone calls happy (Heb. *osher*), WHICH IS BINAH. "...brought you out of Egypt..." designates Jubilee WHICH IS BINAH, CALLED 'ASHER', "WHO HAVE BROUGHT YOU OUT OF THE LAND OF EGYPT," for as we have learned, the aspect of Jubilee WHICH IS BINAH, was the cause of Yisrael's exodus from Egypt. Therefore, this event is mentioned fifty times in the Torah. Fifty days passed from the exodus to the receiving of the Torah, and fifty years had to pass for the liberation of the slaves, FOR ALL THESE EVENTS CORRESPOND TO THE FIFTY GATES OF BINAH.

390. מִבֵּית עֲבָדִים: כְּמָה דִּכְתִיב הִכָּה כָּל בְּכוֹר בְּאֶרֶץ מִצְרַיִם. וְתָנֵינָן

אִלֵּין כִּתְרִין תַּתָּאִין, דְּאִתְרְחִיצוּ בְּהוּ מִצְרָאֵי. כְּמָה דְּאִית בֵּיתָא לְעֵילָא, אִית בֵּיתָא לְתַתָּא. בֵּיתָא קַדִּישָׁא לְעֵילָא, דִּכְתִיב, בְּחָכְמָה יִבָּנֶה בָּיִת. בֵּיתָא תַּתָּאָה לְתַתָּא, דְּלָא קַדִּישָׁא, כְּמָה דִּכְתִיב מִבֵּית עֲבָדִים.

390. "…out of the house of bondage…" as it is written: "Hashem smote all the firstborn in the land of Egypt" (Shemot 12:29). We have learned that this signifies the lower crowns in which the Egyptians had faith. As there is a house above, there is one below, a holy House above as it is said: "through wisdom a house is built" (Mishlei 24:3) and an unholy house below, IN THE KLIPOT, as it is written, "out of the house of bondage."

391. תָּאנָא, בְּשַׁעֲתָא דְּאִתְּמַר אָנֹכִי, כָּל אִינוּן פִּקּוּדֵי אוֹרַיְיתָא, דְּמִתְאַחֲדָן בְּמַלְכָּא קַדִּישָׁא עִלָּאָה, בְּסִטְרָא דָּא, כֻּלְּהוּ הֲוָה כְּלִילָן בְּהַאי מִלָּה.

391. We have learned that when the "I" was proclaimed, all those commandments of the Torah which were united with the Supernal Holy King, WHICH IS ZEIR ANPIN, were comprised in this word "I."

392. כְּמָה דִּתְנֵינָן, כָּל פִּקּוּדֵי אוֹרַיְיתָא, מִתְאַחֲדָן בְּגוּפָא דְּמַלְכָּא. מִנְהוֹן בְּרֵישָׁא דְּמַלְכָּא, וּמִנְהוֹן בְּגוּפָא, וּמִנְהוֹן בִּידֵי מַלְכָּא, וּמִנְהוֹן בְּרַגְלוֹי, וְלֵית מַאן דְּנָפִיק מִן גּוּפָא דְּמַלְכָּא לְבַר. וּבְגִין כָּךְ, מַאן דְּפָשַׁע בְּחַד פִּקּוּדֵי אוֹרַיְיתָא, כְּמַאן דְּפָשַׁע בְּגוּפָא דְּמַלְכָּא, כְּמָה דִּכְתִיב וְיָצְאוּ וְרָאוּ בְּפִגְרֵי הָאֲנָשִׁים הַפּוֹשְׁעִים בִּי. בִּי מַמָּשׁ. וַוי לְחַיָּיבַיָּא, דְּעַבְרִין עַל פִּתְגָּמֵי אוֹרַיְיתָא, וְלָא יַדְעִין מַאי קָא עַבְדִין.

392. As we have already learned, all the commandments of the Torah clung to the body of the King, WHICH IS ZEIR ANPIN, some of them to His head, some to His hands and some to His feet, and none of them ever step out and become separate from the body of the King. Therefore, he who transgresses even one of the commandments of the Torah is as though he transgresses against the body of the King, as it is written: "And they shall go forth and

look upon the carcasses of the men that have rebelled against Me" (Yeshayah 66:24) – "against Me," literally. Woe to the wicked who break the words of the Torah, and do not know what they do.

393. דְּאָמַר ר' שִׁמְעוֹן, הַהוּא אֲתָר דְּאִיהוּ חָב לְגַבֵּיהּ, הַהוּא אֲתָר מַמָּשׁ גַּלֵּי חוֹבֵיהּ. חָב בְּקוּדְשָׁא בְּרִיךְ הוּא, קוּדְשָׁא בְּרִיךְ הוּא גַּלֵּי חוֹבֵיהּ, דִּכְתִּיב יְגַלּוּ שָׁמַיִם עֲוֹנוֹ וְאֶרֶץ מִתְקוֹמָמָה לוֹ. יְגַלּוּ שָׁמַיִם עֲוֹנוֹ: דָּא קוּדְשָׁא בְּרִיךְ הוּא. וְאֶרֶץ מִתְקוֹמָמָה לוֹ: דָּא כ"י.

393. Thus said Rabbi Shimon: The very place against which a sinner has committed a sin, reveals the sin. When a sin has been committed against the Holy One, blessed be He, AS MENTIONED ABOVE, the Holy One, blessed be He, reveals his sin, as it is written: "The heaven shall reveal his iniquity and the earth shall rise up against him" (Iyov 20:27). "The heaven shall reveal his iniquity," signifies the Holy One, blessed be He, MEANING, ZEIR ANPIN CALLED 'HEAVEN', and "the earth shall rise up against him," signifies the Congregation of Yisrael, NAMELY MALCHUT WHICH IS CALLED 'EARTH'.

394. תָּנֵינָא, שָׁמַיִם גַּלְּיָין חוֹבֵיהּ דְּבַר נָשׁ. וּבְשַׁעֲתָא דְּאִיהוּ גַּלְיָא חוֹבֵיהּ, אֶרֶץ עָבֵיד דִּינָא דְּבַר נָשׁ, דִּכְתִּיב וְאֶרֶץ מִתְקוֹמָמָה לוֹ, לְמֶעְבַּד דִּינָא בֵּיהּ. אָמַר ר' יוֹסֵי, תָּנֵינָן מִשְּׁמֵיהּ דְּר' שִׁמְעוֹן, בְּשַׁעֲתָא דְּאִתְיְהִיבַת אוֹרַיְיתָא, אִימָא וּבְנִין בִּשְׁלֵימוּתָא אִשְׁתְּכָחוּ, דִּכְתִּיב אֵם הַבָּנִים שְׂמֵחָה.

394. We have learned that "the heaven," ZEIR ANPIN, reveals a man's sin and at that time "the earth," WHICH IS MALCHUT, executes Judgment on the sinner, as it is written: "And the earth shall rise up against him," to punish him. Rabbi Yosi said in the name of Rabbi Shimon that when the Torah was given, the Mother, WHICH IS BINAH, and the Children, WHICH ARE MALE AND FEMALE, were in perfect harmony, as it is written: "and be a joyful mother of children" (Tehilim 113:9).

395. אָנֹכִי יְיָ' אֱלֹהֶיךָ. אָנֹכִי, כְּמָה דְּתָנֵינָן, בַּת הָיְתָה לוֹ לְאַבְרָהָם

אָבִינוּ, הִיא שְׁכִינְתָּא. וְדָא בַּת. יְיָ' אֱלֹהֶיךָ, דִּכְתִיב בְּנִי בְכוֹרִי יִשְׂרָאֵל. וּכְתִיב עֵץ חַיִּים הִיא לַמַּחֲזִיקִים בָּהּ, הָא בֵן.

395. "I am Hashem your Elohim." "I" is, as we have learned, that Abraham the Patriarch had a daughter. It is the Shechinah who is a Daughter. "Hashem your Elohim," SIGNIFIES ZEIR ANPIN WHICH IS CALLED 'YISRAEL', as it is written: "Yisrael is My son, My firstborn" (Shemot 4:22). It is also written: "She is the Tree of Life to those who lay hold on her" (Mishlei 3:18). THIS SIGNIFIES ZEIR ANPIN, WHICH IS CALLED 'THE TREE OF LIFE'. This is the son.

396. אֲשֶׁר הוֹצֵאתִיךָ מֵאֶרֶץ מִצְרַיִם, דִּכְתִיב יוֹבֵל הִיא קֹדֶשׁ תִּהְיֶה לָכֶם, וּכְתִיב אֵם הַבָּנִים שְׂמֵחָה. וְקִדַּשְׁתֶּם אֶת שְׁנַת הַחֲמִשִּׁים שָׁנָה וּקְרָאתֶם דְּרוֹר, הָא אִימָּא וּבְנִין. יָתְבָא אִימָּא יַתְבִין בְּנִין. כֻּלְּהוּ בְּחֶדְוָה בִּשְׁלִימוּתָא. וְעַ"ד כְּתִיב, אֵם הַבָּנִים שְׂמֵחָה. מִתְעַבְרָא אִימָּא, כֻּלְּהוּ מִתְעַבְּרָן בְּדוּכְתַּיְיהוּ. וּכְתִיב, לֹא תִקַּח הָאֵם עַל הַבָּנִים. וְתָנֵינָן, לָא יַעֲבִיד בַּר נָשׁ חוֹבֵי לְתַתָּא, בְּגִין דְּאִתְעֲבָר אִימָּא מֵעַל בְּנִין.

396. "Who have brought you out of the land of Egypt." It is as it is written: "For it is a Jubilee; it shall be holy to you" (Vayikra 25:12), NAMELY, BINAH. IT IS ALSO WRITTEN: "And be a joyful mother of children," and, "And you shall hallow the fiftieth year and proclaim liberty" (Ibid. 10). THIS IS BINAH WHICH IS CALLED 'THE FIFTIETH YEAR', AND ALSO CALLED 'IMA'. Thus, there are mother and children. THE MOTHER HAS BEEN BROUGHT TO US FROM THE LAND OF EGYPT AND THE CHILDREN, "I" THE DAUGHTER, AND "HASHEM YOUR ELOHIM" THE SON, AS MENTIONED ABOVE. Thus, the mother and children were there, all in joy and completeness. Of this it is written: "a joyful mother of children." When the mother is gone, everybody is gone from their place, as written: "You shall not take the mother bird together with the young" (Devarim 22:6). We have learned that THE MEANING OF THIS VERSE IS THAT a man should be careful not to sin below, as THAT CAUSES the removal of the mother from the children.

397. אָמַר ר' יִצְחָק, כֹּלָּא קוּדְשָׁא בְּרִיךְ הוּא. כֹּלָּא הוּא. כֹּלָּא חַד.

וּמִלִּין אִלֵּין, לְמֶחְצְדֵי חַקְלָא אִתְגַּלְיָין. זַכָּאִין אִינוּן בְּעָלְמָא דֵין, וּבְעָלְמָא דְּאָתֵי.

397. Rabbi Yitzchak said that all THE SFIROT MENTIONED ABOVE refer to the Holy One, blessed be He, who is everything. And this thing is disclosed to the reapers of the field, MEANING TO THOSE WHO ALREADY HAVE THE MERIT TO KNOW THE SECRETS OF THE TORAH AND WHO "SHALL REAP IN JOY" (TEHILIM 126:4), MEANING THOSE WHO HAVE RECEIVED THEIR GRADES FROM MALCHUT WHICH IS CALLED 'FIELD'. Happy they are in this world and in the world to come.

398. תָּאנֵי אָמַר ר' אֶלְעָזָר, כְּתִיב, בְּרֵאשִׁית בָּרָא אֱלֹהִים אֵת הַשָּׁמַיִם וְאֵת הָאָרֶץ. וּכְתִיב, בְּיוֹם עֲשׂוֹת יְיָ' אֱלֹהִים אֶרֶץ וְשָׁמָיִם. בְּמַאי אוֹקִימְנָא הָנֵי קְרָאֵי, הָא תָּנֵינָן, דְּתַרְוַויְיהוּ כַּחֲדָא אִתְבְּרִיאוּ. מְלַמֵּד, שֶׁנָּטָה הַקּוּדְשָׁא בְּרִיךְ הוּא קַו יְמִינוֹ וּבָרָא הַשָּׁמַיִם, וּנְטָה קַו שְׂמֹאלוֹ, וּבָרָא אֵת הָאָרֶץ. בְּקַדְמֵיתָא אֵת הַשָּׁמַיִם וְאֵת הָאָרֶץ, וּלְבָתַר אֶרֶץ וְשָׁמָיִם.

398. Rabbi Elazar said: It is written, "In the beginning Elohim created the heaven and the earth" (Beresheet 1:1), THE HEAVEN PRECEDING THE EARTH, and, "in the day that Hashem Elohim made the earth and the heavens" (Beresheet 2:4), THE EARTH PRECEDING THE HEAVEN. How can we reconcile these verses WHICH CONTRADICT EACH OTHER? HE ANSWERS: We learned that both were created together. We have learned that the Holy One, blessed be He, stretched out His right hand and created the heavens, and then He stretched out His left hand and created the earth. THEREFORE, it first says, "the heaven and the earth," and later, "the earth and the heavens."

399. תְּנָן, כְּתִיב, בַּיוֹם הַהוּא אֶעֱנֶה נְאֻם יְיָ' אֶעֱנֶה אֶת הַשָּׁמַיִם וְהֵם יַעֲנוּ אֶת הָאָרֶץ. אֶעֱנֶה אֶת הַשָּׁמַיִם, שָׁמַיִם מַמָּשׁ. דִּכְתִיב הַשָּׁמַיִם כִּסְאִי. וְהֵם יַעֲנוּ אֶת הָאָרֶץ. הָאָרֶץ מַמָּשׁ, דִּכְתִיב וְהָאָרֶץ הֲדוֹם רַגְלָי. שָׁמַיִם שָׁמַיִם עִלָּאִין. וְאֶרֶץ אֶרֶץ עִלָּאָה. דְּתַנְיָא, כַּד אִתְּקַן שָׁמַיִם דָּא בְּתִיקּוּנוֹי, אִתְּקַן לְקַבְלֵיהּ דְּהַאי אֶרֶץ, וְתֵיאוּבְתֵּיהּ לְקַבְּלָהּ, בְּחַד דַּרְגָּא

דְּאִקְרֵי צַדִּיק. כְּמָה דִּכְתִיב וְצַדִּיק יְסוֹד עוֹלָם, וְאִתְדָּבַּק בְּהַאי אֶרֶץ.

399. It is written: "'And it shall come to pass on that day, that I will respond,' says Hashem. 'I will answer the heavens and they shall answer the earth'" (Hoshea 2:23). "I will answer the heavens," NAMELY the heavens themselves, ZEIR ANPIN, as it is written: "Heaven is My throne" (Yeshayah 66:1), FOR BINAH SAYS: ZEIR ANPIN IS MY THRONE. "...and they shall answer the earth..." the earth herself, MALCHUT, as it is written: "and the earth is My footstool" (Ibid.). "The heaven," refer to the supernal heavens, ZEIR ANPIN, and "the earth" to the supernal earth, WHICH IS MALCHUT, for as we have learned, when the heavens were created, they longed for the earth. This occurs in the grade called 'Righteous', as it is written: "The righteous is an everlasting (lit. 'of the world') foundation" (Mishlei 10:25). And it cleaved to that earth.

400. וּמֵרֵישָׁא דְּמַלְכָּא, עַד הַהוּא אֲתָר דְּשָׁארֵי הַאי צַדִּיק, אָתֵי חַד נַהֲרָא קַדִּישָׁא, מְשְׁחָא דִּרְבוּת, וְאָטִיל בִּסְגִיאוּת תִּיאוּבְתָּא, בְּהַאי אֶרֶץ קַדִּישָׁא, וְנַטִיל כֹּלָּא הַאי אֶרֶץ. וּלְבָתַר, מֵהַאי אֶרֶץ אִתְּזַן כֹּלָּא, עִילָאֵי וְתַתָּאֵי. כְּדוּגְמָא דָּא, כַּד תִּיאוּבְתֵּיהּ לְאִתְדָּבְּקָא בְּנוּקְבָּא, דְּאַפִּיק זַרְעָא דִּרְבוּת, מֵרֵישָׁא דְּמוֹחָא, בְּהַהוּא אָמָה, וְאָטִיל בְּנוּקְבָּא, וּמִנֵּיהּ מִתְעַבְּרָא נוּקְבָּא, אִשְׁתְּכַח, דְּכֻלְּהוּ שַׁיְיפִין דְּגוּפָא, כֻּלְּהוּ מִתְדַּבְּקָן בְּנוּקְבָּא, וְנוּקְבָּא אֲחִידָא כֹּלָּא. כְּדוּגְמָא דָּא תָּנֵינָן, כָּל דְּאַשְׁלִים לַעֲשָׂרָה קַדְמָאֵי דְּבֵי כְּנִישְׁתָּא, נוֹטֵל אֲגַר כֻּלְּהוּ. ר' יוֹסֵי אוֹמֵר, לָקֳבְלֵי דְּכֻלְּהוּ.

400. A holy river of the oil of anointment COMES from the head of the King, THE THREE FIRST SFIROT OF ZEIR ANPIN, to the place wherein this Righteous dwells, WHO IS YESOD OF ZEIR ANPIN, and pours itself out in fullness of desire upon this earth, WHICH IS MALCHUT. The earth, having received it thence, nourishes all, both above and below. This happens the same way as the male, having the desire to unite with the female, brings out of the top of his head a seed of propagation into the male organ and injects it in the female, from which she conceives. Thus, all parts of the body cleave to the female, and the female receives everything. According to this model we have learned, that the one who completes the first ten people who come

to pray in a synagogue receives their merits. Rabbi Yosi says that he is considered as ten, FOR THEY CORRESPOND TO THE TEN SFIROT, AND HE CORRESPONDS TO MALCHUT, NAMELY THE NUKVA WHO RECEIVES ALL, AS MENTIONED ABOVE.

401. ר' יִצְחָק אָמַר, כְּתִיב וַיֵּט שָׁמַיִם וַיֵּרַד, וּכְתִיב וְיֵרַד יְיָ' לְעֵינֵי כָל הָעָם עַל הַר סִינַי, וַיֵּט שָׁמַיִם וַיֵּרַד, לְאָן נַחַת. אִי תֵּימָא דְּנַחַת לְסִינַי, עַל הַר סִינַי כְּתִיב וְלָא כְּתִיב בְּהַר סִינַי.

401. Rabbi Yitzchak said: It is written, "He bowed the heavens also, and came down" (II Shmuel 22:10), AND IN THE TORAH it is written, "And Hashem will come down in the sight of all the people upon Mount Sinai" (Shemot 19:11). When He "came down," to where did He go down? You may think it was to Sinai, AS WRITTEN IN THE TORAH, yet it says, "upon (lit. 'above') Mount Sinai" and not 'on Mount Sinai'.

402. אֶלָּא, וַיֵּט שָׁמַיִם וַיֵּרַד, לְאָן נַחַת. אָמַר ר' יוֹסֵי, נָחִית בְּדַרְגּוֹי, מִדַּרְגָּא לְדַרְגָּא, וּמִכִּתְרָא לְכִתְרָא, עַד דְּאִתְדַּבַּק בְּהַאי אֶרֶץ, וּכְדֵין אִתְנְהַר סִיהֲרָא, וְקַיְימָא בְּאַשְׁלָמוּתָא. הה"ד וַיֵּט שָׁמַיִם וַיֵּרַד, לְהַאי אֶרֶץ. וּכְדֵין כְּתִיב, עַל הַר סִינַי. מַה קַיְימָא עַל הַר סִינַי, הֲוֵי אֵימָא דָּא שְׁכִינְתָּא.

402. HE EXPLAINS: "He bowed the heavens also, and came down." To where did He descend? Rabbi Yosi said: He descended down His grades, from grade to grade, from crown to crown, until He reached this earth, WHICH IS MALCHUT. Then the moon, MALCHUT, shone and stood in its fullness. Therefore, it is written: "He bowed the heaven also, and came down" to this earth. Then it says "upon Mount Sinai." Who stood upon Mount Sinai? The Shechinah did, AND HE DESCENDED TOWARDS HER.

403. ר' אַבָּא אָמַר מֵהָכָא, מִפְּנֵי אֲשֶׁר יָרַד עָלָיו יְיָ' בָּאֵשׁ. וּכְתִיב כִּי יְיָ' אֱלֹהֶיךָ אֵשׁ אוֹכְלָה הוּא. וּכְתִיב, וַיְיָ' הִמְטִיר עַל סְדוֹם וְעַל עֲמוֹרָה גָּפְרִית וָאֵשׁ מֵאֵת ה' מִן הַשָּׁמָיִם. וַיְיָ' הִמְטִיר דָּא הוּא אֶרֶץ מַאן אֲתָר נָטִיל הַאי, סוֹפֵיהּ דִּקְרָא מוֹכַח, דִּכְתִיב מֵאֵת יְיָ' מִן הַשָּׁמָיִם, מִן

הַשָּׁמַיִם מַמָּשׁ. רַבִּי חִיָּיא אָמַר מֵהָכָא, וַיְדַבֵּר אֱלֹהִים אֵת כָּל, כָּל,
כְּלָלָא דְכֹלָּא, דְהָא בְּהַאי תַּלְיָא כֹּלָּא.

403. Rabbi Aba said: From the following verses WE LEARN THAT HE DESCENDED TOWARDS THE SHECHINAH, for it is written, "Because Hashem descended upon it in fire" (Shemot 19:18), and, "For Hashem your Elohim is a consuming fire" (Devarim 4:24), WHICH IS THE SHECHINAH, TOWARDS WHOM HE DESCENDED. HE QUESTIONS FURTHER: Yet it says, "Then Hashem rained upon Sodom and upon Gomorrah brimstone and fire from Hashem out of heaven" (Beresheet 19:24). THUS, ZEIR ANPIN HIMSELF IS THE FIRE, PART OF WHICH RAINED UPON SODOM. HE ANSWERS: "Then Hashem rained" signifies the earth, WHICH IS THE SHECHINAH, FOR "THEN (AND) HASHEM" INDICATES HE AND HIS COURT-HOUSE, WHICH IS THE SHECHINAH FROM WHICH THE FIRE WAS ISSUED UPON SODOM. Whence did she receive it? The second part of the verse, "from Hashem out of heaven," explained that she received from heaven itself, BEING ZEIR ANPIN, AND WHATEVER THE SHECHINAH HAS, SHE RECEIVES FROM ZEIR ANPIN. "From Hashem out of heaven," the heaven themselves, WHICH IS ZEIR ANPIN, FOR WHATEVER THE SHECHINAH HAS SHE RECEIVES FROM ZEIR ANPIN. Rabbi Chiya said that this verse SIGNIFIES THAT HE DESCENDED AND BECAME UNITED WITH THE SHECHINAH. "And Elohim spoke all these words saying..." (Shemot 20:1) "ELOHIM" IS THE SHECHINAH; "all" MEANS the inclusion of everything, BEING ZEIR ANPIN upon whom everything and everyone depends. HENCE, ZEIR ANPIN DESCENDED AND UNITED WITH THE SHECHINAH.

23. "You shall not have"

A Synopsis

We learn that when a man is circumcised he enters into the covenant established by Abraham. However this is only a beginning, for he must also obey the commandments of the Torah in order to enter the grade of Adam. Rabbi Yehuda and Rabbi Chizkiyah speak about how vital to their understanding is the wisdom of Rabbi Shimon, who is such a light to everyone. Rabbi Shimon, when encountered, teaches them that the prayer of the poor man is more effective than all others, for the poor are nearer to God than anyone else is. He says that God dwells in broken vessels, in those who are broken hearted and humble, and that if we harm the poor we wrong the Shechinah.

404. לֹא יִהְיֶה לְךָ אֱלֹהִים אֲחֵרִים עַל פָּנָי. רַבִּי יִצְחָק אָמַר, אֱלֹהִים אֲחֵרִים, לְאַפָּקָא שְׁכִינְתָּא. עַל פָּנָי, לְאַפָּקָא אַפֵּי מַלְכָּא. דְּבְהוּ אִתְחֲזֵי מַלְכָּא קַדִּישָׁא, וְאִינּוּן שְׁמֵיהּ. וְהוּא אִינּוּן. הוּא שְׁמֵיהּ, דִּכְתִיב אֲנִי יְיָ' הוּא שְׁמִי. הוּא וּשְׁמֵיהּ חַד הוּא בְּרִיךְ שְׁמֵיהּ לְעָלַם וּלְעָלְמֵי עָלְמַיָּא.

404. "You shall have no other Elohim beside Me" (Shemot 20:3). According to Rabbi Yitzchak, "other Elohim" excludes the Shechinah, and thus, "YOU SHALL HAVE NO OTHER ELOHIM" THAN THE SHECHINAH, CALLED "ELOHIM." "...beside Me (lit. 'My face')..." excludes the face of the King upon which the Holy King is manifested. It is His Name and His Name is it; THE VISIBLE FACE IS HIS NAME, WHICH IS MALCHUT, AND HIS NAME IS THE VISIBLE FACE. He is His Name, AND ZEIR ANPIN IS HIS NAME, WHICH MEANS THEY ARE ONE, as it is written: "I am Hashem, that is My Name" (Yeshayah 42:8). He and His Name are one. Blessed be His Name for ever and ever.

405. תָּאנֵי רַבִּי שִׁמְעוֹן, זַכָּאִין אִינּוּן יִשְׂרָאֵל, דְּקוּדְשָׁא בְּרִיךְ הוּא קָרָא לוֹן אָדָם, דִּכְתִיב וְאַתֵּן צֹאנִי צֹאן מַרְעִיתִי אָדָם אַתֶּם, אָדָם כִּי יַקְרִיב מִכֶּם. מַאי טַעֲמָא קָרָא לוֹן אָדָם. מִשּׁוּם דִּכְתִיב וְאַתֶּם הַדְּבֵקִים בַּיְיָ' אֱלֹהֵיכֶם. אַתֶּם וְלֹא שְׁאַר עַמִּין עכו"ם. וּבְג"כ אָדָם אַתֶּם, אַתֶּם קְרוּיִין אָדָם, וְאֵין עכו"ם קְרוּיִין אָדָם.

405. Rabbi Shimon taught: Blessed are Yisrael, for the Holy One, blessed be He, called them 'men', as it is written: "But you My flock, the flock of My pasture, are men" (Yechezkel 34:31), AND ALSO, "If a man of you bring an offering" (Vayikra 1:2). Why are they called "men"? The reason is found in the verse: "You that did cleave to Hashem your Elohim" (Devarim 4:4) – you and not the heathen nations. Therefore, you are called "men" and they are not.

406. דְּתַנְיָא, אָמַר ר' שִׁמְעוֹן, כֵּיוָן דְּבַר נָשׁ יִשְׂרָאֵל אִתְגְּזַר, עָאל בִּבְרִית דְּגָזַר קוּדְשָׁא בְּרִיךְ הוּא בְּאַבְרָהָם, דִּכְתִיב בֵּרַךְ אֶת אַבְרָהָם בַּכֹּל. וּכְתִיב חֶסֶד לְאַבְרָהָם. וְשָׁארֵי לְמֵיעָאל בְּהַאי אֲתָר. כֵּיוָן דְּזָכָה לְקַיְימָא פִּקוּדֵי אוֹרַיְיתָא, עָאל בֵּיהּ בְּהַאי אָדָם, וְאִתְדְּבַּק בְּגוּפָא דְמַלְכָּא, וּכְדֵין אִקְרֵי אָדָם.

406. Rabbi Shimon continued with his explanations: When a Jewish boy is circumcised he enters into the Covenant which the Holy One, blessed be He, made with Abraham, as it says: "And Hashem had blessed Abraham in all things" (Beresheet 24:1), and, "loyal love to Abraham" (Michah 7:20). Thus, he begins to enter into that place, and when he commences to keep the precepts of the Torah he enters the grade of Adam (man), THAT OF THE SUPERNAL CHARIOT, and becomes attached to the body of the King. Then he is called 'man'.

407. וְזַרְעָא דְיִשְׂרָאֵל אִקְרוּן אָדָם. ת"ח, כְּתִיב בֵּיהּ בְּיִשְׁמָעֵאל, וְהוּא יִהְיֶה פֶּרֶא אָדָם. פֶּרֶא אָדָם, וְלֹא אָדָם. פֶּרֶא אָדָם, מִשׁוּם דְּאִתְגְּזַר. וְשֵׁירוּתָא דְּאָדָם הֲוָה בֵּיהּ, דִּכְתִיב וְיִשְׁמָעֵאל בְּנוֹ בֶּן שְׁלֹשׁ עֶשְׂרֵה שָׁנָה בְּהִמּוֹלוֹ אֶת בְּשַׂר עָרְלָתוֹ, כֵּיוָן דְּאִתְגְּזַר, עָאל בְּהַאי שֵׁירוּתָא, דְּאִקְרֵי כָּל. הה"ד וְהוּא יִהְיֶה פֶּרֶא אָדָם, וְלֹא אָדָם. יָדוֹ בַכֹּל, יָדוֹ בַכֹּל וַדַּאי, וְלֹא יַתִּיר, מִשׁוּם דְּלָא קַבִּיל פִּקוּדֵי אוֹרַיְיתָא. שֵׁירוּתָא הֲוָה בֵּיהּ, בְּגִין דְּאִתְגְּזַר, וְלָא אִשְׁתְּלִים בְּפִקוּדֵי אוֹרַיְיתָא. אֲבָל זַרְעָא דְיִשְׂרָאֵל, דְּאִשְׁתְּלִימוּ בְּכֹלָּא, אִקְרוּן אָדָם מַמָּשׁ, וּכְתִיב כִּי חֵלֶק יְיָ' עַמּוֹ יַעֲקֹב חֶבֶל נַחֲלָתוֹ.

407. The seed of Yisrael is called 'man'. Come and behold: of Ishmael it is written: "And he will be a wild man" (Beresheet 16:12). "...a wild man..." and not 'a man'. HE WAS CALLED "a wild man" because he was circumcised, and therefore he had the beginnings of being "a man," as it is written: "And Ishmael his son was thirteen years old when he was circumcised in the flesh of his foreskin" (Beresheet 17:25). Since his circumcision he entered to the grade which is called 'all', WHICH IS YESOD. Hence, he was not called 'a man' but "a wild man". "His hand will be against every man (lit. 'in all')" (Beresheet 16:12). Assuredly, "in all" and no more, because he did not accept the commandments of the Torah. He had the start, being circumcised, but was not perfected through the commandments of the Torah. But the seed of Yisrael, who were perfected in all things, is called "men" in the full sense, as it is written: "For Hashem's portion is His people, Jacob is the lot of His inheritance" (Devarim 32:9).

408. א״ר יוֹסֵי, בג״ד, כָּל פַּרְצוּפִין שָׁרוּ, בַּר מִפַּרְצוּפָא דְּאָדָם. ר׳ יִצְחָק אָמַר, כַּד אִתְעֲבַד, אִתְחֲזֵי דִּגְלִיפָא גּוֹ גְּלִיפִין דְּאַשְׁלָמוּתָא. א״ר יְהוּדָה, הַיְינוּ דְּאַמְרֵי אִינְשֵׁי קִיטְרוֹי בְּזִיקָא, בְּטִפְסָא שְׁכִיחֵי.

408. Rabbi Yosi said: Therefore, the engraving and painting of all faces is permitted, except the face of a man. Rabbi Yitzchak said that when A HUMAN FORM is represented, it looks engraved with an engraving of perfection, THAT IS, A SPECIAL PERFECTION IS PERCEIVED THEREIN. Rabbi Yehuda said: This accords with the popular saying: 'the form of the spirit is in the image', MEANING THAT ACCORDING TO THE IMAGE OF THE MAN FORMED, HIS CONNECTION WITH THE SPIRIT WITHIN HIM IS RECOGNIZED.

409. רַבִּי יְהוּדָה הֲוָה אָזִיל מִקַּפּוֹטְקִיָּא לְלוּד, לְמֶחֱמֵי לְרַבִּי שִׁמְעוֹן, דַּהֲוָה תַּמָּן, וַהֲוָה רַבִּי חִזְקִיָּה אָזִיל עִמֵּיהּ. אָמַר רַבִּי יְהוּדָה לְר׳ חִזְקִיָּה, הָא דִּתְנֵינָן, קָמֵי ר׳ שִׁמְעוֹן, וְהוּא יִהְיֶה פֶּרֶא אָדָם, וַדַּאי כָּךְ הוּא. וְדָא הוּא בְּרִירָא דְמִלָּה. סוֹפֵיהּ דִּקְרָא דִּכְתִיב, וְעַל פְּנֵי כָל אֶחָיו יִשְׁכּוֹן. מַהוּ וְעַל פְּנֵי כָל אֶחָיו יִשְׁכּוֹן.

409. Rabbi Yehuda was once going from Cappadocia to Lod to see Rabbi Shimon who was there, and Rabbi Chizkiyah accompanied him. Rabbi

Yehuda said to Rabbi Chizkiyah: What Rabbi Shimon taught us concerning the meaning of the term "wild man" is perfectly true and quite clear, BUT what is the meaning of the second part of the verse which says: "And he shall dwell in the presence of all his brethren" (Beresheet 16:12).

410. אָמַר לֵיהּ, לָא שְׁמַעְנָא, וְלָא אֵימָא. דְּהָא אוֹלִיפְנָא, כְּתִיב וְזֹאת הַתּוֹרָה אֲשֶׁר שָׂם מֹשֶׁה. אֲשֶׁר שָׂם מֹשֶׁה, אַתָּה יָכוֹל לוֹמַר. דְּלָא שָׂם מֹשֶׁה, אִי אַתָּה יָכוֹל לוֹמַר.

410. He replied: I have heard no interpretation and I shall not give any, for we learned that, "And this is the Torah which Moses set Yisrael" (Devarim 4:44). That "which Moses set" you can speak of, but what Moses did not set, MEANING WHAT WAS NOT TAUGHT BY ONE'S TEACHER, one can not tell.

411. פָּתַח ר׳ יְהוּדָה וְאָמַר, כִּי הוּא חַיֶּיךָ וְאֹרֶךְ יָמֶיךָ. מַאן דְּזָכֵי בְּאוֹרַיְיתָא, וְלָא אִתְפְּרַשׁ מִינָהּ, זָכֵי לִתְרֵין חַיִּין, חַד בְּעָלְמָא דֵּין, וְחַד בְּעָלְמָא דְּאָתֵי. דִּכְתִיב חַיֶּיךָ, תְּרֵי. וְכָל מַאן דְּיִתְפְּרַשׁ מִינָהּ, כְּמַאן דְּמִתְפְּרַשׁ מִן חַיֵּי, וּמַאן דְּמִתְפְּרַשׁ מֵר׳ שִׁמְעוֹן, כְּאִילּוּ מִתְפְּרַשׁ מִכֹּלָּא.

411. Rabbi Yehuda opened the discussion with that verse: "For He is your life, and the length of your days" (Devarim 30:20). He who is worthy of the Torah and does not separate himself from her is worthy of two lives, life in this world and life in the World to Come, as it is written, "your life," LITERALLY, IN A PLURAL FORM, WHICH MEANS two. He who separates himself from her, separates himself from life, and he who separates himself from Rabbi Shimon, separates himself from all things.

412. וּמַה בְּהַאי קְרָא דְּאִיהוּ פָּתַח פִּתְחָא, לָא יָכִילְנָא לְמֵיעָאל בָּהּ. פִּתְגָּמֵי אוֹרַיְיתָא דִּסְתִּימִין, עַל אַחַת כַּמָּה וְכַמָּה. וַוי לְדָרָא, דְּר׳ שִׁמְעוֹן בֶּן יוֹחָאי יִסְתָּלִיק מִנֵּיהּ. דְּכַד אֲנַן קַיְימִין קַמֵּי דְּר׳ שִׁמְעוֹן, מַבּוּעִין דְּלִבָּא פְּתִיחִין לְכָל עִיבָר, וְכֹלָּא מִתְגַּלְיָא. וְכַד אִתְפְּרַשְׁנָא מִנֵּיהּ. לָא יָדַעְנָא מִידִי, וְכָל מַבּוּעִין סְתִימִין.

412. Here is a verse to which Rabbi Shimon already opened a door, yet we

can not enter it. How much more difficult will it be for us to understand these words of the Torah. Woe to the generation from which Rabbi Shimon will be removed, for as long as we are in his presence the springs of the heart are open on every direction and everything is revealed, but as soon as we separate ourselves from him we know nothing and all the springs are closed.

413. אָמַר ר' חִזְקִיָּה, הַיְינוּ דִּכְתִיב, וַיָּאצֶל מִן הָרוּחַ אֲשֶׁר עָלָיו וַיִּתֵּן עַל שִׁבְעִים אִישׁ הַזְּקֵנִים, כְּבוּצִינָא דָּא, דְּנָהֲרִין מִינֵּהּ כַּמָּה בּוּצִינִין, וְהוּא בְּקִיּוּמֵיהּ שְׁכִיחַ. כָּךְ ר' שִׁמְעוֹן בֶּן יוֹחַאי, מָארֵי דְּבוּצִינִין, הוּא נָהִיר לְכֹלָּא, וּנְהוֹרָא לָא אַעְדֵּי מִנֵּיהּ, וְאִשְׁתְּכַח בְּקִיּוּמֵיהּ. אָזְלוּ עַד דְּמָטוּ לְגַבֵּיה.

413. Rabbi Chizkiyah said: As it is written, "And he took the spirit that was upon him, and gave it to the seventy elders" (Bemidbar 11:25). It was like a light of a candle from which many lights are kindled; it remains whole AND ITS LIGHT STANDS IN ITS FULLNESS EVEN THOUGH MANY CANDLES WERE LIT BY IT. Rabbi Shimon bar Yochai is such a light. He illuminates everyone and yet his light is not diminished, but remains steadfast in its full splendor. They walked on until they reached his dwelling.

414. כַּד מָטוּ גַּבֵּיהּ, אַשְׁכְּחוּהוּ, דַּהֲוָה יָתִיב וְלָעֵי בְּאוֹרַיְיתָא, וַהֲוָה אָמַר, תְּפִלָּה לְעָנִי כִי יַעֲטֹף וְלִפְנֵי יְיָ' יִשְׁפֹּךְ שִׂיחוֹ. כָּל צְלוֹתָא דְּיִשְׂרָאֵל צְלוֹתָא, וּצְלוֹתָא דְּעָנִי עִלָּאָה מִכֻּלְּהוּ. מַאי טַעֲמָא. מִשּׁוּם דְּהַאי סַלְקָא עַד כּוּרְסֵי יְקָרָא דְּמַלְכָּא, וְאִתְעַטָּר בְּרֵישֵׁיהּ. וְקוּדְשָׁא בְּרִיךְ הוּא מִשְׁתַּבַּח בְּהַהִיא צְלוֹתָא וַדַּאי. תְּפִלָּה דְּעָנִי, תְּפִלָּה אִקְרֵי.

414. When they reached him, they found him studying the Torah. He was saying: "A prayer of the afflicted (lit. 'poor') when he faints and pours out his complaint before Hashem" (Tehilim 102:1). He said: All prayers of Yisrael are effective, but the prayer of the poor man is more effective than all others. Why? Because it reaches the Throne of Glory and becomes a garland for His head, and the Holy One, blessed be He, is praised by this prayer. THEREFORE, a prayer of a poor man is called 'a prayer'.

415. כִּי יַעֲטֹף. עֲטוּפָא דָא, לָאו עֲטוּפָא דְּכַסּוּ הוּא, דְּהָא לֵית לֵיהּ.
אֶלָּא, כְּתִיב הָכָא כִּי יַעֲטֹף. וּכְתִיב הָתָם, הָעֲטוּפִים בְּרָעָב. וְלִפְנֵי יְיָ'
יִשְׁפֹּךְ שִׂיחוֹ, דְּיִקַבֵּל קַמֵּי מָארֵיהּ, וְדָא נִיחָא לֵיהּ קַמֵּי קוּדְשָׁא בְּרִיךְ
הוּא, מִשּׁוּם דְּעָלְמָא מִתְקַיְימָא בֵּיהּ, כַּד לָא אִשְׁתְּכָחוּ שְׁאָר קַיְימֵי
עָלְמָא בְּעָלְמָא. וַוי לְמַאן דְּהַהוּא מִסְכְּנָא יְקַבֵּל עֲלוֹהִי לְמָארֵיהּ, מִשּׁוּם
דְּמִסְכְּנָא קָרִיב לְמַלְכָּא יַתִּיר מִכֻּלְּהוּ, דִּכְתִיב וְהָיָה כִּי יִצְעַק אֵלַי
וְשָׁמַעְתִּי כִּי חַנּוּן אָנִי.

415. "…when he faints (Heb. *ya'atof*; also Eng. 'wraps')…" This wrapping
is not that of garments, for he has no GARMENT, but the word "*ya'atof*" has
the same significance here as the words in the verse: "That faint (Heb.
atufim) for hunger" (Eichah 2:19). IN THIS VERSE AS WELL, HE IS
CLOTHED IN HUNGER. "He pours out his complaints before Hashem." He
should cry before his Master because this is pleasing to the Holy One,
blessed be He, for the world is sustained him. Woe to him against whom a
poor man complains to his Master, for the poor man is nearer to the King
than anyone else, as it is written: "when he cries to Me, that I will hear"
(Shemot 22:26).

416. וְלִשְׁאָר בְּנֵי עָלְמָא, זִמְנִין דְּשָׁמַע, זִמְנִין דְּלָא שָׁמַע. מ"ט. מִשּׁוּם
דְּדִיּוּרֵיהּ דְּמַלְכָּא בְּהָנֵי מָאנֵי תְּבִירֵי, דִּכְתִיב, וְאֶת דַּכָּא וּשְׁפַל רוּחַ.
וּכְתִיב קָרוֹב יְיָ' לְנִשְׁבְּרֵי לֵב. לֵב נִשְׁבָּר וְנִדְכֶּה אֱלֹהִים לֹא תִבְזֶה.

416. As for other people, sometimes He hears them, and sometimes He does
not. What is the reason for this? The Holy One, blessed be He, dwells in
broken vessels, as it is written: "yet with him also that is of a contrite and
humble spirit" (Yeshayah 57:15), and: "Hashem is near to them who are of
a broken heart" (Tehilim 34:19), and also: "A broken and a contrite heart,
Elohim, You will not despise" (Tehilim 51:19).

417. מִכָּאן תָּנֵינָן, מַאן דְּנָזִיף בְּמִסְכְּנָא, נָזִיף בִּשְׁכִינְתָּא, דִּכְתִיב וְאֶת
דַּכָּא וּשְׁפַל רוּחַ. וּכְתִיב כִּי יְיָ' יָרִיב רִיבָם וְגוֹ'. בְּגִין דְּאַפּוֹטְרוֹפָא דִּלְהוֹן
תַּקִּיפָא, וְשַׁלִּיטָא עַל כֹּלָּא, דְּלָא אִצְטְרִיךְ סַהֲדֵי, וְלָא אִצְטְרִיךְ לְדַיָּינָא
אָחֳרָא, וְלָא נָטִיל מַשְׁכּוֹנָא, כִּשְׁאָר דַּיָּינָא. וּמַה מַשְׁכּוֹנָא נָטִיל, נִשְׁמָתִין

דְּבַר נָשׁ, דִּכְתִיב וְקָבַע אֶת קוֹבְעֵיהֶם נָפֶשׁ.

417. Hence, we have learned that he who wrongs a poor man wrongs the Shechinah, as it is written: "yet with him also that is of a contrite and humble spirit," and also, "For Hashem will plead their cause" (Mishlei 22:23). For Hashem is their Protector and He rules everywhere and needs no witnesses, and no other judge. He does not accept pledges like other judges, except those of the souls, as it is written: "And rob of life those who rob them" (Mishlei 22:23).

418. תּוּ אָמַר תְּפִלָּה לְעָנִי, כָּל אֲתָר דְּאִקְרֵי תְּפִלָּה, מִלָּה עִלָּאָה הִיא, דְּהִיא סַלְקָא לַאֲתָר עִלָּאָה. תְּפִלָּה דְּרֵישָׁא, אִינּוּן תְּפִלֵּי דְּמַלְכָּא, דְּאָנַח לְהוּ.

418. He continued with his explanations: "A prayer (Heb. tfilah) of the afflicted." Wherever the word "Tfilah" is mentioned, it signifies something supernal, for it ascends to a supernal place. Tfilah (Eng. 'phylactery') of the head is the Tefilin which the King puts, NAMELY THE MOCHIN OF ZEIR ANPIN, WHICH ARE CALLED 'HEAD TEFILIN'.

419. ר' שִׁמְעוֹן אַסְחַר רֵישֵׁיה, וְחָמָא לְר' יְהוּדָה וּלְר' חִזְקִיָּה, דִּמְטוּ גַּבֵּיה. בָּתַר דְּסַיֵּים אִסְתָּכַּל בְּהוּ. אָמַר לְהוּ, סִימָא הֲוָה לְכוּ וְאִתְאֲבִיד מִנַּיְיכוּ. אָמְרוּ לֵיה, וַדַּאי דְּפִתְחָא עִלָּאָה פָּתַח מַר, וְלָא יָכִילְנָא לְמֵיעָאל בָּה.

419. Rabbi Shimon turned his head and saw Rabbi Yehuda and Rabbi Chizkiyah approaching him. When he had finished he looked at them and said: You look as if you have lost something valuable. FOR THEY HAD HEARD WORDS OF TORAH WHICH THEY FORGOT. They replied: Yes, for the master opened a precious door and yet we can not enter into it.

420. אָמַר, מַאי הִיא. אָמְרוּ לֵיה, וְהוּא יִהְיֶה פֶּרֶא אָדָם, וְסוֹפֵיה דִּקְרָא בָּעֵינָא לְמִנְדַּע, דִּכְתִיב וְעַל פְּנֵי כָל אֶחָיו יִשְׁכּוֹן, מַהוּ עַל פְּנֵי כָל אֶחָיו. דְּהָא בְּרִירָא דְּכוּלֵיה קְרָא יְדַעְנָא, וְהַאי לָא יָדַעְנָא, דְּסֵיפֵיה דִּקְרָא, לָא

אִתְחֲזֵי כְּרֵישֵׁיהּ.

420. What is it? He asked. They said to him: What is the meaning of the last part of the verse, "And he will be a wild man," which is, "and he shall dwell in the presence of all his brethren"? The beginning of the verse is clear to us, but what of this? The end does not seem to suit the beginning.

421. אָמַר לוֹן, חַיֵּיכוֹן, כֹּלָּא חַד מִלָּה הִיא, וּבְחַד דַּרְגָּא סַלְקָא. תָּאנָא, כַּמָּה פָּנִים לַפָּנִים, אִית לֵיהּ לְקוּדְשָׁא בְּרִיךְ הוּא. פָּנִים דְּנַהֲרִין. פָּנִים דְּלָא נַהֲרִין. פָּנִים תַּתָּאִין. פָּנִים רְחִיקִין. פָּנִים קְרִיבִין. פָּנִים דִּלְגוֹ. פָּנִים דִּלְבַר. פָּנִים דִּימִינָא. פָּנִים דִּשְׂמָאלָא.

421. Then Rabbi Shimon replied: Upon your life, both parts of the verse have one significance and point to the same truth. We know that the Holy One, blessed be He, has many aspects (faces) upon aspects. There is a shining aspect, a dull aspect, a low aspect, a distant aspect, an external aspect, an inner aspect, the right aspect, and the left aspect.

422. תָּא חֲזֵי, זַכָּאִין אִינּוּן יִשְׂרָאֵל קָמֵיהּ דְּקוּדְשָׁא בְּרִיךְ הוּא, דַּאֲחִידָן בְּאַנְפִּין עִלָּאִין דְּמַלְכָּא. בְּאִינּוּן פָּנִים דְּהוּא וּשְׁמֵיהּ אֲחִידָן בְּהוּ, וְאִינּוּן וּשְׁמֵיהּ חַד הוּא. וּשְׁאַר עַמִּין אֲחִידָן בְּאִינּוּן פָּנִים רְחִיקִין, בְּאִינּוּן פָּנִים תַּתָּאִין. וּבְגִינֵי כָּךְ אִינּוּן רְחִיקִין מִגּוּפָא דְּמַלְכָּא, דְּהָא חֲמֵינָא כָּל אִינּוּן דְּמִצְרָאִים, קְרִיבוֹי דְּיִשְׁמָעֵאל, כַּמָּה אַחִין וּקְרִיבִין הֲווֹ לֵיהּ, וְכֻלְּהוּ הֲווֹ בְּאַנְפִּין תַּתָּאִין, בְּאִינּוּן פָּנִים רְחִיקִין.

422. Come and behold: happy are Yisrael before the Holy One, blessed be He, for they are united with the most supernal aspect of the King, with the aspect in which He and His Name are one, while other nations are united with the most distant aspect, the lower aspect, and therefore they are at a great distance from the body of the King. For we see that all those Egyptians who are related to Ishmael, and his many kin and relatives, were all connected with the lower and distant aspects.

423. וּבְגִינֵיהּ דְּאַבְרָהָם, כַּד אִתְגְּזַר יִשְׁמָעֵאל, זָכָה, דְּשַׁוֵּי מָדוֹרֵיהּ

וְחוּלָקֵיהּ בַּאֲתַר דְּשַׁלִּיטָא עַל כָּל אִינּוּן פָּנִים רְחִיקִין וְתַתָּאִין, עַל כָּל אִינּוּן פָּנִים דִּשְׁאַר עַמִּין. הה"ד יָדוֹ בַכֹּל, וּבְגִינֵי כַּךְ עַל פְּנֵי כָל אֶחָיו יִשְׁכּוֹן, כְּלוֹמַר, וְשַׁוֵּי מָדוֹרֵיהּ וְחוּלָקֵיהּ לְעֵילָּא מִכֻּלְּהוּ, דִּכְתִיב יָדוֹ בַכֹּל, דְּשַׁלְּטָא עַל כָּל שְׁאַר פָּנִים דִּלְתַתָּא. וּבג"כ עַל פְּנֵי כָל אֶחָיו וַדַּאי, דְּלָא זָכוּ כְּוָותֵיהּ.

423. Ishmael, however, when he was circumcised, had the privilege, for Abraham's sake, of having his dwelling place and his portion in the sphere which dominated all those distant and lower aspects, rather than in the aspects of the other nations. Therefore it says of him: "His hand will be against every man (lit. 'in all')." THE WORD "ALL" SIGNIFIES YESOD, therefore "he shall dwell in the presence (lit. 'above the face') of all his brethren," meaning that he will be in a superior dwelling to any of them, as "in all" rules over all the aspects that are below. Hence, "above the face of all his brethren," for they had no such merit.

424. אָתוּ רַבִּי יְהוּדָה וְר' חִזְקִיָּה, וְנָשְׁקוּ יְדוֹי. א"ר יְהוּדָה, הַיְינוּ דְּאַמְרֵי אִינָשֵׁי, חַמְרָא בְּדַרְדְּיָא, וּנְבִיעָא דְּבֵירָא, בְּקִטִּירָא דְּקִיזְרָא אִתְעַטָּר. וַוי לְעָלְמָא, כַּד יִסְתַּלַּק מַר מִנֵּיהּ. וַוי לְדָרָא, דְּיִתְעָרַע בְּהַהוּא זִמְנָא. זַכָּאָה דָּרָא דְּאִשְׁתְּמוֹדְעוּן לֵיהּ לְמַר. זַכָּאָה דָּרָא דְּאִיהוּ שָׁרֵי בְּגַוֵּיהּ.

424. Then Rabbi Yehuda and Rabbi Chizkiyah approached him and kissed his hands. Rabbi Yehuda said: This is an illustration of the proverb, 'Wine settled on its lees and a bubbling spring is a crown over earth and dross,' FOR IT COVERS IT AND WHEN THE SPRING IS ABOUT TO BREAK THROUGH THE EARTH IT BECOMES MORE POWERFUL. THUS ISHMAEL RULED POWERFULLY OVER THE DROSS OF HIS BROTHERS, WHO WERE CONNECTED WITH THE LOWER AND DISTANT ASPECTS, AS MENTIONED ABOVE. Woe to the world when the master is gone from it. Woe to the generation in which time it will happen. Happy is the generation that is privileged to know him and in which he lives.

425. אָמַר רַבִּי חִזְקִיָּה, הָא תָּנֵינָן, גִּיּוֹרָא כַּד אִתְגְּזַר, אִקְרֵי גֵּר צֶדֶק, וְלָא יַתִּיר. וְהָכָא אָמַר מַר יָדוֹ בַכֹּל. אָמַר ר"ש, כֹּלָּא אִתְקְשָׁר בְּחַד.

אֲבָל גִּיּוֹרָא תָּנֵינָן. שָׁאנֵי יִשְׁמָעֵאל, דְּלָאו גִּיּוֹרָא הוּא. בְּרֵיהּ דְּאַבְרָהָם הֲוָה, בְּרֵיהּ דְּקַדִּישָׁא הֲוָה. וּכְתִיב בֵּיהּ בְּיִשְׁמָעֵאל, הִנֵּה בֵּרַכְתִּי אוֹתוֹ. כְּתִיב הָכָא, בֵּרַכְתִּי אוֹתוֹ. וּכְתִיב הָתָם, וַיְיָ׳ בֵּרַךְ אֶת אַבְרָהָם בַּכֹּל. וְעַל כַּךְ כְּתִיב, יָדוֹ בַכֹּל.

425. Rabbi Chizkiyah said: We have learned that a proselyte, when circumcised, is merely called "a proselyte of Righteousness" and nothing more, and yet, according to your interpretation of this verse, master, "His hand will be against every man (lit. 'in all')," MEANING THAT HE HAD THE MERIT TO DWELL IN YESOD, WHICH IS CALLED "ALL." Rabbi Shimon replied: All is attached to the same place. Yet we were speaking of converts. Ishmael was not merely a proselyte for he was a son of Abraham, a son of a holy man, and of Ishmael it says "Behold, I have blessed him" (Beresheet 17:20). It says here "I have blessed him," and elsewhere "And Hashem blessed Abraham in all" (Beresheet 24:1). THIS BLESSING HERE, TOO, IS IN "ALL." Therefore of Ishmael it is written "his hand in all."

426. וּבְגִינֵי כַּךְ כְּתִיב, עַל פְּנֵי כָל אֶחָיו יִשְׁכּוֹן. דְּאִי שְׁאָר קְרִיבוֹי אִתְגַּיָּירוּ אִקְרוּן גֵּירֵי צֶדֶק, וְלָא יַתִּיר, וְהוּא יַתִּיר וְעִלָּאָה מִכֻּלְּהוּ. כ״ש אִינּוּן דְּלָא אִתְגְּזָרוּ, דְּקַיְימִין בְּאִינּוּן אַפִּין רְחִיקִין, בְּאִינּוּן אַפִּין תַּתָּאִין. וְאִיהוּ, מָדוֹרֵיהּ לְעֵילָּא מִכָּל פָּנִים דִּידְהוּ, וּמִכָּל פָּנִים דְּעַמִּין עעכו״ם, הֲדָא הוּא דִכְתִּיב, עַל פְּנֵי כָל אֶחָיו יִשְׁכּוֹן. א״ר יְהוּדָה, קוּדְשָׁא בְּרִיךְ הוּא בְּגִין כַּךְ אַכְרִיז וְאָמַר, לֹא יִהְיֶה לְךָ אֱלֹהִים אֲחֵרִים עַל פָּנַי, דְּדָא הוּא מְהֵימְנוּתָא דִּילֵיהּ.

426. Therefore it is written: "And he shall dwell in the presence of all his brethren." For proselytes from among other nations, Ishmael's kin, would be called "proselytes of righteousness" and no more, but he is superior to them all. Moreover, he dwells higher than the aspects of those who were not circumcised and were connected with the distant and lower aspects, and the aspects of the heathen nations. Therefore, it is written: "And he shall dwell in the presence (lit. 'above the faces') of all his brethren." Rabbi Yehuda said: Hence the proclamation of the Holy One, blessed be He: "You shall have no other Elohim beside Me (lit. 'over My face')," FOR HIS FACE IS MALCHUT, CALLED 'FACE'.

24. "You shall not make"

A Synopsis
"You shall not make for yourself any carved idol, or any likeness." In this section we are reminded not to attach interpretations to the Torah without knowing the correct meaning or without having learned them from our teacher; we are reminded not to be false to the Holy Name, and not to be false to the Covenant of Abraham by bringing it into a foreign domain.

427. לֹא תַעֲשֶׂה לְךָ פֶּסֶל וְכָל תְּמוּנָה. הָא אִתְּמַר. וְאָמַר רַבִּי יוֹסִי, כָּל פַּרְצוּפִין שָׁרֵי, בַּר מִפַּרְצוּפָא דְּאָדָם, דְּהָא הַאי פַּרְצוּפָא שָׁלִיט בְּכֹלָּא.

427. "You shall not make for yourself any carved idol, or any likeness" (Shemot 20:4). This was already explained. Rabbi Yosi added any form of a face one can make, except that of a man, for a man's face rules over all things.

428. דָּבָר אַחֵר, לֹא תַעֲשֶׂה לְךָ פֶּסֶל וְכָל תְּמוּנָה. רַבִּי יִצְחָק פָּתַח, אַל תִּתֵּן אֶת פִּיךָ לַחֲטִיא אֶת בְּשָׂרֶךָ. כַּמָּה אִית לֵיהּ לְבַר נָשׁ לְאִזְדַּהֲרָא עַל פִּתְגָּמֵי אוֹרַיְיתָא, כַּמָּה אִית לֵיהּ לְאִזְדַּהֲרָא דְּלָא יִטְעֵי בְּהוּ, וְלָא יָפִיק מֵאוֹרַיְיתָא מַה דְּלָא יָדַע, וְלָא קַבִּיל מֵרַבֵּיהּ. דְּכָל מַאן דְּאָמַר בְּמִלֵּי דְּאוֹרַיְיתָא מַה דְּלָא יָדַע, וְלָא קַבִּיל מֵרַבֵּיהּ, עֲלֵיהּ כְּתִיב לֹא תַעֲשֶׂה לְךָ פֶּסֶל וְכָל תְּמוּנָה. וְקוּדְשָׁא בְּרִיךְ הוּא זַמִּין לְאִתְפָּרְעָא מִנֵּיהּ, בְּעָלְמָא דְּאָתֵי, בְּזִמְנָא דְּנִשְׁמָתֵיהּ בַּעְיָא לְמֵיעָאל לְדוּכְתָּא, דַּחְיָין לָהּ לְבַר, וְתִשְׁתְּצֵי מֵהַהוּא אֲתָר דִּצְרִירָא בִּצְרוֹרָא דְּחַיֵּי דִּשְׁאַר נִשְׁמָתִין.

428. There is also another explanation of the verse: "You shall not make any carved idol or any likeness." Rabbi Yitzchak opened the discussion with the verse: "Do not let your mouth cause your flesh to sin" (Kohelet 5:5). How careful one must be not to err in regard to the meaning of the words of the Torah, and not to attach interpretations to the Torah without knowing the correct meaning or having learned them from his teacher, for of whoever speaks of scripture without knowledge or learning from his Rabbi, it says: "You shall not make any carved idol or any likeness." The Holy One, blessed be He, will punish him in the World to Come, when his soul shall

desire to enter its place. It will then be repelled and it will be cut off from that region which is bound up with the bundle of life, wherein are the other souls.

429. רַבִּי יְהוּדָה אוֹמֵר מֵהָכָא כְּמָה דִּתְנֵינָן, לָמָה יִקְצֹף הָאֱלֹהִים עַל קוֹלֶךָ. קוֹלֶךָ: דָּא הִיא נִשְׁמָתֵיהּ דְּבַר נָשׁ. אָמַר רַבִּי חִיָּיא, ע"ד כְּתִיב, כִּי יְיָ' אֱלֹהֶיךָ אֵל קַנָּא. מ"ט. מִשּׁוּם דְּקַנֵּי לִשְׁמֵיהּ בְּכֹלָּא. אִי בְּגִין פַּרְצוּפִין מְקַנֵּי לִשְׁמֵיהּ, מִשּׁוּם דִּמְשַׁקֵּר בִּשְׁמֵיהּ. אִי מִשּׁוּם אוֹרַיְיתָא.

429. Rabbi Yehuda said: From this we understand the verse: "Why should the Elohim be angry at your voice?" (Kohelet 5:5). "Your voice" signifies a soul of a man. Rabbi Chiya said: Of this it is written, "For I Hashem your Elohim am a jealous El" (Shemot 20:5). He is zealous above all for His Name when He sees an image of a face, or one who is false to His name, or when the Torah IS MISINTERPRETED WITH AN EXPLANATION ONE HAD NOT LEARNED FROM HIS TEACHERS.

430. תָּנֵינָן, אוֹרַיְיתָא כֹּלָּא שְׁמָא קַדִּישָׁא הִיא, דְּלֵית לָךְ מִלָּה בְּאוֹרַיְיתָא דְּלָא כָּלִיל בִּשְׁמָא קַדִּישָׁא. וּבְגִינֵי כַּךְ, בָּעֵי לְאִזְדַּהֲרָא, בְּגִין דְּלָא יִטְעֵי בִּשְׁמֵיהּ קַדִּישָׁא, וְלָא יְשַׁקֵּר בֵּיהּ. וּמַאן דִּמְשַׁקֵּר בְּמַלְכָּא עִלָּאָה, לָא עָאלִין לֵיהּ לְפַלְטְרוֹי דְּמַלְכָּא, וְיִשְׁתְּצֵי מֵעָלְמָא דְּאָתֵי.

430. We have learned that the whole Torah is a Holy Name, for there is not a word written which is not included in the Holy Name. Therefore, one must beware of erring in regard to His Holy Name, and one must not be false to it. He who is false to the Supernal King will not be allowed to enter the King's palace, and will be driven away from the World to Come.

431. אָמַר רַבִּי אַבָּא, כְּתִיב הָכָא לֹא תַעֲשֶׂה לְךָ פֶסֶל וְכָל תְּמוּנָה. וּכְתִיב הָתָם, פְּסָל לְךָ שְׁנֵי לֻחֹת אֲבָנִים. כְּלוֹמַר, לֹא תַעֲשֶׂה לְךָ פֶסֶל, לָא תַעֲבֵד לָךְ אוֹרַיְיתָא אַחֲרָא דְּלָא יַדְעַת, וְלָא אָמַר לָךְ רַבָּךְ. מַאי טַעֲמָא. כִּי אָנֹכִי יְיָ' אֱלֹהֶיךָ אֵל קַנָּא, אֲנָא הוּא דְּזַמִּין לְאִתְפָּרְעָא מִינָךְ בְּעָלְמָא דְּאָתֵי, בְּשַׁעֲתָא דְּנִשְׁמָתָא בַּעְיָא לְמֵיעָאל קַמָּאי, כַּמָּה זְמִינִין לְשַׁקְרָא בָּהּ, וּלְעַיְּילָא לָהּ גּוֹ גֵּיהִנָּם.

431. Rabbi Aba cited the verse: "You shall not make for yourself any carved idol (Heb. *pesel*)," and in another place it is written: "Hew (Heb. *pesol*) for yourself two tablets of stone" (Shemot 34:1), MEANING you shall not hew another Torah which you neither know, nor have learned from your master. Why? Because "I Hashem your Elohim am a jealous El" and I shall punish you in the World to Come, MEANING it is I who will punish you in the World to Come when your soul shall long to stand in My Presence. How many emissaries will then be ready to frustrate its desire and thrust it into Gehenom.

432. תָּנֵיָא, אָמַר ר' יִצְחָק, לֹא תַעֲשֶׂה לְךָ וְגוֹ', דְּבָעֵי בַּר נָשׁ דְּלָא לְשַׁקְּרָא בִּשְׁמָא דְקוּדְשָׁא בְּרִיךְ הוּא דְקַשְׁרָא קַדְמָאָה, דְּאִתְקַשָּׁרוּ יִשְׂרָאֵל בְּקוּדְשָׁא בְּרִיךְ הוּא, כַּד אִתְגְּזָרוּ. וְדָא הוּא קְיוּמָא קַדְמָאָה דְּכֹלָּא, לְמֵיעָאל בִּבְרִית דְּאַבְרָהָם, דְּהוּא קֶשֶׁר דִּשְׁכִינְתָּא. וּבָעֵי בַּר נָשׁ, דְּלָא לְשַׁקְּרָא בְּהַאי בְּרִית, דְּמַאן דִּמְשַׁקֵּר בְּהַאי בְּרִית, מְשַׁקֵּר בְּקוּדְשָׁא בְּרִיךְ הוּא. מַאי שִׁקְרָא הוּא. הוּא, דְּלָא יֵיעוּל הַאי בְּרִית בִּרְשׁוּתָא אַחֲרָא. כְּמָה דְאַתְּ אָמַר וּבָעַל בַּת אֵל נֵכָר.

432. Rabbi Yitzchak said: "You shall not make..." means that one should not be false to the Name of the Holy One, blessed be He, for Yisrael entered into the first Covenant and union with the Holy One, blessed be He, when they circumcised, for this was the first condition to enter the Covenant of Abraham, the bond with the Shechinah. And one must not be false to that Covenant, for he that is false to that Covenant, is false to the Holy One, blessed be He. What is this falsehood? The bringing of the covenant into a foreign domain, as it is written: "And has married the daughter of a strange El" (Malachi 2:11).

433. ר' יְהוּדָה אָמַר מֵהָכָא, בַּיְיָ' בָּגָדוּ כִּי בָנִים זָרִים יָלָדוּ. מַאן דִּמְשַׁקֵּר בְּהַאי בְּרִית, מְשַׁקֵּר בְּקֻבָּ"ה. מִשּׁוּם דְּהַאי בְּרִית בְּקֻבָּ"ה אֲחִידָא, וּכְתִיב לֹא תַעֲשֶׂה לְךָ פֶסֶל וְכָל תְּמוּנָה אֲשֶׁר בַּשָּׁמַיִם מִמַּעַל וְגוֹ'.

433. Rabbi Yehuda said: Hence, "They have dealt treacherously against Hashem, for they have begotten strange children" (Hoshea 5:7). Whoever is

false to the Covenant is false to the Holy One, blessed be He, because the Covenant is united with Him. Therefore, it is written: "You shall not make for yourself any carved idol, or any likeness of any thing that is in heaven above..."

25. "You shall not bow down to them"

A Synopsis
Rabbi Elazar explains why it is forbidden to marry any woman from a heathen nation, for the result is always rebellious children who inherit the taint of idolatry. We are reminded that we who keep the commandments of the Torah are the children of Hashem.

434. לֹא תִשְׁתַּחֲוֶה לָהֶם וְלֹא תָעָבְדֵם. ר' אֶלְעָזָר הֲוָה אָזִיל בְּאָרְחָא, וַהֲוָה ר' חִיָּיא עִמֵּיה. אָמַר ר' חִיָּיא, כְּתִיב וְרָאִיתָ בַּשִּׁבְיָה אֵשֶׁת יְפַת תֹּאַר וְגוֹ', מַאי טַעְמָא. וְהָא כְּתִיב לֹא תִתְחַתֵּן בָּם. אָמַר לֵיה, בְּעוֹד דִּבְרָשׁוּתַיְיהוּ קַיְימֵי.

434. "You shall not bow down to them, nor serve them" (Shemot 20:5). Rabbi Elazar was once walking in company with Rabbi Chiya. Rabbi Chiya said: It is written, "And you see among the captives a beautiful woman..." (Devarim 21:11). Why DOES THE TORAH ALLOW MARRIAGE TO HER? Is it written: "you shall not make marriages with them" (Devarim 7:3). He replied to him: THIS ONLY APPLIED to women independent in their own land. HERE IT INDICATES A CAPTIVE WOMAN WHO COMES UNDER THE RULE OF YISRAEL. THEREFORE, SHE IS PERMITTED BY THE TORAH TO BE TAKEN AS A WIFE.

435. וְתָא חֲזֵי, לֵית לָךְ אִנְתּוּ בְּעַמִּין עעכו"ם כְּשֵׁרָה כַּדְקָא חֲזֵי. דִּתְנֵינָן, אֲמַאי אַסְמִיךְ פַּרְשְׁתָּא דָא, לְבֶן סוֹרֵר וּמוֹרֶה. אֶלָּא בְּוַדַּאי, מַאן דְּנָסִיב הַאי אִתְּתָא, בֶּן סוֹרֵר וּמוֹרֶה יָרִית מִינָה. מַאי טַעְמָא. מִשּׁוּם דְּקָשֶׁה לְמֶעְבַּר זוּהֲמָא מִינָה, וְכָל שֶׁכֵּן הַהִיא דְּאִתְנְסִיבַת בְּקַדְמֵיתָא, דְּדִינָא בְּדִינָא אִתְדְּבַק, וְאִסְתָּאֲבַת בָּה, וְקַשְׁיָא זוּהֲמָא לְמֶעְבַּר מִינָה, וְהַיְינוּ דְּאָמַר מֹשֶׁה בְּנְשֵׁי מִדְיָן, וְכָל אִשָּׁה יוֹדַעַת אִישׁ לְמִשְׁכַּב זָכָר הֲרוֹגוּ.

435. Come and behold: there is no woman among the heathen nations who is free from taint, therefore this section concerning the captive woman is immediately followed by that of the rebellious son, to indicate that whoever marries such a woman, begets rebellious children. What is the reason for

this? The impurity of idolatry inherited by the mother is difficult to remove, and this is even the more so if she has already been married to a heathen, for Judgment cleaves to Judgment, and she is tainted. Therefore, Moses commanded the extermination of the Midianite women, as it is written: "Kill every woman that has known man by lying with him" (Bemidbar 31:17).

436. זַכָּאָה חוּלָקֵיה, דְּהַהוּא בַּר נָשׁ דִּירִית אַחֲסַנְתָּא דָּא, וְנָטִיר לָהּ. דִּבְהַהוּא אַחֲסָנָא קַדִּישָׁא אִתְדְּבַק בַּר נָשׁ בְּקוּדְשָׁא בְּרִיךְ הוּא, כָּל שֶׁכֵּן אִי זָכֵי בְּפִקּוּדֵי אוֹרַיְיתָא, דְּהָא פָּשִׁיט מַלְכָּא יְמִינֵיה לְקַבְּלֵיה, וְאִתְדְּבַק בְּגוּפָא קַדִּישָׁא. וְעַל דָּא כְּתִיב בְּהוּ בְּיִשְׂרָאֵל, וְאַתֶּם הַדְּבֵקִים בַּיְיָ' אֱלֹהֵיכֶם. וּכְתִיב בָּנִים אַתֶּם לַיְיָ'. בָּנִים אַתֶּם מַמָּשׁ. דִּכְתִיב בְּנִי בְכוֹרִי יִשְׂרָאֵל. וּכְתִיב יִשְׂרָאֵל אֲשֶׁר בְּךָ אֶתְפָּאָר.

436. Happy is the portion of the man who keeps this heritage in purity, THAT OF THE HOLY COVENANT, for in this holy possession he unites himself with the Holy One, blessed be He. This is all the more so if he keeps the commandments of the Torah. Then the King stretches out His right hand to receive him, and he cleaves to the Holy Body, NAMELY, ZEIR ANPIN. Therefore it is written of Yisrael: "But you that did cleave to Hashem your Elohim" (Devarim 4:4), and: "You are the children of Hashem your Elohim" (Devarim 14:1) – literally children, as it is written: "Yisrael is My son, My firstborn" (Shemot 4:22), and "Yisrael, in whom I will be glorified" (Yeshayah 49:3).

26. "You shall not take the Name"

26. "You shall not take the Name"

A Synopsis

Rabbi Shimon tells us that the supernal blessing requires something to bless, that it cannot dwell on an empty place. One cannot say a blessing over an empty table. The discussion turns to "A good name is better than precious ointment," which Rabbi Elazar says represents the supernal mountains of pure balsam. It is vital never to take the Name of the Holy One in vain, and that Name must be uttered only after a preceding word. Rabbi Yosi tells us that the blessing is the Holy Name itself, the source of blessing for the whole universe.

437. לֹא תִשָּׂא אֶת שֵׁם וְגוֹ'. ר' שִׁמְעוֹן פָּתַח, וַיֹּאמֶר אֵלֶיהָ אֱלִישָׁע מָה אֶעֱשֶׂה לָךְ הַגִּידִי לִי מַה יֶשׁ לָךְ בַּבָּיִת. אָמַר לָהּ אֱלִישָׁע, כְּלוּם אִית לָךְ עַל מַה דְּתִשְׁרֵי בִּרְכָתָא דְּקוּדְשָׁא בְּרִיךְ הוּא, דְּתָנֵינָן אָסוּר לֵיהּ לְבַר נָשׁ, לְבָרְכָא עַל פָּתוֹרָא רֵיקָנְיָא. מ"ט. מִשּׁוּם דְּבִרְכָתָא דִּלְעֵילָא, לָא שַׁרְיָא בַּאֲתָר רֵיקַנְיָא.

437. "You shall not take the Name..." (Shemot 20:7). Rabbi Shimon cited the verse: "And Elisha said to her, 'What shall I do for you? Tell me, what have you in the house?'" (II Melachim 4:2). He explained: What Elisha meant was: Have you aught upon which the blessing of the Holy One, blessed be He, could rest? For one should not say the blessing after the meal over an empty table. Why? Because the supernal blessing can not rest on an empty place.

438. וּבְגִינֵי כַּךְ, בָּעֵי בַּר נָשׁ לְסַדְּרָא עַל פָּתוֹרֵיהּ, חַד נַהֲמָא, אוֹ יַתִּיר, לְבָרְכָא עֲלוֹי. וְאִי לָא יָכִיל, בָּעֵי לְשַׁיְּירָא מֵהַהוּא מְזוֹנָא דְּאָכַל, עַל מַה דִּיבָרֵךְ. וְלָא יִשְׁתְּכַח דִּיבָרֵךְ בְּרֵיקַנְיָא.

438. Therefore, it is necessary to put a loaf or more on the table before one says his grace, and in case one has not MUCH TO PUT ON the table, he must put at least the remnants of his meal, IN ORDER THAT THERE WILL BE SOMETHING to bless, so that he will not say a blessing over an empty TABLE.

439. כֵּיוָן דְּאָמְרָה, אֵין לְשִׁפְחָתְךָ כֹל בַּבַּיִת כִּי אִם אָסוּךְ שָׁמֶן. אָמַר
וַדַּאי הָא בִּרְכָתָא שְׁלֵימָתָא בְּהַאי, דִּכְתִיב טוֹב שֵׁם מִשֶּׁמֶן טוֹב. דִּשְׁמָא
קַדִּישָׁא מִשֶּׁמֶן נָפְקָא, לְאִתְבָּרְכָא, לְאַדְלְקָא בּוֹצִינִין קַדִּישִׁין. מַאי שֶׁמֶן
דָא. ר' יִצְחָק אָמַר, כְּמָה דְּאַתְּ אָמַר, כַּשֶּׁמֶן הַטּוֹב עַל הָרֹאשׁ וְגוֹ'. ר'
אֶלְעָזָר אוֹמֵר, אָלֵין טוּרֵי דַּאֲפַרְסְמוֹנָא דַּכְיָא.

439. When she said: "Your handmaid has nothing in the house, except a pot of oil" (Ibid.), he said, "This is fit to receive a perfect blessing," as it is written: "A good name is better than (lit. 'from') precious ointment" (Kohelet 7:1), for the Holy Name comes forth from oil, to bless and to kindle the Holy Lights. HE ASKED: What is this oil? and Rabbi Yitzchak said: It represents the same oil as described in the scripture: "It is like the precious ointment upon the head" (Tehilim 133:2), MEANING THE SUPERNAL PLENTY. Rabbi Elazar said: It represents the supernal mountains of pure balsam, MEANING THE PLENTY OF THE SUPERNAL BINAH.

440. אָמַר ר' שִׁמְעוֹן, טוֹב שֵׁם, כַּמָּה טָבָא שְׁמָא עִלָּאָה, דְּבוֹצִינִין
עִלָּאִין קַדִּישִׁין, כַּד כֻּלְּהוּ נַהֲרִין מִשֶּׁמֶן טוֹב, כְּמָה דַּאֲמֵינָא. וְאָסִיר לֵיהּ
לְבַר נָשׁ, לְאַדְכְּרָא שְׁמֵיהּ דְּקוּדְשָׁא בְּרִיךְ הוּא בְּרֵיקַנְיָא. דְּכָל מַאן
דְּאַדְכַּר שְׁמָא דְּקב"ה בְּרֵיקַנְיָא, טָב לֵיהּ דְּלָא אִתְבְּרֵי.

440. Rabbi Shimon interpreted the verse: "A good name is better." How good is the Supernal Name of the Supernal Holy Lights, for they radiate כרמצ "precious ointment," and a man must not mention the Name of the Holy One, blessed be He, in vain, for he who does so would have been better not to have been born.

441. ר' אֶלְעָזָר אָמַר, לָא אִצְטְרִיךְ לְמִדְכַּר שְׁמָא קַדִּישָׁא אֶלָּא בָּתַר
מִלָּה. דְּהָא שְׁמָא קַדִּישָׁא, לָא אִדְכַּר בְּאוֹרַיְיתָא, אֶלָּא בָּתַר תְּרֵין מִלִּין,
דִּכְתִיב בְּרֵאשִׁית בָּרָא אֱלֹהִים.

441. Rabbi Elazar said: One should utter the Holy Name only after a preceding word, as in the Torah it is mentioned for the first time after two words: "In the beginning Elohim created (Heb. *Beresheet-bara-Elohim*)."

442. רַבִּי שִׁמְעוֹן אָמַר, לָא אִדְכַּר שְׁמָא קַדִּישָׁא, אֶלָּא עַל עוֹלָם שָׁלֵם. דִּכְתִּיב בְּיוֹם עֲשׂוֹת יְיָ' אֱלֹהִים אֶרֶץ וְשָׁמָיִם. מִכָּאן, דְּלָא לְאַדְכְּרָא שְׁמֵיה קַדִּישָׁא בְּרֵיקַנְיָא. וּכְתִיב לֹא תִשָּׂא אֶת שֵׁם יְיָ' אֱלֹהֶיךָ לַשָּׁוְא.

442. Rabbi Shimon said: The Holy Name is mentioned only in connection with a completed world, NAMELY, YUD HEI VAV HEI, as it is written: "In the day that Hashem Elohim made the earth and the heavens" (Beresheet 2:4). From this it follows that one should not mention the Holy Name in vain, as it is written: "You shall not take the Name of Hashem your Elohim in vain" (Shemot 20:7).

443. וְתָנֵינָן, אָמַר רַבִּי יוֹסִי, מַהוּ בְּרָכָה. שְׁמָא קַדִּישָׁא. בְּגִין דְּמִינֵיה מִשְׁתְּכַח בִּרְכָתָא, לְכָל עָלְמָא. וּבִרְכְתָא לָא אִשְׁתְּכַח עַל אֲתַר רֵיקַנְיָא, וְלָא שַׁרְיָיא עֲלוֹי, הֲדָא הוּא דִכְתִיב לֹא תִשָּׂא אֶת שֵׁם יְיָ' אֱלֹהֶיךָ לַשָּׁוְא.

443. Rabbi Yosi said: What is the blessing? It is the Holy Name, being the source of blessing for the whole universe. A blessing does not dwell in an empty place, nor rests upon it, and therefore it is written: "You shall not take the Name of Hashem your Elohim in vain."

27. "Remember the Shabbat day, to keep it holy"

A Synopsis

This very long section tells of the blessings and joy that accrue from observing the three Sabbath meals properly. He who blemishes one of these meals will be made to bear three burdens: judgment in Gehenom, Armageddon, and pre-Messianic tribulations. We are told that on festivals and holidays one must share with the poor. Because all the Faith is centered in the Sabbath, a man is given an additional soul on this day, and all judgments are withheld. Rabbi Yehudah tells us that the Sabbath is of equal importance to the Torah, and that one who keeps the Sabbath is considered as having fulfilled the Torah. Rabbi Shimon tells about the verse "For thus says Hashem to the eunuchs," explaining that those who study Torah are like eunuchs for six nights but on the Sabbath they have conjugal union, this being the right time to unite the Matron with the King; then they are blessed with good and holy children.

444. זָכוֹר אֶת יוֹם הַשַּׁבָּת לְקַדְּשׁוֹ. רַבִּי יִצְחָק אָמַר, כְּתִיב וַיְבָרֶךְ אֱלֹהִים אֶת יוֹם הַשְּׁבִיעִי, וּכְתִיב בַּמָּן שֵׁשֶׁת יָמִים תִּלְקְטֻהוּ וּבַיּוֹם הַשְּׁבִיעִי שַׁבָּת לֹא יִהְיֶה בּוֹ. כֵּיוָן דְּלָא מִשְׁתְּכַח בֵּיהּ מְזוֹנֵי, מַה בִּרְכָתָא אִשְׁתְּכַח בֵּיהּ.

444. "Remember the Shabbat day to keep it holy" (Shemot 20:8). Rabbi Yitzchak cited the verse: "And Elohim blessed the seventh day" (Beresheet 2:3). Of the manna, it is written: "Six days you shall gather it but on the seventh day, which is Shabbat, on it there shall be none" (Shemot 16:26). HE ASKS: If there was no food on that day, what blessing is attached to it?

445. אֶלָּא הָכִי תָּאנָא, כָּל בִּרְכָאן דִּלְעֵילָא וְתַתָּא, בְּיוֹמָא שְׁבִיעָאָה תַּלְיָין. וְתָאנָא, אֲמַאי לָא אִשְׁתְּכַח מָנָא בְּיוֹמָא שְׁבִיעָאָה, מִשּׁוּם דְּהַהוּא יוֹמָא, מִתְבָּרְכָאן מִינֵּיהּ כָּל שִׁיתָא יוֹמִין עִלָּאִין, וְכָל חַד וְחַד יָהִיב מְזוֹנֵיהּ לְתַתָּא, כָּל חַד בְּיוֹמוֹי, מֵהַהִיא בְּרָכָה דְּמִתְבָּרְכָאן בְּיוֹמָא שְׁבִיעָאָה.

445. We have learned that all blessing from above and from below depend

-211-

upon the seventh day, and we have also learned that there was no manna on the seventh day because all the six supernal days – WHICH ARE CHESED, GVURAH, TIFERET, NETZACH, HOD AND YESOD – derive their blessing from it, and each of them sends forth nourishment to the world below from the blessing it received from the seventh day.

446. וּבְגִינֵי כַּךְ, מַאן דְּאִיהוּ בְּדַרְגָּא דִּמְהֵימְנוּתָא, בָּעֵי לְסַדְּרָא פָּתוֹרָא, וּלְאַתְקְנָא סְעוּדָתָא בְּלֵילְיָא דְּשַׁבְּתָא, בְּגִין דְּיִתְבָּרֵךְ פָּתוֹרֵיהּ, כָּל אִינוּן שִׁיתָא יוֹמִין, דְּהָא בְּהַהוּא זִמְנָא, אִזְדַּמַּן בְּרָכָה, לְאִתְבָּרְכָא כָּל שִׁיתָא יוֹמִין דְּשַׁבְּתָא, וּבִרְכָתָא לָא אִשְׁתְּכַח בְּפָתוֹרָא רֵיקַנְיָא. וְעַל כַּךְ, בָּעֵי לְסַדְּרָא פָּתוֹרֵיהּ בְּלֵילְיָא דְּשַׁבְּתָא, בְּנַהֲמֵי וּבִמְזוֹנֵי.

446. Therefore, he who has attained the grade of Faith must prepare a table and a meal on Shabbat eve so that his table may be blessed all through the other six days. For at that time, blessing is prevalent for all the six week days, for no blessing is found at an empty table. Therefore, one should make ready the table on Shabbat eve with bread and other foods, IN ORDER TO DERIVE BLESSINGS FOR ALL THE SIX DAYS.

447. רַבִּי יִצְחָק אָמַר, אֲפִילוּ בְּיוֹמָא דְּשַׁבְּתָא נָמֵי. רַבִּי יְהוּדָה אָמַר, בָּעֵי לְאִתְעַנְּגָא בְּהַאי יוֹמָא, וּלְמֵיכַל תְּלַת סְעוּדָתֵי בְּשַׁבְּתָא, בְּגִין דְּיִשְׁתְּכַח שָׂבְעָא וְעֹנֶג בְּהַאי יוֹמָא בְּעָלְמָא.

447. Rabbi Yitzchak said: Also on Shabbat day ONE SHOULD PREPARE THE TABLE WITH MEALS AND DRAW BLESSING FOR THE OTHER SIX DAYS. Rabbi Yehuda added: One must enjoy himself on this day with three meals, in order that there will be satisfaction and pleasure in the world on that day.

448. רַבִּי אַבָּא אָמַר, לְאִזְדַּמְּנָא בִּרְכָתָא בְּאִינוּן יוֹמִין דִּלְעֵילָא, דְּמִתְבָּרְכָאן מֵהַאי יוֹמָא. וְהַאי יוֹמָא, מַלְיָא רֵישֵׁיהּ דִּזְעֵיר אַנְפִּין, מִטַּלָּא דְּנָחִית מֵעַתִּיקָא קַדִּישָׁא סְתִימָא דְּכֹלָּא, וְאָטִיל לְחַקְלָא דְּתַפּוּחִין קַדִּישִׁין, תְּלַת זִמְנֵי, מִכַּד עָיֵיל שַׁבְּתָא, דְּיִתְבָּרְכוּן כֻּלְּהוּ כַּחֲדָא.

448. Rabbi Aba explained that THE REASON FOR PREPARING THREE

MEALS FOR SHABBAT IS in order that blessings may spread to the supernal days – CHESED, GVURAH, TIFERET, NETZACH, HOD AND YESOD – which receive their blessing from that day, WHICH IS THE SHECHINAH, THE SEVENTH ATTRIBUTE. On this day the head of Zeir Anpin, MEANING THE THREE FIRST SFIROT, is filled with the dew, MEANING PLENTY, which descends from the most hidden Atika Kadisha (the Holy Ancient One). He causes it to descend into the field of holy apple trees, WHICH IS THE SHECHINAH, three times after the entrance of the Shabbat, in order that all may enjoy the blessing.

449. וְעַל דָּא בָּעֵי בַּר נָשׁ, לְאִתְעַנְּגָא תְּלַת זִמְנִין אִלֵּין, דְּהָא בְּהָא תַּלְיָא מְהֵימָנוּתָא דִּלְעֵילָא, בְּעַתִּיקָא קַדִּישָׁא, וּבִזְעֵיר אַפִּין, וּבְחַקְלָא דְּתַפּוּחִין. וּבָעֵי בַּר נָשׁ לְאִתְעַנְּגָא בְּהוּ, וּלְמֶחֱדֵי בְּהוּ. וּמַאן דְּגָרַע סְעוּדָתָא מִנַּיְיהוּ, אַחְזֵי פְּגִימוּתָא לְעֵילָא וְעוֹנְשֵׁיהּ דְּהַהוּא בַּר נָשׁ סַגִּי.

449. Therefore, a man should enjoy these three times, for therein depends the true Faith, in Atika Kadisha, in Zeir Anpin and the field of holy apple trees, MEANING THAT ZEIR ANPIN RECEIVES FROM ATIKA AND TRANSFERS IT TO MALCHUT, AS IS MENTIONED ABOVE. He who lessens the number of the meals exposes a blemish into the regions above, and his punishment will be great.

450. בְּגִינֵי כָּךְ, בָּעֵי לְסַדְּרָא פָּתוֹרֵיהּ, תְּלַת זִמְנֵי, מִכַּד עָיֵיל שַׁבְּתָא, וְלָא יִשְׁתְּכַח פָּתוֹרֵיהּ רֵיקַנְיָא, וְתִשְׁרֵי בִּרְכְתָא עָלֵיהּ, כָּל שְׁאָר יוֹמֵי דְּשַׁבְּתָא. וּבְהַאי מִלָּה, אַחְזֵי, וְתָלֵי מְהֵימָנוּתָא לְעֵילָא.

450. Therefore, it is necessary to prepare the table with three meals after the entrance of the Shabbat, and his table must not be empty. Thus, blessing will rest upon it during all the other week days, for therein depends the true Faith above.

451. רַבִּי שִׁמְעוֹן אָמַר, הַאי מַאן דְּאַשְׁלִים תְּלַת סְעוּדָתֵי בְּשַׁבְּתָא, קָלָא נָפִיק וּמַכְרְזָא עָלֵיהּ, אָז תִּתְעַנַּג עַל יְיָ', דָּא סְעוּדָתָא חֲדָא, לָקֳבֵל עַתִּיקָא קַדִּישָׁא דְּכָל קַדִּישִׁין. וְהִרְכַּבְתִּיךָ עַל בָּמֳתֵי אָרֶץ, דָּא סְעוּדָתָא

תְּנִיָּינָא, לָקֳבֵל חַקְלָא דְּתַפּוּחִין קַדִּישִׁין. וְהַאֲכַלְתִּיךָ נַחֲלַת יַעֲקֹב אָבִיךָ, דָּא הוּא שְׁלִימוּ דְּאִשְׁתְּלִים בִּזְעֵיר אַפִּין.

451. Rabbi Shimon said: When a man has completed the three meals on Shabbat, a voice comes forth and proclaims of him: "Then shall you delight yourself in Hashem" (Yeshayah 58:14). This is in reference to one meal, which corresponds to the most Holy Ancient One among the holy. "And I will cause you to ride upon the high places of the earth" (Ibid.), is the second meal, which corresponds to the field of holy apple trees, WHICH IS MALCHUT. "And feed you with the heritage of Jacob your father" (Ibid.), is the perfection it reaches in Zeir Anpin, IN THE THIRD MEAL.

452. וּלְקֳבְלַיְיהוּ בָּעֵי לְאַשְׁלְמָא סְעוּדָתֵיה, וּבָעֵי לְאִתְעַנְּגָא בְּכֻלְּהוּ סְעוּדָתֵי, וּלְמֶחֱדֵי בְּכָל חַד וְחַד מִנַּיְיהוּ, מִשּׁוּם דְּאִיהוּ מְהֵימָנוּתָא שְׁלֵימְתָא. וּבְגִין כָּךְ, שַׁבְּתָא אִתְיָקַר, מִכָּל שְׁאָר זִמְנִין וְחַגִּין, מִשּׁוּם דְּכֹלָּא בֵּיה אִשְׁתְּכַח, וְלָא אִשְׁתְּכַח הָכִי בְּכֻלְּהוּ זִמְנֵי וְחַגֵּי. אָמַר רַבִּי חִיָּיא, בְּג״כ, מִשּׁוּם דְּאִשְׁתְּכַח כֹּלָּא בֵּיה, אִידְכַר תְּלַת זִמְנִין. דִּכְתִיב, וַיְכַל אֱלֹהִים בַּיּוֹם הַשְּׁבִיעִי. וַיִּשְׁבּוֹת בַּיּוֹם הַשְּׁבִיעִי. וַיְבָרֶךְ אֱלֹהִים אֶת יוֹם הַשְּׁבִיעִי.

452. Corresponding to this, one should complete the meals and find joy in each and all of them because this is a manifestation of perfected Faith. Therefore, Shabbat is more precious than all other times and holidays because it contains all in itself, whereas no other times or holidays do so. Rabbi Chiya said: Because all things are in it, it is mentioned three times: "And by the seventh day Elohim ended His work which He had done... And He rested on the seventh day from all His work which He had done... And Elohim blessed the seventh day and sanctified it" (Beresheet 2:2-3).

453 רַבִּי אַבָּא, כַּד הֲוָה יָתִיב בִּסְעוּדָתָא דְּשַׁבְּתָא, הֲוֵי חַדֵּי, בְּכָל חַד וְחַד, וַהֲוָה אָמַר, דָּא הִיא סְעוּדָתָא קַדִּישָׁא, דְּעַתִּיקָא קַדִּישָׁא סְתִימָא דְּכֹלָּא. בִּסְעוּדָתָא אַחֲרָא הֲוָה אָמַר, דָּא הִיא סְעוּדָתָא דְּקוּדְשָׁא בְּרִיךְ הוּא. וְכֵן בְּכֻלְּהוּ סְעוּדָתֵי, וַהֲוָה חַדֵּי בְּכָל חַד וְחַד. כַּד הֲוָה אַשְׁלִים

סְעוּדָתַי, אָמַר אַשְׁלִימוּ סְעוּדָתֵי דִּמְהֵימָנוּתָא.

453. When Rabbi Aba sat at his Shabbat meals, he used to rejoice in each one of them and he would say: This is the holy meal of the Holy Ancient, hidden to all. Over another he would say: This is the meal of the Holy One, blessed be He, NAMELY, ZEIR ANPIN, and so in each and every meal. And when he came to the last one, he would say: The meals of the Faith are completed.

454. רַבִּי שִׁמְעוֹן, כַּד הֲוָה אָתֵי לִסְעוּדָתָא, הֲוָה אָמַר הָכִי, אַתְקִינוּ סְעוּדָתָא דִּמְהֵימְנוּתָא עִלָּאָה, אַתְקִינוּ סְעוּדָתָא דְּמַלְכָּא, וַהֲוָה יָתִיב וְחַדֵּי. כַּד אַשְׁלִים סְעוּדָתָא תְּלִיתָאָה, הֲוֵוֹ מַכְרְזֵי עָלֵיהּ, אָז תִּתְעַנַּג עַל יְיָ׳ וְהִרְכַּבְתִּיךָ עַל בָּמֳתֵי אָרֶץ וְהַאֲכַלְתִּיךָ נַחֲלַת יַעֲקֹב אָבִיךָ.

454. When Rabbi Shimon sat at his meals, he would say: Prepare the meal of the supernal Faith! Prepare the meal of the King! And then he would sit and rejoice. When the third meal was completed, it was proclaimed of him: "Then shall you delight yourself in Hashem and I will cause you to ride upon the high places of the earth and feed you with the heritage of Jacob your father."

455. אָמַר רַבִּי אֶלְעָזָר לְאֲבוּי, אִלֵּין סְעוּדָתֵי הֵיךְ מִתְתַּקְנָן. אָמַר לֵיהּ, לֵילְיָא דְּשַׁבַּתָּא, כְּתִיב, וְהִרְכַּבְתִּיךָ עַל בָּמֳתֵי אָרֶץ. בֵּיהּ בְּלֵילְיָא, מִתְבָּרְכָא מַטְרוֹנִיתָא, וְכֻלְּהוּ חֲקַל תַּפּוּחִין, וּמִתְבָּרְכָא פָּתוֹרֵיהּ דְּבַר נָשׁ, וְנִשְׁמְתָא אִתּוֹסְפַת, וְהַהוּא לֵילְיָא, חֶדְוָה דְּמַטְרוֹנִיתָא הֲוֵי. וּבְעֵי בַּר נָשׁ לְמֶחֱדֵי בְּחֶדְוָותָא, וּלְמֵיכַל סְעוּדָתָא דְּמַטְרוֹנִיתָא.

455. Rabbi Elazar said to his father: How are those three meals prepared? Rabbi Shimon replied: At Shabbat eve, as it is written: "And I will cause you to ride upon the high places of the earth." In this night the Matron is blessed and the whole field of apples, WHICH IS MALCHUT, is also blessed, and the man's table is blessed and a soul is added TO A MAN. This night signifies the rejoicing of the Matron, and therefore a man should rejoice and partake in the meal of the Matron, WHICH IS MALCHUT.

456. בְּיוֹמָא דְשַׁבַּתָּא, בִּסְעוּדָתָא תִּנְיָינָא, כְּתִיב אָז תִּתְעַנַּג עַל יְיָ׳. עַל
יְיָ׳ וַדַּאי. דְּהַהִיא שַׁעֲתָא אִתְגַּלְיָא עַתִּיקָא קַדִּישָׁא, וְכֻלְּהוּ עָלְמִין
בְּחֶדְוָותָא, וּשְׁלִימוּ וְחֶדְוָותָא דְּעַתִּיקָא עַבְדֵּינָן, וּסְעוּדָתָא דִּילֵיהּ הוּא
וַדַּאי.

456. Concerning the second meal of Shabbat day, it is written: "Then shall you delight yourself in (lit. 'above') Hashem." Most assuredly "above Hashem," WHICH MEANS ABOVE ZEIR ANPIN, for at that hour the Holy Ancient One reveals Himself and all the worlds are in joy. And we, in participating in this meal, contribute to that joy and completeness of Atika (the Ancient One) for, assuredly, this is His meal.

457. בִּסְעוּדָתָא תְּלִיתָאָה דְּשַׁבַּתָּא, כְּתִיב וְהַאֲכַלְתִּיךְ נַחֲלַת יַעֲקֹב
אָבִיךְ. דָּא הִיא סְעוּדָתָא דִּזְעֵיר אַפִּין, דְּהַוֵי בִּשְׁלֵימוּתָא. וְכֻלְּהוּ שִׁיתָא
יוֹמִין, מֵהַהוּא שְׁלִימוּ מִתְבָּרְכָן. וּבָעֵי בַּר נָשׁ לְמֶחֱדֵי בִּסְעוּדָתֵיהּ,
וּלְאַשְׁלְמָא אִלֵּין סְעוּדָתֵי, דְּאִינּוּן סְעוּדָתֵי מְהֵימְנוּתָא שְׁלֵימָתָא,
דְּזַרְעָא קַדִּישָׁא דְּיִשְׂרָאֵל, דִּי מְהֵימְנוּתָא עִלָּאָה, דְּהָא דִּילְהוֹן הִיא, וְלָא
דְּעַמִּין עעכו"ם. וּבְגִינֵי כַּךְ אָמַר, בֵּינִי וּבֵין בְּנֵי יִשְׂרָאֵל.

457. Concerning the third meal of Shabbat, it is written: "And feed you with the heritage of Jacob your father." This is the meal of Zeir Anpin, who is then in perfection, from which all the six days receive their blessing. Therefore, a man must rejoice in these meals and complete his meals, for they are meals of the perfect Faith of the holy seed of Yisrael, the supernal Faith, which is theirs and not that of the heathen nations. Hence, it is written: "It is a sign between Me and the children of Yisrael" (Shemot 31:17).

458. ת"ח, בִּסְעוּדָתֵי אִלֵּין, אִשְׁתְּמוֹדְעוּן יִשְׂרָאֵל, דְּאִינּוּן בְּנֵי מַלְכָּא.
דְּאִינּוּן מֵהֵיכְלָא דְּמַלְכָּא, דְּאִינּוּן בְּנֵי מְהֵימְנוּתָא, וּמַאן דְּפָגִים חַד
סְעוּדָתָא מִנַּיְיהוּ, אַחְזֵי פְּגִימוּתָא לְעֵילָא, וְאַחְזֵי גַּרְמֵיהּ דְּלָאו מִבְּנֵי
מַלְכָּא עִלָּאָה הוּא, דְּלָאו מִבְּנֵי הֵיכְלָא דְּמַלְכָּא הוּא דְּלָאו מִזַּרְעָא
קַדִּישָׁא דְּיִשְׂרָאֵל הוּא. וְיַהֲבִין עֲלֵיהּ חוּמְרָא דִּתְלַת מִלִּין, דִּינָא

-216-

דְּגֵיהִנָּם וגו'.

458. Come and behold: by these meals Yisrael are distinguished as the King's children, belonging to the palace of the King as people of Faith. And he who blemishes one of these meals shows an incompleteness above, and he testifies of himself that he is not one of the King's sons, not part of the palace of the King, and not of the holy seed of Yisrael. He will be made to bear the burden of three things: the punishment in Gehenom, THE WAR OF GOG AND MAGOG (ARMAGEDDON) AND PRE-MESSIANIC TRIBULATIONS.

459. וְתָא חֲזֵי, בְּכֻלְּהוּ שְׁאַר זִמְנִין וְחַגִּין, בָּעֵי בַּר נָשׁ לְחֶדֵי, וּלְמֶחֱדֵי לְמִסְכְּנֵי. וְאִי הוּא חַדֵי בִּלְחוֹדוֹי, וְלָא יָהִיב לְמִסְכְּנֵי, עוֹנָשֵׁיהּ סַגִּי, דְּהָא בִּלְחוֹדוֹי חַדֵי, וְלָא יָהִיב חֲדוּ לְאַחֲרָא. עֲלֵיהּ כְּתִיב, וְזֵרִיתִי פֶרֶשׁ עַל פְּנֵיכֶם פֶּרֶשׁ חַגֵּיכֶם. וְאִי אִיהוּ בְּשַׁבַּתָּא חַדֵי, אע"ג דְּלָא יָהִיב לְאַחֲרָא, לָא יַהֲבִין עֲלֵיהּ עוֹנָשָׁא, כִּשְׁאַר זִמְנִין וְחַגִּין, דִּכְתִיב פֶּרֶשׁ חַגֵּיכֶם. פֶּרֶשׁ חַגֵּיכֶם קָאָמַר, וְלָא פֶּרֶשׁ שַׁבַּתְּכֶם. וּכְתִיב חָדְשֵׁיכֶם וּמוֹעֲדֵיכֶם שָׂנְאָה נַפְשִׁי. וְאִלּוּ שַׁבָּת לָא קָאָמַר.

459. Come and behold: on all festivals and holidays a man must both rejoice himself and give joy to the poor. If he rejoices alone and does not share with the poor his punishment will be great, for he rejoices himself and does not make others happy. Of him it is written: "And spread dung upon your faces, even the dung of your feasts" (Malachi 2:3) but he is not punished if he rejoices on Shabbat and does not give a share to another. For it is written: "the dung of your feasts" and not 'the dung of your Shabbat,' and it is also written, "Your new moons and your appointed feasts My soul hates" (Yeshayah 1:14), but Shabbat is not mentioned.

460. וּבְגִינֵי כַּךְ כְּתִיב, בֵּינִי וּבֵין בְּנֵי יִשְׂרָאֵל. וּמִשּׁוּם דְּכָל מְהֵימָנוּתָא אִשְׁתְּכַח בְּשַׁבָּתָא, יַהֲבִין לֵיהּ לְבַר נָשׁ נִשְׁמָתָא אַחֲרָא, נִשְׁמָתָא עִלָּאָה, נִשְׁמָתָא דְּכָל שְׁלִימוּ בָּהּ, כְּדוּגְמָא דְּעָלְמָא דְּאָתֵי. וּבְגִינֵי כַּךְ אִקְרֵי שַׁבָּת. מַהוּ שַׁבָּת. שְׁמָא דְּקוּדְשָׁא בְּרִיךְ הוּא. שְׁמָא דְּאִיהוּ שְׁלִים מִכָּל סִטְרוֹי.

460. Therefore it is written: "Between Me and the children of Yisrael," and because all the Faith is centered in Shabbat, man is given an additional soul on this day, a supernal soul, a soul in which all perfection exists, resembling that of the World to Come. Therefore, this day is called Shabbat. What does the word Shabbat mean? This is the Name of the Holy One, blessed be He, WHICH IS MALCHUT, the Name which is perfect on all sides ON SHABBAT DAY.

461. אָמַר רַבִּי יוֹסִי, וַדַּאי כָּךְ הוּא. וַוי לֵיהּ לְבַר נָשׁ, דְּלָא אַשְׁלִים חֶדְוָותָא דְּמַלְכָּא קַדִּישָׁא. וּמַאן חֶדְוָותָא דִּילֵיהּ. אִלֵּין תְּלַת סְעוּדָתֵי מְהֵימָנוּתָא. סְעוּדָתֵי דְּאַבְרָהָם יִצְחָק וְיַעֲקֹב כְּלִילָן בְּהוּ. וְכֻלְּהוּ חֲדוּ עַל חַדוּ מְהֵימָנוּתָא שְׁלֵימוּתָא, מִכָּל סִטְרוֹי.

461. Rabbi Yosi said: It is indeed so. Woe to a man who does not complete the joy of the Holy King. And what is His joy? Those three meals of the Faith, the meals wherein Abraham, Isaac and Jacob participate and express joy upon joy, and the Faith, MALCHUT, is perfect on all sides.

462. תָּאנָא, בַּהֲדֵין יוֹמָא מִתְעַטְּרָן אֲבָהָן, וְכָל בְּנִין יַנְקִין, מַה דְּלָאו הָכִי בְּכָל שְׁאַר חַגִּין וּזְמַנִּין. בַּהֲדֵין יוֹמָא, חַיָּיבַיָּא דְּגֵיהִנָּם נַיְיחִין. בַּהֲדֵין יוֹמָא, כָּל דִּינִין אִתְכַּפְיָין, וְלָא מִתְעָרִין בְּעָלְמָא. בַּהֲדֵין יוֹמָא אוֹרַיְיתָא מִתְעַטְּרָא בְּעִטְרִין שְׁלֵימִין. בַּהֲדֵין יוֹמָא, חֶדְוָותָא וְתַפְנוּקָא אִשְׁתְּמַע, בְּמָאתָן וְחַמְשִׁין עָלְמִין.

462. We have learned that on this day the Fathers, WHO ARE CHESED, GVURAH AND TIFERET, are crowned, FOR THEY BECOME THE FIRST THREE SFIROT, and all the children, NETZACH, HOD AND YESOD, suckle from them differently than on other festive and holy days. On this day all Judgments are held back and are not aroused, BUT THEY BECOME THE FIRST THREE SFIROT. On this day, the sinners rest in Gehenom. On this day the Torah, WHICH IS ZEIR ANPIN, is crowned with perfect crowns, MEANING THE SUPERNAL ABA AND IMA. On this day joy and gladness resound throughout two hundred and fifty worlds.

463. תָּא חֲזֵי, בְּכָל שִׁיתָא יוֹמֵי דְּשַׁבַּתָּא, כַּד מָטָא שַׁעֲתָא דִּצְלוֹתָא

דְּמִנְחָה, דִּינָא תַּקִּיפָא שַׁלְטָא, וְכָל דִּינִין מִתְעָרִין. אֲבָל בְּיוֹמָא דְשַׁבַּתָּא, כַּד מָטָא עִדָּן דִּצְלוֹתָא דְמִנְחָה, רַעֲוָא דְרַעֲוִין אִשְׁתְּכַח, וְעַתִּיקָא קַדִּישָׁא גַּלְיָא רָצוֹן דִּילֵיהּ, וְכָל דִּינִין מִתְכַּפְיָין, וּמִשְׁתְּכַח רְעוּתָא וְחֶדוּ בְּכֹלָּא.

463. Come and behold: on all six days of the week, when the hour of Minchah (the Afternoon Prayer) arrives, Stern Judgment rules and all the chastisements are aroused. But on Shabbat, at the time of Minchah, the will of all wills is present, and Atika Kadisha (the Holy Ancient One) shows goodwill, and all the Judgments rest, and gladness and joy are everywhere.

464. וּבְהַאי רָצוֹן, אִסְתַּלָּק מֹשֶׁה, נְבִיאָה מְהֵימָנָא קַדִּישָׁא מֵעָלְמָא. בְּגִין לְמִנְדַּע, דְּלָא בְּדִינָא אִסְתַּלָּק, וְהַהִיא שַׁעֲתָא בִּרְצוֹן דְּעַתִּיקָא קַדִּישָׁא נָפַק נִשְׁמָתֵיהּ, וְאִתְטַמַּר בֵּיהּ. בְּגִין כָּךְ, וְלֹא יָדַע אִישׁ אֶת קְבֻרָתוֹ כְּתִיב. מַה עַתִּיקָא קַדִּישָׁא, טְמִירָא מִכָּל טְמִירִין, וְלָא יַדְעִין עִלָּאִין וְתַתָּאִין. אוֹף הָכָא, הַאי נִשְׁמָתָא דְּאִתְטַמַּר בְּהַאי רָצוֹן, דְּאִתְגַּלְיָא בְּשַׁעֲתָא דִּצְלוֹתָא דְמִנְחָה דְּשַׁבַּתָּא, כְּתִיב וְלֹא יָדַע אִישׁ אֶת קְבֻרָתוֹ וְהוּא טָמִיר מִכָּל טְמִירִין דְּעָלְמָא, וְדִינָא לָא שַׁלְטָא בֵּיהּ. זַכָּאָה חוּלָקֵיהּ דְּמֹשֶׁה.

464. In this time of goodwill, Moses, the holy faithful prophet, passed away from this world, in order that it should be known that he was not taken away in time of Judgment. At that hour his soul departed by the will of the Holy Ancient One, and was treasured in Him. Therefore, it is written: "No man knows his grave" (Devarim 34:6). As the Holy Ancient One is the most hidden of all, whom neither those above nor those below can comprehend, so this soul was hidden by the will OF THE HOLY ANCIENT ONE at the hour of Shabbat Afternoon Prayer. This soul of which it is written: "No man knows his grave," is the most hidden of all hidden things in the world, and Judgment does not rule over it. Happy is the portion of Moses.

465. תָּאנָא, בְּהַאי יוֹמָא, דְּאוֹרַיְיתָא מִתְעַטְּרָא בֵּיהּ, מִתְעַטְּרָא בְּכֹלָּא, בְּכָל אִינּוּן פִּקּוּדִין בְּכָל אִינּוּן גְּזֵרִין וְעוֹנָשִׁין, בְּשַׁבְעִין עֲנָפִין דִּנְהוֹרָא,

דְּזָהֲרִין מִכָּל סְטְרָא וְסִטְרָא. מַאן חָמֵי, עֲנָפִין דְּנָפְקִין מִכָּל עֲנָפָא
וְעֲנָפָא, חַמְשָׁא קַיְימִין בְּגוֹ אִילָנָא, כֻּלְּהוּ אַנְפִּין בְּהוּ אֲחִידָן. מַאן חָמֵי,
אִינוּן תַּרְעִין דְּמִתְפַּתְּחָן בְּכָל סְטָר וּסְטָר, כֻּלְּהוּ מִזְדַּהֲרִין וְנַהֲרִין,
בְּהַהוּא נְהוֹרָא דְּנָפִיק וְלָא פָּסַק.

465. We have learned that on this SHABBAT day with which the Torah crowned itself, it crowns itself with everything: with all those commandments, with all those decrees and punishments, and with seventy branches of light which illuminate all sides – FOR THE SEVEN SFIROT ARE CHESED, GVURAH, TIFERET, NETZACH, HOD, YESOD AND MALCHUT, AND EACH ONE OF THEM INCLUDES TEN SFIROT, AND ALL OF THEM TOGETHER ARE SEVENTY. Who saw the twigs which emanate from each branch OF THE SEVENTY BRANCHES, five of which are within the tree itself – MEANING THE FIVE SFIROT: CHESED, GVURAH, TIFERET, NETZACH AND HOD OF ZEIR ANPIN, CALLED A 'TREE', WHICH RECEIVES THEM FROM BINAH. All the aspects are attached to them. Who saw all those gates which open to each and every side OF THEM, AS EACH ONE INCLUDES TEN, SO THAT TOGETHER THEY ARE FIFTY GATES. They all shine and glow by that never-ending stream of light.

466. קָל כָּרוֹזָא נָפִיק, אִתְּעָרוּ קַדִּישֵׁי עֶלְיוֹנִין, אִתְּעָרוּ עַמָּא קַדִּישָׁא,
דְּאִתְבְּחַר לְעֵילָּא וְתַתָּא. אִתְּעָרוּ חֶדְוָותָא לְקָדָמוּת מָארֵיכוֹן. אִתְּעָרוּ
בְּחֶדְוָותָא שְׁלֵימָתָא. אִזְדְּמָנוּ בִּתְלַת חֶדְוָון, דִּתְלַת אֲבָהָן. אִזְדְּמָנוּ
לְקָדָמוּת מְהֵימְנוּתָא, דְּחֶדְוָוה דְּכָל חֶדְוָותָא. זַכָּאָה חוּלָקְכוֹן, יִשְׂרָאֵל
קַדִּישִׁין, בְּעָלְמָא דֵּין וּבְעָלְמָא דְּאָתֵי. דָּא הוּא יָרוּתָא לְכוֹן, מִכָּל עַמִּין
עעכו"ם. וְעַל דָּא כְּתִיב, בֵּינִי וּבֵין בְּנֵי יִשְׂרָאֵל.

466. A voice proclaims: Awake supernal saints! Awake holy people chosen from above and from below! Raise joy before your Master! Awake in perfect joy! Prepare yourselves in the threefold joy of the three Fathers, MEANING THE THREE MEALS OF SHABBAT! Prepare yourselves for the Faith, the joy of all joys. Happy is your portion, holy Yisrael, in this world and in the World to Come. This is your heritage OVER AND ABOVE that of all heathen nations. Hence, it is written: "between Me and the children of Yisrael."

467. אָמַר ר' יְהוּדָה, הָכִי הוּא וַדַּאי. וְעַ"ד כְּתִיב זָכוֹר אֶת יוֹם הַשַּׁבָּת
לְקַדְּשׁוֹ וּכְתִיב קְדוֹשִׁים תִּהְיוּ כִּי קָדוֹשׁ אֲנִי יְיָ'. וּכְתִיב, וְקָרָאתָ לַשַּׁבָּת
עֹנֶג לִקְדוֹשׁ יְיָ מְכוּבָּד.

467. Rabbi Yehuda said: It is indeed so, and therefore it is written, "Remember the Shabbat day to keep it holy" (Shemot 20:8), and: "You shall be holy, for I Hashem your Elohim am holy" (Vayikra 19:2), and, "And call the Shabbat a delight, the holy day of Hashem."

468. תָּאנָא, בְּהַאי יוֹמָא, כָּל נִשְׁמָתֵיהוֹן דְּצַדִּיקַיָּיא, מִתְעַדְּנִין בְּתַפְנוּקֵי
עַתִּיקָא קַדִּישָׁא, סְתִימָא דְּכָל סְתִימִין. וְרוּחָא חֲדָא מֵעֲנוּגָא דְּהַהוּא
עַתִּיקָא קַדִּישָׁא מִתְפַּשְּׁטָא בְּכֻלְּהוּ עָלְמִין, וְסַלְקָא וְנַחְתָּא, וּמִתְפַּשְּׁטָא
לְכֻלְּהוּ בְּנֵי קַדִּישִׁין, לְכֻלְּהוּ נָטוּרֵי אוֹרַיְיתָא, וְנַיְיחִין בְּנַיְיחָא שְׁלִים,
מִתְנְשֵׁי מִכֻּלְּהוּ, כָּל רוּגְזִין, כָּל דִּינִין, וְכָל פּוּלְחָנִין קָשִׁין. הה"ד בְּיוֹם
הָנִיחַ יְיָ' לָךְ מֵעָצְבְּךָ וּמֵרָגְזֶךָ וּמִן הָעֲבוֹדָה הַקָּשָׁה.

468. We have learned that on this SHABBAT day all the souls of the righteous feast on the delights of Atika Kadisha (the Holy Ancient One), the most hidden of all, KETER. One spirit of this delight of Atika Kadisha, is extended through all the worlds. It ascends and descends and spreads abroad to all the holy children, to all the guardians of the Torah, so that they enjoy perfect rest, forgetting all cares, all penalties and all hard work, as it is written: "And it shall come to pass on the day that Hashem shall give you rest from your sorrow and from your fear, and from the hard bondage in which you were made to serve" (Yeshayah 14:3).

469. בְּגִינֵי כַּךְ, שָׁקִיל שַׁבְּתָא לָקֳבֵל אוֹרַיְיתָא, וְכָל דְּנָטִיר שַׁבְּתָא,
כְּאִילוּ נָטִיר אוֹרַיְיתָא כֹּלָּא. וּכְתִיב אַשְׁרֵי אֱנוֹשׁ יַעֲשֶׂה זֹאת וּבֶן אָדָם
יַחֲזִיק בָּהּ שׁוֹמֵר שַׁבָּת מֵחַלְּלוֹ וְשׁוֹמֵר יָדוֹ מֵעֲשׂוֹת כָּל רָע. אִשְׁתְּמַע,
דְּמַאן דְּנָטִיר שַׁבָּת, כְּמַאן דְּנָטִיר אוֹרַיְיתָא כֹּלָּא.

469. Therefore the Shabbat is equal in importance to the Torah, and he who keeps the Shabbat is regarded as one who fulfills the whole Torah. It is

written: "Happy is the man that does this, and the son of man that lays hold on it, that keeps the Shabbat and does not profane it, and keeps his hand from doing any evil" (Yeshayah 56:2). From this we understand that he who keeps the Shabbat is as if he kept the whole Torah.

470. ר׳ יוּדָאי שָׁאִיל לֵיהּ לְרַ׳ שִׁמְעוֹן, יוֹמָא חַד דְּאַעְרַע עִמֵּיהּ בְּאָרְחָא, אָמַר לֵיהּ, ר׳, הָא כְּתִיב בְּפָרְשָׁתָא דָא שַׁבָּת, דְּאָמַר יְשַׁעְיָה, דִּכְתִיב כֹּה אָמַר יְיָ׳ לַסָּרִיסִים אֲשֶׁר יִשְׁמְרוּ אֶת שַׁבְּתוֹתַי וְגוֹ׳, וְנָתַתִּי לָהֶם בְּבֵיתִי וּבְחוֹמוֹתַי וְגוֹ׳. מַה קָא מַיְירֵי.

470. One day Rabbi Yudai met Rabbi Shimon on the road and asked him to explain a verse concerning the weekly portion, wherein Isaiah says: "For thus says Hashem: 'To the eunuchs that keep My Shabbatot and choose the things that please Me, and take hold of My Covenant. To them will I give, in My house and within My walls...'" (Ibid. 4-5). What does this mean?

471. א״ל, קַפּוֹטְקָאָה, חֲמָרָךְ קְטַרֵי בְּטִיפְסָא, וּנְחִית, דְּמִלָּה דְּאוֹרַיְיתָא בָּעֵי צָחוּתָא. אוֹ אַפְכֵי לַאֲחוֹרָךְ, וְזִיל אֲבַתְרָאי, וּתְכַוֵּון לִבָּךְ. א״ל, בְּגִינֵיהּ דְּמַר עֲבִידְנָא אָרְחָא, וּבַתְרֵיהּ דְּמַר אֶסְתַּכַּל בִּשְׁכִינְתָּא.

471. Rabbi Shimon said: Cappadocian! – NAMING HIM AFTER THE NAME OF THE CITY HE LIVED IN – Fasten your donkey to a fence and alight, for words of Torah require attentiveness. Turn around and follow me, and pay attention. He replied: It is for the master's sake that I have come all this long way, and in following him I shall behold the Shechinah.

472. א״ל, ת״ח, מִלָּה דָא הָא אוּקְמוּהָ חַבְרַיָּיא, וְלָא פְּרִישׁוּ מִלָּה. כֹּה אָמַר יְיָ׳ לַסָּרִיסִים. מַאן סָרִיסִים. אַלֵּין אִינּוּן חַבְרַיָּיא, דְּמִשְׁתַּדְּלֵי בְּאוֹרַיְיתָא, וּמְסָרְסֵי גַּרְמַיְיהוּ כָּל שִׁיתָא יוֹמִין דְּשַׁבַּתָּא, וְלָעָאן בְּאוֹרַיְיתָא, וּבְלֵילְיָא דְּשַׁבַּתָּא מִזְרְזֵי גַּרְמַיְיהוּ בְּזִוּוּגָא דִּלְהוֹן, מִשּׁוּם דְּיַדְעֵי רָזָא עִלָּאָה, בְּשַׁעְתָּא דְּמַטְרוֹנִיתָא אִזְדַּוְוגַת בְּמַלְכָּא.

472. He said to him: Come and behold. This verse has already been considered by the friends but they have not explained it sufficiently. "For

thus says Hashem: To the eunuchs." Who are these "eunuchs"? These are students of the Torah who study Torah and make themselves "eunuchs" during the six days of the week. And on Shabbat night they hasten to have their conjugal union, for they know the supernal secret of the right time when the Matron is united with the King.

473. וְאִינּוּן חַבְרַיָּיא דְּיַדְעִין רָזָא דָא, מְכַוְּונִין לִבַּיְיהוּ לִמְהֵימָנוּתָא דְּמָארֵיהוֹן וּמִתְבָּרְכָאן בְּאִיבָּא דִּמְעֵיהוֹן בְּהַהוּא לֵילְיָא. וְדָא הוּא דִּכְתִיב, אֲשֶׁר יִשְׁמְרוּ, כְּמָה דְּאַתְּ אָמַר, וְאָבִיו שָׁמַר אֶת הַדָּבָר.

473. Those students who know this secret concentrate their hearts on the Faith of their Master and are blessed with offspring on that night. Therefore, it is written: "That keep My Shabbatot," as it is said in the verse: "But his father kept the matter in mind" (Beresheet 37:11).

474. וְאִקְרוּן סָרִיסִים וַדַּאי, בְּגִין לְחַכָּאה לְשַׁבְּתָא לְאַשְׁכְּחָא רַעֲוָא דְּמָארֵיהוֹן, דִּכְתִיב וּבָחֲרוּ בַּאֲשֶׁר חָפָצְתִּי. מַאי בַּאֲשֶׁר חָפָצְתִּי. דָּא זִוּוּגָא דְּמַטְרוֹנִיתָא. וּמַחֲזִיקִים בִּבְרִיתִי, כֹּלָּא חַד, בִּבְרִיתִי סְתָם. זַכָּאה חוּלָקֵיהּ דְּמַאן דְּאִתְקַדָּשׁ בִּקְדוּשָׁה דָא, וְיָדַע רָזָא דָא.

474. They are called "eunuchs" because they wait for the Shabbat in order to please their Master, as it is written: "and choose the things that please Me," meaning His union with the Matron; "and take hold of My Covenant" amounts to the same, AS IT ALSO MEANS A UNION. "My Covenant" without attribute IS THE SUPERNAL YESOD WHO IS UNITED WITH THE MATRON. Happy is the man who is sanctified in this Holiness and knows this secret.

475. תָּא חֲזִי, כְּתִיב שֵׁשֶׁת יָמִים תַּעֲבֹד וְעָשִׂיתָ כָּל מְלַאכְתֶּךָ וְיוֹם הַשְּׁבִיעִי שַׁבָּת לַיְיָ' אֱלֹהֶיךָ וְגוֹ', כָּל מְלַאכְתֶּךָ, בְּאִינּוּן שִׁיתָא יוֹמֵי עֲבִידְתַּיְיהוּ דִּבְנֵי נָשָׁא וּבְגִין הַאי מִלָּה. לָא מִזְדַּוְוגֵי חַבְרַיָּיא, בַּר בְּזִמְנָא דְּלָא יִשְׁתְּכַח מֵעֲבִידְתַּיְיהוּ דִּבְנֵי נָשָׁא, אֶלָּא עֲבִידְתֵּיהּ דְּקוּדְשָׁא בְּרִיךְ הוּא. וּמַאי עֲבִידְתֵּיהּ. זִוּוּגָא דְּמַטְרוֹנִיתָא, לְאַפָּקָא נִשְׁמָתִין קַדִּישִׁין לְעָלְמָא.

475. Come and behold: in the verse, "Six days shall you labour, and do all your work, but the seventh day is a Shabbat to Hashem your Elohim" (Shemot 20:9), the words "all your work" indicate that in those six days man must work, and therefore those who study the Torah have their conjugal union only at a time when they do not work, but when the Holy One, blessed be He, works – MEANING, IN SHABBAT, WHEN MAN'S WORK IS FORBIDDEN. Then His work is the union with the Matron, MALCHUT, in order to bring forth holy souls into the world.

476. וּבְג"כ, בְּהַאי לֵילְיָא חַבְרַיָּיא מִתְקַדְּשֵׁי בִּקְדוּשָׁה דְּמָארֵיהוֹן, וּמְכַוְּונֵי לְבַיְיהוּ, וְנָפְקֵי בְּנֵי מַעֲלֵי, בְּנִין קַדִּישִׁין, דְּלָא סָטָאן לִימִינָא וְלִשְׂמָאלָא, בְּנִין דְּמַלְכָּא וּמַטְרוֹנִיתָא. וְעַל אִלֵּין כְּתִיב, בָּנִים אַתֶּם לַיְיָ' אֱלֹהֵיכֶם, לַיְיָ' אֱלֹהֵיכֶם וַדַּאי. בְּגִין דְּאִלֵּין אִקְרוּן בְּנִין דִּילֵיהּ, בְּנִין לְמַלְכָּא וּלְמַטְרוֹנִיתָא.

476. Therefore, the companions sanctify themselves on this night in the Holiness of their Master and concentrate their hearts, and begot good and holy children who turn neither to the right nor to the left, children of the King and the Matron. Of them it is written: "You are the children of Hashem your Elohim" (Devarim 14:1). Assuredly, of "Hashem your Elohim," for they are called "His children," the children of the King and the Matron.

477. וְהָא דַּעְתַּיְיהוּ דְּחַבְרַיָּיא דְּיַדְעִין רָזָא דָא, בְּדָא מִתְדַּבְּקָן. וּבְגִין כַּךְ אִקְרוּן בְּנִין לְקוּדְשָׁא בְּרִיךְ הוּא. וְהָנֵי אִינוּן דְּעָלְמָא מִתְקַיְּימָא בְּגִינַיְיהוּ. וְכַד סָלִיק עָלְמָא בְּדִינָא, אִסְתְּכַּל קוּדְשָׁא בְּרִיךְ הוּא בְּאִינוּן בְּנוֹי, וּמְרַחֵם עַל עָלְמָא. וְעַל דָּא כְּתִיב כֻּלֹּה זֶרַע אֱמֶת. זֶרַע אֱמֶת וַדַּאי. מַהוּ אֱמֶת. עִזְקָא קַדִּישָׁא שְׁלֵימָתָא. כד"א תִּתֵּן אֱמֶת לְיַעֲקֹב. וְכֹלָּא חַד. וּבְגִינֵי כַּךְ, זֶרַע אֱמֶת וַדַּאי.

477. Those who study the Torah know this secret and cling to it, therefore they are called 'the children of the Holy One, blessed be He', and the world is sustained by their merit. And when the world is placed on trial, the Holy One, blessed be He, looks on His children and has mercy on the world.

Therefore, it is written: "an entirely right seed" (Yirmeyah 2:21). It is a "right (lit. 'true') seed," indeed. And what does "true" mean? This is the perfect and holy circle. This is expressed in the verse: "You will show truth to Jacob" (Michah 7:20); JACOB IS THE SECRET OF THE CENTRAL COLUMN, and all these verses refer to the same thing. Hence, it is assuredly a true seed.

478. אָמַר לֵיה ר׳ יוּדָאי, בְּרִיךְ רַחֲמָנָא דְּשַׁדְּרַנִי הָכָא, בְּרִיךְ רַחֲמָנָא, דְּהָא מִלָּה דָּא שְׁמַעֲנָא מִפּוּמָךְ. בָּכָה רַבִּי יוּדָאי. אָמַר לֵיה ר׳ שִׁמְעוֹן, אֲמַאי קָא בָּכִית. אָמַר לֵיה, בָּכֵינָא, דַּאֲמֵינָא דְּוַוי לְאִינוּן בְּנֵי עָלְמָא, דְּאָרְחֵיהוֹן כִּבְעִירֵי, וְלָא יַדְעֵי וְלָא מִסְתַּכְּלֵי, דְּטַב לוֹן דְּלָא אִתְבְּרִיאוּ. וַוי לְעָלְמָא כַּד יִפּוּק מֹר מִנֵּיה, דְּמַאן יָכִיל לְגַלָּאָה רָזִין, וּמַאן יִנְדַע לוֹן, וּמַאן יִסְתָּכַּל בְּאָרְחֵי אוֹרַיְיתָא.

478. Rabbi Yudai said to him: Blessed be the Merciful One who sent me here! Blessed be the Merciful One for allowing me to come and hear your words! Rabbi Yudai wept. Rabbi Shimon asked: Why do you weep? He answered: I weep because of those people whose ways are the ways of beasts, without knowledge and observation. It would have been better for them not to have been created. Woe to the world when you, master, will depart from it, for who will then reveal the secrets and who will then comprehend the ways of the Torah?

479. אָמַר לֵיה, חַיֶּיךָ, לֵית עָלְמָא אֶלָּא לְאִינוּן חַבְרַיָּיא, דְּמִשְׁתַּדְּלֵי בְּאוֹרַיְיתָא וְיַדְעִין סְתִימֵי אוֹרַיְיתָא. וַדַּאי בִּקְשׁוֹט גָּזְרוּ חַבְרַיָּיא עַל עַמָּא דְּאַרְעָא, דִּמְחַבְּלִין אָרְחַיְיהוּ, וְלָא יַדְעִין בֵּין יְמִינָא לִשְׂמָאלָא, דְּהָא אִינוּן כִּבְעִירֵי, דְּיָאוֹת לְמֶעְבַּד בְּהוּ דִּינָא, אֲפִילּוּ בְּיוֹם הַכִּפּוּרִים. וְעַל בְּנַיְיהוּ כְּתִיב, כִּי בְנֵי זְנוּנִים הֵמָּה, בְּנֵי זְנוּנִים מַמָּשׁ.

479. He said to him: Upon your life, the world is created only for those who are occupied in Torah and know its secrets. Assuredly, the sages have decreed that the ignorant corrupt their ways, not knowing their right hand from their left, and are like cattle. And so it is fitting to punish them even on Yom Kippur (the Day of Atonement). Of their children, it is written: "For they are the children of harlotry" (Hoshea 2:6), actual children of harlotry.

480. אָמַר לֵיהּ, ר', הַאי קְרָא בָּעֵי לְאִתְיַישְׁבָא בְּאָרְחוֹי. כְּתִיב וְנָתַתִּי לָהֶם בְּבֵיתִי וּבְחוֹמוֹתַי יָד וָשֵׁם טוֹב מִבָּנִים וּמִבָּנוֹת שֵׁם עוֹלָם אֶתֵּן לוֹ. אֶתֵּן לָהֶם מִבָּעֵי לֵיהּ, מַהוּ אֶתֵּן לוֹ.

480. He said to him: Rabbi, this verse should have been explained further by more explanation, for it is written: "And to them will I give in My house and within My walls, a memorial better than sons and daughters. I will give him an everlasting name". HE ASKS: Why is it written, "I will give him an everlasting name" (Yeshayah 56:5)? It should have been written: 'I will give them', NAMELY, TO THE EUNUCHS.

481. אָמַר לֵיהּ, תָּא חֲזֵי, וְנָתַתִּי לָהֶם בְּבֵיתִי, מַהוּ בֵּיתִי. כְּמָה דְאַתְּ אָמַר בְּכָל בֵּיתִי נֶאֱמָן הוּא. וּבְחוֹמוֹתַי, כד"א עַל חוֹמוֹתַיִךְ יְרוּשָׁלַם הִפְקַדְתִּי שׁוֹמְרִים יָד וָשֵׁם, כְּלוֹמַר דְּיִשְׁלְפוּן נִשְׁמָתִין קַדִּישִׁין מִדּוּכְתָּא דָּא. וְהַהוּא יָד, חוּלַק בְּאַשְׁלָמוּתָא. טַב, מַלְיָא מִבָּנִין וּמִבְּנָתָן. שֵׁם עוֹלָם אֶתֵּן לוֹ, לְהַהוּא חוּלַק שָׁלִים. אֲשֶׁר לֹא יִכָּרֵת לְדָרֵי דָּרִין. דָּבָר אַחֵר אֶתֵּן לוֹ לְהַהוּא דְּיָדַע רָזָא דְּמִלָּה, וְיִתְכַּוָּון בְּמָה דְּבָעֵי לְכַוְּונָא.

481. He said to him: Come and behold. It is written: "And to them will I give in My house." What does "my house" signify? It signifies the same meaning as in the verse: "For he is trusted one in all My house" (Bemidbar 12:7), MEANING THE SHECHINAH, WHICH IS CALLED 'A HOUSE'. "…and within My walls…" is as it is written: "I have set watchmen upon your walls, O Jerusalem" (Yeshayah 62:6), MEANING THE EXTERNAL ASPECT OF THE SHECHINAH. "A memorial" (lit. 'a hand and a name') means that they would draw holy souls from this place, THE SHECHINAH, and that 'hand' MEANS a portion of perfection. The word "better" MEANS abundant with sons and daughters. "I will give him an everlasting name," meaning to this part of perfection WHICH IS CALLED 'A HAND'. "That shall not be cut off" (Ibid. 5) for all generations. Another explanation is that "I will give him," MEANS to him who knows this secret "OF THE EUNUCHS WHO KEEP MY SHABBATOT," with appropriate intention.

482. תּוּ אָמַר ר' שִׁמְעוֹן, כְּתִיב, לֹא תְבַעֲרוּ אֵשׁ בְּכָל מוֹשְׁבוֹתֵיכֶם בְּיוֹם הַשַּׁבָּת. מַאי טַעְמָא. בְּגִין דְּלָא אִתְחֲזֵי דִינָא בְּהַאי יוֹמָא. וְאִי תֵּימָא

הָא לַגְבוֹהַ סַלְקָא. בְּכָל מוֹשְׁבוֹתֵיכֶם קָאמַר, וְלָא לַגְבוֹהַ. וְהַהוּא
דְּסַלְקָא לַגְבוֹהַ, לְאַכְפְיָא לְדִינָא אַחֲרָא סַלְקָא. דִּתְנֵינָן, אִית אֶשָּׁא
אָכְלָא אֶשָּׁא. וְאֶשָּׁא דְּמַדְבְּחָא, אָכְלָא אֶשָּׁא אַחֲרָא.

482. Rabbi Shimon continued by citing the verse: "You shall kindle no fire
throughout your habitations on the Shabbat day" (Shemot 35:3), and he
explained that the reason for it is that there is no Judgment on that day, AND
HE WHO KINDLES A FIRE AROUSES JUDGMENT. You may protest that it
rises high, REFERRING TO THE FIRE ON THE ALTAR WHICH BURNS ON
SHABBAT AS WELL. HE ANSWERS: It is written "throughout your
habitations," and not, 'high above', for that FIRE which ascends high, rises
to subdue another Judgment. For as we have learned, there is a fire which
consumes a fire, and the fire of the altar consumes the other fire, NAMELY,
IT SUBDUES THE OTHER JUDGMENT SO IT WILL NOT RULE ON THE DAYS
OF THE WEEK.

483. וּבְגִינֵי כַּךְ, אִתְגַּלְיָא עַתִּיקָא קַדִּישָׁא בְּהַאי יוֹמָא, מִכָּל שְׁאַר
יוֹמִין. וּבְזִמְנָא דְּאִתְגַּלְיָא עַתִּיקָא, לָא אִתְחֲזֵי דִּינָא כְּלָל. וְכָל עִלָּאִין
וְתַתָּאִין מִשְׁתַּכְּחִין בְּחֶדְוָותָא שְׁלֵימָתָא, וְדִינָא לָא שַׁלְטָא.

483. Therefore, Atika Kadisha reveals Himself on that day MORE than on
any other day. And when He reveals Himself, Judgment is not in evidence at
all, and all the upper and lower beings are in perfect joy, and Judgment has
no dominion.

484. תָּאנָא, כְּתִיב כִּי שֵׁשֶׁת יָמִים עָשָׂה יְיָ' אֶת הַשָּׁמַיִם וְאֶת הָאָרֶץ.
שֵׁשֶׁת יָמִים וַדַּאי, וְלָא בְּשֵׁשֶׁת. וְהָנֵי יוֹמִין קַדִּישִׁין עִלָּאִין, אִקְרוּן יוֹמֵי
דִּשְׁמָא קַדִּישָׁא אִתְכְּלִיל בְּהוּ, וְאִינּוּן אִתְכְּלִילָן בֵּיהּ. זַכָּאָה חוּלְקֵהוֹן
דְּיִשְׂרָאֵל מִכָּל עַמִּין עעכו"ם, עָלַיְיהוּ כְּתִיב, וְאַתֶּם הַדְּבֵקִים בַּיְיָ'
אֱלֹהֵיכֶם חַיִּים כֻּלְּכֶם הַיּוֹם.

484. We have learned from the verse: "For (in) six days Hashem made
heavens and earth" (Shemot 31:17), that it was assuredly "six days," WHICH
ARE CHESED, GVURAH, TIFERET, NETZACH, HOD AND YESOD, FROM

WHICH THE HEAVENS AND EARTH, BEING MALE AND FEMALE, WERE CREATED. Therefore, it is not written, 'within six days'. Those supernal holy days are called days in which the Holy Name, MALCHUT, WHICH IS CALLED 'EARTH', is included. And they are contained in it. Happy is the portion of Yisrael above all the heathen nations; of them it is written: "But you that did cleave to Hashem your Elohim are alive every one of you this day" (Devarim 4:4).

28. "Honor your father and your mother"

A Synopsis

Rabbi Chiya and Rabbi Aba explain that "father" is the spring of the holy fountain which feeds the river from Eden, and that Eden itself is called "father." Rabbi Shimon adds that the words "Honor your father" refer to the Holy One, Zeir Anpin, and "your mother" refers to the Congregation of Yisrael, Malchut. From here the discussion turns to the first five of the Ten Commandments, showing us that they include the second five within them; then they are paired and analyzed at some length. Rabbi Elazar explains that all the laws of the Torah are engraved in the Ten Commandments, for the Torah is the Name of the Holy One, blessed be He.

485. כַּבֵּד אֶת אָבִיךְ וְאֶת אִמֶּךְ. רַבִּי חִיָּיא פָּתַח, וְנָהָר יוֹצֵא מֵעֵדֶן וְגוֹ'. וְנָהָר, דָּא נְבִיעוּ דְּמַבּוּעָא, דְּנָפִיק תָּדִיר וְלָא פָּסִק. וּמִנַּהֲרָא דְּמַבּוּעָא דָּא, אִתְשַׁקְיָא כָּל גִּנְתָּא דְּעֵדֶן. וְהַהוּא נַהֲרָא דְּמַבּוּעָא קַדִּישָׁא, אִקְרֵי אָ"ב. מַאי טַעֲמָא. מִשּׁוּם דְּאִיהוּ נְבִיעָא לְאִתְזְנָא לְגִנְתָּא.

485. "Honor your father and your mother" (Shemot 20:12). Rabbi Chiya opened the discussion with the verse: "And a river went out of Eden..." (Beresheet 2:10). "And a river," is the spring of the fountain which flows constantly and never stops, and whence the whole Garden of Eden is watered. And this spring of the holy fountain is called 'father' because it maintains the Garden.

486. רַבִּי אַבָּא אָמַר, עֵדֶן מַמָּשׁ אִקְרֵי אָב. מִשּׁוּם דְּהַאי עֵדֶן, מִשְׁתְּכַח מֵהַהוּא אֲתָר, דְּאִקְרֵי אַיִן. וּבְגִינֵי כַּךְ, אִקְרֵי אָב. וְהָא אוּקִימְנָא, מֵאֲתָר דְּשָׁארֵי לְאִתְמַשְּׁכָא כֹּלָּא, אִקְרֵי אַתָּה, וְאִקְרֵי אָב. כְּמָה דְּאַתְּ אָמַר, כִּי אַתָּה אָבִינוּ.

486. Rabbi Aba said that Eden itself is called 'father', because it issues from a place called "Ayin" (lit. 'naught'), THE KETER OF ARICH ANPIN, OF WHICH NO ONE CAN CONCEIVE. It is therefore called 'father'. We have already explained that the place whence everything issues is called '*Atah*' (lit. 'you'), and is called '*Av*' (lit. 'Father'), as it is written: "You are our father" (Yeshayah 63:16).

487. ר' אֶלְעָזָר אָמַר, כַּבֵּד אֶת אָבִיךָ, דָּא קוּדְשָׁא בְּרִיךְ הוּא. וְאֶת
אִמֶּךָ, דָּא כְּנֶסֶת יִשְׂרָאֵל. אֶת אָבִיךָ, אֶת דַּיְּיקָא, לְאַכְלְלָא שְׁכִינְתָּא
עִלָּאָה. רַבִּי יְהוּדָה אָמַר, כַּבֵּד אֶת אָבִיךָ, סְתָם. וְאֶת אִמֶּךָ, סְתָם. דְּהָא
כֹּלָּא הֲוָה בְּמִנְיָינָא. אֶת, לְרַבּוֹת כָּל מַה דִּלְעֵילָּא וְתַתָּא.

487. Rabbi Shimon said: The words "Honor your father" allude to the Holy
One, blessed be He, NAMELY ZEIR ANPIN; "your mother" alludes to the
Congregation of Yisrael, NAMELY, MALCHUT; the particle "*Et*" before
"your" alludes to the Supernal Shechinah, WHICH IS THE NUKVA, IS FROM
THE CHEST ABOVE OF ZEIR ANPIN. Rabbi Yehuda said that "Honor your
Father" is unspecified, and "your mother" is unspecified, because they
account for everything, THEY SIGNIFY CHOCHMAH AND BINAH, AND ALSO
ZEIR ANPIN AND THE NUKVA, SINCE THE WORDS ARE NOT SPECIFIC, and
the article "*Et*" adds all that is above and all that is below, BOTH ABA AND
IMA, AND MALE AND FEMALE.

488. רַבִּי יוֹסֵי אָמַר, הַאי דְּאָמַר רַבִּי אַבָּא, מֵאֲתָר דְּשָׁאֲרֵי לְאִתְמַשְּׁכָא
כֹּלָּא, אִקְרֵי אַתָּה, שַׁפִּיר. דְּהָא אוֹלִיפְנָא, הַהוּא דְּטָמִיר וְלָא אִית בֵּיה
שֵׁירוּתָא, קָרֵינָן הוּא. מֵאֲתָר דְּשֵׁירוּתָא אִשְׁתְּכַח, קָרֵינָן אַתָּה. וְאִקְרֵי
אָב. וְכֹלָּא חַד. בְּרִיךְ שְׁמֵיה לְעָלַם וּלְעָלְמֵי עָלְמַיָּא אָמֵן.

488. Rabbi Yosi referred to Rabbi Aba's remark that the place whence
everything begins is called 'you', for we have learned that what is hidden
and has no beginning, OF BESTOWING MOCHIN, is called 'he', NAMELY,
THE THIRD PERSON. The place whence there is a beginning, OF
BESTOWING MOCHIN, is called 'you', and is also called 'father', and it is
all one. Blessed Be His Name for ever and ever. Amen.

489. רַבִּי חִזְקִיָּה אָמַר, וַדַּאי כֹּלָּא חַד. כַּבֵּד אֶת אָבִיךָ, דָּא קוּדְשָׁא
בְּרִיךְ הוּא. וְאֶת אִמֶּךָ, דָּא כְּנֶסֶת יִשְׂרָאֵל. דְּהָא תְּנָן, אר"ש, כְּתִיב בָּנִים
אַתֶּם לַיְיָ' אֱלֹהֵיכֶם, הַהוּא אֲתָר דְּאִקְרֵי בָּנִים. וּבְגִינֵי כַּךְ סְתִימָא
דְּמִלָּה, כַּבֵּד אֶת אָבִיךָ וְאֶת אִמֶּךָ, לְאַכְלְלָא כֹּלָּא, דִּלְעֵילָּא וְתַתָּא. ר'
יִצְחָק אָמַר, לְאַכְלְלָא בֵּיה רַבְיָה, דְּהוּא אָעִיל לֵיה לְעָלְמָא דְּאָתֵי. אָמַר
רַבִּי יְהוּדָה, בִּכְלָלָא דְּקוּדְשָׁא בְּרִיךְ הוּא הֲוֵי.

489. Rabbi Chizkiyah said: Assuredly, they are all one. "Honor your father," indicates the Holy One, blessed be He, NAMELY, ZEIR ANPIN; "your mother," indicates the Congregation of Yisrael, NAMELY, MALCHUT, for we have learned from Rabbi Shimon that the verse "You are the children of Hashem your Elohim" (Devarim 14:1) alludes to the place called 'children', WHICH ARE MALE AND FEMALE. Therefore, the verse: "Honor your father and your mother," includes all, MEANING ABA AND IMA, above and below. Rabbi Yitzchak said that it includes one's teacher of the Torah, who ushers one to the World to Come. Rabbi Yehuda said that THE TEACHER is included in the Holy One, blessed be He.

490. תָּאנָא, בְּהָנֵי חָמֵשׁ אֲמִירָן, כָּלִיל כֹּלָּא. בְּהָנֵי חָמֵשׁ אֲמִירָן, אִתְגְּלִיפוּ חָמֵשׁ אַחֲרָנִין, וַדַּאי חָמֵשׁ גּוֹ חָמֵשׁ. הָא כֵּיצַד. אָנֹכִי יְיָ' אֱלֹהֶיךָ, לָקֳבֵל לֹא תִּרְצַח. דְּתָנֵינָן, תְּרֵין אִלֵּין, בִּכְלָלָא חֲדָא אִתְכְּלִילָן, דְּמַאן דְּקָטִיל, אַזְעִיר דְּמוּתָא וְצַלְמָא דְּמָארֵיהּ. דִּכְתִּיב, כִּי בְּצֶלֶם אֱלֹהִים עָשָׂה אֶת הָאָדָם. וּכְתִיב וְעַל דְּמוּת הַכִּסֵּא דְּמוּת כְּמַרְאֵה אָדָם.

490. We have learned that the first five commandments IN THE RIGHT SIDE are all inclusive. In these five commandments the second five OF THE LEFT are engraved, five within five. How? The first commandment, "I am Hashem your Elohim" (Shemot 20:2) corresponds to, "You shall not murder," for as we learned, these two are under one principle. For one who murders diminishes the image and likeness of his Master, because according to the scripture, "in the image of Elohim made He man" (Beresheet 9:6), and: "And upon the likeness of the throne was the likeness as the appearance of a man" (Yechezkel 1:26).

491. אָמַר ר' חִיָּיא, כְּתִיב שָׁפֵךְ דַּם הָאָדָם בָּאָדָם דָּמוֹ יִשָּׁפֵךְ וְגוֹ', מַאן דְּשָׁפִיךְ דָּמָא, כְּאִלּוּ אַזְעִיר דְּמוּתָא וְצַלְמָא דִּלְעֵילָּא, כְּלוֹמַר, לָא אַזְעַר דְּמוּתָא דָּא, אֶלָּא דְּמוּתָא אַחֲרָא, מַשְׁמַע דִּכְתִּיב שָׁפֵךְ דַּם הָאָדָם בָּאָדָם דָּמוֹ יִשָּׁפֵךְ. בְּאָדָם עִלָּאָה, מָטֵי הַאי פְּגִימוּתָא, מֵהַהוּא דָּמָא דְּאוֹשִׁיד. מַאי טַעְמָא. מִשּׁוּם כִּי בְּצֶלֶם אֱלֹהִים עָשָׂה אֶת הָאָדָם. וּבְגִין כָּךְ, הָא בְּהָא תַּלְיָא.

491. Rabbi Chiya said: It is written, "Whoever sheds man's blood by man, his blood shall be shed" (Beresheet 9:6). He who sheds blood is considered as if he diminishes the supernal image and likeness above, meaning that he does not diminish the image of the man BELOW, but another image, and this is the interpretation of the verse: "Whoever sheds man's blood by man, his blood shall be shed". The damage he does by shedding blood reaches the supernal man. Why? "...for in the image of Elohim made He man." Therefore, they are interdependent, THE FIRST COMMANDMENT DEPENDS ON "YOU SHALL NOT MURDER."

492. לֹא יִהְיֶה לְךָ, לָקֳבֵל לֹא תִּנְאָף דָּא מְשַׁקֵּר בִּשְׁמָא דְקוּדְשָׁא בְּרִיךְ הוּא, דְּאִתְרְשִׁים בֵּיהּ בְּבַר נָשׁ. וּבְדָא, כַּמָּה וְכַמָּה חוֹבִין וְגִזְרִין וְעוֹנָשִׁין, תַּלְיָין. וּמַאן דִּמְשַׁקֵּר בְּהַאי, מְשַׁקֵּר בֵּיהּ בְּמַלְכָּא, דִּכְתִיב בַּיְיָ' בָּגְדוּ כִּי בָנִים זָרִים יָלָדוּ. וּכְתִיב לֹא תִשְׁתַּחֲוֶה לָהֶם וְלֹא תָעָבְדֵם, וְהָא בְּהָא תַּלְיָא.

492. "You shall have no other Elohim beside Me," corresponds to, "You shall not commit adultery." THE ADULTERER is false to the Name of the Holy One, blessed be He, which is impressed upon man, a sin including many other sins and entailing corresponding punishments. He who is unfaithful in this, is unfaithful towards the King, as it is written: "They have dealt treacherously against Hashem, for they have begotten strange children" (Hoshea 5:7), and, "You shall not bow down to them, nor serve them." One is the result of the other. THUS, "YOU SHALL HAVE NO OTHER ELOHIM" IS CONNECTED WITH, "YOU SHALL NOT COMMIT ADULTERY."

493. לֹא תִשָּׂא לָקֳבֵל לֹא תִגְנוֹב. וּכְתִיב חוֹלֵק עִם גַּנָּב שׂוֹנֵא נַפְשׁוֹ אָלֶה יִשְׁמַע וְלֹא יַגִּיד. וַדַּאי הָא בְּהָא תַּלְיָא, דְּהָא גַּנָּבָא לְדָא אִזְדְּמַן, לְאוֹמָאָה בְּשִׁקְרָא. מַאן דְּעָבֵיד דָּא, עָבֵיד דָּא.

493. "You shall not take the name of Hashem your Elohim in vain," corresponds to "You shall not steal." For a thief is inclined to swear falsely because he who steals also lies, as it is written: "Whoever is partner with a thief is his own enemy, he hears the adjuration of witnesses, but discloses nothing" (Mishlei 29:24).

494. זָכוֹר אֶת יוֹם הַשַּׁבָּת, לָקֳבֵל לֹא תַעֲנֶה בְרֵעֲךָ עֵד שָׁקֶר. דְּאָמַר ר׳
יוֹסִי, שַׁבָּת סַהֲדוּתָא אִקְרֵי. וּבָעֵי בַּר נָשׁ לְסַהֲדָא, עַל הָא דִכְתִיב כִּי
שֵׁשֶׁת יָמִים עָשָׂה יְיָ׳ וְגו׳. וְשַׁבָּת כְּלָלָא דְכֹלָּא. וְאָמַר ר׳ יוֹסִי, מַאי
דִכְתִיב תִּתֵּן אֱמֶת לְיַעֲקֹב, כְּמָה דְאַתְּ אָמַר וְשָׁמְרוּ בְנֵי יִשְׂרָאֵל אֶת
הַשַּׁבָּת, וּמַאן דְּאַסְהִיד שִׁקְרָא, מְשַׁקֵּר בְּשַׁבָּת, דְּהִיא סַהֲדוּתָא דִּקְשׁוֹט,
וּמַאן דִּמְשַׁקֵּר בְּשַׁבָּת, מְשַׁקֵּר בְּאוֹרַיְיתָא כֹּלָּא. וּבְג״כ, הָא בְּהָא תַּלְיָא.

494. "Remember the Shabbat day to keep it holy," corresponds to, "You shall not bear false witness against your neighbor," for as Rabbi Yosi said, the Shabbat day is called 'a witness', and man should bear testimony to the verse: "in six days Hashem made heaven and earth." And Shabbat comprises everything. Rabbi Yosi said that he who bears false witness against his neighbor lies against the Shabbat, which is the true witness, and the verse, "You will show truth to Jacob" (Michah 7:20), refers to the same motive which is expressed in the verse: "Wherefore the children of Yisrael shall keep the Shabbat" (Shemot 31:16). Therefore, he who lies against the Shabbat lies against the whole Torah. Hence, they are interdependent. THUS, "REMEMBER" IS CONNECTED TO "YOU SHALL NOT BEAR FALSE..."

495. כַּבֵּד אֶת אָבִיךָ, לָקֳבֵל לֹא תַחְמֹד אֵשֶׁת רֵעֶךָ. וְאָמַר ר׳ יִצְחָק, כַּבֵּד
אֶת אָבִיךָ, אָבִיךָ מַמָּשׁ. דְּהָא מַאן דְּחָמִיד אִתְּתָא, וְאוֹלִיד בַּר, הַהוּא
אוֹקִיר לְאַחֲרָא, דְּלָא אֲבוּי. וּכְתִיב כַּבֵּד אֶת אָבִיךָ וְגו׳, לֹא תַחְמֹד בֵּית
רֵעֶךָ שָׂדֵהוּ. וּכְתִיב הָכָא, עַל הָאֲדָמָה אֲשֶׁר יְיָ׳ אֱלֹהֶיךָ נוֹתֵן לָךְ. הַהוּא
דִּיָהַב לָךְ, יְהֵא דִילָךְ, וְלֹא תַחְמֹד אַחֲרָא. וַדַּאי הָא בְּהָא תַּלְיָא.

495. "Honor your father and your mother," corresponds to, "You shall not covet your neighbor's wife." According to the explanation of Rabbi Yitzchak, "Honor your father," refers to one's own father; for when he who covets a woman begets a child, the child will honor another who is not his own father. It is written: "Honor your father and your mother," and, "neither shall you desire your neighbor's house, his field" (Devarim 5:18). The second part OF THE FORMER is, "that your days may be long in the land which Hashem your Elohim gives you," MEANING that whatever is given to you shall

be yours, and you shall not covet another. Assuredly, they are interdependent. THUS, "HONOR..." IS CONNECTED WITH "YOU SHALL NOT COVET."

496. וְאִלֵּין חָמֵשׁ קַדְמָאֵי, כְּלִילָן חָמֵשׁ אַחֲרָנִין. וּבְגִינֵי כַּךְ, מִימִינוֹ אֵשׁ דָּת לָמוֹ. דְּכֹלָּא אִתְעֲבֵיד יְמִינָא. וְעַל הָא, בַּחֲמִשָּׁה קָלִין אוֹרַיְיתָא אִתְיְיהִיבַת. אָמַר ר' יְהוּדָה, כֻּלְּהוּ הֲווֹ חָמֵשׁ גּוֹ חָמֵשׁ. לָקֳבְלֵיהוֹן חֲמִשָּׁה חוּמְשֵׁי תּוֹרָה.

496. These first five COMMANDMENTS ON THE RIGHT SIDE include the second five. Therefore: "From His right hand went a fiery law for them," (Devarim 33:2) for all was included in the right, and the Torah was proclaimed in five voices. Rabbi Yehuda said that the whole TEN COMMANDMENTS were folded in such a way that five were within five, corresponding to the five Books of the Torah.

497 תָּאנֵי ר' אֶלְעָזָר, בְּאִלֵּין עֶשֶׂר אֲמִירָן, אִתְגְּלִיפוּ כָּל פִּקּוּדֵי אוֹרַיְיתָא, גְּזִירִין וְעוֹנָשִׁין. דַּכְיָא וּמְסָאֲבָא. עַנְפִין וְשָׁרָשִׁין. אִילָנִין וּנְטִיעִין. שְׁמַיָּא וְאַרְעָא. יַמָּא וּתְהוֹמֵי. דְּהָא אוֹרַיְיתָא שְׁמָא דְּקוּדְשָׁא בְּרִיךְ הוּא הֲוֵי, מַה שְׁמָא דְּקוּדְשָׁא בְּרִיךְ הוּא אִתְגְּלִיף בְּעֶשֶׂר אֲמִירָן, אוּף אוֹרַיְיתָא אִתְגְּלִיפָא בְּעֶשֶׂר אֲמִירָן. אִלֵּין עֶשֶׂר אֲמִירָן אִינּוּן שְׁמָא דְּקוּבָּ"ה. וְאוֹרַיְיתָא כֹּלָּא שְׁמָא חַד הֲוֵי, שְׁמָא קַדִּישָׁא דְּקוּדְשָׁא בְּרִיךְ הוּא מַמָּשׁ.

497. Rabbi Elazar explained that in the ten commandments were engraved all the laws of the Torah, all the decrees and punishments, all the laws concerning purity and impurity, all the branches and the roots, trees and plants, heavens and earth, seas and depths, for the Torah is the Name of the Holy One, blessed be He. As the Name of the Holy One, blessed be He, is engraved in the ten commandments, the ten commandments are the Name of the Holy One, blessed be He. So is the whole Torah engraved in them, and the whole Torah is thus one Name, the Holy Name of the Holy One, blessed be He, indeed.

498. זַכָּאָה חוּלָקֵיה, דְּמַאן דְּזָכֵי בָּה. מַאן דְּזָכֵי בְּאוֹרַיְיתָא, זָכֵי בִּשְׁמָא

קַדִּישָׁא. ר׳ יוֹסִי אָמַר, בְּקוּדְשָׁא בְּרִיךְ הוּא מַמָּשׁ זָכֵי, דְּהָא הוּא וּשְׁמֵיהּ חַד הוּא, בְּרִיךְ שְׁמֵיהּ לְעָלַם וּלְעָלְמֵי עָלְמִין אָמֵן.

498. Blessed is the one who is worthy of the Torah, for he will be worthy of the Holy Name. Rabbi Yosi said that he will be worthy of the Holy One, blessed be He, Himself, as He and His Name are one. Blessed be His Name, for ever and ever. Amen.

29. "You shall not make with Me"

A Synopsis

Rabbi Yitzchak says that the two colors gold and silver are engraved in Yisrael, which is the central column that includes and balances them. Mercy and judgment are imprinted upon God, whose garments are the colors of Chesed and Gvurah. Righteousness, Malchut, has those two colors engraved in her as well. Rabbi Yosi closes by telling of the four kinds of joy that correspond to the four exiles of the children of Yisrael.

499. לֹא תַעֲשׂוּן אִתִּי אֱלֹהֵי כֶסֶף וֵאלֹהֵי זָהָב. אָמַר ר' יוֹסִי, מ"ט. מִשּׁוּם דִּכְתִיב, לִי הַכֶּסֶף וְלִי הַזָּהָב, אע"ג דְּלִי הַכֶּסֶף וְלִי הַזָּהָב, לֹא תַעֲשׂוּן אִתִּי, אִתִּי: כְּלוֹמַר אוֹתִי.

499. "You shall not make with Me Elohim of silver, neither shall you make for yourselves Elohim of gold" (Shemot 20:20). Rabbi Yosi gave his interpretation of this verse by saying that although, "The silver is Mine and the gold is Mine" (Chagai 2:8), "you shall not make with Me," that is, 'make Me.'

500. אָמַר ר' יִצְחָק, כְּתִיב מֵאֵין כָּמוֹךָ יְיָ' גָּדוֹל אַתָּה וְגָדוֹל שִׁמְךָ בִּגְבוּרָה וְגוֹ', גָּדוֹל אַתָּה, הַיְינוּ לִי הַכֶּסֶף. וְגָדוֹל שִׁמְךָ בִּגְבוּרָה, הַיְינוּ וְלִי הַזָּהָב. אִלֵּין תְּרֵין גְּווֹנִין לָא מִתְחַזְיָין, וְלָא מִתְפָּאֲרָן, בַּר כַּד אִינּוּן גְּלִיפִין בַּאֲתָר חַד, בְּאָן אֲתָר אִתְגְּלִיפוּ. בְּיִשְׂרָאֵל. כָּאן אִתְחֲזוּן גְּווֹנִין לְאִתְפָּאֲרָא, כד"א יִשְׂרָאֵל אֲשֶׁר בְּךָ אֶתְפָּאָר.

500. Rabbi Yitzchak cited the verse: "For as much as there is none like You, Hashem, You are great, and Your Name is great in might" (Yirmeyah 10:6). The verse, "You are great," corresponds to, "The silver is Mine," BEING CHESED, THE RIGHT COLUMN, while, "Your name is great in might," corresponds to "The gold is Mine," WHICH IS GVURAH, THE LEFT COLUMN. These two colors are only visible in their full beauty when they are engraved in one place, namely Yisrael, BEING THE CENTRAL COLUMN, TIFERET, WHICH INCLUDES AND BALANCES BOTH OF THEM. Here the colors are seen in their beauty, as it is written: "You are My servant, Yisrael, in whom I will be glorified" (Yeshayah 49:3).

501. ר' יְהוּדָה פָּתַח, שׂוֹשׂ אָשִׂישׂ בה' תָּגֵל נַפְשִׁי בֵאלֹהַי וְגוֹ', זַכָּאָה
חוּלָקֵהוֹן דְּיִשְׂרָאֵל, מֵעַמִּין עעכו"ם, דְּחֶדְוָותָא וְתַפְנוּקָא דִּלְהוֹן
בְּקוּדְשָׁא בְּרִיךְ הוּא, דִּכְתִיב שׂוֹשׂ אָשִׂישׂ בַּיְיָ'. כֵּיוָן דְּאָמַר בַּיְיָ', אֲמַאי
כְּתִיב בֵאלֹהַי. אֶלָּא הָכִי אָמְרוּ יִשְׂרָאֵל, אִי בְּרַחֲמֵי אָתֵי עָלָנָא, שׂוֹשׂ
אָשִׂישׂ בַּיְיָ'. אִי בְּדִינָא, תָּגֵל נַפְשִׁי בֵאלֹהַי.

501. Rabbi Yehuda opened his discourse with the verse: "I will greatly
rejoice in Hashem, my soul shall be joyful in my Elohim, for He has clothed
me with the garments of salvation" (Yeshayah 61:10). Blessed is the portion
of Yisrael above all heathen nations, for they have their joy in the Holy One,
blessed be He, as it is written: "I will greatly rejoice in Hashem". As it says,
"Hashem," why add, "my Elohim"? Yisrael said that when He comes with
Mercy, "I will greatly rejoice in Hashem," WHICH IS MERCY, and when He
comes in Judgment, then "My soul shall be joyful in my Elohim," WHICH IS
JUDGMENT.

502. מ"ט. מִשּׁוּם דְּאִלֵּין בֵּיהּ אִתְגְּלִיפוּ, דִּכְתִיב כִּי הִלְבִּישַׁנִי בִּגְדֵי
יֶשַׁע. מַהוּ בִּגְדֵי יֶשַׁע. גַּוְונִין, דְּאִתְגְּלִיפוּ לְאִסְתַּכְּלָא בֵּיהּ. כד"א, יִשְׁעוּ
וְגוֹ' אֶל יְיָ'. יֶשַׁע אִסְתַּכְּלוּתָא הוּא. מַאן דְּבָעֵי לְאִסְתַּכְּלָא בִּי, בְּגַוְונִין
דִּילִי יִסְתַּכַּל. מַאי טַעֲמָא. מִשּׁוּם דִּכְתִיב מְעִיל צְדָקָה יְעָטָנִי, צְדָקָה
מַמָּשׁ, דִּגְוָונִין בֵּיהּ אִתְגְּלִיפוּ. כְּחָתָן יְכַהֵן פְּאֵר, הָא גַּוְונָא חַד. וְכַכַּלָּה
תַּעְדֶּה כֵלֶיהָ, הָא גַּוְונָא אַחֲרָא. וְכַד גַּוְונִין מִתְחַבְּרָן, בֵּיהּ שַׁעֲתָא
אִתְחֲזֵיִין, וְכֻלְּהוּ תְּאִיבִין לְאַחֲזָאָה, וּלְאִסְתַּכְּלָא בֵּיהּ.

502. Why DO YISRAEL REJOICE IN TIMES OF MERCY AS WELL AS IN
THOSE OF JUDGMENT? For these two are imprinted upon Him, THE HOLY
ONE, BLESSED BE HE, as indicated by the words: "for He has clothed me
with the garments of salvation," meaning that these "garments of salvation"
are the colors OF CHESED AND GVURAH, so imprinted that one can gain a
perception of Him, NAMELY, DERIVE CHOCHMAH. It is written: "They
looked, but there was none to save, to Hashem..." (II Shmuel 22:42).
Hence, salvation means looking. 'Whoever wishes to behold Me, let him
behold My colors OF CHESED AND GVURAH'. What is the reason? It is
found in the verse: "He has covered me with the robe of righteousness"
(Ibid.), exactly righteousness, NAMELY MALCHUT, CALLED

"RIGHTEOUSNESS," has those two colors engraved in her, FOR CHOCHMAH IS DRAWN ONLY BY MALCHUT. "As a bridegroom decks himself with a garland" (Yeshayah 61:10), is one color, CHESED, "and as a bride adorns herself with her jewels"(Ibid.), is the other color, GVURAH. And when both colors are united IN THE CENTRAL COLUMN, they are visible and all are aflame to behold Him.

503. ר' יוֹסֵי אָמַר, שׂוֹשׂ אָשִׂישׂ בַּיְיָ', תְּרֵין חֶדְוָון. בַּיְיָ': בְּרַחֲמֵי. תָּגֵל נַפְשִׁי, הָא בְּדִינָא. אָמַר ר' יְהוּדָה, בְּכֹלָּא חֶדְוָה עַל חֶדְוָה. וְחֶדְוָה דְּצִיּוֹן, זַמִּין קוּדְשָׁא בְּרִיךְ הוּא לְאַחְדָאָה לְיִשְׂרָאֵל, בְּחֶדְוָותָא יַתִּיר מִכֹּלָּא, דִּכְתִיב וּפְדוּיֵי יְיָ' יְשׁוּבוּן וּבָאוּ צִיּוֹן בְּרִנָּה וְגו'. וּפְדוּיֵי יְיָ' יְשׁוּבוּן, הָא חַד. וּבָאוּ צִיּוֹן בְּרִנָּה, הָא תְּרֵי. וְשִׂמְחַת עוֹלָם עַל רֹאשָׁם, הָא תְּלַת. שָׂשׂוֹן וְשִׂמְחָה יַשִּׂיגוּ, הָא אַרְבַּע. לָקֳבְלֵיהוֹן דְּאַרְבַּע זִמְנִין דְּאִתְפְּזָרוּ יִשְׂרָאֵל בֵּינֵי עֲמַמְיָא. וּכְדֵין כְּתִיב וַאֲמַרְתֶּם בַּיּוֹם הַהוּא הוֹדוּ לַיְיָ' קִרְאוּ בִשְׁמוֹ וְגו'.

503. Rabbi Yosi said that the words, "I will greatly rejoice in Hashem," refer to two kinds of joy. One joy is in "Hashem," meaning in Mercy, and, "my soul shall be joyful IN MY ELOHIM," is in Judgment. Rabbi Yehuda said: THEY REJOICE BOTH IN MERCY AND IN JUDGMENT, and in each joy there is joy upon joy. However, the joy which the Holy One, blessed be He, will bring upon Yisrael in the future, the joy in Zion, will excel them all, as it is written: "And the ransomed of Hashem shall return and come to Zion with songs..." (Yeshayah 35:10). "And the ransomed of Hashem shall return," signifies one joy; "and come to Zion with songs," signifies the second; "and everlasting joy upon their heads," the third; and "they shall obtain joy and gladness" is the fourth joy. THESE ARE four kind of joy which correspond to the four exiles of Yisrael among the nations. Then, "in that day shall you say, 'Praise Hashem, call upon His name...'" (Yeshayah 12:4).

30. "I am Hashem your Elohim," part two

A Synopsis

We learn that Malchut, the moon, was in perfect unity with Zeir Anpin, equal with Him and under the same crown. After the moon was diminished she received light only from the sun, and her own aspect is hidden. This section then tells of the meaning of "I," Anochi, the secret that contains everything. It closes by saying that souls are punished for sins they committed in earlier incarnations.

504. וַיְדַבֵּר אֱלֹהִים אֵת כָּל הַדְּבָרִים הָאֵלֶּה. כָּל הַדְּבָרִים, כְּלָלָא דָא, הוּא כְּלָלָא דְּכֹלָּא, כְּלָלָא דִּלְעֵילָא וְתַתָּא.

504. "And Elohim spoke all these words, saying..." (Shemot 20:1); "...all these words..." means that THE TEN COMMANDMENTS contain everything that there is, above and below.

505. אָנֹכִי, רָזָא דְּעָלְמָא עִלָּאָה, בְּרָזָא דִּשְׁמָא קַדִּישָׁא יה״ו. אָנֹכִי, אִתְגַּלְיָא וְאִתְגְּנִיז. אִתְגַּלְיָא בְּרָזָא קַדִּישָׁא דְּכֻרְסְיָיא, דְּסִיהֲרָא קַיְּימָא בִּשְׁלִימוּ כַּחֲדָא, כַּד שִׁמְשָׁא שַׁלְטָא, וְסִיהֲרָא אִתְנְהִירַת, וְלֵית לָהּ שְׁבָחָא, בַּר שְׁבָחָא דִּנְהוֹרָא דְּנָהִיר עֲלָהּ.

505. "I," signifies the mystery of the supernal world, NAMELY, THE NUKVA WHICH IS PLACED FROM THE CHEST ABOVE OF ZEIR ANPIN. This is the secret of the Holy Name, *Yud-Hei-Vav*, BEING THE THREE COLUMNS CHESED, GVURAH AND TIFERET, WHICH THE NUKVA RECEIVES FROM ZEIR ANPIN. "I," MALCHUT, was first revealed and LATER concealed. She was revealed in the Holy Secret of the Throne, BINAH, FOR MALCHUT WAS THE FOURTH LEG OF THE THRONE, and the moon, MALCHUT, was then in perfect unity WITH ZEIR ANPIN – WHICH MEANS THAT BOTH MALCHUT AND ZEIR ANPIN WERE EQUAL AND WERE UNDER THE SAME CROWN. AND SHE IS HIDDEN when the sun, ZEIR ANPIN, rules. And the moon receives its light from it, not having THEN any praise OF ITS OWN, except the praise of light which ZEIR ANPIN radiates upon it, THUS ITS OWN ASPECT IS HIDDEN. THIS HAPPENED AFTER THE MOON WAS DIMINISHED.

506. אָנֹכִי, בְּאַשְׁלָמוּת רָזִין דְּשְׁלִימוּ דְּכוּרְסְיָיא לְתַתָּא, וְאִסְתַּלְּקוּ חַיִּין

קַדִּישִׁין, וְאִיהִי אִתְתַּקְנַת בְּתִקּוּנָהָא. וְכַד אִיהִי שַׁפִּירָא בְּחֵיזוּ, וּבַעֲלָה אָתֵי לְגַבָּהָא, כְּדֵין אִקְרֵי אָנֹכִי.

506. "I," SIGNIFIES MALCHUT WHEN SHE IS completing part of the perfection of the Lower Throne – MEANING THAT AFTER SHE WAS DIMINISHED AND DESCENDED FROM ABOVE THE CHEST TO BELOW THE CHEST, AND WAS ESTABLISHED THERE AS THE PRINCIPLE OF THE LOWER THRONE, all the holy living creatures departed from her. Then, being in perfection and beauty, when her Husband, ZEIR ANPIN, comes to her, she is called "I."

507. אָנֹכִי, רָזָא דְּכֹלָּא כַּחֲדָא, בִּכְלָלָא דְּכָל אַתְוָון, בִּשְׁבִילֵי אוֹרַיְיתָא, דְּנַפְקוּ מִגּוֹ רָזָא עִלָּאָה, בְּהַאי אָנֹכִי, תַּלְיָין רָזִין עִלָּאִין וְתַתָּאִין. אָנֹכִי, רָזָא לְמֵיהַב אֲגַר טַב לְצַדִּיקַיָּא, דְּקָא מְחַכָּאן לֵיהּ וְנַטְרֵי פִּקּוּדֵי אוֹרַיְיתָא, בְּהַאי, אִית לוֹן בִּטְחוֹנָא כַּדְקָא חֲזֵי לְעָלְמָא דְּאָתֵי, וְסִימָנִיךְ אֲנִי פַרְעֹה.

507. "I" is the secret WHICH CONTAINS everything together, BY INCLUDING ALL THE 22 LETTERS, AND THE 32 PATHS OF CHOCHMAH, WHICH MEANS all THE 22 letters in the 32 paths of the Torah that permeate from the supernal secret, NAMELY FROM CHOCHMAH. From this "I" all the upper and lower secrets are suspended. "I" contains the secret of the reward kept for the righteous who are the Torah keepers and await Him. Through this "I," they have faith in the world to come. This is derived from, "I am Pharaoh" (Beresheet 41:44), THESE WORDS SAID IN ORDER TO ASSURE JOSEPH THAT HIS PROMISE WILL BE KEPT.

508. אָנֹכִי וְלֹא יִהְיֶה לָךְ, אִתְּמַר בְּרָזָא דְּאוֹרַיְיתָא, וְדָא אִיהוּ זָכוֹר וְשָׁמוֹר. אָנֹכִי, רָזָא סְתִימָא וְגָנִיז, בְּכָל אִינּוּן דַּרְגִּין דְּעָלְמָא עִלָּאָה, בִּכְלָלָא חֲדָא. וְכֵיוָן דְּאִתְּמַר אָנֹכִי, אִתְחַבַּר כֹּלָּא כַּחֲדָא, בְּרָזָא חֲדָא.

508. The two commandments "I" (Heb. *Anochi*), and, "You shall have no" (Shemot 20:3), contain the secret of the Torah which is "Remember the Shabbat" (Shemot 20:8), and "Keep the Shabbat" (Devarim 5:12). "I" SIGNIFIES THE SECRET OF "REMEMBER," AND "YOU SHALL HAVE NO," SIGNIFIES THE SECRET OF "KEEP." "I" contains the concealed and kept

secret of all the grades of the supernal world, BEING THE YUD, HEI AND VAV united together, AS MENTIONED ABOVE. And when the word "I" had been uttered, all were united within one secret, FOR "I" SIGNIFIES THE UNITY OF ALL THE GRADES.

509. אָנֹכִי, רָזָא דִּתְרֵין כֻּרְסָוָון. אֲנִי כֻּרְסְיָיא חֲדָא. כ', כֻּרְסְיָיא אַחֲרָא עִלָּאָה.

509. The word "I (Heb. *Anochi*)" contains the secret of the two thrones WHICH ARE THE SUPERNAL THRONE, BINAH HAVING MALCHUT AS A FOURTH LEG, AND THE LOWER THRONE, BEING MALCHUT HERSELF AFTER BECOMING DIMINISHED, AS MENTIONED ABOVE. *Ani, Aleph Nun-Yud* (*Ani*=I) OF "*ANOCHI*," ALLUDES to the Lower Throne, and the letter *Caf* of the word "*Anochi*," ALLUDES to the Supernal Throne.

510. אָנֹכִי, דְּקָא אִתְדַּכֵּי מַקְדְּשָׁא, וְנוּכְרָאָה לָא אִתְקְרַב בַּהֲדֵיהּ, וּמַקְדְּשָׁא נָהִיר בִּלְחוֹדוֹי, דְּקָא אִתְבַּטַּל בְּהַהִיא שַׁעֲתָא יֵצֶר הָרָע מֵעָלְמָא, וְקוּדְשָׁא בְּרִיךְ הוּא אִסְתַּלָּק בִּיקָרֵיהּ בִּלְחוֹדוֹי, וּכְדֵין אִתְּמַר אָנֹכִי יְיָ' אֱלֹהֶיךָ. רָזָא שְׁלִים, בִּשְׁמָא קַדִּישָׁא. א': לְיַחֲדָא רָזָא דִּשְׁמָא קַדִּישָׁא בְּדַרְגּוֹי, לְמֶהֱוֵי חַד. בְּגִין דְּרָזָא דִּילֵיהּ אִיהוּ ו'. נ': רָזָא לְמִדְחַל מִקּוּדְשָׁא בְּרִיךְ הוּא, וּלְמִנְדַּע דְּאִית דִּין וְאִית דַּיָּין, וְאִית אֲגַר טַב לְצַדִּיקַיָּיא וּפוּרְעָנוּת לְרַשִׁיעַיָּא, בְּגִין דְּרָזָא דִּילֵיהּ ה' תַּתָּאָה.

510. The word "*Anochi*" INDICATES that the Temple is purified, WHICH IS MALCHUT, and that no stranger has approached it. The Temple alone radiated its light, for then the Evil Inclination was removed from the world and the Holy One, blessed be He, alone was exalted in glory. Then the words, "I am Hashem your Elohim," were uttered, having the complete secret folded in His Holy Name. The letter *Aleph* OF "*ANOCHI*" INDICATES the unification of the secret of the Holy Name together with its grades into one, as its secret is the letter *Vav* OF YUD HEI VAV HEI. The letter *Nun* IN THE WORD "*ANOCHI*" INDICATES the secret of standing in awe of the Holy One, blessed be He, knowing that there is a judge and Judgment, the righteous will be rewarded, and the wicked will be punished, for its secret is the lower *Hei* IN THE NAME YUD HEI VAV HEI.

511. כ': לְקַדְּשָׁא שְׁמָא קַדִּישָׁא בְּכָל יוֹמָא, לְאִתְקַדְּשָׁא בְּדַרְגִּין קַדִּישִׁין, וּלְצַלָּאָה צְלוֹתָא לְגַבֵּיה בְּכָל זִמְנָא, לְאִסְתַּלְּקָא כִּתְרָא עִלָּאָה, רָזָא דְּכֻרְסַיָּיא עִלָּאָה, עַל גַּבֵּי חֵיוָון עִלָּאִין, כַּדְקָא יֵאוֹת, וְרָזָא דִּילֵיה ה' עִלָּאָה.

511. The letter *Caf* IN THE WORD *"ANOCHI"* signifies that one should sanctify the Holy Name daily, sanctify oneself through holy grades, and say the everyday prayers to Him to raise the supreme crown, the secret of the Upper Throne, NAMELY BINAH, in a proper manner above the supernal living creatures – WHICH ARE CHESED AND GVURAH, TIFERET AND MALCHUT, FROM THE CHEST ABOVE OF ZEIR ANPIN, AND THE FOUR LEGS OF THE THRONE, WHOSE FOURTH LIVING CREATURE AND FOURTH LEG IS MALCHUT. Its secret is the supernal *Hei* OF THE NAME YUD HEI VAV HEI, WHICH IS BINAH. SINCE MALCHUT IS THE FOURTH LEG OF THE SUPERNAL THRONE, WHICH IS BINAH, SHE IS CONSIDERED AS PERTAINING TO BINAH AND TO THE UPPER *HEI* OF YUD HEI VAV HEI.

512. י': לְאִשְׁתַּדְּלָא בְּאוֹרַיְיתָא יְמָמָא וְלֵילֵי, וּלְמִגְזַר גְּזִירוּ, בְּרָזָא לִתְמַנְיָא יוֹמִין, וּלְקַדְּשָׁא בּוּכְרָא. וּלְאַנָּחָא תְּפִילִין וְצִיצִית וּמְזוּזָה. וּלְמִמְסַר נַפְשָׁא לְגַבֵּי קוּדְשָׁא בְּרִיךְ הוּא, וּלְאִתְדַּבְּקָא בֵּיה. אִלֵּין אִינּוּן תְּרֵיסַר פְּקוּדִין עִלָּאִין, דִּכְלִילָן רל"ו פְּקוּדִין אַחֲרָנִין דְּאִינּוּן בְּרָזָא דְּאָנֹכִי, כְּלָלָא דִּזְכוֹר. וְאַתְּ דָּא, לָא אִתְחַלַּף בְּאֲתָר אַחֲרָא, דָּא בְּגִין דְּאִיהִי י', רָזָא עִלָּאָה, כְּלָלָא דְּאוֹרַיְיתָא, וּבְאִלֵּין תְּרֵיסַר, אִית תְּרֵיסַר מְכִילִין דְּרַחֲמֵי, דְּתַלְיָין מִנַּיְיהוּ, וְחַד דְּשַׁלְטָא לְמֶהֱוֵי תְּלֵיסַר.

512. The letter *Yud* IN THE WORD *"ANOCHI"* INDICATES that one should study the Torah day and night, and circumcise his son on the eighth day, and sanctify the firstborn, and put on Tefilin, and wear the fringes (Heb. *tzitzit*), and affix a Mezuzah, and surrender his life to cleave to the Holy One, blessed be He, with his whole heart. These are the twelve supernal commandments – WHICH ARE ALLUDED TO BY THE WORD *"ANOCHI,"* which include 236 other commandments, BRINGING IT TO 248 POSITIVE COMMANDMENTS – which are included in the words "Remember the Shabbat." FOR "REMEMBER" INCLUDES 248 POSITIVE COMMANDMENTS, AND "KEEP" INCLUDES THE 365 NEGATIVE COMMANDMENTS. This letter

is not interchangeable with another place, AS THE *ALEPH, NUN* AND *CAF* OF *ANOCHI*, WHICH ARE INTERCHANGEABLE WITH *HEI, VAV* AND *HEI* OF YUD HEI VAV HEI. For the letter *Yud* signifies the supernal secret of the whole Torah, MEANING THAT IT IS THE SECRET OF THE LOWER CHOCHMAH WHICH UNITES WITH THE LETTER *YUD* OF YUD HEI VAV HEI, THE SECRET OF THE UPPER CHOCHMAH. THEREFORE, THIS IS NOT A CHANGE OF PLACE. Those twelve COMMANDMENTS include the twelve attributes of Mercy which are derived from them. And one rules THEM ALL, WHICH IS THE ESSENCE OF MALCHUT WHICH IS CALLED "ANOCHI," bringing it to thirteen, CORRESPONDING TO THE THIRTEEN ATTRIBUTES OF MERCY.

513. לֹא יִהְיֶה לְךָ, רָזָא דְּשָׁמוֹר, בִּתְלַת מְאָה וְשִׁתִּין וְחָמֵשׁ פִּקּוּדֵי אוֹרַיְיתָא. ל': רָזָא דְּלָא לְמֵיהַב יְקָר וּרְבוּ לְאֱלָהָא אַחֲרָא. ל': מִגְדְּלָא דְּפָרַח וְסָלִיק בַּאֲוִירָא, דְּלָא יִסְטֵי לִבָּא, לְמִבְנֵי לָהּ לְאֱלָהָא אַחֲרָא, כְּמָה דְּאִית רָזָא, דְּבוֹנֶא מִגְדְּלָא. ל': דְּלָא לְמִפְנֵי בְּדִיּוּקְנָא דע"ז, דְּלָא לְהַרְהֲרָא אֲבַתְרָהָא, דְּלָא לְסַגְדָּא, וְלָא לְאַכְפְּיָא גַּרְמֵיהּ לְאֱלָהָא אַחֲרָא.

513. The commandment "You shall have no other Elohim" (Shemot 20:3), signifies the secret of "keep," which includes the 365 NEGATIVE PRECEPTS in the Torah. The letter *Lamed* IN "YOU SHALL HAVE NO (HEB. *LO*, LAMED-ALEPH)" contains the secret of not worshipping or paying respect to other Elohim. The letter *Lamed* has the form of a tower rising up in the air. One should not be tempted to build A CASTLE to other Elohim, in the secret of building a tower, AS IN THE TIME OF THE GENERATION OF THE TOWER OF BABYLON. *Lamed* shows that one should not look at the images of idol worshipping, nor think about it, neither bowing, nor subduing oneself to other Elohim.

514. א': דְּלָא לְחַלְּפָא יְחוּדָא דְּמָרֵיהּ, בְּגִין טַעֲוָון אַחֲרָנִין. א': דְּלָא לְהַרְהֲרָא דְּאִית אֱלָהָא אַחֲרָא בַּר מִנֵּיהּ. א': דְּלָא לְמִסְטֵי בָּתַר בְּיָדִין וּדְכוּרוֹ, בְּרָזָא דְּדִיּוּקְנָא דְּאָדָם, וְלָא בְּדִיּוּקְנָא אַחֲרָא. א': דְּלָא לְמִשְׁאַל מִן מֵתַיָּיא, וְלָא לְמֶעְבַּד חַרְשִׁין. א': דְּלָא יוֹמֵי בְּפוּמוֹי, בִּשְׁמָא דֶּאֱלָהָא

אַחֲרָא. עַד הָכָא, תְּרֵיסַר אַחֲרָנִין, דְּאִינּוּן פִּקוּדֵי שָׁמוֹר. וּבְאִלֵּין תְּרֵיסַר, תַּלְיָין תְּלַת מְאָה וְחַמְשִׁין וּתְלַת פִּקוּדֵי דְּשָׁמוֹר אַחֲרָנִין, דִּכְלִילָן בְּאִלֵּין תְּרֵיסַר, וְרָזָא דָּא אָנֹכִי.

514. The letter *Aleph* IN THE COMMANDMENT, "YOU SHALL HAVE NO OTHER ELOHIM," indicates that one should not replace his Master with other Elohim; he should not even meditate on the existence of another deity besides Him; he should not take counsel from a necromancer or a soothsayer through the medium of the image of man or any other form; he is not to ask of the dead; he is not to practice magic; and he should not swear in another deity's name. Up to this point are the other twelve COMMANDMENTS, the precepts INCLUDED in "keep." From them come the other 353 precepts of "keep," included in these twelve, BRINGING IT TO 365. This is the secret of the word "*Anochi*," AND, "YOU SHALL HAVE NO."

515. אר"ש, תּוּ תָּנֵינָן, אָנֹכִי כְּלָלָא דִּעֵילָּא וְתַתָּא, כְּלָלָא דְּעֶלְאִין וְתַתָּאִין, כְּלָלָא דְּחֵיוָן קַדִּישִׁין, דִּכְלִילָן בֵּיהּ, כֹּלָּא הוּא בְּרָזָא דְּאָנֹכִי. לֹא יִהְיֶה לְךָ לְתַתָּא, רָזָא דִּתְרֵיסַר חֵיוָן תַּתָּאִין.

515. Rabbi Shimon said: We have learned that the word "*Anochi*" (lit. 'I') includes the above and the below, the upper and lower beings. It includes the holy living creatures. All is included in the secret of "*Anochi*." "You shall have no," refers to the secret below, of the twelve lower living creatures IN MALCHUT.

516. לֹא תַעֲשֶׂה לְךָ פֶסֶל. פְּסִלוּ מֵהַהוּא אֲתָר עִלָּאָה, מֵהַהוּא אֲתָר קַדִּישָׁא. פֶּסֶל. פְּסוֹלֶת דִּקְדוּשָׁא דְּאִיהוּ רָזָא דְּטַעֲוָא אַחֲרָא. וְרָזָא דָּא, כד"א וָאֵרֶא וְהִנֵּה רוּחַ סְעָרָה בָּאָה מִן הַצָּפוֹן וְגוֹ'. וְכָל תְּמוּנָה הה"ד וְאֵשׁ מִתְלַקַּחַת. כִּי אָנֹכִי יְיָ' אֱלֹהֶיךָ, בְּגִין לְאִתְעָרָא לִבָּא לְגַבֵּי עֵילָּא, וְלָא לְנַחְתָּא לְתַתָּא וְלָא לְמִקְרַב לִתְרַע בֵּיתָא. אֵל קַנָּא, דְּקַנְאָה אִיהוּ בְּהַהוּא אֲתָר.

516. "You shall not make for yourself any carved idol (Heb. *pesel*)," alludes

to the dross (Heb. *pesolet*) of that lofty place, NAMELY, THE LEFT SIDE OF HOLINESS, *pesel* being the refuse of Holiness, the secret of other Elohim, as it is written: "And I looked and behold, a storm wind came out of the north" (Yechezkel 1:4). THE NORTH IS THE SECRET OF THE LEFT SIDE OF HOLINESS. "...any likeness of any thing..." (Shemot 20:4) as it is written, "a fire flaring up" (Yechezkel 1:4). "For I Hashem your Elohim," so that your heart should be directed upwards, and it should not descend below and approach the portal OF THE OTHER SIDE. He is "a jealous El," for in that place lies jealousy.

517. וְרָזָא דָּא, תַּחַת שָׁלֹשׁ רָגְזָה אֶרֶץ. וְאִיהוּ לֹא תַעֲשֶׂה לְךָ, חַד. פֶּסֶל, תְּרֵין. וְכָל תְּמוּנָה, תְּלַת. וְאֶרֶץ דָּא, עַל דָּא אִתְרְגִיזַת.

517. This is the secret of, "For three things the earth is disquieted" (Mishlei 30:21), which are: "You shall not make for yourself," "A carved idol," and, "any likeness of any thing." For these "the earth is disquieted."

518. פָּקַד עֲוֹן אָבוֹת עַל בָּנִים עַל שִׁלֵּשִׁים וְעַל רִבֵּעִים. אִלָּנָא חֲדָא, דְּאִינְצִיב חֲדָא, וּתְרֵין זִמְנִין, וּתְלַת זִמְנִין, וְאַרְבַּע זִמְנִין, וְאִתְפְּקַד עַל חוֹבֵי קַדְמָאֵי, אָב וּבֵן. שְׁלִישִׁי וּרְבִיעִי חַד הוּא כַּד לָא אִתְתַּקַּן, וְלָא חָיִישׁ לְאִתְתַּקְּנָא, וְכֵן בְּהִפּוּכָא דְּדָא, לְאִילָנָא דְּאִיהוּ אִתְתַּקַּן כַּדְקָא חֲזִי, וְקָאִים עַל קִיּוּמֵיהּ וְעוֹשֶׂה חֶסֶד וְגו'.

518. It is written: "Punishing the iniquity of the fathers upon the children to the third and fourth generation" (Shemot 20:5). HE WAS PRESENTED WITH THE DIFFICULTY OF THE WORDS: "NOR THE CHILDREN BE PUT TO DEATH FOR THE FATHERS" (II MELACHIM 14:6). AND HE ANSWERS THAT this is the same tree, THE SAME SOUL coming once, twice, thrice, four times, WHICH MEANS IT HAD BEEN INCARNATED AND COME IN FOUR BODIES, being punished for the first sins IN THE FOURTH REINCARNATION. For the father, the son, the third and fourth generations, NAMELY THESE FOUR INCARNATIONS, are one, BEING ONE SOUL that has not done its correction or cared to attend to it. IT IS THEREFORE PUNISHED FOR THE SINS IN THE FIRST INCARNATIONS. The reverse is also true. A tree well established THROUGH INCARNATIONS stands firm, AND OF IT, IT IS WRITTEN: "But showing mercy..." (Shemot 20:5).

31. "You shall not take the name of Hashem your Elohim in vain"

A Synopsis

We learn that at the time that God created the world He placed a stone with His name engraved upon it into the deep waters. This stone flows up to receive the oath of those who swear on the Truth; then it returns to the deep waters. If the oath is false, the waters flow up but the stone retreats without receiving the oath, and the letters on the stone disperse in the deep, until God invites Azriel to engrave the Holy Letters as they were before, and the world is settled by them.

519. לֹא תִשָּׂא, רָזָא דָּא הָא אוּקְמוּהָ חַבְרַיָּיא. בְּגִין דְּקוּדְשָׁא בְּרִיךְ הוּא
כַּד שָׁתִיל עָלְמָא, אַטְבַּע גּוֹ תְּהוֹמֵי, צְרוֹרָא חֲדָא, חָקִיקָא בִּשְׁמָא
קַדִּישָׁא, וְאַטְבַּע לֵהּ לְגוֹ תְּהוֹמָא. וְכַד מַיָּא בָּעָאן לְסַלְּקָא, חָמָאן רָזָא
דִּשְׁמָא קַדִּישָׁא, חָקִיק עַל הַהוּא צְרוֹרָא, וְתַיְיבִין וּמִשְׁתַּקְּעִין, וְהַדְרִין
לַאֲחוֹרָא, וּשְׁמָא דָּא קַיְּימָא עַד יוֹמָא דָּא, גּוֹ תְּהוֹמָא.

519. "You shall not take the name of Hashem your Elohim in vain" (Shemot 20:7). This secret has already been interpreted by the friends. When the Holy One, blessed be He, planted the world, He planted into the deep waters His Name engraved UPON A STONE. Since then, when the water desires to rise, INTENDING TO DROWN THE WORLD, it sees the Holy Name engraved on that stone and retreats and returns to its place, and the Holy Name remains in the deep waters to this day.

520. וּבְשַׁעֲתָא דְּאוֹמִין בְּנֵי נָשָׁא עַל קְשׁוֹט, בְּקִיּוּמָא דִּקְשׁוֹט, הַהוּא
צְרוֹרָא סַלְּקָא, וּמְקַבְּלָא הַהוּא אוֹמָאָה, וְאַהֲדָר וְאִתְקַיַּים עַל תְּהוֹמָא,
וְעָלְמָא אִתְקַיַּים, וְהַהוּא אוֹמָאָה דִּקְשׁוֹט קַיָּים עָלְמָא.

520. At the time when men take a true oath, firmly attached to the Truth, that rock flows up and receives that oath, and then it returns to its place in the deep waters. And the world is maintained by that true oath.

521. וּבְשַׁעֲתָא דְּאוֹמוּ בְּנֵי נָשָׁא אוֹמָאָה לְשִׁקְרָא, הַהוּא צְרוֹרָא סַלְּקָא
לְקַבְּלָא לֵהּ לְהַהִיא אוֹמָאָה, כֵּיוָן דְּחָזֵי דְּאִיהוּ דְּשִׁקְרָא. כְּדֵין הַהוּא

צְרוֹרָא דַּהֲוָה סָלִיק, תָּב לַאֲחוֹרָא, וּמַיָּין אַזְלִין וְשָׁטִין, וְאַתְוָון דְּהַהוּא
צְרוֹרָא, פָּרְחָן גּוֹ תְּהוֹמֵי, וְאִתְבַּדְּרָן, וּבָעָאן מַיָּא לְסַלְּקָא לְחַפְיָיא
עָלְמָא, וּלְאַהֲדָרָא לֵיהּ כְּמִלְּקַדְמִין.

521. When men take a false oath, that rock flows up, intending to receive that oath, but when it sees that this oath was taken in vain, it retreats and all the waters flow up. And the letters of that stone soar inside the deep and disperse. And the waters wish to cover the world and return it to its former state OF WATER.

522. עַד דְּזַמִּין קוּדְשָׁא בְּרִיךְ הוּא, לְחַד מְמָנָא, יְעַזְרִיאֵ"ל, דִּי מְמָנָא
עַל שַׁבְעִין מַפְתְּחָן, בְּרָזָא דִּשְׁמָא קַדִּישָׁא, וְעָאל לְגַבֵּיהּ דְּהַהוּא צְרוֹרָא,
וְחָקִיק בֵּיהּ אַתְוָון כְּמִלְּקַדְמִין, וּכְדֵין אִתְקַיָּים עָלְמָא, וְאַהֲדְרוּ מַיָּין
לְדוּכְתַּיְיהוּ. וְעַ"ד כְּתִיב לֹא תִשָּׂא אֶת שֵׁם ה' אֱלֹהֶיךָ לַשָּׁוְא.

522. Then the Holy One, blessed be He, invites Ye'azriel the Minister, who is in charge of seventy keys of the secret of the Holy Name. He then engraves the Holy Letters as they were before, and the world is settled by them, and the deep waters return to their place. Of that it is written: "You shall not take the Name of Hashem your Elohim in vain" (Shemot 20:7).

A Synopsis

We learn that the twelfth commandment is to swear by God's name truthfully, for he who takes a true oath combines himself with the supernal seven grades. He who takes a false oath causes Malchut to be disturbed. Taking a vow is a stricter act than taking an oath, for it is connected higher.

רעיא מהימנא

523. פְּקוּדָא י"ב, לְאוֹמָאָה בִּשְׁמֵיהּ בְּאֹרַח קְשׁוֹט. וּמַאן דְּאוֹמֵי שְׁבוּעָה,
הוּא כָּלִיל גַּרְמֵיהּ, בְּאִינּוּן ז' דַּרְגִּין עִלָּאִין, דִּשְׁמָא דְּקוּדְשָׁא בְּרִיךְ הוּא
אִתְכְּלִיל בְּהוּ. וְהָא שִׁיתָא אִינּוּן. הַהוּא בַּ"נ דְּאוֹמֵי אוֹמָאָה דִּקְשׁוֹט
עַ"פ בַּ"ד, כָּלִיל גַּרְמֵיהּ בְּהוּ, וְהוּא שְׁבִיעָאָה, לְקַיְּימָא שְׁמָא קַדִּישָׁא

בְּדוּכְתֵּיהּ. וְעַ״ד כְּתִיב, וּבִשְׁמוֹ תִּשָּׁבֵעַ. וּמַאן דְּאוֹמֵי אוֹמָאָה לִמַגְּנָא וּלְשַׁקְרָא, גָּרִים לְהַהוּא אֲתָר דְּלָא יִתְקַיֵּים בְּדוּכְתֵּיהּ.

Ra'aya Meheimna (the Faithful Shepherd)

523. The twelfth commandment is to swear in His name in a truthful way. And he who takes an oath combines himself with the supernal seven grades in which the Name of the Holy One, blessed be He, WHICH IS MALCHUT, is included. Thus, there are six grades: CHESED, GVURAH, TIFERET, NETZACH, HOD AND YESOD, and when man take a true oath, he then includes himself with them by becoming a seventh, CORRESPONDING TO MALCHUT, so as to maintain the Holy Name, WHICH IS MALCHUT, in its place. Therefore, it is written: "And shall swear by His Name" (Devarim 6:13). And he who takes a false oath causes that place, MALCHUT, to be disturbed in its abode.

524. אוֹמָאָה לְקַיְּימָא פְּקוּדָא דְּמָארֵיהּ, דָּא אִיהוּ שְׁבוּעָה דִּקְשׁוֹט, כַּד הַהוּא יֵצֶר הָרָע מְקַטְרֵג לְבַר נָשׁ, וּמְפַתֵּה לֵיהּ לְמֶעֱבַר עַל פְּקוּדָא דְּמָארֵיהּ. דָּא אִיהוּ אוֹמָאָה דְּמָארֵיהּ אִשְׁתְּבַח בֵּיהּ, וְאִצְטְרִיךְ לֵיהּ לְבַר נָשׁ לְאוֹמָאָה בְּמָארֵיהּ עַל דָּא, וְאִיהוּ שְׁבָחָא דִּילֵיהּ. וְקוּדְשָׁא בְּרִיךְ הוּא מִשְׁתְּבַח בֵּיהּ. כְּגוֹן בּוֹעַז, דִּכְתִּיב חַי יְיָ' שִׁכְבִי עַד הַבֹּקֶר. דְּהָא יֵצֶר הָרָע הֲוָה מְקַטְרֵג לֵיהּ, וְאוֹמֵי עַל דָּא.

524. The oath to keep one's Master's commandment is a true oath, and the Evil Inclination denounces him and tempts this man to transgress his Master's commandment. Such is an oath with which his Master praises himself, and it is proper for man to take a true oath in the Name of his Master, for then the Holy One, blessed be He, is praised by this oath, as Boaz did, as written: "As Hashem lives, lie down until the morning" (Rut 3:13). He took an oath, for the Evil Inclination was, then, denouncing him. He therefore swore to it.

525. נֶדֶר אִיהוּ לְעֵילָּא, וְאִינּוּן חַיֵּי מַלְכָּא, רָזָא דִּרְמַ״ח שַׁיְיפִין, וּתְרֵיסַר קְטִירִין, כְּחוּשְׁבַּן נֶדֶ״ר. וְעַל דָּא חָמִיר מִשְׁבוּעָה. חַיֵּי דְּמַלְכָּא אִלֵּין, דְּיָהִיב חַיִּין לְכָל אִלֵּין שַׁיְיפִין, וְאִקְרוּן הָכִי בְּגִין אִינּוּן חַיִּין, וְאִינּוּן חַיִּין

-248-

נַחְתִּין מֵעֵילָא לְתַתָּא. לְהַהוּא מְקוֹרָא דְּחַיִּין. וּמֵהַהוּא מְקוֹרָא נַחְתִּין
לְתַתָּא, לְכָל אִינּוּן שַׁיְיפִין.

525. A vow (Heb. *neder*) is connected higher and is the King's life,
MEANING THE MOCHIN OF MALCHUT IN BINAH, the secret of 248 limbs
and twelve ties, WHICH ARE THE FOUR SFIROT: CHESED AND GVURAH,
TIFERET AND MALCHUT. EACH ONE OF THESE SFIROT INCLUDES THE
THREE COLUMNS. Thus, they amount to the numerical value of "*neder*"
(=254) AS 248 PLUS TWELVE AMOUNTS TO 254. Therefore, taking a vow
is a stricter act than taking a oath. This King's Life maintains all the 248
limbs and it is called 'THE KING'S LIFE' for indeed it gives life, and this life
descends from above, FROM THE ENDLESS LIGHT downwards, to the
source of life, WHICH IS BINAH from which it descends TO MALCHUT, to
all the 248 limbs.

526. שְׁבוּעָה לְקַיְּימָא דַּרְגָּא דִלְתַתָּא, רָזָא דִּשְׁמָא קַדִּישָׁא. וְדָא אִקְרֵי
מֶלֶךְ עַצְמוֹ, דְּרוּחָא עִלָּאָה וְגוּפָא דִּילֵיהּ, לְמִשְׁרֵי בְּגַוֵּיהּ, וּלְדַיְּירָא בֵּיהּ,
כְּרוּחָא דְּשָׁארֵי גּוֹ גוּפָא. וּבְגִין כַּךְ, מַאן דְּאוֹמֵי בִּקְשׁוֹט, הוּא מְקַיֵּים
לְהַהוּא אֲתָר, וְכַד קָאֵי הַאי אֲתָר מְקוּיְּים, מְקַיֵּים כָּל עָלְמָא. נֶדֶר שַׁרְיָא
עַל כֹּלָּא, עַל מִצְוָה, וְעַל רְשׁוּתָא דְּלָאו הָכִי בִּשְׁבוּעָה, וְהָכִי אוּקְמוּהָ
חַבְרַיָּיא.

ע"כ רעיא מהימנא

526. An oath maintains the lower grade, the secret of the Holy Name,
WHICH IS MALCHUT, called the King Himself, whose supernal spirit within
His body COMES to dwell in it and stay in it as a spirit dwelling in a body –
WHICH MEANS THAT THE MOCHIN ARE ALREADY PLACED IN THE VESSEL
OF MALCHUT, WHICH IS CALLED 'BODY'. FOR IT IS HIDDEN ABOVE IN
BINAH, AND IS REVEALED ONLY IN MALCHUT. Therefore, he who takes a
true oath maintains that place and by doing so, the whole world is
maintained. A vow applies to both that which is obligatory and optional. But
an oath is not so, AS IT DOES NOT APPLY TO PRECEPTS. This has been
explained by the friends.

End of Ra'aya Meheimna (the Faithful Shepherd)

32. "Remember the Shabbat day to keep it holy," part two

A Synopsis
We are reminded that the Sabbath includes the whole Torah, and he who keeps the Sabbath is considered to have kept the entire Torah.

527. זָכוֹר אֶת יוֹם הַשַׁבָּת לְקַדְּשׁוֹ דָּא אִיהוּ רָזָא דִּבְרִית קַדִּישָׁא. וּבְגִין דִּבְהַאי בְּרִית קַיְימִין כָּל מְקוֹרִין דְּשַׁיְיפֵי גוּפָא, וְאִיהוּ כָּלַל כֹּלָּא. כְּגַוְונָא, דָּא שַׁבָּת אִיהוּ כְּלָלָא דְּאוֹרַיְיתָא, וְכָל רָזִין דְּאוֹרַיְיתָא בֵּיהּ תַּלְיָין, וְקִיּוּמָא דְּשַׁבָּת, כְּקִיּוּמָא דְּכָל אוֹרַיְיתָא, מַאן דְּנָטִיר שַׁבָּת, כְּאִילּוּ נָטִיר אוֹרַיְיתָא כֹּלָּא.

527. "Remember the Shabbat day, to keep it holy" (Shemot 20:8). This is the secret of the Holy Covenant, WHICH IS YESOD, for in this Covenant lie all the sources of the limbs of the body, and it comprises everything. In the same manner, the Shabbat day includes all the Torah, all of its secrets originate in it. And he who keeps the Shabbat is considered as one who keeps the whole Torah.

A Synopsis
This section talks about 'remember' and 'keep', and the three grades – the supernal Sabbath, the Sabbath day, and Sabbath night – that include all the secrets of the whole Torah: The Law, the Prophets and the Writings.

רעיא מהימנא

528. פְּקוּדָא כ"ד, לְמֶהֱוֵי דָּכִיר יוֹם הַשַׁבָּת, כד"א זָכוֹר אֶת יוֹם הַשַׁבָּת לְקַדְּשׁוֹ. רָזָא דְּשַׁבָּת, הָא אוּקִימְנָא בְּכָל אִינּוּן דּוּכְתֵּי, יוֹמָא דּוּכְרָנָא דְּנַיְיחָא דְּעָלְמָא וְאִיהוּ כְּלָלָא דְּאוֹרַיְיתָא. וּמַאן דְּנָטִיר שַׁבָּת, כְּאִילּוּ נָטִיר אוֹרַיְיתָא כֹּלָּא. וְהָא אִתְּמַר, דּוּכְרָנָא דְּשַׁבָּת, לְקַדְשָׁא לֵיהּ בְּכָל זִינֵי קְדוּשִׁין. מַאן דְּאָדְכַּר לְמַלְכָּא, אִצְטְרִיךְ לְבָרְכָא לֵיהּ, מַאן דְּאָדְכַּר שַׁבָּת, צָרִיךְ לְקַדְשָׁא לֵיהּ וְהָא אִתְּמַר.

Ra'aya Meheimna (the Faithful Shepherd)

528. The twenty-fourth commandment is to remember the Shabbat day, as written: "Remember the Shabbat day, to keep it holy." We have explained the secret of Shabbat in many places. It is to be remembered as the day of the world's rest, and it includes the whole Torah, and he who keeps the Shabbat is considered as one who keeps the whole Torah. We have already learned that a man who remembers the Shabbat has to sanctify it in all manners of sanctifications. He who remembers the King has to praise Him, and he who remembers the Shabbat day, has to sanctify it, as we have already learned.

529. זָכוֹר לִדְכוּרָא אִיהוּ. שָׁמוֹר אִיהוּ לְנוּקְבָּא. יוֹם שַׁבָּת, רָזָא דְכָל מְהֵימָנוּתָא, דְּתַלְיָא מֵרֵישָׁא עִלָּאָה, עַד סוֹפָא דְּכָל דַּרְגִּין, שַׁבָּת אִיהוּ כֹּלָא.

529. "Remember" applies to the Male, WHICH IS ZEIR ANPIN, and "keep" applies to the Female, WHICH IS MALCHUT. The Shabbat day is the secret of the whole Faith which is suspended from the supernal head, WHICH IS KETER, to the bottom of all the grades. Shabbat is everything.

530. תְּלַת דַּרְגִּין אִינּוּן, וְכֻלְּהוּ אִקְרוּן שַׁבָּת. שַׁבָּת עִלָּאָה. שַׁבָּת דְּיוֹמָא. שַׁבָּת דְּלֵילְיָא. וְכֻלְּהוּ חַד וְאִקְרֵי כֹּלָא שַׁבָּת. וְכָל חַד, כַּד אִיהוּ שַׁלְטָא, נָטִיל לְחַבְרוֹי, וְזַמִּין לוֹן בַּהֲדֵיהּ, בְּהַהוּא שׁוּלְטָנוּ דִּילֵיהּ. וְכַד הַאי אָתֵי לְעָלְמָא כֻּלְּהוּ אַתְיָין וְזַמִּינִין בַּהֲדֵיהּ.

530. There are three grades and all of them are called Shabbat. These are the supernal Shabbat, WHICH IS BINAH, Shabbat day, WHICH IS ZEIR ANPIN, and Shabbat night, WHICH IS MALCHUT. All of them are called Shabbat, and when the time comes for one of them to rule, all the others are invited to rule with it. And when it is manifested in the world, all come to be with it.

531. כַּד אָתֵי לֵילְיָא, זַמִּין בַּהֲדֵיהּ לְשַׁבָּת דְּיִמָּמָא, וְזַמִּין לֵיהּ בְּהֵיכָלֵיהּ, וְאִתְטְמַּר בַּהֲדֵיהּ. כֵּיוָן דְּהַאי אַתְיָא, שַׁבָּת עִלָּאָה אִתְמְשָׁךְ עֲלֵיהּ, וְכֻלְּהוּ גְּנִיזִין בְּהֵיכְלָא דְּלֵילְיָא וּבְג״ד סְעוּדָתָא דְּלֵילְיָא חֲמוּר כִּדְבִימָמָא.

531. When the time of SHABBAT night comes, it invites the Shabbat day to

its palace, and they are both hidden. Once it comes, the supernal Shabbat is drawn over it, and all of them are concealed in the palace of the SHABBAT night. Therefore, the meal on SHABBAT night is as significant as the one during the Shabbat day.

532. כַּד אָתֵי יְמָמָא, זַמִּין בַּהֲדֵיה לִתְרֵין אִלֵּין אַחֲרָנִין, דַּרְגָּא עִלָּאָה וְדַרְגָּא תַּתָּאָה, דָּא דְּאַנְהִיר לֵיה, וְדָא דְּאִתְנְהִיר מִנֵּיה. וְכֹלָּא כַּחֲדָא אִקְרֵי שַׁבָּת, וְשָׁלְטִין בְּיוֹמָא דְּשַׁבָּת. וְאִלֵּין תְּלַת דַּרְגִּין, אִינּוּן כְּלָלָא וְרָזָא דְּכָל אוֹרַיְיתָא, תּוֹרָה שֶׁבִּכְתָב, נְבִיאִים וּכְתוּבִים. מַאן דְּנָטִיר שַׁבָּת, נָטִיר אוֹרַיְיתָא כֹּלָּא.

532. When the time of SHABBAT day comes, WHICH IS ZEIR ANPIN, it invites the other two, the supernal and the lower grades – the one which illuminates, NAMELY BINAH, and the one which is illuminated from it, NAMELY MALCHUT. All these three grades together are called 'Shabbat' and rule on the day of Shabbat, and they include and are the secrets of the whole Torah: The Law, the Prophets and The Writings. And he who keeps the Shabbat keeps the whole Torah.

33. Two pearls

A Synopsis

We read of two pearls, a supernal pearl – Binah – and a lower pearl – Malchut – which are separated by a curtain that is made of the 22 letters that comprise the whole Torah. There is a long description of the engravings and movement and meaning of all the letters in the Names of God, and of the twelve tribes, illuminated by and joins to the supernal pearl, and both of them become one the seventy branches and the ten sayings. The lower pearl is.

533. תְּרֵין מַרְגְּלָן אִינּוּן, וְחַד סִיכְתָא בַּהֲדַיְיהוּ, בְּגַוְוייהוּ, דְּקָאִים בֵּין הַאי וּבֵין הַאי. מַרְגְּלָא עִלָּאָה לֵית בֵּיה גָּוֶון, לֵית בֵּה חֵיזוּ בְּאִתְגַּלְיָיא.

533. There are two pearls and there is a curtain between them. The supernal pearl is hidden and has no visible color.

534. הַאי מַרְגְּלָא, כַּד שָׁארֵי לְאִתְגַּלְיָיא, נַהֲרִין, ז' אַתְוָון גְּלִיפִין, בַּלְטִין וְנָצְצִין וּבָקְעִין בְּקִיעִין וְקַסְטִירִין, וְנַהֲרִין כָּל חַד וְחַד. וְאִינּוּן ז' אַתְוָון, אִינּוּן תְּרֵין שְׁמָהָן מְחַקְּקִין בְּהַהוּא מַרְגְּלָא. וּבְיוֹמָא דְּשַׁבָּת, נָצְצִין וְנַהֲרִין, וּפַתְחִין פַּתְחִין, וְנַפְקֵי וְשַׁלְטֵי. וְאִינּוּן אֲדי"ד יד"ו, מִתְנָצְצֵי אַתְוָון, וּבְנְצִיצוּ דִּלְהוֹן, עָאלִין דָּא בְּדָא, וְנַהֲרִין דָּא בְּדָא.

534. When the supernal pearl is about to be revealed, seven shining engraved letters come out, piercing through palaces, and illuminate each one of them. These seven letters are the two names which are engraved upon the pearl. On the Shabbat day they sparkle and shine, and they come out through doorways and rule. These are *Aleph-Hei-Yud-Hei* and *Yud-Hei-Vav*. The letters glitter, and by their glitter they intermingle and shine, the one within the other.

535. וְכַד עָאלִין דָּא בְּדָא, נָהֲרִין דָּא מִגּוֹ דָּא, בִּתְרֵין גְּווֹנִין. חַד גָּוֶון חִוָּור, וְחַד גָּוֶון סוּמָק. וּמֵאִינּוּן תְּרֵין גְּווֹנִין, אִתְעֲבִידוּ תְּרֵין שְׁמָהָן אַחֲרָנִין, עַד דְּסַלְּקִין אַתְוָון לְשֶׁבַע שְׁמָהָן.

535. When these letters are combined, they illuminate from within each

other by two colors: white, WHICH IS RIGHT, and red, WHICH IS LEFT –
MEANING THAT THEY DO NOT REALLY BECOME ONE GRADE BUT THE
ALEPH-HEI-YUD-HEI TURNS TO BE THE RIGHT SIDE AND *YUD-HEI-VAV*
TURNS TO BE THE LEFT ONE – AND THEY ARE BOTH UNITED. Of these
two colors, two other names are formed, until the letters produce seven
names, FOR EACH ONE OF THE LETTERS OF *ALEPH-HEI-YUD-HEI* AND
YUD-HEI- VAV BECOMES ONE NAME.

536. א׳ נָפִיק וְנָצִיץ, וְעָאל בְּאָת ו׳, וְנַהֲרִין תַּרְוַוייהוּ, בִּתְרֵין גְּווֹנִין,
וְאִינּוּן תְּרֵין שְׁמָהָן, חַד אִקְרֵי יְדוָ״ד, וְחַד אִקְרֵי אֵ״ל, וְנַהֲרִין כַּחֲדָא. ה׳
נָפִיק וְנָצִיץ, וְעָאל בְּאָת ה׳ וְנַהֲרִין תַּרְוַוייהוּ, בִּתְרֵין גְּווֹנִין, וְאִינּוּן תְּרֵין
שְׁמָהָן, חַד אִקְרֵי יְדֹוִד רָזָא דֶּאֱלֹהִים. וְחַד אִקְרֵי אֱלֹהִים. וְנַהֲרִין
כַּחֲדָא. י׳ עָאל בִּי׳, וְנַהֲרִין וּנְצִיצִין כַּחֲדָא, וְעָאלוּ דָא בְּדָא, וְנַהֲרִין
תַּרְוַוייהוּ, גְּלִיפִין מְחַקְּקָן כַּחֲדָא, וְאִינּוּן זַקְפָן רֵישָׁא, נְהִירִין מְנַצְצִין
עַנְפִּין סַלְקִין מֵהַאי סִטְרָא, וּמֵהַאי סִטְרָא, וְאִינּוּן חַד סָרֵי עַנְפִּין.

536. HE EXPLAINS HOW THE SEVEN LETTERS BECOME SEVEN NAMES.
HE SAYS THAT the letter *Aleph* OF THE NAME *ALEPH-HEI-YUD-HEI* comes
out shining and enters into the letter *Vav* OF THE NAME *YUD-HEI-VAV*. And
they illuminate in two colors, WHITE AND RED – AS MENTIONED ABOVE,
and become two Names: one Name is called Yud Hei Vav Hei and the other
one is called '*Aleph-Lamed*' (meaning: *El*), and both of them shine together.
The letter *Hei* OF THE NAME *ALEPH-HEI-YUD-HEI* comes out shining and
enters and combines with the letter *Hei* OF THE *NAME YUD-HEI-VAV*. And
they illuminate in two colors, WHITE AND RED, and become two Names.
One is called 'Yud Hei Vav Hei', in the secret of THE VOWELING OF
Elohim, IN WHICH THE LETTER *YUD* IS VOWELED WITH A SEMIVOWEL
(*CHATAF-SEGOL (E)*), AND THE *HEI* WITH THE VOWEL *CHOLAM (O)*, AND
THE *VAV* WITH *CHIRIK (I)*). And one is called 'Elohim', and the letters shine
together. *Yud* OF *ALEPH-HEI-YUD-HEI* enters into the *Yud* OF *YUD-HEI-VAV*
and they both shine, penetrating each other, imprinted upon and engraved
together. And they lift their head, MEANING THAT THEY ATTAIN THE THREE
FIRST SFIROT, shining and glittering. And eleven branches shoot forth from
each side, THE RIGHT AND THE LEFT, AND TOGETHER THEY ARE
TWENTY-TWO BRANCHES, THE SECRET OF THE TWENTY-TWO LETTERS.

537. וְאִלֵּין תְּרֵין אַתְוָון דְּנַהֲרָן, מִתְחַבְּקָן דָּא בְּדָא, אִינּוּן יְדוֹ״ד יְדוֹ״ד מַצפָּץ מַצפָּץ, בְּרָזָא דִּתְלֵיסָר מְכִילָן דְּרַחֲמֵי. וְאִלֵּין תְּרֵין אַתְוָון, כַּד עָאלִין דָּא בְּדָא, וְכַד מִתְחַבְּקָן דָּא בְּדָא, זַקְפִין רֵישָׁא, וְנָהֲרָן וּמְנַצְצָן עַל כֹּלָּא, בְּאִינּוּן חַד סָרֵי עַנְפִּין, דְּנָפְקִין בְּכָל סְטָר.

537. Those two shining letters – THE *YUD* OF *ALEPH-HEI-YUD-HEI* AND THE *YUD* OF *YUD-HEI-VAV* – embracing each other are Yud Hei Vav Hei, Yud Hei Vav Hei, *Mem-Tzadi-Pe-Tzadi, Mem-Tzadi-Pe-Tzadi,* in the secret of the thirteen attributes of Mercy. When these two letters interpenetrate, and embrace each other, and lift their heads, ATTAINING THE FIRST THREE SFIROT, they shine and glitter upon all, with eleven branches shooting forth from each side, ELEVEN FROM THE LEFT AND ELEVEN FROM THE RIGHT. AND TOGETHER THEY ARE THE 22 LETTERS OF THE TORAH, AS MENTIONED ABOVE, FOR THE WHOLE TORAH AND WISDOM ARE REVEALED BY THE 22 LETTERS.

538. ה׳ דְּאִשְׁתְּאַר, אִיהִי סַלְקָא בִּשְׁמָא חַד, לְאִתְחַבְּרָא בַּהֲדַיְיהוּ, וְאִיהִי אֲדֹנָי. וְכָל אִלֵּין שְׁמָהָן, בַּלְטִין וְנָצְצִין וְנָפְקֵי וְשַׁלְטֵי בְּהַאי יוֹמָא. כֵּיוָן דְּאִלֵּין שַׁלְטֵי, נָפַק הַהוּא מַרְגְּלָא עִלָּאָה, בַּלְטָא מְנַצְצָא. וּמִגּוֹ נְצִיצוּ דִּילָהּ, לָא אִתְחֲזֵי בָּהּ גַּוְון.

538. The remaining *Hei* OF *ALEPH-HEI-YUD-HEI* is raised by one Name, *Aleph-Dalet-Nun-Yud*, to join with them. FROM THEN ON HE EXPLAINS THAT THIS LETTER DESCENDED FROM THERE TO THE LOWER PEARL. And all those raised, shining Names issue and rule on that SHABBAT day. Since they rule, the supernal pearl, THE FIRST THREE SFIROT OF BINAH, comes out, protruding and shining without any color.

539. כַּד נָפְקָא, בָּטַשׁ בְּאִלֵּין שְׁמָהָן, חַד שְׁמָא מִנַּיְיהוּ אֲדֹנָי, דְּאִיהוּ שְׁבִיעָאָה, מִתְעַטְּרָא וְעָאל בְּמַרְגְּלָא תַּתָּאָה, וְאִתְיַישַׁב שְׁמָא אַחֲרָא תְּחוֹתֵיהּ, וְאִיהוּ י״ה. וְאִסְתְּחַר הַהוּא מַרְגְּלָא עִלָּאָה בֵּיהּ, וּמִתְעַטְּרָא הַהוּא נְצִיצוּ דְּנָצִיץ, בְּהַאי שְׁמָא.

539. When THE PEARL comes out, it unites with AND GIVES PLENTY TO those Names, *ALEPH-HEI-YUD-HEI,* AND *YUD-HEI-VAV,* WHICH ARE ITS

SEVEN LOWER SFIROT. Then, one of the Names, *Aleph-Dalet-Nun-Yud*, WHICH IS MALCHUT FROM THE CHEST AND BELOW, which is the seventh, is crowned and enters the lower pearl, WHICH IS MALCHUT. Then another Name replaces *ALEPH-DALET-NUN-YUD*. This is *Yud-Hei*, NAMELY CHOCHMAH AND BINAH. Then the supernal pearl is settled by the name OF *YUD-HEI*, and it is adorned by the radiation of the light of this Name.

540. לְבָתַר דְּבָטַשׁ בְּהָנֵי שְׁמָהָן, נָפְקִין מִינַיְיהוּ שִׁבְעִים עַנְפִּין לְכָל סְטָר, וּמִתְחַבְּרָן כֻּלְּהוּ כַּחֲדָא, וְאִתְעֲבֵיד רְתִיכָא וְכֻרְסְיָיא חֲדָא, לְהַהוּא מַרְגְּלָא עִלָּאָה, וְשַׁלְטָא בְּעִטְרוֹי, מַלְכָּא בְּכֻרְסְיָיא, בְּיוֹמָא דָא, וְחַדֵּי כֹּלָּא. כֵּיוָן דְּחַדֵּי כֹּלָּא, יָתִיב מַלְכָּא עַל כֻּרְסְיָיא, וְסָלִיק בְּשַׁבְעִין עַנְפִּין כֻּרְסְיָיא, כִּדְקָאמְרָן.

540. After THE SUPERNAL PEARL unites with AND IS BESTOWED WITH PLENTY BY those Names, *ALEPH-HEI-YUD-HEI* AND *YUD-HEI-VAV* AS MENTIONED ABOVE, seventy branches shoot forth from all the sides, WHICH ARE ZEIR ANPIN. And all of them join together and become a Chariot and a Throne to the supernal pearl. And the King, WHICH IS CHOCHMAH, is crowned on that day and rules, and all rejoice. Since all rejoice, the King sits on His Throne, which is raised by seventy branches as we have mentioned – FOR THE SEVENTY BRANCHES ARE ZEIR ANPIN, WHOSE CHESED, GVURAH, TIFERET AND MALCHUT BECOME ITS FOUR LEGS.

541. וְאִינּוּן תְּרֵין אַתְוָון, סַלְקִין וְנַחְתִּין, וְנַהֲרִין וּמִתְעַטְּרִין אַתְוָון כ״ב, כְּלָלָא דְאוֹרַיְיתָא. בַּטְשֵׁי בִּתְרֵי אַתְוָון קַדְמָאֵי, וְסַלְקֵי לְחַד, בְּשִׁית שִׁבְטִין, וּלְחַד בְּשִׁית שִׁבְטִין אַחֲרָנִין. וְאִלֵּין אִינּוּן י״ב שִׁבְטִין דְּיִשְׂרָאֵל עִלָּאָה.

541. Those two letters, NAMELY, THE TWO *YUD'S* OF THE NAMES *ALEPH-HEI-YUD-HEI* AND *YUD-HEI-VAV* ascend and descend, and illuminate, and adorn the 22 letters, being the whole Torah. They unite with the two first letters OF THE 22 LETTERS, NAMELY THE *TAV* AND THE *SHIN,* IN REVERSE ALPHABETICAL ORDER. And they ascend THROUGH THEIR LIGHT, the one to the six tribes, and the other to the other six tribes.

These are the twelve tribes of supernal Yisrael, NAMELY YISRAEL-SABA, THE SECRET OF THE FOUR GRADES – CHESED AND GVURAH, TIFERET AND MALCHUT, EVERY ONE OF WHICH INCLUDES THE THREE COLUMNS, BRINGING TOGETHER THE TWELVE.

542. תּוּ, אִלֵּין תְּרֵין אַתְוָון, סַלְּקִין וְנַחְתִּין, וּבַטְשֵׁי בִּתְרֵין אַתְוָון, דְּסֵיפָא דכ"ב אַתְוָון. וְסַלְּקֵי, חַד בְּחָמֵשׁ דַּרְגִּין, וְחַד בְּחָמֵשׁ דַּרְגִּין. וְאִלֵּין עֲשַׂר אֲמִירָן לְאַכְלְלָא לְכ"ב אַתְוָון, י"ב שְׁבָטִין בִּתְרֵין אַתְוָון, וַעֲשַׂר אֲמִירָן דִּתְרֵין אַתְוָון דְּסֵיפָא, הָא כ"ב אַתְוָון, כְּלָלָא דְּאוֹרַיְיתָא. וְרָזָא דָּא, יָרִית מַרְגְּלָא עִלָּאָה, בְּהַהוּא כֻּרְסְיָיא דְּע"ב, וְנָהֲרִין כ"ב אַתְוָון.

542. Those two letters, THE TWO YUD'S IN THE NAMES ALEPH-HEI-YUD HEI AND YUD-HEI-VAV, ascend and descend and unite with the two last letters of the 22 letters WHEN ARRANGED IN REVERSE ORDER OF TAV -SHIN-RESH-KOF, NAMELY, BET AND ALEPH. They ascend AND ILLUMINATE five grades each, CORRESPONDING TOGETHER TO TEN SAYINGS. These ten sayings include the 22 letters. The twelve tribes EMERGED BY the two letters TAV AND SHIN, TOGETHER WITH the ten sayings of the last two letters, BET AND ALEPH, which are the whole Torah, NAMELY, ZEIR ANPIN WHICH IS CALLED 'TORAH' AND WHICH IS CREATED FROM THOSE 22 LETTERS. The supernal pearl inherits this secret upon a throne of 72, and the 22 letters shine.

543. מַרְגְּלָא תַּתָּאָה, בְּשַׁעֲתָא דְּיָתִיב מַרְגְּלָא עִלָּאָה בְּהַהוּא כֻּרְסְיָיא דְּע"ב, וְנָהֲרִין כ"ב אַתְוָון. כְּדֵין הַהוּא מַרְגְּלָא תַּתָּאָה דְּהוּא בַּחֲשׁוֹכָא, מִסְתַּכֵּל בְּהַהוּא נְהִירוּ, בְּחֵילָא דְּתוּקְפָּא דְּאִינּוּן אַתְוָון, דְּאִתְרְשִׁים בְּהוֹן, דְּאִקְרוּן אֲדֹנָי, וּכְדֵין אִתְנְהִיר וְסָלִיק הַהוּא נְהוֹרָא, וְנָטִיל כָּל אִינּוּן כ"ב אַתְוָון עִלָּאִין, וְשָׁאִיב לוֹן הַהוּא מַרְגְּלָא בְּגַוֵּיהּ, וְנָהִיר נְהִירוּ דְּנִצִיץ לְע"ב עִיבָר.

543. When the supernal pearl sits upon the throne of the 72 and the 22 letters illuminate, then the lower pearl, which is in the darkness, observes

the illumination OF THE 22 LETTERS through the letters imprinted upon it – which are called *Aleph-Dalet-Nun-Yud*. Then that light ascends and shines and receives all those 22 supernal letters, and the lower pearl draws them. And then it shines in 72 directions.

544. כֵּיוָן דְּהַאי מַרְגְּלָא, נָצִיץ וְשָׁאִיב לְאִינוּן אַתְוָון בַּהֲדָה, כְּדֵין מַרְגְּלָא עִלָּאָה אִתְמְשַׁךְ בַּהֲדַיְיהוּ, וְאִתְדַּבָּק מַרְגְּלָא בְּמַרְגְּלָא, וַהֲוֵי כֹּלָּא חַד. וְדָא אִיהוּ רָזָא חֲדָא דְּתוּשְׁבַּחְתָּא, וְהָא אוֹקִימְנָא.

544. Since that LOWER pearl shines and derives all those letters from it, the supernal pearl is then attracted to them, and pearl cleaves to pearl. THE LOWER PEARL, WHICH IS MALCHUT, CLINGS TO THE SUPERNAL PEARL, WHICH IS BINAH. AND BOTH OF THEM become one. This is the secret of a certain praise which we already expounded upon, THE SONG OF PRAISE 'EL ADON', WHICH IS SAID ON SHABBAT DAY.

545. אַתְוָון, כַּד נָצְצִין מֵהַאי סִטְרָא, וּמֵהַאי סִטְרָא, דָּא אִיהוּ סִיבְתָא דִּי בְּגַוַוייהוּ, בֵּין מַרְגְּלָא לְמַרְגְּלָא, כְּדֵין אִתְעֲבֵידוּ רָזָא דִּשְׁמָא קַדִּישָׁא דְמ"ב אַתְוָון. בְּכֹלָּא רָזָא דִּשְׁמָא קַדִּישָׁא דְע"ב אַתְוָון, דִּרְתִיכָא עִלָּאָה, וְכֹלָּא, הַאי וְהַאי, אִתְקְרֵי שַׁבָּת, וְדָא אִיהוּ רָזָא דְּשַׁבָּת.

545. The 22 letters which shine on both sides, TO THE RIGHT SIDE AND TO THE LEFT, are the curtain between THE SUPERNAL pearl and THE LOWER pearl. And they become the secret of the Holy Name of *Mem-Bet* (= 42) letters, and this is the secret of the Holy Name of *Ayin-Bet* (= 72) letters of the supernal Chariot. And both THE NAME OF *MEM-BET* AND THE NAME OF *AYIN-BET* are called 'Shabbat', and this is the secret of Shabbat.

End of Ra'aya Meheimna (the Faithful Shepherd)

A Synopsis
We read of the meaning of "remember," that is Zeir Anpin, above which there is no forgetfulness. We are reminded to remember the Sabbath day.

546. זָכוֹר רָזָא דִּדְכוּרָא אִיהוּ, רָזָא דִּדְכוּרָא דְּנָקִיט כָּל שַׁיְיפֵי דְּעָלְמָא עִלָּאָה. אֶת יוֹם הַשַּׁבָּת, לְאַסְגָּאָה מַעֲלֵי שַׁבַּתָּא, דְּאִיהוּ לַיְלָה, וְדָא אִיהוּ אֶת. לְקַדְּשׁוֹ, דְּאִצְטְרִיךְ קְדוּשָׁה מִגּוֹ עַמָּא קַדִּישָׁא, וּלְאִתְעַטְּרָא בְּהוּ כַּדְקָא חֲזֵי.

546. "Remember" is the secret of the Male, WHICH IS ZEIR ANPIN, which receives all the limbs, NAMELY, THE WHOLE MOCHIN of the supernal world, NAMELY BINAH. "The (Heb. 'et') Shabbat day" includes Shabbat eve, which is night, NAMELY, MALCHUT WHICH IS CALLED 'NIGHT'. The word "Et" expresses it, FOR MALCHUT IS CALLED "ET." It is necessary "to keep it holy," for it must receive Holiness from the Holy Nation and be crowned by them, as is proper.

547. זָכוֹר, אֲתָר דְּלֵית לֵיהּ שִׁכְחָה, וְלָא קַיְימָא בֵּיהּ שִׁכְחָה דְּהָא לֵית שִׁכְחָה בַּאֲתָר דִּבְרִית עִלָּאָה, וְכָ"שׁ לְעֵילָּא. וּלְתַתָּא, אִית שִׁכְחָה, אֲתָר דְּאִצְטְרִיךְ לְאַדְכְּרָא, וְעַ"ד כְּתִיב, יִזָּכֵר עֲוֹן אֲבוֹתָיו וְגוֹ'. וְאִית תַּמָּן מְמָנָן, דְּאַדְכְּרָן זַכְיָין דְּבַר נָשׁ, וְחוֹבוֹי.

547. "Remember" comes from a place wherein there is no forgetfulness, for there is no forgetfulness in the place of the supernal Covenant, WHICH IS YESOD, and all the more so above IN ZEIR ANPIN. Below, IN MALCHUT, there is forgetfulness, for this is the place wherein men should be reminded, as it is written: "May the iniquity of his fathers be remembered" (Tehilim 109:14).

548. וְלֵית שִׁכְחָה קָמֵי כֻּרְסְיָיא קַדִּישָׁא, מַה דְּאִיהוּ קָמֵיהּ. וּמַאן אִיהוּ קָמֵיהּ. זָכוֹר. וְכָ"שׁ לְעֵילָּא. בְּגִין דְּכֹלָּא רָזָא דִּדְכוּרָא אִיהוּ, וְתַמָּן אִתְגְּלִיף רָזָא דִּשְׁמָא קַדִּישָׁא יְדֹ"ו. וּלְתַתָּא, אִצְטְרִיךְ לְאִתְקַדְּשָׁא, וּבַמֶּה אִתְקַדַּשׁ. בְּזָכוֹר, דְּהָא מִנֵּיהּ נָטִיל כָּל קְדוּשָׁן וְכָל בִּרְכָּאן. וְדָא, כַּד מִתְעַטְּרֵי מַעֲלֵי שַׁבַּתָּא, עַל עַמָּא קַדִּישָׁא כַּדְקָא יָאוֹת, בִּצְלוֹתִין וּבִבְעוּתִין, וּבְסִדּוּרָא דַּחֲדְוָה.

548. There is no forgetfulness before the Holy Throne, that is, she who stands in front of the Holy Throne, NAMELY, BINAH. And who stands

before the Throne? "Remember," NAMELY, ZEIR ANPIN, FOR ZEIR ANPIN STANDS BEFORE BINAH AND RECEIVES FROM HER. OF ZEIR ANPIN IT IS SAID: "THERE IS NO FORGETFULNESS BEFORE THE THRONE OF YOUR HONOR." Above ZEIR ANPIN THERE IS NO FORGETFULNESS, for there lies the whole secret of the Male, wherein the secret of the Holy Name, *Yud-Hei-Vav,* is engraved. Below, NAMELY, IN MALCHUT, men should be sanctified by fulfilling the commandment "remember" (the Shabbat day), WHICH IS ZEIR ANPIN from which MALCHUT derives all her blessings and Holiness. Then Shabbat eve, NAMELY, MALCHUT, is crowned, as it should be, by the prayers of the Holy Nation and by joyful preparations.

549. וְאִי תֵּימָא, זָכוֹר, לָא אִצְטְרִיךְ לְאִתְקַדְּשָׁא, דְּהָא מִנֵּיהּ נָפְקִין כָּל קְדוּשִׁין דְּעָלְמָא. לָאו הָכִי. דְּהָא דָא אִצְטְרִיךְ לְאִתְקַדְּשָׁא בִּימָמָא, וְדָא אִצְטְרִיךְ לְאִתְקַדְּשָׁא בְּלֵילְיָא, וְכָל קְדוּשִׁין נַטְלִין לוֹן יִשְׂרָאֵל לְבָתַר, וְאִתְקַדְּשָׁן בְּקַדּוּשֵׁי דְקוּדְשָׁא בְּרִיךְ הוּא.

549. You might say that "remember," NAMELY ZEIR ANPIN, does not need to be sanctified BY YISRAEL, for all THE BLESSINGS AND Holiness in the world come from it. This is not so, for ZEIR ANPIN should be sanctified on the SHABBAT day AND MALCHUT on the SHABBAT night, and only then Yisrael are sanctified by the Holiness of the Holy One, blessed be He.

34. "Honor your father and your mother"

A Synopsis

We are told to honor the Holy One, blessed be He, who is our father, and Malchut, who is our mother, by studying the Torah and observing the commandments. A man is created from two drops of seed – one from his father and one from his mother, and the parents have an obligation to teach their children to learn Torah and good deeds. There are three partners in creating a man: the father and mother, who gave him his body, and God, who gave him his soul. A man must honor all three of them. He must also perform correct actions with all of his heart and desire, with the correct intentions.

550. כַּבֵּד אֶת אָבִיךָ וְאֶת אִמֶּךָ, בְּכָל זִינֵי יְקָר, לְמֶחְדֵי לוֹן בְּעוֹבָדֵי דְּכַשְׁרָאָן, כד״א גִּיל יָגִיל אֲבִי צַדִּיק, וְדָא אִיהוּ יְקָרָא דַּאֲבוֹי וּדְאִמֵּיה.

550. "Honor your father and your mother" (Shemot 20:12). HONOR THEM with respect, and gladden them with good deeds, as it is written: "The father of the righteous shall greatly rejoice" (Mishlei 23:24), for this is the way one should honor his father and mother.

רעיא מהימנא

551. כַּבֵּד אֶת אָבִיךָ וְאֶת אִמֶּךָ. כַּבְּדֵהוּ בִּכְסוּת נְקַיָּיה, דְּהַיְינוּ כַּנְפֵי מִצְוָה, כַּבֵּד אֶת ה' מֵהוֹנֶךָ, דָּא תּוֹרָה וּמִצְוֹת. הה״ד, אוֹרֶךְ יָמִים בִּימִינָהּ בִּשְׂמֹאלָהּ וְגוֹ'. דְּעָנִי לָאו אִיהוּ בַּר נָשׁ, אֶלָּא מִן הַתּוֹרָה וּמִן הַמִּצְוֹת, אִשְׁתְּמוֹדַע, דְּבָתַר דְּאוּקְמוּהָ מָארֵי מַתְנִיתִין אֵין עָנִי אֶלָּא מִן הַתּוֹרָה וּמִן הַמִּצְוֹת, דְּעַתְרָא דְּבַר נָשׁ אוֹרַיְיתָא וּמִצְוֹת.

Ra'aya Meheimna (the Faithful Shepherd)

551. "Honor your father and your mother." Honor THE HOLY ONE, BLESSED BE HE, WHICH IS CALLED "YOUR FATHER," AND MALCHUT WHICH IS CALLED "YOUR MOTHER," by a clean fringed garment, MEANING, A NICE PRAYING SHAWL (HEB. *TALIT*) WHICH IS CALLED 'AN ARTICLE FOR FULFILLING A COMMANDMENT'. "Honor Hashem with your substance"

(Mishlei 2:8), meaning, by studying the Torah and fulfilling the commandments, as it is written: "Length of days is in her right hand, and in her left hand are riches and honor" (Mishlei 3:15). A man is considered poor when he does not study the Torah or fulfill the commandments. It is known, since it has been explained by the sages of the Mishnah, that poverty is the lack of the Torah and the precepts, which are a man's wealth.

552. וּבְגִין דָּא, כַּבֵּד אֶת יְיָ' מֵהוֹנֶךָ, וְלָא תִּשְׁתַּדֵּל בְּאוֹרַיְיתָא, כְּדֵי לְהִתְגַּדֵּל בָּה. כְּמָה דְאוּקְמוּהָ חַבְרַיָּיא, וְאַל תַּעֲשֵׂם עֲטָרָה לְהִתְגַּדֵּל בָּהֶם, וְלֹא תֹאמַר אַקְרָא בַּעֲבוּר שֶׁיִּקְרָאוּנִי רַבִּי, אֶלָּא גַּדְּלוּ לַיְיָ' אִתִּי. כַּבֵּד אֶת יְיָ' מֵהוֹנֶךָ, כְּבֶן דְּאִיהוּ חַיָּיב בִּיקָרָא דַּאֲבוֹי וְאִמֵּיהּ.

552. Therefore, "Honor Hashem with your substance," and do not study the Torah in order to magnify yourself. As the students of the Torah said: Do not make them into a wreath, wherewith to magnify yourself. And do not say: I will study the Torah so I will be called "Rabbi," but rather, "O magnify Hashem with me" (Tehilim 34:4). "Honor Hashem with your substance," as a child must honor his father and mother.

553. בְּגִין דְּאִיהוּ מְשׁוּתָּף מִתְרֵין טִפִּין, דְּמִנְּהוֹן נוֹצַר בַּר נָשׁ. מִטִפָּה דְאַבוּהָ, חַוָּורוּ דְעַיְינִין, וְגַרְמִין וְאֶבְרִין. וּמִטִפָּה דְאִמֵּיהּ, שָׁחוֹר דִי בְעַיְינִין, וְשַׂעֲרָא וּמַשְׁכָא וּבִשְׂרָא. וְרַבִּיאוּ לֵיהּ בְּאוֹרַיְיתָא, וְעוֹבְדִין טָבִין.

553. A man is created from two drops of seed. From his father's sperm the bones of the body and the whiteness of the eyes ARE CREATED, and from his mother's the blackness of the eyes, the skin and the flesh ARE CREATED. And both of them raise the child to learn the Torah and good deeds.

554. דְּבַר נָשׁ חַיָּיב לְלַמֵּד בְּנוֹ תּוֹרָה, דִּכְתִיב וְשִׁנַּנְתָּם לְבָנֶיךָ. וְאִי לָא אוֹלִיף לֵיהּ אוֹרַיְיתָא וּפִקוּדִין, כְּאִילוּ עָבֵיד לֵיהּ פֶּסֶל, וּבְגִין דָּא לֹא תַעֲשֵׂה לְךָ פֶסֶל. וְעָתִיד לִהְיוֹת בֵּן סוֹרֵר וּמוֹרֶה, וּמְבַזֶּה אָבוּי וְאִמֵּיהּ, וְגוֹזֵל מִנֵּיהּ כַּמָּה בִּרְכָּאן. דְּהוֹאִיל וְאִיהוּ עַם הָאָרֶץ, חָשִׁיד אִיהוּ עַל כֹּלָּא, וַאֲפִילוּ עַל שְׁפִיכוּת דָּמִים, וְגִילוּי עֲרָיוֹת, וע״ז. דְּמַאן דְּאִיהוּ עַם

הָאָרֶץ. וְאָזִיל לַאֲתַר דְּלָא אִשְׁתְּמוֹדְעוּן לֵיהּ, וְלָא יָדַע לְבָרְכָא, חַשְׁדִינָן לֵיהּ דְּאִיהוּ עע״ז.

ע״כ רעיא מהימנא

554. A man should teach his son Torah, as it is written: "And you shall teach them diligently to your children" (Devarim 6:7), otherwise he is as if he makes him idols. Therefore, it is written: "You shall not make for yourself any carved idol" (Shemot 20:4). The ignorant son is destined to be an unruly child who treats his father and mother with contempt and robs them of many blessings. For since he is ignorant, he is suspected to transgress in everything, even idolatry, incest and bloodshed. For when the ignorant goes where he is not known and does not know how to say a benediction, he is believed to be an idol worshipper.

End of Ra'aya Meheimna (the Faithful Shepherd)

555. כַּבֵּד אֶת אָבִיךָ כד״א כַּבֵּד אֶת יְיָ׳ מֵהוֹנֶךָ. מֵהוֹנֶךָ: מִמָּמוֹנָךְ. מֵהוֹנֶךָ: מֵחִנָּךָ. בְּחֶדְוָה דִּנְגּוּנָא, לְמֶחֱדֵי לִבָּא, דְּהָא דָא חֶדְוָה דְּלִבָּא, כְּגַוְונָא דָא נִגּוּנָא דְּכָל עָלְמָא. עוֹבָדִין דְּכַשְׁרָאָן דְּהַהוּא בְּרָא, חַדֵּי לִבָּא דְּאָבוּהָ וּדְאִמֵּיהּ. מֵהוֹנֶךָ, מִמָּמוֹנָךְ לְכָל מַה דְּאִצְטְרִיכוּ.

555. "Honor your father" MEANS the same as "Honor Hashem with your substance." "...your substance..." means your money. And "your substance" means your grace, MEANING, with a joyful tune, for then the heart is gladdened as when any melody is sounded. The son's good deeds gladden the hearts of his father and mother. Thus, "with your substance," means with your money, for anything necessary.

556. כְּגַוְונָא דְּבַר נָשׁ אוֹקִיר לְקוּדְשָׁא בְּרִיךְ הוּא, הָכִי אִצְטְרִיךְ לְאַבָּא וּלְאִמָּא, בְּגִין דְּשׁוּתָּפוּתָא חֲדָא אִית לוֹן בְּקוּדְשָׁא בְּרִיךְ הוּא עָלֵיהּ. וּכְמָה דְּאִצְטְרִיךְ לְמִדְחַל לְקוּדְשָׁא בְּרִיךְ הוּא, הָכִי אִצְטְרִיךְ לְמִדְחַל לְאָבוּהָ וּלְאִמֵּיהּ, וּלְאוֹקִיר לוֹן כַּחֲדָא, בְּכָל זִינֵי יְקָר.

556. As a man honors the Holy One, blessed be He, so should he HONOR his father and mother, for they are in partnership over him with the Holy One,

.blessed be He. FOR THERE ARE THREE PARTNERS IN CREATING MAN: THE HOLY ONE, BLESSED BE HE, THE FATHER, AND MOTHER. HIS FATHER AND MOTHER GIVE HIM THE BODY, AND THE HOLY ONE, BLESSED BE HE, GIVES HIM THE SOUL. As a man should have great fear of the Holy One, blessed be He, so should he respect his father and mother, and honor them by all the means he has.

557. לְמַעַן יַאֲרִיכוּן יָמֶיךָ, בְּגִין דְּאִית יוֹמִין לְעֵילָא, דְּתַלְיָין בְּהוּ חַיֵּי בַּר נָשׁ בְּהַאי עָלְמָא. וְאוֹקִימְנָא עַל אִינּוּן יוֹמִין דְּבַר נָשׁ בְּהַהוּא עָלְמָא לְעֵילָא, וְכֻלְּהוּ קַיְימִין קָמֵי קוּדְשָׁא בְּרִיךְ הוּא, וּבְהוּ אִשְׁתְּמוֹדְעָן חַיֵּי דְּבַר נָשׁ.

557. "…that your days may be long…" (Shemot 20:12); For there are days above – NAMELY, THE SEVEN SFIROT: CHESED, GVURAH, TIFERET, NETZACH, HOD, YESOD AND MALCHUT – on which a man's life in this world depends. We have explained that these are man's days in that world above, THE SEVEN SFIROT, which are placed before the Holy One, blessed be He. And by them man's life is known.

558. עַל הָאֲדָמָה אֲשֶׁר יְיָ' אֱלֹהֶיךָ נוֹתֵן לָךְ. אַבְטָחוּתָא לְאִתְהַנְיָא בְּאַסְפָּקְלַרְיָא דְּנַהֲרָא, וְרָזָא דָּא עַל הָאֲדָמָה, דָּא אַסְפַּקְלַרְיָא דְּנַהֲרָא, בְּאִינּוּן יוֹמִין עִלָּאִין, דְּנַהֲרִין מִגּוֹ מַבּוּעָא דְּכֹלָּא.

558. "…in the land which Hashem your Elohim gives you…" (Ibid.); this is a promise given to enjoy the shining mirror. "…in the land…" is the mirror which shines upon the supernal days – CHESED, GVURAH, TIFERET, NETZACH, HOD, YESOD AND MALCHUT OF ZEIR ANPIN – and which shines from the fount of everything, WHICH IS BINAH.

559. מַאי שְׁנָא, בְּאִלֵּין תְּרֵין פִּקּוּדִין דְּאוֹרַיְיתָא, דִּכְתִּיב בְּהוּ לְמַעַן יַאֲרִיכוּן יָמֶיךָ, בְּדָא, וּבְשִׁלּוּחַ הַקֵּן. אֶלָּא תְּרֵין פִּקּוּדִין אִלֵּין, כֻּלְּהוּ תַּלְיָין לְעֵילָא. אַבָּא וְאִמָּא, רָזָא דְּזָכוֹר וְשָׁמוֹר כַּחֲדָא. וּבְגִינֵי כַּךְ כְּתִיב לְמַעַן יַאֲרִיכוּן יָמֶיךָ. וּבְשִׁלּוּחַ הַקֵּן, דִּכְתִּיב שַׁלֵּחַ תְּשַׁלַּח אֶת הָאֵם וְאֶת הַבָּנִים תִּקַּח לָךְ לְמַעַן יִיטַב לָךְ וְגוֹ', רָזָא דְּעָלְמָא עִלָּאָה, דְּלָא

אִתְיְיהִיב בֵּיה רְשׁוּ לְאִסְתַּכְּלָא, וְאִצְטְרִיךְ לְשַׁלַּח מִגּוֹ שְׁאֶלְתָּא וְאִסְתַּכְּלוּתָא בֵּיה.

559. HE ASKS: What is the difference between the two commandments of the Torah, of which it is written: "that your days may be long," this one and the other which refers to driving away the mother-bird from the nest? HE ANSWERS: Both of the commandments refer to the world above. Aba and Ima are the secret of "remember" and "keep" in one, BEING ZEIR ANPIN AND MALCHUT. Therefore, it is written: "that your days may be long." In regards to letting the mother-bird go from the nest, it is written: "but you shall surely let the mother go, and take the young to you; that it may be well with you, and that you may prolong your days" (Devarim 22:7). This is the secret of the supernal world, WHICH IS BINAH BEING CALLED 'MOTHER', MEANING that no permission is given to look at her, and one should steer away from asking any questions or looking at her.

560. וְאֶת הַבָּנִים תִּקַּח לָךְ, דִּכְתִיב, כִּי שְׁאַל נָא לְיָמִים רִאשׁוֹנִים וְגוֹ' מִקְצֵה הַשָּׁמַיִם וְעַד קְצֵה הַשָּׁמָיִם. אֲבָל לְעֵילָא מִקְצֵה הַשָּׁמַיִם, שַׁלַּח תְּשַׁלַּח מֵרַעְיוֹנֶיךְ לְמִשְׁאַל.

560. "...and take the young to you..." HERE, "THE YOUNG" ARE ZEIR ANPIN AND MALCHUT, as it is written: "For ask now of the days that are past, which were before you since the day that Elohim created man upon the earth and from the one side of heaven to the other" (Devarim 4:32) – MEANING THAT ONE CAN ASK A QUESTION OF AND LOOK AT HEAVEN, WHICH IS ZEIR ANPIN CALLED 'HEAVEN', WHICH CAN BE INVESTIGATED AND OBSERVED. But above the heaven, ZEIR ANPIN, you not should let your thoughts investigate.

561. וּבְדָא כְּתִיב, לְמַעַן יִיטַב לָךְ וְהַאֲרַכְתָּ יָמִים, לְמַעַן אִיטַב לָךְ לָא כְּתִיב, אֶלָּא לְמַעַן יִיטַב לָךְ. וְיַאֲרִיכוּן יָמֶיךְ לָא כְּתִיב, אֶלָּא וְהַאֲרַכְתָּ יָמִים. לְמַעַן יִיטַב לָךְ, הַהוּא אֲתַר דְּאוֹטִיב לְכֹלָּא, וְאִיהוּ עָלְמָא דְּסָתִים וְגָנִיז. וְהַאֲרַכְתָּ יָמִים, כְּמָה דִּכְתִיב, תִּקַּח לָךְ, בִּרְשׁוּתָא דְּבַר נָשׁ אִיהוּ.

561. Therefore, it is written: "that it may be well with you and that you may prolong your days." It says, "that it may be well with you," in the third

person. It is not written: 'that your days may be long', but rather, "that you may prolong your days." "…it may be well with you…" refers to the place from which goodness issues for everyone, and this is the hidden and unrevealed world, BINAH. "…that you may prolong your days…" meaning, BY YOUR OWN STRENGTH, as it is written: "and take the young to you," for one is capable OF CLINGING TO THE CHILDREN, WHICH ARE ZEIR ANPIN AND MALCHUT. FOR THROUGH THEM ONE HAS A LENGTH OF DAYS.

562. וְאִי אִזְדְּמַן לֵיהּ עוֹבָדָא וִיכַוֵּון בֵּיהּ, זַכָּאָה אִיהוּ. וְאַף עַל גַּב דְּלָא מְכַוֵּון בֵּיהּ, זַכָּאָה אִיהוּ, דְּעָבֵיד פִּקּוּדָא דְּמָרֵיהּ. אֲבָל לָא אִתְחֲשִׁיב כְּמַאן דְּעָבֵיד רְעוּתָא לִשְׁמָהּ, וִיכַוֵּון בֵּיהּ, בִּרְעוּתָא דְּאִסְתַּכְּלוּתָא בִּיקָרָא דְּמָרֵיהּ, כְּמַאן דְּלָא יָדַע לְמִסְבַּר סְבָרָא, דְּהָא בִּרְעוּתָא תַּלְיָא מִלָּה לִשְׁמָהּ. וּבְעוֹבָדָא דִּלְתַתָּא לִשְׁמָהּ, אִסְתַּלָּק עוֹבָדָא לְעֵילָא, וְאִתְתָּקַן כַּדְקָא יָאוֹת.

562. If one has the opportunity to perform A PRECEPT and he does so attentively, then he is considered as a righteous man. And even if this is not his intention, he is still considered righteous because he fulfills the commandment of his Master – FOR PERFORMING A PRECEPT DOES NOT REQUIRE AN INTENTION. Yet he who does not understand the reason is not considered as he who directs his will for the sake of doing it and meditates upon it, with the wish to behold the glory of his Master. This is because an intentional deed depends upon the wish. Such a deed below arouses a corresponding act above, WHICH IS MALCHUT, CALLED 'AN ACT', and is properly rectified.

563. כְּגַוְונָא דָּא, בְּעוֹבָדָא דְּגוּפָא, אִתְתָּקַן עוֹבָדָא דְּנַפְשָׁא, בְּהַהוּא רְעוּתָא. דְּהָא קוּדְשָׁא בְּרִיךְ הוּא בָּעֵי לִבָּא, וּרְעוּתָא דְּבַר נָשׁ. וַאֲפִילוּ הָכִי, אִי לָאו תַּמָּן רְעוּתָא דְּלִבָּא דְּאִיהוּ עִקָּרָא דְּכֹלָּא, עַל דָּא צַלֵּי דָוִד וְאָמַר, וּמַעֲשֵׂה יָדֵינוּ כּוֹנְנָה עָלֵינוּ וְגוֹ'. דְּהָא לֵית כָּל בַּר נָשׁ חַכִּים, לְשַׁוָּאָה רְעוּתָא וְלִבָּא, לְתַקָּנָא כֹּלָּא וְיַעֲבִיד עוֹבָדָא דְּמִצְוָה. עַל דָּא צַלֵּי צְלוֹתָא דָּא, וּמַעֲשֵׂה יָדֵינוּ כּוֹנְנָה עָלֵינוּ.

563. As in a physical action, an act of the soul is also manifested through that intention, for the Holy One, blessed be He, desires the heart and

intention of man. If a person does not fulfill the commandment with his heart, which is the most essential quality, of this prayed David: "and establish the work of our hands upon us; O prosper it, the work of our hands" (Tehilim 90:17), for not everyone has the capability to be mindful and to direct his heart, to correct everything, and perform a precept. He therefore said this prayer, "and establish the work of our hands upon us."

564. מַאי כּוֹנְנָה עָלֵינוּ. כּוֹנְנָה, וְאַתְקִין תִּקּוּנָךְ לְעֵילָא כַּדְקָא יֵאוֹת. עָלֵינוּ, אַף עַל גַּב דְּלֵית אֲנָן יַדְעֵי לְשַׁוָּאָה רְעוּתָא, אֶלָּא עוֹבָדָא בִּלְחוֹדוֹי. מַעֲשֵׂה יָדֵינוּ כּוֹנְנֵהוּ. לְמַאן. לְהַהוּא דַּרְגָּא דְּאִצְטְרִיךְ לְאִתְתַּקְנָא. כּוֹנְנֵהוּ, בְּחִבּוּרָא חֲדָא בַּאֲבָהָן, לְמֶהֱוֵי מִתַּתְקְנָא בְּהוֹן, בְּהַאי עוֹבָדָא, כַּדְקָא יֵאוֹת.

564. HE ASKS FOR THE MEANING OF: "and establish the work of our hands upon us," AND HE ANSWERS THAT "establish" MEANS accomplish your establishment properly above. "..upon us..." although we know only how to act, but not how to direct the right intentions of the heart. "O prosper it, the work of our hands". HE ASKS: Prosper whom? AND ANSWERS: The grade that needs establishing, NAMELY MALCHUT. It must prosper so that it can be united with the fathers – WHICH ARE CHESED, GVURAH AND TIFERET OF ZEIR ANPIN – and in whom it will be properly established, through this deed.

35. "You shall not murder. You shall not commit adultery"

A Synopsis

This section tells us that in specific instances killing may be prohibited or permitted, in order to kill those who transgress the law. Intercourse may be prohibited or allowed for correct reasons like procreation. The text goes on to tell how the tonal pause in each commandment allows for the possibility of prohibition or permission under certain circumstances. However, "You shall not bear false witness against your neighbor" is always forbidden. "You shall not covet" is always forbidden except for the desire of the Torah. In truth, the Ten Commandments contain the essence of all celestial and terrestrial commandments, and through their engraving on the tablets of stone they were revealed to all the children of Yisrael. At that time the bodies of the children of Yisrael became lucent, with no impurity, and their souls were bright as they beheld the glory of their Master. The Holy One, blessed be He, was made known both above and below, and He was exalted over all.

565. לֹא תִרְצַח. לֹא תִנְאָף. לֹא תִגְנֹב. לֹא. פָּסְקָא טַעֲמָא בְּכָל הָנֵי תְלָת. וְאִי לָא דְּפָסְקָא טַעֲמָא, לָא הֲוֵי תִקּוּנָא לְעָלְמִין, וְיְהֵא אָסִיר לָן לְקַטְלָא נַפְשָׁא בְּעָלְמָא, אע"ג דְּיַעֲבוֹר עַל אוֹרַיְיתָא. אֲבָל בְּמַה דְּפָסְקָא טַעֲמָא, אָסִיר, וְשָׁרֵי.

565. "You shall not murder. You shall not commit adultery. You shall not steal" (Shemot 20:13-15). UNDER the word "shall not (Heb. *lo*)" in all three commandments, there is a tonal pause, for in the absence of this interruptive mark, harmony would be unattainable in the world. It would be forbidden to kill even one who transgresses the law. However, the presence of the pause TEACHES that in specific instances, killing may be prohibited or permitted.

566. לֹא תִנְאָף. אִי לָאו דְּפָסְקָא טַעֲמָא, אָסִיר אֲפִילוּ לְאוֹלָדָא, אוֹ לְמֶחֱדֵי בְּאִתְּתֵיהּ חֶדְוָה דְּמִצְוָה. וּבַמֶּה דְּפָסְקָא טַעֲמָא, אָסִיר וְשָׁרֵי. לֹא תִגְנֹב. אִי לָאו דְּפָסְקָא טַעֲמָא, הֲוָה אָסִיר אֲפִילוּ לְמִגְנַב דַּעְתָּא דְרַבֵּיהּ בְּאוֹרַיְיתָא. אוֹ דַעְתָּא דְחָכָם, לְאִסְתַּכְּלָא בֵּיהּ. אוֹ דַּיָּינָא דְדָאִין דִּינָא לְפוּם טַעֲנָה, דְּאִצְטְרִיךְ לֵיהּ לְמִגְנַב דַּעְתָּא דְּרַמָּאָה, וּלְמִגְנַב דַּעְתָּא

דְּתַרְוַויְיהוּ, לְאַפְקָא דִינָא לִנְהוֹרָא. וּבַמֶּה דְּפָסְקָא טַעֲמָא, אָסִיר וְשָׁרֵי.

566. "You shall not commit adultery": in the absence of this tonal pause, it would be prohibited to engage in the commandments of procreation or to enjoy marital intercourse. The inclusion of the trope INDICTATES the possibility of prohibition or permission. "You shall not steal": in the absence of the interruptive mark, it would be forbidden to deceive one's Torah teacher or a Torah scholar in order to gaze upon him. Furthermore, it would be prohibited for a judge to trick a swindling claimant or two disputants in order to clarify the truth. However, once again the punctuation INDICTATES that it is permitted or prohibited.

567. לֹא תַעֲנֶה בְרֵעֲךָ עֵד שָׁקֶר. הָכָא לָא פָּסְקָא טַעֲמָא, בְּגִין דְּאָסִיר הוּא כְּלָל כְּלָל. וּבְכָל מִילֵי דְאוֹרַיְיתָא, קוּדְשָׁא בְּרִיךְ הוּא שַׁוֵּי רָזִין עִלָּאִין, וְאוֹלִיף לִבְנֵי נָשָׁא אָרְחָא, לְאִתְתַּקָּנָא בָּהּ, וּלְמֶהַךְ בָּהּ. כְּמָה דְּאַתְּ אָמַר, אֲנִי יְיָ' אֱלֹהֶיךָ מְלַמֶּדְךָ לְהוֹעִיל מַדְרִיכְךָ בְּדֶרֶךְ תֵּלֵךְ.

567. "You shall not bear false witness against your neighbor" (Shemot 20:13). Here there is no tonal pause, indicating that this is always forbidden. The Holy One, blessed be He, has placed supernal mysteries in all the words of Torah and instructed mankind how to strive towards perfection through it, as it is written: "I am Hashem your Elohim who teaches you for your profit, who leads you by the way that you should go" (Yeshayah 48:17).

568. אוּף הָכִי, לֹא תַחְמֹד, לָא פָּסִיק טַעֲמָא כְּלָל. וְאִי תֵּימָא, אֲפִילוּ חֶמְדָּא דְאוֹרַיְיתָא אָסִיר, כֵּיוָן דְּלָא פָּסְקָא. ת"ח, בְּכֻלְּהוּ עֲבַדַת אוֹרַיְיתָא כְּלָל, וּבְהַאי עֲבַדַת פְּרָט. בֵּית רֵעֲךָ שָׂדֵהוּ וְעַבְדוֹ וְגוֹ', בְּכָל מִילֵי דְעָלְמָא. אֲבָל אוֹרַיְיתָא, אִיהִי חֲמוּדַת תָּדִיר, שַׁעֲשׁוּעִים, גִּנְזֵי דְחַיֵּי, אַרְכָּא דְיוֹמִין, בְּעָלְמָא דֵין וּבְעָלְמָא דְּאָתֵי.

568. Also in the commandment: "You shall not covet" (Ibid. 17), the tonal pause is absent. If you say that even desiring Torah is forbidden, due to the absence of the punctuation, come and behold: the previous prohibitions were stated in a general manner. However, specific details were stated in

regards to this prohibition, as it is written: "Your neighbor's house, his field, or his manservant..." (Devarim 5:18). The prohibition extends ONLY towards material possessions, thus excluding the Torah, which is forever desirable. It is delight and eternal life in this world and the World to Come.

569. הָנֵי עֶשֶׂר אֲמִירָן דְּאוֹרַיְיתָא, אִינּוּן כְּלָלָא דְּכָל פִּקּוּדֵי אוֹרַיְיתָא, כְּלָלָא דִּעֵילָּא וְתַתָּא, כְּלָלָא דְּכָל עֲשַׂר אֲמִירָן דִּבְרֵאשִׁית. אִלֵּין אִתְחָקְקוּ עַל לוּחֵי אַבְנִין, וְכָל גְּנִזִין דַּהֲווֹ בְּהוּ, אִתְחָזוּן לְעֵינַיְיהוּ דְּכֹלָּא, לְמִנְדַּע וּלְאִסְתַּכְּלָא בְּרָזָא דְּתרי"ג פִּקּוּדִין דְּאוֹרַיְיתָא דִּכְלִילָן בְּהוּ, כֹּלָּא אִתְחָזֵי לְעֵינִין, כֹּלָּא אִיהוּ בְּסָכְלְתָנוּ, לְאִסְתַּכְּלָא בְּלִבָּא דְיִשְׂרָאֵל כֻּלְּהוּ, וְכֹלָּא הֲוָה נָהִיר לְעֵינַיְיהוּ.

569. The Ten Commandments of the Torah contain the essence of all celestial and terrestrial commandments, the essence of the ten sayings of Creation. They were engraved on tablets of stone and all the hidden things in them were seen by everybody's eyes, so as to conceive and behold the secret of the 613 commandments of the Torah. Everything was revealed to their eyes, through understanding, to the attentive hearts of all of Yisrael. Everything shone before their eyes.

570. בְּהַהוּא שַׁעֲתָא, כָּל רָזִין דְּאוֹרַיְיתָא, וְכָל רָזִין עִלָּאִין וְתַתָּאִין, לָא אַעֲדֵי מִינַּיְיהוּ. בְּגִין דַּהֲווֹ חָמָאן עֵינָא בְּעֵינָא, זִיו יְקָרָא דְּמָרֵיהוֹן, מַה דְּלָא הֲוָה בְּהַהוּא יוֹמָא, מִיּוֹמָא דְּאִתְבְּרֵי עָלְמָא, דְּקוּדְשָׁא בְּרִיךְ הוּא אִתְגְּלֵי בִּיקָרֵיהּ עַל טוּרָא דְסִינַי.

570. At that hour, all the mysteries of the Torah were revealed. No mystery of heaven and earth was held back from them, for they saw the splendor of the glory of their Master; that which has never occurred since the creation of the world: the revelation of the glory of the Holy One, blessed be He, upon Mount Sinai.

571. וְאִי תֵּימָא, הָא תָּנֵינָן דְּחָמָאת שִׁפְחָה עַל הַיָּם, מַה דְּלָא חָמָא יְחֶזְקֵאל נְבִיאָה, יָכוֹל בְּהַהוּא יוֹמָא דְּקַאִימוּ יִשְׂרָאֵל עַל טוּרָא דְסִינַי.

לָאו הָכִי. בְּגִין דְּהַהוּא יוֹמָא דְּקַיְימוּ יִשְׂרָאֵל עַל טוּרָא דְּסִינַי, אַעֲבַר
זוּהֲמָא מִנַּיְיהוּ, וְכָל גּוּפִין הֲווֹ מְצַחְצְחָן, כְּצַחְצְחָא דְּמַלְאָכִין עִלָּאִין,
כַּד מִתְלַבְּשָׁן בִּלְבוּשֵׁי מְצַחְצְחָן, לְמֶעְבַּד שְׁלִיחוּתָא דְּמָרֵיהוֹן.

571. You might say that we learned that upon the crossing of the Red Sea,
even a maid-servant saw more than the prophet Ezekiel – THAT IT
RESEMBLED the day when Yisrael stood upon Mount Sinai. This is not so.
For on this day all the dross was removed from them, and their bodies
became as lucent as the angels above when they are clothed in radiant
garments for the accomplishments of their Master's mission.

572. וּבְהַהוּא מַלְבּוּשָׁא מְצַחְצְחָא, עָאלִין לְאֶשָּׁא, וְלָא דַּחֲלִין. כְּגַוְונָא
דְּהַהוּא מַלְאָכָא דְּמָנוֹחַ, כַּד אִתְחֲזֵי לֵיהּ, וְעָאל בְּשַׁלְהוֹבָא, וְסָלִיק
לִשְׁמַיָּא, דִּכְתִיב, וַיַּעַל מַלְאַךְ יְיָ' בְּלַהַב הַמִּזְבֵּחַ. וְכַד אַעֲבַר מִנַּיְיהוּ
הַהוּא זוּהֲמָא, אִשְׁתְּאָרוּ יִשְׂרָאֵל גּוּפִין מְצוּחְצָחִין בְּלָא טִנּוּפָא כְּלָל,
וְנִשְׁמָתִין לְגוֹ כְּזוֹהֲרָא דִּרְקִיעָא, לְקַבְּלָא נְהוֹרָא.

572. They penetrated fire without fear wearing those radiant garments, as
we have read concerning the angel who appeared to Manoach, who entered
a flame and ascended to heaven, as it is written: "The angel of Hashem
ascended in the flame of the altar" (Shoftim 13:20). When all the impurity
was removed from Yisrael, their bodies became lucent, without any
impurity whatsoever, and the souls within the bodies were as bright as the
splendor of the sky, ready to receive light.

573. הָכִי הֲווֹ יִשְׂרָאֵל, דַּהֲווֹ חָמָאן וּמִסְתַּכְּלָן גּוֹ יְקָרָא דְּמָרֵיהוֹן, מַה
דְּלָא הֲוֵי הָכִי עַל יַמָּא, דְּלָא אִתְעֲבַר זוּהֲמָא מִנַּיְיהוּ בְּהַהוּא זִמְנָא.
וְהָכָא בְּסִינַי דְּפָסְקָא זוּהֲמָא מִגּוּפָא, אֲפִילוּ עוּבָּרִין דִּבְמְעֵי אָמֵן, הֲווֹ
חָמָאן וּמִסְתַּכְּלָן בִּיקָרָא דְּמָרֵיהוֹן. וְכֻלְּהוּ קַבִּילוּ כָּל חַד וְחַד, כְּדְקָא חֲזֵי
לֵיהּ.

573. Such was the state of Yisrael when they beheld the glory of their
Master. It was not thus at the Red Sea, when the filth had not yet been

removed from them. There, at Mount Sinai, when impurity was removed from their bodies, even the embryos in their mother's wombs could observe their Master's glory, and everyone received according to his worth.

574. וְהַהוּא יוֹמָא, הֲוָה חֶדְוָה קֵמֵי קוּדְשָׁא בְּרִיךְ הוּא, יַתִּיר מִיוֹמָא דְּאִתְבְּרֵי עָלְמָא, בְּגִין דְּיוֹמָא דְּאִתְבְּרֵי עָלְמָא, לָא הֲוָה בְּקִיוּמָא, עַד דְּקַבִּילוּ יִשְׂרָאֵל אוֹרַיְיתָא, דִּכְתִיב אִם לֹא בְרִיתִי יוֹמָם וְלַיְלָה חֻקּוֹת שָׁמַיִם וָאָרֶץ לֹא שָׂמְתִּי.

574. On that day the Holy One, blessed be He, rejoiced more than on any previous day since He had created the world, for the world had no proper existence before Yisrael received the Torah, as it is written: "If my Covenant be not day and night, it is as if I had not made the ordinances of heaven and earth" (Yirmeyah 33:25).

575. כֵּיוָן דְּקַבִּילוּ יִשְׂרָאֵל אוֹרַיְיתָא עַל טוּרָא דְּסִינַי, כְּדֵין אִתְבַּסַּם עָלְמָא, וְאִתְקְיָּימוּ שְׁמַיָּא וְאַרְעָא, וְאִשְׁתְּמוֹדַע קב"ה עֵילָא וְתַתָּא, וְאִסְתַּלָּק בִּיקָרֵיהּ עַל כֹּלָּא. וְעַל הַהוּא יוֹמָא כְּתִיב יְיָ׳ מָלַךְ גֵּאוּת לָבֵשׁ לָבֵשׁ יְיָ׳ עֹז הִתְאַזָּר. וְאֵין עֹז, אֶלָּא תוֹרָה. שֶׁנֶּאֱמַר יְיָ׳ עֹז לְעַמּוֹ יִתֵּן יְיָ׳ יְבָרֵךְ אֶת עַמּוֹ בַשָּׁלוֹם.

575. Once Yisrael received the Torah on Mount Sinai, the world was completely sweetened and heaven and earth received a proper foundation. And the Holy One, blessed be He, was made known both above and below, and He was exalted in His glory over all. Concerning that day it is written: "Hashem reigns, He is clothed with majesty, Hashem is robed, he has girded Himself with strength" (Tehilim 92:1), and "strength" is the Torah, as it is written: "Hashem gives strength to His people, Hashem blesses His people with peace" (Tehilim 29:11).

MISHPATIM

Names of articles

1. "And these are the judgments which you shall set before them"

A Synopsis
Rabbi Shimon says that the title verse refers to the rules concerning reincarnation – the judgments of souls that are to be sentenced according to their punishable acts.

א. פָּתַח ר' שִׁמְעוֹן וְאָמַר, וְאֵלֶּה הַמִּשְׁפָּטִים אֲשֶׁר תָּשִׂים לִפְנֵיהֶם, תַּרְגוּם, וְאִלֵּין דִּינַיָּא דִּתְסַדֵּר קָדָמֵיהוֹן. אִלֵּין אִינּוּן סִדּוּרִין דְּגִלְגּוּלָא, דִּינִין דְּנִשְׁמָתִין, דְּאִתְדָנוּ כָּל חַד וְחַד לְקַבֵּל עוֹנְשֵׁיהּ.

1. Rabbi Shimon opened with the words, "And these are the judgments which you shall set before them" (Shemot 21:1). ALSO IN THE ARAMAIC TRANSLATION, IT SPEAKS OF JUDGMENTS. These are the rules concerning reincarnation, NAMELY, the judgments of souls that INCARNATE AGAIN IN THIS WORLD to be sentenced each according to its punishable acts.

2. "If you buy a Hebrew servant..."

A Synopsis

Rabbi Shimon continues by saying that unperfected souls are forced to be born again until they have finished correcting the six levels of Chesed, Gvurah, Tiferet, Netzach, Hod and Yesod. Only when they are from the aspect of the seventh, the Shechinah, are they allowed to go free. We learn of the three souls: the one called a maidservant, the one called a handmaid, and the one called the King's daughter. Rabbi Shimon also speaks of the maidservant, that is the Neshamah of Briyah, the manservant, that is the Ruach of Yetzirah, and the handmaid of the King's daughter, that is the Nefesh of Asiyah. A righteous man can also be given a Nefesh of Atzilut and a Ruach of Atzilut and even a Neshamah from the aspect of Aba and Ima. If he has more merit he is given Yud Hei Vav Hei which is the secret of man in the upper way of Atzilut. Then he is named after the image of his Master, and will "have dominion over the fish of the sea." He will have power throughout the firmaments.

2. כִּי תִקְנֶה עֶבֶד עִבְרִי שֵׁשׁ שָׁנִים יַעֲבֹד וּבַשְּׁבִיעִית יֵצֵא לַחָפְשִׁי חִנָּם. חַבְרַיָּיא, עִידָן הָכָא, לְגַלָּאָה כַּמָּה רָזִין טְמִירִין דְּגִלְגּוּלָא. כִּי תִקְנֶה עֶבֶד עִבְרִי שֵׁשׁ שָׁנִים יַעֲבֹד. כַּד נִשְׁמָתָא אִתְחַיְּיבַת בְּגִלְגּוּלָא, אִם הִיא מִסִּטְרָא דְּהַהוּא עֶבֶד מְטַטְרוֹן, דְּאִיהוּ כָּלִיל שִׁית סְטְרִין, כְּתִיב בֵּיהּ שֵׁשׁ שָׁנִים יַעֲבֹד, גִּלְגּוּלִין דִּילָהּ לָא מִתְחַיְּיבָא אֶלָּא שִׁית שְׁנִין, עַד דְּאַשְׁלִימַת שֵׁשׁ דַּרְגִּין, מֵהַהוּא אֲתַר דְּאִתְנְטִילַת.

2. "If you buy a Hebrew servant, six years he shall serve, and in the seventh he shall go out free" (Shemot 21:2). RABBI SHIMON SAID TO THEM, friends, the time has come to reveal some hidden mysteries concerning incarnation. "If you buy a Hebrew servant, six years he shall serve," NAMELY, the soul is required to incarnate, EITHER BECAUSE OF SINS, OR BECAUSE IT HAD NOT COMPLETELY FULFILLED DURING ITS LIFETIME THE TORAH AND THE PRECEPTS. IT IS FORCED TO COME BACK TO THIS WORLD AND DON A BODY, THAT IS, TO BE BORN AGAIN AND FINISH WHAT WAS IMPOSED ON IT FOR THE SEVENTY YEARS OF LIFE IN THIS WORLD. If it is of the aspect of THE ANGEL Metatron IN THE WORLD OF BRIYAH, which comprises six levels OF CHESED, GVURAH, TIFERET, NETZACH, HOD, AND YESOD, it is written of it, "six years he shall serve." It is

required to incarnate only until IT FINISHES correcting the six levels, CHESED, GVURAH, TIFERET, NETZACH, HOD, AND YESOD, of the same place whence it was taken, NAMELY METATRON.

3. אֲבָל אִם נִשְׁמָתָא הִיא מִסִּטְרָא דִּשְׁכִינְתָּא, דְּאִיהִי שְׁבִיעִית וַדַּאי מַה כְּתִיב, וּבַשְּׁבִיעִית יֵצֵא לַחָפְשִׁי חִנָּם, דְּצַדִּיק, וַדַּאי לֵית בֵּיהּ מְלָאכָה, כֵּיוָן דְּלֵית בֵּיהּ מְלָאכָה, לֵית בֵּיהּ שִׁעְבּוּד. וְנִשְׁמָתָא דְּאִיהִי מִתַּמָּן, אִתְּמַר בָּהּ וּבַשְּׁבִיעִית יֵצֵא לַחָפְשִׁי חִנָּם, לֵית בָּהּ שִׁעְבּוּדָא.

3. But if the soul is from the aspect of the Shechinah, which is seventh, NAMELY MALCHUT OF ATZILUT THAT IS SEVENTH TO CHESED, GVURAH, TIFERET, NETZACH, HOD, AND YESOD, surely it is written OF IT, "and in the seventh he shall go out free." For no work pertains to a righteous man, WHO MERITS A SOUL FROM MALCHHUT OF ATZILUT, AS HE IS OF THE ASPECT OF SHABBAT, TO WHICH NO WORK, NAMELY EXTRACTING MOCHIN, APPLIES. Since no work or enslavement are affixed to him, it says of the soul that originates there, "and in the seventh he shall go out free;" no enslavement binds it.

4. אַדְהָכִי, הָא סָבָא נָחַת לְגַבֵּיהּ, א"ל, אִי הָכִי, רַבִּי, מַה תּוֹסֶפֶת לְנִשְׁמָתָא דְּאִיהִי מִנָּהּ, דְּאִתְּמַר בָּהּ, לֹא תַעֲשֶׂה כָל מְלָאכָה אַתָּה וּבִנְךָ וּבִתֶּךָ וְעַבְדְּךָ וְגו'.

4. In the meanwhile, behold an old sage coming down to him. He said to him, Rabbi, if this is so, what about the addition of the soul that is derived from it, of which it says, "in it you shall not do any work, you, nor your son, nor your daughter, your manservant, nor your maidservant..." (Shemot 20:10)?

5. א"ל, סָבָא סָבָא, וְאַתְּ שָׁאִיל דָּא, דְּוַדַּאי הַאי עַל נִשְׁמָתָא דְּצַדִּיק אִתְּמַר, דְּאע"ג דְּאִתְחַיָּיב לְאַחְתָא בְּגִלְגּוּלָא בְּכָל אִלֵּין, אֲפִילּוּ בְּעֶבֶד וְאָמָה, וּבְעִירָן דְּאִינּוּן אוֹפַנִּים, אוֹ בְּכָל חַיָּין, דְּמִנְּהוֹן נִשְׁמָתִין דִּבְנֵי נָשָׁא, כְּתִיב בָּהּ לֹא תַעֲשֶׂה כָל מְלָאכָה. וְהַאי אִיהוּ, לֹא תַעֲבֹד בּוֹ עֲבוֹדַת עָבֶד, בְּצַדִּיק דְּאִיהוּ יוֹם הַשַּׁבָּת, לֹא תַעֲבֹד בּוֹ עֲבוֹדַת עָבֶד,

-277-

דְּאִיהוּ יוֹם דְּחוֹל.

5. RABBI SHIMON said to him, old man, do you ask this?! Assuredly it was said of the soul of a righteous man, WHICH IS FROM ATZILUT, that though it had to come down to incarnate in all these, NAMELY, even in a manservant or a maidservant, or cattle, which are Wheels, NAMELY IN THE WORLD OF ASIYAH, or in any other living creatures whence human souls originate, it is written of it, "you shall not do any work." This is the meaning of, "you shall not compel him to work as a bondservant" (Vayikra 25:39), NAMELY you shall not compel a righteous man, who is Shabbat, to work as a bondservant, METATRON, who is a weekday.

6. אֲבָל סָבָא סָבָא, שַׁבָּת דְּאִיהִי בַּת יְחִידָה, וְאִיהִי בַּת זוּגֵיהּ דְּצַדִּיק, דְּאִיהוּ שַׁבָּת. מַאי אִם אַחֶרֶת יִקַּח לוֹ. א"ל הָא וַדַּאי הַבְדָּלָה, חוּלוֹ שֶׁל שַׁבָּת, דְּאִית אַחֲרָא דְּלָא אִתְקְרִיאַת חוּלוֹ שֶׁל שַׁבָּת, אֶלָּא חוּלוֹ שֶׁל טֻמְאָה שִׁפְחָה. א"ל. וְהָא חוּלוֹ שֶׁל שַׁבָּת מַאי הִיא. א"ל, דָּא אֲמָתָא, דְּאִיהִי גּוּפָא דְּבַת יְחִידָה דְּעָלָה אִתְּמַר, אִם אַחֶרֶת יִקַּח לוֹ.

6. Yet old man, Shabbat is an only daughter, NAMELY MALCHUT, and the soulmate of the righteous, who is ALSO Shabbat, NAMELY, ACCORDING TO THE VERSE, "AND IN THE SEVENTH HE SHALL GO OUT FREE." If this is so, what is the meaning of, "If he take another wife" (Shemot 21:10)? He said to him, a distinction should be made there. She is the secular part of Shabbat, AND THE VERSE, "IF HE TAKE ANOTHER WIFE," REFERS TO IT. For there is another KIND OF NON-HOLINESS that is not the secular part of Shabbat but of the impure handmaid. He said to him, so what is the secular part of Shabbat? He said to him, it is the maidservant IN BRIYAH, who is the body of the only daughter, as the only daughter, WHO IS MALCHUT OF ATZILUT, IS CLOTHED IN IT AS A SOUL IN A BODY. It is of it that it says, "If he take another wife."

7. תָּא חֲזִי, נִשְׁמָתָא אִית דְּאִתְקְרִיאַת אָמָה, וְאִית נִשְׁמָתָא דְּאִתְקְרִיאַת שִׁפְחָה, וְנִשְׁמָתָא אִית דְּאִתְקְרִיאַת בְּרַתָּא דְּמַלְכָּא. הָכָא אִית אִישׁ, דְּאִתְּמַר בֵּיהּ יְיָ' אִישׁ מִלְחָמָה. וְאִית אִישׁ, דְּאִתְּמַר בֵּיהּ וְהָאִישׁ גַּבְרִיאֵל.

7. Come and see, there is a soul called a maidservant, a soul that is called a handmaid and a soul that is called the King's daughter. EACH IS NAMED AFTER THE PLACE WHENCE IT ORIGINATES, OR WHERE IT INCARNATES. There is a man here, NAMELY, A MAN THAT SELLS HIS DAUGHTER FOR A MAIDSERVANT, of whom it says, "Hashem is a man of war" (Shemot 15:3), NAMELY ZEIR ANPIN OF ATZILUT, and a man, of whom it says, "and the man Gabriel" (Daniel 9:21) IN THE WORLD OF BRIYAH. THIS IS THE MEANING OF, "AND IF A MAN," THAT IS THE HOLY ONE, BLESSED BE HE, "SELL HIS DAUGHTER TO BE A MAIDSERVANT" (SHEMOT 21:7), NAMELY, THE SOUL OF ATZILUT CALLED "THE ONLY ONE OF HER MOTHER" (SHIR HASHIRIM 6:9), TO INCARNATE IN THE WORLD OF BRIYAH, TO WHICH BELONGS THE ASPECT OF THE BODY OF THE SHECHINAH THAT IS CALLED A MAIDSERVANT.

‏8. וּבְגִין דָּא, נִשְׁמְתָא דְּאִיהִי מְחַיְיבָא בְּגִלְגּוּל, אִם הִיא בְּרָתָא דְּקוּדְשָׁא בְּרִיךְ הוּא, אִי תֵּימָא דְּאִזְדְּבָן בְּגוּפָא נוּכְרָאָה, דְּתַמָּן שָׁלְטָנוּתָא דְּיֵצֶר הָרָע דְּאִיהוּ מִסִּטְרָא דְּסָמָאֵ״ל. ח״ו. דְּהָא כְּתִיב, אֲנִי יְיָ׳ הוּא שְׁמִי וּכְבוֹדִי לְאַחֵר לֹא אֶתֵּן דְּאִיהוּ יֵצֶר הָרָע.

8. For this reason, if the soul that requires incarnation is the daughter of the Holy One, blessed be He, NAMELY, DRAWN FROM MALCHUT OF ATZILUT, it must not be thought of that it would be sold to a foreign body OF THE KLIPAH, where the Evil Inclination of the aspect of Samael rules. Heaven forbid ONE WOULD SAY SO, for it is written, "I am Hashem, that is My name; and My glory will I not give to another" (Yeshayah 42:8), which is the Evil Inclination. FOR IF THE SOUL IS FROM ATZILUT, EVEN THOUGH IT INCARNATES INTO THE WORLD OF BRIYAH, NO WORK OR ENSLAVEMENT TO THE KLIPOT APPLIES TO IT, AS MENTIONED.

‏9. וְהַהוּא גוּפָא, דְּשַׁרְיָא בְּרָתָא דְּמַלְכָּא, אִי תֵּימָא דְּאִזְדְּבָן בְּכִתְרִין תַּתָּאִין דִּמְסָאֲבוּ, חֲלִילָה וְחָס. עָלָהּ אִתְּמַר וְהָאָרֶץ לֹא תִּמָּכֵר לִצְמִיתוּת כִּי לִי הָאָרֶץ. מַאן גּוּפָא דִּבְרָתָא דְּמַלְכָּא. דָּא מְטַטְרוֹן. וְהַאי גוּפָא אִיהוּ אָמָה דִּשְׁכִינְתָּא, אע״ג דְּאִיהִי נִשְׁמְתָא דְּאִיהִי בְּרָתָא דְּמַלְכָּא שְׁבוּיָה תַּמָּן, בְּגִלְגּוּלָא אַתְיָא מַה כְּתִיב בָּהּ וְכִי יִמְכּוֹר אֶת בִּתּוֹ לְאָמָה לֹא תֵצֵא כְּצֵאת הָעֲבָדִים.

9. And if you ask whether the body where the King's daughter abides, WHICH IS CALLED A MAIDSERVANT, is sold to the lower crowns of impurity, heaven forbid! It says of it, "the land shall not be sold for ever; for the land is Mine" (Vayikra 25:23). The body of the King's daughter is Metatron, and the body is the Shechinah's maidservant, WHICH THE SHECHINAH DONS. And though the King's daughter's soul is trapped there, incarnating there, it is written of it, "And if a man sell his daughter to be a maidservant, she shall not go out as the menservants do."

10. וְעוֹד וְכִי יִמְכּוֹר אִישׁ, דָּא קוּדְשָׁא בְּרִיךְ הוּא. אֶת בִּתּוֹ: אִלֵּין יִשְׂרָאֵל, דְּאִינּוּן מִסִּטְרָא דְּבַת יְחִידָה, אִתְקְרִיאוּ בִּתּוֹ. וְאִי תֵּימָא דְיִפְּקוּן, כְּגַוְונָא דְּאִלֵּין מִסִּטְרָא דְּעֶבֶד, דְּאִיהוּ מְטַטְרוֹ"ן, דְּנַפְקוּ בִּמְנוּסָה מִמִּצְרַיִם, לֹא תֵצֵא כְּצֵאת הָעֲבָדִים, הה"ד, כִּי לֹא בְחִפָּזוֹן תֵּצֵאוּ וּבִמְנוּסָה לֹא תֵלֵכוּן.

10. Also, "And if a man sell" refers to the Holy One, blessed be He, and "his daughter" is Yisrael, who are from the aspect of the only daughter. THAT IS, SINCE THEY ARE DRAWN FROM MALCHUT, they are called His daughter. And if you argue that they will go out IN THE FUTURE like those WHO LEFT EGYPT, WHO WERE from the aspect of the servant Metatron, who were fleeing Egypt, IT SAYS OF IT, "she shall not go out as the menservants do." This is the meaning of, "For you shall not go out with haste, nor go by flight" (Yeshayah 52:12).

11. תָּא חֲזֵי, ב"נ כַּד אִתְיְלִיד, יָהֲבִין לֵיהּ נַפְשָׁא מִסִּטְרָא דִּבְעֵירָא, מִסִּטְרָא דְּדַכְיוּ, מִסִּטְרָא דְּאִלֵּין דְּאִתְקְרוּן אוֹפַנֵּי הַקּוֹדֶשׁ. זָכָה יַתִּיר, יַהֲבִין לֵיהּ רוּחָא, מִסִּטְרָא דְּחַיּוֹת הַקּוֹדֶשׁ. זָכָה יַתִּיר, יַהֲבִין לֵיהּ נִשְׁמְתָא, מִסִּטְרָא דְּכֻרְסְיָיא. וּתְלַת אִלֵּין, אִינּוּן אָמָה עֶבֶד וְשִׁפְחָה דִּבְרַתָּא דְמַלְכָּא.

11. Come and see, when a man is born, he is given a Nefesh of the animal element from the side of purity, from those that are called the holy Wheels, NAMELY FROM THE WORLD OF ASIYAH. If he gains further merit, he is given a Ruach from the aspect of the holy living creatures, NAMELY FROM THE WORLD OF YETZIRAH. If he merits further, he is given a Neshamah

from the part of the throne, NAMELY FROM THE WORLD OF BRIYAH. These three are the maidservant, the manservant and the handmaid of the King's daughter. THEY ARE NESHAMAH, RUACH AND NEFESH FROM THE EXPANDING OF MALCHUT THROUGH BRIYAH, YETZIRAH AND ASIYAH. THE MAIDSERVANT IS THE NESHAMAH OF BRIYAH, THE MANSERVANT THE RUACH OF YETZIRAH AND THE HANDMAID IS THE NEFESH OF ASIYAH.

12. זָכָה יַתִּיר, יַהֲבִין לֵיה נַפְשָׁא בְּאֹרַח אֲצִילוּת, מִסִּטְרָא דְּבַת יְחִידָה, וְאִתְקְרִיאַת אִיהִי בַּת מֶלֶךְ. זָכָה יַתִּיר, יַהֲבִין לֵיה רוּחָא דְּאֲצִילוּת. מִסִּטְרָא דְּעַמּוּדָא דְּאֶמְצָעִיתָא, וְאִקְרֵי בֵּן לְקוּדְשָׁא בְּרִיךְ הוּא, הה"ד בָּנִים אַתֶּם לַיְיָ' אֱלֹהֵיכֶם. זָכָה יַתִּיר, יַהֲבִין לֵיה נִשְׁמָתָא, מִסִּטְרָא דְּאַבָּא וְאִמָּא. הה"ד, וַיִּפַּח בְּאַפָּיו נִשְׁמַת חַיִּים. מַאי חַיִּים. אֶלָּא אִינּוּן י"ה, דְּעָלַיְיהוּ אִתְּמַר, כָּל הַנְּשָׁמָה תְּהַלֵּל יָהּ, וְאִשְׁתְּלִים בֵּיה ידו"ד.

12. If he gains further merit, he is given a Nefesh of the path of Atzilut, from the part of the only daughter called the King's daughter, NAMELY MALCHUT OF ATZILUT. If he is more meritorious, he is given Ruach of Atzilut from the side of the Central Pillar THAT IS ZEIR ANPIN and he is called a child of the Holy One, blessed be He. That is the meaning of, "You are the children of Hashem your Elohim" (Devarim 14:1). If he has more merit he is given a Neshamah from the aspect of Aba and Ima, WHICH ARE BINAH, as written, "and breathed into his nostrils the breath (lit. 'NESHAMAH') of life" (Beresheet 2:7). What is life? It is Yah, WHICH ARE ABA AND IMA, of whom it says, "Let everything that has breath (lit. 'NESHAMAH') praise Yah (Yud Hei)" (Tehilim 150:6). With them, the name of Yud Hei Vav Hei is completed. FOR RUACH AND NEFESH OF ATZILUT ARE VAV HEI AND NESHAMAH OF ATZILUT IS YUD HEI, THUS FORMING TOGETHER YUD HEI VAV HEI.

13. זָכָה יַתִּיר, יַהֲבִין לֵיה ידו"ד בִּשְׁלִימוּ דְּאַתְוָון, יו"ד ה"א וָא"ו ה"א, דְּאִיהוּ אָדָם, בְּאֹרַח אֲצִילוּת דְּעֵילָּא, וְאִתְקְרֵי בִּדְיוּקְנָא דְּמָארֵיה. וְעֲלֵיה אִתְּמַר, וּרְדוּ בִּדְגַת הַיָּם וְגוֹ'. וְהַאי אִיהוּ שׁוּלְטָנוּתֵיה בְּכָל רְקִיעִין, וּבְכָל אוֹפַנִּים וּשְׂרָפִים וְחֵיוָון, וּבְכָל חַיָּילִין וְתוּקְפִין דִּלְעֵילָּא

וְתַתָּא. וּבג"ד, כַּד ב"נ זָכֵי בְּנֶפֶשׁ מִסְטְרָא דְּבַת יְחִידָה, אִתְּמַר בֵּיהּ, לֹא תֵצֵא כְּצֵאת הָעֲבָדִים.

13. If he has more merit, he is given Yud Hei Vav Hei fully spelled THUS: Yud Vav Dalet, Hei ALEPH, Vav ALEPH Vav, Hei ALEPH, which is the secret of man, WHICH NUMERICAL VALUE IS 45, in the upper way of Atzilut. THAT IS ZEIR ANPIN WHEN HE IS A GARMENT TO SUPERNAL ABA AND IMA, WHICH ARE THE SECRET OF CHOCHMAH, WHICH IS SPELLED WITH THE SAME LETTERS AS THOSE OF 'THE POWER OF (HEB. *KO'ACH*) MEM HEI'. And he is named after the image of his Master, and it says of him, "and have dominion over the fish of the sea..." (Beresheet 1:28). He has power throughout the firmaments, over all the Wheels, Serafim and living creatures, and over all the hosts and legions above and below. Hence, when one merits the Nefesh of the aspect of the only daughter, it says of him, "she shall not go out as the menservants do."

3. The old sage (Saba)

A Synopsis

Rabbi Yosi recounts to Rabbi Chiya a number of annoying riddles that had been posed to him by an old merchant with whom he had traveled on a voyage. The two rabbis call for the merchant to speak to them. The merchant says that there are matters of wisdom hidden in every subject of the Torah, all of which require interpretation. He goes on to speak about the verse "And if a priest's daughter be married to a stranger," telling how the soul is drawn from Binah and clothed with Chesed that puts them into the Tree of Life; then the souls soar from there and enter the treasury, Malchut. He says that it is important to know how to be careful when attracting a soul into a body during intercourse. During our lives we must conduct ourselves to the good side so that the great scales are balanced and tipped to the good side.

14. רַבִּי חִיָּיא וְרַבִּי יוֹסִי אִעֲרָעוּ חַד לֵילְיָא בְּמִגְדַּל דְּצוֹר. אִתְאָרְחוּ תַּמָּן וְחַדוּ דָּא בְּדָא. אָמַר רַבִּי יוֹסִי, כַּמָּה חַדֵּינָא דַּחֲמֵינָא אַנְפֵּי שְׁכִינְתָּא, דְּהַשְׁתָּא בְּכָל אָרְחָא דָא, אִצְטַעַרְנָא בַּחֲדָא סָבָא, טַיְיעָא, דַּהֲוָה שָׁאִיל לִי כָּל אָרְחָא.

14. Rabbi Chiya and Rabbi Yosi met one night in a tower in Tyre and lodged there. They rejoiced in each other. Rabbi Yosi said, how glad I am to have seen the face of the Shechinah, for the whole way I was annoyed by a certain old merchant, who questioned me throughout the voyage.

15. מַאן הוּא נָחָשָׁא, דְּפָרַח בַּאֲוִירָא, וְאָזִיל בִּפְרוּדָא, וּבֵין כַּךְ וּבֵין כַּךְ, אִית נַיְיחָא לְחַד נִמָלָה, דְּשָׁכִיב בֵּין שִׁנּוֹי. שָׁרֵי בְּחִבּוּרָא וְסַיֵּים בִּפְרוּדָא. וּמַאי אִיהוּ נִשְׁרָא, דְּקָא מְקַנְּנָא, בְּאִילָן דְּלָא הֲוָה. בְּנוֹי דְּאִתְגְּזָלוּ, וְלָאו מִן בִּרְיָין. דְּאִתְבְּרִיאוּ בַּאֲתָר דְּלָא אִתְבְּרִיאוּ. כַּד סַלְקִין נַחְתִּין, כַּד נַחְתִּין סַלְקִין. תְּרֵין דְּאִינוּן חַד, וְחַד דְּאִינוּן תְּלָתָא. מַהוּ עוּלֵימָתָּא שַׁפִּירְתָּא, וְלֵית לָהּ עַיְינִין, וְגוּפָא טְמִירְתָּא וְאִתְגַּלְיָא, אִיהִי נַפְקַת בְּצַפְרָא, וְאִתְכַּסִּיאַת בִּימָמָא. אִתְקַשְּׁטַת בְּקִשּׁוּטִין דְּלָא הֲווֹ.

15. HE ASKED ME who is the serpent that soared in the air and goes on in

separation so that in the meantime there is rest to a certain ant that lies in its jaws. It starts connected and ends up divided. And what is an eagle that nests in a tree that does not exist; its stolen young are not creatures, because there were created where they were not created. When they go up they go down and when they go down they go up; two that are one and one that is three. What is a beautiful eyeless maiden, whose body is hidden yet revealed, who goes out during the morning and covers herself during the day, and adorns herself with nonexistent adornment.

16. כָּל דָּא שָׁאִיל בְּאָרְחָא, וְאִצְטַעֲרְנָא. וְהַשְׁתָּא אִית לִי נַיְיחָא. דְּאִילוּ הֲוֵינָא כַּחֲדָא, אִתְעַסַּקְנָא בְּמִלֵּי דְּאוֹרַיְיתָא, מַה דַּהֲוֵינָן בְּמִלִּין אַחֲרָנִין דְּתַהוּ. אָמַר רִבִּי חִיָּיא, וְהַהוּא סָבָא טַיְיעָא, יָדְעַת בֵּיה כְּלוּם. אָמַר לֵיה, יָדַעְנָא, דְּלֵית מַמָּשׁוּ בְּמִלּוֹי. דְּאִילוּ הֲוָה יָדַע, יִפְתָּח בְּאוֹרַיְיתָא, וְלָא הֲוָה אָרְחָא בְּרֵיקַנְיָיא. אָמַר רִבִּי חִיָּיא, וְהַהוּא טַיְיעָא אִית הָכָא, דְּהָא לְזִמְנִין בְּאִינּוּן רֵיקָנִין, יִשְׁכַּח גְּבַר זַגִּין דְּדַהֲבָא. אָמַר לֵיה, הָא הָכָא אִיהוּ, וְאַתְקִין חֲמָרֵיה בְּמֵיכְלָא.

16. He asks me all that along the way and I was annoyed. Now I have rest. Had we been together, we would have delved into the words of the Torah, instead of my dealing with other vain things. Rabbi Chiya said, do you know that old merchant? He said to him, I know that his words are senseless, for had he known he would have expounded with the Torah and the way would not have been spent aimlessly. Rabbi Chiya said, the merchant is here. Sometimes one may find golden bells, THAT IS, GOLDEN TONGUES in vain people. He said to him, he is here and gives his donkey fodder.

17. קָרוּ לֵיה, וְאָתָא לְקַמַּיְיהוּ. אָמַר לוֹן, הַשְׁתָּא תְּרֵין אִינּוּן תְּלַת, וּתְלַת אִינּוּן כְּחַד. אָמַר רִבִּי יוֹסִי, לָא אֲמֵינָא לָךְ, דְּכָל מִלוֹי רֵיקָנִין, וְאִינּוּן בְּרֵיקַנְיָיא יָתִיב קַמַּיְיהוּ.

17. They called for him and he came before them. He said to them, now two are three, BECAUSE AFTER JOINING THEM THERE ARE THREE; and three are as one, AS THEY JOINED TOGETHER. Rabbi Yosi said, did I not tell you that his words are senseless and empty? He sat before them.

18. אָמַר לוֹן רַבָּנָן, אֲנָא טַיָּיעָא אִתְעֲבִידְנָא, וּמִיּוֹמִין זְעִירִין, דְּהָא בְּקַדְמֵיתָא לָא הֲוֵינָא טַיָּיעָא, אֲבָל בְּרָא חַד זְעִירָא אִית לִי, וְיָהֲבִית לֵיהּ בְּבֵי סַפְרָא, וּבָעֵינָא דְּיִשְׁתַּדַּל בְּאוֹרַיְיתָא. וְכַד אֲנָא אַשְׁכַּחְנָא חַד מֵרַבָּנָן דְּאָזִיל בְּאָרְחָא, אֲנָא טָעִין אֲבַתְרֵיהּ, וְהַאי יוֹמָא, חֲשִׁיבְנָא דְּאֶשְׁמַע מִלִּין חַדְתִּין בְּאוֹרַיְיתָא, וְלָא שְׁמַעְנָא מִדִי.

18. He said to them, gentlemen, I have become a merchant but a while ago. At first I was not a merchant but I had a young child, whom I placed in school and wanted him to study Torah. THEREFORE I BECAME A MERCHANT SO I COULD SUPPORT HIM. When I find one of the sages travelling, I lead my donkeys after him. Today I have thought I would hear new expositions of the Torah, but have heard nothing.

19. אָמַר ר' יוֹסֵי, בְּכָל מִלִּין דְּשָׁמַעְנָא דְּקָאמַרְתְּ, לָא תַּוְוהֲנָא, אֶלָּא מֵחַד. אוֹ אַנְתְּ בִּשְׁטוּתָא אָמַרְתְּ, אוֹ מִלִּין רֵיקָנִין אִינּוּן. אָמַר הַהוּא סָבָא, וּמַאן אִיהִי. אָמַר עוּלֵימְתָּא שַׁפִּירְתָּא וְכוּ'.

19. Rabbi Yosi said, in all your words, I wondered about one only. Either you spoke in jest or these words are worthless. The old man asked, what is that? RABBI YOSI SAID, a beautiful eyeless maiden, etc.

20. פָּתַח הַהוּא סָבָא וְאָמַר, יְיָ' לִי לֹא אִירָא מַה יַּעֲשֶׂה לִי אָדָם. יְיָ' לִי בְּעֹזְרָי וְגוֹ'. טוֹב לַחֲסוֹת בַּיְיָ' וְגוֹ'. כַּמָּה טָבִין וּנְעִימִין וְיַקִּירִין וְעִלָּאִין מִלִּין דְּאוֹרַיְיתָא, וַאֲנָא הֵיכִי אֵימָא קָמֵי רַבָּנָן, דְּלָא שְׁמַעְנָא מִפּוּמַיְיהוּ עַד הַשְׁתָּא, אֲפִילוּ מִלָּה חֲדָא. אֲבָל אִית לִי לְמֵימַר, דְּהָא לֵית בְּסוֹפָא כְּלָל לְמֵימַר מִלֵּי דְּאוֹרַיְיתָא קָמֵי כֹּלָּא.

20. The old man opened with, "Hashem is on my side: I will not fear: what can a man do to me? Hashem takes my part with those who help me…It is better to take refuge in Hashem…" (Tehilim 118:6-8). How goodly, pleasant, precious and lofty are the words of Torah. And I, how could I say before these sages that I have heard from them not even one word until

now? Yet I should speak up, because I am not ashamed to speak words of Torah in public.

21. אִתְעַטָּף הַהוּא סָבָא, פָּתַח וְאָמַר, וּבַת כֹּהֵן כִּי תִהְיֶה לְאִישׁ זָר הִיא בִּתְרוּמַת הַקֳּדָשִׁים לֹא תֹאכֵל. הַאי קְרָא אַקְרָא אַחֲרָא סָמִיךְ, וּבַת כֹּהֵן כִּי תִהְיֶה אַלְמָנָה וּגְרוּשָׁה וְזֶרַע אֵין לָהּ וְשָׁבָה אֶל בֵּית אָבִיהָ כִּנְעוּרֶיהָ מִלֶּחֶם אָבִיהָ תֹּאכֵל וְכָל זָר לֹא יֹאכַל בּוֹ. הָנֵי קְרָאֵי כְּמַשְׁמָעָן. אֲבָל מִלִּין דְּאוֹרַיְיתָא מִלִּין סְתִימִין אִינּוּן.

21. That old man wrapped himself, and spoke, "And if a priest's daughter be married to a stranger, she may not eat of an offering of the holy things" (Vayikra 22:12). This verse is followed by another, "But if a priest's daughter be a widow, or divorced, and have no child, and has returned to her father's house, as in her youth, she shall eat of her father's bread: but no stranger shall eat of it" (Ibid. 13). These verses may be understood literally, yet the words of the Torah are undisclosed, AS THERE ARE SECRETS IN EACH AND EVERY MATTER.

22. וְכַמָּה אִינּוּן מִלִּין דְּחָכְמְתָא דִּסְתִּימִין בְּכָל מִלָּה וּמִלָּה דְּאוֹרַיְיתָא, וְאִשְׁתְּמוֹדְעָן, אִינּוּן לְגַבֵּי חַכִּימִין, דְּיַדְעִין אָרְחִין דְּאוֹרַיְיתָא. דְּהָא אוֹרַיְיתָא לָאו מִלִּין דְּחֶלְמָא אִינּוּן, דְּקָא אִתְמַסְרָן לְמַאן דְּפָשַׁר לוֹן, וְאִתְמַשְׁכָן בָּתַר פּוּמָא, וע"ד אִצְטְרִיכוּ לְמִפְשַׁר לוֹן לְפוּם אָרְחוֹי. וּמַה אִי מִלִּין דְּחֶלְמָא אִצְטְרִיכוּ לְמִפְשַׁר לוֹן לְפוּם אָרְחוֹי, מִלִּין דְּאוֹרַיְיתָא דְּאִינּוּן שַׁעֲשׁוּעִין דְּמַלְכָּא קַדִּישָׁא, עַל אַחַת כַּמָּה וְכַמָּה דְּאִצְטְרִיכוּ לְמֵהַךְ בְּאֹרַח קְשׁוֹט בְּהוּ, דִּכְתִיב כִּי יְשָׁרִים דַּרְכֵי יְיָ' וְגוֹ'.

22. And many are the matters of wisdom hidden in each and every subject in the Torah, which are known to the wise who know the ways of the Torah. For the Torah is not the context of dreams handed to those who interpret them, or follow the mouth of the interpreter, yet they have to be interpreted according to their ways. And if dream matters need interpreting according to their ways, how much more so the words of the Torah, the delights of the Holy King, needs to be followed in the true path, as written, "for the ways of Hashem are right..." (Hoshea 14:10).

23. הַשְׁתָּא אִית לְמֵימַר, וּבַת כֹּהֵן, דָּא נִשְׁמְתָא עִלָּאָה, בְּרַתֵּיהּ דְּאַבְרָהָם אָבִינוּ קַדְמָאָה לַגִּיּוֹרִין, וְאִיהוּ מָשִׁיךְ, לָהּ לְהַאי נִשְׁמְתָא מֵאֲתַר עִלָּאָה. מַה בֵּין קְרָא דְּאָמַר וּבַת אִישׁ כֹּהֵן, וּבֵין קְרָא דְּאָמַר וּבַת כֹּהֵן, וְלָא כְּתִיב אִישׁ. אֶלָּא, אִית כֹּהֵן דְּאִקְרֵי אִישׁ כֹּהֵן, וְלֹא כֹּהֵן מַמָּשׁ. וְעַל אָרְחָא דָּא, הֲוָה כֹּהֵן, וַהֲוָה סְגָן, וַהֲוָה כה״ג, וַהֲוָה כֹּהֵן דְּלָאו אִיהוּ גָּדוֹל. כֹּהֵן סְתָם, רַב וְעִלָּאָה יַתִּיר מֵאִישׁ כֹּהֵן. וע״ד אִית נִשְׁמְתָא, וְאִית רוּחָא, וְאִית נֶפֶשׁ.

23. Now we should say, "a priest's daughter" is the supernal Neshamah, the daughter of the patriarch Abraham, the first of converts, WHO IS CHESED. He attracts this Neshamah from a supernal place, THAT IS BINAH. HE ASKS, what is the difference between the verses, "And the daughter of any priest" (Vayikra 21:9), and "And if a priest's daughter"? HE ANSWERS, some priests are called 'any priest' but not a real priest. In the same way, there is a priest, an aid and a high priest, and a priest that is not high. A mere priest is higher than any priest. THEREFORE THERE ARE GRADES TO THE SOUL, there are Neshamah, Ruach and Nefesh. THE HIGH PRIEST IS THE NESHAMAH, A PRIEST IS RUACH AND ANY PRIEST IS NEFESH.

24. וּבַת כֹּהֵן כִּי תִהְיֶה לְאִישׁ זָר, דָּא נִשְׁמְתָא קַדִּישָׁא, דְּאִתְמַשְּׁכַת מֵאֲתַר עִלָּאָה, וְעָאלַת לְגוֹ סְתִימוּ דְּאִילָנָא דְּחַיֵּי. וְכַד רוּחָא דְּכַהֲנָא עִלָּאָה נָשְׁבָא, וְיָהִיב נִשְׁמָתִין בְּאִילָנָא דָּא, פַּרְחִין מִתַּמָּן אִינּוּן נִשְׁמָתִין, וְעָאלִין בְּאוֹצָר חַד.

24. "And if a priest's daughter be married to a stranger": this is the holy Neshamah that is drawn from a lofty place, WHICH IS BINAH, and enters into the closure of the Tree of Life, WHICH IS ZEIR ANPIN. And when the Ruach (or 'wind') of the high priest, WHICH IS CHESED OF ZEIR ANPIN, blows and bestows souls, THAT IS, CLOTHES THE SOULS WITH CHESED AND PUTS THEM in that tree, WHICH IS ZEIR ANPIN, the souls soar from them and enter a treasury, WHICH IS MALCHUT.

25. וַוי לְעָלְמָא, דְּלָא יַדְעִין בְּנֵי נָשָׁא לְאִסְתַּמְּרָא, דְּקָא מַשְׁכִין מְשִׁיכוּ בַּהֲדֵי יֵצֶר הָרָע, דְּאִיהוּ אִישׁ זָר, וְהַאי בַּת כֹּהֵן פַּרְחַת לְתַתָּא, וְאַשְׁכַּח

בְּנְיָינָא בְּאִישׁ זָר. וּבְגִין דְּאִיהוּ רְעוּתָא דְּמָרָהּ, עָאלַת תַּמָּן וְאִתְכַּפְיַאת, וְלָא יָכִילַת לְשַׁלְטָאָה, וְלָא אִשְׁתְּלִימַת בְּהַאי עָלְמָא. כַּד נַפְקַת מִנֵּיהּ, הִיא בִּתְרוּמַת הַקֳּדָשִׁים לֹא תֹאכֵל, כִּשְׁאָר כָּל נִשְׁמָתִין, דְּאִשְׁתְּלִימוּ בְּהַאי עָלְמָא.

25. Woe to the world, for people do not know how to be careful when attracting A SOUL INTO A BODY DURING INTERCOURSE by means of the Evil Inclination, which is a stranger. And that priest's daughter, WHICH IS THE SOUL, flies down and finds an edifice, NAMELY A BODY, in a strange man. Since this is the will of its Master, it goes in there to be subdued and has no power, and is not perfected in this world upon its leaving it. It "may not eat of an offering of the holy things," like the other souls that reached perfection in this world.

26. תּוּ אִית בְּהַאי קְרָא, וּבַת כֹּהֵן כִּי תִהְיֶה לְאִישׁ זָר. עֲלוּבְתָא אִיהִי נִשְׁמָתָא קַדִּישָׁא, כִּי תִהְיֶה לְאִישׁ זָר, דְּקָא אִתְמַשְׁכַת, עַל גִּיּוֹרָא דְּאִתְגַּיַּיר, וּפָרְחַת עֲלֵיהּ מג"ע בְּאֹרַח סָתִים, עַל בִּנְיָינָא דְּאִתְבְּנֵי מֵעָרְלָה מְסָאֲבָא, דָּא הֲוַת לְאִישׁ זָר.

26. There is something else to this verse, "And if a priest's daughter be married to a stranger." The holy soul is ashamed to be married to a stranger, that is, it is drawn upon a converted proselyte and flies to it from the Garden of Eden in a hidden way, to the edifice, NAMELY THE BODY, that is built of the impure foreskin, SINCE ITS FATHERS WERE NOT CIRCUMCISED. This is the meaning of "a stranger."

27. וְדָא הוּא רָזָא עִלָּאָה יַתִּירָא מִכֹּלָּא. בְּעַמּוּדָא דְּקַיְּימָא לְטִקְלִין, גּוֹ אֲוֵירָא דְּנָשְׁבַת, אִית טִיקְלָא חֲדָא בְּהַאי סִטְרָא, וְאִית טִיקְלָא אָחֳרָא בְּהַאי סִטְרָא. בְּהַאי סִטְרָא מֹאזְנֵי צֶדֶק. וּבְהַאי סִטְרָא מֹאזְנֵי מִרְמָה. וְהַאי טִיקְלָא, לָא שָׁכִיךְ לְעָלְמִין, וְנִשְׁמָתִין סַלְקִין וְנַחְתִּין עָאלִין וְתָבִין, וְאִית נִשְׁמָתִין עֲשִׁיקִין, כַּד שַׁלְטָא אָדָם בְּאָדָם, דִּכְתִיב עֵת אֲשֶׁר שָׁלַט הָאָדָם בְּאָדָם לְרַע לוֹ, לְרַע לוֹ וַדַּאי.

27. This is the loftiest secret. On a pillar set for weighing, in the midst of the

blowing air, there are scales on the one side, THE RIGHT, and other scales on the other, THE LEFT; true scales on this RIGHT side, and false scales on that LEFT side. These scales are never quiet. The souls go up and down, come and return BY MEANS OF THESE SCALES. Some souls are wronged, when the man OF THE OTHER SIDE has power over the man OF HOLINESS, as written, "a time when one man rules over another to his own hurt" (Kohelet 8:9), assuredly to his own hurt.

28. אֲבָל הַאי נִשְׁמְתָא, דַּהֲוַת לְסִטְרָא אַחֲרָא, אִישׁ זָר, וְאִתְעֲשָׁקַת מִנֵּיהּ, דָּא אִיהִי לְרַע לוֹ. לוֹ: לְהַהוּא אִישׁ זָר, וְאִיהִי בִּתְרוּמַת הַקֳּדָשִׁים לֹא תֹאכֵל, עַד דְּעָבֵיד בָּהּ קוּדְשָׁא בְּרִיךְ הוּא מַה דְּעָבֵיד, אָתָא קְרָא וְאָמַר וּבַת כֹּהֵן כִּי תִהְיֶה לְאִישׁ זָר הָכִי הוּא.

28. But the soul that was married to the Other Side CALLED a stranger and was wronged by it, it is "to his own hurt," that of the stranger. And it, "may not eat of an offering of the holy things," AS THE OTHER SOULS, until the Holy One, blessed be He, does with it that which is to be done, THAT IS, HE CORRECTS IT, AS SHALL BE EXPLAINED. CONCERNING THIS the verse says, "And if a priest's daughter be married to a stranger," it shall be so, THAT IT "MAY NOT EAT OF AN OFFERING OF THE HOLY THINGS."

29. הָכָא אִית רָזָא, הֵיךְ מִתְעַשְׁקָן נִשְׁמָתִין. אֶלָּא הַאי עָלְמָא אִתְנְהַג כֹּלָּא, בְּאִילָנָא דְּדַעַת טוֹב וָרָע. וְכַד אִתְנַהֲגָן בְּנֵי עָלְמָא בְּסִטְרָא דְּטוֹב, טִיקְלָא קַיְימָא וְאַכְרַע לְסִטְרָא דְּטוֹב. וְכַד אִתְנַהֲגָן בְּסִטְרָא דְּרַע, אַכְרַע לְהַהוּא סִטְרָא. וְכָל נִשְׁמָתִין דַּהֲווֹ בְּהַהִיא שַׁעֲתָא בְּטִיקְלָא, הֲוָה עָשִׁיק לוֹן, וְנָטִיל לוֹן.

29. There is a secret here about the way souls are wronged. For everything in this world is guided by the Tree of Knowledge of Good and Evil, WHICH IS MALCHUT. When people in the world conduct themselves according to the good side, RECONCILED BY THE CENTRAL COLUMN, the scales are balanced and are tipped to the good side. When they conduct themselves according to the Evil Side, the scales tip to that side, THE OTHER SIDE, which takes all the souls that were on the scales at that time and wrongs them.

30. אֲבָל לְרַע לוֹ, דְּאִינּוּן נִשְׁמָתִין כַּפְיָין לְכָל מַה דְּאִשְׁתְּכַח מִסִּטְרָא

בִּישָׁא, וְשֵׁיצִיאָן לֵיהּ. וְסִימָנָא לְדָא, אֲרוֹנָא קַדִּישָׁא, דְּאִתְעֲשָׁק גּוֹ פְּלִשְׁתִּים, וּשְׁלִיטוּ בֵּיהּ, לְרַע לוֹן. אוֹף הָכִי. הָנֵי נִשְׁמָתִין אִתְעֲשָׁקִין מִסִּטְרָא אַחֲרָא לְרַע לוֹן.

30. But it is "to his own hurt," THE OTHER SIDE'S, because those souls subdue all they find of the Evil Side and consume it. And indicative for that is the holy Ark, which was violated by the Philistines who had power over it to their own hurt, SINCE THEY AND THEIR DEITIES WERE PLAGUED BY IT. Here too, the souls wronged by the Other Side, it is to its own hurt.

31. מָה אִתְעֲבִידוּ מֵאִינּוּן נִשְׁמָתִין. חֲמֵינָן בְּסִפְרֵי קַדְמָאֵי, דְּמִנַּיְיהוּ הֲווֹ אִינּוּן חֲסִידֵי אוּמוֹת הָעוֹלָם. וְאִינּוּן מַמְזְרֵי תַּלְמִידֵי חֲכָמִים, דְּקַדְמָן לְכַהֲנָא רַבָּא עַמָּא דְּאַרְעָא, וְחָשׁוּב בְּעָלְמָא, אַף עַל גַּב דְּעָאל לְפְנַי וְלְפְנִים. בָּכָה הַאי סָבָא רִגְעָא חֲדָא, תַּוְוהוּ חַבְרַיָּיא, וְלָא אָמְרוּ מִדִי.

31. We have seen in ancient books what had come of these wronged souls. Some of them were righteous of the nations. These are bastard scholars, and bastard scholars are better than ignorant high priests, and are more valuable in the world, even though THE HIGH PRIEST enters the innermost HOLY OF HOLIES. The old man wept for a moment. The friends were amazed and said nothing.

32. פָּתַח הַהוּא סָבָא וְאָמַר, אִם רָעָה בְּעֵינֵי אֲדֹנֶיהָ אֲשֶׁר לֹא יְעָדָהּ וְהֶפְדָּהּ לְעַם נָכְרִי וְגוֹ'. הַאי פַּרְשָׁתָּא עַל רָזָא דָּא אִתְּמַר, וְכִי יִמְכֹּר אִישׁ אֶת בִּתּוֹ לְאָמָה לֹא תֵצֵא כְּצֵאת הָעֲבָדִים אִם רָעָה וְגוֹ'. מָארֵיהּ דְּעָלְמָא מַאן לָא יִדְחַל מִינָךְ, דְּאַנְתְּ שַׁלִּיט עַל כָּל מַלְכִין דְּעָלְמָא, כד"א מִי לֹא יִרָאֲךָ מֶלֶךְ הַגּוֹיִם כִּי לְךָ יָאָתָה וְגוֹ'.

32. The old man opened with, "If she please not her master, who has designated her for himself, then shall he let her be redeemed, to sell her to a strange nation..." (Shemot 21:8). This passage was said in relation to this hidden matter OF WRONGED SOULS, "And if a man sell his daughter to be a maidservant, she shall not go out as the menservants do. If she pleases not..." (Ibid. 7). Master of the Universe, who will not fear You, who

governs all the kings in the world, as written, "Who would not fear You, O King of the nations? For to You it is fitting..." (Yirmeyah 10:7).

33. כַּמָה אִינוּן בְּנֵי נָשָׁא בְּעָלְמָא, דְּקָא מִשְׁתַּבְּשָׁן בְּהַאי קְרָא, וְכֻלְּהוּ אַמְרֵי, אֲבָל קְרָא דָּא לָא אִתְיַישָּׁר בְּפוּמַיְיהוּ. וְכִי קוּדְשָׁא בְּרִיךְ הוּא מֶלֶךְ הַגּוֹיִם אִיהוּ, וַהֲלֹא מֶלֶךְ יִשְׂרָאֵל אִיהוּ, וְהָכִי אִקְרֵי, דְּהָא כְּתִיב, בְּהַנְחֵל עֶלְיוֹן גּוֹיִם וְגוֹ'. וּכְתִיב כִּי חֵלֶק יְיָ' עַמּוֹ. וע"ד אִקְרֵי מֶלֶךְ יִשְׂרָאֵל. וְאִי תֵּימָא דְּאִיהוּ מֶלֶךְ הַגּוֹיִם אִקְרֵי, הָא שְׁבָחָא דִּלְהוֹן דְּקוּדְשָׁא בְּרִיךְ הוּא מֶלֶךְ הוּא עֲלַיְיהוּ, וְלָא כְּמָה דְּאַמְרִין דְּאִתְמַסְרִין לְשַׁמָּשִׁין וְלִמְמָנָן דִּילֵיהּ.

33. How many people in the world read wrong and err in this verse. They all recite it, yet they do not rightly explain the verse. Is the Holy One, blessed be He, called the King of the nations? Yet He is the King of Yisrael. And He is also named in the verse, "When the most High divided to the nations their inheritance" (Devarim 32:8), and, "For Hashem's portion is His people" (Ibid. 9). So He is called the King of Yisrael. If you argue that He is called the King of the nations, it is to their advantage that the Holy One, blessed be He, reigns over them instead, as it is said, that they were given to His ministers and appointed officers.

34. וְתוּ סֵיפָא דִּקְרָא, דִּכְתִיב כִּי בְּכָל חַכְמֵי הַגּוֹיִם וּבְכָל מַלְכוּתָם מֵאַיִן כָּמוֹךְ. כָּל הַאי, שְׁבָחָא אִיהוּ לִשְׁאָר עַמִּין, וּתְוָוהָא אִיהוּ, הֵיךְ לָא מִסְתַּלְּקֵי בְּהַאי קְרָא לְרוּם רְקִיעָא. אֶלָּא, דְּקוּדְשָׁא בְּרִיךְ הוּא סָמָא עֵינַיְיהוּ, וְלָא יַדְעֵי בֵּיהּ כְּלָל, דְּהָא מַה דַּאֲנַן אַמְרֵי דְּכֻלְּהוּ אַיִן, וָאֶפֶס, וָתֹהוּ. דִּכְתִיב כָּל הַגּוֹיִם כְּאַיִן נֶגְדּוֹ מֵאֶפֶס וָתֹהוּ נֶחְשְׁבוּ לוֹ, הָא עִקְּרָא עִלָּאָה רַבָּא וִיקִירָא שַׁוֵּי לוֹן קְרָא דָּא.

34. Moreover, the end of the passage states, "for among all the wise men of the nations, and in all their kingdoms, there is none like You..." (Yirmeyah 10:7). All this praise is directed to the other nations. It is wonder that they are not raised in this verse to the highest heaven. AS THE VERSE GIVES THEIR SAGES AND KINGDOMS SOME RELATION TO THE HOLY ONE,

BLESSED BE HE, THAT IT IS NECESSARY TO SAY THAT HE IS GREATER
THAN THEY. But the Holy One, blessed be He, blinds their eyes so they do
not know Him at all, which is what we say that they are all nothing, less
than nothing and vanity, as written, "All nations before Him are as nothing;
and they are counted to Him less than nothing, and vanity" (Yeshayah 40:7).
Yet the verse gives them great and precious importance IN SAYING THAT
AMONG ALL THE SAGES OF THE NATIONS AND THROUGHOUT THEIR
KINGDOM THERE IS NONE LIKE YOU.

A Synopsis

The merchant talks about the greatness of God, and how he is
falsely compared to the sages of the various nations. We hear of
the names Elohim, Yud Hei Vav Hei fully spelled out, King of the
Nations, and Hashem. "For among all the wise men of the nations,
and in all their kingdoms, there is none like You."

35. אָמַר לֵיהּ ר' חִיָּיא וְהָא כְּתִיב מָלַךְ אֱלֹהִים עַל גּוֹיִם וְגוֹ'. אָמַר לֵיהּ,
אֲנָא חֲמֵינָא דְּבָתַר כּוֹתְלַיְיהוּ הֲוֵית, וְנָפְקַת בְּהַאי קְרָא לְסַיְּיעָא לוֹן, הֲוָה
לִי לְאָתָבָא בְּקַדְמֵיתָא, עַל מַה דַּאֲמֵינָא. אֲבָל כֵּיוָן דְּאַשְׁכַּחְנָא לָךְ
בְּאָרְחָא, אַעְבַּר לָךְ מִתַּמָּן, וּמִתַּמָּן אֵיהָךְ לְאַעְבְּרָא כֹּלָּא.

35. Rabbi Chiya said to him, yet it is written, "Elohim reigns over the
nations…" (Tehilim 47:9). He told him, I see that you were behind their
wall, and came out with this verse to support them. I should have answered
first to all that I said, but since I have found you on the way, I will remove
you from there and thence I will move everything.

36. ת"ח, כָּל שְׁמָהָן, וְכָל כִּנּוּיִין דִּשְׁמָהָן, דְּאִית לֵיהּ לְקוּדְשָׁא בְּרִיךְ
הוּא, כֻּלְּהוּ מִתְפַּשְּׁטָן לְאָרְחַיְיהוּ, וְכֻלְּהוּ מִתְלַבְּשִׁין אַלֵּין בְּאַלֵּין, וְכֻלְּהוּ
מִתְפַּלְּגִין לְאָרְחִין וּשְׁבִילִין יְדִיעָן. בַּר שְׁמָא יְחִידָאָה, בָּרִיר דְּכָל שְׁאַר
שְׁמָהָן, דְּאַחֲסִין לְעַמָּא יְחִידָאָה, בָּרִיר מִכָּל שְׁאַר עַמִּין, וְאִיהוּ יוּ"ד
הֵ"א וָא"ו הֵ"א, דִּכְתִיב כִּי חֵלֶק יְיָ' עַמּוֹ. וּכְתִיב וְאַתֶּם הַדְּבֵקִים בַּיְיָ'
בִּשְׁמָא דָּא מַמָּשׁ, יַתִּיר מִכָּל שְׁאַר שְׁמָהָן.

36. Come and see, all these names and appellations to the names of the Holy
One, blessed be He, expand to their paths, and are clothed in each other, and

separate into specific ways and paths except for one name, that is more refined than any other name, which He bequeathed to the unique people, the most purified of the other nations. It is Yud Vav Dalet, Hei Aleph, Vav Aleph Vav, Hei Aleph, as written, "For Hashem's portion is His people," and "But you that did cleave of Hashem" (Devarim 4:4), CLEAVING to this very name more than to any other name.

37. וּשְׁמָא חַד מִכָּל שְׁאַר שְׁמָהָן דִּילֵיהּ, הַהוּא דְּאִתְפְּשַׁט וְאִתְפְּלַג לְכַמָּה אָרְחִין וּשְׁבִילִין, וְאִקְרֵי אֱלֹהִים. וְאַחֲסִין שְׁמָא דָא, וְאִתְפְּלַג לְתַתָּאֵי דְּהַאי עָלְמָא, וְאִתְפְּלַג שְׁמָא דָא, לְשַׁמָּשִׁין וְלִמְמָנָן דִּמְנַהֲגֵי לִשְׁאַר עַמִּין. כד"א, וַיָּבֹא אֱלֹהִים אֶל בִּלְעָם לַיְלָה. וַיָּבֹא אֱלֹהִים אֶל אֲבִימֶלֶךְ בַּחֲלוֹם הַלָּיְלָה. וְכֵן כָּל מְמָנָא וּמְמַנָּא דְּאַחֲסִין לוֹן קוּדְשָׁא בְּרִיךְ הוּא לִשְׁאַר עַמִּין, בִּשְׁמָא דָא כְּלִילָן. וַאֲפִילוּ ע"ז בִּשְׁמָא דָא אִקְרֵי. וּשְׁמָא דָא מָלַךְ עַל גּוֹיִם, וְלָא הַהוּא שְׁמָא, דָּא הַהוּא דְּמָלַךְ עַל יִשְׂרָאֵל, דְּאִיהוּ יְחִידָאָה, לְעַמָּא יְחִידָאָה, לְעַמָּא דְיִשְׂרָאֵל, עַמָּא קַדִּישָׁא.

37. There is one name, of all His names, that extends into several ways and paths, called Elohim. He bequeathed this name, and it was divided among the lower beings in this world. This name was divided among the ministers and the appointed officers that lead the other nations, as written, "And Elohim came to Bilaam at night" (Bemidbar 22:20), and "But Elohim came to Abimelech in a dream by night" (Beresheet 20:3). Also every minister that the Holy One, blessed be He, had designated to the other nations, are part of this name. Even idolatry is called by this name. And this name reigned over the nations, and not the name that reigned over Yisrael, WHICH IS THE NAME YUD HEI VAV HEI, which is unique to the unique nations, the people of Yisrael, the holy nation.

38. וְאִי תֵּימָא, עַל אָרְחָא דָא נוֹקִים קְרָא דִּכְתִיב מִי לֹא יִרָאֲךָ מֶלֶךְ הַגּוֹיִם, דְּדָא אִיהוּ שְׁמָא דְּקָא מָלַךְ עַל גּוֹיִם, אֱלֹהִים דְּהָא דְּחִילוּ בֵּיהּ שַׁרְיָא וְדִינָא בֵּיהּ שַׁרְיָא. לָאו הָכִי, וְלָאו עַל דָּא אִתְּמַר, דְּאִי הָכִי אֲפִילוּ ע"ז בִּכְלָלָא דָּא אִיהוּ.

38. But if you argue that we can explain the verse, "Who would not fear You, O King of the nations?" that the name that is king of the nations is Elohim, as fear pertains to it, and Judgment abides in it, this is not so. It was not said in this context, for otherwise even idolatry would be included in that, IN "WHO WOULD NOT FEAR YOU," AS EVEN IDOLATRY IS CALLED ELOHIM.

39. אֲבָל כֵּיוָן דִּכְתָלָא דַּהֲוֵית סָמִיךְ אֲבַתְרֵיהּ, אִתְנְסָח, קְרָא קָאֵים עַל קִיּוּמָא, בְּאִסְתַּכְּלוּתָא זְעֵיר. מִי לֹא יִרְאֲךָ מֶלֶךְ הַגּוֹיִם, וְאִי תֵּימָא דְּמֶלֶךְ הַגּוֹיִם עַל קוּדְשָׁא ב״ה אִתְּמַר, לָאו הָכִי. אֶלָּא, מַאן הוּא מֶלֶךְ הַגּוֹיִם דְּלָא יִרְאֲךָ, דְּלָא דָחִיל מִינָךְ, וְלָא יִזְדַעֲזַע מִינָךְ. מִי מֶלֶךְ הַגּוֹיִם דְּלָא יִרְאֲךָ. כְּגַוְונָא דָא הַלְלוּיָהּ הַלְלוּ עַבְדֵי יְיָ' הַלְלוּ אֶת שֵׁם יְיָ'. מַאן דְּשָׁמַע לֵיהּ, לָא יָדַע מַאי קָאֲמַר, כֵּיוָן דְּאָמַר הַלְלוּיָהּ, אוּף הָכִי הַלְלוּ עַבְדֵי יְיָ', דַּהֲוָה לֵיהּ לְמִכְתַּב, עַבְדֵי יְיָ' הַלְלוּ אֶת שֵׁם יְיָ'. אוּף הָכָא. הֲוָה לֵיהּ לְמִכְתַּב, מִי מִמֶּלֶךְ הַגּוֹיִם דְּלָא יִרְאֲךָ. אֶלָּא כֹּלָּא עַל תִּקּוּנֵיהּ אִתְּמַר.

39. But once the wall behind which you were leaning is torn down, the verse prevails after some observation. "Who would not fear You, O King of the nations?" If you would say it refers to the Holy One, blessed be He, as the King of the nations, it is not so. But THE EXPLANATION IS, What king of the nations would not fear You, nor be in awe of You or tremble before You? IT IS AS IF IT WERE WRITTEN, 'What king of the nations would not fear You?' Similarly, "Haleluyah! Give praise, O servants of Hashem, praise the name of Hashem" (Tehilim 113:1). Whoever hears it does not know what it means. After saying Haleluyah, IT SAYS also, "Give praise, O (or: 'to') servants of Hashem." It should have been written, 'Servants of Hashem, praise the name of Hashem'. BUT YET IT IS NECESSARY, FOR THOUGH IT FIRST SAYS HALELUYAH, THE SUBJECT IS THE SERVANTS OF HASHEM. Here too, THOUGH IT SAYS FIRST "WHO WOULD NOT FEAR YOU," THE SUBJECT IS 'THE KING OF THE NATIONS'. IT IS AS IF it were written, 'Who among the kings of the nations would not fear You'. It was all said properly.

40. כִּי בְּכָל חַכְמֵי הַגּוֹיִם וּבְכָל מַלְכוּתָם מֵאֵין כָּמוֹךָ, מַהוּ מִלָּה דְּאִתְפָּשַׁט בֵּינַיְיהוּ בְּחָכְמְתָא דִּלְהוֹן, מֵאֵין כָּמוֹךָ וְכֻלְּהוּ אוֹדָאן עַל דָּא, כַּד חָמָאן בְּחָכְמְתָא דִּלְהוֹן עוֹבָדָךְ וּגְבוּרְתָּךְ, אִתְפָּשַׁט מִלָּה דָא בֵּינַיְיהוּ,

וְאַמְרֵי מֵאֵין כָּמוֹךְ בְּכָל חַכְמֵי הַגּוֹיִם וּבְכָל מַלְכוּתָם. מֵאֵין כָּמוֹךְ אַמְרֵי, וְאִתְפָּשַׁט בֵּינַיְיהוּ. חַדּוּ חַבְרַיָּיא, וּבְכוּ וְלָא אָמְרוּ מִדִי. אוּף הָכִי בְּכָה אִיהוּ כְּמִלְּקַדְּמִין.

40. "For among all the wise men of the nations, and in all their kingdoms, there is none like You…" means, what is the phrase spread among them in their wisdom – it is "there is none like You," and they all acknowledge that. When they see in their wisdom Your deeds and mighty actions, this phrase spreads among them and they say, "there is none like You." THE LESSON OF THE VERSE IS THAT among all the sages of the nations and throughout their kingdoms, they say "there is none like You," and it is known among them. The friends rejoiced and wept, but said nothing. He too wept again.

A Synopsis

We learn about idolatry and about the soul that incarnates for evil deeds in the world, as alluded to in "And if a man sell his daughter to be a maidservant". When God sees that a child will turn bad later in life he gathers it in to Himself while it is still young and fragrant. The merchant says that when God created the world he also created all the souls that would later be incarnated into bodies, and that even when souls do not wish to come to the world he makes them do so, since that is why they were created. When the time comes to depart from the world the soul must be free, refined and cleansed so that God can be pleased with it and reward it in the Garden of Eden. The souls are entered into the King's book, where they are recorded with their names. If the soul was soiled, and not worthy, it is met by strange camps of demons who bring it to Gehenom. Pure souls are protected by the garment that is spread on them, which is the name Eloha. We hear that the souls of the beloved enter into the chamber of love, which is situated underneath the Holy of Holies of Briyah, in the hidden firmament. The Holy One, blessed be He, finds that holy soul there, and raises it with up with Him in delight.

41. פָּתַח וְאָמַר וַתֹּאמֶר לְאַבְרָהָם גָּרֵשׁ הָאָמָה הַזֹּאת וְאֶת בְּנָהּ וְגוֹ', חַבְרַיָּיא אִתְּעָרוּ, דְּבָעָאת שָׂרָה לְפַנָּאָה ע״ז מִבֵּיתָא, וע״ד כְּתִיב כָּל אֲשֶׁר תֹּאמַר אֵלֶיךָ שָׂרָה שְׁמַע בְּקוֹלָהּ. הָכָא כְּתִיב וְכִי יִמְכֹּר אִישׁ אֶת בִּתּוֹ, דָּא נִשְׁמְתָא בְּגִלְגּוּלֵי עַל עוֹבָדִין בִּישִׁין דְּעָלְמָא. לְאָמָה: הַהוּא סִטְרָא אַחֲרָא בְּגִלְגּוּלָא בִּישָׁא דְּטִיקְלָא, דְּאַהֲדָר, וְהָא אִתְעַשְּׁקַת,

לְאַפָּקָא לָה מִתַּמָּן. וַדַּאי לֹא תֵצֵא כְּצֵאת הָעֲבָדִים, כָּל אִינּוּן נִשְׁמָתִין דְּמִתְעַשְׁקָן.

41. He opened with, "So she said to Abraham, Cast out this bondwoman and her son…" (Beresheet 21:10). The friends have remarked that Sarah wanted to remove idolatry from the house. Therefore it is written, "all that Sarah has said to you, hearken to her voice" (Ibid. 12), AS THE BONDWOMAN IS CONSIDERED IDOLATRY. Here it is written, "And if a man sell his daughter to be a maidservant" (Shemot 21:7), namely, the soul that incarnates for evil deeds in the world. "To be a maidservant" refers to that other side of the evil incarnation of the scales that reverted INTO FALSE SCALES AS MENTIONED, and it is wronged BY THE OTHER SIDE. In taking it out of there, it "shall not go out as the menservants do" (Ibid. 8), which are the wronged souls, BUT IT RECEIVES A CROWN ON ITS HEAD, AS WILL BE SAID.

42. מַאן אִינּוּן הָכָא. אִיהוּ רָזָא, אִלֵּין אִינּוּן נִשְׁמָתִין דִּינוֹקִין זְעִירִין, כַּד אִינּוּן יַנְקֵי מִגּוֹ תּוּקְפָּא דְּאִמְּהוֹן. וְקוּדְשָׁא בְּרִיךְ הוּא חָמֵי, דְּאִי יִתְקַיְּימוּן בְּעָלְמָא, יְבַאֲשׁוּן רֵיחֵיהוֹן, וְיַחְמְצוּן כְּחוֹמֶץ דָּא. לָקִיט לוֹן זְעִירִין, בְּעוֹד דְּיַהֲבֵי רֵיחָא.

42. HE ASKS, who are THE SOULS mentioned here, AND ANSWERS, this is a secret. These are the souls of young children, who suckle on their mothers' strength. The Holy One, blessed be He, sees that if they will live in the world they will be bad smelling and turn sour like vinegar. THEREFORE He gathers them when they are still young and emit good fragrance.

43. מַה עָבֵיד. שָׁבִיק לוֹן לְאִתְעַשְּׁקָא בִּידָא דְּהַהִיא אָמָה, וְדָא אִיהִי לִילִית דְּכֵיוָן דְּאִתְיְיהִיבוּ בִּרְשׁוּתָה, חַדְאַת בְּהַהוּא יְנוֹקָא, וַעֲשִׁיקַת לֵיה, וְאַפִּיקַת לֵיה מֵעָלְמָא, כַּד אִיהוּ יָנִיק בְּתוּקְפָּא דְּאִמֵּיה.

43. What does THE HOLY ONE, BLESSED BE HE, do He allows them to be wronged by the hands of the bondwoman, who is Lilit. Once they are placed under her power, she rejoices in that child and oppresses him. She takes him away from the world while he is still suckling on his mother's strength.

44. וְאִי תֵּימָא, אִינּוּן נִשְׁמָתִין דְּיַעַבְדוּן טַב לְעָלְמָא. לָאו הָכִי. דִּכְתִיב

אִם רָעָה בְּעֵינֵי אֲדֹנֶיהָ, דְּיַחֲמִיץ הַהוּא גַּבְרָא בָּהּ לְבָתַר יוֹמִין, אִי
אִתְקַיַּים בָּהּ. דָּא אִתְעֲשָׁקַת, וְאַחֲרָא לָא אִתְעֲשָׁקַת. וְעַל אִלֵּין כְּתִיב,
וָאֶרְאֶה אֶת כָּל הָעֲשׁוּקִים וְגוֹ' וְהַיְינוּ אִם רָעָה בְּעֵינֵי אֲדֹנֶיהָ.

44. If you argue that these souls will do good in the world, it is not so, as written, "If she please not her master" (Shemot 21:8), as that man will turn sour by it after some time, if he will go on living. This soul is oppressed, while another is not. Of these it is written, "and considered all the oppressions" (Kohelet 4:1). That is the meaning of, "If she please not her master."

45. אֲשֶׁר לֹא יְעָדָהּ, לֹא בְּאָלֶף כְּתִיב. אִי תֵּימָא, דְּהָא בְּהַהוּא סִטְרָא
אַחֲרָא, אַזְמִין לָהּ קוּדְשָׁא בְּרִיךְ הוּא מִיּוֹמָא דַּהֲוַת. לָא. וְהַשְׁתָּא
בְּגִלְגּוּלֵי טִיקְלָא, לוֹ יְעָדָהּ בְּוָא"ו. מַה דְּלָא הֲוַת מִקַּדְמַת דְּנָא.

45. "Who has designated her for himself (Heb. *lo*)" (Shemot 21:8). The word 'lo' is spelled with Aleph to mean not. If you say the Holy One, blessed be He, gave it to the Other Side from the first day of its existence, it is not so. For now with the turnings of the scales, He "has designated her for himself," 'lo' being pronounced as with Vav to mean for himself, which it was not before.

46. וְהֶפְדָּהּ, מַאי וְהֶפְדָּהּ. פָּרִיק לָהּ קוּדְשָׁא בְּרִיךְ הוּא הַשְׁתָּא, דְּסַלְקָא
רֵיחָא, עַד לָא תַּחֲמִיץ, וְסָלִיק לָהּ לְרוּמֵי מְרוֹמִים, בִּמְתִיבְתָּא דִּילֵיהּ,
וְאִי תֵּימָא כֵּיוָן דְּאִתְעֲשָׁקַת מֵהַהוּא סִטְרָא אַחֲרָא, יָהִיב לָהּ, כְּמָה
דְּאָמְרוּ לַחֲסִידֵי שְׁאָר עַמִּין, וּלְאִינוּן מַמְזֵרֵי ת"ח. אָתָא קְרָא וְאוֹכַח,
לְעַם נָכְרִי לֹא יִמְשׁוֹל לְמָכְרָהּ וַדַּאי, בְּבִגְדוֹ בָהּ, דְּעָשִׁיק לָהּ בַּעֲשִׁיקוּ
דְּגִלְגּוּלָא דְּטִיקְלָא, אֶלָּא לְיִשְׂרָאֵל וַדַּאי, וְלָא לְאַחֲרָא. וְכַד נָפְקַת מִן
טִיקְלָא, לֹא תֵצֵא כְּצֵאת הָעֲבָדִים, אֶלָּא מִתְעַטְּרָא בְּעִטְרָהָא בְּאַרְמָא
עַל רֵישַׁיהּ.

46. "Then shall he let her be redeemed" (Ibid.). What is the meaning of that? HE ANSWERS, the Holy One, blessed be He, redeems it now, WHILE it still

emits GOOD fragrance, before it turns sour. He raises it to the highest skies to His Yeshivah. If you say that since it was wronged by the Other Side, He hands it, as was said, to scholarly bastards and to the righteous of the nations, the verse proves that, "to sell her to a strange nation he shall have no power, seeing he has dealt deceitfully with her" (Ibid.), as He oppressed it with the turning of the scales. But assuredly He will give it to Yisrael and to no other. When it emerges from the scales, it "shall not go out as the menservants do," but is given a crown high on its head.

47. וְאִי תֵּימָא, דְּהַאי סִטְרָא עָאלַת לָהּ בְּהַהוּא יַנּוּקָא. לָאו הָכִי. אֶלָּא נַטְלַת לָהּ, וְחֶדְוָאת בַּהֲדָהּ, וּפַרְחַת מִן יְדָהָא, וְעָאלַת בְּהַהוּא אֲתָר, וְאִיהִי פְּקִידַת לְהַהוּא יַנּוּקָא, וְחֶדְוָאת בֵּיהּ, וְחַיְיכַת בֵּיהּ, וְתָאִיבַת לְהַהוּא בָּשָׂר עַד דִּלְבָתַר נָטִיל קוּדְשָׁא בְּרִיךְ הוּא נִשְׁמָתֵיהּ, וְהִיא לְגוּפָא. וּלְבָתַר כֹּלָּא אִיהוּ בִּרְשׁוּתָא דְּקוּדְשָׁא בְּרִיךְ הוּא.

47. If you say that that side comes in the child, WHICH MEANS IT HAS POWER OVER HIS SOUL, it is not so. But it takes the soul and rejoices in it. He flies out of its hands and enters that place OF THE OTHER SIDE, where it visits that child. It is delighted with it and mocks it, lusting after that flesh, so that the Holy One, blessed be He, takes its soul while it TAKES its body. After that everything is under the control of the Holy One, blessed be He.

48. ת"ח, לֹא תֵצֵא כְּצֵאת הָעֲבָדִים, מַאי הוּא. אֶלָּא, בְּשַׁעֲתָא דְּנָפְקַת מִן טִיקְלָא וְהַהוּא סִטְרָא בְּחֶדוּ, רָשִׁים לָהּ לְקוּדְשָׁא בְּרִיךְ הוּא, וְחָתִים לָהּ בְּחַד גּוּשְׁפַּנְקָא, וּפָרִישׂ עָלָהּ לְבוּשׁ יְקָר דִּילֵיהּ, וּמַאן אִיהוּ. שְׁמָא קַדִּישָׁא דְּאִקְרֵי אֱלוֹהַּ. וְדָא הוּא בְּבִגְדוֹ בָהּ, לְבוּשָׁא יַקִּירָא דְּמַלְכָּא פָּרִישׂ עָלָהּ וּכְדֵין אִיהִי נְטִירָא, דְּלָא אִתְמַסְרַת לְעַם נָכְרִי, אֶלָּא לְיִשְׂרָאֵל לְחוּד.

48. Come and see, "she shall not go out as the menservants do." HE ASKS, what is the meaning of, "GO OUT AS THE MENSERVANTS," AND ANSWERS, when it leaves the scales and that side with joy, the Holy One, blessed be He marks it and seals it with a certain ring, spreads on it His precious garment, which is the Holy Name Eloha. That is the meaning of, "he has dealt deceitfully with her (also: 'his garment is with her')," that is, while the

precious garment of the King is on it. Since His garment is upon it, it is written, "to sell her to a strange nation he shall have no power."

49. וְדָא אִיהוּ דִּכְתִּיב, כִּימֵי אֱלוֹהַ יִשְׁמְרֵנִי, וְעַל רָזָא דָא כְּתִיב הָכָא, לְעַם נָכְרִי לֹא יִמְשֹׁל לְמָכְרָהּ בְּבִגְדוֹ בָהּ, בְּעוֹד דִּלְבוּשׁ יְקָר דְּמַלְכָּא בָהּ. כֵּיוָן דְּבִגְדוֹ בָהּ, כְּתִיב לְעַם נָכְרִי לֹא יִמְשֹׁל לְמָכְרָהּ.

49. This is the meaning of, "as in the days when Eloha preserved me" (Iyov 29:2), WHICH REFERS TO THE PRECIOUS GARMENT CALLED ELOHA, AS MENTIONED. It is in reference to this secret that it is written here, "to sell her to a strange nation he shall have no power, seeing that his garment is with her." It is because the precious garment of the King is upon it, since "His garment is with her" then "to sell her to a strange nation he shall have no power."

50. מַה רְשׁוּ אִית לְהַהוּא סִטְרָא בָהּ. תָּ"ח, כָּל בְּנֵי עָלְמָא כֻּלְּהוּ, בִּרְשׁוּתֵיהּ דְּמַלְכָּא קַדִּישָׁא, וְכֻלְּהוּ אִית לוֹן זִמְנָא בְּהַאי עָלְמָא, עַד דְּאִיהוּ בָּעֵי לְסַלְּקָא לוֹן מִן עָלְמָא, וְדָא לֵית לֵיהּ זִמְנָא, וְעַ"ד אִיהִי חַיְּיכָת בְּהוּ, וְחַדָּאת בְּהוּ.

50. HE ASKS, what of the dominion that side has over that soul. FOR HE SAID THAT THE HOLY ONE, BLESSED BE HE, GIVES PERMISSION TO THE OTHER SIDE TO WRONG THAT SOUL. HE ANSWERS, come and see, the people in the world are all under the dominion of the holy King; they all have time TO LIVE in this world until He wishes to raise them from the world. THE OTHER SIDE IS NOT ALLOWED TO HARM THEM BEFORE THAT TIME. Yet as for it, it has not SET time TO LIVE. THEREFORE it mocks and delights in that soul AND TAKES IT AWAY FROM THIS WORLD. THUS, SINCE IT WAS NOT ALLOTTED TIME, THE OTHER SIDE IS GIVEN PERMISSION TO OPPRESS IT.

51. תּוּ, אַזְהָרוּתָא לְבַר נָשׁ אִית בְּהָנֵי קְרָאֵי, וְכַמָּה עֵיטִין טָבִין עִלָּאִין אִינוּן, בְּכָל מִילֵי דְאוֹרַיְיתָא, וְכֻלְּהוּ קְשׁוֹט, בְּאֹרַח קְשׁוֹט, וְאִשְׁתְּמוֹדְעָן לְגַבֵּי חַכִּימִין, דְּיַדְעֵי וְאַזְלֵי בְּאֹרַח קְשׁוֹט. בְּזִמְנָא דְּבָעָא קוּדְשָׁא בְּרִיךְ הוּא לְמִבְרֵי עָלְמָא, סָלִיק בִּרְעוּתָא קַמֵּיהּ, וְצִיֵּיר כָּל נִשְׁמָתִין דְּאִינוּן

זְמִינִין לְמֵיהָב בִּבְנֵי נָשָׁא לְבָתַר, וְכֻלְּהוּ אִתְצַיָּירוּ קַמֵּיהּ בְּהַהוּא צִיּוּרָא מַמָּשׁ, דְּזְמִינִין לְמֶהֱוֵי בִּבְנֵי נָשָׁא לְבָתַר, וְחָמָא כָּל חַד וְחַד.

51. Moreover, these verses contain admonitions to people, and much good lofty advice is present in all the words of the Torah, which are all true and of a true way. They are known to the wise, who know and walk the path of truth. When the Holy One, blessed be He, wished to create the world, He so desired it and fashioned all the souls that will be placed in people afterwards. And they were all fashioned before Him in the very shape they will have later in people, and He saw each and every one.

52. וְאִית מִנְּהוֹן דְּזְמִינִין לְאַבְאָשָׁא אָרְחַיְיהוּ בְּעָלְמָא, וּבְשַׁעֲתָא דְּמָטָא זִמְנַיְיהוּ, קָרֵי קוּדְשָׁא בְּרִיךְ הוּא לְהַהִיא נִשְׁמָתָא, אָמַר לָהּ, זִילִי עוּלִי בְּדוּךְ פְּלָן. בְּגוּף פְּלָן. אֲתִיבַת קַמֵּיהּ, מָארֵיהּ דְּעָלְמָא, דֵּי לִי בְּעָלְמָא דָּא דַּאֲנָא יָתְבָא בֵּיהּ, וְלָא אֵיהַךְ לְעָלְמָא אַחֲרָא, דְּיִשְׁתַּעְבְּדוּן בִּי, וְאֶהֵא מְלוּכְלְכָא בֵּינַיְיהוּ. אָמַר לָהּ קוּדְשָׁא בְּרִיךְ הוּא, מִן יוֹמָא דְּאִתְבְּרִיאַת, ע״ד אִתְבְּרִיאַת לְמֶהֱוֵי בְּהַהוּא עָלְמָא. כֵּיוָן דְּחָמָאת נִשְׁמָתָא כָּךְ, בְּעַל כָּרְחָהּ נַחֲתַת וְעָאלַת תַּמָּן.

52. Some of them will befoul their ways in the world. When their time comes TO DESCEND INTO THE WORLD, the Holy One, blessed be He, summons that soul and says to it, go, enter a certain place, a certain body. It replies to Him, Master of the Universe, I am satisfied with the world I dwell in and shall not go into another world, where I shall be enslaved and soiled in their midst. The Holy One, blessed be He, said to it, ever since you were created, this is the reason why you were created, to be in that world IN A BODY. When the soul sees that, it descends despite itself and there enters A BODY.

53. אוֹרַיְיתָא דְּיָהֲבַת עֵיטָא לְכָל עָלְמָא חָמָאת הָכִי, אַזְהִירַת לִבְנֵי עָלְמָא, וְאָמְרַת, חָמוּ כַּמָּה חָס קוּדְשָׁא בְּרִיךְ הוּא עָלַיְיכוּ, מַרְגְּלִיתָא טָבָא דַּהֲוַת לֵיהּ, זַבִּין לְכוּ לְמַגָּנָא, דְּתִשְׁתַּעְבְּדוּן בָּהּ בְּהַאי עָלְמָא.

53. The Torah that gives advice to all who realize that, admonishes the

people in the world, saying, See how much the Holy One, blessed be He, has compassion for you. He sold for free the good gem He had, NAMELY THE SOUL, so that you will cultivate it in this world.

54. וְכִי יִמְכֹּר אִישׁ: דָּא קוּדְשָׁא בְּרִיךְ הוּא. אֶת בִּתּוֹ: דָּא נִשְׁמָתָא קַדִּישָׁא. לְאָמָה: לְמֶהֱוֵי אָמָה מִשְׁתַּעְבְּדָא בֵּינַיְיכוּ בְּהַאי עָלְמָא. בְּמָטוּ מִנַּיְיכוּ, בְּשַׁעֲתָא דְּמָטֵי זִמְנָא לְנָפְקָא מֵהַאי עָלְמָא, לֹא תֵצֵא כְּצֵאת הָעֲבָדִים, לָא תִּפּוּק מִתְטַנְּפָא בְּחוֹבִין, תִּפּוּק בַּת חוֹרִין, בְּרִירָה נְקִיָּה, בְּגִין דְּיֶחֱדֵי בָּהּ מָארָה וְיִשְׁתָּבַח בָּהּ וְיָהִיב לָהּ אֲגַר טָב, בְּצַחְצוּחֵי דְּגִנְתָא דְּעֵדֶן. כד"א וְהִשְׂבִּיעַ בְּצַחְצָחוֹת נַפְשֶׁךָ, וַדַּאי כַּד תִּפּוּק בְּרִירָה נְקִיָּה כַּדְקָא יֵאוֹת.

54. "And if a man sell," the Holy One, blessed be He, "his daughter," the holy soul; "to be a maidservant," to be an enslaved maidservant among you in this world. I pray you, when its time comes to depart from this world, that "she shall not go out as the menservants do," not soiled with iniquities, but free, refined and cleansed, so that its Master will be happy with it, praise Himself with it and give it good reward in the brightness of the Garden of Eden. This is the meaning of, "and satisfy your soul in drought (also: 'brightness')" (Yeshayah 58:11). THIS IS surely when the soul emerges properly clear and clean.

55. אֲבָל אִם רָעָה בְּעֵינֵי אֲדֹנֶיהָ, כַּד נָפְקַת מְלוּכְלְכָא בְּטִנּוּפֵי חוֹבִין, וְלָא אִתְחֲזִיאַת קַמֵּיהּ כַּדְקָא יֵאוֹת, וַוי לְהַהוּא גוּפָא, דְּאִתְאֲבִיד מֵהַהִיא נִשְׁמָתָא לְעָלְמִין. בְּגִין, דְּכַד נִשְׁמָתִין סַלְּקִין בְּרִירָן, וְנָפְקִין נְקִיִּין מֵהַאי עָלְמָא, כָּל נִשְׁמָתָא וְנִשְׁמָתָא, עָאלַת בְּסִפְרָא דְּאָחְמָתָא דְּמַלְכָּא, וְכֻלְּהוּ בִּשְׁמָהָן, וְאָמַר דָּא הִיא נִשְׁמָתָא דִּפְלָנְיָא, זְמִינַת תְּהֵא לְהַהוּא גוּפָא דְּשַׁבְקַת, וּכְדֵין כְּתִיב, לוֹ יְעָדָהּ, בּוֹ'.

55. But "If she please not her master," emerging soiled with the filth of transgressions, and it not presentable before Him as it should, woe to that body that was lost to the soul forever. For when the souls ascend clear and come out cleansed from this world, each soul enters the book in the King's bag. They are all RECORDED with names, which says that the soul of so and

so is designated to the body it left. Then it is written, "who has designated her for himself."

56. וְכַד נַפְקַת רָעָה בְּעֵינֵי אֲדֹנֶיהָ, דְּקָא אִסְתְּאָבָא בְּחוֹבִין, וּבְטִנּוּפָא דְּחַטָּאִין, כְּדֵין לֹא יְעָדָהּ בָּא׳. וְאִתְאֲבִיד הַהוּא גּוּפָא מִינָהּ וְאִיהִי לָא אִזְדַּמְנַת לְגַבֵּיהּ בַּר הַהִיא דְּמָארָהּ אִתְרָעֵי, וְתָב בְּתִיוּבְתָּא דְּגוּפָא בָּהּ, כְּדֵין כְּתִיב, וְהֶפְדָּהּ. כד״א פָּדָה נַפְשׁוֹ מֵעֲבוֹר בַּשַּׁחַת. וְהֶפְדָּהּ, הַאי אִיהוּ בְּבַר נָשׁ, דְּעֵיטָא דִּילֵיהּ, דְּיִפְרוֹק לָהּ, וְיֵתוּב בְּתִיוּבְתָּא, וְלִתְרֵין סִטְרִין קָאָמַר קוּדְשָׁא בְּרִיךְ הוּא, וְהֶפְדָּהּ בְּתִיוּבְתָּא. לְבָתַר דְּתָב בְּתִיוּבְתָּא, פָּדָא לָהּ מֵאוֹרְחָא דְּגֵיהִנָּם.

56. But when it comes out not pleasing its Master, soiled in the iniquities and filth of sins, then, "who has designated her for himself (Heb. *lo,* Lamed Vav)" is pronounced as "not (Heb. *lo,* Lamed Aleph) designated her," and the body is lost to it and it is not designated for it. The exception is the soul, which Master desires, as the body repented. Then it is written, "redeemed," as in, "Thus he will redeem his soul from going into the pit" (Iyov 33:28). "Redeemed" refers to man, whose advice is to redeem it and repent. And to both sides THE VERSE SAYS, "THEN SHALL HE LET HER BE REDEEMED." THE FIRST IS the Holy One, blessed be He, "THEN SHALL HE LET HER BE REDEEMED" FROM GEHENOM. THE SECOND CONCERNS MAN, who shall "let her be redeemed" by repentance, for after he repents, the Holy One, blessed be He, redeems them from the way to Gehenom.

57. לְעַם נָכְרִי לֹא יִמְשֹׁל לְמָכְרָהּ. מַאן עַם נָכְרִי. עֲלוּבְתָּא אִיהִי נִשְׁמָתָא, דְּכַד נַפְקַת מֵעָלְמָא, וּבַר נָשׁ אַסְטֵי אָרְחֵיהּ בַּהֲדָהּ, הִיא בָּעָאת לְסַלְּקָא לְעֵילָא, גּוֹ מַשְׁרְיָין קַדִּישִׁין, בְּגִין דְּמַשְׁרְיָין קַדִּישִׁין קַיְימִין בְּהַהוּא אָרְחָא דְּג״ע, וּמַשְׁרְיָין נוּכְרָאִין קַיְימִין בְּהַהוּא אָרְחָא דְּגֵיהִנָּם.

57. "To sell her to a strange nation he shall have no power." HE ASKS, what is the strange nation, AND ANSWERS, the soul is ashamed when it departs from the world, if the man deviated from the way together with it. It seeks to rise up to the holy camps, for holy camps are situated on the way to the Garden of Eden and strange camps, THAT IS, DEMONS, stand on the way to Gehenom.

‏58. זָכְתָה נִשְׁמְתָא, וְהַהוּא נְטִירוּ, וּפְרִישׂוּ דִּלְבוּשָׁא יַקִּירָא עָלָהּ. כַּמָּה מַשְׁרְיָין קַדִּישִׁין, קָא מִתְעַתְּדָן לָהּ, לְאִתְחַבְּרָא בַּהֲדָהּ, וּלְמֵיעָאל לָהּ לג״ע. לָא זָכְתָה, כַּמָּה מַשְׁרְיָין נוּכְרָאִין מִתְעַתְּדָן לְמֵיעַל לָהּ בְּאָרְחָא דְּגֵיהִנָּם. וְאִינוּן מַשְׁרְיָין דְּמַלְאֲכֵי חַבָּלָה זְמִינִין לְמֶעְבַּד בָּהּ נוּקְמִין, אָתָא קְרָא וְאוֹכַח, לְעַם נָכְרִי לֹא יִמְשֹׁל לְמָכְרָהּ, אִלֵּין מַלְאֲכֵי חַבָּלָה. בְּבִגְדוֹ בָהּ, אִיהוּ נְטִירוּ, דְּקוּדְשָׁא בְּרִיךְ הוּא עָבֵיד לָהּ נְטִירָא, דְּלָא יִשְׁלֹוט בָּהּ עַם נָכְרִי, בְּהַהוּא פְּרִיסוּ דִּנְטִירוּ עָלָהּ.

58. If that soul is worthy and the precious garment is spread on it, NAMELY THE NAME ELOHA, many holy camps meet it to join it and bring it to the Garden of Eden. If it is not worthy, many strange camps meet it to bring it to Gehenom. The camps of demons will wreak vengeance on it. For that the verse instructs, "To sell her to a strange nation he shall have no power," to the demons, "seeing that his garment is on her," which is the protective GARMENT, as the Holy One, blessed be He, protects it so that a strange nation will not rule over it through that protection spread over it, WHICH IS THE NAME ELOHA.

‏59. וְאִם לִבְנוֹ יִיעָדֶנָּה, ת״ח כַּמָּה אִית לֵיהּ לב״נ לְאִזְדַּהֲרָא דְּלָא יִסְטֵי אָרְחוֹי בְּהַאי עָלְמָא, דְּאִי זָכָה ב״נ בְּהַאי עָלְמָא, וְנָטִיר לָהּ לְנִשְׁמְתָא כַּדְקָא יֵאוֹת, הַאי אִיהוּ ב״נ דְּקוּדְשָׁא בְּרִיךְ הוּא אִתְרְעֵי בֵּיהּ, וְאִשְׁתְּבַח בֵּיהּ בְּכָל יוֹמַיָּא, בְּפָמַלְיָיא דִּילֵיהּ, וְאָמַר, חֲמוּ בְּרָא קַדִּישָׁא דְּאִית לִי בְּהַהוּא עָלְמָא, כָּךְ וְכָךְ עָבֵיד, כָּךְ וְכָךְ עוֹבָדוֹי מִתַּתְקְנָן.

59. "And if he designated her for his son" (Shemot 21:9): come and see how much a man should beware of not turning aside from his ways in this world. For if a man gains merit in this world and properly guards his soul, such is a man whom the Holy One, blessed be He, desires and is praised with every day before His retinue, saying, see the holy child I have in that world. He did such and such, these deeds of his are well done.

‏60. וְכַד הַאי נִשְׁמְתָא, נָפְקַת מֵהַאי עָלְמָא, זַכְיָיא נְקִיָּיה בְּרִירָה, קוּדְשָׁא בְּרִיךְ הוּא אַנְהִיר לָהּ בְּכַמָּה נְהוֹרִין, בְּכָל יוֹמָא קָארֵי עָלָהּ, דָּא

הִיא נִשְׁמְתָא דִפְלַנְיָא בְּרִי, נְטִירָא לֶיהֱוֵי לֵיהּ לְהַהוּא גּוּפָא דְּשָׁבַק.

60. When this soul emerges from this world pure, clean and refined, the Holy One, blessed be He, shines upon it many lights and announces daily of it, 'this it the soul of so and so my child, a keeping shall be provided for the body it left.'

‏61. וְדָא הוּא דִּכְתִיב, וְאִם לִבְנוֹ יִיעָדֶנָּה כְּמִשְׁפַּט הַבָּנוֹת יַעֲשֶׂה לָהּ, מַאי כְּמִשְׁפַּט הַבָּנוֹת. הָכָא אִית רָזָא לְחַכִּימִין, בְּגוֹ טִנָּרָא תַּקִּיפָא, רְקִיעָא טְמִירָא, אִית הֵיכָלָא חֲדָא, דְּאִקְרֵי הֵיכַל אַהֲבָה. וְתַמָּן אִינּוּן גִּנְזִין טְמִירִין, וְכָל נְשִׁיקִין דִּרְחִימוּ דְּמַלְכָּא אִינּוּן תַּמָּן, וְאִינּוּן נִשְׁמָתִין רְחִימָאן דְּמַלְכָּא עָאלִין תַּמָּן.

61. This is the meaning of, "And if he designated her for his son, he shall deal with her after the manner of daughters." What is "the manner of daughters"? Here is a secret to the wise. Within the strong rock, WHICH IS THE WORLD OF BRIYAH, in the hidden firmament, ABOVE EVERY OTHER FIRMAMENT THERE, there is a certain chamber called the chamber of love, WHICH IS SITUATED UNDERNEATH THE HOLY OF HOLIES OF BRIYAH. There are hidden treasures there, and all the kisses of the King's love are there. All the souls beloved of the King enter there.

‏62. כֵּיוָן דְּמַלְכָּא עָאל בְּהַהוּא הֵיכָלָא דְּמַלְכָּא, תַּמָּן כְּתִיב, וַיִּשַּׁק יַעֲקֹב לְרָחֵל, וְקוּדְשָׁא בְּרִיךְ הוּא אַשְׁכַּח תַּמָּן לְהַהִיא נִשְׁמְתָא קַדִּישָׁא, קָדִים מִיַּד וְנָשִׁיק לָהּ, וְגָפִיף לָהּ, וְסָלִיק לָהּ בַּהֲדֵיהּ, וְאִשְׁתַּעֲשַׁע בָּהּ.

62. When the King enters that King's chamber, it is written of that, "And Jacob kissed Rachel" (Beresheet 29:11), AS THE UNION OF KISSES LIES THERE. The Holy One, blessed be He, finds that holy soul there, and immediately hastens to kiss and embrace it, and raises it with Him to be delighted with it.

‏63. וְדָא הוּא כְּמִשְׁפַּט הַבָּנוֹת יַעֲשֶׂה לָהּ, כְּדִינָא דְּאַבָּא עָבִיד לִבְרַתֵּיהּ, דְּאִיהִי חֲבִיבָא לְגַבֵּיהּ, דְּנָשִׁיק לָהּ, וְגָפִיף לָהּ, וְיָהִיב לָהּ מַתְּנָן. כַּךְ

קוּדְשָׁא בְּרִיךְ הוּא עָבִיד, לְנִשְׁמְתָא זַכָּאָה בְּכָל יוֹמָא, כְּמָה דִּכְתִּיב
כְּמִשְׁפַּט הַבָּנוֹת יַעֲשֶׂה לָהּ.

63. This is the meaning of, "he shall deal with her after the manner of daughters," like a father would do to his favorite daughter, kissing her, embracing her and giving her gifts. Thus the Holy One, blessed be He, does to the worthy soul every day, as written, "he shall deal with her after the manner of daughters."

64. הַיְינוּ דִּכְתִּיב יַעֲשֶׂה לְמְחַכֵּה לוֹ, כְּמָה דְּהַאי בְּרַתָּא, אַשְׁלִימַת
עֲשִׂיָּיה בְּהַאי עָלְמָא. אוּף הָכִי קוּדְשָׁא בְּרִיךְ הוּא אַשְׁלִים לָהּ עֲשִׂיָּיה
אָחֳרָא בְּעָלְמָא דְּאָתֵי, דִּכְתִּיב, עַיִן לֹא רָאָתָה אֱלֹהִים זוּלָתְךָ יַעֲשֶׂה
לְמְחַכֵּה לוֹ. וְהָכָא כְּתִיב יַעֲשֶׂה לָהּ. ע״כ. הַהוּא סָבָא אִשְׁתַּטַּח, וְצַלֵּי
צְלוֹתָא. בָּכָה כְּמִלְקַדְמִין.

64. Hence it is written, "should do such a thing for him that waits for Him" (Yeshayah 64:3). Just as the daughter, NAMELY THE SOUL, finished its doing in this world, so the Holy One, blessed be He, finishes a different kind of action in the World to Come, as written, "neither has the eye seen, that an Elohim, beside You should do such a thing for him that waits for Him," while here it is written, "he shall deal (do) with her." THERE IS AN ANALOGY BETWEEN THE WORDS 'DO' IN THE VERSES. THE EYE CANNOT SEE THE DOING IN THE SECOND VERSE AS WELL. So far. The old man prostrated himself ON THE GROUND and prayed. He wept again.

65. וְאָמַר אִם אַחֶרֶת יִקַּח לוֹ וְגוֹ', מַאי אִם אַחֶרֶת, וְכִי נִשְׁמְתָא אָחֳרָא
זַמִּין קוּדְשָׁא בְּרִיךְ הוּא לְאָתָבָא לְצַדִּיקַיָּיא בְּהַאי עָלְמָא, וְלָאו הַאי
נִשְׁמְתָא דְּאַשְׁלִימַת בְּהַאי עָלְמָא רְעוּתָא דְּמָארָהּ, אִי הָכִי לֵית
אַבְטָחוּתָא לְצַדִּיקַיָּיא כְּלָל. מַאי אִם אַחֶרֶת יִקַּח לוֹ.

65. He said, "If he take another" (Shemot 21:10). HE ASKS, what does that mean, did the Holy One, blessed be He, prepare another soul to return to the righteous in this world? Is it not the same soul who filled to completion in this world the wishes of its Master? In that case there is no surety to the righteous at all. What is the meaning of, "If he take another"?

66. פָּתַח הַהוּא סָבָא וְאָמַר, וְיָשֹׁוב הֶעָפָר עַל הָאָרֶץ כְּשֶׁהָיָה וְהָרוּחַ
תָּשׁוּב אֶל הָאֱלֹהִים אֲשֶׁר נְתָנָה. הַאי קְרָא אוּקְמוּהָ חַבְרַיָּיא, בְּחָרְבַּן בֵּי
מַקְדְּשָׁא. וְיָשׁוֹב הֶעָפָר עַל הָאָרֶץ כְּשֶׁהָיָה. הָכָא אִיהוּ מַאי דִּכְתִּיב,
וְהַכְּנַעֲנִי אָז בָּאָרֶץ, כְּשֶׁהָיָה וַדַּאי. וְהָרוּחַ תָּשׁוּב אֶל הָאֱלֹהִים אֲשֶׁר
נְתָנָה, מַאי וְהָרוּחַ תָּשׁוּב. דָּא שְׁכִינְתָּא, דְּאִיהִי רוּחַ קַדִּישָׁא. כַּד חָמָאת
שְׁכִינְתָּא, בְּאִינּוּן עֶשֶׂר מַסָּעוֹת דְּקָא נַטְלָא, וְלָא בָּעוּן יִשְׂרָאֵל לְאָתָבָא
בִּתְיוּבְתָּא קָמֵי קוּדְשָׁא בְּרִיךְ הוּא, וְשָׁלְטָא סִטְרָא אַחֲרָא עַל אַרְעָא
קַדִּישָׁא, וְאוּקְמוּהָ חַבְרַיָּיא.

66. The old man opened with, "and the dust returns to the earth as it was; and the spirit returns to Elohim who gave it" (Kohelet 12:7). The friends ascribed this verse to the destruction of the Temple. "And the dust returns to the earth as it was" here accords with the verse, "And the Canaani was then in the land" (Beresheet 12:6). FOR AFTER THE DESTRUCTION THE LAND RETURNED TO BE UNDER THE RULE OF THE KLIPAH OF CANAAN AS BEFORE. "and the spirit returns to Elohim who gave it." What does it mean, "the spirit returns"? This is the Shechinah, which is the Holy Spirit. When the Shechinah saw in the ten journeys She took that Yisrael do not want to repent before the Holy One, blessed be He, and that the Other Side rules over the Holy Land, THE SHECHINAH DEPARTED AND RETURNED TO ELOHIM. The friends have explained it.

67. תָּא חֲזֵי, רוּחָא דְּבַר נָשׁ זַכָּאָה, אִתְעַטָּר בְּדִיּוּקְנָא בג״ע דִּלְתַתָּא,
וּבְכָל שַׁבָּתֵי וּמוֹעֲדֵי וְרֵישֵׁי יַרְחֵי, מִתְעַטְּרָן רוּחֵי, וּמִתְפַּשְׁטָן, וְסַלְּקִין
לְעֵילָא. כְּמָה דְּעָבִיד קוּדְשָׁא בְּרִיךְ הוּא, בְּהַהִיא נִשְׁמְתָא עִלָּאָה
קַדִּישָׁא לְעֵילָא, ה״נ עָבִיד בְּהַאי רוּחָא, לְתַתָּא בג״ע לְתַתָּא, דְּקָא
סַלְּקַת קַמֵּיהּ. וְאָמַר דָּא אִיהִי רוּחָא דִּפְלַנְיָא גוּפָא, מִיָּד מְעַטְּרָא לָהּ
קוּדְשָׁא בְּרִיךְ הוּא לְהַאי רוּחָא בְּכַמָּה עִטְרִין, וְאִשְׁתַּעֲשַׁע בָּהּ.

67. Come and see, the spirit of a righteous man is crowned with an image in the lower Garden of Eden. On every Shabbat, holiday and first day of the month, the spirits are crowned and take off THEIR IMAGE OF THE LOWER GARDEN OF EDEN, and rise up TO THE UPPER GARDEN OF EDEN. Just as

the Holy One, blessed be He, does to the holy soul above, so He does with this spirit below in the lower Garden of Eden that rose before Him. He says, this is the spirit of the body of so and so. Immediately the Holy One, blessed be He crowns that spirit with many crowns and delights in it.

68. וְאִי תֵּימָא, דְּהָא בְּגִין רוּחָא דָּא, שָׁבִיק קוּדְשָׁא בְּרִיךְ הוּא מַה דְּעָבִיד לְנִשְׁמָתָא. לָאו הָכִי. אֶלָּא שְׁאֵרָה כְּסוּתָה וְעֹנָתָהּ לֹא יִגְרָע, אִלֵּין אִינּוּן תְּלַת שְׁמָהָן עִלָּאִין, דְּעַיִן לֹא רָאֲתָה אֱלֹהִים זוּלָתְךָ.

68. If you wonder if the Holy One, blessed be He, leaves His dealings with the soul for that spirit it is not so, but, "her food, her clothing, and her duty of marriage, shall he not diminish" (Shemot 21:10). These are the three lofty names, as "neither has the eye seen, that an Elohim, beside You," WHICH IS THE SECRET OF BINAH.

69. וְכֻלְּהוּ בְּעָלְמָא דְּאָתֵי וְאִתְמַשְּׁכוּ מִתַּמָּן. חַד מִנַּיְיהוּ שְׁאֵרָה, מְשִׁיכוּ דִּנְצִיצוּ וּנְהִירוּ, דְּנָהִיר בְּאֹרַח, סָתִים, מְזוֹנָא דְּזָן כֹּלָּא, וְאִקְרֵי יהו"ד בְּנְקוּדַת אֱלֹהִים. שְׁאֵרָה בְּהִפּוּךְ אַתְוָון, אֲשֶׁר ה', וְדָא מֵאָשֵׁר שְׁמֵנָה לַחְמוֹ, וְדָא הוּא שְׁאֵרָה.

69. They all abide in the World to Come, WHICH IS BINAH, and flow from there. One of them is "her food," which is a flowing of radiance and light, WHICH ARE RETURNING LIGHT AND STRAIGHT LIGHT that shines in an obscure way. It is sustenance that nourishes everything and is called Yud Hei Vav Hei with the vowels of Elohim, WHICH IS THE NAME OF BINAH. *She'erah* (Eng. 'her food'), with the letters in a different order, becomes 'Asher Hei'. ASHER IS BINAH, WHICH IS THE FIRST HEI OF YUD HEI VAV HEI. This is the meaning of, "Out of Asher his bread shall be fat" (Beresheet 49:20), FOR FOOD FLOWS FROM IT. This is the meaning of, "her food."

70. כְּסוּתָה: פְּרִישׂוּ דְּמַלְכָּא. דָּא מְשִׁיכוּ אַחֲרָא, דְּנָהִיר וְנָטִיר לָהּ תָּדִיר, פְּרִישׂוּ דִּלְבוּשָׁא דְּמַלְכָּא, דְּפָרַשׂ עָלָהּ אֱלוֹהַּ. דָּא בְּבִגְדוֹ בָהּ תָּדִיר, דְּלָא אִתְעָדֵי מִינָהּ, וְהַאי אִיהוּ כְּסוּתָה.

70. "Her clothing" is the covering the King SPREADS OVER IT, NAMELY

THE PRECIOUS GARMENT OF THE NAME ELOHA. This is another shining flow, which always protects THE SOUL. It is the covering of the garment of the King that Eloha spreads over it. This is the meaning of, "he has dealt deceitfully with her (also: 'his garment is with her')" (Shemot 21:8) always, never absent from it. This is the meaning of, "her clothing."

71. וְעֹנָתָהּ, מַאן אִיהוּ. דָּא מְשִׁיכוּ דְּעָלְמָא דְּאָתֵי, דְּבֵיהּ כֹּלָּא. יְיָ' צְבָאוֹת אִיהוּ, וְדָא אִיהוּ דְּנָהִיר בְּכָל נְהוֹרִין סְתִימִין עִלָּאִין דְּאִילָנָא דְּחַיֵּי, דְּבֵיהּ עוֹנָה טְמִירָא, דְּמִתַּמָּן נַפְקַת. וְכָל דָּא בְּעֶדּוּנָא וְכִסּוּפָא דְּעָלְמָא דְּאָתֵי.

71. What is "her duty of marriage"? It is a flow from the World to Come, WHICH IS BINAH that contains everything. It is Yud Hei Vav Hei Tzva'ot THAT IS THE NAME IN NETZACH AND HOD IN BINAH. It shines with all the high hidden lights of the Tree of Life, where the duty of marriage is hidden and whence it comes out with the pleasure and yearning of the World to Come, WHICH IS BINAH.

72. תְּלָתָא הָנֵי לֹא יִגְרַע לָהּ, כַּד אִיהִי זַכָּאת כַּדְקָא יֵאוֹת. וְאִי לָאו אִיהִי כַּדְקָא יֵאוֹת, הָנֵי תְּלָתָא גַּרְעָאן מִנָּהּ, דְּלָא יִתְעֲבִיד לָהּ עֲטָרָה אֲפִילוּ מֵחַד מִנַּיְיהוּ, תָּא חֲזֵי, מַה כְּתִיב, וְאִם שְׁלָשׁ אֵלֶּה לֹא יַעֲשֶׂה לָהּ, דְּלָא זָכָאת בְּהוּ, וְיָצְאָה חִנָּם אֵין כָּסֶף תִּפוּק מִקַּמֵּיהּ, וְדַחְיָין לָהּ לְבַר. אֵין כָּסֶף, לֵית לָהּ כִּסּוּפָא, וְלֵית לָהּ עֶדּוּנָא כְּלָל.

72. These three must He not diminish, when it is properly worthy. If it is not as it should be, these three are taken from it, as not even one becomes a crown for it. Come and see, it is written, "And if he do not these three to her" (Ibid. 11), that is, it is not worthy of them, "then shall she go out free without money" (Ibid.), go out from Him. It is pushed out. It is "without money," without yearning, OR LONGING, and derives no pleasure at all.

73. עַד כָּאן אוֹכְּחַת אוֹרַיְיתָא, דְּכָל עֵיטִין בָּהּ תַּלְיָין, וְיָהִיבַת עֵיטָא טָבָא לִבְנֵי נָשָׁא. מִכָּאן וּלְהָלְאָה נֶהְדַּר לְמִלִּין קַדְמָאִין, בְּהַהוּא נְטִירוּ עִלָּאָה, דְּקָא פָּרִישׁ עֲלָהּ קוּדְשָׁא בְּרִיךְ הוּא, בְּגִין דְּלָא תְּהֵא לְעַם נָכְרִי,

דְּהָא בִּגְדוּ בָהּ, וּנְטִירוּ אִיהוּ לָהּ תָּדִיר.

73. Up to here the Torah admonishes, from which come every kind of advice, and gives good advice to people. From now on, let us return to the first subject of the lofty protection the Holy One, blessed be He, spreads over it, THE SOUL, so it shall not be to a strange nation, because "his garment is with her," and always protects it.

74. וְאִם לִבְנוֹ יִיעָדֶנָּה כְּמִשְׁפַּט הַבָּנוֹת יַעֲשֶׂה לָהּ. אָמַר הַהוּא סָבָא, חַבְרַיָּיא, כַּד תְּהַכוּן לְגַבֵּי הַהוּא טִינָרָא דְּעָלְמָא סָמִיךְ עֲלֵיהּ, אִמְרוּ לֵיהּ, דְּיִדְכַּר יוֹמָא דְּתַלְגָּא דְּאִזְדְּרָעוּ פּוֹלִין לְחַמְשִׁין וּתְרֵין גַּוְונִין, וַהֲדַר אַקְרֵינָן הַאי קְרָא, וְהוּא יֵימָא לְכוֹן.

74. "And if he designated her for his son, he shall deal with her after the manner of daughters." The old man said, friends, when you go to that rock that supports the world, THAT IS, RABBI SHIMON, tell him to remember the snowy day when beans were sown in 52 ways. Then shall you recite this verse and he will tell you ITS MEANING.

A Synopsis

The merchant turns to the question of who is the son of the Holy One, blessed be He, explaining that at the age of thirteen a boy is considered a son to the Congregation of Yisrael, and at the age of twenty a man is considered to be a son of the Holy One, blessed be He. The merchant tells of the additional soul that is attained by the righteous on the Sabbath.

75. אָמְרוּ בְּמָטוּ מִינָךְ מַאן דְּשָׁארֵי מִלָּה הוּא יֵימָא. אָמַר לוֹן, וַדַּאי דְּיָדַעְנָא דְּזַכָּאִין אַתּוּן, וְאִית לְרַמְזָא לְכוּ רְמָזָא דְּחַכִּימִין, וְעַל מַה דַּאֲנָא אֵימָא, כַּד תִּדְכְּרוּן לֵיהּ סִימָנָא דָּא, הוּא יַשְׁלִים עַל דָּא. הַשְׁתָּא אִית לוֹמַר, מַאן הוּא דְּאִקְרֵי בֵּן לְקוּדְשָׁא בְּרִיךְ הוּא.

75. The said to him, if you please, whoever opened the discussion, let him tell it. He said to them, assuredly I knew that you were righteous, and that you are to be intimated to as the sages are. As for my words TO YOU, when you mention this sign TO RABBI SHIMON, he will finish it, THAT IS, FINISH MY WORDS. Now let us say who he is that is called the son of the Holy One,

blessed be He.

76. תַּ"ח כָּל הַהוּא דְּזָכֵי לִתְלֵיסַר שְׁנִין וּלְהָלְאָה, אִקְרֵי בֵּן לכ"י. וְכָל מַאן דְּאִיהוּ מִבֶּן עֶשְׂרִין שְׁנִין וּלְעֵילָא וְזָכֵי בְּהוּ, אִקְרֵי בֵּן לְקוּדְשָׁא בְּרִיךְ הוּא וַדַּאי בָּנִים אַתֶּם לַיְיָ' אֱלֹהֵיכֶם.

76. Come and see, whoever reached thirteen years and on is considered a son to the Congregation of Yisrael, WHICH IS MALCHUT. Whoever is twenty years old or older and gains merit in them, is considered a son of the Holy One, blessed be He, NAMELY ZEIR ANPIN, as written, "You are the children of Hashem your Elohim" (Devarim 14:1).

77. כַּד מָטָא דָּוִד לִתְלֵיסַר שְׁנִין, וְזָכָה בְּהַהוּא יוֹמָא דְּעָאל לְאַרְבֵּיסַר, כְּדֵין כְּתִיב, יְיָ' אָמַר אֵלַי בְּנִי אַתָּה אֲנִי הַיּוֹם יְלִדְתִּיךָ. מ"ט. דְּהָא מִקַּדְמַת דְּנָא לָא הֲוָה לֵיהּ בְּרָא, וְלָא שָׁרָאת עָלֵיהּ נִשְׁמְתָא עִלָּאָה, דְּהָא בִּשְׁנֵי עָרְלָה הֲוָה, וּבג"כ, אֲנִי הַיּוֹם יְלִדְתִּיךָ, הַיּוֹם וַדַּאי יְלִדְתִּיךָ. אֲנִי, וְלָא סִטְרָא אַחֲרָא, כְּמָה דַּהֲוָה עַד הַשְׁתָּא, אֲנִי בִּלְחוֹדָאי. בַּר עֶשְׂרִין שְׁנִין, מַה כְּתִיב בִּשְׁלֹמֹה, כִּי בֵן הָיִיתִי לְאָבִי, לְאָבִי מַמָּשׁ וַדַּאי.

77. When David was thirteen years old and gained merit on the day he entered his fourteenth year, he wrote, "Hashem has said to me, You are my son; this day have I begotten you" (Tehilim 2:7). What is the reason for it? Before that, he was not His son, as the supernal soul did not dwell on him, since he lived during the Orlah years. Therefore it is written, "this day have I begotten you." Assuredly I have begotten you, I and not the Other Side, as it was until now. BUT NOW it is I alone. Upon his reaching his twentieth year, it is written of Solomon, "For I was my father's son" (Mishlei 4:3), my own father's NAMELY THE SON OF THE HOLY ONE, BLESSED BE HE. FOR AT THE AGE OF TWENTY HE MERITED THE MOCHIN OF CHAYAH, WHICH MADE HIM A SON OF THE HOLY ONE, BLESSED BE HE, NAMELY TO ZEIR ANPIN.

78. וְאִם לִבְנוֹ יִיעָדֶנָּה. בַּר תְּלֵיסַר שְׁנִין וּלְהָלְאָה, דְּהָא נַפְקָא מֵרְשׁוּ דְּסִטְרָא אַחֲרָא דְּאִזְדַּמְּנַת לֵיהּ, מַה כְּתִיב כְּמִשְׁפַּט הַבָּנוֹת יַעֲשֶׂה לָּהּ. מַהוּ כְּמִשְׁפַּט הַבָּנוֹת. תָּנֵינָן, בְּכָל יוֹמָא וְיוֹמָא, חָמֵי קוּדְשָׁא בְּרִיךְ הוּא

לְהַהוּא יְנוֹקָא דְּקָאֵי בִּרְשׁוּ דְּעָרְלָה, וְאִיהוּ נָפִיק מִינָהּ, וְאִתְמְשַׁךְ לְבֵי סָפְרָא, וְתַבַּר לָהּ, וְאָזִיל לְבֵי כְּנִישְׁתָּא, וְתַבַּר לָהּ. מַה עָבִיד קוּדְשָׁא בְּרִיךְ הוּא לְהַהִיא נִשְׁמָתָא. אָעִיל לָהּ לְאִדְרָא דִּילֵיהּ, וְיָהִיב לָהּ מַתְּנָן, וּנְבִזְבְּזָן סַגִּיאִין, וְקָשִׁיט לָהּ בְּקִשׁוּטִין עִלָּאִין, עַד זִמְנָא דְּאָעִיל לָהּ לַחוּפָּה בְּהַהוּא בַּר, מִתְּלֵיסַר שְׁנִין וּלְעֵילָא.

78. "And if he designated her for his son," that is, since he is thirteen years old or more, when he is no longer under the dominion of the Other Side that comes his way. Then it is written, "he shall deal with her after the manner of daughters." What is the manner of daughters? HE ANSWERS, we learned that the Holy One, blessed be He, sees daily that child under the rule of the Orlah. When he comes out of it and goes to school to break it, goes to the synagogue to break it, the Holy One, blessed be He, takes that soul into His room where He gives it many gifts and offerings and adorns it with supernal adornments until the time comes when He brings it under the canopy into that son, NAMELY HE CLOTHES IT WITH HIM, after his thirteenth year.

79. אִם אַחֶרֶת יִקַּח לוֹ. הָכָא אִית רָזָא דְּרָזִין, לְחַכִּימִין אִתְמְסָרֵי, וְאִית לְאוֹדְעָא בְּקַדְמֵיתָא מִלָּה חֲדָא. ת"ח, בְּיוֹמָא דְּשַׁבַּתָּא בְּשַׁעֲתָא דְּאִתְקַדָּשׁ יוֹמֵי, נַפְקֵי נִשְׁמָתִין מִגּוֹ אִילָנֵי דְּחַיֵּי, וּמְנַשְּׁבָן אִינּוּן נִשְׁמָתִין קַדִּישִׁין לְתַתָּאֵי, וְנַיְיחִין בְּהוּ כָּל יוֹמָא דְּשַׁבַּתָּא. וּלְבָתַר דְּנָפִיק שַׁבַּתָּא, סַלְּקִין כֻּלְּהוּ נִשְׁמָתִין וּמִתְעַטְּרָן בְּעִטְרִין קַדִּישִׁין לְעֵילָא. אוֹף הָכִי, קוּדְשָׁא בְּרִיךְ הוּא אַזְמִין לְהַהוּא בַּר נָשׁ, וְדָא הוּא נִשְׁמָתָא אַחֶרֶת, וְאע"ג דְּדָא זְמִינָא לֵיהּ, נִשְׁמָתָא דַּהֲוָת לֵיהּ בְּקַדְמֵיתָא, שְׁאָרָה דְּקַדְמֵיתָא, כְּסוּתָהּ וְעֹנָתָהּ לֹא יִגְרָע, כְּמָה דְּאִתְּמַר.

79. "If he take another": WHAT IS ANOTHER? Here there are secret mysteries given to the sages. First I have to inform you of something. Come and see, on Shabbat, when the day is sanctified, souls emerge from the Tree of Life, NAMELY ZEIR ANPIN. These souls blow on the lower beings, who rest for it throughout the Shabbat day. THEY ARE THE SECRET OF THE ADDITIONAL SOUL THAT THE RIGHTEOUS ATTAIN ON SHABBAT DAY. At the end of Shabbat, all the souls go up AGAIN to be crowned with holy crowns above. HERE too the Holy One, blessed be He, summons for that

man ON THE DAY OF SHABBAT AN ADDITIONAL SOUL. This is the other
soul, OF WHICH THE VERSE SAYS, "IF HE TAKE ANOTHER." And though
this soul came to him, as for the soul he had before, the food of the first one,
"her clothing, and her duty of marriage, shall he not diminish," THE
MEANING OF WHICH IS according to the explanation given.

80. בָּכָה הַהוּא סָבָא כְּמִלְּקַדְמִין, וְאָמַר אִיהוּ לְנַפְשֵׁיהּ, סָבָא סָבָא,
כַּמָּה יָגַעְתָּ לְאַדְבְּקָא מִלִּין קַדִּישִׁין אִלֵּין, וְהַשְׁתָּא תֵּימָא לוֹן בְּרִגְעָא
חֲדָא. אִי תֵּימָא דְּתֵיחָס עָלַיְיהוּ עַל אִינוּן מִלִּין וְלָא תֵּימָא לוֹן, הָא
כְּתִיב אַל תִּמְנַע טוֹב מִבְּעָלָיו בִּהְיוֹת לְאֵל יָדְךָ לַעֲשׂוֹת.

80. The old man wept again and said to himself, old, old man, how much
have you toiled to attain these holy matters, and now you say them in an
instance. If you contemplate sparing these matters and not disclosing them,
yet it says, "Withhold not good from those to whom it is due, when it is in
the power of your hand to do it" (Mishlei 3:27).

81. מַאי אַל תִּמְנַע טוֹב מִבְּעָלָיו. אֶלָּא, קוּדְשָׁא בְּרִיךְ הוּא וכ"י אִינוּן
הָכָא. דְּהָא בְּכָל אֲתָר דְּמִלִּין דְּאוֹרַיְיתָא אַמְרִין, קוּדְשָׁא בְּרִיךְ הוּא וכ"י
אִינוּן תַּמָּן, וְצַיְיתֵי לוֹן. וּכְדֵין, הַהוּא אִילָנָא דְּטוֹב וָרָע, בְּשַׁעֲתָא
דְּאַזְלִין מִתַּמָּן, וְצַיְיתוּ אִינוּן מִלִּין, הַהוּא סִטְרָא דְּטוֹב אִתְגַּבַּר,
וְאִסְתַּלַּק לְעֵילָא, וְקוּדְשָׁא בְּרִיךְ הוּא וכ"י מִתְעַטְּרָן בְּהַהוּא טוֹב, וְאִלֵּין
אִינוּן בְּעָלָיו דְּהַהוּא טוֹב.

81. What is THE MEANING OF, "Withhold not good from those to whom it is
due"? HE SAYS, the Holy One, blessed be He, and the Congregation of
Yisrael, WHICH IS MALCHUT, are here. For wherever words of the Torah
are spoken, the Holy One, blessed be He, and the Congregation of Yisrael
are present, and hearken to them. Then, when THE HOLY ONE, BLESSED
BE HE, AND THE CONGREGATION OF YISRAEL go away from the Tree of
Knowledge of Good and Evil, WHICH IS MALCHUT, to listen to words of
Torah, its good side is elevated and rises high, and the Holy One, blessed be
He, and the Congregation of Yisrael are crowned with that goodness. They
are those to whom it is due. THEREFORE "WITHHOLD NOT GOOD FROM

THOSE TO WHOM IT IS DUE" REFERS TO THE HOLY ONE, BLESSED BE HE, AND THE CONGREGATION OF YISRAEL.

‎82. סָבָא סָבָא, אַתְּ אָמַרְתְּ מִלִּין אִלֵּין, וְלָא יָדַעְתְּ אִי קוּדְשָׁא בְּרִיךְ הוּא הָכָא, וְאִי אִלֵּין דְּקַיְימֵי הָכָא זַכָּאִין לְמִלִּין אִלֵּין. לָא תִּדְחַל סָבָא, דְּהָא הֲוֵית בְּכַמָּה קְרָבִין דְּגַבְרִין תַּקִיפִין, וְלָא דָחִילַת, וְהַשְׁתָּא אַנְתְּ דָחִיל, אֵימָא מִילָּךְ, דְּהָא וַדַּאי הָכָא אִיהוּ קוּדְשָׁא בְּרִיךְ הוּא וכ"י, וְזַכָּאִין אִינוּן אִלֵּין דְּהָכָא. וְאִי לָאו הָכִי, לָא אַעֲרַעְנָא בְּהוּ, וְלָא שָׁרֵינָא בְּאִלֵּין מִלִּין. אֵימָא מִלּוּלָךְ סָבָא, אֵימָא בְּלָא דְחִילוּ.

82. AGAIN HE SAID TO HIMSELF, old, old man, you have spoken these words, yet you did not know whether the Holy One, blessed be He, is here, and whether those present here are worthy of these words. Do not fear, old man, for you have participated in several wars with mighty men yet you had no fear, yet now you fear. Speak up, for assuredly the Holy One, blessed be He, and the Congregation of Yisrael are here, and those present are righteous. Otherwise, I would not have met them, or began with these words. Speak up, old man, speak without fear.

A Synopsis

We hear an explanation of "Hashem my Elohim, You are very great, You are clothed with glory and majesty," "who covers Himself with light as with a garment," "who stretches out the heavens," "who lays the beams of His chambers in the waters," "who makes the clouds His chariots," "who walks upon the wings of the wind," who "makes the winds His messengers." Next we learn about the souls of converts that soar from the Garden of Eden.

‎83. פָּתַח וְאָמַר, יי' אֱלֹהַי גָּדַלְתָּ מְאֹד הוֹד וְהָדָר לָבָשְׁתָּ. יי' אֱלֹהַי: דָּא שֵׁירוּתָא דִּמְהֵימְנוּתָא, סְלִיקוּ דְמַחֲשָׁבָה, וְעָלְמָא דְּאָתֵי, רָזָא חֲדָא בְּלָא פְּרוּדָא. גָּדַלְתָּ: דָּא שֵׁירוּתָא, יוֹמָא קַדְמָאָה, וְאִינוּן יוֹמִין עַתִּיקִין, סְטָרָא דִּימִינָא. מְאֹד: דָּא הוּא סְטָרָא דִּשְׂמָאלָא.

83. He opened up with the words, "Hashem my Elohim You are very great, You are clothed with glory and majesty" (Tehilim 104:1). "Hashem my Elohim" is the beginning of Faith: the rising of thought, WHICH IS

CHOCHMAH, and the World to Come, WHICH IS BINAH, ARE PART OF the same secret, without separation. FOR ABA AND IMA, WHICH ARE CHOCHMAH AND BINAH, ARE TWO FRIENDS THAT NEVER SEPARATE. "You are very great" is the beginning OF THE SEVEN LOWER SFIROT, the first day, WHICH IS THE FIRST SFIRAH, CHESED. They are ancient days, NAMELY, IT RECEIVES FROM THE SFIROT OF ATIK, and is the right side. "Very" is the left side, NAMELY GVURAH.

84. הוֹד וְהָדָר לָבַשְׁתָּ: אִלֵּין תְּרֵין בַּדֵּי עֲרָבוֹת. עַד הָכָא, כֵּיוָן דְּמָטָא לְגוֹ אִילָנָא דְּחַיֵּי, אִתְטָמַר, וְלָא אִסְתַּלָּק לְמֶהֱוֵי בְּמִנְיָינָא, בְּגִין הַהוּא מְאֹד. מַאי מְאֹד. שְׂמָאלָא, דְּכָל עַנְפִּין דִּלְתַתָּא וּבִכְלָלָא עֲנָפָא מְרִירָא חֲדָא. וְעַל דָּא אִתְטָמַר הַהוּא אִילָנָא דְּחַיֵּי, וְלָא בָּעָא לְמֶהֱוֵי בְּמִנְיָינָא דָּא, עַד דְּאַהֲדַר כְּמִלְּקַדְמִין, וְשַׁבַּח בְּגַוְונָא אַחֲרָא.

84. "You are clothed with glory and majesty": these are the two branches of willow, WHICH ARE NETZACH AND HOD. IT SPOKE until here; once it reached the Tree of Life, WHICH IS TIFERET, it hid and could not be counted, because of "very." What is "very?" It is the left, as all the lower branches, among which is one bitter branch, WHICH IS SAMAEL, ARE INCLUDED IN THE LEFT. Therefore the Tree of Life hid, and did not wish to be part of the count, until it again praised in a different manner.

85. וְאָמַר, עֹטֶה אוֹר כְּשַׁלְמָה דָּא שֵׁירוּתָא דְּיוֹמָא קַדְמָאָה. נוֹטֶה שָׁמַיִם, הָכָא אִתְכְּלִיל שְׂמָאלָא, וְלָא אָמַר מְאֹד, אִתְכְּלִיל שְׂמָאלָא בִּימִינָא, לְמֶהֱוֵי נָהִיר בִּכְלָלָא דִּשְׁמַיִם. הַמְקָרֶה בַּמַּיִם עֲלִיּוֹתָיו, הָכָא נָפִיק בְּחֶדְוָה הַהוּא אִילָנָא דְּחַיֵּי, נָהָר דְּנָפִיק מֵעֵדֶן, וְאִשְׁתְּרָשׁוּ בֵּיהּ בְּמֵימוֹי אִינּוּן תְּרֵי בַּדֵּי עֲרָבוֹת, דְּאִינּוּן גַּדְלִין בְּמֵימוֹי, הה״ד הַמְקָרֶה בַמַּיִם עֲלִיּוֹתָיו. מַאן עֲלִיּוֹתָיו. אִלֵּין בַּדֵּי עֲרָבוֹת.

85. It says, "Who covers Himself with light as with a garment" (Ibid. 2): this is the beginning of the first day, NAMELY THE FIRST SFIRAH, CHESED. "Who stretches out the heavens" (Ibid.) IS TIFERET THAT IS CALLED HEAVENS. Here the left side, WHICH IS GVURAH, is included, yet it does not say 'very', for the left is included in the right so it illumines throughout

the heaven, THAT IS TIFERET. "Who lays the beams of His chambers in the waters" (Ibid. 3). Here the Tree of Life gladly emerged, which is the tree that went out of Eden, NAMELY TIFERET. The two branches of willow, WHICH ARE NETZACH AND HOD, were rooted in its waters, where they grow. This is the meaning of, "Who lays the beams of His chambers in the waters." What are His chambers? They are the two branches of willow, NETZACH AND HOD.

86. וְדָא הוּא דִּכְתִּיב, וְעַל יוּבַל יְשַׁלַּח שָׁרָשָׁיו. וְדָא הוּא רָזָא דִּכְתִּיב נָהָר פְּלָגָיו יְשַׂמְּחוּ עִיר אֱלֹהִים. מַאן פְּלָגָיו. אִלֵּין אִינּוּן שָׁרָשָׁיו. וְהָכִי אִקְרוּן, עֲלִיּוֹתָיו, שָׁרָשָׁיו, פְּלָגָיו, כֻּלְּהוּ אִשְׁתְּרָשׁוּ בְּאִינּוּן מַיִין דְּהַהוּא נָהָר.

86. This is the meaning of, "and that spreads out its roots by the river" (Yirmeyah 17:8). This is a secret mentioned in, "There is a river, whose streams make glad the city of Elohim" (Tehilim 46:5). Who are the streams? They are His roots, NAMELY NETZACH AND HOD. They are so called, His beams, roots and streams. They all grew roots in the water of the river, WHICH IS TIFERET.

87. הַשָּׂם עָבִים רְכוּבוֹ. דָּא מִיכָאֵל וְגַבְרִיאֵל, אִלֵּין הֵם עָבִים. הַמְהַלֵּךְ עַל כַּנְפֵי רוּחַ, לְמֵיהַב אַסְוָותָא לְעָלְמָא, וְדָא אִיהוּ רְפָאֵל. מִכָּאן וּלְהָלְאָה עוֹשֶׂה מַלְאָכָיו רוּחוֹת וְגוֹ'. סָבָא סָבָא, אִי כָּל הַנֵּי יָדַעְתְּ, אֵימָא וְלָא תִּדְחַל, אֵימָא מִילָךְ וְיִנְהֲרוּן מִלִּין דְּפוּמָךְ. חֲדוּ חַבְרַיָּיא, וַהֲווֹ צַיְּיתִין בְּחֶדְוָה לְמִלּוֹי קַדִּישִׁין. אָמַר אִי סָבָא אִי סָבָא, בְּמָה עָיֵילַת גַּרְמָךְ, עָאלַת בְּיַמָּא רַבָּא, אִית לָךְ לְשַׁטְטָא וּלְנַפְקָא מִתַּמָּן.

87. "Who makes the clouds His chariots" (Tehilim 104:3): these are Michael and Gabriel, who are clouds. "Who walks upon the wings of the wind" (Ibid.) to give healing to the world. This is Refael. From now on, He "makes the winds His messengers…" (Ibid. 4). Old, old man, since you know these matters, speak and do not be afraid, speak up and let the words of your mouth shine forth. The friends rejoiced and were listening with joy to his holy words. THE OLD MAN said TO HIMSELF, Oh old man, what have

you got yourself into? You have come into the great sea, and now you should swim to get out of there.

אם אַחֶרֶת יַקַּח לוֹ, כַּמָּה גִּלְגּוּלִין עַתִּיקִין הָכָא, דְּלָא אִתְגַּלְּוֹן עַד .88
הָאִידָנָא, וְכֻלְּהוּ קְשׁוֹט כַּדְקָא יֵאוֹת, דְּלֵית לְאַסְטָאָה מֵאֹרַח קְשׁוֹט,
אֲפִילוּ כִּמְלֹא נִימָא. בְּקַדְמֵיתָא אִית לְאִתְעָרָא, נִשְׁמָתִין דְּגִיּוֹרִין כֻּלְּהוּ,
פָּרְחָן מִגּוֹ גִּנְתָּא דְּעֵדֶן בְּאֹרַח סָתִים, כַּד מִסְתַּלְּקָן מֵהַאי עָלְמָא,
נִשְׁמָתְהוֹן דְּקָא רְוָוחָא מִגּוֹ גִּנְתָּא דְּעֵדֶן, לְאָן אֲתַר תַּיְּיבִין.

88. "If he take another" (Shemot 21:10). How many ancient incarnations are here that were not yet revealed, which are all properly true, for one should not turn from the true path even a hairbreadth. First it should be commented that all the souls of the converts soar from the Garden of Eden by a hidden path TO BE CLOTHED IN CONVERTS. HE ASKS, once they depart from this world, to where do the souls the converts merited return? THAT IS, WHO RAISES THEM BACK TO THE PLACE FROM WHENCE THEY CAME, NAMELY THE GARDEN OF EDEN?

אֶלָּא תָּנֵינָן, מַאן דְּנָטִיל וְאָחִיד בְּנִכְסֵי גִּיּוֹרִין בְּקַדְמֵיתָא, זָכֵי בְּהוּ. .89
אוּף הָכִי כָּל אִינּוּן נִשְׁמָתִין קַדִּישִׁין עִלָּאִין, דְּקָא זַמִּין לוֹן קוּדְשָׁא
בְּרִיךְ הוּא לְתַתָּא כִּדְקָאַמְרַן, כֻּלְּהוּ נָפְקִין לְזִמְנִין יְדִיעָן. בְּגִין
לְאִשְׁתַּעְשְׁעָא בַּג״ע, וּפַגְעָן בְּאִינּוּן נִשְׁמָתִין דְּגִיּוֹרִין, מַאן דְּאָחִיד בְּהוּ
מֵאִלֵּין נִשְׁמָתִין, אָחִיד בְּהוּ וְזָכֵי בְּהוּ, וּמִתְלַבְּשָׁן בְּהוּ, וְסַלְּקִין. וְכֻלְּהוּ
קַיְּימֵי בְּהַאי לְבוּשָׁא וְנַחְתּוּ גּוֹ גִּנְתָּא בִּלְבוּשָׁא דָא. בְּגִין דִּבְגִנְתָּא דְּעֵדֶן,
לָא קַיְּימָאן תַּמָּן, אֶלָּא בִּלְבוּשָׁא, כָּל אִינּוּן דְּקַיְּימֵי תַּמָּן.

89. But we learned that whoever seizes and takes first the possessions of a convert WHO HAS NO HEIRS gets them. Here too, all these holy supernal souls that the Holy One, blessed be He, summons to come down as we said, emerge in specific times, NAMELY ON SHABBAT, HOLIDAYS AND THE FIRST DAY OF THE MONTH, to enjoy in the Garden of Eden where they meet the souls of the converts. Whichever of the souls they take, they merit and clothe themselves with it and rise. They all remain in that garment and descend into the Garden of Eden in that garment, since all those who stay

there do so only in a garment. THUS, THOSE SOULS RAISE THE SOULS OF THE CONVERTS BACK TO THE GARDEN OF EDEN.

90. אִי תֵּימָא, דִּבְגִין הַאי לְבוּשָׁא, גַּרְעָן אִינּוּן נִשְׁמָתִין מִכָּל עֲנוּגָא דַּהֲוָה לוֹן בְּקַדְמֵיתָא. הָא כְּתִיב, אִם אַחֶרֶת יִקַּח לוֹ שְׁאֵרָהּ כְּסוּתָהּ וְעוֹנָתָהּ לֹא יִגְרָע. בְּגִנְתָּא קַיְימֵי בִּלְבוּשֵׁי דָּא, דְּקַדְמָן לְאַחֲדָא בְּהוּ וְזָכֵי בְּהוּ, וְכַד סַלְּקִין לְעֵילָא, מִתְפַּשְׁטָן מִנֵּיהּ, דְּהָא תַּמָּן לָא קַיְימָן בִּלְבוּשָׁא.

90. If you say that for that garment OF THE CONVERTS' SOULS, their former delight is diminished, it is written of it, "If he take another wife, her food, her clothing, and her duty of marriage, shall he not diminish." They remain in the Garden of Eden in that garment that they were the first to take and get, NAMELY THE GARMENT MADE OF CONVERTS' SOULS. When they rise, they strip themselves from it, because there, ABOVE, they are not clothed.

91. בָּכָה הַהוּא סָבָא כְּמִלְּקַדְמִין, וְאָמַר לְנַפְשֵׁיהּ, סָבָא סָבָא, בְּוַדַּאי אִית לָךְ לְמִבְכֵּי, בְּוַדַּאי אִית לָךְ לְאוֹשָׁדָא דִּמְעִין, עַל כָּל מִלָּה וּמִלָּה, אֲבָל גַּלֵּי קֳמֵי קוּדְשָׁא בְּרִיךְ הוּא וּשְׁכִינְתֵּיהּ קַדִּישָׁא, דַּאֲנָא בִּרְעוּ דְּלִבָּא, וּבְפוּלְחָנָא דִּלְהוֹן קָאמֵינָא, בְּגִין דְּאִינּוּן בְּעָלַיו דְּכָל מִלָּה, וּמִתְעַטְּרָן בְּהוּ.

91. The old man cried as before, and said to himself: Old, old man, most certainly, you have reason to cry! Surely you have justification to shed tears for each and every word. Yet it is revealed to the Holy One, blessed be He, and His sacred Shechinah, that it is willingly and for their worship that I speak, since they are the owners of every word, and are adorned with them.

92. כָּל אִינּוּן נִשְׁמָתִין קַדִּישִׁין, כַּד נַחְתֵּי לְהַאי עָלְמָא, בְּגִין לְמִשְׁרֵי כָּל חַד עַל דּוּכְתַּיְיהוּ, דְּאִתְחֲזוּן בְּהוּ, לִבְנֵי נָשָׁא. כֻּלְּהוּ נַחְתֵּי מִתְלַבְּשָׁן בְּאִינּוּן נִשְׁמָתִין דְּקָא אַמְרָן, וְהָכִי עָאלִין בְּזַרְעָא קַדִּישָׁא. וּבְמַלְבּוּשָׁא דָּא, קַיְימֵי לְאִשְׁתַּעֲבְּדָא מִנַּיְיהוּ בְּהַאי עָלְמָא. וְכַד אִשְׁתָּאבָן אִינּוּן

מַלְבּוּשִׁין מִמַּלִּין דְּהַאי עָלְמָא, אִינּוּן נִשְׁמָתִין קַדִּישִׁין, אִתְזָנָן מֵרֵיחָא דְּקָא אֲרִיחָא, מִגּוֹ לְבוּשֵׁיהוֹן אִלֵּין.

92. All those sacred souls, when they have descended to this world, come with a view to finding their proper resting place within the human being. They all come clothed with these souls OF CONVERTS, as we have stated, and in this manner pass into the holy seed. And with this raiment they are ready to be provided for in this world, WITH THE PRECEPTS AND GOOD DEEDS; and when these vestments have been satiated with the things of this world, NAMELY, THE PRECEPTS, then these sacred souls take pleasure in the fragrances that exude from their attire.

93. קוּדְשָׁא בְּרִיךְ הוּא כָּל מִלִּין סְתִימִין דְּאִיהוּ עָבִיד, עָאל לוֹן בְּאוֹרַיְיתָא קַדִּישָׁא, וְכֹלָּא אִשְׁתְּכַח בְּאוֹרַיְיתָא, וְהַהִיא מִלָּה סְתִימָא גַּלֵּי לָהּ אוֹרַיְיתָא, וּמִיַּד אִתְלַבְּשָׁא בִּלְבוּשָׁא אַחֲרָא, וְאִתְטַמַּר תַּמָּן, וְלָא אִתְגַּלֵּי. וְחַכִּימִין דְּאִינּוּן מַלְיָין עַיְינִין, אע״ג דְּהַהִיא מִלָּה אַסְתִּים בִּלְבוּשָׁהּ, חָמָאן לָהּ מִגּוֹ לְבוּשָׁא, וּבְשַׁעֲתָא דְּאִתְגְּלֵי הַהִיא מִלָּה עַד לָא תֵּיעוּל בִּלְבוּשָׁא, רָמָאן בָּהּ פְּקִיחוּ דְּעֵינָא, ואע״ג דְּמִיָּד אַסְתִּים, לָא אִתְאֲבִיד מֵעֵינַיְיהוּ.

93. All the esoteric functions that the Holy One, Blessed be He, performs are committed to the sacred Torah, and all are found therein. All concealed matters are revealed by the Torah, and immediately thereafter are clothed with another vestment, to be secreted therein and never to be revealed. Yet the sagacious scholars, whose eyes are filled, even though a matter is concealed in its vestment, can see it inside its garment. And when the matter is revealed, before it again is concealed in its vestment, they behold it fully; and even though it immediately passes from sight, it is never lost to their eyes.

94. בְּכַמָּה דּוּכְתִּין אַזְהַר קוּדְשָׁא בְּרִיךְ הוּא עַל גִּיּוֹרָא, דְּזַרְעָא קַדִּישָׁא, יִזְדַּהֲרוּן בֵּיהּ, וּלְבָתַר נָפִיק מִלָּה סְתִימָא מְנַרְתְּקָהּ. וְכֵיוָן דְּאִתְגְּלֵי אַהְדָּר לְנַרְתְּקָהּ מִיַּד, וְאִתְלַבַּשׁ תַּמָּן.

94. In many places, the Holy One, blessed be He, cautioned the holy seed,

NAMELY YISRAEL, to beware of the convert, since afterwards the hidden thing came out of its case, NAMELY ITS COVERING. Immediately after being revealed, it returned to its sheath to be covered there.

95. כֵּיוָן דְּאַזְהַר עַל גִּיּוֹרָא בְּכָל אִינּוּן דּוּכְתִּין, נָפַק מִלָּה מִנַּרְתְּקָהּ וְאִתְגְּלֵי, וְאָמַר, וְאַתֶּם יְדַעְתֶּם אֶת נֶפֶשׁ הַגֵּר. מִיָּד עָאלַת לְנַרְתְּקָהּ, וְאִהֲדָרַת בִּלְבוּשָׁהּ וְאִתְטַמְּרַת, דִּכְתִּיב כִּי גֵרִים הֱיִיתֶם בְּאֶרֶץ מִצְרָיִם, דְּחָשִׁיב קְרָא, דִּבְגִין דְּאִתְלְבַּשׁ מִיָּד, לָא הֲוָה מַאן דְּאַשְׁגַּח בָּהּ. בְּהַאי נֶפֶשׁ הַגֵּר, יַדְעַת נִשְׁמְתָא קַדִּישָׁא בְּמִלִּין דְּהַאי עָלְמָא, וְאִתְהֲנִיאַת מִנַּיְיהוּ.

95. Since He cautioned in relation to the convert so many times, the matter came out of its sheath, was revealed and said, "for you know the heart of the stranger (also: 'convert')" (Shemot 23:9), THAT IS, BY MEANS OF THE SOULS CLOTHED IN HIM AS MENTIONED. Immediately it is inserted in its sheath, dons its garment and hides, as written, "seeing you were strangers in the land of Egypt" (Ibid.), WHICH IS A SECONDARY EXPLANATION. The verse reckons that since it is immediately clothed, none would notice it. Through the Nefesh of the convert, the Neshamah is made aware of worldly matters and enjoys them, BEING AN INTERMEDIARY BETWEEN THE SOUL AND THE BODY. HENCE IT SAYS, "FOR YOU KNOW..."

A Synopsis
The merchant says that "And Moses went into the midst of the cloud, and went up into the mountain" means that the rainbow, that is the secret of Malchut, stripped off her three colors and gave them to Moses, in which garment he ascended the mountain. The old man reminds us that the Torah reveals its secrets subtly and fleetingly to those who love it and who pursue it with heart and soul.

96. פָּתַח הַהוּא סָבָא וְאָמַר, וַיָּבֹא מֹשֶׁה בְּתוֹךְ הֶעָנָן וַיַּעַל אֶל הָהָר וְגוֹ', עָנָן דָּא מַאי הִיא. אֶלָּא דָּא הוּא דִּכְתִּיב, אֶת קַשְׁתִּי נָתַתִּי בֶּעָנָן. תָּנֵינָן, דְּהַהוּא קֶשֶׁת אַשְׁלַחַת לְבוּשׁוֹי, וְיָהִיב לוֹן לְמֹשֶׁה, וּבְהַהוּא לְבוּשָׁא סָלִיק מֹשֶׁה לְטוּרָא וּמִנֵּיהּ חָמָא מַה דְּחָמָא, וְאִתְהֲנֵי מִכֹּלָּא. עַד הַהוּא אֲתָר, אָתוּ אִינּוּן חַבְרַיָּיא, וְאִשְׁתַּטָּחוּ קַמֵּיהּ דְּהַהוּא סָבָא, וּבָכוּ וְאָמְרוּ,

אִלְמָלֵא לָא אֲתֵינָא לְעָלְמָא, אֶלָּא לְמִשְׁמַע מִלִּין אִלֵּין מִפּוּמָךְ דַּי לָן.

96. The old man opened with the verse, "And Moses went into the midst of the cloud, and went up into the mountain…" (Shemot 24:18). HE ASKS, what is this cloud, AND ANSWERS, it accords with the verse, "I have set my bow in the cloud" (Beresheet 9:13). We have learned that this rainbow, WHICH IS THE SECRET OF MALCHUT WHEN RECEIVING THE THREE COLORS, WHITE, RED AND GREEN, FROM THE THREE COLUMNS OF ZEIR ANPIN, stripped of her clothes, THE THREE COLORS, WHITE, RED AND GREEN, and gave them to Moses. In that garment Moses ascended to the mountain, and from within it he saw all that he saw and took delight in all. WHEN THE OLD MAN reached this place, the friends came to him, NAMELY RABBI CHIYA AND RABBI YOSI, and prostrated before him. They said, had we come into the world only to listen to these words out of your mouth, it would have sufficed us.

97. אָמַר הַהוּא סָבָא, חַבְרַיָּיא, לָאו בְּגִין דָּא בִּלְחוֹדוֹי שָׁרֵינָא מִלָּה, דְּהָא סָבָא כְּגִינִי, לָאו בְּמִלָּה חֲדָא עָבֵיד קִישׁ קִישׁ, וְלָא קָרֵי, כַּמָּה בְּנֵי עָלְמָא בְּעִרְבּוּבְיָא בְּסָכְלְתָנוּ דִּלְהוֹן, וְלָא חָמָאן בְּאֹרַח קְשׁוֹט בְּאוֹרַיְיתָא, וְאוֹרַיְיתָא קָרֵי בְּכָל יוֹמָא בִּרְחִימוּ לְגַבַּיְיהוּ, וְלָא בָּעָאן לְאַתְבָא רֵישָׁא.

97. The old man said, friends, I have not started speaking for that alone, for an old man like me does not make ado for one thing and does not cry out TO MAKE HIMSELF KNOWN. THAT IS, UNLIKE THE NATURE OF AN IGNORANT PERSON, WHO, WHEN HE KNOWS SOMETHING, CREATES A COMMOTION AND MAKES A NAME FOR HIMSELF, ACCORDING TO THE PROVERB, 'AN EMPTY VESSEL RATTLES THE MOST'. How confused are the people in the world, and do not regard the Torah in the true way. The Torah calls to them daily with love, but they do not care to turn their heads TO LISTEN TO IT.

98. וְאע"ג דַּאֲמֵינָא, דְּהָא אוֹרַיְיתָא מִלָּה נָפְקָא מִנַּרְתְּקָה, וְאִתְחֲזִיאַת זְעֵיר, וּמִיָּד אִתְטַמְּרַת. הָכִי הוּא וַדַּאי. וּבְזִמְנָא דְּאִתְגַּלְיַאת מִגּוֹ נַרְתְּקָה וְאִתְטַמְּרַת מִיָּד, לָא עָבְדַת דָּא, אֶלָּא לְאִינוּן דְּיַדְעִין בָּהּ, וְאִשְׁתְּמוֹדְעָאן בָּהּ.

98. And though I said that in the Torah the matter comes out of its sheath to be seen little by little, and immediately hides, it is certainly so that when it does come out of its sheath to hide forthwith, THE TORAH does it but to those who have knowledge of it and become knowledgeable in it.

99. מָשָׁל למה"ד, לִרְחִימָתָא, דְּאִיהִי שַׁפִּירְתָּא בְּחֵיזוּ, וּשְׁפִירְתָּא בְּרֵיוָא, וְאִיהִי טְמִירְתָּא בִּטְמִירוּ גּוֹ הֵיכָלָא דִּילָהּ, וְאִית לָהּ רְחִימָא יְחִידָאָה, דְּלָא יַדְעִין בֵּיהּ בְּנֵי נָשָׁא, אֶלָּא אִיהוּ בִּטְמִירוּ. הַהוּא רְחִימָא, מִגּוֹ רְחִימָא דְּרָחִים לָהּ עָבַר לְתַרְעָא דְּבֵיתָהּ תָּדִיר, זָקִיף עֵינוֹי לְכָל סְטַר. אִיהִי, יַדְעַת דְּהָא רְחִימָא אַסְחַר תַּרְעָא דְּבֵיתָהּ תָּדִיר, מָה עַבְדַת, פָּתְחַת פִּתְחָא זְעֵירָא בְּהַהוּא הֵיכָלָא טְמִירָא, דְּאִיהִי תַּמָּן, וּגְלִיאַת אַנְפָּהָא לְגַבֵּי רְחִימָאָה, וּמִיָּד אִתְהַדְרַת וְאִתְכַּסִּיאַת. כָּל אִינוּן דַּהֲווֹ לְגַבֵּי רְחִימָא, לָא חָמוּ וְלָא אִסְתַּכָּלוּ, בַּר רְחִימָא בִּלְחוֹדוֹי, וּמֵעוֹי וְלִבֵּיהּ וְנַפְשֵׁיהּ אָזְלוּ אֲבַתְרָהּ. וְיָדַע דְּמִגּוֹ רְחִימוּ דִּרְחִימַת לֵיהּ, אִתְגְּלִיאַת לְגַבֵּיהּ רִגְעָא חֲדָא, לְאִתְעָרָא רְחִימוּ לֵיהּ. הָכִי הוּא מִלָּה דְּאוֹרַיְיתָא, לָא אִתְגְּלִיאַת, אֶלָּא לְגַבֵּי רְחִימָאָה. יַדְעַת אוֹרַיְיתָא, דְּהַהוּא חַכִּימָא דְּלִבָּא אַסְחַר לְתַרְעָא דְּבֵיתָא כָּל יוֹמָא, מָה עַבְדַת, גְּלִיאַת אַנְפָּהָא לְגַבֵּיהּ, מִגּוֹ הֵיכָלָא, וְאַרְמִיזַת לֵיהּ רְמִיזָא, וּמִיָּד אֲהַדְרַת לְאַתְרָהּ וְאִתְטַמְּרַת. כָּל אִינוּן דְּתַמָּן, לָא יַדְעֵי, וְלָא מִסְתַּכְּלֵי, אֶלָּא אִיהוּ בִּלְחוֹדוֹי, וּמֵעוֹי וְלִבֵּיהּ וְנַפְשֵׁיהּ אָזִיל אֲבַתְרָהּ. וְע"ד, אוֹרַיְיתָא אִתְגְּלִיאַת וְאִתְכַּסִּיאַת, וְאַזְלַת בִּרְחִימוּ לְגַבֵּי רְחִימְהָא, לְאִתְעָרָא בַּהֲדֵיהּ רְחִימוּ.

99. This is likened to a beautiful and good-looking beloved, who hides in the secret of her chamber. She has a lover unknown to men, who is in hiding. That lover, for the love he bears her, passes always around the gate to her house and looks everywhere. She knows that her lover always goes around her house's gate so she opens a small aperture in that hidden chamber when she stays, and reveals her face to her lover. Then immediately she is concealed again. None of those who were with the lover looked or observed, save the lover alone, whose entrails, heart and soul go out to her. And he knows that for the love she has for him, she is revealed to him for a moment to arouse the love of him. It is so with the Torah that is revealed only to its lover. The Torah knows that the wise-hearted paces

around its gate every day, so it reveals its face to him from within the chamber and immediately return to its place to be hidden again. None of those with him knew or beheld it but he himself, and his entrails, heart and soul go after it. Hence the Torah is revealed and concealed and lovingly goes to its lover to arouse love with him.

100. ת״ח, אָרְחָא דְּאוֹרַיְיתָא כַּךְ הוּא, בְּקַדְמֵיתָא כַּד שַׁרְיָא לְאִתְגַּלְּאָה לְגַבֵּי בַּר נָשׁ, אַרְמִיזַת לֵיהּ בִּרְמִיזוּ, אִי יָדַע טָב. וְאִי לָא יָדַע, שָׁדְרַת לְגַבֵּיהּ, וְקַרְאַת לֵיהּ פֶּתִי. וְאָמְרַת אוֹרַיְיתָא, לְהַהוּא דִּשְׁדָרַת לְגַבֵּיהּ, אִמְרוּ לְהַהוּא פֶּתִי, דְּיִקְרָב הָכָא, וְאִשְׁתָּעֵי בַּהֲדֵיהּ. הה״ד, מִי פֶתִי יָסֻר הֵנָּה חֲסַר לֵב וְגוֹ׳. קָרִיב לְגַבָּהּ, שָׁרִיאַת לְמַלְּלָא עִמֵּיהּ, מִבָּתַר פָּרוֹכְתָּא דְּפַרְסָא לֵיהּ, מִלִּין לְפוּם אָרְחוֹי, עַד דְּיִסְתַּכַּל זְעֵיר זְעֵיר, וְדָא הוּא דְּרָשָׁא.

100. Come and see: such is the way of the Torah. At first, when it begins to be revealed to man, it gives him a slight hint. If he recognizes it, well, but if he does not, it sends for him and calls him a fool. The Torah says to whoever it sends for, 'Tell that fool to come here so I can talk to him'. This is the meaning of, "Whoever is simple, let him turn in here: and as for him that lacks understanding…" (Mishlei 9:16). THAT MAN approaches, and it begins by speaking to him from behind the veil that it spreads before him, of matters according to his understanding, until little by little he will pay attention. This is homiletic interpretation.

101. לְבָתַר, תִּשְׁתָּעֵי בַּהֲדֵיהּ, מִבָּתַר שׁוֹשִׁיפָא דָּקִיק, מִלִּין דְּחִידָה, וְדָא אִיהוּ הַגָּדָה. לְבָתַר דְּאִיהוּ רָגִיל לְגַבָּהּ, אִתְגַּלְיַאת לְגַבֵּיהּ אַנְפִּין בְּאַנְפִּין, וּמְלִילַת בַּהֲדֵיהּ כָּל רָזִין סְתִימִין דִּילָהּ, וְכָל אָרְחִין סְתִימִין, דַּהֲווֹ בְּלִבָּאהּ טְמִירִין, מִיּוֹמִין קַדְמָאִין. כְּדֵין אִיהוּ בַּר נָשׁ שְׁלִים, בַּעַל תּוֹרָה וַדַּאי, מָארֵי דְּבֵיתָא, דְּהָא כָּל רָזִין דִּילָהּ גְּלִיאַת לֵיהּ, וְלָא רְחִיקַת, וְלָא כַּסִּיאַת מִינֵּיהּ כְּלוּם.

101. Afterwards it speaks with him in riddles from behind a thin sheet. This is Hagadah. When he frequents it, it is revealed to him face to face, and tells him all the obscure secrets and obscure ways that were hidden in its heart

since primordial days. Then that man is a ruler, man of the Torah, the master of the house, since it revealed to him all its secrets and has not kept or concealed from him anything.

102. אָמְרָה לֵיהּ, חָמֵית מִלָּה דִּרְמִיזָא דְּקָא רָמִיזְנָא לָךְ בְּקַדְמֵיתָא, כַּךְ וְכָךְ רָזִין הֲווֹ, כַּךְ וְכָךְ הוּא. כְּדֵין חָמֵי, דְּעַל אִינּוּן מִלִּין לָאו לְאוֹסָפָא, וְלָאו לְמִגְרַע מִנַּיְיהוּ. וּכְדֵין פְּשָׁטֵיהּ דִּקְרָא, כְּמָה דְּאִיהוּ, דְּלָאו לְאוֹסָפָא וְלָא לְמִגְרַע אֲפִילּוּ אָת חַד. וְע"ד, בְּנֵי נָשָׁא אִצְטְרִיכוּ לְאִזְדַּהֲרָא, וּלְמִרְדַּף אֲבַתְרָהּ דְּאוֹרַיְיתָא, לְמֶהֱוֵי רְחִימִין דִּילָהּ, כְּמָה דְּאִתְּמַר.

102. THE TORAH said to him, have you seen the allusion I gave you in the beginning ?Tt contained such and such secrets, this is the way it is. He then sees that one must not add or diminish from the words in the Torah. Then the literal meaning is as it is, so that not even one letter must be added or taken away. Therefore the people in the world must take heed to chase after the Torah and love it, as we learned.

103. ת"ח אִם אַחֶרֶת יִקַּח לוֹ, גִּלְגּוּלִין דְּמִתְגַּלְגְּלָן בְּהַאי קְרָא, כַּמָּה רַבְרְבִין וְעִלָּאִין אִינּוּן, דְּהָא כָּל נִשְׁמָתִין עָאלִין בְּגִלְגּוּלָא. וְלָא יַדְעִין בְּנֵי נָשָׁא אָרְחוֹי דְּקוּדְשָׁא בְּרִיךְ הוּא, וְהָאֵיךְ קַיְּימָא טִיקְלָא, וְהֵיךְ אִתְדָּנוּ בְּנֵי נָשָׁא בְּכָל יוֹמָא, וּבְכָל עִידָן, וְהֵיךְ נִשְׁמָתִין עָאלִין בְּדִינָא, עַד לָא יֵיתוּן לְהַאי עָלְמָא, וְהֵיךְ עָאלִין בְּדִינָא, לְבָתַר דְּנַפְקֵי מֵהַאי עָלְמָא.

103. Come and see: "If he take another" (Shemot 21:10). The incarnations in this verse are great and lofty, as all souls incarnate. Yet people do not know the ways of the Holy One, blessed be He, and how the scales are placed and men judged every day at every season, and how souls are sentenced before they come into this world and sentenced after leaving this world.

104. כַּמָּה גִּלְגּוּלִין, וְכַמָּה עוֹבָדִין סְתִימִין, עָבֵיד קוּדְשָׁא בְּרִיךְ הוּא בַּהֲדֵי כַּמָּה נִשְׁמָתִין עַרְטִילָאִין, וְכַמָּה רוּחִין עַרְטִילָאִין אַזְלִין בְּהַהוּא

עָלְמָא, דְּלָא עָאלִין לְפַרְגּוֹדָא דְּמַלְכָּא. וְכַמָּה עָלְמִין אִתְהַפַּךְ בְּהוּ
וְעָלְמָא דְּאִתְהַפַּךְ בְּכַמָּה פְּלִיאָן סְתִימִין. וּבְנֵי נָשָׁא לָא יַדְעִין, וְלָא
מַשְׁגִּיחִין וְהֵיךְ מִתְגַּלְגְּלִין נִשְׁמָתִין, כְּאַבְנָא בְּקוּסְפִּיתָא. כְּד"א, וְאֵת
נֶפֶשׁ אוֹיְבֶיךָ יְקַלְּעֶנָּה בְּתוֹךְ כַּף הַקָּלַע.

104. How many incarnations and obscure deeds does the Holy One, blessed
be He, bestow upon naked Neshamot WITHOUT A GARMENT OF THE
TORAH AND THE PRECEPTS. And how many naked Ruchot walk about that
world, not entering the presence of the King, and how many worlds are
turned for their sakes, THAT IS, THE ARRANGEMENT OF THE GRADES,
CALLED WORLDS, IS CHANGED FOR THEM. AND THE WORLD is turned
around in many obscure wondrous ways. Yet people do not know nor
observe. And how do souls roll (incarnate) as a stone in a sling, as written,
"and the souls of your enemies, them shall he sling out, as out of the hollow
of a sling" (I Shmuel 25:29)!

A Synopsis

He now reveals that all the Neshamot emerge from the great strong
tree that is the river that comes out of Eden, that is Zeir Anpin, and
all the Ruchot emerge from another smaller tree that is Malchut.
They join together as male and female, and when they unite they
are called a candle as they shine forth a great light. The Neshamah
is enveloped in the Ruach so as to be there above in the Supernal
Garden of Eden in the hidden chamber; the Nefesh does not come
there, but when the Neshamah and Ruach descend to the lower
Garden of Eden they are clothed in another spirit, the soul of a
convert. The explanation turns to the concept of Levirate marriage
following the death of a man who left no children. The merchant
tells of the seven lands: Eretz (Land), Adamah (Ground), Gai
(Valley), Nishyah (Forgetfulness), Tziyah (Wilderness), Tevel
(World) and Arka.

105. הַשְׁתָּא אִית לְגַלָּאָה, דְּהָא כָּל נִשְׁמָתִין, מֵאִילָנָא רַבְרְבָא וְתַקִּיפָא
דְּהוּא נָהָר דְּנָפִיק מֵעֵדֶן נַפְקֵי. וְכָל רוּחִין, מֵאִילָנָא אַחֲרָא זְעֵירָא
נַפְקִין. נִשְׁמָה מִלְּעֵילָא רוּחַ מִלְתַתָּא, וּמִתְחַבְּרָן כַּחֲדָא, כְּגַוְונָא דִּדְכַר
וְנוּקְבָּא. וְכַד מִתְחַבְּרָן כַּחֲדָא, כְּדֵין נְהִירִין נְהִירוּ עִלָּאָה. וּבְחִבּוּרָא
דְּתַרְוַויְיהוּ אִקְרֵי נֵר. נֵר יְיָ' נִשְׁמַת אָדָם. מַהוּ נ"ר. נְשָׁמָה רוּחַ. וְעַל

חֲבוּרָא דְּתַרְוַויְיהוּ כַּחֲדָא אִקְרֵי נֵר, דִּכְתִּיב נֵר יְיָ' נִשְׁמַת אָדָם.

105. Now is the time to reveal that all the Neshamot emerge from the great strong tree, which is the river that comes out of Eden, NAMELY ZEIR ANPIN, and all the Ruchot emerge from another, small tree, WHICH IS MALCHUT. A Neshamah emerges from above and a Ruach from below, and they join together as male and female. When they unite they shine forth a lofty light. The joining of the two is called a candle (Heb. *ner*), WHICH IS MADE OF THE INITIALS OF NESHAMAH RUACH, AS WRITTEN, "The soul of man is the candle of Hashem" (Mishlei 20:27). What is the candle? Neshamah Ruach. The joining of the two together is called a candle, as written OF THEM, "The soul of man is the candle of Hashem."

106. נִשְׁמָה וְרוּחַ: דְּכַר וְנוּקְבָּא לְאַנְהֲרָא כַּחֲדָא, וְדָא בְּלָא דָא, לָא נְהִירִין, וְלָא אִקְרֵי נֵר, וְכַד מִתְחַבְּרָן כַּחֲדָא, אִקְרֵי כֹּלָּא נֵר. וּכְדֵין אִתְעַטָּף נִשְׁמָה בְּרוּחַ, לְקַיְימָא תַּמָּן לְעֵילָא, בְּהֵיכְלָא טְמִירָא, דִּכְתִּיב כִּי רוּחַ מִלְפָנַי יַעֲטוֹף. יִתְעַטֵּף לָא כְּתִיב, אֶלָּא יַעֲטוֹף. מ"ט. בְּגִין דְּנִשְׁמוֹת אֲנִי עָשִׂיתִי, תַּמָּן לְעֵילָא בְּגִנְתָּא, בְּהֵיכְלָא טְמִירָא, אִתְעַטָּף וְאִתְלַבַּשׁ נִשְׁמָה בְּרוּחַ כְּמָה דְּאִתְחֲזֵי.

106. The Neshamah and Ruach are male and female that shine together. They do not shine without each other, and when they join, the whole is called a candle. Then the Neshamah is enveloped in a Ruach in order to be there above IN THE SUPERNAL GARDEN OF EDEN in the hidden chamber, as written, "but the spirit...should faint (or: 'envelop') before Me" (Yeshayah 57:16). It is not written, 'be enveloped' but "envelop," WHICH MEANS IT ENVELOPS OTHERS. The reason is that the Neshamah that I have made there, in the UPPER Garden OF EDEN, in the hidden chamber, is enveloped and clothed in the Ruach, as it should be.

107. וְכֵיוָן דִּבְהַהוּא הֵיכָלָא, לָא הֲוֵי, וְלָא אִשְׁתַּמַּשׁ אֶלָּא בְּרוּחַ וּנְשָׁמָה, נֶפֶשׁ לָא אָתֵי לְתַמָּן, אֶלָּא מִתְלַבַּשׁ בְּהַהוּא רוּחַ תַּמָּן, וְכַד נַחְתָּא לְגוֹ ג"ע דִּלְתַתָּא, אִתְלַבַּשׁ בְּהַהוּא רוּחָא אַחֲרָא דְּאֲמֵינָא, הַהוּא דְּנָפִיק מִתַּמָּן, וַהֲוָה מִתַּמָּן וּבְכֻלְּהוּ שַׁרְיָא בְּהַאי עָלְמָא, וְאִתְלַבַּשׁ בְּהוּ.

107. Since this chamber has, and employs, only the Neshamah and Ruach, the Nefesh does not come there. Only THE NESHAMAH is clothed in the Ruach there. When it descends to the lower Garden of Eden, it is clothed in another spirit that emerges from there that dwelt there, THAT IS, THE SOULS OF THE CONVERTS. THE NESHAMAH dwells in this world in them all and is clothed in them, THAT IS, BOTH IN ITS OWN RUACH AND THE SOULS OF THE COVERTS.

108. הַהוּא רוּחַ דְּנָפִיק מֵהַאי עָלְמָא, דְּלָא אִתְרַבֵּי וְלָא אִתְפָּשַׁט בְּהַאי עָלְמָא. אַזְלָא בְּגִלְגּוּלָא, וְלָא אַשְׁכַּח נַיְיחָא, אָתֵי בְּגִלְגּוּלָא בְּעָלְמָא, כְּאַבְנָא בְּקוּסְפִיתָא, עַד דְּיִשְׁכַּח הַהוּא פָּרוּקָא דְּיִפְרוֹק לֵיה, וְאַיְיתֵי לֵיה בְּהַהוּא מָאנָא מַמָּשׁ, דַּהֲוָה אִיהוּ אִשְׁתַּמַּשׁ בֵּיה, וְדָבִיק בֵּיה תָּדִיר רוּחֵיה וְנַפְשֵׁיה, וַהֲוַת בַּת זוּגֵיה, רוּחָא בְּרוּחָא, וְהַהוּא פָּרוּקָא בָּנֵי לֵיה כְּמִלְּקַדְּמִין.

108. That Ruach that comes out of this world, having neither grown nor expanded in this world, THAT IS, HAD NO CHILDREN, incarnates and finds no rest. It incarnates in this world as a stone in a sling, until he finds a redeemer to redeem him, THAT IS A KINSMAN TO MARRY HIS WIFE, and places him in the very vessel he employed and cleft to in Ruach and Nefesh, and which used to be his spouse, spirit to spirit, NAMELY HIS WIFE. That redeemer establishes him as before, THAT IS, BRINGS HIM INTO THE SON BORN FROM HIS WIDOW, SO HE COMES BACK TO LIFE IN THIS WORLD AS BEFORE.

109. וְהַהוּא רוּחָא דְּשָׁבַק וְאִתְדְּבַק בְּהַהוּא מָאנָא, לָא אִתְאֲבִיד. דְּהָא לֵית מִלָּה אֲפִילוּ זְעֵירָא בְּעָלְמָא, דְּלָא הֲוֵי לֵיה אֲתָר וְדוּכְתָּא לְאִתְטַמְּרָא וּלְאִתְכַּנְשָׁא תַּמָּן, וְלָא אִתְאֲבִיד לְעָלְמִין. וּבְג״כ, הַהוּא רוּחָא דְּשָׁבַק בְּהַהוּא מָנָא, תַּמָּן הוּא, וַדַּאי רָדִיף בָּתַר עִקְרָא וִיסוֹדָא דִּילֵיה, דְּקָא נָפִיק מִינֵּיה, וְאַיְיתֵי לֵיה, וּבָנֵי לֵיה בְּדוּכְתֵּיה, בַּאֲתָר דְּהַהוּא רוּחַ בַּת זוּגֵיה, דְּנָפְקַת בַּהֲדֵיה, וְאִתְבְּנֵי תַּמָּן כְּמִלְּקַדְּמִין. וְדָא אִיהוּ בְּרִיָּה חַדְתָּא הַשְׁתָּא בְּעָלְמָא, רוּחָא חַדְתָּא וְגוּפָא חַדְתָּא.

109. The spirit he left WITH HER IN HIS PRIOR LIFE, AS SHALL BE SAID

THAT THE HUSBAND LEAVES IN HIS WIFE A SPIRIT IN HIS PRIOR LIFE, that cleaves to that vessel, NAMELY HIS WIFE, AS IT IS NEVER ABSENT FROM HER EVEN AFTER HIS DEMISE, is not lost. For there is nothing in the world, be it ever so small, that has no place or stand to hide in and go there, and it is never lost. The spirit he left in that vessel is therefore there, and it surely follows its root and foundation whence it came, NAMELY, THE HUSBAND WHO DIED CHILDLESS. It brings him and establishes him in his place, that is, the place of the spirit, which is his spouse that went out with him, THAT IS, HIS WIFE. There he is newly built, and is now a new creature in the world, a new spirit and a new body.

110. וְאִית תֵּימָא, רוּחַ דָּא הוּא מַה דַּהֲוָה. הָכִי הוּא אֲבָל לָא אִתְבְּנֵי, אֶלָּא בְּגִין הַהוּא רוּחָא אַחֲרָא דְּקָא שָׁבַק בְּהַהוּא מָאנָא, הָכָא אִית רָזָא דְרָזִין. בְּסִפְרָא דַּחֲנוֹךְ, בִּנְיָינָא דָא דְּאִתְבְּנֵי, לָא אִתְבְּנֵי, אֶלָּא בְּהַהוּא רוּחָא אַחֲרָא דְּשָׁבִיק תַּמָּן, בְּהַהוּא מָאנָא. וְכַד שָׁרֵי לְאִתְבְּנָאָה, דָּא מָשִׁיךְ אֲבַתְרֵיהּ דְּהַהוּא רוּחַ דְּאָזִיל עַרְטִילָאָה, וּמָשִׁיךְ לֵיהּ לְגַבֵּיהּ, וְתַמָּן תְּרֵי רוּחוֹת דְּאִינּוּן חַד. לְבָתַר, דָּא אִיהוּ רוּחַ, וְדָא אִיהוּ נִשְׁמָה, וְתַרְוַויְיהוּ חַד.

110. You may argue that the spirit IN THE BORN BABY is what it used to be, NAMELY, THE MAN HIMSELF AND NOT THE SPIRIT HE LEFT WITH HER WHEN HE INCARNATED BEFORE, WHICH IS BUT A PART OF HIM. HE ANSWERS, it is so, but he is established IN THE BORN SON only by means of the other spirit he left in that vessel, HIS WIFE. Here is the most secret of mysteries, in the book of Enoch. The edifice BUILT IN THE SON BORN TO THE LEVIRATE MARRIAGE is built only by means of the other spirit he left in that vessel, NAMELY HIS WIFE IN THE PRIOR LIFE. When it begins to be built, THE SPIRIT attracts the naked CHILDLESS spirit and draws it to itself. So two spirits are made there into one. Afterwards the one becomes a Ruach and the other Neshamah, both being one.

111. אִי זָכָה לְאִתְדַּכְּאָה כַּדְקָא יָאוּת, תַּרְוַויְיהוּ אִינּוּן חַד, לְאִתְלַבְּשָׁא בְּהוּ נִשְׁמְתָא אַחֲרָא עִלָּאָה. כְּמָה דְאִית לִשְׁאָר בְּנֵי עָלְמָא, רוּחַ, דְּזַכָּאִין בְּהוּ נִשְׁמָתִין, אִינּוּן דְּקַדְמָן וְאַחִידָן בְּהוּ, וְרוּחָא אַחֲרָא

מִלְעֵילָא. וְנִשְׁמָתָא קַדִּישָׁא אִתְלַבְּשָׁא בְּהוּ. אוּף הָכִי נָמֵי, מִדִּילֵיהּ
מַמָּשׁ אִית תְּרֵין רוּחִין, בְּגִין לְאִתְלַבְּשָׁא בְּהוּ נִשְׁמָה עִלָּאָה.

111. If he merits to be properly purified, the two become one, so that another, supernal Neshamah will be clothed in them. Just as other people in the world have a spirit that the Neshamot that come first hold on to, THAT IS, TO THE SOULS OF THE CONVERTS, and another spirit above, and the holy Neshamah above is clothed in both, so he too has two spirits, HIS OWN AND THE SPIRIT HE LEFT IN HIS WIFE IN A FORMER LIFETIME, so that the supernal Neshamah will be clothed in them.

112. יְהֵא לְדֵין גּוּפָא אַחֲרָא, דְּקָא אִתְבְּנֵי הַשְׁתָּא חַדְתָּא, הַהוּא גּוּפָא
קַדְמָאָה דְּשָׁבַק, מָה אִתְעֲבֵיד מִנֵּיהּ. אוֹ הַאי בְּרֵיקַנְיָּיא, אוֹ הַאי
בְּרֵיקַנְיָּיא. לְפוּם סָכְלְתָנוּ דב"נ אִשְׁתְּמַע, דְּהַאי קַדְמָאָה דְּלָא אִשְׁתְּלִים
בְּקַדְמֵיתָא, אִתְאֲבֵיד, הוֹאִיל וְלָא זָכָה. אִי הָכִי, לְמַגָּנָא אִשְׁתַּדַּל
בְּפִקּוּדֵי אוֹרַיְיתָא, אוֹ אֲפִילוּ בְּחַד מִנַּיְיהוּ. וְהָא אֲנָן יַדְעֵינָן, דַּאֲפִילוּ
רֵיקָנִין שֶׁבְּיִשְׂרָאֵל, כֻּלְּהוּ מַלְיָין מִצְוֹת כְּרִמּוֹן. וְגוּפָא דָּא, אע"ג דְּלָא
אִשְׁתְּלִים, לְאִתְרַבְּאָה, וּלְמִזְכֵּי וּלְמִסְגֵּי בְּעָלְמָא, פִּקּוּדִין אַחֲרָנִין
דְּאוֹרַיְיתָא נָטַר, דְּלָא אִתְאֲבִידוּ מִנֵּיהּ, וְכִי לְמַגָּנָא הֲוֹו.

112. HE ASKS, NOW THAT he has a body newly built BY LEVIRATE MARRIAGE, what is made of the first body he left? Either the one or the other is in vain. According to human understanding it seems that the earlier body that was not completed first is lost, because it did not acquire merit. If so, in vain was it occupied in the precepts of the Torah, even if it dealt with but one of them. Yet we know that even the most ignorant people of Yisrael are full to the brim with precepts. So this one, though it was not made whole in procreating and meriting and growing in the world, yet kept other precepts of the Torah, and did not lose them, was it for nothing?

113. חַבְרַיָּיא חַבְרַיָּיא, פְּקִיחוּ עֵינַיְיכוּ, דְּהָא אֲנָא יָדַעְנָא, דְּהָכִי אַתּוּן
סַבְרִין וְיַדְעִין, דְּכָל אִינּוּן גּוּפִין, צִיּוּנִין אִינּוּן בְּרֵיקַנְיָּיא, דְּלָא אִית לוֹן
קִיּוּמָא לְעָלְמִין. לָאו הָכִי, וְחַס לָן לְאִסְתַּכְּלָא בְּאִלֵּין מִלִּין.

113. Friends, friends, open up your eyes, for I know that you think and know that all those bodies are noted FOR DISTINCTION in vain, that they have no everlasting existence. This is not so, we must not look into these matters.

114. פָּתַח סָבָא וְאָמַר, מִי יְמַלֵּל גְּבוּרוֹת יְיָ' יַשְׁמִיעַ כָּל תְּהִלָּתוֹ. מַאן הוּא בְּעָלְמָא, דְּיָכִיל לְמַלְּלָא גְּבוּרָן, דְּעָבֵיד קוּדְשָׁא בְּרִיךְ הוּא בְּעָלְמָא תָּדִיר. הַהוּא גּוּפָא קַדְמָאָה דְּשָׁבַק, לָא אִתְאֲבִיד, וְקִיּוּמָא לֶהֱוֵי לֵיהּ לְזִמְנָא דְּאָתֵי. דְּהָא עוֹנְשֵׁיהּ סָבַל בְּכַמָּה זִמְנִין, וְקוּדְשָׁא בְּרִיךְ הוּא לָא מְקַפַּח אַגְרָא דְּשׁוּם בִּרְיָין דְּבָרָא, בַּר אִינוּן דְּנַפְקוּ מִגּוֹ מְהֵימְנוּתָא דִּילֵיהּ, וְלָא הֲוָה בְּהוּ טָב לְעָלְמִין. וּבַר מֵאִינוּן דְּלָא כָּרְעוּ בְּמוֹדִים, דְּהֵנֵי קוּדְשָׁא בְּרִיךְ הוּא עָבֵיד מִנַּיְיהוּ בִּרְיָין אַחֲרָנִין, בְּגִין דְּלָא יִתְבְּנֵי הַהוּא גּוּפָא דְּיוּקְנָא דְּבַר נָשׁ, וְלָא יְקוּם לְעָלְמִין. אֲבָל הָנֵי לָאו הָכִי.

114. The old man opened with, "Who can utter the mighty acts of Hashem? Who can declare all His praise" (Tehilim 106:2). Who in the world can speak of the mighty acts the Holy One, blessed be He, constantly performs in the world? The first body he left is not lost. It will exist in the future to come, for it already received punishment in several manners. And the Holy One, blessed be He, does not withhold the reward of any creature He created, except those who came away from the faith in Him, and never had anything good in them, and those who did not bow at 'Modim' IN THE AMIDAH PRAYER. From these, the Holy One, blessed be He, makes other creatures, as that body will not be built in a human form and will never resurrect. But it is not so for those WHO DIED CHILDLESS.

115. מַה עָבֵד קוּדְשָׁא בְּרִיךְ הוּא. אִי הַהוּא רוּחַ, זָכֵי לְאִתְתַּקְּנָא בְּהַאי עָלְמָא, בְּהַהוּא גּוּפָא אַחֲרָא, מֶה עָבֵיד קוּדְשָׁא בְּרִיךְ הוּא. הַהוּא פְּרוּקָא דְּקָא פָּרִיק לֵיהּ, הַהוּא רוּחַ דִּילֵיהּ דְּקָא אָעִיל תַּמָּן, וְשָׁתַף וְעָרַב בְּהַהוּא רוּחַ דַּהֲוָה בְּהַהוּא מָאנָא, וַדַּאי לָא אִתְאֲבִיד, וּמַה אִתְעֲבֵיד, דְּהָא תְּלַת רוּחִין תַּמָּן, חַד, דַּהֲוָה בְּהַהוּא מָאנָא, וְאִשְׁתְּאַר תַּמָּן. וְחַד, הַהוּא דְּאִתְמְשַׁךְ תַּמָּן דַּהֲוָה דְּהַהוּא עַרְטִילָאָה. וְחַד, הַהוּא דְּאָעִיל תַּמָּן הַהוּא פְּרוּקָא, וְאִתְעֲרַב בְּהוּ. לְמֶהֱוֵי בִּתְלַת רוּחִין אִי אֶפְשָׁר. וּמַה אִתְעֲבֵיד.

115. If the spirit attained improvement in this world in that other body, what did the Holy One, blessed be He, do? The spirit of the redeemer who redeemed him, NAMELY, HIS BROTHER, that he put in there and mixed with the spirit that was in that vessel, WHICH HIS BROTHER LEFT IN HIS FORMER LIFE, is surely not lost. What is to become of it, seeing there are three spirits there – the first is THE SPIRIT that was in the vessel and remained there, THAT IS, THAT HIS DEAD BROTHER LEFT BEHIND IN HIS LAST LIFE. Another IS THE SPIRIT OF THE DEAD BROTHER ITSELF that is drawn there, which was naked, CHILDLESS. Yet another is the spirit that the redeemer put in, NAMELY THE KINSMAN, and mixed with them. For three spirits to be there is impossible, what is to be done?

116. אֶלָּא, כָּךְ אִינּוּן גְּבוּרָן עִלָּאִין, דְּעָבֵיד קוּדְשָׁא בְּרִיךְ הוּא. הַהוּא רוּחָא דְּאָעִיל תַּמָּן הַהוּא פָּרוֹקָא, בֵּיהּ אִתְלָבַּשׁ הַהִיא נִשְׁמְתָא, בַּאֲתָר דִּלְבוּשָׁא דְּגִיּוֹרֵי, וְהַהוּא רוּחָא עַרְטִילָאָה, דְּתָב תַּמָּן לְאִתְבַּנְּאָה, לֶהֱוֵי לְבוּשָׁא לְנִשְׁמְתָא עִלָּאָה. וְהַהוּא רוּחַ דַּהֲוָה בְּקַדְמֵיתָא, דְּאִשְׁתְּאַר בְּהַהוּא מָנָא, פָּרַח מִתַּמָּן. וְקוּדְשָׁא בְּרִיךְ הוּא אַזְמִין לֵיהּ אֲתָר, בְּגוֹ רָזִין כַּוִּין דְּטִנָרָא, דְּבָתַר כִּתְפוֹי דְּג"ע, וְאִתְטַמַּר תַּמָּן. וְאִסְתַּלָּק לְהַהוּא גּוּפָא קַדְמָאָה, דְּהַהוּא בְּקַדְמֵיתָא. וּבְהַהוּא רוּחַ יְקוּם הַהוּא גּוּפָא, וְדָא אִיהוּ חַד דְּאִינּוּן תְּרֵין, דְּקָא אֲמֵינָא.

116. These are the lofty mighty acts the Holy One, blessed be He, performs. The Soul is clothed with the spirit the redeemer put in there, instead of the garment of converts' souls. The DEAD MAN'S spirit, naked AND CHILDLESS, that returned there to be built ANEW, will serve as a garment to the supernal Soul. The spirit that was there before, which remained in that vessel, NAMELY THE SPIRIT HER DEAD HUSBAND LEFT IN HER FROM HIS PRIOR LIFE, flies away from there, and the Holy One, blessed be He, arranges a place within the secret of the window in the rock behind the back of the Garden of Eden where it hides. It rises to the former body that HE WHO DIED CHILDLESS had before. With that spirit, that body will rise AT THE RESURRECTION OF THE DEAD. This is the one that is two, which I mentioned.

117. אֲבָל הַהוּא גּוּפָא, עַד דְּלָא יְקוּם, עוֹנְשֵׁיהּ סַגְיָא דְּהָא בְּגִין דְּלָא

זָכָה לְאִתְרַבְּאָה, נַחְתֵּי לֵיהּ לְגוֹ אֲדָמָה, דְּסָמִיךְ לְאַרְקָא. וְאִתְדָן תַּמָּן, וּלְבָתַר סַלְקִין לֵיהּ לְהַאי תֵּבֵל. הַשְׁתָּא נָחִית, וְהַשְׁתָּא סָלִיק, הָא סָלִיק, וְהָא נָחִית, לֵית לֵיהּ שְׁכִיכוּ בַּר בְּשַׁבָּתֵי, וּבְיוֹמִין טָבִין וּבְרֵישֵׁי יַרְחֵי.

117. But the punishment of that body, until it rises AND RESURRECTS, is great, since it did not merit growth BY CHILDREN, so it is brought down into Adamah, close to Arka. FOR THERE ARE SEVEN LANDS, ERETZ (LAND), ADAMAH (GROUND), GAI (VALLEY), NISHYAH (FORGETFULNESS), TZIYAH (WILDERNESS), TEVEL (WORLD). There he is punished. Then it is brought up to Tevel, WHERE WE ARE, and it descends BACK TO ADAMAH. Now it rises and now it descends. It has no rest, save on Shabbatot, holidays, and the first days of months.

118. וְאִלֵּין דְּמִיכִין בְּאַדְמַת עָפָר, אַדְמַת, מֵאֲדָמָה. עָפָר מִתֵּבֵל. וְעַל אִלֵּין כְּתִיב, וְרַבִּים מִיְשֵׁנֵי אַדְמַת עָפָר יָקִיצוּ אֵלֶּה לְחַיֵּי עוֹלָם וְאֵלֶּה לַחֲרָפוֹת וּלְדִרְאוֹן עוֹלָם. אִי זָכָה הַהוּא רוּחָא עַרְטִילָאָה, דְּתָב כְּמִלְּקַדְמִין, לְאִתְתַּקְּנָא. זַכָּאָה אִיהוּ, דְּהָא הַהוּא רוּחָא דְּאִתְּמַר בֵּיהּ, דְּאִתְטְמַר בְּטִנָרָא, יִתְתְּקַן בְּהַהוּא גּוּפָא קַדְמָאָה. וְעַל אִלֵּין כְּתִיב אֵלֶּה לְחַיֵּי עוֹלָם וְאֵלֶּה לַחֲרָפוֹת וְגוֹ'. כָּל אִינּוּן דְּלָא זָכוּ לְאִתְתַּקְּנָא.

118. These are those that sleep in the dust of the ground. Ground IS SO CALLED since it is from Adamah, dust IS SO CALLED since it is from Tevel. Of those it is written, "And many of those who sleep in the dust of the earth (Heb. *adamah*) shall awake, some to everlasting life, and some to shame and everlasting contempt" (Daniel 12:2). If the naked spirit, NAMELY THE SPIRIT OF HE WHO DIED CHILDLESS, was worthy of coming back into the world as before IN THE CHILD BORN TO THE LEVIRATE MARRIAGE to perfect itself, it is meritorious. For the spirit HE LEFT IN HIS WIFE IN THE FORMER LIFE, of which we said it was hid in the rock, will be corrected in the former body THAT THE CHILDLESS DECEASED LEFT BEHIND. Of these it is written, "some to everlasting life, and some to shame…", NAMELY, all those who did not attain perfection.

119. וְאִלֵּין אִינּוּן גְּבוּרָן עִלָּאִין, דְּמַלְכָּא עִלָּאָה קַדִּישָׁא, וְלָא אִתְאֲבִיד

כְּלוּם. אֲפִילוּ הֶבֶל דְּפוּמָא אֲתָר וְדוּכְתָּא אִית לֵיהּ, וְקוּדְשָׁא בְּרִיךְ הוּא עָבֵיד מִינֵהּ מַה דְּעָבֵיד. וַאֲפִילוּ מִלָּה דְּבַר נָשׁ, וַאֲפִילוּ קָלָא, לָא הֲוֵי בְּרֵיקַנְיָיא, וַאֲתָר וְדוּכְתָּא אִית לְהוּ לְכֻלָּא.

119. These are the lofty mighty acts of the holy supernal King, that nothing is lost. Even a breath has a place and rank, and the Holy One, blessed be He, does something from it. Even a man's word, even a voice are not in vain. Everything has place and station.

120. הַאי דְּאִתְבְּנֵי הַשְׁתָּא, וְנָפַק לְעָלְמָא בְּרִיָה חַדְתָּא, לֵית לֵיהּ בַּת זוּג. וְעַ"ד לָא מַכְרִיזֵי, דְּהָא בַּת זוּגֵיהּ אִתְאֲבִידַת מִנֵּיהּ, בַּת זוּגֵיהּ דַּהֲוַת לֵיהּ, אִתְעֲבֵידַת אִמֵּיהּ, וְאָחוּהָ אָבוּהָ.

120. He who was just built, NAMELY THE CHILDLESS DEAD MAN, WHO INCARNATED IN THE CHILD BORN TO THE LEVIRATE MARRIAGE, and came into the world a new creature, has no soulmate. This is why HIS SOULMATE is not announced BEFORE HE IS BORN, because he lost his soulmate, who became his mother, while his brother became his father.

A Synopsis
The merchant, during these expositions, constantly berates and questions himself about the propriety of revealing these secrets, but then regains strength and sureness of purpose, and continues.
Now he speaks of "Go forth, O daughters of Zion, and behold King Solomon", saying that Zeir Anpin calls Malchut daughter, sister and mother – everything is in her. The merchant explains at length the complicated arrangement of souls in the dead husband, the widow and the children of a Levirate marriage. The question of the role of soulmates in this instance is also addressed.

121. סָבָא סָבָא, מַה עֲבַדְת, טַב הֲוָה לָךְ שְׁתִיקָא, סָבָא סָבָא, הָא אֲמֵינָא דְּעָאלַת בְּיַמָּא רַבָּא, בְּלָא חַבְלִין, וּבְלָא דִּגְלָא. אִי תֵּימָא דְּתִסְלַק לְעֵילָא, לָא תִּיכוֹל. אִי תֵּימָא דְּתֵיחוֹת לְתַתָּא, הָא עִמְקָא דִּתְהוֹמָא רַבָּא, מַה תַּעֲבֵיד. אִי סָבָא אִי סָבָא, לָא אִית לָךְ לְאַהֲדָרָא לַאֲחוֹרָא. בְּעֶדָּנִין אִלֵּין, לָא הֲוֵית, וְלָא אִתְרְגִּילַת, לְאִתְחַלְּשָׁא בְּתוּקְפָּךְ,

דְּהָא יַדְעַת, דְּבַר נָשׁ אַחֲרָא בְּכָל דָּרָא דָא, לָא עָאל בְּאַרְבָּא בְּעֲמִיקָא
דָּא דְּאַנְתְּ תַּמָּן.

121. He said to himself, old, old man, what have you done? Silence would have been good for you. Old, old man, I have told you that you entered the great sea without ropes or a flag. What shall you do? If you mean to rise up, you cannot. If you intend to descend, behold the depth of the great abyss. What shall you do? Woe, old man, woe, it is not for you to turn back. In such times you were not wont to weaken in strength, for you knew that no other man in the generation would enter in a ship to the depth where you are.

122. בְּרֵיהּ דְּיוֹחַאי יָדַע לְאִסְתַּמְּרָא אָרְחוֹי, וְאִי עָאל בְּיַמָּא עֲמִיקָא, אַשְׁגַּח בְּקַדְמֵיתָא, הֵיךְ יַעֲבַר בְּזִמְנָא חֲדָא, וְיִשׁוֹטֵט בְּיַמָּא, עַד לָא יֵיעוּל וְאַנְתְּ סָבָא, לָא אַשְׁגַּחַת בְּקַדְמֵיתָא. הַשְׁתָּא סָבָא, הוֹאִיל וְאַנְתְּ תַּמָּן, לָא תֶּחֱלַשׁ בְּתוּקְפָּךְ, לָא תִּשְׁבּוֹק כָּל אָרְחָךְ, לְמִשְׁטְטָא לִימִינָא וְלִשְׂמָאלָא, לְאָרְכָּא וּלְפוּתְיָיא, לְעָמְקָא וּלְרוּמָא, לָא תִּדְחַל. סָבָא סָבָא, אִתְתַּקַּף בְּתֶקְפָּךְ, כַּמָּה גֻּבְרִין תַּקִּיפִין תָּבַרְתְּ בְּתֶקְפֵיהוֹן, וְכַמָּה קְרָבִין נָצַחְתְּ.

122. The son of Yochai, NAMELY RABBI SHIMON, knows how to guard his paths. Had he entered the deep sea, he would pay attention, before entering, how he is to pass in a certain time and then roam in the sea. Yet you, old man, have not looked first. Now, old man, since you are there, do not weaken in strength, nor leave your path to roam right or left, to the length of width, to the depth or height. Do not fear, old man, strengthen yourself in your power. How many mighty men of strength have you broken, in how many wars have you conquered.

123. בָּכָה, פָּתַח וְאָמַר, צְאֶינָה וּרְאֶינָה בְּנוֹת צִיּוֹן בַּמֶּלֶךְ שְׁלֹמֹה בַּעֲטָרָה שֶׁעִטְּרָה לּוֹ אִמּוֹ בְּיוֹם חֲתֻנָּתוֹ וּבְיוֹם שִׂמְחַת לִבּוֹ. הַאי קְרָא אוּקְמוּהָ, וְהָכִי הוּא. אֲבָל צְאֶינָה וּרְאֶינָה, וְכִי מַאן יָכִיל לְמֶחֱמֵי בַּמֶּלֶךְ שְׁלֹמֹה, דְּהוּא מַלְכָּא דִשְׁלָמָא דִילֵיהּ, וְהָא סָתִים הוּא, מִכָּל חֵילֵי

מְרוֹמִין דִּלְעֵילָּא, בְּהַהוּא אֲתָר, דְּעַיִן לָא רָאֲתָה אֱלֹהִים זוּלָתְךָ. וְאַתְּ
אָמַרְתְּ צְאֶינָה וּרְאֶינָה בְּנוֹת צִיּוֹן בַּמֶּלֶךְ שְׁלֹמֹא. וְתוּ, דְּהָא כָּבוֹד דִּילֵיהּ,
כֻּלְּהוּ מַלְאֲכֵי עִלָּאֵי שָׁאֲלֵי וְאָמְרֵי, אַיֵּה מְקוֹם כְּבוֹדוֹ.

123. He wept, then and opened with the verse, "Go forth, O daughters of Zion, and behold King Solomon with the crown with which his mother crowned him on the day of his wedding, and on the day of the gladness of his heart" (Shir Hashirim 3:11). This verse has been expounded and it is so, yet go forth and behold – who could behold King Solomon (Heb. *Shlomo*), that is, the King that peace (Heb. *shalom*) is His, NAMELY ZEIR ANPIN. For He is concealed from all the celestial high armies that are in that place that, "neither has the eye see, (that) an Elohim, beside you" (Yeshayah 64: 3), WHICH IS BINAH. Yet you say, "Go forth, O daughters of Zion, and behold King Solomon." Moreover, as His glory, all the celestial angels ask, saying, 'where is the place of His glory', WHICH IS THE CONCEALMENT, SO WHAT IS THE GOOD OF "GO FORTH…"?

124. אֶלָּא, מַה דְּאָמַר צְאֶינָה וּרְאֶינָה בְּנוֹת צִיּוֹן בַּמֶּלֶךְ שְׁלֹמֹה, בַּעֲטָרָה
כְּתִיב, וְלָא כְּתִיב וּבַעֲטָרָה דְּכָל מַאן דְּחָמֵי הַהוּא עֲטָרָה, חָמֵי נֹעַם
מַלְכָּא דִשְׁלָמָא דִילֵיהּ. שֶׁעִטְּרָה לוֹ אִמּוֹ, הָא תָּנֵינָן, קָרֵי לָהּ בַּת, וְקָרֵי
לָהּ אָחוֹת, קָרֵי לָהּ אֵם, וְכֹלָּא אִיהוּ. וְכֹלָּא הֲוֵי, מַאן דְּיִסְתַּכַּל וְיִנְדַּע
בְּהַאי, יִנְדַּע חָכְמְתָא יַקִּירָא.

124. HE ANSWERS, yet in the words, "Go forth, O daughters of Zion, and behold King Solomon," it is written, "with the crown," instead of 'and the crown'. For whoever sees that crown, WHICH IS MALCHUT, sees the pleasantness of the King that the peace is His. "with which his mother crowned him," REFERS TO MALCHUT THAT SURROUNDS ZEIR ANPIN, for we have learned that he calls her daughter, sister and mother. She is all that and everything is in her. Whoever looks to know it, MALCHUT, will have knowledge of precious wisdom.

125. הַשְׁתָּא מָה אַעֲבִיד, אִי אֵימָא, רָזָא סְתִימָא דָּא, לָא אִצְטְרִיךְ
לְגַלָּאָה. אִי לָא אֵימָא, יִשְׁתָּאֲרוּן זַכָּאִין אִלֵּין, יַתְמִין מֵהַאי רָזָא, נָפַל
הַהוּא סָבָא עַל אַנְפּוֹי, וְאָמַר, בְּיָדְךָ אַפְקִיד רוּחִי פָּדִיתָ אוֹתִי יְיָ' אֶל

אֱמֶת. מָאנָא דַּהֲוָה לְתַתָּא, הֵיךְ יִתְעֲבִיד לְעֵילָּא, בַּעְלָהּ דַּהֲוָה לְעֵילָּא,
הֵיךְ יִתְהַפֵּךְ וַהֲוָה לְתַתָּא. בַּת זוּגֵיהּ אִתְעֲבִידַת אִמֵּיהּ. תְּוָוהָא עַל
תְּוָוהָא. אֲחוּהָ אֲבוּהָ. אִי אֲבוּהָ דְּקַדְמֵיתָא, יִפְרוֹק לֵיהּ, יֵאוֹת, אֲבָל
אֲחוּהָ דִּלֶיהֱוֵי אֲבוּהָ, וְכִי לָא תְּוָוהָא אִיהוּ דָּא. עָלְמָא בְּהִפּוּכָא אִיהוּ.
וַדַּאי עֶלְאִין לְתַתָּא, וְתַתָּאִין לְעֵילָּא.

125. THE OLD MAN SAID TO HIMSELF, what shall I do now, if I say, yet this obscure secret must not be revealed. If I do not speak, these righteous men will remain bereaved of this secret. The old man fell on his face and said, "Into Your hand I commit my spirit: You have redeemed me, Hashem El of truth" (Tehilim 31:6). The vessel below, NAMELY THE WIDOW WHO USED TO BE THE DEAD CHILDLESS MAN'S WIFE, AND WAS UNDER HIM, how could it be above, AND BECOME HIS MOTHER? Her husband, NAMELY HE WHO DIED CHILDLESS, who was above her, how could he turn to be under, BECOMING HER SON? His spouse turns into his mother. Wonder upon wonder, his brother is his father. If the father of the former, HIS WIFE, would have redeemed him, AND MARRY HIS WIFE, it would have been well. But that his brother would be his father, is not it a wonder? Assuredly it is a world turned upside down, the upper below and the lower above.

126. אֶלָּא, לֶהֱוֵא שְׁמֵיהּ דִּי אֱלָהָא מְבָרַךְ מִן עָלְמָא וְעַד עָלְמָא דִּי
חָכְמְתָא וּגְבוּרְתָּא דִּילֵיהּ הִיא. וְהוּא מְהַשְׁנֵא עִדָּנַיָּא וְזִמְנַיָּא וְגו' יָדַע
מָה בַּחֲשׁוֹכָא וּנְהוֹרָא עִמֵּיהּ שָׁרָא. תָּא חֲזֵי, מַאן דְּשָׁרֵי בִּנְהוֹרָא, לָא
יָכִיל לְאִסְתַּכְּלָא וּלְמֶחֱמֵי בַּחֲשׁוֹכָא. אֲבָל קוּדְשָׁא בְּרִיךְ הוּא לָאו הָכִי,
יָדַע מָה בַּחֲשׁוֹכָא, אע"ג דִּנְהוֹרָא עִמֵּיהּ שָׁרָא. מִגּוֹ נְהוֹרָא, אִסְתַּכַּל
בַּחֲשׁוֹכָא, וְיָדַע כָּל מַה דְּתַמָּן.

126. But, "Blessed be the name of Elohim for ever and ever: for wisdom and might are His: and He changes the times and the seasons... He knows what is in the darkness, and the light dwells with Him" (Daniel 2:20-22). Come and see, whoever is in a lighted place, cannot look to see what is in the darkness. But it is not so with the Holy One, blessed be He. He knows what is in the darkness, even though light dwells with Him, and from within the light regards the darkness and knows all that exists there.

127. הָכָא, אִית לְאַקְדְּמָא בְּקַדְמֵיתָא, מִלָּה חֲדָא, דְּאָמְרוּ קַדְמָאֵי, בְּאִינּוּן חֶזְוֵי לֵילְיָא. דִּתְנָן, מַאן דְּאָתֵי עַל אִמֵּיהּ בְּחֶלְמָא, יְצַפֶּה לְבִינָה. דִּכְתִיב, כִּי אִם לַבִּינָה תִקְרָא, הָכָא אִית לְאִסְתַּכְּלָא, אִי בְּגִין דְּאִיהִי אֵם יֵאוֹת, וַהֲוָה לֵיהּ לְמִכְתַּב הָכִי, דְּמַאן דְּחָמָא אִמֵּיהּ בְּחֶלְמָא, יִזְכֵּי לַבִּינָה. אֲבָל מַאן דְּאָתֵי עַל אִמֵּיהּ אֲמַאי.

127. Here we should first introduce something the ancient people said in regard to visions at night. We learned that whoever comes into his mother (Heb. *em*) in a dream should expect Binah, as written, "if (Heb. *im*) you cry after wisdom (Binah)" (Mishlei 2:3). We should check this. If the reason for this is that it is a mother THAT HE SHOULD EXPECT BINAH, it is well. BUT it should have said that he who sees his mother in a dream should attain Binah, but not he who comes into his mother. Wherefore IS THAT?

128. אֶלָּא רָזָא עִלָּאָה אִיהוּ, בְּגִין דְּאִתְהַפַּךְ וְסָלִיק מִתַּתָּא לְעֵילָּא. בְּרָא הֲוָה בְּקַדְמֵיתָא, כֵּיוָן דְּסָלִיק לְעֵילָּא, אִתְהַפַּךְ אִילָנָא, וְאִתְעֲבֵיד אִיהוּ מֵעָלְמָא עִלָּאָה, וְשַׁלִּיט עֲלָהּ, וְזָכֵי לַבִּינָה.

128. HE ANSWERS, this is a high mystery. For he turned and rose from below upwards. At first he was a son, NAMELY BELOW HER; once he rose up AND CAME IN TO HER, the tree turned over so he became part of the supernal world and ruler over her, and attained Binah.

129. בְּקַדְמֵיתָא כַּד סָלִיק אֵינָשׁ לִי"ג שְׁנִין, מַה כְּתִיב, יְיָ' אָמַר אֵלַי בְּנִי אַתָּה אֲנִי הַיּוֹם יְלִדְתִּיךָ, כְּדֵין אִיהוּ לְתַתָּא מִינָהּ. כֵּיוָן דְּסָלִיק עֲלָהּ, הַאי אִיהוּ מֵעָלְמָא עִלָּאָה. דְּהָא אִסְתַּלַּק בְּדַרְגָּא דְּיוֹסֵף, וְדָא וַדַּאי זָכֵי לַבִּינָה.

129. HE EXPLAINS HIS WORDS: at first, when a man reaches his thirteenth year, it is written, "Hashem has said to me, You are my son; this day have I begotten you" (Tehilim 2:7), FOR HE BECAME A SON OF MALCHUT, AND MALCHUT HIS MOTHER. Then he is under her. Once he came over her AND BECAME HER HUSBAND, he is of the supernal world, ZEIR ANPIN, because he rose to the grade of Joseph, WHO IS YESOD OF ZEIR ANPIN. Assuredly he merits Binah, LIKE ZEIR ANPIN THAT HAS MOCHIN OF BINAH.

130. אוּף הָכִי הַאי מָאנָא, בְּקַדְמֵיתָא אִיהוּ הֲוָה בְּדַרְגָּא דְּיוֹסֵף, בַּעַל אִילָנָא תַּתָּאָה, קַיְּימָא בִּרְעוּתֵיה, וְשָׁלִיט עָלֵיה, דְּהָא כָּל נוּקְבָּא, בְּדִיּוּקְנָא דְּנוּקְבָּא אִילָנָא תַּתָּאָה קַיְּימָא. כֵּיוָן דְּאִיהוּ לָא בָּעָא לְקַיְּימָא בְּהַהוּא דַּרְגָּא דְּיוֹסֵף, וְלָא אִתְקְיַים לְשַׁמְּשָׁא בֵּיה, וּלְאַפָּשָׁא בְּעָלְמָא, וּלְמֶעְבַּד תּוֹלְדִין, כְּדֵין נָחִית לְתַתָּא, וְאִתְעֲבֵידַת אִיהִי אִמֵּיה. וְהַהוּא פָּרוֹקָא, יָרִית יָרוּתָא דְּיוֹסֵף, דַּהֲוָה הוּא בְּקַדְמֵיתָא וְאִיהוּ נָחִית לְתַתָּא.

130. It the same with the vessel, THE WIDOW. At first he, HER DEAD HUSBAND, was of the grade of Joseph, YESOD OF ZEIR ANPIN, THAT IS, the husband of the lower tree, MALCHUT. She obeys his wishes and he rules over her, because every woman is fashioned in the shape of the Nukva, WHICH IS the lower tree, MALCHUT. Since he did not wish to abide in the grade of Joseph, and did not live to use it and multiply in the world and beget offspring, BUT DIED CHILDLESS, he went down, AND INCARNATED IN THE CHILD BORN TO THE LEVIRATE MARRIAGE, while she, HIS WIFE, becomes his mother. The redeemer, HIS BROTHER, received the inheritance of Joseph that he, HIS BROTHER, had before, while he descended AND INCARNATED IN THE BORN CHILD.

131. כֵּיוָן דְּנָחִית לְתַתָּא, כְּדֵין אִתְקַיַּים בֵּיה, יְיָ' אָמַר אֵלַי בְּנִי אַתָּה אֲנִי הַיּוֹם יְלִדְתִּיךָ. אִתְהַפָּךְ אִילָנָא, מַה דַּהֲוָה תְּחוֹתֵיה וְאִיהוּ שָׁלִיט עָלֵיה, אִתְהַדָּר וְשָׁלִיט הַהוּא אִילָנָא עָלֵיה, וְאִיהוּ נָחִית לְתַתָּא. כֵּיוָן דְּאִיהוּ נָחִית לְתַתָּא, הַהוּא דְּיָרִית אֲתָר דְּיוֹסֵף, אֲבוֹי אִקְרֵי, אֲבוֹי הֲוֵי וַדַּאי, כֹּלָּא אִיהוּ עַל תִּקּוּנֵיה וַדַּאי כַּדְקָא יֵאוֹת.

131. Since he descended, it was fulfilled in him, "Hashem has said to me, You are my son; this day have I begotten you," FOR HE BECAME HER SON. The tree turned over, whatever was below that he had power over AS A HUSBAND OVER HIS WIFE, now that he descended TO INCARNATE IN THE CHILD BORN TO THE LEVIRATE MARRIAGE, he, who inherited the place of Joseph, NAMELY HIS BROTHER THE REDEEMER, is called is father, and is his father. Everything is now in place, as it should be.

132. בְּקַדְמֵיתָא הֲוָה מֵעָלְמָא דִּדְכוּרָא, וְהָא אִתְעַקַּר מִתַּמָּן, וְהַשְׁתָּא

אִיהוּ מֵעָלְמָא דְּנוּקְבָּא. וּמַה דַּהֲוָה אִיהוּ שָׁלִיט עֲלָה, שַׁלְטָא אִיהִי
עֲלֵיהּ, וְאִתְהַדָּר לְמֶהֱוֵי בְּעָלְמָא דְּנוּקְבָּא. וְעַל דָּא לֵית לֵיהּ בַּת זוּג
כְּלָל. וְלָא מַכְרִיזֵי עֲלֵיהּ, עַל נוּקְבָּא. דְּהָא מֵעָלְמָא דְּנוּקְבָּא אִתְהַדָּר
אִיהוּ.

132. Before he was of the world of the male, THE ASPECT OF JOSEPH. But he was uprooted there and is now of the world of the female, WHICH IS MALCHUT. He used to rule her but now she rules him and he is back in the world of the female. Therefore he has no spouse at all, and no proclamation regarding spouse is made on his behalf, AS IS DONE FOR ANY MAN BEFORE HE IS BORN, 'THE DAUGHTER OF SO AND SO TO SO AND SO'. For he was returned to the world of the female.

133. וְהַהוּא גוּפָא קַדְמָאָה דְּשָׁבַק, אִלְמָלֵא יִנְדְּעוּן וְיִסְתַּכְּלוּן בְּנֵי
עָלְמָא, צַעֲרָא דְּאִית לֵיהּ, כַּד יִתְעֲקַר מֵעָלְמָא דִּדְכוּרָא, וְאִתְהַדָּר
לְעָלְמָא דְּנוּקְבָּא. יִנְדְּעוּן, דְּהָא לֵית צַעֲרָא בְּעָלְמָא, כְּהַהוּא צַעֲרָא. בַּת
זוּג לֵית לֵיהּ, דְּהָא לָא קַיְימָא בְּאֲתָר דִּדְכוּרָא. לָא מַכְרִיזֵי עֲלֵיהּ, עַל
נוּקְבָּא, דְּהָא מֵעָלְמָא דְּנוּקְבָּא אִיהוּ. וְאִי אִית לֵיהּ בַּת זוּג, הֲוֵי בְּרַחֲמֵי,
אִעֲרַעַת בַּהֲדֵי נוּקְבָּא, דְּעַד כְּעַן לָא אִית לָהּ בַּר זוּג. וְעַל דָּא תָּנֵינָן,
דִּילְמָא יְקַדְּמֶנּוּ אַחֵר בְּרַחֲמִים. אַחֵר תְּנָן. וְכֹלָּא אִיהוּ עַל תִּקּוּנֵיהּ.

133. If people would know the grief of the first body, which he WHO DIED CHILDLESS left, when it is uprooted from the world of the male and returned to the world of the female, they would know that no grief equals that grief. He has no spouse since he is not in the place of the male. No wife is proclaimed for him, because he is of the world of the female. If he does have a wife, it is with mercy THROUGH PRAYER that he meets a woman, who until now had no husband. In relation to that we learned that 'maybe another will precede him through mercy', the meaning of another IS THAT HE WHO DIED CHILDLESS IS CALLED OTHER. And everything is in order.

134. וְעַל דָּא כְּתִיב וּבַת כֹּהֵן כִּי תִהְיֶה אַלְמָנָה וּגְרוּשָׁה וְזֶרַע אֵין לָהּ
וְשָׁבָה אֶל בֵּית אָבִיהָ כִּנְעוּרֶיהָ. וּבַת כֹּהֵן, הָא אוֹקִימְנָא מִלָּה דָּא.

אַלְמָנָה, מֵהַהוּא גּוּפָא קַדְמָאָה. וּגְרוּשָׁה, דְּלָא עָאלַת לְפַרְגּוֹדָא
דְּמַלְכָּא, דְּכָל אִינּוּן דְּלָא קַיְימֵי בְּעָלְמָא דִּדְכוּרָא, לָא אִית לְהוּ בֵּיהּ
חוּלָקָא. הוּא אִשְׁתְּמִיט וְאַעֲקַר גַּרְמֵיהּ מֵעָלְמָא דִּדְכוּרָא, לָא אִית לֵיהּ
חוּלָקָא בֵּיהּ וְעַל דָּא אִיהִי גְרוּשָׁה. וְזֶרַע אֵין לָהּ, דְּאִי הֲוָה לָהּ זֶרַע, לָא
אִתְעֲקַר מִנֵּיהּ, וְלָא הֲוָה נָחִית לְעָלְמָא דְּנוּקְבָא.

134. Regarding this it is written, "But if a priest's daughter be a widow, or divorced, and have no child, and has returned to her father's house, as in her youth" (Vayikra 22:13). We have explained the phrase 'a priest's daughter' AS THE SOUL. It is a widow from the former body OF THE CHILDLESS DEAD MAN, 'divorced' because it does not enter the King's curtain, because all those not of the world of the male have no share in it. He has gone and uprooted himself from the world of the male, so he has no share IN THE KING, ZEIR ANPIN. Hence it is divorced; "and have no child," for had it had a child, it would not be uprooted FROM THE WORLD OF THE MALE, nor had it descended to the world of the female.

135. וְשָׁבָה אֶל בֵּית אָבִיהָ, מַאן בֵּית אָבִיהָ. דָּא עָלְמָא דְּנוּקְבָא,
דְּהַהוּא עָלְמָא בֵּית אָבִיהָ אִקְרֵי, וְהַהוּא מָאנָא דַּהֲוָה אִתְתָּקַן
לְאִשְׁתַּמְּשָׁא בֵּיהּ, אִתְהַפַּךְ וְאִיהוּ נָחִית לְתַתָּא, וְהַהוּא מָאנָא סָלִיק
לְעֵילָא. כִּנְעוּרֶיהָ, כְּהַהוּא זִמְנָא דִּכְתִיב, אֲנִי הַיּוֹם יְלִדְתִּיךָ, יְלִדְתִּיךָ
וַדַּאי, יָשׁוּב לִימֵי עֲלוּמָיו, כְּמָה דַּהֲוָה מִתְּלֵיסַר שְׁנִין וּלְעֵילָא.

135. "And has returned to her father's house": what is her father's house? HE ANSWERS, it is the world of the female, as that world is called her father's house. The vessel, HIS WIFE that was prepared for his use, turned; he came down while the vessel rose up, AS MENTIONED. "as in her youth," as in the time of which it is written, "this day have I begotten you" (Tehilim 2:7), AS HE BECAME THE SON OF THE FEMALE, WHICH IS MALCHUT. Assuredly "have I begotten you" and "he shall return to the days of his youth" (Iyov 33:25), as he used to be from his thirteenth year on.

136. אִי זָכָאת לְאִתְתַּקְנָא, הוֹאִיל וְשָׁבָה אֶל בֵּית אָבִיהָ, מִלֶּחֶם אָבִיהָ
תֹּאכֵל, תִּתְעַנַּג מֵהַהוּא עִנּוּגָא. דְּעָלְמָא דְּנוּקְבָא, דְּאַכְלֵי מִנַּהֲמָא

דְּאַבִּירִים, דְּנָחִית מִלְּעֵילָא. אֲבָל לְאַסְתַּכְּלָא וּלְאִתְהֲנֵי בְּמַה דְּאִתְהֲנוּן שְׁאַר צַדִּיקַיָּיא, לָא יַכְלָא בְּגִין דַּהֲוָה זָר לְתַמָּן. וְעַל דָּא לָא אָכִיל קֹדֶשׁ אֲבָל אָכִיל תְּרוּמָה, דְּאִיהוּ יָתִיב בְּעָלְמָא דְנוּקְבָּא.

136. If it merited perfecting itself, once it "has returned to her father's house...she shall eat of her father's bread," and partake of the delight of the world of the female where one eats of the bread of the noble that descends from above, FROM ZEIR ANPIN. But it cannot behold and enjoy what the rest of the righteous enjoy, because it is a stranger there, AS WRITTEN OF IT, "NO STRANGER SHALL EAT OF THE HOLY THING" (VAYIKRA 22:10), SINCE THE HOLY THINGS ARE IN THE WORLD OF THE MALE. But it does eat of the heave-offering, because it dwells in the world of the female.

137. וּמִגּוֹ דְּאִיהוּ מֵעָלְמָא דְנוּקְבָּא, לָא אָכִיל לֵיהּ אֶלָּא בַּלַּיְלָה, דִּכְתִּיב, וּבָא הַשֶּׁמֶשׁ וְטָהֵר וְאַחַר יֹאכַל מִן הַקֳּדָשִׁים כִּי לַחְמוֹ הוּא. דְּהָא קֹדֶשׁ דְּאִיהוּ מֵעָלְמָא דִּדְכוּרָא, לָא אִתְאֲכִיל אֶלָּא בַּיּוֹם. בְּגִינֵי כַּךְ קֹדֶשׁ יִשְׂרָאֵל לַיְיָ' רֵאשִׁית תְּבוּאָתָה, שֵׁירוּתָא עִלָּאָה דְּכָל עָלְמָא דִּדְכוּרָא, קֹדֶשׁ אִיהוּ, וּמַה דְּסָלִיק בֵּיהּ, בַּקֹּדֶשׁ יִשְׂרָאֵל הֲוָה, וּבְגִינֵי כַּךְ קֹדֶשׁ יִשְׂרָאֵל לַיְיָ' רֵאשִׁית תְּבוּאָתָה.

137. Since it is of the world of the female, it eats it only at night, WHEN THE NUKVA, MALCHUT, REIGNS, as written, "And when the sun is down, he shall be clean, and shall afterwards eat of the holy things; because it is his food" (Ibid. 7). For the holy things that are from the world of the male are eaten only by day, THE TIME OF THE REIGN OF THE MALE, ZEIR ANPIN. Hence IT IS WRITTEN, "Yisrael is holy to Hashem, the first fruits of His increase" (Yirmeyah 2:3). IT IS CALLED FIRST, because the highest beginning of the whole world of the male is holy, NAMELY SUPERNAL ABA AND IMA THAT ARE THE MOCHIN OF ZEIR ANPIN. Whatever came out of holiness is Yisrael, NAMELY ZEIR ANPIN, and hence, "Yisrael is holy to Hashem, the first fruits of His increase."

138. כַּד רוּחִין פְּקִידָאן, בְּאִינּוּן זִמְנִין דְּפַקְדִין לְבֵי קִבְרֵי, אִינּוּן לָא פַקְדִין, דְּהָא לָא זְכָאן לְעָלְמָא דְּקֹדֶשׁ, דִּכְתִּיב וְכָל זָר לֹא יֹאכַל קֹדֶשׁ.

וְאִי לָא זָכָה הַהוּא רוּחָא לְאִתְתַּקְּנָא כַּדְקָא יָאוֹת, כֵּיוָן דְּאַהֲדָר בְּגִלְגּוּלָא, אֲפִילוּ בְּהַהוּא אֲתַר, בִּתְרוּמָה לָא אָכִיל, וְזָר אִקְרֵי, אֲפִילוּ לְעָלְמָא תַתָּאָה וְלָא אָכִיל בָּה. עַד הָכָא בְּרָזָא דָא.

138. When spirits visit the cemetery at appointed times, NAMELY FROM NIGHTFALL UNTIL MIDNIGHT, they do not visit those WHO DIED WITHOUT CHILDREN, since they do not attain the world of holiness, as written, "No stranger shall eat of the holy thing," AND THEIR SPIRITS HAVE NO ABUNDANCE TO BESTOW UPON THE BODY IN THE CEMETERY. And if the spirit did not attain proper correction, once it reincarnates, even in that place OF THE WORLD OF THE FEMALE, it does not eat of the heave-offering and is considered a stranger even to the lower world, THE FEMALE WORLD, and does not eat in it. Up to here concerning the secret OF LEVIRATE MARRIAGE.

139. סָבָא סָבָא, כֵּיוָן דְּשָׁרִיאַת לְשַׁטְּטָא בְּיַמָּא רַבָּא, זִיל בִּרְעוּתָךְ, לְכָל סִטְרִין דְּיַמָּא. הַשְׁתָּא אִית לְגַלָּאָה, דְּהָא אֲמֵינָא, דְּהַאי פָּרוֹקָא כַּד אָתֵי, עָאל גַּבֵּי הַהוּא מָאנָא, דְּקָא אֲמֵינָא, אָעִיל תַּמָּן, וְדָבִיק תַּמָּן רוּחָא דִּילֵיהּ בְּהַהוּא מָאנָא וְלָא אִתְאֲבִיד כְּלוּם, אֲפִילוּ הֶבֶל דְּפוּמָא, יָאוֹת הוּא וְכָךְ הוּא. סָבָא סָבָא, אִי תֵּימָא וּתְגַלֵּי, אֵימָא בְּלָא דְּחִילוּ.

139. HE SAID TO HIMSELF, old, old man, once you started to sail in the wide sea, go as you wish in every direction in the sea. It is now the time to reveal, for I have said that the redeemer, NAMELY THE KINSMAN, when he comes and enters the vessel I mentioned, NAMELY THE WIDOW, brings his spirit there and causes it to cleave to that vessel. Thus nothing is lost, not even a breath. It is well and it is so. Old man, if you talk and reveal, speak without fear.

140. שְׁאָר בְּנֵי נָשָׁא דְּעָלְמָא, דְּקָא מִסְתַּלְּקֵי מִנֵּיהּ, וְהָא יְדַעְנָא, דְּרוּחַ דִּילֵיהּ שָׁבִיק בְּהַהִיא אִתְּתָא דַּהֲוַת לֵיהּ, וְרוּחָא אָעִיל תַּמָּן, מַה אִתְעֲבֵיד מֵהַהוּא רוּחַ. וְאִי נַסְבָא הַאי אִתְּתָא, אוֹף הָכִי, מַה אִתְעֲבֵיד מֵהַהוּא רוּחַ דְּשָׁבַק בָּהּ בַּעְלָהּ קַדְמָאָה, דְּהָא גְּבַר אַחֲרָא אָתֵי עֲלָהּ.

140. As for other people who depart from the world, we know that the spirit

one left in the wife he had, the spirit he placed there IN FORMER LIFE, what has become of that spirit? And if the wife remarries, what becomes of the spirit her first husband left in her, seeing that another man came in to her?

141. לְאִתְקַיְּימָא רוּחַ בְּרוּחַ לָא אֶפְשָׁר, דְּהָא הַאי דְּאָתֵי עָלָה הַשְׁתָּא, רוּחַ אָעִיל בָּהּ. וְכֵן הַהוּא קַדְמָאָה דְּאִסְתָּלִיק, רוּחַ אָעִיל בָּהּ. הַהוּא קַדְמָאָה דְּאִסְתַּלַּק בְּנִין הֲווֹ לֵיהּ, וְדָא דְּהַשְׁתָּא לָאו פָּרוֹקָא אִיהוּ, רוּחַ דְּשָׁבַק הַהוּא קַדְמָאָה בְּהַהוּא מָאנָא, וְאָתָא הַאי אַחֲרָא וְאָעִיל בָּהּ רוּחַ, וַדַּאי לָא יַכְלֵי תַּרְוַויְיהוּ לְאִתְקַיְּימָא בְּהַהוּא גּוּפָא דְּאִתְּתָא כַּחֲדָא, אִי נֵימָא דְּאִתְאֲבִיד, אִי אֶפְשָׁר, מָה אִתְעֲבֵיד מִנֵּיהּ.

141. For a spirit to coexist with a spirit is impossible. For the one who just came in to her inserted a spirit in her, and also the first one who is gone placed a spirit in her. The first who is gone had children, so the current man is not a redeemer. Hence, the spirit the first husband left in the vessel and the spirit the other who came and brought in to her ALSO, surely cannot coexist in the body of that woman. If you say it is lost, this is impossible, AS NOTHING IS LOST. SO what has become of it?

142. אוּף הָכִי אִי אִיהִי לָא אִתְנְסִיבַת, הַהוּא רוּחָא דְּשָׁבַק בָּהּ בַּעְלָהּ, מַאי אִתְעֲבֵיד מִנֵּיהּ. אִי נֵימָא דְּאִתְאֲבִיד לָאו הָכִי. כָּל דָּא צָרִיךְ לְגַלָּאָה הַשְׁתָּא. סָבָא סָבָא, חֲמֵי מָה עֲבַדְתְּ, וּבַמֶּה אָעִילַת גַּרְמָךְ. קוּם סָבָא, אָרִים דִּגְלָךְ. קוּם סָבָא, וְאַשְׁפִּיל גַּרְמָךְ קַמֵּי מָארָךְ.

142. Also, if she does not remarry, what becomes of the spirit her husband left in her? If you argue it is lost, it is not so. All this has to be revealed now. HE SAID TO HIMSELF, old, old man, see what you have done, what you have got yourself into. Arise, old man, raise your banner. Rise, old man and humble yourself before your Master.

A Synopsis

The talk turns to "Hashem, my heart is not haughty", and we are reminded how important it is to be humble of heart before the Holy King, however powerful we are in the world. The merchant then begins a section about divorce and the rules about remarriage. We

hear of persons mentioned in scripture who were reincarnations of
other named persons; for example, the merchant says that Boaz
was a reincarnation, and that good often emerges from what had
been evil.

143. פָּתַח הַהוּא סָבָא וְאָמַר, יְיָ' לֹא גָבַהּ לִבִּי וְלֹא רָמוּ עֵינַי וְגוֹ'. דָּוִד
מַלְכָּא אָמַר דָּא, בְּגִין דַּהֲוָה מַלְכָּא עִלָּאָה, וְשַׁלִּיטָא עַל כָּל מַלְכִין
עִלָּאִין, וְשַׁלִּיטִין דְּאִית מִמִּזְרָח וְעַד מַעֲרַב, וְלָא סָלִיק עַל לִבֵּיהּ
לְאַסְטָאָה מֵאָרְחָא, וְתָדִיר שָׁפִיל לְבֵּיהּ קַמֵּי מָארֵיהּ, וְכַד הֲוָה לָעֵי
בְּאוֹרַיְיתָא, הֲוָה מִתְגַּבַּר כְּאַרְיָא, וְעֵינוֹי תָּדִיר מְאִיכִין בְּאַרְעָא, מִדְחִילוּ
דְּמָארֵיהּ. וְכַד הֲוָה אָזִיל בֵּין עַמָּא, לָא הֲוָה בֵּיהּ גַּסּוּת רוּחָא כְּלָל.

143. The old man began with the verse, "Hashem, my heart is not haughty,
nor my eyes lofty…" (Tehilim 131:1). King David said that, because he was
a high king, ruler over all high kings and rulers from east to west, THAT IS,
THEY WERE AFRAID OF HIS POWER. Yet it did not enter his mind to deviate
from the way, and he always humbled his heart before his Master. When he
was occupied with the Torah, he became strong as a lion, and his eyes were
always cast to the ground for fear of his Master. When he walked among the
people, he had no arrogance at all.

144. וְעַל דָּא כְּתִיב, יְיָ' לֹא גָבַהּ לִבִּי וְגוֹ', לֹא גָבַהּ לִבִּי, אע"ג דַּאֲנָא
מַלְכָּא שַׁלִּיטָא עַל כָּל שְׁאַר מַלְכִין דְּעָלְמָא. וְלֹא רָמוּ עֵינַי, בְּזִמְנָא
דַּאֲנָא קַיְימָא קַמָּךְ, לָעֵי בְּאוֹרַיְיתָא. וְלֹא הִלַּכְתִּי בִּגְדוֹלוֹת וּבְנִפְלָאוֹת
מִמֶּנִּי, בְּשַׁעֲתָא דַּאֲנָא אָזִיל בֵּין עַמָּא. וְאִי דָּוִד מַלְכָּא אָמַר הָכִי, שְׁאַר
בְּנֵי עָלְמָא עַל אַחַת כַּמָּה וְכַמָּה. וַאֲנָא כַּמָּה אֲנָא שָׁפִיל לְבָּא, וּמָאִיךְ
עֵינָא קַמֵּי מַלְכָּא קַדִּישָׁא. וְחָס לִי, דִּבְמִלִּין קַדִּישִׁין דְּאוֹרַיְיתָא, יְרוֹם
לְבָּאי. בָּכָה וְדִמְעוֹי נַפְלִין עַל דִּיקְנֵיהּ.

144. Therefore it is written, "Hashem, my heart is not haughty…" My heart
is not haughty though I am a king and ruler over all the other kings in the
world. "Nor my eyes lofty" when I am before You, delving in the Torah.
"Nor do I exercise myself in great matters, or in things too high for me"
(Ibid.), when I walk among the people. If King David said so, how much

more so the rest of the people in the world! And I, how humble of heart I am and lowering my eyes before the holy King. Far be it for me to be proud in the holy matters of the Torah! He wept and his tears fell on his beard.

145. אָמַר, סָבָא לָאֵי בְּחֵילָא, כַּמָּה שַׁפִּירָאן דְמָעִין עַל דִּיקְנָךְ, כְּמָה דַּהֲוָה שַׁפִּיר מִשְׁחָא טָבָא, כַּד הֲוָה נָחִית עַל דִּיקְנָא דְסָבָא טָבָא דְּאַהֲרֹן. אֵימָא מִילָךְ סָבָא דְּהָא מַלְכָּא קַדִּישָׁא הָכָא. שְׁאַר בְּנֵי נָשָׁא דְּעָלְמָא, דְּקָא אִסְתָּלָקוּ מִנֵּיה, וְשָׁבְקוּ רוּחָא בְּהַהוּא מָאנָא, דַּהֲווֹ מִשְׁתַּמְּשֵׁי בֵּיה, וְאִתְנְסִיבַת, וְאָתָא אַחֲרָא וְאָעִיל בְּהַהוּא מָאנָא רוּחָא אַחֲרָא, מָה אִתְעֲבֵיד מֵהַהוּא קַדְמָאָה, כְּמָה דְּאִתְּמַר.

145. He said TO HIMSELF, old man, weary and powerless, how becoming are the tears on your beard, the good old man as becoming as the precious ointment running down on the beard of Aaron. Speak up, old man, for the holy King is here. Other people, when they depart from the world, leaving a spirit in the vessel they used, NAMELY THEIR WIVES, what happens to the first spirit, if she remarries and another comes and puts another spirit in that vessel, as I mentioned?

146. תָּא חֲזֵי, כַּמָּה עִלָּאִין גְּבוּרָאן דְּמַלְכָּא קַדִּישָׁא, דְּקָא עָבֵיד, וּמַאן יָכִיל לְמַלְּלָא לוֹן. כַּד הַאי בַּעְלָה תִּנְיָינָא, אָתֵי וְאָעִיל רוּחָא בְּהַהוּא מָאנָא, רוּחָא קַדְמָאָה, מְקַטְרְגָא בְּהַאי רוּחַ דְּעָאל, וְלָא אִתְיַישְׁבָן כַּחֲדָא.

146. Come and see how lofty the mighty acts the holy King performs are. Who could tell them? When the second husband comes and inserts a spirit in that vessel, IN THE WIFE, the first spirit OF THE FIRST HUSBAND denounces the coming spirit, and they do not get along together.

147. וּבְגִינֵי כַּךְ, אִתְּתָא לָא אִתְיַישְׁבַת כַּדְקָא יֵאוֹת, בַּהֲדֵי בַּעְלָה תִּנְיָינָא, בְּגִין דְּרוּחָא קַדְמָאָה מְכַשְׁכְּשָׁא בָּה, וּכְדֵין אִיהִי דְּכִירַת לֵיה תָּדִיר, וּבָכַאת עֲלֵיה, אוֹ אִתְאַנְּחַת עֲלֵיה, דְּהָא רוּחָא דִּילֵיה, מְכַשְׁכְּשָׁא בִּמְעָהָא כְּחִוְיָא, וּמְקַטְרְגָא בַּהֲדֵי רוּחַ אַחֲרָא, דְּעָאל בָּה מִבַּעְלָה תִּנְיָינָא. עַד זְמָן סַגִּי מְקַטְרְגִין דָּא בְּדָא.

147. For that reason the woman does not get along well with the second husband, since the spirit of the first is tapping inside her. She then remembers him always, weeps for him or sighs for him, since his spirit taps in her innards like a snake, and speaks ill of the other spirit that came from the second husband. They assail each other a long time.

148. וְאִי אַעְבַּר דָּא דְּעָאל, לְהַהוּא דַּהֲוָה קַדְמָאָה, דָּא קַדְמָאָה נָפִיק וְאָזִיל לֵיהּ. וּלְזִמְנִין, דְּדָחֵי דָּא קַדְמָאָה לְהַהוּא תִּנְיָינָא, וְאִתְעֲבֵיד לֵיהּ מְקַטְרְגָא, עַד דְּאַפִּיק לֵיהּ מֵעָלְמָא. וְעַל דָּא תָּנֵינָן, דְּמִתְּרֵין וּלְהָלְאָה, לָא יִסַּב בַּר נָשׁ לְהַאי אִתְּתָא, דְּהָא מַלְאַךְ הַמָּוֶת אִתְתָּקַף בָּהּ, וּבְנֵי עָלְמָא לָא יַדְעִין, דְּהָא רוּחָא בֵּיוָן דְּאִתְתָּקַף וְקָא נָצַח לְהַהוּא רוּחָא אָחֳרָא תִּנְיָינָא, מִכָּאן וּלְהָלְאָה לָא יִתְעָרַב בַּר נָשׁ אָחֳרָא בַּהֲדָהּ.

148. If the one coming FROM THE SECOND HUSBAND removes the former spirit OF THE FIRST HUSBAND, it leaves and goes away. At times the first pushes away the second and attacks it, until it takes it out of the world. In relation to this we learned that from two or more, THAT IS, AFTER HER TWO HUSBANDS DIED, a man should not marry this woman, because the Angel of Death is strong in her. But people do not know that once the spirit OF THE FIRST HUSBAND prevailed and overcame the other, second spirit, AND PUSHED IT OUT OF THE WORLD, from now on no one should mix with her.

149. חַבְרַיָּיא, הָא יְדַעְנָא דְּבַאֲתָר דָּא אִית לְכוּ לְמִקְשֵׁי, וְלֵימָא אִי הָכִי לָא מִית בְּדִינָא הַאי תִּנְיָינָא, וְלָא דַּיְינִין לֵיהּ מִלְעֵילָא. תָּא חֲזֵי, כֹּלָּא אִיהוּ בְּדִינָא, דְּיִנְצַח פְּלוֹנִי לִפְלוֹנִי אוֹ דְּלָא יְקַטְרֵג עֲלֵיהּ פְּלוֹנִי לִפְלוֹנִי. וּמַאן דְּנָסִיב אַרְמַלְתָּא, כְּמַאן דְּעָאל בְּיַמָּא, בְּרוּחִין תַּקִּיפִין, בְּלָא חַבְלִין, וְלָא יָדַע אִי יַעְבַּר בִּשְׁלָם, אִי יִטְבַּע גּוֹ תְּהוֹמֵי.

149. Friends, I do know that now you should raise a question and say that in this case, the second husband died unlawfully and was not judged from above, BUT WAS REJECTED BY THE SPIRIT OF THE FIRST HUSBAND. Come and see, everything is according to law, BECAUSE IT HAS BEEN DECREED ABOVE that either one would overcome one, or that one would not attack one. He who marries a widow is like he who enters the sea with strong

winds BLOWING, without ropes, and does not know whether he will pass in peace or drown in the deep.

150. וְאִי דָא דְּעָאל הַהוּא רוּחָא תִּנְיָינָא, אִתְתָּקִיף וְנָצַח לְהַהוּא קַדְמָאָה, הַהוּא קַדְמָאָה נָפַק מִתַּמָּן וְאָזִיל לֵיהּ. לְאָן אֲתָר אָזִיל לֵיהּ, וּמָה אִתְעָבֵיד. סָבָא סָבָא מָה עֲבַדְתְּ. חָשַׁבְתְּ דִּתְמַלֵּל זְעֵיר, וְנַפְקַת לְהַאי, הָא עָאלַת בַּאֲתָר דְּלָא עָאל בַּר נָשׁ אַחֲרָא, מִן יוֹמָא דְּדוֹאֵג וַאֲחִיתוֹפֶל עָבְדוּ בַּעְיָין אִלֵּין, בְּאִינּוּן אַרְבַּע מְאָה בַּעְיֵי, דַּהֲווֹ בָּעָאן עַל מִגְדְּלָא דְּפָרַח בַּאֲוִירָא, וְלָא אָתִיב עֲלַיְיהוּ בַּר נָשׁ, עַד דְּאָתָא שְׁלֹמֹה מַלְכָּא, וּבֵירֵר לוֹן כָּל חַד וְחַד עַל תִּקּוּנֵיהּ. סָבָא סָבָא, רָזָא עִלָּאָה דַּהֲוָה טְמִירָא, אָתִית לְגַלָּאָה, מָה עֲבַדִית.

150. If the second spirit that JUST entered prevails and overcomes the first SPIRIT, the first goes away from there and goes its way. HE ASKS, whither does it go, and what becomes OF IT? HE SAID TO HIMSELF, old, old man, what have you done? You thought you would speak a little and come away, but you have entered a place where no one else has entered since the day Do'eg and Achitofel formed these questions of the four hundred questions they were asking about the tower soaring in the air. None had answered them until King Solomon came, who properly clarified each one. Old, old man, you have come to reveal a concealed lofty secret, what have you done?

151. סָבָא סָבָא, בְּקַדְמֵיתָא הֲוָה לָךְ לְנַטְרָא אָרְחָךְ, וְתִסְתַּכַּל בְּרֵישָׁךְ. אֲבָל הַשְׁתָּא, לָאו שַׁעֲתָא לְאִתְטַמְּרָא. סָבָא, אַהֲדַר בְּתִקְפָךְ. הַהוּא רוּחַ דְּנָפַק, לְאָן אָזַל. בָּכָה וְאָמַר, חַבְרַיָּא, כָּל הָנֵי בְּכָיָין דְּקָא בָּכֵינָא, לָאו בְּגִינַיְיכוּ הוּא, אֶלָּא דְּחִילְנָא לְמָארֵי עָלְמָא, דְּגַלֵּינָא אָרְחִין סְתִימִין, בְּלָא רְשׁוּ. אֲבָל גַּלֵּי קָמֵי קוּדְשָׁא בְּרִיךְ הוּא, דְּלָא לִיקָרָא דִּילִי עֲבִידְנָא, וְלָא לִיקָרָא דְּאַבָּא, אֲבָל רְעוּתִי לְפוּלְחָנָא דִּילֵיהּ, וַאֲנָא חֲמֵינָא, יְקָרָא דְּחַד מִנַּיְיכוּ, בְּהַהוּא עָלְמָא, וְאַחֲרָא יָדַעְנָא דְּהָכִי הוּא. אֲבָל לָא גַּלֵּי קַמָּאי, וְהַשְׁתָּא חֲמֵינָא.

151. Old, old man, you should have guarded your path in the beginning and

observed when you started, but now is not the time to hide. Old man, answer with your might. Whither does the spirit go, which left? He wept and said, friends, all these tears I wept were not for your sakes, but I feared the Master of the universe, for revealing hidden ways without permission. But it is known before the Holy One, blessed be He, that is not for my own glory or the glory of my father, but my wish is to serve Him. And I have seen the preciousness of one of you in that world, and I know it is the same with the other, though it has not been disclosed to me. But now I see.

152. תָּנֵינָן, דְּחַיָּין גַּבְרָא מקַמֵּי גַּבְרָא, בְּכַמָּה אָרְחִין סְתִימִין אִתְדַּחְיָין. הַהוּא רוּחָא קַדְמָאָה, דְּאִתְדַּחֵי מקַמֵּי הַהוּא תִּנְיָינָא, לְאָן אָזִיל. הַהוּא רוּחָא, נָפִיק וְאָזִיל, וּמְשַׁטְּטָא בְּעָלְמָא, וְלָא יְדִיעַ, וְאָזִיל לְגוֹ קִבְרָא דְּהַהוּא בַּר נָשׁ, וּמִתַּמָּן מְשַׁטְּטָא בְּעָלְמָא, וְאִתְחֲזֵי בְּחֶלְמָא לִבְנֵי נָשָׁא, וְחָמָאן בְּחֶלְמָא דִּיּוּקְנָא דְּהַהוּא בַּר נָשׁ, וְאוֹדַע לוֹן מִלִּין לְפוּם אָרְחֵיהּ דְּהַהוּא רוּחַ קַדְמָאָה, דְּקָא אִתְמְשַׁךְ מִנֵּיהּ, כְּמָה דְּאִיהוּ בְּהַהוּא עָלְמָא, הָכִי מְשַׁטְּטָא הַאי, וְאוֹדַע בְּהַאי עָלְמָא.

152. We have learned that a man is pushed aside for another, and they are rejected in many hidden ways. The first spirit that was pushed aside before the second, where does it go? HE ANSWERS, the spirit leaves and goes to roam the world unbeknownst, and goes to the grave of that man, from whence it goes about the world, to be seen to people in dreams. They see in a dream the image of that man, who informs them of things according to the way of the first spirit that came out of him. As things are in that world, it goes about and informs so in this world.

153. וְהָכִי אָזִיל וּמְשַׁטְּטָא בְּעָלְמָא, וּפַקְדַת תָּדִיר לְהַהוּא קִבְרָא, עַד זִמְנָא דְּרוּחוֹת פַּקְדָן לְגַבֵּי קַבְרַיְיהוּ דְּגוּפִין. כְּדֵין, הַאי רוּחָא, אִתְחַבַּר בְּהַהוּא רוּחַ דִּילֵיהּ, וְאִתְלָבַשׁ בֵּיהּ, וְאָזִיל לֵיהּ. כַּד עָאל לְדוּכְתֵּיהּ, אִתְפָּשַׁט מִנֵּיהּ. וְדוּכְתָּא אִית לֵיהּ בְּאִינוּן הֵיכָלִין דְּגַן עֵדֶן, אוֹ לְבַר, לְפוּם אָרְחוֹי דְּכָל חַד וְחַד, וְתַמָּן אִתְטַמַּר.

153. In this manner it goes about the world, always visiting that grave, when spirits visit the graves of the bodies. THEN THE SPIRIT ITSELF OF THE

FIRST HUSBAND GOES TO THE GRAVE TO VISIT ITS BODY. Then this spirit, WHICH IS JUST A PART OF THE MAIN SPIRIT, joins its MAIN spirit, which is clothed in it and goes its way. And when THE SPIRIT enters its place, it is divested of it. And it has place in the chambers in the Garden of Eden, or outside, according to the way of each individual. There it hides.

154. וְכַד רוּחִין פַּקְדָן לְהַאי עָלְמָא, דְּמֵתִין נִזְקָקִין לְגַבֵּי חַיִּין, לָא נִזְקָקִין אֶלָּא בְּהַהוּא מְשִׁיכוּ דְרוּחָא, וּבֵיהּ אִתְלָבַשׁ רוּחָא אַחֲרָא. וְאִי תֵּימָא, אִי הָכִי, תּוֹעַלְתָּא אִיהוּ, לְרוּחָא, וְהַאי אִתְּתָא תּוֹעַלְתָּא עַבְדַת לְכֹלָּא. לָאו הָכִי, דְּאִלְמָלֵא לָא אִתְנְסִיבַת לְגַבֵּי אַחֲרָא, וְהַאי רוּחָא קַדְמָאָה לָא מִתְדַּחְיָיא מִקַּמֵּי הַאי גַּבְרָא אָחֳרָא, תּוֹעַלְתָּא אַחֲרָא הֲוָה לֵיהּ, בְּגַוְונָא אַחֲרָא, וְלָא יְהֵא לָאֵי בְּעָלְמָא, כְּמָה דְּהֲוֵי, וְלָא יִזְדַּקֵּק לְגַבֵּי חַיִּין דְּהַאי עָלְמָא, כְּמָה דְּהֲוֵי מְשַׁטְּטָא הָכָא וְהָכָא.

154. And when the spirits visit this world, the dead are engaged with the living only by means of the attraction of that spirit, NAMELY THE SPIRIT THE HUSBAND LEAVES IN HIS WIFE IN THE PREVIOUS LIFE, in which the other, MAIN spirit is clothed. If it is said that it is for the good of the spirit, and the woman does good in every way, BECAUSE BY MEANS OF THE SPIRIT HER HUSBAND LEFT IN HER – THE SPIRIT IS ATTACHED TO THE LIVING, it is not so. For had she not married another, and had the first spirit not been rejected before the other man, THE SECOND HUSBAND, he would have derived benefit in another way, and not TOIL in that world as he does, nor be attached to the living in this world, roaming to and fro.

155. אִי הָכִי זוּוּגָא תִּנְיָינָא דְּהַאי אִתְּתָא, לָא הֲוֵי מִלְּעֵילָּא. וְאַתְּ אֲמַרְתְּ דְּאִתְדַּחְיָיא גְּבַר מִקַּמֵּי גְּבַר, וַאֲמֵינָא דְּהַאי בַּעֲלָהּ תִּנְיָינָא, דְּנָסִיב לְאִתְּתָא דָא, אִיהוּ בַּת זוּגֵיהּ מַמָּשׁ. וְהַהוּא קַדְמָאָה לָאו בַּר זוּגֵיהּ מַמָּשׁ הֲוָה. וְהַאי תִּנְיָינָא דִּילֵיהּ הֲוָה, וְכַד מָטָא זִמְנֵיהּ, אִתְדַּחְיָיא דָא מִקַּמֵּיהּ. וַדַּאי הָכִי הוּא, דְּהָא לָא אִתְדַּחְיָיא הַהוּא רוּחָא קַדְמָאָה, דְּהֲוָה בְּהַאי אִתְּתָא. אֶלָּא בְּגִין דְּהַאי תִּנְיָינָא, דְּאִיהוּ בַּר זוּגָהּ.

155. HE ASKS, if so, the second marriage of the woman is not decreed from above, because you said one man is rejected before another. HE ANSWERS,

yet I say that the second husband who married this woman, she is his very soulmate, while the first is not her real soulmate. Therefore she is of the second, and when his time comes AND HE MARRIES HER, the first is pushed aside from before him. Assuredly it is so, because the spirit of the first that was in that woman is rejected only because the second is her soulmate. THUS THE SECOND MARRIAGE IS FROM HEAVEN.

156. וְכָל אִינּוּן תִּנְיָינִין, דְּאִתְדַּחְיָין מִקַּמֵּי קַדְמָאִין. קַדְמָאִין הֲוֹו בְּנֵי זוּגַיְיהוּ, וְלָא הָנֵי. וּבְגִין כָּךְ, לָא אִית לוֹן קִיּוּמָא בַּהֲדַיְיהוּ, וְאִתְדַּחְיָיא רוּחַ תִּנְיָינָא מִקַּמֵּי רוּחָא קַדְמָאָה. וּבְגִין כָּךְ, מַאן דְּנָסִיב אַרְמַלְתָּא, קָרֵינָן עָלֵיהּ, וְלֹא יָדַע כִּי בְנַפְשׁוֹ הוּא. כִּי חִנָּם מְזוֹרָה הָרָשֶׁת וְגוֹ' וְלָא יְדִיעַ אִי הִיא בַּת זוּגֵיהּ מַמָּשׁ אִי לָאו.

156. All those second HUSBANDS rejected before the first HUSBANDS, the first ones were their soulmates while the latter were not. This is why they do not live with them, and the second spirit is pushed from before the first spirit. Hence one says of he who marries a widow, "and knows not that it is for his life" (Mishlei 7:23), "For no heed is taken of the net" (Mishlei 1:17), since it is not known if she is his real soulmate or not.

157. אַרְמַלְתָּא דְּלָא נְסִיבַת, אע"ג דְּאָתֵי בַּר זוּגָהּ, וְאִיהִי לָא בָּעָאת לְאִתְנַסְּבָא, קוּדְשָׁא בְּרִיךְ הוּא לָא כַּיִּיף לָהּ מִן דִּינָא, וְקוּדְשָׁא בְּרִיךְ הוּא אַזְמִין לְהַהוּא בַּר נָשׁ אִתְּתָא אַחֲרָא, וְלָא עָאלַת בְּדִינָא כְּהַאי בְּהַהוּא עָלְמָא, וְאַף עַל גַּב דְּלֵית לָהּ בַּר, דְּהָא אִתְּתָא לָא אִתְפַּקְּדַת אַפְרְיָיה וּרְבִיָּה, כְּמָה דְּאוּקִמוּהָ.

157. An unmarried widow, who does not wish to marry even if her soulmate comes, the Holy One, blessed be He, does not force her to by law. And the Holy One, blessed be He, arranges that man another wife, and THE WIDOW is not judged for this in that world, even if she does not have a child, since a woman is not commanded to be fruitful and multiply, as we explained.

158. אִתְּתָא דָּא דְּלָא אִתְנְסִיבַת זִמְנָא תִּנְיָינָא, הַהוּא רוּחַ דְּשָׁבַק בָּהּ בַּעְלָהּ מָה אִתְעֲבֵיד מִנֵּיהּ. יָתִיב תַּמָּן תְּרֵיסַר יַרְחֵי, וּבְכָל לֵילְיָא

וְלֵילְיָא, נָפִיק וּפַקְדָּא לְנַפְשָׁא, וְאִתְהַדָּר לְאַתְרֵיהּ. לְבָתַר תְּרֵיסַר יַרְחֵי,
דְּקָא אִסְתַּלָּק דִּינָא דְּהַהוּא גַּבְרָא, דְּהָא כָּל אִינּוּן תְּרֵיסַר יַרְחֵי, הָא
רוּחָא אִתְכַּפְיָיא בַּעֲצִיבוּ כָּל יוֹמָא. לְבָתַר תְּרֵיסַר יַרְחֵי, נָפִיק מִתַּמָּן,
וְאָזִיל וְקַיְימָא לְתַרְע גַּן עֵדֶן, וּפַקְדָּא לְהַאי עָלְמָא, לְגַבֵּי הַהוּא מָאנָא,
דְּנָפִיק מִנֵּיהּ. וְכַד הַאי אִתְּתָא אִסְתַּלְּקַת מֵעָלְמָא, הַהוּא רוּחַ נָפִיק
וְאִתְלָבַשׁ בְּהַהוּא רוּחַ דִּילָהּ, וְזָכָאת בֵּיהּ לְגַבֵּי בַּעְלָהּ, וְנַהֲרִין תַּרְוַויְיהוּ,
כַּדְקָא יָאוֹת, בְּחִבּוּרָא חֲדָא.

158. What becomes of the spirit in this woman, who does not remarry, whose husband left in her IN HIS LAST LIFE? HE ANSWERS, it remains there, IN THE WIFE, twelve months, and every night it comes out, visits the Nefesh and returns to its place. After twelve months, the sentence is alleviated from that man, NAMELY HER HUSBAND, for during the twelve months the spirit is downcast with sadness the whole day. After twelve months it goes away from there, FROM THE WIFE, and goes to stand at the gate of the Garden of Eden, and visits in this world that vessel, THE WOMAN, which it left. When the woman leaves the world, that spirit comes out and is clothed in her spirit, OF THE WIFE, and she gains it by her husband, and they both illuminate worthily, united into one.

159. כֵּיוָן דְּאָתֵינָא לְהַאי אֲתָר, הַשְׁתָּא אִית לְגַלָּאָה אָרְחִין סְתִימִין,
דְּמָארֵי עָלְמָא, לָא יַדְעִין בְּהוּ בְּנֵי נָשָׁא. וְכֻלְּהוּ אַזְלִין בְּאֹרַח קְשׁוֹט,
כד"א כִּי יְשָׁרִים דַּרְכֵי יְיָ' וְצַדִּיקִים יֵלְכוּ בָם וּפוֹשְׁעִים יִכָּשְׁלוּ בָם. וּבְנֵי
נָשָׁא לָא יַדְעִין, וְלָא מַשְׁגִּיחִין, כַּמָּה אִינּוּן עִלָּאִין, עוֹבָדִין דְּקוּדְשָׁא
בְּרִיךְ הוּא, וְכַמָּה מְשַׁנְיָין אִינּוּן, וּבְנֵי עָלְמָא לָא יַדְעִין, וְכֻלְּהוּ בְּאֹרַח
קְשׁוֹט, דְּלָא סָטָאן לִימִינָא וְלִשְׂמָאלָא.

159. Having come to this place, it is now proper to reveal the hidden ways of the Master of the universe, which people do not know of. They all follow the true path, as written, "for the ways of Hashem are right, and the just do walk in them: but the transgressors shall stumble in them" (Hoshea 14:10). But people do not know nor care how lofty the deeds of the Holy One, blessed be He, are and how diverse, yet the people in the world do not know it. They are all in the path of truth, not turning right or left.

160. הָנֵי דְּמִתְגַּלְגְּלִין, דְּקָא אִתְתְּרָכוּ בְּתֵרוּכִין מֵהַהוּא עָלְמָא, וְלֵית לוֹן בַּת זוּג. בַּת זוּג דְּקָא מִזְדַּוְּוגָן בְּהַאי עָלְמָא, מַאן אִינוּן, אִינוּן נָשִׁין, דְּקָא מִזְדַּוְּוגָן בַּהֲדַיְיהוּ בְּהַאי עָלְמָא. דְּהָא לְכֻלְּהוּ בְּנֵי נָשָׁא, אִית לוֹן בַּת זוּג, בַּר מֵהַאי.

160. As for those incarnated, who were driven out (divorced) of that world and have no spouse, HE ASKS, the spouses they marry in this world, who are the women whom they marry in this world? For any man has a spouse except him WHO INCARNATES.

161. חֲמוּ הַשְׁתָּא, כַּמָּה אִינוּן רַבְרְבִין וְעִלָּאִין גְּבוּרָן דִּילֵיהּ. תָּנֵינָן, מַאן דִּמְתָרֵךְ אִתְּתֵיהּ קַדְמָאָה, מַדְבְּחָא אָחִית עֲלוֹי דִּמְעִין. מַדְבְּחָא אֲמַאי. אֶלָּא, הָא אֲמֵינָא, דְּכָל נָשִׁין דְּעָלְמָא בְּדִיּוּקְנָא דְּהַאי מִזְבֵּחַ קַיְימֵי, וְעַל דָּא יָרְתָאן אִינוּן שֶׁבַע בִּרְכָאן, דְּכֻלְּהוּ מִכְּנֶסֶת יִשְׂרָאֵל אִינוּן. וְאִי אִיהוּ מְתָרֵךְ לָהּ, אַהֲדָר אַבְנָא דְּמַדְבְּחָא עִלָּאָה לְגִרְעוֹנָא. מ"ט. בְּגִין דְּמִתְחַבְּרָן תֵּרוּכִין בַּהֲדֵי הֲדָדֵי.

161. See now how great and lofty His mighty acts are. We learned that whoever divorces his first wife, the altar sheds tears for him. HE ASKS, why the altar, AND ANSWERS, I say that all the women in the world are fashioned in the shape of the altar, WHICH IS MALCHUT, AS EVERY WOMAN'S ROOT IS IN MALCHUT. They therefore inherit seven blessings, all from the Congregation of Yisrael, WHICH IS MALCHUT. And if he divorces her, HIS FIRST WIFE, the stone OF THE SUPERNAL ALTAR, NAMELY, THE ROOT OF THAT WOMAN, WHICH IS IN MALCHUT, reverts to a state of deficiency and lack. What is the reason for this? IT IS because the two divorcees are united. JUST AS SHE WAS DIVORCED FROM HER HUSBAND, IT IS DIVORCED FROM ITS ROOT IN MALCHUT.

162. וְרָזָא דָּא דִּכְתִּיב, וְכָתַב לָהּ סֵפֶר כְּרִיתוּת וְנָתַן בְּיָדָהּ וְגוֹ', וְיָצְאָה מִבֵּיתוֹ וְהָלְכָה וְהָיְתָה לְאִישׁ אַחֵר. מִמַּשְׁמַע דְּאָמַר, וְהָלְכָה וְהָיְתָה לְאִישׁ, לָא יְדַעְנָא דְּלֵיתֵיהּ דְּהַהוּא דְּתָרִיךְ לָהּ, מַאי אַחֵר. אֶלָּא כְּמָה דְּאִתְּמַר, אַחֵר תְּנָן, וְאַחֵר כְּתִיב, וְאַחֵר קָרֵינָן לֵיהּ, דִּכְתִּיב וּמֵעָפָר אַחֵר

יִצְמָחוּ. וְתָרוּכִין מִתְחַבְּרָן כַּחֲדָא, תָּרוּכִין דְּהַהוּא עָלְמָא, וְתָרוּכִין דְּהַאי
עָלְמָא. וּמַה דַּהֲוַת הַאי אִתְּתָא, בְּדִיּוּקְנָא עִלָּאָה, הָא אִשְׁתַּעְבְּדָא
לְדִיּוּקְנָא תַּתָּאָה, קָרֵינָא לֵיהּ אַחֵר.

162. This is the secret of the words, "then let him write her a bill of divorce, and give it in her hand...And when she is departed out of his house, she may go and be another man's wife" (Devarim 24:1). HE ASKS, seeing that "she may go and be another man's wife," do I not know he is not the one who divorced her? Why DOES IT SAY "another"? HE ANSWERS, it is as we learned it, we learned of the other, and it is written of "another," and he is called another, as written, "and out of the earth shall others spring" (Iyov 8:19). HENCE THE INCARNATED IS CALLED 'ANOTHER'. And the divorcees are joined together, he who is divorced from that world, NAMELY THE INCARNATED MAN WHO HAS NO SPOUSE, WHO IS DRIVEN AWAY FROM THAT WORLD INTO THIS WORLD, WHO MARRIED THE DIVORCED WOMAN, and the divorced WOMAN in this world FROM HER HUSBAND, as this woman who had the supernal shape OF MALCHUT, is now enslaved to the lower shape, NAMELY TO THE INCARNATED MAN WITHOUT A SPOUSE, WHO MARRIED HER, who is called another, AS MENTIONED BEFORE. FOR HE CLEAVED TO ANOTHER EL, FOR WHICH REASON HE AGAIN INCARNATED IN THIS WORLD.

163. וְקָרֵינָן לֵיהּ אַחֲרוֹן, אַחֲרוֹן מִנָּלָן. דִּכְתִיב, וְאַחֲרוֹן עַל עָפָר יָקוּם.
וְהָכָא כְּתִיב וּשְׂנֵאָהּ הָאִישׁ הָאַחֲרוֹן. אוֹ כִּי יָמוּת הָאִישׁ הָאַחֲרוֹן.
אַחֲרוֹן, שֵׁנִי מִבָּעֵי לֵיהּ. וְאִי תֵּימָא, דְּלָא תִּזְדַּוְּוג אֲפִילוּ לַעֲשָׂרָה, דָּא
בָּתַר דָּא. לָאו הָכִי. וְכִי לְבַעְלָהּ דָּא תִּזְדַּוְּוג, וְלָא לְאַחֲרָא, מַאי אַחֲרוֹן.

163. And he is called 'last'. Whence do we know he is called latter? From the words, "and that he who outlives all things (lit. 'latter'), will rise" (Iyov 19:25). SO THE INCARNATED MAN IS CALLED LATTER. And here it is written, "And if the latter husband hate her" (Devarim 24:3), or, "or if the latter...should die" (Ibid.). HE ASKS, it says latter, while it should have said 'second'. If you say THE PURPOSE OF THE VERSE IS TO FORBID that she would marry ten one after the other, it is not so. For she would marry this husband and no other, WHEREFORE SHOULD SHE BE FORBIDDEN TO ANOTHER? Why is he then called 'last'?

164. אֶלָּא דָּא אִיהוּ הַאי אַחֵר דְּקָאָמְרָן, וְאִיהוּ אַחֵר, וְאִיהוּ אַחֲרוֹן. הַשְׁתָּא אַבְנָא מִתְגַּלְגְּלָא בְּקוּסְפְתָּא. אַחֵר אֲמַאי אִקְרֵי הָכִי דְּהָא כָּל בִּנְיָינָא נָפַל, וְאִתְהַדָּר לְעַפְרָא, אִיהוּ הֲוָה מַה דַּהֲוָה, וְלָא אַחֲרָא. אֲמַאי קָרֵינָן לֵיהּ אַחֵר. אוּף הָכִי אֲמַאי אִקְרֵי אַחֲרוֹן, וְכִי אַחֲרוֹן אִיהוּ, וְהָא אִי יִתְיַישֵׁר יֵאוֹת, וְאִי לָא, יֶהְדָּר וְיִתְגַּלְגֵּל וְיִתְנְטַע כְּמִלְּקַדְמִין, אֲמַאי אִקְרֵי אַחֲרוֹן.

164. HE ANSWERS, this is the last we mentioned. He is another and is last. For now the stone turns in the sling, WHICH MEANS THAT IN RELATION TO THE FIRST BODY THAT DIED, THE INCARNATED IN THE SLING, WHO CAME AGAIN INTO THE WORLD IS CALLED BY THE NAME 'ANOTHER' AND 'LATTER (LAST)'. SINCE HE HAS NO SPOUSE HE MARRIES THE DIVORCEE AND HENCE THE VERSE CALLS HIM 'ANOTHER' AND 'LAST'. HE ASKS, why is he called another IN RELATION TO THE FIRST BODY THAT DIED, seeing that the whole edifice, NAMELY THE FIRST BODY, collapsed and returned to the dust AND IS AS IF IT NEVER EXISTED, and that THE INCARNATED is what THE FIRST BODY was and not another. Why then is he called another, and also why latter? If he is the latter because he straightens his ways AND IMPROVES, it is well, BECAUSE HE IS LAST AND INCARNATES NO LONGER. But if not, he incarnates again to be planted as before. Why then is he called last?

165. אֲבָל תָּא חֲזֵי, כְּתִיב וַיַּרְא אֱלֹהִים אֶת כָּל אֲשֶׁר עָשָׂה וְהִנֵּה טוֹב מְאֹד, מַאי טוֹב. תָּנֵינָן, דָּא מַלְאָךְ דְּטוֹב. מְאֹד, דָּא מַלְאַךְ הַמָּוֶת. וּלְכֹלָּא קוּדְשָׁא בְּרִיךְ הוּא אַזְמִין תִּקּוּנוֹי.

165. Yet come and see, it is written, "And Elohim saw everything that He had made, and, behold, it was very good" (Beresheet 1:31). What is 'good'? It is the Angel of Good; 'very' is the Angel of Death. The Holy One, blessed be He, summons ways of correcting for everyone, SO THAT EVEN THE ANGEL OF DEATH REVERTS TO BEING VERY GOOD.

166. ת"ח, כְּתִיב וְנָהָר יוֹצֵא מֵעֵדֶן לְהַשְׁקוֹת אֶת הַגָּן, נָהָר דָּא, לָא שָׁכִיךְ לְעָלְמִין, מְלַאַפְּשָׁא וּלְמִסְגֵּי וּלְמֶעְבַּד פֵּירִין, וְאֵל אַחֵר אִסְתָּרַס,

וְלֵית לֵיהּ תִּיאוּבְתָּא לְעָלְמִין, וְלָא אָפִישׁ, וְלָא עָבֵיד פֵּירִין, דְּאִלְמָלֵי עָבֵיד פֵּירִין, יְטַשְׁטֵשׁ לְכָל עָלְמָא.

166. Come and see, "And a river went out of Eden to water the garden" (Beresheet 2:10), WHICH IS ZEIR ANPIN THAT WATERS MALCHUT THAT IS CALLED GARDEN. This river never ceases from multiplying, increasing and producing fruit, while another El is sterile and never has any desire, does not fertilize or produce fruit. For had it produced fruit, it would have troubled the world.

167. וּבְג״כ, בַּר נָשׁ דְּגָרִים לְהַהוּא סְטַר דְּיִפּוּשׁ בְּעָלְמָא, אִקְרֵי רַע, וְלָא חָמֵי אַפֵּי שְׁכִינְתָּא לְעָלְמִין, דִּכְתִיב לֹא יְגֻרְךָ רָע. הַאי בַּר נָשׁ, דְּמִתְגַּלְגְּלָא בְּגִלְגּוּלָא, אִי אִיהוּ עָבַר וְאִתְדַּבָּק בְּהַהוּא אֵל אַחֵר, דְּלָא עָבֵיד פֵּירִין, וְלָא אָפִישׁ בְּעָלְמָא, בְּגִין כָּךְ אִקְרֵי אַחֵר, וּשְׁמָא גָּרִים לֵיהּ, אִיהוּ הוּא, וְאַחַר אִקְרֵי, אַחַר וַדַּאי.

167. This is why the man who caused that side to increase in the world is called evil and never beholds the face of the Shechinah, as written, "nor shall evil dwell with You" (Tehilim 5:5). An incarnated man, who transgresses and cleaves to another El, which does not produce fruit nor multiplies in the world, is therefore called another. The name OF THE OTHER SIDE brought it upon him that even if he, THE DEAD MAN, is THE INCARNATED ONE, he is called another LIKE THE OTHER SIDE, another surely.

168. אַחֲרוֹן: מִקַּדְמָאָה וְאֵילָךְ, אַחֲרוֹן קָרֵינָן לֵיהּ, וְאַחֲרוֹן אִקְרֵי. תִּנְיָינָא אִיהוּ, וּמִיַּד אִקְרֵי אַחֲרוֹן, וְהָכִי קָרֵי לֵיהּ קוּדְשָׁא בְּרִיךְ הוּא אַחֲרוֹן, בְּגִין דְּיִתְתָּקַן לְמֶהֱוֵי אַחֲרוֹן, וְלָא יְתוּב כְּמִלְּקַדְמִין. תְּלִיתָאָה אוּף הָכִי. וְכֵן בְּכָל זִמְנִין, מִקַּדְמָאָה וְאֵילָךְ. הָכִי אִקְרֵי אַחֲרוֹן, וְהָכִי אִצְטְרִיךְ לְמִקְרֵי אַחֲרוֹן, דְּאִלְמָלֵא אִתְקְרֵי מִיַּד תִּנְיָינָא, הָא פְּתִיחוּ דְּפוּמָא לְאַהֲדָרָא כְּמִלְּקַדְמִין, וְהַהוּא בִּנְיָינָא אִסְתְּתַר.

168. "Latter": he is called latter since from the first time onward one is always called latter, and named latter IN THE TORAH. Be he second, he is

called latter forthwith, and the Holy One, blessed be He, calls him thus, latter, so that he will be perfected IN THIS INCARNATION and be last and come back no longer TO INCARNATE AGAIN. The third too IS CALLED LATTER, and so each time HE INCARNATES after the first time, he is called latter. And he should be called latter, for were he called second, an excuse WOULD BE GIVEN for him TO INCARNATE again, and for the current edifice to collapse.

169. מְנָלָן. מִבַּיִת שֵׁנִי דְּאִקְרֵי אַחֲרוֹן, דִּכְתִיב גָּדוֹל יִהְיֶה כְּבוֹד הַבַּיִת הַזֶּה הָאַחֲרוֹן מִן הָרִאשׁוֹן. דְּהָא מִקַּדְמָאָה וְאֵילָךְ, אַחֲרוֹן אִקְרֵי, דְּהָא לָא יְהֵא פְּתִיחוּ דְּפוּמָא, דְּהַהוּא בִּנְיָינָא יִנְפּוֹל, וְיִתְהַדָּר כְּמִלְּקַדְמִין.

169. Whence do we know that? From the second Temple that is called latter, as written, "The glory of this latter house shall be greater than that of the former (first)" (Chagai 2:9). For from the first onward it is called latter, so there will be no excuse that the edifice will collapse and will BE BUILT again as before.

170. אוֹף הָכִי דָא, אַחֲרוֹן קָרֵינָן לֵיהּ. וּבְגִין כָּךְ כְּתִיב, לֹא יוּכַל בַּעְלָהּ הָרִאשׁוֹן אֲשֶׁר שִׁלְּחָהּ לָשׁוּב לְקַחְתָּהּ. לֹא יוּכַל, לֹא יִקָּחֶנָּה מִבָּעֵי לֵיהּ, מַאי לֹא יוּכַל. אֶלָּא כֵּיוָן דְּהַאי אִתְּתָא אִתְדַּבְּקַת בְּאַחֵר, וְנַחְתַּת לְאִשְׁתַּעְבְּדָא בְּדַרְגָּא תַּתָּאָה, לָא בָּעֵי קוּדְשָׁא בְּרִיךְ הוּא, דְּאִיהוּ יְתוּב מִדַּרְגָּא דִּילֵיהּ, לְמֵיהַב אִיבָּא, וּלְאִתְדַּבְּקָא בְּהַהוּא דַּרְגָּא דְּלָאו דִּילֵיהּ.

170. In this case too, the incarnated man also is called last, LIKE THE SECOND TEMPLE. Hence it is written, "her former husband, who sent her away, may not take her again to be his wife" (Devarim 24:4). HE ASKS, why "may not"? It should have been 'will not take her.' HE ANSWERS, once the woman cleaved to another and went down to be enslaved to the lower grade OF THE OTHER SIDE, the Holy One, blessed be He, does not wish the former to descend from his grade and produce fruit and cleave to a grade that is not his.

171. וְת"ח, אִי הַאי אִתְּתָא לָא אִתְנְסִיבַת, אֲפִילוּ תִּזְנֶה בְּכָל גּוּבְרִין דְּעָלְמָא, אִי בָּעֵי בַּעְלָהּ יְתוּב לְגַבָּהּ, אֲבָל אִי אִתְדַּבְּקַת בְּנִשּׂוּאִין לְאַחֵר,

דָּא לֹא יוּכַל לָשׁוּב לְדַרְגָּא קַדְמָאָה, דַּהֲוָה בְּקַדְמֵיתָא לְגַבָּה. לֹא יוּכַל
וַדַּאי לְאָתָבָא לְהַהוּא דַרְגָּא לְעָלְמִין.

171. And come and see, if that woman does not marry, even if she whores
with all the men in the world, if her husband wishes to, he may return to her.
But if she cleaved in marriage to another, she cannot return to the former
grade she had. HENCE IT IS WRITTEN, "MAY NOT"; assuredly he may never
return to that grade.

172. אַחֲרֵי אֲשֶׁר הֻטַּמָּאָה. תָּנֵינָן, דְּהַטַּמָּאָה בְּלִבֵּיה. אִי הָכִי, אֲפִילוּ אִי
תִּתְרַחֵק וְתִזְנֶה בְּלָא נִשּׂוּאִין. אֶלָּא, כֵּיוָן דְּאִתְדַּבְּקַת לְאַחֵר, הָא קַבִּילַת
עֲלָה חוּלָקָא דְּהַהוּא סִטְרָא, וּבַעְלָה קַדְמָאָה דְּאִיהוּ מִסִּטְרָא אַחֲרָא
טָבָא דְּטוֹב, לָא יְהֵא לֵיהּ בָּהּ חוּלָקָא לְעָלְמִין, וְלָא יַפִּישׁ כְּלָל לְהַהוּא
אָתָר. הָא אִם שִׁלְּחָהּ הָאִישׁ הָאַחֲרוֹן, אוֹ כִּי יָמוּת הָאִישׁ הָאַחֲרוֹן,
לְקַדְמָאָה אֲסוּרָה, אֲבָל לִשְׁאָר בְּנֵי נָשָׁא, תִּשְׁתְּרֵי. דִּילְמָא תִּשְׁכַּח
אַתְרָא כְּמִלְּקַדְּמִין, וְאַחֲרוֹן יָקוּם דְּיִזְדַּוַּוג בַּהֲדָהּ.

172. "After she is defiled" (Ibid.). We learned that she is defiled in his heart.
HE ASKS, if this is so, even if she goes out to whore without marriage SHE
SHOULD BE FORBIDDEN. HE ANSWERS, once she cleaves to the other, she
accepts upon her the portion of that EVIL side. Her first husband is of the
other, good side, BUT she shall never have a portion of that good, and he
must not increase that place at all. Hence, if the latter man sends her out or
"if the latter husband...should die" (Ibid. 3), she is forbidden to the first
one. But she is permitted to other men; perhaps she will find a place again
and a latter one to come and marry her.

173. מַאן דְּאִית לֵיהּ בְּנִין מֵאִתְּתֵיה קַדְמֵיתָא, וְאָעִיל הַאי לְגוֹ בֵּיתֵיה,
הַהוּא יוֹמָא אִתְדַּבַּק בְּחַרְבָּא קַשְׁיָא דְּמִתְהַפְּכָא, בְּגִין תְּרֵין סִטְרִין. חַד,
דְּהָא תְּרֵין דְּחַת לוֹן לְבַר, וְהַשְׁתָּא אִיהוּ תְּלִיתָאָה. וְתוּ, מָאנָא
דְּאִשְׁתַּתַּף בֵּיהּ אַחֵר, הֵיךְ יֵיתֵי אִיהוּ לְמֵיהַב בֵּיהּ רוּחָא דִּילֵיהּ,
וְיִשְׁתַּתַּף בַּהֲדָהּ, וְיִתְדַּבַּק בָּהּ. לָאו דְּאִיהִי אֲסוּרָה, אֲבָל וַדַּאי שׁוּתָפָא
בִּישָׁא אִיהוּ לְגַרְמֵיה.

173. Whoever has children from the first wife, yet brings this WOMAN into his house, cleaves that day to the relentless revolving sword for two reasons. The first is that she has already rejected two men, and he is the third. Another is that how could he put his spirit in a vessel that another had joined, to join her and cleave to her, not because she is forbidden but it is a bad alliance for himself.

174. רַבִּי לְוִיטַס אִישׁ כְּפַר אוֹנוֹ, הֲוָה חַיָּיךְ וּמִתְלוֹצֵץ עַל אִתְּתָא דָא, כַּד חָמֵי מַאן דְּאִזְדַּוַּג בַּהֲדָהּ, וַהֲוָה אָמַר, וַתִּשְׂחַק לְיוֹם אַחֲרוֹן כְּתִיב, מַאן דְּאִתְדַּבְּקַת בֵּיהּ בְּאִישׁ אַחֲרוֹן, חִיּוּכָא אִיהִי לְבָתַר.

174. Rabbi Levitas, the leader of Kfar Ono, used to laugh and joke about such a woman, when he saw someone marrying her. He would say, it is written, "and she laughs at the time to come" (Mishlei 31:25); if she marries a latter man, he later becomes a laughing stock.

175. הַשְׁתָּא, אִית לְאַהֲדָרָא וּלְעַיְּינָא, עַל אֲתָר חַד רַב וְעִלָּאָה, דַּהֲוָה בְּעָלְמָא, וְגִזְעָא וְשָׁרְשָׁא דִּקְשׁוֹט, וְאִיהוּ עוֹבֵד אֲבִי יִשַׁי אֲבִי דָוִד. דְּהָא אִתְּמַר דְּאַחֲרוֹן הֲוָה, הֵיךְ נָפַק שָׁרְשָׁא דִּקְשׁוֹט, מִגּוֹ אֲתָר דָּא.

175. Let us come back and contemplate a certain great and lofty place that was in the world, a true stock and root. It is Oved, the father of Yishai, father of David. We learned that THE INCARNATED is the latter, AND OVED WAS AN INCARNATION OF MACHLON, WHO DIED CHILDLESS. How could a true root come from such a place?

176. אֶלָּא, עוֹבֵד אִתְתָּקַּן בְּתִקּוּנָא עִלָּאָה, וְאַהֲדָר שָׁרְשָׁא דְּאִילָנָא דְּקָא אִתְהַפָּךְ, עַל תִּקּוּנֵיהּ, וְאִסְתְּלִיק בֵּיהּ, וְאִתְתָּקַּן כַּדְקָא יָאוֹת, וְע"ד אִקְרֵי עוֹבֵד. מַה דְּלָא זָכוּ הָכִי, שְׁאַר בְּנֵי עָלְמָא.

176. HE ANSWERS, but Oved was improved by lofty correction, and the root of the inverted tree, WHERE THE WIFE BECOMES THE MOTHER, was set aright again. And he rose in it and was duly perfected. Hence he is called Oved, DERIVED FROM WORK, something that none of the people in the world merited.

177. אָתָא אִיהוּ, פָּלַח וְאַעֲדָר עִקָּרָא וְשָׁרְשָׁא דְּאִילָנָא, וְנָפַק מֵאַנְפִּין מְרִירָן, וְאַהֲדָר וְאַתְקַן בְּנוֹפָא דְּאִילָנָא אַחֲרָא עִלָּאָה, אָתָא יִשַׁי בְּרֵיהּ, וְאַחֲסִין לֵיהּ, וְתָקִין לֵיהּ, וְאִתְאֲחַד בְּעַנְפּוֹי דְּאִילָנָא אַחֲרָא עִלָּאָה, וְחִבֵּר אִילָנָא בְּאִילָנָא, וְאִסְתְּבָכוּ דָּא בְּדָא. כֵּיוָן דְּאָתָא דָּוִד, אַשְׁכַּח אִילָנִין מִסְתַּבְּכָן וּמִתְאַחֲדָן דָּא בְּדָא, כְּדֵין יָרִית שֻׁלְטָנוּ בְּאַרְעָא, וְעוֹבֵד גָּרִים דָּא.

177. OVED came, cultivated (Heb. *avad*) and hoed the trunk and root of the tree, came out of the bitter face and again improved the branches of the tree, MALCHUT. Yishai his son came, strengthened and fixed it, and held to the boughs of another, higher tree, ZEIR ANPIN. He joined one tree to another and they intertwined. When David came, he found the trees, ZEIR ANPIN AND MALCHUT, intertwined and bound to each other. He then inherited dominion in the land. All this Oved brought about.

178. בָּכָה הַהוּא סָבָא וְאָמַר, אִי סָבָא סָבָא, וְלָא אֲמֵינָא לָךְ, דְּעַלַּת בְּיַמָּא רַבָּא, הַשְׁתָּא אַנְתְּ הוּא גּוֹ תְּהוֹמֵי רַבְרְבִין, אִתְתַּקַּן לְסַלְּקָא. סָבָא סָבָא, אַנְתְּ גַּרְמַתְּ דָּא, דְּאִלְמָלֵא הֲוֵית שָׁתִיק בְּקַדְמֵיתָא, הֲוָה יָאוֹת לָךְ, אֲבָל הַשְׁתָּא לָא יָכִילַת וְלֵית מַאן דְּאָחִיד בִּידָךְ, אֶלָּא אַנְתְּ בִּלְחוֹדָךְ. קוּם סָבָא וְאִסְתַּלָּק בִּסְלִיקוּ.

178. The old man wept and said TO HIMSELF, Woe old man, have not I told you that you entered the great sea. Now you are in the great deeps. Prepare to rise. Old, old man, you have brought all this about. Had you been quiet before, it would have become you, but now you cannot, and there is none to hold your hand save you alone. Arise old man, and rise up.

179. עוֹבֵד דָּא, אִתְתַּקַּן וְנָפַק מִגּוֹ חֲקַל בִּישָׁא, דְּגוּבִין בִּישִׁין. אָתָא יִשַׁי בְּרֵיהּ, וְאַתְקִין וְאַעֲדָר אִילָנָא, וְעַכְּ״ד, דָּא רָזָא דְּרָזִין, וְלָא יְדַעְנָא אִי אֵימָא, אִי לָא אֵימָא. אֵימָא מֵילָךְ סָבָא, וְדַאי אֵימָא, בְּדָא יְדִיעָאן כָּל שְׁאַר בְּנֵי גִּלְגוּלָא. עוֹבֵד עַכְּ״ד אִילָנָא אַתְקִין. כַּד אָתָא דָּוִד מַלְכָּא, בְּאִילָנָא תַּתָּאָה דְּנוּקְבָּא אִשְׁתְּאַר, וְאִצְטְרִיךְ לְקַבְּלָא חַיִּין מֵאַחֲרָא, וּמַה

אִי הַאי דְּאִתְתָּקַן, וְאַתְקִין כֹּלָּא, הָכִי. שְׁאַר בְּנֵי עָלְמָא דְּאַתְיָין בְּגִלְגּוּלָא, דְּלָא יַכְלִין לְאִתְתַּקְּנָא הָכִי, עאכ״ו.

179. Oved was corrected and came out of the evil field of evil cisterns. His son Yishai came and fixed and hoed the tree. Nevertheless, this is the most secret of mysteries, and I do not know whether I should tell it or not. Speak up, old man, assuredly I say that in this way are recognized all the incarnated. Though Oved fixed the tree, when King David came, he remained in the lower tree of the female, WHICH IS MALCHUT, and had to receive life from another, for of himself he had no life. And if this is so for he, who was perfected and perfected everything, this is much more so for other people, who cannot be thus perfected.

A Synopsis
The merchant tells the rabbis about the levels Chesed, Gvurah, Tiferet and Malchut attaching to the grades Reuben, Shimon, Levi and Judah, and how this relates to barrenness. He speaks a great deal about Judah, and about the twelve tribes of Judah, saying that they are celestial shapes after the supernal shape; since they were real people in this world, the Shechinah was perfected by them.

180. בְּכָל סִטְרִין אִתְהַפַּךְ בְּגִלְגּוּלָא. פֶּרֶץ הָכִי הֲוָה. בֹּעַז הָכִי הֲוָה. עוֹבֵד הָכִי הֲוָה. וּבְכֹלָּא נָפִיק אִילָנָא מִסִּטְרָא דְּרַע, וְאִתְדְּבַק לְבָתַר בְּסִטְרָא דְּטוֹב. בְּקַדְמֵיתָא, וַיְהִי עֵר בְּכוֹר יְהוּדָה רַע. מַחְלוֹן אוּף הָכִי, וְלָאו כ״כ. אֲבָל בְּהָנֵי אִתְעַכַּל רַע, וְנָפִיק טוֹב לְבָתַר, הַהוּא דִּכְתִיב בֵּיהּ, וְטוֹב רֹאִי. וַיְיָ׳ עִמּוֹ. הָכָא קַיְימָא אִילָנָא תַּתָּאָה עַל תִּקּוּנֵיהּ, וּמֶלֶךְ אֱלֹהִים עַל גּוֹיִם.

180. In every respect this turns to incarnation. Peretz was so, AN INCARNATION OF ER; Boaz was so, AN INCARNATION OF JUDAH; Oved was so, AN INCARNATION OF MACHLON. In them all, the tree came out of the evil side and then cleaved to the good. At first, "And Er, Judah's firstborn, was wicked in the sight of Hashem" (Beresheet 38:7). Machlon was also evil, though not as much. But in these, evil was consumed, and good then emerged, THAT IS, him of whom it is written, "good looking" (I Shmuel 16:12), AND "Hashem was with him" (Ibid. 18). Here the lower

tree, MALCHUT, reached completion, and "Elohim reigns over the nations" (Tehilim 47:9).

181. בְּשֵׁירוּתָא דְּכֹלָּא, מֵעָקָרָא וִיסוֹדָא עִלָּאָה, אִשְׁתָּרְשׁוּ דַּרְגִּין, רְאוּבֵן שִׁמְעוֹן לֵוִי יְהוּדָה, מַה כְּתִיב בֵּיה, הַפַּעַם אוֹדֶה אֶת יְיָ', וּכְתִיב וַתַּעֲמוֹד מִלֶּדֶת. הַיְינוּ רָנִּי עֲקָרָה לֹא יָלָדָה. בְּגִין דְּכַד אִתְיְלִיד יְהוּדָה, נָפְקַת נוּקְבָּא מִתְדַּבְּקָא בִּדְכוּרָא, וְלָא הֲוַת עַל תִּקּוּנָהָא אַנְפִּין בְּאַנְפִּין, וְלָא אִתְכַּשְׁרַת לְאוֹלָדָא. כֵּיוָן דְּנָסַר לָהּ קוּדְשָׁא בְּרִיךְ הוּא וְאַתְקִין לָהּ כְּדֵין אִתְכַּשְׁרַת לְאִתְעַבְּרָא וּלְאוֹלָדָא.

181. In the very beginning, the grades, Reuben, Shimon, Levi and Judah struck root in the supernal essence and foundation. THEY ARE CHESED, GVURAH, TIFERET AND MALCHUT. It is written of him, "Now I will praise Hashem...and she left off bearing" (Beresheet 29:35). This is the meaning of, "Sing, O barren one, you that did not bear" (Yeshayah 54:1), since when Judah was born, the Nukva, MALCHUT, came out attached to the Male, ZEIR ANPIN, but there were not well set face to face, and MALCHUT was not capable of bearing. When the Holy One, blessed be He, sawed her, THAT IS, DETACHED HER FROM THE BACK OF THE MALE, and fixed her, she became capable of conceiving and bearing, AS WILL BE EXPLAINED.

182. וּבְסִפְרָא דַּחֲנוֹךְ, וַתַּעֲמוֹד מִלֶּדֶת, לָאו עַל לֵאָה אִתְּמַר, אֶלָּא עַל רָחֵל אִתְּמַר, הַהִיא דִּמְבַכָּה עַל בְּנֶיהָ, הַהִיא דְּאִשְׁתָּרָשַׁת בִּיהוּדָה: יה"ו ד"ה. וַתַּעֲמוֹד מִלֶּדֶת, דְּהָא לָא אִתְתַּקְּנָא.

182. In the book of Enoch it is written that, "she left off bearing" does not refer to Leah, WHO IS THE NUKVA OF ZEIR ANPIN ABOVE THE CHEST, but to Rachel, who is "weeping for her children" (Yirmeyah 31:14). It is she, THE NUKVA OF ZEIR ANPIN BELOW THE CHEST, who struck root in Judah, who is composed of the letters Yud-Hei-Vav and Dalet-Hei. "And she left off bearing," because she is not yet corrected.

183. בְּקַדְמֵיתָא, דִּיּוּקְנָא דִּלְעֵילָא הֲוָה כֹּלָּא רְאוּבֵן: או"ר בֵּ"ן. וַיֹּאמֶר אֱלֹהִים יְהִי אוֹר, יְמִינָא אוֹר. שִׁמְעוֹן שְׂמָאלָא אוֹר בְּהַהוּא סִיגָא

דְּדַהֲבָא בַּהֲדֵיהּ שֵׁם עָוֹן. לֵוִ"י: חֲבוּרָא דְּכֹלָּא, לְאִתְחַבְּרָא מִתְּרֵין
סִטְרִין. יְהוּדָה: נוּקְבָא בַּהֲדֵי דְכוּרָא מִתְדַּבְּקַת, יְהֹ"וּ, דָּא דְּכוּרָא. דָ"ה,
דָּא נוּקְבָא דַּהֲוַת בַּהֲדֵיהּ.

183. At first, everything had the upper form, AND EVEN RACHEL ASCENDED ABOVE THE CHEST. Reuben is composed of the segments *Or* (Eng. 'light') *Ben* (Eng. 'son'), which is the secret of, "And Elohim said, Let there be light" (Beresheet 1:3), which is right, NAMELY CHESED OF ZEIR ANPIN. Shimon is the left, and is light together with the oars of gold, because Shimon is composed of the segments *Shem Avon* (Eng. 'name of iniquity'), WHICH IS THE LEFT, GVURAH OF ZEIR ANPIN. Levi is overall unity, the joining of the two aspects, BEING THE CENTRAL COLUMN THAT UNITES THE RIGHT WITH THE LEFT. HE IS TIFERET OF ZEIR ANPIN. AFTER THE EMERGENCE OF CHESED, GVURAH AND TIFERET ABOVE THE CHEST, THE NUKVA CALLED RACHEL CAME OUT. That is Judah, WHO IS THE NUKVA. The Female cleaves to the Male, WHO IS CHESED, GVURAH AND TIFERET OF ZEIR ANPIN; Yud Hei Vav is the Male, NAMELY CHESED, GVURAH AND TIFERET; Dalet and Hei are the Nukva, RACHEL who was with him, WITH THE MALE.

184. דָ"ה, אֲמַאי דָ"ה. אֶלָּא ד', בְּאִתְדַּבְּקוּתָא דְרַע בַּהֲדָהּ, אִיהִי
דְּלֵ"ת, מִסְכְּנָא אִיהִי, וְאִצְטְרִיךְ לְאָתָבָא בְּגִלְגּוּלָא, לְאִתְעַבְּדָא הַהוּא
רַע, וּלְמִתְבְּלֵי בְּעַפְרָא. וּלְבָתַר לְצַמְחָא בְּסִטְרָא דְטוֹב, וּלְנָפְקָא מִמִּסְכְּנוּ
לַעֲתִירוּ, וּכְדֵין ה'. וְעַל דָּא, יְהֹ"וּ דָ"ה.

184. HE ASKS, THE NUKVA IS ALLUDED TO IN THE LETTERS Dalet Hei. Why Dalet Hei? HE ANSWERS, THE NUKVA IS CALLED Dalet while evil cleaves to her, NAMELY WHEN SHE IS OF THE QUALITY OF THE LEFT ONLY, AND IS ATTACHED TO THE BACK OF THE MALE. She is Dalet, which means she is poor (Heb. *dalah*), and needs to reincarnate, REFERRING TO THE INCARNATIONS FROM JUDAH TO KING DAVID, to destroy that evil, wither in the dust and grow again on the good side, NAMELY BY BUILDING ABA AND IMA ANEW, ACCORDING TO THE SECRET OF THE VERSE, "AND OF THE SIDE, WHICH HASHEM ELOHIM HAD TAKEN FROM THE MAN, HE MADE A WOMAN" (BERESHEET 2:22), to emerge from poverty to wealth. She is then called Hei, and hence JUDAH IS COMPOSED OF THE LETTERS

Yud-Hei-Vav and Dalet-Hei, YUD-HEI-VAV BEING CHESED, GVURAH, AND TIFERET OF THE MALE, AND DALET AND HEI ARE THE NUKVA IN HER TWO STATES MENTIONED BEFORE THAT UNITES WITH THE MALE.

185. פּוּק סָבָא, מִגּוֹ תְּהוֹמֵי, לָא תִּדְחַל, כַּמָּה אַרְבִּין זְמִינִין לָךְ, בְּשַׁעֲתָא דְּתִשׁוֹטֵט יַמָּא, בְּגִין לְנַיְיחָא בְּהוּ. בָּכָה כְּמִלְקַדְמִין וְאָמַר, מָארֵי דְּעָלְמָא, דִּילְמָא יֵימְרוּן מַשִׁרְיָין עִלָּאִין, דַּאֲנָא סָבָא, וּבָכֵי כְּינוֹקָא. גַּלֵּי קַמָּךְ, דְּעַל יְקָרָךְ אֲנָא עָבֵיד, וְלָא עֲבִידְנָא עַל יְקָרָא דִּילִי, דְּהָא בְּקַדְמֵיתָא הֲוָה לִי לְאִסְתַּמְּרָא, דְּלָא אֵיעוּל בְּיַמָּא רַבָּא, וְהַשְׁתָּא כֵּיוָן דַּאֲנָא בֵּיהּ, אִית לִי לְשַׁטְטָא בְּכָל סִטְרִין, וּלְנָפְקָא מִנֵּיהּ.

185. HE SAID TO HIMSELF, come, old man, out of the depth, have no fear. How many ships are waiting for you when you sail in the sea, to rest in. He wept again and said, Master of the universe, lest the celestial camps shall say that I am old and cry like a child, it is known before You that for Your glory I do that, and not for my own glory. For at first I should have kept from entering the great sea, yet now that I am in it, it behooves me to sail in every direction and come out.

186. יְהוּדָה אַתָּה יוֹדוּךְ אַחֶיךָ, הַיְינוּ דַּאֲנַן אַמְרִין בָּרוּךְ אַתָּה. אִיהוּ בָּרוּךְ וְאִיהִי אַתָּה, לְכֻלְּהוּ בְּנוֹי לָא אָמַר יַעֲקֹב אַתָּה, אֶלָּא לַאֲתָר דְּאִצְטְרִיךְ. דָּא אִיהוּ אַתָּה.

186. "Judah you are he whom your brethren shall praise" (Beresheet 49:8), that is, when we say, 'blessed are you', he is blessed, WHEN YESOD OF ZEIR ANPIN POURS CHASSADIM UPON MALCHUT, IT IS CALLED 'BLESSED' and she 'you'. MALCHUT IS CALLED 'YOU', SINCE THE NAME 'YOU' ALLUDES TO CHASSADIM, AS IN, "YOU SHALL BE A PRIEST" (TEHILIM 110:4), AS SHALL BE SAID. Jacob mentioned 'you' in relation to none of his sons, except the needed place. FOR MALCHUT IS DRAWN FROM THE LEFT SIDE, WHERE CHOCHMAH ILLUMINES WITHOUT CHASSADIM. SHE NEEDS THE NAME 'YOU', WHICH IS CHASSADIM, WITH WHICH TO CLOTHE CHOCHMAH. FOR WITHOUT CHASSADIM, CHOCHMAH DOES NOT SHINE, AND IS IN THE SECRET OF DARKNESS. This is WHY HE SAID TO JUDAH 'you'.

187. שְׁמָא דָּא, יוֹדוּךְ אַחֶיךָ, כֻּלְּהוּ אוֹדָן לָךְ עַל שְׁמָא דָּא, וַדַּאי אַתָּה
יוֹדוּךְ אַחֶיךָ, עַל שְׁמָא דָּא, אִסְתַּלָּק וְאִתְכַּפְיָא סְטַר אַחֲרָא, בְּגִין דְּכַד
אִתְקְרֵי וְאִדְכַּר, הָא נָפְקַת סִטְרָא אַחֲרָא בַּהֲדָהּ. כֵּיוָן דְּאָמְרֵי אַתָּה,
שֻׁלְטָנוּ וְרַבְרְבָנוּ אִית לָהּ, וְסִטְרָא אַחֲרָא אִתְכַּפְיָיא, וְלָא אִתְחֲזִיאַת
תַּמָּן. וַדַּאי בִּשְׁמָא דָּא אִתְרְשִׁים וְאִתְבְּרִיר מִסִּטְרָא אַחֲרָא. וְדָא
אִסְתַּלְּקוּ וְשֻׁלְטָנוּ דִּילֵיהּ, וּתְבִירוּ וּבִישׁ לְסִטְרָא אַחֲרָא. כֵּיוָן דְּיוֹדוּךְ
אַחֶיךָ עַל שְׁמָא דָּא, אַתָּה, כְּדֵין יָדְךָ בְּעֹרֶף אוֹיְבֶיךָ, מִיָּד אִתְכַּפְיָין
לְגַבָּךְ, וּשְׁמָא דָּא גָּרִים.

187. "He whom your brethren shall praise," they shall all praise you for that name; assuredly, "you are he whom your brethren shall praise," for it is due to that name that the other side was gone and subdued. This is because when THE NAME JUDAH is called and mentioned, the Other Side comes out with it, NAMELY, IN THE DALET OF JUDAH, THAT ALLUDES TO ITS FIRST STATE, WHEN SHE IS DRAWN FROM THE LEFT ALONE, WHERE THE OTHER SIDE FEEDS, DUE TO THE LACK OF CHASSADIM IN THE RIGHT. Once 'you' is uttered, WHICH IS THE DRAWING CHASSADIM FROM THE RIGHT, she has power and greatness and the Other Side is subdued and not seen there. Assuredly it is by means of this name that she is marked and extracted from the Other Side, BECAUSE WHEN SHE IS CLOTHED WITH CHASSADIM, THE OTHER SIDE IS DISTANCED FROM HER. This is the elevation and power OF MALCHUT and breaking and evil to the Other Side. Once "your brethren shall praise" you for the name 'you', then "your hand shall be on the neck of your enemies" (Ibid.); immediately THE OTHER SIDE is subdued before you, which is brought about by that name.

188. יָדַעְנָא חַבְרַיָּיא יָדַעְנָא, דְּהָא אַתָּה שְׁמָא דָּא, אַתּוּן אָמְרִין לַאֲתַר
אַחֲרָא עִלָּאָה, דִּכְתִיב אַתָּה כֹהֵן לְעוֹלָם, בִּימִינָא עִלָּאָה. שַׁפִּיר אִיהוּ,
דְּהָא כֵּיוָן דְּרִבִּי שִׁמְעוֹן אוֹדָן לֵיהּ עִלָּאִין וְתַתָּאִין, וְזָכָה לְכֹלָּא, כָּל מַה
דְּאִיהוּ אָמַר, הָכִי אִיהוּ וְשַׁפִּיר.

188. I know, friends, I do know that you ascribe the name 'you' to another, higher place, as written, "you shall be a priest forever" (Tehilim 110:4), which is at the supernal right, NAMELY CHOCHMAH. It is well because since

the high and low praise Rabbi Shimon, and he attained everything, everything he said is so, and is well.

189. אֲבָל כַּד תֶּהֱווֹן מָטָאן לְגַבֵּיה, אִמְרוּ לֵיה, וְאַדְכְּרוּ לֵיה, יוֹמָא דְתַלְגָּא, כַּד זְרַעְנָא פּוֹלִין, לְחַמְשִׁין וּתְרֵין גַּוְונִין. דְּהָא אַתָּה כֹהֵן, הָכָא אִתְקְשַׁר כּוֹס דְּבִרְכָתָה בִּימִינָא, בְּלָא פֵּרוּדָא כְּלָל. וּבְגִין כָּךְ, אַתָּה כֹהֵן לְעוֹלָם, הָכָא אִתְקְשַׁר כּוֹס בִּימִינָא, כַּדְקָא יָאוֹת.

189. But when you arrive at his place, tell and remind him of the snowy day, when we planted fifty-two kinds of beans. For "you shall be a priest" MEANS THAT here the cup of blessing, WHICH IS MALCHUT CALLED YOU, is attached to the right, WHICH IS CHESED CALLED PRIEST, without any separation. Hence, "you shall be a priest forever," for here the cup, WHICH IS MALCHUT, is properly attached, AND SO ENDURES FOREVER.

190. וְעַל דָּא אָמַר קְרָא, יְהוּדָה אַתָּה, לְהַאי אַתָּה יוֹדוּךְ אַחֶיךָ, וְלָא כְּתִיב יְהוּדָה יוֹדוּךְ אַחֶיךָ, וְלָא יַתִּיר, אֶלָּא עַל שְׁמָא דְאַתָּ"ה. אַתָּה, אֲתָר דָּא, אִצְטְרִיךְ לִשְׁמָא דָּא, וְלָא אַחֲרָא.

190. In regard to this, the verse says, "Judah you," and to 'you' "your brethren shall praise." For it is not written just, 'Judah is he whom your brethren shall praise,' but the name 'you' HIS BRETHREN WILL PRAISE. This place, MALCHUT, needs the name 'you' and none other.

191. יְהוּדָה, אַבָּא קַדְמָאָה, וְאַבָּא תִּנְיָינָא, וְלָא הֲוָה בֵּיה חִלּוּפָא לְעָלְמִין. וּבג"כ פֶּרֶץ אִתְתַּקַּף בֵּיה בְּתוּקְפוֹי, מַה דְּלָא הֲוָה הָכִי לְכָל בְּנֵי עָלְמָא. וְע"ד בִּנְיָינָא דְּדָוִד, שָׁארֵי חֻשְׁבָּנָא מִפֶּרֶץ, וְלָא מִבֹּעַז, דַּהֲוָה בֵּיה שְׁנוּיָא. חַבְרַיָּיא, אִי תַּשְׁגְּחוּן, לָאו מִלִּין בִּסְתִימוּ קָא אֲמֵינָא, וְאע"ג דִּסְתִימִין אִינּוּן.

191. Judah is the father first OF ER AND ONAN, and father a second time TO PERETZ AND ZERACH, WHO ARE THE INCARNATIONS OF ER AND ONAN. He was never exchanged, AS THE GRADE NEVER CHANGED BY THE BROTHER BECOMING THE FATHER. FOR THE CHILDLESS DEAD

INCARNATES IN THE SON BORN TO HIS BROTHER, WHO BECOMES HIS FATHER, WHICH IS CONSIDERED A DESCENT IN GRADES AND A BLEMISH. BUT THERE WAS NO CHANGE AND DESCENT OF GRADE IN JUDAH, BECAUSE HE WAS ALSO THE FIRST FATHER OF ER AND ONAN, WHO INCARNATED IN PERETZ AND ZERACH. This is why Peretz was very forceful, AS WRITTEN OF HIM, "WHY HAVE YOU MADE SUCH A BREACH FOR YOURSELF" (BERESHEET 38:29). THIS IS BECAUSE HIS GRADE DID NOT DESCEND, which is not the case for any other man in the world WHO INCARNATES, WHO DESCENDS, AS THE BROTHER BECOMES HIS FATHER. Therefore the establishment of David begins to be counted with Peretz and not with Boaz, who suffered a change, NOT BEING THE FIRST FATHER OF THE INCARNATED MAN, WHO IS MACHLON. Friends, if you observe my words, such words are not spoken vaguely WITHOUT POSSIBILITY OF UNDERSTANDING THEM, though they are vague.

192. וְע"ד, יְהוּדָה רָוַוח שְׁמָא דָא, דְּאִקְרֵי אַתָּה. קָם עַל בּוּרְיֵהּ זִמְנָא קַדְמָאָה, וְזִמְנָא תִּנְיָינָא, וְלָא אִשְׁתַּנֵּי לְעָלַם. וּבְנוֹי דְּיהוּדָה וְזַרְעָא דִּילֵיהּ, אוֹדָן וְאָמְרִין כִּי אַתָּה אָבִינוּ. מַה דְּלֵית הָכִי לִשְׁאַר בְּנֵי גִלְגוּלָא לְעָלְמִין. שְׁאַר בְּנֵי גִלְגוּלָא, תְּרֵין אֲבָהָן, תְּרֵין אִמָּהָן, אִית לוֹן גַּוְון לְבִנְיָינָא. וְרָזִין אִלֵּין, בְּעִמְקֵי יַמָּא, בְּלִבָּא דִּתְהוֹמֵי אִינּוּן, מַאן יָכִיל לְאַפָּקָא לוֹן. קוּם סָבָא, אִתְגַּבַּר וְאִתָּקַף בְּתוּקְפָּךְ, אַפִּיק מַרְגְּלָן מִגּוֹ תְּהוֹמֵי.

192. Hence Judah achieved the name called 'you'. He was properly established the first time WITH ER AND ONAN and the second time WITH PERETZ AND ZERACH and never changed. His children and descendants praise and say, "You are our father" (Yeshayah 63:16), SINCE THEY DID NOT SUFFER A DESCENT, WHEN THE BROTHER BECOMES THE FATHER. This is not so with other incarnated in the world. Other people who incarnate, two fathers and two mothers have a party in their edifice. FOR IN ADDITION TO HIS FIRST FATHER, HIS BROTHER BECOMES HIS FATHER, SO HE HAS TWO FATHERS, AND ALSO TWO MOTHERS, AS IN ADDITION TO HIS FIRST MOTHER, HIS WIFE BECOMES HIS MOTHER. These mysteries are in the depths of the sea, in the middle of the abyss. Who could take them out of there? Arise, old man, grow strong with your might, and draw pearls out of the depths.

193. בֹּעַז, אִתְחֲזֵי דַּהֲוָה בֵּיה שְׁנוּיָא, כַּד אוֹלִיד לְעוֹבֵד, דְּהָא עוֹבֵד בִּשְׁנוּיָא הוּא. לָאו הָכִי. אִבְצָן הוּא בֹּעַז, הוּא אַבָּא קַדְמָאָה, דְּלָא עָבֵד שְׁנוּיָא. וְאִי תֵּימָא, אִיהוּ הֲוָה, וַדַּאי כַּד אִתְעַר לְעוֹבָדָא דָּא, בֵּיה הֲוָה, מַאן דְּהוּא תַּקִּיף כְּאַרְיָא וּכְלֵיתָא בֵּיה הֲוָה. בְּגִין דְּלָא לֶהֱוֵי שְׁנוּיָא בֵּיה בְּדָוִד, וְאִתְהַדַּר מִלָּה לְעִקָּרָא קַדְמָאָה, בְּגִין דִּיהֵא כֹּלָא מֵאַבָּא חֲדָא, וְשַׁלְשְׁלָא חֲדָא. וְכֹלָּא חַד, וְלָא הֲוָה שְׁנוּיָא בְּגִלְגּוּלָא דְּזַרְעָא דְּדָוִד. וְעַל דָּא, אַתָּה מֵרֵישָׁא וְעַד סוֹפָא, בְּלָא שְׁנוּיָיא כְּלָל.

193. Boaz seems to have changed when he begot Oved, since Oved is changed, FOR HE IS HIS SECOND FATHER. HE SAYS, it is not so, Ivtzan is Boaz. WHY IS HE CALLED BOAZ? BBECAUSE he is the first father to bring no change, NAMELY, JUDAH, WHO IS THE FIRST FATHER, INCARNATED IN HIM. You may argue that it was he himself, AND NO INCARNATION OF JUDAH, YET surely when he was roused to perform the act OF LEVIRATE MARRIAGE, he who was fierce as a lion and a lion's whelp, THAT IS, JUDAH was present in him. HENCE HE WAS CALLED BOAZ, DERIVED FROM *Bo Az* (ENG. 'FIERCENESS IS IN HIM'), WHO REFERS TO JUDAH. THIS WAS so that there will be no change in David. AND SINCE JUDAH INCARNATED IN HIM, the matter reverted to the former root, so that all will originate in one father and lineage. It is all the same, and there was no change in the incarnation of David's seed. Thus you, from beginning to end, are entirely without change.

194. הַשְׁתָּא, נָפְקַת סָבָא, מֵעֻמְקֵי לִבָּא דְּיַמָּא. יְהוּדָה אַתָּה, וַדַּאי מֵרֵישָׁא וְעַד סוֹפָא וְלָא אִתְחֲזֵי לְכָל שְׁאָר בְּנִין, לְאִתְקְרֵי אַתָּה, אֶלָּא לֵיה בִּלְחוֹדוֹי. זַכָּאָה חוּלָקֵיה דְּדָוִד, דְּהָכִי אִתְבְּרִיר, וְאִסְתַּלַּק מִשְּׁאָר עִקָּרָא דִּבְנֵי נָשָׁא בְּאַרְעָא.

194. Now, old man, you have come out of the depths of the sea. Judah is 'you' surely, from beginning to end. It is not worthy to name none of the sons 'you' except him alone. Happy is the portion of David, who was so extracted and rose above other roots of people in the land.

195. יוֹדוּךָ אַחֶיךָ, יוֹדוּךָ כָּל בְּנֵי עָלְמָא מִבְּעֵי לֵיה, מַ"ט אַחֶיךָ. אֶלָּא

אֹרַח כָּל בְּנֵי עָלְמָא, לָא מִתְיַבְּמִין לְגִלְגּוּלָא, אֶלָּא מִסְטְרָא דְּאַחִין,
וְאָחָא אִזְדַּמַּן לְיַבּוּמָא, וְאַתָּה בְּגַרְמָךְ, אִזְדַּמַּנְתְּ לְיַבּוּמָא. וְהָכָא כֻּלְּהוּ
אַחֶיךָ יוֹדוּךְ, דְּלָא יִשְׁתַּלְשֵׁל מִנַּיְיהוּ, וְלָא מֵחַד מִנַּיְיהוּ, שַׁלְשׁוּלָא
דְּמַלְכוּ, אֶלָּא אַתָּה בִּלְחוֹדָךְ. אַתָּה, מֵרֵישָׁא וְעַד סוֹפָא אַתָּה עֲבַדְתְּ,
וּמִינָךְ נָפַק, כָּל שַׁלְשׁוּלָא וְגִזְעָא דְּאַרְיֵה.

195. "Your brethren shall praise." HE ASKS, it should have said, 'all the people in the world should praise'. Why DOES IT SAY, "your brethren"? HE ANSWERS, it is not the custom in the world to perform levirate marriage for the sake of incarnation OF THE CHILDLESS DEAD, except for kinsmen. The brother would perform levirate marriage, and you yourself performed levirate marriage. Here all your brethren praise you, that the lineage of kingship did not come from them, from none of them, but from you alone. It is you, who performed it from beginning to end, and from you the whole lineage and race of the lion emerged.

196. בָּנֶיךָ, בְּנֵי אַרְיֵה, דְּלָא אִתְעֲבָרוּ לְשִׁנּוּיָא דְּאָחֶיךָ, לָא אִתְחַלְּפוּ
לְטָלֶה, וְלָא לְשׁוֹר, וְלָא לִגְדִי, וְלָא לְשׁוּם דְּיוּקְנָא אַחֲרָא, אֶלָּא אַרְיֵה
שָׁארֵי לְמִבְנֵי, וְאַרְיֵה סִיֵּים בְּנָיָנָא. כָּל שַׁלְשׁוּלָךְ, בְּנֵי אַרְיֵה נִינְהוּ.
דְּאִלְמָּלֵא אָתָא גִלְגּוּלָא מִסְטְרָא דְּאַחוּךְ, יִתְחַלְּפוּן כָּל דִּיוּקְנִין,
וְיִתְעָרְבוּן אִלֵּין בְּאִלֵּין. וְעַל דָּא יוֹדוּךְ אַחֶיךָ, דְּלָא הֲוָה חַד מִנְּהוֹן,
בְּגִלְגּוּלָא דְּשַׁלְשְׁלָאָה דִּבְנָךְ. יָדְךָ זְקִיף, דְּלָא הֲוָה בָּךְ עִרְבּוּבְיָא אַחֲרָא
מִנַּיְיהוּ.

196. Your descendants are lion cubs, who have not turned into your brothers, nor changed into a lamb, an ox, or a kid. FOR THERE ARE TWELVE SHAPES IN THE TWELVE CONSTELLATIONS, WHICH CORRESPOND TO THE TWELVE TRIBES. THE CHILDREN OF JUDAH HAD ALL THE IMAGE OF A LION, NOT THE IMAGE OF OTHER TRIBES. A lion began to establish and a lion concluded the edifice. Your whole lineage is of lion cubs, for had anyone on the side of your brothers incarnated INTO YOUR CHILDREN, the images would have changed and mixed with each other. For that "your brethren shall praise," that none of them incarnated into your descendants' ancestry. Raise your hand for none of them was mingled.

197. וְהַיְינוּ מִטֶּרֶף בְּנִי עָלִיתָ, דְּלָא הֲוָה טַרְפָּא לְאַחֲרָא עַל פָּתוֹרָךְ. כָּרַע, בְּמִיתַת עֵר. רָבַץ, בְּמִיתַת אוֹנָן. לְבָתַר אִתְגַּבַּר כַּאֲרִי, לְאָקָמָא לְפֶרֶץ. וּכְלָבִיא, לְאָקָמָא לְזֶרַח. מִי יְקִימֶנּוּ, דִּכְתִיב וְלֹא יָסַף עוֹד לְדַעְתָּהּ. וְתַרְגּוּם וְלָא פָּסַק. מִי יְקִימֶנּוּ, מַאן הוּא דְּיֵימָא, אֲסוּרָה אִתְּתָא דָא. מַאן הוּא דְּיֵימָא, הוֹאִיל וְאַשְׁלִימַת אָרְחָהָא, לָא אִצְטְרִיכָא לָךְ יַתִּיר, יְבָמָה דָא, כֵּיוָן דְּאַשְׁלִימַת אָרְחָהָא, לָא אִצְטְרִיכַת לָךְ יַתִּיר, וְאִתְחֲזִיאַת לְאִתְפָּרְשָׁא מִינָהּ, אֲבָל מִי יְקִימֶנּוּ, וַדַּאי מִתַּמָּן וּלְהָלְאָה אִיהִי דִּילֵיהּ. דְּהָא אַפִּין מַאן דִּמְכַשְׁכֵּשׁ בִּמְעָהָא.

197. This is the meaning of, "from the prey, my son, you are gone up" (Beresheet 49:9), for there is no prey OR FOOD for another on your table. "He stooped down" when Er died, "he couched" when Onan died. He then got stronger "as a lion" to sire Peretz, "and as a lioness" to raise up Zerach. "Who shall rouse him up?" (Ibid.), as written, "And he knew her again no more" (Beresheet 38:26), which is translated into Aramaic as, "and he stopped not." This is the meaning of, "Who shall rouse him up?" Who can say this woman is forbidden, who can say that once she completed her practices, you need her no longer, that once the widow has finished her practices, she is of no more use to you, and you are beholden to withdraw from her. But, "Who shall rouse him up?" From now on she is his, because she bore him, who was moving about in her belly, NAMELY THE SPIRIT OF HER FIRST HUSBAND, WHICH HE LEFT IN HER IN HIS FORMER LIFE. IT WAS MOVING IN HER BELLY, AND NOW SHE BORE IT.

198. רָזָא סְתִימָא הָכָא, אָחוּהָ דְּבַר נָשׁ אֲמַאי. תּוּ יְהוּדָה דַּהֲוָה אֲבוֹי אֲמַאי. אֶלָּא, הַהוּא דִּמְכַשְׁכֵּשָׁא בִּמְעָהָא, חָמֵי דְּמַאן דַּהֲוָה נָטִיר לֵיהּ, מְקַטְרֵג לֵיהּ קַטְרוּגִין, בְּכָל סִטְרִין. בָּעֵי לְאַפָּקָא. כֵּיוָן דְּנָפִיק, זַמִּין לְאַחֲרָא הַהוּא רוּחַ אַחֲרָא, וְאַתְיָין לְאַעְלָא כְּמִלְּקַדְמִין, עַד דְּאִתְבְּנֵי כְּמִלְּקַדְמִין, בְּחֵילָא דְּקַטְרוּגָא תַּקִּיף דְּקָא מְקַטְרֵג בַּאֲחוּהָ. מִתַּמָּן וּלְהָלְאָה שָׁרִיאַת אִתְּתָא דָא לֵיהּ.

198. There is a hidden mystery here. Why SHOULD a man's brother MARRY

HIS WIDOW, and moreover, why SHOULD Judah his father MARRY HIS WIDOW, INSTEAD OF A STRANGER WHO IS NOT A KINSMAN? HE ANSWERS, because he who moves about in the belly OF THE WIDOW, NAMELY, THE SPIRIT HER DEAD HUSBAND LEFT IN HER, sees him who keeps him, THAT IS, HIS KINSMAN, and charges against him in every manner. HAD HE BEEN A STRANGE MAN, HE WOULD HAVE REJECTED HIM, BUT HE DOES NOT WISH TO PUSH AWAY HIS KINSMAN. Hence he wishes to go away FROM THERE. Once he leaves, he summons the other, NAMELY the other, MAIN spirit OF THE DEAD, and the TWO enter THE WOMAN'S BELLY again, until he is newly established, NAMELY, INCARNATES IN THE SEMEN OF THE KINSMAN. THIS CAME ABOUT by means of the fierce denouncement against his brother, FOR WHICH REASON HE DECIDED TO GO AWAY FROM HER. From now on the woman is permitted to him, SINCE THE DENOUNCING SPIRIT HAS ALREADY LEFT HER. THIS IS WHY THE KINSMAN SHOULD MARRY HER, BECAUSE A STRANGE MAN, WHO IS NOT A RELATIVE, WOULD HAVE BEEN REJECTED BY THE SPIRIT.

199. זַכָּאָה חוּלָקָא דִיהוּדָה, בְּקַדְמֵיתָא הֲוָה גוּר. לְבָתַר אַרְיֵה, דְּקָא אִתְגַּבָּר וְאִתְפָּשַׁט בְּחֵילֵיה אַרְיֵה. וְסִיֵּים בְּלָבִיא. כָּל שְׁאַר בְּנֵי עָלְמָא לָאו הָכִי, וְעַל דָּא יְהוּדָה כִּדְקָאֲמָרָן.

199. Happy is the portion of Judah. At first he was a whelp, then a lion, as he grew greater and stronger as a lion. He finished as a lioness. It is not so with other people in the world. Hence 'Judah YOU', like we said.

200. רְאוּבֵן שִׁמְעוֹן לֵוִי, הָא תְּלָתָא, כִּדְקָאֲמָרָן. יְהוּדָה אִתְחַבָּר בַּהֲדַיְיהוּ, וְכֹלָּא כִּדְקָא יֵאוֹת. יִשָּׂשכָר זְבוּלוּן, תְּרֵין יַרְכִין. אֲתָר דְּיַנְקֵי נְבִיאֵי קְשׁוֹט. יִשָּׂשכָר יַרְכָא יְמִינָא, כְּתִיב וּמִבְּנֵי יִשָּׂשכָר יוֹדְעֵי בִינָה לָעִתִּים וּכְתִיב, שְׂמַח זְבוּלוּן בְּצֵאתֶךָ, וּבְשִׁעוּרָא רַבְרְבָא, כְּתִיב, זְבוּלוּן לְחוֹף יַמִּים יִשְׁכֹּן וְהוּא לְחוֹף אֳנִיּוֹת. מ"ט. בְּגִין דְּוַיַרְכָתוֹ עַל צִידוֹן. שִׁיעוּרָא דְּיָרֵךְ דִּידֵיה עַד צִידוֹן.

200. Reuben, Shimon and Levi are a threesome, as we said THAT THEY ARE CHESED, GVURAH AND TIFERET. Judah, WHO IS MALCHUT, joined them, SO EVERYTHING IS AS IT SHOULD BE. Issachar and Zebulun are the two

thighs, NETZACH AND HOD, whence the true prophets are sustained. Issachar is the right thigh, WHICH IS NETZACH. It is written, "And of the children of Issachar, men who had understanding of the times" (I Divrei Hayamim 12:33), WHICH MEANS THAT NETZACH DRAWS THE LIGHT OF BINAH TO MALCHUT CALLED 'TIMES'. And it is written, "Rejoice, Zebulun, in your going out" (Devarim 33:18), WHICH MEANS THAT HOD IS THE LAST OF THE FIVE SFIROT, CHESED, GVURAH, TIFERET, NETZACH AND HOD, WHICH IS THE MEASURE OF THE EXPANDING OF THE LIGHT OF BINAH. FROM IT DOWN IT IS CONSIDERED GOING OUT OF THE GRADES. In the greater reckoning, THERE ARE SEVEN SFIROT, CHESED, GVURAH, TIFERET, NETZACH, HOD, YESOD AND MALCHUT. THEN it is written, "Zebulun shall dwell at the shore of the sea; and he shall be a haven for ships" (Beresheet 49:13), NAMELY, DOWN TO MALCHUT THAT IS CALLED BOTH A SEA AND A SHIP. What is the reason HE DWELLS ALL THE WAY TO MALCHUT – IT IS because "his border (or thigh) shall be at Tzidon" (Ibid.), as the measure of his thigh, HOD, EXPANDS to MALCHUT THAT IS CALLED Tzidon.

201. בִּנְיָמִין, אִשְׁתְּאַר לְעֵילָא בֵּין יַרְכִין, דְּהָא יוֹסֵף הֲוָה דְּיוּקְנֵיהּ בְּאַרְעָא, וּלְאִשְׁתַּמְּשָׁא בְּעָלְמָא דָא, וְעַמֵּיהּ אִשְׁתְּמַּשׁ מֹשֶׁה, דִּכְתִיב וַיִּקַּח מֹשֶׁה אֶת עַצְמוֹת יוֹסֵף עִמּוֹ. בִּנְיָמִין אִסְתַּלָּק לְעֵילָא, בִּנְיָמִין צַדִּיקוּ דְּעָלְמָא.

201. Benjamin remained above, between the thighs, BEING YESOD. AND THOUGH JOSEPH IS YESOD, Joseph was its image on earth, WHICH IS MALCHUT, for use in this world, WHICH IS MALCHUT. Moses used him, as written, "And Moses took the bones of Joseph with him" (Shemot 13:19). Benjamin rose up TO YESOD OF ZEIR ANPIN, and Benjamin is the Righteous one of the world, BEING YESOD.

202. מְבָרְכִין לְתַתָּא, דָּן וְנַפְתָּלִי גָּד וְאָשֵׁר. בְּיַרְכָא שְׂמָאלָא, דָּן עַד פִּרְקָא דְּרַגְלָא. פִּרְקָא דְּרַגְלָא נַפְתָּלִי. וּבג״כ, נַפְתָּלִי אַיָּלָה שְׁלוּחָה, קָל בְּרַגְלוֹי. בְּיַרְכָא יְמִינָא. גָּד, וְהוּא יָגוּד עָקֵב, עַד פִּרְקָא דְּעָקֵב. אָשֵׁר פִּרְקָא דְּעָקֵב יְמִינָא. וְטוֹבֵל בַּשֶּׁמֶן רַגְלוֹ. וּכְתִיב בַּרְזֶל וּנְחֹשֶׁת מִנְעָלֶיךָ. כָּל אִלֵּין, אִינּוּן דְּיוּקְנִין עִלָּאִין, דְּיוּקְנָא דִּלְעֵילָא. וּבְגִין דַּהֲווֹ בִּרְיָין

מַמָּשׁ בְּהַאי עָלְמָא, אִתְתַּקְנַת בְּהוּ שְׁכִינְתָּא, בְּאִלֵּין תְּרֵיסַר פִּרְקִין,
תְּרֵיסַר מְתִיחִין, דְּאִתְמְתָחוּ מִיִּשְׂרָאֵל מַמָּשׁ. דִּכְתִיב כָּל אֵלֶּה שִׁבְטֵי
יִשְׂרָאֵל שְׁנֵים עָשָׂר. מְתִיחִין דְּיִשְׂרָאֵל, אֵלֶּה אִקְרוֹן. לְאִתְמַתְּחָא שְׁמָא
דְּמִ״י, לְמֶהֱוֵי בִּנְיָינָא כַּדְקָא יָאוּת, לְמֶהֱוֵי יִשְׂרָאֵל בִּכְלָלָא דִּשְׁמָא
דֶּאֱלֹהִים. אֵלֶ״ה אִיהוּ יִשְׂרָאֵל בִּכְלָל. מִ״י חִבֵּר אֵלֶּה בַּהֲדֵיהּ, וַהֲוָה
בִּנְיָינָא שְׁלִים עַל תִּקּוּנֵיהּ, שְׁמָא חֲדָא מַמָּשׁ.

202. Below the knees THERE ARE TWO MORE PARTS. They are Dan and
Naftali, Gad and Asher. In the left leg, Dan reaches the joint of the foot,
NAMELY THE MIDDLE PART, Naftali is the foot segment, NAMELY, THE
LOWER SECTION. Hence, "Naftali is a hind let lose" (Beresheet 49:21),
being light footed. In the right leg is Gad, who "shall overcome at last"
(Ibid. 19), that is, down to the heel joint, WHICH IS THE MIDDLE PART;
Asher is in the section of the right heel, NAMELY THE LOWER PART. Hence,
"let him dip his foot in oil. Your shoes shall be iron and brass" (Devarim
33:24). THUS, IN THE THREE SEGMENTS OF THE RIGHT LEG ARE
ISSACHAR IN THE UPPER, GAD IN THE MIDDLE AND ASHER IN THE
LOWER PART. IN THE THREE PARTS OF THE LEFT LEG ARE ZEBULUN IN
THE UPPER, DAN IN THE MIDDLE AND NAFTALI IN THE LOWER PART. All
these TWELVE TRIBES are celestial shapes after the supernal shape. Since they
were real people in this world, the Shechinah was perfected by them, through
the twelve parts, which are the twelve flows that were drawn from Yisrael
himself, WHO IS ZEIR ANPIN, as written, "All these (Heb. *eleh*) are the twelve
tribes of Yisrael" (Beresheet 49:28). The flows from Yisrael are called 'Eleh'
FROM WHICH the name 'mi' spreads out, to make the building fit, so that
Yisrael will be included in the name Elohim (ALEPH LAMED HEI YUD MEM).
Eleh (ALEPH LAMED HEI) is Yisrael in general and Mi (MEM YUD) unites
Eleh with it, to make the building duly whole, into one real name.

203. הֲדָא הוּא דְּאָמַר לֵיהּ לְיַעֲקֹב, הַהוּא מְמָנָא דְּעֵשָׂו, דִּכְתִיב כִּי
שָׂרִיתָ עִם אֱלֹהִים, לְעֵילָא, בְּתִקּוּנָא קַדְמָאָה, בְּבִנְיָינָא קַדְמָאָה. כָּל
אֵלֶּה, וַדַּאי בִּנְיָינָא קַדְמָאָה אִיהוּ.

203. This is what the minister of Esau said to Jacob, as written, "for you
have contended with Elohim" (Beresheet 32:29), THAT IS, above, SINCE HE

ROSE WITH THE LETTERS OF ELEH OF MALE AND FEMALE TO BE INCLUDED IN THE NAME ELOHIM, WHICH WAS THERE JOINED AND MADE WHOLE through the first correction in the first establishment. "All these (Heb. *eleh*) ARE THE TWELVE TRIBES OF YISRAEL." Surely this is the first edifice, WHERE THE JOINING OF MI WITH ELEH IS EFFECTED.

204. וְעַל דָּא, לֵית שְׁצִיאוּ לְיִשְׂרָאֵל, לְעָלַם וּלְעָלְמֵי עָלְמִין. וְחַס וְשָׁלוֹם אִלְמָלֵא יִשְׁתְּצִיאוּ, שְׁמָא דָא לָא הֲוֵי, הה"ד וְהִכְרִיתוּ אֶת שְׁמֵנוּ מִן הָאָרֶץ וּמַה תַּעֲשֵׂה לְשִׁמְךָ הַגָּדוֹל. שְׁמָא גָדוֹל, דָּא, בִּנְיָינָא קַדְמָאָה, שְׁמָא קַדְמָאָה אֱלֹהִים. וְהַשְׁתָּא דְּיִשְׂרָאֵל אִינּוּן בְּגָלוּתָא, כִּבְיָכוֹל כָּל בִּנְיָינָא נָפַל. לְזִמְנָא דְאָתֵי, כַּד יִפְרוֹק קוּדְשָׁא בְּרִיךְ הוּא לִבְנוֹי מִגָּלוּתָא, מִ"י וְאֵלֶ"ה דַּהֲוָה בְּפֵרוּדָא בְּגָלוּתָא, יִתְחַבְּרוּן כַּחֲדָא, וּשְׁמָא דֶּאֱלֹהִים יְהֵא שְׁלִים עַל תִּקּוּנֵיהּ, וְעָלְמָא יִתְבַּסַּם. הה"ד, מִי אֵלֶה כָּעָב תְּעוּפֶינָה וְכַיּוֹנִים אֶל אֲרֻבּוֹתֵיהֶם.

204. Therefore Yisrael will never ever perish. Had they perished, heaven forbid, the name Elohim would not have existed. This is the meaning of, "and cut off our name from the earth: and what will You do for Your great name?" (Yehoshua 7:9), NAMELY this great name, the first establishment, the first name Elohim. Now that Yisrael are in exile it is as if the whole establishment collapsed. In the future to come, when the Holy One, blessed be He, will redeem His children from exile, Mi and Eleh that were apart in exile will join and the name Elohim will be duly whole and the world would be scented. This is the meaning of, "Who (Heb. *mi*) are these (Heb. *eleh*) that fly as a cloud, and as the doves to their windows?" (Yeshayah 60:8).

205. וּבְגִין דְּאִיהוּ שְׁמָא חֲדָא, לָא כְּתִיב מִי וְאֵלֶה, אֶלָּא מִי אֵלֶה, שְׁמָא חֲדָא, בְּלָא פֵּרוּדָא, וְהוּא אֱלֹהִים. דְּהַשְׁתָּא בְּגָלוּתָא, אִסְתַּלָּק מִי לְעֵילָא, כִּבְיָכוֹל אִימָּא מֵעַל בְּנִין. וּבְנִין נָפְלוּ. וּשְׁמָא דַּהֲוָה שְׁלִים, דְּהוּא שְׁמָא עִלָּאָה רַבְרְבָא קַדְמָאָה, נָפִיל.

205. Since the name is one whole, it is not written, 'Mi and Eleh THAT FLY AS A CLOUD', but 'Mi eleh' as an indivisible name. This is the name Elohim. For now in exile Mi has gone up so to speak INTO MALCHUT, and

the mother, NAMELY MALCHUT, is gone from the children, YISRAEL. The children fell and the name ELOHIM, which used to be whole, being the first great name, collapsed.

206. וְעַל דָּא, אֲנָן מְצַלָּן, וּמְקַדְּשָׁן בְּבָתֵּי כְּנֵסִיּוֹת, עַל שְׁמָא דָּא, דְּיִתְבְּנֵי כְּמָה דַּהֲוָה. וְאַמְרֵי יִתְגַּדַּל וְיִתְקַדַּשׁ שְׁמֵיהּ רַבָּא. אָמֵן יְהֵא שְׁמֵיהּ רַבָּא מְבָרַךְ. מַאן שְׁמֵיהּ רַבָּא. הַהוּא קַדְמָאָה דְּכֹלָּא, בְּגִין דְּלֵית לֵיהּ בִּנְיָינָא אֶלָּא בַּהֲדָן. מ"י לָא יִתְבְּנֵי לְעוֹלָם, אֶלָּא בְּאֵלֶּה. וְעַל דָּא, בְּהַהוּא זִמְנָא, מִי אֵלֶּה כָּעָב תְּעוּפֶינָה. וְיֶחֱמוּן כָּל עָלְמָא, דְּהָא שְׁמָא עִלָּאָה אִתְתָּקַן עַל תִּקּוּנֵיהּ.

206. For this we pray and sanctify in synagogues the name ELOHIM, so it would be established like it used to, and we recited the KADDISH – 'May His great name grow exalted and sanctified… Amen. May His great name be blessed forever and ever'. What is His great name – it is the first one, NAMELY THE NAME ELOHIM THAT WAS COMPLETED IN THE FIRST ESTABLISHMENT. For it is established only in us, as Mi will be only built with the letters of Eleh. Therefore at that time, "Mi Eleh that fly as a cloud," and the whole world will see that the celestial name is well composed.

207. וְאִי שְׁמֵיהּ רַבָּא דָּא אִתְתַּקַּן, וְאִתְבְּנֵי עַל תִּקּוּנֵיהּ, הָא יִשְׂרָאֵל שַׁלִּיטִין עַל כֹּלָּא, וְכָל שְׁאַר שְׁמָהָן יִתְהַדְּרוּן עַל תִּקּוּנַיְיהוּ, וְיִשְׂרָאֵל שַׁלִּיטִין עַל כֹּלָּא, דְּהָא כֻּלְּהוּ תַּלְיָין בִּשְׁמֵיהּ רַבָּא, קַדְמָאָה לְכָל בִּנְיָינִין.

207. And if His great name Elohim is corrected and well built, Yisrael rule over everything, and all the other names reach perfection. And Yisrael have power over everything, since they all depend on His great name, the first of all establishments.

208. רָזָא דָּא, כַּד בָּרָא קוּדְשָׁא בְּרִיךְ הוּא עָלְמִין. קַדְמָאָה לְכָל בִּנְיָינִין, שְׁמָא דָּא אִתְבְּנֵי. דִּכְתִיב שְׂאוּ מָרוֹם עֵינֵיכֶם וּרְאוּ מִי בָרָא אֵלֶּה, בָּרָא שְׁמֵיהּ עַל תִּקּוּנֵיהּ, וְכַד בָּרָא אֵלֶּה, בָּרָא לֵיהּ בְּכָל חֵילִין דְּיִתְחֲזוּן לֵיהּ, לְמֶהֱוֵי שְׁמֵיהּ עַל תִּקּוּנֵיהּ כַּדְקָא יֵאוֹת, דִּכְתִיב הַמּוֹצִיא בְמִסְפָּר צְבָאָם.

208. The secret behind it is that when the Holy One, blessed be He, WHO IS BINAH, created the worlds, MALE AND FEMALE, this name was built as the first establishment, as written, "Lift up your eyes on high, and behold who (Heb. *mi*) has created these (Heb. *eleh*)" (Yeshayah 40:26), has created His name ELOHIM well formed. When He created Eleh, He created it with all the powers proper to it, to be His name suitably formed, as written, "that brings out their host by number" (Ibid.).

209. מַאי בְּמִסְפָּר. אֶלָּא בְּרָא חַד דְּנָהִיר מִסַּיְיפֵי עָלְמָא עַד סַיְיפֵי עָלְמָא, אִית לֵיהּ לְקוּדְשָׁא בְּרִיךְ הוּא, וְהוּא אִילָנָא רַבָּא וְתַקִּיף. רֵישֵׁיהּ מָטֵי לְצֵית שְׁמַיָּא, וְסוֹפֵיהּ מַתְחָן שָׁרְשׁוֹי, וְאִשְׁתַּרְשָׁן בְּעָפָר קַדִּישָׁא, וּמִסְפָּר שְׁמֵיהּ. וְתַלְיָא בַּשָּׁמַיִם עִלָּאִין, וְחָמֵשׁ רְקִיעִין תַּלְיָין מִנֵּיהּ, עַד הַאי מִסְפָּר, וְכֻלְּהוּ נַטְלִין שְׁמָא דָא בְּגִינֵיהּ דִּכְתִיב הַשָּׁמַיִם מְסַפְּרִים, בְּגִין הַאי מִסְפָּר, כֻּלְּהוּ שָׁמַיִם רְוִוחִין שְׁמָא דָא בְּגִינֵיהּ, וְעַל דָּא הַמּוֹצִיא בְמִסְפָּר צְבָאָם, דְּאִלְמָלֵא מִסְפָּר דָּא, לָא יִשְׁתַּכְּחוּן חַיָּילִין וְתוֹלְדִין לְעָלְמִין.

209. HE ASKS, what is "by number," IN "THAT BRINGS OUT THEIR HOST BY NUMBER," AND ANSWERS, the Holy, One, blessed be He, has a son that shines from one end of the world to the other. He is a great and strong tree, YESOD OF ZEIR ANPIN. His top reaches the height of heaven, WHICH IS ZEIR ANPIN THAT IS CALLED HEAVEN, and at his ending his roots spread and strike root in the holy earth, WHICH IS MALCHUT, ACCORDING TO THE VERSE, "FOR ALL THAT IS IN HEAVEN AND ON EARTH" (I DIVREI HAYAMIM 29:11). His name is number. He originates in the upper heaven, THAT IS ZEIR ANPIN, and five firmaments hang IN HEAVEN, WHICH ARE CHESED, GVURAH, TIFERET, NETZACH AND HOD down to this number, WHICH IS THE SIXTH FIRMAMENT, NAMELY YESOD. All the FIRMAMENTS receive the name 'NUMBER (HEB. *MISPAR*)' for YESOD, as written, "The heavens declare (Heb. *MESAPRIM*)" (Tehilim 19:2). Due to that number, the whole heaven, THE FIVE FIRMAMENTS, attain this name for its sake. Hence, "that brings out their host by number," for were it not for that number, there would never be hosts and generations, SINCE YESOD PRODUCES OFFSPRING.

A Synopsis

We hear an explanation of "Who can count the dust of Jacob, and the number of the fourth part of Yisrael," and "and many of those who sleep in the dust of the earth shall awake". The merchant says that the "dust of the earth" was seen in the Book of Enoch as the letters floating in the air. "The dust" is the first dust, that is the body of the childless dead man, and "the earth" is the second, corrected one, the body of the incarnated man which corrects the first. In the time to come those who are corrected are destined to live forever, and the other side will be removed from the world. Repentance breaks many sentences and verdicts, and nothing withstands repentance; God accepts everyone who repents, as He is full of compassion and mercy. The Holy One, blessed be He, sees the ways of one who walks in evil, and He holds his hand, and gives him healing, and leads him in the true path.

210. וְעַל דָּא כְּתִיב, מִי מָנָה עֲפַר יַעֲקֹב וּמִסְפָּר אֶת רֹבַע יִשְׂרָאֵל, תְּרֵין אִינּוּן, דְּמָנוּ עָאנָא, וְעָאלוּ בְּחוּשְׁבָּנָא עַל יְדַיְיהוּ, בְּגִין דְּלָא שַׁלְטָא בְּהוּ עֵינָא בִּישָׁא. מִי מָנָה עֲפַר יַעֲקֹב, הָא חַד, דְּעָבֵיד חוּשְׁבָּנָא. וּמִסְפָּר אֶת רֹבַע יִשְׂרָאֵל, הָא מוֹנֶה אַחֲרָא.

210. In relation to this it is written, "Who can count the dust of Jacob, and the number of the fourth part of Yisrael" (Bemidbar 23:10). There were two who counted the flock that was numbered by them, because the evil eye had no power over them. "Who can count the dust of Jacob" refers to one who counts. "The number of the fourth part of Yisrael" is the second enumerator.

211. וְעַל תְּרֵין אִלֵּין לָא שַׁלְטָא בְּהוּ עֵינָא בִּישָׁא, דְּהָא מִי מָנָה לְעָפַר יַעֲקֹב, אִלֵּין אִינּוּן אֲבָנִין קַדִּישִׁין, אֲבָנִין מְפוּלָמִין, דְּמִנְּהוֹן נַפְקֵי מַיִין לְעָלְמָא. וְעַל דָּא כְּתִיב וְהָיָה זַרְעֲךָ כַּעֲפַר הָאָרֶץ מַה הַהוּא עָפָר, עָלְמָא. מִתְבָּרֵךְ בְּגִינֵיה. אוּף הָכִי וְהִתְבָּרֲכוּ בְזַרְעֲךָ כָּל גּוֹיֵי הָאָרֶץ. כַּעֲפַר הָאָרֶץ מַמָּשׁ. וּמִסְפָּר דְּאִיהוּ מוֹנֶה תִּנְיָינָא, מָנָה לְרֹבַע כָּל אִינּוּן נוּקְבִין, מַרְגְּלָן עִלָּאִין, דְּמַטֶּה דְּשָׁכִיב עֲלֵיה יִשְׂרָאֵל.

211. Over these two the evil eye has no power, for "Who can count the dust of Jacob" refers to the holy stones, strong stones, from which water sprouts

into the world. Of this it is written, "and your seed shall be as the dust of the earth" (Beresheet 28:14). As the dust of the world is blessed for his sake, so, "and in your seed shall all the nations of the earth be blessed" (Beresheet 22:18), like the very dust of the earth. 'Number' is the second enumerator, who counted so as to cause all those females, the celestial pearls, to rest on the bed on which Jacob was lying, WHICH IS MALCHUT.

212. וּמִתַּמָּן וּלְהָלְאָה, אִיהוּ מוֹנֶה לְכֹלָּא, בְּגִין דְּאִיהוּ טוֹב עַיִן. הֲדָא הוּא דִכְתִּיב, מוֹנֶה מִסְפָּר לַכּוֹכָבִים. מַאן הוּא מוֹנֶה לַכּוֹכָבִים. מִסְפָּר. מוֹנֶה מִסְפָּר לַכּוֹכָבִים, עַל יְדוֹי עַבְרִין כֻּלְּהוּ בְּחֻשְׁבָּנָא, וּלְזִמְנָא דְּאָתֵי, עוֹד תַּעֲבוֹרְנָה הַצֹּאן עַל יְדֵי מוֹנֶה, וְלָא יַדְעִינָן מַאן הוּא. אֶלָּא בְּגִין דִּבְהַהוּא זִמְנָא, יְהֵא כֹּלָּא בְּיִחוּדָא בְּלָא פְּרוּדָא, כֹּלָּא לֶיהֱוֵי מוֹנֶה חַד.

212. From then onward, it counts everything, because it, YESOD, has a good eye. Hence it is written, "He counts the number of the stars" (Tehilim 147:4), WHICH MEANS that they are all reckoned by it. In the future to come it is written, "shall the flocks pass again under the hands of him that counts them" (Yirmeyah 33:13), yet we do not know who that is, WHETHER THE FIRST OR SECOND ONE. But since at that time everything will be together indivisible, all will be conducted by one enumerator.

213. קוּם סָבָא, אִתְּעַר וְאִתְגַּבַּר בְּחֵילָךְ, וְשׁוּט יַמָּא. פָּתַח וְאָמַר, מִי מָנָה עֲפַר יַעֲקֹב וּמִסְפָּר אֶת רֹבַע יִשְׂרָאֵל. בְּשַׁעְתָא דְּיִתְּעַר קוּדְשָׁא בְּרִיךְ הוּא לְאַחֲיָיא מֵתַיָּא, הָנֵי דְּאִתְהַדְרוּ בְּגִלְגּוּלָא, תְּרֵין גּוּפִין בְּרוּחָא חֲדָא, תְּרֵין אֲבָהָן, תְּרֵין אִמָּהָן, כַּמָּה גִּלְגּוּלִין מִתְגַּלְגְּלָן עַל דָּא, אע"ג דְּאִתְּמַר, וְהָכִי הוּא, אֲבָל מִי מָנָה עֲפַר יַעֲקֹב, וְאִיהוּ עָפָר יַתְקִין כֹּלָּא, וְלָא יִתְאֲבִיד כְּלוּם, וְכֹלָּא יְקוּם.

213. HE SAID TO HIMSELF, rise, old man, wake up and grow strong to sail in the sea. He opened with the verse, "Who can count the dust of Jacob, and the number of the fourth part of Yisrael." When the Holy One, blessed be He, will awaken to raise the dead, those who were incarnated, who are two bodies with one spirit, NAMELY THE BODY OF THE DEAD MAN AND THE BODY OF THE INCARNATED, WHO BOTH HAVE BUT ONE SPIRIT. They have

two fathers, THE FATHER OF THE DEAD AND THAT OF THE INCARNATED BODY, and also two mothers. How many incarnations do they undergo for that UNTIL ONE IS CORRECTED. For though we learned THIS and it is so, yet "Who can count the dust of Jacob," WHICH IS THE FIRST ONE TO COUNT that will amend everything, ALL THE INCARNATED BODIES, and nothing will be lost, so everything will rise TO RESURRECT.

214. וְהָא אִתְּמַר, וְרַבִּים מִיְשֵׁנֵי אַדְמַת עָפָר יָקִיצוּ. אַדְמַת עָפָר הָנֵי, כְּמָה דְּאִתְּמַר בְּסִפְרָא דַּחֲנוֹךְ, כַּד חַבְרַיָּיא אִסְתַּכָּלוּ בְּאִינּוּן אַתְוָון דְּטָסִין בַּאֲוִירָא בֵּיהּ, וְאִינּוּן אע"ד פמת"ר, הַיְינוּ, אדמ"ת עָפָ"ר.

214. We have studied, "And many of those who sleep in the dust of the earth shall awake" (Daniel 12:2). The dust of the earth IS as was said in the book of Enoch that the friends looked at the letters floating in the air, which are Aleph Ayin Dalet Pei Mem Tav Resh, WHICH FORM 'dust of the earth'.

215. הַיְינוּ וְשַׁבֵּחַ אֲנִי אֶת הַמֵּתִים שֶׁכְּבָר מֵתוּ, אַדְמַת עָפָר אִינּוּן אַתְוָון וְקָלָא אִתְּעַר וְאוֹדַע וְהָכִי אָמַר בְּבִנְיָינָא תִּנְיָינָא. עָפָר, עָפָר קַדְמָאָה. אַדְמַת תִּנְיָינָא, דְּאִתְתָּקַן עִקָּר קַדְמָאָה פְּסוֹלֶת לְגַבֵּיהּ.

215. Hence, "So I praised the dead that are already dead" (Kohelet 4:2), which are the letters of 'dust of the earth', THAT IS, BOTH THE DEAD OF THE ASPECT OF DUST AND THE DEAD OF THE ASPECT OF EARTH. A voice is roused to inform, saying so during the second edifice, WHICH IS THE BODY OF THE INCARNATED, WHICH CORRECTS BOTH THE BODY OF THE DEAD OF THE ASPECT OF DUST, AND THE BODY ITSELF, WHICH IS THE ASPECT OF EARTH. IT IS IT THAT SAYS, "SO I PRAISED THE DEAD," THAT IS, FIXES THEM. The dust is the first dust, WHICH IS THE BODY OF THE DEAD MAN, the earth is the second, corrected one, THE BODY OF THE INCARNATED MAN, TO WHICH the sterile, first one is refuse. FOR THE BODY OF THE CHILDLESS DEAD MAN, WHICH IS STERILE, IS AS REFUSE IN RELATION TO THE INCARNATED BODY, WHICH CORRECTS IT. HENCE IT SAYS, "SO I PRAISED THE DEAD," THAT IS, FIXES THEM.

216. אַדְמַת עָפָר כֻּלְּהוּ, יָקִיצוּ. אֵלֶּה דְּאִתְתָּקְנוּ, לְחַיֵּי עוֹלָם. מַאן עוֹלָם. דָּא עוֹלָם דִּלְתַתָּא דְּהָא לָא זָכוּ לְמֶהֱוֵי בְּעוֹלָם דִּלְעֵילָא. וְאֵלֶּה דְּלָא

זָכוּ, לַחֲרָפוֹת וּלְדִרְאוֹן עוֹלָם. מַאי לַחֲרָפוֹת, אֶלָּא בְּגִין דְּסִטְרָא אַחֲרָא יִתְעֲבַר מֵעָלְמָא, וְקוּדְשָׁא בְּרִיךְ הוּא אִלֵּין דַּהֲווֹ מִנְבִּיעוּ דְּהַהוּא סִטְרָא, יַשְׁאַר לוֹן, לְתַוְוהָא בְּהוֹן כָּל בְּנֵי עָלְמָא.

216. Those sleeping in the dust of the earth shall all wake up. Those that were corrected are destined to live forever (lit. 'for the world'). Which world is that? It is the lower world, NAMELY MALCHUT, for they did not merit being in the upper world BUT DESCENDED TO THE FEMALE WORLD. Those who did not merit CORRECTING will be "to shame and everlasting contempt" (Daniel 12:2). HE ASKS, what is contempt, AND SAYS that the other side will be removed from the world, and the Holy One, blessed be He, will leave those who flowed from that side for people to wonder about. THIS IS THE MEANING OF, "TO SHAME AND EVERLASTING CONTEMPT."

217. כָּל דָּא מַאן גָּרִים, הַהוּא דְּלָא בָּעֵי לְאַפָּשָׁא בְּעָלְמָא, וְלָא בָּעֵי לְקַיְּימָא בְּרִית קַדִּישָׁא, עַל דָּא גָּרִים כָּל מַה דְּגָרִים, וְכָל הָנֵי גִּלְגּוּלִין דְּקָא אֲמֵינָא עֲלָהּ עַד הָכָא. עַד כָּאן סָבָא. שָׁתִיק רִגְעָא חֲדָא, וְחַבְרַיָּיא הֲווֹ תְּווֹהִין, וְלָא הֲווֹ יַדְעִין, אִי הֲוָה יְמָמָא, אִי הֲוָה לֵילְיָא, אִי קַיְימֵי תַּמָּן, אִי לָא קַיְּימֵי.

217. Who brought all this about? THE MAN who did not want to be fruitful and to procreate in the world or to uphold the holy covenant. He thus brought about all that, and all the incarnations I mentioned until now. HE SAID TO HIMSELF, up to here, old man. He was silent for a moment. The friends were stupefied and did not know whether it was day or night, or whether they were THERE or not.

218. פָּתַח הַהוּא סָבָא וְאָמַר, כִּי תִקְנֶה עֶבֶד עִבְרִי שֵׁשׁ שָׁנִים יַעֲבֹד וּבַשְּׁבִיעִית וְגוֹ'. קְרָא דָא אוֹכַח, עַל כָּל מַה דְּאִתְּמַר. ת"ח, כָּל דְּכוּרָא, קָאֵים בְּדִיּוּקְנָא, בְּעָלְמָא דִּדְכוּרָא. וְכָל נוּקְבָּא קָאֵים בְּדִיּוּקְנָא, בְּעָלְמָא דְּנוּקְבָּא. בְּעוֹד דְּאִיהוּ עֲבַדָּא דְּקוּדְשָׁא בְּרִיךְ הוּא אִתְדַּבַּק בֵּיהּ, בְּאִינּוּן שֵׁשׁ שָׁנִים קַדְמוֹנִיּוֹת, וְאִי אִתְעַקַּר גַּרְמֵיהּ מִפּוּלְחָנֵיהּ, יַעֲקַר לֵיהּ קוּדְשָׁא בְּרִיךְ הוּא מֵאִינּוּן שֵׁשׁ שָׁנִים, דְּעָלְמָא דִּדְכוּרָא, וְאִתְמְסַר לְב"נ, דְּאִיהוּ

מְשִׁית סְטְרִין, יִפְלַח לֵיהּ שִׁית שְׁנִין, וְיִתְעֲקַר מְשִׁית שְׁנִין דִּלְעֵילָא.

218. The old man started with, "If you buy a Hebrew servant, six years he shall serve: and in the seventh..." (Shemot 21:2). This verse proves all that we have said. Come and see, every male is in the image of the male world, WHICH IS ZEIR ANPIN, and every female is in the image of the female world, WHICH IS MALCHUT. When one is the servant of the Holy One, blessed be He, he cleaves to the six primordial years, NAMELY CHESED, GVURAH, TIFERET, NETZACH, HOD AND YESOD OF ZEIR ANPIN. But if he tears himself away from WORSHIPPING Him, the Holy One, blessed be He, tears him from the six years of the male world, NAMELY CHESED, GVURAH, TIFERET, NETZACH, HOD AND YESOD OF ZEIR ANPIN, and he is given to the man of six extremities, CHESED, GVURAH, TIFERET, NETZACH, HOD AND YESOD, whom he serves for six years, torn away from the supernal six years OF ZEIR ANPIN.

219. לְבָתַר נָחִית מִתַּמָּן, וְאִתְמְסַר בְּעָלְמָא דְּנוּקְבָּא. הוּא לָא בָּעָא לְקַיְימָא בִּדְכוּרָא, נָחִית וְקַיְימָא בְּנוּקְבָּא. אָתָאת נוּקְבָּא, דְּאִיהִי שְׁבִיעִית, וְנָטְלָא לֵיהּ, הָא מִכָּאן וּלְהָלְאָה, מֵעָלְמָא דְּנוּקְבָּא אִיהוּ.

219. After that, he descends from there and is given to the female world. He who did not want to dwell in the male, goes down to dwell in the female, WHICH IS MALCHUT. The Nukva comes, which is the seventh SFIRAH, and takes him. OF HER IT IS SAID, "AND IN THE SEVENTH HE SHALL GO OUT FREE" (IBID.). From now on he is of the female world.

220. לָא בָּעָא לְקַיְימָא בָּהּ, וּבְפִירוּקָא דִּילָהּ, נָחִית לְתַתָּא, וְאִתְדָּבַק לְתַתָּא, וְאִתְאַחִיד בְּסִטְרָא אַחֲרָא. מִכָּאן וּלְהָלְאָה, אִתְעֲקַר מֵעָלְמָא דִּדְכוּרָא, וּמֵעָלְמָא דְּנוּקְבָּא. הָא אִתְאֲחַד, בְּאִינוּן עֲבָדִים דְּאִינוּן מִסִּטְרָא אַחֲרָא.

220. If he did not want to be maintained by her or her redemption, SAYING, "I LOVE MY MASTER...I WILL NOT GO OUT FREE" (IBID. 5), he goes down to cleave below, attaching himself to the Other Side. From now on he is torn from the world of the male and the world of the female, because he has joined the servants of the Other Side.

221. הַשְׁתָּא כֵּיוָן דְּהָכִי הוּא, אִיצְטְרִיךְ פְּגָם, וּלְמֶעְבַּד בֵּיהּ רְשִׁימוּ דִּפְגַם, דְּהָא כָּל פְּגָם דְּסִטְרָא אַחֲרָא אִיהוּ, וּמִיוֹבֵל וּלְהָלְאָה אִתְהַדַּר לְגִלְגּוּלָא, וְתָב לְעָלְמָא כְּמִלְּקַדְמִין. וְאִתְדַּבַּק בְּהַהוּא עָלְמָא דְּנוּקְבָּא, וְלָא יַתִּיר. זָכָה עָבֵיד תּוֹלְדִין בְּעָלְמָא דְּנוּקְבָּא, וְכֻלְּהוּ רָזָא דִּכְתִיב בְּתוּלוֹת אַחֲרֶיהָ רְעוֹתֶיהָ מוּבָאוֹת לָךְ. וְזַכָּאָה אִיהוּ כַּד אִתְתָּקַן וְזָכֵי לְכָךְ.

221. Now that it is so, AND HE IS ATTACHED TO THE OTHER SIDE, he needs a blemish, to be branded with a mark of blemish, NAMELY, "AND HIS MASTER SHALL BORE HIS EAR THROUGH WITH AN AWL" (IBID. 6), since every blemish pertains to the Other Side. THEN, "HE SHALL SERVE HIM FOREVER (LIT. 'TO THE WORLD')" (IBID.), THAT IS, UNTIL JUBILEE CALLED WORLD. From the Jubilee on, he incarnates again and goes back into the world as before, cleaving no further than the female world. If he attains merit, he begets offspring in the world of the female, WHICH IS MALCHUT, which are all described in the verse, "the virgins, her companions that follow her, shall be brought to you" (Tehilim 45:15). He is worthy, when he perfects himself to attain that.

222. וְאִי לָא זָכָה אֲפִילוּ בְּגִלְגּוּלָא דְּיוֹבְלָא, הָא אִיהוּ כְּלָא הֲוָה אִתְהַדַּר, וְלָא אַשְׁלִימוּ יוֹמוֹי, לְאִתְנַסְבָא בְּעָלְמָא, וּלְמֶעְבַּד תּוֹלְדִין. מַה כְּתִיב, אִם בְּגַפּוֹ יָבֹא בְּגַפּוֹ יֵצֵא. אִי יְחִידָאי יֵעוּל בְּהַהוּא עָלְמָא בְּלָא תּוֹלְדִין, וְלָא בָּעָא לְאִשְׁתַּדְּלָא בְּהַאי, וְנָפַק מֵהַאי עָלְמָא יְחִידָאי, בְּלָא זַרְעָא, אָזִיל כְּאַבְנָא בְּקוֹסְפִיתָא, עַד הַהוּא אֲתָר דְּטִנָּרָא תַּקִּיפָא, וְעָאל תַּמָּן וּמִיַּד נָשַׁב רוּחָא דְּהַהוּא יְחִידָאי, דְּקָא אִשְׁתְּבִיק מִנּוּקְבֵּיהּ, וְאָזִיל יְחִידָאי, כְּחִוְיָא דְּלָא אִתְחַבַּר בְּאַחֲרָא בְּאוֹרְחָא, וְנָשִׁיב בֵּיהּ.

222. If he has no merit, even when he incarnates at the Jubilee he is as if he never was, for HE INCARNATED again, yet did not perfect his life by marrying in the world and siring offspring. It is then written, "If he came in by himself, he shall go out by himself" (Shemot 21:3). If he entered the world alone, without children, and did not care to strive after that but left the world alone without children, he moves like a stone in a sling up to that place in the strong rock BEHIND THE GARDEN OF EDEN. There he enters,

but the lone spirit blows at once that left his wife AND CAME THERE. THIS IS THE SPIRIT THAT REMAINED IN THE WIFE BY HER FIRST HUSBAND, which goes solitary like a snake that does not keep company on the road. FOR IT IS SEPARATED FROM THE TWO SPIRITS IN THE WOMAN AND GOES ALONE. It blows on him, ON THE SPIRIT OF THE CHILDLESS DEAD MAN THAT JUST CAME THERE, THAT IS, PUSHES IT AWAY FROM THERE, SO IT WILL INCARNATE AND PERFECT ITSELF.

223. וּמִיָּד נָפַק מִגּוֹ הַהוּא אֲתָר דְּטִנָּרָא תַּקִּיפָא, הוּא בִּלְחוֹדוֹי, וְאָזִיל וּמְשַׁטְּטָא בְּעָלְמָא, עַד דְּקָא אַשְׁכַּח פָּרוֹקָא לְאָתָבָא. וְהַיְינוּ אִם בְּגַפּוֹ יָבֹא בְּגַפּוֹ יֵצֵא, הַאי דְּלָא בָּעָא לְאִתְנַסְבָא, לְמֶהֱוֵי לֵיהּ תּוֹלְדִין.

223. Whereupon he leaves that place of the strong rock, alone WITHOUT A WIFE, and roams in the world until he finds a redeemer TO BRING HIM BACK TO THIS WORLD for his improvement. That is, "If he came in by himself, he shall go out by himself" WITHOUT A WIFE, he who did not wish to marry and have children. SINCE HE HAS NO SPOUSE HE HAS TO MARRY A DIVORCED WOMAN.

224. אֲבָל אִם בַּעַל אִשָּׁה הוּא, דְּקָא אִתְנְסִיב, וְאִשְׁתַּדַּל בְּאִתְּתֵיהּ, וְלָא יָכִיל, הַהוּא לָא אִתְתָּרַךְ כְּהַהוּא אַחֲרָא, לָא יֵיעוּל יְחִידָאִי, וְלָא נָפִיק יְחִידָאִי, אֶלָּא אִם בַּעַל אִשָּׁה הוּא, קוּדְשָׁא בְּרִיךְ הוּא לָא מְקַפַּח אֲגַר כָּל בִּרְיָין, אע"ג דְּלָא זָכוּ בִּבְנֵי, מַה כְּתִיב וְיָצְאָה אִשְׁתּוֹ עִמּוֹ. וְתַרְוַוייהוּ אַתְיָין בְּגִלְגּוּלָא, וְזַכְיָין לְאִתְחַבְּרָא כַּחֲדָא כְּמִלְּקַדְמִין. וְהַאי לָא נָסִיב אִתְּתָא דְּתִרוּכִין, אֶלָּא הַהִיא דְּאִשְׁתַּדַּל בָּהּ בְּקַדְמֵיתָא, וְלָא זָכוּ, הַשְׁתָּא יִזְכּוּ כַּחֲדָא, אִי יְתַקְּנוּן עוֹבָדִין, וע"ד וְיָצְאָה אִשְׁתּוֹ עִמּוֹ.

224. But, "if he is married" (Ibid.); he who did marry and tried with her but could not BEGET CHILDREN, such a man is not driven away like the other, nor comes out alone. But, "if he is married," the Holy One, blessed be He, does not withhold reward from anyone. Even though he did not have children, it is written, "then his wife shall go out with him" (Ibid.). The two incarnate, and are able to unite again. He does not marry a divorced woman, like the other who has no spouse, but marries the same woman with whom he tried before yet they had no children. Now they shall attain it together, if they act

well. Hence it is written, "then his wife shall go out with him."

225. אִם אֲדוֹנָיו יִתֶּן לוֹ אִשָּׁה וְגוֹ'. אַהֲדָר קְרָא לְמִלִּין אַחֲרָנִין, לְהַהוּא דְּנָפִיק יְחִידָאִי בְּלָא נוּקְבָּא כְּלָל, וַיִּפְרוֹק לֵיהּ הַהוּא דּוּכְתָּא דְּאִקְרֵי שְׁבִיעִית. וְהַהוּא שְׁבִיעִית אִקְרֵי אֲדוֹנָיו, אֲדוֹן כָּל הָאָרֶץ אִיהוּ. אִם דָּא אֲדוֹנָיו חָס עָלֵיהּ, וְאָתִיב לֵיהּ לְהַאי עָלְמָא יְחִידָאִי כְּמָה דַּהֲוָה, וְיָהִיב לֵיהּ אִתְּתָא הַהִיא דְּמִזְבֵּחַ אֲחִיתַת עֲלוֹי דִּמְעִין, וְאִתְחַבְּרָא כַּחֲדָא. וְיָלְדָה לוֹ בָנִים אוֹ בָנוֹת הָאִשָּׁה וִילָדֶיהָ תִּהְיֶה לַאֲדֹנֶיהָ כְּמָה דְּאִתְּמַר.

225. "If his master has given him a wife" (Ibid. 4): the verse returns to another subject, to him who went out alone, without any wife. The place called seventh, NAMELY MALCHUT, shall redeem him, and that seventh is considered his master; it is the master of the whole earth. If his master has compassion for him and brings him back to the world solitary as he was and gives him a woman, for whom the altar sheds tears, NAMELY A DIVORCED WOMAN, they marry and she bears him boys or girls, "the wife and her children shall be her master's" (Ibid.), OF HOLY MALCHUT, as we learned.

226. דְּהָא אִי תָּב, וְאַתְקִין הַהוּא אֲתָר דְּפָגִּים בְּחַיּוֹי, אִתְקַבַּל קַמֵּי מַלְכָּא קַדִּישָׁא, נָטִיל לֵיהּ, וְאַתְקִין לֵיהּ עַל תִּקּוּנוֹי לְבָתַר. וְדָא אִקְרֵי בַּעַל תְּשׁוּבָה, דְּהָא יָרִית מוֹתְבֵיהּ, דְּהַהוּא אֲתָר, דְּהַהוּא נָהָר דְּנָגִיד וְנָפִיק, וְאַתְקִין גַּרְמֵיהּ מִמַּה דַּהֲוָה בְּקַדְמֵיתָא. כֵּיוָן דְּאִתְתַּקַּן וְתָב בִּתְיוּבְתָּא, הָא סָלִיק עַל תִּקּוּנֵיהּ. דְּלֵית מִלָּה בְּעָלְמָא, וְלֵית מַפְתְּחָא בְּעָלְמָא, דְּלָא תָּבַר הַהוּא דְּתָב בִּתְיוּבְתָּא.

226. For if he repented and corrected the place he blemished during his life, he is accepted before the holy King, who receives him and then sets him aright. He is considered a penitent, since he inherited a dwelling in that place of the flowing river, NAMELY MALCHUT. FOR THE RIVER THAT COMES OUT AND FLOWS IS YESOD, ITS BED IS MALCHUT. He improves his former state. Once he is corrected and has repented, he achieves perfection, for there is nothing in the world, no key in the world that the penitent cannot break.

227. מַאי יֵצֵא בְגַפּוֹ. הָא אִתְּמַר, אֲבָל תּוּ רָזָא אִית בֵּיהּ, יֵצֵא בְגַפּוֹ, כְּמָה דְאַתְּ אָמַר, עַל גַּפֵּי מְרוֹמֵי קָרֶת, מַה לְהָתָם עֲלַוְויָא וְסָלִיקוּ, אוּף הָכָא עֲלַוְויָא וְסָלִיקוּ, אָתָר דְמָרֵיהוֹן דִתְיוּבְתָּא סַלְקִין, אֲפִילוּ צַדִּיקִים גְּמוּרִים לָא יַכְלִין לְמֵיקָם תַּמָּן. וּבְג"כ כֵּיוָן דְתָב בִּתְיוּבְתָּא, קוּדְשָׁא בְּרִיךְ הוּא מְקַבֵּל לֵיהּ וַדַּאי מִיָּד.

227. HE ASKS, what is the meaning of, "he shall go out by himself (Heb. gapo)"? HE ANSWERS, we have already studied it, yet it contains another hidden meaning. "He shall go out by himself (Heb. gapo)" is the same as in, "the highest (Heb. gapei) places of the city" (Mishlei 9:3). As in the latter, GAPEI IS AN EXPRESSION OF exaltation and praise, here too GAPO HAS THE MEANING OF exaltation and praise. In the place to which the penitent rise, even the most accomplished righteous cannot dwell. Therefore, once he repented, the Holy One, blessed be He, accepts him.

228. תָּנֵינָן, לֵית מִלָה בְּעָלְמָא דְקַיְּימָא קַמֵּי תְּשׁוּבָה, וּלְכֹלָּא קוּדְשָׁא בְּרִיךְ הוּא מְקַבֵּל וַדַּאי. וְאִי תָּב בִּתְיוּבְתָּא הָא אִזְדָּמַן לְקָבְלֵיהּ אֹרַח חַיִּים, וְאַף ע"ג דְפָגִים מַה דְפָגִים, כֹּלָּא אִתְתָּקַן, וְכֹלָּא אִתְהַדַּר עַל תְּקוּנֵיהּ, דְהָא אֲפִילוּ בְּמַה דְאִית בֵּיהּ אוֹמָאָה, קוּדְשָׁא בְּרִיךְ הוּא מְקַבֵּל, דִכְתִּיב חַי אֲנִי נְאָם יְיָ' כִּי אִם יִהְיֶה כָּנְיָהוּ וְגוֹ' וּכְתִיב כִּתְבוּ אֶת הָאִישׁ הַזֶּה עֲרִירִי וְגוֹ'. וּבָתַר דְתָב בִּתְיוּבְתָּא כְּתִיב, וּבְנֵי יְכָנְיָה אַסִּיר בְּנוֹ וְגוֹ', מִכָּאן דִתְשׁוּבָה מִתְבַּר כַּמָּה גְזָרִין וְדִינִין, וְכַמָּה שַׁלְשְׁלָאִין דְפַרְזְלָא, וְלֵית מַאן דְקַיְּימָא קַמֵּי דִתְיוּבְתָּא.

228. We have learned that nothing in the world withstands repentance, and the Holy One, blessed be He, surely accepts everyone. If one repents, the way of life is prepared for him. Even though he made any blemish, everything is mended and becomes corrected. For even having uttered an oath, the Holy One, blessed be He, accepts him, as written, "As I live, says Hashem, though Konyahu…" (Yirmeyah 22:24), and "Write this man childless" (Ibid. 30). But after he repented, it is written, "And the sons of Yechonyah: Assir…" (I Divrei Hayamim 3:17). From here we conclude that repentance breaks many sentences and verdicts and many iron chains, and that nothing withstands repentance.

229. וְעַל דָּא כְּתִיב, וְיָצְאוּ וְרָאוּ בְּפִגְרֵי הָאֲנָשִׁים הַפּוֹשְׁעִים בִּי. אֲשֶׁר פָּשְׁעוּ בִּי, לָא כְּתִיב, אֶלָּא הַפּוֹשְׁעִים בִּי, דְּלָא בָּעָאן לְאָתָבָא, וּלְאִתְנַחֲמָא עַל מַה דְּעָבְדוּ. אֲבָל כֵּיוָן דְּאִתְנַחֲמוּ, הָא מְקַבֵּל לוֹן קוּדְשָׁא בְּרִיךְ הוּא.

229. In relation to that it is written, "And they shall go forth, and look upon the carcasses of the men that rebel against Me" (Yeshayah 66:24). It does not say, 'that rebelled against Me', but "rebel against Me," NAMELY THOSE who did not want to repent and regret what they have done. But if they regretted AND REPENTED, the Holy One, blessed be He, accepts them.

230. בְּגִין כָּךְ, בַּר נָשׁ דָּא, אַף עַל גַּב דְּפָשַׁע בֵּיה, וּפָגִים בְּאַתְרָא דְּלָא אִצְטְרִיךְ, וְתָב לְקַמֵּיה, מְקַבֵּל לֵיה, וְחָס עָלֵיה, דְּהָא קוּדְשָׁא בְּרִיךְ הוּא מָלֵא רַחֲמִין אִיהוּ, וְאִתְמְלֵי רַחֲמִים עַל כָּל עוֹבָדוֹי, כד"א וְרַחֲמָיו עַל כָּל מַעֲשָׂיו. אֲפִילוּ עַל בְּעִירֵי וְעוֹפֵי מָאטוּן רַחֲמוֹי. אִי עֲלַיְיהוּ מָאטוּן רַחֲמוֹי, כָּל שֶׁכֵּן עַל בְּנֵי נָשָׁא, דְּיַדְעִין וְאִשְׁתְּמוֹדְעָאן לְשַׁבְּחָא לְמָארֵיהוֹן, דְּרַחֲמוֹי מָאטוּן עֲלַיְיהוּ, וְשָׁרָאן עֲלַיְיהוּ. וְע"ד אָמַר דָּוִד, רַחֲמֶיךָ רַבִּים יְיָ' כְּמִשְׁפָּטֶיךָ חַיֵּינִי.

230. Therefore such a man, even though he rebelled against Him, and blemished where he must not have blemished, but repented before Him, He accepts him and has pity on him. For the Holy One, blessed be He, is full of compassion, and is filled with compassion for all His works, as written, "and His tender mercies are over all His works" (Tehilim 145:9). His mercy reaches even beasts and fowls. So if His mercy reaches them, all the more so people who recognize and know how to praise their Master, when His mercy reaches them and dwells on them. Regarding this David said, "Great are Your compassions, Hashem: give me life as is Your wont" (Tehilim 119:156).

231. אִי עַל חַיָּיבִין מָאטוּן רַחֲמוֹי, כ"ש עַל זַכָּאִין. אֶלָּא מַאן בָּעֵי אַסְוָתָא, אִינוּן מָארֵי כְּאֵבִין, וּמַאן אִינוּן מָארֵי כְּאֵבִין. אִלֵּין אִינוּן חַיָּיבִין, אִינוּן בָּעָאן אַסְוָותָא וְרַחֲמֵי, דְּקוּדְשָׁא בְּרִיךְ הוּא רַחֲמֵי עֲלַיְיהוּ, דְּלָא יְהוֹן שְׁבִיקִין מִנֵּיה, וְאִיהִי דְּלָא אִסְתְּלַק מִנַּיְיהוּ, וְיתוּבוּן לְקַבְּלֵיה.

כַּד מְקָרֵב קוּדְשָׁא בְּרִיךְ הוּא, בִּימִינָא בְּקָרֵב. וְכַד דָּחֵי, בִּשְׂמָאלָא דָּחֵי. וּבְשַׁעֲתָא דְּדָחֵי, יְמִינָא מְקָרֵב. מִסִּטְרָא דָּא דָּחֵי, וּמִסִּטְרָא דָּא מְקָרֵב, וְקוּדְשָׁא בְּרִיךְ הוּא לָא שָׁבִיק רַחֲמוֹי מִנַּיְיהוּ.

231. And if His mercy reaches the wicked, the righteous all the more. But who needs healing? Those who suffer pains. Who suffer pain? The wicked, who need healing and mercy, for the Holy One, blessed be He, takes pity on them so they will not be forsaken by Him, and He does not go away from them so they will return IN REPENTANCE before Him. When the Holy One, blessed be He, beckons, He does so with the right, and when He repels, He does so with the left. When He repels, the right beckons; He repels with one side and beckons with the other. The Holy One, blessed be He does not withdraw His mercy from them.

232. ת"ח, מַה כְּתִיב וַיֵּלֶךְ שׁוֹבָב בְּדֶרֶךְ לִבּוֹ. וּכְתִיב בַּתְרֵיהּ, דְּרָכָיו רָאִיתִי וְאֶרְפָּאֵהוּ וְאַנְחֵהוּ וַאֲשַׁלֵּם נִחֻמִים לוֹ וְלַאֲבֵלָיו. וַיֵּלֶךְ שׁוֹבָב, אע"ג דְּחַיָּיבִין עַבְדִין, כָּל מַה דְּעַבְדִין בְּזָדוֹן דְּאַזְלִין בְּאָרְחָא דִּלְבַיְיהוּ, וְאַחֲרָנִין עַבְדִין בְּהוּ הַתְרָאָה, וְלָא בָּעָאן לְצַיְּיתָא לוֹן. בְּשַׁעֲתָא דְּתָבִין בִּתְיוּבְתָּא, וְנַטְלִין אָרְחָא טָבָא דִּתְיוּבְתָּא, הָא אַסְוָותָא זְמִינָא לְקַבְּלַיְיהוּ.

232. Come and see, "but he went perversely in the way of his heart," followed by, "I have seen his ways, and will heal him: I will lead him also, and bestow comforts on him and on his mourners" (Yeshayah 457:17-18). HE EXPLAINS, "but he went perversely" MEANS though the wicked do what they do willfully and follow the way of their heart, and others admonish them but they care not to listen to them, NEVERTHELESS, when they repent and take the good path of repentance, remedy awaits them.

233. הַשְׁתָּא אִית לְאִסְתַּכְּלָא, אִי עַל חַיָּיא אָמַר קְרָא, אוֹ עַל מֵתַיָּיא אָמַר קְרָא. דְּהָא רֵישָׁא דִּקְרָא, לָאו אִיהוּ סֵיפָא. וְסֵיפָא, לָאו אִיהוּ רֵישָׁא. רֵישָׁא דִּקְרָא, אַחְזֵי עַל חַיָּיא. וְסוֹפֵיהּ אַחְזֵי עַל מֵתַיָּיא. אֶלָּא, קְרָא אָמַר, בְּעוֹד דְּבַר נָשׁ אִיהוּ בְּחַיּוֹי, וְהָכִי הוּא, וַיֵּלֶךְ שׁוֹבָב בְּדֶרֶךְ לִבּוֹ, בְּגִין דְּיֵצֶר הָרַע דְּבֵיהּ, תַּקִּיף וְאִתְתַּקַּף בֵּיהּ, וְע"ד אָזַל שׁוֹבָב, וְלָא

בָּעֵי לְאָתָבָא בִּתְיוּבְתָּא.

233. We should observe now whether the verse refers to the living or the dead, for the beginning of the verse is not as its ending, nor the ending the beginning. The first part of the verse points at the living, SAYING, "BUT HE WENT PERVERSELY...", yet the latter part points to the dead, SAYING, "AND BESTOW COMFORTS ON HIM AND ON HIS MOURNERS." HE ANSWERS, the verse speaks of living man, and it is thus: "he went perversely in the way of his heart," because the Evil Inclination within him is strong and gains power. Hence "he went perversely," and does not care to repent.

234. קוּדְשָׁא בְּרִיךְ הוּא חָמֵי אָרְחוֹי, דְּקָא אַזְלִין בְּבִישׁ, בְּלָא תּוֹעַלְתָּא, אָמַר קוּדְשָׁא בְּרִיךְ הוּא, אֲנָא אִצְטְרִיכְנָא לְאַתְקְפָא בִּידֵיהּ, הה"ד דְּרָכָיו רָאִיתִי, דְּקָא אַזְלִין בְּחָשׁוֹכָא, אֲנָא בָּעֵי לְמֵיהַב לֵיהּ אַסְוָתָא הה"ד וְאֶרְפָּאֵהוּ, קוּדְשָׁא בְּרִיךְ הוּא אִיהוּ אָעִיל בְּלִבֵּיהּ אָרְחֵיהּ דִּתְיוּבְתָּא וְאַסְוָתָא לְנִשְׁמָתֵיהּ. וְאַנְחֵהוּ, מַאי וְאַנְחֵהוּ. כד"א לֵךְ נְחֵה אֶת הָעָם. אַנְהִיג לֵיהּ קוּדְשָׁא בְּרִיךְ הוּא בְּאֹרַח מֵישָׁר, כְּמַאן דְּאַתְקִיף בִּידָא דְּאַחֲרָא, וְאַפְּקֵיהּ מִגּוֹ חֲשׁוֹכָא.

234. The Holy One, blessed be He, sees his ways, that he walks in evil to no use. He says, I need to hold his hand, as written, "I have seen his ways" walking in the darkness; I wish to give him healing, as written, "and will heal him." The Holy One, blessed be He, brings into his heart the path of repentance and healing for his soul. "I will lead him also" – what does this mean? It resembles the words, "go, lead the people" (Shemot 32:34), and the Holy One, blessed be He, leads him in the true path as one holding someone's hand, leading him out of darkness.

235 וַאֲשַׁלֵּם נְחוּמִים לוֹ וְלַאֲבֵלָיו, הָא אִתְחֲזֵי דְּמִיתָא אִיהוּ, אִין וַדַּאי מֵיתָא אִיהוּ, וְקַיְּימָא בַּחַיִּין דְּהוֹאִיל וְאִיהוּ רָשָׁע, מֵיתָא אִקְרֵי. מַהוּ וַאֲשַׁלֵּם נְחוּמִים לוֹ וְלַאֲבֵלָיו. אֶלָּא קוּדְשָׁא בְּרִיךְ הוּא עָבֵיד טִיבוּ עִם בְּנֵי נָשָׁא, דְּכֵיוָן דְּעָאל מי"ג שְׁנִין וּלְהָלְאָה, פָּקִיד עַמֵּיהּ תְּרֵין מַלְאָכִין נְטוּרִין דְּנָטְרֵי לֵיהּ, חַד מִימִינֵיהּ, וְחַד מִשְּׂמָאלֵיהּ.

235. "And bestow comforts on him and on his mourners": HE ASKS, it seems as if he is dead, NOT AS IN THE FIRST PART OF THE VERSE. HE ANSWERS, assuredly he is dead; even though he is alive, since he is wicked, he is considered dead. What is the meaning of, "and bestow comforts on him and on his mourners"? HE SAYS, the Holy One, blessed be He, acts kindly with people. Ever since one's thirteenth birthday, He gives two guardian angels to be with him, and they guard him, one to his right and one to his left.

236. כַּד אָזִיל בַּר נָשׁ בְּאֹרַח מֵישָׁר, אִינּוּן חַדָּאן בֵּיהּ, וְאַתְקִיפוּ עֲמֵיהּ בְּחֶדְוָה, מַכְרְזָן קַמֵּיהּ וְאַמְרִין, הָבוּ יְקַר לְדִיּוּקְנָא דְּמַלְכָּא. וְכַד אָזִיל בְּאֹרַח עֲקִימוּ, אִינּוּן מִתְאַבְּלָן עָלֵיהּ, וּמִתְעַבְּרָן מִנֵּיהּ. כֵּיוָן דְּאַתְקִיף בֵּיהּ קוּדְשָׁא בְּרִיךְ הוּא, וְאַנְהִיג לֵיהּ בְּאֹרַח מֵישָׁר, כְּדֵין כְּתִיב, וַאֲשַׁלֵּם נְחוּמִים לוֹ וְלַאֲבֵלָיו. וַאֲשַׁלֵּם נְחוּמִים לוֹ בְּקַדְמֵיתָא, דְּאִיהוּ אִתְנְחַם עַל מַה דְּעָבַד בְּקַדְמֵיתָא, וְעַל מַה דְּעָבַד הַשְׁתָּא, וְתָב בִּתְיוּבְתָּא. וּבָתַר כֵּן וְלַאֲבֵלָיו, אִינּוּן מַלְאָכִין דַּהֲווֹ מִתְאַבְּלָן עָלֵיהּ כַּד אִתְעֲבָרוּ מִנֵּיהּ, וְהַשְׁתָּא דְּאִתְהַדָּרוּ בַּהֲדֵיהּ, הָא וַדַּאי נְחוּמִים לְכָל סִטְרִין.

236. When man walks the right path they rejoice in him and uphold him with joy, announcing before him saying, Give honor to the image of the King. But when he treads the crooked path, they mourn for him and leave him. When the Holy One, blessed be He, holds him and leads him in the right way, it is written, "and bestow comforts on him and on his mourners." First I will "bestow comforts on him," for he regrets all that he did formerly and what he has done now and repents. Then, "on his mourners," who are the angels that mourned him when they departed from him. Now that they have returned there are consolations (Heb. *nichumim*) in every aspect, HE BOTH REGRETS (HEB. *MITNACHEM*) HIS DEEDS AND TAKES COMFORT (HEB. *MITNACHEM*) FOR HIS TROUBLES AND MOURNING.

237. וְהַשְׁתָּא אִיהוּ חַי וַדַּאי. חַי בְּכָל סִטְרִין, אָחִיד בְּאִילָנָא דְּחַיֵּי, וְכֵיוָן דְּאָחִיד בְּאִילָנָא דְּחַיֵּי, כְּדֵין אִקְרֵי בַּעַל תְּשׁוּבָה, דְּהָא כְּנֶסֶת יִשְׂרָאֵל, תְּשׁוּבָה אוּף הָכִי אִקְרֵי. וְאִיהוּ בַּעַל תְּשׁוּבָה אִקְרֵי. וְקַדְמָאֵי אָמְרוּ, בַּעַל תְּשׁוּבָה מַמָּשׁ. וְע"ד, אֲפִילוּ צַדִּיקִים גְּמוּרִים אֵינָם יְכוֹלִים לַעֲמוֹד,

בִּמְקוֹם שֶׁבַּעֲלֵי תְּשׁוּבָה עוֹמְדִים.

237. Now he is surely alive, he is living in every respect, holding to the Tree of Life. Since he is attached to the Tree of Life, he is called a penitent, for the Congregation of Yisrael, WHICH IS MALCHUT, is also called penitence. FOR REPENTANCE (HEB. *TESHUVAH*) IS COMPOSED OF THE SEGMENTS, LET VAV RETURN (HEB. *TASHUV*) TO HEI. THE VAV IS THE TREE OF LIFE, ZEIR ANPIN, AND HEI IS MALCHUT. HENCE MALCHUT IS CALLED REPENTANCE. And he is called a repentant, and the ancient sages called him man of repentance literally, NAMELY, THE HUSBAND OF MALCHUT CALLED REPENTANCE, WHICH MEANS HE BESTOWS PLENTY ON HER. Therefore, even the wholly righteous cannot dwell where the penitents do.

A Synopsis

The old merchant talks about David's situation when he took Bath-Sheva to wife and when he slew her husband, Uriah, with the sword of the children of Amon. He says that David did no sin when he took Bath-Sheva, but that he should have killed Uriah when he rebelled against the kingdom rather than using the Amonites to kill him. Some sins are against other men, and some are just against God.

238. דָּוִד מַלְכָּא אָמַר, לְךָ לְבַדְּךָ חָטָאתִי וְהָרַע בְּעֵינֶיךָ עָשִׂיתִי וְגוֹ', לְךָ לְבַדְּךָ, מַאי לְךָ לְבַדְּךָ. אֶלָּא, בְּגִין דְּאִית חוֹבִין, דְּחָטֵי ב"נ לְקוּדְשָׁא בְּרִיךְ הוּא וְלִבְנֵי נָשָׁא. וְאִית חוֹבִין דְּחָטָא לִבְנֵי נָשָׁא, וְלָא לְקוּדְשָׁא בְּרִיךְ הוּא. וְאִית חוֹבִין דְּחָטֵי לְקוּדְשָׁא בְּרִיךְ הוּא בִּלְחוֹדוֹי וְלָא לִבְנֵי נָשָׁא. דָּוִד מַלְכָּא, חָב לְקוּדְשָׁא בְּרִיךְ הוּא בִּלְחוֹדוֹי, וְלָא לִבְנֵי נָשָׁא.

238. King David said, "Against You, You alone, have I sinned and done that which is evil in Your sight" (Tehilim 51:6). What is the meaning of, "You alone"? HE ANSWERS, there are sins man commits against the Holy One, blessed be He, and against people, sins against people but not the Holy One, blessed be He, and sins against the Holy One, blessed be He, but not against people. King David sinned against the Holy One, blessed be He, alone, but not against people. HENCE HE SAID, "AGAINST YOU, YOU ALONE, HAVE I SINNED."

239. וְאִי תֵּימָא הָא חָב הַהוּא חוֹבָה דְּבַת שֶׁבַע, וְתָנֵינָן, מַאן דְּאָתֵי עַל

-388-

עֶרְוָה אָסְרָה עַל בַּעְלָהּ, וְחָב לְחַבְרֵיהּ, וְחָב לְקוּדְשָׁא בְּרִיךְ הוּא. לָאו
הָכִי הוּא דְּהַהוּא דְּאַתְּ אָמַר. בְּהֶיתֵּרָא הֲוָה, וְדָוִד דִּילֵיהּ נָקַט, וְגֵט הֲוָה
לָהּ מִבַּעְלָהּ, עַד לָא יֵהַךְ לִקְרָבָא, דְּהָכִי הֲוָה מִנְהֲגָא דְּכָל יִשְׂרָאֵל,
דְּיַהֲבִין גֵּט זְמַן לְאִתְּתֵיהּ, כָּל דְּנָפִיק חֵילָא. וְכֵן עָבַד אוּרִיָּה לְבַת שֶׁבַע.
וּלְבָתַר דְּעָבַר זְמַן וַהֲוַת פְּטוּרָא לְכֹלָּא, נָטַל לָהּ דָּוִד. וּבְהֶיתֵּרָא עָבַד כָּל
מַה דְּעָבַד.

239. HE ASKS, yet if you argue that he did commit that sin by Bathsheba, we learned that whoever commits a sexual transgression with a man's wife, renders her forbidden to her husband, and THUS sins against his neighbor and against the Holy One, blessed be He. HE ANSWERS, this is not so. The sin you mentioned was permitted and David took that which was his, for she had a letter of divorce from her husband before he went to war. It was then the custom that men in Yisrael, who went to war, gave their wives a letter of divorce applicable after a certain time. Uriah did the same with Bathsheba. After the time had elapsed she was permitted to any man, and David married her. Whatever he did was permitted.

240. דְּאִלְמָלֵא לָאו הָכִי, וּבְאִסּוּרָא הֲוָה, לָא שַׁבְקָהּ קוּדְשָׁא בְּרִיךְ הוּא
לְגַבֵּיהּ. וְהַיְינוּ דִּכְתִיב לְסָהֲדוּתָא, וַיְנַחֵם דָּוִד אֵת בַּת שֶׁבַע אִשְׁתּוֹ.
סָהֲדוּתָא דְּאִשְׁתּוֹ הִיא, וַדַּאי אִשְׁתּוֹ, וּבַת זוּגוֹ הֲוַת, דְּאִזְדַּמְּנַת לְגַבֵּיהּ,
מִיּוֹמָא דְּאִתְבְּרֵי עָלְמָא. הָא סָהֲדוּתָא דְּלָא חָב דָּוִד חוֹבָה דְּבַת שֶׁבַע
כִּדְקָאמָרָן.

240. For had not it been so, but prohibited, the Holy One, blessed be He, would not have let her stay with him. Thus it is written as testimony, "And David comforted Bathsheba his wife" (II Shmuel 12:24). This is the testimony that she was his wife. Assuredly she was his wife and soulmate, ready for him from the day the world was created. This testifies that David did not commit sin by Bathsheba, as we said.

241. וּמַה הִיא חוֹבָה דְּחָב, לְקוּדְשָׁא בְּרִיךְ הוּא בִּלְחוֹדוֹי, וְלָא לְאָחֳרָא.
דְּקָטַל לְאוּרִיָּה בַּחֶרֶב בְּנֵי עַמּוֹן, וְלָא קַטְלֵיהּ אִיהוּ בְּשַׁעֲתָא דְּאָמַר לֵיהּ

וַאֲדֹנִי יוֹאָב, דְּהָא דָוִד הֲוָה רִבּוֹן עֲלֵיהּ, וְקָרָא אוֹכַח, דִּכְתִיב וְאֵלֶּה
שְׁמוֹת הַגִּבּוֹרִים אֲשֶׁר לְדָוִד, וְלֹא אֲשֶׁר לְיוֹאָב, וְלֹא קַטְלֵיהּ הַהִיא
שַׁעֲתָא, וְקַטְלֵיהּ בְּחֶרֶב בְּנֵי עַמּוֹן.

241. What was the sin he committed against the Holy One, blessed be He, and not against another? It is that he slew Uriah with the sword of the children of Amon, instead of killing him when he said to him, "and my lord Joab" (II Shmuel 11:11), seeing that he himself was his master. This the verse proves in the words, "These are the names of David's warriors" (II Shmuel 23:8), and not 'Joab's warriors'. THUS HE IS A REBEL AGAINST THE KINGDOM, WHICH IS PUNISHABLE BY DEATH. Yet he did not slay him at that time, but rather by the sword of Amon.

242. וְקָרָא אָמַר, וְלֹא נִמְצָא אִתּוֹ דָבָר, רַק בִּדְבַר אוּרִיָּה הַחִתִּי. רַק
לְמָעוּטֵי קָא אָתֵי, בִּדְבַר אוּרִיָּה, וְלָא בְּאוּרִיָּה. וְקוּדְשָׁא בְּרִיךְ הוּא אָמַר,
וְאוֹתוֹ הָרַגְתָּ בְּחֶרֶב בְּנֵי עַמּוֹן, וְכָל חֶרֶב בְּנֵי עַמּוֹן, הֲוָה חָקִיק בֵּיהּ חִוְיָא
עֲקִים, דִּיּוּקְנָא דְּדַרְקוֹן, וְאִיהוּ ע"ז דִּלְהוֹן. אָמַר קוּדְשָׁא בְּרִיךְ הוּא,
יָהַבְתְּ חֵילָא לְהַהוּא. שִׁקּוּץ. בְּגִין דִּבְשַׁעֲתָא דְּקַטְלוּ בְּנֵי עַמּוֹן לְאוּרִיָּה,
וְסַגִּיאִין מִבְּנֵי יִשְׂרָאֵל עִמֵּיהּ, וְאִתְגַּבַּר בְּהַהִיא שַׁעֲתָא חֶרֶב בְּנֵי עַמּוֹן,
כַּמָּה תֶּקְפָּא אִתְתַּקַּף הַהִיא ע"ז שִׁקּוּץ.

242. The text says that there was no fault found in him, "save only in the matter of Uriah the Hittite" (I Melachim 15:5). "Save only" indicates exclusion, that HE SINNED in the matter of Uriah, and not SINNED by Uriah HIMSELF. The Holy One, blessed be He, said, "and have slain him with the sword of the children of Amon" (I Shmuel 12:9). On each of the swords of the children of Amon, a crooked serpent was engraved, an image of a dragon, which is their idol. The Holy One, blessed be He, said, you have empowered that abomination. For when the children of Amon killed Uriah together with many of the children of Yisrael, the sword of the children of Amon grew strong at that time, and much strength was added to that idol and abomination.

243. וְאִי תֵּימָא, אוּרִיָּה לָא הֲוָה זַכַּאי, כֵּיוָן דִּכְתִיב עֲלֵיהּ אוּרִיָּה הַחִתִּי.
לָאו הָכִי, זַכָּאָה הֲוָה, אֶלָּא דְּשִׁמָא דְּאַתְרֵיהּ הֲוָה חִתִּי. כד"א וַיִּפְתַּח

הַגִּלְעָדִי, עַל שׁוּם אַתְרֵיהּ אִתְקְרֵי הָכִי.

243. You may say that Uriah was no righteous man, since it is written of him that he is Uriah the Hittite. But it is not so, he was righteous, only he was Hittite after his place, just like, "Yiftach the Gil'adite" (Shoftim 11:1), was so named after his place. THE SAME APPLIES TO URIAH THE HITTITE.

244. וְעַל דָּא בִּדְבַר אוּרִיָּה הַחִתִּי, דְּשִׁקּוּץ בְּנֵי עַמּוֹן אִתְגַּבָּר עַל מַחֲנֵה אֱלֹהִים, דְּמַשִׁרְיָתָא דְּדָוִד, דְּיוּקְנָא מַמָּשׁ דִּלְעֵילָּא הֲווֹ. וּבְהַהוּא שַׁעֲתָא דְּפָגִים דָּוִד מַשִׁרְיָתָא דָּא, פָּגִים לְעֵילָּא מַשִׁירָתָא אַחֲרָא. וְעַל דָּא אָמַר דָּוִד, לְךָ לְבַדְּךָ חָטָאתִי. לְבַדְּךָ, וְלָא לְאַחֲרָא. דָּא הֲוָה הַהוּא חוֹבָה דְּחָב לְגַבֵּיהּ. וְדָא הוּא בִּדְבַר אוּרִיָּה. וְדָא הוּא בְּחֶרֶב בְּנֵי עַמּוֹן.

244. Hence it is written, "in the matter of Uriah the Hittite," AND NOT AGAINST URIAH HIMSELF, FOR HE WAS ALREADY LIABLE TO DEATH PENALTY FOR REBELLING AGAINST THE KINGDOM, AS MENTIONED. THIS IS BECAUSE HE CAUSED the abomination of the children of Amon to prevail against the camp of Elohim of David's army, who had the very shape of above, OF THE HOSTS OF SUPERNAL MALCHUT. When David caused a defect in his camp, he caused a defect above in another camp. David therefore said, "Against You, You alone, have I sinned"; against "You alone" and none other was the sin he committed. Hence THE VERSE SAYS, "in the matter of Uriah the Hittite," and hence, "with the sword of the children of Amon," WHICH MEANS THAT THE SIN WAS NOT AGAINST URIAH HIMSELF BUT IN THE MATTER OF URIAH, BY GIVING POWER TO THE SWORD OF THE CHILDREN OF AMON.

245. כְּתִיב, כִּי יְיָ' עֵינָיו מְשׁוֹטְטוֹת בְּכָל הָאָרֶץ, אַלֵּין נוּקְבִין. וּכְתִיב עֵינֵי יְיָ' הֵמָּה מְשׁוֹטְטִים, אַלֵּין דְּכוּרִין, וְהָא יְדִיעָן אִינּוּן. דָּוִד אָמַר וְהָרַע בְּעֵינֶיךָ עָשִׂיתִי. בְּעֵינֶיךָ, לְפְנֵי עֵינֶיךָ מִבָּעֵי לֵיהּ. אֶלָּא מַאי בְּעֵינֶיךָ, אָמַר דָּוִד, בְּהַהוּא אֲתָר דְּחַבְנָא, בְּעֵינֶיךָ הֲוָה. דַּהֲוֵינָא יָדַע, דְּהָא עֵינֶיךָ הֲווֹ זְמִינִין, וְקַיְימִין קַמַּאי, וְלָא חֲשִׁיבְנָא לוֹן, הֲרֵי חוֹבָא דְּחַבְנָא, וְעַבְדָּנָא, בְּאָן אֲתָר הֲוָה, בְּעֵינֶיךָ.

245. It is written, "For the eyes of Hashem run to and fro throughout the whole earth" (II Divrei Hayamim 16:9), which are female, AS 'RUN' HAS A FEMININE SUFFIX. And it is written, "the eyes of Hashem, they rove to and fro through the whole earth" (Zecharyah 4:10), which are male, AS 'ROVE' IS MASCULINE. So they are distinct, SOME OF THEM ARE CONSIDERED MALE AND SOME FEMALE. David said, "and done that which is evil in Your sight (eyes)" (Tehilim 51:6). HE ASKS, it says, "in Your eyes," while it should have been 'before Your eyes'. HE ANSWERS, yet THE REASON FOR SAYING "in Your eyes" IS THAT David said, the place against which I have sinned was in Your eyes, because I knew your eyes were ready and set before me, yet I was not mindful of them. Thus the sin I committed was against Your eyes.

246. לְמַעַן תִּצְדַּק בְּדָבְרֶךָ תִּזְכֶּה בְשָׁפְטֶךָ, וְלֹא יְהֵא לִי פִּתְחוֹן פֶּה לְמֵימָר קַמָּךְ. ת״ח, כָּל אוּמָנָא, כַּד מַלִּיל, בְּאוּמָנְתֵיהּ מַלִּיל. דָּוִד בְּדִיחָא דְּמַלְכָּא הֲוָה, וְאע״ג דַּהֲוָה בְּצַעֲרָא, כֵּיוָן דַּהֲוָה קַמֵּי מַלְכָּא, תָּב לִבְדִיחוּתֵיהּ, כְּמָה דַּהֲוָה, בְּגִין לְבַדְּחָא לְמַלְכָּא.

246. "So that You are justified in Your sentence, and clear in Your judgment" (Ibid.), and he will have no excuse to say before You, "EXAMINE ME, HASHEM, AND PROVE ME" (TEHILIM 26:2). Come and see, every artist speaks of his craft. David was the King's jester, and even though he was grieved, when he was before the King, he employed his jests as before, to amuse the King.

247. אָמַר, מָארֵי דְעָלְמָא, אֲנָא אֲמֵינָא, בְּחָנֵנִי יְיָ' וְנַסֵּנִי, וְאַתְּ אָמַרְתְּ דְּלָא אִיכוּל לְקַיְּימָא בְּנִסְיוֹנָךְ. הָא חָבְנָא, לְמַעַן תִּצְדַּק בְּדָבְרֶךָ, וִיהֵא מִילָךְ קְשׁוֹט, דְּאִלְמָלֵא לָא חָבְנָא, יְהֵא מִלָּה דִילִי קְשׁוֹט, וִיהֵא מִילָךְ בְּרֵיקַנְיָא, הַשְׁתָּא דְּחָבְנָא, בְּגִין דְּלֶהֱוֵי מִילָךְ קְשׁוֹט, יָהִיבְנָא אֲתַר לְצַדְּקָא מִילָךְ, בְּגִין כַּךְ עֲבִידְנָא, לְמַעַן תִּצְדַּק בְּדָבְרֶךָ תִּזְכֶּה בְשָׁפְטֶךָ. אַהְדָּר דָּוִד לְאוּמָנוּתֵיהּ, וְאָמַר גּוֹ צַעֲרֵיהּ מִלִּין דִּבְדִיחוּתָא לְמַלְכָּא.

247. He said, Master of the universe, I said, "Examine me, Hashem, and prove me," and you said I cannot withstand the test. Here I have sinned "so that You are justified in Your sentence," and your words prove right. For

had I not sinned, my word would be true and Yours vain. Now that I have sinned, I did it so that Your sentence will be true. I have allowed place to justify Your sentence, which I did, "so that You are justified in Your sentence, and clear in Your judgment." For David reverted to his craft, and said in his grief words of jest to the King.

248. תָּנֵינָן, לָאו דָּוִד אִתְחֲזֵי לְהַהוּא עוֹבָדָא, דְּהָא אִיהוּ אָמַר, וְלִבִּי חָלָל בְּקִרְבִּי הָכִי הוּא. אֲבָל אָמַר דָּוִד, בְּלִבָּא אִית תְּרֵין הֵיכָלִין, בְּחַד דָּמָא, וּבְחַד רוּחָא, הַהוּא חַד דְּמַלְיָיא דָּמָא, בֵּיהּ דִּיּוּרָא לְיֵצֶר הָרָע. וְלִבִּי לָאו הָכִי, דְּהָא רֵיקָן אִיהוּ, וְלָא יָהֲבִית דִּיּוּרָא לְדָמָא בִּישָׁא, לְשַׁכְנָא בֵּיהּ יֵצֶר הָרָע, וְלִבִּי וַדַּאי חָלָל אִיהוּ, בְּלָא דִּיּוּרָא בִּישָׁא, וְכֵיוָן דְּהָכִי הוּא, לָא אִתְחֲזֵי דָּוִד לְהַהוּא חוֹבָה דְּחָב אֶלָּא, בְּגִין לְמֵיהַב פִּתְחוֹ דְּפוּמָא לְחַיָּיבַיָּא, דְּיֵימְרוּן, דָּוִד מַלְכָּא חָב וְתָב בִּתְיוּבְתָּא, וּמָחַל לֵיהּ קוּדְשָׁא בְּרִיךְ הוּא, כ"ש שְׁאַר בְּנֵי נָשָׁא. וע"ד אָמַר אֲלַמְּדָה פוֹשְׁעִים דְּרָכֶיךָ וְחַטָּאִים אֵלֶיךָ יָשׁוּבוּ.

248. We learned that the deed was not becoming of David, as he said, "and my heart is wounded (or: 'empty') within me" (Tehilim 109:22). It is so, as David said, there are two chambers in the heart, one with blood and the other with air. The one filled with blood is an abode for the Evil Inclination, yet my heart is not so, because it is empty, and I have not given place for the evil blood to allow the Evil Inclination to dwell in it. My heart is surely clear, without an evil dweller. Since it is so, it was not befitting David to commit that sin, only to give a pretext for the wicked to say that if King David sinned and the Holy One, blessed be He, forgave him, how much more so the rest of the people in the world. Hence David said, "Then I will teach transgressors Your ways; and sinners shall return to You" (Tehilim 51:15).

249. וּכְתִיב, וְדָוִד עֹלֶה בְמַעֲלֵה הַזֵּיתִים עוֹלֶה וּבוֹכֶה וְרֹאשׁ לוֹ חָפוּי וְהוּא הוֹלֵךְ יָחֵף. רֹאשׁ לוֹ חָפוּי, וְיָחֵף אֲמַאי. אֶלָּא, נָזוּף הֲוָה, עֲבַד גַּרְמֵיהּ נָזוּף, לְקַבְּלָא עָנְשָׁא. וְעַמָּא הֲווֹ רְחִיקִין מִנֵּיהּ ד' אַמּוֹת. זַכָּאָה עַבְדָּא דְּהָכִי פָּלַח לְמָארֵיהּ, וְאִשְׁתְּמוֹדַע בְּחוֹבֵיהּ, לְאָתָבָא מִנֵּיהּ בִּתְיוּבְתָּא שְׁלֵימָתָא.

249. And it is written, "And David went up by the ascent of the Mount of Olives, and wept as he went up, and had his head covered, and he went barefoot" (II Shmuel 15:30). HE ASKS, wherefore was "his head covered, and he went barefoot"? AND HE ANSWERS, he was reprimanded; he made himself reprimanded in order to receive punishment, and the people were four cubits apart from him. Happy is the servant who serves his Master this way, and makes known his sin, in order to wholly repent it.

250. ת״ח, יַתִּיר הֲוָה, מַה דְּעָבֵד לֵיהּ שִׁמְעִי בֶּן גֵּרָא, מִכָּל עַקְתִּין דְּעָבְרוּ עָלֵיהּ עַד הַהוּא יוֹמָא, וְלָא אָתִיב דָּוִד לְקַבְלֵיהּ מִלָּה דְּהָכִי הֲוָה יָאוֹת לֵיהּ, וּבְדָא אִתְכַּפָּרוּ חוֹבוֹי.

250. Come and see, what Shim'i the son of Gera did to him was greater than all the troubles he had until that day, yet David did not answer back anything, for so it became him and thus his iniquities were atoned for.

251. הַשְׁתָּא אִית לְאִסְתַּכְּלָא, שִׁמְעִי ת״ח הֲוָה, וְחָכְמְתָא סַגִּיאָה הֲוַת בֵּיהּ, אֲמַאי נָפִיק לְגַבֵּי דָּוִד, וְעָבֵד לֵיהּ כָּל מַה דְּעָבַד. אֶלָּא מֵאֲתָר אַחֲרָא הֲוָה מִלָּה, וְאָעִיל לֵיהּ בְּלִבֵּיהּ מִלָּה דָּא. וְכָל דָּא לְתוֹעַלְתָּא דְּדָוִד. דְּהָא הַהוּא דְּעָבַד לֵיהּ שִׁמְעִי, גָּרְמָא לֵיהּ לְמֵיתַב בִּתְיוּבְתָּא שְׁלֵימָתָא, וְתָבַר לְבֵּיהּ בִּתְבִירוּ סַגִּי, וְאוֹשִׁיד דְּמָעִין סַגִּיאִין, מִגּוֹ לְבֵּיהּ קֳדָם קוּדְשָׁא בְּרִיךְ הוּא, וְעַל דָּא אָמַר, כִּי יְיָ׳ אָמַר לוֹ קַלֵּל. יָדַע, דְּהָא מֵאֲתָר עִלָּאָה אַחֲרָא נָחַת מִלָּה.

251. We should now observe this. Shim'i was a sage and had great wisdom. Why did he come to David and do what he did to him? HE ANSWERS, this came from a different place that put it into him. Whatever he did was for David's benefit. For what Shim'i did to him caused him to wholly repent, and broke his heart greatly, so he shed many tears from his heart before the Holy One, blessed be He. Hence it says, "because Hashem had said to him, curse" (II Shmuel 16:10). He knew that this has come down from another, high place.

252. תְּרֵין פִּקּוּדִין, פָּקִיד דָּוִד לִשְׁלֹמֹה בְּרֵיהּ, חַד דְּיוֹאָב, וְחַד דְּשִׁמְעִי, עִם שְׁאַר פִּקּוּדִין דְּפָקִיד לֵיהּ. דְּיוֹאָב, דִּכְתִיב: וְגַם אַתָּה יָדַעְתָּ אֵת אֲשֶׁר

עָשָׂה לִי יוֹאָב בֶּן צְרוּיָה. מִלָּה סְתִימָא הֲוָה, דַּאֲפִילוּ שְׁלֹמֹה לָא הֲוָה
לֵיהּ לְמִנְדַּע, אֶלָּא בְּגִין דְּיַדְעוּ אַחֲרָנִין, אִתְגְּלֵי לִשְׁלֹמֹה. וְעַל דָּא אָמַר,
וְגַם אַתָּה יָדַעְתָּ וְגוֹ'. מַה דְּלָא אִתְחֲזֵי לָךְ לְמִנְדַּע.

252. David bade his son Solomon do two things, one concerning Joab, the other Shim'i, among the other commands he bade him. One concerned Joab, as written, "Moreover you know also what Joab the son of Tzruyah did to me" (I Melachim 2:5). It was something unknown that even Solomon could not have known. But since others knew, Solomon found out. Hence he said, "Moreover you know," what he was not supposed to have known.

253. דִּשְׁמְעִי: כְּתִיב, וְהִנֵּה עִמְּךָ שִׁמְעִי בֶן גֵּרָא. מַאי וְהִנֵּה עִמְּךָ, זַמִּין
הוּא עִמְּךָ תָּדִיר, רַבּוֹ הֲוָה. וּבְגִין כַּךְ לָא אָמַר עַל יוֹאָב וְהִנֵּה עִמְּךָ
יוֹאָב. אֲבָל שִׁמְעִי דָּא, דְּאִשְׁתְּכַח עִמֵּיהּ תָּדִיר, אָמַר וְהִנֵּה עִמְּךָ.

253. One concerned Shim'i, as written, "And, behold, you have with you Shim'i the son of Gera" (Ibid. 8). What is the meaning of, "with you"? HE ANSWERS, he is always at your disposal, since he was his teacher. This is why he did not say of Joab, 'And, behold, you have Joab with you'. But of Shim'i, who was constantly by him, he said, "And, behold, you have with you."

254. וַיִּשְׁלַח הַמֶּלֶךְ וַיִּקְרָא לְשִׁמְעִי וַיֹּאמֶר בְּנֵה לְךָ בַיִת בִּירוּשָׁלַיִם. אָן
הוּא חָכְמְתָא דִּשְׁלֹמֹה מַלְכָּא בְּהַאי. אֶלָּא כֹּלָּא בְּחָכְמְתָא עָבַד, וּלְכָל
סִטְרִין אַשְׁגַּח, דְּהָא חַכִּים הֲוָה שִׁמְעִי, וְאָמַר שְׁלֹמֹה, בְּעֵינָא דְּיִסְגֵּי
אוֹרַיְיתָא בְּאַרְעָא עַל יְדוֹי דִּשְׁמְעִי, וְלָא יִפּוֹק לְבַר.

254. "And the king sent and called for Shim'i, and said to him, Build you a house in Jerusalem" (Ibid. 36). HE ASKS, where was King Solomon's wisdom in doing this? AND HE ANSWERS, he did everything wisely and noticed every aspect, that Shim'i was a sage. Solomon said, I want Torah to increase in this land by Shim'i, and that he shall not leave it.

255. תּוּ מִלָּה אַחֲרָא אַשְׁגַּח שְׁלֹמֹה בְּחָכְמְתָא, דִּכְתִיב, יֵצֵא יָצֹא

וַיְקַלֵּל. מַאי יָצֹא יָצָא תְּרֵי זִמְנֵי, וַיֵּצֵא וַיְקַלֵּל סַגִּי. אֶלָּא, חַד יְצִיאָה,
דְּנָפַק מִבֵּי מִדְרָשָׁא לְגַבֵּי דָוִד. וְחַד יְצִיאָה, דְּנָפַק מִירוּשְׁלֵם, לְגַבֵּי
עַבְדּוֹי דְּמִית עֲלוֹי. יְצִיאָה חֲדָא לְגַבֵּי מַלְכָּא, וִיצִיאָה תִּנְיָינָא לְגַבֵּי
עַבְדִּין. וְכָל דָּא חָמָא שְׁלֹמֹה, וְאַשְׁגַּח בְּרוּחַ קוּדְשָׁא, הַהוּא יְצִיאָה
תִּנְיָינָא. וְעַל דָּא אָמַר, וְהָיָה בְיוֹם צֵאתְךָ, יָדַע דְּבִיצִיאָה יָמוּת.

255. Another thing is that Solomon observed wisely the words, "he came out, cursing as he came" (II Shmuel 16:5). Why does it say 'came' twice, 'he came out cursing' should have sufficed. AND HE ANSWERS, once he came out of the study hall TO CURSE David, and once he came out of Jerusalem for his servants, for which he died. He came out once for the king and once for his servants. Solomon saw all this and looked through the Holy Spirit at the second coming out. Hence he said, "For it shall be, that on the day you go out" (I Melachim 2:37), he knew that he will die going out.

256. וְעָפָר בֶּעָפָר מַהוּ. אָמַר שְׁלֹמֹה לְגַבֵּי אַבָּא בֶּעָפָר הֲוָה. לְגַבֵּי שִׁמְעִי
בְּמַיָּא, דִּכְתִיב וְהָיָה בְיוֹם צֵאתְךָ וְעָבַרְתָּ אֶת נַחַל קִדְרוֹן. עָפָר הָתָם,
וְהָכָא מַיָּא. תַּרְוַוייהוּ דָן שְׁלֹמֹה, לְמֶהֱוֵי עָפָר וּמַיָּא כְּסוֹטָה, לְמַאן
דְּאַסְטִין אָרְחָא לְגַבֵּי אֲבוֹי.

256. "And cast dust" (II Shmuel 16:5). HE ASKS, What does it mean, "and cast dust"? AND HE ANSWERS, it was dust by my father, and water by Shim'i, as written, "For it shall be, that on the day you go out, and pass over the wadi of Kidron." It was dust there and water here. Solomon took account of them both so that he will be PUNISHED by dust and water like a Sota (a wife suspected of adultery), he who accused his father by the way.

257. כְּתִיב וְהוּא קִלְלַנִי קְלָלָה נִמְרֶצֶת. וּכְתִיב וָאֶשָּׁבַע לוֹ בַּיְיָ' לֵאמֹר
אִם אֲמִיתְךָ בֶּחָרֶב. מַאי בֶּחָרֶב. וְכִי שִׁמְעִי טִפְשָׁא הֲוָה, דְּאִילּוּ הָכִי
אוֹמֵי לֵיה, דְּלָא יֵימָא בְּחֶרֶב לָא. אֲבָל בַּחֲנִית אוֹ בְּגִירָא אִין.

257. It is written, "who cursed me with a grievous curse…and I swore to him by Hashem, saying, I will not put you to death with the sword" (I Melachim 2:8). HE ASKS, what is "with the sword"? Was Shim'i a fool

THAT HE DID NOT UNDERSTAND that had he sworn this way, he may not say later, not with the sword, but with a spear or an arrow.

258. אֶלָּא תְּרֵין מִלִּין הָכָא. חַד אָמַר יְנוֹקָא, בְּרֵיה דְּנוּנָא רַבָּא הַהוּא דְּקַשְׂקְשׂוֹי סָלְקִין לְרוּם עֲנָנִין. אוֹמָאָה דְּדָוִד מַלְכָּא, כַּד הֲוָה בָּעֵי לְאוֹמָאָה, אַפִּיק חַרְבָּא דִּילֵיה, דְּתַמָּן הֲוָה חָקִיק שְׁמָא גְּלִיפָן, וְתַמָּן אוֹמֵי. וְכַךְ עָבִיד לְשִׁמְעִי, דִּכְתִיב וָאֶשָּׁבַע לוֹ בַיְיָ׳ לֵאמֹר אִם אֲמִיתְךָ בֶּחָרֶב. בְּמַאי הֲוָה אוֹמָאָה דָּא. בֶּחָרֶב. בֶּחָרֶב אוֹמֵי. וּמִלָּה אַחֲרָא, דָּן שְׁלֹמֹה, אָמַר, בִּקְלָלָה אָתָא לְגַבֵּי אַבָּא, בְּמִלִּין, הָא מִלִּין לְגַבֵּיה, וּבְשֵׁם הַמְּפוֹרָשׁ קַטְלֵיה, וְלָא בֶּחָרֶב. וּבְגִין דָּא עָבַד שְׁלֹמֹה הָכִי.

258. HE ANSWERS, there are two matters here. The child, the son of the great fish whose scales rise to the height of the clouds, spoke of the first. When David wanted to swear an oath, he would draw his sword, on which the engraved name was imprinted, and thus swore it. So he did with Shim'i, as written, "and I swore to him by Hashem, saying, I will not put you to death with the sword." How did he swear – with the sword. The other MATTER IS THAT Solomon considered, and said, he came cursing to my father, THAT IS, words, so I TOO HAVE words for him. So he slew him with the Tetragrammaton, and not with the sword. This is why Solomon acted this way.

259. הַשְׁתָּא אִית לְאִסְתַּכְּלָא, דְּכֵיוָן דְּאוֹמֵי לֵיה דָּוִד, אֲמַאי קַטְלֵיה, דְּאִתְחֲזֵי דְּהָא אוֹמָאָה דָּא בַּעֲלִילָה הֲוָה, דְּהָא לִבָּא וּפוּמָא לָא הֲווֹ כַּחֲדָא. אֶלָּא וַדַּאי דָּוִד לָא קַטְלֵיה, וְהָא יְדִיעָא, כָּל שַׁיְיפִין דְּגוּפָא מְקַבְּלִין כֹּלָּא, וְלִבָּא לָא מְקַבְּלָא אֲפִילוּ כְּחוּטָא דְּנֵימָא דְּשַׂעֲרָא. דָּוִד מַלְכָּא לִבָּא הֲוָה, וְקַבִּיל מַה דְּלָא אִתְחֲזֵי לֵיה לְקַבְּלָא, וּבְגִין כָּךְ, וְיָדַעְתָּ אֶת אֲשֶׁר תַּעֲשֶׂה לוֹ כְּתִיב. וְתוּ, דְּהָא אִילָנָא גָּרִים לְמֶהֱוֵי נָטִיר וְנוֹקֵם כְּחִוְיָא.

259. We should now observe. If David swore to him, why did he kill him, for it seems as if this oath was false, since he did not speak his mind. HE ANSWERS, surely David did not kill him. It is known that every body part receives, but the heart does not receive even a hairsbreadth. King David was

the heart OF YISRAEL, but received what was not befitting for him to receive, NAMELY, SHIM'I THROWING STONES AND CASTING DUST AT HIM. Therefore, "know what you ought to do to him" (Ibid. 9). Moreover, THE TREE, NAMELY HIS BEING OF THE ASPECT OF MALCHUT, THE SMALL TREE, caused him to be vindictive and grudging as a snake.

260. כְּתִיב כִּי לֹא תַחְפּוֹץ זֶבַח וְאֶתֵּנָה עוֹלָה לֹא תִרְצֶה. זִבְחֵי אֱלֹהִים רוּחַ נִשְׁבָּרָה לֵב נִשְׁבָּר וְנִדְכֶּה אֱלֹהִים לֹא תִבְזֶה. כִּי לֹא תַחְפּוֹץ זֶבַח, וְכִי לָא בָּעֵי קוּדְשָׁא בְּרִיךְ הוּא דְּיִקְרְבוּן קַמֵּיהּ קָרְבָּנָא, וְהָא אִיהוּ אַתְקִין לְגַבֵּי חַיָּיבַיָּא קָרְבָּנָא, דְּיִקְרְבוּן וְיִתְכַּפַּר לְהוּ חוֹבַיְיהוּ. אֶלָּא דָּוִד לְקָמֵי שְׁמָא דֶּאֱלֹהִים אָמַר, וְקָרְבָּנָא לָא קָרְבִין לִשְׁמָא דֶּאֱלֹהִים, אֶלָּא לִשְׁמָא דְּיוּ"ד הֵ"א וָא"ו הֵ"א. דְּהָא לְגַבֵּי דִּינָא קַשְׁיָא מִדַּת הַדִּין, לָא מְקָרְבִין קָרְבָּנָא. דִּכְתִיב אָדָם כִּי יַקְרִיב מִכֶּם קָרְבָּן לַיְיָ'. לַיְיָ', וְלָא לִשְׁמָא דֶּאֱלֹהִים. וְכִי תַקְרִיב. קָרְבָּן מִנְחָה לַיְיָ'. זֶבַח תּוֹדָה לַיְיָ'. זֶבַח שְׁלָמִים לַיְיָ'.

260. It is written, "For You desire not sacrifice; or else I would give it: You delight not in burnt offering. The sacrifices of Elohim are a broken spirit: a broken and a contrite heart, Elohim, You will not despise" (Tehilim 51:18-19). HE ASKS, "For You desire not sacrifice": does not the Holy One, blessed be He, desire a sacrifice to be offered Him? He did decree that the wicked would sacrifice an offering so their iniquities would be atoned for. AND HE ANSWERS, But David addressed that to the name Elohim, WHICH IS THE ATTRIBUTE OF JUDGMENT. A sacrifice is not brought to the name Elohim, but to the name Yud-Vav-Dalet, Hei-Aleph, Vav-Aleph-Vav, Hei-ALEPH. For a sacrifice is not brought to severe Judgment, the attribute of Judgment, as written, "If any man of you bring your offering to Hashem" (Vayikra 1:2), to Yud Hei Vav Hei, and not to the name Elohim. IT IS ALSO WRITTEN, "And when any will offer a meal offering to Hashem" (Vayikra 2:1), "a sacrifice of peace offerings to Hashem" (Vayikra 22:21), and "a sacrifice of thanks-giving to Hashem" (Ibid. 29), YET THE NAME ELOHIM IS NOT MENTIONED.

261. וּבְגִין כָּךְ, כֵּיוָן דְּדָוִד מַלְכָּא, לְגַבֵּי אֱלֹהִים אָמַר. אִצְטְרִיךְ לְמִכְתַּב, כִּי לֹא תַחְפּוֹץ זֶבַח וְאֶתֵּנָה עוֹלָה לֹא תִרְצֶה. דְּהָא לִשְׁמָא דָּא לָא

מְקָרְבִין, אֶלָּא רוּחַ נִשְׁבָּרָה. דִּכְתִיב זִבְחֵי אֱלֹהִים רוּחַ נִשְׁבָּרָה. קָרְבְּנָא דֶּאֱלֹהִים, עֲצִיבוּ, וּתְבִירוּ דְלִבָּא. וּבְגִין כָּךְ, מַאן דְּחָלַם חֶלְמָא בִּישָׁא, עֲצִיבוּ אִצְטְרִיךְ לְאַחֲזָאָה, דְּהָא בְּמִדַּת אֱלֹהִים קַיְּמָא, וְזֶבַח דְּמִדַּת דִּינָא, עֲצִיבוּ אִצְטְרִיךְ וְרוּחַ נִשְׁבָּרָה, וְהַהוּא עֲצִיבוּ מִסְתַּיֵּיהּ לְחֶלְמָא בִּישָׁא, וְלָא שַׁלְטָא דִּינָא עֲלוֹי. דְּהָא זֶבַח דְּאִתְחֲזֵי לְמִדַּת דִּינָא, אַקְרִיב קַמֵּיהּ.

261. Therefore, since King David addressed the name Elohim, it had to be written, "For You desire not sacrifice; or else I would give it: You delight not in burnt offering," for to that name only a broken spirit is offered, as written, "The sacrifices of Elohim are a broken spirit." A sacrifice to Elohim is sadness and a broken heart. Hence whoever had a bad dream needs to look sad, because he is under the attribute of Elohim and the sacrifice to the attribute of Judgment needs TO BE sadness and a broken spirit. Sadness is useful for bad dreams, so judgment has no power over him, for he offered the proper sacrifice to the attribute of Judgment.

262. לֵב נִשְׁבָּר וְנִדְכֶּה אֱלֹהִים לֹא תִבְזֶה, מַאי לֹא תִבְזֶה, מִכְּלָל דְּאִיכָּא לֵב דְּאִיהוּ בּוּזֶה. אִין. הַיְינוּ לֵב דְּאִיהוּ גֵּאֶה, לֵב בְּגַסּוּת רוּחָא, הַיְינוּ לֵב דְּאִיהוּ בּוּזֶה, אֲבָל לֵב נִשְׁבָּר וְנִדְכֶּה אֱלֹהִים לֹא תִבְזֶה.

262. "A broken and a contrite heart, Elohim, You will not despise" (Tehilim 51:19). HE ASKS, Is, "you will not despise," indicative that there exists a heart to be despised? HE ANSWERS, Yes, namely a heart that is haughty, a heart that is presumptuous. Such is a heart He despises, but a broken and contrite heart, Elohim will not despise.

263. הֵיטִיבָה בִרְצוֹנְךָ אֶת צִיּוֹן תִּבְנֶה חוֹמוֹת יְרוּשָׁלָיִם. מַאי הֵיטִיבָה, אִתְחֲזֵי דְּהָא טִיבוּ אִית בָּהּ, וְהַשְׁתָּא הֵיטִיבָה עַל הַהוּא טִיבוּ. וַדַּאי הָכִי הוּא, דְּהָא מִן יוֹמָא דְּקוּדְשָׁא בְּרִיךְ הוּא אִשְׁתַּדַּל בְּבִנְיַן בֵּי מַקְדְּשָׁא לְעֵילָּא, עַד כְּעַן, הַהוּא הֲטָבָה דִּרְצוֹן, לָא שַׁרְיָיא עַל הַהוּא בִּנְיָן, וְעַל דָּא לָא אִשְׁתַּכְלַל. דְּהָא בְּשַׁעֲתָא דִּרְצוֹן דִּלְעֵילָּא יִתְּעַר, יֵיטִיב וְיַדְלִיק נְהוֹרִין דְּהַהוּא בִּנְיָן, וְהַהוּא עֲבִידְתָּא, דַּאֲפִילוּ מַלְאָכִין דִּלְעֵילָּא, לָא

יֵיכְלוּן לְאִסְתַּכְּלָא בְּהַהוּא בֵּי מַקְדְּשָׁא, וְלָאו בְּהַהוּא בִּנְיָן. וּכְדֵין בֵּי מַקְדְּשָׁא, וְכָל עוֹבָדָא אִשְׁתַּכְלַל.

263. "Do good in your favor to Zion: build you the walls of Jerusalem" (Ibid. 20). HE ASKS: What is meant by "Do good"? Is it not apparent that there already exists something good in it? Thus, WHY DO WE NEED TO PRAY to do good to that which is good? ANSWER: It is certain THAT PRAYER IS NEEDED FOR THE PURPOSE OF DOING BETTER, as from the day that the Holy One, blessed be He, was involved with the construction of the supernal Temple until this day, no good will dwell in that edifice, and so it was never completed. But when the moment arrives when His favor on high is aroused, He will do good and kindle the lights of that edifice which shall project to such an extent that even the angels on High will not be able to gaze at that edifice, that Temple. Then the Temple with its auxiliary tasks will be completed. CONCERNING THIS, HE PRAYED, "DO GOOD IN YOUR FAVOR TO ZION."

264. תִּבְנֶה חוֹמוֹת יְרוּשָׁלַיִם, וְכִי מִן יוֹמָא דְּאִשְׁתַּדַּל בְּבִנְיָן בֵּי מַקְדְּשָׁא עַד כְּעַן, לָא בָּנָה לוֹן. אִי חוֹמוֹת יְרוּשָׁלַם עַד כְּעַן לָא בָּנָה, בֵּי מַקְדְּשָׁא עַל אַחַת כַּמָּה וְכַמָּה. אֶלָּא קוּדְשָׁא בְּרִיךְ הוּא, כָּל עוֹבָדוֹי, לָאו כְּעוֹבָדֵי דְּב"נ. בְּנֵי נָשָׁא כַּד בָּנוּ בֵּי מַקְדְּשָׁא לְתַתָּא, בְּקַדְמֵיתָא עָבְדוּ שׁוּרֵי קַרְתָּא, וּלְבַסּוֹף עָבְדוּ בֵּי מַקְדְּשָׁא. שׁוּרֵי קַרְתָּא בְּקַדְמֵיתָא, בְּגִין לְאַגָּנָא עֲלַיְיהוּ, וּלְבָתַר בִּנְיָינָא דְּבֵיתָא. קוּדְשָׁא בְּרִיךְ הוּא לָאו הָכִי, אֶלָּא בָּנֵי בֵּי מַקְדְּשָׁא בְּקַדְמֵיתָא, וּלְבַסּוֹף, כַּד יָחִית לֵיהּ מִשְּׁמַיָּא, וְיוֹתִיב לֵיהּ עַל אַתְרֵיהּ, כְּדֵין יִבְנֶה חוֹמוֹת יְרוּשָׁלַם דְּאִנּוּן שׁוּרִין דְּקַרְתָּא. וְע"ד אָמַר דָּוִד ע"ז, הֵיטִיבָה בִרְצוֹנְךָ אֶת צִיּוֹן בְּקַדְמֵיתָא, וּלְבָתַר תִּבְנֶה חוֹמוֹת יְרוּשָׁלַם.

264. "build You the walls of Jerusalem." HE ASKS: Is it possible that, from the day that He endeavored to build the Temple to the present, He did not construct them? If the walls of the Temple were not built, then surely the Temple WAS NOT BUILT, AND SO WHY DOES HE SAY TO "DO GOOD IN YOUR FAVOR TO ZION," MEANING, THE TEMPLE? NORMALLY WALLS ARE BUILT FIRST THEN THE TEMPLE ITSELF. ANSWER: The works of the Holy One, blessed be He, are not similar to those of man. When building the

Temple below, man first constructs the walls of the city, then the Temple. The walls of the city must first protect them, then work can be done with the Temple. This is not so with the Holy One, blessed be He. First He constructs the Temple and later, after lowering it from Heaven and placing it upon its site, He builds the walls of Jerusalem which are actually the walls of the city. Therefore, David, may he rest in peace, said, "Do good in your favor to Zion," first, and then, "build You the walls of Jerusalem."

265. הָכָא אִית רָזָא, כָּל עוֹבָדִין דְּעָבֵיד קוּדְשָׁא בְּרִיךְ הוּא, בְּקַדְמֵיתָא אַקְדִּים הַהוּא דִּלְבַר, וּלְבָתַר מוֹחָא דִּלְגוֹ, וְהָכָא לָאו הָכִי. ת"ח, כָּל אִינּוּן עוֹבָדִין דְּעָבֵיד קוּדְשָׁא בְּרִיךְ הוּא, וְאַקְדִּים הַהוּא דִּלְבַר, מוֹחָא אַקְדִּים בְּמַחֲשָׁבָה, וּבְעוֹבָדָא הַהוּא דִּלְבַר, דְּהָא כָּל קְלִיפָה מִסִּטְרָא אַחֲרָא הֲוֵי, וּמוֹחָא מִן מוֹחָא, וְתָדִיר סִטְרָא אַחֲרָא אַקְדִּים וְרַבֵּי וְאַגְדִיל וְנָטִיר אִיבָּא. כֵּיוָן דְּאִתְרַבֵּי, זַרְקִין לֵיהּ לְבַר, וְיָכִין רָשָׁע וְצַדִּיק יִלְבַּשׁ, וְזַרְקִין לְהַהִיא קְלִיפָה, וּמְבָרְכִין לְצַדִּיקָא דְּעָלְמָא.

265. Here there is a secret. Generally, in all doings of the Holy One, blessed be He, at the outset He proceeds to work upon what is on the outside, and then He proceeds to the inner part within. Yet here it is not so, SINCE HE PROCEEDED WITH THE CONSTRUCTION OF THE TEMPLE PRIOR TO CONSTRUCTING THE WALLS, WHICH ARE IN THE EXTERIOR. WHY? HE ANSWERS Come and behold: In all doings where the Holy One, blessed be He, proceeds with the outer work, in the planning stage He begins with the inner, MEANING THE INNERMOST. However, in actual doing, He proceeds with that which is found in the outside – just as the Klipah, MEANING THE SHELL OUTSIDE, stems from the Other Side, yet the inner part is drawn from the inner part, MEANING THE SIDE OF HOLINESS. The Other Side proceeds consistently, and it grows and protects the fruit. Once the fruit ripens, THE SHELL is cast aside, "the evil may prepare it, but the just shall put it on" (Iyov 27:17). The shell is thrown away and the righteous of the world are blessed.

266. אֲבָל הָכָא, בְּבִנְיָינָא דְּבֵי מַקְדְּשָׁא, דְּסִטְרָא בִּישָׁא יִתְעֲבַר מֵעָלְמָא, לָא אִצְטְרִיךְ, דְּהָא מוֹחָא וּקְלִיפָה דִּילֵיהּ הֲוֵי. אַקְדִּים מוֹחָא, דִּכְתִּיב הֵיטִיבָה בִּרְצוֹנְךָ אֶת צִיּוֹן בְּקַדְמֵיתָא, וּלְבָתַר תִּבְנֶה חוֹמוֹת

יְרוּשָׁלַם. הַהִיא חוֹמָה דִּלְבַר, דְּאִיהִי קְלִיפָּה, דִּילֵיהּ הִיא מַמָּשׁ. דִּכְתִּיב, וַאֲנִי אֶהְיֶה לָהּ נְאָם יְיָ׳ חוֹמַת אֵשׁ סָבִיב. אֲנִי וְלָא סִטְרָא בִּישָׁא.

266. But here, concerning the construction of the Temple OF THE FUTURE when the Evil Side will be removed from the world, there will not be a need TO BEGIN WITH THE OUTSIDE because the inner part and the shell will both be His, so that He will commence with the inner part, as it is written, "Do good in Your favor to Zion," first, and then, "build You the walls of Jerusalem." For the outside wall, the shell, will be His own, as written: "'for I', says Hashem, 'will be to her a wall of fire round about,'" (Zecharyah 2:9) "I" and not the side of evil.

267. יִשְׂרָאֵל, אִינּוּן מוֹחָא, עִלָּאָה דְּעָלְמָא. יִשְׂרָאֵל סְלִיקוּ בְּמַחֲשָׁבָה בְּקַדְמֵיתָא, עַמִּין עעכו״ם, דְּאִינּוּן קְלִיפָּה, אַקְדִּימוּ. דִּכְתִּיב וְאֵלֶּה הַמְּלָכִים אֲשֶׁר מָלְכוּ בְּאֶרֶץ אֱדוֹם לִפְנֵי מְלָךְ מֶלֶךְ לִבְנֵי יִשְׂרָאֵל. וְזַמִּין קוּדְשָׁא בְּרִיךְ הוּא, לְאַקְדְּמָא מוֹחָא, בְּלָא קְלִיפָּה. דִּכְתִּיב קֹדֶשׁ יִשְׂרָאֵל לַיְיָ׳ רֵאשִׁית תְּבוּאָתָה, מוֹחָא קָדִים לִקְלִיפָּה. וְאע״ג דְּמוֹחָא יְקוּם בְּלָא קְלִיפָּה, מַאן הוּא דְּיוֹשִׁיט יְדָא לְמֵיכָל מִנֵּיהּ, בְּגִין, דְּכָל אוֹכְלָיו יֶאְשָׁמוּ רָעָה תָּבֹא אֲלֵיהֶם נְאָם יְיָ׳.

267. Yisrael is the supernal core of the world, as the thought of Yisrael came first – AS IN THOUGHT, THE INNERMOST PRECEDED THE SHELL, AS MENTIONED BEFORE. The heathen nations are like the shell TO YISRAEL. They came first IN DEED, BECAUSE IN ACTION THE SHELL COMES BEFORE THE INNER PART OF THE FRUIT AS LISTED EARLIER, as written: "And these are the kings that reigned in the land of Edom, before there reigned any king over the children of Yisrael" (Beresheet 36:31). In the future, the Holy One, blessed be He, will bring forth the fruit without the shell, as written: "Yisrael is holy to Hashem, the first fruits of His increase" (Yirmeyah 2:3), MEANING that the fruit comes before the shell. Even though the fruit will stay without a shell, who would dare extend his hand to eat of it, because of the verse "all that devour him shall be held guilty; evil shall come upon them, says Hashem" (Ibid.).

268. בְּהַהוּא זִמְנָא, אָז תַּחְפּוֹץ זִבְחֵי צֶדֶק. בְּגִין, דְּהָא בְּדֵין, יִתְחַבַּר

כְּלָא בְּחִבּוּרָא חֲדָא, וִיהֵא שְׁמָא שְׁלִים בְּכָל תִּקּוּנֵיהּ. וּכְדֵין קָרְבְּנָא לֶהֱוֵי שְׁלִים, לַיְיָ׳ אֱלֹהִים. דְּהַשְׁתָּא אֱלֹהִים לָא אִתְחַבָּר לְקוֹרְבָּנָא, דְּאִלְמָלֵא אִתְחַבָּר בֵּיהּ, כַּמָה אֱלֹהִים יְסַלְּקוּן אוֹדְנִין לְאִתְחַבְּרָא תַּמָּן. אֲבָל בְּהַהוּא זִמְנָא, כִּי גָדוֹל אַתָּה וְעוֹשֵׂה נִפְלָאוֹת אַתָּה אֱלֹהִים לְבַדֶּךָ. וְאֵין אֱלֹהִים אַחֲרָא.

268. Of that time, IT IS WRITTEN: "Then shall You be pleased with the sacrifices of righteousness" (Tehilim 51:21), because then all will be enjoined into one and the Name will be whole in all its aspects, and there will be a whole sacrifice to Hashem Elohim. Presently, Elohim is not enjoined with the sacrifice, for if He was enjoined with it, numerous other Elohim would raise their ears in an attempt to join AND NURTURE FROM HOLINESS, HEAVEN FORBID. However, in the future time, IT IS WRITTEN, "For You are great, and do wondrous things, You are Elohim alone" (Tehilim 86:10), without any other deities.

A Synopsis
At the time of resurrection, we are told, all those who have not died will experience death from the Holy One, blessed be He, and will then immediately rise back to life; this is in order that none of the impurity in the world will remain, and that the new world will be brought about from the workings of God.

269. וּבְהַהוּא זִמְנָא כְּתִיב, רְאוּ עַתָּה כִּי אֲנִי אֲנִי הוּא וְאֵין אֱלֹהִים עִמָּדִי רְאוּ כִּי אֲנִי אֲנִי הוּא סַגִּי, מַאי עַתָּה. אֶלָּא דְּלָא הֲוָה קֹדֶם לָכֵן, וְהַהוּא זִמְנָא לֶיהֱוֵי. אָמַר קוּדְשָׁא בְּרִיךְ הוּא, עַתָּה רְאוּ, מַה דְּלָא תֵּיכְלוּן לְמֶיחֱמֵי מִקַּדְמַת דְּנָא.

269. At that time, it is written: "See now that I, even I, am He, and there is no Elohim with Me" (Devarim 32:39). HE ASKS: "See now that I, even I, am He"; THIS WOULD BE sufficient, so why MENTION THE WORD "now"? ANSWER: This situation never existed before, but from this time on, it will exist. The Holy One, blessed be He, said: 'See now what you were unable to see before.'

270. כִּי אֲנִי אֲנִי, תְּרֵי זִמְנֵי אֲמַאי. אֶלָּא לְדַיְיקָא, דְּהָא לֵית תַּמָּן

אֱלֹהִים, אֶלָּא הוּא. דְּהָא כַּמָּה זִמְנִין, דְּאִתְּמַר אֲנִי זִמְנָא חֲדָא, וְלָא יַתִּיר, וַהֲוָה תַּמָּן סִטְרָא אַחֲרָא. אֲבָל הַשְׁתָּא אֲנִי אֲנִי הוּא וְאֵין אֱלֹהִים עִמָּדִי, דְּהָא כָּל סִטְרָא אַחֲרָא אִתְעֲבַר, וְדַיְיקָא אֲנִי אֲנִי.

270. "That I, even I, am He..." HE ASKS: Why is "I" written twice? ANSWER: It is to stress that there is no other Elohim but Him THERE. Sometimes where it writes "I" once and not more, there may be the Other Side, but now, "I, even I, am He, and there is no Elohim with Me," for the Other Side has vanished, stressing exclusively that 'I alone am HE'.

271. אֲנִי אָמִית וַאֲחַיֶּה, עַד הַשְׁתָּא מוֹתָא הֲוַת מִסִּטְרָא אַחֲרָא, מִכָּאן וּלְהָלְאָה, אֲנִי אָמִית וַאֲחַיֶּה, מִכָּאן דִּבְהַהוּא זִמְנָא, כָּל אִינּוּן דְּלָא טַעֲמֵי טַעֲמָא דְּמוֹתָא. מִנֵּיהּ תְּהֵא לוֹן מוֹתָא, וְיָקִים לוֹן מִיָּד. אֲמַאי. בְּגִין דְּלָא יִשְׁתְּאַר מֵהַהוּא זוּהֲמָא בְּעָלְמָא כְּלָל, וְיְהֵא עָלְמָא חַדְתָּא, בְּעוֹבְדֵי יְדוֹי דְּקוּדְשָׁא בְּרִיךְ הוּא.

271. "I cause death and bring life..." (Ibid.). Until this moment, death was brought about via the Other Side; from this time on, "I will cause death and give life," MEANING from that time on – MEANING AT TIME OF RESURRECTION – all those who did not experience the taste of death from Him, FROM THE HOLY ONE, BLESSED BE HE, will then experience death and rise immediately back TO LIFE. DEATH WILL BE BROUGHT ABOUT BY THE HOLY ONE, BLESSED BE HE, in order that none of that impurity in the world will remain. There shall be a new world brought about from the workings of the Holy One, blessed be He.

272. וְאִם אָמֹר יֹאמַר וְגוֹ' לֹא אֵצֵא חָפְשִׁי. כְּמָה דְּאִתְּמַר כְּדֵין פָּגִים לֵיהּ פְּגִימוּ. אִם בְּגַפּוֹ יָבֹא, מַהוּ בְּגַפּוֹ. תָּנֵינָן, כְּתַרְגוּמוֹ, בִּלְחוֹדוֹי. יָאוֹת הוּא. אֲבָל הָא תָּנֵינָן, כָּל עָלְמָא, לָא קַיְימִין, אֶלָּא עַל גַּפָּא חֲדָא, דִּלְוָיָתָן.

272. "And if the servant plainly said... I will not go out free" (Shemot 21:5). As we explained, then he is impaired with a blemish, MEANING, "HIS MASTER SHALL BORE HIS EAR WITH AN AWL." "If he came in by himself" (Ibid. 3). What is meant by "by himself"? We learned with the Aramaic translation that this "alone" is a fine translation. However, we did learn that

the world maintains itself with only one fin of the Leviathan.

273. וְרָזָא דָא, בְּשַׁעֲתָא דְּקַיְימָא דְּכַר וְנוּקְבָּא, דִּדְכַר וְנוּקְבָּא בְּרָא לוֹן קוּדְשָׁא בְּרִיךְ הוּא, וּבְכָל מַה דְּאַזְלִין, עָלְמָא מִזְדַּעְזַע, וְאִלְמָלֵא דְּסָרֵס קוּדְשָׁא בְּרִיךְ הוּא דְּכוּרָא, וְצַנֵּן יַת נוּקְבָּא, הֲווֹ מְטַשְׁטְשִׁין עָלְמָא. וְע"ד לָא עַבְדִין תּוֹלְדִין, אִם בְּגַפּוֹ יָבֹא, תְּחוֹת הַהוּא גַּפָּא, דְּלָא עָבֵיד תּוֹלְדִין עָאל. וְהוֹאִיל וְכֵן, בְּגַפּוֹ יֵצֵא, לְתַמָּן. אִתְדַּחְיָא, וְלָא עָאל לְפַרְגּוֹדָא כְּלָל, וְאִתְדַּחְיָא וְאִתְטְרִיד מֵהַהוּא עָלְמָא. בְּגַפּוֹ יֵצֵא, בְּגַפּוֹ יֵצֵא וַדַּאי.

273. This is its secret: where there was both male and female LEVIATHAN, as the Holy One, blessed be He, created them as male and female, wherever they went they caused the earth to tremble. Had not the Holy One, blessed be He, sterilized the male and cooled down the female, they would have disturbed the earth. As a result, they do not produce offspring. THIS IS THE ESSENCE OF: "If he came in by himself (Heb. *gapo*)" MEANING IF HE COMES under the wing (Heb. *gaf*) OF THE LEVIATHAN, that is, if he produces no offspring, "he shall go out by himself." He is thrust away there, and can not enter in the vicinity OF THE KING at all. He is thrust away and caused to be lost from that world. Thus, "he shall go out by himself," truly alone.

274. ת"ח, מַה כְּתִיב, עֲרִירִים יָמוּתוּ עֲרִירִים כְּלָל דְּכַר וְנוּקְבָּא. בְּרָזָא דִּדְכוּרָא עָאל, וּבְרָזָא דְּנוּקְבָּא יִפּוּק. עָאל בְּהַאי, וְיִפּוּק בְּהַאי. וְהַאי אִיהוּ אֲתָר, דְּקָא אִתְדַּבַּק בֵּיהּ בְּהַהוּא עָלְמָא, דְּהָא קוּדְשָׁא בְּרִיךְ הוּא לָא בָּעֵי דְּיֵיעוֹל קַמֵּיהּ, מַאן דִּמְסָרֵס גַּרְמֵיהּ בְּהַאי עָלְמָא.

274. Come and behold: it is written, "They will die childless" (Vayikra 20:20). The word "childless" comprises male and female. He arrives through the secret of the male, and departs by the secret of the female. He arrives with one and departs with the other. This is that place that he clings to in that world, MEANING IN MALCHUT. The Holy One, blessed be He, does not want anyone to come before Him who sterilized himself in this world.

275. תָּא חֲזֵי, מִן קָרְבְּנָא. דְּלָא הֲווֹ מְקָרְבִין קַמֵּיהּ סֵרוּסָא, וְאַפִּיקוּ לֵיהּ, דְּלָא יִתְקְרַב לְקַמֵּיהּ, וּפָקִיד וְאָמַר, וּבְאַרְצְכֶם לֹא תַעֲשׂוּ. וְכֵן לְדָרֵי דָּרִין אָסִיר לְסָרוּסֵי בִּרְיָין, דְּבָרָא קוּדְשָׁא בְּרִיךְ הוּא בְּעָלְמָא. דְּהָא כָּל סֵרוּסָא, דְּסִטְרָא אַחֲרָא אִיהוּ.

275. Come and behold: this is the example of the sacrifice. They did not offer before Him that which has been castrated. They would remove it so as not to offer it before Him. He commanded: "neither shall you do thus in your land" (Vayikra 22:24). And so unto all generations it is prohibited to emasculate any creature created by Hashem, as emasculation stems from the Other Side.

276. וְאִי אִיהוּ אִשְׁתָּדַּל, וְנָסִיב אִיתְּתָא, וְלָא עָבִיד תּוֹלְדִין, וְלָא בָּעָא, וְאע"ג דְּאִית לֵיהּ אִיתְּתָא, אוֹ אִי הִיא לָא בָּעָאת, וְעָאל לְהַהוּא עָלְמָא, בְּלָא תּוֹלְדִין, מַה כְּתִיב. אִם בַּעַל אִשָּׁה הוּא, וְלָא אַשְׁגָּחוּ לְפַעַל יְדוֹי דְּמָארֵיהוֹן, וְיָצְאָה אִשְׁתּוֹ עִמּוֹ, אִיהוּ יֵעוּל בְּגַפּוֹ דִּדְכוּרָא, וְאִיהִי בְּנוּקְבָא. בְּגַפּוֹ יָבֹא בְּגַפּוֹ יֵצֵא כְּמָה דְּאִתְּמַר, כֹּלָּא עַל תִּקּוּנֵיהּ.

276. If he endeavored and married and did not produce offspring, or he did not want to although married, or she did not want to produce offspring and later came to that world childless, we find the verse says: "if he is married," and he did not give proper attention to to the work of the Holy One, blessed be He, TO HAVE CHILDREN, "then his wife shall go out with him." He enters under the wing of the male and she under the wing of the female, DENOTING MALCHUT, AND EACH ONE OF THEM who "came in by himself... shall go out by himself (also: 'his wing')" as we explained. Everything fits in well.

277. אִם אֲדֹנָיו יִתֶּן לוֹ אִשָּׁה, כְּמָה דְּאִתְּמַר, אִם אֲדֹנָיו, דָּא אִיהוּ אָדוֹן כָּל הָאָרֶץ. יִתֶּן לוֹ אִשָּׁה, מֵהָכָא, דְּלָאו בִּרְשׁוּתָא דְּבַר נָשׁ קַיְּימָא לְמֵיסַב אִתְּתָא. אֶלָּא כֹּלָּא בְּמֹאזְנַיִם לַעֲלוֹת. יִתֶּן לוֹ אִשָּׁה, דְּהָא לָאו בִּרְשׁוּתֵיהּ אִיהוּ. וּמַאן אִיהוּ. הַהִיא דְּלָאו דִּילֵיהּ, וְלָא אִזְדַּמְּנַת לְגַבֵּיהּ, וּמַאן אִיהִי. הַהִיא דַּהֲוַת זְמִינָא לְאַחֲרָא, וְאַקְדִּים הַאי בְּרַחֲמֵי, וְנָטִיל לָהּ, דָּא אִתְיְיהִיבַת לֵיהּ, דְּלָא אִתְחֲזִיאַת לֵיהּ.

277. "If his master has given him a wife…" As we learned, "if his master," refers to the Master of the universe, NOTABLY MALCHUT, who "has given him a wife." We see here that man does not have the complete authority to marry a woman. All depends on the scale, MEANING ACCORDING TO THE MEASURE OF HIS MERITS, and so, He "has given him a wife," as this is not under his authority. Who is she? She is not his, NOT HIS MATE, and not set for him. Who is she? She is a WOMAN designated for someone else, but through mercy, he won her first and married her. This woman was given to him though she was not the proper one for him.

278. וְקוּדְשָׁא בְּרִיךְ הוּא חָמֵי מֵרָחִיק, וְחָמֵי לְהַהִיא אִתְּתָא, דִּזְמִינַת לְאַפָּקָא תּוֹלְדִין בְּעָלְמָא. אַקְדִּים הַאי בְּרַחֲמֵי, וְאִתְיְיהִיבַת לֵיהּ, וְעָבֵיד אִיבִין, וְזָרַע זַרְעָא, בְּאִתְּתָא דְּלָאו דִּילֵיהּ, בְּג"כ, הָאִשָּׁה וִילָדֶיהָ תִּהְיֶה לַאדֹנֶיהָ, וְהוּא יֵצֵא בְּגַפּוֹ. אִי עַנְיָיא מִסְכְּנָא, כַּמָּה אִשְׁתַּדַּל בְּרֵיקַנְיָא, לֵאָה וְאִשְׁתַּדַּל לְמֶעְבַּד פֵּירִין, בְּגִנְתָּא דְּלָאו אִיהִי דִּילֵיהּ, וְנָפַק בְּרֵיקַנְיָא.

278. The Holy One, blessed be He, sees this from afar, that this woman is poised to bring offspring into the world. AND AFTER this man initiated with pleas of mercy she was given to him; he thus had offspring and planted a seed with the woman that was not his. Therefore, "the wife and her children shall remain her master's and he shall go out by himself." See how a wretched poor man toiled for naught to bring forth fruit in a garden that was not his, and departed empty-handed.

279. סָבָא סָבָא, בְּעִדָּנִין אִלֵּין, לָא הֲוֵית בְּרַגְלָיךְ דָּחֵי לְתַרְעָא, כְּמַאן דְּשָׁכִיב בְּאַרְעָא בְּלָא תּוּקְפָּא, דְּהָא אִתְחֲלַשׁ וּמֵחַלְשָׁא סַגִּי, דְּלָא יָכִיל, דָּחֵי בְּרַגְלוֹי. אִתְתְּקַף סָבָא, וְלָא תִּדְחַל. הָא עַנְיָיא מִסְכְּנָא, דְּאִשְׁתַּדַּל בְּרֵיקַנְיָא, אֵימָא אֲמַאי. אִי בְּגִין דְּזָרַע בְּגִנְתָּא אַחֲרָא דְּלָאו דִּילֵיהּ, יָאוֹת. אֲבָל הָכָא קוּדְשָׁא בְּרִיךְ הוּא יָהִיב לֵיהּ הַהוּא גִּנְתָּא לְמִזְרַע בָּהּ, דְּהָא אִיהוּ לָא נָטִיל לָהּ.

279. HE SAYS TO HIMSELF: Old man, in a time such as this, you were not as one who pushes the gate open with his feet, as one who lies on the ground

without strength, and as a result of his weakness, he is unable to OPEN THE GATE so he pushes on it with his feet. Have courage, old man, do not fear. This poor unfortunate toiled for naught – why? Is it because he did not plant in a garden of his own? Then we could understand. But here, the Holy One, blessed be He, gave him this garden to plant; he did not take it ON HIS OWN INITIATIVE.

280. אֶלָּא ת"ח, כָּל מִלִּין דְּקוּדְשָׁא בְּרִיךְ הוּא עָבִיד, כֻּלְּהוּ בְּדִינָא אִינוּן, וְלָא הֲוָה מִלָּה בְּרֵיקַנְיָא. הַאי דְּקוּדְשָׁא בְּרִיךְ הוּא יָהַב לֵיהּ אִתְּתָא, וְעָבֵיד בָּהּ פֵּירִין וְאֵיבִין, לָאו הַאי כִּשְׁאָר בְּנֵי גִּלְגוּלָא, וְלָא דָּמֵי מַאן דְּאִשְׁתַּדַּל בְּהַאי עָלְמָא לְאַסְגָּאָה אִילָנָא, וְלָא יָכִיל לְמַאן דְּלָא בָּעָא לְאַסְגָּאָה לְאִשְׁתַּדְּלָא, וְאַעְקַר וְאֲפִיל טַרְפִּין דְּאִילָנָא, וְאַזְעַר אִיבָּא דִּילֵיהּ.

280. But, come and behold: all the things the Holy One, blessed be He, has done are according to the Law; there is nothing found wanting. If the Holy One, blessed be He, gave him a wife, and he produced fruits and plants, he is not like other incarnated ones. One who endeavors in this world to enlarge the tree but is unable is not the same as one who makes no effort to enlarge, but instead uproots, causes leaves to fall from the tree and diminishes its fruits.

281. הַאי דַּאֲדֹנָיו יָהִיב לֵיהּ אִתְּתָא, בְּגִין לְמֶעְבַּד אֵיבִין, הָא אִשְׁתַּדַּל בְּקַדְמֵיתָא בְּגִין לְאַסְגָּאָה אִילָנָא, וְלָא יָכִיל. זַכְיָין כָּל כַּךְ לֵית לֵיהּ, דְּאִי הֲוָה זַכָּאָה כַּדְקָא יֵאוֹת, לָא הֲוָה תָּב בְּגִלְגּוּלָא, דְּהָא כְּתִיב, וְנָתַתִּי לָכֶם בְּבֵיתִי וּבְחוֹמוֹתַי יָד וָשֵׁם טוֹב מִבָּנִים וּמִבָּנוֹת. וְהַשְׁתָּא דְּלָא זָכָה, קוּדְשָׁא בְּרִיךְ הוּא חָמֵי, דְּהָא אִשְׁתַּדַּל וְלָא יָכִיל, הַאי, אֲדֹנָיו יִתֶּן לוֹ אִשָּׁה, כְּמָה דְּאִתְּמַר. וְכֵיוָן דְּחָס עָלֵיהּ קוּדְשָׁא בְּרִיךְ הוּא, וְיָהַב לֵיהּ בְּרַחֲמֵי, קוּדְשָׁא בְּרִיךְ הוּא גַּבֵּי מִדִּידֵיהּ בְּקַדְמֵיתָא, וְנָטִיל מַה דְּגָרַע הַהוּא מַבּוּעָא, וּבג"כ, הָאִשָּׁה וִילָדֶיהָ תִּהְיֶה לַאדֹנֶיהָ, וּלְבָתַר יֵיתוּב, וְיִשְׁתַּדַּל עַל גַּרְמֵיהּ, לְאַשְׁלוּמֵי גִּרְעוֹנֵיהּ. עַד הָכָא רָזָא דִּקְרָא.

281. He whose Master gave him a wife to produce offspring, who strove before to enlarge the tree, but was unable, does not possess many merits.

Had he possessed the proper merits, he would not need to reincarnate, as it is written: "And to them will I give in my house and within My walls a memorial better than sons and daughters" (Yeshayah 56:5). But now that he does not merit, the Holy One, blessed be He, sees that he tried to have children and was unable. Then "his Master has given him a wife," as we learned, and as a result of the Holy One, blessed be He, showing mercy, that He gives him A WIFE out of mercy, He takes His own back, He takes what caused that well to diminish FROM BEFORE THIS. For this reason, "the wife and her children shall be her master's." Later, he must return and work on himself to compensate for his loss. Here ends the secret of the verse.

282. סָבָא סָבָא, אַתְּ אֲמַרְתְּ ע״ד, דִּבְרֵיקָנְיָא אִשְׁתָּדַּל, וְלָא אַשְׁגַּחַת עֲלָךְ, דִּבְרֵיקָנְיָא אַתְּ אָזִיל בְּמָה דַּאֲמַרְתְּ, דְּהָא קְרָא רָדִיף אֲבַתְרָךְ, דְּסָתִיר כָּל בִּנְיָינָא דְּבָנִית עַד הַשְׁתָּא, וְאַתְּ חָשִׁיב דְּאַנְתְּ מְשַׁטְטָא יַמָּא לִרְעוּתָךְ. וּמַאי אִיהוּ. דִּכְתִיב, וְאִם אָמֹר יֹאמַר הָעֶבֶד אָהַבְתִּי אֶת אֲדוֹנִי אֶת אִשְׁתִּי וְגוֹ'.

282. HE SAID TO HIMSELF: Old man, you are saying that he toiled in vain TO BEGET CHILDREN. But you really did not pay attention to yourself that you walk in vain, for in regard to what you said, there is a verse that contradicts your entire construction, and you thought that you were swimming in the sea to your heart's content. What is this VERSE? It is written, "If the servant plainly says, 'I love my master, my wife and children...'" (Shemot 21:5), WE SEE THAT HE AGAIN MERITS THEM, AND SO HE DID NOT TOIL IN VAIN.

283. אִי סָבָא סָבָא, לָאֵי חֵילָא, מַה תַּעֲבֵיד, חָשַׁבְתְּ דְּלָא לֶיהֱוֵי מַאן דִּרְדִיף אֲבַתְרָךְ, הָא הַאי קְרָא רָדִיף אֲבַתְרָךְ, וְנָפִיק מִבָּתַר כְּתָלָא, כְּאַיָּלָה בְּחַקְלָא, מְדַלֵּג דִּלּוּגִין אֲבַתְרָךְ, תְּלֵיסַר דִּילּוּגִין דָּלֵיג אֲבַתְרָךְ וְאַדְבִּיק לָךְ, מַה תַּעֲבִיד סָבָא. הַשְׁתָּא אִית לָךְ לְאִתְגַּבְּרָא בְּחֵילָךְ. דְּהָא גִיבָּר תַּקִּיף הֲוֵית עַד יוֹמָא. סָבָא סָבָא, הֲוֵי דָּכִיר יוֹמָא דְּתַלְגָּא, כַּד זַרְעָנָא פּוֹלִין, וַהֲווֹ כַּמָּה גּוּבְרִין בְּנֵי חֵילָא, לָקֳבְלָךְ, וְאַנְתְּ בִּלְחוֹדָךְ, נָצַחְתְּ תְּלֵיסַר גַּבְרִין תַּקִּיפִין, בְּנֵי חֵילָא, דְּכָל חַד מִנַּיְיהוּ קָטִיל אַרְיָא, עַד לָא יֵיכוּל.

283. Woe, old man, weary without strength, what shall you do? You thought that there was no one pursuing you, but there is a verse pursuing you, coming out from behind the wall like a doe in the field. THAT IS, THAT HE DID NOT REMEMBER BEFORE, BUT SUDDENLY REMEMBERED, as if His hopping after you with thirteen hops behind you, DENOTING THE THIRTEEN WORDS IN THE VERSE FROM, "IF THE SERVANT PLAINLY SAYS" UNTIL THE WORD "FREE" (WITH THE LAST WORD NOT INCLUDED). It did reach you. What should you do, old man? Now, strengthen yourself because you were a mighty person until now. Old man! Remember the snowy day we planted beans and there were mighty warriors against you, and you alone defeated thirteen warriors who had each slain a hungry lion.

284. אִי לְאִינוּן תְּלֵיסַר גּוּבְרִין נָצַחְתְּ, הָנֵי תְּלֵיסַר דְּלֵית בְּהוּ חֵילָא, אֶלָּא מִלִּין, עאכ״ו. אָמַר יֹאמַר כְּתִיב. אֶלָּא קוּדְשָׁא בְּרִיךְ הוּא אָרְחֵיהּ לְמֶעְבַּד דִּינָא לְכֹלָּא. כַּד מָטָא זִמְנָא דְּהַאי אִתְּתָא לְאַשְׁכְּחָא בַּר זוּגֵיהּ מַה עָבִיד קָטִיל לְדֵין, וְנָטִיל לָהּ הַהוּא בַּר זוּגָא, וְאִיהוּ נָפִיק מֵהַאי עָלְמָא בִּלְחוֹדוֹי יְחִידָאָה.

284. If these thirteen mighty ones have you defeated, then how much more so these thirteen WORDS IN THE VERSE, "IF THE SERVANT PLAINLY SAYS..." which have no more power than words. It is written, "He will surely say." The way of the Holy One, blessed be He, is to execute His Judgment with all. When the time arrives for that woman THAT THE SERVANT TOOK to find her real mate, what does THE HOLY ONE, BLESSED BE HE, do? He slays THE SERVANT THAT MARRIED HER, NOT BEING HER REAL MATE, and her real mate takes her, and THE SERVANT departs this world alone.

285. וְאִם אָמֹר יֹאמַר, הָא אוּקְמוּהָ חַבְרַיָּיא כְּפְשָׁטֵיהּ דִּקְרָא. וְאִם אָמַר, בְּשֵׁירוּתָא דְּשִׁית שְׁנִין, יֹאמַר, בְּסוֹפָא דְּשִׁית שְׁנִין, עַד לָא יֵעוּל שְׁבִיעָאָה, דְּהָא אִי אָמַר, כַּד אִיהוּ אֲפִילוּ בְּיוֹמָא חַד מִשְּׁבִיעָאָה, מִלּוֹי בְּטֵלִין. מ״ט. הָעֶבֶד כְּתִיב, בְּעוֹד דְּאִיהוּ עֶבֶד, בְּשַׁתָּא שְׁתִיתָאָה. אָמַר בְּשֵׁירוּתָא דְּשִׁית שְׁנִין, וְלָא אָמַר בְּסוֹפָא דְּשִׁית שְׁנִין, לָאו כְּלוּם הוּא, וּבְגִין כָּךְ, תְּרֵי זִמְנֵי אָמֹר יֹאמַר.

285. "And if the servant shall plainly say (lit. 'speaks, saying')" The friends have maintained according to the literal meaning of the verse: and if he speaks at the beginning of the sixth year, he will be saying at the end of the sixth year just before the entry of the seventh year. If he made this declaration even one day into the seventh year, his words would be void. What is the proof? It states "the servant," as long as he is a servant, meaning in the sixth year. If he spoke in the beginning of the sixth year and did not repeat at the end of the sixth year, it would be meaningless. For this reason, it writes twice, "speaks, saying."

286. וְהָכָא, בְּעוֹד דְּאִיהוּ בְּהַאי אִתְּתָא, אַסְגֵּי צְלוֹתִין וּבָעוּתִין בְּכָל יוֹמָא, לְגַבֵּי מַלְכָּא קַדִּישָׁא, כְּמָה דַּהֲוָה שֵׁירוּתָא בְּרַחֲמֵי, הָכִי הוּא סוֹפָא בְּרַחֲמֵי, וְדָא הוּא אָמֹר יֹאמַר. אֱמוֹר בְּקַדְמֵיתָא, כַּד אַקְדִּים בְּרַחֲמֵי. יֹאמַר בְּסוֹפָא וְיִתְקַבֵּל בְּרַחֲמֵי. וּמַה יֹאמַר. אָהַבְתִּי אֶת אֲדוֹנִי, דִּבְג"ד, וּבְסַגִּיאוּ דִּצְלוֹתִין, רָחִים לֵיהּ לְקוּדְשָׁא בְּרִיךְ הוּא. אַתְקִין עוֹבָדוֹי, וְאָמַר אָהַבְתִּי אֶת אֲדוֹנִי אֶת אִשְׁתִּי וְאֶת בָּנַי לֹא אֵצֵא חָפְשִׁי. וְקוּדְשָׁא בְּרִיךְ הוּא קַבִּיל לֵיהּ, בְּהַהוּא תְּיוּבְתָּא, וּבְאִינּוּן סַגִּיאוּ דִּצְלוֹתִין.

286. Here, CONTINUING WITH OUR SUBJECT, while the servant is still with his wife, he intensifies his prayer and requests daily before the Holy King. Just as he acquired her through mercy, so too the ending is with pleas for mercy. This is the essence of "speaks, saying." He speaks at the beginning to hasten the taking of her through mercy and later PLEADS THAT HE SHOULD NOT BE SHUNTED ASIDE BEFORE HER REAL MATE, AND THAT HIS PETITION be received with mercy. He says: "I love my master." Because of his numerous prayers, he is beloved by the Holy One, blessed be He. He amends his actions, saying, "I love my master, my wife and my children: I will not go out free." The Holy One, blessed be He, receives his penance and manifold prayers.

287. מַה עָבֵיד קוּדְשָׁא בְּרִיךְ הוּא, מַה דַּהֲוָה זַמִּין לְאַהֲדָרָא לֵיהּ בְּגִלְגּוּלָא, וּלְמִסְבַּל עוֹנָשִׁין בְּהַאי עָלְמָא, עַל מַה דְּעָבַד, לָא אַהֲדָר לֵיהּ לְהַאי עָלְמָא. וּמֶה עָבִיד, קָרִיב לֵיהּ לְבֵי דִּינָא דִּמְתִיבְתָּא דִּרְקִיעָא, וְדַיְינִין לֵיהּ, וּמַסְרִין לֵיהּ לְבֵי מַלְקִיּוּתָא, וְאַרְשִׁים לֵיהּ קוּדְשָׁא בְּרִיךְ

הוּא, הֵיךְ אִתְמְסַר לְבֵי עוֹנְשָׁא, וּפָגִים לֵיהּ, לְמֶהֱוֵי תְּחוֹת שָׁלְטָנֵיהּ
דְּעָרְלָה, עַד זְמַן יְדִיעָא, וּבָתַר פָּרִיק לֵיהּ.

287. What does the Holy One, blessed be He, do? Though he was prepared to reincarnate him and cause him to endure punishment in this world for his actions, He does not return him to this world. What does He do? He brings him near to the Heavenly Council, they judge him, submit him to the house of punishment, and the Holy One, blessed be He, brands him WITH THE AWL. He is handed over to punishment house to remain under the dominion of the uncircumcised until a specific time, and then He redeems him.

288. אִי בְּהַהוּא זִמְנָא דְּקָא עַבְדִין לֵיהּ פְּגִימוּ, אִי מָטָא יוֹבְלָא, אֲפִילוּ
יוֹמָא חַד לְיוֹבְלָא, אִתְחֲשַׁב כְּמָה דְּאַשְׁכַּח זִמְנָא עַד יוֹבְלָא, הָכִי
אִתְעֲנַשׁ וְלָא יַתִּיר. אָתָא יוֹבְלָא, וְאַפְרוּק, וְעָאלִין לֵיהּ גּוֹ פַּרְגּוֹדָא. עַד
הָכָא. אַסְתִּים עֵינוֹי הַהוּא סָבָא, רִגְעָא חֲדָא.

288. If at that time when he is being marked WITH THE AWL the Jubilee has arrived, and even if it is one day until Jubilee it is thus considered as if he spent the full time until Jubilee. This is the penalty and no more. With the arrival of Jubilee he is redeemed and brought into the presence OF THE HOLY ONE, BLESSED BE HE. The old man closed his eye for one moment.

A Synopsis
The merchant now begins a long section to do with strength, speaking about strong mountains, about the strong foundations of the earth, about King Solomon and about the mighty patriarchs. This leads to the issue of the birthright that Jacob took from Esau, and Jacob's strength over his brother. The serpent was able to seduce Adam because Adam lacked strength and might; that quality first appeared in Seth. Jacob's strength already existed in the form of Joseph.

289. פָּתַח וְאָמַר, שִׁמְעוּ הָרִים אֶת רִיב יְיָ' וְהָאֵיתָנִים מוֹסְדֵי אָרֶץ כִּי
רִיב לַייָ' עִם עַמּוֹ וְגוֹ'. אִי סָבָא, עַד הַשְׁתָּא הֲוֵית בְּעִמְקֵי יַמָּא, וְהַשְׁתָּא
דְּלָגַת בְּטוּרִין תַּקִּיפִין, לְמֶעְבַּד עִמְּהוֹן קְרָבָא. אֶלָּא וַדַּאי עַד כְּעַן,
בְּיַמָּא תַּקִּיפָא אַנְתְּ, אֲבָל עַד דְּאַזְלַת בְּעִמְקֵי יַמָּא, פָּגַעַת בְּאִינּוּן טוּרִין

תַּקִּיפִין, דִּי בְּגוֹ יַמָּא, וְאַעֲרָעַת בְּהוּ. הַשְׁתָּא אִית לָךְ לְאַגָּחָא קְרָבָא
בְּעִמְקֵי יַמָּא, וּבְהַנְהוּ טוּרִין.

289. He began and said, "Hear, O mountains, Hashem's controversy, and
you, strong foundations of the earth: for Hashem has controversy with His
people" (Michah 6:2). HE THEN SAID TO HIMSELF: Old man, until now you
were in the depths of the sea, and now you have skipped over the powerful
mountains to wage war with them. Until now, surely, you were in the strong
sea, but prior to coming into the deep sea, you met these powerful
mountains that are located in the midst of the sea. Now you need to wage
war against the depths of the sea and these mountains.

290. סָבָא לָאֵי חֵילָא, מַאן יָהֲבָךְ בְּדָא, הֲוֵית בִּשְׁלָם, וּבָעִית לְכָל הַאי,
אַנְתְּ עֲבַדְתְּ, אַנְתְּ סָבִיל. הַשְׁתָּא לֵית לָךְ, אֶלָּא לְאַגָּחָא קְרָבָא, וּלְנַצְחָא
כֹּלָּא, וְלָא לְמֶהֱדַר לַאֲחוֹרָא. אִתְקַּף בְּחֵילָךְ, חֲגוֹר חַרְצָךְ, וְלָא תִדְחַל,
לְתַבְרָא הָנֵי טוּרִין, דְּלָא יִתְתַּקְּפוּן לְגַבָּךְ. אֵימָא לוֹן, טוּרִין רָמָאִין,
טוּרִין תַּקִּיפִין, הֵיךְ אַתּוּן מִתְתַּקְּפִין.

290. Weary old man without strength, who put you into this. You were in a
state of peace, but you wanted this; you caused this, you are going to suffer.
Now there is no other way for you but to wage war and conquer everything,
and not turn back. Be strong, gird your loins, and do not fear to smash these
mountains so they do not overpower you. Say to them: high mountains,
mighty peaks, how strong you became.

291. תְּרֵי קְרָאֵי כְּתִיבֵי, חַד כְּתִיב, קוּם רִיב אֶת הֶהָרִים וְתִשְׁמַעְנָה
הַגְּבָעוֹת קוֹלֶךָ. וְחַד כְּתִיב, שִׁמְעוּ הָרִים אֶת רִיב יְיָ'. אֶלָּא אִית טוּרִין,
וְאִית טוּרִין. אִית טוּרִין, דְּאִינּוּן טוּרִין רָמָאִין לְעֵילָא לְעֵילָא, לְאִלֵּין
כְּתִיב, שִׁמְעוּ הָרִים אֶת רִיב יְיָ'. וְאִית הָרִים, דְּאִינּוּן טוּרִין תַּתָּאִין
לְתַתָּא מִנַּיְיהוּ, לְאִלֵּין כְּתִיב, קוּם רִיב אֶת הֶהָרִים. דְּהָא רָדִיף מָצוּתִין,
אִית לְגַבַּיְיהוּ. וְעַל דָּא אִית טוּרִין וְאִית טוּרִין.

291. Two verses are written. One writes, "Arise, contend before the
mountains, and let the hills hear your voice" (Ibid. 1). Another writes,

"Hear, O mountains, Hashem's controversy." There are mountains, and there are other mountains. There are mountains, very lofty, DENOTING CHESED, GVURAH AND TIFERET. About these, it is written, "Hear O mountains, Hashem's controversy." There are other mountains whose heights are somewhat lower, DENOTING NETZACH, HOD AND YESOD. Regarding these, it is written, "Arise, contend before the mountains," because the pursuer of quarrels is upon them, MEANING, THERE ARE JUDGMENTS IN THEM. Hence, there are different mountains.

292. וְאִי תֵּימָא, סָבָא, הָא כְּתִיב וְתִשְׁמַעְנָה הַגְּבָעוֹת, אִלֵּין גְּבָעוֹת כָּל אִנּוּן דִּלְתַתָּא, וְהַשְׁתָּא אַנְתְּ עָבִיד לוֹן הָרִים. אֶלָּא הָכִי הוּא, לְגַבֵּי אִנּוּן טוּרִין רָמָאִין, אִקְרוּן גְּבָעוֹת. כַּד אִנּוּן בִּלְחוֹדַיְיהוּ אִנּוּן הָרִים אִקְרוּן.

292. You may say that yet it writes, "let the hills hear your voice." These hills are below and you make mountains of them. HE ANSWERS: It is so. When compared to the lofty mountains, these are called hills, but by themselves, they are called mountains.

293. תָּא חֲזֵי, כְּתִיב וְהָאֵיתָנִים מוֹסְדֵי אָרֶץ, כֵּיוָן דִּכְתִּיב שִׁמְעוּ הָרִים, מַאן אִנּוּן הָרִים, וּמַאן אִנּוּן אֵיתָנִים. אֶלָּא, הָרִים, וְאֵיתָנִים כֻּלְּהוּ חַד. אֲבָל אִנּוּן תְּלַת עִלָּאִין לְעֵילָא עַל רֵישַׁיְיהוּ. וְאִנּוּן תְּלַת לְתַתָּא מִנַּיְיהוּ. וְכֻלְּהוּ חַד. הָרִים לְעֵילָא, וְעָלַיְיהוּ אָמַר דָּוִד אֶשָּׂא עֵינַי אֶל הֶהָרִים. וְאִלֵּין אִנּוּן תְּלַת קַדְמָאֵי. וְהָאֵיתָנִים מוֹסְדֵי אָרֶץ, אִלֵּין אִנּוּן תְּלַת בַּתְרָאֵי, לְתַתָּא מִנַּיְיהוּ, תְּרֵי סַמְכֵי בֵּיתָא, וְחַד חֶדְוָה דְּבֵיתָא, וְאִלֵּין אִקְרוּן מוֹסְדֵי אָרֶץ. אֵיתָנִים אִנּוּן, וְאֵיתָנִים אִקְרוּן.

293. Come and behold: it is written, "and you strong foundations of the earth." HE ASKS: If it wrote, "Hear, O mountains," who then are these strong ones? HE ANSWERS: Mountains and strong ones are really the same. However, mountains are the three upper ones overtop OF THE STRONG ONES, DENOTING CHESED, GVURAH AND TIFERET. The STRONG ONES are three lower ones, NAMELY NETZACH, HOD AND YESOD. It is all one. Concerning the upper mountains, David said: "I lift my eyes to the mountains" (Tehilim 121:1). These refer to the three primary ones, NAMELY CHESED, GVURAH AND TIFERET; "strong foundations of the earth," refer

to the three secondary ones below the primary, WHICH ARE the supports of the Temple, NAMELY NETZACH AND HOD, and one is the joy of the Temple, NAMELY YESOD. These are called 'the foundations of the land'; they are strong and are called 'strong'.

294. סָבָא סָבָא, הָא יָדַעְתְּ, מַאן דְּאַגָּח קְרָבָא, אִי לָא יָדַע לְאִסְתַּמְּרָא, לָא יְנַצַּח קְרָבִין, אִצְטְרִיךְ לְמָחָאָה בִּידֵיהּ, וּלְאִסְתַּמְּרָא בְּרַעְיוֹנֵיהּ, מַה דִּיהֵא חָשִׁיב אַחֲרָא, דִּיהֵא חָשִׁיב אִיהוּ, וְיַד יְמִינָא זְמִינָא תָּדִיר לְמָחָאָה. וּמַחֲשָׁבוֹי וִידָא שְׂמָאלִית, זְמִינָא תָּדִיר לְקַבְּלָא וּלְאִסְתַּמְּרָא, וִימִינָא כֹּלָא.

294. HE SAID TO HIMSELF: Old man, you are aware that he who wages war, if he is not on guard, can not win wars. He needs to strike with his hand, and be on guard in his thoughts. Whatever the other plans, he must anticipate AND BE ON GUARD. The right hand is designated at all times to strike, and his left hand and his thoughts to receive and be on guard – THE THOUGHTS TO BE ON GUARD, THE LEFT HAND TO RECEIVE BLOWS FROM THE ADVERSARY. The right serves in any THING.

295. הַשְׁתָּא אָמַרְתְּ וְהָאֵיתָנִים, אֵיתָנִים אִינּוּן לְתַתָּא, וְהָרִים לְעֵילָּא. אִסְתַּמַּר סָבָא, דְּהָא רַעְיוֹנָא אַחֲרָא לָקֳבְלָךְ, דִּכְתִּיב מַשְׂכִּיל לְאֵיתָן הָאֶזְרָחִי. וְדָא אִיהוּ אַבְרָהָם סָבָא, וְאִקְרֵי אֵיתָן, וְאִי אַבְרָהָם אִיהוּ אֵיתָן, יִצְחָק וְיַעֲקֹב אֵיתָנִים אִקְרוּן. קוּם סָבָא, דְּהָא יָדַעְתְּ רַעְיוֹנָא דָא הֲוֵי מָחֵי לְרַעְיוֹנָךְ.

295. Now you speak of the strong ones. The strong ones (Heb. eitanim) are below, DENOTING NETZACH, HOD, AND YESOD, and mountains above DENOTE CHESED, GVURAH, AND TIFERET. Be on guard, old man, as there is another thought that conflicts with yours, as written, "A maskil of Eitan the Ezrachite" (Tehilim 89:1), referring to old Abraham, called Eitan. So if Abraham is known as 'Eitan' then Isaac and Jacob must be referred to as eitanim (lit. 'strong ones') AND WE KNOW THAT THE FATHERS DENOTE CHESED, GVURAH, AND TIFERET, FOR CHESED, GVURAH AND TIFERET ARE REFERRED TO AS 'STRONG'. Rise, old man, as you see that this thought conflicts with your thought.

296. וְיִשָּׂא מְשָׁלוֹ וַיֹּאמַר אֵיתָן מוֹשָׁבֶךָ וְשִׂים בַּסֶּלַע קִנֶּךָ. אֵיתָן: דָּא בֹּקֶר דְּאַבְרָהָם. וְהַיְינוּ, הַבֹּקֶר אוֹר. דָּא עַמּוּדָא, דְּכָל עָלְמָא קַיְימָא עֲלֵיהּ, וּנְהִירוּ דִּילֵיהּ מֵאַבְרָהָם יָרִית. נָהָר הַיּוֹצֵא מֵעֵדֶן אִקְרֵי. אִי סָבָא סָבָא, הָא רַעְיוֹנָא אַחֲרָא לְקָבְלָךְ, וְלָא יָדַעְתְּ לְאִסְתַּמְּרָא, הֵיכִי מַגִּיחִין קְרָבָא. סָבָא, אָן הוּא תּוּקְפָּא דִּילָךְ, וַדַּאי לֹא לַגִּבּוֹרִים הַמִּלְחָמָה.

296. "...and took up his discourse, and said, 'Strong is your dwelling place...'" (Bemidbar 24:21) '*Eitan*' refers to the morning of Abraham, as written "As soon as the morning was light" (Beresheet 44:3). This refers to the pillar, DENOTING YESOD, that the entire earth, DENOTING MALCHUT, leans upon. Its light is received from Abraham, DENOTING CHESED. The river exiting Eden is so called, DENOTING YESOD, AND SO YESOD IS REFERRED TO AS '*EITAN*'. HE SAID TO HIMSELF: Old man, one thought is in opposition to you, and you are unable to be on your guard. How can one wage war, old man, where is your strength? Surely "nor the battle to the strong" (Kohelet 9:11).

297. כְּתִיב מַשְׂכִּיל לְאֵיתָן הָאֶזְרָחִי, וּכְתִיב מַשְׂכִּיל לְדָוִד, דָּא נָהָר הַיּוֹצֵא מֵעֵדֶן, דְּאִיהוּ תּוּרְגְּמָן לְדָוִד, לְאוֹדְעָא לֵיהּ, מֵאִינּוּן מִלִּין סְתִימִין עִלָּאִין. אִי מַשְׂכִּיל אִיהוּ נָהָר דְּנָפִיק מֵעֵדֶן. אֵיתָן הָאֶזְרָחִי אַבְרָהָם, אִיהוּ לְעֵילָּא וַדַּאי, הָא יְדַעְנָא. וְאע״ג דַּאֲנָא סָבָא, עַל רַעְיוֹנָא דָּא מָחֵינָא. אֵיתָן הָאֶזְרָחִי, תְּרֵין דַּרְגִּין אִינּוּן. כד״א, בֹּקֶר אוֹר. אוֹר, הוּא אַבְרָהָם. בֹּקֶר הוּא נָהָר. אוּף הָכִי, אֵיתָן הָאֶזְרָחִי, אֶזְרָח, הוּא אַבְרָהָם. אֵיתָן, כְּמָה דְאִתְּמַר, דָּא הַהוּא נָהָר דְּנָגֵיד וְנָפִיק מֵעֵדֶן.

297. It is written "A *maskil* of Eitan the Ezrachite," and there is a verse, "A *maskil* of David," denoting the river that flows from Eden, ALLUDING TO YESOD, that clarifies David, REPRESENTING MALCHUT, to inform him of these concealed heavenly matters, AND SO YESOD BECOMES REFERRED TO AS '*MASKIL*' (ENG. 'ERUDITE'). Now if *maskil* alludes to the river flowing from Eden, MEANING YESOD THAT IS BELOW, IN NETZACH, HOD, AND YESOD, then Eitan the Ezrachite ALLUDES TO Abraham, whom I know to be above, WITH CHESED, GVURAH AND TIFERET. And though I am an old man, I overcome this thought. BUT Eitan the Ezrachite points to

two grades, as the verse says: "As soon as the morning was light." "Light" denotes Abraham, WHO IS CHESED; "morning" is the river, WHICH IS YESOD. So in relation to Eitan the Ezrachite, 'Ezrachite' alludes to Abraham and 'Eitan' is, as we said, that river flowing from Eden, NAMELY YESOD.

298. הַשְׁתָּא סָבָא, קוּם קָאֵים עַל רְתִיכָךְ, דְּהַשְׁתָּא תִּנְפּוֹל וְלָא תִיכוּל לְמֵיקָם. הָא שְׁלֹמֹה מַלְכָּא, אָתֵי בְּחֵילוֹי וּרְתִיכוֹי וְגִבְרוֹי וּפָרָשׁוֹי, וְאָתֵי לְקַבְלָךְ, קוּם פּוּק מִן חַקְלָא, דְּלָא יִשְׁכַּח לָךְ תַּמָּן. כְּתִיב וַיִּקָּהֲלוּ אֶל הַמֶּלֶךְ שְׁלֹמֹה כָּל אִישׁ יִשְׂרָאֵל בְּיֶרַח הָאֵיתָנִים בֶּחָג וְגוֹ'. יֶרַח דְּאִתְיְלִידוּ בֵּיהּ הָאֵיתָנִים, וּמַאן אִינּוּן. אֲבָהָן, וְאִינּוּן אֵיתָנֵי עוֹלָם. וַיֶּרַח דָּא, אִיהוּ תִּשְׁרֵי. דְּאַלְפָּא בֵּיתָא אַהֲדַר לְמִפְרַע מִתַּתָּא לְעֵילָא.

298. Now, old man, stand upon your chariot, as you will now fall and will not be able to rise. Behold King Solomon. He came with his hosts, chariots, warriors, and cavaliers and they come towards you. Rise, and leave the field so they will not find you there. It is written, "And all the men of Yisrael assembled themselves to king Solomon at the feast in the month of *etanim*" (I Melachim 8:2). THIS MEANS the month that the *eitanim* (lit. 'strong ones') were born. Who are these? They are the Fathers, who are the mighty ones of the earth. This month is *Tishrei*, in which the alphabet is in reverse order, from below upwards, MEANING PROCEEDING FROM TAV TO SHIN-RESH-KOF. SO ALSO THE LETTERS OF TISHREI REPRESENT THE LETTERS GOING BACKWARD, FOR THE EITANIM ARE THE FATHERS, WHO ARE CHESED, GVURAH, AND TIFERET.

299. וְתוּ מִמִּילָךְ, יֵאוֹת דְּתִפּוֹק מִן חַקְלָא, וְלָא תִּשְׁתְּכַח תַּמָּן. אִילוּ כְּתִיב מַשְׂכִּיל אֵיתָן הָאֶזְרָחִי כִּדְקָאָמַרְתְּ. הַשְׁתָּא דִּכְתִיב מַשְׂכִּיל לְאֵיתָן הָאֶזְרָחִי. לֵית קָרְבָּךְ כְּלוּם, וְתִפּוֹק מִן חַקְלָא, בְּעַל כָּרְחָךְ וְלָא תִּתְחֲזֵי תַּמָּן.

299. Furthermore, from your OWN words, SAYING THAT EITAN THE EZRACHITE REPRESENTS TWO LEVELS, you had better leave the field and not be found, for had the verse said, "A *maskil* Eitan the Ezrachite," then

things would be FINE, since as you maintained, IT REPRESENTS TWO
LEVELS. But now that it writes, 'A *maskil* of Eitan the Ezrachite,' your
fight is meaningless, BECAUSE NOW IT APPEARS THAT IT IS ONE LEVEL,
NOT TWO. Depart the field unwillingly, and do not be seen.

300. אִי סָבָא עַנְיָא מִסְכְּנָא, הֵיכִי תִּפּוֹק. אִי הָכִי, יִנְצְחוּן לָךְ וְתִעֲרוֹק
מִן חַקְלָא, כָּל בְּנֵי עָלְמָא יִרְדְּפוּן אֲבַתְרָךְ, וְלֵית לָךְ אַנְפִּין לְאִתְחֲזָאָה
קַמֵּי בַּר נָשׁ לְעָלְמִין. הָכָא אוֹמֵינָא, דְּלָא אֶפּוֹק מִן חַקְלָא, וְהָכָא
אִתְחֲזֵי אַנְפִּין בְּאַנְפִּין בִּשְׁלֹמֹה מַלְכָּא, וְכָל אִישׁ יִשְׂרָאֵל, וְגוּבְרִין
וּפָרָשִׁין וּרְתִיכִין דִּילֵיהּ. קוּדְשָׁא בְּרִיךְ הוּא יְסַיֵּיעַ לָךְ סָבָא, דְּהָא לָאֵי
חֵילָא אַנְתְּ. קוּם סָבָא אִתְגַּבָּר בְּחֵילָךְ וְאִתְתַּקַּף, דְּעַד יוֹמָא דָּא הֲוֵית
גִּיבָּר תַּקִּיף בְּגוּבְרִין.

300. O poor unfortunate old man, how are you going to leave THE FIELD? If
you do, they will be victorious over you and you will have fled the field.
Everybody will chase you and you will never have courage to see anyone.
No, now I swear that I will not leave the field, I will see King Solomon face
to face, and any man of Yisrael with the warriors, cavaliers, and chariots.
The Holy One, blessed be He, will help you, old man, as you are weary and
without strength. Arise, old man, have courage, for until now you were a
mighty force.

301. פָּתַח וְאָמַר, מַשְׂכִּיל לְאֵיתָן הָאֶזְרָחִי. אֵלּוּ כְּתִיב מַשְׂכִּיל לְדָוִד,
כִּדְקָאָמַרְתְּ, אֲבָל מַשְׂכִּיל לְאֵיתָן, אִית מַשְׂכִּיל וְאִית מַשְׂכִּיל. אִית
מַשְׂכִּיל לְעֵילָא, וְאִית מַשְׂכִּיל לְתַתָּא. מַשְׂכִּיל לְאֵיתָן בְּזִמְנָא דְּהַהוּא
נָהָר, קָם בְּתִאוּבְתָּא כָּל שַׁיְּיפִין חַדָּאן וּמִתְחַבְּרָן לְגַבֵּיהּ, וְאִי הוּא סָלִיק,
עַד דְּמוֹחָא עִלָּאָה אִתְפַּיַּיס לְגַבֵּיהּ, וְחַדֵּי לְקַבְּלֵיהּ. וּכְדֵין מַשְׂכִּיל לְאֵיתָן
הָאֶזְרָחִי, מַשְׂכִּיל לֵיהּ, וְאוֹדַע לֵיהּ עַל יְדָא דְּאַבְרָהָם רְחִימוֹי, כָּל מַה
דְּאִצְטְרִיךְ, וְהַהוּא מוֹחָא עִלָּאָה מַשְׂכִּיל לְאֵיתָן. וְכַד דָּוִד מַלְכָּא,
אִתְתַּקַּן בְּתִיאוּבְתָּא לְגַבֵּיהּ, אִיהוּ מַשְׂכִּיל לְדָוִד. כְּמָה דַּהֲוָה מוֹחָא
עִלָּאָה, מַשְׂכִּיל לֵיהּ. וְעַל דָּא, אִית מַשְׂכִּיל, וְאִית מַשְׂכִּיל.

301. He commenced: it is written, "A *maskil* of Eitan the Ezrachite." Had it

been written 'A *maskil* of David', the explanation would have been as you said, REFLECTING YESOD THAT OFFERS BOUNTY TO MALCHUT, CALLED 'DAVID'. But IT IS WRITTEN "A *maskil* of Eitan." HE ANSWERS: There is *maskil* and there is *maskil*, a *maskil* on high and one below. *Maskil* of Eitan is to tell us when that river, YESOD, rises with yearning, all limbs rejoice and join with him. If it rises to the point that that supernal mind, CHESED BECOMING CHOCHMAH, is favored to him and rejoices in him, then you have a *maskil* of Eitan the Ezrachite. For it instructs (Heb. *maskil*) Eitan the Ezrachite, instructing YESOD, and informs him through Abraham his beloved, REPRESENTING CHESED THAT ROSE TO BECOME CHOCHMAH, with all that is necessary. That supernal mind, BEING CHOCHMAH, is *maskil* of Eitan, DENOTING YESOD. When king David, DENOTING MALCHUT, is established with yearning TO YESOD, YESOD informs (*maskil*) David, just as the supernal mind *maskil* TO YESOD. So there is *maskil* and *maskil*.

302. בְּיֶרַח הָאֵיתָנִים, דְּאִתְיְלִידוּ בְּהָא יֶרַח אֵיתָנִים, בִּנְיָנָא לְתַתָּא אִיהוּ כְּגַוְונָא דִלְעֵילָא, וְאִתְיְלִידוּ בֵּיהּ הָרִים וְאֵיתָנִים. הָרִים סְתִימִין. אֵיתָנִים: יַרְכִין תַּקִּיפִין כִּנְחָשָׁא, וְהַהוּא אֵיתָן בֵּינַיְיהוּ.

302. "…the month of *etanim*…" For in this month were born the *eitanim* (lit. 'strong ones'). The edifice below, NETZACH, HOD, AND YESOD, is similar to that above, CHESED, GVURAH, AND TIFERET, and so were four mountains and strong ones born in it. The mountains, BEING CHESED, GVURAH, AND TIFERET, are concealed, AS CHOCHMAH IS CONCEALED AND DOES NOT ILLUMINATE. The strong ones, the thighs, NETZACH AND HOD, are strong as copper; *eitan* (lit. 'strong', sing) is between them, DENOTING YESOD THAT AFFECTS THE ILLUMINATION OF CHOCHMAH.

303. קוּם סָבָא, הֲוֵי מָחֵי לְכָל סִטְרִין, בְּשַׁעֲתָא דְּסָלִיק מֹשֶׁה לְקַבְּלָא אוֹרַיְיתָא, מָסַר לֵיהּ קוּדְשָׁא בְּרִיךְ הוּא שַׁבְעִין מַפְתְּחָן דְּאוֹרַיְיתָא. כַּד מָטָא לְתִשְׁעָה וְחַמְשִׁין, הֲוָה חַד מַפְתְּחָא גָּנִיז וְסָתִים, דְּלָא הֲוָה מָסַר לֵיהּ, אִתְחֲנָן לְקַמֵּיהּ. אָמַר לֵיהּ, מֹשֶׁה, כָּל מַפְתְּחָן עִלָּאִין וְתַתָּאִין בְּהַאי מַפְתְּחָא תַּלְיָין. אָמַר לְקַמֵּיהּ, מָארֵיהּ דְּעָלְמָא, מַה שְׁמֵיהּ. אָמַר לֵיהּ אֵיתָן. וְכָל אִינּוּן אֵיתָנִים בֵּיהּ תַּלְיָין, וּבֵיהּ קַיְימָן לְבַר מִגּוּפָא

דְּתוֹרָה שֶׁבִּכְתָב אִיהוּ. אוֹדַע לֵיהּ, וּמַשְׂכִּיל לֵיהּ, אִיהוּ עָקָרָא וּמַפְתְּחָא דְּתוֹרָה שֶׁבִּכְתָב.

303. Rise, old man, strike out on all sides. At the time Moses ascended to receive Torah, the Holy One, blessed be He, handed him seventy keys of the Torah, NAMELY SEVEN SFIROT: CHESED, GVURAH, TIFERET, NETZACH, HOD, YESOD, AND MALCHUT, EACH POSSESSED ITS OWN TEN SFIROT, TOTALING SEVENTY. When he reached 59, MEANING YESOD WITHIN THE TEN SFIROT OF THE OVERALL YESOD, there was one hidden, concealed key, NAMELY MALCHUT WITHIN THE TEN SFIROT OF THE OVERALL YESOD, KNOWN AS THE DIADEM OF YESOD, that was not handed to him. It pleaded before him, saying, 'Moses, all the upper and lower keys are dependent upon this key'. Moses said, 'Master of the World, what is its name?' He replied, 'Eitan and all other *Eitanim* are dependent upon it.' Within it are maintained NETZACH, HOD, AND YESOD, which are outside of the body of the written Torah, WHICH IS ZEIR ANPIN, It, ZEIR ANPIN, informs it, MEANING, FLOWING WITH KNOWLEDGE, and instructs it. And it, THE DIADEM OF YESOD, is the principal and the key of the written Torah, ZEIR ANPIN.

304. וְכַד אִתְתַּקְנַת תּוֹרָה שֶׁבְּעַל פֶּה לְגַבֵּיהּ, הוּא מַפְתְּחָא דִּילָהּ, וַדַּאי כְּדֵין מַשְׂכִּיל לְדָוִד. וּמִגּוֹ דְּיָרְתָא תּוֹרָה שֶׁבְּעַל פֶּה, אַתְוָון לְמַפְרֵעַ. עַל דָּא אִקְרֵי תִּשְׁרֵ"י תש"ר אִיהוּ, אֲבָל בְּגִין דְּאִיהוּ רָזָא דִּשְׁמָא קַדִּישָׁא חָתִים בֵּיהּ קוּדְשָׁא בְּרִיךְ הוּא, אָת דִּשְׁמֵיהּ י'. בַּמִּזְבֵּחַ, חָתִים בֵּיהּ ה' הָרֶשֶׁת עַד חָצֵי הַמִּזְבֵּחַ. אָתַת דִּבוֹרָה, וְחָתִים בֵּיהּ ו', וְהַיְינוּ דִּכְתִיב וַתָּשַׁר דְּבוֹרָה. וּבַאֲתַר דָּא, חָתִימוּ דִּשְׁמָא קַדִּישָׁא, דְּאַחְתִּים בֵּיהּ.

304. And when Oral Torah, WHICH IS MALCHUT, affixes itself to it, then, it, THE DIADEM OF YESOD, becomes its key, MEANING OF YESOD OF MALCHUT, then surely YESOD is referred to as 'A *maskil* of David', WHO IS MALCHUT. And due to the fact that the Oral Torah inherits it, AND IT BECOMES ITS YESOD, CALLED '*RESH-SHIN-TAV*', THAT ILLUMINATES FROM DOWN UPWARDS. SO IN IT, the letters are in reverse order, and as a result, ITS YESOD IS CALLED '*Tishrei*', IN WHICH THE LETTERS ARE IN REVERSE ORDER, THAT IS, *TAV-SHIN-RESH-KOF*. The letters are *Tav-Shin-Resh*, but being the secret of the Holy Name, NAMELY MALCHUT,

the Holy One, blessed be He, imprinted a letter of His name, *Yud*, THUS CALLED '*TISHREI*' (*TAV-SHIN-RESH-YUD*). Upon the altar, ALSO A NAME OF MALCHUT, He added IN ITS YESOD the letter *Hei* OF YUD HEI VAV HEI, such as the *Hei* of: "that the net (Heb. *hareshet* – Hei-Resh-Shin-Tav) may reach the midst of the altar" (Shemot 27:5). Deborah came, ALSO BEING A NAME OF MALCHUT, AND He placed in her *Vav*, as it is written, "Then sang (Heb. *vatashar* – Vav-Tav-Shin-Resh) Deborah." And in this place, YESOD OF MALCHUT, the seal of the Holy Name is imprinted upon it.

305. וְהַהוּא מַפְתְּחָא, כַּד פְּתִחָא בַּתּוֹרָה שֶׁבְּעַל פֶּה, בָּעֵינָן לְאִשְׁתְּמוֹדְעָא לֵיהּ, וְדָא אִיהוּ תַּנְיָא, אֵיתָן מוֹשָׁבֶךְ, בָּרַיְיתָא לְבַר מִגּוּפָא. אֵיתָנִים: אִינּוּן תַּנָּאִים. עַמּוּדִים סַמְכִין, לְבַר מִגּוּפָא. הַשָּׁתָּא אִית לְאוֹדְעָא מִלָּה, בְּזִמְנָא דְּאִלֵּין לְגַבֵּי תּוֹרָה שֶׁבִּכְתָב, אִקְרוּן אֵיתָנִים. לְגַבֵּי תּוֹרָה שֶׁבְּעַל פֶּה, אִקְרוּן תַּנָּאִים. אֵיתָן, לְגַבֵּי תּוֹרָה שֶׁבִּכְתָב. תַּנְיָא, לְגַבֵּי תּוֹרָה שֶׁבְּעַל פֶּה. וְכֹלָּא כַּדְקָא יָאוּת.

305. When that key, THE DIADEM OF YESOD, opens the Oral Torah, MEANING WHEN IT IS AFFIXED TO ITS YESOD, it is necessary to understand it. This is the meaning of *Tanya* (lit. 'it has been taught in the *Baraita*') CONSISTING OF THE LETTERS IN *EITAN*, AND THEN APPLIES, "Strong (Heb. *eitan*) is your dwelling place" (Bemidbar 24:21), AS MALCHUT IS CALLED 'DWELLING PLACE'. WHEN IT RECEIVES FROM THE DIADEM OF YESOD, IT IS MENTIONED REGARDING IT, "STRONG IS YOUR DWELLING PLACE," CALLED '*BARAITA*' MEANING SOMETHING outside of the body OF ZEIR ANPIN. *BARAITA* STEMS FROM THE WORD 'OUTSIDE', WHICH IS EXTERNAL. *Eitanim* IN THE WRITTEN TORAH, ZEIR ANPIN, becomes the *Tanaim* OF THE ORAL TORAH, MALCHUT. These are supporting pillars outside of the body, MEANING NETZACH, HOD AND YESOD. Now it needs to be known that when these, NETZACH, HOD AND YESOD, are called with regard to the written Torah, ZEIR ANPIN, *Eitanim*, then with regard to the Oral Torah they are called *Tanaim*, which is spelled with the same letters. *Eitan* is used with regard to the written Torah, *Tanya* with the Oral Torah, and everything is as it should be.

306. חַבְרַיָּיא, הָא אֲנָא בְּחַקְלָא. שְׁלֹמֹה מַלְכָּא, וְגוּבְרִין תַּקִּיפִין דִּילֵיהּ. יֵיתֵי וְיִשְׁכַּח חַד סָבָא, לָאֵי בְּחֵילָא, תַּקִּיף גִּיבָּר, נָצַח קְרָבִין. הָא יְדַעְנָא

דְּאָתָא, וְקַיְימָא לְבָתַר טִינָרָא דְּחַקְלָא, וְהוּא אַשְׁגַּח בִּי, וְהֵיךְ גְּבוּרְתִּי
קַיְימָא בְּחַקְלָא, בִּלְחוֹדוֹי אַשְׁגַּח, דְּאִיהוּ אִישׁ שָׁלוֹם, מָארֵיהּ דִּשְׁלָמָא,
וְאָזַל לֵיהּ. הַשְׁתָּא סָבָא, גְּבוּרְתָּךְ עֲלָךְ, וְאַנְתְּ בִּלְחוֹדָךְ בְּחַקְלָא, תּוּב
לְאַתְרָךְ. וְשָׁארֵי זֵינָךְ מֵעֲלָךְ.

306. Friends, behold, I am in the field. King Solomon the king and his mighty warriors will come and find an old weary man who is strong, a warrior, victor of wars. I know that he will come, standing behind the rock in the field. He watches me, how my strength abides in the field. He alone watches me, he is a man of peace, who has peace. Go now old man, with your strength, you are alone in the field. Return to your place. Remove your weapons from yourself.

307. שִׁמְעוּ הָרִים אֶת רִיב יְיָ' וְהָאֵתָנִים מוֹסְדֵי אָרֶץ. שִׁמְעוּ הָרִים
כִּדְקָאמְרָן. וְהָאֵיתָנִים מוֹסְדֵי אָרֶץ, מוֹסְדֵי אָרֶץ וַדַּאי, דְּהָא מִנַּיְיהוּ
אִתְזָן, וּמִנַּיְיהוּ קַבִּיל כָּל יוֹמָא, וְאִינּוּן מוֹסְדֵי אָרֶץ.

307. "Hear, O mountains, Hashem's controversy, and you, strong foundations of the earth." "Hear, O mountains," is TO BE EXPLAINED as we have said. "…and you, strong foundations of the earth…" is the foundations of the earth indeed, WHICH IS MALCHUT, REFERRED TO AS 'EARTH'. For from them, THE STRONG ONES – NETZACH, HOD AND YESOD – MALCHUT is nurtured and receives bounty daily. THEREFORE they are the foundations of the earth.

308. כִּי רִיב עִם לַה' עַמּוֹ, מַאן הוּא דְּיָכִיל לְמֵיקָם בְּרִיב דְּקוּדְשָׁא
בְּרִיךְ הוּא בְּיִשְׂרָאֵל. וְעַל דָּא אָמַר לְאִלֵּין, שִׁמְעוּ הָרִים אֶת רִיב ה', דָּא
אִיהוּ מַצוּתָא חֲדָא. קוּם רִיב אֶת הֶהָרִים, מַצוּתָא תִּנְיָינָא. דְּנָצַח בְּהוּ
קוּדְשָׁא בְּרִיךְ הוּא, כָּל אִלֵּין רִיבוֹת לְיִשְׂרָאֵל, וְכָל אִינּוּן תּוֹכָחוֹת, כֻּלְּהוּ
כְּאַבָּא דְּאוֹכַח לִבְרֵיהּ, וְהָא אוּקְמוּהָ.

308. "…for Hashem has controversy with His people…" Who can stand his ground when the Holy One, blessed be He, quarrels with Yisrael, regarding which He says to them, "Hear, O mountains, Hashem's controversy." This is one dispute. "Arise, contend before the mountains," is the second dispute.

The Holy One, blessed be He, won in all disputes with Yisrael; and all the admonitions are as a father admonishes his son. So we have explained it.

309. בְּיַעֲקֹב כְּתִיב, בְּשַׁעֲתָא דְּבָעָא לְנַצְחָא בַּהֲדֵיהּ, מַה כְּתִיב, וְרִיב לַיְיָ' עִם יְהוּדָה וְלִפְקוֹד עַל יַעֲקֹב. מָה רִיב אִיהוּ, כְּמָה דִּכְתִיב, בַּבֶּטֶן עָקַב אֶת אָחִיו. עַל הַאי מִלָּה אָתָא תּוֹכַחָה, וְכָל אִינּוּן רִיבוֹת. וְכִי לָאו מִלָּה רַבְרְבָא אִיהוּ, בַּבֶּטֶן עָקַב אֶת אָחִיו וְגוֹ'. הַאי לָאו מִלָּה זְעֵירָא אִיהוּ, מַאי דְּעָבֵיד בַּבֶּטֶן. וְכִי עוּקְבָא עָבֵיד בַּבֶּטֶן אִין וַדַּאי.

309. About Jacob, it is written concerning the time he came to be victorious over him: "Hashem has also a controversy with Judah, and will punish Jacob" (Hoshea 12:3). What is the controversy? It is as it is written: "He took his brother by the heel in the womb" (Ibid. 4). And this resulted in the admonition and all these controversies. This is an important matter that "He took his brother by the heel in the womb." What he did in the belly is not a simple matter. HE ASKS: Was he deceitful in the belly? HE ANSWERS: Assuredly so.

310. וְהָא אִתְּמַר בְּכֹלָּא, דָּחָה יַעֲקֹב לְעֵשָׂו אָחוּי, בְּגִין דְּלָא יְהֵא לֵיהּ חוּלָקָא כְּלָל. עֵשָׂו לָא הִתְרַעַם אֶלָּא מֵחַד דְּאִינּוּן תְּרֵין, דִּכְתִיב וַיַּעְקְבֵנִי זֶה פַעֲמַיִם. פַעֲמַיִם מִבָּעֵי לֵיהּ, מַאי זֶה. אֶלָּא, חַד דְּאָקִישׁ לִתְרֵין. חַד דְּנָפַק לִתְרֵין. וּמַאי נִיהוּ. בְּכֹרָתִי אִתְהַפְּכוּ אַתְוָון, וַהֲוָה בִּרְכָתִי. זֶה פַעֲמַיִם: חַד, דְּאִתְקַשׁ לִתְרֵין.

310. So we learned that in every way, Jacob rejected Esau so that he would not have any share IN HOLINESS. Esau complained only about one which equaled two, as it is written, "for he has supplanted me these two times" (Beresheet 27:36). It should have been written, 'he has supplanted me two times'. What is the meaning of the word "these (Heb. zeh, lit. 'this')"? HE ANSWERS: HE WAS INSINUATING about one thing which has the value of two, one that turned into two. What is it? When rearranging the letters of "my birthright (Heb. bechorati)" it becomes "my blessing (Heb. birchati)." "...this two times..." MEANS one item equaling two.

311. וְלָא יָדַע עֵשָׂו מַה דְּעָבֵד לֵיהּ בַּבֶּטֶן, אֲבָל רַב מְמָנָא דִּילֵיהּ יָדַע

הֲוָה, וְקוּדְשָׁא בְּרִיךְ הוּא אַרְגִּישׁ שְׁמַיָּא וְחֵיילַיְיהוּ לְקָלָא דָא, דְּהָא
בְּרָכָה וּבְכוֹרָה לָא תָבַע מִמָּנָא דִּילֵיהּ, וְלָא אָמַר. דְּהָא בְּרָכָה הֲוָה לֵיהּ
לְמִתְבַּע, וְלָא תָבַע. אָחוּהָ הָא תָבַע וַדַּאי, דִּכְתִיב וּמִבְּשָׂרְךָ לֹא תִתְעַלָּם
וְלָא בָּעָא יַעֲקֹב לְמֵיהָב לֵיהּ לְמֵיכַל, עַד דְּנָטַל מִנֵּיהּ בְּכוֹרָתָא דִּילֵיהּ.

311. Esau did not know what Jacob did to him in the belly, but his Appointed Minister knew. The Holy One, blessed be He, caused the heavens and the hosts to tremble from the sound of the voice OF THE ACCUSATION OF THE MINISTER OF ESAU. He could have claimed blessing and birthright, but said nothing. He should have put in a claim for the blessing, but did not; he claimed brotherhood, as it is written, "and that you hide not yourself from your own flesh" (Yeshayah 58:7). Jacob did not want to give him any food before he took the birthright from him.

312. מַאי בְּכוֹרָה נָטַל מִנֵּיהּ, הַבְּכוֹרָה דִּלְעֵילָא וְתַתָּא. בְּכֹרָה חָסֵר ו'.
כְּדֵין עָקַב אֶת אָחִיו, וַדַּאי דְּעָבֵד לֵיהּ עוּקְבָא, וְאַרְמֵי לֵיהּ לַאֲחוֹרָא.
מַאי אֲחוֹרָא. אַקְדִּים לֵיהּ, דְּיִפּוֹק בְּקַדְמֵיתָא לְהַאי עָלְמָא. אָמַר יַעֲקֹב
לְעֵשָׂו, טוֹל אַתָּה הַאי עָלְמָא בְּקַדְמֵיתָא, וַאֲנָא לְבָתַר.

312. What birthright did he take? He took from him the birthright of above and below, MEANING THE HOLY BIRTHRIGHT ON HIGH, TO OFFER SACRIFICE, AND THE BIRTHRIGHT BELOW TO RECEIVE TWO SHARES. The word 'bechorah' ('birthright') IS WRITTEN minus a Vav. He then supplanted (Heb. ikev) his brother and made a heel (Heb. akev) of him and threw him backwards. What is backwards? He caused Esau to precede him into this world. Said Jacob to Esau: 'You take this world first, and I will follow.'

313. ת"ח, מַה כְּתִיב, וְאַחֲרֵי כֵן יָצָא אָחִיו וְיָדוֹ אֹחֶזֶת בַּעֲקֵב עֵשָׂו. מַאי
בַּעֲקֵב עֵשָׂו. וְכִי ס"ד דַּהֲוָה אָחִיד יְדֵיהּ בְּרַגְלֵיהּ, לָאו הָכִי. אֶלָּא, יָדוֹ
אֹחֶזֶת בְּמַאן דְּהַהוּא דַּהֲוָה עָקַב, וּמַנוּ עֵשָׂו. דְּהָא עֵשָׂו עָקַב אִקְרֵי,
מִשַּׁעֲתָא דְּעָקַב לֵיהּ לְאָחוּי, וּמִיּוֹמָא דְּאִתְבְּרֵי עָלְמָא עָקַב קָרֵי לֵיהּ
קוּדְשָׁא ב"ה, דִּכְתִיב הוּא יְשׁוּפְךָ רֹאשׁ וְאַתָּה תְּשׁוּפֶנּוּ עָקֵב. אַנְתְּ
דְּאִקְרֵי עָקֵב, תְּשׁוּפֶנּוּ בְּקַדְמֵיתָא. וּלְבַסּוֹף הוּא דְּיִמְחֵי רֵישָׁךְ מֵעָלָךְ.

וּמַנּוּ. סָמָאֵ״ל. דְּאִיהוּ רֵישָׁא דְּחִוְיָא, דְּמָחֵי בְּהַאי עָלְמָא.

313. Come and behold: It is written, "And after that came out his brother, and his hand took hold of Esau's heel" (Beresheet 25:26). What is meant by Esau's heel? Do you really believe that his hand was grasping the other's leg? Not so. His hand was grasping someone who is a heel. And who may that be? It is Esau. Esau is known as the heel. From the time that Jacob followed him and from the day of Creation, the Holy One, blessed be He, called him 'heel', AS ESAU IS OF THE ASPECT OF THE SERPENT, as it is written concerning him, "it shall bruise your head, and you shall bruise his heel" (Beresheet 3:15), MEANING you who are called 'heel' will bite first and in the end he will bruise your head. Who is HIS HEAD? IT IS Samael, the head of the serpent that strikes in this world.

314. וְעַל דָּא בַּבֶּטֶן עָקַב אֶת אָחִיו, שַׁוֵּי עֲלֵיהּ לְמֶהֱוֵי עָקֵב, וְנָטַל עֵשָׂו הַאי עָלְמָא בְּקַדְמֵיתָא, וְדָא רָזָא דִּכְתִּיב, וְאֵלֶּה הַמְּלָכִים אֲשֶׁר מָלְכוּ בְּאֶרֶץ אֱדוֹם לִפְנֵי מְלָךְ מֶלֶךְ לִבְנֵי יִשְׂרָאֵל. וְדָא אִיהוּ רָזָא דְּאָמַר שְׁלֹמֹה מַלְכָּא, נַחֲלָה מְבוֹהֶלֶת בָּרִאשׁוֹנָה וְאַחֲרִיתָהּ לֹא תְבוֹרָךְ, בְּסוֹף עָלְמָא.

314. And so in the womb he was insidious, and deceitful to his brother, and so Esau took first this world as the verse writes, "And these are the kings that reigned in the land of Edom, before there reigned any king over the children of Yisrael" (Beresheet 36:31). This secret is alluded to by King Solomon who says, "An estate may be gotten hastily at the beginning; but its end shall not be blessed" (Mishlei 20:21), by the end of the world.

315. וְעַל דָּא בַּבֶּטֶן עָקַב אֶת אָחִיו וּבְאוֹנוֹ שָׂרָה אֶת אֱלֹהִים. מַאי וְאוֹנוֹ. הָכִי אָמְרוּ בְּחֵילָא וְתוּקְפָּא דִּילֵיהּ יָאוֹת, אֲבָל לָאו הָכִי. בְּרִירוּ דְּמִלָּה, יַעֲקֹב דְּיוּקְנָא עִלָּאָה הֲוָה, וְגוּפָא קַדִּישָׁא. דְּלֵית גּוּפָא מִיּוֹמָא דַּהֲוָה אָדָם הָרִאשׁוֹן, כְּגוּפָא דְּיַעֲקֹב, וְשׁוּפְרֵיהּ דְּאָדָם הָרִאשׁוֹן, הַהוּא שׁוּפְרֵיהּ מַמָּשׁ הֲוָה לֵיהּ לְיַעֲקֹב. וְדִיּוּקְנֵיהּ דְּיַעֲקֹב, דִּיּוּקְנָא דְּאָדָם הָרִאשׁוֹן מַמָּשׁ.

315. And so, "He took his brother by the heel in the womb, and by his strength he strove with Elohim." HE ASKS: what is meant by "his strength"? HE ANSWERS: They explained it as his might, and this is well; but actually it is not so. The true clarification of the matter is that Jacob was a supernal image and holy body to the extent that since Adam, there was no body AND BEAUTY as that of Jacob. The beauty of Adam was literally the beauty of Jacob, and the image of Jacob was actually the image of Adam.

316. אָדָם הָרִאשׁוֹן, בְּשַׁעֲתָא דְּאָתָא חִוְיָא וְאִתְפַּתָּה עַל יְדוֹי, יָכִיל חִוְיָא לֵיהּ. מ"ט. בְּגִין דְּלָא הֲוָה תּוּקְפָּא לְאָדָם הָרִאשׁוֹן, וְעַד כְּעָן לָא אִתְיְלִיד מַאן דַּהֲוָה תּוּקְפָּא דִּילֵיהּ. וּמַנוּ תּוּקְפָּא דְּאָדָם הָרִאשׁוֹן. דָּא שֵׁת, דַּהֲוָה בְּדִיּוּקְנָא דְּאָדָם הָרִאשׁוֹן מַמָּשׁ, דִּכְתִיב וַיּוֹלֶד בִּדְמוּתוֹ כְּצַלְמוֹ וַיִּקְרָא אֶת שְׁמוֹ שֵׁת. מַאי בִּדְמוּתוֹ כְּצַלְמוֹ. דַּהֲוָה מָהוּל. וְכַד אָתָא מְמָנָא דְּעֵשָׂו לְגַבֵּי דְּיַעֲקֹב, כְּבָר אִתְיְלִיד תּוּקְפָּא דְּיַעֲקֹב, דְּאִיהוּ יוֹסֵף. וְזֶהוּ וּבְאוֹנוֹ שָׂרָה אֶת אֱלֹהִים.

316. When the Serpent came and seduced Adam, the serpent was able to overcome him as Adam lacked strength or might, as up until that day, he who was comprised of his strength and might was not born. And who is Adam's strength and might? This was Seth, who possessed the identical image of Adam, as it is written, "and begot a son in his own likeness, after his image; and called his name Seth" (Beresheet 5:3). What is the meaning of, "in his own likeness, after his image"? It means born circumcised. So when the Minister of Esau came to Jacob, Jacob's strength and substance already existed in the form of Joseph. This is the meaning of, "and by his strength he strove with Elohim," AS JOSEPH WAS HIS STRENGTH.

317. הַאי קָלָא דְּאִתְּתָא, דְּיַכְלָא קָלָא דְּחִוְיָא לְאַחֲדָא בָּהּ, כְּכַלְבָּא בְּכַלְבְּתָא, מַאן אִיהוּ. אֶלָּא תָּא חֲזֵי, דְּלֵית בְּכָל קָלִין דְּנָשִׁין דְּעָלְמָא, דְּיַכְלָא קָלָא דְּחִוְיָא לְאִתְדַּבְּקָא בָּהּ, וּלְאִתְאַחֲדָא בָּהּ, וּלְאִשְׁתַּתְּפָא בָּהּ. אֶלָּא תְּרֵין נָשִׁין אִינוּן דְּיַכְלָא קָלָא דְּחִוְיָא לְאִתְאַחֲדָא בְּהוֹן, חֲדָא. הַאי דְּלָא נְטִירַת סוֹאֲבוּת נִדּוּתָהּ, וְיִמֵּי לְבוּנָהּ, כַּדְקָא יֵאוֹת, אוֹ דְּאַקְדִּימַת יוֹמָא חֲדָא לִטְבוֹל. וַחֲדָא, הַאי אִתְּתָא דִּמְאַחֶרֶת עוֹנָה דִּילָהּ לְמֶעְבַּד צַעֲרָא לְבַעְלָהּ, בַּר אִי אִיהוּ לָא חַיָּישׁ, וְלָא אַשְׁגַּח לְדָא.

-426-

317. What is the sound of the woman, which the sound of the snake can join with, as do a male a female dog? HE ANSWERS: The serpent's voice can not cling to any voice of a woman, but there are two kinds of women with whom he can unite. One is a woman who does not observe the days of her menstrual impurity and the day of cleansing, and purifies by immersion a day too early, or a woman who delays the marital visits to spite her husband, unless her husband does not mind or does not care about it.

318. אֵלֵין אִינּוּן תְּרֵין נָשִׁין, דְּהָא כְּמָה דְּאַקְדִּימוּ, הָכִי אִינּוּן מִתְאַחֲרָן, לְגַבֵּי קָלָא דְּנָחָשׁ, עַד דְּאַדְבִּיק קָלָא בְּקָלָא, וּכְמָה דְּמִתְאַחֲרָן לְמֶעְבַּד צַעֲרָא לְבַעְלָהּ בְּעִכּוּבָא דְּמִצְוָה, הָכִי אַקְדִּים קָלָא דְּנָחָשׁ, לְאִתְדַּבְּקָא בְּהַהִיא קָלָא דְּאִתְּתָא. וְאֵלֵין אִינּוּן תְּרֵין נָשִׁין, דְּקָלָא דְּנָחָשׁ אָחִיד בְּקָלָא דִּלְהוֹן, כְּכַלְבָּא בְּכַלְבְּתָא, סָאוּבְתָּא בָּתַר סָאוּבְתָּא, זִינָא בָּתַר זִינֵיהּ.

318. With these two women, as one hastens TO IMMERSE BEFORE THE PROPER TIME, one also tarries with the voice of the serpent, until the voices merge. Just as she delays her marital visit to distress her husband, in postponing the performance of a precept, so the voice of the serpent advances to merge with the voice of the woman. These two women with whom the sound of the serpent is caught up are comparable to the union of the male and female dog. Uncleanliness follows uncleanliness, a species seeks out its own.

319. וְא״ת, מָה אִיכְפַּת לָן, אִי אָחִיד קָלָא בְּקָלָא, אִי לֹא אָחִיד. וַוי דְּהָכִי מִתְאַבְּדָן בְּנֵי עָלְמָא בְּלֹא דַּעְתָּא. הַאי קָלָא דְּאִתְּתָא, כַּד אִתְעֲרַב וְאִשְׁתַּתַּף בַּהֲדֵי קָלָא דְּנָחָשׁ, בְּשַׁעֲתָא דְּחַיָּיבַת וּמַרְשַׁעַת נָפְקַת מִגּוֹ אֵיפָה וּמִשַׁטְטָא בְּעָלְמָא, אִי עַרְעַת בְּהָנֵי תְּרֵין קַלִּין, קָלָא דְּנָחָשׁ, וְקָלָא דְּאִתְּתָא, וְאִתְּתָא אִתְחַמְּמַת בְּהוּ, וְאִינּוּן בָּהּ, וְכֵיוָן דְּאִתְחַמְּמַת, מִתְעַבְּדִין רוּחָא, וְאַזְלִין בַּהֲדָהּ, עַד דְּמִשַׁטְטָא, וְעָאל בִּמְעָהָא דְּהַאי אִתְּתָא.

319. One may ask why it should bother us if one voice is caught up with another, or not? HE ANSWERS: Woe that the people in the world perish

unknowingly. If the woman's voice mingles and joins with the voice of the serpent, when sinful evil LILIT comes out of her lair, when she meets these two voices, the voice of the serpent and the voice of the woman, the woman LILIT is heated by them, and they by her. Thus she conceives and a spirit is formed, and they follow it until THE SPIRIT invades the intestines of that woman.

320. וְהַאי יָנוֹקָא דְּיִלִידַת, כַּד אָתֵאת הַהִיא חַיָּיבְתָּא, פְּקִידַת לֵיה לְהַהוּא רוּחָא, דְּאִיהוּ חֲבוּרָא בִּישָׁא, קָלָא דְּנָחָשׁ, דִּמְכַּשְׁכְּשָׁא בָּה, וְאִיהוּ מְחַיְּיכָא בִּינוֹקָא, עַד דְּאָתַת הַהִיא חַיָּיבְתָּא, כְּאִתְּתָא דְּפָקֵידַת בְּרָא לְאִתְּתָא אַחֲרָא, וּמְפַטְפֵּט לֵיה וְחַיֵּיכַת לֵיה, בִּפְטִפּוּטָא עַד דְּתֵיתֵי אִמֵּיה. כַּךְ עָבְדָּא הַאי רוּחָא. וְזִמְנִין סַגִּיאִין, דְּאִיהוּ שְׁלִיחָא דְּהַהִיא חַיָּיבְתָּא, וְקָטְלָא לֵיה, הֲדָא הוּא דִכְתִיב וּמִיַּד עוֹשְׁקֵיהֶם כֹּחַ. וְלָא כְּמָה דְּאַתּוּן אַמְרִין. אֶלָּא הַהוּא כֹּחַ דְּהַהוּא רוּחָא, וְעַל דָּא, תְּרֵין זִמְנִין כְּתִיב בְּהַאי קְרָא, וְאֵין לָהֶם מְנַחֵם. חַד מִלִּילִית חַיָּיבְתָּא, וְחַד מֵהַהוּא רוּחָא.

320. The sinful LILIT comes and visits the spirit, of this child that is born, which came about from this awful merger with the sound of the serpent that rattles inside her. This SPIRIT plays with the child until the evil LILIT arrives, just as a woman might visit another woman's child and prattle with it until its mother arrives. Many times, this SPIRIT, a messenger of the evil LILIT, may kill it. The verse writes, "and on the side of their oppressors there was power" (Kohelet 4:1). The explanation OF THE VERSE is not as you suggest, but ITS EXPLANATION IS AS FOLLOWS. The strength of that spirit OPRESSES HIM. And so twice is written in the verse, "but they had no comforter" (Ibid.), from the wicked Lilit and from that spirit.

321. אִי סָבָא, הַשָּׁתָּא אִית לָךְ רְחִימִין, וְאַתְּ מִשְׁתָּעֵי, כְּמַאן דְּלָא חָמֵית אִינוּן מַגִּיחֵי קְרָבָא, הָא כֻּלְּהוּ בִּשְׁלָמָא עִמָּךְ. הַשָּׁתָּא מִכָּאן וּלְהָלְאָה, לָא אַעֲדֵי מִנַּאי מָאנֵי קְרָבָא בְּדִיל לְאַדְכְּרָא שְׁמֵי.

321. HE SAID TO HIMSELF: Old man, now you have friends, you speak like one who never saw war wagers. They are at peace with you. From now on I

will not remove from me weapons of war in order to make my name remembered.

322. הַהוּא חַטָאת רוֹבֵץ, קָאִים עַל פִּתְחָא כְּכַלְבָּא. בְּזִמְנָא דְקָלָא בַּתְרַיְיתָא, דְּיָהִיבַת אִתְּתָא, נָפִיק, אִיהוּ דָּלִיג מֵעַל פִּתְחָא וְאִתְעֲבַר מִתַּמָן, וְאָזִיל אֲבַתְרָה. מ"ט. בְּגִין דְקוּדְשָׁא בְּרִיךְ הוּא שָׁדַר חַד מַפְתְּחָא דִּילֵיהּ, וְקָלָא פֶּרְחָא, וּמַפְתְּחָא אַתְיָא, וְחִוְיָא אָזַל בָּתַר קָלָא דְּהוּא נָפִיק לְעָלְמָא, וְעַד טוּרָא דְּבִטְנָא אָזִיל, וּמִכַשְׁכְּשָׁא, עַד עִידָן דְּאִתְנְקִיאַת, מֵהַהוּא זוּהֲמָא, דְּנַשְׁכִין דְּחִוְיָא בִּישָׁא. וְקוּדְשָׁא ב"ה, מְסַבֵּב סְבוּבִין, וְעָבֵיד עוֹבָדִין כַּדְקָא יָאוֹת.

322. That sin that lies in wait, MEANING THE SERPENT ABOUT WHOM IT IS WRITTEN, "SIN CROUCHES AT THE DOOR" (BERESHEET 4:7), BEING THE DOOR OF MALCHUT, stands by the door like a dog. When the last sound is emitted, when the woman about to give birth cries, JUST BEFORE BIRTH, he skips from the door and goes after the woman. Why? Because the Holy One, blessed be He, sends a key TO OPEN THE WOMB and when the voice flies forth, the key comes. The serpent follows the voice that is emitted and goes to the hill of the stomach – DENOTING YESOD, AS NETZACH, HOD AND YESOD ARE CALLED 'THE LOWER MOUNTAINS' – IT BITES THAT PLACE, OPENS THE WOMB, and knocks there until such time that she is cleansed from the filth of the bite of that evil serpent. The Holy One, blessed be He, brings about situations and performs fitting actions.

323. וְכָל דָּא, בְּגִין דְּהַהוּא בֶּטֶן אִתְדַּחְיָא. הָא וַדַּאי, אִתְדַּחְיָא מֵהַהוּא בֶּטֶן, וְלֵית לֵיהּ חוּלָקָא, וְאִתְדָּחֵי מִבֶּטֶן דִּלְתַתָּא, דְּשָׁאַר נָשִׁין דְּעָלְמָא, דְּאע"ג דְּעָבֵיד צַעַר, לָא אִתְיְהִיב לֵיהּ רְשׁוּ לְשַׁלְטָאָה בֵּיהּ. וּמַאן בֶּטֶן אִתְיְיהִיב לֵיהּ, וְאִיהוּ שָׁלִיט עֲלֵיהּ. הַהוּא בֶּטֶן דְּסוֹטָה, דִּכְתִּיב וְצָבְתָה בִטְנָהּ, בְּגִין דְּהַאי בֶּטֶן, עָבִיד בֵּיהּ נוּקְמִין לִרְעוּתֵיהּ, וְהַאי בֶּטֶן דִּילֵיהּ אִיהוּ, וְקוּדְשָׁא בְּרִיךְ הוּא יָהִיב לֵיהּ בְּגִין דְּלָא אִתְדָּחֵי מִכֹּלָּא. הַשְׁתָּא רְחִימִין דִּילִי, אֲצִיתוּ. לָא חֲמֵינָא לְכוּ, וּמַלִּילְנָא לְכוּ. כָּל הַדְּבָרִים יְגֵעִים, לָא יָכִיל אֱינָשׁ לְמַלְּלָא, אֲפִילּוּ מִלִּין דְּאוֹרַיְיתָא יְגֵעִים אִינּוּן.

323. All this NURTURING OF THE SERPENT comes because that belly was rejected. It is sure THAT THE SERPENT was shunted from that belly and has no part IN IT. ALSO, he is shunted from the belly below of other women in the world, AS WOMEN BELOW ARE BRANCHES OF THE SUPERNAL NUKVA. So even though he can distress them, he has no right to dominate them. Which belly does he have authority to dominate? It is the belly of the *sotah* (lit. 'a married woman suspected of adultery') about whom it is written: "and her belly will swell" (Bemidbar 5:27). With this belly, he acts with vengeance as this belly is his to do with what he wishes, and the Holy One, blessed be He, allowed him this in order that he not be totally shunted. My friends, listen! I have not seen you or spoken to you, "All things are full of weariness" (Kohelet 1:8); no one can speak, even Torah words are wearisome.

324. כְּתִיב, וַיִּוָּתֵר יַעֲקֹב לְבַדּוֹ וַיֵּאָבֵק אִישׁ עִמּוֹ, וּכְתִיב וַיַּרְא כִּי לֹא יָכוֹל לוֹ וַיִּגַּע בְּכַף יְרֵכוֹ. וְהַהוּא יָרֵךְ דְּרָוַוח מִיַּעֲקֹב. וְהַהוּא יָרֵךְ בַּחֲלִישׁוּ דִּילֵיהּ עַד דְּאָתָא שְׁמוּאֵל. מַאי בַּחֲלִישׁוּ דְּלָא מָשִׁיךְ נְבוּאָה. כַּד אָתָא שְׁמוּאֵל, נָטַל הַהוּא יָרֵךְ, וְסַלְקֵיהּ מֵהַהוּא אֲתָר, וְחָטַף לֵיהּ מִנֵּיהּ, וּמֵהַהוּא זִמְנָא אִתְעֲדֵי מִנֵּיהּ, וְלָא הֲוָה לֵיהּ חוּלָקָא בִּקְדוּשָׁה כְּלָל.

324. It is written: "And Jacob was left alone, and there wrestled a man with him" (Beresheet 32:25), and, "And when he saw that he did not prevail against him, he touched the hollow of the thigh." From that hollow did THE OTHER SIDE profit FROM JACOB. That thigh was in a state of weakness until Samuel came. What is its weakness? It did not draw THE LIGHT OF prophecy. When Samuel arrived, he took that thigh and removed it from the place OF THE OTHER SIDE and snatched it away from it. From that time that it was removed from it, it had no part of Holiness at all.

325. קוּדְשָׁא בְּרִיךְ הוּא לָא קַפַּח, וְלָא דָּחֵי לֵיהּ מִכֹּלָּא, בְּגִין דְּנָטַל שְׁמוּאֵל יָרֵךְ דִּילֵיהּ, אֶלָּא יָהִיב לֵיהּ חוּלָקָא חֲדָא. מַאי אִיהִי. יָהִיב לֵיהּ הַהוּא יָרֵךְ וּבֶטֶן דְּסוֹטָה, חֲלַף הַהוּא יָרֵךְ וּבֶטֶן, דְּאַעֲדֵי מִנֵּיהּ. וְעַל דָּא תַּרְוַויְיהוּ יָהִיב לֵיהּ קוּדְשָׁא בְּרִיךְ הוּא, לְמֶהֱוֵי אַתְרָא דְּקַדְשָׁא פָּנוּי מִכָּל סָאֲבוּתָא.

325. The Holy One, blessed be He, did not withhold or reject it totally when Samuel took the thigh, but gave it one portion. He gave it the thigh and belly of the *Sotah*, in exchange for the thigh and belly taken from him. Both things, the Holy One, blessed be He, gave to the Other Side so that the place of Holiness would be free of it altogether.

326. וְלַנְפִּיל יָרֵךְ. מַהוּ וְלַנְפִּיל, וְנָפְלָה יְרֵכָה וְלַצְבּוֹת, וְצָבְתָה מִבָּעֵי לֵיהּ. אֶלָּא, כְּמַאן דְּאַשְׁדֵי גַּרְמָא לְכַלְבָּא, וְאָמַר לֵיהּ, טוֹל הַאי לְחוּלָקָךְ. וּמִכֹּלָּא לָא אַבְאִישׁ קַמֵּיהּ, אֶלָּא דְּגָזְלוּ מִנֵּיהּ יָרֵךְ, בְּגִין דְּאִיהוּ יָגַע וְלָאֵי עָלֵיהּ, וְרָוַוח לֵיהּ וְאַפִּיקוּ לֵיהּ מִנֵּיהּ. וְעַל דָּא, קוּדְשָׁא בְּרִיךְ הוּא אַפִּיל לֵיהּ, גַּרְמָא דָּא דְּסוֹטָה, וְאַפִּיק לֵיהּ כִּדְקָאמְרָן, וּבְדָא אִיהוּ רָוֵי וְחַדֵי.

326. It is written, "and your thigh to fall away" (Bemidbar 5:22). HE ASKS: IT SHOULD READ, 'and her thigh shall fall away'. It is written, "to make the belly to swell" (Ibid.), yet it should be written, 'and her belly shall swell'. HE ANSWERS: This is similar to one who throws a bone to a dog and tells him: This is your share. HENCE, THE VERSE SAYS, "TO SWELL...TO FALL AWAY." Nothing hurt it so much as when it was deprived of the thigh for which it struggled, AS INDICATED FROM THE VERSE: "AND THERE WRESTLED A MAN WITH HIM..." It earned it, yet it was taken from it, so the Holy One, blessed be He, threw it the bone of the *Sotah,* as we said, and with that it was happy and satisfied.

327. כָּל אִינּוּן רְתִיכִין וְסִיַּיעְתָּא דִּילֵיהּ, בָּעָאן תָּדִיר יָרֵךְ, וְאַזְלֵי בְּכְסוֹפָא אֲבַתְרֵיהּ. וּבג״ד, הָנֵי בִּרְכֵי דְּרַבָּנָן דְּשַׁלְהֵי, מִן דָּא אִיהוּ. דְּכָל בְּסוֹפָא דִּלְהוֹן, בָּתַר יָרֵךְ אִיהוּ, וְכָל שֶׁכֵּן יָרֵךְ דְּרַבָּנָן, וְכָל מִלָּה אַהְדָּר לְאַתְרֵיהּ, וְקוּדְשָׁא בְּרִיךְ הוּא לָא גָּרַע כְּלוּם, מִכָּל מַה דְּאִצְטְרִיךְ, וְלָא בָּעָא דְּיִקְרַב לְקְדוּשָׁה, בַּר עִמֵּיהּ וְעַדְבֵיהּ חוּלְקֵיהּ וְאַחֲסַנְתֵּיהּ. כְּמָה דְּעָבֵיד קוּדְשָׁא בְּרִיךְ הוּא לְעֵילָּא, הָכִי עַבְדֵי יִשְׂרָאֵל לְתַתָּא, וְהָכִי אִצְטְרִיךְ לְמֶעְבַּד, וְהָכִי תָּנֵינָן, אָסִיר לֵיהּ לְיִשְׂרָאֵל, לְמֵילַף אוֹרָיְיתָא לְעכו״ם, דִּכְתִיב, מַגִּיד דְּבָרָיו לְיַעֲקֹב וְגו׳, לֹא עָשָׂה כֵן לְכָל גּוֹי וְגו׳.

327. All these Chariots and its companions always desire the thigh and

yearn for it. As a result the knees of the sages are weary from THE OTHER SIDE, as all its yearning is for the thigh, and particularly for the sage's thigh. Everything is returned to its place and the Holy One, blessed be He, lacks nothing, and He wishes that only His people, His lot, His portion, shall approach Holiness. As the Holy One, blessed be He, does above, so the children of Yisrael do below, and so it should be. As we learned, the children of Yisrael are prohibited from teaching Torah to the heathen, as it is written, "He declares his word to Jacob… He has not dealt so with any other nation" (Tehilim 147:19-20), FOR IT IS NECESSARY TO DISTANCE THEM FROM SANCTITY.

328. וְעַל דָּא דָּחֵי לֵיה יַעֲקֹב, וְדָחֵי לֵיה שְׁמוּאֵל, דְּלָא יְהֵא לֵיה חוּלָקָא בְּקוּדְשָׁא. וּבג״ד, כָּל נְטִירוּ דְּבָבוּ לְיִשְׂרָאֵל, עַל דָּא אִיהוּ. לְכַלְבָּא דְּחָטִיף עוֹפָא דַּכְיָא מִן שׁוֹקָא, וְאַיְיתֵי לֵיה, וְעַד לָא אִתְּבַר, אָתָא חַד בַּר נָשׁ וְחָטְפָא מִנֵּיה, לְבָתַר יָהִיב לֵיה חַד גַּרְמָא גְּרִירָא בְּלָא תּוֹעַלְתָּא.

328. And so Jacob and Samuel shunted it aside so that it would have no part of Holiness. For this reason, all the preservation of hatred towards the children of Yisrael is about this. It is SIMILAR to a dog that seized a clean bird from the market, and before HE HAD A CHANCE to shatter it, a man came, snatched it from him, and later gave him a useless bone to carry about.

329. כַּךְ לְשָׂרוֹ עַל עֵשָׂו, אַפִּיקוּ לֵיה מֵהַהוּא בֶּטֶן, חָטִיפוּ מִנֵּיה הַהוּא יָרֵךְ. לְבָתַר יָהֲבוּ לֵיה גַּרְמָא חַד, הַהוּא בֶּטֶן וְהַהוּא יָרֵךְ דְּסוֹטָה, וְלָא אָחֳרָא. הָא גַּרְמָא, דְּקָא יָהֲבוּ לֵיה לְחוּלָקֵיה וְעַדְבֵיה, וְעָרַב לֵיה. וּבג״כ, כָּל דִּינִין דְּקוּדְשָׁא בְּרִיךְ הוּא דִּינִין דִּקְשׁוֹט אִינּוּן, וּבְנֵי נָשָׁא לָא יַדְעִין, וְלָא מַשְׁגִּיחִין לְקוּדְשָׁא בְּרִיךְ הוּא. וְכֻלְּהוּ בְּאֹרַח קְשׁוֹט. הִיא אַסְטְיאַת גַּרְמָהּ מִבַּעֲלָהּ, כד״א הָעוֹזֶבֶת אַלּוּף נְעוּרֶיהָ וְגוֹ׳, אוּף הָכִי אִתְּתָא, כְּגַוְונָא דִּילָהּ בְּאַרְעָא.

329. So it is with the Minister of Esau. He was removed from the womb, the thigh taken from him and later given a bone, namely, the stomach and thigh of the Sotah, and of none other. This is the bone given to him as his share and lot, and this was delightful to him. All Judgments of the Holy One,

blessed be He, are truthful, yet people do not realize or pay attention to the Holy One, blessed be He. However, all is with Truth. She, THE OTHER SIDE, deviated from her husband, as the verse says, "who forsakes the friend of her youth" (Mishlei 2:17), and so too the corresponding wife on earth, MEANING THE *SOTAH,* IS HANDED OVER TO HER.

330. ת"ח, מַאן דְּאַשְׁכַּח חַבְרָא כְּוָותֵיהּ, דְּעָבֵיד כְּעוֹבָדוֹי בְּעָלְמָא, רָחִים לֵיהּ, וְאִתְדָּבַּק בַּהֲדֵיהּ, וְעָבֵיד עִמֵּיהּ טִיבוּ. אֲבָל סִטְרָא אָחֳרָא לָאו הָכִי, כֵּיוָן דְּאַשְׁכַּח מַאן דְּשָׁבַק סִטְרָא דְּקֻדְשָׁה דְּקוּדְשָׁא בְּרִיךְ הוּא, וְעָבֵיד כְּעוֹבָדוֹי, וְאִתְדָּבַּק בָּהּ, כְּדֵין בַּעְיָא לְשֵׁיצָאָה וּלְאַפָּקָא לֵיהּ מֵעָלְמָא. הַאי אִתְּתָא, עֲבַדַת כְּעוֹבָדָהָא, וְאִתְדַּבְּקַת בָּהּ, חֲזֵי מַה דְּעָבְדַת בָּהּ, וְצַבְתָה בִטְנָהּ וְנָפְלָה יְרֵכָהּ. קוּדְשָׁא בְּרִיךְ הוּא לָאו הָכִי, מַאן דְּשָׁבִיק לְסִטְרָא אָחֳרָא, וְאִתְדָּבַּק בֵּיהּ בְּקוּדְשָׁא בְּרִיךְ הוּא, כְּדֵין רָחִים לֵיהּ, וְעָבֵיד לֵיהּ כָּל טִיבוּ דְּעָלְמָא. הַשְׁתָּא סָבָא אַתְקִין גַּרְמָיךְ, דְּהָא חִוְיָא אָזִיל לֵיהּ, וּבָעָא לְאִתְגָּרָא בַּהֲדָךְ, וְלָא יָכִיל.

330. Come and behold: one who finds a friend like himself, who acts like him, will love him, cling to him and favor him with kindness. However, the Other Side is not so. When it finds someone who has left the holy side of the Holy One, blessed be He, and behaves like it, and clings to it, then it attempts to destroy him. This woman imitated its way and clung to it. Look what it did to her. "...and her belly shall swell, and her thigh shall fall away." The Holy One, blessed be He, is not so. He will love that person who leaves the Other Side and clings to the Holy One, blessed be He, and He will dispense every kindness in the world to him. HE SAID TO HIMSELF: Now, old man, prepare yourself as the serpent tries to entice you but is unable.

A Synopsis

The old man's talk returns repeatedly to the issue of one who has no offspring. He says that God does not want anyone who practices evil to produce future generations that might devastate the world. The merchant tells the story of King Solomon riding on the eagle four hundred parasangs until arriving at the mountains of darkness. There, in the area of the olive tree, King Solomon learned the foreign wisdom that he was interested in, and then

went aboard the eagle again and returned home. Then he contemplated that wisdom that he had learned. He knew of the many oppressions of the world.

331. פָּתַח וְאָמַר מַה יִתְרוֹן לָאָדָם בְּכָל עֲמָלוֹ שֶׁיַעֲמוֹל תַּחַת הַשָּׁמֶשׁ, וְכִי לָא אָתָא שְׁלֹמֹה אֶלָּא לְאוֹלָפָא מִלָּה דָּא. אֵלּוּ אָמַר בַּעֲמָלוֹ שֶׁיַעֲמוֹל יֵאוֹת, דְּהָא אִשְׁתְּאַר עָמָל, דְּאִית בֵּיהּ יִתְרוֹן. אֶלָּא כֵּיוָן דִּכְתִיב בְּכָל עֲמָלוֹ, הָא כְּלָלָא דְּכֹלָא, דְּלָא אִשְׁתְּאַר כְּלוּם דְּאִית בֵּיהּ יִתְרוֹן.

331. He began to say, "What profit has a man of all his labor wherein he labors under the sun" (Kohelet 1:3). HE ASKS: Is Solomon trying to teach us only this? Had he said "in his labor that he does," I would understand that there is work that brings profit. However, when he writes, "of all his labor," that includes everything, that nothing has profit.

332. אֶלָּא, לָאו לְכָל אָדָם אָמַר שְׁלֹמֹה מִלָּה דָּא, אֶלָּא אָדָם אִית בְּעָלְמָא, דְּאִיהוּ מִשְׁתַּדֵּל תָּדִיר בְּבִישׁ וּלְאַבְאָשָׁא, וְלָא אִשְׁתַּדַּל בְּטָב אֲפִילוּ רִגְעָא חֲדָא. וְעַ"ד כְּתִיב עֲמָלוֹ, וְלָא כְּתִיב יְגִיעוֹ. עֲמָלוֹ: כד"א, יָשׁוּב עֲמָלוֹ בְּרֹאשׁוֹ. וְלֹא רָאָה עָמָל בְּיִשְׂרָאֵל. יְגִיעוֹ: כד"א יְגִיעַ כַּפֶּיךָ כִּי תֹאכֵל וְגוֹ'. וּכְתִיב וְאֶת יְגִיעַ כַּפִּי רָאָה אֱלֹהִים. אֲבָל עֲמָלוֹ, כְּתִיב, עָמָל וָכַעַס. אִשְׁתַּדְּלוּתֵיהּ הוּא תָּדִיר לְבִישׁ, וְעַ"ד אִיהוּ תַּחַת הַשָּׁמֶשׁ.

332. HE ANSWERS: Solomon did not make his statement regarding all people. There are people that are constantly busy doing evil and harming others, and do nothing positive at all. Therefore, the verse uses the expression, "his labor," instead of 'his toil'. "...his labor (Heb. amalo)..." MEANS IN EVIL DEEDS, as a verse writes, "His mischief (Heb. amalo) shall return upon his own head" (Tehilim 7:17), or, "nor has he seen perverseness (Heb. amal) in Yisrael" (Bemidbar 23:21). The word 'toil' IS USED TO IMPLY POSITIVE ACTS, as the verse says, "For you shall eat the toil (Heb. yegia) of your hands" (Tehilim 128:2), and, "Elohim has seen my affliction and the labor (Heb. yegia) of my hands" (Beresheet 31:42). But of 'amal' it says, "mischief and spite" (Tehilim 10:14). Hence, HE SAID, "WHAT PROFIT HAS A MAN OF ALL HIS LABOR WHEREIN HE LABORS UNDER THE

SUN," for it is under the sun, ALLUDING TO THE OTHER SIDE, WHICH IS BELOW THE SUN.

333. בְּשַׁעֲתָא דְּהַאי אָדָם אִשְׁתַּדַּל בְּבִישׁ, עַל הַאי כְּתִיב, לָא נִין לוֹ וְלָא נֶכֶד בְּעַמּוֹ וְגוֹ', דְּהָא קוּדְשָׁא בְּרִיךְ הוּא בָּעֵי, דְּלָא יַעֲבִיד תּוֹלְדִין, דְּאִלְמָלֵא יַעֲבִיד תּוֹלְדִין, הֲוָה מְטַשְׁטְשָׁא עָלְמָא. וְעַ"ד כְּתִיב, מַה יִּתְרוֹן לָאָדָם בְּכָל עֲמָלוֹ. וּמַאן דְּלָא יִשְׁתַּדַּל לְמֶעְבַּד תּוֹלְדִין, אִתְדָּבַק בְּהַאי סִטְרָא דְּאָדָם בִּישָׁא וְעָאל תְּחוֹת גַּדְפּוֹי.

333. When man practices evil, the verse writes, "He will have no child nor offspring among his people" (Iyov 18:19). The Holy One, blessed be He, does not want him to produce future generations, for if he produced offspring, he would devastate the world. And so it says, "What profit has a man of all his labor"; one who does not try to have offspring becomes part of this evil man and finds himself under his wing.

334. רוּת אָמְרָה, וּפָרַשְׂתָּ כְנָפֶיךָ עַל אֲמָתְךָ, בְּגִין לְאִזְדַּוְּוגָא בַּהֲדֵיהּ דְּצַדִּיק, לְמֶעְבַּד תּוֹלְדִין, וְקוּדְשָׁא בְּרִיךְ הוּא פָּרִישׂ גַּדְפּוֹי עַל בַּר נָשׁ, בְּגִין לְאַפָּשָׁא בְּעָלְמָא. לְמַאן דְּלָא בָּעֵי לְמֶעְבַּד תּוֹלְדִין, בְּגַפּוֹ יָבֹא, בְּגַפּוֹ דְּהַהוּא בִּישׁ, דְּאִיהוּ אָזִיל עֲרִירִי, כְּחִוְיָא דָא, דְּאָזִיל יְחִידָאי. בְּגַפּוֹ יֵצֵא, אִיהוּ דְּלָא אִשְׁתַּדַּל לְמֶעְבַּד תּוֹלְדִין, הָא אִתְּמַר כָּל מַה דְּאִצְטְרִיךְ.

334. Ruth said "spread therefore your skirt (also: 'wing') over your handmaid" (Rut 3:9) so that she would mate with the righteous man to produce offspring. And the Holy One, blessed be He, spread His wings over people in order that they should be fruitful. BUT the one who refuses to produce offspring, "he came in by himself (also: 'in his wing')" the wing of the evil man who remains childless, as the serpent who operates alone. "...he shall go out by himself..." refers to one who did not try to have offspring. We have already discussed THIS sufficiently.

335. רִיב דְּעָבֵד קוּדְשָׁא בְּרִיךְ הוּא, הָא אִתְּמַר, רִיב: דִּכְתִיב, קוּם רִיב אֶת הֶהָרִים. מַאי אִיהוּ. אֶלָּא, אִינּוּן טוּרִין דִּלְתַתָּא. אֲמַאי רִיב דָּא.

בְּגִין דְּבְהוּ תַּלְיָא, כָּל חוֹבָא דְּעַבְדִין יִשְׂרָאֵל, לְגַבֵּי אֲבוּהוֹן דְּבִשְׁמַיָּא. מַאי טַעֲמָא. בְּגִין דְּיִשְׂרָאֵל הֲווֹ יַדְעִין שִׁמּוּשָׁא דְּכָל מַלְאָכִין עִלָּאִין דְּבִשְׁמַיָּא, וְלָא אָנִיס לְהוּ, אֲפִילוּ שְׁמָא דְּחַד מִנַּיְיהוּ, וְכָל שִׁמּוּשָׁא דִּלְהוֹן.

335. The dispute that the Holy One, blessed be He, engaged with, we have learned, is as the verse says, "Arise, contend before the mountains." Who are they? They are the mountains below, NAMELY NETZACH, HOD, AND YESOD. What is the essence of this contention? With them are intertwined all sins that Yisrael commit before their Heavenly Father. How is that? Yisrael knew of the worship, THE CONJURING of the heavenly angels. Not even one name of theirs was unknown to them, nor their worshipping.

336. וּבִתְרֵין סִטְרִין הֲוֵי טָעָאן אֲבַתְרַיְיהוּ. חַד, דַּהֲווֹ יַדְעִין לְאַמְשָׁכָא חֵילָא דִּלְהוֹן, דְּכֹכְבַיָּא וּמַזָּלֵי בְּאַרְעָא. וְחַד, דַּהֲווֹ יַדְעֵי לְאוּמָאָה לוֹן, בְּכָל מַה דְּאִצְטְרִיכוּ. וְעַל דָּא בָּעָא קוּדְשָׁא בְּרִיךְ הוּא לְמֶעְבַּד בְּהוּ רִיב וְדִינָא. וְכֵיוָן דִּבְּהוֹן לֶהֱוֵי רִיב וְדִינָא, כָּל שִׁלְשׁוּלָא נָפַל דְּהָא לָא יֶהֱוֵי בֵּיהּ תּוֹעַלְתָּא. וּבְגִין כָּךְ, קוּם רִיב וְגוֹ'. וְתִשְׁמַעֲנָה הַגְּבָעוֹת קוֹלֶךָ. מַאן גְּבָעוֹת. אִלֵּין אִינּוּן אִמָּהוֹת, דַּרְגִּין דְּאִקְרוּן בְּתוּלוֹת אַחֲרֶיהָ וְגוֹ', וּבְגִין כָּךְ וְתִשְׁמַעֲנָה הַגְּבָעוֹת קוֹלֶךָ. דְּהָכִי הֲווֹ עַבְדֵי יִשְׂרָאֵל, עַד דְּאִשְׁתַּתָּפוּ בְּדַרְגִּין תַּתָּאִין.

336. In two ways, they used to whore after them. 1) They knew how to draw the powers of the stars and constellations on earth, and 2) they knew how to cause them to call upon them in all that is needed. For this, the Holy One, blessed be He, was to engage in contention and Judgment against them, THE MOUNTAINS, AS ALL ANGELS AND HEAVENLY MINISTERS RECEIVE THEIR POWER FROM NETZACH, HOD AND YESOD, REFERRED TO AS 'MOUNTAINS'. Inasmuch as they are subject to contention and Judgment, THEIR LIGHTS WILL BE BLURRED; the entire chain, MEANING THE ANGELS OF BRIYAH, YETZIRAH AND ASIYAH, shall fall as they will be of no use, SINCE THEIR POWERS HAVE BEEN MADE VOID. And therefore, it says, "Arise, and contend..." "and let the hills hear your voice." HE ASKS: Who are the hills? HE ANSWERS: These are the mothers, NAMELY THE SEVEN

CHAMBERS IN BRIYAH, who are levels called "the virgins…that follow her" (Tehilim 45:15), MEANING SEVEN MAIDENS THAT SERVICE MALCHUT. So did Yisrael do until they took part with the lower levels. He said to himself: Old man, return to the earlier words.

337. ת״ח, דְּאִית לְאַהֲדְּרָא סָבָא, בְּמִלִּין קַדְמָאִין, יָרֵךְ דְּקָא אַמְרָן, סַגִּי אַתְקִיפוּ לוֹן יִשְׂרָאֵל, בְּהַהוּא יָרֵךְ. מָרְדְּכַי הֲוָה אַחֲמֵי לְהַהוּא רָשָׁע דְּהָמָן הַהוּא יָרֵךְ דִּילֵיהּ, וְעַל דָּא הֲוָה רָגִיז, מִלָּה דְּאִתְחֲזֵי לֵיהּ, וְאִיהוּ אַרְגִּיז לֵיהּ בַּהֲדֵיהּ. חָמוּ חַבְרַיָּיא, מַה כְּתִיב, וַתִּקַּח רִבְקָה אֶת בִּגְדֵי עֵשָׂו בְּנָהּ הַגָּדוֹל הַחֲמוּדוֹת וְגוֹ'. בְּאִלֵּין לְבוּשִׁין דִּילֵיהּ, גֵּזֵל דִּילֵיהּ, וְאַפִּיק לֵיהּ מִכָּל בִּרְכָאן דִּילֵיהּ, וּמִבְּכֵרוּתָא.

337. Yisrael sharply struck THE OTHER SIDE with this thigh that we spoke of. Mordechai showed the evil Haman his thigh, for which reason he became furious, claiming it was his, THAT HE EARNED IT FROM JACOB. Mordechai incensed him, SHOWING HIM THAT IT WAS ALREADY SNATCHED FROM HIM. Behold friends, it is written, "And Rivkah took the best clothes of her elder son Esau" (Beresheet 27:15). With these garments, Jacob was able to snatch all his blessings and birthright.

338. וּבְגִין, כַּךְ, עִילָּה דְּקָא אַשְׁכָּחוּ רְתִיכִין דִּילֵיהּ, לְרַבָּנָן, אִיהוּ דְּחוּפְיָא דִּלְהוֹן לְמָאנֵי דְּרַבָּנָן תָּדִיר. לְיַרְכִין דִּלְהוֹן. וּלְמָאנִין דִּלְהוֹן. וְאִלֵּין תְּרֵין מִלִּין דִּסְטַר אַחֲרָא הֲווֹ, וְכָל דָּא בְּגִין דְּגָזְלוּ לוֹן מִנֵּיהּ. לֵית לְהוּ עִילָּה אֶלָּא לְרַבָּנָן. וּבְגִין כַּךְ, הָנֵי מָאנֵי דְּרַבָּנָן דְּקָא בְּלוּ מֵחוּפְיָא דִּלְהוֹן אִיהוּ, וְהָנֵי בִּרְכֵי דְּשַׁלְהֵי, מִנַּיְיהוּ הוּא וַדַּאי. וּמִדִּלְהוֹן הֲווֹ, וּמִנְּהוֹן נַטְלֵי עִילָּה, וּמִמַּה דַּהֲווֹ מִנַּיְיהוּ. בָּעָאן לְרַבָּנָן, דְּאִינּוּן כְּלָלָא דְּהַהוּא יוֹשֵׁב אֹהָלִים, וְעַל דָּא לֵית עִילָּה בְּלָא עִילָּה, וְעַל דָּא לֵית מִלָּה, בְּלָא דִּינָא, וְכָל מִלָּה תָּב לְאַתְרֵיהּ.

338. For this reason, chariots OF THE OTHER SIDE found a reason to be hostile to the sages. They robbed the garments of the sages at every chance – MEANING, their thighs and garments, as these two items belonged to the Other Side. Their anger was primarily due to the theft of these items. AND

SO, they can complain only to the sages. For this reason, the sages' garments wither from rubbing against them. The weakening in the knees is due to them, and in this way they show their grievance against THE SAGES and demand what is theirs. They are seeking from the sages that which is theirs. Why the sages? They represent he who is sitting in the tent, JACOB; there is no accusation without a cause, nothing happens without justice and judgment, and so everything returns to its place.

339. שְׁלֹמֹה אָמַר, וְשַׁבְתִּי אֲנִי וָאֶרְאֶה אֶת כָּל הָעֲשׁוּקִים אֲשֶׁר נַעֲשׂוּ תַּחַת הַשָּׁמֶשׁ וְהִנֵּה דִּמְעַת הָעֲשׁוּקִים וְאֵין לָהֶם מְנַחֵם וּמִיַּד עוֹשְׁקֵיהֶם כֹּחַ וְאֵין לָהֶם מְנַחֵם. הַאי קְרָא אַרְמִיזְנָא בֵּיהּ, וְאִתְּמַר. אֲבָל שַׁבְתִּי אֲנִי, וְכִי מֵאָן אֲתָר תָּב שְׁלֹמֹה. אִי נֵימָא, לְבָתַר דְּאָמַר מִלָּה דָּא, תָּב כְּמִלְּקַדְמִין, וְאָמַר מִלָּה אָחֳרָא, יָאוֹת אֲבָל שַׁבְתִּי וָאֶרְאֶה.

339. Solomon said, "So I returned, and considered all the oppressions that are done under the sun: and behold the tears of such as were oppressed, and they had no comforter; and on the side of their oppressors there was power: but they had no comforter" (Kohelet 4:1). We have spoken of what he is hinting at. The verse says, "I returned." From where did Solomon return? One may conclude THAT it MEANS, after this matter, he repeated something else, AND SO HE MEANS 'I HAVE GONE BACK'. This is fine, but if so HE SHOULD HAVE SAID, 'returned, and considered'; WHY DOES HE SAY, "I RETURNED"?

340. תַּמָּן תְּנֵינָן, בְּכָל יוֹמָא הֲוָה אַקְדִּים שְׁלֹמֹה בִּצַפְרָא, וַהֲוֵי שַׁוֵּי אַנְפּוֹי לְסְטַר מִזְרָח, וְחָמֵי מַה דְּחָמֵי, וּלְבָתַר תָּב לְסְטַר דָּרוֹם, וְחָמֵי מַה דְּחָמֵי וְהָדַר תָּב לְסְטַר צָפוֹן, וְקָאִים תַּמָּן. מָאִיךְ עֵינוֹי וְזָקִיף רֵישֵׁיהּ.

340. There we learned that daily Solomon would rise early, turn his face eastward, NAMELY TO TIFERET AND THE CENTRAL COLUMN, and see what he saw. Later he would turn to the south, NAMELY CHESED AND THE RIGHT COLUMN, and see what he saw. Later he would turn northward, BEING GVURAH AND THE LEFT COLUMN, stand there, lower his eyes, and raise his head.

341. בְּהַאי שַׁעֲתָא, הָא עַמּוּדָא דְּאֶשָּׁא וְעַמּוּדָא דַּעֲנָנָא, הֲווֹ אַתְיָין,

וְעַל הַהוּא עַמּוּדָא דַּעֲנָנָא, הֲוָה אָתֵי נִשְׁרָא חֲדָא. וְהַהוּא נִשְׁרָא הוּא
רַבְרְבָא וְתַקִּיף, וְכֵן הֲוָה אָתֵי, גַּדְפָּא יְמִינָא, עַל גַּבֵּי עַמּוּדָא דְּאֶשָּׁא,
וְגוּפָא וְגַדְפָּא שְׂמָאלָא, עַל גַּבֵּי עַמּוּדָא דַּעֲנָנָא. וְהַהוּא נִשְׁרָא הֲוֵי
מַיְיתֵי תְּרֵין טַרְפִּין בְּפוּמֵהּ, אָתָא עַמּוּדָא דַּעֲנָנָא, וְעַמּוּדָא דְּאֶשָּׁא,
וְהַהוּא נִשְׁרָא עֲלַיְיהוּ, וְסַגְדִּין לְקָמֵיהּ דִּשְׁלֹמֹה מַלְכָּא.

341. At that moment, a pillar of fire and pillar of cloud would come. On the cloud pillar was an eagle, large and powerful. In this manner DID THE EAGLE APPROACH; the right wing was over the pillar of fire, its body and left wing on the cloud pillar. That eagle brought two leaves in its mouth. All three, the pillar of cloud, pillar of fire, and the eagle bowed before King Solomon.

342. אָתָא נִשְׁרָא, וּמָאִיךְ לְקָמֵיהּ, וְיָהִיב לֵיהּ אִינּוּן טַרְפִּין, נָטִיל לוֹן
שְׁלֹמֹה מַלְכָּא, וַהֲוָה מֵרִיחַ בְּהוּ, וַהֲוָה יָדַע בְּהוֹן סִימָן, וְאָמַר דָּא אִיהוּ
דְּנוֹפֵל, וְדָא אִיהוּ דִּגְלוּי עֵינַיִם. בְּשַׁעֲתָא דִּתְרֵין טַרְפִּין הֲווֹ, הֲוָה יָדַע,
דְּתַרְוַויְיהוּ, נוֹפֵל וּגְלוּי עֵינַיִם בָּעָאן לְאוֹדְעָא לֵיהּ מִלִּין.

342. The eagle came, bent before him, and presented him with the leaves. King Solomon took them, smelled them, and recognized the sign. He said that one is from "falling down," and the other is of "having his eyes open" (Bemidbar 24:16). When the two leaves were before him, he realized that both "falling down" and "having his eyes open" wished to reveal something to him.

343. מַה עָבִיד, חָתִים כֻּרְסָיֵּיהּ בְּגוּשְׁפַנְקָא, דַּהֲוָה חָקִיק בֵּיהּ שְׁמָא
קַדִּישָׁא. וְאִיהוּ נָטִיל עִזְקָא דְּחָקִיק עֲלֵיהּ שְׁמָא קַדִּישָׁא, וְסָלִיק לְאַגְרָא,
וְרָכִיב עַל הַהוּא נִשְׁרָא, וְאָזִיל לֵיהּ. וְהַהוּא נִשְׁרָא, הֲוָה מִסְתַּלַּק, לְרוּם
עֲנָנִין, וּבְכָל אֲתָר דְּאִיהוּ עָבַר, הֲוָה אִתְחֲשָׁךְ נְהוֹרָא. חַכִּימֵי דַּהֲווֹ
בְּהַהוּא אֲתָר דְּאִתְחֲשָׁךְ נְהוֹרָא, הֲווֹ יַדְעֵי, וַהֲווֹ אַמְרֵי, שְׁלֹמֹה מַלְכָּא
הָא אָזִיל, וְאַעֲבַר הָכָא, וְלָא יַדְעֵי לְאָן אֲתָר הֲוָה אָזִיל. טִפְּשִׁין דַּהֲווֹ
תַּמָּן, הֲווֹ אַמְרֵי עֲנָנִין הֲווֹ אִינּוּן, דְּקָא אַזְלֵי וְחָשִׁיךְ עָלְמָא.

343. What did he do? He stamped his throne with the same seal in which the Holy Name was engraved. He took the ring that was engraved with the Holy Name and went up to the attic. He rode on top of the eagle and took off. The eagle climbed to the highest clouds and wherever he passed, the light dimmed. The wise men where the light dimmed understood and said that King Solomon was passing by, but they did not know where he was going. The fools said the clouds are causing the darkness.

344. גְּבַהּ נִשְׂרָא בַּהֲדֵיהּ, וּפָרַח אַרְבַּע מְאָה פַּרְסִין, עַד דְּמָטָא לְטוּרֵי חָשׁוֹךְ. וְתַמָּן אִיהוּ תַּרְמוּד בַּמִּדְבָּר בְּהָרִים, וְאִיהוּ נָחִית תַּמָּן. זָקִיף רֵישֵׁיהּ, וְחָמֵי טוּרָא חָשׁוֹךְ, וַהֲוָה יָדַע תַּמָּן כָּל מַה דְּאִצְטְרִיךְ. וַהֲוָה יָדַע דְּתַמָּן יֵעוּל. הֲוָה רָכִיב עַל נִשְׂרָא כְּמִלְקַדְמִין, וְטָאס וְעָאל לְגוֹ טוּרִין, עַד הַהוּא אֲתָר דַּחֲזֵיתָא תַּמָּן, קָרָא בְּחֵילָא וְאָמַר, יְיָ׳ רָמָה יָדְךָ בַּל יֶחֱזָיוּן וְגוֹ׳.

344. The eagle lifted a bird with him and flew four hundred parasangs until arriving at the mountains of darkness. There Tarmod lies amidst the wilderness in the mountains. He descended there, raised his head, saw the mountains of darkness and knew all that was needed. He realized that he MUST enter there. He rode the eagle again and flew into the mountains to that place where the olive tree is located. He cried loudly, "Hashem, when Your hand is lifted up, they will not see" (Yeshayah 26:11).

345. עָאל תַּמָּן, עַד דְּקָרִיב לְהַהוּא אֲתָר, שַׁוֵּי עִזְקָא קַמַּיְיהוּ, וְקָרִיב, וְתַמָּן הֲוָה יָדַע כָּל מַה דְּבָעֵי מֵאִינּוּן חָכְמְתָן נוּכְרָאִין, דְּבָעֵי לְמִנְדַּע. כֵּיוָן דַּהֲווֹ אַמְרִין לֵיהּ כָּל מַה דְּבָעֵי, כְּדֵין הֲוָה רָכִיב עַל הַהוּא נִשְׂרָא, וְתָב לְאַתְרֵיהּ. כֵּיוָן דַּהֲוָה יָתִיב עַל כּוּרְסְיֵיהּ, אִתְיַישַּׁב בְּדַעְתֵּיהּ וַהֲוָה מְמַלֵּל בְּדַעְתֵּיהּ מִלִּין דְּחָכְמְתָא יַקִּירָא. בְּהַהִיא שַׁעְתָּא הֲוָה אָמַר, וְשַׁבְתִּי אֲנִי וָאֶרְאֶה, שַׁבְתִּי וַדַּאי מֵהַהוּא אָרְחָא, שַׁבְתִּי מֵהַהִיא חָכְמְתָא, וְאִתְיַישַּׁבְת בְּלִבַּאי וּבְדַעְתָּאי. וּכְדֵין וָאֶרְאֶה אֶת כָּל הָעֲשׁוּקִים.

345. He entered and approached the area OF THE OLIVE TREE, placed the ring before them, and approached. There he learned whatever he wished of

the foreign wisdom that interested him. Once told what he needed, he again boarded the eagle and returned to his place. Once again sitting on his throne, he thought of and discussed this precious wisdom with himself. He then said, "So I returned, and considered," MEANING, I have returned from that trip, I have brought back this wisdom and I have assembled it in my mind, and considered then "all the oppressions that are done."

346. סָלְקָא דַעְתָּךְ דְּכָל עֲשִׁיקִין דַּהֲווֹ בְּעָלְמָא, הֲוָה חָמֵי שְׁלֹמֹה מַלְכָּא. אֶלָּא, מַאי עֲשׁוּקִים אִלֵּין דְּהוּא אָמַר. אִינּוּן יְנוֹקִין דְּמֵתִין בְּתוּקְפָּא דְּאִמְּהוֹן, דְּקָא עֲשׁוּקִים מִכַּמָּה סִטְרִין, עֲשׁוּקִים בַּאֲתַר עִלָּאָה דִּלְעֵילָּא, וַעֲשׁוּקִים לְתַתָּא. וְהָא חַבְרַיָּיא אִתְּעֲרוּ, וְהָכִי הוּא, אֲבָל סַגִּיאִין אִינּוּן. קוּם סָבָא, אִתְּעַר בְּחֵילָךְ. סָבָא אֵימָא מִילָךְ, דְּוַדַּאי בְּלָא דְחִילוּ תֵּימָא.

346. Do you really believe that all the oppressed in the world were seen by King Solomon, THAT THE VERSE SAYS THAT I "CONSIDERED ALL THE OPPRESSIONS"? HE ANSWERS: But the oppressed mentioned are the children dying while on the knees of their mother, deprived in several ways: oppressed in the supernal area above, FROM THE STANDPOINT OF THEIR SPIRIT, and oppressed below, FROM THE PHYSICAL STANDPOINT. The friends have commented about this. Yet there are many OPRESSED BESIDES THESE. HE SAID TO HIMSELF: Old man, rise, be alert, speak your words, for surely you will speak without fear.

347. לֵית עָשׁוּק כְּאִינּוּן עֲשׁוּקִים, דַּהֲוָה אִיהוּ עָשִׁיק בְּקַדְמֵיתָא, אוֹ מִתַּלְתָּא לְאָחֳרָא, כְּמָה דִכְתִיב, פּוֹקֵד עֲוֹן אָבוֹת עַל בָּנִים וְעַל בְּנֵי בָנִים עַל שִׁלֵּשִׁים וְעַל רִבֵּעִים.

347. There is no one so oppressed as those whom one oppressed previously BY SINNING, or IF DUE TO HIS SIN, the third generation TO THE FOURTH after him ARE PUNISHED; THE CHILDREN DIE WITHOUT SIN AND SO THEIR OPPRESSION IS NOT THAT HARSH. THIS IS NOT SO IF THEY THEMSELVES, THEIR FATHERS, OR THEIR GRANDFATHERS SIN. As it is written: "punishing the iniquity of the fathers upon the children unto the third and fourth generation" (Shemot 20:5).

348. הֵיךְ הֲוָה עָשִׁיק. שְׁלֹמֹה מַלְכָּא צָוַוח וְאָמַר אָדָם עָשׁוּק בְּדָם נָפֶשׁ

עַד בּוֹר יָנוּס אַל יִתְמְכוּ בוֹ. כֵּיוָן דְּהוּא עָשׁוּק, בְּדַם נֶפֶשׁ, הוּא, אוֹ בְּנוֹ,
אוֹ בֶּן בְּנוֹ, יְהוֹן עֲשׁוּקִין בְּטִיקְלָא, דִּכְתִיב עַד בּוֹר יָנוּס אַל יִתְמְכוּ בוֹ.
עַד הַהוּא בּוֹר רַק יָנוּס מֵאֲתַר קַדִּישָׁא, וְאַל יִתְמְכוּ בוֹ בְּהַאי עָלְמָא.
כֵּיוָן דְּאִיהוּ עָשׁוּק בְּדַם נֶפֶשׁ, אִיהוּ אוֹ זַרְעֵיה, לֶהֱווֹ עֲשׁוּקִים מֵהַהוּא
סִטְרָא אַחֲרָא.

348. HE ASKS: How would he oppress? WHAT WAS HIS SIN? HE
ANSWERS: King Solomon cried out, "A man that is burdened with the blood
of any person shall flee to the pit; let none support him" (Mishlei 28:17).
Now that he is oppressed WITH THE SIN OF SHEDDING the blood of the
soul, he, his son or grandson will be held hostage upon the scale BY THE
OTHER SIDE, as it is written, "shall flee to the pit; let none support him."
So to the pit OF THE OTHER SIDE let him flee from Holiness without
support in this world. Once guilty of THE SIN OF blood of any person, he or
his seed will be oppressed by the Other Side.

349. אִית עָשׁוּק, מִשְּׁאָר עֲשׁוּקִים, כד״א לֹא תַעֲשׁוֹק אֶת רֵעֲךָ. אִיהוּ
עָבַר וְעָשַׁק, אִיהוּ עָשׁוּק בִּבְנוֹי, מֵהַהוּא סִטְרָא אַחֲרָא. וּבְג״כ אָמַר, אֶת
כָּל הָעֲשׁוּקִים. אָמַר שְׁלֹמֹה, קָאִימְנָא בְּכָל אִינּוּן עֲשׁוּקִים, בְּכָל סִטְרִין
דַּעֲשָׁק.

349. There are those oppressed more than others. They are OPPRESSED
BECAUSE OF THE SIN OF: "YOU SHALL NOT DEFRAUD," WHICH HIS
FATHER, OR GRANDFATHER, HAS TRANSGRESSED, as written "You shall
not defraud your neighbor" (Vayikra 19:13). He transgressed and
oppressed, SO HE IS REPAID MEASURE FOR MEASURE. Thus, he becomes
oppressed via his sons through the hands of the Other Side. Therefore
Solomon says, 'of "all the oppressions (also: 'oppressed')" I am aware, AND
KNOW of every oppression, from whatever side it comes'. IT WAS NOT
NECESSARY THAT HE SAW EVERY OPPRESSION IN THE WORLD.

350. וְאַמַאי אִינּוּן עֲשׁוּקִים. אֲשֶׁר נַעֲשׂוּ תַּחַת הַשֶּׁמֶשׁ. אֲשֶׁר נַעֲשׂוּ,
אֲשֶׁר גָּרוּ מִבְּעֵי לֵיה, מַאי אֲשֶׁר נַעֲשׂוּ. אִי עֲשִׂיָּיה אִיהִי לִשְׁבָחָא, לָאו
עֲשִׂיָּיה דִּלְהוֹן אֶלָּא לְעֵילָּא מִן שִׁמְשָׁא.

350. HE ASKS: Why in the verse, "the oppressions (also: 'oppressed') that are done under the sun" does it say "that are done," when it should have been 'that dwelt'? Also, if the doing is praiseworthy, then their doing is above the sun, WHERE BENEFIT AND CORRECTION TAKE PLACE, BUT HERE THE VERSE MENTIONS "BENEATH THE SUN."

351. אֲבָל וַדַּאי נַעֲשׂוּ. הֵיךְ נַעֲשׂוּ. אֶלָּא כֵּיוָן דַּעֲשׁוּקִים מֵרוּחֵיהוֹן תַּמָּן, אֲמַאי אַתְיָין לְהַאי עָלְמָא. אֶלָּא רוּחִין וַדַּאי נַעֲשׂוּ, אִתְעֲבֵידוּ בְּרוּחִין וּבְגוּפָא בְּהַאי עָלְמָא, כֵּיוָן דְּאִשְׁתַּכְלַל גּוּפָא דִּלְהוֹן, וְאִתְעֲבֵיד הַהוּא רוּחָא בְּגוּפָא זַךְ וְנָקִי בְּלָא לִכְלוּכָא דְּחוֹבִין, בְּהַאי עָלְמָא, כְּדֵין אִתְעֲשַׁק גּוּפָא, כְּמָה דְּאִתְעֲשַׁק רוּחָא. וְהַאי אִיהוּ גּוּפָא, דְּאִתְהֲנֵי בֵּיהּ יַתִּיר מִכֹּלָּא. וַעֲשׁוּקִין אַחֲרָנִין אִית, בְּכַמָּה זִינִין מֵרוּחִין תַּמָּן, וְלָא נַעֲשׂוּ בְּגוּפִין. אֲבָל אִלֵּין, אִינּוּן עֲשׁוּקִים אֲשֶׁר נַעֲשׂוּ.

351. HE ANSWERS: Assuredly they "are done," but howso? If they are deprived of their spirit, why come to this world THROUGH REINCARNATION? THE EXPRESSION 'DOING (HEB. *ASIYAH*)' APPLIES TO THE BODY, WHICH IS IN THE WORLD OF ASIYAH. Spirits are surely completed, fashioned with spirit and body in this world. When the body is perfected, and that spirit is fashioned AND CLOTHED in a pure, clean body without the soil of sin in this world, then the body becomes as deprived as the spirit. This is the body that THE OTHER SIDE enjoys above all others. There are other oppressed SPIRITS of various types not fashioned into bodies, NEVER INCARNATED IN THIS WORLD. But these are "the oppressed that are done" WITH BODIES, AND SO THE VERSE IS WRITTEN, "THAT ARE DONE."

352. אִית אַחֲרָנִין, אֲשֶׁר נַעֲשׂוּ, וְאִטְרָחוּ בְּנֵי נָשָׁא לְמָארֵיהוֹן. וּמַאן אִיהוּ. מַאן דְּעָשִׁיק אִתְּתָא דְּחַבְרֵיהּ בְּטָמִירוּ, אוֹ בְּאִתְגַּלְיָיא. וְהַהוּא וַלְדָּא דְּאִתְיְלִיד מִנַּיְיהוּ, עָשׁוּק אִיהוּ, בְּלָא רְעוּתָא דְּמָארֵיהוֹן, וְלָא יָדַע בַּעֲלָהּ דְּאִתְּתָא, אִינּוּן עוֹבָדִין עֲשׁוּקִין אִינּוּן, וְאִטְרָחוּ לְקוּדְשָׁא בְּרִיךְ הוּא לְמֶעְבַּד לוֹן גּוּפָא, וּלְצַיְּירָא לוֹן צוּרָה, אִלֵּין עֲשׁוּקִים אֲשֶׁר נַעֲשׂוּ. אֲשֶׁר נַעֲשׂוּ וַדַּאי גּוּפִין דִּלְהוֹן, עַל כָּרְחָא. בְּג״כ, שְׁלֹמֹה מַלְכָּא אָמַר,

וָאֶרְאֶה אֶת כָּל הָעֲשׁוּקִים, בְּכָל זִינֵי עֲשׁוּקִים קָאִימְנָא, אִינּוּן אֲשֶׁר
נַעֲשׂוּ וְאִתְעֲבִידוּ בַּעֲשִׂיָּיה.

352. There are others that were made where people implored their Master. Who are they? The child born from one who oppressed his neighbor's wife secretly or openly is oppressed, as the consent of their Master was not obtained and it was without knowledge of the husband of the woman. These creations are oppressions, and they make it imperative that the Holy One, blessed be He, provide them with a body, and design an image. There are "the oppressions that are made," since their bodies are made by compulsion. For this reason, King Solomon said: 'I "considered all the oppressions," I am aware and know of many kinds of oppression made in Asiyah.'

353. כְּמָה דְּהָנֵי אִינּוּן עֲשׁוּקִין, דִּכְבָר נַעֲשׂוּ בְּעָרְלָה רַבֵּי וְנָטִיל וְגָדִיל
גּוּפָא, וְעָבֵיד לֵיהּ, וּלְבָתַר עַשְׁקִין לוֹן מִנֵּיהּ, וְנַטְלִין לוֹן, הֲרֵי עֲשׁוּקִים
אֲשֶׁר נַעֲשׂוּ, וְעַל כֹּלָּא קָאֵים שְׁלֹמֹה מַלְכָּא וְאָמַר, קָאִימְנָא עַל כָּל
הָעֲשׁוּקִים אֲשֶׁר נַעֲשׂוּ.

353. Like these, there are oppressions that were done by the foreskin, that took, caused the body to grow, made it, and later, UPON BECOMING BAR-MITZVAH, they snatch it from it. This is another example of "oppressions that are done." About all these, King Solomon said: 'I am aware AND KNOW of all "the oppressions that are done."'

354. וְהִנֵּה דִּמְעַת הָעֲשֻׁקִים, כֹּלָּא אוֹשְׁדִין דִּמְעִין, עִם טַעֲנָה קַמֵּי
קוּדְשָׁא בְּרִיךְ הוּא. הָנֵי אוֹשְׁדִין דִּמְעִין, דְּהָא עָרְלָה רַבֵּי לוֹן, וְגָדִיל
לוֹן, עַד י"ג שְׁנִין, וּלְבָתַר עַשְׁקִין לוֹן מֵעָרְלָה, וְנָטִיל לוֹן קוּדְשָׁא בְּרִיךְ
הוּא, הָא לָךְ עֲשׁוּקִין אֲשֶׁר נַעֲשׂוּ כְּבָר.

354. "and behold the tears of such as were oppressed." Everybody shed tears with complaints before the Holy One, blessed be He, because the foreskin, THE OTHER SIDE, caused them to reach thirteen years and then later they were taken from the foreskin, and the Holy One, blessed be He, takes them. These are oppressions that were already done.

355. עָבַר עֲבֵירָה קַטְלִין לֵיהּ. לוֹן אִית טַעֲנָה, וְזַמְּנִין לוֹמַר, מָארֵי
דְעָלְמָא, תִּינוֹק בַּר יוֹמֵיהּ דְּחָב, דַּיְינִין לֵיהּ דִּינָא. אֲנָא בַּר יוֹמֵיהּ
הֲוֵינָא, דְּהָא מֵהַהוּא יוֹמָא קָרֵי לֵיהּ קוּדְשָׁא בְּרִיךְ הוּא בֵּן, דִּכְתִיב יְיָ'
אָמַר אֵלַי בְּנִי אַתָּה אֲנִי הַיּוֹם יְלִדְתִּיךָ, מָארֵיהּ דְּעָלְמָא, יְלִיד בַּר יוֹמָא,
דִּינָא עַבְדִּין לֵיהּ, הֲרֵי דִּמְעַת אִינּוּן הָעֲשׁוּקִים וְאֵין לָהֶם מְנַחֵם.

355. A THIRTEEN YEAR AND A DAY OLD that committed a sin FOR WHICH THE PENALTY IS DEATH, is put to death. These people have reason to complain and may in the future say: Master of the Universe, a child one day old who has sinned is SO judged?! I am like a child one day old, AS RIGHT AFTER BAR-MITZVAH, the Holy One, blessed be He, called me son, as it is written, "Hashem said to me, 'you are My son, this day I have begotten you'" (Tehilim 2:7). Master of the universe, is a child who is one day old to be so judged? These are "the tears of such as were oppressed, and they had no comforter."

356. וְאִית עָשׁוּק אַחֵר, הַהוּא עָשׁוּק דְּאִקְרֵי מַמְזֵר, כַּד נָפַק מֵעָלְמָא,
מִיָּד מַפְרִישִׁין לֵיהּ מִקְּהִלָּתָא דְּעַמָּא קַדִּישָׁא. הַהוּא מַמְזֵר, עַנְיָא
מִסְכְּנָא, אוֹשִׁיד דִּמְעִין קָמֵי קוּדְשָׁא בְּרִיךְ הוּא, וְאַטְעִין קַמֵּיהּ, מָארֵיהּ
דְעָלְמָא, אִי אֲבָהָתַי חָאבוּ, אֲנָא מַה חוֹבָא עֲבִידְנָא, הָא עוֹבָדַאי,
מִתְתַּקְנָן לְקַמָּךְ הֲווֹ, וְהִנֵּה דִּמְעַת הָעֲשׁוּקִים וְאֵין לָהֶם מְנַחֵם. וְכֵן לְכָל
אִינּוּן עֲשׁוּקִים, אִית לוֹן טַעֲנָה קָמֵי קוּדְשָׁא בְּרִיךְ הוּא, וּמֵהַהִיא טַעֲנָה
לֵית לוֹן מְנַחֵם, וְלֵית דְּיָתִיב מִלָּה עַל לִבְּהוֹן.

356. There is another example of oppressed. This oppressed one is called a bastard. When he is deceased, he is set apart from the holy congregation. This poor, unfortunate bastard [this refers to a real bastard, born to illicit relationship] pours out tears before the Holy One, blessed be He, with the following complaint: Master of the Universe, if my forebearers sinned, what wrong have I done, my actions are proper before you! Here are "the tears of such as were oppressed, and they had no comforter." It is the same with all these oppressed who have reason to complain to the Holy One, blessed be He; with this complaint there is no comforter and no one to soothe their hearts.

357. וּמַה דְּאָמַר וְהִנֵּה דִּמְעַת הָעֲשׁוּקִים, אִלֵּין אִינוּן דְּמֵתִין בְּתוּקְפָּא דְּאִמְּהוֹן, אִלֵּין עַבְדִּין לְאוֹשָׁדָא דִמְעִין, לְכָל בְּנֵי עָלְמָא, בְּגִין דְּלֵית דִּמְעִין דְּנַפְקֵי מִלִּבָּא, כְּהָנֵי דִמְעִין, דְּכָל בְּנֵי עָלְמָא תָּוְוהִין וְאַמְרִין, דִּינִין דְּקוּדְשָׁא בְּרִיךְ הוּא קְשׁוֹט אִינוּן, וְעַל אֹרַח קְשׁוֹט אַזְלֵי. הָנֵי מַסְכְּנֵי יְנוּקֵי דְּלָא חָאבוּ, אֲמַאי מִיתוּ. אָן דִּינָא דִּקְשׁוֹט, דְּעָבֵיד מָארֵי עָלְמָא. אִי בְּחוֹבֵי אֲבָהַתְהוֹן אִסְתַּלְּקֵי מֵעָלְמָא, אֲמַאי. וַדַּאי אֵין לָהֶם מְנַחֵם.

357. This that says, "behold the tears of the oppressed," refers to those who die in the bosom of their mother. These are bound to shed tears for mankind, for there are no other tears from the heart like these tears. For all the people in the world stand in wonder and say: But the Judgments of the Holy One, blessed be He, are True and follow a truthful course; why do these innocent children die? Where is the Judgment of Truth, that the Holy One, blessed be He, practices? If it is due to the sins of the parents, why is this so? Assuredly, "they had no comforter."

358. תּוּ, וְהִנֵּה דִּמְעַת הָעֲשׁוּקִים, הַהוּא דִּמְעָה דִּלְהוֹן בְּהַהוּא עָלְמָא, דְּקָא מְגִינִין עַל חַיָּיא. דִּתְנַן אֲתָר אִית מִתְתַּקְּנָא לוֹן בְּהַהוּא עָלְמָא, דַּאֲפִילוּ צַדִּיקִים גְּמוּרִים לָא יַכְלִין לְקַיְּימָא תַּמָּן, וְקוּדְשָׁא בְּרִיךְ הוּא רָחִים לוֹן, וְאִתְדָּבַּק בְּהוּ, וְאַתְקִין בְּהוּ, מְתִיבְתָּא עִלָּאָה דִּילֵיהּ. וַעֲלַיְיהוּ כְּתִיב מִפִּי עוֹלְלִים וְיוֹנְקִים יִסַּדְתָּ עֹז. וּמַאי תּוֹעַלְתָּא עַבְדִּין תַּמָּן, וַאֲמַאי סַלְּקִין תַּמָּן. דִּכְתִיב לְמַעַן צוֹרְרֶיךָ לְהַשְׁבִּית אוֹיֵב וּמִתְנַקֵּם. וְכֵן אִית אֲתָר אָחֳרָא לְבַעֲלֵי תְּיוּבְתָּא.

358. Moreover, "behold the tears of such as were oppressed" refers to their tears in that world that protects the living. We learned there is a designated place in that world, where even the completely pious have no standing. And the Holy One, blessed be He, loves them, clings to them and places them in His supernal Yeshiva. About them it is written: "Out the mouths of babes and sucklings have you founded strength" (Tehilim 8:3). What is the gain from their being there, and why do they ascend there? AS THE VERSE CONTINUES, "because of your enemies, that you may silence the enemy and the avenger." There is also another place for those who repent.

A Synopsis

The merchant says that prior to the Sabbath, the letters, the written alphabet and the tablets had already been created. These were the work of Elohim, and it is only after the completion of Creation that we find the full name "Hashem Elohim". "engraved upon the tablets" means freedom from everything – from the Angel of Death, from the subjection of nations. It is the seal of the World to Come.

359. תָּנֵינָן, עֲשָׂרָה דְּבָרִים אִתְבְּרִיאוּ בְּע"ש וְכוּ'. הַכְּתָב וְהַמִּכְתָּב וְהַלּוּחוֹת. דִּכְתִיב וְהַלֻּחֹת מַעֲשֵׂה אֱלֹהִים הֵמָה וְהַמִּכְתָּב מִכְתַּב אֱלֹהִים הוּא. מַאי אִירְיָא מִדְּהָכִי דְּע"ש הֲוָה, וְדִילְמָא אֶלֶף שְׁנִין לְבָתַר, אוֹ בְּשַׁעְתָּא דְּקַיִּימוּ יִשְׂרָאֵל עַל טוּרָא דְּסִינַי. אֶלָּא, וַדַּאי הָכִי הוּא דִּבְע"ש הֲוָה. ת"ח, בְּכָל עוֹבָדָא דִּבְרֵאשִׁית, לָא אִתְּמַר שֵׁם מָלֵא, אֶלָּא אֱלֹהִים אֱלֹהִים, בְּכָל מַה דְּאִתְבְּרֵי. וְכֻלְּהוּ שֵׁם אֱלֹהִים, עַד דְּכָל עוֹבָדָא אִשְׁתְּכְלַל בְּע"ש. מִדְּאִשְׁתְּכְלָלוּ כָּל עוֹבָדָא, אִקְרֵי יְיָ' אֱלֹהִים, שֵׁם מָלֵא.

359. We learned of ten things which were created just prior to the Shabbat: the letters, the written alphabet, and the tablets, as it is written, "And the tablets were the work of Elohim, and the writing was the writing of Elohim" (Shemot 32:16). HE ASKS: wherein do we see that they were created just before Shabbat? Perhaps they were created a thousand years later or at the time Yisrael stood at Mount Sinai? HE ANSWERS: It surely was just before Shabbat. Come and behold: throughout Creation we do not find the full Name, but only Elohim. That Name is found throughout until Creation is completed at Shabbat eve. Only after the completion of Creation, do we find the full Name: "Hashem Elohim."

360. וְאע"ג דִּבְשֵׁם אֱלֹהִים אִתְבְּרֵי כֹּלָּא, לָא אִשְׁתְּכְלַל בַּעֲשִׂיָּה, כָּל מַה דְּאִתְבְּרֵי, עַד ע"ש. בְּהַהִיא שַׁעְתָּא אִשְׁתְּכְלַל כֹּלָּא בַּעֲשִׂיָּה, דִּכְתִיב מְלַאכְתּוֹ אֲשֶׁר עָשָׂה. מִכָּל מְלַאכְתּוֹ אֲשֶׁר עָשָׂה. וְקַיְימָא בְּמַעֲשֶׂה. וְע"ד כְּתִיב, וְהַלֻּחֹת מַעֲשֵׂה אֱלֹהִים, כַּד אִשְׁתְּכְלַל עָלְמָא, בְּשֵׁם אֱלֹהִים בְּמַעֲשֶׂה, וְלָא לְבָתַר, דִּכְתִיב יְיָ' אֱלֹהִים וּבְדָא אִשְׁתְּכְלַל עָלְמָא, וְקַיְימָא עַל קִיּוּמֵיהּ.

360. Even though with the name Elohim He created all, it did not go into effect until just prior to Shabbat. Only then was the work completely done, as it is written, "His work which He had done" (Beresheet 2:2), and, "from all His work, which Elohim had created" (Ibid. 3) MEANING, only then did it go into effect. And so the verse, "And the tablets were the work of Elohim," MEANS when the world was completed and done with the Name of Elohim, WHICH WAS AT SHABBAT EVE and not later, as when the verse refers to Hashem Elohim, then completion came to the world and it was set.

361. ת״ח, בְּהַהִיא שַׁעֲתָא דְּתָבַר מֹשֶׁה הַלּוּחוֹת, דִּכְתִּיב וַיְשַׁבֵּר אוֹתָם תַּחַת הָהָר. צָף אוֹקְיָינוֹס מֵאַתְרֵיה, וְסָלִיק לְשַׁטְפָא עָלְמָא. חָמָא מֹשֶׁה דְּאוֹקְיָינוֹס סָלִיק לְגַבַּיְיהוּ, וַהֲוָה בָּעֵי לְשַׁטְפָא עָלְמָא, מִיָּד וַיִּקַּח אֶת הָעֵגֶל אֲשֶׁר עָשׂוּ וַיִּשְׂרוֹף אוֹתוֹ בָּאֵשׁ וְגוֹ׳, וַיִּזֶר עַל פְּנֵי הַמַּיִם. קָם מֹשֶׁה עַל מֵי אוֹקְיָינוֹס וְאָמַר, מַיָא מַיָא מָה אַתּוּן בָּעָאן. אָמְרוּ וְכִי אִתְקַיָּים עָלְמָא אֶלָּא בְּאוֹרַיְיתָא דִּלּוּחוֹת, וְעַל אוֹרַיְיתָא דְּשָׁקְרוּ בָּהּ יִשְׂרָאֵל וְעָבְדוּ עֶגְלָא דְּדַהֲבָא, אֲנָן בָּעָאן לְשַׁטְפָא עָלְמָא.

361. Come and behold: at the time Moses smashed the tablets, as it is written, "and broke them at the foot of the mountain" (Shemot 32:19), the ocean rose from its position to flood the universe, and at once, "he took the calf which they had made, and burnt it in the fire… and scattered it upon the water" (Ibid. 20). Moses rose against the ocean and said: 'Waters, waters, what do you want?' They replied: 'The universe can only survive through the Torah upon the tablets, but the children of Yisrael have rejected the Torah and made a golden calf instead. We wish to inundate the world.'

362. מִיָּד אָמַר לוֹן, הָא כָּל מַה דְּעָבְדוּ בְּחוֹבָא דְּעֶגְלָא, הָא מָסִיר לְכוֹן, וְלָא דַּי כָּל אִינּוּן אַלְפִין דְּנָפְלוּ מִנַּיְיהוּ, מִיָּד וַיִּזֶר עַל פְּנֵי הַמַּיִם. לָא הֲווֹ מִשְׁתַּכְּחֵי מַיָּא, עַד דְּנָטִיל מַיָּא מִנַּיְיהוּ וְאַשְׁקֵי לוֹן, מִיָּד אִשְׁתְּקַע אוֹקְיָינוֹס בְּאַתְרֵיה.

362. Immediately, he said to them: 'All that transpired with the sin of the golden calf is known to you. Is it not enough the thousands that perished because of it?' Immediately, he "scattered it upon the water," but the waters

were not pacified until he took water from them, FROM THE OCEAN, and caused the children of Yisrael to drink of it. Then the ocean sank to its position.

363. דְּהָא בְּהַהוּא מִדְבָּר לָא הֲווֹ מַיָּא, דִּכְתִיב לֹא מְקוֹם זֶרַע וְגוֹ'. וּמַיִם אַיִן לִשְׁתּוֹת. וְאִי תֵּימָא, לְבֵירָא דְּמִרְיָם אַרְמִי לֵיהּ. ח״ו, דְּתַמָּן שָׁדֵי מֹשֶׁה דִּכְרָנָא בִּישָׁא דָּא לְמִשְׁתֵּי לְבָתַר. וְתוּ, דְּעַד כָּאן לָא הֲוָה לְהוּ בֵּירָא, עַד דְּאָתוּ לְמִדְבַּר מַתָּנָה, דִּכְתִיב בְּאֵר חֲפָרוּהָ שָׂרִים וְגוֹ'. וּמִמִּדְבָּר מַתָּנָה. מִתַּמָּן יַרְתוּ בֵּירָא. כְּתִיב הָכָא עַל פְּנֵי הַמַּיִם, וּכְתִיב הָתָם עַל פְּנֵי תְהוֹם.

363. For in the wilderness, there was no water, as it is written, "it is no place of seed... nor is there any water to drink" (Bemidbar 20:5), SO HE MUST HAVE USED THE WATERS OF THE OCEAN. One may think that he threw THE ASHES into the well of Miriam, but heaven forbid that Moses would throw a memorial of this terrible act there, and drink of it afterwards. Furthermore, at that point they did not have that well, it was only when arriving at the wilderness of Matana, as it is written, "the well dug by the prince... and from the wilderness they went to Matana" (Bemidbar 21:18); at that point they acquired the well. It is written here, "upon the water" (Shemot 32:20), and it is written elsewhere, "upon the face of the deep" (Beresheet 1:2); JUST AS THERE THE REFERENCE IS TO THE OCEAN, SO IT IS HERE TOO.

364. חָרוּת עַל הַלֻּחֹת, מַאי חָרוּת עַל הַלֻּחֹת. הָכִי אוּקְמוּהָ, חֵירוּ מִמַּלְאַךְ הַמָּוֶת, חֵירוּ מִשִׁעְבּוּד מַלְכְיוֹת, חֵירוּ מִכֹּלָּא, הָכִי הוּא. וּמַאי חָרוּת. גּוּשְׁפַּנְקָא דְּעָלְמָא דְּאָתֵי, דְּבֵיהּ הֲוָה חֵירוּת, בְּכָל מִינֵי חֵירוּת. וְאִלְמָלֵא לָא אִתְבָּרוּ, כָּל מַה דִּאָתָא לְעָלְמָא לְבָתַר, לָא אָתָא, וַהֲווֹ יִשְׂרָאֵל דִּיּוּקְנָא דְּמַלְאָכִין עִלָּאִין דִּלְעֵילָּא. וְעַל דָּא אַבְרִיז קְרָא וְאָמַר, וְהַלֻּחֹת מַעֲשֵׂה אֱלֹהִים וְגוֹ', לָא תֵּימָא דִּלְבָתַר דְּעָלְמָא אִשְׁתַּכְלַל, וְאִדְכַּר שֵׁם מָלֵא הֲווֹ, אֶלָּא בְּשַׁעֲתָא דְּאִשְׁתְּכַלַּל בְּשֵׁם אֱלֹהִים, עַד לָא יֵיעוּל שַׁבָּת.

364. "engraved upon the tablets." What is meant by, "engraved (Heb.

charut) upon the tablets"? HE ANSWERS: We have that it means freedom (Heb. *cherut*) from the Angel of Death, freedom from subjection of nations, freedom from everything. What is freedom? It is the seal of the World to Come, wherein there is freedom expressed in all kinds of freedoms. Had Moses not broken THE TABLETS, what followed in the world would not have happened; Yisrael would have retained an angelic image above and below. This is what the verse proclaimed, "And the tablets were the work of Elohim." Do not say that once the world was completed, and the complete name OF YUD HEI VAV HEI ELOHIM was mentioned, then THE TABLETS came about. It is not so, but rather when the world was completed with the name of Elohim prior to the Shabbat.

365. הֵמָּה, מַאי הֵמָּה. הֲפוֹךְ מה"ה הָווּ. מִתְּרֵין סִטְרִין הָווּ. חֲדָא בְּעוֹבָדָא, וַחֲדָא דְּחֵירוּת לְעֵילָּא, רָשִׁים לְעֵילָּא לְנַטְרָא לְכֹלָּא. וְעַל דָּא המ"ה. וְהַמִּכְתָּב מִכְתַּב אֱלֹהִים הוּא, אֶשָּׁא אוּכְמָא עַל גַּבֵּי אֶשָּׁא חִוַּרָא. מִכְתַּב אֱלֹהִים הוּא, הַיְינוּ דִכְתִּיב, וְעָבַד הַלֵּוִי הוּא. חָרוּת כְּמָה דְּאִתְּמַר, דְּהָא יוֹבֵל קָרֵי חָרוּת, וְעָבֵיד חֵירוּת לְכָל עָלְמִין.

365. HE ASKS: IT IS WRITTEN, "WERE (HEB. *HEMAH*) THE WORK OF ELOHIM." What is meant by *hemah*, WHICH IS SUPERFLUOUS? HE ANSWERS: Switch its letters into *mehah* (lit. 'from *Hei-Hei'*) MEANING from two sides, THE TWO *HEI'S* OF THE NAME YUD HEI VAV HEI, BINAH AND MALCHUT. One, in deed – NAMELY THE LAST *HEI*, MALCHUT – one of the freedom above, WHICH IS THE FIRST *HEI*, BINAH, registered above IN BINAH to watch over everything. Hence it is written, "*hemah*." "…the writing is the writing of Elohim…" MEANING black fire on white fire. "…is (Heb. *hu*) the writing of Elohim…" resembles the verse, "the Levites shall do the service of the Tent (lit. 'of him', *hu*)" (Bemidbar 18:23) REFERRING TO BINAH CALLED '*HU*', DENOTING freedom, as we said, for Jubilee DENOTING BINAH, is also called 'freedom' as it proclaims freedom to all.

A Synopsis
The old merchant now reveals himself to be Yeva Saba (the elder), and Rabbi Chiya and Rabbi Yosi prostrate themselves before him and weep. They said to him: "May we be favored that our image be engraved in your heart as your seal is engraved in our heart."

366. ע"כ חַבְרַיָּיא. מִכָּאן וְהָלְאָה תִּנְדְּעוּן, דְּהָא סִטְרָא בִּישָׁא, לָא

שַׁלְטָא עֲלַיְיכוּ וַאֲנָא יֵיבָא סָבָא, קָאִימְנָא קָמַיְיכוּ, לְאִתְּעָרָא מִלִּין אִלֵּין, קָמוּ אִינּוּן, כְּמַאן דְּאִתְּעַר מִשֵּׁינָתֵיהּ, וְאִשְׁתְּטָחוּ קָמֵיהּ, וְלָא הֲווֹ יַכְלִין לְמַלְּלָא. לְבָתַר שַׁעֲתָא בָּכוּ.

366. Until this point ARE MY WORDS. From here on, be advised that the evil side will not have any hold on you. I, Yeva Saba (the elder) stand before you to make you aware of these things. RABBI CHIYA AND RABBI YOSI arose as one who had awakened from sleep, prostrated before him, unable to speak. After some time they wept.

367. פָּתַח רִבִּי חִיָּיא וְאָמַר, שִׂימֵנִי כַחוֹתָם עַל לִבֶּךָ כַּחוֹתָם עַל זְרוֹעֶךָ וְגוֹ', שִׂימֵנִי כַחוֹתָם, בְּשַׁעֲתָא דְּאִתְדַּבְּקָא כְּנֶסֶת יִשְׂרָאֵל בְּבַעֲלָהּ, אִיהִי אַמְרַת שִׂימֵנִי כַחוֹתָם, אָרְחָא דְּחוֹתָם, כֵּיוָן דְּאִתְדַּבָּק בְּהַהוּא אֲתָר דְּאִתְדַּבַּק שָׁבִיק בֵּיהּ כָּל דִּיּוּקְנֵיהּ, אַף עַל גַּב דְּהַהוּא חוֹתָם אָזִיל הָכָא וְהָכָא, וְלָא קַיְּימָא תַּמָּן, וְהָא אִתְעֲבַר מִנֵּיהּ, כָּל דִּיּוּקְנֵיהּ שָׁבִיק תַּמָּן, וְתַמָּן קַיְּימָא. אוֹף הָכִי אַמְרַת כ"י, כֵּיוָן דְּאִתְדַּבְּקְנָא בָּךְ, כָּל דִּיּוּקְנִי לֶיהֱוֵי חָקִיק בָּךְ, דְּאַף עַל גַּב דְּאֵיזִיל הָכָא אוֹ הָכָא, תִּשְׁכַּח דִּיּוּקְנִי חָקִיק בָּךְ, וְתִדְכַּר לִי.

367. Rabbi Chiya commenced the discussion: "Set me as a seal upon your heart, as a seal upon your arm..." (Shir Hashirim 8:6). "Set me as a seal"; when the Congregation of Yisrael, MALCHUT, clung to her husband, ZEIR ANPIN, she said, "Set me as a seal." The way of a seal is as follows: Once it comes in contact with something, it leaves its mark even though the seal itself moves about and does not remain there. It left its shape there, and there remains ITS SHAPE. The Congregation of Yisrael says the same: once I have clung to You, my mark will be engraved with You even though I move from place to place, my mark will remain with You and you will thus remember me.

368. וְכַחוֹתָם עַל זְרוֹעֶךָ, כְּמָה דִּכְתִיב שְׂמֹאלוֹ תַּחַת לְרֹאשִׁי וִימִינוֹ תְּחַבְּקֵנִי, אוֹף הָכִי, תְּהֵא דִּיּוּקְנִי חָקִיק תַּמָּן. וּבְכֵן אֶהֱא בָּךְ מִתְדַּבְּקָא לְעָלְמִין, וְלָא אִתְנְשֵׁי מִינָךְ. כִּי עַזָּה כַמָּוֶת אַהֲבָה, תַּקִּיפָא כַּמָּוֶת

אַהֲבָה, בְּתוּקְפָּא תַּקִּיף, כְּהַהוּא אֲתָר דְּשַׁרְיָא בֵּיה מוֹתָא. אַהֲבָה, הַהוּא אֲתָר דְּאִקְרֵי אַהֲבַת עוֹלָם.

368. "…as a seal upon your arm…" like the verse, "His left hand is under my head, and his right hand embraces me" (Shir Hashirim 2:6). So here, my mark will be engraved, and so I will always adhere to You and not be forgotten by You. "…for love is as strong as death…" mighty as that place where death dwells. Love is the place known as eternal love.

369. קָשָׁה כִשְׁאוֹל קִנְאָה, אוּף הָכִי, דְּהָא אִלֵּין שְׁמָהָן, מֵהַהוּא סִטְרָא אִינוּן. רְשָׁפֶיהָ רִשְׁפֵּי אֵשׁ, מַאן אִינוּן רִשְׁפֵּי אִלֵּין. אִינוּן אַבְנִין וּמַרְגְּלָן טָבָאן, דְּאִתְיְלִידוּ מֵהַהוּא אֵשׁ. שַׁלְהֶבֶת יָהּ. מֵהַהוּא שַׁלְהוֹבָא, דְּנָפְקָא מֵעָלְמָא עִלָּאָה, וְאִתְאַחֲדָא בִּכְנֶסֶת יִשְׂרָאֵל, לְמֶהֱוֵי כֹּלָּא חַד יְחוּדָא, וַאֲנָן, הָא אַהֲבָה וּרְשָׁפִין דְּשַׁלְהוֹבָא דְּלִבָּא אֲבַתְרָךְ, יְהֵא רַעֲוָא, דְּדִיּוּקְנָא דִילָן, תְּהֵא חֲקוּקָה בְּלִבָּךְ, כְּמָה דְּדִיּוּקְנָא דִילָךְ חַקִּיק בְּלִבָּן. נָשַׁק לוֹן, וּבָרִיךְ לוֹן וְאַזְלוּ.

369. "…jealousy is cruel as Sheol…" The same is here, AS MENTIONED EARLIER WITH LOVE. These names, SUCH AS LOVE, JEALOUSY, stem from that side, MEANING THE LEFT SIDE. "…the coals thereof are coals of fire." HE ASKS: What are these coals? HE ANSWERS: These refer to precious stones and pearls formed from this fire, REPRESENTING SUPERNAL LEVELS – MEANING from these flames emanating from the supernal world, FROM THE LEFT SIDE, BINAH takes hold of the Congregation of Yisrael to become one unity. AND HE SAID TO THE OLD MAN: As for us, our love and flaming heart is with you. May we be favored that our image be engraved in your heart as your seal is engraved in our heart. THE OLD MAN kissed them, blessed them and they left.

370. כַּד מָטוּ לְגַבֵּי דְּרַבִּי שִׁמְעוֹן, וְסָחוּ לֵיה כָּל מַה דְּאִירַע לוֹן, חַדִּי וְתַוָּוהּ, אָמַר, זַכָּאִין אַתּוּן דְּזָכִיתוּן לְכָל הַאי, וּמַה הֲוֵיתוּן בַּהֲדֵי אַרְיָא עִלָּאָה, גִּיבָּר תַּקִּיף, דְּלָא הֲווֹ כַּמָּה גִּיבָּרִין לְגַבֵּיה כְּלוּם, וְלָא יְדַעְתּוּן לְאִשְׁתְּמוֹדְעָא לֵיה מִיַּד. תַּוָּוהְנָא, אֵיךְ אִשְׁתְּזַבְתּוּן מֵעוֹנָשָׁא דִּילֵיה,

אֶלָּא קוּדְשָׁא בְּרִיךְ הוּא בָּעָא לְשֵׁזָבָא לְכוֹן, קָרָא עֲלַיְיהוּ, וְאֹרַח צַדִּיקִים כְּאוֹר נֹגַהּ הוֹלֵךְ וָאוֹר עַד נָכוֹן הַיּוֹם. בְּלֶכְתְּךָ לֹא יֵצֵר צַעֲדֶךָ וְאִם תָּרוּץ לֹא תִכָּשֵׁל. וְעַמֵּךְ כֻּלָּם צַדִּיקִים לְעוֹלָם יִרְשׁוּ אָרֶץ נֵצֶר מַטָּעַי מַעֲשֵׂה יָדַי לְהִתְפָּאֵר. ע"כ מן רב ייבא סבא.

370. When they reached Rabbi Shimon, they told him what transpired. He stood in awe and said: How fortunate are you to have merited this, you were with this supernal lion, this mighty hero compared to whom all mighty people are nothing, and you did not recognize him at first. I wonder how you were saved from his penalty – but the Holy One, blessed be He, wished to protect you. He said about them: "But the path of just men is like the gleam of sunlight, that shines ever more brightly until the height of noonday" (Mishlei 4:18). "When you go, your steps shall not be confined: and when you run, you shall not stumble" (Ibid. 12) "Your people also shall be all Righteous: they shall inherit the land for ever; they shall be the branch of My planting, the work of My hands, that I may be glorified" (Yeshayah 60:21). UNTIL THIS POINT ALL COMES FROM RAV YEVA SABA (THE ELDER).

4. "If men strive"

A Synopsis

The title verse is explained as saying that if Michael, representing holiness, and Samael, representing defilement, strive and hurt the congregation of Yisrael, Samael will be punished by the Holy One, blessed be He.

רעיא מהימנא

371. כִּי יִנָּצוּ אֲנָשִׁים. אִלֵּין, מִיכָאֵל וְס"מ. וְנָגְפוּ אִשָּׁה הָרָה, דָּא כ"י. וְיָצְאוּ יְלָדֶיהָ, בְּגָלוּתָא. עָנוֹשׁ יֵעָנֵשׁ, דָּא ס"מ, כַּאֲשֶׁר יָשִׁית עָלָיו בַּעַל הָאִשָּׁה, דָּא קוּדְשָׁא בְּרִיךְ הוּא.

Ra'aya Meheimna (the Faithful Shepherd)

371. "If men strive..." (Shemot 21:22) These are Michael and Samael- MICHAEL REPRESENTS HOLINESS, SAMAEL, DEFILEMENT. "...and hurt a woman with child..." (Ibid.) This is the Congregation of Yisrael, DENOTING MALCHUT; "so that her children depart from her," refers to the exile; "he shall be surely punished," refers to Samael; "according as the woman's husband will lay upon him" refers to the Holy One, blessed be He.

5. Returning that which was lost

A Synopsis

Rabbi Shimon says that the thing that was lost was Malchut, that Moses lost when the tablets broke. Malchut can rise only with the aid of her husband, Moses, and this is the lost thing returned. He tells Moses that the Torah was revealed to him because it is like the waters of a well; the well is said to be Malchut, which recognizes its master. All the waters of the universe are gathered within her, as it is endless, and "broader than the sea." Drawing water from this well brings all the world's wisdom. Rabbi Shimon says that in the future God will set aside cities of refuge for Moses, as in every generation there is the incarnation and expression of Moses.

372. פְּקוּדָא בָּתַר דָּא, לְהָשִׁיב אֲבֵדָה. וַאֲבַתְרֵיה לְהָשִׁיב הַגְּזֵל. אָמַר בּוּצִינָא קַדִּישָׁא, קוּדְשָׁא בְּרִיךְ הוּא עָתִיד לְאַהֲדָרָא לָךְ, אֲבֵדָה דְּאָבְדַת בְּגִין עֶרֶב רַב, וְדָא כַּלָה דִּילָךְ, דִּבְזִמְנָא דְּעָבְדוּ עֶרֶב רַב יַת עֶגְלָא, נָפְקַת כַּלָה דִּילָךְ, הה"ד וַיַּשְׁלֵךְ מִיָּדָו אֶת הַלֻחֹת.

372. The following precept is regarding returning lost articles, and to return that which was stolen. The Holy Luminary, MEANING RABBI SHIMON, SAID TO MOSES: The Holy One, blessed be He, will in the future return the article you lost because of the mixed multitudes. This is your bride, DENOTING MALCHUT, AS MOSES IS CONSIDERED THE HUSBAND OF THE MATRON. When the mixed multitudes made the calf, your bride fell, as the verse states, "he threw the tablets out of his hands" (Shemot 32:19), ALLUDING TO MALCHUT.

373. וְאִתְּמַר בָּךְ לֶךְ רֵד, הָתָם קָא רָמִיז נְחִיתוּ דִּילָךְ, בְּגָלוּתָא רְבִיעָאָה, לֶךְ: כְּגוֹן לֶךְ לְךָ מֵאַרְצְךָ וְגוֹ'. הָכָא שׁ, הֵן כָּל אֵלֶה יִפְעַל אֵל פַּעֲמִים שָׁלֹשׁ עִם גָּבֶר. הָכָא קָא רָמִיז לָךְ, לָךְ ג' זִמְנִין בְּגָלוּתָא. רְבִיעָאָה רֵד, בְּגִין בַּת יְחִידָה, כַּלָה דִּילָךְ, דְּנָפְלָה. הה"ד, נָפְלָה לֹא תוֹסִיף קוּם. וּמִיַּד דְּאַנְתְּ נָחִית בְּגִינֵיה, תָּקוּם עֲלָךְ וְהַאי אִיהוּ הַשָּׁבַת אֲבֵדָה דִּילָךְ.

373. It is mentioned with you, "Go, get you down" (Ibid. 7). That verse alludes to your demotion into the fourth exile. "Go" – ITS EXPLANATION IS

similar to "Get you out of your country" (Beresheet 12:1), MEANING ENTERING INTO EXILE. HERE, IN THE NAME OF MOSES, there is a *Shin*, CONSISTING OF THREE LINES, IN THE SECRET OF "Lo, El does all these things twice or three times with a man" (Iyov 33:29). Here, IN THE THREE LINES OF THE *SHIN*, it is indicated to you, Yisrael, to go three times in exile, WHILE WITH the fourth EXILE, "get you down" on behalf of YOUR only daughter, MEANING MALCHUT, who is really your bride that fell, as it says, "...is fallen; she shall no more rise" (Amos 5:2) but as soon as you descend on her behalf, she will rise with you. SHE WILL NOT BE ABLE TO RISE ON HER OWN, BUT ONLY WITH THE AID OF HER HUSBAND, NAMELY MOSES. This is your lost thing returned.

374. דְּלַאו לְמַגָּנָא אִתְגַּלְיָא לָךְ אוֹרַיְיתָא, יַתִּיר מִכָּל יִשְׂרָאֵל, וְאִסְתַּלָּקַת לְגַבָּךְ, כְּמַיָא דְּבֵאר דְּאִסְתַּלָּקוּ לְגַבָּךְ, וְלָא לַאֲבָהָן, וְלָא לְבַר נָשׁ, דְּהָא בֵּאר מַכֶּרֶת אֲדוֹנֶיהָ. וְאוֹרַיְיתָא דָּא, אִתְּמַר עֲלָהּ, וּמִשָּׁם בְּאֵרָה הִיא הַבְּאֵר וְגוֹ'. הַבְּאֵר הִיא מַלְיָא, וְלָא נָפְקִין מֵימוֹי לְבַר. וְאִיהוּ בֵּאר מַיָא דְּאוֹרַיְיתָא, דְּאַפִּיק כָּל מַיִין, וְכָל מַיִין דְּעָלְמָא עָאלִין בֵּיהּ, וְלָא נָפְקִין מֵימוֹי לְבַר.

374. It was not for naught that the Torah was revealed to you more than all Yisrael, and it went to meet you as the waters of the well that rose towards you, but not to the fathers or any other person. The well, WHICH IS MALCHUT, recognizes its master, and about this Torah it is said, "And from thence they went to Beer (lit. 'well') that is the well" (Bemidbar 21:16). The well is full, its waters do not spill out; it is the well of water of Torah, AS TORAH IS REFERRED TO AS 'WATER', that produced all waters, MEANING THE ENTIRE TORAH. And all waters in the universe enter within it and its waters do not spill out, BUT RATHER THEY ARE GATHERED WITHIN HER.

375. וְאִיהוּ בֵּאר דַּאֲפִילוּ כָּל בְּנֵי עָלְמָא שָׁאֲבִין מִנֵּיהּ מַיָא, וַאֲפִילוּ כָּל עֲנָנֵי עָלְמָא, לָא חַסְרִין מִנֵּיהּ, אֲפִילוּ כְּחוּט הַשַּׂעֲרָה. בְּגִין דִּבְאֵר דָּא, לֵית לֵיהּ סוֹף, יַתִּיר עָמוֹק הוּא מִדְּאוֹרַיְיתָא, דְּאִתְּמַר בָּהּ וּרְחָבָה מִנִּי יָם. וּבְכַד דִּילֵיהּ, מַאן דְּשָׁאֲבֵי מִנֵּיהּ מַיָא, אִיהוּ בָּלַע כָּל חָכְמָתִין דְּעָלְמָא, כָּל שֶׁכֵּן בֵּאר עַצְמוֹ.

-456-

375. Even if all mankind were to draw the water of this well, and even if all the clouds did, it would not miss even a hairsbreadth of it. This well is endless, deeper than the Torah, as it is written, "and broader than the sea" (Iyov 11:9). One who draws water with the pitcher (Heb. *kad*, Caf Dalet) OF THE WELL, MEANING OF THE TWENTY-FOUR (CAF DALET) HOLY SCRIPTURES, absorbs all the world's wisdom and surely the well itself.

376. וְכֵן עָתִיד קוּדְשָׁא בְּרִיךְ הוּא לְאָהַדְרָא לָךְ גֶּזֶל דִּילָךְ, דְּאִיהוּ מַטֶּה, דְּאִתְּמַר בֵּיה וַיִּגְזוֹל אֶת הַחֲנִית מִיַּד הַמִּצְרִי, דְּעָלָךְ אִתְּמַר אִישׁ מִצְרִי. וּבְגָלוּתָא דִּילָךְ וּבְגִלְגּוּלָא דִּילָךְ, יַפְרִישׁ לָךְ עָרֵי מִקְלָט, לְשֵׁזָבָא, מִכַּמָּה דְּרַדְפִין אֲבַתְרָךְ, דְּלֵית לְהוֹן סוֹף.

376. And so in the future, the Holy One, blessed be He, will return that which was stolen from you, namely the staff, as it is written, "and plucked the spear out of the hand of the Egyptian" (II Shmuel 23:21) for it was you who was referred to as an Egyptian man. In your exile and your incarnation, AS IN EVERY GENERATION THERE IS THE EXPRESSION OF MOSES, He will set aside for you cities of refuge to save yourself from your endless pursuers.

6. Setting aside cities of refuge

A Synopsis

Rabbi Shimon continues to speak to Moses, telling him that he has merited the last Hei, Malchut, due to his seeking it with repentance, returning it to his Master, leading it out of exile and not seeking any reward. God put His name in Moses and he put His thoughts with Moses. Moses endeavored his whole life with Truth, so God allowed him to be raised with the Torah of Truth and to be incorporated with all its qualities and letters – with the Holy Name, Yud Hei Vav Hei.

377. וְהַאי אִיהוּ פִּקּוּדָא, לְהַפְרִישׁ עָרֵי מִקְלָט, לְמַאן דְקָטֵל, בְּגִין הַהוּא מִצְרִי דְקָטַלְתְּ בְּמִצְרַיִם, דְתַמָּן הֲוָה נָחָשׁ הַקַּדְמוֹנִי וְכָל מַשְׁרְיָיתֵיה, דַהֲווֹ סַחֲרִין לֵיה, וְקַטַלְתְּ לֵיה בְּלָא זִמְנֵיה, וְלָא דָחַלְתָּ מֵרוֹדְפִין דִילֵיה, דִבְכַמָּה אַתְרִין רָדְפוּ אֲבַתְרָךְ, כַּמָּה נָשִׁין בְּנַעֲרוּתָךְ, דְאִינוּן נַעֲמָ"ה אַגְרָ"ת לִילִי"ת אוּכְמָא. וְקוּדְשָׁא בְּרִיךְ הוּא יָהִיב לָךְ עָרֵי מִקְלָט, לְאִשְׁתְּזָבָא מִנְּהוֹן, וְאִינוּן שַׁעֲרֵי תְּשׁוּבָה.

377. Now we have the commandment of setting aside cities of refuge for one who killed, due to the Egyptian man you slew in Egypt who contained within him the primordial serpent and his encampment that surrounded him. You killed him prematurely and you did not fear his followers. Numerous women pursued you in your youth – THE KLIPOT, Na'amah, Agrat – black Lilit. And the Holy One, blessed be He, gave cities of refuge to save you from them. These are the gates of repentance.

378. בְּגִין דְאַתְּ בֵּן יָה, בְּרָא דְאַבָּא וּדְאִמָּא. בָּתַר דְהַדְרַת בְּהֵ"א בִּתְיוּבְתָּא, אִסְתְּלָקַת בַּבִּינָה, יה"ו, אִילָנָא דְחַיֵּי, וּבְגִינָהּ אַתְּ זָכֵי לְאָת ה', בְּגִין דְאַעִילַת גַּרְמָךְ אֲבַתְרָהָא, בִּתְיוּבְתָּא לְאַהַדְרָא לָהּ לְמָרָךְ, וּלְסַלְקָא לָהּ מִגָלוּתָא, וְלָא לְקַבְּלָא אַנְתְּ אַגְרָא.

378. This is because you are a son of *Yud-Hei*, AS MOSES WAS AT THE LEVEL OF *VAV*, DENOTING ZEIR ANPIN, being the son of Aba and Ima, WHO ARE CHOCHMAH AND BINAH, *YUD-HEI*. And after you returned with repentance with the LAST *Hei* OF THE NAME YUD HEI VAV HEI, you

ascended to Binah AND MERITED NOW THE NAME *Yud-Hei-Vav*, which is the Tree of Life – FOR BINAH IS CALLED 'LIVING ELOHIM', AND ZEIR ANPIN THAT ASCENDS TO BINAH IS CALLED THE 'TREE OF LIFE', and therefore you have merited the LAST *Hei*, WHICH IS MALCHUT. All this is due to your bringing yourself after it with repentance, returning it to your Master, leading it out of exile, and not seeking reward.

379. וְקוּדְשָׁא בְּ"ה, שַׁוֵּי שְׁמֵיה בָּךְ, וּבְגִין דְּמַחֲשָׁבָה דִּילָךְ הֲוַת לְעִלַּת הָעִלּוֹת, שַׁוֵּי בָּךְ מַחֲשַׁבְתֵּיה, דְּאִיהִי יוּ"ד הֵ"א וָא"ו הֵ"א. וְעִלַּת הָעִלּוֹת, אִיהוּ מְיַחֵד אִלֵּין אַתְוָון בָּךְ, לְאִשְׁתְּמוֹדְעָא לֵיה בְּאִלֵּין אַתְוָון.

379. And the Holy One, blessed be He, put His name in you, and since your thoughts were with the cause of causes, NOTABLY KETER, He put His thoughts with you – DENOTING THE SECRET OF CHOCHMAH, which is YUD HEI VAV HEI, FULLY SPELLED WITH *ALEPH'S*, WITH THE NUMERICAL VALUE OF *MEM-HEI* (= 45) AS CHOCHMAH (*CHET-CAF-MEM-HEI*) CONSISTS OF THE FORCE (*CAF-CHET*) OF 45 (*MEM-HEI*). FOR THROUGH THE NAME OF *MEM-HEI* WHICH IS THE CENTRAL COLUMN OF THE MOCHIN, WHICH IS CHOCHMAH REVEALED, the Cause of all causes unifies all these letters within you in order to reorganize and know Him through these letters.

380. וּבְגִין דְּאַתְּ הֲוֵית גּוֹמֵל חֶסֶד עִם שְׁכִינְתָּא, דְּכָל פִּקּוּדִין דִּילָךְ לְקַיְּימָא, אֵיזֶהוּ חָסִיד הַמִּתְחַסֵּד עִם קוֹנוֹ. יָהַב לָךְ מִדַּת חֶסֶד. וּבְגִין דְּנָטַרְתְּ פִּקּוּדִין דְּלָא תַעֲשֶׂה, וַהֲוָה לָךְ לְאִתְגַּבְּרָא עַל יִצְרָךְ, לְמִקְשַׁר לֵיה תְּחוֹת יְדָךְ, וְלָא אִשְׁתַּדְּלַת בְּהַאי פְּקוּדָא, אֶלָּא לְקַשְּׁרָא סָמָאֵ"ל תְּחוֹת יְדָא דְּקוּדְשָׁא בְּרִיךְ הוּא. וּבַת זוּגֵיה דְּאִיהִי שִׁפְחָתָא בִּישָׁא, תְּחוֹת יַד גְּבִירְתָּא. לוֹן וּלְכָל מְמָנָן וּלְכָל מַשִׁרְיָין דִּלְהוֹן. קוּדְשָׁא בְּרִיךְ הוּא יָהַב לָךְ, מִדַּת גְּבוּרָה דִּילֵיה, לְמֶהֱוֵי בְּסִיַּיעְתָּךְ דְּיִתְחַלְחָלוּן וִידַחֲלוּן מִינָךְ, סָמָאֵ"ל וּבַת זוּגֵיה, וְכָל מְמָנָן וּמַשִׁרְיָין דִּלְהוֹן, וִיהוֹן קְשׁוּרִים בְּשַׁלְשְׁלָאֵי תְּחוֹת יְדָךְ.

380. AFTER BEING INCLUDED IN THOUGHT, WHICH IS THE SECRET OF THE FIRST THREE SFIROT, HE GOES ON TO EXPLAIN HOW HE RECEIVED

THE OTHER SIX SFIROT, AND SAYS: Since you dispensed kindness with the Shechinah, as all the precepts are yours with which to provide for the pious (Heb. *chasid*) man, who is pious to his Possessor, so He gave you the quality of Chesed. You observed the negative commandments and had to overcome your inclinations to tie it under you, and you strove with this precept only to tie up Samael under the Holy One, blessed be He, and to have the mate OF SAMAEL, who is an evil maidservant, bound under her mistress, NAMELY MALCHUT, and THEN all their appointees and their hosts. Therefore, the Holy One, blessed be He, has given you the quality of Gvurah, that will be at your assistance to cause Samael, his mate and all their hosts to fear and be tied in a chain under you.

381. וּבְגִין דְּהַדְרַת בִּתְיוּבְתָּא, בְּאוֹת בְּרִית, נָחִית בִּינָה יה"ו, לְאִתְחַבְּרָא בְּצַדִּיק. בְּגִינָךְ, קוּדְשָׁא בְּרִיךְ הוּא יָהִיב לָךְ אוֹת בְּרִית צַדִּיק דִּילֵיהּ. וּבְגִין דְּמַחֲשָׁבָה טוֹבָה עָבַדְתְּ כֹּלָּא, הָכִי נָחִית שְׁמָא מְפֹרָשׁ עָלָךְ, וּמִתַּמָּן, נָחִית עָלָךְ.

381. And since you repented with the sign of the Covenant, NAMELY YESOD, Binah descended, BEING THE LETTERS *Yud-Hei-Vav*, to join with the Righteous, NAMELY YESOD, for your sake. And so the Holy One, blessed be He, gave you the sign of the Covenant of the righteous, NAMELY, YESOD. As you did everything with a pure thought, so descended the explicit name upon you, and from there, FROM THE THOUGHT, WHICH IS THREE FIRST SFIROT, did it descend on you.

382. וּבְגִין דְּאַנְתְּ תִּשְׁתְּדַּל בְּכָל יוֹמָא, בִּתְרֵין שִׂפְוָון דִּילָךְ בִּצְלוֹתָא, לְשַׁבְּחָא לְמָרָךְ, בַּאֲדֹנָי שְׂפָתַי תִּפְתָּח, בִּתְרֵין שִׂפְוָון דִּילָךְ. בִּנְבִיאִים וּבִכְתוּבִים. וּבְכָל מִינֵי זְמָר וְנִגּוּן בִּצְלוֹתָא. קוּדְשָׁא בְּרִיךְ הוּא נָחִית לוֹן בְּשִׂפְוָון דִּילָךְ. כָּל שֶׁכֵּן דַּרְגָּא דִּילָךְ, עַמּוּדָא דְּאֶמְצָעִיתָא, וּבֵיהּ אִשְׁתְּדַּלְתְּ בְּכָל יוֹמִין דִּילָךְ בִּקְשׁוֹט, קוּדְשָׁא בְּרִיךְ הוּא יָהֲבֵיהּ לָךְ, לְסַלְּקָא לָךְ בֵּיהּ, בְּתוֹרַת אֱמֶת, כְּלִילָא מִכָּל מִדּוֹת וְאַתְוָון. בִּשְׁמָא מְפֹרָשׁ, בַּד' אַתְוָון.

382. And because you strive daily, with both of your lips in prayer to extol your Master with, "Adonai, open my lips," utilizing both lips with words of

the prophets and the writings and all types of song and tune in prayer, the Holy One, blessed be He, lowers them through your two lips, NETZACH AND HOD. Even more so in your level, being the middle pillar, NAMELY TIFERET, with which you endeavored all your life with Truth; the Holy One, blessed be He, allowed you to be raised with the Torah of Truth, incorporated with all qualities and letters – SUCH AS CHESED, GVURAH, TIFERET, NETZACH, HOD AND YESOD – with the explicit Name consisting of four letters, YUD HEI VAV HEI, WHICH IS THE FIRST THREE SFIROT.

383. דְּקֶדֶם דְּחָזַרְתְּ בְּתִיוּבְתָּא לָא הֲוֵית, אֶלָּא בְּאִילָנָא דְּטוֹב וָרָע, עֶבֶד וְנַעַר הֲוָה שְׁמָךְ בְּקַדְמֵיתָא, וְהִנֵּה נַעַר בּוֹכֶה, עֶבֶד נֶאֱמָן, הה"ד לֹא כֵן עַבְדִּי מֹשֶׁה בְּכָל בֵּיתִי נֶאֱמָן הוּא. וְהַהוּא רַע, שׁוּתָּפָא דְּעֶבֶד, גָּרַם לָךְ לְמֶחֱטֵי בַּסֶּלַע, בְּגִין דְּמַטֶּה דְּאִתְּמְסַר לָךְ, הֲוָה דְּאִילָנָא דְּטוֹב וָרָע, מְטַטְרוֹ"ן טוֹב. סָמָאֵ"ל רַע.

383. Before you repented, you were associated with the Tree of Knowledge of Good and Evil. Servant and child were your original names, as it is written: "and, behold, a weeping boy" (Shemot 2:6), or a devoted servant, as written, "My servant Moses is not so, for he is the trusted one in all My house" (Bemidbar 12:7). The evil, that is the partner of a servant, caused you to sin by the rock, as the staff handed you came from the Tree of Knowledge of Good and Evil, MEANING METATRON AND SAMAEL. Metatron is good, and Samael is evil.

7. *Mem-Tet* and *Mot* ('the rod')

A Synopsis

Rabbi Shimon tells Moses that the staff given to him will be a Tree of Life, denoting Vav, which will become a rod. He explains that two precepts were validated: "you shall surely help him to lift them up again" and "You shall surely unload it with him." These allude to Messiah the son of David and Messiah the son of Joseph. The third precept is that of the gleaning, the forgotten sheaf and the poor man's tithe. The rising, meaning redemption, is in Moses' level.

384. וּכְעָן, דְּהָדַרְתְּ בְּתִיוּבְתָּא, וְאִתְדַּבְּקַת בְּאִילָנָא דְּחַיֵּי, הָא נַפְקַת מֵעֶבֶד, וְאִתְהַדַּרְתְּ בֵּן לְקוּדְשָׁא בְּרִיךְ הוּא. וּמַטֶּה דְּאִתְמְסַר בִּידָךְ, יְהֵא עֵץ חַיִּים, ו', דְּאִיהוּ בֵּן יָ"ה, וְתֵיעוּל בְּמ"ט אַנְפִּין דִּילָךְ בְּאוֹרַיְיתָא, וְיִתְעֲבֵד מוֹט. וְיִתְקַיָּים בָּךְ, לֹא יִתֵּן לְעוֹלָם מוֹט לַצַּדִּיק. מ"ט אַנְפִּין, מ"ט אַתְוָון דִּשְׁמַע יִשְׂרָאֵל, וּבָרוּךְ שֵׁם, שִׁית תֵּיבִין דְּיִחוּדָא עִלָּאָה, ו' עִלָּאָה תִּפְאֶרֶת. שִׁית תֵּיבִין תִּנְיָינִין, דְּבָרוּךְ שֵׁם, ו' תִּנְיָינָא צַדִּיק. מ"ט. בְּאֶמְצָעִיתָא א. וַיִּשָׂאֻהוּ בַמּוֹט בִּשְׁנָיִם.

384. And now that you have repented and enjoined yourself with the Tree of Life, and you have relinquished the role of servant and returned to be a son to the Holy One, blessed be He, the staff (Heb. *mateh*) given to you will be a Tree of Life – denoting *Vav*, which is the son of *Yud Hei*. THE *VAV* will penetrate the *Mem-Tet* (= 49) aspects you have in Torah, and will become a rod (Heb. *mot*: *Mem-Vav-Tet*) and as such can be fulfilled with the verse: "He shall never suffer the righteous to be moved (Heb. *mot*)" (Tehilim 55:23). The 49 aspects ARE THE SECRET OF the 49 letters in 'Sh'ma Yisrael' and 'Blessed is the Name OF YOUR GLORIOUS KINGDOM FOREVER', REPRESENTING the six words of supernal unity, pointing to the supernal *Vav* (= 6) denoting Tiferet. And then the six words of "Blessed is the Name" is a second group OF LOWER UNITY, meaning to point to the second *Vav* IN THE LETTER *VAV* FULLY SPELLED (*VAV-ALEPH-VAV*) denoting the Righteous, REFLECTING YESOD. AND THEY ARE a rod (Heb. *mot*). We find in the middle OF TWO *VAV*'S there is an *Aleph*, the secret of the verse, "and they carried it between two on a pole" (Bemidbar 13:24), MEANING TWO *VAVS*.

385. בְּלָא וָא״ו בְּאֶמְצָעִיתָא, אִיהוּ מ״ט. וְצַדִּיק מ״ט לִפְנֵי רָשָׁע. וּמַאן גָּרַע דָּא. א׳. אֶחָד מֵחֲמִשִׁים. דְּחַמְשִׁין תַּרְעִין אִתְיְהִיבוּ לָךְ, חָסֵר חַד, כְּמָה דְּאוּקְמוּהָ מָארֵי מַתְנִיתִין, חַמְשִׁים שַׁעֲרֵי בִּינָה נִמְסְרוּ לְמֹשֶׁה, חוּץ מֵאֶחָד. וְהַאי אִיהוּ א׳, דְּחָסֵר מֵחַמְשִׁין, וְאִשְׁתְּאַר מ״ט, וְדָא גָּרִים לָךְ צַדִּיק מ״ט לִפְנֵי רָשָׁע. מַאי רָשָׁע. דָּא סָמָאֵ״ל.

385. If it lacks a *Vav* in the middle, the word becomes *Mem-Tet*, MEANING the righteous bends (Heb. *mat*) before the villain. What caused this? *Aleph* (= 1) one of fifty, as fifty gates minus one were given to you; as the masters of the Mishnah explain, fifty gates minus one of Binah were given to Moses. This is the missing *Aleph* from the fifty, so only *Mem-Tet* (= 49) remained. This is why the righteous bends before the villain. Who is the villain? It is Samael.

386. וְהַאי אִיהוּ מ״ט, מִן מַטֶּה דִּילָךְ, דְּאִתְּמַר בֵּיהּ וּמַטֵּה הָאֱלֹהִים בְּיָדִי. מַטֶּה דִּילָךְ הוּא מַטֵּה דְּמֹשֶׁה, וּבְגִין דָּא א׳, דְּאִיהִי בִּינָה, חוֹזֶרֶת לָךְ, כְּמָה דְּאוּקְמוּהָ בְּמַתְנִיתִין, אָלֶף בִּינָה. דְּחָזֶרֶת לָךְ בִּתְיוּבְתָּא, וְתֵיעוּל בֵּין וָ״ו, וְאִתְעֲבֵיד וָא״ו, לְקַיֵּים בָּךְ לְיִשְׂרָאֵל, וּבְרַחֲמִים גְּדוֹלִים אֲקַבְּצֵךְ. מִתַּמָּן וְאֵילָךְ יִתְקַיֵּים בָּךְ, לֹא יִתֵּן לְעוֹלָם מוֹט לַצַּדִּיק.

386. This *Mem-Tet* stems from your staff (Heb. *mateh*: Mem-Tet-Hei) as it is written: "with the rod (Heb. *mateh*) of the Elohim in my hand" (Shemot 17:9). Your staff is that of Moses, and therefore the letter *Aleph,* which is Binah, comes back to you, as recorded in the Mishnah; *Aleph* is Binah. It returns to you as a result of repentance, and enters between the two *Vav's* to become *Vav-Aleph-Vav*. Thus is fulfilled in you the verse: "but with great mercies will I gather you" (Yeshayah 54:7) for the sake of Yisrael. From this point will be fulfilled: "He shall never suffer the righteous to be moved (Heb. *mot*)."

387. בְּהַהוּא זִמְנָא, יִתְקַיְּימוּ בָּךְ תְּרֵין פִּקּוּדִין. חַד, הָקֵם תָּקִים עִמּוֹ. תִּנְיָינָא, עָזוֹב תַּעֲזוֹב עִמּוֹ. הָקֵם עִם ו׳ עִלָּאָה, מָשִׁיחַ רִאשׁוֹן. תָּקִים עִם ו׳ תִּנְיָינָא. עִמּוֹ, דָּא בֶן עַמְרָם, דְּסָלִיקַת לַבִּינָה דְּאִיהִי א׳.

387. At that time two precepts were validated. 1) "you shall surely help him to lift (lit. 'lifting will you lift') them up again" (Devarim 22:4), and 2) "You shall surely unload it with him" (Shemot 23:5). "Surely help" lift together with the supernal *Vav*, alludes to the first Messiah NAMELY MESSIAH, THE SON OF DAVID; and in helping with the second *Vav*, NAMELY THE SECOND MESSIAH, BEING MESSIAH THE SON OF JOSEPH. "Him" refers to the son of Amram, that ascended to Binah – which is equal to *Aleph*, SITUATED BETWEEN THE TWO *VAVS*, AS MENTIONED. THEY REFER TO THE *VAV*, WRITTEN OUT FULLY AS *VAV* (*VAV-ALEPH-VAV*).

388. וּלְמַאן הָקֵם תָּקִים. לְאָת ה'. דְּנַפְלַת בְּאָלֶף חֲמִשָׁאָה, בָּתַר ע"ב, כְּמִנְיָן עֲזוֹ"ב תַּעֲזוֹב עִמּוֹ. עָזוֹב: ע"ב ז"ו. וְדָא ע"ב שְׁמָהָן, וַיִּסַּע וַיָּבֹא וַיֵּט. דָא וָא"ו מִן וה"ו, תַּמָּן עֵזֶר, וְלָא קִימָה, וְהָאי אִיהוּ עָזוֹב תַּעֲזוֹב, תַּמָּן בְּעַת"ו יוֹרֶה וּמַלְקוֹשׁ וְאָסַפְתָּ דְגָנֶךָ וְתִירֹשְׁךָ וְיִצְהָרֶךָ, דְּאִינּוּן יִשְׂרָאֵל. לֶקֶט שִׁכְחָה וּפֵאָה, לֶעָנִי וְלַגֵּר תַּעֲזוֹב אוֹתָם. הָכָא אוֹלִיפְנָא. פְּקוּדָא תְּלִיתָאָה.

388. Whom shall you help to rise? It refers to the letter *Hei*, NAMELY MALCHUT, that fell in the fifth millennium after seventy-two YEARS, according to the count in "You shall surely unload (Heb. *azov*) it with him." "*Azov*" (*Ayin-Zayin-Vav-Bet*) EQUALS THE LETTERS *Ayin-Bet, Zayin-Vav; Ayin-Bet* (= 72) refers to the 72 names derived from: "And removed...and it came... And...stretched" (Shemot 14:19-21). *ZAYIN*-VAV MEANS THE INITIALS OF 'THIS IS (HEB. *ZEH*) VAV', the *Vav* from *Yud-Hei-Vav* EQUALING ZEIR ANPIN. There, IN THE YEAR FIVE THOUSAND AND SEVENTY-TWO, he helped, HELPING THE FALLEN *HEI,* but did not lift, FOR THE TIME OF RISING AND REDEMPTION HAS NOT ARRIVED. Hence, it says, "You shall surely unload it with him" – JUST HELPING. There IS PRACTICED "in its due season, the early rain and the late rain, that you may gather in your corn, and your wine, and your oil" (Devarim 11:14). This alludes to Yisrael. "CORN" REFERS TO YISRAEL, "WINE" REFERS TO THE LEVITES, AND "OIL" TO THE PRIESTS. AND SO APPLY THE CUSTOM OF the gleaning, the forgotten sheaf, and the poor man's tithe – "you shall leave them for the poor and strange" (Vayikra 19:10). So here we learn about the third precept OF THE GLEANING, THE FORGOTTEN SHEAF AND THE POOR MAN'S TITHE.

389. וְצָרִיךְ לְאַחֲזָרָא עָלַיְיהוּ, דְּהָא מִסִּטְרָא דְצַדִּיק, עָנִי, עָזוֹב תַּעֲזוֹב, צַדִּיק. עִמּוֹ, דָּא בֶּן עַמְרָם. וְהַאי אִיהוּ לֶעָנִי וְלַגֵּר תַּעֲזוֹב אוֹתָם. גֵּר אַנְתְּ כְּגַוְונָא דְּאִתְּמַר בָּךְ בְּקַדְמֵיתָא עַם עָנִי, גֵּר הָיִיתִי בְּאֶרֶץ נָכְרִיָּה.

389. You must seek them TO SUPPORT THEM, as the poor are from the aspect of the Righteous, MEANING YESOD. "You shall surely unload it," YESOD, the Righteous; "with him," refers to the son of Amram. This is the meaning of, "you shall leave them for the poor and strange." You are a stranger, a poor nation, as it is written about you at the start, "I have been an alien in a strange land" (Shemot 18:3).

390. אֲבָל הֲקָמָה, בְּדַרְגָּא דִּילָךְ, הָקֵם ו' תַּתָּאָה. תָּקִים עִמּוֹ: עִם בֶּן עַמְרָם, בְּדַרְגָּא עִלָּאָה דִּילָךְ, תִּפְאֶרֶת. בְּמַ"ה דִּילָךְ, שְׁמָא מְפָרַשׁ בִּשְׁלִימוּ. בָּתַר קַ' קַ' דְּהָקֵם תָּקִים, אִשְׁתְּאַר תִּים. מַאי קָא אַחֲזֵי. יַעֲקֹב אִישׁ תָּם. עִמּוֹ: עִם בֶּן עַמְרָם, יוֹקִים. הָקֵם: צַדִּיק. תָּקִים: תָּם.

390. But the rising, MEANING REDEMPTION, is in your level – lifting points to the lower Vav, the FULFILLMENT OF VAV, DENOTING YESOD. "…lift with him…" with the son of Amram, with your level, being Tiferet, USING THE NAME Mem-Hei of yours, BEING YUD HEI VAV HEI FULLY SPELLED WITH ALEPH'S THAT NUMERICALLY REACH MEM-HEI, which is the explicit Name in its completeness. Following the two Kuf's of "lifting… lift (Heb. hakem-takim: Tav-Kof-Yud-Mem)" remain Tav-Yud-Mem. HE ASKS: What does this teach? HE REPLIES: It points to, "Jacob was a plain (Heb. tam: Tav-Mem) man" (Beresheet 25:27), DENOTING TIFERET, SO THE EXPLANATION OF THE VERSE IS, "with him," MEANING with the son of Amram he will rise. "…lifting…" refers to the Righteous, MEANING YESOD. "…lift…" refers to the plain one, MEANING TIFERET.

8. Redeeming a Hebrew servant

A Synopsis

This section tells us that we must strive to serve our Master to become His servant. A person who toils in Torah in order to merit the World to Come is called 'an acquisition', as in "when you acquire a Hebrew servant, six years he shall serve." After the acquisition, he will achieve redemption. Rabbi Shimon speaks of the Kriat Sh'ma, and says that the cantor can fulfill a man's obligation for one who is incapable of praying. The six years correspond to the three initial and the three concluding blessings of the Amidah prayer. Rabbi Shimon closes by saying that in the World to Come one will not be able to find redemption through another: "If I am not for myself, who is for me?"

391. פְּקוּדָא בָּתַר דָּא לִפְדּוֹת עֶבֶד עִבְרִי וְאָמָה הָעִבְרִיָּה, לְיַעֵד אָמָה הָעִבְרִיָּה, לָדוּן בְּקִנְיַן עֶבֶד עִבְרִי, הַעֲנֵק תַּעֲנִיק לוֹ. הה"ד, כִּי תִקְנֶה עֶבֶד עִבְרִי שֵׁשׁ שָׁנִים יַעֲבֹד. מַאי שֵׁשׁ שָׁנִים יַעֲבֹד. וּמַאי קִנְיָן דִּילֵיהּ. אֶלָּא בְּסִתְרֵי תוֹרָה, מְטַטְרוֹ"ן עֶבֶד יְיָ', כָּלִיל שִׁית סִטְרִין, כְּחוּשְׁבָּן שִׁית אַתְוָון דִּילֵיהּ, שִׁית סִדְרֵי מִשְׁנָה. וּבְהוֹן אִית לֵיהּ לְבַר נָשׁ לְמִפְלַח לְמָארֵיהּ, לְמֶהֱוֵי לֵיהּ עֶבֶד, לְמֶעְבַּד קִנְיָן כַּסְפּוֹ, דְּכֶסֶף יְמִינָא, דְּאַבְרָהָם חֶסֶד דַּרְגָּא דִּילֵיהּ, אוֹרַיְיתָא מִתַּמָּן אִתְיְהִיבַת.

391. The precept that follows is to redeem the Hebrew servant and the Hebrew maidservant, to marry off the Hebrew maidservant, and to contemplate the method of acquisition of the Hebrew slave: "you shall furnish him liberally" (Devarim 15:14). As the verse reads, "when you acquire a Hebrew servant, six years he shall serve" (Shemot 21:2). HE ASKS: What is meant by, "six years he shall serve," and how is he to be purchased? HE ANSWERS: With the secrets of Torah. The ANGEL Metatron IS the servant of Hashem, incorporating the six ends, NAMELY CHESED, GVURAH, TIFERET, NETZACH, HOD, AND YESOD, with the same number of the six letters, BEING THE SECRET OF the six orders of the Mishnah. With them one should strive to serve his Master to become His servant. Money represents the right and Abraham, whose level is Chesed, and Torah was given from them.

392. וּמַאן דְּאִשְׁתַּדַּל בָּהּ, בְּגִין לְזַכָּאָה לְעָלְמָא דְּאָתֵי, אִקְרֵי קִנְיָן.

כַּסְפּוֹ: עָלְמָא דְּכִסּוּפָא. קִנְיָן: עַל שֵׁם אֵל עֶלְיוֹן קוֹנֶה שָׁמַיִם וָאָרֶץ. קְנֵה חָכְמָה קְנֵה בִינָה.

392. One who toils IN TORAH in order to merit the world to come is called 'an acquisition'; his money refers to the world of pleasure, the buying is derived from to "the most high El, the possessor of heaven and earth" (Beresheet 14:22); "Get wisdom, get understanding" (Mishlei 4:5).

393. בָּתַר דְּקָנָה לוֹ, גְּאוּלָה תִּהְיֶה לוֹ. אִית דְּאִיהוּ קָנוּי לְעוֹלָם, וְאִית דְּאִיהוּ קָנוּי לֵיהּ שִׁית שְׁנִין. מַאן דְּאִיהוּ קָנוּי לֵיהּ לְעוֹלָם, כְּתִיב בֵּיהּ, וְרָצַע אֲדוֹנָיו אֶת אָזְנוֹ בַּמַּרְצֵעַ וַעֲבָדוֹ לְעוֹלָם. לֵית עוֹלָם, אֶלָּא עוֹלָמוֹ שֶׁל יוֹבֵל, דְּאִינּוּן חַמְשִׁין. וְדָא קְרִיאַת שְׁמַע, דְּתַמָּן כ"ה כ"ה אַתְוָון, עַרְבִית וְשַׁחֲרִית. נ' תַּרְעִין דְּבִינָה.

393. After he acquires him, redemption will come to him. There are those bought forever, and others bought for six years. Of those bought forever, the verse writes, "His master will bore his ear with an awl and work for him forever" – forever, meaning Jubilee DENOTING BINAH REFERRED TO AS JUBILEE which amounts to fifty. This alludes to the reading of Sh'ma, which contains 25 and 25 letters, of the morning and evening services, which are the fifty gates of Binah.

394. בָּתַר דְּמִיַּחֵד בְּהוֹן בַּר נָשׁ לְקוּדְשָׁא בְּרִיךְ הוּא, דְּאִיהוּ עֶבֶד דִּילֵיהּ, בְּעוֹל תְּפִלִּין עַל רֵישֵׁיהּ. וְאָזֶן דִּילֵיהּ רְצִיעָא פְּתִיחָא לְמִשְׁמַע קְרִיאַת שְׁמַע, דִּשְׁמַע, בְּכָל לָשׁוֹן שֶׁאַתָּה שׁוֹמֵעַ, דְּהַיְינוּ מַשְׁמָעוּת.

394. After man joins the Holy One, blessed be He, through their means, becoming His servant through the yoke of Tefilin on his head, and his ear pierced, MEANING open to hear Kriat Sh'ma – as the word Sh'ma means in any language that you hear – HEAR means 'meaning' (Heb. mashmaut) AS ONE MUST UNDERSTAND THE READING OF SH'MA SINCE IT IS THE SECRET OF THE UNITY.

395. דְּמַאן דְּפִדְיוֹן דִּילֵיהּ תְּלוּיָה בִּקְרִיאַת שְׁמַע, דְּאִיהוּ רָזָא דְּחַמְשִׁין,

לֵית לֵיהּ פִּדְיוֹן עַל יַד אַחֲרָא בְּגִלְגּוּלָא, דִּמְרוּצָע הוּא לְמָארֵיהּ, הָכָא לָא אִתְּמַר אוֹ דוֹדוֹ אוֹ בֶן דּוֹדוֹ יִגְאָלֶנּוּ. דִּבְצְלוֹתָא דְּבַר נָשׁ, אִיהוּ כְּעֶבֶד, דְּאִתְּמַר בֵּיהּ שֵׁשׁ שָׁנִים יַעֲבֹד. וְאֵין עֲבוֹדָה, אֶלָּא תְּפִלָּה. שֵׁשׁ שָׁנִים יַעֲבֹד: ג' רִאשׁוֹנוֹת, וְג' אַחֲרוֹנוֹת דְּשָׁלִיחַ צִבּוּר אַפִּיק לֵיהּ לְבַר נָשׁ יְדֵי חוֹבָתוֹ, לְמַאן דְּלָא יָדַע לְצַלָּאָה בְּהוּ דְּצַדִּיק חַי עָלְמָא, אִתְקְרֵי בְּהוּ, עַל שְׁמֵיהּ. בֹּעַז, צַדִּיק, גּוֹאֵל, קָרוֹב, וְנֶאֱמָן.

395. For that person whose redemption is dependent on the reading of Sh'ma, which is the secret of fifty, ALLUDING TO BINAH, there can be no redemption through the intervention of someone else, as he is pierced only for his Master. In this verse, we do not find mentioned "one of his brethren may redeem him" (Vayikra 25:49). In regard to man's prayer, he can be like a slave, as it is written, "six years shall he toil." Here, toil means prayer. "Six years shall he toil" POINTS TO the first three and last three blessings OF THE AMIDAH, with which the cantor can fulfill man's obligation for one who is not capable of praying. IN THIS CASE, THERE IS REDEMPTION THROUGH SOMEONE ELSE INASMUCH AS THE CANTOR REDEEMS HIM, as the Righteous who lives forever – DENOTING YESOD, REFERRING TO THE CANTOR – is then called by the names of Boaz: Righteous, Kinsman, Near Kinsman, Faithful. THE MESSAGE FROM THOSE NAMES ILLUSTRATES THAT THEY REDEEM ONE WHO CAN NOT HELP HIMSELF, WHICH IS THE SECRET OF THE LAW OF THE LEVIRATE MARRIAGE AND INCARNATION.

396. קָרוֹב יְיָ' לְכָל קוֹרְאָיו. וְטָב לֵיהּ לְבַר נָשׁ, שֶׁכֵּן קָרוֹב מֵאָח רָחוֹק, דְּהַיְינוּ עַמּוּדָא דְּאֶמְצָעִיתָא, דְּאִיהוּ בֶּן יָהּ, דְּאִסְתַּלָּק לְעֵילָא דְּאִיהוּ בִּינָה, דְּעוֹלָם דָּא, עוֹלָמוֹ שֶׁל יוֹבֵל, דְּאִיהוּ חַמְשִׁין אַתְוָון דְּיִחוּדָא. דִּבְעָלְמָא, דֵּין, יָכִיל בַּר נָשׁ, לְמֶהֱוֵי לֵיהּ פִּדְיוֹן בְּצַדִּיק, ו' שְׁנִין דְּכָלִיל תְּלַת קַדְמָאִין, וּתְלַת בַּתְרָאִין דִּצְלוֹתָא. ו' זְעֵירָא, אִיהוּ שִׁית שְׁנִין יַעֲבֹד.

396. "Hashem is near to all those who call upon Him" (Tehilim 145:18). It is better for man to be "a neighbor that is near than a brother far off" (Mishlei 27:10), meaning the middle pillar, DENOTING TIFERET – AS YESOD IS CALLED 'A CLOSE NEIGHBOR' AND TIFERET IS CALLED 'A

DISTANT BROTHER' that is considered as the son of *Yud-Hei* that ascended above to Binah. This world is the world of Jubilee consisting of the fifty letters of the unity OF *KRIAT SH'MA*, BEING THE FIFTY GATES OF BINAH, AS EXPLAINED ABOVE. In this world, NAMELY MALCHUT, man can redeem himself through the righteous, DENOTING YESOD, BEING six years that incorporates the three initial and three concluding blessings OF THE AMIDAH PRAYER; THIS IS THE SECRET OF the small *Vav*, DENOTING YESOD. This is the meaning of, "six years he shall toil."

397. אֲבָל בְּעָלְמָא דְאָתֵי, דְּאִיהוּ עוֹלָמוֹ שֶׁל יוֹבֵל, דְּתַמָּן נ' אַתְוָון דְּק"ש, לֵית ש"צ אַפִּיק לֵיה מֵחוֹבָה. בְּגִין דְּלֵית לֵיה פִּדְיוֹן ע"י אֲחֵרִים. וּבְג"ד שְׁמַע, בְּכָל לָשׁוֹן שֶׁאַתָּה שׁוֹמֵעַ. וּבְג"ד קָא רָמִיז, אִם אֵין אֲנִי לִי מִי לִי. מִ"י: וַדַּאי עוֹלָמוֹ שֶׁל יוֹבֵל.

397. However, in the world to come, the world of Jubilee DENOTING BINAH, where there is present the fifty letters of *Kriat Sh'ma*, the cantor can not exempt another from his duty, as there is no redemption through others, so hear (Heb. *sh'ma*) in whatever language you understand, BUT IT IS CRITICAL THAT YOU READ IT YOURSELF. Present here is the hint, "If I am not for myself, who is for me". "I" DENOTES MALCHUT; "who" (Heb. *mi*) refers to the world of Jubilee DENOTING BINAH. THIS INSINUATES ABOUT SH'MA WHERE "I" DOES NOT APPLY, BUT "*MI*" DOES.

9. A two edged sword

A Synopsis

The head Rabbis of the Yeshiva have descended with Rabbi
Shimon and are addressing Moses. They speak about the verse,
"The high praises of El are in their throats, and a two edged sword
in their hand." They tell Moses that he is the mouthpiece of the
higher and lower Shechinah, with which God spoke to him mouth
to mouth. For this reason, they tell him, Elijah has been delayed
above and cannot come down because, while he would bring
wealth, the poverty of Moses is a redemption for Yisrael. Moses
replies that he releases him from his oath, and that they should all
work to release Elijah so that he may descend to them.

398. מִיַּד דְּשָׁמְעוּ מִלִּין אִלֵּין, מָארֵי מְתִיבָתָאן דַּהֲווֹ נַחְתֵּי עִם בּוּצִינָא
קַדִּישָׁא, פָּתְחוּ וְאָמְרוּ, רַעְיָא מְהֵימָנָא, פִּי שְׁכִינְתָּא עִלָּאָה וְתַתָּאָה,
דְּבִתְרַוְויְיהוּ קוּדְשָׁא בְּרִיךְ הוּא אֵל פֶּה אֶל פֶּה מַלִּיל עִמָּךְ בְּק״ש, דְּאִתְּמַר
בֵּיהּ, רוֹמְמוֹת אֵל בִּגְרוֹנָם וְחֶרֶב פִּיפִיּוֹת בְּיָדָם. דְּהָא וַדַּאי, י׳, רֵישָׁא
דְחַרְבָּא, דְּאַסְחַר שָׂפָה דִּילָךְ. ו׳, לִישָׁנָא דְּחַרְבָּא דִּילָךְ. ה׳, ה׳, תְּרֵין
פִּיפִיּוֹת, בִּתְרֵין שִׂפְוָון דִּילָךְ. וְהָא וַדַּאי, שְׁמָא דְמָרָךְ, מְמַלֵּל בְּפוּמָךְ.
יו״ד ה״א וָא״ו ה״א, אִיהוּ בְּמַחֲשַׁבְתָּךְ דְּאַפִּיק אִלֵּין חַמְשִׁין מִפּוּמָךְ.

398. As soon as THESE head Rabbis of the Yeshivas, who descended with
the Holy Luminary, RABBI SHIMON, heard these things, they commenced to
say TO MOSES: 'Faithful Shepherd, YOU ARE the mouthpiece of the higher
and lower Shechinah, BEING BINAH AND MALCHUT, with which the Holy
One, blessed be He, spoke to you, mouth to mouth, through *Kriat Sh'ma* –
as it is written: "The high praises of El are in their throats, and a two edged
sword in their hand" (Tehilim 149:6) – as the *Yud* OF YUD HEI VAV HEI is
the top of the sword surrounding your lip. The *Vav* OF YUD HEI VAV HEI is
like the tongue of your sword. The two *Hei's* OF YUD HEI VAV HEI are two
edges in your two lips. And surely the Name of your Master, BEING THE
SHECHINAH, speaks through your mouth. *Yud Vav Dalet, Hei Aleph, Vav
Aleph Vav, Hei Aleph* is in your thought, that produced these fifty GATES of
BINAH from your mouth.

399. בְּוַדַּאי, בְּגִין מִלִּין אִלֵּין, אֵלִיָּהוּ אִתְעַכָּב לְעֵילָּא, דְּתָפִיס אִיהוּ.

דְּלָא נָחִית לְגַבָּךְ, דְּהָא בְּכַמָּה עִתְרָא הֲוָה נָחִית לְגַבָּךְ. וְאִיהוּ תָּפִיס
לְעֵילָא, דְּלָא נָחִית לְגַבָּךְ. בְּגִין דַּעֲנִיּוּתָא דִּילָךְ, אִיהוּ פְּרוֹקָא לְיִשְׂרָאֵל.
וּבְג״ד מָשִׁיחַ אָמַר, עַד דְּיֵיתֵי עָנִי, וְהַאי אִיהוּ דִּכְתִּיב וּבַחֲבוּרָתוֹ נִרְפָּא
לָנוּ.

399. Surely for these reasons CITED ABOVE, THEIR ROOT IS TO PERFECT
MALCHUT IN BINAH AND PLACE THEM SIDE BY SIDE, AND BECAUSE OF
THIS Elijah has been delayed above, where he is confined, AS IN PRISON.
And he does not descend to you because he would have come down with
wealth for you, but he is confined above and descends not, as your poverty
is in reality a redemption for Yisrael. Hence the Messiah says: 'Until a poor
man comes', as the verse says, "and by his injury we are healed" (Yeshayah
53:5).

400. אָמַר לוֹן, אִי הָכִי, נַעֲבֵד לֵיהּ הַתָּרָה, וְיֵהֵא נָחִית לְגַבָּאי, דְּחָשִׁיב
הוּא גַּבָּאי, מִכָּל מָמוֹנָא דְּעָלְמָא. וְהָא אֲנָא מָחִיל וְשָׁרֵי לֵיהּ, וּמַתִּיר
לֵיהּ אוֹמָאָה. וְאַתּוּן אוּף הָכִי שָׁרוּ לֵיהּ וְאִי צָרִיךְ הַתָּרָה יַתִּיר, נִשְׁתַּדֵּל
בַּהֲתָּרָתֵיהּ, דְּיֵהֵא נָחִית גַּבָּאי.

400. He said to them: 'If so, let us give him a release so that he can descend,
as he is more precious to me than all silver in the world. Behold, I pardon
him, free him and release him of the oath. You, too, release him; if he needs
pardon, pardon him. Let us work to release him so he may descend to us.

10. A vow and an oath

A Synopsis

Rabbi Shimon says that Hashem's oath is the Shechinah, the only daughter, and that three people are required to release one from an oath. A vow is superior to an oath because, while an oath can take effect only on something of substance, a vow can take effect even on something insignificant; a vow is considered as being made on the Life of the King. Moses reminds the Head Rabbis that from darkness emanates light, and that "Elohim has made the one as well as the other." He says that vows stemming from the World to Come, being Binah, surpass the oaths, which are considered only of this world. Anyone who swears by the Name of Hashem falsely is considered as though he is demolishing the construction of heaven and earth and restoring the world to void and formlessness. Moses says that falsehood abides in Samael's place, and that the false oath can be compared to building heaven and earth on a base of falsehood; falsehood can not prevail, as it must become void, and therefore he has demolished the structure and caused the fall of heaven and earth. At the end the Yeshiva heads say that they will ask God to lower Elijah to Moses, laden with riches for him.

401. אָמַר לֵיהּ בּוּצִינָא קַדִּישָׁא, שְׁבוּעַת יְיָ', אִיהִי שְׁכִינְתָּא, בַּת יְחִידָה. וְלָא לְמַגָּנָא תַּקִּינוּ תְּלַת בְּנֵי נָשָׁא, לְמִפְטַר לֵיהּ. אֶלָּא, ש', דְּשַׁבָּת, תְּלַת עַנְפֵי אֲבָהָן, בַּת יְחִידָה. שְׁבוּעָה. דְּאִשְׁתְּתָפַת בְּהוּ.

401. The holy Luminary said to him: Hashem's oath is the Shechinah, the only daughter, CALLED 'HASHEM'S OATH'. It is not for naught that it was decided that three people are needed to release one FROM THE OATH; IT IS THE SECRET OF the letter *Shin* of Shabbat that three branches of THE LETTER *SHIN* IMPLY the THREE fathers, NAMELY CHESED, GVURAH, AND TIFERET, AND THE THICK LINE UNITES THE THREE BRANCHES OF THE BOTTOM. Thus, IT IS an only daughter CALLED *shevuah* (lit. 'oath') as it joins THE THREE BRANCHES OF THE *SHIN*.

402. בְּוַדַּאי, שְׁבוּעָה לָא חָלָה אֶלָּא עַל דָּבָר שֶׁיֵּשׁ בּוֹ מַמָּשׁ. נֶדֶר חָל, אֲפִילוּ עַל דָּבָר שֶׁאֵין בּוֹ מַמָּשׁ. וְהָא אוּקְמוּהָ בְּמַתְנִיתִין. וְלֹא עוֹד, אֶלָּא יַתִּיר אָמְרוּ, נְדָרִים ע״ג שְׁבוּעוֹת עוֹלִין, וְכָל הַנִּשְׁבַּע כְּאִלּוּ נִשְׁבַּע בְּמֶלֶךְ עַצְמוֹ. וְכָל הַנּוֹדֵר, כְּאִילּוּ נוֹדֵר בְּחַיֵּי הַמֶּלֶךְ.

402. It is sure that an oath can only take effect on something of substance, but a vow can take effect even on an insignificant thing, and so it is established in the Mishnah. Furthermore, they said that a vow is superior to an oath in that the one uttering the oath swears by the King himself, DENOTING MALCHUT, whereas a vow is considered making the vow by the Life of the King, DENOTING BINAH FROM WHENCE LIFE IS DRAWN, NAMELY MOCHIN, TO MALCHUT.

403. אָמַר לוֹן ר״מ, מָארֵי דִּמְתִיבְתָּאן, וְיִדְעָנָא בְּכוּ, דְּאַתּוּן יַדְעִין, אֲבָל הַהוּא דִּמְחַדֵּשׁ בְּכָל יוֹם תָּמִיד מַעֲשֵׂה בְּרֵאשִׁית, יְחַדֵּשׁ לוֹן חִדּוּשִׁין, דְּהָא וַדַּאי אָמַר קֹהֶלֶת, אֵין כָּל חָדָשׁ תַּחַת הַשָּׁמֶשׁ, אֲבָל לְמַעְלָה מִן הַשֶּׁמֶשׁ, יֵשׁ לוֹ. וּבְסִתְרֵי תוֹרָה אֲנָא בָּעֵינָא לְמֵימַר, שֶׁמֶשׁ וּמָגֵן יְיָ׳ אֱלֹהִים צְבָאוֹת, בְּעָלְמָא דִּילֵיהּ, וְלָא בְּעָלְמָא דְּהֶדְיוֹט, אַף עַל גַּב דְּזֶה לְעוּמַת זֶה עָשָׂה הָאֱלֹהִים, מִגּוֹ חֲשׁוֹכָא, נָפִיק נְהוֹרָא.

403. The Faithful Shepherd replied: Head Rabbis of the Yeshivas. I am certain that you are well aware of THE TOPIC OF OATHS AND VOWS. However, He who renews daily the act of creation will make us aware of new insights, for though Kohelet said, "and there is nothing new under the sun" (Kohelet 1:9) DENOTING ZEIR ANPIN, above the sun there is. Regarding the secrets of Torah, I wish to say that from "For Hashem Elohim is a sun and shield" (Tehilim 84:12), it IS TO BE INFERRED THAT HE ILLUMINATES AND SHIELDS EVEN BELOW THE SUN. THIS IS TRUE in His world, MEANING THE WORLD OF ATZILUT, but not in the Common world, MEANING THE THREE WORLDS OF BRIYAH, YETZIRAH, AND ASIYAH, WHICH CONTAIN KLIPOT, THAT DENY HIS UNITY. This is so even though "Elohim has made the one as well as the other" (Kohelet 7:14), MEANING THAT THE KLIPOT ARE ALSO THE WORK OF ELOHIM. For from darkness, WHICH IS THE KLIPOT, emanates light, WHEN PEOPLE OVERCOME THEM. THIS IS UNTIL THEY ARE CONSIDERED AS COMMON WORLD, AND THE LIGHT OF THE SUN, THAT IS ZEIR ANPIN OF ATZILUT, DOES NOT EXTEND TO SHIELD THEM.

404. וּבְוַדַּאי עָלְמָא דְּאָתֵי, בִּינָה, אִיהִי לְמַעְלָה מֵהַשֶּׁמֶשׁ, דְּאִיהוּ עַמּוּדָא דְּאֶמְצָעִיתָא. נְדָרִים מִתַּמָּן, עַל גַּבֵּי שְׁבוּעָה עוֹלִים, וְחָלִין עַל דָּבָר שֶׁאֵין בּוֹ מַמָּשׁ, בְּגִין דִּשְׁבוּעָה אִיהוּ עָלְמָא דֵּין, דְּלֵית לֵיהּ קִיּוּמָא,

-473-

אֶלָּא עַל יְסוֹד, הה"ד וְצַדִּיק יְסוֹד עוֹלָם.

404. Most certainly, the world to come, being Binah, is above the sun, being the middle pillar, DENOTING ZEIR ANPIN. Thus, vows stemming from there surpass the oaths and take effect even in insignificant matters. An oath is considered of this world, DENOTING MALCHUT, which survives only through Yesod, as the verse writes, "but the righteous is an everlasting foundation" (Mishlei 10:25), SO IT CAN ONLY TAKE EFFECT ON A MATTER OF SUBSTANCE.

405. וּבֵיהּ אוֹמָאָה, דִּכְתִּיב, חַי יְיָ' שְׁכְבִי עַד הַבֹּקֶר. דִּשְׁכִינְתָּא תַּתָּאָה, כּוֹתֶל מַעֲרָבִי, דִּיּוּרָא דִּילֵיהּ. עַל שֵׁם דְּאִיהוּ תֵּל שֶׁהַכֹּל פּוֹנִים בּוֹ. כ"ו תֵּ"ל, יְדֹנָ"ד כ"ו, וַדַּאי שְׁכִינְתָּא, אִיהוּ תֵּל דִּילֵיהּ. עַל שֵׁם, קְוּוצוֹתָיו תַּלְתַּלִּים שְׁחֹרוֹת כָּעוֹרֵב וְאוּקְמוּהָ עַל כָּל קוֹץ וְקוֹץ תִּלֵּי תִּלִּים שֶׁל הֲלָכוֹת. ד' מִן אֶחָד, תֵּל שֶׁהַכֹּל פּוֹנִים בּוֹ. וְהַאי קוֹץ, הוּא אָחִיד בֵּין א"ח, וּבֵין ד', הה"ד, כִּי כֹל בַּשָּׁמַיִם וּבָאָרֶץ, וְת"י, דְּאָחִיד בִּשְׁמַיָּא וּבְאַרְעָא.

405. WITHIN YESOD are oaths made, as it is written, "as Hashem lives: lie down until the morning" (Rut 3:13). "LIVES" IS CALLED 'YESOD', as the lower Shechinah is called the 'western wall', BEING MALCHUT, His dwelling, being the mount (Heb. *tel,* Tav Lamed) which all turn to. The WALL (HEB. *KOTEL*) IS SPELLED *Caf-Vav Tav-Lamed* – Yud Hei Vav Hei, DENOTING ZEIR ANPIN, NUMERICALLY equals *Caf-Vav.* And surely the Shechinah is the mound (Heb. *tel*) OF ZEIR ANPIN based on the verse: "his locks (Heb. *kevutzotav*) are wavy (Heb. *taltalim*) and black as the raven" (Shir Hashirim 5:11). It was established that every tip (Heb. *kotz*) of any letter contains heaps (Heb. *tel*) of rules. The *Dalet* of 'one '(Heb. *echad,* Aleph-Chet-Dalet) is a hill that all turn to, DENOTING MALCHUT. This tip OF THE *DALET* THAT DIFFERENTIATES IT FROM THE *RESH* FORM, WHICH DENOTES YESOD, is caught between the *Aleph* and *Chet* of the word *echad,* DENOTING ZEIR ANPIN, and the *Dalet* of *echad,* DENOTING MALCHUT. THUS THE VERSE, "for all that is in heaven and on earth" (I Divrei Hayamim 29:11); as Targum Yonatan reads, 'it is caught between heaven and earth', MEANING THAT "ALL" IS ANOTHER NAME FOR YESOD, AND IT

IS HELD BETWEEN ZEIR ANPIN, REFERRED TO AS 'HEAVEN', AND
MALCHUT, REFERRED TO AS 'EARTH'.

406. וְעָלֵיהּ אוּקְמוּהָ מָ"מ בַּחֲגִיגָה, עַל מַה הָעוֹלָם עוֹמֵד, עַל עַמּוּד
אֶחָד שֶׁשְּׁמוֹ צַדִּיק, שֶׁנֶּאֱמַר וְצַדִּיק יְסוֹד עוֹלָם. וּבְוַדַּאי אִיהוּ בְּרִית
דִּשְׁבוּעָה, דַּעֲלֵיהּ קַיְימִין א"ח ד', דְּאִינּוּן שְׁמַיָּא וְאַרְעָא, דִּכְתִּיב אִם
לֹא בְרִיתִי יוֹמָם וָלַיְלָה חֻקּוֹת שָׁמַיִם וָאָרֶץ לֹא שָׂמְתִּי. א"ח שָׁמַיִם,
הה"ד, וְאַתָּה תִּשְׁמַע הַשָּׁמַיִם. ד', הָאָרֶץ. הה"ד, וְהָאָרֶץ הֲדוֹם רַגְלָי.

406. Upon it, YESOD, have the masters of the Mishnah stated in Tractate
Chagigah: "...on what does the world stand?" On one pillar whose name is
Righteous, MEANING YESOD, or as it is written, "but the Righteous is an
everlasting foundation," surely it is the covenant in the oath, DENOTING
MALCHUT. Upon this pillar stands *Aleph-Chet* and *Dalet*, which are heaven
and earth, as it is written: "If My covenant be not day and night, it would be
as if I have not established the ordinances of heaven and earth" (Yirmeyah
33:25). *Aleph-Chet* point to heaven, as written, "then hear you IN heaven" (I
Melachim 8:32), WHICH REFERS TO ZEIR ANPIN, and *Dalet* points to earth
as the verse reads, "and the earth is my footstool" (Yeshayah 66:1),
DENOTING MALCHUT.

407. וּבְגִין דִּבְרִית אָחִיד בֵּין שְׁמַיָּא וְאַרְעָא, וּבֵיהּ שְׁבוּעָה, הה"ד, חַי
יְיָ' שִׁכְבִי עַד הַבֹּקֶר. מַאן דְּאוּמֵי בִּשְׁמֵיהּ לְשַׁקְרָא, כְּאִילּוּ הָרַס בִּנְיָינָא
דִּשְׁמַיָּא וְאַרְעָא, וְאַהֲדָּר עָלְמָא לְתֹהוּ וָבֹהוּ. דְּאִי בַּר נָשׁ יַעֲדֵי קוֹצָא דִּד'
מִן אֶחָד יִשְׁתְּאָר אַחֵר, סָמָאֵל בַּאֲתָרֵיהּ שָׁקֶר. וּכְאִילּוּ הַהוּא בַּר נָשׁ בָּנֵי
שְׁמַיָּא וְאַרְעָא שֶׁל שָׁקֶר. וְקוּשְׁטָא קָאֵי, שִׁקְרָא לָא קָאֵי. הָרַס בִּנְיָינָא,
וְנָפְלוּ שְׁמַיָּא וְאַרְעָא.

407. And since the covenant, DENOTING YESOD, is held between heaven
and earth, DENOTING MALE AND FEMALE, and contains an oath, BEING
MALCHUT, where the verse reads: "as Hashem lives: lie down until the
morning," SO AN OATH IS DEPENDENT UPON YESOD, REFERRED TO AS
'LIVING'. One who swears by His Name falsely is considered like one who
demolishes the construction of heaven and earth, and restores the world to

void and formlessness. When man removes the tip, BEING YESOD, from the *Dalet* of *echad*, BEING MALCHUT, what remains is an other (Heb. *acher*, Aleph Chet Resh) namely Samael – REFERRED TO AS 'THE OTHER', in whose place abides falsehood. This can be compared to building heaven and earth on a base of falsehood. Truth prevails; falsehood can not, as it must become void. As such he has demolished the structure and caused the fall of heaven and earth.

408. וְהַאי אִיהוּ כְּאִילוּ הִשְׁלִיךְ מִשָּׁמַיִם אֶרֶץ תִּפְאֶרֶת יִשְׂרָאֵל. דְּמַאן יָהִיב אֶרֶץ בַּשָּׁמַיִם, דְּקָאָמַר הִשְׁלִיךְ מִשָּׁמַיִם אֶרֶץ אֶלָּא וַדַּאי דָא שְׁכִינְתָּא, וְתִפְאֶרֶת עִמָּהּ, דְּלָא אִתְפְּרַשׁ מִינָה בְּנְפִילוּ דִּילָה, לְקַיֵּים בָּהּ אֲנִי יְיָ׳ הוּא שְׁמִי וּכְבוֹדִי לְאַחַר לֹא אֶתֵּן. וּמְנָלָן דֶּאֱמֶת נָפַל עִמָּהּ, דִּכְתִיב וְתַשְׁלֵךְ אֱמֶת אַרְצָה. וּמַאן דְּאוֹמֵי קוּשְׁטָא, הוּא מְקַיֵּים אֱ"מֶת מֵ"אֶרֶץ תִּ"צְמָח, דְּאִיהוּ עַמּוּדָא דְּאֶמְצָעִיתָא, דְּבֵיהּ אִיהוּ קַיְימָא בִּנְיָינָא. הה"ד בָּרָ"א אֱלֹהִי"ם א"ת, וּלְבָתַר הַשָּׁמַיִם וְאֵת הָאָרֶץ.

408. This one, WHO SWEARS FALSELY, is like the verse "He threw earth from the heavens, the glory (Heb. *tiferet*) of Yisrael" (Eichah 2:1). HE ASKS: Who placed earth in heaven so that it could be cast out from there? HE ANSWERS: It points to the Shechinah, CALLED 'EARTH', and Tiferet, CALLED 'HEAVEN' (HEB. *SHAMAYIM*) is with her, as it did not part from her EVEN at her downfall. This concept is found in the verse "Hashem is My Name and My glory, I shall give to another" (Yeshayah 42:8). How do we know that truth, DENOTING ZEIR ANPIN, fell with her – as it is written, "and it cast down the truth to the ground" (Daniel 8:12). SO WE SEE THAT WHICH CAUSES THE FALL OF MALCHUT LIKEWISE CAUSES THE FALL OF ZEIR ANPIN, AND SO HE WHO SWEARS FALSELY CAUSES THE DOWNFALL OF HEAVEN AND EARTH. One who swears truthfully fulfills the verse: "Truth will spring out of the earth" (Tehilim 85:12), THE INITIALS OF WHICH SPELL OUT *EMET* ('TRUTH'), which is the middle pillar – MEANING ZEIR ANPIN THAT IS CALLED 'TRUTH' upon which stands the structure, as written, "Elohim created the" (Beresheet 1:1), THE LAST LETTERS OF WHICH SPELL OUT *EMET*. Then the verse continues, "the heaven and the earth," SO WE SEE THAT THE STRUCTURE OF HEAVEN AND EARTH IS BASED ON TRUTH.

409. וּבְגִין דִּשְׁבוּעָה, אִיהוּ בִּנְיָינָא דְּעָלְמָא דָא, לֵית לֵיהּ קִיּוּמָא בְּלָא

יְסוֹד, דָּבָר שֶׁיֵּשׁ בּוֹ מַמָּשׁ. נֶדֶר, דְּאִיהוּ עָלְמָא דְּאָתֵי, עַל גַּבֵּי שְׁבוּעָה
סְלִיקַת, וְאִיהוּ חָלָה עַל דָּבָר שֶׁאֵין בּוֹ מַמָּשׁ, דְּלָא צְרִיכָה יְסוֹד לְקַיְּימָא
עֲלֵיהּ, דְּאִיהוּ בְּרִית, דְּבֵיהּ תַּשְׁמִישׁ הַמִּטָּה. וּבְגִין דָּא, בְּיוֹם הַכִּפּוּרִים,
עָלְמָא דְּאָתֵי, דְּבֵיהּ תַּקִּינוּ כָּל נִדְרֵי, אָסוּר בְּתַשְׁמִישׁ הַמִּטָּה.

409. As the oath is the edifice of this world, MALCHUT, it having no continuity without Yesod, which is a matter of substance, a vow, alluding to the world to come, BINAH, supersedes the oath and can take effect even on matters lacking substance, AS in order to prevail, BINAH does not require Yesod, the male organ which pertains to marital relations. For IN THE FIRST THREE SFIROT, CHOCHMAH DOES NOT NEED CHASSADIM WITH WHICH TO BE CLOTHED, AS ALSO MENTIONED EARLIER. Hence, on Yom Kippur (Day of Atonement), signifying the World to Come, BINAH, FOR which the prayer *Kol Nidre* (lit. 'all the vows') was composed – AS THE VOW STEMS FROM BINAH – prohibits marital relations, AS THE MATING OF YESODOT IS NOT PRACTICED IN BINAH, AS INDICATED.

410. תַּמָּן אוֹת בְּרִית, י׳ אִיהִי תָּגָא עַל ס״ת צַדִּיק, כְּמָה דְּאוּקְמוּהָ
הָעוֹלָם הַבָּא, אֵין בּוֹ, לֹא אֲכִילָה, וְלֹא שְׁתִיָּה, וְלֹא תַּשְׁמִישׁ הַמִּטָּה,
אֶלָּא צַדִּיקִים יוֹשְׁבִים וְעַטְרוֹתֵיהֶם בְּרָאשֵׁיהֶם.

410. There, IN BINAH, the letter of the Covenant, *Yud* – MEANING YESOD OF BINAH is the crown of the Torah scroll, namely the righteous, DENOTING YESOD OF ZEIR ANPIN, as explained. In the World to Come there is no eating, drinking, and no marital intercourse, but only righteous people sitting, with their crowns on their heads.

411. וּבְגִין דְּלֵית שִׁמּוּשׁ בְּעָלְמָא דֵין בְּתָגָא, אוּקְמוּהָ מָארֵי מַתְנִיתִין,
כָּל הַמִּשְׁתַּמֵּשׁ בְּתָגָא חֲלָף. דְּתָגָא לְתַתָּא, בְּעָלְמָא דֵין אִיהִי. נְקוּדָה
שִׁמּוּשָׁא דְּאַתְוָון. אֲבָל בְּעָלְמָא דְּאָתֵי, לֵית שִׁמּוּשָׁא בְּאַתְוָון, וּבְגִין דָּא
ס״ת לֵית בֵּיהּ נְקוּדָה בְּאַתְווֹי, אֶלָּא תָּגָא, וּבְגִין דָּא, מַאן דְּמִשְׁתַּמֵּשׁ
בְּסֵפֶר תּוֹרָה חֲלָף. וְהָכִי, מַאן דְּמִשְׁתַּמֵּשׁ בְּמִי שֶׁשּׁוֹנֶה הֲלָכוֹת, עָלֵיהּ
אוּקְמוּהָ רַבָּנָן, דְּאִשְׁתַּמֵּשׁ בְּתָגָא חֲלָף.

411. And since there can be no use made in this world, NAMELY MALCHUT, with the crown – BEING THE CROWN ON THE HEAD OF THE RIGHTEOUS, PRACTICED ONLY WITH BINAH – so the masters of the Mishnah have announced that all who make use of the crown shall depart FROM THIS WORLD. The crown in this world is below YESOD AND NOT AT THE HEAD OF THE RIGHTEOUS. The vowels are to be used by the letters. However, in the world to come, BEING BINAH, there will be no use of the letters, WHICH INSINUATE MALE AND FEMALE. Hence, in the Torah scroll, there are no vowels but crowns, DRAWN FROM BINAH, AND THEY ARE THE CROWN ON TOP OF THE LETTERS, BEING MALE AND FEMALE. So, he who makes use of a Torah scroll will depart THIS WORLD, and also one who makes use of one who studies Halachah, the Rabbis predicted, will die.

412. אָתוּ כֻּלְּהוּ מָארֵי מְתִיבְתָּאן, וְאִשְׁתְּטָחוּ קָמֵיהּ, וְאָמְרוּ וַדַּאי קוּדְשָׁא בְּרִיךְ הוּא מַלִּיל בְּפוּמָךְ, וְלֵיהּ אֲנָן סַגְדִּין. וַאֲנָן אִשְׁתְּמוֹדְעִין בְּמִלִּין אִלֵּין, דְּלֵית יְלוּד אִשָּׁה אַחֲרָא בַּר מִינָךְ, יָכִיל לְמַלְּלָא לוֹן. וַדַּאי מִלִּין אִלֵּין, קָא סָהֲדִין בָּךְ, דְּאַנְתְּ הוּא דְּאִתְּמַר בֵּיהּ, פֶּה אֶל פֶּה אֲדַבֶּר בּוֹ. לֵית לְעַכְּבָא לְאֵלִיָּהוּ גַּבָּךְ, אֶלָּא לְפַיְּיסָא לֵיהּ לְקוּדְשָׁא בְּרִיךְ הוּא, לְנַחְתָּא לֵיהּ לְגַבָּךְ, מַלְיָא עוּתְרָא, מַלְיָיא סְגוּלוֹת לְגַבָּךְ.

412. All the Yeshiva heads prostrated before him and said: Surely the Holy One, blessed be He, speaks through your mouth, and to Him do we bend. We realize from these words that no human being beside yourself could utter them. These prove the verse which testifies about you: "With him I speak mouth to mouth" (Bemidbar 12:8). Elijah must not be withheld from you, we must ask of the Holy One, blessed be He, to lower him to you, laden with riches and treasures for you.

11. The threshing flour and the winepress

A Synopsis

We are told that the Hebrew letters of 'winepress' are the initials of unison, holiness and blessing – this is the Shechinah, the blessing of God. God is always with one who is well versed in the Torah and the Halachah. Moses speaks of the two worlds, and says that for those who are clothed with the lowly body the spirit can not see what is above it, but that one should 'Know what is above you – a watchful eye, an attentive ear, and all your deeds are recorded in a book.' He who is in the body has no permission to look at the angels or the Shechinah or the Holy One, blessed be He. Due to their sins, men are separated from God, who covers Himself with His wings. Yet in the time to come "yet your teacher shall not withdraw himself any more, your eyes shall see your teacher."

413. רַעְיָא מְהֵימְנָא, עֶבֶד נֶאֱמָן, לְגַבָּךְ עֶבֶד עִבְרִי, הַעֲנֵק תַּעֲנִיק לוֹ. הַעֲנֵק לֵיהּ, תַּעֲנִיק לִבְנוֹי, בְּמִלִּין גְּנִיזִין אִלֵּין. וּמִגָּרְנְךָ: גָּרְנָה שֶׁל תּוֹרָה דִּילָךְ. וּמִיָּקְבֶךָ, בְּגֹרֶן וְיֶקֶב קְרָא מְמַלֵּל, כְּמָה דְּאוּקְמוּהָ מָארֵי מַתְנִיתִין, בִּפְסֹלֶת גֹּרֶן וְיֶקֶב הַכָּתוּב מְדַבֵּר.

413. A Faithful Shepherd, loyal servant, in relation to you IT WAS SAID OF the Hebrew slave "You shall furnish him liberally" (Devarim 15:14). You shall furnish him, and be liberal to his sons with these concealed things: "out of your threshing flour" (Ibid.), the threshing flour of your Torah, "and out of your winepress." The verse refers to the threshing flour and to the winepress, the same way as the scholars of the Mishnah established, namely, to the residue of the threshing floor and the winepress.

414. יֶקֶ"ב: יִ"חוּד. קְ"דוּשָׁה. בְּ"רָכָה דְּקוּדְשָׁא בְּרִיךְ הוּא. וְדָא שְׁכִינְתָּא, דְּאִיהִי בְּרָכָה, דְּקוּדְשָׁא בְּרִיךְ הוּא, מִימִינָא. וְאִיהִי קְדוּשָׁה מִשְּׂמָאלֵיהּ. וְאִיהִי יִחוּדֵיהּ, בְּאֶמְצָעִיתָא. וְקוּדְשָׁא בְּרִיךְ הוּא, הָכִי סָלְקִין אַתְוֵוי דִּילֵיהּ, יַבְּ"ק. כְּגַוְונָא דָא, הַקוּדְשָׁא בְּרִיךְ הוּא: בְּחֻשְׁבָּן יַבְּ"ק.

414. The winepress (Heb. *yekev*, Yud-Kof-Bet) ARE THE INITIALS OF *yichud* (lit. 'unison') *kedushah* ('holiness') and *berachah* ('blessing') of the

Holy One, blessed be He. This is the Shechinah, DENOTING MALCHUT, being the blessing of the Holy One, blessed be He, WHEN SHE IS THE SECRET of the right, NAMELY CHASSADIM. It is the Holiness OF THE HOLY ONE, BLESSED BE HE, WHEN SHE FINDS HERSELF in His left, MEANING IN CHOCHMAH. She is the unison OF THE HOLY ONE, BLESSED BE HE, WHEN IT IS FOUND IN THE Central COLUMN. The letters of the Holy One, blessed be He, equal 112 (*Yud-Bet-Kof*) BEING also the letters *Yud-Kof-Bet*. FOR THE HOLY ONE, BLESSED BE HE, IS ZEIR ANPIN, AND THE NUKVA IS THE SECRET OF THE NUMEROLOGY OF ZEIR ANPIN.

415. וּמַאן דְּאִיהוּ בָּקִ"י בַּהֲלָכָה דִּילֵיהּ, דְּאִיהִי שְׁכִינְתָּא, קוּדְשָׁא בְּרִיךְ הוּא עִמֵּיהּ. דִּבְגִינָה לָא יָזוּז מִנֵּיהּ לְעָלַם. דְּאִית הֲלָכָה דְּאִיהִי נַעֲרָה דִּילָהּ, מִסְטְרָא דְּנַעַר, וּבְגִינָה אִתְּמַר הֲלָכָה כִּפְלוֹנִי. אֲבָל הֲלָכָה דִּילָךְ, רַעְיָא מְהֵימְנָא, אִיהִי דְּאִתְּמַר בָּהּ, הֲלָכָה לְמֹשֶׁה מִסִּינַי, מִפִּי הַגְּבוּרָה, יָהִיב לָךְ קוּדְשָׁא בְּרִיךְ הוּא, בְּרָתָא דִּילֵיהּ.

415. The Holy One, blessed be He, is with one who is well versed (Heb. *baki, Bet-Kof-Yud*), WHICH IS SPELLED WITH *YUD-KOF-BET*, in the Halachah, denoting the Shechinah. For her sake, He will never forsake him. There is Halachah, which is a SERVING maiden of the Halachah from the standpoint of the lad – MEANING METATRON OF BRIYAH – and there we say that the Halachah is according to so and so, AS IT ALLUDES TO ITS MAIDEN. But of your Halachah, Faithful Shepherd, it is written: "The tradition attributed to Moses hails from Sinai"; by divine command did the Holy One, blessed be He, give you His daughter, NAMELY THE SHECHINAH.

416. וּבְגִין דָּא, עַל הֲלָכוֹת אַחֲרָנִין אִתְּמַר, רַבּוֹת בָּנוֹת עָשׂוּ חָיִל. עַל הֲלָכָה דִּילָךְ אִתְּמַר, וְאַתְּ עָלִית עַל כֻּלָּנָה. דְּאִתְגַּבְּרַת עַל כֻּלְּהוּ, בִּגְבוּרָה. יְיָ' עִמְּךָ גִּבּוֹר הֶחָיִל. אַתְקִין בָּךְ, וְאַשְׁלִים בְּנְיָינָא דְּמַלְכָּא, וְאִיהוּ בָּנֵי בְּנְיָינֵיהּ עַל פּוּמָךְ, וְעַל יְדָךְ, זַכָּאָה חוּלָקָךְ.

416. For this reason, concerning other Halachot, we read, "Many daughters have done virtuously" (Mishlei 31:29), but with your Halachah, it reads "but you excel them all" (Ibid.), as yours overpowers them all, with might.

"Hashem is with you, you mighty man of valor" (Shoftim 6:12). The edifice of the King, DENOTING SHECHINAH, is fixed and completed as He builds His edifice through your mouth and hands. How fortunate is your lot.

417. פָּתַח רַעְיָא מְהֵימָנָא וְאָמַר, הַמַּלְאָךְ הַגּוֹאֵל אוֹתִי מִכָּל רָע, דְּאִיהִי שְׁכִינְתָּא, דְּאִתְּמַר בָּהּ, וַיִּסַּע מַלְאַךְ הָאֱלֹהִים. יְבָרֵךְ לְכוּ בְּעָלְמָא דְּאָתֵי. וְיִדְגּוּ לָרֹב בְּקֶרֶב הָאָרֶץ, בְּעָלְמָא דֵּין. לְמֶהֱוֵי שָׁלְטָנוּתְכוֹן בִּתְרֵין עָלְמִין, דְּאַתּוּן חַיִּין. דְּמַאן דְּאִיהוּ מֵעָלְמָא דָּא, חַי אִתְקְרֵי. כְּמָה דִּכְתִּיב, עֵץ חַיִּים הִיא לַמַּחֲזִיקִים בָּהּ. חַיִּים תַּמָּן, חַיִּים הָכָא.

417. The Faithful Shepherd commenced to say: "the angel who redeemed me from all evil" (Beresheet 48:16), refers to the Shechinah, of whom it is written, "the angel of the Elohim… removed" (Shemot 14:19). He will bless you in the world to come, WHICH IS BINAH. "…and let them grow into a multitude in the midst of the earth…" referring to this world, NAMELY MALCHUT, so your governance shall be in two worlds where you live. One who is from this world, MALCHUT is called 'living', as it is written, "She is a Tree of Life to those who lay hold on her" (Mishlei 3:8) – life there, IN BINAH, and life here, IN MALCHUT.

418. מַה דְּלָאו הָכִי, מַאן דְּאִיהוּ מְלוּבָּשׁ בְּאִלֵּין קְלִיפִין, דְּעוֹר וּבְשַׂר וַעֲצָמוֹת וְגִידִים דְּגוּפָא שְׁפָלָא, דְּרוּחָא הוּא מִית תַּמָּן. מַה מֵּיתָא, לָא חָמֵי וְלָא שָׁמַע וְלָא מְמַלֵּל וְלֵית לֵיהּ תְּנוּעָה בְּכָל אֵבָרִין דִּילֵיהּ. הָכִי רוּחָא, לָא חָזָא דִּלְעֵיל מִנֵּיהּ. דְּאִתְּמַר בְּאוֹרַיְיתָא עָלַיְיהוּ, דָּא מַה לְמַעְלָה מִמָּךְ, עַיִן רוֹאָה וְאֹזֶן שׁוֹמַעַת, וְכָל מַעֲשֶׂיךָ בְּסֵפֶר נִכְתָּבִים.

418. This is not so with whoever is clothed with the Klipot of the skin, flesh, bone and sinews of the lowly body. His spirit dies there. Just as a corpse sees not, hears not, speaks not, and has no limb movements, so the spirit sees not what is above it, as it is written of them in the Torah: 'Know what is above you – a watchful eye, an attentive ear and all your deeds are recorded in a book'.

419. דְּכַמָּה מַלְאָכִין אַזְלִין עִמֵּיהּ, דְּאִתְּמַר בְּהוֹן, כִּי מַלְאָכָיו יְצַוֶּה לָךְ.

וְלֵית לֵיהּ רְשׁוּ בְּהַאי גוּפָא, לְאִסְתַּכְּלָא בְּהוֹן, וּלְמִשְׁמַע בְּקַלַּיְיהוֹן, דְּאִינּוּן חַיָּין דְּאֶשָׁא, מְמַלְלָן וּמְקַדְּשָׁן וּמְבָרְכָן וּמְיַחֲדַן לְקוּדְשָׁא בְּרִיךְ הוּא, עִם יִשְׂרָאֵל כַּחֲדָא. כָּל שֶׁכֵּן לִשְׁכִינְתָּא, דְּאִיהִי עֲלַיְיהוּ. כָּל שֶׁכֵּן קוּדְשָׁא בְּרִיךְ הוּא דְּאִיהוּ לְעֵילָּא מִן שְׁכִינְתֵּיהּ, דְּבָהּ מְקַבֵּל צְלוֹתִין דְּיִשְׂרָאֵל.

419. Numerous angels accompany him, as it is written: "For He shall give His angels charge over you" (Tehilim 91:11), but he who is in the body has no permission to look at them or hear their voices, as they are fiery creatures that speak, sanctify and bless both the Holy One, blessed be He, together with Yisrael. This is all the more so with regards to the Shechinah that is above them, and even more so with the Holy One, blessed be He, who is above the Shechinah, that receives the supplications of Yisrael.

420. וּבְגִין חוֹבִין, הֲווֹ מִתְלַבְּשִׁין בְּאִלֵּין קְלִיפִין. כְּגַוְונָא דְּאָדָם, דְּחוֹבֵי אֲבָהַתְהוֹן בִּידַיְיהוּ. וְהַאי אִיהוּ דְּאוּקְמוּהָ מָארֵי מַתְנִיתִין, כְּשֶׁאוֹחֲזִין מַעֲשֵׂה אֲבוֹתֵיהֶם בִּידֵיהֶם. וּבְגִין אִלֵּין קְלִיפִין דְּחוֹבִין, אָמַר קְרָא, כִּי אִם עֲוֹנוֹתֵיכֶם הָיוּ מַבְדִּילִים בֵּינֵיכֶם לְבֵין אֱלֹהֵיכֶם. וּבְגִין אִלֵּין קְלִיפִין, קוּדְשָׁא בְּרִיךְ הוּא מִתְכַּסְיָא בְּכַמָּה גַּדְפִין. דְּאִתְּמַר בְּהוֹן, בִּשְׁתַּיִם יְכַסֶּה פָנָיו וּבִשְׁתַּיִם יְכַסֶּה רַגְלָיו וְגו'.

420. Due to sins, they were clothed with these Klipot like people who possess the sins of their fathers, or as the sages of the Mishnah expressed, 'when they maintain the sins of their fathers.' Due to these Klipot, STEMMING FROM THE SINS, the verse says: "but your iniquities have made a separation between you and your Elohim" (Yeshayah 59:2). And as a result of these Klipot, the Holy One, blessed be He, covers Himself with numerous wings, as it is written: "with two He covers his face, and with two He covers his feet..." (Yeshayah 6:2).

421. לֶעָתִיד לָבֹא, וְלֹא יִכָּנֵף עוֹד מוֹרֶיךָ וְהָיוּ עֵינֶיךָ רוֹאוֹת אֶת מוֹרֶיךָ. דְּאַתּוּן בְּהַאי עָלְמָא, דְּלֵית לְכוֹן קְלִיפִין וְעוֹרִין, אִית לְכוֹן רְשׁוּ לְאִסְתַּכְּלָא בִּבְנֵי עָלְמָא, וּבְנֵי עָלְמָא אִית לוֹן רְשׁוּ לְאִסְתַּכְּלָא בְּכוּ.

וּבְגִין דָּא, עֲלַיְיכוּ אִתְּמַר דְּאַתּוּן חַיִּין, וְעָלְמָא דִּלְכוֹן, עוֹלָם הַחַיִּים.
אֲבָל עָלְמָא שְׁפָלָא, דָּא עוֹלָם הַמֵּתִים, דְּכָל אֱלָהוּת דְּאוּמִין דְּעָלְמָא,
מִבַּלְעֲדֵי יְיָ', כֻּלְּהוֹן מֵתִים.

421. In the time to come, THE VERSE SAYS: "yet your teacher shall not withdraw himself (lit. 'be winged') any more, your eyes shall see your teacher" (Yeshayah 30:20). When you are in this world, MALCHUT, where you have no Klipot, skins, then you may look at other humans, and they at you. Thus, you are called 'living' and your world is the world of living. But this lowly world is the world of the dead, as all the deities of the nations are dead except Hashem.

12. "He looks in at the windows"

A Synopsis

Rabbi Shimon tells Moses that Moses can see everything with the wisdom of his heart – the inhabitants of the World to Come, angels, the Holy One, blessed be He, and the Shechinah. A prophet can see only with his eyes, but the wise man who perceives with his heart is better. "And in the hearts of all that are wise hearted I have put wisdom": such is not so with eyes. He says that for one who possesses a heart that sees more than a prophet, surely his thoughts which are endless can see Him who is endless – that which could not be perceived with eyes. "He looks in at the windows" means the windows of the eyes, ears, nostrils and mouth; with prayer, the soul ascends through these seven openings.

422. אמ"ל רַבִּי שִׁמְעוֹן, רַעְיָא מְהֵימְנָא, עִם כָּל דָּא, דְּאַנְתְּ לָא יָכִיל לְאִסְתַּכְּלָא בִּבְנֵי עָלְמָא דְּאָתֵי, בְּעַיְינִין, וְלָא בְּמַלְאֲכַיָּא, כָּל שֶׁכֵּן בְּקוּדְשָׁא בְּרִיךְ הוּא וּבִשְׁכִינְתֵּיהּ, אֲבָל בְּעֵין הַשֵּׂכֶל דְּלִבָּךְ, אַתְּ חֲזֵי בְּכֹלָּא בִּבְנֵי עָלְמָא דְּאָתֵי, וּבְמַלְאָכִין וּבְקוּדְשָׁא בְּרִיךְ הוּא וּשְׁכִינְתֵּיהּ. דְּסַחֲרִין לָךְ. וּבְגִין דָּא אָמַר שְׁלֹמֹה, דִּכְתִּיב בֵּיהּ וַיֶּחְכַּם מִכָּל הָאָדָם, וְלִבִּי רָאָה הַרְבֵּה חָכְמָה וָדָעַת.

422. Rabbi Shimon said to him: Faithful servant, with your eyes you are not able to see the inhabitants of the world to come, nor angels, certainly not the Holy One, blessed be He, nor His Shechinah, but with the wisdom of your heart you can see everything: the inhabitants of the world to come, angels, the Holy One, blessed be He, and the Shechinah. Therefore, Solomon, about whom it is written, "For he was wiser than all men" (I Melachim 5:11), said, "for my heart has seen much wisdom and knowledge" (Kohelet 1:16), NAMELY, THROUGH HIS MIND'S EYES.

423. אֲבָל בִּנְבוּאָה, לֵית רְשׁוּ לְאִסְתַּכְּלָא בֵּיהּ נָבִיא בְּעֵין הַשֵּׂכֶל, אֶלָּא בְּעַיְינִין, דְּאִיהִי מַרְאֶה וְחֶזְיוֹן דְּעַיְינִין, הה"ד, בַּמַּרְאָה אֵלָיו אֶתְוַדַּע. וְעוֹד בְּחֶזְיוֹן לַיְלָה, מַרְאֶה בִּימָמָא, חֶזְיוֹן בְּלֵילְיָא, וְכֹלָּא בְּעַיְינִין, וְלָא בְּעֵין הַשֵּׂכֶל דְּלִבָּא. וְעַיְינִין אִינּוּן תְּרֵי סַרְסוֹרֵי דְּלִבָּא, וּמְשַׁמְּשִׁין דִּילֵיהּ. וְאִיהוּ מַלְכָּא בֵּינַיְיהוּ וּבְגִין דָּא, חַכָּם עָדִיף מִנָּבִיא. וְהָכִי הוּא

תְּרֵין אוּדְנִין, תְּרֵין שַׁמָּשֵׁי דְלִבָּא.

423. But when it comes to prophecy, a prophet can not see through his mind's eyes but with his eyes alone, as it is written, "I, Hashem, make Myself known to him in a vision" (Bemidbar 12:6) – that is, a sight by night or a vision by day, both by eye. The TWO eyes serve as two agents of the heart that mediate BETWEEN THE EVIL INCLINATION OF THE HEART AND MAN and serve it, and it is their king. For this reason, the wise man WHO PERCEIVES WITH HIS HEART'S EYES is better than the prophet WHO SEES WITH HIS EYES. And similarly, the two ears are two agents of the heart.

424. וּבג״ד אוּקְמוּהָ רַבָּנָן, הַלֵּב רוֹאֶה, וְהַלֵּב שׁוֹמֵעַ. וְלֹא עוֹד, אֶלָּא דְּאִתְּמַר בַּלֵּב, הַלֵּב מֵבִין, הַלֵּב יוֹדֵעַ. וּבְלֵב כָּל חָכַם לֵב נָתַתִּי חָכְמָה. הֲרֵי חָכְמָה וּתְבוּנָה וָדַעַת בְּלִבָּא. דִּבְהוֹן אִתְעֲבִידוּ שְׁמַיָּא וְאַרְעָא, וּתְהוֹמִין. וּבְהוֹן אִתְעֲבִיד מַשְׁכְּנָא, הה״ד, וָאֲמַלֵּא אוֹתוֹ רוּחַ אֱלֹהִים בְּחָכְמָה בִּתְבוּנָה וּבְדַעַת. מַה דְּלֵית כּוּלֵי הַאי בְּעַיְינִין.

424. For this reason, the sages have declared that a heart sees, hears, understands, knows, "and in the hearts of all that are wise hearted I have put wisdom" (Shemot 31:6). So we see that wisdom, understanding, and knowledge are in the heart, with which heaven, earth, and the deeps were made. Also it says, "and I have filled him with the spirit of Elohim, in wisdom, and in understanding and in knowledge" (Ibid. 3). Such is not so with eyes.

425. וְרַעְיָא מְהֵימָנָא, מַאן דְּכוּלֵי הַאי בְּלִבֵּיה, יַתִּיר חֲזֵי מִן נָבִיא, כָּל שֶׁכֵּן מַחֲשַׁבְתָּא דִּילָךְ. דְּלֵית לָה סוֹף, וּבָה תִּסְתָּכַּל, בְּהַהוּא, דְּלֵית בֵּיה סוֹף, מַה דְּלָא הֲוָה לָךְ רְשׁוּ בְּקַדְמֵיתָא לְאִסְתַּכְּלָא בְּעַיְינִין. הה״ד, וְרָאִיתָ אֶת אֲחוֹרָי וּפָנַי לֹא יֵרָאוּ.

425. Faithful servant, one who possesses such a heart that sees more than a prophet, surely your thoughts which are endless can see Him who is endless – that which you could not perceive with eyes. As it is written: "and you shall see My back, but My face shall not be seen" (Shemot 33:23).

426. אַלֵּין טִפְּשֵׁי דְלִבָּא, אִינּוּן מֵתִין, וְסוּמִין בְּאַלֵּין קְלִיפִין. אֲבָל לְגַבָּךְ, לָאו אִינּוּן חֲשִׁיבִין כְּלוּם, וְלָא מַפְסִיקִין בֵּינָךְ לְבֵין קוּדְשָׁא בְּרִיךְ הוּא וּשְׁכִינְתֵּיה, וְכָל בְּנֵי עָלְמָא דְאָתֵי, וּמַלְאָכִין, דְּהָכִי יֵיעוּל לְגַבָּךְ בְּאִינּוּן חַלּוֹנִין, דְעַיְינִין, וְאוּדְנִין, וְנוּקְבֵי חוֹטָמָא, וּפוּמָא. כְּמַלְכָּא דְּיֵיעוּל בְּאִתְכַּסְיָיא לְחַדְרֵי חֲדָרִים, לְמַלְּלָא עִם בְּרֵיה. וּבְג"ד, מְצַלֵּין יִשְׂרָאֵל בֵּיה בִּצְלוֹתָא דִּלְהוֹן, אַתָּה חוֹפֵשׁ כָּל חַדְרֵי בֶטֶן רוֹאֶה כְּלָיוֹת וָלֵב וְאֵין כָּל דָּבָר נֶעְלָם מִמְּךָ.

426. The foolish-hearted people are dead, blind with the Klipot OF THE BODY. With you these do not matter and do not act as an obstruction between you and the Holy One, blessed be He, and His Shechinah, members of the world to come, and angels. He will come to you through the windows of the eyes, ears, nostrils and mouth, as a king who enters a secret compartment to speak with his son. Such is the prayer of Yisrael – 'you may search all the inward parts of the belly, examine the kidneys and heart, and nothing is hidden from you'.

427. וְהַיְינוּ דְּאָמַר שְׁלֹמֹה, מַשְׁגִּיחַ מִן הַחַלּוֹנוֹת וְגו'. וְאַלֵּין אִינּוּן חַלּוֹנוֹת, דְעַיְינִין וְאוּדְנִין וְנוּקְבֵי חוֹטָמָא וּפוּמָא בְּאַלֵּין שִׁבְעָה נוּקְבִּין, נִשְׁמָתָא סְלִיקַת, בְּשִׁבְעָה מִינֵי בּוּסְמִין, וְהָכִי צְלוֹתָא סְלִיקַת בְּאַלֵּין ז' בּוּסְמִין, דְּאִינּוּן נֵרְדְּ וְכַרְכֹּם קָנֶה וְקִנָּמוֹן עִם כָּל עֲצֵי לְבוֹנָה מֹר וַאֲהָלוֹת עִם כָּל רָאשֵׁי בְשָׂמִים. בְּהַהוּא זִמְנָא דִּצְלוֹתָא הָכִי סְלִיקַת, מְקֻטֶּרֶת מֹר וְכוּ'. הַקּוּדְשָׁא בְּרִיךְ הוּא שָׁאִיל הוּא עָלֵה, מִי זֹאת עוֹלָה מִן הַמִּדְבָּר מְקֻטֶּרֶת מֹר וּלְבֹנָה וְגו'. מִי זֹאת וַדַּאי, מִסִּטְרָא דְּמִ"י אִיהוּ וַדַּאי בִּינָה, כְּלִילָא מִשִּׁבְעָה מִינֵי בּוּסְמִין.

427. Thus spoke Solomon: "he looks in at the windows" (Shir Hashirim 2:9). These are the windows of the eyes, ears, nostrils and mouth. Through these seven openings does the soul ascend with seven types of spice. And so does prayer rise with these seven types of spice, which are: "Nard and saffron; calamus and cinnamon, with all trees of frankincense; myrrh and aloes, with all the chief spices" (Shir Hashirim 4:14). At the time the prayer so rises, "perfumed with myrrh..." (Shir Hashirim 3:6), the Holy One,

blessed be He, asks about it: "Who is this coming out of the wilderness like columns of smoke, perfumed with myrrh...?" Assuredly, "Who (Heb. *mi*) is this," indeed, from the side of *mi* that represents Binah which incorporates the seven types of spice – WHICH ARE CHESED, GVURAH, TIFERET, NETZACH, HOD, YESOD AND MALCHUT THAT ILLUMINATE IN THE SECRET OF FRAGRANCE OF THE ILLUMINATION OF CHOCHMAH.

428. וְדָא ק״ש, כְּלִילָא מֵחַמְשִׁין תַּרְעִין, דְּאִינּוּן כ״ה כ״ה. כְּלִילָא מִשִּׁבְעָה בִּרְכָּאן, בַּשַּׁחַר שְׁתַּיִם לְפָנֶיהָ, וְאַחַת לְאַחֲרֶיהָ, וּבְעֶרֶב שְׁתַּיִם לְפָנֶיהָ, וּשְׁתַּיִם לְאַחֲרֶיהָ. וְאִינּוּן, הַגְּדוּלָה וְהַגְּבוּרָה וְהַתִּפְאֶרֶת וְהַנֵּצַח וְהַהוֹד, עַד לְךָ יְיָ' הַמַּמְלָכָה, דְּאִיהִי מַלְכוּת. דְּאִיהִי כְּלִילָא מִתְּלַת בּוּסְמִין. מְקֻטֶּרֶת מֹר, דָּא כֶּתֶר. וּלְבוֹנָה, דָּא חָכְמָה. מִכֹּל אַבְקַת רוֹכֵל, דָּא בִּינָה. קוּם אַשְׁלִים פִּקּוּדִין דְּמָרָךְ.

428. *Kriat Sh'ma* is composed of the fifty gates OF BINAH, consisting of 25 plus 25 letters, 25 FROM THE MORNING SH'MA AND 25 FROM THE EVENING SH'MA. It is composed of the seven blessings: in the morning, two before and one following; in the evening, two before and two following. They are THE SEVEN SFIROT, "the greatness, and the power (*Gvurah*) and the glory (*Tiferet*) and the victory (*Netzach*) and the majesty (*Hod*): FOR ALL THAT IS IN HEAVEN AND ON EARTH, (DENOTES YESOD)...Yours is the kingdom" (I Divrei Hayamim 29:11), denoting Malchut; she consists of three spices; "perfumed with myrrh," denotes Keter, "frankincense" denotes Chochmah, and the "powders of the merchant" denotes Binah. Come and complete the precepts of your Master.

13. "You shall not follow a multitude to do evil"

A Synopsis

We are told that a judge who does not render a truthful verdict is equivalent to having given dominion of the world to Samael. When a judge is about to render judgment, Gehenom is open before him on the left, a sword (the Angel of Death) is at his neck, Samael stands behind him, the Garden of Eden is open to the right, and the Tree of Life is open above his head. Depending on his judgment he is killed and punished, or rewarded, as appropriate. We learn that the judgment of the kingdom is the law, the law that is in the heart, and as we have already been told, 'the heart sees'. The eyes of God, the Judge, are open upon man, and "he looks in at the windows."

429. לֹא תִהְיֶה אַחֲרֵי רַבִּים לְרָעוֹת וְגוֹ', אַחֲרֵי רַבִּים לְהַטּוֹת. אַחֲרֵי רַבִּים לְהַטּוֹת, לֵית רַבִּים פָּחוּת מִג' וְאִי לֵית בֵּית דִין בְּג', לֵית לְהַטּוֹת בַּתַר דִּינֵיהּ. בֵּית דִין: שְׁכִינְתָּא. בְּג': תְּלַת חֵיוָן דְּמֶרְכַּבְתָּא דִילָהּ, וְאִיהִי דִין תּוֹרָה דִין אֱמֶת, עַמּוּדָא דְּאֶמְצָעִיתָא. וְכָל דַּיָין דְּלָא דָן דִין אֱמֶת לַאֲמִתּוֹ, דָּא אִיהוּ כְּאִילוּ אַשְׁלִיט סָמָאֵ"ל בְּעָלְמָא. וַתַּשְׁלֵךְ אֱמֶת אַרְצָה, וַאֲפִילּוּ שְׁכִינְתָּא עִמֵּיהּ, וְיָקִים גֵּיהִנָּם, בַּת זוּגֵיהּ דְּסָמָאֵ"ל, עִם סָמָאֵ"ל. בַּאֲתָר דְּדִין אֱמֶת, יוֹקִים שְׂפַת שָׁקֶר. דִין אֱמֶת, עַמּוּדָא דְּאֶמְצָעִיתָא. שְׂפַת שָׁקֶר גֵּיהִנָּם וְסָמָאֵ"ל.

429. "You shall not follow a multitude to do evil...to incline after a multitude to pervert justice" (Shemot 23:2). HE EXPLAINS: A multitude is no less than three. If the judicial court lacks three members, you are not bound by its judicial decisions. The court represents the Shechinah; with three are the living creatures of the Chariot, NAMELY CHESED, GVURAH, AND TIFERET. THE SHECHINAH IS CALLED THE 'Law of Torah', Truthful law, the middle pillar, NAMELY ZEIR ANPIN REFERRED TO AS 'TRUTH'; SHECHINAH IS HIS PROMULGATED LAW. A judge that does not render a truthful verdict is equivalent to having given dominion of the world to Samael. "...and it cast down the truth to the ground..." (Daniel 8:12) REFERRING TO ZEIR ANPIN who cast the Shechinah with him, causing Gehenom (which is the mate of Samael) to rise with Samael. Instead of rendering true justice, he encourages falsehood. The truthful Justice is considered the middle pillar, while falsehood is Gehenom and Samael.

430. וּבג"ד, כַּד דַּיָּין דָּן דִּין, גֵּיהִנָּם פְּתוּחָה לְפָנָיו מִשְּׂמֹאלוֹ, בַּת זוּגֵיהּ דְּסָמָא"ל. וְחֶרֶב עַל צַוָּארוֹ, מַלְאַךְ הַמָּוֶת. סָמָא"ל מֵאֲחוֹרוֹי מֵעַל צַוָּארֵיהּ. וְגַן עֵדֶן פָּתוּחַ לִימִינֵיהּ, וְעֵץ הַחַיִּים פָּתוּחַ לְקַמֵּיהּ, עַל רֵישֵׁיהּ.

430. As a result, when a judge is about to render judgment, the Gehenom lies open before him on the left, being the mate of Samael. A sword is by his neck, which is the Angel of Death. Samael stands behind his neck; the Garden of Eden is open to the right, and the Tree of Life is open above his head.

431. אִי דָּן דִּינָא דְּשִׁקְרָא, שַׁלִּיט עֲלֵיהּ מַלְאַךְ הַמָּוֶת, וְשָׁחִיט לֵיהּ, וּלְבָתַר אוֹקִיד לֵיהּ בַּגֵּיהִנָּם. וְאִי דָּן דִּין אֱמֶת, קוּדְשָׁא בְּרִיךְ הוּא יֵיעוֹל לֵיהּ לְגַן עֵדֶן, וְאַטְעִים לֵיהּ מֵאִילָנָא דְּחַיֵּי, דִּכְתִּיב עֲלֵיהּ, וְלָקַח גַּם מֵעֵץ הַחַיִּים וְאָכַל וָחַי לְעוֹלָם. דְּאִתְבְּרֵי בְּאוֹרַיְיתָא, דְּאִתְּמַר בָּהּ, עֵץ חַיִּים הִיא לַמַּחֲזִיקִים בָּהּ. עֵץ חַיִּים, תִּפְאֶרֶת. חַיִּים דִּילֵיהּ חָכְמָה וּבִינָה. חַיֵּי הַמֶּלֶךְ וַדַּאי.

431. If he delivers a false judgment, the Angel of Death seizes him and slays him and later burns him in Gehenom. If he judges truthfully, the Holy One, blessed be He, brings him into the Garden of Eden and gives him a taste of the Tree of Life, as it is written about him: "and take also of the Tree of Life, and eating, live for ever" (Beresheet 3:22). "For ever," as it is created by the Torah, of which it is written: "She is a Tree of Life to those who lay hold on Her" (Mishlei 3:18); a Tree of Life, Tiferet – its life is Chochmah and Binah, the life of the king indeed.

432. וּלְעוֹלָם, דִּינָא דְּמַלְכוּתָא, דִּינָא. וְדִינָא בַּלֵּב, וְאִתְּמַר בֵּיהּ, הַלֵּב רוֹאֶה. וּבְגִין דָּא, אֵין לוֹ לַדַּיָּין אֶלָּא מַה שֶּׁעֵינָיו רוֹאוֹת. וְהָכָא לֵית דַּיָּין, אֶלָּא קוּדְשָׁא בְּרִיךְ הוּא. מַה שֶּׁעֵינָיו רוֹאוֹת, כִּי יְיָ' עֵינָיו מְשׁוֹטְטוֹת. עֵינָיו עַל דַּרְכֵי אִישׁ.

432. Forever the Judgment of the kingdom is the law, the law that is in the heart, and it is said regarding it, 'the heart sees'. Therefore, the Judge has only what his eyes observe. The Judge is none other than the Holy One,

blessed be He, and his eyes observe, "For the eyes of Hashem run to and fro throughout the whole earth" (II Divrei Hayamim 16:9). "For His eyes are upon the ways of man" (Iyov 34:21).

433. וּבְהוֹן, מַשְׁגִּיחַ מִן הַחַלּוֹנוֹת. בְּז' נוּקְבִין דְּבַר נָשׁ, בִּתְרֵין עַיְינִין, וּתְרֵין אוּדְנִין, וּתְרֵין נוּקְבִין דְּחוֹטָמָא, וּפוּמָא. הָא ז' דְּאִמָּא עִלָּאָה. וְהָכִי בְּעוֹבָדוֹי אִסְתַּכַּל בְּשֶׁבַע, מִסְּטְרָא דִּשְׁכִינְתָּא תַּתָּאָה, בְּב' יְדִין וְצַוָּאר תְּלַת, וְגוּף וּבְרִית תְּרֵין, הָא חֲמֵשׁ. תְּרֵין רַגְלִין, הָא שֶׁבַע. יָ"ה, יוּ"ד הֵ"א, בְּשֶׁבַע אַתְוָון דִּילֵיהּ, אִסְתַּכַּל בְּשֶׁבַע נוּקְבִין דְּרֵישָׁא, נְקָבִים: עַל שֵׁם נְקָבָה, דְּנִקְבֵיהָ פְּתוּחוֹת לְקַבֵּל. ו"ה, וא"ו ה"א, בְּשֶׁבַע אַתְוָון דִּילֵיהּ, אִסְתַּכַּל בְּשִׁבְעָה אֵבָרִין דִּלְתַתָּא, דְּאִינּוּן תִּקּוּנָא דְּגוּפָא, דִּבְהוֹן עֲשִׂיַּית הַמִּצְוֹת.

433. Through them "…He looks in at the windows…" (Shir Hashirim 2:9) MEANING through the seven openings of man, two eyes, two ears, two nostrils and mouth. Behold the seven SFIROT of supernal Ima. So He examines deeds with seven from the standpoint of the lower Shechinah: the two hands and neck, WHICH ARE three, with body and the sex organ, NAMELY TIFERET AND YESOD, are five, and WITH two legs, seven – BEING THE SEVEN SFIROT OF THE LOWER SHECHINAH. TWO LETTERS OF THE NAME *Yud-Hei* THAT ARE IN THE FIRST THREE, FULLY SPELLED AS *Yud-Vav-Dalet, Hei-Aleph*, EQUAL SEVEN LETTERS. With these seven letters He examines the seven openings of the head. They are called openings after the female (derived from aperture), DENOTING THE SUPERNAL IMA whose openings are open to receive. The two letters *Vav-Hei* IN THE BODY, MEANING LOWER SHECHINAH, FULLY SPELLED AS *VAV-ALEPH-VAV, HEI-ALEPH*, EQUAL SEVEN LETTERS. With these seven letters, He examines the seven lower limbs; HANDS, NECK, AND SO ON. They compliment the body with which to perform the precepts.

434. אִשְׁתּוֹ כְּגוּפוֹ דַּמְיָא. וְעַל שֵׁם פְּקוּדִין, אִתְקְרִיאוּ אֵבָרִים. עַל שֵׁם שְׁכִינְתָּא, גּוּפָא. דְּמִסְּטְרָא אַחֲרָא לְבוּשָׁא, דְּאִינּוּן עוֹר וּבָשָׂר. הה"ד, עוֹר וּבָשָׂר תַּלְבִּישֵׁנִי וּבַעֲצָמוֹת וְגִידִים תְּסוֹכְכֵנִי, בַּאֲתָר דְּלֵית שְׁכִינְתָּא, הַהוּא גּוּפָא לָא אִתְקְרֵי, אֶלָּא לְבוּשָׁא דְּאָדָם. דְּאִיהוּ תּוֹרָה, זֹאת

הַתּוֹרָה אָדָם כִּי יָמוּת בְּאֹהֶל. כְּתִפְאֶרֶת אָדָם לָשֶׁבֶת בָּיִת. וּבַאֲתַר דְּתַמָּן
מִצְוָה, אִתְקְרֵי גּוּפָא דְּאָדָם, כְּגוֹן גּוּפֵי הֲלָכוֹת, וּפְסְקֵי דִינִין.

434. The wife OF ZEIR ANPIN, DENOTING SHECHINAH, is like the body –
AS THE BODY OF MAN BELOW IS DRAWN FROM HER – and after the
precepts, it is called 'limbs', DENOTING THE TWO HUNDRED AND
FORTY-EIGHT LIMBS. After the Shechinah, it is called 'body'. Because
from the Other Side THE BODY MEANS ONLY the garments, such as skin and
flesh, as written, "You have clothed me with skin and flesh, and have knit
me together with bones and sinews" (Iyov 10:11). Wherever the Shechinah
is not, the body OF LOWER MAN is called but 'the garment of man',
DENOTING ZEIR ANPIN, alluding to Torah CALLED 'MAN', as it is written,
"This is the Torah: when a man dies in a tent" (Bemidbar 19:14), and,
"according to the beauty of a man; that it may remain in the house"
(Yeshayah 44:13). Where there is a precept, DENOTING SHECHINAH, SO
THE BODY OF LOWER MAN is called "the body of man" – just as we find the
expression, the essentials of Halachah and sentences of laws, WHICH ARE
NAMES OF THE SHECHINAH.

435. קוּדְשָׁא בְּרִיךְ הוּא שׁוֹפֵט, עַמּוּדָא דְּאֶמְצָעִיתָא. מִסְּטְרָא דְּבִינָה,
דְּאִיהוּ יְדֹנָ"ד. דַּיָּין, מִסְּטְרָא דְּמַלְכוּת. שׁוֹטֵר, הוּא שַׁלִּיט, וְיוֹסֵף הוּא
הַשַּׁלִּיט. וְכָל סְפִירִין, אִינּוּן שׁוֹפְטִים, מִסְּטְרָא דְּאִמָּא עִלָּאָה, דְּתִפְאֶרֶת
שׁוֹפֵט. וְאִינּוּן שׁוֹטְרִים, מִסְּטְרָא דְּמַלְכוּת. דְּצַדִּיק מִתַּמָּן שׁוֹטֵר וּמוֹשֵׁל.

435. The Holy One, blessed be He, is Judge – DENOTING the Central
Column, BEING ZEIR ANPIN, from the standpoint of Binah, MEANING THE
MOCHIN OF THE FIRST THREE SFIROT DRAWN FROM BINAH – being Yud
Hei Vav Hei, he is REFERRED TO AS MAGISTRATE. Judge IS CALLED SO
from the aspect of Malchut. An officer is the ruler, as it is written: "And
Joseph was the governor" (Beresheet 42:6). All the Sfirot are Judges from
the standpoint of Ima Supernal, BEING BINAH, wherein ARE THE MOCHIN
as Tiferet, THAT IS DRAWN FROM IT is the Judge, WHEREIN ARE INCLUDED
ALL SFIROT. These ARE officers from Malchut, FROM WHICH COMES
RULERSHIP, and the righteous rules from there.

14. "Keep you far from a false matter"

A Synopsis

The commandment is to treat the protagonists equally and be far from falsehood. This section explores the issue of 'the evil man – goodness befalls him' and 'the righteous – evil befalls him'. Even in the evil man there is still goodness existing somewhere; perhaps he will repent and overpower his inclination. When evil befalls the righteous it stems from the Tree of Knowledge of Good and Evil; the Good Inclination controls him and so he is righteous, although there is evil present in him which is under domination. The perfect righteous who has no evil inclination stems from the Tree of Life.

436. מִדְּבַר שֶׁקֶר תִּרְחָק וְנָקִי וְצַדִּיק אַל תַּהֲרוֹג וְגוֹ'. פְּקוּדָא לְהַשְׁווֹת הַבַּעֲלֵי דִינִין, וּלְהִתְרַחֵק מִדְּבַר שֶׁקֶר, דְּלָא יֵימְרוּן מַשׂוֹא פָנִים. דְּקוּדְשָׁא בְּרִיךְ הוּא אִתְּמַר בֵּיהּ, אֲשֶׁר לֹא יִשָּׂא פָנִים. וְל"א יִקַּ"ח שֹׁחַ"ד, בְּסוֹפֵי תֵּיבוֹת אֶחָד. הַאי דַּיָּין, צָרִיךְ לְמֶהֱוֵי כְּגַוְונָא דְּאֶחָד, דְּאִיהוּ יְדֹוָ"ד אֶחָד, דְּלָא יִקַּח שֹׁחַד, דִּיהֵא אִיהוּ בְּדִיּוּקְנֵיהּ.

436. "Keep you far from a false matter" (Shemot 23:7). The commandment is to treat equally the protagonists and be far from falsehood, so that no one will say there is favoritism IN THE MATTER. Regarding the Holy One, blessed be He, it is written: "who favors no person, and takes no bribe" (Devarim 10:17). The last letter of these words equals One (Heb. *echad*). A judge must be like the "One"-One Yud Hei Vav Hei, without bribe, so as to be in His image.

437. וּבְדִינָא לְהַשְׁווֹת תַּרְוַויְיהוּ כְּאֶחָד, וְלָא יַטֶּה דִינָא לְדָא יַתִּיר מִן דָּא, אֶלָּא בְּתִקְלָא חַד, עַד דִּיקַבְּלוּן דִּינָא. וּלְבָתַר, כָּל חַד אִתְדָּן, כְּפוּם עוֹבָדוֹי.

437. So in judgment, one should treat both protagonists the same, and not bend the law to favor one over the other, but give them similar importance, until they receive judgment. Later each is judged according to his deeds.

438. וְאוֹקְמוּהָ מָארֵי מַתְנִיתִין, צַדִּיק יֵצֶר הַטּוֹב שׁוֹפְטוֹ. רָשָׁע, יֵצֶר הָרַע שׁוֹפְטוֹ. בֵּינוֹנִי, זֶה וְזֶה שׁוֹפְטוֹ. מַאן דְּאִיהוּ מֵאִילָנָא דְּחַיֵּי, לֵית

לֵיהּ דִּינָא כְּלָל, לֵית לֵיהּ יֵצֶר הָרָע, וְדָא צַדִּיק גָּמוּר, וְדָא צַדִּיק וְטוֹב
לוֹ. וְלֵית טוֹב, אֶלָּא תּוֹרָה. הה״ד. כִּי לֶקַח טוֹב נָתַתִּי לָכֶם תּוֹרָתִי אַל
תַּעֲזוֹבוּ. וְצַדִּיק וְרַע לוֹ, מִסְטְרָא דְּעֵץ הַדַּעַת טוֹב וָרָע. וְאַמַאי אִתְקְרֵי
צַדִּיק בָּתַר דְּרַע לוֹ, דְּאִיהוּ יֵצֶר הָרָע. אֶלָּא, בְּגִין דְּטוֹב שַׁלִּיט עֲלֵיהּ,
אִתְקְרֵי צַדִּיק וְרַע לוֹ. דְּהַהוּא רָע אִיהוּ תְּחוֹת רְשׁוּתֵיהּ.

438. The masters of the Mishnah have established that the righteous is judged by the Good Inclination, and the evil man by the Evil Inclination. The intermediate man is judged by both. The one who stems from the Tree of Life, WHICH IS DRAWN FROM ZEIR ANPIN, has no Judgment at all, no Evil Inclination. Such is the perfect righteous, 'the righteous-goodness befalls him', and goodness means only the Torah, as it is written, "For I give you a good doctrine, forsake not My Torah" (Mishlei 4:2). 'The righteous- evil befalls him', stems from the Tree of Knowledge of Good and Evil, DENOTING MALCHUT. Why is he called righteous if he has evil, which is the Evil Inclination, REFERRED TO AS EVIL? The answer is that the Good Inclination controls him and so he is a righteous man even though there is evil present which is under domination.

439. רָשָׁע וְטוֹב לוֹ, אַמַאי אִתְקְרֵי רָשָׁע. בְּגִין דְּאִיהוּ אִסְתַּלָּק לְמֶהֱוֵי
רֵישָׁא יצה״ר דִּילֵיהּ, וְטוֹב אִיהוּ תְּחוֹת רְשׁוּתֵיהּ, כְּעַבְדָּא תְּחוֹת רַבֵּיהּ.
וְאע״ג דְּרָשָׁע אִיהוּ מַכְתִּיר אֶת הַצַּדִּיק, וְיָכִיל צַדִּיק גָּמוּר לְאַעֲנָשָׁא
לֵיהּ, גַּם עֲנוֹשׁ לַצַּדִּיק לֹא טוֹב, בְּגִין הַהוּא טוֹב דְּאִיהוּ תְּחוֹת רַגְלוֹי
דְּרָשָׁע, לֵית לְאַעֲנָשָׁא לֵיהּ, דְּאוּלַי יַחֲזוֹר בִּתְשׁוּבָה וְיִתְגַּבֵּר עַל יִצְרֵיהּ,
וִיהֵא עָפָר תְּחוֹת רַגְלוֹי.

439. HE ASKS: 'The wicked-goodness befalls him', REFERS TO TORAH THAT IS CALLED 'GOOD', AS MENTIONED. IF SO, why is he called 'evil'? HE ANSWERS: He is at the head of his Evil Inclination. Goodness is under his control, like a servant serving under his master. Even though the evil one crowns the righteous, and the perfect righteous can punish him, "Neither is it good to punish an innocent man (lit. 'the righteous')" (Mishle 17:26); because of that goodness that still exists beneath the feet of the evil man, perhaps he will repent and overpower his inclination, and THE EVIL INCLINATION will become as dust beneath his feet.

440. דְּמִסְטְרָא דְּרָשָׁע וְטוֹב לוֹ, שְׁכִינְתָּא שְׁכִיבַת, וַתְּגַל מַרְגְּלוֹתָיו וַתִּשְׁכָּב. הַאי אִיהוּ וְשִׁפְחָה כִּי תִירַשׁ גְּבִירְתָּהּ. שִׁפְחָה, יֵצֶר הָרָע נוּקְבָּא. יֵצֶר הָרָע, דְּכַר. בְּגִינֵיהּ אִתְּמַר, וּכְבוֹדִי לְאַחֵר לֹא אֶתֵּן. וְהַזָּר הַקָּרֵב יוּמָת.

440. From the aspect of: 'the evil man-goodness befalls him', the Shechinah lies, AS THE VERSE SAYS: "and uncovered his feet, and laid herself down" (Rut 3:7). This is in essence, "and a handmaid that is heir to her mistress" (Mishlei 30:23). The maid is considered the female of the Evil Inclination. The Evil Inclination is male, and so it says, "and My glory will I not give to another" (Yeshayah 42:8), and it says, "and the stranger that comes near shall be put to death" (Bemidbar 1:51). FOR THE EVIL INCLINATION IS CALLED 'ANOTHER' AND 'A STRANGER'.

441. וּמִסְטְרָא דְּצַדִּיק וְרַע לוֹ, שְׁכִינְתָּא אִיהִי עֲטָרָה עַל רֵישָׁא דְּבַר נָשׁ, וְשִׁפְחָה יֵצֶר הָרָע, אִתְכַּפְיָיא תְּחוֹת גְּבִירְתָּהּ. וּמִסְטְרָא דְּצַדִּיק גָּמוּר, לֵית זָר, וְלֵית יֵצֶר הָרָע. וּמִסְטְרָא דְּרָשָׁע גָּמוּר, לֵית לֵיהּ חוּלְקָא בִּשְׁכִינְתָּא, דְּלֵית חוּלְקָא לְב״נ בִּשְׁכִינְתָּא, אֶלָּא מִסְטְרָא דְּטוֹב.

441. From the aspect of: 'the righteous-evil befalls him', the Shechinah here is like a crown on the head of man. The maid, the Evil Inclination, is subjugated beneath Her mistress. From the standpoint of the perfect righteous, there is neither a stranger, nor an Evil Inclination here. From the aspect of the completely evil man, he has no part with the Shechinah because man can only have a share in the Shechinah from the Good Side.

442. וְלֵית כָּל שְׁכִינְתָּא שְׁקִילִין, דְּהָא שְׁכִינְתָּא דְּאִילָנָא דְּטוֹב וָרַע, אִיהוּ כֻּרְסַיָּיא, אֲבָל שְׁכִינְתָּא דְּאִילָנָא דְּחַיֵּי, עָלָהּ אִתְּמַר, לֹא יְגוּרְךָ רָע. אֲבָל בְּגִין דְּאִתְּמַר בָּהּ, וּמַלְכוּתוֹ בַּכֹּל מָשָׁלָה, מַאן דְּפָגִים אֲתַר דִּילָהּ, אִתְחֲשִׁיב כְּאִילוּ עָבִיד בְּמַטְרוֹנִיתָא קְלָנָא. דְּקָלָנָא דְּמַטְרוֹנִיתָא אִיהוּ, מַאן דְּמִזְדַּזֵּל בְּאַתְרָהָא. וּקְלָנָא דְּמַטְרוֹנִיתָא, דְּמַלְכָּא אִיהוּ.

442. Not all of the Shechinah is the same. The Shechinah of the Tree of Knowledge of Good and Evil is considered a throne, SITUATED IN THE

WORLD OF BRIYAH OR 'BODY OF MAN'. But of the Shechinah of the Tree of Life, BEING THE WORLD OF ATZILUT, it is written: "nor shall evil dwell with You" (Tehilim 5:4). But since it is written, "and His kingdom rules over all" (Tehilim 103:19), one who causes a defect in Her site, IN BRIYAH OR 'BODY OF MAN', is considered as one who causes dishonor in the Matron herself, IN ATZILUT. Dishonor of the Matron is considered of one who cheapens Her in Her abode. Dishonor of the Matron is equivalent to disgrace of the King, ZEIR ANPIN, AND RESULTS IN DISGRACE TO ZEIR ANPIN.

443. כָּל שֶׁכֵּן מַאן דְּאַעְבַּר לָה מֵאַתְרָהָא, וְשַׁוֵּי שִׁפְחָה בְּאַתְרָהָא. דִּבְכָל אֲתָר דְּאִיהוּ פָּגִים, מַטְרוֹנִיתָא לָא שַׁרְיָא תַּמָּן, אֶלָּא שִׁפְחָה, דְּאִיהִי פְּגִימָא, שַׁרְיָא בְּאֲתָר פָּגִים. וּפְגִימוּ דְּבַר נָשׁ דְּחוֹבוֹי, פָּגִים בְּכָל אֶבְרִין דִּילֵיהּ, עַד דְּלָא אַשְׁכְּחַת מַטְרוֹנִיתָא אֲתָר לְשַׁרְיָא תַּמָּן. וְלֵית לֵיהּ תִּקּוּנָא עַד דְּיַחֲזִיר לָה עַל כָּל אֶבְרִין דִּילֵיהּ.

443. Even more so for the one who causes Her to move from Her position IN BRIYAH, and appoints the maid in Her stead, for wherever he dishonors Her, the Matron does not abide, but rather the maid, who is defected and dwells in a defected place. The defect of man due to his sins causes defects to all his limbs to the extent that the Matron finds no place to dwell. There is no remedy for him until he returns Her all his limbs, MEANING HE REPENTS HIS SINS.

444. אָמַר בּוּצִינָא קַדִּישָׁא, רַעְיָא מְהֵימָנָא, בְּגִין דָּא, אַנְתְּ מְתַקֵּן, בְּחִבּוּרָא דָּא, דִּרְמַ"ח פִּקּוּדִין. לְאַמְלְכָא לְקוּדְשָׁא בְּרִיךְ הוּא עַל כָּל אֶבְרִים דִּשְׁכִינְתָּא, בְּכָל פִּקּוּדָא וּפִקּוּדָא, וְלֵית אַנְתְּ חַיָּישׁ לִיקָרָךְ. זַכָּאָה חוּלָקָךְ, דִּכְגַוְונָא דְּאַנְתְּ מַמְלִיךְ לְקוּדְשָׁא בְּרִיךְ הוּא בְּכָל אֶבְרִים דִּשְׁכִינְתָּא, דְּאִינּוּן בַּעֲלֵי מִדּוֹת, דְּכָל יִשְׂרָאֵל. מָארֵי מִדּוֹת אִינּוּן אֶבְרִים דִּשְׁכִינְתָּא, הָכִי עָבֵיד קוּדְשָׁא בְּרִיךְ הוּא לְשַׁרְיָא שְׁמֵיהּ עָלָךְ, וְיַמְלִכִינָךְ, עַל כָּל מַשְׁרְיָין עִלָּאִין וְתַתָּאִין.

444. The Holy Luminary, RABBI SHIMON, said: Faithful Shepherd, you therefore make ready, with this composition of 248 precepts, the means to

coronate the Holy One, blessed be He, upon all the limbs of the Shechinah, in each and every precept, and you are not concerned about your honor. Happy is your lot! As you coronate the Holy One, blessed be He, over the limbs of the Shechinah – that are the men of virtue of all Yisrael, inasmuch as the men of virtue are the Shechinah's limbs – so does the Holy One, blessed be He, cause His name to dwell upon you and coronate you over the upper and lower encampments.

15. The order of laws in Tractate *Nezikin* (cause of injuries)

A Synopsis

Here we learn about the judgments regarding the laws of damage; the four primary causes of injury are the ox, the pit, crop destroying beast, and fire. Lastly there is man, who is always prone to harm. Moses says that the letters of Adonai, when rearranged, form Dina, which is judgment. All judgments are executed by that Name. Moses lists other laws which require judgment, and he talks about damage, idleness, shame and weakness. We are reminded of the blessings that were stolen from Yisrael through heavy tax burdens, different kinds of harsh judgments, and Temple sacrifices deprived from the Shechinah. The bull that has gored thrice has devastated everything with sin and destruction, anger and wrath. Moses also speaks about the exile of the children of Yisrael. He tells us that there are angels that serve the body, and angels that serve the soul, and there is a difference between them. Every lower level receives from the higher. In man there is division between body and soul, one being material and the other mental, one being Life and the other Death. But the Holy One, blessed be He, is Life and His Shechinah is also Life.

445. קוּם רַעְיָא מְהֵימָנָא, לְסַדְּרָא דִּינִין בְּהִלְכוֹת נְזִקִין, בְּסִדּוּרָא דִּשְׁמָא דָּא, הֲוָיָ"ה. דְּאִיהוּ, רֶכֶב אֱלֹהִים רִבּוֹתַיִם אַלְפֵי שִׁנְאָן, דְּאִינּוּן, שׁוֹר נֶשֶׁר אַרְיֵה אָדָם, דְּהָא מִסִּטְרָא דִּימִינָא, דְּתַמָּן יְדֹוָ"ד, ד' חֵיוָון הָכִי אִיהוּ סִדּוּרָא דִּלְהוֹן, אָדָם אַרְיֵה נֶשֶׁר שׁוֹר. וּכְפוּם שִׁנּוּיִין דְּהֲוָויִין, הָכִי אִיהוּ תְּנוּעָה וְסִדּוּרָה דְּחֵיוָון. וְחֵיוָן דְּסִטְרָא אַחֲרָא, דְּאִינּוּן נְזִיקִין דִּשְׂמָאלָא, הָכִי סִדּוּרַיְיהוּ, שִׁנְאָן. וּבְגִין דָּא, הַתְחָלָה דִּלְהוֹן, הַשּׁוֹר. קָשׁוּר בַּד' אָבוֹת נְזִיקִין, הַשּׁוֹר וְהַבּוֹר וְהַמַּבְעֶה וְהַהֶבְעֵר וְסִיּוּמָא דִּלְהוֹן אָדָם, מוּעָד.

445. Arise, Faithful Shepherd, to arrange the Judgments regarding the laws of damage in the order of the name Yud Hei Vav Hei, being: "The chariot of Elohim are twice ten thousand, thousands upon thousands (lit. '*shin'an*')" (Tehilim 68:18), that is, the ox, eagle, lion and man. From the right side where there is Yud Hei Vav Hei, such is the order of the four living creatures: man, lion, eagle, ox, MEANING THAT OX, BEING GVURAH, IS LISTED LAST, and according to the changes that take place in them, so is

their movement and order. The animals on the Other Side are the caves of injuries on the left, '*shin'an* ('thousand', also: 'angel')', MEANING THE INITIALS OF OX, EAGLE, LION, MAN. Hence it starts with ox, which is connected with the four primary causes of injury: the ox, the pit, crop destroying beast, and fire. Their last one is man, WHO IS ALWAYS prone to harm.

446. קוּם אִתְּעַר בְּדִינִין. פָּתַח רַעְיָא מְהֵימָנָא וְאָמַר, אֲדֹנָי שְׂפָתַי תִּפְתָּח וּפִי יַגִּיד תְּהִלָּתֶךָ. אֲדֹנָ"י, בְּהִפּוּךְ אַתְוָון דִּינָ"א. וּבְג"ד, אָמְרוּ מָארֵי מַתְנִיתִין, דִּינָ"א דְּמַלְכוּתָא דִּינָא. כָּל דִּינִין בְּהַאי שְׁמָא אִתְדָּנוּ בְּד', בְּג', בְּד': שְׁכִינְתָּא לָקֳבֵל תְּלַת אֲבָהָן. עַמּוּדָא דְּאֶמְצָעִיתָא, דַּיָּין אֱמֶת, וְהוּא דַּיָּין, לָדוּן מִסִּטְרָא דַּאֲדֹנָ"י, דְּתַמָּן אִיהוּ דַיָּין אֱמֶת. וּמִסִּטְרָא דְּשֵׁם אֱלֹהִים, שׁוֹפֵט. הֲדָא הוּא דִכְתִּיב, כִּי אֱלֹהִים שׁוֹפֵט.

446. Arise, awaken with Judgment. The Faithful Shepherd commenced to say: "Adonai, open my lips; and my mouth shall rehearse Your praise" (Tehilim 51:17). *Adonai*, when rearranged, spells *Dina* (lit. 'judgment'). So Mishnah masters said: The law of the kingdom is the law, SINCE MALCHUT IS CALLED 'ADONAI', THE LETTERS OF *DINA* (ENG. 'LAW'). All Judgments are executed by that Name, and are executed by the letters *Dalet* and *Gimel*. The *Dalet* alludes to the Shechinah corresponding with the *Gimel* (= 3) patriarchs, TO WHOM SHE BECOMES THE FOURTH. GIMEL REPRESENTS the Central Column, MEANING ZEIR ANPIN, WHO INCORPORATES CHESED, GVURAH, AND TIFERET, which is a True Judge, Judging from the side of Adonai – DENOTING MALCHUT where the true judge abides. From the side of the Name of Elohim, DENOTING BINAH, there is a magistrate as it says: "but Elohim is the Judge" (Tehilim 75:7).

447. וּמַה דִּינִין אִינּוּן. חַד, לָדוּן בְּנִזְקֵי שׁוֹר. תִּנְיָינָא, לָדוּן בְּנִזְקֵי בּוֹר. תְּלִיתָאָה, לָדוּן בְּנִזְקֵי אֵשׁ. רְבִיעָאָה, לָדוּן בְּנִזְקֵי אָדָם. וַאֲבַתְרַיְיהוּ, לָדוּן בְּדִינֵי אַרְבַּע שׁוֹמְרִים. שׁוֹמֵר חִנָּם. וְשׁוֹמֵר שָׂכָר. וְהַשּׁוֹאֵל. וְנוֹשֵׂא שָׂכָר. לָקֳבְלַיְיהוּ, דִּינִין אַרְבְּעָה. דִּין חֲלוּקַת הַשּׁוּתָּפִים. דִּין חֲלוּקַת קַרְקָעוֹת. דִּינֵי עֲבָדִים וּשְׁפָחוֹת. דִּינֵי תוֹבֵעַ וְנִתְבַּע, בְּכַמָּה מִינֵי תְּבִיעוֹת דְּחִיּוּב מָמוֹן, וְגֵזֶל, וְאֲבֵדָה, אוֹ שֶׁמַּזִּיק לַחֲבֵרוֹ, וְהוֹרְגוֹ בְּאֶחָד מֵאַרְבַּע מִיתוֹת

בֵּית דִּין.

447. What are these Judgments? First to judge the damages by the ox, secondly, damage of the pit, thirdly, fire damage, fourth, damage by man. Later, the law of the four watches, namely he who watches free of charge, he who watches for a fee, the borrower, and the renter. These correspond to four laws: the law of division between partners, division of lands, laws of male and female slaves, laws of a claimant and a respondent in matters of money, theft, lost articles, injury to fellow man and the four types of death penalty through court.

448. אָדוֹן אִיהוּ קוּדְשָׁא בְּרִיךְ הוּא, בַּאֲדֹנָ"י. לָדוּן בְּכָל מִינֵי דִינִין, לְשִׁפְחָה בִּישָׁא, כִּי תִירַשׁ גְּבִירְתָּה. דְּמִינָהּ כָּל נְזִיקִין אִשְׁתְּכָחוּ, דְּאִינּוּן מַלְאֲכֵי חַבָּלָה, דְּמִנַּיְיהוּ נִשְׁמָתְהוֹן שֶׁל רְשָׁעִים, כְּמָה דְּאוּקְמוּהָ מָארֵי מַתְנִיתִין, נִשְׁמוֹת הָרְשָׁעִים הֵן הֵן הַמַּזִּיקִים בָּעוֹלָם. אֵל אַחֵר, מַזִּיק, גַּזְלָן רָשָׁע. וּבַת זוּגֵיהּ, סַם הַמָּוֶת.

448. The Holy One, blessed be He, is Master (Heb. *adon*) through Adonai, AS *ADON* STEMS FROM *DIN* (LIT. 'LAW'), to judge with various judgments against the wicked maidservant who is heir to her mistress, from whom stems all harm, being demons, and from whom come the souls of the wicked as established by the masters of the Mishnah, that the souls of the wicked cause havoc in the world. Another El IS harmful, a thief, evil, and Another El's mate is deadly poison.

449. נֶזֶק שֶׁבֶת וּבֹשֶׁת וְרִפּוּי, לִשְׁכִינְתָּא וּבְנָהָא. שֶׁבֶת, דְּבַטּוּלָא דְּאוֹרַיְיתָא, דְּבַטִּילַת לִבְנָהָא. וְרִפּוּי, דְּגַרְמַת לוֹן דְּמִתְרַפִּין מִדִּבְרֵי תוֹרָה. נֶזֶק, בְּכַמָּה נְזִיקִין דְּמַלְאֲכֵי חַבָּלָה, מָארֵי מַשְׁחִית אַף וְחֵימָה. וּבֹשֶׁת, דַּהֲווֹ מְבַזִּין לִשְׁכִינְתָּא בכו"ם, שִׁקְרָא דִּלְהוֹן, וַהֲווֹ אַמְרִין אֵלֶּה אֱלֹהֶיךָ. וְכַמָּה גְּזֵלוֹת מִן שִׁפְחָה בִּישָׁא, דְּאִתְּמַר בָּהּ גְּזֵלַת הֶעָנִי בְּבָתֵּיכֶם.

449. Damage, idleness, shame and weakness MUST BE PAID to the Shechinah and her children, THE CHILDREN OF YISRAEL. HE EXPLAINS:

Idleness means idleness from studying Torah, WHICH THE OTHER SIDE brings upon the children; weakness, because it causes them to be slack from the words of the Torah; damage, the various injuries by damaging demons, anger and wrath; shame, because they shamed the Shechinah with their idols and asked: 'Where is your Elohim?' So much plunder did the evil maidservant pilfer, as it is written: "the robbery of the poor in your house" (Yeshayah 3:14).

450. כַּמָה בִּרְכָאן, גְּזֵלַת לִשְׁכִינְתָּא, שִׁפְחָא בִּישָׁא. בְּכוֹבֶד הַמַּס, וּבְכוֹבֶד כַּמָה דִּינִין מְשׁוּנִים עַל בְּנָהָא, וְכַמָה קָרְבָּנִין דְּבֵי מַקְדְּשָׁא, דְּבָטִילַת לְמַטְרוֹנִיתָא. וּבֹשֶׁת דְּמַטְרוֹנִיתָא, דְּאִשְׁתְּאָרַת עֲרוּמָה, מַד' בִּגְדֵי זָהָב דְּנָהֲרִין, מַד' טוּרֵי אָבֶן, בִּי"ב אַבְנִין מַרְגְּלָן. מְעִיל בְּכַמָה זַגִין וְרִמּוֹנִים. וְאַרְבַּע בִּגְדֵי לָבָן, דְּבְהוֹן הֲוַת מַטְרוֹנִיתָא, מִתְקַשְּׁטָא קָדָם מַלְכָּא. הה"ד, וּרְאִיתִיהָ לִזְכֹּר בְּרִית עוֹלָם. וְגָזְלַת לָה לִגְבִרְתָּה, כַּמָה מַאֲכָלִין דְּקָרְבָּנִין.

450. So many blessings did the evil maidservant steal from the Shechinah through heavy tax burdens, different kinds of harsh judgments against the SHECHINAH'S children, numerous Temple sacrifices deprived from the Matron, the shaming of the Matron, who remained deprived of: her four golden garments sparkling from the four rows of precious stones – MEANING CHESED, GVURAH, TIFERET, AND MALCHUT – on the twelve gems – AS EACH OF THE CHESED, GVURAH, TIFERET, AND MALCHUT, IS PART OF THREE COLUMNS EQUALING TWELVE; the cloak with bells and ornaments; four garments of white with which the Matron adorns Herself before the King, as the verse says: "and I will look upon it, that I may remember the everlasting covenant" (Beresheet 9:16), and also the stealing from the mistress, NAMELY THE SHECHINAH, of numerous sacrificial offerings.

451. שׁוֹר מוּעָד בַּעֲלָה, עָאל לְבֵי מַלְכָּא רְבּוֹנֵיה, בְּאַרְבַּע אֲבוֹת נְזִיקִין דִּילֵיה, דְּאִינוּן, עָוֹן וּמַשְׁחִית אַף וְחֵמָה, דְּכֻלְהוּ מוּעָדִין לְקַלְקֵל. בְּגוּפָא דִּילֵיה, הִרְבִּיץ עַל הַכֵּלִים, מִזְבֵּחַ מְנוֹרָה שֻׁלְחָן וּשְׁאָר מָאנִין, רָבַץ עֲלַיְיהוּ וְשַׁבְּרָתָן. וּבְשֵׁן דִּילֵיה, אָכִיל כָּל קָרְבָּנִין דְּמַאֲכָלִים דְּפָתוֹרָא,

וְשַׁאֲרָא בְּרַגְלוֹי רַפְסָא. וּבְקֶרֶן דִּילֵיהּ, קָטַל כַּהֲנֵי וְלֵיוָאֵי. הָרַס כֹּלָּא, חִלֵּל מַמְלָכָה וְשָׂרֶיהָ.

451. The bull that has gored thrice, the husband OF THE EVIL MAID, enters the abode of his Master, the King, with his four primary causes of injury, namely: sin and destruction, anger and wrath, all calculated to destroy. With his body, he crushes the vessels, altar, menorah, table and other vessels; he lies upon them and destroys them. With his tooth, he consumes the sacrificial offerings on the table; the rest he tramples with his feet. With his horn, he gores the priests and Levites, and devastates everything, "he has profaned the kingdom and its princes" (Eichah 2:2).

452. הַבּוֹר, נוּקְבָּא בִּישָׁא, לִילִית, בְּבֵיתָ דִּילָהּ, דְּאִיהִי בֵּית הַסֹּהַר, תְּפִיסַת לְמַטְרוֹנִיתָא וּבְנָהָא, שִׁפְחָה בִּישָׁא, בְּגָלוּתָא דִּילָהּ, וְשַׁוְּיָיאן לוֹן, בְּכַמָּה שַׁלְשְׁלָאִין וַאֲסוּרִין לִבְנָהָא מְהַדְּקָן לַאֲחוֹרָא. הִיא יָשְׁבָה בַּגּוֹיִם לֹא מָצְאָה מָנוֹחַ. וְלֹא עוֹד אֶלָּא כָּל מְכַבְּדֶיהָ הִזִילוּהָ כִּי רָאוּ עֶרְוָתָהּ גַּם הִיא נֶאֶנְחָה וַתָּשָׁב אָחוֹר.

452. The pit represents the evil wife, Lilit, in her house, namely the prison. The evil maid seized the Matron and her children, NAMELY THE CHILDREN OF YISRAEL, put them in her exile, placed them in twisted chains, and tied their hands to the back; "she dwells among the nations, she finds no rest" (Eichah 1:3). Furthermore, "all that honored her despise her, because they have seen her nakedness: she herself also sighs, and turns backward" (Ibid. 8).

453. וְלֹא עוֹד, אֶלָּא זוֹנָה דְּאִיהִי הַבְּעֵר, דְּהַיְינוּ אֵשׁ, וַיַּצֶּת אֵשׁ בְּצִיּוֹן. לְבָתַר קָם אָדָם בְּלִיַּעַ"ל רָשָׁע, רְבִיעִי לַאֲבוֹת נְזִיקִין, דְּאִתְּמַר בֵּיהּ אָדָם מוּעָד לְעוֹלָם, בֵּין עֵר בֵּין יָשֵׁן, וְשָׁלַח אֶת בְּעִירוֹ, וְאָכִיל וְשֵׁצֵי וְגָדַע כְּרָמִים וּפַרְדֵּסִים דִּירוּשְׁלֵם, וְשֵׁצֵי כֹּלָּא.

453. And in addition to this is the EVIL KLIPAH, the harlot, the Consuming Fire, as it is written, "a fire engulfed Zion" (Ibid.). Later, a vile man came fourth in the series of principal damages, WHICH IS THE DAMAGE OF CROP DESTROYING ANIMAL, as it says regarding man that he is eternally liable

whether awake or asleep. "He sent in his cattle to graze," MEANING HIS LEGIONS, which ate, consumed, pillaged the vineyards and orchards of Jerusalem and devastated everything.

454. רִבּוֹן עָלְמָא, אַנְתְּ קְשׁוֹט, וְאוֹרַיְיתָךְ קְשׁוֹט, יָהֲבַת לָן מִצְוַת תְּפִילִין, לַצַּדִּיקִים גְּמוּרִים אִיהוּ אַגְרָא כְּפוּם עוֹבָדַיְיהוּ, פְּאֵר עַל רֵישַׁיְיהוּ. וּמְשַׁמְּשִׁין לַאֲבוּהוֹן וְאִמְּהוֹן, כְּגַוְונָא דְגוּפָא, דְּכָל אֵבָרִים דִּילֵיהּ מְשַׁמְּשִׁין לְרֵישָׁא. הָכִי אִתְּתָא, מְשַׁמְּשָׁא לְבַעְלָהּ.

454. Master of the Universe. You are True, your Torah is truth. You gave us the precept of Tefilin, for the perfect Righteous it serves as reward for their deeds, an article of beauty upon their heads, and they serve their Father and Mother WITH THIS, BEING MALE AND FEMALE, such as the body, where all limbs serve the head. And so the woman, DENOTING MALCHUT AND THE HAND TEFILIN, serves her husband, MEANING ZEIR ANPIN.

455. וְאִית מַלְאָכִין דְּאִינּוּן מְשַׁמְּשִׁין לְגוּפָא, וּמַלְאָכִין דִּמְשַׁמְּשִׁין לְנִשְׁמְתָא. וּכְגַוְונָא דְּאִית אַפְרָשׁוּתָא בֵּין גּוּפָא לְנִשְׁמְתָא, הָכִי אִית אַפְרָשׁוּתָא בֵּין מַלְאָכִין דְּגוּפָא, לְמַלְאָכִין דְּנִשְׁמְתָא. וְאִית נִשְׁמְתָא לְנִשְׁמְתָא. וּמַלְאָכִין לְמַלְאָכִין, כִּי גָבוֹהַּ מֵעַל גָּבוֹהַּ שֹׁמֵר וּגְבוֹהִים עֲלֵיהֶם. וְאִלֵּין דְּאִינּוּן נִשְׁמְתָא לְנִשְׁמְתָא, כֻּלְּהוּ חַד. וְאע"ג דְּאָרַח מַתְלָא, אִינּוּן כְּגוּפָא אֵצֶל נִשְׁמְתָא אִלֵּין לְאִלֵּין, בְּגִין דִּמְקַבְּלִין אִלֵּין מֵאִלֵּין. הָכִי שְׁכִינְתָּא, אע"ג דְּאִיהִי לָקֳבֵל שְׁאַר נְהוֹרִין דִּבְרִיאָה, כְּנִשְׁמְתָא אֵצֶל גּוּפָא, לָקֳבֵל קוּדְשָׁא בְּרִיךְ הוּא חֲשִׁיבָא כְּגוּפָא. אֲבָל כֹּלָּא חַד. הָכָא גּוּפָא וְנִשְׁמְתָא כֹּלָּא חַד. מַה דְּלָאו הָכִי בְּבַר נָשׁ, דְּגוּפֵיהּ וְנִשְׁמְתֵיהּ בְּפֵרוּדָא. דָּא חוֹמֶר, וְדָא שֵׂכֶל. דָּא חַיֵּי, וְדָא מוֹתָא. אֲבָל קוּדְשָׁא בְּרִיךְ הוּא חַיִּים, וּשְׁכִינְתֵּיהּ חַיִּים, הה"ד, עֵץ חַיִּים הִיא לַמַּחֲזִיקִים בָּהּ.

455. There are angels that serve the body, and angels that serve the soul. Just as there is a distinction between body and soul, so there is a difference between angels of the body and angels of the soul. There is a soul over the

soul and angels over the angels, as it says, "for there is one high one who watches over him that is high; and there are yet higher ones over them" (Kohelet 5:7). This is the soul of a soul, COMING FROM ATZILUT, all of them one, NO DIVISION AMONG THEM AT ALL. Even though metaphorically EVERY LOWER LEVEL COMPARED TO A HIGHER ONE is like a body compared to soul, it is because they receive one from another. So the Shechinah, when compared to other lights in the world of Briyah, is like the soul to body, but when compared to the Holy One, blessed be He, ZEIR ANPIN, She is considered like a body. But it is all one, the body and soul. Not so with man, where there is division between the body and soul. One is material, the other mental; one is Life, the other Death, but the Holy One, blessed be He, is Life and His Shechinah is Life, as written, "She is a Tree of Life to those who lay hold on Her" (Mishlei 3:18).

16. Those marked with the signs of the Holy One, blessed be He, and His Shechinah

16. Those marked with the signs of the Holy One, blessed be He, and His Shechinah

A Synopsis

We are told that God marked Yisrael so that they will be recognizable to the angels. Those who have Torah in them are marked on the right with Chesed; those that did precepts are marked on the left with Gvurah; those who keep Tefilin, Shabbat and the Covenant are marked with the Righteous, Yesod. The evil-doers are without any markings of purity; their punishment is poverty. Yet when that spirit blesses and sanctifies and unifies God, then He descends to that spirit with many hosts.

456. וְכָל אִינּוּן דִּרְשִׁימִין בְּסִימָנִין דְּקוּדְשָׁא בְּרִיךְ הוּא וּשְׁכִינְתֵּיה, אִינּוּן רְשִׁימִין בְּיוֹמִין דְּחוֹל, בְּאוֹת דִּתְפִלִּין, וּבְאוֹת דְּמִילָה. וּרְשִׁימִין בְּזָכוֹר וְשָׁמוֹר בְּשַׁבָּת. רְשִׁימִין בַּתּוֹרָה שֶׁבִּכְתָב, דְּאִתְיְהִיבַת מִימִינָא. וּבַתּוֹרָה שבע"פ, דְּאִתְיְהִיבַת מִשְּׂמָאלָא. וְקוּדְשָׁא בְּרִיךְ הוּא, זָכוֹר מִימִינָא, וְשָׁמוֹר מִשְּׂמָאלָא. וּשְׁכִינְתָּא, זְכִירָה מִימִינָא, וּשְׁמִירָה מִשְּׂמָאלָא. אִינּוּן תְּפִלִּין דְּרֵישָׁא דב"נ, וּתְפִלִּין דְּיָד. וְהָכִי שְׁכִינְתָּא, תּוֹרַת יְיָ' תְּמִימָה, וּמִצְוָה דִּילֵיהּ. וְהַאי מִסִּטְרָא דְּעַמּוּדָא דְּאֶמְצָעִיתָא, דְּאִיהוּ כָּלִיל דִּינָא וְרַחֲמֵי. זָכוֹר וְשָׁמוֹר. אִתְקְרִיאַת אִיהִי זְכִירָה שְׁמִירָה. וּבְכָל פִּקּוּדִין אִיהִי שְׁקִילָה לְגַבֵּיהּ בְּמַדְרֵגָה.

456. All those that are marked with the signs of the Holy One, blessed be He, and His Shechinah: with the sign of Tefilin and the sign of circumcision during the week days, and are marked with 'remember' and 'keep' on the Shabbat, and they are marked by the written Torah given from the right and the Oral Torah given from the left. With the Holy One, blessed be He, 'remember' is from the right and 'keep' from the left. Also with the Shechinah 'remembering' is from the right and 'keeping' from the left. So also the Head Tefilin OF MAN STEMS FROM THE RIGHT. And the Tefilin of the hand, FROM THE LEFT. So the Shechinah is called "The Torah of Hashem is perfect" (Tehilim 19:8), FROM ITS RIGHT SIDE, and precept FROM ITS LEFT. This is all from the direction of the Central Column, NAMELY ZEIR ANPIN, that comprises Judgment and Mercy, BEING 'remember' and 'keep'. AND FROM ITS POSITION, MALCHUT is also called

'remembering' and 'keeping', for from the standpoint of the precepts she is on an equal level with him.

457. אֲבָל מִסִּטְרָא דְחֶסֶד, קוּדְשָׁא בְּרִיךְ הוּא זָכוֹר, וּשְׁכִינְתָּא שָׁמוֹר. כְּמָה דְּאוּקְמוּהָ מָארֵי מַתְנִיתִין, זָכוֹר לְזָכָר, וְשָׁמוֹר לְכַלָּה. בְּגִין דְּבִימִינָא וּבִשְׂמָאלָא עַנְפִּין מִתְפָּרְדִין, כְּגַוְונָא דְּכַנְפֵי רֵיאָה, דְּאִינּוּן פְּרוּדוֹת מִלְמַעְלָה. לָקֳבְלַיְיהוּ חֵיוָן, וּפְנֵיהֶם וְכַנְפֵיהֶם פְּרוּדוֹת מִלְמַעְלָה. וְלָקֳבֵל פְּתוּחוֹת דִּס"ת. לְתַתָּא תַּרְוַויְיהוּ בְּיִחוּדָא חֲדָא, כְּגוֹן סְתוּמוֹת דִּס"ת, דְּלֵית תַּמָּן פְּרוּדָא. וּבְגִין דָּא, בַּאֲתָר דְּיִחוּדָא, דְּאִיהוּ גוּפָא, דּוּמֶה לַשִׂדְרָה דְלוּלָב, אִם נִפְרְצוּ, אוֹ נִפְרְדוּ עָלָיו פָּסוּל.

457. But from the aspect of Chesed, the Holy One, blessed be He, is considered 'remember' and the Shechinah 'keep'. The Mishnah masters have established 'remember' is applicable to the male and 'keep' to the bride. Within the right and left, FROM THE CHEST AND UP OF ZEIR ANPIN, the branches separate like the wing-like lung where they separate above. Correspondingly, the living creatures OF WHICH IT IS WRITTEN, "Thus were their faces: and their wings were divided upwards" (Yechezkel 1:11), correspond to the open Torah scroll. Now below, MEANING, FROM THE CHEST DOWN, IS FOUND THE NUKVA CALLED 'PRECEPT', both ZEIR ANPIN AND MALCHUT are together in one unity like the closed chapters in the Torah scroll, where there is no separation. SO THEY ARE BOTH EVEN, JUST AS ZEIR ANPIN IS CALLED 'REMEMBER', SO ALSO SHE IS CALLED 'REMEMBERING' AND 'KEEPING', AS MENTIONED. IT IS NOT SO ABOVE THE CHEST, RIGHT AND LEFT, WHERE MALCHUT IS CALLED ONLY 'KEEP' BUT NOT 'REMEMBER'. As a result, at the place of unity, the body, MALCHUT, is similar to the spine-like stalk of the Lulav: if it breaks or splits it is rejected.

458. בְּכַמָּה רְשִׁימִין רָשִׁים קוּדְשָׁא בְּרִיךְ הוּא לְיִשְׂרָאֵל, לְאִשְׁתְּמוֹדְעָא לְגַבֵּי מַלְאָכִין. אִלֵּין דְּיָמִינָא, דְּתַלְיָין מִקּוּדְשָׁא בְּרִיךְ הוּא. אוֹ אִלֵּין דִּשְׂמָאלָא, דְּתַלְיָין מִשְּׁכִינְתָּא. אוֹ אִלֵּין דְּתַלְיָין מִקּוּדְשָׁא בְּרִיךְ הוּא. וּשְׁכִינְתֵּיהּ בְּיִחוּדָא חֲדָא. וְדַאי אִלֵּין דְּאִית בְּהוֹן תּוֹרָה, רְשִׁימִין בְּחֶסֶד. וְאִלֵּין דְּאִית בְּהוֹן מִצְוָה, רְשִׁימִין בִּגְבוּרָה. וְאִלֵּין מָארֵי דִּתְפִלִּין, וְאוֹת

16. Those marked with the signs of the Holy One, blessed be He, and His Shechinah

שַׁבָּת, וְאוֹת בְּרִית, רְשִׁימִין בְּצַדִּיק.

458. In several markings did the Holy One, blessed be He, mark Yisrael, so they will be recognizable to the angels. Those OF YISRAEL THAT DRAW from the right, are dependent upon the Holy One, blessed be He; those that draw from the left are dependent on the Shechinah; those dependent on the Holy One, blessed be He, and His Shechinah are in one unity. HE EXPLAINS: Those who have Torah in them are marked ON THE RIGHT with Chesed; those that did precepts are marked ON THE LEFT with Gvurah. Those who keep Tefilin, Shabbat and the Covenant are marked with the Righteous, NAMELY YESOD.

459. וּבְעִירָן, עַמֵּי הָאָרֶץ, אִינּוּן רְשִׁימִין בְּאַעְבְּרוּ דְּעָרְלָה וּפְרִיעָה. עוֹפִין, בְּזֶפֶק וּבְקַרְקְבָן נִקְלָף, בְּאַעְבְּרוּ דְּזֶפֶק, וּקְלִיפָה דְּקַרְקְבָן, אִינּוּן רְשִׁימִין עוֹפִין לְמֵיכַל וּבְעִירָן, בִּתְרֵי סִימָנִין, מַעֲלַת גֵּרָה, וּמַפְרֶסֶת פַּרְסָה. כֻּלְּהוּ רְשִׁימִין בִּתְרֵי סִימָנִין, כְּגַוְונָא דְּעָרְלָה וּפְרִיעָה, דְּמִתְעַבְּרָן מֵעַמָּא קַדִּישָׁא.

459. Those OF YISRAEL that are beasts and ignorant are marked by the symbol of the removal of the foreskin and the splitting of the corona, BEING TWO SIGNS OF PURITY, AND SO ARE fowl also with two signs, the crop and the peeled stomach – the removal of the crop and peel of the stomach being the signs permitting the fowl to be eaten. The two signs in animals are chewing the cud and split hoofs. All are marked with two signs, such as the foreskin and the uncovering of the corona that are removed from the holy people.

460. אֲבָל תַּלְמִידֵי חֲכָמִים, כֻּלְּהוֹן רְשִׁימִין מִנְהוֹן, בְּכַרְסְיָיא. וּמִנְהוֹן, בְּמַלְאֲכֵי, בְּאַרְבַּע חֵיוָן דְּכַרְסְיָיא. מִנְהוֹן בְּכֹכְבַיָּא וּבְמַזָּלֵי. וּמִנְהוֹן רְשִׁימִין, דְּמַדּוֹת דְּקוּדְשָׁא בְּרִיךְ הוּא אִשְׁתְּמוֹדְעִין. וְאִינּוּן דְּמִתְעַסְּקִין בְּאוֹרַיְיתָא וּבְמִצְוֹת, לִשְׁמָא דְּקוּדְשָׁא בְּרִיךְ הוּא וּשְׁכִינְתֵּיה, שֶׁלֹּא עַל מְנָת לְקַבֵּל פְּרָס, אֶלָּא כִּבְרָא דְּאִיהוּ מְחוּיָּיב בִּיקָרָא דַּאֲבוֹהִי וְאִמֵּיה, דָּא אִתְקְשָׁר וַדַּאי וְאִתְרְשִׁים, בְּעַמּוּדָא דְּאֶמְצָעִיתָא וּשְׁכִינְתֵּיה, כְּאִילּוּ

בֵּיהּ הֲווֹ חַד. וּמַאן דְּאִית בֵּיהּ תּוֹרָה בְּלָא מִצְוָה, אוֹ מִצְוָה בְּלָא תּוֹרָה, כִּבְיָכוֹל כְּאִילוּ הֲווֹ בֵּיהּ בִּפְרוּדָא. אֲבָל בְּדָא וְדָא, כְּאִילָנָא, דְּעַנְפוֹי מִתְפָּרְדִין לִימִינָא וְלִשְׂמָאלָא, וְאִילָנָא יִחוּדָא דְּתַרְוַוְיְיהוּ, בְּאֶמְצָעִיתָא.

460. But the students of the Torah are listed ABOVE, some in the throne, DENOTING MALCHUT, some with the angels, the four living creatures carrying the throne, some with stars and planets. Some are marked with the measures, NAMELY THE SFIROT, through which the Holy One, blessed be He, is made known. Those involved in the Torah and the precepts for the sake of the Holy One, blessed be He, and His Shechinah, not seeking any recompense but rather like a son duty bound in honor of his parents, are indeed bound. And so this is marked in the central pillar, NAMELY THE HOLY ONE, BLESSED BE HE, and His Shechinah becoming as One. One who has Torah without precepts, or precepts without Torah, so to speak, is as if there is a split within him. However, when there is both, TORAH AND THE PRECEPTS, he is comparable to a tree whose branches spread to the right and left, but the tree itself is the unifying factor in the center.

461. רַשִּׁיעַיָּא, אִינּוּן רְשִׁימִין בְּלָא סִימָנִין דְּטָהֲרָה, אִינּוּן דְּלֵית לְהוֹן תְּפִלִּין עַל רֵישָׁא, וּדְרוֹעָא. וְאִינּוּן דְּלָא רְשִׁימִין בַּתּוֹרָה וּבַמִּצְוֹת. וְאִלֵּין דְּלָא נַטְרִין זָכוֹר וְשָׁמוֹר. וְלָא רְשִׁימִין בִּתְכֵלֶת וְלָבָן דְּצִיצִית. וְאִלֵּין דְּלָא רְשִׁימִין בְּאִלֵּין סִימָנִין, שֶׁקֶץ הֵם לָכֶם, לָאו אִינּוּן יִשְׂרָאֵל אֶלָּא עַמֵּי הָאָרֶץ. מַה אִלֵּין שֶׁקֶץ וְשָׁרַץ, אוֹף אִינּוּן כֵּן, שֶׁקֶץ וְשֶׁרֶץ. כְּמָה דְּאוּקְמוּהָ מָארֵי מַתְנִיתִין, עַמֵּי הָאָרֶץ הֵם שֶׁרֶץ, וּנְשׁוֹתֵיהֶם שֶׁקֶץ. וְעַל בְּנוֹתֵיהֶם אִתְּמַר, אָרוּר שׁוֹכֵב עִם כָּל בְּהֵמָה.

461. The evil-doers are without any markings of purity, they have neither head nor arm Tefilin, and are not marked by the Torah and the precepts, or by 'remember' and 'keep', or by the blue and white of the *Tzitzit* ('the fringes'). Those lacking these markings are an abomination to you, not pertaining to Yisrael, but to the ignorant. Just like those LACKING CLEAN MARKINGS are abominable and detested insects, so also these people are detestable. As the Mishnah masters have established, the ignorant masses are abominable, their wives detestable and of their daughters it is written, "Cursed be he that lies with any manner of beast" (Devarim 27:21).

16. Those marked with the signs of the Holy One, blessed be He, and His Shechinah

462. וּמִיתַתְהוֹן מִיתָה בְּאִתְגַּלְיָא, וְלֵית מִיתָה אֶלָּא עֲנִיּוּתָא, וּמִיתָה דַעֲנִיּוּתָא דִּלְהוֹן, לָא יְהֵא בְּאִתְכַּסְיָא, כְּעוֹפִין דְּרַמְיָין לְמָארֵי פִּקוּדִין, אֶלָּא בְּאִתְגַּלְיָיא, לְעֵינֵי עַמָּא, דְּעָנִי חָשׁוּב כְּמֵת. וְאִית עֲנִיּוּתָא בְּאִתְכַּסְיָא, מֵעֵינֵי בְּנֵי נָשָׁא. וְאִית עֲנִיּוּתָא, לְעֵינֵי כֹּלָּא. כִּזְרִיקוּ דְּדָם דִּבְהֵמָה, וּזְרִיקָתָה לְעֵינֵי כֹּלָּא, דְּשַׁפְכִין דָּמָא קַמֵי כֹּלָּא. הָכִי עֲנִיִּין שַׁפְכִין דָּמוֹי בְּאַנְפַּיְיהוּ, לְעֵינֵי בְּנֵי נָשָׁא, וְאִתְהַדְרִין יְרוֹקִין כַּמֵּתִין.

462. Their demise is a public one, demise meaning poverty. Their punishment of poverty is not to be kept secret, like the case of fowl, which hints at those who perform the precepts – FOR THEIR BLOOD IS COVERED, but here it is public for the eyes of all. He EXPLAINS: A pauper is considered like a dead man. Some poverty is hidden from the eyes of man, and some is public knowledge such as the sprinkling of cattle blood where the blood is shed before all. So there are paupers whose blood is shed publicly, and they become green as corpses.

463. וְאִי הַדְרִין בְּתִיוּבְתָּא, וְלָא פַּתְחִין פּוּמְהוֹן לְהַטִּיחַ דְּבָרִים כְּלַפֵּי מַעְלָה וּמִיתָה דִּלְהוֹן בִּסְתִימוּ דְּפוּמָא, כִּבְעִירָא דְּאִיהִי מֵיתָא, וְלֵית לָהּ קוֹל וְדִבּוּר. וּבְוִידוּי הָכִי יֵימָא אִיהוּ, אֵין לִי פֶּה לְהָשִׁיב, וְלֹא מֵצַח לְהָרִים רֹאשׁ, וְיִתְוַדֶּה וּמְיַיחֵד לְקוּדְשָׁא בְּרִיךְ הוּא בְּכָל יוֹמָא, לְמֶהֱוֵי מִיתָתֵיהּ בְּאֶחָד. כְּגַוְונָא דִּשְׁחִיטַת בְּהֵמָה, בִּתְרֵיסַר בְּדִיקוֹת דְּסַכִּין, וּבְסַכִּין דְּאִינוּן אֶחָ"ד.

463. If they repent, do not complain before heaven, and accept death without a murmur like cattle experiencing death without a sound, and they confess saying, 'I am speechless to speak back, nor can I lift my head in arrogance'. If they will confess and declare the unity of the Holy One, blessed be He, AND ACCEPT UPON THEMSELVES to die, pronouncing 'one (Heb. *echad*)' with the twelve checks with the SLAUGHTERING knife of animals, PLUS the knife ITSELF NOW THIRTEEN EQUALING, THE FIGURE *echad* (= 13).

464. וּמְבָרֵךְ וּמְקַדֵּשׁ לְקוּדְשָׁא ב"ה בְּכָל יוֹמָא, בְּבָרְכוּ וּבִקְדוּשָׁא, וּבְכָל

אֲכִילָה וּשְׁתִיָּה דִּילֵיהּ. כְּגַוְונָא דִּמְבָרֵךְ כַּהֲנָא, בָּרוּךְ אַתָּה, הָא בְּרָכָה. אֲשֶׁר קִדְּשָׁנוּ, הָא קְדוּשָׁה. כַּד רוּחָא מְבָרַךְ לְקוּדְשָׁא בְּרִיךְ הוּא, בְּכָל יוֹמָא בְּבָרוּךְ, וּמְקַדֵּשׁ לֵיהּ בִּקְדוּשָׁא דִּילֵיהּ, וּמְיַחֵד לֵיהּ בְּיִחוּדָא דְּאִיהוּ שְׁכִינְתֵּיהּ. קוּדְשָׁא בְּרִיךְ הוּא נָחִית עַל הַהוּא רוּחָא בְּכַמָּה מַשְׁרְיָין.

464. And if he blesses and sanctifies the Holy One, blessed be He, daily with the *barchu* ('Bless Hashem') and *kedushah* ('sanctification'). And when eating or drinking, such as when the priest blesses, WHO IS CHESED 'Blessed are you' represents blessing, 'that sanctified us' represents sanctification. When the spirit blesses the Holy One, blessed be He, daily with 'blessed' and sanctifies Him with the sanctification, and unifies Him with unification, which is His Shechinah, the Holy One, blessed be He, descends to that spirit with many hosts.

17. A spirit ascends and descends every night

A Synopsis

They who offers their spirits as an offering to Hashem are happy, and every night their spirits ascend to Him. They who ascend by a precept, meaning the precept of Tefilin, are happy. We read about the connection of deed, speech and thought, and about the seventy words in the psalm, "May Hashem hear you in the day of trouble". Among the masters of Torah there are two grades: morning and dawn. The morning of Abraham, Chesed, appears on the Day of Redemption, but the dawn precedes the Day of Redemption, being Netzach, as the Shechinah from this aspect is called the star of dawn. The morning alludes to the right hand of Abraham, which alludes to Messiah the son of David.

465. אֵלִיָּהוּ, וַדַּאי בַּר נָשׁ דִּמְבָרֵךְ וּמְקַדֵּשׁ וּמְיַחֵד לְמַטְרוֹנִיתָא, כַּמָּה מַשִׁרְיָין דְּמַטְרוֹנִיתָא סַלְקִין עִמֵּיה, וּמַשִׁרְיָין דְּמַלְכָּא, נַחְתִּין לְגַבֵּיה. וְכֻלְּהוּ לְנַטְרָא לֵיה, וּלְאוֹדָעָא לֵיה לְהַהוּא רוּחָא, כַּמָּה חִידוּשִׁין וַעֲתִידוֹת, בְּחֶלְמִין דִּנְבוּאָה, וְכַמָּה סְתָרִים. כְּגַוְונָא דְּיַעֲקֹב, דְּאִתְּמַר בֵּיה, וְהִנֵּה מַלְאֲכֵי אֱלֹהִים עוֹלִים וְיוֹרְדִים בּוֹ. וְעַל מַשִׁרְיָין דְּמַלְכָּא וּמַטְרוֹנִיתָא אִתְּמַר, וַיִּקְרָא שֵׁם הַמָּקוֹם הַהוּא מַחֲנָיִם. אֲבָל מַלְכָּא וּמַטְרוֹנִיתָא לָא נַחְתִּין תַּמָּן.

465. THE FAITHFUL SHEPHERD SAID TO ELIJAH: Elijah, certainly WHEN EVEN ORDINARY PEOPLE bless and sanctify and unite the Matron, numerous hosts of the Matron ascend with him, and hosts of the King descend to him and all with the purpose to guard him, to make known to that spirit many novel ideas, and forecasts within the dream of prophecy and many hidden matters. An example is Jacob, about whom is written, "and behold the angels of Elohim ascending and descending on it" (Beresheet 28:12). Regarding the hosts of the King and the Matron are written: "and he called the name of that place *Machanaim* (lit. 'two camps')" (Beresheet 32:2). However the King and Matron THEMSELVES do not descend there, WHEREAS WITH REGARD TO A REPENTANT, THE HOLY ONE, BLESSED BE HE, PERSONALLY DESCENDS TO THAT SPIRIT, AS DISCUSSED.

466. אָמַר אֵלִיָּהוּ, רַעְיָא מְהֵימְנָא, הָכִי הוּא וַדַּאי. אֲבָל בְּגִין דִּבְכָל

פְּקוּדָא וּפְקוּדָא, הֲוָה אִשְׁתַּדְּלוּתָא דִּילָךְ, לְיַחֲדָא קוּדְשָׁא בְּרִיךְ הוּא וּשְׁכִינְתֵּיה, בְּכָל מַשִּׁרְיָין דְּעֵילָא וְתַתָּא, הָכִי קוּדְשָׁא בְּרִיךְ הוּא וּשְׁכִינְתֵּיה, וְכָל מַשִּׁרְיָיתֵיה עֵילָא וְתַתָּא, מִתְיַחֲדִין בְּרוּחָא דִּילָךְ, בְּכָל פְּקוּדָא וּפְקוּדָא, כִּבְרָא דְמַלְכָּא, דְּאַבָּא וְאִמָּא רַחֲמִין לֵיה, וְנַשְׁקִין לֵיה, וּבַחֲבִיבוּ דִּילֵיה, לָא הֵמְנִין לֵיה בְּמַשִּׁרְיָין דִּלְהוֹן, אֶלָּא אִינּוּן גּוּפַיְיהוּ, נַטְרִין לֵיה.

466. Elijah said: Faithful Shepherd, so it is. As a result of your efforts in every precept to unify the Holy One, blessed be He, and His Shechinah with all the hosts above and below, so the Holy One, blessed be He, and His Shechinah and all Her hosts above and below unify with your spirit, with every precept done. As a prince whose parents love and kiss him, they do not rely on their hosts, but choose to guard him themselves.

467. בְּגִין דְּהַהוּא רוּחָא דִּילָךְ, מִסִּטְרָא דְעַמּוּדָא דְּאֶמְצָעִיתָא אִיהוּ, דְּאִיהוּ ו' כָּלִיל אַבָּא וְאִמָּא, דְּאִינּוּן י"ה. נֶפֶשׁ דִּילָךְ. בַּת יְחִידָא, מִסִּטְרָא דְּאָת ה', שְׁכִינְתָּא תַּתָּאָה, לָא זָזַת מִינָךְ. וּכְגַוְונָא דְּאַבָּא וְאִמָּא נַטְרִין בְּרָא, הָכִי נַטְרִין בְּרַתָּא. בְּמַשִּׁרְיָין עִלָּאִין, דְּאִינּוּן מַחֲנַיִם. וּבְמַחֲשָׁבָה עִלָּאָה, סַלְקִין לְרוּחָא דִּילָךְ, כְּמָה דְּאוּקְמוּהָ, יִשְׂרָאֵל עָלָה בְּמַחֲשָׁבָה, יו"ד ה"א וא"ו ה"א. וְאֵימָתַי רוּחָא דִּילָךְ סְלִיקַת בְּמַחֲשָׁבָה. כַּד אִיהִי שְׁלֵימָא, וְאִתְּמַר בָּה, כֹּל הַנְּשָׁמָה תְּהַלֵּל יָהּ. וּבְנַפְשָׁא דְּאִיהִי ה'.

467. EXPLANATION: Your spirit stems from the central pillar, NAMELY ZEIR ANPIN, being the *Vav* that comprises Aba and Ima, which are *Yud-Hei*. Your soul is an only daughter from the aspect of the letter *Hei*, the lower Shechinah, NAMELY MALCHUT, that does not move from you. Just as Aba and Ima guard the son, NAMELY ZEIR ANPIN, so they guard the daughter, NAMELY MALCHUT, in the supernal hosts, the two camps. With the supernal thought, WHICH IS CHOCHMAH, they raise your spirit, as was stated. The thought of Yisrael came to mind, being Yud Hei Vav Hei. When does your spirit come up in thought? When it is complete. It is said about it: "Let everything that has breath (lit. 'every soul') praise Yah" (Tehilim 150:6),

and with the Nefesh too, being the *Hei* OF YUD HEI VAV HEI, MEANING
THE SOUL ASCENDS WITH THE SPIRIT.

468. רוּחַ יְיָ׳ אִתְּמַר בֵּיהּ, כֹּה אָמַר יְיָ׳ מֵאַרְבַּע רוּחוֹת בֹּאִי הָרוּחַ.
וְאִינּוּן, רוּחַ יְיָ׳, רוּחַ חָכְמָה וּבִינָה, רוּחַ עֵצָה וּגְבוּרָה וְגוֹ׳, שְׁלִים
בְּאַרְבַּע אַתְוָון, סָלִיק בְּמַחֲשָׁבָה, וְעִלַּת הָעִלּוֹת מְעַטֵּר לֵיהּ בְּכֶתֶר. בְּכָל
הַאי יְקָר, רוּחָא דִּילָךְ, סָלִיק וְנָחִית בְּכָל לֵילְיָא. וְכָל מִלִּין דְּאִתְגַּלְיָין
לָךְ בְּחֶסֶד וַעֲלַיְיהוּ אִתְּמַר וְאַתֶּם הַדְּבֵקִים בַּיְיָ׳, אַתֶּם, וְלָא אוּמִין
עכו״ם. וּבְג״ד, זֹבֵחַ לָאֱלֹהִים יָחֳרָם, אֱלֵיהֶם אֲחֵרִים. בִּלְתִּי לַיְיָ׳ לְבַדּוֹ.

468. Regarding the spirit of Hashem, it is written, "Come from the four
winds (also: 'spirits') O breath (also: 'spirit')" (Yechezkel 37:9). WHEN
COMPOSED OF THE FOUR SPIRITS, IT IS CALLED 'THE SPIRIT OF YUD HEI
VAV HEI'; that is: "and the spirit of Hashem shall rest upon him, the spirit
of wisdom and understanding, the spirit of counsel and might..." (Yeshayah
11:2). If he is perfect with the four letters OF YUD HEI VAV HEI, the
thought of him occurs, NAMELY CHOCHMAH, and the Cause of all Causes
adorns him with the crown. Within all this glory, your spirit ascends and
descends nightly. All things are revealed to you with Chesed, of which the
verse says, "But you that did cleave of Hashem" (Devarim 4:4); you, but not
the nations of the world. Hence, "He that sacrifices to any Elohim," other
Elohim, "save to Hashem only, he shall be utterly destroyed" (Shemot
22:19).

469. זַכָּאָה עַמָּא קַדִּישָׁא, דְּאִתְקְרִיאוּ עָאנָא דְּקוּדְשָׁא בְּרִיךְ הוּא,
לְמִקְרַב גַּרְמַיְיהוּ קָרְבְּנִין קַמֵּיהּ. כְּמָה דְּאִתְּמַר, כִּי עָלֶיךָ הוֹרַגְנוּ כֹּל
הַיּוֹם נֶחְשַׁבְנוּ כְּצֹאן טִבְחָה. וְקָרְבִּין גַּרְמַיְיהוּ כְּעָאנִין, בְּתַעֲנִיתָא.
דִּמְעוּט חֶלְבָּא וְדָמָא, דְּתַעֲנִיתָא, אִיהוּ חָשִׁיב יַתִּיר מִקָּרְבְּנָא דִּבְעִירָן,
דַּהֲוָה מִתְמַעֵט דָּמָא וְחֶלְבָּא וְכָל אִינּוּן אֵמוּרִין וּפַדְרִין, דְּמִתְאַכְּלִין כָּל
לֵילְיָא.

469. Fortunate is the Holy Nation that are called 'sheep of the Holy One,
blessed be He', ready to offer themselves as a sacrifice for Him, as it is
written: "But for Your sake are we killed all the day long; we are reckoned

as sheep for the slaughter" (Tehilim 44:23). They would sacrifice themselves as sheep by fasting. Diminishing one's own fat and blood during a fast takes on more importance than animal sacrifice, where the diminishing of animal fat and blood takes place, as well as the nightly burning of the limbs and parts OF THE SACRIFICES.

470. זַכָּאִין אִינּוּן, דִּמְקָרְבִין רוּחִין דִּלְהוֹן, קָרְבְּנִין קָדָם יְיָ'. וּבְכָל לֵילְיָא וְלֵילְיָא, דְּרוּחָא דִּלְהוֹן הִיא הָעוֹלָה לְגַבֵּיה, אִי סָלִיק לָה, בַּתּוֹרָה וּמִצְוָה, בַּתּוֹרָה, דְּאִיהִי עֶשֶׂר אֲמִירָן, דְּאִתְיְיהִיבוּ מֵאָת י' דִּבְעֶשֶׂר דִּבְּרָן, מֵאַתְוָון ה"ה. בּוֹ', בְּשִׁית חוּמְשֵׁי תּוֹרָה בְּסֵפֶר בְּרֵאשִׁית. חֲמִשָּׁה אִינּוּן דְּאִתְקְרִיאוּ חֲמִשָּׁה חוּמְשֵׁי תּוֹרָה. שְׁתִיתָאָה סֵפֶר בְּרֵאשִׁית אִקְרֵי. וּבְמַחֲשָׁבָה דְּאִיהוּ יוּ"ד ה"א וָא"ו ה"א, דְּאִתְּמַר בֵּיה, יִשְׂרָאֵל עָלָה בְּמַחֲשָׁבָה. וּלְאָן אֲתָר סָלִיק. לְגַבֵּי כֶּתֶר דְּתַמָּן עִלַּת הָעִלּוֹת, מוּפְלָא וּמְכוּסָה.

470. Happy are they that offer their spirits as an offering to Hashem, and nightly their spirits ascend to Him. If it ascends with Torah and the precepts, meaning the Ten Commandments that were given by the *Yud* OF YUD HEI VAV HEI, AS THE NUMBER OF the Ten Commandments are from the letter *Hei* (= 5) OF YUD HEI VAV HEI, ADDING TO TEN. Now with the *Vav* OF YUD HEI VAV HEI, with six books of Torah with the book of Beresheet, five are called the Five Books – AS HE COUNTS TWO VERSES OF "AND IT CAME TO PASS, WHEN THE ARK SET FORWARD..." (BEMIDBAR 10:35) AS AN INDEPENDENT BOOK, AS TOLD BY OUR SAGES OF BLESSED MEMORY. SO THERE ARE FIVE BOOKS, BEGINNING WITH THE BOOK OF SHEMOT. Beresheet is considered the sixth Book. If it occurs to thought, being Yud Hei Vav Hei OF THE FIRST THREE SFIROT, it is written: "Yisrael occurred to mind (lit. 'Yisrael ascended with thought)"; to where does he ascend? To Keter, the site of the most wondrous, concealed cause of all causes.

471. זַכָּאָה מַאן דְּסָלִיק לֵיה בַּמִּצְוָה, דְּאִיהִי מִצְוַת תְּפִילִין, דִּבְהוֹן אַרְבַּע פָּרְשִׁיוֹת, דִּבְהוֹן שֵׁם יְדֹוָ"ד. י': קַדֶּשׁ לִי. ה': וְהָיָה כִּי יְבִיאֲךָ. ו': שְׁמַע יִשְׂרָאֵל. ה': וְהָיָה אִם שָׁמוֹעַ. בְּמַחֲשָׁבָה. לְקַשְׁרָא לָה בְּיָד, דִּשְׁכִינְתָּא וְאִיהִי כְּלִילָא מִמַּעֲשֶׂה דְּאִיהִי ה'. וְדִבּוּר דְּאִיהִי בִּינָה,

כְּלִילָא ו' סְפִירָאן. וּבְמַחֲשָׁבָה, דְּאִיהוּ יוּ"ד הֵ"א וָא"ו הֵ"א, יְדוֹ,ֵ יִ"ד אַתְוָון, כְּחוּשְׁבָּן יָד. וְאִתְרְמִיזוּ בְּאַרְבַּע פָּרְשִׁיָין, וּבֵיתָא דִּתְפִלִּין א', וּתְרֵין רְצוּעֵי דְּרֵישָׁא, שָׁבַע. דִּתְרֵין שִׁינִין תֵּשַׁע. וְקֶשֶׁר דִּרְצוּעָה עֶשֶׂר. וְד' פָּרְשִׁיָין דִּיָד, הֲרֵי יַ"ד. יַד דִּשְׁכִינְתָּא, יַד יְדוֹ,ֵ"ד.

471. Happy is he who ascends by a precept, meaning the precept of Tefilin, containing the four chapters containing the name Yud Hei Vav Hei. *Yud* OF YUD HEI VAV HEI is the portion: "Sanctify to me" (Shemot 13:2). *Hei* OF YUD HEI VAV HEI alludes to: "And it shall be when Hashem shall bring you" (Ibid. 11). *Vav* OF YUD HEI VAV HEI, in "Hear, O Yisrael" (Devarim 6:4); and the last *Hei* OF YUD HEI VAV HEI: "And it shall come to pass, of you shall hearken" (Devarim 28:1). ALL ARE INCLUDED in thought, MEANING THE FIRST THREE SFIROT, IN THE HEAD, to connect thought with the hand – ALLUDING TO THE SHECHINAH, REFERRED TO AS THE HAND TEFILIN. THE SHECHINAH IS COMPOSED OF DEED, SPEECH, THE SIX SFIROT, AND THOUGHT. She is composed of Deed, being the *Hei*, ALLUDING TO HER MALCHUT; of speech, being Her Binah; composed of six Sfirot, BEING HER TIFERET – and composed of thought, being *Yud-Vav- Dalet, Hei-Aleph, Vav-Aleph-Vav, Hei-Aleph* – Yud Hei Vav Hei EQUALING fourteen letters, equaling the numerical value of *Yad* (Lit. 'Hand') WHICH IS HER FIRST THREE SFIROT. THE NUMBER FOURTEEN alludes to four chapters and one compartment of HAND Tefilin, with two straps – now we have seven – two *Shin's* ON THE RIGHT AND LEFT OF THE TEFILIN COMPARTMENT – NOW equal nine – WITH the knot of the strap – NOW ten – with the four chapters of the hand TEFILIN – which equal fourteen. So that is why the Shechinah is called 'hand', 'the hand of Yud Hei Vav Hei'.

472. בְּגִינָה אִתְּמַר, בְּיָדְךָ אַפְקִיד רוּחִי וְגוֹ'. רוּחַ אִתְפְּקַד לַיְדוֹ,ֵ"ד. וְקוּדְשָׁא בְּרִיךְ הוּא נָחִית לְגַבֵּיהּ, לְקַבְּלָא לֵיהּ לְגַבֵּי שְׁכִינְתָּא. וְנַטְרֵי לֵיהּ קוּדְשָׁא בְּרִיךְ הוּא וּשְׁכִינְתֵּיהּ. וּמַאן גָּרִים דָּא. מַאן דִּבְכָל מִצְוָה וּמִצְוָה, סָלִיק שְׁכִינְתָּא לְגַבֵּי קוּדְשָׁא בְּרִיךְ הוּא.

472. About Her it is written: "Into Your hand I commit my spirit..." (Tehilim 31:6). The spirit is deposited with Yud Hei Vav Hei, and the Holy One, blessed be He, descends to receive it and place it by the Shechinah. For the Holy One, blessed be He, and His Shechinah guard it. Who brought

this about? He who with every precept lifted the Shechinah to the Holy One, blessed be He.

473. וְעַ' תֵּיבִין דְּיַעַנְךָ יְיָ' בְּיוֹם צָרָה. וּבְמַאי צְוֹוַחַת. אֶלָּא וַדַּאי יִשְׂרָאֵל אִית בְּהוֹן מָארֵי תּוֹרָה, מַלְאָכִים, מִסִּטְרָא דְּאַיֶּלֶת הַשַּׁחַר, דְּאִיהִי שְׁכִינְתָּא. וּתְרֵין דַּרְגִּין אִינוּן, בֹּקֶר וְשַׁחַר, וַעֲלַיְיהוּ אִתְּמַר, נְעִימוֹת בִּימִינְךָ נֶצַח. בֹּקֶר דְּאַבְרָהָם, דְּאִיהוּ חֶסֶ"ד, דָּא סָלִיק יַתִּיר בְּיוֹמָא דְּפוּרְקָנָא, אֲבָל שַׁחַר אַקְדִּים לְיוֹמָא דְּפוּרְקָנָא. וּמַאי אִיהוּ. נֶצַח, דִּשְׁכִינְתָּא מִסִּטְרֵיה אִתְקְרִיאַת אַיֶּלֶת הַשַּׁחַר.

473. The seventy words IN THE PSALM: "May Hashem hear you in the day of trouble" (Tehilim 20:2), ALLUDE TO THE SEVENTY SOUNDS MADE BY THE EXPECTANT MOTHER ABOUT TO GIVE BIRTH, BEING ALSO THE SEVENTY SOUNDS GIVEN OUT BY THE SHECHINAH FOR THE DISTRESS OF THE CHILDREN OF YISRAEL PRIOR TO REDEMPTION – CONSIDERED THEN "A DAY OF TROUBLE." HE ASKS: Why does She cry out? HE ANSWERS: It is known that among Yisrael there are masters of Torah and kings from the aspect of the star of dawn, namely the Shechinah. There are two grades: morning and dawn, about which it is said: "at Your right hand are pleasure for evermore (*Netzach*)" (Tehilim 16:11). The morning of Abraham, Chesed, appears on the ACTUAL Day of Redemption. But the dawn precedes the Day of Redemption, being *Netzach*, as the Shechinah from this aspect is called 'the star (or dow) of dawn'.

474. וּבְגִין דָּא, ל"מ נֶצַ"ח, תַּמָּן נֶצַ"ח, תַּמָּן ל"מ. דְּאִינוּן ע' קָלִין דְּצַוְוחַת אַיֶּלֶת הַשַּׁחַר עַל בְּנָהָא, דְּאִתְתַּקַּף עֲלַיְיהוּ קַדְרוּתָא בְּגָלוּתָא, שַׁחֲרוּת הַשַּׁחַר בְּע' שְׁנִין בַּתְרָאִין, בְּהַהוּא זִמְנָא יִתְקַיֵּים בְּיִשְׂרָאֵל, כְּמוֹ הָרָה תַּקְרִיב לָלֶדֶת תָּחִיל תִּזְעַק בַּחֲבָלֶיהָ כֵּן הָיִינוּ מִפָּנֶיךָ יְיָ'. וְעַל כֵּן נְקַוֶּה לָךְ יְיָ' אֱלֹהֵינוּ.

474. Hence, "the chief musician (Heb. *lamenatzeach*)," WRITTEN BEFORE, "MAY HASHEM HEAR YOU IN THE DAY OF TROUBLE," is spelled *Netzach* and *Lamed-Mem,* AS THE WORD *LAMNATZEACH* IS SPELLED *LAMED-MEM-NETZACH,* SINCE THE PREVALENCE OF DAWN IS FOREVER (HEB. *NETZACH*). THE NUMERICAL VALUE OF *LAMED-MEM* IS SEVENTY, which

are the seventy sounds that the dow of dawn cries out for her children when
the darkness of the exile overcomes them, NAMELY the darkness (Heb.
shacharut) of dawn (Heb. *shachar*) taking place at the last seventy years. At
that time will be fulfilled in Yisrael: "Like a woman with child, that draws
near the time of her delivery, is in pain, and cries out in her pangs; so have
we been in Your sight, Hashem" (Yeshayah 26:17). And SO SINCE THE
SHECHINAH SUFFERS WITH US, "And therefore we hope for You, Hashem
our Elohim," THAT YOU WILL REDEEM US.

475. וּבְהוֹן אַיֶּלֶת אֲעֵילַת רֵישָׁהָא בֵּין בִּרְכָּהָא. רֵישָׁא, אִיהוּ צַדִּיק יְסוֹד
עוֹלָם. בֵּין בִּרְכָּהָא דְּאִינּוּן נֶצַח וְהוֹד. וְאוֹמֵי לָהּ בֵּיהּ, לְמִפְרַק לִבְנָהָא
בַּבֹּקֶר, דְּאִיהוּ אַרְיֵה בֹּקֶר יְמִינָא דְּאַבְרָהָם, מָשִׁיחַ בֶּן דָּוִד דְּנָפִיק
מִיהוּדָה, דְּאִתְּמַר בֵּיהּ, גּוּר אַרְיֵה יְהוּדָה. וּבְג"ד, חַי יְיָ' שִׁכְבִי עַד
הַבֹּקֶר.

475. And with them, MEANING THE SEVENTY SOUNDS OF THE DOW,
BEING THE SHECHINAH, She places Her head between Her knees. Her
head is the righteous, the Foundation of the World, and between Her knees
are Netzach and Hod; and he takes an oath BY THE RIGHTEOUS to redeem
Her children in the morning, which is a lion, NAMELY CHESED REFERRED
TO AS 'LION'. The morning alludes to the right hand of Abraham,
DEPICTING CHESED, ALLUDING TO Messiah, the son of David, who stems
from Judah, about whom it is written, "Judah is a lion's whelp" (Beresheet
49:9). For this reason, THE VERSE SAYS, "as Hashem lives: lie down until
the morning" (Rut 3:13), UNTIL THE APPEARANCE OF MESSIAH, THE SON
OF DAVID, WHO IS CALLED 'A LION', AND IS MORNING, NAMELY THE
LIGHT OF CHESED.

476. וּבָהּ מוֹלִיךְ לִימִין מֹשֶׁה זְרוֹעַ תִּפְאַרְתּוֹ בּוֹקֵעַ מַיִם וְגוֹ', בְּגִין
דְּתִפְאֶרֶת דַּרְגָּא דְּמֹשֶׁה גּוּפָא, וְחֶסֶד דְּרוֹעָא דִּילֵיהּ, וּמֹשֶׁה אִתְקְשַׁר
בְּע"ב דְּאִיהוּ חֶסֶד, דַּרְגָּא דְּאַבְרָהָם. דְּהָכִי סָלִיק בְּחוּשְׁבָּן ח"י. וו"ו מִן
וַיִּסַּע וַיָּבֹא וַיֵּט, תְּלַת עַנְפֵי אֲבָהָן. שׁ, דְּאִתְקְשַׁר בְּשׁ' שֶׁל מֹשֶׁה. דְּאִתְּמַר
בְּהוֹן וּפְנֵי אַרְיֵה אֶל הַיָּמִין לְאַרְבַּעְתָּן וּפְנֵי שׁוֹר מֵהַשְּׂמֹאל וְגוֹ', וּפְנֵי
נֶשֶׁר לְאַרְבַּעְתָּן. מ"ה מִן מֹשֶׁה, וּדְמוּת פְּנֵיהֶם פְּנֵי אָדָם.

476. "That caused His glorious (*tiferet*) arm to go at the right hand of Moses, dividing the water..." (Yeshayah 63:12) since Tiferet, the level of Moses, is considered a body THAT INCLUDES ALL SIX SFIROT – CHESED, GVURAH, TIFERET, NETZACH, HOD, AND YESOD. Chesed is His RIGHT arm. Moses is bound by THE NAME *Ayin-Bet,* Chesed, WHICH IS the level of Abraham, AS *AYIN-BET* is the numerical total of FOUR TIMES eighteen ('living') – three *Vav's* (= 18) AT THE BEGINNING OF THE THREE VERSES OF "And the angel...removed...and it came... And Moses stretched out" (Shemot 14:19-21), BEING THE SECRET OF THE NAME *AYIN-BET,* containing the three branches of the fathers, CHESED, GVURAH, AND TIFERET, AS "AND REMOVED" DENOTES CHESED; "AND CAME" DENOTES GVURAH, AND "AND STRETCHED OUT" DENOTES TIFERET. THEY ARE THREE TIMES EIGHTEEN BOUND with the *Shin* of Moses THAT CONTAINS THREE BRANCHES, WHICH IS THE SECRET OF THE THREE FACES, LION-OX-EAGLE. As it is said about them: "and the four had the face of a lion, on the right side: the face of an ox on the left side, and also had the face of an eagle" (Yechezkel 1:10); THEY DENOTE CHESED, GVURAH, AND TIFERET. The *Mem-Hei* of the name Moses IS "As for the likeness of their faces, they had the face of a man" (Ibid.), DENOTING MALCHUT AS "ADAM ('MAN')", WHICH EQUALS *MEM-HEI,* BEING THE FOURTH EIGHTEEN – THIS BEING THE SECRET OF "AS HASHEM LIVES (HEB. *CHAI*=EIGHTEEN): LIE DOWN UNTIL THE MORNING" (RUTH 3:13). THROUGH THE MORNING LIGHT IS COMPLETED THE FOURTH EIGHTEEN, WHICH IS MALCHUT, AND THE NAME *AYIN BET* THAT ENCOMPASSES FOUR TIMES EIGHTEEN IN THE FOUR FACES OF THE CHARIOT INDICATED WITH THE *SHIN* OF MOSES AND WITH THE *MEM-HEI* OF MOSES.

18. Two Messiahs

A Synopsis

This section begins by telling of Messiah son of Ephraim. Later it says that the verse, "May He have dominion also from sea to sea, and from the river to the ends of the earth," will be fulfilled in Messiah. The flag of Messiah son of David will come, and the flag of Messiah son of Joseph will come; the flag of Moses will be in the middle or central column. Messiah son of Joseph will consume the ministers of world nations, and Messiah son of David will divide the spoils for the children of Yisrael. At that time, no more converts will be accepted. Yisrael is compared to the five grains, crushed during the exile; once they are sorted from the straw, i.e. the other nations, they will assemble at the place called Jerusalem. After leaving exile they are compared to apples and other fragrant things.

477. דְּרוֹעָא שְׂמָאלָא, אִתְּמַר בֵּיהּ, שְׂמֹאל דּוֹחָה, וְיָמִין מְקָרֶבֶת. דְּאַף עַל גַּב דְּאַקְדִּים בְּתִשְׁרֵי, דְּאוֹקְמוּהָ בֵּיהּ מָארֵי מַתְנִיתִין, בְּתִשְׁרֵי עֲתִידִין לְהִגָּאֵל. תְּהֵא דּוֹחָה, בְּגִין דְּלָא יָמוּת מָשִׁיחַ בֶּן אֶפְרַיִם, דּוֹחָה מִתִּשְׁרֵי דְּאִיהִי שְׂמֹאל. עַד דְּיִקְרַב יָמִין, פֶּסַח דְּרוֹעָא יְמִינָא. לְקַיֵּים בָּהּ, כִּימֵי צֵאתְךָ מֵאֶרֶץ מִצְרַיִם אַרְאֶנּוּ נִפְלָאוֹת וְהַאי אִיהוּ בְּנִיסָן נִגְאֲלוּ וּבְנִיסָן עֲתִידִין לְהִגָּאֵל. לְקַיֵּים בְּהוֹן וּבְחֶסֶד עֶלְיוֹן רַחֲמָתִיךְ אָמַר גּוֹאֲלֵךְ יְיָ'.

477. Of the left arm, DENOTING GVURAH, it is written: "the left pushes aside, the right brings near"; even though he sped up THE TIME FOR REDEMPTION to the month of *Tishrei*, as the masters of Mishnah have posited that in *Tishrei* shall be the Redemption, SINCE *TISHREI* IS CONSIDERED THE LEFT SIDE OF MONTHS, it will delay THE REDEMPTION in order that the Messiah, son of Ephraim, will not die BY THE JUDGMENTS OF THE LEFT. FOR MESSIAH, SON OF EPHRAIM, IS THE REINCARNATION OF YARAVAM WHO HAS ACCUSERS UPON HIM FOR SINNING AND CAUSING OTHERS TO SIN. So it was deferred from *Tishrei* until the approach of the right, namely *Pesach* (Passover) considered the right arm, DENOTING CHESED. THEN WILL THEY BE REDEEMED to fulfill the verse, "As in the days of your coming out of the land of Egypt I will show him marvelous things" (Michah 7:15). Hence, it is stated: "they were redeemed

in Nissan, and in Nissan will they again be redeemed," to fulfill the prophecy, "but with everlasting faithful Love will I have Mercy on you, says your Redeemer, Hashem" (Yeshayah 54:8).

478. וּלְבָתַר נַטְלֵי כֻּלְהוּ מִגְּבוּרָה, דְּמִנֵּיהּ מָשִׁיחַ בֶּן אֶפְרַיִם, לְנַטְלָא נוּקְמָא מִשַּׂנְאוֹי. דְּהָכִי בָּעֵי לְנַקָאָה עִבּוּרָא, דְּאִינּוּן יִשְׂרָאֵל, בִּימִינָא. וּלְבָתַר לְאוֹקְדָא קַשׁ, בִּשְׂמָאלָא. הַה״ד, וְהָיָה בֵית יַעֲקֹב אֵשׁ וּבֵית יוֹסֵף לֶהָבָה וּבֵית עֵשָׂו לְקַשׁ וְדָלְקוּ בָּהֶם וַאֲכָלוּם. וּכְנִישׁוּ דְּעִבּוּרָא, דָּא עַמּוּדָא דְּאֶמְצָעִיתָא. בֵּיהּ וַיֵּאָסֶף. לְאָן אֲתַר. לְבֵיתָא, דָּא שְׁכִינְתָּא.

478. And later, all are taking from Gvurah, whence comes Messiah, the son of Ephraim, to avenge his enemies. So it is necessary first to cleanse the grain, namely Yisrael, with the right. Later, it is necessary to burn the stubble which is with the left. As it is written: "The House of Jacob shall be fire, and the House of Joseph flame, and the House of Esau for stubble, and they shall kindle in them, and devour them" (Ovadyah 1:18). The gathering of the grain will be with the Central Column, where IT IS SAID, "and was gathered" (Beresheet 25:8). Where ASSEMBLED to? To the House, which is the Shechinah.

479. אֲבָל בְּדַרְגָּא דִּמְשִׁיחַ בֶּן יוֹסֵף, אִיהוּ דְּקָא רָמִיז, עַתָּה יְלַחֲכוּ הַקָּהָל אֶת כָּל סְבִיבֹתֵינוּ כִּלְחֹךְ הַשּׁוֹר אֵת יֶרֶק הַשָּׂדֶה. דַּעֲלַיְיהוּ אִתְּמַר, בִּפְרֹחַ רְשָׁעִים כְּמוֹ עֵשֶׂב וְגוֹ'. מִפֶּסַח וְעַד תִּשְׁרֵי, יְהֵא פּוּרְקָנָא דְּאִיהוּ עַד. וּמִתַּמָּן וְאֵילָךְ יְהֵא הַשְׁמָדָה דִּלְהוֹן, לְהִשָּׁמְדָם עֲדֵי עַד. כַּד מָטוּ לְתִשְׁרֵי דְּאִיהוּ שׁוֹר, בֵּיהּ כִּלְחֹךְ הַשּׁוֹר.

479. But of the level of Messiah, son of Joseph, it is indicated: "Now shall this company lick up all that are round about us, as the ox licks up the grass of the field" (Bemidbar 22:4), REFERRING TO MESSIAH, THE SON OF JOSEPH, CALLED 'Ox'. About them it is written: "When wicked spring like grass" (Tehilim 92:8). From *Pesach* until *Tishrei* will be the Redemption CALLED 'forever'; from then on will come their destruction, as written, "that they shall be destroyed forever" (Ibid.), until *Tishrei* arrives, being an ox. Then it will be fulfilled, "as the ox licks."

480. וּסְמִיכָה דִּלְהוֹן דְּיִשְׂרָאֵל, בִּימִינָא דְּאִיהוּ אַרְיֵה. אֲבָל קִימָה

דִּלְהוֹן בְּגוּפָא דְּאִילָנָא. וְהַאי אִיהוּ כָּל הַכּוֹרֵעַ כּוֹרֵעַ בְּבָרוּךְ, צַדִּיק. דְּאִתְּמַר בֵּיהּ בְּיוֹסֵף הַצַּדִּיק, וְהִנֵּה תְּסֻבֶּינָה אֲלֻמֹּתֵיכֶם וַתִּשְׁתַּחֲוֶיןָ לַאֲלֻמָּתִי. וְהַאי אִיהוּ, חַי יְיָ' שְׁכְבִי עַד הַבֹּקֶר. וְכָל הַזּוֹקֵף זוֹקֵף בְּשֵׁם, דַּרְגָּא דְּמֹשֶׁה רַבֵּינוּ לְעֵילָא. וּמֹשֶׁה לְתַתָּא, בֵּיהּ יְקוּמוּן כָּל יִשְׂרָאֵל, כְּאַבְרִין דְּגוּפָא, דְּבֵיהּ כֻּלְּהוּ זְקִיפִין בַּעֲמִידָה. וּבְהַאי אִיהוּ כָּל הַזּוֹקֵף, זוֹקֵף בְּשֵׁם, בְּגִין דְּעָלֵיהּ אִתְּמַר, וָאֵדָעֲךָ בְּשֵׁם.

480. The support of Yisrael DURING THE EXILE is with the right, namely the lion, CHESED, but their rising, THEIR REDEMPTION, is in the trunk of the tree, DENOTING ZEIR ANPIN. Therefore, kneeling is always with the mention of 'blessed be', DENOTING THE RIGHTEOUS, MEANING YESOD, as it is written: "and, behold, your sheaves stood round about, and bowed to my sheaf" (Beresheet 37:7). This is what is written: "as Hashem lives: lie down until the morning" (Rut 3:13). FOR IN THEIR SITUATION OF KNEELING AND LYING, THEY REQUIRE SUPPORT OF CHASSADIM FROM YESOD. Rising is at the mention of "name," being the level of the Moses above, DENOTING DA'AT. With Moses below, DENOTING TIFERET, will all the children of Yisrael rise as the limbs of the body. When all line up at the time of standing, with this all who straighten themselves do so by the "name," about which it is written: "and I know you by name" (Shemot 33:17).

481. יְהוֹן מָשִׁיחַ מִן דָּוִד, דְּאִיהוּ אַרְיֵה, מִימִינֵיהּ. וּמָשִׁיחַ בֶּן יוֹסֵף, דְּאִיהוּ שׁוֹר, מִשְּׂמָאלֵיהּ. מִימִינָא אַבְרָהָם, מִשְּׂמָאלָא יִצְחָק, וְאִיהוּ נֶשֶׁר בְּאֶמְצָעִיתָא. שַׁלְשֶׁלֶת דִּלְהוֹן, מִסִּטְרָא דְיַעֲקֹב. שׁ' דְּמֹשֶׁה, קְדוּשָׁה לְךָ יְשַׁלֵּשׁוּ. מִסִּטְרָא דְּאַרְיֵה, ג' אַנְפִּין דַּאֲבָהָן, אִתְקְרִיאוּ אֲרָיוֹת. בָּקָר. מִסִּטְרָא דִשְׂמָאלָא אִתְקְרִיאוּ פָּרִים מְנַגְּחִים. וּמִסִּטְרָא דְּאֶמְצָעִיתָא, אִתְקְרִיאוּ נְשָׂרִים. וַעֲלַיְיהוּ אִתְּמַר וָאֶשָּׂא אֶתְכֶם עַל כַּנְפֵי נְשָׁרִים וָאָבִיא אֶתְכֶם אֵלָי. הָא אִינּוּן ט'. עֲשִׂירָאָה, וּרְבִיעָאָה, אָדָם מַה בִּשְׁמוֹ דְּמֹשֶׁה דְּרָכִיב עַל תְּלַת חֵיוָון.

481. Messiah, the son of David, designated as the lion, CHESED, will be to the right of Moses and Messiah, the son of Joseph, designated as an Ox, GVURAH, to his left – MEANING WITHIN THE SECRET OF THE THREE

COLUMNS, where on the right stands Abraham, DEPICTING CHESED, to the left Isaac, DEPICTING GVURAH, and Moses himself depicted as an eagle, TIFERET, stands in the middle. Their chain, MEANING THE THREE COLUMNS REFERRED TO AS 'CHAIN', stems from Jacob, MEANING THREE COLUMNS INCORPORATED IN JACOB BEING TIFERET. This is the secret of the *Shin* in the name Moses, ALLUDING TO THE THREE COLUMNS INCORPORATED IN MOSES, BEING THE CENTRAL COLUMN. DA'AT, THE SECRET OF 'thrice repeat holy unto You'; MEANING THAT EVERY COLUMN IS COMPOSED OF ALL THE THREE. From the side of the lion, DENOTING CHESED, there are three facets of the fathers, CHESED, GVURAH, AND TIFERET, and all THREE are called 'lions'. The cattle, MEANING FROM THREE FACETS in the left, THE THREE are called 'goring oxen'. NOW THE THREE FACETS INCLUDED in the central Column, WHICH IS MOSES AND JACOB, are called 'eagles'. Of them it is said: "I bore you on the wings of eagles and brought you to Myself" (Shemot 19:4). THE RESULT IS THAT THE THREE COLUMNS become nine, AS EACH IS COMPOSED OF THREE. The tenth, or the fourth OF THE THREE ENCOMPASSING COLUMNS, is Adam ('man') who is the *Mem-Hei* of the name Moses, riding over the three living creatures, LION, OX, EAGLE – BEING THREE BRANCHES OF THE *SHIN* IN THE NAME OF MOSES.

482. וְאִתְּמַר בְּיִשְׂרָאֵל, וְיִרְדוּ בִדְגַת הַיָּם, מִמְּנָן דְּיַמָּא, בְּסִטְרָא דְּנָחָשׁ, דַּהֲוָה שָׂרָה דְּמִצְרַיִם, דְּאִתְפָּשַׁט בְּגָלוּתָא בַּתְרָאָה, מַיִם עַד יָם. וּבְעוֹף הַשָּׁמַיִם, עִרְבּוּבְיָא בִּישָׁא. עֲמָלֵקִים, נְפִילִים, תַּעֲרוֹבֶת דְּכָל אוּמִין, בְּכָל סִטְרָא, בְּגָלוּתָא בַּתְרָאָה, בֵּין בְּיִשְׂרָאֵל, בֵּין בְּיִשְׁמָעֵאל, בֵּין בְּעֵשָׂו. וּבַבְּהֵמָה, אִלֵּין בְּנֵי עֵשָׂו. דְּשׁוּלְטָנִתְהוֹן בְּכָל הָאָרֶץ.

482. It is written regarding Yisrael: "and let them have dominion over the fish of the sea" (Beresheet 1:26), MEANING the ministers in the sea from the sphere of the serpent, the Minister of Egypt that will expand with the last exile, from sea to sea. "...and over the birds of the air..." (Ibid.) refers to the evil crowd of giant Amalekites, a mixture of all nations in the last exile from all spheres, either Yisrael, Ishmael or Esau. "...and over the cattle..." refers exclusively to the children of Esau, whose dominion is over all the earth.

483. וְיִתְקַיֵּים בְּמָשִׁיחַ, וְיֵרְדְּ מִיָּם עַד יָם וּמִנָּהָר עַד אַפְסֵי אָרֶץ. וְהָכִי

בְּב' מְשִׁיחִין, וְהָכִי בְּיִשְׂרָאֵל, וְכֹלָּא בִּזְכוּת מ"ה דְּמֹשֶׁה. וְיֵיתוּן, נֵס
דִּמְשִׁיחַ בֶּן דָּוִד, מִיהוּדָה, אַרְיֵה רָשִׁים עָלֵיהּ, וְנֵס דִּמְשִׁיחַ בֶּן יוֹסֵף, שׁוֹר
רָשִׁים עָלֵיהּ. וְנֵס דְּשִׁילֹה, אַרְיֵה לִימִינָא, שׁוֹר לִשְׂמָאלָא, נֶשֶׁר
בְּאֶמְצָעִיתָא, וְאָדָם עַל כֻּלְּהוּ. וְד' אַנְפִּין לְכָל חַד. ד' שִׁבְטִין דְּג' חֵיוָן,
י"ב. וּלְגַבֵּי אָדָם, דְּאִיהוּ מַה שְׁמוֹ, בְּנֵי מֹשֶׁה, דִּבְהַהוּא זִמְנָא יִתְקַיֵּים
בְּמֹשֶׁה וְאֶעֱשֶׂה אוֹתְךָ לְגוֹי גָּדוֹל וְעָצוּם מִמֶּנּוּ. בְּהַהוּא זִמְנָא, מַ"ה
שֶׁ"הָיָה הוּ"א שֶׁיִּהְיֶה. וַאֲשֶׁר לִהְיוֹת כְּבָר הָיָה.

483. The verse, "May He have dominion also from sea to sea, and from the river to the ends of the earth" (Tehilim 72:8), will be fulfilled in Messiah. And so with the two Messiahs, and so with the children of Yisrael, all through the merit of the *Mem-Hei* in the name of Moses (*Mem-Shin-Hei*), BEING THE FACE OF MAN. The flag of Messiah, the son of David, will come, BEING of Judah, with a lion marked upon it, and the flag of Messiah, the son of Joseph, on which is the mark of an ox, and the flag of Shilo, BEING MOSES, AS HIS NAME NUMERICALLY EQUALS *SHILO*. And so, we have the lion to the right, ox to the left, and eagle in the middle, AS MOSES IS THE SECRET OF THE EAGLE, NAMELY, THE CENTRAL COLUMN THAT INCORPORATES WITHIN IT RIGHT AND LEFT. The man is above all, AS IN EACH OF THE THREE FACES A MAN IS INCLUDED, as each OF THREE CREATURES has four faces – BEING THE SECRET of the four tribes, each having three living creatures, LION, OX, AND EAGLE, totaling twelve. By the FACE OF man, which is the *Mem-Hei* of his name, MEANING THE VALUE OF WHAT (HEB. *MAH, MEM-HEI*) WILL BE the sons of Moses; for at that time, will be fulfilled in Moses, "and will make of you a greater nation and mightier than they" (Bemidbar 14:12). At that time "That (Heb. *mah, Mem-Hei*) which (*Shin*) has been, it is that which shall be" (Kohelet 1:9), MEANING MOSES WAS THE REDEEMER IN EGYPT, AND HE WILL BE THE FUTURE REDEEMER. "...and that which is to be has already been..." (Kohelet 3:15) MEANING THE TWO MESSIAHS, SON OF JOSEPH AND SON OF DAVID, AS JOSEPH AND DAVID ALREADY EXISTED.

484. וְהָאֱלֹהִים יְבַקֵּשׁ אֶת נִרְדָּף, יִשְׂרָאֵל דְּאִתְּמַר בְּהוֹן, וְאַתֵּן צֹאנִי
צֹאן מַרְעִיתִי אָדָם אַתֶּם, הֲווֹ נִרְדָּפִים קֳדָם עֵרֶב רַב, דְּאִבִים בִּישִׁין, הָא
בִּנְיָמִין זְאֵב יִטְרָף לְגַבַּיְיהוּ, דְּטָרִיף לוֹן, וְיִתְקַיֵּים בְּהַהוּא זִמְנָא, בַּבֹּקֶר

יֹאכַל עַד. דְּהַיְינוּ עַד כִּי יָבֹא שִׁילֹה, וְדָא בֹּקֶר דְּאַבְרָהָם. וְלָעֶרֶב יְחַלֵּק שָׁלָל דָּא עֶרֶב דְּיִצְחָק, דְּתַמָּן תְּרֵין מְשִׁיחִין. בְּחַד יֵיכוּל מְמָנָא דְּאוּמִּין דְּעָלְמָא. וּבְחַד יְחַלֵּק לוֹן לְיִשְׂרָאֵל.

484. "...and only the Elohim can find the fleeting..." (ibid.) NAMELY the children of Yisrael, of whom it is said: "But you my flock, the flock of my pasture, are men" (Yechezkel 34:31). They were the pursued before the motley crowd, evil wolves. "Benjamin is a ravenous wolf" (Beresheet 49:27) against them, that rends them. And then will be fulfilled: "in the morning he shall devour the prey (Heb. *ad*)" (Ibid.), meaning "until (Heb. *ad*) Shiloh comes" (Ibid. 11), REFERRING TO MOSES – the morning being the morning of Abraham, DEPICTING CHESED, MEANING, IN THE MORNING, WHEN THE GREAT CHESED BECOMES REVEALED, THEN *Ad*, WHO IS MOSES, WILL BE REVEALED. "...and at night he shall divide the spoil..." refers to the evening of Isaac, MALCHUT BUILT FROM THE LEFT COLUMN, where both Messiahs are located – TO HER RIGHT, MESSIAH, THE SON OF DAVID, TO HER LEFT MESSIAH, THE SON OF JOSEPH. One will consume AND DEVASTATE the ministers of world nations, THIS BEING THE ONE FROM THE HOUSE OF JOSEPH, and the other will divide the spoils for the children of Yisrael, THIS BEING THE ONE FROM THE HOUSE OF DAVID.

485. יִשְׂרָאֵל דְּאִינּוּן אַיֶּלֶת, נִרְדְּפִין קֳדָם רַשִׁיעַיָּא אַרְיָוֹת. וְיִתְעַר נַפְתָּלִי, דְּאִיהוּ אַיָּלָה שְׁלוּחָה הַנּוֹתֵן אִמְרֵי שָׁפֶר. יִתְעַר בִּימִינָא דְּאִיהוּ אַרְיֵה מְשִׁיחַ בֶּן דָּוִד, דְּאִתְּמַר בֵּיהּ, גּוּר אַרְיֵה יְהוּדָה מִטֶּרֶף בְּנִי עָלִיתָ. וְיַחֲזוֹר עַל אוּמִּין דְּעָלְמָא, כָּרַע שָׁכַב עֲלַיְיהוּ, לְמִטְרַף לוֹן מִי יְקִימֶנּוּ, בְּהַהוּא זִמְנָא נֶחֱזֵי מַאן הוּא אֱלָהּ אַחֲרָא, דְּיָקִים לֵיהּ מִלְּטָרוֹף עֲלַיְיהוּ, אוֹ אוּמָה וְלִישָׁן.

485. Yisrael, who are as a doe, are pursued by the wicked, who are lions. This will alert Naftali, who is "a hind let loose: he gives goodly words" (Ibid. 21). It will alert on the right the lion, Messiah, the son of David, about whom it is written: "Judah is a lion whelp from the prey, my son, you have gone up" (Ibid. 9), and he will go around to the nations of the world. "...he stooped down, he crouched..." upon them, to devour them; "who shall rouse

him up," MEANING at that time, what deity can rouse him AND NOT PERMIT HIM to devour them, or what nation WILL BE ABLE TO RISE TO STOP HIM FROM EATING THEM.

486. וְיִשְׂרָאֵל דַּהֲווֹ כַּיּוֹנָה, נִרְדְּפִין קֳדָם נֶשֶׁר, מִסִּטְרָא דְּעוֹפִין דְּאוּמִין דְּעָלְמָא. בְּהַהוּא זִמְנָא, יִתְּעַר נֶשֶׁר, וְיִתְפְּרַשׁ גַּדְפָהָא, עַל עִרְבּוּבְיָא דְּאוּמִין, וְעֵשָׂו וְיִשְׁמָעֵאל, דְּאִינּוּן עֲמָלֵקִים, וְעִרְבּוּבְיָא בִּישָׁא דְּיִשְׂרָאֵל, וְטָרִיף לוֹן, דְּלָא יִשְׁתְּאַר חַד מִנַּיְיהוּ, לְקַיֵּים מַה שֶׁנֶּאֱמַר בְּיִשְׂרָאֵל, יְיָ' בָּדָד יַנְחֶנּוּ וְאֵין עִמּוֹ אֵל נֵכָר.

486. And Yisrael are like a dove pursued by the eagle, representing the birds of the nations of the world. At that time will be aroused the eagle OF HOLINESS. He shall spread his wings upon the mixed multitudes, Esau, Ishmael, Amalekites, and the evil multitudes of Yisrael, and devour them. And not one will remain, to fulfill that which is written about Yisrael: "so Hashem alone did lead him, and there was no strange El with him" (Devarim 32:12).

487. מִתַּמָּן וְאֵילָךְ, אֵין מְקַבְּלִים גֵּרִים, כְּמָה דְּאוּקְמוּהָ מָארֵי מַתְנִיתִין אֵין מְקַבְּלִים גֵּרִים לִימוֹת הַמָּשִׁיחַ. וְאוּמִין עכו"ם דְּעָלְמָא דְּיִשְׁתָּאֲרוּן, יִתְּעַר קוּדְשָׁא בְּרִיךְ הוּא חַיָּה דְּאָדָם, לְשַׁלְטָאָה עָלַיְיהוּ. לְקַיְּימָא בְּהוֹן, כִּי הַגּוֹי וְהַמַּמְלָכָה אֲשֶׁר לֹא יַעַבְדוּךְ יֹאבֵדוּ. לְקַיֵּים בְּיִשְׂרָאֵל, וְיִרְדּוּ בִדְגַת הַיָּם וְגוֹ'. וּמוֹרַאֲכֶם וְחִתְּכֶם וְגוֹ'.

487. From that time on, no converts will be accepted, as the masters of the Mishnah have expressed it: At the days of Messiah, no converts will be accepted. The nations of the world that will remain will see the Holy One, blessed be He, stir upon them the beasts of man, to fulfill the words of the prophet: "For the nation and kingdom that will not serve you shall perish" (Yeshayah 60:12), and to fulfill with Yisrael: "and let them have dominion over the fish of the sea..." "And the fear of you and the dread of you..." (Beresheet 9:2).

488. וּמִסִּטְרָא דִּתְבוּאוֹת, ה' מִינֵי נָהֲמָא, תְּבִירִין מִכֻּלְּהוּ. וְאִינּוּן, חִטָּה, וּשְׂעוֹרָה, וּכְסֶמֶת, וְשִׁבֹּלֶת שׁוּעָל, וְשִׁיפוֹן. אִמְתִיל לוֹן לְיִשְׂרָאֵל, הֲה"ד,

קֹדֶשׁ יִשְׂרָאֵל לַיְיָ' רֵאשִׁית תְּבוּאָתֹה, בְּה'. כַּד יִפְּקוּן מִגָּלוּתָא, הָכִי יְהוֹן תְּבִירִין, עַד דְּיִתְבְּרִיר אוֹכֵל מִתּוֹךְ פְּסֹלֶת, דְּהַיְינוּ קַשׁ, עֵרֶב רַב, עַד דְּיִתְבָּרְרוּ וְיִשְׁתְּמוֹדְעוּ יִשְׂרָאֵל בֵּינַיְיהוּ, כְּבָר, דְּאִתְבְּרִיר מִגּוֹ מוֹץ וָתֶבֶן.

488. Now from the subject of grain, five types of bread that are the most broken of them all, WITH THE THRESHING AND MELTING, are wheat, barley, spelt, rye, and oats. Yisrael have been compared to them, as it says: "Yisrael is holy to Hashem, the firstfruits of his increase (Heb. *tevuatoh*, also: 'grain')" (Yirmeyah 2:3). *Tevuatoh* is written with *Hei* (= 5) TO ALLUDE TO THE FIVE TYPES OF BREAD. When YISRAEL will exit the exile, they will be broken so that the edible will be collected from the refuse, the straw, which is the mixed multitude, until Yisrael will be picked and recognizable from them, already picked from the straw and hay.

489. וְעַד דְּיִתְבְּרִירוּ מִנַּיְיהוּ, י' דְּאִיהוּ מַעֲשֵׂר, לָא שַׁרְיָא עַל ה', דְּאִיהוּ נַהֲמָא, דְּה' מִינִין, לְקַיְּימָא אוּמָאָה, כִּי יָד עַל כֵּס יָ"ה. וּבְגִין דָּא, מוֹץ וָתֶבֶן, אֵינוּ מְחוּיָּיב בְּמַעֲשֵׂר, עַד דְּיִתְבְּרִיר. לְבָתַר דְּיִתְבְּרִיר, מִתְכַּנְּשִׁין לְהַהוּא אֲתָר דְּאִקְרֵי יְרוּשָׁלֶם. כְּמָה דְחִטָּה, דְּבָתַר דְּאִתְבְּרִיר קַשׁ וָתֶבֶן, מַכְנִיסִין לָהּ לְאוֹצָר. הָכִי יִתְכַּנְּשׁוּן יִשְׂרָאֵל, דְּאִינּוּן בַּר, לִירוּשְׁלֵם, דְּאִיהִי בְּנוּיָה עַל הַר יְיָ', דְּאִתְּמַר בָּהּ, מִי יַעֲלֶה בְהַר יְיָ' וּמִי יָקוּם בִּמְקוֹם קָדְשׁוֹ נְקִי כַפַּיִם וּבַר לְבָב. נָקִי כַּבָּר, דְּאִיהִי עֲבוּרָא כַּד בָּרִיר מִגּוֹ פְּסֹלֶת. בְּהַהוּא זִמְנָא, נַשְׁקוּ בַר כְּדִבְקַדְמֵיתָא, דְּאִתְּמַר בֵּיהּ, יִשָּׁקֵנִי מִנְּשִׁיקוֹת פִּיהוּ. בַּר תַּרְגּוּם בֵּן, בְּהַהוּא זִמְנָא דִּיהוֹן נְקִיִּים כַּבָּר, מִגּוֹ קַשׁ וָתֶבֶן. שַׁרְיָא שְׁמֵיהּ עָלַיְיהוּ, וְקָרָא לוֹן, בְּנִי בְכוֹרִי יִשְׂרָאֵל.

489. Until they are sorted, the *Yud* OF THE NAME YUD HEI VAV HEI, which INDICATES THE tithe, does not rest upon the *Hei* OF YUD HEI VAV HEI, which HINTS AT THE bread of the five kinds, thus fulfilling the oath: "Because Yah has sworn by his throne" (Shemot 17:16) – THE OATH BEING THAT THE NAME AND THE THRONE REMAIN INCOMPLETE UNTIL THE ERADICATION OF THE SEED OF AMALEK. Therefore, chaff and straw are not subject to tithing until it is all sorted. After THE CHILDREN OF YISRAEL are picked, they will assemble at that place called Jerusalem. Like wheat

after the removal of chaff and straw is brought into the storehouse, so Yisrael will gather, which are grains, to Jerusalem that is built on the mountain of Hashem, as it is written; "Who shall ascend into the mountain of Hashem? Or who stand in His holy place? He that has clean hands, and a pure (Heb. *bar*) heart" (Tehilim 24:3-4). "…clean…" is the corn (Heb. *bar*), meaning grain after it was sorted out of the chaff. At that time, his kisses are clean (Heb. *bar*) as the verse says, "Let him kiss me with the kisses of his mouth" (Shir Hashirim 1:2). *Bar* is Aramaic for son meaning at that time after being cleansed from chaff and straw (Heb. *bar*) His name will hover over them and will call them, "Yisrael is My son, My firstborn" (Shemot 4:22).

490. וְהָכִי מִכָּל אִילָנִין, לֵית תְּבִיר כַּגֶּפֶן. בִּנְטִיעוּ דִּילֵיהּ תְּבִיר, בַּעֲנָבִים דִּילֵיהּ תְּבִיר, דְּאִינּוּן כְּתִישִׁין בֵּין רַגְלִין. וְהָכִי זַיִת זֵיתִים דִּילָהּ כְּתִישִׁין. בְּגָלוּתָא אַמְתִּילוּ יִשְׂרָאֵל בְּהוֹן, הה"ד, גֶּפֶן מִמִּצְרַיִם תַּסִּיעַ. וְכֵן בְּגָלוּת רְבִיעָאָה, כִּי כֶרֶם יְיָ' צְבָאוֹת בֵּית יִשְׂרָאֵל. וּכְגַוְונָא דָא לַזַּיִת מְשׁוּלִים יִשְׂרָאֵל, זַיִת רַעֲנָן יְפֵה פְרִי תֹאַר. וּבְגִין דָּא, אֶשְׁתְּךָ כְּגֶפֶן פּוֹרִיָּה בְּיַרְכְּתֵי בֵיתֶךָ בָּנֶיךָ כִּשְׁתִילֵי זֵיתִים. סָמִיךְ דָּא לְדָא, בְּגִין דְּאִינּוּן תְּבִירִין בְּגָלוּתָא.

490. And so with the trees, no tree is so broken like the vine. In planting, it is hammered, AS IT HAS NO STRENGTH TO STAND BUT LAY ON THE GROUND. Its grapes are broken, crushed under feet. And so the olive is crushed. Yisrael is compared to them in the exile, as written: "You have brought a vine out of Egypt" (Tehilim 80:9). And so in the fourth exile, "For the vineyard of Hashem Tzevaot is the House of Yisrael" (Yeshayah 5:7). And likewise Yisrael is likened to the olive, as it is written, "A green olive tree, fair with goodly fruit" (Yirmeyah 11:16). Therefore, IT IS WRITTEN, "Your wife shall be like a fruitful vine in the recesses of your house: your children like olive plants" (Tehilim 128:3). They here are side by side, because YISRAEL becomes broken LIKE THEM in the exile.

491. וּלְבָתַר דִּיהוֹן נְקִיִּים מִגּוֹ פְּסוֹלֶת, יִתְקַדְּשׁוּן לְבֵי מַקְדְּשָׁא, בְּיַיִן לְנַסְּכָא עַל גַּבֵּי מַדְבְּחָא, וְזֵיתִים לְאַדְלְקָא בּוֹצִינָא שְׁרָגִין לִמְנַרְתָּא. וּמַאן זָכָה לְהַאי. יַיִן דְּלָא יִתְנְסַךְ לכו"ם. דְּעֶרֶב רַב אִינּוּן יַיִן דְּנִתְנְסַךְ לכו"ם, וּמִנְּהוֹן מְשׁוּמָּדִים, מִינִים, אֶפִּיקוֹרְסִים מְשׁוּמָּדִים לַעֲבֵירוֹת

שֶׁבְּכָל הַתּוֹרָה כּוּלָה.

491. After THE GRAPES AND OLIVES are cleaned from all refuse, they become sanctified for the Temple: wine for libation upon the altar, the olives for kindling the candle, MEANING the candles of the lamp. Who merits this? Wine not libated in idolatry. The mixed multitudes are like wine poured for idol worship, among them are apostates and non-believers, that transgress the whole Torah.

492. וְיִשְׂרָאֵל דְּאִתְּמַר בְּהוֹן וַיִּתְעָרְבוּ בַגּוֹיִם וַיִּלְמְדוּ מַעֲשֵׂיהֶם. עַד דְּיהוֹן דְּרוּכִין בֵּין רַגְלַיְיהוּ, בְּגָלוּתָא לָא אִתְבְּרִירוּ מִנַּיְיהוּ. וּבְגִינַיְיהוּ אָמַר דָּוִד ע"ה, לָמָה אִירָא בִּימֵי רָע עֲוֹן עֲקֵבַי יְסַבֵּנִי. וְעָלַיְיהוּ אָמַר שְׁלֹמֹה, צְאִי לָךְ בְּעִקְבֵ"י הַצֹּאן. בְּיַעֲקֹ"ב. דְּעָלֵיה אִתְּמַר, לְגַבֵּי נָחָשׁ הַקַּדְמוֹנִי דְּפַתֵּי לְחַוָּה, הוּא יְשׁוּפְךָ רֹאשׁ וְאַתָּה תְּשׁוּפֶנּוּ עָקֵב. בָּתַר דְּיִפְּקוּן מִן גָּלוּתָא, נִמְשְׁלִים לְתַפּוּחִים, וּלְכָל רֵיחִין טָבִין. כְּגַוְונָא דְּמַפְּקָנוּ דְּמִצְרַיִם, דִּכְתִיב בֵּיה תַּחַת הַתַּפּוּחַ עוֹרַרְתִּיךָ.

492. About Yisrael, it is written, "but were mingled among the nations, and learned their works" (Tehilim 106:35), and until they are trampled under their feet in the exile, they can not be sorted out from them. About them, David of blessed memory said. "Why should I fear in the days of evil, when the iniquity of my persecutors (also: 'heels') compasses me about?" (Tehilim 49:6). About them Solomon said "Go your way forth by the footsteps (Heb. *ikvei*, lit. 'heels') of the flock" (Shir Hashirim 1:8); IKVEI ARE THE SAME LETTERS as Jacob, about him is written concerning the original serpent who seduced Eve, "it shall bruise your head, and you shall bruise his heel" (Beresheet 3:15). After leaving exile, they are compared to apples and all matters of fragrance, as happened when departing Egypt, as it says "I roused you under the apple tree" (Shir Hashirim 8:5).

19. Concerning tithing

A Synopsis

The precept discussed here is to offer the first fruit, then to confess by the first fruit and later to publicly announce the crop by tithing. The question that arises is whether to tithe before or after the fruits and grains are formed. Yisrael are compared to the tree and to grain; they are called a large powerful tree with sustenance for all within it. The Torah is sustenance on high and prayer is sustenance for those below. Even the sustenance for angels comes only through Yisrael because of their Torah study and their following of the precepts. The Torah is compared to water and to fire, both of which are required to ripen fruit (the sun being fire). Those who study the Torah, the Tree of Life, follow the blossoming, and so they are tithed because Chochmah dwells in them.

493. פְּקוּדָא בָּתַר דָּא, לְהָבִיא בִּכּוּרִים, וַאֲבַתְרֵיה לְהִתְוַדּוֹת עַל הַבִּכּוּרִים, וַאֲבַתְרֵיה לְהִתְוַדּוֹת עַל הַמַּעֲשֵׂר. וּמָארֵי מַתְנִיתִין, מַקְשִׁים עַל הַמַּעֲשֵׂר, דְּאִי יְהֵא קֹדֶם לְקִיטָתוֹ, אוֹ אַחַר לְקִיטָתוֹ עִשׂוּרוֹ. כְּגוֹן אֶתְרוֹג, דְּאִתְּמַר בֵּיה בְּאִילָן, הָלַךְ אַחַר חֲנָטָה. אִית מַאן דְּאָמַר, אַחַר בִּשׁוּל הַפֵּירוֹת. וְאֶתְרוֹג מִקְצָתוֹ דּוֹמֶה לְאִילָן, וּמִקְצָתוֹ לַתְּבוּאָה, דְּאִינּוּן זְרָעִים, דְּאִתְּמַר בְּהוֹן, דִּלְאַחַר לְקִיטָתוֹ עִשׂוּרוֹ. דְּאִילָן לָאו אִיהוּ, אֶלָּא עַד אַחַר גְּמַר בִּשׁוּלוֹ.

493. The following precept is to offer the first fruit, and then to confess by the first fruit, later to publicly announce the crop by tithing. The masters of the Mishnah question IN ORDER TO UNDERSTAND concerning tithing, if tithing should take place prior to its gleaning, MEANING FROM TIME OF ITS FORMING SO TITHE ACCORDING TO THAT YEAR or after gleaning. Like the Etrog, where the Rabbis said: In regard to fruits of the tree, you tithe according to the forming of the fruit; some say WITH ETROG, you follow the ripening of the fruits, as the Etrog is similar somewhat to the tree and somewhat to grain, namely seeds, where you tithe according to its forming, and not like trees that follow the rule of ripening, THAT FOLLOWS ITS FORMING GRAIN.

494. וּבג"ד, תַּקִּינוּ הַמּוֹצִיא מֵאַתַר דְּבִשׁוּלוֹ יָפֶה. לְאַפָּקָא פַּת שָׂרוּף,

אֶלָּא מִמָּקוֹם שֶׁהוּא מוּטְעָם. וְהָכִי תְּבוּאָה, בָּתַר לְקִיטָתוֹ, אִיהוּ כְּבִשׁוּל פֵּירוֹת.

494. And because they postulated TO SAY blessing over bread, on that which is well cooked, excluding burnt bread, but rather which tastes good. So with grain, you follow its forming, which is equivalent to ripe fruit. THEN IT IS TASTY.

495. וְיִשְׂרָאֵל, אִינוּן מְשׁוּלִים לְאִילָן וְלַתְּבוּאָה, דְּאִתְּמַר בְּהוֹן רֵאשִׁית בִּכּוּרֵי אַדְמָתְךָ תָּבִיא בֵּית יְיָ' אֱלֹהֶיךָ. וְהָכִי רֵאשִׁית גֵּז צֹאנְךָ תִּתֶּן לוֹ. דְּאִינוּן יִשְׂרָאֵל. דְּאִתְּמַר בְּהוֹן, וְאַתֵּן צֹאנִי. וְהָכִי יִשְׂרָאֵל, קֹדֶשׁ יִשְׂרָאֵל לַיְיָ' רֵאשִׁית תְּבוּאָתֹה, לְאַחַר לְקִיטָתוֹ מִן גָּלוּתָא, עָשׂוּר. וְאִתְקְרִיאוּ קֹדֶשׁ לַיְיָ'.

495. Yisrael are compared to the tree and to grain LIKE ETROG IS TO THE TREE as it is written: "The first of the firstfruits of your land you shall bring to the house of Hashem your Elohim" (Shemot 23:19), and so also, "and the first of the fleece of your sheep shall give him" (Devarim 18:4), HINTING to the children of Yisrael, about whom it is written, "But you My flock" (Yechezkel 34:31). And so Yisrael ARE COMPARED TO GRAIN, AS IT IS WRITTEN "Yisrael is holy to Hashem, the firstfruits of His increase" and so after being picked up from exile, is the term for His tithing; THEN they are called "holy to Hashem."

496. וְיִשְׂרָאֵל אִתְקְרִיאוּ אִילָנָא רַבָּא וְתַקִּיף, וּמָזוֹן לְכֹלָּא בֵּיהּ. בֵּיהּ אוֹרַיְיתָא, דְּאִיהִי מְזוֹנָא לְעֵילָא. בֵּיהּ צְלוֹתָא, דְּאִיהִי מְזוֹנָא לְתַתָּא. וַאֲפִילּוּ מַלְאָכִין לֵית לוֹן מְזוֹנָא, אֶלָּא בְּיִשְׂרָאֵל. דְּאִי לָאו דְּיִשְׂרָאֵל יִתְעַסְּקוּן בְּאוֹרַיְיתָא, לָא הֲוָה נָחִית לוֹן מְזוֹנָא, מִסְטַר דְּאוֹרַיְיתָא, דְּאַמְתִילָא לְעֵץ, הַה"ד, עֵץ חַיִּים הִיא לַמַּחֲזִיקִים בָּהּ. וּלְאִיבָּא, דְּאִיהִי מִצְוָה.

496. And Yisrael are called a large powerful tree with sustenance for all within it. Within is the Torah being sustenance on high, FROM THE ASPECT

OF ZEIR ANPIN. Within is prayer, sustenance for those below, FROM THE ASPECT OF NUKVA. Even the sustenance for angels comes only through Yisrael, for were it not for Yisrael studying the Torah, sustenance would not have come from the Torah that is compared to a tree, as is written, "She is a Tree of Life to those who lay hold on her" (Mishlei 3:18), and also from the fruit OF THE TORAH, namely the precepts.

497. וְהָכִי אוֹרַיְיתָא אַמְתִּי לָא לְמַיָּא. וְהָנֵי לְאֶשָּׁא. וְלָא הֲוָה נָחִית מַיָּא מִלְעֵילָא, וְחַמָּה דְּאִיהִי אֶשָּׁא, לָא הֲוָה נָחִית לְבַשְּׁלָא פֵּירוֹת הָאִילָן. אֶלָּא, בְּגִין יִשְׂרָאֵל. וּבְגִין דָּא אִתְּמַר בְּיִשְׂרָאֵל, הַתְּאֵנָה חָנְטָה פַגֶּיהָ, אִלֵּין מָארֵי מִצְוֹת. וְהַגְּפָנִים סְמָדַר נָתְנוּ רֵיחַ, כַּד פַּתְחִין בִּתְיוּבְתָּא, וּמִיַד אִתְּמַר בְּיִשְׂרָאֵל, קוּמִי לָךְ רַעְיָתִי יָפָתִי וּלְכִי לָךְ, מִן גָּלוּתָא.

497. And so the Torah is compared to water, and so to fire. The waters would not descend, and the sun, being fire, would not come to ripen the fruit of the trees, only because of Yisrael. For this reason, it is written concerning Yisrael, "the fig puts forth her green figs" (Shir Hashirim 2:13), referring to the doer of precepts, "and the vines in blossom give their scent" (Ibid.), when people commence to repent. Immediately it writes about Yisrael, "Arise, my love, my fair one, and come away" (Ibid.), from out of exile.

498. וּבְגִין דָּא בְּאִילָן, דְּאִיהוּ עֵץ הַחַיִּים, בְּאוֹרַיְיתָא, בְּאִלֵּין דְּמִשְׁתַּדְּלִין בָּהּ, אָזְלִין בָּתַר חֲנָטָה, וּמְעַשְּׂרִין לֵיהּ, דְּשַׁרְיָא יוּ״ד עֲלַיְיהוּ, דְּאִיהִי חָכְמָ״ה, א׳ מִי׳ וּבָהּ מִתְכַּנְּשִׁין ה״ה, דְּאִינוּן פֵּירוֹת הָאִילָן. וּמַאן אִילָן. ו׳. אֲבָל שְׁאָר עַמָּא, אַחַר לְקִיטָתוֹ מִן גָּלוּתָא, עַשּׂרוּ. אִינּוּן צַדִּיקִים דְּאִתְּמַר בְּהוֹן, וּלְקַחְתֶּם לָכֶם בַּיוֹם הָרִאשׁוֹן פְּרִי עֵץ הָדָר. הָדָר בְּעוֹבָדֵיהוֹן, דַּאֲחִידָאן בְּמָארֵי תוֹרָה וּמִצְוֹת, וְאַחַר חֲנָטָה אָזְלֵינָן לְגַבַּיְיהוּ בְּאִילָן.

498. By the tree, the Tree of Life, MEANING Torah, BEING ZEIR ANPIN, those who study it, THE TORAH, follow the blossoming, MEANING AS THEY START STUDYING IT, and they are tithed, because the *Yud*, being Chochmah, dwells upon them, AND SO THEY ARE TITHED one out of *Yud* (= 10). With it

is gathered from exile the last *'Hei'* OF YUD HEI VAV HEI BEING YISRAEL, the fruit of the tree, WHICH IS THE TORAH. And what is the tree? This is Vav, NAMELY ZEIR ANPIN BEING THE SECRET OF TORAH. The rest of the nation are tithed following their being plucked from exile. HOWEVER, Righteous men, of whom it is written, "And you shall take for yourselves on the first day the fruit of the tree hadar" (Vayikra 23:40), namely, glory (Heb. *hadar*) in the deeds attached to AND PERFORMED BY students of Torah who perform precepts. With this group, we follow the blossoming, as in a tree, AND SO IT SAYS REGARDING THEM, "THE FIRST DAY" AS THEY DO NOT NEED TO WAIT UNTIL BEING PLUCKED FROM EXILE.

499. וּבְגִין דָּא אוּקְמוּהָ בְּמַסֶּכֶת קִדּוּשִׁין, קמ"ל דְּאֶתְרוֹג כְּיָרָק, מַה יָרָק דַּרְכּוֹ לִיגָּדֵל עַל כָּל מַיִם, וּבְשַׁעַת לְקִיטָתוֹ עִשּׂוּרוֹ. אוּף אֶתְרוֹג נָמֵי דַּרְכּוֹ לִיגָּדֵל וְכוּ' וּמִסִּטְרָא דְּחָכְמָה, אֵין מַיִם אֶלָּא תּוֹרָה. וּבְאֲתַר אַחֲרָא לְעֵילָא, וְהָא דִּתְנָן, אֶתְרוֹג שָׁוֶה לָאִילָן בִּשְׁלֹשָׁה דְּרָכִים, הָא אֶתְרוֹג, אָחִיד ב' סְטְרִין, וְאֶתְרוֹג אִיהוּ דְּיוּקְנָא דְּלִבָּא, דְּאָחִיד לְעֵילָא וְאָחִיד לְתַתָּא. אָחִיד לְעֵילָא, הַלֵּב רוֹאֶה. אָחִיד לְתַתָּא, בְּדַעַת. כְּמָה דְּאוּקְמוּהָ, הַלֵּב יוֹדֵעַ. דַּעַת אִיהִי אִילָנָא, תּוֹרָה אִיבָּא דִּילֵיהּ. עַיְינִין דְּאִינּוּן פְּקוּדִין, דִּבְּהוֹן הַלֵּב רוֹאֶה.

(ע"כ רעיא מהימנא)

499. And so it was established in Tractate *Kidushin*, Etrog's law is that of a vegetable. Just as a vegetable can thrive from all sources of water, and its tithing depends on time of picking it, so the Etrog thrives on all sources of water... AND SO ALSO YISRAEL HAS THE SIMILARITY TO ETROG IN THAT IT ALSO THRIVES UPON ALL SOURCES OF WATER, as from the aspect of Chochmah, water can mean only Torah, on which YISRAEL THRIVES. In another place before we learned that Etrog is similar to a tree in three ways, MEANING Etrog, DEPICTING MALCHUT, is held on two sides, CHESED AND GVURAH, CONSISTING OF TWO WAYS; 'Etrog' ITSELF has a shape of a heart held above and below; held above means to imply that the Heart sees, BEING CHOCHMAH REFERRED TO AS 'SEEING'; it is held below, meaning with Da'at (Eng. 'knowledge') as expressed: 'the heart knows'. NOW A THIRD WAY: Da'at is a tree, THE INTERNAL ZEIR ANPIN; Torah, WHICH IS

THE BODY OF ZEIR ANPIN, is the fruit OF DA'AT, SPREADING FROM DA'AT. The eyes are the precepts with which the heart sees.

End of Ra'aya Meheimna (the Faithful Shepherd)

20. "And you shall be holy men to Me"

A Synopsis

Rabbi Yehuda says that God told Yisrael that they should be to Him "a kingdom of priests," "a holy nation," "a holy people," and "holy men". He considers the verse, "But where shall wisdom be found? And where is the place of understanding?" saying that the Torah emanated from Chochmah from the place called 'holiness', and that Chochmah emanated from the place called 'Holy of Holies'. The law to do with "neither shall you eat any meat that is torn of beasts in the field" is explored; it is prohibited for those called 'holiness' to eat of it. Rabbi Aba concludes by telling us that this law is considered one of the most difficult laws of the Torah, and that all difficult matters of the Torah were given only to those fearing sin who keep God's commandments, not to the other nations.

500. וְאַנְשֵׁי קֹדֶשׁ תִּהְיוּן לִי וְגוֹ'. רַבִּי יְהוּדָה פָּתַח, וְהַחָכְמָה מֵאַיִן תִּמָּצֵא וְאֵיזֶה מְקוֹם בִּינָה. זַכָּאִין אִינּוּן יִשְׂרָאֵל, דְּקוּדְשָׁא בְּרִיךְ הוּא בָּעֵי לְיַקְּרָא לוֹן, יַתִּיר עַל כָּל שְׁאָר בְּנֵי עָלְמָא. בְּקַדְמֵיתָא אָמַר לוֹן, וְאַתֶּם תִּהְיוּ לִי מַמְלֶכֶת כֹּהֲנִים. לָא אַעֲדֵי רְחִימוּתָא סַגִּיאָה מִנְּהוֹן, עַד דְּקָרָא לוֹן וְגוֹי קָדוֹשׁ דְּאִיהִי יַתִּיר. לָא אַעֲדֵי רְחִימוּתָא מִנְּהוֹן, עַד דְּקָרָא לוֹן כִּי עַם קָדוֹשׁ אַתָּה. לָא אַעֲדֵי רְחִימוּתָא מִנְּהוֹן, עַד דְּקָרָא לוֹן וְאַנְשֵׁי קֹדֶשׁ תִּהְיוּן לִי דְּאִיהוּ יַתִּיר מִכֹּלָּא.

500. "And you shall be holy men to Me" (Shemot 22:30): Rabbi Yehuda commenced: "But where shall wisdom be found? And where is the place of understanding?" (Iyov 28:12). Fortunate are Yisrael as the Holy One, blessed be He, desired to honor them above all mankind. First He said to them, "and you shall be to Me a kingdom of priests" (Shemot 19:6). He never removed from them His great love, so much so that He called them, "a holy nation" (Ibid.), considered a more WORTHY STATEMENT. Love was not removed until He called them "For you are a holy people" (Devarim 14:2). He did not remove His love until He called them, "And you shall be holy men (lit. 'men of holiness') to Me," the most worthy statement.

501. כְּתִיב וְהַחָכְמָה מֵאַיִן תִּמָּצֵא. אוֹרַיְיתָא מֵחָכְמָה נַפְקַת, מֵאֲתָר

דְּאִקְרֵי קֹדֶשׁ. וְהַחָכְמָה נַפְקַת, מֵאֲתַר דְּאִקְרֵי קֹדֶשׁ הַקֳּדָשִׁים. ר׳ יִצְחָק אָמַר, וְכֵן יוֹבְלָא אִתְקְרֵי קֹדֶשׁ. דִּכְתִּיב, יוֹבֵל הִיא קֹדֶשׁ תִּהְיֶה לָכֶם. וְיִשְׂרָאֵל כְּלִילָן מִנַּיְיהוּ, הה״ד וְאַנְשֵׁי קֹדֶשׁ תִּהְיוּן לִי.

501. It is written, "But where shall wisdom be found?" The Torah emanated from Chochmah from the place called 'holiness', DENOTING CHOCHMAH. Chochmah emanated from the place called 'Holy of Holies' DENOTING KETER. Rabbi Yitzchak said: So is Jubilee DENOTING BINAH, called 'holiness', as written, "For it is the Jubilee; it shall be holy (lit. 'holiness') to you" (Vayikra 25:12). Yisrael is composed of them, CHOCHMAH AND BINAH, as in the verse; "And you shall be men of holiness to Me."

502. בְּקַדְמֵיתָא קָדוֹשׁ, וְהַשְׁתָּא קֹדֶשׁ. מַה בֵּין הַאי לְהַאי. א״ר יוֹסֵי, דָּא לְעֵילָא לְעֵילָא, וְדָא לָאו הָכִי. דִּכְתִּיב, וְהָיָה הַנִּשְׁאָר בְּצִיּוֹן וְהַנּוֹתָר בִּירוּשָׁלַם קָדוֹשׁ יֵאָמֶר לוֹ. בְּהַאי אֲתַר אִקְרֵי קָדוֹשׁ וּלְעֵילָא לְעֵילָא קֹדֶשׁ.

502. At first, THE HOLY ONE, BLESSED BE HE, called them 'holy', now He call them 'holiness'. What is the difference? Rabbi Yosi said 'HOLINESS' is most high, IN CHOCHMAH AND BINAH AS MENTIONED, 'HOLY' is not so, AS 'HOLY' POINTS TO MALCHUT, as it is written, "And it shall come to pass, that he that is left in Zion, and he that remains in Jerusalem shall be called holy" (Yeshayah 4:3). In this place, ZION AND JERUSALEM, it is called 'holy', with the most High WHEN IN CHOCHMAH AND BINAH it is called 'holiness'.

503. רַבִּי אַבָּא הֲוָה אָזִיל בְּאָרְחָא, וַהֲווֹ אָזְלֵי עִמֵּיהּ ר׳ יוֹסֵי וְר׳ חִיָּיא, אָמַר ר׳ חִיָּיא, וְאַנְשֵׁי קֹדֶשׁ תִּהְיוּן לִי, מְנָלָן. א״ל, הָא ר׳ יוֹסֵי וְכֻלְּהוּ חַבְרַיָּיא שַׁפִּיר קָאַמְרוּ, וְהָכִי הוּא. מְנָלָן. דִּכְתִּיב, קֹדֶשׁ יִשְׂרָאֵל לַיְיָ׳ רֵאשִׁית תְּבוּאָתֹה, רֵאשִׁית: וְדַאי חָכְמָה אִקְרֵי רֵאשִׁית, דִּכְתִּיב רֵאשִׁית חָכְמָה יִרְאַת יְיָ׳.

503. Rabbi Aba was walking and Rabbi Yosi and Rabbi Chiya went along. Rabbi Chiya spoke: "And you shall be men of holiness to Me" WAS

EXPLAINED TO MEAN CHOCHMAH. Whence do we know this? He replied: Rabbi Yosi and all the scholars already said, IT MEANS CHOCHMAH, and it is, because it is written, "Yisrael is holiness to Hashem, the firstfruits of His increase" (Yirmeyah 2:3), first being Chochmah called 'first' as it is written: "The fear of Hashem is the beginning of wisdom" (Tehilim 111:10).

504. וּמִשׁוּם דְּיִשְׂרָאֵל אִקְרוּן קֹדֶשׁ בִּשְׁלִימוּ דְּכֹלָּא, כְּתִיב וּבָשָׂר בַּשָּׂדֶה טְרֵפָה לֹא תֹאכֵלוּ. דְּהָא יִשְׂרָאֵל דְּאִינּוּן שְׁלֵמִין עַל כֹּלָּא, לָא יַנְקִין מִסִּטְרָא דְּדִינָא קַשְׁיָא. לַכֶּלֶב תַּשְׁלִיכוּן אוֹתוֹ. לַכֶּלֶב וַדַּאי, דְּהוּא דִּינָא חֲצִיפָא תַּקִּיפָא עַל כֹּלָּא. כֵּיוָן דְּדִינָא תַּקִּיפָא שַׁרְיָא עֲלוֹי, וְאָטִיל זוּהֲמָא בֵּיהּ, אָסִיר לְהוּ לְאִינּוּן דְּאִקְרוּן קֹדֶשׁ. אֶלָּא לַכֶּלֶב תַּשְׁלִיכוּן אוֹתוֹ וַדַּאי, דְּאִיהוּ דִּינָא חֲצִיפָא, דִּינָא תַּקִּיפָא יַתִּיר מִכֹּלָּא, דִּכְתִיב וְהַכְּלָבִים עַזֵּי נֶפֶשׁ.

504. Now that Yisrael is called 'holiness', which comprises every perfection, the verse says "neither shall you eat any meat that is torn of beasts in the field" (Shemot 22:30), as Yisrael are in a state of perfection, they do not nurture from the aspect of harsh judgment, TO WHICH TORN MEAT ALLUDES, "you shall cast it to the dogs" (Ibid.): surely to the dog, which symbolizes insolent judgment to all, so since the harsh judgment dwells upon THE TORN MEAT and inserted foulness within, it is prohibited for those called 'holiness' TO EAT OF IT. THIS IS THE ESSENCE OF THE VERSE, "AND YOU SHALL BE MEN OF HOLINESS TO ME: NEITHER SHALL YOU EAT ANY MEAT THAT IS TORN OF BEASTS IN THE FIELD," SO WE SEE THE CONNECTION BETWEEN THE PROHIBITION OF TORN MEAT AND PEOPLE OF HOLINESS. But "you shall cast it to the dogs" where insolent judgment and harsh judgment apply as the verse says "the dogs are greedy" (Yeshayah 56:11).

505. תּ"ח, כַּד אִדְכַּר נְבֵלָה בְּאוֹרַיְיתָא, כְּתִיב בְּיִשְׂרָאֵל קָדוֹשׁ, וְלֹא קֹדֶשׁ. הָכָא כְּתִיב, וְאַנְשֵׁי קֹדֶשׁ תִּהְיוּן לִי וּבָשָׂר בַּשָּׂדֶה טְרֵפָה לֹא תֹאכֵלוּ. וְהָתָם בִּנְבֵלָה כְּתִיב, לֹא תֹאכְלוּ כָל נְבֵלָה לַגֵּר אֲשֶׁר בִּשְׁעָרֶיךָ תִּתְּנֶנָּה וְגוֹ', כִּי עַם קָדוֹשׁ אַתָּה. קָדוֹשׁ וְלֹא קֹדֶשׁ, דְּהָא נְבֵלָה מִסִּטְרָא דְּיִשְׂרָאֵל אִתְעֲבֵיד, דְּלָא פָּסִיל הַאי אֶלָּא יִשְׂרָאֵל. וְסַגִּיאָן גְּוֵונִין, אִית

בָּהּ בִּנְבֵלָה. כְּמָה דְּאוֹקִימְנָא.

505. Come and see, when the Torah mentions 'a thing that dies of itself', it refers to Yisrael as holy, not holiness. It says here "And you shall be men of holiness to me: neither shall you eat any meat that is torn of beasts in the field." There, with regard to a thing that dies of itself, it writes "You shall not eat of any thing that dies of itself: you shall give it to the stranger who is in your gates…for you are a holy people" (Devarim 14:20) – 'holy' and not 'holiness'. A thing that dies of itself is caused by one of Yisrael, IT BECAME SO FROM AN IMPROPER SLAUGHTER BY ONE OF YISRAEL, SO THAT it became forbidden to be eaten because of Yisrael. SO THE LAW IS NOT SO STRINGENT; HOWEVER WITH THE TORN MEAT THAT IS REJECTABLE DUE TO BEING RIPPED BY WILD BEASTS, THE LAW IS MORE STRINGENT, SO DISTANCE FROM TORN MEAT IS CALLED 'HOLINESS', FROM ANY THING THAT DIES OF ITSELF IS CALLED 'HOLY'. There are other shades of meaning in relation to a thing that dies of itself, as we explained.

506. אר"ש, כְּתִיב הָכָא וְאַנְשֵׁי קֹדֶשׁ תִּהְיוּן לִי, וּכְתִיב הָתָם כִּי עַם קָדוֹשׁ אַתָּה לַיְיָ', אֱלֹהֶיךָ. לַיְיָ' אֱלֹהֶיךָ, לִי מִבָּעֵי לֵיהּ. אֶלָּא הָכָא לְעֵילָא לְעֵילָא. וְהָתָם שְׁכִינְתָּא. וּכְתִיב, וְהָיָה הַנִּשְׁאָר בְּצִיּוֹן וְהַנּוֹתָר בִּירוּשָׁלַם קָדוֹשׁ יֵאָמֶר לוֹ וְלָא קֹדֶשׁ. בְּכַאן קָדוֹשׁ, וּלְעֵילָא קֹדֶשׁ. כְּתִיב קֹדֶשׁ יִשְׂרָאֵל לַיְיָ' רֵאשִׁית תְּבוּאָתֹה, בְּה"א כְּמָה דְּאוֹקִימְנָא. וְע"ד וְאַנְשֵׁי קֹדֶשׁ תִּהְיוּן לִי וַדַּאי.

506. Rabbi Shimon said: It is written here, "And you shall be men of holiness to Me." It is written there, "for you are a holy people to Hashem your Elohim." HE ASKS: Why does it write; "to Hashem your Elohim" instead of "to Me." HE ANSWERS, the verse here speaks about the ultimate high, NAMELY OF CHOCHMAH AND BINAH, while there, it refers to the Shechinah NAMELY MALCHUT SO IT WRITES "TO HASHEM YOUR ELOHIM" AS MALCHUT IS REFERRED TO AS ELOHIM. It is written, "And it shall come to pass, that he that is left in Zion, and he that remains in Jerusalem shall be called holy," rather than 'holiness', because here IN MALCHUT ALSO CALLED ZION AND JERUSALEM is considered 'holy', while above IN CHOCHMAH AND BINAH, we say 'holiness'. It is also written, "Yisrael is holiness to Hashem, the firstfruits of his increase (Heb. *tevuatoh*)"

(Yirmeyah 2:3), the word 'tevuatoh' written with an EXTRA Hei, HINTING ABOUT BINAH BEING THE FIRST 'HEI' OF YUD HEI VAV HEI, AND FIRST ALLUDES TO CHOCHMAH, AS WE ESTABLISHED, therefore "And you shall be men of holiness to me."

507. רַבִּי יִצְחָק הֲוָה יָתִיב קַמֵּיהּ דר״ש, א״ל הָא כְּתִיב קֹדֶשׁ יִשְׂרָאֵל לַיְיָ׳ סוֹפֵיהּ דִּקְרָא כְּתִיב כָּל אוֹכְלָיו יֶאֱשָׁמוּ, מַאי קָא מַיְירֵי. א״ל ר״ש, שַׁפִּיר קָא אָמַר, כָּל אֹכְלָיו יֶאֱשָׁמוּ, הַיְינוּ דִכְתִיב, וְאִישׁ כִּי יֹאכַל קֹדֶשׁ בִּשְׁגָגָה וְגו׳. וּכְתִיב, וְכָל זָר לֹא יֹאכַל קֹדֶשׁ. וּמִשּׁוּם דְּיִשְׂרָאֵל אִקְרוּן קֹדֶשׁ, כְּתִיב כָּל אֹכְלָיו יֶאֱשָׁמוּ. אָתָא ר׳ יִצְחָק וְנָשִׁיק יְדוֹי, אָמַר, אִי לָא אַתֵּינָא הָכָא אֶלָּא לְמִשְׁמַע מִלָּה דָּא סַגֵּי.

507. Rabbi Yitzchak was sitting before Rabbi Shimon. He said to him, it is written, "Yisrael is holiness to Hashem," and the end of the verse reads, "all that devour him shall be held guilty." What does it mean? Rabbi Shimon replied, it speaks well when it says: "all that devour him shall be held guilty", as there is a verse, "And if a man eat of the holy thing (lit. 'holiness') unwittingly..." (Vayikra 22:14) and there is a verse, "No stranger shall eat of the holy thing (lit. 'holiness')" (Ibid. 10). Since Yisrael are called holiness, it follows that "all that devour him shall be held guilty." Rabbi Yitzchak kissed his hand, said, if I came only to hear this, it is worth it.

508. א״ל רַבִּי, הָא תָּנֵינָן, דְּקֹדֶשׁ, יַתִּיר לְעֵילָּא מִן קָדוֹשׁ. אִי הָכִי, הָא כְּתִיב ק׳ ק׳ ק׳ יְיָ׳ צְבָאוֹת, וְדָא שְׁלִימוּ דְּכֹלָּא. א״ל ת״ח, כַּד מִתְחַבְּרָן כַּחֲדָא, כֻּלְּהוּ אִתְעֲבִידוּ חַד בֵּיתָא, וְהַאי בֵּיתָא, אִקְרֵי קֹדֶשׁ. כְּלָלָא דְּכֻלְּהוּ קָדוֹשׁ וּבְגִינֵי כַּךְ קֹדֶשׁ, הוּא כְּלָלָא, דְּכֹלָּא אִתְכְּלִיל בֵּיהּ. וְיִשְׂרָאֵל כַּד אִתְכְּלִיל בְּהוּ מְהֵימְנוּתָא שְׁלֵימָתָא קֹדֶשׁ אִקְרוּן, כְּלָלָא דְּכֹלָּא, דִּכְתִיב קֹדֶשׁ יִשְׂרָאֵל לַיְיָ׳. וּבְגִינֵי כַּךְ, וְאַנְשֵׁי קֹדֶשׁ תִּהְיוּן לִי.

508. RABBI YITZCHAK said to him, Rabbi, we learned that 'holiness' is considered higher than 'holy'. If so, there is a verse, "Holy, holy, holy is Hashem Tzevaot" (Yeshayah 6:3), which expresses perfection, AND YET IT IS WRITTEN 'HOLY'. He said to him, come and see, when you enjoin THREE 'HOLY' together, it becomes one house, and this house is called 'holiness',

being the sum total of the three 'holy', THUS BECOMING TOTAL PERFECTION. As a result, 'holiness' is a generalization that includes all; when Yisrael incorporates within the total Faith, they are called 'holiness', which is the sum of all, as it is written: "Yisrael is holiness to Hashem." Hence it is written, "And you shall be men of holiness to Me."

509. לִגְיוֹן חַד שָׁאִיל לְר' אַבָּא, א"ל, לָא כְּתִיב וּבָשָׂר בַּשָּׂדֶה טְרֵפָה לֹא תֹאכֵלוּ, אִי הָכִי, מַאי דִּכְתִיב, טֶרֶף נָתַן לִירֵאָיו. טֶרֶף נָתַן לַכְּלָבִים מִבָּעֵי לֵיהּ, אֲמַאי נָתַן לִירֵאָיו. א"ל, רֵיקָא, מִי כְּתִיב טְרֵפָה נָתַן לִירֵאָיו, טֶרֶף כְּתִיב. וְאִי תֵּימָא, טֶרֶף כִּטְרֵפָה. נָתַן לִירֵאָיו וַדַּאי דְּמִלָה דָּא, לָא יָהֲבֵיהּ לְאַזְדַּהֲרָא בֵּיהּ, אֶלָּא לְאִינּוּן דַּחֲלֵי שְׁמֵיהּ, וְדַחֲלִין לֵיהּ. בְּג"כ הַאי מִלָּה לָא יָהִיב לְכוּ, דְּהָא יָדַע דְּאַתּוּן לָא דַחֲלִין לֵיהּ, וְלָא נַטְרִין פִּקּוּדוֹי, וּבְגִין דְּהַאי מִלָּה חוּמְרָא דְּאוֹרַיְיתָא, וּבָעֵי לְאִזְדַּהֲרָא בָּהּ, נָתַן לִירֵאָיו, לִירֵאָיו וַדַּאי, וְלָא לְאָחֳרֵי. וְכָל חוּמְרֵי דְּאוֹרַיְיתָא, לָא יָהִיב לוֹן קוּדְשָׁא בְּרִיךְ הוּא, אֶלָּא לְאִינּוּן דַּחֲלֵי חַטָאָה, לְאִינּוּן דַּחֲלֵי פִּקּוּדוֹי וְלָא לְכוּ.

509. A legionnaire, NAMELY A GENERAL, asked Rabbi Aba: Is it not written, "neither shall you eat any meat that is torn (Heb. *trefah*) of beasts in the field"? yet there is a verse, "He has given food (Heb. *teref*) to those that fear Him" (Tehilim 111:5). Teref should go to dogs, why does it say "to those that fear Him"? He replied, fool, does it write "He has given trefah to those that fear Him?" "Teref" is written MEANING SUSTENANCE. And even if you say Teref is the same as Trefah, assuredly He gave it "to those that fear Him." THE MEANING CONVEYED IS THEY SHOULD BE CAREFUL OF IT AND NOT EAT IT, AND WHAT IT MENTIONS means that none can be careful in this, save those who hold His name in awe, who fear Him; and that is why this law was not given to you, as He knows that you do not revere Him nor keep His commandments. This law is considered one of the difficult laws of the Torah, and requires care, He gave it to those that fear Him and not to others. And all difficult matters of the Torah, the Holy One, blessed be He, gave to those fearing sin, these that are careful TO KEEP His commandments, not to you.

21. "And you shall be men of holiness to Me"

A Synopsis

Rabbi Elazar teaches that since Yisrael are called 'holiness' and because they are 'holiness', no one must call his neighbor a shameful name, nor should he make up a name for him, because there is a great penalty for it. As a result of bad talk, illnesses come into the world. Rabbi Aba says that Yisrael are fortunate, because God did not call them just 'like holiness', but actual 'holiness'.

510. תָּאנֵי ר' אֶלְעָזָר, כְּתִיב וְאַנְשֵׁי קֹדֶשׁ תִּהְיוּן לִי, מַהוּ וְאַנְשֵׁי. וּלְבָתַר קֹדֶשׁ, אֶלָּא וְאַנְשֵׁי קֹדֶשׁ וַדַּאי. דְּתָנֵינָן, לָא נָפְקוּ יִשְׂרָאֵל לְחֵירוּ, אֶלָּא מִסִּטְרָא דְּיוֹבְלָא. בָּתַר דְּנָפְקוּ לְחֵירוּ, נָקִיט לוֹן הַאי יוֹבְלָא בְּגַדְפּוֹי, וְאִקְרוּן גּוּבְרִין דִּילֵיהּ. בְּנִין דִּילֵיהּ, וּכְתִיב בֵּיהּ בְּיוֹבְלָא, יוֹבֵל הִיא קֹדֶשׁ תִּהְיֶה לָכֶם, קֹדֶשׁ וַדַּאי, לָכֶם וַדַּאי. וּבְגִינֵי כָּךְ, וְאַנְשֵׁי קֹדֶשׁ תִּהְיוּן לִי, אַנְשֵׁי קֹדֶשׁ וַדַּאי, גּוּבְרִין דִּילֵיהּ מַמָּשׁ.

510. Rabbi Elazar taught, it is written, "And you shall be men of holiness to Me." Why write "men" and then "holiness," IT WOULD SUFFICE TO SAY 'YOU SHALL BE HOLY TO ME? HE ANSWERS: good reason to write "men of holiness," we learned, Yisrael had won freedom only as a result of Jubilee DENOTING BINAH; after gaining freedom, Jubilee accepted them under its wings and they are thus called its people, its children, and about Jubilee, it is written, "For it is the Jubilee; it shall be holy (lit. 'holiness') to you" (Vayikra 25:12). Hence it says "And you shall be men of holiness to Me," its men in deed.

511. וְקוּדְשָׁא בְּרִיךְ הוּא אָמַר דָּא, וְעַל דָּא זָכוּ יִשְׂרָאֵל לְאִתְקְרֵי אַחִים לְקוּדְשָׁא בְּרִיךְ הוּא, דִּכְתִיב, לְמַעַן אַחַי וְרֵעָי וְגוֹ'. לְבָתַר אִקְרוּן קֹדֶשׁ מַמָּשׁ. דִּכְתִיב, קֹדֶשׁ יִשְׂרָאֵל לַיְיָ' רֵאשִׁית תְּבוּאָתֹה, קֹדֶשׁ וְלָא אַנְשֵׁי קֹדֶשׁ, בְּגִינֵי כָּךְ כָּל אֹכְלָיו יֶאְשָׁמוּ, וּכְתִיב, וְכָל זָר לֹא יֹאכַל קֹדֶשׁ. וְאִישׁ כִּי יֹאכַל קֹדֶשׁ בִּשְׁגָגָה.

511. And the Holy One, blessed be He, said this, "AND YOU SHALL MEN OF HOLINESS TO ME." And so Yisrael merited to be called brothers of the

Holy One, blessed be He, as it is written: "For my brethren and companions'
sakes" (Tehilim 122:8), AS YISRAEL ARE SONS TO JUBILEE, BEING
BINAH, AND ZEIR ANPIN IS SON OF BINAH, THE RESULT BEING THAT
THEY ARE ALSO BROTHERS TO ZEIR ANPIN. Then they get called
'holiness' literally, as it says, "Yisrael are holiness to Hashem, the firstfruits
of His increase." Here it is written holiness, not 'men of holiness', and
therefore "all that devour him shall be held guilty," and, "No stranger shall
eat of the holiness" "And if a man eat of the holiness unwittingly..."

512. תָּאנָא, יִשְׂרָאֵל אִקְרוּן קֹדֶשׁ, וּבְגִין דְּאִינּוּן קֹדֶשׁ, אָסִיר לֵיהּ
לְאֵינָשׁ, לְמִקְרֵי לְחַבְרֵיהּ בִּשְׁמָא דִּגְנַאי, וְלָא לְכַנָּאָה שְׁמָא לְחַבְרֵיהּ,
וְעוֹנְשֵׁיהּ סַגִּי. וְכָל שֶׁכֵּן בְּמִלִּין אַחֲרָנִין. תָּאנָא, כְּתִיב נְצוֹר לְשׁוֹנְךָ מֵרָע
וְגוֹ'. מַהוּ מֵרָע. דִּבְגִין לִישָׁנָא בִּישָׁא, מַרְעִין נַחְתִּין לְעָלְמָא.

512. So we learned, Yisrael are called 'holiness', and because they are
'holiness', no one must call his neighbor a shameful name, and not make up
a name for him, as there is a great penalty, all the more so in other matters.
We learned, "Keep your tongue from evil" (Tehilim 34:14). What is meant
by evil? As a result of bad talk, illnesses come to the world.

513. אָמַר ר' יוֹסִי כָּל מַאן דְּקָרֵי לְחַבְרֵיהּ בִּשְׁמָא דְּלֵית בֵּיהּ, וְגַנֵּי לֵיהּ,
אִתְפַּס בְּמָה דְּלֵית בֵּיהּ, דְּאָמַר ר' חִיָּיא אָמַר ר' חִזְקִיָּה, כָּל מַאן דְּקָרֵי
לְחַבְרֵיהּ רָשָׁע, נַחְתִּין לֵיהּ לַגֵּיהִנָּם. וְנַחְתִּין לֵיהּ לְעֵלָּעוֹי, בַּר אִינּוּן
חֲצִיפִין דְּאוֹרַיְיתָא, דְּשָׁרֵי לֵיהּ לְאִינִישׁ לְמִקְרֵי לְהוּ רָשָׁע.

513. Rabbi Yosi said, one who calls another with a name that is not proper
and shames him, he is brought TO JUDGMENT for something he did not do,
as Rabbi Chiya said in the name of Rabbi Chizkiyah: One who calls his
neighbor a villain, is lowered to Gehenom, and he is slapped on his cheek,
the exception being those acting insolently to the Torah, whom one may call
villains.

514. הַהוּא גַּבְרָא, דְּלָיֵיט לְחַבְרֵיהּ, אַעֲבַר ר' יֵיסָא, אָמַר לֵיהּ כְּרָשָׁע
עֲבַדְתְּ. אַתְיֵיהּ לְקָמֵיהּ דְּר' יְהוּדָה, א"ל רָשָׁע לָא קָאֲמֵינָא לֵיהּ, אֶלָּא

כְּרָשָׁע, דְּאַחֲזֵי מִלּוֹי כְּרָשָׁע, וְלָא אֲמֵינָא דְּאִיהוּ רָשָׁע. אָתָא ר' יְהוּדָה, וְשָׁאִיל לְעוֹבָדָא קַמֵּיהּ דְּרַבִּי אֶלְעָזָר, אָמַר לֵיהּ, וַדַּאי לָא אִתְחַיָּיב. מְנָלָן. דִּכְתִיב, הָיָה יְיָ' כְּאוֹיֵב, וְלָא אוֹיֵב. דְּאִי לָאו הָכִי, לָא אִשְׁתְּאַר מִיִּשְׂרָאֵל גִּזְעִין בְּעָלְמָא. כְּגַוְונָא דָּא, הָיְתָה כְּאַלְמָנָה, וְלָא אַלְמָנָה, כְּאַלְמָנָה דְּאָזִיל בַּעְלָהּ לְעַבְרָא דְּיַמָּא, וּמְחַכָּאת לֵיהּ.

514. A man cursed his neighbor, and Rabbi Yesa passed by and said to him: "you acted like a villain." The person came before Rabbi Yehuda with a complaint. He said to him, I did not say to him, that he is a villain, but acts like a villain exhibiting cruel behavior, but I did not call him a villain. Rabbi Judah came and asked about this case of Rabbi Elazar. He told him: Surely he is not liable, and the proof, there is a verse, "Hashem was like an enemy" (Eichah 2:5), but not an actual enemy. Were it now so, nothing would have remained of the race of Yisrael in the world. Similarly, "like a widow" (Eichah 1:1), not actual widow, but like a widow whose husband went overseas and she awaits him, AND BEING ALONE WITHOUT A HUSBAND SHE IS LIKENED TO A WIDOW.

515. אָמַר ר' חִיָּיא, וּמֵהָכָא מַשְׁמַע, מֵהָתָם מַשְׁמַע, דְּהוּא עִקְרָא דְּכֹלָּא, דִּכְתִיב, וְעַל דְּמוּת הַכִּסֵּא דְּמוּת כְּמַרְאֵה אָדָם. כְּמַרְאֵה אָדָם, וְלָא מַרְאֵה אָדָם. א״ר יִצְחָק, כְּתִיב, כְּתַפּוּחַ בַּעֲצֵי הַיַּעַר וְגוֹ', כְּתַפּוּחַ וְלָא תַּפּוּחַ. כְּתַפּוּחַ: דְּמִתְפָּרְשָׁא בִּגְוָונוֹי, וּבִגְוָונִין אִתְאַחֲדָא מִלָּה. אָמַר רַבִּי יְהוּדָה, אִלּוּ לָא אֲתֵינָא הָכָא אֶלָּא לְמִשְׁמַע מִלִּין אִלֵּין, דַּיִּי.

515. Rabbi Chiya said, is the proof from here? IS IT NOT from there which is the principal, MEANING THE PROHIBITION OF IMAGE, as it is written: "and upon the likeness of the throne was the likeness as the appearance of a man" (Yechezkel 1:26), again, it writes "like the appearance of man," not "the appearance of man," EVIDENTLY 'LIKE THE APPEARANCE' IS NOT SIMILAR TO 'THE APPEARANCE'. Rabbi Yitzchak said: it is written, "Like the apple among the trees of the wood" (Shir Hashirim 2:3), meaning, "like the apple," but not 'the apple', to be understood, like the apple is recognizable by its colors, and unified through its colors, AS THE UNITY OF THE HOLY ONE, BLESSED BE HE, IS THE SECRET OF THE THREE COLUMNS BEING THE SECRET OF WHITE, RED, AND GREEN AS EXISTING WITH THE APPLE,

TO BE UNDERSTOOD AS CHESED, JUDGMENT, MERCY. Rabbi Yehuda said, if I came only to hear this, it was worth it.

516. תָּאנָא כְּתִיב, וְהָיָה הַנִּכְשָׁל בָּהֶם בַּיּוֹם הַהוּא כְּדָוִד. כְּדָוִד, וְלָא דָוִד. כְּדָוִד, דְּאָמַר, וְהִנֵּה בְעָנְיִי הֲכִינוֹתִי לְבֵית יְיָ'. וּכְתִיב, כִּי עָנִי וְאֶבְיוֹן אָנִי. וְהוּא מַלְכָּא עַל מַלְכִין הֲוָה, וַהֲוָה קָרֵי לְגַרְמֵיהּ הָכִי. אָמַר רִבִּי אַבָּא, זַכָּאִין אִינּוּן יִשְׂרָאֵל, דְּקוּדְשָׁא בְּרִיךְ הוּא לָא קָרָא לוֹן כְּקֹדֶשׁ, אֶלָּא קֹדֶשׁ מַמָּשׁ, דִּכְתִיב קֹדֶשׁ יִשְׂרָאֵל לַיְיָ', וּבג"כ כָּל אֹכְלָיו יֶאְשָׁמוּ וְגוֹ'.

516. We learned, it is written: "and he that stumbles among them at that day shall be like David" (Zecharyah 12:8), MEANING like David but not David, for he says, "Now, behold, in my trouble I have prepared for the house of Hashem" (I Divrei Hayamim 22:14), and it is written, "for I am poor and needy" (Tehilim 86:1). And he was at the time a king over kings, and yet referred to himself so. Rabbi Aba said, fortunate are Yisrael, that the Holy One, blessed be He, did not call them "like holiness" but actually "holiness," as it is written: "Yisrael is holiness to Hashem," the end of the verse reads, "all that devour him shall be held guilty," LIKE A STRANGER EATING OF THE HOLINESS.

22. "Execute judgment in the morning"

A Synopsis

We learn that the laws were instituted after the ten commandments because the earth can survive only with law; consequently the world was created with law, and so it survives. Rabbi Aba talks about "execute judgment in the morning," saying that it means to judge before the judge has a chance to eat or drink, so he will render a truthful verdict. Rabbi Yehuda says that the institutions of the King are those mentioned in "who exercise faithful love, justice, and righteousness, in the earth."

517. תָּאנָא, אָמַר ר' יוֹסֵי, מַאי קָא חָמָא קוּדְשָׁא בְּרִיךְ הוּא, לְמֵיהַב דִּינִין לְיִשְׂרָאֵל, בָּתַר עֲשַׂר אֲמִירָן. אֶלָּא הָכִי תְּנֵינָן, מִסִּטְרָא דִּגְבוּרָה, אִתְיְיהִיבַת אוֹרַיְיתָא לְיִשְׂרָאֵל. בְּגִינֵי כַּךְ, בָּעָא לְמֵיתַן שְׁלָמָא בֵּינַיְיהוּ, בְּגִין דְּאוֹרַיְיתָא תְּהֵא נְטִירָא מִכָּל סִטְרוֹי. דְּאָמַר רַבִּי אַבָּא אָמַר רַבִּי יִצְחָק, לֵית עָלְמָא מִתְקַיְּימָא, אֶלָּא עַל דִּינָא, דְּאִלְמָלֵא דִּינָא, לָא מִתְקַיְּימָא. וּבְג"כ עָלְמָא בְּדִינָא אִתְבְּרֵי, וְאִתְקַיַּים.

517. We learned, Rabbi Yosi said, why did the Holy One, blessed be He, see fit to place the chapters of laws, MEANING THE PORTION OF JUDGMENTS, after the ten commandments? HE ANSWERS: we have learned that from the aspect of Gvurah Torah was given to Yisrael. As a result, it is important to establish harmony among them, THROUGH LOWER AND JUDGMENT, in order that the Torah be the guardian from all sides. Rabbi Aba said on behalf of Rabbi Yitzchak, the earth can survive only with law; without law, the world cannot survive, so consequently the world was created with law and so it survives.

518. תָּאנָא, ר' אַבָּא, כְּתִיב דִּינוּ לַבֹּקֶר מִשְׁפָּט. וְכִי לַבֹּקֶר, וְלָאו בְּכָל יוֹמָא. אֶלָּא לַבֹּקֶר, עַד לָא יֵיכְלוּן דַּיָּינִין, וְלָא יִשְׁתּוּן, דְּכָל מַאן דְּדָאִין דִּינָא בָּתַר דְּאָכַל וְשָׁתָה, לָאו דִּינָא דְּקַשׁוֹט הוּא, דִּכְתִיב לֹא תֹאכְלוּ עַל הַדָּם. מַאי עַל הַדָּם. אַזְהָרָה לְדַיָּינֵי, דְּלָא יֵיכְלוּן עַד דְּדַיְינֵי דִּינָא, דְּכָל מַאן דְּדָאִין דִּינָא בָּתַר דְּאָכִיל וְשָׁתֵי, כְּאִלּוּ חַיָּיב דָּמָא דְּחַבְרֵיהּ לְאַחֲרָא, דְּהָא דָּמֵיהּ מַמָּשׁ יָהִיב לְאַחֲרָא. הַאי בְּמָמוֹנָא, כ"ש בְּדִינֵי

נַפְשׁוֹת, דְּבָעוּ דַּיָּינֵי לְאִסְתַּמְּרָא, דְּלָא לְמֵידָן דִּינָא אֶלָּא קֹדֶם דְּאַכְלוּ
וְשָׁתוּ, וְעַל דָּא כְּתִיב דִּינוּ לַבֹּקֶר מִשְׁפָּט וּכְתִיב, אֲנִי יְיָ' עוֹשֶׂה חֶסֶד
וּמִשְׁפָּט וּצְדָקָה בָּאָרֶץ כִּי בְאֵלֶּה חָפַצְתִּי נְאֻם יְיָ'.

518. Rabbi Aba taught, it is written, "Execute judgment in the morning" (Yirmeyah 21:12). HE ASKS: Why only in the morning and not all day? HE ANSWERS: "Morning" MEANS, to judge before the judges has a chance to eat or drink, for we know that one who judge after consuming food or drink does not render a truthful verdict, as it is written, "You shall not eat anything with the blood" (Vayikra 19:26). What is meant "with the blood"? It is a warning to judges that they not eat before judging, for one who judges a case after food and drink is considered causing the loss of blood of the individual and giving it to another, as he is literally transferring blood to another, THROUGH THE MEANS OF FALSE JUDGMENT. If this holds true in monetary matters, then how much more so in capital matters. Judges must be careful to judge only before food or drink is consumed. So that is why it is written: "Execute judgment in the morning" and it writes "that I am Hashem who exercise faithful love, justice, and righteousness, in the earth: for in these things I delight, says Hashem" (Yirmeyah 9:23).

519. תָּנֵינָא, אָמַר ר' יְהוּדָה, מַאן דִּמְשַׁקֵּר בְּדִינָא, מְשַׁקֵּר בְּתִקּוּנֵי
מַלְכָּא. מַאן תִּקּוּנֵי מַלְכָּא. אִינּוּן דְּאִתְּמַר, דִּכְתִּיב עוֹשֶׂה חֶסֶד מִשְׁפָּט
וּצְדָקָה בָּאָרֶץ. וּכְתִיב כִּי בְאֵלֶּה חָפַצְתִּי נְאֻם יְיָ'. וְכֻלָּא הַאי בְּהַאי
תַּלְיָא. ר' יוֹסֵי אָמַר, אִלֵּין אִינּוּן תִּקּוּנֵי כֻּרְסְיָיא, דִּכְתִּיב צֶדֶק וּמִשְׁפָּט
מְכוֹן כִּסְאֶךָ. וּכְתִיב וְהוּכַן בַּחֶסֶד כִּסֵּא.

519. Rabbi Yehuda said, He who falsifies judgment, is false to the institutions of the King. What are the institutions of the King? They are those of which we learned, "who exercise faithful love, justice, and righteousness, in the earth" and further "for in these things I delight, says Hashem." And all these, FAITHFUL LOVE, JUSTICE, AND RIGHTEOUSNESS, are intertwined. Rabbi Yosi said, these are the institutions of the throne, DENOTING MALCHUT, as it is written, "Righteousness and Justice are the foundation of Your throne" (Tehilim 89:15), and, "And in mercy a throne was established" (Yeshayah 16:5).

23. The assembly discussing the tabernacle

A Synopsis

Here follows a long metaphorical exposition of the features of the head and body of the King, Zeir Anpin: hairs, forehead, eyes, eyebrows, nose, ears, face, lips, the mouth, the palate, the body, the legs and the kidneys – linking them all to the various aspects and combinations of the Sfirot. The text turns to the issue of judgment, telling us that when judgments are not rendered below then the same occurs above; all arrangements do not work properly. Then the mighty serpent controls, and the righteous cannot draw from the Nukva because she is not blessed. Rabbi Aba recalls that Rabbi Shimon told him that the river flowing out of Eden is Binah, and that it came out to water the Garden, Malchut, to nurture it.

כאן מתחיל אידרא דמשכנא

520. תָּנֵינָא בְּרָזָא דְרָזִין, רֵישָׁא דְמַלְכָּא, אִתְתָּקַן בְּחֶסֶד וּבִגְבוּרָה. בְּהַאי רֵישָׁא, תַּלְיָין שַׂעֲרֵי, נִימִין עַל נִימִין, דְּאִינּוּן כֹּל מְשִׁיכוּתָא דְמִתְאַחֲדָן בְּהוּ עִלָּאֵי וְתַתָּאֵי. מָארֵי דְמָארִין, מָארֵי דְקַשּׁוֹט, מָארֵי דְמִתְקְלָא, מָארֵי דִיבָבָא, מָארֵי דִילָלָה, מָארֵי דְדִינָא, מָארֵי דְרַחֲמֵי, וְטַעֲמֵי אוֹרַיְיתָא, וְרָזֵי אוֹרַיְיתָא דַכְיָין, מִסָאֲבָן, כֻּלְּהוּ אִקְרוּן שַׂעֲרֵי דְמַלְכָּא, כְּלוֹמַר מְשִׁיכוּתָא דְאִתְמְשַׁךְ מִמַּלְכָּא קַדִּישָׁא, וְכֹלָּא נָחִית מֵעַתִּיקָא סְתִימָאָה.

Here begins the discussion of the tabernacle

520. We learned in the utmost secret, that the head of the King is arranged with Chesed and Gvurah. From that head OF ZEIR ANPIN hairs come down, hairs upon hairs, which are all flows, through which the supernal and lower GRADES are united. THIS MEANS, THAT THROUGH THEM, EACH LOWER GRADE RISES TO THE UPPER, AND THEY BECOME ONE. FROM FEW OF THE HAIRS ARE DRAWN men of power, men of truth, men of weight, who sigh, who weep, who judge, who are compassionate, who possess secrets of the Torah about kinds of purity and impurities. They are all called the King's hairs, that is, those which are drawn from the holy King. And

everything descends from the most ancient concealed one, WHICH IS ARICH ANPIN.

521. מִצְחָא דְמַלְכָּא, פְּקִידוּתָא דְחַיָּבַיָּא, כַּד אִתְפַּקְדָן בְּעוֹבָדַיְיהוּ, וְכַד אִתְגַּלְיָין חוֹבַיְיהוּ, כְּדֵין אִקְרֵי מִצְחָא דְמַלְכָּא. כְּלוֹמַר, גְּבוּרָה אִתְתָּקַּף בְּדִינוֹי, וְאִתְפָּשַׁט בְּסִטְרוֹי, וְדָא אִשְׁתָּנֵי מִמִּצְחָא דְעַתִּיקָא קַדִּישָׁא, דְּאִקְרֵי רָצוֹן.

521. The forehead of the King, DENOTING ZEIR ANPIN, brings to mind the remembrance of the wicked. When their deeds are remembered and their sins exposed, this is called 'Forehead of the king' meaning that Gvurah becomes reinforced in its judgments and extends itself. This change comes from the forehead of Atika Kadisha called will.

522. עַיְינִין דְּמַלְכָּא, אַשְׁגָּחוּתָא דְכֹלָּא, אַשְׁגָּחוּתָא דְּעֶלְאִין וְתַתָּאִין, וְכָל אִינּוּן מָארֵי אַשְׁגָּחוּתָא הָכִי אִקְרוּן. בְּעַיְינִין, גַּוְונִין אִתְאַחֲדָן, וְאִינּוּן גַּוְונִין אִקְרוּן, כָּל אִינּוּן מָארֵי אַשְׁגָּחוּתָא דְּמַלְכָּא, כָּל חַד כְּפוּם אָרְחֵיהּ, וְכֻלְּהוּ גַּוְונִין דְּעֵינָא אִקְרוּן. כְּמָה דְּאִתְחֲזֵי אַשְׁגָּחוּתָא דְּמַלְכָּא, הָכִי גַּוְונִין מִתְעָרִין.

522. The eyes of the King MEANS the overall supervision, supervision over the upper and lower. All these supervisors OF THE KING are called so, EYES. With the eyes the colors are unified, MEANING WHITE, RED, GREEN. By these colors are named all the supervisors of the King, each in his own way, all called colors of the eye. As appears the supervision of the King, so are the colors stirred. IF THE SUPERVISION IS OF CHESED, THEN IT IS WHITE; IF OF JUDGMENT, IT IS RED; IF OF MERCY, IT IS GREEN.

523. גְּבִינֵי דְעַיְינִין, אִקְרוּן, אֲתָר דְּיַהֲבִין אַשְׁגָּחוּתָא, לְכֻלְּהוּ גַּוְונִין מָארֵי אַשְׁגָּחוּתָא. הָכִי גְּבִינִין, לְגַבֵּי דִלְתַתָּא, גְּבִינִין לְאַשְׁגָּחוּתָא מֵהַהוּא נַהֲרָא דְּנָגִיד וְנָפִיק, אֲתָר לְאִתְמַשְּׁכָא מֵהַהוּא נַהֲרָא, לְאִסְתַּחֲאָה בְּחִוָּורָא דְּעַתִּיקָא, מֵחַלְבָּא דְּנָגִיד מֵאִמָּא, דְּכַד גְּבוּרָה

מִתְפַּשְּׁטָא, וְעַיְינִין מְלַהֲטָן בְּגָוֵון סוּמָקָא, נָהִיר עַתִּיקָא קַדִּישָׁא חִיוָּרָא
דִּילֵיהּ, וְלָהֲטָא בְּאִמָּא, וְאִתְמַלְּיָיא מֵחֲלָבָא, וְיַנְקָא לְהָנֵי, וְאִסְתְּחָן
כֻּלְּהוּ עַיְינִין, בְּהַהוּא חֲלָבָא דְּאִמָּא, דְּאִתְנְגִיד וְנָפִיק תָּדִיר. הֲהֲ"ד,
רוֹחֲצוֹת בֶּחָלָב. בַּחֲלָב דְּאִמָּא, דְּנָגִיד תָּדִירָא וְלָא פָּסִיק.

523. The eyebrows is the name of the place that the supervisor gives to all colors of the lower supervisors. These eyebrows in relation downwards, MEANING CORRESPONDING TO THE EYES, ARE eyebrows to look AND MOVE ON from that river that flows, NAMELY BINAH. This is the place to draw from that river so as to bathe in the whiteness of Atika, MEANING THE LIGHT OF CHASSADIM, from the milk flowing from Ima. HE EXPLAINS, when Gvurah, BEING THE LEFT COLUMN, extends itself; and the eyes, BEING THE SECRET OF CHOCHMAH, become inflamed with the color of red FROM THE ABUNDANCE OF JUDGMENT, BEING CHOCHMAH MINUS CHASSADIM, then Atika Kadisha, BEING KETER, shines upon its white BEING THE LIGHT OF CHASSADIM, kindles Ima, MEANING ABA AND IMA SUPERNAL, and she is filled with milk, DENOTING LIGHT OF CHASSADIM THAT SHE RECEIVED FROM KETER and she nurtures these EYES, THAT wash themselves with the milk of SUPERNAL Ima that flows constantly. CHOCHMAH THAT IS THE EYES ADORNS ITSELF WITH THOSE CHASSADIM. This is the essence of the verse, "washed with milk" (Shir Hashirim 5:12), MEANING, "HIS EYES ARE LIKE DOVES BY THE WATER COURSES, WASHED with milk" of Ima that flows constantly without stop, AS THE MERGER OF ABA AND IMA SUPERNAL IS AN UNINTERRUPTED UNITY AS EXPRESSED IN THE ADJACENT PARAGRAPH.

524. חוֹטָמָא דְּמַלְכָּא קַדִּישָׁא, תִּקּוּנָא דְּפַרְצוּפָא, כַּד מִתְפַּשְּׁטָן גְּבוּרָן,
וּמִתְאַחֲדָן כַּחֲדָא, אִינּוּן חוֹטָמָא דְּמַלְכָּא קַדִּישָׁא. וְאִינּוּן גְּבוּרָן מֵחַד
גְּבוּרָה אֲחִידָן וְנָפְקִין. וְכַד דִּינִין מִתְעָרִין, וְנָפְקִין מִסִּטְרַיְיהוּ, לָא
מִתְבַּסְּמָן, אֶלָּא בִּתְנָנָא דְּמַדְבְּחָא. וּכְדֵין כְּתִיב, וַיָּרַח יְיָ' אֶת רֵיחַ
הַנִּיחֹחַ. שָׁאנֵי חוֹטָמָא דְּעַתִּיקָא, דְּלָא אִצְטְרִיךְ, דְּחוֹטָמָא דְּעַתִּיקָא,
אֶרֶךְ אַפַּיִם בְּכֹלָּא אִקְרֵי, וְהַהוּא נְהִירוּ דְּחָכְמְתָא סְתִימָאָה, אִקְרֵי
חוֹטָמָא דִּילֵיהּ. וְהַיְינוּ תְּהִלָּה, דִּכְתִיב, וּתְהִלָּתִי אֶחֱטָם לָךְ. וְעַל דָּא
אִתְּעַר דָּוִד מַלְכָּא, תְּהִלָּה לְדָוִד וְגוֹ'.

524. The nose of the Holy King, DENOTING ZEIR ANPIN, is the arrangement of the face. When Gvurot expand and unite, they are the nose of the Holy King. These Gvurot with one act of Gvurah join together and come out. When judgments are stirred and EACH steps from their side, they are scented only by the smoke of the altar. Then we find written: "And Hashem smelled the sweet savor" (Beresheet 8:21). The nose of Atika, BEING ARICH ANPIN, is different, however, since it does not need THE SMOKE OF THE ALTAR and it is considered wholly 'long suffering (lit. 'long nosed'), and the light of concealed Chochmah is called its nose (Heb. *chotem*); this is the meaning of the word 'praise', as it is written, "and for my praise will I refrain (Heb. *echetom*) for you" (Yeshayah 48:9). Regarding this David commented in "A praise of David..." (Tehilim 145:1).

525. אוּדְנִין דְּמַלְכָּא, כַּד רַעֲוָא אִשְׁתְּכַח, וְאִמָּא יָנְקָא, וּנְהִירוּ דְּעַתִּיקָא קַדִּישָׁא אִתְנְהִיר, מִתְעֲרִין נְהִירוּ דִּתְרֵין מוֹחֵי, וּנְהִירוּ דְּאַבָּא וְאִמָּא, כָּל אִינּוּן דְּאִקְרוּן מוֹחֵי דְּמַלְכָּא, וּמִתְלַהֲטִין כַּחֲדָא. וְכַד מִתְלַהֲטָן כַּחֲדָא, אִקְרוּן אָזְנֵי יְיָ'. דְּהָא אִתְקַבִּילַת צְלוֹתְהוֹן דְּיִשְׂרָאֵל. וּכְדֵין אִתְעָרוּתָא לְטָב וּלְבִישׁ, וּבְאִתְעָרוּתָא דָּא, מִתְעֲרִין מָארֵי דְּגַדְפִין, דְּנַטְלִין קָלִין דְּעָלְמָא, וְכֻלְּהוּ אִקְרוּן אָזְנֵי יְיָ'.

525. The ears of the King exist with the presence of goodwill, Ima nurtures ZEIR ANPIN WITH LIGHT OF CHASSADIM, and the light of Atika Kadisha shines; the illumination of two hemispheres of the brain is roused, and the light of Aba and Ima and all those known as the hemispheres of the brains of the King, and they enflame together. And when they enflame together, they are called the ears of Hashem. Then the prayers of Yisrael are received, and consciousness then enlists for good or bad, and with this stirring are awakened the winged ones that receive the voices of the earth; all are called ears of Hashem.

526. אַנְפּוֹי דְּמַלְכָּא, נְהִירוּ דְּאַבָּא וְאִמָּא, וְאִתְפַּשְׁטוּתָא דִּלְהוֹן, דְּנַהֲרִין וְסַחֲרִין, וְלָהֲטִין בְּהַאי רֵישָׁא דְּמַלְכָּא. וּכְדֵין סַהֲדוּתָא אִסְתְּהַד בְּמַלְכָּא מִנַּיְיהוּ. דִּיּוּקְנָא דְּמַלְכָּא, יַקִּירוּתָא מִכֹּלָּא. מֵרֵישָׁא שָׁארֵי חֶסֶד עִלָּאָה, וּגְבוּרָה. וּנְהִירוּ דְּאַבָּא וְאִמָּא אִתְפְּלַג, נְהִירוּ דְּאַבָּא בִּתְלַת נְהוֹרִין, וְאִמָּא בִּתְרֵין, הָא חֲמִשָּׁה. חֶסֶד וּגְבוּרָה בְּחַד נְהוֹרָא, הָא שִׁיתָא.

לְבָתַר, אִתְעַטָּר חֶסֶ״ד, וְאִתְלְהִיט וְאִתְנְהִיר בִּתְרֵין נְהוֹרִין וְאִינּוּן
תְּמַנְיָיא. לְבָתַר אִתְעַטָּר, וּגְבוּרָה, אִתְנְהִיר בְּחַד, הָא תִּשְׁעָה. וְכַד
מִתְחַבְּרָן כֻּלְּהוּ נְהוֹרִין כַּחֲדָא, אִקְרוֹן דִּיּוּקְנָא דְּמַלְכָּא, וּכְדֵין כְּתִיב, יְיָ'
כַּגִבּוֹר יֵצֵא כְּאִישׁ מִלְחָמוֹת יָעִיר קִנְאָה וְגוֹ'.

526. The face of the King, BEING ZEIR ANPIN, is the light of Aba and Ima and their extension, IN THE ORDER OF THE THREE DOTS-CHOLAM-SHURUK-CHIRIK-that give light IN THE CHOLAM, go around THE SHURUK and glow IN THE CHIRIK, in the head of the King. Then flows from them the testimony, MEANING THE ILLUMINATIONS OF CHOCHMAH, testifying for the King, NAMELY ZEIR ANPIN. The image of the King is the most cherished. Within the head, dwells supernal Chesed and Gvurah. The light of Aba and Ima divides itself thus: The light of Aba in three lights, THE LIGHT OF Ima in two lights, total of five LIGHTS. Chesed and Gvurah included in one light, now total six. Later Chesed adorns itself and kindles in two lights, now total eight; Gvurah kindles one LIGHT, now nine LIGHTS. When all lights join, they are called the image of the King. Then the verse writes, "Hashem shall go forth as a mighty man, He shall stir up ardor like a man of war" (Yeshayah 42:13), AS THE ILLUMINATION OF CHOCHMAH IS DRAWN ONLY THROUGH GVURAH.

527. שִׂפְוָון דְּמַלְכָּא, הָכִי תָּאנָא, כַּד אִתְנְהִיר נְהִירוּ דְּאַבָּא, נָהִיר
בִּתְלַת נְהוֹרִין. מֵחַד נְהוֹרָא, נָהִיר חֶסֶד עִלָּאָה. מֵחַד נְהוֹרָא, אִתְנְהִיר
נְהִירוּ דְּאִקְרֵי מוֹחָא דְּמַלְכָּא. וְחַד נְהוֹרָא, הֲוָה תָּלֵי, עַד דְּאִתְנְהִיר
נְהִירוּ דְּאִמָא. וְכַד אִתְנְהִיר אִתְנְהִיר בְּחָמֵשׁ נְהוֹרִין.

527. The lips of the King: We learned that when the light of Aba, NAMELY ABA AND IMA SUPERNAL, sheds light, it does so with three lights; from one light, CHOCHMAH, kindles supernal Chesed; from one light, BINAH, a light shines called the brain of the King. One light, DA'AT remains suspended until the light of Ima ignites, YISRAEL SABA AND TEVUNAH. When the light RETURNS, it shines with five lights.

528. בְּמַאי אִתְנְהִיר מֵחַד שְׁבִילָא, דְּטָמִיר וְגָנִיז, דְּאִתְדַּבַּק בֵּיה אַבָּא,

דִּכְתִיב, נָתִיב לֹא יְדָעוֹ עָיְט וְגוֹ'. כְּמָה דְּאִתְדַּבַּק דְּכוּרָא בְּנוּקְבָא,
וְאִתְעַבְּרַת, וְאוֹלִידַת, וְאַפִּיקַת חָמֵשׁ נְהוֹרִין. וּמֵאִינוּן חָמֵשׁ נְהוֹרִין,
אִתְגְּלִיפוּ חַמְשִׁין תַּרְעִין, דִּנְהוֹרִין סַגִּיאִין. חַמְשִׁין אִינוּן, לָקֳבְלֵיהוֹן,
מ"ט פָּנִים טָהוֹר, מ"ט פָּנִים טָמֵא, בְּאוֹרַיְיתָא, אִשְׁתְּאַר חַד, וְהַאי חַד
אִתְנְהִיר בְּכֹלָּא, וְהַהוּא דְּאַבָּא, הֲוָה תָּלֵי. כַּד מִתְחַבְּרָן כַּחֲדָא,
וּמִתְיַישְּׁבָן בְּמַלְכָּא, אִקְרוּן שִׂפְווֹן דְּמַלְכָּא. בְּגִינֵי כַּךְ, גָּזַר מִלִּין דִּקְשׁוֹט.

528. HE ASKS: From what does IMA give light? HE ANSWERS: From one concealed path that Aba clings to, as the verse writes, "There is a path which no bird of prey knows" (Iyov 28:7), as the male clings to female. And she conceives and gives forth five lights. From these five lights are engraved fifty gates of manifold lights BEING KETER, CHOCHMAH, BINAH, TIFERET, AND MALCHUT WITH EACH COMPOSED OF TEN SFIROT. They are fifty, facing them are 49 pure aspects and 49 impure aspects of the Torah. There remains one NOT IN THIS COUNT, NAMELY THE FIFTIETH GATE. The one sheds lights to all, BEING THE SECRET OF THE PATH OF ABA ABOUT WHOM IT IS WRITTEN: "A PATH WHICH NO BIRD OF PREY KNOWS," MEANING MOSES REFERRED TO AS 'BIRD OF PREY', AS HE TOO WAS NOT GIVEN THE FIFTIETH GATE. THE LIGHT OF Aba remains suspended. When ABA AND IMA join and become clothed with the King, ZEIR ANPIN, they are called lips of the King, AS ABA IS CLOTHED WITH A SUPERNAL LIP AND IMA WITH THE LOWER LIP, and as a result, He decrees truthfully.

529. וּפוּמָא, בְּהוּ תַּלְיָיא, פְּתִיחוּתָא דְּפוּמָא. מַאי פוּמָא. אֶלָּא דַּעַת
גָּנִיז בְּפוּמָא דְּמַלְכָּא, דְּאִקְרֵי ת"ת. פְּשִׁיטוּתָא דְּתִפְאֶרֶת, דְּכָל אוֹצְרִין
וְכָל גְּווֹנִין אִתְאַחֲדָן בֵּיהּ. דִּכְתִיב, וּבְדַעַת חֲדָרִים יִמָּלְאוּ. וְהַהוּא דַּעַת,
הוּא גָּנִיז, בְּפוּמָא דְּמַלְכָּא. וּמַלְיָיא כָּל אִדְּרִין וְאַכְסַדְרָאִין. וְכַד אִתְּעַר
נְהִירוּ דְּבֵיהּ וְנָפִיק, כְּדֵין אִקְרֵי פֶּה יְיָ'. וְשִׂפְווֹן דְּאִינוּן תְּרֵין נְהוֹרִין
מֵאַבָּא וּמֵאִימָּא, בְּשַׁעֲתָא דְּאִתְעַרְעָן בְּהַהִיא נְהִירוּ דְּדַעַת, מִתְחַבְּרָן
כַּחֲדָא, וּמִלִּין אִתְגְּזָרוּ בִּקְשׁוֹט, בְּחָכְמָה בִּתְבוּנָה וּבְדַעַת. וּכְדֵין, כָּל
מִלִּין דְּקוּדְשָׁא בְּרִיךְ הוּא, בְּאִלֵּין אִתְגְּזָרוּ.

529. The mouth OF ZEIR ANPIN; THE LIPS allow for a mouth opening. HE ASKS: what is the mouth? HE ANSWERS: Da'at is concealed in the mouth of the King, called Tiferet, NAMELY ZEIR ANPIN AS DA'AT IS the extension of Tiferet, NAMELY ZEIR ANPIN, BEING THE SECRET OF ZEIR ANPIN THAT ASCENDED AND BECAME THE CENTRAL COLUMN TO LINK ABA AND IMA WITH EACH OTHER. All treasures and colors are united within, IN DA'AT BEING THE CENTRAL COLUMN, as it is written, "and by knowledge (*Da'at*) are the chambers filled" (Mishlei 24:4). This Da'at is concealed in the mouth of the King and fills all the chambers and porches, MEANING IT EXPANDS IN CHESED, GVURAH, TIFERET, NETZACH, HOD AND YESOD, OF ZEIR ANPIN AS CHESED, GVURAH AND TIFERET ARE CALLED CHAMBERS AND NETZACH HOD YESOD THE PORCHES. When the light of Da'at is stirred and emerges, it is then referred to as 'the mouth of Hashem' and the lips, being the two lights of Aba and Ima, when they meet the light of Da'at, they join BY IT together, and the matter is pronounced in truth, through Chochmah, Tevunah, and Da'at. Then all words of the Holy One, blessed be He, are pronounced WITH CHOCHMAH, BINAH AND DA'AT.

530. נַהֲרִין תְּלַת אִלֵּין, וְעָיְילִין בְּגוֹ לְגוֹ, וְאִתְעַטְּרוּ בְּחַד. וְכַד מִתְחַבְּרָן בְּעִטּוּרָא חַד, כְּדֵין אִקְרוּן חִכּוֹ מַמְתַּקִּים. וְאִינּוּן חֵיךְ דְּמַלְכָּא, וְאִקְרוּן, מְתִיקָא דְּמַלְכָּא. וְעַל הַאי כְּתִיב, טַעֲמוּ וּרְאוּ כִּי טוֹב יְיָ'. וּבְהַאי חֵיךְ, תַּלְיָין כָּל אִינּוּן שְׁלִיטִין וְהוּרְמָנִין דְּמַלְכָּא, דִּכְתִּיב, וּבְרוּחַ פִּיו כָּל צְבָאָם.

530. These three, CHOCHMAH, BINAH, DA'AT, shed light and enter in the most inner areas, MEANING THE HEAD OF ZEIR ANPIN WITH THE ASPECT OF IMA AND FROM THERE THEY EXPAND and adorn with the one, MEANING THE BODY OF ZEIR ANPIN, AS A RESULT OF THE REASONING GIVEN ABOVE; SINCE THE THREE OF IMA ARE DERIVED FROM ONE, FROM TIFERET THAT ASCENDED THERE WITH THE ASPECT OF THE CENTRAL COLUMN, SO ONE, BEING TIFERET EXISTS IN THREE. When CHOCHMAH, BINAH, DA'AT joins in one crown, then THE CROWN is called "His mouth is most sweet" (Shir Hashirim 5:16). They are the palate of the King FOUND AT THE BEGINNING OF THE BODY and called the sweetness of the King, and so it writes; "O taste and see that Hashem is good" (Tehilim 34:9), SINCE THE SENSE OF TASTE IS IN THE PALATE. And to this palate

are linked all the appointees and officials of the King, as it is written, "and all the hosts of them by the breath of His mouth" (Tehilim 33:6).

531. בְּהַאי חֵיךְ שְׁלֵימוּתָא דְּכֹלָּא אִשְׁתְּכַח. וּבְגִינֵי כַּךְ, כָּל אַתְוָון דְּאִינוּן בְּהַאי אֲתָר שְׁלֵימוּתָא אִתְחַזְיָיא בְּהוּ. אֹהֹחֹ"ע, א', נְהִירוּ דְּעַתִּיקָא קַדִּישָׁא סְתִימָאָה דְּכָל סְתִימִין. ח', נְהִירוּ דְּחָכְמְתָא, דְּלָא אִשְׁתְּכַח וְלָא אִתְדְּבַּק דִּכְתִּיב, לָא יָדַע אֱנוֹשׁ עֶרְכָּה. ה', נְהִירוּ דְּאִימָּא, דְּנָהִיר וְנָגִיד וְנָפִיק, וּמַשְׁקֵי לְכֹלָּא, וְיָנְקָא לִבְנִין, עַד דְּמָטֵי הַהוּא רְבוּת, וּמַלֵּי לַצַּדִּיק, וְאִיהוּ אִתְקַטֵּר בְּנוּקְבָא תַּתָּאָה, וְאִתְבָּרְכָא מִנֵּיהּ, וְלָא מִתְפָּרְשִׁין דָּא מִן דָּא. חִוָּור מִגּוֹ סוּמָק, דִּכְתִּיב הַר הַמּוֹר גִּבְעַת הַלְּבוֹנָה. ע', נְהִירוּ דְּע' אַנְפִּין, דְּאִתְזָנוּ מֵהַאי רוּחָא, דְּנָפִיק מִן פּוּמָא, כְּדֵין ע' שְׁמָהָן דְּקוּדְשָׁא בְּרִיךְ הוּא. לָקֳבְלֵהוֹן בְּאַרְעָא, כָּל הַנֶּפֶשׁ לְבֵית יַעֲקֹב הַבָּאָה מִצְרַיְמָה שִׁבְעִים. דְּהָא יַעֲקֹב אִילָנָא בְּאַרְעָא, וְאִינוּן ע' נֶפֶשׁ, ע' עַנְפִּין.

531. Within the palate, all perfection is present, so the perfection of all letters found in this place, is discernible. FOUR LETTERS Aleph, Chet, Hei, Ayin ARE ARTICULATED IN THE THROAT. THEIR SECRET IS AS FOLLOWS: Aleph is the light of the most concealed Atika Kadisha, NAMELY KETER. *Chet* is light of Chochmah, not found nor grasped, as it is written, "Man cannot know its price" (Iyov 28:13). Hei is the light of Ima, that sheds light, comes out, waters everything, nurtures the children, NAMELY MALE AND FEMALE, until the HOLY anointing comes and fills the Righteous, BEING YESOD, then joins the lower Nukva, BEING MALCHUT, that is blessed from it, and they do not separate from each other. THE BOUNTY OF IMA IS white from within the red, MEANING THAT THE LEFT CALLED RED IS INCORPORATED IN THE RIGHT CALLED WHITE, as it is written: "the mountain of myrrh, and to the hill of frankincense" (Shir Hashirim 4:6). THIS VERSE REFERS TO IMA WHERE MYRRH SPICE IS RED AND FRANKINCENSE IS WHITE. Ayin refers to the light of seventy 'faces', nourished from the breath departing from the mouth, they are the seventy names of the Holy One, blessed be He, ZEIR ANPIN, corresponding on earth to, "all the souls of the house of Jacob who came into Egypt were seventy" (Beresheet 46:27). Jacob is the tree on earth, CORRESPONDING TO ZEIR ANPIN; his seventy souls are the seventy branches OF THE TREE.

532. מֵאִלֵּין אַתְוָון, נְהִירִין אַרְבַּע אָחֲרָנִין. מָא' נָהִיר גִּימֶ"ל, דְּאִיהִי
אֲגַר טָב לְצַדִּיקַיָּיא, דְּאִקְרֵי גְּמוּל, וְעַל דָּא כְּתִיב אָז תִּתְעַנַּג עַל יְיָ'.
מֵח' נָהִיר יוּ"ד, דְּהִיא חָכְמָה, כְּלָּא אַסְתִּים בְּיוּ"ד, דְּאִיהִי סְתִימָא מִכָּל
סִטְרוֹי, וּבְג"כ, לָא אִשְׁתְּכַח, דִּכְתִיב, וְלֹא תִמָּצֵא בְּאֶרֶץ הַחַיִּים. מֵה',
נָהִיר כָּ"ף. דְּאִיהוּ נְהִירוּ וּמְשַׁח רְבוּת, דְּאִתְפָּרַק מֵאִימָּא, לְהַהוּא אֲתָר
דְּאִתְקְרֵי קֶרֶן, וְאִקְרֵי קֶרֶן הַיּוֹבֵל. וְדָא מַלְכוּת דָּוִד. וּבְגִין כָּךְ, לֵית
מְשִׁיחָא, אֶלָּא בְּרָזָא דְכַ"ף.

532. From these FOUR letters, ALEPH-CHET-HEI-AYIN, FOUR other LETTERS SHINE, GIME-YUD-CAF-KOF THAT EMANATE FROM THE PALATE. From the Aleph OF THE ALEPH-CHET-HEI-AYIN GROUP-Gimel shines OF THE GIMEL-YUD-CAF-KOF GROUP being good reward (Heb. *gemul*) to the Righteous, called '*Gemul*' NAMELY GIMEL; about this is written "Then shall you delight yourself in Hashem" (Yeshayah 58:14). From *Chet* OF THE ALEPH-CHET-HEI-AYIN GROUP, *Yud* shines OF THE GIMEL-YUD-CAF-KOF GROUP, which is Chochmah, that becomes entirely enclosed within the *Yud*, as it is closed on all sides, CONTAINING NO WHITE, SO CHOCHMAH is not to be found, as the verse writes, "nor is it found in the land of the living" (Iyov 28:13), AS EXPLAINED. From Hei OF THE CHET-HEI-AYIN GROUP *Caf* shines OF GIMEL-YUD-CAF-KOF being the light and anointing oil poured from Ima to that place called 'horn' and called "ram's (Jubilee's) horn" AS 'HORN' ALLUDES TO MALCHUT AND JUBILEE TO BINAH. AND WHEN MALCHUT RECEIVES BOUNTY FROM BINAH, SHE IS NAMED RAM'S HORN. This is a Kingdom of David. Hence, so anointing of kings needs to be with the secret of Caf.

533. ק' מֵע' נָהִיר ק', כְּמָה דְע' שַׁבְעִין, כַּךְ ק' מֵאָה, דְּאִינּוּן שְׁלִימוּ,
וְהָכִי הוּא, וּבְגִין כָּךְ, בְּהַאי חֵיךְ שְׁלִימוּ דְכֹלָּא. וְכָל מַאן דְּיָדַע רָזָא דָא,
וְאִזְדְּהַר בֵּיהּ, זַכָּאָה חוּלְקֵיהּ.

533. The *Kof* OF GIMEL-YUD-CAF-KOF shines from the *Ayin* OF THE ALEPH-CHET-HEI-AYIN GROUP. Just as Ayin is seventy, CONTAINING THE SEVEN SFIROT OF CHESED, GVURAH, TIFERET, NETZACH, HOD, YESOD AND MALCHUT WHERE EACH POSSESSES TEN SFIROT, so the Kof

is one Hundred, AS IT POSSESSES ALSO THE THREE FIRST SFIROT CHOCHMAH, BINAH, DA'AT, the completion OF THE TEN SFIROT. It is so because the palate has the total perfection. Whoever is familiar with this secret and is mindful of it, happy is his portion.

534. גּוּפָא דְמַלְכָּא, אִתְפַּשְׁטוּתָא דְּתִפְאֶרֶת, דִּגְוָונִין בֵּיהּ מִתְחַבְּרָן. דְרוֹעִין דְמַלְכָּא, נְהִירוּ דְחֶסֶד וּגְבוּרָה. וּבְגִין כַּךְ יָמִין וּשְׂמָאל. מְעוֹי בְּדַעַת אִתְתַּקָּנָן, עָיֵיל בְּרֵישָׁא, אִתְתָּקַּן וְאִתְפַּשַּׁט לְגוֹ, וּבְגוֹ גּוּפָא.

534. The body of the King is the extension of THE SFIRAH OF Tiferet wherein the colors WHITE AND RED are linked, BEING TWO COLUMNS, RIGHT AND LEFT, THE BODY BEING THE CENTRAL COLUMN THAT UNIFIES THEM. The arms of the King are the lights of Chesed and Gvurah; they are therefore THE TWO COLUMNS Right and Left, WITH THE BODY AS THE CENTRAL COLUMN THAT UNITES THEM. The intestines, MEANING THE INTERIOR are arranged with Da'at that enters through the head AND SETS IN BETWEEN THE TWO COLUMNS CHOCHMAH AND BINAH, and extends to the interior within the body, DENOTING TIFERET.

535. שׁוֹקִין אִתְאַחֲדָן בִּתְרֵין נְהוֹרִין, וְאִינּוּן תְּרֵין נְהוֹרִין מַמָּשׁ. שׁוֹקִין וּתְרֵין כֻּלְיָין. כֻּלְּהוּ מִתְחַבְּרָן בְּאֲתָר חַד, דְּתַמָּן אִתְכְּנַשׁ כָּל רְבוּת, וְכָל מְשִׁחָא דְגוּפָא. וּמִתַּמָּן, שַׁרְיָין כָּל הַהוּא רְבוּת, לַאֲתָר דְּאִתְקְרֵי יְסוֹד עוֹלָם. יְסוֹד, מֵהַהוּא אֲתָר דְּאִקְרֵי עוֹלָם. וּמַאן אִיהוּ. נֶצַח וְהוֹד, וְעַל כֵּן, יְיָ' צְבָאוֹת שְׁמוֹ ב"ה בְּרִיךְ שְׁמֵיהּ לְעָלַם וּלְעָלְמֵי עָלְמִין.

535. The legs join with two lights, literally two lights, MEANING NETZACH AND HOD. The legs and two kidneys join in one place, AS THE TWO KIDNEYS ARE ALSO NETZACH AND HOD. There gather the anointment and all oil of the body, and from there, FROM NETZACH AND HOD flows all HOLY anointing oil to a place called the foundation of the world, MEANING Yesod, from that place called 'world'. What is this? It is Netzach and Hod and so, Hashem Tzevaot is His name, AS NETZACH AND HOD are CALLED TZEVAOT, Blessed be He and His name to all eternity.

536. כָּל הָנֵי תִּקּוּנִין, אַתְיָין לְאִתְחַבְּרָא בְּחַד, עַד דְכָל רְבוּת קַדְשָׁא,

נָטִיל כֹּלָּא הַאי יְסוֹד, וְאַשְׁדֵּי לְנוּקְבָּא, וּמִתְבָּרְכָא מִנֵּיהּ. אֵימָתַי
מִתְבָּרְכָא מִנֵּיהּ. בְּשַׁעֲתָא דְּאִתְתַּקְנוּ דִּינִין דִּלְתַתָּא. וְכַד דִּינִין מִתְתַּקְנִין
לְתַתָּא, מִתְתַּקְנִין לְעֵילָּא, וְכָל תִּקּוּנִין דְּמַלְכָּא, בְּחֶדְוָותָא, בִּשְׁלִימוּ,
דְּאִינּוּן שְׁמָא קַדִּישָׁא, וַהֲוָה כֹּלָּא חַד. וּכְדֵין הוּא שָׁארֵי בְּגַוַּויְיהוּ,
דִּכְתִיב אֱלֹהִים נִצָּב בַּעֲדַת אֵל בְּקֶרֶב אֱלֹהִים יִשְׁפֹּט.

536. All these arrangements join in the one, MEANING NUKVA, until Yesod receives all the holy anointing oil and pours it to Nukva, NAMELY MALCHUT, which is blessed from it. When is she blessed from it? When judgments are arranged below; and when judgments are rendered below, they are arranged above. All adornments of the King, which are the Holy Name, are with joy and perfection. Then He dwells in their midst, as it is written, "Elohim stands in the Congregation of El; He judges among the judges" (Tehilim 82:1). THEREFORE JUDGMENTS ARE COMPARED TO FIRE. JUST AS FIRE IN A PROPER VESSEL GIVES FORTH LIGHT AND COOKS, BUT WHEN IMPROPERLY USED, CONSUMES AND DESTROYS, SO IT IS WITH JUDGMENTS.

537. וְכַד דִּינִין לָא מִתְתַּקְנָן לְתַתָּא, כִּבְיָכוֹל הָכִי לְעֵילָּא. דְּכָל תִּקּוּנִין
לָא מִתְיַשְּׁרָן הָכִי, דְּהָא אִימָּא אִסְתָּלְקַת מֵעַל בְּנִין, וּבְנִין לָא יַנְקֵי,
דְּהָא יְסוֹד לָא אַשְׁדֵּי בְּנוּקְבָּא, וְכָל דִּינִין מִתְעָרִין, וְחִוְיָא תַּקִּיפָא
שָׁלְטָא. כִּבְיָכוֹל, תִּקּוּנֵי מַלְכָּא עַל דִּינָא אִסְתָּלְקוּ, דְּכֵיוָן דְּהַאי נוּקְבָּא
לָא מִתְבָּרְכָא, וְצַדִּיק לָא נָטִיל. וְחִוְיָא תַּקִּיפָא שָׁלְטָא. וַוי לְעָלְמָא
דְּיַנְקָא מִנַּיְיהוּ.

537. When judgments are not rendered below, so to speak, the same occurs above, that all arrangements are not working properly, ACCORDING TO THE MANNER WE DESCRIBED EARLIER. Ima then deserts the children, THEY BEING MALE AND FEMALE; the children do not suckle, Yesod does not pour into the Nukva, WHICH IS MALCHUT, judgments are stirred up, and the mighty serpent controls; the adornments of the King are removed due to the Judgment. Since the Nukva is not blessed, the righteous, BEING YESOD, does not receive FOR OF HER, the mighty serpent has power. Woe to the world that is nurtured from them.

538. אָמַר ר' אֶלְעָזָר, כָּל הָנֵי תִקּוּנִין, אַבָּא גַּלֵי לוֹן, בְּגִין דְּלָא יֵיעוֹל בְּכִסוּפָא לְעָלְמָא דְּאָתֵי. הַשְׁתָּא אֲמַאי אִצְטְרִיכוּ לְאִתְגַּלָּאָה. אָמַר לֵיהּ ר' אַבָּא, הַהוּא דַּאֲנָא כָּתַבְנָא מִבּוּצִינָא קַדִּישָׁא, אֲמֵינָא לְגַבֵּי חַבְרַיָּא, דְּהָא אִינּוּן יַדְעִין מִלִּין, וְהָא אִצְטְרִיךְ לְמִנְדַּע, דִּכְתִיב, וִידַעְתֶּם כִּי אֲנִי יְיָ'. וּכְתִיב וְיָדְעוּ כִּי אֲנִי יְיָ'. בְּגִין דְּאִתְיַישְּׁבָן מִלִּין. וּמִכָּאן וּלְהָלְאָה, סְתִימִין מִלִּין בְּגַוָּון. זַכָּאָה חוּלָקָנָא בְּהַאי עָלְמָא, וּבְעָלְמָא דְּאָתֵי, דְּהָא עַד כְּעַן בּוּצִינָא קַדִּישָׁא אִתְעַטָּר, בְּמִלִּין דִּבְגַוָּון.

538. Rabbi Elazar said, my father revealed all these arrangements, so he will not enter the World to Come in shame. But why is it necessary now to reveal? Rabbi Aba replied: This is what I wrote from the Holy LUMINARY, I said it is for the friends as they know AND UNDERSTAND these matters. It is important to know them as it is written, "that you may know that I am Hashem" (Shemot 10:2), and, "And they shall know that I am Hashem" (Shemot 29:46). Thus we understand the things said. From this point on, the matters are treasured among us. Fortunate is our lot in this world and the world to come. Until this point, the Holy Luminary was adorned with this matter among us.

539 ת"ח, אֲנָא חָזֵינָא לֵיהּ בְּחֶלְמָא, וְשָׁאִילְנָא קַמֵּיהּ דְּרַבִּי שִׁמְעוֹן, הָא אוֹלִיפְנָא קַמֵּיהּ דְּמַר, י' דְּאִיהִי חָכְמָה, וְהָכִי הוּא וַדַּאי. ה' אֲמַאי אִיהוּ בִּינָה. אָמַר לִי, ת"ח, הָא כְּתִיב וְנָהָר יוֹצֵא מֵעֵדֶן לְהַשְׁקוֹת אֶת הַגָּן. מָאן הוּא נָהָר דְּיוֹצֵא מֵעֵדֶן דָּא בִּינָה. וּבְג"כ הַהוּא נָהָר, י' סָתִים בְּגַוֵּיהּ. וְיוֹ"ד פָּשִׁיט נַהֲרָא דָּא מִכָּל סִטְרוֹי. וְדָא הִיא ד', לְבָתַר אֲפִיקַת בֵּן תְּחוֹתָהּ דְּאִיהוּ ו', כְּגַוְונָא דָּא ה'. בג"כ הוּא יָ"ה. לְבָתַר אוֹלִידַת וְאַפִּיקַת הַאי בֵּן, וְשַׁוְּיֵהּ לְקַמָּהּ, וּבְגִין כַּךְ יה"ו, דְּהָא ו' לְקַמָּהּ יָתִיב, לְיַנְקָא לֵיהּ. וְעַל כַּךְ תָּנֵינָן בְּמַתְנִיתָא דִּילָן, ה' ד' הֲוַת, מִדְּאִתְחַבַּר דְּכוּרָא עִמָּהּ אִתְעַבְּרַת מֵחַד בֵּן, וְאִקְרֵי ה'. לְבָתַר אוֹלִידַת וְאַפִּיקַת ו' הַהוּא בֵּן, וְקָאִים לְקַמָּהּ. וְעַל הַאי כְּתִיב, וְנָהָר יוֹצֵא מֵעֵדֶן, מִנֵּיהּ נָפִיק וַדַּאי, לְהַשְׁקוֹת אֶת הַגָּן, לְיַנְקָא לֵיהּ.

539. Come and behold. When I had seen him in a dream, I asked Rabbi Shimon: Master, I learned that *Yud* OF THE NAME YUD HEI VAV HEI represents Chochmah. And this is assuredly so. Hei OF YUD HEI VAV HEI, why is it Binah? He told me: Come and behold. It is written, "And a river went out of Eden to water the Garden" (Beresheet 2:10). What is this river flowing from Eden? It is Binah, THAT EXISTS FROM EDEN WHICH IS CHOCHMAH. As a result, the Yud MEANING CHOCHMAH, is enclosed within that river. This Yud spreads this light OF BINAH on all sides, MEANING ABOVE, THE SECRET OF RIGHT, AND BELOW, THE SECRET OF LEFT. It is now a *Dalet*. Later Binah begets a son beneath her, a Vav, MEANING THE CENTRAL COLUMN, THUS becoming now like a Hei. Now it is *Yud-Hei*, MEANING CHOCHMAH AND BINAH. Later, she brings forth that son before her. Now we have *Yud-Hei-Vav*; the *Vav* sat before her in order to suckle. About this we learned in our *Baraita* that the *Hei* was ORIGINALLY a *Dalet*. When the male, BEING CHOCHMAH, merged with it, it became pregnant with one son, and is called Hei; later it gave birth to the *Vav* OUTSIDE ITSELF and placed it before itself. Thus writes the verse, "And a river went out of Eden", WHICH IS BINAH THAT COMES OUT OF CHOCHMAH CALLED 'EDEN', it surely came out to water the Garden, BEING MALCHUT, to nurture it.

540. הַוֵינָא אָחִיד בִּידֵיהּ, וְנָשִׁיק בִּידוֹי. אֲנָא בְּהַאי עִדּוּנָא אִתְּעַרְנָא, בָּכֵי וְחַיֵּיךְ, וַהֲווֹ תְּלָתָא יוֹמִין דְּלָא אֲכִילְנָא מִידִי. חַד מֵחֶדְוָותָא, וְחַד דְּלָא זָכֵינָא לְמֶחֱמֵי לֵיהּ זִמְנָא אַחֲרָא. וְעִם כָּל דָּא, בֵּיהּ אִתְקַשַּׁרְנָא תָּדִירָא. דְּהָא כַּד נְהִירָא לִי שְׁמַעַתְּתָא, חֲמֵינָא דְּיוּקְנֵיהּ, דְּאִתְּעַר קַמָּאי, זַכָּאִין אִינּוּן צַדִּיקַיָּיא, בְּעָלְמָא דֵּין, וּבְעָלְמָא דְּאָתֵי, עֲלַיְיהוּ כְּתִיב, אַךְ צַדִּיקִים יוֹדוּ לִשְׁמֶךָ יֵשְׁבוּ יְשָׁרִים אֶת פָּנֶיךָ.

(ע"כ אידרא דמשכנא)

540. I seized his hand, and kissed it. During this period, I was stirred, cried, laughed, for three days I did not eat anything, because of the ecstasy and also since I merited not to see him again. Still I feel bonded to him. I see his image rising before me. Fortunate are the Righteous in this world and next world. Of them it is written: "Surely the righteous shall give thanks to Your name: the upright shall dwell in Your presence" (Tehilim 140:14).

(End of the assembly of the tabernacle)

24. "And all things that I have said to you be mindful of"

A Synopsis

We are told that it is important to serve God so that He will be mindful that no harm will befall us, and that we must make no mention of the name of other Elohim. Rabbi Yehuda says that the Torah cautions man in numerous places to observe the precepts of the Torah, because the whole Torah is the name of the Holy One, blessed be He.

541. וּבְכָל אֲשֶׁר אָמַרְתִּי אֲלֵיכֶם תִּשָּׁמֵרוּ וְגוֹ'. מַאי תִּשָּׁמֵרוּ, תִּשְׁמוֹרוּ מִבָּעֵי לֵיהּ. אֶלָּא תִּשָּׁמֵרוּ וַדַּאי, מַאי אֲשֶׁר אָמַרְתִּי אֲלֵיכֶם, כְּלוֹמַר דְּאַגְזִימִית לְכוֹן עַל מֵימָר פּוּלְחָנִי. תִּשָּׁמֵרוּ, דְּלָא יִמְטֵי עֲלֵיכוֹן שׁוּם בִּישׁ. תִּשָּׁמֵרוּ מֵהַהִיא שְׁמִירָה וּנְטוּרָא דִּילִי בִּלְבַד. וְשֵׁם אֱלֹהִים אֲחֵרִים לֹא תַזְכִּירוּ, לֹא תַזְכִּירוּ כְּמָה דְּאוֹקִימְנָא. ד"א וְשֵׁם אֱלֹהִים אֲחֵרִים לֹא תַזְכִּירוּ, כְּלוֹמַר, לֹא תְסַבְּבוּן, דְּתִתְפְּלוּן בֵּינֵי עֲמַמְיָא בְּאַרְעָא אַחֲרָא. וִיקוּיַּם בְּכוּ מַה דִּכְתִיב, וַעֲבַדְתָּ שָׁם אֱלֹהִים אֲחֵרִים וְגוֹ'.

541. "And all things that I have said to you be mindful of (Heb. *tishameru*)" (Shemot 23:13). HE ASKS: Why is the passive 'tishameru'? Should it not use the active form? HE ANSWERS: 'tishameru' is correct referring to "all things that I have said to you" meaning, I stressed the point of serving Me, be mindful that no harm will befall you. "tishameru (also: 'be guarded')": by My protection alone. "and make no mention of the name of other Elohim" (Ibid.), is to be understood as we established. Another explanation of the verse "and make no mention of the name of other Elohim" meaning, Do not refer to it, lest you will fall among nations in other lands and may become fulfilled what is written in a verse "and there shall you serve other Elohim... (Devarim 28:36).

542. ד"א וּבְכָל אֲשֶׁר אָמַרְתִּי אֲלֵיכֶם תִּשָּׁמֵרוּ. רַבִּי יְהוּדָה פָּתַח, שְׁמַע עַמִּי וְאָעִידָה בָּךְ וְגוֹ', לֹא יִהְיֶה בְךָ אֵל זָר וְגוֹ'. אָנֹכִי יְיָ' אֱלֹהֶיךָ הַמַּעַלְךָ מֵאֶרֶץ מִצְרַיִם וְגוֹ'. הָנֵי קְרָאן, אֲמָרָן דָּוִד בְּרוּחַ קוּדְשָׁא, וְאִית לְאִסְתַּכָּל בְּהוּ. שְׁמַע עַמִּי בְּכַמָּה אַתְרִין אַזְהִירִין אוֹרַיְיתָא לב"נ. בְּכַמָּה אַתְרִין קוּדְשָׁא בְּרִיךְ הוּא אַזְהִיר בֵּיהּ בְּבַר נָשׁ. וְכֹלָּא לְתוֹעַלְתָּא דְּבַר

נָשׁ. בְּגִין דְּיִנְטַר פִּקוּדֵי אוֹרַיְיתָא, דְּכָל מַאן דְּיִנְטַר אָרְחֵי דְּאוֹרַיְיתָא, וְאִשְׁתָּדַל בָּהּ, כְּמַאן דְּאִשְׁתָּדַל בִּשְׁמָא קַדִּישָׁא.

542. Another explanation for "And all things that I have said to you be mindful of." Rabbi Yehuda commenced, "Hear, My people, and I will testify against you...there shall be no strange El among you... I am Hashem your Elohim who brought you out of the land of Egypt" (Tehilim 81:9-11). David spoke these verses with the Holy Spirit; Let's examine them. "Hear, My people": in numerous places Torah cautions man, in numerous places the Holy One, blessed be He, cautions man and it is for the benefit of man, so he will observe the precepts of the Torah. He who is observant of Torah ways, and is occupied with it, is considered as occupied with the Holy Name.

543. דְּתָנֵינָן, אוֹרַיְיתָא כֹּלָּא שְׁמָא דְּקוּדְשָׁא בְּרִיךְ הוּא. וּמַאן דְּמִשְׁתַּדַל בָּהּ, כְּמַאן דְּמִשְׁתַּדַל בִּשְׁמָא קַדִּישָׁא בְּגִין דְּאוֹרַיְיתָא כֹּלָּא, חַד שְׁמָא קַדִּישָׁא הוּא. שְׁמָא עִלָּאָה, שְׁמָא דְּכָלִיל כָּל שְׁמָהָן. וּמַאן דְּגָרַע אוֹת חַד מִינָה, כְּאִילּוּ עָבִיד פְּגִימוּתָא בִּשְׁמָא קַדִּישָׁא. תָּאנָא, וְשֵׁם אֱלֹהִים אֲחֵרִים לֹא תַזְכִּירוּ, לֹא תּוֹסִיף עַל אוֹרַיְיתָא, וְלֹא תִּגְרַע מִינָּהּ. רַבִּי חִיָּיא אָמַר, וְשֵׁם אֱלֹהִים אֲחֵרִים, דָּא מַאן דְּיִתְעֲסַק בְּסִפְרִין אַחֲרָנִין, דְּלָא מִסִּטְרָא דְּאוֹרַיְיתָא. לָא יִשָּׁמַע עַל פִּיךְ, דְּאָסוּר אֲפִילּוּ לְאַדְכְּרָא לוֹן, וּלְמֵילַף מִנַּיְיהוּ טַעֲמָא, כָּל שֶׁכֵּן עַל אוֹרַיְיתָא.

543. We learned, the whole Torah is the name of the Holy One, blessed be He, and one who is occupied with it is considered to be occupied with the Holy Name, as the whole Torah is one Holy Name, a supernal name, a name incorporating OTHER names. One who deducts one letter from it is considered causing a defect in the Holy Name. We learned, "and make no mention of the name of other Elohim." MEANING, do not add or detract from the Torah, AS HE CAUSES A DEFECT IN THE HOLY NAME AND STRENGTHENS OTHER ELOHIM. Rabbi Chiya said: "the name of other Elohim" refers to those occupied with foreign books not of Torah. "neither let it be heard out of your mouth"; it is forbidden even to mention them, learn from them, especially AN EXPLANATION on the Torah.

544. רַבִּי יְהוּדָה מַתְנֵי הָכִי, מַאי טַעֲמָא כְּתִיב וְשֵׁם אֱלֹהִים אֲחֵרִים, וְסָמִיךְ לֵיהּ אֶת חַג הַמַּצוֹת תִּשְׁמֹר. אֶלָּא, מַאן דְּלָא נָטִיר הַאי, כְּמַאן דְּלָא נָטִיר מְהֵימְנוּתָא דְקוּדְשָׁא בְּרִיךְ הוּא. מַאי טַעֲמָא. מִשּׁוּם דְּבֵיהּ אֲחִידָא מִלָּה. אָמַר רַבִּי יִצְחָק, וְכֵן בְּכָל שְׁאַר זִמְנִין וְחַגִּין, דְּהָא כֻּלְּהוּ אֲחִידָן בִּשְׁמָא קַדִּישָׁא עִלָּאָה. וְעַל דָּא תָּנֵינָן, מַאי דִכְתִיב שָׁלֹשׁ פְּעָמִים בַּשָּׁנָה, מִשּׁוּם דִּבְהוּ תַּלְיָא מְהֵימְנוּתָא.

544. Rabbi Yehuda taught it thus. What is the reason for the verse, "the name of the other Elohim" and adjacent to it is this verse, "You shall keep the feast of unleavened bread" (Shemot 23:15). The explanation is that one who keeps not this, "THE FEAST OF UNLEAVENED BREAD" is equivalent to one who lacks faith in the Holy One, blessed be He. Why? The matter is closely connected to it. Rabbi Yitzchak said: So it is with all other holidays and festivals, as they are all connected with the Holy Name. About this we learned, it is written, "Three times in the year" (Ibid. 17), because from them is Faith suspended, BEING THE SECRET OF THE THREE COLUMNS THAT MALCHUT, CALLED FAITH IS CONSTRUCTED FROM.

25. Every man of Yisrael, who is circumcised, should be presented

A Synopsis
Rabbi Elazar tells us that every circumcised man of Yisrael needs to be seen before the Holy King in order to receive the blessings that flow from the fountain. Through a story he illustrates that Yisrael must remain separated from the unbelievers.

545. יֵרָאֶה כָּל זְכוּרְךָ, אֲמַאי כָּל זְכוּרְךָ. א"ר אֶלְעָזָר כָּל זְכוּרְךָ מַמָּשׁ. בְּגִין דְּנַטְלִין בִּרְכָתָא, מִמַּבּוּעָא דְנַחֲלָא. מִכָּאן תָּנֵינָן, כָּל בַּר יִשְׂרָאֵל דְּאִתְגְּזַר, בָּעֵי לְאִתְחֲזָאָה קַמֵּי מַלְכָּא קַדִּישָׁא, בְּגִין דְּנָטִיל בִּרְכָתָא, מִמַּבּוּעָא דְנַחֲלָא. הה"ד, כְּבִרְכַּת יְיָ' אֱלֹהֶיךָ אֲשֶׁר נָתַן לָךְ. וּכְתִיב אֶל פְּנֵי הָאָדוֹן יְיָ', כְּמָה דְּאוּקִימְנָא, דְּמִתַּמָּן מְרִיקָן בִּרְכָאן, וְנַטְלִין בִּרְכָתָא. זַכָּאָה חוּלָקֵיהוֹן דְּיִשְׂרָאֵל, מִכָּל שְׁאָר עַמִּין.

545. "...all your males shall appear" (Ibid.). HE ASKS: Why "all your males"? Rabbi Elazar said, literally all males for they receive the blessing from the fountain of the spring, DENOTING YESOD. From here we learned that every circumcised Yisrael needs to be seen before the Holy king in order to receive the blessings from the fountain of the spring. This is the essence of the verse "according to the blessing of Hashem your Elohim which he has given you" (Devarim 16:17), and, "before the Master, Hashem." As explained, THE MASTER IS YESOD, because from there the blessings flow, and they receive blessings. Fortunate is the lot of Yisrael above that of other nations.

546. זִמְנָא חֲדָא, סְלִיקוּ יִשְׂרָאֵל לְמֶחַג חַגָּא, וְאִתְעָרְבוּ עעכו"ם בַּהֲדַיְיהוּ, וְהַהוּא שַׁתָּא לָא אִשְׁתְּכַח בִּרְכָתָא בְּעָלְמָא. אָתוּ שָׁאִילוּ לְרַב הַמְנוּנָא סָבָא, אָמַר לְהוּ, חֲמֵיתוּן סִימָנָא בְּקַדְמֵיתָא בְּהַאי א"ל, סִימָנָא חֲמֵינָן, דְּכַד תַּבְנָא מֵהָתָם, כָּל אָרְחִין אִסְתְּימוּ מִמַּיָא, וַעֲנָנָא, וַחֲשׁוֹכָא אִשְׁתְּכַח, דְּלָא יַכְלִין לְמֶהַךְ כָּל אִינּוּן דְּסַלִּיקוּ לְתַמָּן. וְעוֹד, בְּשַׁעֲתָא דְּעָאלָנָא לְאִתְחֲזָאָה אַפֵּי שְׁמַיָא אִתְחַשְּׁכוּ וְאִתְרְגִיזוּ. אָמַר לְהוּ, וַדַּאי אוֹ אִית בֵּינַיְיכוּ בְּנֵי נָשָׁא דְּלָא אִתְגְּזָרוּ, אוֹ עעכו"ם סְלִיקוּ בַּהֲדַיְיכוּ. דְּהָא לָא אִתְבָּרְכָאן בְּהַהִיא שַׁעֲתָא, בַּר מֵאִינּוּן יִשְׂרָאֵל דְּאִתְגְּזָרוּ.

וּבְהַאי אָת קַדִּישָׁא מִסְתַּכֵּל קוּדְשָׁא בְּרִיךְ הוּא, וּבָרִיךְ לוֹן.

546. One time Yisrael made a pilgrimage TO JERUSALEM to celebrate the festival and there were idol worshippers among them. That year no blessings were present in the world. They came and asked Rav Hamnuna Saba. He said to them, did you see any sign TO INDICATE THAT THE PILGRIMAGE WAS INFAVORABLE? They replied, we did see a sign; when we returned from there, all roads were blocked by water, there were clouds and darkness so that none of us who went there were unable TO RETURN. Furthermore, when we came to be seen, the surface of the heavens became dark and stormy. He said to them, for sure either there were among you some uncircumcised people or idol worshippers. For in such moments, the blessing reaches only circumcised Yisrael. The Holy One, blessed be He, looks for that sign and blesses them.

547. לְשַׁתָּא אַחֲרָא סְלִיקוּ, וּסְלִיקוּ אִינּוּן עעכו"ם, דְּאִתְעָרְבוּ בַּהֲדַיְיהוּ, כַּד הֲווֹ אַכְלִין קָרְבְּנַיָּיא, וַהֲווֹ חַדָּאן. וְחָמוּ לְאִינּוּן עעכו"ם, דְּטַפְסָאן בְּקוּטְרַיְיהוּ לְקוּטְרָא דְּכוֹתָלָא. אַשְׁגָּחוּ בְּהוּ דְּכֹלָּא מְבָרְכִין, וְאִינּוּן לָא בְּרִיכוּ. אָתוּ וְאָמְרוּ מִלָּה לְבֵי דִּינָא, אָתוּ וְשָׁאִילוּ לוֹן, אָמְרוּ, הַאי דַּאֲכַלְתּוּן, חוּלָקָא דִּלְכוֹן, מַאן קוּרְבָּנָא הֲוָה. לָא הֲוָה בִּידַיְיהוּ. בָּדְקוּ וְאַשְׁכָּחוּ דְּאִינּוּן עעכו"ם, וְקָטְלוּ לוֹן. אָמְרוּ, בְּרִיךְ רַחֲמָנָא דְּשֵׁזִיב לְעַמֵּיהּ, דְּוַדַּאי לֵית בִּרְכְתָא שַׁרְיָא, אֶלָּא בְּיִשְׂרָאֵל, זַרְעָא קַדִּישָׁא, בְּנֵי מְהֵימְנוּתָא, בְּנֵי קְשׁוֹט. וְהַהִיא שַׁתָּא אִשְׁתְּכַח בִּרְכְתָא בְּעָלְמָא, בִּשְׁלִימוּ. פָּתְחוּ וְאָמְרוּ, אַךְ צַדִּיקִים יוֹדוּ לִשְׁמֶךָ וְגוֹ'.

547. The next year, they made pilgrimage, and idol worshippers were dispersed with them. When they ate of the meat of the sacrifice and were rejoicing, they saw the idol worshippers look like a wall, NAMELY SAD. They watched how everybody made the blessing but they did not. They told this in a court of law. They came and asked them, what part of the sacrifice did you eat? They did not know. Inquiring showed they were idol worshippers and they were slain. They said, blessed is the Merciful One who saved His people. The blessing rests only with Yisrael, holy seed, children of Faith, children of truth. That year the blessing in the world reached its zenith.

They explained, "Surely the Righteous shall give thanks to Your name..." (Tehilim 140:14).

548. ר' חִיָּיא אָמַר, בִּזְכוּת יִשְׂרָאֵל גְּזִירִין, אִתְכַּנְעוּ שַׂנְאֵיהוֹן תְּחוֹתֵיהוֹן, וְיַרְתֵּי אַחֲסַנְתֵּהוֹן. ת"ח מַה כְּתִיב, יֵרָאֶה כָּל זְכוּרְךָ. וּכְתִיב בַּתְרֵיהּ, כִּי אוֹרִישׁ גּוֹיִם מִפָּנֶיךָ וְהִרְחַבְתִּי אֶת גְּבוּלֶךָ. דְּקוּדְשָׁא בְּרִיךְ הוּא עָקַר דִּיּוּרִין מֵאַתְרַיְיהוּ, וְאָתֵיב דִּיּוּרִין, לְאַתְרַיְיהוּ. בְּגִינֵי כַּךְ יֵרָאֶה כָּל זְכוּרְךָ אֶת פְּנֵי הָאָדוֹן יְיָ'. רַבִּי יְהוּדָה אָמַר, הָאָדוֹן, כְּמָה דִכְתִיב, הִנֵּה הָאָדוֹן יְיָ' צְבָאוֹת מְסָעֵף פֻּארָה וְגו', וְיָצָא חוֹטֶר וְגו', וְכֹלָּא חַד, מְעַקַר דִּיּוּרִין וְאָתֵיב דִּיּוּרִין. ר' יִצְחָק אָמַר, אִית אָדוֹן, וְאִית אָדוֹן, וְכֹלָּא בְּחַד תַּלְיָא.

548. Rabbi Chiya said, due to the merit of circumcised Yisrael, the enemy is humbled before them and they inherit their land. Come and behold: it is written, "all you males appear" (Shemot 34:23), MEANING CIRCUMCISED MALES, then it is written: "For I will cast the nations before you, and enlarge your borders" (Ibid. 24). MEANING, IN THE MERIT OF CIRCUMCISION, the Holy One, blessed be He, WHO POSSESSES JUDGMENT AND MERCY, uproots dwellers from their place, REFERRING TO THE ENEMY, and replaces dwellers to their place MEANING THE CHILDREN OF YISRAEL. For this reason, "all you males appear before the master, Hashem," NAMELY THE HOLY ONE, BLESSED BE HE, WHO IS TIFERET POSSESSING JUDGMENT AND MERCY AND SO HE CAN UPROOT SOME AND REPLACE WITH OTHERS. Rabbi Yehuda said, "the master" resembles the words in the verse, "Behold, the master, Hashem Tzevaot, shall lop the bough with terror" (Yeshayah 10:33), WHICH REFERS TO UPROOTING DWELLERS. "And there shall come forth a rod..." (Yeshayah 11:1) REFERS TO BRINGING BACK DWELLERS. It is all the same, JUDGMENT AND MERCY WORKING TOGETHER and he uproots dwellers and settles other dwellers. Rabbi Yitzchak said, there is a master WHICH IS TIFERET, and there is a master (Heb. *adon*) WHICH IS YESOD. All are dependent in one, NAMELY MALCHUT CALLED ADONAI.

26. The Holy One, blessed be He, is called Adonai

A Synopsis
Rabbi Yosi says that Adonai refers to "visions of Elohim," that includes Zeir Anpin and Malchut. Rabbi Yehuda adds that sometimes the celestial are called with names of the lower levels, and sometimes the lower are called by names of the celestial.

549. רַבִּי יְהוּדָה אָמַר, אֲדֹנָי: אָלֶף דְּלֵית נוּן יוֹד, קוּדְשָׁא בְּרִיךְ הוּא אִקְרֵי, וְהַהוּא דְּאִקְרֵי, כְּמָה דְּאִיהוּ כְּתִיב. וּמַאן הוּא. רַבִּי יוֹסֵי אוֹמֵר, מַרְאֹת אֱלֹהִים. מַרְאֹת כְּתִיב. וּמַהוּ מַרְאֹת. שְׁלִימוּ דְכֹלָּא, יוּ"ד הֵ"א וָא"ו הֵ"א. מַרְאֹת לְמַאי אִיהוּ אָלֶ"ף דָּלֵי"ת נוּ"ן יוּ"ד, הַאי אִקְרֵי כְּכְתָבוֹ, וְהַאי לָא אִקְרֵי כְּכְתָבוֹ, וּבְגִינֵי כַּךְ אִקְרֵי בְּהַאי, וְעַל כַּךְ מַרְאֹת אֱלֹהִים כְּתִיב.

549. Rabbi Yehuda said: Adonai, WHEN WRITTEN OUT FULLY, IS SPELLED *Aleph Lamed Pe, Dalet Lamed Tav, Nun Vav Nun, Yud Vav Dalet*, is called 'the Holy One, blessed be He,' DENOTING ZEIR ANPIN, NOT YUD HEI VAV HEI, AS IT IS WRITTEN. That which is pronounced as written IS CALLED 'ADONAI'. Who is it? Rabbi Yosi said: It refers to "visions of Elohim," MEANING MALCHUT, CALLED 'VISION'. HE ASKS: it is written visions, PLURAL NUMBER, why IS IT WRITTEN visions? HE ANSWERS: IT INCLUDES ALSO the entirely of all, *Yud Vav Dalet, Hei Aleph, Vav Aleph Vav, Hei Aleph*, DENOTING ZEIR ANPIN. He asks, Visions of what? IF TO THE NAME YUD HEI VAV HEI, OR THE NAME ADONAI? HE ANSWERS: *Aleph Lamed Pe, Dalet Lamed Tav, Nun Vav Nun, Yud Vav Dalet*, AS BOTH ARE THUS PRONOUNCED. The one, MALCHUT, is pronounced as written, while the other, ZEIR ANPIN, is not pronounced as it is written, WITH THE NAME YUD HEI VAV HEI BUT PRONOUNCE AS THIS NAME *ADONAI*. And so it is written "visions of Elohim," IN THE PLURAL NUMBER FOR IT INCLUDES ZEIR ANPIN AND MALCHUT. FOR THIS REASON, BOTH ARE CALLED BY THE NAME 'ADON ('MASTER')'. THIS IS THE REASON FOR THE WORDS OF RABBI YITZCHAK.

550. רַבִּי יְהוּדָה אָמַר, לְזִמְנִין, עִלָּאִין אִקְרוּן בִּשְׁמָא דְּתַתָּאִין. וּלְזִמְנָא, תַּתָּאִין אִקְרוּן בִּשְׁמָא דְעֶלָּאִין. הָאָדֹן יְיָ', בִּשְׁמָא עִלָּאָה אֲדֹנָי הוּא.

וְהָא אוֹקִימְנָא מִלֵּי. וּבְגַוְונִין סַגִּיאִין אִתְפָּרְשָׁן מִלֵּי, וְכֹלָא חַד. בְּרִיךְ רַחֲמָנָא בְּרִיךְ שְׁמֵיה לְעָלַם וּלְעָלְמֵי עָלְמִין.

550. Rabbi Yehuda ALSO said: Sometimes the celestial are called with terms of the lower, and sometimes the lower are called by names of the celestial. And so it WRITES "the master, Hashem" with a supernal name, ZEIR ANPIN which is Adonai, WHICH IS A LOWER NAME, MALCHUT. In many ways are the words clarified. Blessed is the Merciful One, blessed is His name for ever and ever.

27. The kisses

A Synopsis

Rabbi Yitzchak opens with "Let him kiss me with the kisses of his mouth," and explains that kisses are the clinging of one spirit with another, as the mouth emits and is the source of the breath, or spirit. One whose soul departs through a kiss joins the spirit of the Holy One blessed be He, never to part from Him.

551. הִנֵּה אָנֹכִי שׁוֹלֵחַ מַלְאָךְ לְפָנֶיךָ וְגוֹ'. רַבִּי יִצְחָק פָּתַח, יִשָּׁקֵנִי מִנְּשִׁיקוֹת פִּיהוּ וְגוֹ' אָמְרָה כְּנֶסֶת יִשְׂרָאֵל, יִשָּׁקֵנִי מִנְּשִׁיקוֹת פִּיהוּ. מַאי טַעֲמָא יִשָּׁקֵנִי, יְאֶהֱבֵנִי מִבָּעֵי לֵיהּ, אֲמַאי יִשָּׁקֵנִי. אֶלָּא הָכִי תָּנֵינָן, מַאי נְשִׁיקוֹת אַדְבְּקוּתָא דְּרוּחָא בְּרוּחָא. דִּבְגִינֵי כַּךְ נְשִׁיקָה בַּפֶּה, דְּהָא פּוּמָא אַפְּקוּתָא וּמְקוֹרָא דְּרוּחָא הוּא, וְעַל דָּא נְשִׁיקִין בְּפוּמָא, בַּחֲבִיבוּתָא, וְדַבְקִין רוּחָא בְּרוּחָא, דְּלָא מִתְפָּרְשָׁן דָּא מִן דָּא.

551. "Behold I send an angel before you..." (Shemot 23:20). Rabbi Yitzchak commenced the discussion with: "Let him kiss me with the kisses of his mouth..." (Shir Hashirim 1:2) The Congregation of Yisrael, MEANING THE SHECHINAH says "Let him kiss me." HE ASKS: What is the reason for writing "Let him kiss me?" It should say, 'Let him love me.' Wherefore "Let him kiss me"? HE ANSWERS: we learnt that kisses are the clinging of one spirit with another, so therefore a kiss is by mouth, as the mouth emits and is the source of the breath (also: 'spirit') so a kiss is with the mouth with love, spirits clinging one to another that do not part.

552. וְעַל דָּא מַאן דְּנָפִיק נִשְׁמָתֵיהּ בִּנְשִׁיקָה, מִתְדַּבַּק בְּרוּחָא אַחֲרָא. בְּרוּחָא דְּלָא מִתְפְּרַשׁ מִנֵּיהּ. וְהַיְינוּ אִקְרֵי נְשִׁיקָה. וְעַל דָּא אָמְרָה כְּנֶסֶת יִשְׂרָאֵל, יִשָּׁקֵנִי מִנְּשִׁיקוֹת פִּיהוּ, לְאַדְבְּקָא רוּחָא בְּרוּחָא, דְּלָא יִתְפְּרִישׁ דָּא מִן דָּא.

552. And so, one whose soul departs through a kiss, it joins another spirit, MEANING THE SPIRIT OF THE HOLY ONE, BLESSED BE HE, a spirit never to part from him. This is what is meant by a kiss. So The Congregation of Yisrael said "Let him kiss me with the kiss of his mouth" in order that one spirit cling to the other and never part.

553. כִּי טוֹבִים דּוֹדֶיךָ מִיָּיִן, מַאי בָּעֵי הָכָא יַיִן, וְהָא כְּתִיב וְגַם אֵלֶּה
בַּיַּיִן שָׁגוּ וְגוֹ', וּכְתִיב יַיִן וְשֵׁכָר אַל תֵּשְׁתְּ אַתָּה וּבָנֶיךָ, מַאי טַעְמָא הָכָא
יַיִן. רַבִּי חִיָּיא אָמַר, מֵיְינָהּ דְּאוֹרַיְיתָא. רַבִּי חִזְקִיָּה אָמַר, דָּא דִכְתִיב
וְיַיִן יְשַׂמַּח לְבַב אֱנוֹשׁ, וְעַל דָּא כְּתִיב, כִּי טוֹבִים דּוֹדֶיךָ מִיָּיִן, לְחֶדְוָותָא
דְּלִבָּא. מִיָּיִן, דְּחַדֵּי לִי יַתִּיר מִכֹּלָּא.

553. "for your loves are better than wine" (Ibid.). Why mention here wine? Does it not write, "But they also reel through wine" (Yeshayah 28:7), and "Do not drink wine or strong drink, you, nor your sons with you" (Vayikra 10:9), so why mention wine here? Rabbi Chiya said, it is of the wine of the Torah, MEANING THE MOCHIN OF ZEIR ANPIN CALLED TORAH AND THE MOCHIN OF THE ILLUMINATION OF CHOCHMAH ARE CALLED WINE. Rabbi Chizkiyah said, hence it is written, "and wine that makes glad the heart of man" (Tehilim 104:15), AND THIS REFERS TO WINE OF TORAH. And so it is written: "for your loves are better than wine," AS THEY ARE BETTER for joy of the heart; more than wine that makes me happier than everything else.

554. רַבִּי יְהוּדָה אָמַר, כְּתִיב, וַיִּשַּׁק יַעֲקֹב לְרָחֵל וַיִּשָּׂא אֶת קוֹלוֹ וַיֵּבְךְּ,
אֲמַאי קָא בָכָה. אֶלָּא בְּאִתְדַּבְּקוּתָא דְּרוּחָא בָהּ, לָא יָכִיל לִבָּא לְמִסְבַּל,
וּבָכָה. וְאִי תֵימָא, הָא כְּתִיב, וַיִּשָּׁקֵהוּ וַיִּבְכּוּ. תָּנֵינָן, אֲמַאי נָקוּד
וַיִּשָּׁקֵהוּ, אֶלָּא דְּלָא אִתְדַּבַּק בֵּיהּ רוּחָא כְּלָל, וְעַל דָּא כְּתִיב, וְנַעְתָּרוֹת
נְשִׁיקוֹת שׂוֹנֵא. מַאי וְנַעְתָּרוֹת נְשִׁיקוֹת שׂוֹנֵא. אֶלָּא מַאן דְּנָשִׁיק
בַּחֲבִיבוּתָא, מִתְדַּבַּק רוּחֵיהּ בְּרוּחֵיהּ, בִּדְבֵיקוּתָא דַּחֲבִיבוּתָא וּמַאן דְּלָא
נָשִׁיק בַּחֲבִיבוּתָא, לָאו בִּדְבֵיקוּתָא הוּא, אֶלָּא וְנַעְתָּרוֹת. מַאי נַעְתָּרוֹת.
גַּסּוּתָא, דְּלָא דָבִיק רוּחֵיהּ בְּהַהוּא נְשִׁיקָה. וְלָא אִתְדַּבַּק בֵּיהּ כְּלָל.
וּבְגִינֵי כָּךְ כְּתִיב, יִשָּׁקֵנִי מִנְּשִׁיקוֹת פִּיהוּ, דְּהוּא דְּבֵיקוּתָא רוּחָא בְּרוּחָא.

554. Rabbi Yehuda said, it is written, "And Jacob kissed Rachel, and raised his voice, and wept" (Beresheet 29:11). HE ASKS: why did he cry? HE ANSWERS: when his spirit clung to her, his heart could not hold out, so he wept. One may inquire about: "and kissed him: and they wept" (Beresheet 33:4). HE ANSWERS: As we learned, why are there dots over the word "and

kissed him"? It is because his spirit did not cling to him at all. About this is written, "but the kisses of an enemy are profuse (also: 'deceptive')" (Mishlei 27:6). What is meant by "but the kisses of an enemy are profuse"? but one who kisses with love, spirits cling one to another, clinging with love. One who does not kiss with love, there is no clinging but deception. What is meant by "deceptive"? It is coarseness, as the spirit does not cling with that kiss and it does not cling at all. So therefore it is written: "Let him kiss me with the kisses of his mouth," which is the clinging of spirit to spirit.

28. "Behold I send an angel before you"

A Synopsis

This section talks again about the spirit clinging to Hashem. Moses realized that the angel of "Behold I send an angel before you" would constitute a separation from Yisrael, and he wished the presence of Hashem to be with him. Rabbi Aba says that one should not mix a lower matter with a higher one; the outside should not nurse from an inner level, as the inner represents holiness and the outer represents uncleanness. Rabbi Shimon clarifies the matter by saying that the angel was meant only to guard Yisrael, and it did not mean there would be a separation from Hashem, although other commentators on Torah have disagreed on this point. Rabbi Shimon concludes that Moses did not want an angel, as it is written, "And he said, If now I have found favor in Your sight, Adonai, let my Lord, I pray You, go among us."

555. תָּנָא, כָּל זִמְנָא דְּקוּדְשָׁא בְּרִיךְ הוּא אָזִיל בְּיִשְׂרָאֵל, כִּבְיָכוֹל אִתְדְּבַּק רוּחָא בְּרוּחָא, וְעַל דָּא כְּתִיב, וְאַתֶּם הַדְּבֵקִים בַּייָ', וּבְכָל אִינּוּן גַּוְונֵי דִּבֵיקוּתָא, וְלָא מִתְפָּרְשָׁא דָּא מִן דָּא. בְּשַׁעֲתָא דְּאִתְּמַר הִנֵּה אָנֹכִי שֹׁלֵחַ מַלְאָךְ לְפָנֶיךָ, יָדַע מֹשֶׁה דִּפְרִישׁוּתָא הוּא. אָמַר אִם אֵין פָּנֶיךָ הוֹלְכִים אַל תַּעֲלֵנוּ מִזֶּה.

555. We learned, as long as the Holy One, blessed be He, goes with Yisrael, a spirit, so to speak, clings to a spirit. About this is written, "But you that did cleave to Hashem" (Devarim 4:4), with all types of clinging, with no parting one from another. When it was said, "Behold I send an angel before you" (Shemot 33:2), Moses realized this would constitute a separation FROM YISRAEL so he said, "If Your presence go not with me, carry us not up from here" (Shemot 33:15).

556. רַבִּי אַבָּא אָמַר, מַה כְּתִיב לְעֵילָּא מִן דָּא, רֵאשִׁית בִּכּוּרֵי אַדְמָתְךָ תָּבִיא בֵּית יְיָ' אֱלֹהֶיךָ לֹא תְבַשֵּׁל גְּדִי בַּחֲלֵב אִמּוֹ. מַאי קָא מַיְירֵי. אֶלָּא דְּלָא לְעָרְבָא מִלָּה תַּתָּאָה בְּעִלָּאָה, דְּלָא יָנְקָא סִטְרָא דִּלְבַר, מִסִּטְרָא פְּנִימָאָה. מַה בֵּין הַאי לְהַאי. דָּא דִּלְבַר, מִסִּטְרָא דִּמְסַאֲבָא. וְדָא דִּלְגוֹ,

בְּסִטְרָא קַדִּישָׁא. מַאן אִמּוֹ. דָּא כְּנֶסֶת יִשְׂרָאֵל, דְּאִתְקְרֵי אֵם. בַּחֲלֵב אִמּוֹ, דְּלָא יָנִיק מֵהַאי סִטְרָא, מַאן דְּלָא אִצְטְרִיךְ.

556. Rabbi Aba said, what is written before this verse, "The first of the firstfruits of your land you shall bring to the house of Hashem your Elohim. You shall not boil a kid in its mother's milk" (Shemot 34:26). HE ASKS: what is it trying to imply with these words? HE ANSWERS: do not mix a lower matter with an upper, the outside should not nurse from an inner. What is the difference between them? The outer, MEANING THE KID, represents the aspect of uncleanliness, while the inner, MEANING ITS MOTHER, represents holiness. Who is his mother? It is the Congregation of Yisrael, MALCHUT called 'mother', FOR THE EXTENSION OF MALCHUT REACHES UNTIL THE KLIPOT IN THE SECRET OF "HER FEET GO DOWN TO DEATH" (MISHLEI 5:5). "…its mother's milk…" MEANS that those who are not supposed to, must not suckle from that side.

557. וְהָכָא כְּתִיב, הִנֵּה אָנֹכִי שֹׁלֵחַ מַלְאָךְ לְפָנֶיךָ. אָמַר מֹשֶׁה, הָא קַבִּילְנָא בְּטִחוֹנָא מִינָךְ, דְּלָא תִּתְפְּרַשׁ מִינָן, וַדַּאי אִם אֵין פָּנֶיךָ הוֹלְכִים אַל תַּעֲלֵנוּ מִזֶּה. וּבַמֶּה יִוָּדַע אֵיפוֹא וְגוֹ'.

557. Here is written, "Behold I send my angel before you," SO YISRAEL WHO ARE THE INNERMOST AND ARE CLINGING WITH HASHEM, ARE GIVEN OVER TO THE ANGEL, REPRESENTING THE OUTER ASPECT. Moses said, I received a promise from You, that You would never part from us, FOR AS A RESULT OF THE PRECEPT OF THE FIRSTFRUITS THE OUTER WORLD SHOULD NOT INTERMINGLE WITH THE INNER AS EXPLAINED. Surely, "If Your presence go not with me, carry us not up from here. For in what shall it be known..." ONE MUST NOT INSIST THAT THE LATTER VERSE IS QUOTED FROM KI TISA, AS THERE IS NO CHRONOLOGICAL ORDER IN THE TORAH.

558. אָמַר רַבִּי אֶלְעָזָר, מִלָּה דָּא לָא קָאָמַר קוּדְשָׁא בְּרִיךְ הוּא אֶלָּא בִּרְחִימוּתָא דְּיִשְׂרָאֵל, וּלְאִתְפַּיְּיסָא בַּהֲדַיְיהוּ. לְמַלְכָּא דַּהֲוָה בָּעֵי לְמֵיזַל עִם בְּרֵיהּ. וְלָא בָּעֵי לְשַׁבְקָא לֵיהּ. אָתָא בְּרֵיהּ, וּמִסְתָּפֵי לְמִבְעֵי לֵיהּ לְמַלְכָּא דְּיֵיזִיל בַּהֲדֵיהּ. אַקְדִּים מַלְכָּא וְאָמַר, הָא לִגְיוֹן פְּלָן יֵזִיל

בְּהַדְרָךְ, לְמִנְטַר לָךְ בְּאָרְחָא. לְבָתַר אָמַר אִסְתָּמַר לָךְ מִנֵּיהּ, דְּהָא לָא
גְּבַר שְׁלִים הוּא. אָמַר בְּרֵיהּ, אִי הָכִי, אוֹ אֲנָא אוֹתִיב הָכָא, אוֹ אַתְּ
תֵּזִיל עִמִּי, וְלָא אִתְפְּרַשׁ מִינָךְ. כָּךְ קוּדְשָׁא בְּרִיךְ הוּא, בְּקַדְמֵיתָא אָמַר,
הִנֵּה אָנֹכִי שֹׁלֵחַ מַלְאָךְ לְפָנֶיךָ לִשְׁמָרְךָ בַּדָּרֶךְ. וּלְבָתַר אָמַר הִשָּׁמֶר
מִפָּנָיו וְגו', בֵּיהּ שַׁעֲתָא אָמַר מֹשֶׁה, אִם אֵין פָּנֶיךָ הֹלְכִים וְגו'.

558. Rabbi Elazar said: This statement the Holy One, blessed be He, uttered
out of love for Yisrael and to find favor with them. It is similar to the case
of a king who wanted to go with his son and not forsake him. The son came
but feared to ask the king to go with him. The king spoke up to say, general
so and so will go along to protect you, later he said, be careful of him as he
is not a perfect man. The son said: If so, either I stay here or you go with me
but I will not part from you. So the Holy One, blessed be He, first said, "I
send an angel before you, to keep you in the way." Later He said, be careful
of him... At that moment, Moses said, "If Your presence go not with me..."

559. אָתָא ר"ש, אַשְׁכַּח לְהוּ בְּהַאי. אָמַר, אֶלְעָזָר בְּרִי שַׁפִּיר קָאמַרְתְּ.
אֲבָל ת"ח, בַּאֲתַר דָּא לָא אָמַר מֹשֶׁה מִדִּי, וְלָא אָתִיב מִלָּה לָקֳבְלֵיהּ.
מַאי טַעֲמָא. מִשּׁוּם דְּהָכָא לָא אִשְׁתְּכַח פְּרִישׁוּתָא מִנֵּיהּ. וְהָא אוֹקִימְנָא
מִלָּה דָּא, לְגַבֵּי חַבְרַיָּיא. וְאִית דְּמַתְנֵי אִיפְּכָא וְלָא הָכִי פֵּירוּשׁוּהַ
קַדְמָאֵי. וְכַד יִסְתַּכְּלוּן מִלֵּי כֹּלָּא שַׁפִּיר, וְכֹלָּא בְּחַד מִלָּה אַמְרֵי
טַעֲמַיְיהוּ.

559. Rabbi Shimon arrived, found him, RABBI ELAZAR, SPEAKING THIS
STATEMENT. He said: Elazar, my son, what you are saying is fine. But
come and behold: in this place when the Holy One, blessed be He, said,
"Behold I send an angel..." Moses said nothing, or retorted. Why? At this
point there was no separation from Him, AS THE ANGEL WAS SENT ONLY
TO GUARD THEM, and this matter was established with the friends.
HOWEVER THINGS WERE DIFFERENT REGARDING THE VERSE "AND I
WILL SEND AN ANGEL BEFORE YOU: AND I WILL DRIVE OUT...FOR I WILL
NOT GO UP IN YOUR MIDST..." (SHEMOT 33:2). Others understand these
passages in an opposite fashion; HERE THE VERSE INDICATES SEPARATION
WHEREAS THERE, THERE IS NO SEPARATION. The early commentators did

not see it this way. When you look into the matter, everything turns out to be fine, each based their community using one interpretation.

560. אֵימָתַי אָתִיב מֹשֶׁה. בְּזִמְנָא דְּאָמַר, וְשָׁלַחְתִּי לְפָנֶיךָ מַלְאָךְ. וּכְתִיב כִּי יֵלֵךְ מַלְאָכִי לְפָנֶיךָ, סָתַם וְלָא פָּרִישׁ מִלָּה. וְע"ד כְּתִיב, הָכָא, כִּי אִם שָׁמוֹעַ תִּשְׁמַע בְּקוֹלוֹ וְעָשִׂיתָ כֹּל אֲשֶׁר אֲדַבֵּר. אֲשֶׁר אֲדַבֵּר דַּוְקָא וּכְתִיב וְאָיַבְתִּי אֶת אוֹיְבֶיךָ וְצַרְתִּי אֶת צוֹרְרֶיךָ, וְכֹלָּא בֵּיהּ תַּלְיָא.

560. When did Moses respond? This happened when He said, "and I will send an angel before you" AFTER WHICH IT IS WRITTEN: "FOR I WILL NOT GO UP IN YOUR MIDST." But here it is written: "Behold I send an angel" and the verse does not elaborate WITH THE WORDS "FOR I WILL NOT GO UP IN YOUR MIDST." Hence it says here "But if you shall indeed obey his voice, and do all that I speak" (Shemot 23:22), "all that I speak" exactly, so it writes next to it, "then I will be an enemy to your enemies, and an adversary to your adversaries" (Ibid.). All is dependent upon Him BLESSED BE HE. THERE IS NO SEPARATION HERE SO MOSES DID NOT ANSWER BACK.

561. ר' יְהוּדָה אָמַר, אִי תֵּימָא דְּתַרְוַויְיהוּ מַלְאָךְ מַמָּשׁ, מֹשֶׁה לָא אָתִיב עֲלַיְיהוּ, דְּלָא חָמָא דּוּכְתָּא. אֵימָתַי אָתִיב. בְּזִמְנָא דִּכְתִּיב אִם אֵין פָּנֶיךָ הוֹלְכִים וְגוֹ'. אָמַר ר' שִׁמְעוֹן, כְּלָל דְּכֹלָּא, מֹשֶׁה לָא בָּעָא מַלְאָכָא. דְּהָא כְּתִיב וַיֹּאמֶר אִם נָא מָצָאתִי חֵן בְּעֵינֶיךָ אֲדֹנָי יֵלֶךְ נָא אֲדֹנָי בְּקִרְבֵּנוּ.

561. Rabbi Yehuda said: If you question that in both VERSES we are talking about an actual angel WITH SEPARATION STILL Moses did not reply as he had no strong position SINCE WE SEE THAT EVEN WITH REGARD TO THE VERSE IN THE PORTION OF TISA, "AND I WILL SEND AN ANGEL BEFORE YOU," MOSES DID NOT IMMEDIATELY REACT. When did he answer? When the verse writes, "If Your presence go not with me, carry us not up from here," AS A REACTION TO THE VERSE, "MY PRESENCE SHALL GO WITH YOU, AND I WILL GIVE YOU REST" (SHEMOT 33:14). THERE HE COULD REACT. Rabbi Shimon said: In summary, Moses did not want an angel, as it is written: "And he said, If now I have found favor in Your sight, Adonai, let my lord, I pray You, go among us" (Shemot 34:9).

29. "You shall not boil a kid in its mother's milk"

A Synopsis

Here we learn about the prohibition of eating meat with milk, and other dietary restrictions, all designed to prevent impurity from entering people due to the foods they consume. Like Daniel, those who guard themselves from impurity become perfect in the image of their Master, and cannot be harmed because His image is not removed from them.

562. א"ר יְהוּדָה, הַאי דְּאָמַר ר' אַבָּא, דִּכְתִּיב לֹא תְבַשֵּׁל גְּדִי בַּחֲלֵב אִמּוֹ, בַּחֲלֵב הָאֵם מִבָּעֵי לֵיהּ, מַאי אִמּוֹ. וְאִי תֵּימָא, כְּנֶסֶת יִשְׂרָאֵל אִמּוֹ דְּסִטְרָא דִּמְסָאֲבָא, לָאו הָכִי, דְּהָא שְׁמַעְנָא דְּאָמַר ר' שִׁמְעוֹן, כְּנֶסֶת יִשְׂרָאֵל אִימָא קַדִּישָׁא בְּחוּלָקֵיהּ דְּיִשְׂרָאֵל אִתְאַחֲדָא, דִּכְתִּיב כִּי חֵלֶק יְיָ' עַמּוֹ.

562. Rabbi Yehuda said: Thus spoke Rabbi Aba regarding the verse, "You shall not boil a kid in its mother's milk" (Shemot 34:26): A KID, BEING OF THE OTHER SIDE, SHOULD NOT SUCKLE FROM THE SHECHINAH. It should write in the verse, "the mother's milk." Why write "its mother's milk"? If you say that the Congregation of Yisrael, BEING MALCHUT is the mother of an impure aspect, this is not so. For I have heard from Rabbi Shimon, the Congregation of Yisrael is the saintly mother, joined in the portion of Yisrael as it is written, "For Hashem's portion is His people" (Devarim 32:9).

563. אָמַר ר' שִׁמְעוֹן, שַׁפִּיר קָאֲמַרְתְּ. וְהָא דְּרַבִּי אַבָּא שַׁפִּיר וְכֹלָּא דָּא בְּדָא תַּלְיָא. תָּא חֲזֵי, אִמָּא אִתְאַחֲדָא לְהוּ לְעֵילָּא לְסִטְרָא דָּא וּלְסִטְרָא דָּא, וּתְרֵין אִינּוּן, חֲדָא וִימִינָא, וַחֲדָא לִשְׂמָאלָא. וּבְגִינֵי כַּךְ, מִנְּהוֹן לִימִינָא, וּמִנְּהוֹן לִשְׂמָאלָא. וְכֻלְּהוּ תַּלְיָין בְּהַאי א"ם, אִמָּא קַדִּישָׁא, וְאִתְאַחֲדָן בָּהּ.

563. Rabbi Shimon replied, well spoken, and the words of Rabbi Aba are fine. Things are intertwined. Come and see: Ima, BEING MALCHUT joined

with them above in this aspect OF HOLINESS, and also that aspect OF IMPURITY. There are two, one to the right and one to the left, MEANING, EVERY ASPECT HAS RIGHT AND LEFT, so some of them are of the right and some of the left. They all depend upon that mother, the holy mother, NAMELY MALCHUT and are attached to her.

564. אֵימָתַי אִתְאַחֲדָן בָּהּ. בְּשַׁעֲתָא דְּהַאי אֵם יָנְקָא מִסִּטְרָא אַחֲרָא, וּמַקְדְּשָׁא אִסְתָּאָב, וְחִוְיָא תַּקִּיפָא שָׁארֵי לְאִתְגַּלְּאָה, כְּדֵין גַּדְיָא יַנְקָא מֵחֲלָבָא דְּאִמֵּיהּ, וְדִינִין מִתְעָרִין. וְעַל דָּא, יִשְׂרָאֵל קַדְמִין וְאַיְיתָאן בִּכּוּרִים, וּבְשַׁעֲתָא דְּמַיְיתִין לְהוּ, בַּעְיָין לְמֵימַר וּלְמִפְתַּח בֵּיהּ בְּלָבָן, דִּבְעָא בְּחָרָשׁוֹי אִלֵּין, לְשַׁלְּטָאָה בְּיַעֲקֹב, וּבְזַרְעָא קַדִּישָׁא, וְלָא אִתְיְיהִיבוּ בִּידֵיהּ, וְלָא אִתְמַסְּרָן יִשְׂרָאֵל לְסִטְרָא דָּא. וְעַל דָּא כְּתִיב, רֵאשִׁית בִּכּוּרֵי אַדְמָתְךָ וְגוֹ', לֹא תְבַשֵּׁל גְּדִי בַּחֲלֵב אִמּוֹ. וְלָא יָנְקָא הַהוּא סִטְרָא, מֵחֲלָבָא דְּאִמֵּיהּ, דְּהָא לָא יִסְתְּאָב מַקְדְּשָׁא, וְדִינִין לָא מִתְעָרִין.

564. When are they attached to her? When this mother suckles from the Other Side, and the sanctuary thus becomes unclean, and the mighty serpent begins to reveal himself. Then the kid suckles from the milk of its mother and harsh judgment arouses. So Yisrael need to hasten and come forth with firstfruits, and when they bring them need to commence to speak about Laban, MEANING, THE CHAPTER STARTING WITH THE WORDS, "AN ARAMMIAN ARAMI WISHED TO KILL MY FATHER" (DEVARIM 26:5). He wished through sorcery to control Jacob and his holy seed, but he was not permitted, and Yisrael was not given over to this side, AND SO THEY REMOVE THE POWER OF THE SERPENT SO THE KID WOULD NOT BE ABLE TO SUCKLE THE MILK OF HIS MOTHER. And so it says, "The first of the firstfruits…You shall not boil a kid in its mother's milk," so that side would not suckle on the milk of his mother, BEING MALCHUT, so it would not desecrate the sanctuary and awaken judgments.

565. בְּגִינֵי כָּךְ, לָא יֵיכוּל בִּשְׂרָא בְּחֲלָבָא כָּל זַרְעָא קַדִּישָׁא, וְכָל מַאן דְּאָתֵי מִסִּטְרָא דָּא, דְּלָא יָהִיב דּוּכְתָּא, לְמַאן דְּלָא אִצְטְרִיךְ, דְּהָא בְּעוֹבָדָא תַּלְיָא מִלְּתָא, בְּעוֹבָדָא דִּלְתַתָּא, לְאִתְעֲרָא לְעֵילָא. זַכָּאִין

אִינּוּן יִשְׂרָאֵל מִכָּל עַמִּין עעכו"ם, דְּמָרֵיהוֹן קָרֵי עָלַיְיהוּ, וּבְךָ בָּחַר יְיָ׳ לִהְיוֹת לוֹ לְעַם סְגֻלָּה. וּכְתִיב כִּי עַם קָדוֹשׁ אַתָּה לַיְיָ׳ אֱלֹהֶיךָ וּכְתִיב בָּנִים אַתֶּם לַיְיָ׳ אֱלֹהֵיכֶם וְגוֹ׳.

565. As a result, those of the holy seed do not eat meat with milk, and so also those that trace their lineage from the HOLY aspect in order not to give any opening to that not desired. It depends all on one's actions, as a deed below is NEEDED to stir above. Fortunate is Yisrael more than all idol worshipping nations, for their Master said of them, "and Hashem has chosen you to be a special possession to Himself" (Devarim 14:2); and "For you are a holy people to Hashem your Elohim," and it is written, "You are the children of Hashem your Elohim..." (Ibid. 1).

566. תָּא חֲזֵי, בְּשַׁעֲתָא דְּיִשְׂרָאֵל לָא אִתְכְּשָׁרוּ עוֹבָדַיְיהוּ, מַה כְּתִיב, עַמִּי נוֹגְשָׂיו מְעוֹלֵל וְנָשִׁים מָשְׁלוּ בוֹ. מָשְׁלוּ בוֹ דַּיְיקָא, וְהָא אוֹקִימְנָא מִלֵּי בְּרָזָא דְּסִפְרָא דִּשְׁלֹמֹה מַלְכָּא. וְהָכִי אַשְׁכְּחָן בֵּיה. תּוּ אַשְׁכְּחָן, דְּכָל מַאן דְּאָכִיל הַאי מֵיכְלָא דְּאִתְחַבַּר כַּחֲדָא. בְּשַׁעֲתָא חֲדָא, אוֹ בִּסְעוּדָתָא חֲדָא. אַרְבְּעִין יוֹמִין אִתְחֲזִיָא גַּדְיָא מְקֻלָסָא בְּקַלְפּוֹי, לְגַבֵּי אִינּוּן דִּלְעֵילָא, וְסִיַּעְתָּא מְסָאֲבָא מִתְקָרְבִין בַּהֲדֵיה, וְגָרִים לְאִתְּעָרָא דִּינִין בְּעָלְמָא, דִּינִין דְּלָא קַדִּישִׁין.

566. Come and see, when deeds of Yisrael are unacceptable, the verse writes, "As for my people, children are their oppressors, and women rule over them" (Yeshayah 3:12), literally rule over them. So it is derived from the hidden lore of the text of King Solomon, and so we found therein. We also found, he who consumes food OF MEAT AND MILK during the same hour or in one meal, so they join together, AND HE IS CONSIDERED AS IF HE ATE MEAT AND MILK TOGETHER, forty days a kid roasted with its skin, MEANING ROASTED TOGETHER WITH ITS HEAD, appears to those above. A unit of impurity approaches him, causing unholy judgments to activate in the world.

567. וְאִי אוֹלִיד בַּר בְּאִינּוּן יוֹמִין, אוֹזְפִין לֵיה נִשְׁמָתָא, מִסִּטְרָא אַחֲרָא, דְּלָא אִצְטְרִיכָא. וּכְתִיב וְהִתְקַדִּשְׁתֶּם וִהְיִיתֶם קְדוֹשִׁים וְגוֹ׳. אָתֵי

לְאִסְתַּאֲבָא, מְסָאֲבִין לֵיהּ וַדַּאי. דִּכְתִיב, וְנִטְמֵתֶם בָּם, חָסֵר א',
מְסָאֲבוּתָא אֲטִימָא מִכֹּלָא, דְּלֵית רְשׁוּ לְאִתְדַּכָּאָה הָכִי, כִּשְׁאַר זִינֵי
דִּמְסָאֲבוּתָא דְּמִתְדַּכְּין. וְתוּ, דְּמִסְתָּפֵי מֵחֵיוָן בִּישָׁן, דְּהָא בְּעֵינַיְיהוּ גַּדְיָא
אִשְׁתְּכַח, וְיָכִיל לְאִתְּזְקָא, דְּהָא צֶלְמָא דְּבַר נָשׁ אִתְעֲבָר מִנֵּיהּ.

567. If a son is born to him these days, a soul is borrowed from the Other Side, which is not supposed to be with him, AS IT DEFILES HIM, and the verse says, "you shall therefore sanctify yourselves and be holy..." (Vayikra 11:44). One who wishes to profane himself, he is assuredly defiled, as it is written: "that you should be defiled (Heb. *venitmetem*) by them" (Ibid. 43). Now the word 'venitmetem' is spelled in the verse without an Aleph MEANING a solid impurity more than all other IMPURITIES that he can not ever cleanse himself as with other impurities. Furthermore, he fears dangerous beasts, for he appears before them as a kid and they are capable of harming him because the image of man has been removed from him.

568. רַבִּי יֵיסָא, שָׁרֵי לְמֵיכַל לְתַרְנְגוֹלָא בִּגְבִינָה אוֹ בְּחֶלְבָּא. אָמַר ר'
שִׁמְעוֹן אָסִיר לָךְ דְּלָא יָהִיב אִינִשׁ פִּתְחָא לְזִינִין בִּישִׁין. לֵךְ לֵךְ אַמְרִין
נְזִירָא, סְחוֹר סְחוֹר לְכַרְמָא לָא תִּקְרַב. וַדַּאי אָסִיר לָךְ הוּא, דְּחוּמְרָא
אִית בֵּיהּ, כִּבְעִירָא לִשְׁחִיטָה. וּמַאן דְּשָׁרֵי הַאי, מַה כְּתִיב וַתַּשְׁקוּ אֶת
הַנְּזִירִים יָיִן, מַאן דְּשָׁרֵי הַאי, כְּמַאן דְּשָׁרֵי הַאי. וּכְתִיב לֹא תֹאכַל כָּל
תּוֹעֵבָה, כֹּל, לְאַכְלְלָא כֹּלָּא.

568. Rabbi Yesa permitted to eat chicken with cheese or milk. Rabbi Shimon said, it is prohibited for you. A man should not allow an excuse to evil types, as the expression goes, 'say to the Nazarite, go, go, go around, go around, but don't enter the vineyard.' This item is forbidden for it entails the complex laws of ritual slaughter just like cattle. One who permits this brings to mind the verse, "But you gave the Nazarites wine to drink" (Amos 2:12). One who permits one matter tends to permit other things, AND A DEFECT MADE ABOVE IS ONE OF THEM, and the verse writes, "You shall not eat any abominable thing" (Devarim 14:3); "any" includes everything.

569. תָּאנָא, בְּמָה זָכוּ דָּנִיֵּאל חֲנַנְיָה מִישָׁאֵל וַעֲזַרְיָה, דְּאִשְׁתְּזִיבוּ

מֵאִינּוּן נִסְיוֹנֵי, אֶלָּא בְּגִין דְּלָא אִסְתָּאֲבוּ בְּמֵיכְלֵיהוֹן. אָמַר ר׳ יְהוּדָה, כְּתִיב וַיָּשֶׂם דָּנִיֵּאל עַל לִבּוֹ אֲשֶׁר לֹא יִתְגָּאַל בְּפַת בַּג הַמֶּלֶךְ וְגו׳. וְתָאנָא בְּסְתִימָא דְּמַתְנִיתִין, מֵיכְלָא דְּהַהוּא רָשָׁע, בִּשְׂרָא בְּחַלְבָּא הֲוָה וּגְבִינָה עִם בִּשְׂרָא, בַּר מֵיכְלָן אַחֲרָנִין, וְדָא סָלִיק לֵיהּ בְּפָתוֹרֵיהּ, בְּכָל יוֹמָא.

569. We learned, for what merit were Daniel, Hananiah, Mishael and Azaryah saved from their tests, it is because they did not allow themselves to become unclean due to the foods they consumed. Rabbi Yehuda said? Tt is written "But Daniel purposed in his heart that he would not defile himself with the portion of the king's food..." (Daniel 1:8). And we learned from the secret of Mishnah that the food of that evil NEVUCHADNETZAR was meat in milk, cheese with meat in addition to other foods. This menu was served up daily.

570. וְדָנִיֵּאל דְּאִסְתַּמַּר מֵהַאי, כַּד רָמוּ יָתֵיהּ לְגוּבָּא דְּאַרְיָוָותָא, אִשְׁתְּלִים בְּצוּלְמָא דְמָארֵיהּ, וְלָא שָׁנֵי צוּלְמֵיהּ לְצוּלְמָא אַחֲרָא, וְעַל דָּא דַּחֲלוּ אַרְיָוָותָא מִנֵּיהּ, וְלָא חַבְּלוּהוּ. וְהַהוּא רָשָׁע, בְּשַׁעֲתָא דְּמַלְכוּתָא אִתְעֲדֵי מִנֵּיהּ, וְעִם חֵיוַת בָּרָא הֲוָה מָדוֹרֵיהּ, אַעֲדֵי צוּלְמָא דְּאַנְפּוֹי מִנֵּיהּ, וּמֵהַהוּא יוֹמָא, לָא אִתְחֲזֵי צוּלְמֵיהּ צוּלְמָא דְּבַר נָשׁ, וְכָל בְּעִירָא דְּאָתֵי, אִתְחֲזֵי לֵיהּ, צוּלְמָא דְּזִינֵיהּ, וְנוּקְבֵיהּ, וַהֲווֹ אַתְיָין עֲלֵיהּ כֻּלְּהוּ, וּבְכַמָּה זִמְנִין הֲווֹ אַכְלִין לֵיהּ חֵיוַת בָּרָא, בַּר דְּאִתְגְּזַר הַאי עוֹנָשָׁא עֲלֵיהּ, בְּגִין דִּכְתִיב, וְהוּא בַּמְלָכִים יִתְקַלָּס, בְּגִין כָּךְ, כֹּלָּא יִתְקַלְסוּ בֵּיהּ, כָּל הַהוּא זִמְנָא.

570. Daniel, who guarded himself from it, when he was thrown into the pit of lions, he was perfect in the image of his Master, and his image did not alter to any other image, and so the lions feared him and did not harm him. But that tyrant, when the kingdom was removed from him, and his dwelling was "with the beasts in the field" (Daniel 4:20), the image of his face was removed. From that day, his image did not resemble that of a human, and any animal that approached him, thought it was its own kind, and a female, and so all came in to him. Many times, the beasts of the field would have

attacked him were it not for the penalty decreed for him, as it is written: "And they shall scoff at kings" (Chavakuk 1:10). As a result all denigrated him all that time.

571. תָּא חֲזֵי, מַה כְּתִיב, וּלְמִקְצָת יָמִים עֲשָׂרָה נִרְאָה מַרְאֵיהֶן טוֹב מִכָּל הַיְלָדִים הָאוֹכְלִים אֶת פַּת בַּג הַמֶּלֶךְ. נִרְאָה מַרְאֵיהֶן טוֹב, דְּצוּלְמָא דְּמָארֵיהוֹן לָא אַעֲדִּיאוּ מִנְּהוֹן, וּמֵאַחֲרָנֵי אַעֲדִּיאוּ. מַאן גָּרִים הַאי. בְּגִין דְּלָא אִתְגַּעֲלוּ בְּגִיעוּלֵי מֵיכְלֵיהוֹן. זַכָּאָה חוּלָקֵהוֹן דְּיִשְׂרָאֵל, דִּכְתִיב בְּהוּ, וְאַנְשֵׁי קֹדֶשׁ תִּהְיוּן לִי.

571. Come and see what is written: "And at the end of ten days they appeared fairer and fatter in flesh than all the youths who did eat the portion of the king's fare" (Daniel 1:15). They appeared fairer, MEANING that the image of their Master was not removed from them, but was removed from the others. What caused this? Their not soiling themselves with the soiled food. Praise the lot of children of Yisrael where it is written: "And you shall be men of holiness to Me."

30. "And He said to Moses, Come up to Hashem"

A Synopsis

This section talks about the covenant established when Yisrael were circumcised and the uncovering of the membrane was completed. Then, "there he made for them a statute and an ordinance." Rabbi Yitzchak explains that Moses sprinkled half the blood of the sacrifice on the people and half on the altar. The half that he sprinkled on the people made a bond with the Shechinah, so that the Shechinah and Yisrael were perfected together through Moses. Lastly Rabbi Yitzchak speaks about "and there was under His feet a kind of paved work of sapphire stone," saying that this is like that with which the Holy One, blessed be He, will build the sanctuary.

572. וְאֶל מֹשֶׁה אָמַר עֲלֵה אֶל יְיָ' וְגוֹ'. וְאֶל מֹשֶׁה אָמַר, מַאן אָמַר. דָּא שְׁכִינְתָּא. עֲלֵה אֶל יְיָ', כְּמָה דִּכְתִּיב, וּמֹשֶׁה עָלָה אֶל הָאֱלֹהִים וְגוֹ'. אֲמַאי כָּל דָּא, לְקַיְּימָא עִמְּהוֹן קַיָּים, בְּגִין דְּהָא אִתְפְּרָעוּ, מַה דְּלָא נַפְקוּ הָכִי מִמִּצְרַיִם, דְּאִתְגְּזָרוּ, וְלָא אִתְפְּרָעוּ, וְהָכָא הָא אִתְפְּרָעוּ, וְעָאלוּ בִּבְרִית קַיְּימָא, דִּכְתִּיב שָׁם שָׂם לוֹ חֹק וּמִשְׁפָּט. וְשָׁם נִסָּהוּ, בְּהַאי אָת קַדִּישָׁא, דְּאִתְגַּלְיָיא בְּהוּ, וְהָכָא אִתְקַיָּים בְּהוּ, עַל יְדָא דְמֹשֶׁה גְּזִירָה דְקַיְּימָא, דִּכְתִּיב, וַיִּקַּח מֹשֶׁה אֶת הַדָּם וַיִּזְרֹק עַל הָעָם וְגוֹ'.

572. "And He said to Moses, Come up to Hashem..." (Shemot 24:1). HE ASKS: "And he said"? Who said this? HE ANSWERS: the Shechinah. "Come up to Hashem" as it says, "And Moses went up to the Elohim" (Shemot 19:3). What was all this? It was IN ORDER to establish with them a covenant as they completed the uncovering of the membrane. This did not happen when leaving Egypt where they were circumcised but did not complete the uncovering of the membrane. Now it was done and were complete with the sign of the circumcision, as it is written: "there he made for them a statute and an ordinance" (Shemot 15:25), MEANING THE CIRCUMCISION AND THE UNCOVERING OF THE CORONA. "...and there He tested them..." with the holy sign that revealed itself in them. Now the bond was ratified through Moses, as it is written: "And Moses took the blood and sprinkled it on the people" (Shemot 24:8).

573. א"ר יִצְחָק מַאי דִּכְתִּיב, וַחֲצִי הַדָּם זָרַק עַל הַמִּזְבֵּחַ, בַּמִּזְבֵּחַ לָא

כְּתִיב, אֶלָּא עַל הַמִּזְבֵּחַ דַּיְיקָא. וְהִשְׁתַּחֲוִיתֶם מֵרָחֹק, מַהוּ מֵרָחֹק. כד"א מֵרָחוֹק יְיָ' נִרְאָה לִי. וּכְתִיב, וַתִּתַצַּב אֲחֹתוֹ מֵרָחֹק. תָּאנֵי ר' אַבָּא, דְּקַיְימָא סִיהֲרָא בִּפְגִימוּתָא, וּבֵיהּ שַׁעֲתָא, זָכוּ יִשְׂרָאֵל יַתִּיר בְּחוּלָקָא קַדִּישָׁא, וְגָזְרוּ קַיְימָא קַדִּישָׁא בְּקוּדְשָׁא בְּרִיךְ הוּא.

573. Rabbi Yitzchak said: referring to the verse, "and half of the blood he sprinkled on the altar," the verse does not say "at the altar", AS THE ALTAR HINTS AT MALCHUT, WHEREAS ENACTMENT OF THE COVENANT IS IN YESOD, but the verse writes "on the altar", for an exact purpose, AS ON THE ALTAR HINTS TO YESOD THAT IS ABOVE MALCHUT. "...and bow down afar off..." What is meant by "afar off"? HE ANSWERS: It is as the verse, "Hashem appeared to me from afar" (Yirmeyah 31:2), and "And his sister stood afar off" (Shemot 2:4). Rabbi Aba taught, the moon BEING MALCHUT, remained in its diminished state, AND SO IT IS SAID, "AND BOW DOWN AFAR OFF." At that moment, Yisrael merited more of the holy share and the implementation of the Holy Covenant with the Holy One, blessed be He.

574. וְאֶל מֹשֶׁה אָמַר עֲלֵה אֶל יְיָ'. מ"ט. אָמְרָה לֵיהּ שְׁכִינְתָּא, אִסְתְּלִיק לְעֵילָא, דְּהָא אֲנָא וְיִשְׂרָאֵל, נִשְׁתַּתַּף כַּחֲדָא בִּשְׁלֵימוּתָא עַל יְדָךְ, מַה דְּלָא הֲוָה עַד הָכָא. מַה כְּתִיב וַיִּקַּח מֹשֶׁה חֲצִי הַדָּם וְגוֹ', פָּלַג לֵיהּ לִתְרֵין. חֲצִי הַדָּם זָרַק עַל הָעָם, וַחֲצִי הַדָּם זָרַק עַל הַמִּזְבֵּחַ, כְּמָה דְּאוֹקִימְנָא. וּכְתִיב, הִנֵּה דַם הַבְּרִית אֲשֶׁר כָּרַת יְיָ' עִמָּכֶם. וַיָּשֶׂם בָּאַגָּנֹת, בָּאַגָּנַת כְּתִיב, חָסֵר וָא"ו. כְּמָה דִּכְתִיב, שָׁרְרֵךְ אַגַּן הַסַּהַר אַל יֶחְסַר הַמָּזֶג.

574. "And He said to Moses, Come up to Hashem." HE ASKS: what is the reason for all this? HE ANSWERS: the Shechinah said to him, go up BECAUSE I and the children of Yisrael will together gain perfection through you, something that did not exist until this time. Then the verse writes, "And Moses took half of the blood..." dividing it in two AS IS DONE IN MAKING A COVENANT. Half of the blood he sprinkled on the people, "and half of the blood he sprinkled on the altar", as we explained, THAT ON THE ALTAR INDICATES YESOD. And the verse writes, "Behold the blood of the

covenant, which Hashem has made with you." "…and put it in basins (Heb. *aganot*)…" Aganot is written minus a *Vav*, similar to the verse, "Your navel is like a round goblet (Heb. *agan*) that never lacks blended wine..." (Shir Hashirim 7:4). AGANOT IS MALCHUT, BEING A ROUND GOBLET, AND HENCE IT IS WRITTEN MINUS VAV. SO THE HALF OF BLOOD THAT HE SPRINKLED ON THE PEOPLE, MADE A BOND WITH THE SHECHINAH CALLED 'AGANOT' AND THUS THE SHECHINAH AND YISRAEL WERE PERFECTED TOGETHER THROUGH MOSES.

575. וְנִגַּשׁ מֹשֶׁה לְבַדּוֹ אֶל יְיָ', זַכָּאָה חוּלָקֵיה דְמֹשֶׁה, דְהוּא בִּלְחוֹדוֹי, זָכָה לְמָה דְלָא זָכָה בַּר נָשׁ אַחֲרָא. יִשְׂרָאֵל זָכוּ הַשְׁתָּא, מַה דְלָא זָכוּ עַד הַהִיא שַׁעֲתָא. וְהַהִיא שַׁעֲתָא, אִתְקַיָּימוּ, בְּקִיּוּמָא עִלָאָה קַדִּישָׁא. וּבְהַהוּא שַׁעֲתָא אִתְבַּשָּׂרוּ לְמֶהֱוֵי בֵּינַיְיהוּ מַקְדְּשָׁא, כד"א, וְעָשׂוּ לִי מִקְדָּשׁ וְשָׁכַנְתִּי בְּתוֹכָם.

575. "And Moses alone shall come near Hashem" (Shemot 24:2). Fortunate is Moses' lot that he alone merited what no other man did. Yisrael was now meriting what they did not merit until now. At that moment they lived in a supernal holy existence. At that time they were informed that in their midst shall be the sanctuary, as the verse writes, "And let them make Me a sanctuary: that I may dwell among them" (Shemot 25:8).

576. וַיִּרְאוּ אֵת אֱלֹהֵי יִשְׂרָאֵל וְתַחַת רַגְלָיו כְּמַעֲשֵׂה לִבְנַת הַסַּפִּיר וְגוֹ'. רַבִּי יְהוּדָה פָּתַח, זֹאת קוֹמָתֵךְ דָּמְתָה לְתָמָר וְגוֹ', כַּמָּה חֲבִיבָה כְּנֶסֶת יִשְׂרָאֵל קָמֵי קוּדְשָׁא בְּרִיךְ הוּא, דְלָא מִתְפָּרְשָׁא מִנֵּיה, כְּהַאי תָּמָר, דְלָא פָּרִישׁ דְכַר מִן נוּקְבָּא לְעָלְמִין, וְלָא סָלִיק, הָא בְּלָא דָא. כַּךְ כְּנֶסֶת יִשְׂרָאֵל, לָא מִתְפָּרְשָׁא מִקּוּדְשָׁא בְּרִיךְ הוּא.

576. "and they saw the Elohim of Yisrael: and there was under His feet a kind of paved work of sapphire stone..." (Shemot 24:10): Rabbi Yehuda commenced: "This your stature is like a palm tree" (Shir Hashirim 7:9). How beloved is the Congregation of Yisrael before the Holy One, blessed be He, that she never moves away from Him; like this palm tree where the male never departs from the female, one not growing without the other, so

the Congregation of Yisrael never moves apart from the Holy One, blessed be He.

577. תָּא חֲזֵי, בְּשַׁעֲתָא דְּנָדָב וַאֲבִיהוּא חָמוּ, וְשַׁבְעִין סָבִין. מַה כְּתִיב בְּהוּ. וַיִּרְאוּ אֵת אֱלֹהֵי יִשְׂרָאֵל. דְּאִתְגַּלֵּי עָלַיְיהוּ שְׁכִינְתָּא. רַבִּי יְהוּדָה וְרַבִּי יוֹסֵי אַמְרֵי, אֶת דַּיְיקָא. וְדָא אֶת, הוּא מֵרָחוֹק. אֶת לְאַכְלְלָא מַה דִּי בְּגַוֵּיה.

577. Come and see, when Nadab and Abihu plus the seventy elders saw, the Torah writes, "and they saw the Elohim of Yisrael;" for the Shechinah appeared to them. Rabbi Yehuda and Rabbi Yosi said, "*Et* (Eng. 'the')"; THE VERSE WRITES "THE ELOHIM" is written for a specific reason. "*Et*" TELLS US that it was from a distance. "Et" includes the inner part, MEANING THEY SAW WHAT WAS IN THE INTERNAL PART OF THE SHECHINAH.

578. רַבִּי יִצְחָק אָמַר, וְהָא כְּתִיב הִיא הַחַיָּה אֲשֶׁר רָאִיתִי תַּחַת אֱלֹהֵי יִשְׂרָאֵל בִּנְהַר כְּבָר, מַאן חַיָּה דָא. א"ר יוֹסֵי אָמַר רַבִּי חִיָּיא, חַיָּה זוּטַרְתִּי. וְכִי אִית חַיָּה זוּטַרְתִּי, אִין. חַיָּה זוּטַרְתִּי, וְחַיָּה עִלָּאָה. וְחַיָּה זוּטְרָא דְזוּטַרְתִּי.

578. Rabbi Yitzchak said, it is written, "This is the same living creature that I saw by the river Kevar" (Yechezkel 10:15). What is this living creature? Rabbi Yosi quoted Rabbi Chiya, "a small living creature, DENOTING MALCHUT." Is there such a small living creature? HE ANSWERS: Yes. There is a small living creature, DENOTING MALCHUT and a supernal living creature, WHICH IS IN CHESED, GVURAH, AND TIFERET, FROM THE CHEST UP OF ZEIR ANPIN and also a very small living creature, DENOTING A CREATURE FROM THE WORLD OF YETZIRAH.

579. וַיִּרְאוּ אֵת אֱלֹהֵי יִשְׂרָאֵל, דַּיְיקָא, כְּמָה דַאֲמֵינָא. וְתַחַת רַגְלָיו כְּמַעֲשֵׂה לִבְנַת הַסַּפִּיר, כְּחֵזוּ אֶבֶן טָבָא, דְּזַמִּין קוּדְשָׁא בְּרִיךְ הוּא לְמִבְנֵי מַקְדְּשָׁא, דִּכְתִיב וִיסַדְתִּיךְ בַּסַּפִּירִים.

579. "and they saw the Elohim of Yisrael." "*ET* ('THE')" in the verse is therefore a specific reason as we said. "and there was under His feet a kind

of paved work of sapphire stone," having the appearance of a gem with the like of which the Holy One, blessed be He, will build the sanctuary, as it is written, "and lay your foundations with sapphires" (Yeshayah 54:11).

31. "And upon the nobles of the children of Yisrael"

A Synopsis

When they went to the mountain with Moses, "And upon the nobles of the children of Yisrael he laid not His hand." The verse says "and did eat and drink," and Rabbi Yosi explains that this means they fed their eyes with the light. Rabbi Yehuda adds that they ate actual food and fed from the light and thus connected themselves above. Rabbi Elazar says that Yisrael was proper at that time and the Shechinah was bound to them. And in the future days the Holy One, blessed be He, will reveal Himself to His children and all will see visually His glory.

580. וְאֶל אֲצִילֵי בְּנֵי יִשְׂרָאֵל, דָּא נָדָב וַאֲבִיהוּא. לֹא שָׁלַח יָדוֹ, דְּסָלִיק לוֹן לְבָתַר זִמְנָא, וְלָא אִתְעֲנָשׁוּ הָכָא. רַבִּי יוֹסִי אָמַר, מִלָּה דָּא, לְשַׁבְחָא דִּלְהוֹן, דִּכְתִיב וַיֹּאכְלוּ וַיִּשְׁתּוּ דְּזָנוּ עֵינֵיהוֹן, מִנְּהִירוּ דָּא. רַבִּי יְהוּדָה אָמַר, אֲכִילָה וַדַּאי אָכְלוּ, וְזָנוּ גַּרְמַיְיהוּ, וְהָכָא אִתְקְשָׁרוּ לְעֵילָא, אִי לָא דְּסָטוּ אוֹרְחַיְיהוּ לְבָתַר, כְּמָה דְּאוֹקִימְנָא.

580. "And upon the nobles of the children of Yisrael" (Shemot 24:11), referring to Nadab and Abihu, "he laid not His hand." He led them TO JUSTICE later, but they were not punished now. Rabbi Yosi said, this matter can be interpreted to their credit as the verse says, "and did eat and drink" MEANING they fed their eyes with this light. Rabbi Yehuda said, they ate actual food and fed OF THE LIGHT, and thus connected themselves above, MEANING THEY EXTENDED THE LIGHT FROM BELOW UPWARD; THERE WAS NO SIN IN THIS unless they turned astray later as explained.

581. אָמַר רַבִּי אֶלְעָזָר, וַאֲפִילוּ יִשְׂרָאֵל, בְּהַהִיא שַׁעֲתָא אִתְכַּשָׁרוּ, וְאִתְקְשָׁרַת בְּהוּ שְׁכִינְתָּא. וְדָא קַיְימָא, וְאוֹרַיְיתָא כֹּלָּא, בְּחַד זִמְנָא הֲוָה. וְיִשְׂרָאֵל כְּהַהִיא שַׁעֲתָא לָא חָמוּ לְעָלְמִין. וּלְזִמְנָא דְּאָתֵי, זַמִּין קוּדְשָׁא בְּרִיךְ הוּא לְאִתְגַּלְּאָה עַל בְּנוֹי, וּלְמֶחֱמֵי כֹּלָּא יְקָרָא דִּילֵיהּ עֵינָא בְּעֵינָא, דִּכְתִיב כִּי עַיִן בְּעַיִן יִרְאוּ בְּשׁוּב יְיָ' צִיּוֹן. וּכְתִיב, וְנִגְלָה כְּבוֹד יְיָ' וְרָאוּ כָל בָּשָׂר יַחְדָּו וְגוֹ'.

581. Rabbi Elazar said, Even Yisrael at that time were all proper and the Shechinah was bound to them. This Covenant and the entire Torah took place at one time, MEANING THEY THEN HAD THE LIGHT FROM THE ENTIRE TORAH. Yisrael never did experience a time like that. In the future days, the Holy One, blessed be He, will reveal Himself to His children and all will see visually His glory, as the verse writes, "for they shall see eye to eye, Hashem returning to Zion" (Yeshayah 52:8), and, "and the glory of Hashem shall be revealed, and all flesh shall see it together..." (Yeshayah 40:5).

End of Mishpatim

NOTES

NOTES

NOTES